31399

A HISTORY OF ARCHITECTURE
ON THE COMPARATIVE METHOD

S. Paul's Cathedral, London, from the west (1675–1710).
See p. 906

A HISTORY OF

ARCHITECTURE

ON THE COMPARATIVE METHOD

by

SIR BANISTER FLETCHER

President of the Royal Institute of
British Architects 1929–31

Seventeenth Edition

revised by

R. A. CORDINGLEY

Professor of Architecture in the
University of Manchester

NEW YORK

CHARLES SCRIBNER'S SONS

Published in the U.S.A. by
CHARLES SCRIBNER'S SONS
597 *Fifth Avenue, New York* 17
New York

Reprinted 1963

New material in this edition
© 1961, 1963 *The Royal Institute of British Architects and*
The University of London

The first edition of this book was published
in 1896

Printed in Great Britain by
ROBERT MACLEHOSE AND CO LTD
GLASGOW W3

FOREWORD

UNDER the terms of the Will of Sir Banister Fletcher, who died on 17 August 1953, the Royal Institute of British Architects and the University of London became the joint beneficiaries of a Trust Fund, of which one of the principal assets is the copyright in *A History of Architecture on the Comparative Method*. The income from this Fund, which is shared equally by the Institute and the University, is to be devoted to the furtherance of architectural teaching and appreciation in accordance with the various intentions expressed by Sir Banister Fletcher in his Will.

After reviewing the position of the History of Architecture, the sixteenth edition of which was in the press at the time of its author's death, the Royal Institute of British Architects and the University of London came to the conclusion that the time had arrived for a major revision of the text, which had undergone little change in essentials since the publication of the ninth edition in 1931. They were fortunate in securing the services of Professor R. A. Cordingley, Professor of Architecture in the University of Manchester, as general editor, and they take this opportunity of expressing their gratitude to him for the manner in which he has carried out his arduous task. Professor Cordingley explains in the Preface to this edition the lines upon which the revision has proceeded. The Royal Institute of British Architects and the University of London are confident that the new edition, whilst it incorporates much new material derived from modern historical and archaeological research, at the same time faithfully preserves the spirit, purpose and form, and in great part the actual language, of *A History of Architecture on the Comparative Method* as its distinguished author left it to their care.

The first sixteen editions of the *History of Architecture* were published on behalf of the author by Messrs B. T. Batsford Ltd., whose long and outstandingly successful management of the book has placed generations of readers in their debt. The transfer of the new edition to the Athlone Press of the University of London has been made in compliance with the University's settled policy of using the facilities of its own publishing organisation for important works in respect of which it bears a direct share of responsibility.

WILLIAM G. HOLFORD
President of the Royal Institute of British Architects

BIRKETT
Chairman of the Court of the University of London

PREFACE

THE system which Sir Banister Fletcher devised to give a unity of treatment to his book was thus described by him in his Prefaces to the sixteenth and earlier editions:

'This "History of Architecture on the Comparative Method," of which the short title is "Comparative Architecture," aims at displaying clearly the characteristic features of the architecture of each country by comparing the buildings of each period and by giving due prominence to the influences—geographical, geological, climatic, religious, social, and historical—which have contributed to the formation of particular styles, and which hitherto have not been emphasised systematically in presenting the story of architectural development. . . .

The *analytical* and *comparative* method adopted enables the essentials of individual styles to be easily grasped; thus the character of Gothic is emphasised by comparison with Classic and Renaissance architecture, a similar treatment being followed throughout the book.

Each style is considered under five sections, as follows:

Section 1. **INFLUENCES**

i. **Geographical**	ii. **Geological**
iii. **Climatic**	iv. **Religious**
v. **Social**	vi. **Historical**

These six leading influences help to shape architecture; the first three are physical, the next two civilising, and the last the historical background.

Section 2. **ARCHITECTURAL CHARACTER**

The general appearance and special features of the buildings of each period are in this section described in detail, together with various theories of origin and evolutionary development.

Section 3. **EXAMPLES**

In this section is given a wide range of typical buildings throughout the ages; these are shown both photographically and by specially prepared drawings which latter serve as a key to the size and proportion of the structures, while the text is confined to brief descriptive notes.

Section 4. **COMPARATIVE ANALYSIS**

- A. **Plans,** or general arrangement of buildings.
- B. **Walls,** their construction and treatment.
- C. **Openings,** their character and shape.
- D. **Roofs,** their treatment and development.
- E. **Columns,** their position, structure, and decoration.
- F. **Mouldings,** their form and decoration.
- G. **Ornament,** as applied in general to any building.

This analysis of the characteristic features which resulted from solving certain structural problems enables the student to visualise clearly the main factors which brought about changes in each style.

Section 5. **REFERENCE BOOKS**
The chief books are given to which readers who wish to pursue their studies in greater detail may profitably refer.'

In the text of this, the seventeenth edition, the above system has been scrupulously preserved.

Sir Banister died on 17th August 1953. He had concluded the preface of the previous, sixteenth, edition on Coronation Day of that year. For very many years the book had been internationally renowned, and so familiar to students of architecture everywhere as to be known almost invariably by his own name, rather than by the formal title he gave to it. He received many honours both at home in Britain, where he was President of the Royal Institute of British Architects over the years 1929–31, and abroad—France, Belgium, Greece, Italy, Roumania, Japan, and China —and was the author of other books on the practice and history of architecture as well as this, his most famous work. It was translated in entirety into Spanish and Russian, and is in general use as a text book in the United States of America as in Britain and the British Commonwealth of Nations. In the last of his Prefaces he wrote of the developments since the first publication of 1896: the illustrations comprising specially-prepared drawings, aerial views, restored models, and photographs had been increased from about 100 to over 3,200 in the course of the successive editions. He prided himself on the fact that he had personally visited almost all of the sites and buildings of which he wrote in the text, in whatever part of the world, visiting some of the countries many times.

At every opportunity Sir Banister corrected the book in accordance with the latest investigations; but necessarily, the amendments or additions were made piecemeal, and as a whole, the chapters remained essentially in the form in which they had been conceived originally or as they stood after the last major reassessment of 1931. Thus each represented an interpretation which might or might not still be valid at the present time, in view of the considerable progress made meantime in the archaeological field or in historical research. These latter developments and the passage of time have occasioned changes, too, in informed opinion, affecting certain chapters more strongly than others. His treatment of nineteenth and twentieth century architecture raised questions of another kind.

The revision of the various parts of the book for the seventeenth edition has, in consequence, demanded a varying and flexible approach, and below there is given some brief indication of the different problems involved, and the means adopted towards their solution.

In chapters I and II, on the ancient architectures of Egypt and West Asia, account has had to be taken of much important archaeological research and discovery which has added greatly to our store of knowledge. In particular, the chronologies that had previously served have been replaced or modified, and a greater—though not necessarily final—relative and specific precision has now been given to them. These two chapters therefore have been largely rewritten and much extended.

As regards Greek architecture, it has for some little time been appreciated that a 'dark age' of centuries had intervened between an 'Aegean' culture in Greek lands and the brilliant Hellenic epoch which succeeded it, while the Hellenistic phase to which this gave way in turn has assumed a much greater significance than formerly in linking Greece and Rome in matters of constructional method, civic design and the evolution of building-types as well as in respect of the architectural and decorative arts. Chapter III accordingly has been recast and enlarged sufficiently to allow the Aegean and Hellenistic phases their due identity, and for the rest there has been quite a little rearrangement and amendment of detail. The chapter is about one-tenth longer than previously.

The account of Etruscan and Roman Architecture contained in chapter IV proved to need local rather than extensive revisions, though these have been fairly numerous and have occasioned a modest expansion of the total text. The succeeding series of chapters on Early Christian, Byzantine and Romanesque Architecture (V–X) was found still to be admirably sound in essentials, and the one major change has been to transfer considerations of centrally-planned Italian buildings from the Early Christian to the Byzantine chapter. The same can certainly be said of the 'Mediaeval' or 'Gothic' series of chapters (XI–XVIII), especially the English, which always has been considered the finest part of the book: the earlier editions were produced at a time when the interest in Gothic architecture was keener and more discerning than it is now, and critics always have adjudged the Gothic series to be authoritative and profound. Some fresh elements have been added to the English chapter (XII—to the accounts of timber roofs castles and manor houses) and, in general, other moderate adjustments have been made elsewhere, but only the Belgian and Dutch Gothic chapter (XV) has been entirely rewritten.

The series of chapters on Renaissance architecture has undergone heavy revision. Chapter XIX (European) has been partly rewritten; chapter XX (Italian) almost wholly so, and is now about one-third longer than before; chapter XXI (French) has had considerable local amendment; chapter XXII (German) has been extensively rewritten and moderately extended; chapter XXIII (Belgian and Dutch) is a complete rewriting; chapter XXIV (Spanish) has been partly recast, locally rewritten and slightly extended; while chapter XXV (English) has had many amendments, the more extensive applying to the Georgian elements and as a whole lengthening the chapter by about one-quarter. This Renaissance series of chapters presented special problems to the reviser. Despite intercalations made with the intention of correcting the bias, the treatment in the sixteenth edition remained strongly coloured by the view, common among nineteenth-century architectural historians and the public at large, that the Baroque and Rococo manifestations were despicable and quite unworthy of serious attention. Thus, although the Renaissance period was deemed to extend to about 1830 in Europe, the Italian chapter had little or nothing to say about architecture after *c.* 1600 and the examples selected included only one or two of the more outstanding monuments after this date. There was a similar though less serious unbalance in the accounts of the Renaissance style in other European countries. Much recasting and new writing was required in each case; not solely for this reason but also because terminology raised some difficulties too.

Present-day architectural historians incline to limit the term 'Renaissance' to the initial stages of the adoption of the style in the various European countries, without having substituted another term to embrace as a whole that revived Classicism which, first adopted in the architecture of fifteenth-century Italy, followed a traceable connected course in Europe up to the early nineteenth—to about 1830. Here, in the seventeenth edition, the term 'Renaissance' has been allowed still to carry its former meaning; and the former mode of subdivision of the style into periods in each of the respective European countries also has been almost completely retained. Of necessity there had to be one or two changes. In latter-day writings the term 'Mannerist' frequently is used to denote the more classically-irregular of two alternative architectural expressions which arose in sixteenth-century Italian architecture. It is not, however, a very satisfactory term, if only for the reason that the definitions given are insufficiently broad to embrace all building-designs of the nonconforming type in the period before *c.* 1600, and indeed seem to relate only to practices which arose from the re-discovery of stucco as an architectural medium. Then too, there arose the difficulty that the reflection of Mannerism in other countries than Italy has not yet been adequately traced. Thus, in this seventeenth edition, the term 'Proto-Baroque' is used instead, to stand for all that architecture, which, throwing off the restraint of Classical rule—though not the Classical elements themselves—led more or less directly to the culmination of the whole movement, in Italy at least, in the Baroque. 'High Renaissance' is used for the conforming Italian type over the same period. It was necessary also to coin the term 'Antiquarian' to describe a tendency, evident in Europe from about 1750, to revert to ancient Classical (Greek and Roman) and Mediaeval precedent for inspiration.

It was in the parts of the book dealing with architecture after 1830 that the most considerable amount of revision and expansion was required. Since the origins of the *History of Architecture* lie in the last decade of the nineteenth century, and its growth slowed down after 1931, architecture after 1830 was not treated upon the scale of the earlier chapters, nor did Sir Banister apply to it his own system of chapter organisation. Though material on the nineteenth and twentieth centuries was added from time to time, it was arranged on no discernible plan, and in the sixteenth edition the three chapters devoted to it occupy only 35 pages. They have been replaced in the new edition by four wholly new chapters, occupying 188 pages, in which the system is extended to embrace all Western architecture down to the present day. 'Nineteenth and Twentieth Century Architecture in Britain' is followed by a parallel treatment of 'Nineteenth and Twentieth Century Architecture in Continental Europe', with an intervening short chapter on the 'Architecture of South Africa, Australia and New Zealand'. The whole 'Architecture of the Americas'—South America, the United States and Canada—including the ancient manifestations there, is brought together in a concluding chapter of Part I.

The former general heading ('The Non-Historical Styles') for Part II was anomalous; the architectures of the East are just as historical as those of the West. The historical styles under Part I now are headed 'Ancient Architecture and the Western Succession', and those under Part II, 'Architecture in the East'. All the chapters in Part II have been rewritten, though on the former lines, and the introductions to the two parts and the preliminary chapter on 'Prehistoric Architecture' have been considerably changed.

In the course of the revision it became abundantly clear what a tremendous achievement the book represented. The fruit of a professional lifetime, it had built up to massive proportions over the years. Even so, the former total of 1126 pages has now risen to 1390, and the illustrations from 3232 to 3611. The admirable line diagrams of famous buildings and their details, which have for so long been a distinctive feature of the book, have been retained almost in their entirety, though a certain number, mostly in the earlier part of the book, proved to need small amendments. Over 40 new diagrams have been made; and the 30 maps heading the chapters are entirely new, the old ones having been redrawn on a clearer system. The photographic illustrations have been both revised and very considerably expanded. A large number of those appearing in the sixteenth edition have been replaced by other photographs of the same subjects, and the previous total of 772 individual half tone illustrations has been increased by the addition of new material to 1147. For the reader's convenience, dates are appended to these illustrations as well as page references to the related text.

A2

Every part of the book has been checked, and besides the principal revisions referred to above there have been very many minor corrections, reframings and additions. Wherever feasible, both the commencing and completion dates of buildings now are given, rather than an average date as previously, or a dash indicates which of the two dates has not been forthcoming. The lists of reference books concluding the chapters and the general list at the end of the book have been brought up to date. The glossary contains about twice as many items as formerly, and the very complete index, also much extended, is improved by the addition to the respective items of direct references to the plates, as well as to the text; previously, it was necessary to turn up the text in order to locate particular illustrations. A further improvement is that the principal text reference is distinguished by bolder type from those of a secondary character.

CONTRIBUTORS TO THE SEVENTEENTH EDITION

In the task of revision I have been so fortunate as to secure the assistance of specialists to whom I have been able to confide particular charge of certain of the chapters, and I most gratefully acknowledge their major contribution to the preparation of the new edition. As indicated above, the amount and character of the necessary revision has not been uniform throughout the book; some of these collaborators accordingly have been mainly concerned to amend the existing text in detail, while others have had either to recast or extend it in varying degrees, to rewrite completely or to contribute entirely new chapters. Their names and the parts undertaken by each are listed below, following the chapter order of the book.

MR. CECIL STEWART, M.A., D.A.(Edin.), F.R.I.B.A., A.M.T.P.I., A.I.L.A.: chapters V to X (Early Christian, Byzantine, Romanesque in Europe, Italian Romanesque, French Romanesque, German Romanesque).

MR. MICHAEL DAVID BEASLEY, A.R.I.B.A., A.A. DIPLOMA: chapter XV (Belgian and Dutch Gothic) and chapter XXIII (Belgian and Dutch Renaissance).

MR. FRANK ILLTYD JENKINS, B.ARCH., M.A. (Durham), M.S.(ARCH.)(Illinois), A.R.I.B.A.: chapter XXVII (Architecture of South Africa, Australia and New Zealand) and chapter XXIX (Architecture of the Americas).

MR. JOHN TERRY, F.R.I.B.A., A.A. DIPLOMA: chapter XXX (Architecture in India and Pakistan).

MR. HOWARD KELLY, F.R.I.B.A.: chapter XXXI (Chinese Architecture).

MR. WILLIAM ARTHUR SHERRINGTON, F.R.I.B.A., F.R.I.C.S., A.R.C.A. (London): chapter XXXII (Japanese Architecture).

MR. MARTIN SHAW BRIGGS, F.R.I.B.A.: chapter XXXIII (Muslim Architecture).

For the detailed revision of the remainder of the text as, of course, for the general plan of the edition, I am responsible.

Several other authorities have given generous help and advice regarding elements of the text. Professor R. R. Betts (London University) made a preliminary check of the facts contained in the historical preambles of the Mediaeval and Renaissance chapters of the sixteenth edition, supplying many useful comments and corrections. Mr. Alan Rowe (Manchester University) took an unflagging interest in the reorganisation of the Egyptian material, contributing a flow of factual information and ideas gained in his long years of experience in archaeological excavation and research in Egypt and Cyrenaica. Mr. W. C. Brice (Manchester University), deeply informed regarding the circumstances of ancient Anatolia and the early

Aegean, gave unstinted help in the framing of the text relative to those areas. Dr. J. F. Healy (Manchester University) made productive comments on the drafts of the revised Greek chapter. Professor Peter Collins (McGill University), contributed outline suggestions for the French Renaissance section. Professor Thomas Howarth (Toronto University) took an important part in the initial framing of the Americas chapter, giving further guidance and advice in the later stages. Thanks particularly are due to the members of the staff of the Athlone Press, upon whom extremely heavy and exacting labours have fallen. In the processes of production of a book of this character, used extensively for reference as well as general reading, laden with factual statements and sewn with multitudinous cross-references, great demands have been made upon their vigilance; on points of detail of every nature, numerous fruitful suggestions have been forthcoming.

The prodigious index, which already in the sixteenth edition filled 56 close-knit double-column pages, has been expertly revised and extended on the new principle by Mr. G. Norman Knight, M.A., M.S.IND., with the assistance of Mr. L. M. Harrod, F.L.A., M.S.IND., and Mr. Terence Miller, M.S.IND.

By far the greater part of the full-page line illustrations are those prepared for the earlier editions under the supervision of Sir Banister. Among the persons importantly concerned in the actual drawing of these admirable diagrams was Mr. Herbert Tilley, L.R.I.B.A., F.R.I.C.S., who was for many years closely associated with Sir Banister and whose advice regarding the system employed has been most helpful in ensuring continuity in the present edition. For the preparation of the new diagrams and such amendments of the older ones as it has been necessary to make I am particularly indebted to Mr. Denis J. Cox, M.A., A.R.I.B.A., and Mr. Leslie Parker, but also to Mr. E. Atherden, Mr. J. S. Anderson, Mr. G. H. Broadbent, Mr. A. D. Gardiner, Mr. A. Rigby, Mr. C. H. Simon, Mr. D. G. Woodcock and Dr. R. B. Wood-Jones, who at various times have lent their architectural skills to the work. All the maps in the seventeenth edition were drawn by Mrs. E. Wilson.

15th February 1961   R. A. CORDINGLEY

CONTENTS

PART II

ARCHITECTURE IN THE EAST

LINE DIAGRAMS

THE illustrations and text are paged consecutively. Every illustration can be found in the Index (p. 1275) under the name of the building or feature. A list of *the full-page line illustrations only* is also given below, since some of these bear general titles which may be more conveniently traced in this form.

NOTE

*Information about the supply of large-scale Lecture Diagrams
may be obtained from the publishers*

SOURCES OF ILLUSTRATIONS

THE PUBLISHERS wish to express their thanks to the great number of institutions, commercial firms and private persons who have supplied photographs for use in this book or who have given permission for copyright material to be used in the preparation of plans and drawings. The following list relates primarily to new material in the seventeenth edition; for illustrations derived from earlier editions a source is given only where it is of special interest or where a specific request for acknowledgment in this edition has been made. Enquiries about the sources of illustrations not acknowledged should be addressed to the publishers.

Where acknowledgment is made to a published work mentioned in the lists of reference books appended to each chapter the number in parentheses refers to the page of the *History of Architecture* where the full title may be found.

FRONTISPIECE
ii, A. F. Kersting.

PREHISTORIC ARCHITECTURE
1, Crown Copyright, reproduced by permission of the Ministry of Works.

EGYPTIAN ARCHITECTURE
6, Lehnert and Landrock; 12, from Lange and Hirmer (p. 58, Phaidon Press Ltd, 3rd ed. 1961, original German edition by Hirmer Verlag, Munich); 24A, after Emery, 1939 (p. 58); 24B, after Garstang (p. 58); 24C, after Badawy (p. 58); 24D, after (i) F. Benoit, *L'Architecture d'antiquité*, H. Laurens, Paris 1911, (ii) A. Rowe, *Museum Journal of the University of Philadelphia*, xxii, No. 1, Philadelphia 1931, (iii) A. Scharff, *Handbuch der Archäologie, Ägypten*, 1939; 24G, after Lange and Hirmer (p. 58); 24H, after Borchardt, 1928 (p. 58); 24J, after Reisner, 1935 (p. 59); 24K, L, after (i) D. Holscher, *Das Grabdenkmal des Konigs Chephren*, Leipzig, 1921, (ii) Badawy (p. 58), (iii) Edwards (p. 58); 24N, after Borchardt, 1910-13, and Edwards (p. 58); 28, drawings and reconstructions by J.-Ph. Lauer; 29, after J.-Ph. Lauer, E. Drioton, O. M. Firth and J. E. Quibell (p. 58); 31A, Aerofilms and Aeropictorial Ltd; 31B, from G. Jéquier, *Les Temples memphites et thébains des origines à la XVIIIe dynastie*, Editions Albert Morancé, Paris 1920; 32F, in part after Edwards (p. 58); 37A, after H. Ricke, *Beitrage zur Ägyptischen Bauforschung und Altertumskunde*, Cairo 1950, and Baedeker, *Egypt and the Sudan*, Allen and Unwin Ltd, London 1908; 37B, after A. M. Calverley, *The Temple of King Sethos I at Abydos*, ed. Sir Alan Gardiner, vol. i, 1933, by permission of the Egypt Exploration Society and the Oriental Institute, University of Chicago; 37C-F, after Baedeker, *Egypt and the Sudan*, Allen and Unwin Ltd, London 1908 and 1929 editions; 37G, after Lange and Hirmer (p. 58); 41A, Metropolitan Museum of Art, New York, bequest of Levi Hale Willard, 1883; 42A, from Lange and Hirmer (p. 58); 46A, Aerofilms and Aeropictorial Ltd; 48A, Oriental Institute, University of Chicago; 48B, Lehnert and Landrock; 51B, A. F. Kersting; 52A, Royal Institute of British Architects; 52B, Egypt Exploration Society; 59, from Carter and Mace (p. 58).

WEST ASIATIC ARCHITECTURE
67A, Oriental Institute, University of Chicago, reconstruction by Hamilton Darby; 67B, Oriental Institute, University of Chicago, reconstruction by H. D. Hill; 68A, after (i) Parrot, 1946 (p. 87), (ii) Frankfort, 1954 (p. 87), (iii) Noldeke and others, *Vorläufiger Bericht*

über die Ausgrabungen in Uruk-Warka, Berlin 1937; 68B, after Parrot, 1946 (p. 87) and Sir Leonard Woolley, *Ur Excavations V, The Ziggurat and its Surroundings*, London 1939; 68C, R. Ghirshman; 71A, from Layard, *Monuments of Nineveh*, 2nd series, London 1853; 71B, from Loud (p. 87) by permission of the Oriental Institute, University of Chicago; 71C, from R. Koldewey, *Excavations at Babylon*, Macmillan and Co., London 1914; 72F, after Luschan (p. 87); 72G, after *Mitteilungen aus den Orientalischen Sammlungen, Heft XXV; Ausgrabungen in Sendschirli IV*, Königliche Museum, Berlin 1911; 74C, after Loud (p. 87) by permission of the Oriental Institute, University of Chicago; 76C, after Schmidt (p. 88) by permission of the Oriental Institute, University of Chicago; 77A, B, Oriental Institute, University of Chicago; 77C, from Ghirshman, 1954 (p. 87); 83A, after Lloyd, 1956, and Puchstein (p. 87); 83B, after Gurney and Puchstein (p. 87); 83C, Oriental Institute, University of Chicago; 83D, after K. Bittel, R. Naumann, H. Otto, *Yazilikaya*, Leipzig 1941; 83E, after K. Bittel, *Die Ruinen von Bogazköy*, Berlin 1937.

GREEK ARCHITECTURE
99B, after Sir Arthur Evans (p. 160, Macmillan); 100A, B, after Dinsmoor (p. 158, Batsford) and Piet de Jong; 100C, after Lawrence (p. 161); 103A, Agora Excavations, American School of Classical Studies, Athens/photo Alison Frantz; 106A, Metropolitan Museum of Art, New York, Dodge Fund, 1930; 106B, model of the reconstruction in the Wellcome Historical Medical Museum; 109, in part after Dinsmoor (p. 158, Batsford), and T. Wiegand, *Achter vorläufiger Bericht über die von den Staatlichen Museen in Milet und Didyma unternommenen Ausgrabungen*, Berlin 1924; 110F, after Dinsmoor (p. 158, Batsford); 117E, after Fürtwangler (p. 158, Bayerische Akademie der Wissenschaften); 118A, from D'Espouy, *Monuments antiques*, vol. i (p. 158); 118B, Agora Excavations, American School of Classical Studies, Athens; 124 B, C, F, in part after Lawrence (p. 161) and F. Krischen, *Die Griechische Stadt*, Berlin 1938; 127A–C, 134F, after Dinsmoor (p. 158, Batsford) and Anderson and Spiers, *Architecture of Ancient Greece and Rome*, Batsford, London 1907; 135A, Agora Excavations, American School of Classical Studies, Athens/photo Alison Frantz; 135B, Beaux-Arts Restorations, Paris; 136, Greek Embassy Information Office, London; 141N, after T. Wiegand (as 109); 142G, after Dinsmoor (p. 158, Batsford); 144A, J. D. Starling; 144B, Agora Excavations, American School of Classical Studies, Athens/photo Alison Frantz; 144C, Foto Marburg; 145B, after Dorpfeld (p. 158); 145C, after Overbeck, *Pompeii*, 1884; 145E, after Durm, *Handbuch der Architektur*, Stuttgart, 1905; 153A, B, after Homolle (p. 158) by permission of the Ecole française, Athens, and Editions Boccard, Paris; 154A, from Wiegand (p. 161, Walter de Gruyter and Co., Berlin); 154B, after Fürtwangler (p. 158, Bayerische Akademie der Wissenschaften); 158, *The Times*; 161, R. D. Gentle.

ROMAN ARCHITECTURE
166A, A. F. Kersting; 166B, Alinari; 171B, Alinari; 172A, B, 182A, from Gatteschi, *Restauri della Roma Imperiale*, Rome 1924; 182B, after plan by H. C. Bradshaw from Anderson, Spiers and Ashby (p. 248, Batsford); 185A–F, R. D. L. Felton; 186, R. A. Cordingley; 195A, after Anderson, Spiers and Ashby (p. 248, Batsford); 196A, Anderson; 208A, after Gatteschi (as 172A, B); 208B, from D'Espouy (p. 248); 214A, Oreste Onestinghel, Verona; 219A–C, Alinari; 220E–G, after Pierce (p. 248); 226B, A. F. Kersting; 234C, E, after Robertson (p. 248), T. Wiegand and H. Schrader, *Priene*, Berlin 1904; 237A, model by Gismondi/photo Alinari; 237B, after Cordingley and Richmond (p. 248); 237C, after Pierce (p. 248); 238A, Metropolitan Museum of Art, New York; 241A–F, R. D. L. Felton; 242A, Alinari; 245A, drawing by Gatteschi/Fototeca Unione, Rome; 245B, C, Alinari; 249F, after Overbeck (as 145C); 251, Anderson.

EARLY CHRISTIAN ARCHITECTURE
252B, 256A, B, 263B, Alinari; 268A, from H. Decker, *Venice*, Anton Schroll and Co., Vienna 1953; 268B, C, A. F. Kersting; 269A, Alinari; 269B, Anderson; 270, Testolini.

BYZANTINE ARCHITECTURE
273, from D. Talbot Rice, *The Art of Byzantium*, Thames and Hudson, London 1959; 274, from Fossati (p. 302); 282A, from M. Hürlimann, *Istanbul*, Thames and Hudson, London 1959; 282B, A. F. Kersting; 282C, Mansell Collection; 282D, Josephine Powell;

286B, from Schultz and Barnsley (p. 302); 286C, from Gurlitt (p. 302); 287A, Press Attaché, Turkish Embassy, London; 287B, Agora Excavations, American School of Classical Studies, Athens; 291A, Alinari; 291B, 292A, from L. Price, *Interiors and Exteriors in Venice*, London 1843; 292B, from H. Decker (as 268A above); 294A, from Schultz and Barnsley (p. 302); 294B, from D. R. Buxton, *Russian Mediaeval Architecture*, Cambridge 1934; 299A, from Gurlitt (p. 302); 299B, Alinari; 299C, Omniafoto, Turin; 302, Spyros Meletzis, Athens.

ROMANESQUE ARCHITECTURE IN EUROPE
310A, Archives photographiques, Paris.

ITALIAN ROMANESQUE
317A–C, 317B, 318A, Alinari; 318B, 321A, Brogi; 321B, C, Alinari; 325A, Omniafoto, Turin; 326A, Alinari; 326B, Anderson; 326C, J. B. Price; 327A, B, Alinari; 327C, D, Brogi; 333, Alinari.

FRENCH ROMANESQUE
346B, Courtauld Institute of Art/photo G. C. Druce.

ENGLISH MEDIAEVAL ARCHITECTURE
378, A. F. Kersting; 391B, Radio Times Hulton Picture Library; 395A, Aerofilms and Aeropictorial Ltd; 395B, Photo Precision Ltd; 396A, C, 400A, A. F. Kersting; 400C, National Buildings Record/Weaver; 403B, 422B, A. F. Kersting; 428, National Buildings Record; 439A, B, 440A–C, 441A–F, Aerofilms and Aeropictorial Ltd; 449H, 450B, after Garner and Stratton (p. 513, Batsford); 453A, from J. Nash, *The Mansions of England in the Olden Time*, London 1839; 453B, National Buildings Record; 454A, Aerofilms and Aeropictorial Ltd; 454B, National Buildings Record; 454C, *Country Life*; 455A, from Nash (as 453A); 455B, C, *Country Life*; 456A, National Buildings Record/photo F. H. Crossley; 456B, National Buildings Record; 456C, *Country Life*; 457A–C, National Buildings Record; 458C, after Garner and Stratton (p. 513, Batsford); 460B, after Belcher and Macartney (p. 979, Batsford); 462A, Royal Commission on Historical Monuments, by permission of the Controller of H.M. Stationery Office; 462B, *Country Life*; 464B, G, H, after Garner and Stratton (p. 513, Batsford); 464C, after Davie and Dawber, *Old Cottages and Farmhouses in Kent and Sussex*, Batsford, London 1900; 464D, E, after B. Oliver, *Old Houses and Village Buildings in East Anglia*, Batsford, London 1912; 465A, B, 466A, B, Royal Commission on Historical Monuments, by permission of the Controller of H.M. Stationery Office; 467A, J. Allan Cash; 467B, F. C. Morgan; 468, A. F. Kersting; 475A, B, Aerofilms and Aeropictorial Ltd; 476, from D. Loggan, *Cantabrigia illustrata*, Cambridge 1690; 477A, B, Aerofilms and Aeropictorial Ltd; 482A, A. F. Kersting; 482B, Royal Commission on Historical Monuments, by permission of the Controller of H.M. Stationery Office; 484B, J, M, after Garner and Stratton (p. 513, Batsford); 484F, G, H, L, after Davie and Dawber (as 464C, Batsford); 484N, after Gotch, 1891–4 (p. 979, Batsford); 485D, E, G, after Garner and Stratton (p. 513, Batsford); 485F, after Parkinson and Ould, *Old Cottages and Farmhouses and other Half-Timbered Buildings in Shropshire, Herefordshire and Cheshire*, Batsford, London 1904; 488A, B, A. F. Kersting; 497M, after Vallance, 1912 (p. 514, Batsford); 500G, after Garner and Stratton (p. 513, Batsford); 516K, after Bond, 1905 (p. 513, Batsford).

SCOTTISH AND IRISH ARCHITECTURE
523A, A. F. Kersting; 524A–C, Crown Copyright, Ministry of Works; 526A, B, Thomas H. Mason and Sons Ltd.

FRENCH GOTHIC
532A, B, Foto Marburg; 532C, Cathedral of S. John the Divine, New York; 535A, D, 536B, A. F. Kersting; 539C, Foto Marburg; 546C, Giraudon; 546D, Archives photographiques, Paris; 548B, D, A. F. Kersting; 554B, Archives photographiques, Paris; 556B, Giraudon.

BELGIAN AND DUTCH GOTHIC
575A–C, Rijksdienst voor de Monumentenzorg; 576B, copyright A.C.L. Brussels; 582, Netherlands Embassy, London.

GERMAN GOTHIC
585A, D, Foto Marburg; 597, from L. Haghe, *Sketches of Belgium and Germany*, 2nd series, London 1840–50.

ITALIAN GOTHIC
598C, 605A, B, 606A, Alinari; 606C, Anderson; 609A–C, 610A–C, Alinari; 615B, A. F. Kersting; 615C, Brogi; 618A, B, Alinari; 619A, B, A. F. Kersting; 619C, 620A, B, 621A, 622B, 625C, Alinari; 626A, A. F. Kersting; 626C, Anderson; 632A, A. F. Kersting; 632B, Alinari.

SPANISH MEDIAEVAL ARCHITECTURE
652B–D, A. F. Kersting.

RENAISSANCE IN EUROPE
664, Anderson.

ITALIAN RENAISSANCE
675A, Brogi; 675B, C, Alinari; 682A, A. F. Kersting; 682B–E, Alinari; 686A, Brogi; 689A–C, Alinari; 689D, Brogi; 692B–F, 693A–F, 694A, B, Alinari; 697A, Cassa di Risparmio delle Provincie Lombarde; 697B, Alinari; 697C, D, Brogi; 706A–F, 709A, 712A, Alinari; 712B, Brogi; 715A–C, 716A, B, 720A, Alinari; 720B, Piranesi; 724A–D, Alinari; 724E, A. F. Kersting; 724F, 727A, Anderson; 727B–D, Alinari; 728A, Anderson; 728B, C, 730A, 736A, B, 739B, C, Alinari; 744A, E, G–J, after A. Haupt, *Renaissance Palaces of North Italy and Tuscany*, vol. ii, Batsford, London 1931; 746A, Alinari; 746B, Anderson; 756, Alinari.

FRENCH RENAISSANCE
764A, Giraudon; 764B, after Ward, 1909 (p. 805, Batsford); 771G, after Ward, 1926 (p. 805, Batsford); 776B, A. F. Kersting; 778B, Foto Marburg; 778C, D, Archives photographiques, Paris; 782A, Robin, Richelieu; 782B, 784B, 786A, Foto Marburg; 786B, Giraudon; 786C, Archives photographiques, Paris; 787A, B, 790A, B, Foto Marburg; 790C, from T. Shotter Boys, *Picturesque Architecture in Paris and other places*, London 1839; 794A, Archives photographiques, Paris; 795B, C, 796B, 797B, Foto Marburg; 797D, A. F. Kersting.

GERMAN RENAISSANCE
810B, 813A, B, D–F, 814A–C, Foto Marburg; 816A, Bundesdenkmalamt, Vienna/photo Eva Frodl-Kraft; 816B, 819B, C, 820A, Foto Marburg; 820B, Bundesdenkmalamt, Vienna/photo Eva Frodl-Kraft; 821A–C, Foto Marburg; 821D, from Mencl (p. 825); 822A–D, Foto Marburg; 825A, C. N. P. Powell; 825B, Foto Marburg.

BELGIAN AND DUTCH RENAISSANCE
826A, B, Rijksdienst voor de Monumentenzorg; 829A, Belgian Embassy, London, Press Bureau; 829B, 833A–D, copyright A. C. L. Brussels; 833E, F, 834A, Rijksdienst voor de Monumentenzorg; 834B, 837A, copyright A. C. L. Brussels; 837B, Rijksmuseum, Amsterdam/Photo-Commissie; 837C, copyright A. C. L. Brussels; 837D, 840A, B, Rijksdienst voor de Monumentenzorg.

SPANISH RENAISSANCE
843A, 844A–C, 847A, C, 848A, B, 849A, B, 850B, Mas; 854A, B, after Prentice (p. 862, Batsford); 857A–C, 858A, Mas; 858B, A. F. Kersting; 858C, D, 859C, D, Mas; 860A–E, after Prentice (p. 862, Batsford); 861A, A. F. Kersting.

ENGLISH RENAISSANCE
879A, Royal Commission on Historical Monuments, by permission of the Controller of H.M. Stationery Office; 879B, E, A. F. Kersting; 879C, National Buildings Record; 883A, B, Aerofilms and Aeropictorial Ltd; 884A, National Buildings Record; 884B, 887A, A. F. Kersting; 887B, *Country Life*; 888A, Crown Copyright, reproduced from the Ministry of Works's *Official Guide Book to Kirby Hall*, 1955, by permission of the Controller of H.M. Stationery Office; 888B, *Country Life*; 890A, B, Aerofilms and Aeropictorial Ltd; 890C, A. F. Kersting; 891B, C, 893A, National Buildings Record; 894A, A. F. Kersting; 894D, *Country Life*; 895A, B, A. F. Kersting; 895C, D, Royal Commission on Historical Monuments, by permission of the Controller of H.M. Stationery Office; 896A, National Maritime Museum; 896B, 900A, B, A. F. Kersting; 901B, D, E, 902E, F, after Belcher and Macartney

(p. 979, Batsford); 903A, E, National Buildings Record; 903B, C, *Country Life*; 903D, Royal Commission on Historical Monuments, by permission of the Controller of H.M. Stationery Office; 907A, B, *Country Life*; 907C, National Buildings Record; 908B, A. F. Kersting; 908C, Royal Commission on Historical Monuments, by permission of the Controller of H.M. Stationery Office; 908D, Warburg Institute; 909A, Aerofilms and Aeropictorial Ltd; 915C, D, A. F. Kersting; 917D, after Birch (p. 979, Batsford); 920A, B, D, A. F. Kersting; 921A, C, E, National Buildings Record; 921B, Royal Commission on Historical Monuments, by permission of the Controller of H.M. Stationery Office; 921D, F, 922A, A. F. Kersting; 922B, *Country Life*; 922C, Royal Commission on Historical Monuments, by permission of the Controller of H.M. Stationery Office; 923A, Aerofilms and Aeropictorial Ltd; 923B, A. F. Kersting; 923C, Royal Commission on Historical Monuments, by permission of the Controller of H.M. Stationery Office; 924A, B, E. J. Farmer; 924D, National Buildings Record and the Wren Society; 927F, after Belcher and Macartney (p. 979, Batsford); 933A, Aerofilms and Aeropictorial Ltd; 933B, *Country Life*; 934A, C, E, A. F. Kersting; 934B, D, National Buildings Record; 935A–C, *Country Life*; 936A, D, A. F. Kersting; 936B, J. B. Price; 936E, Aerofilms and Aeropictorial Ltd; 940A, C–E, after Belcher and Macartney (p. 979, Batsford); 941A, A. F. Kersting; 941B, Crown Copyright, by permission of the Controller of H.M. Stationery Office; 942A–C, 943A, B, *Country Life*; 944A, A. F. Kersting; 944B, *Country Life*; 944C, D, National Buildings Record; 945A, from Neale, *Views of the Seats of Noblemen and Gentlemen*, 2nd series, vol. i, London 1824/ National Buildings Record; 945B, *Country Life*; 946A, Aerofilms and Aeropictorial Ltd; 947A, National Buildings Record; 947B–D, 951A, B, D, A. F. Kersting; 951C, from *Survey of London*, vol. xxvii, Athlone Press 1957, by permission of London County Council; 952A, Birmingham Post and Mail Ltd; 952B, D, A. F. Kersting; 953A, National Buildings Record; 953B, National Buildings Record/photo Gerald Cobb; 953C, 954A–C, A. F. Kersting; 954D, 957A, National Buildings Record; 957B, E, Judges Ltd; 957C, 958A, B, A. F. Kersting; 958C, Raphael Tuck and Sons Ltd; 958D, the Trustees of Sir John Soane's Museum; 959A, A. F. Kersting; 959B, National Buildings Record; 961A, A. F. Kersting; 961B, Radio Times Hulton Picture Library; 962B, A. F. Kersting; 962D, British Museum; 965A, after Gotch, *Old Halls and Manor Houses of Northamptonshire*, Batsford, London 1936; 965B, C, after Gotch, 1914 (p. 979, Batsford); 965E–J, after Gotch, 1891–4 (p. 979, Batsford); 966A–E, after Belcher and Macartney (p. 979, Batsford); 969B–D, after Gotch, 1891–4 (p. 979, Batsford); 971A–D, H, after Belcher and Macartney (p. 979, Batsford); 975D, 976E, after Gotch, 1891–4 (p. 979, Batsford); 977A, B, D, after G. P. Bankart, *The Art of the Plasterer*, Batsford, London 1908.

NINETEENTH AND TWENTIETH CENTURY BRITISH

982, A. F. Kersting; 993A, *Country Life*; 993B, 994A, A. F. Kersting; 994B, D, E, National Buildings Record; 994C, F. Frith & Co; 994F, *Country Life*; 997A, from Pevsner (p. 1118); 997B, A. F. Kersting; 998A, Crown Copyright/Victoria and Albert Museum; 998B, E, F, *Country Life*; 998C, National Buildings Record; 998D, A. F. Kersting; 1001A, Sanderson and Dixon; 1001B, from Pevsner (p. 1118); 1001C, D, F, from Howarth (p. 1056, Routledge); 1001E, *Country Life*; 1002A, R.I.B.A. Library, by permission of C. Cowles-Voysey; 1002B, T. and R. Annan; 1003A, Margaret Tomlinson; 1003B, *Architectural Review*; 1004A, B, C, *Country Life*; 1005A, B, 1006A, *Architectural Review*/photos Dell and Wainwright; 1006B, Denys Lasdun; 1006C, Director of Housing, Liverpool/photo John Mills Ltd; 1006D, Aerofilms and Aeropictorial Ltd; 1009A, National Buildings Record; 1009B–D, 1010A, A. F. Kersting; 1010B, Friends of Lancing Chapel/Sussex Photo Agency; 1010C, R. A. Cordingley; 1013A, T. and R. Annan; 1013B, A. F. Kersting; 1013C, The Administrator, Westminster Cathedral/photo Valentine and Sons Ltd; 1014A, Elsam, Mann and Cooper; 1014B, Stewart Bale Ltd; 1014C, *Country Life*; 1015A–C, Eric de Maré; 1016B, *Country Life*; 1016C, *Industrial Architecture*/photo Sydney W. Newbery; 1016D, *The Architect and Building News*/photo Herbert Felton; 1017B, Basil Spence and Partners/photo de Burgh Galwey; 1018A–C, Basil Spence and Partners; 1021A, A. F. Kersting; 1021B, E, National Buildings Record; 1021C, D, from *Survey of London*, vol. xxx, Athlone Press 1960, by permission of London County Council; 1021F, Royal College of Physicians, Edinburgh; 1022A, City Art Gallery, Manchester/photo Elsam, Mann and Cooper; 1022B, from W. H. Pyne, *The History of the Royal Residences*, vol. iii, London 1819; 1022C, D, 1023A, B, A. F.

Kersting; 1024A, National Buildings Record; 1024C, 1027A, A. F. Kersting; 1027B, National Buildings Record; 1028A, Elsam, Mann and Cooper; 1028B, A. F. Kersting; 1029A, B, National Buildings Record; 1029D, *Architectural Review*/photo Dell and Wainwright; 1030A–C, T. and R. Annan; 1031B, Aerofilms and Aeropictorial Ltd; 1032C, P.A.-Reuter Photos Ltd; 1033B, *The Field*; 1033C, *Architectural Review*/photo de Burgh Galwey; 1034A, National Buildings Record; 1034B, *Architectural Review*/photo de Burgh Galwey; 1034C, *Architectural Review*/photo Dell and Wainwright; 1037A, Drake and Lasdun; 1037B, J. Allan Cash; 1038A, from T. Rose, *Westmorland, Cumberland, Durham, and Northumberland*, 1831–2; 1038B, from *Builder*, 29 Sept. 1849; 1038C, A. F. Kersting; 1038D, British Railways; 1039A, B, National Buildings Record; 1039C, Gerald Sanville; 1039D, A. F. Kersting; 1040A, *Country Life*; 1040B, Sir John Summerson; 1040C, by permission of the British Transport Commission; 1043A, National Buildings Record; 1043B, Fox Photos Ltd; 1044A, T. and R. Annan; 1044B, National Buildings Record; 1044C, Cadena Cafés Ltd; 1045A, B, Eric de Maré; 1046A, A. F. Kersting; 1046B, *Architectural Review*/photo Newbery; 1046C, Birmingham Post and Mail Ltd; 1046D, J. Allan Cash; 1049B, *Architectural Review*/photo Newbery; 1049C, *Daily Express*; 1049D, 1050A, National Buildings Record; 1050B, Gollins, Melvin, Ward and Partners/photo Colin Westwood; 1050C, Skinner and Bailey; 1053A, H. Tempest Ltd; 1053B, *Architectural Review*/photo de Burgh Galwey.

SOUTH AFRICA, AUSTRALIA AND NEW ZEALAND
1057, The Michaelis Collection/photo Arthur English.

NINETEENTH AND TWENTIETH CENTURY EUROPEAN
1060, Pier Luigi Nervi/Foto Vasari, Rome; 1069A, J. Allan Cash; 1069B, F, Viollet; 1069C, Mas; 1069D, from Pevsner (p. 1118); 1069E, Netherlands Government Information Service/photo E. M. van Ojen; 1070A, Austrian Embassy, London; 1070B, C, Mas; 1073A, Chevojon; 1073B, copyright A.C.L. Brussels; 1073C, from H. Kulka, *Adolf Loos*, Anton Schroll and Co., Vienna 1931; 1073D, Koninklijke Maatschappij tot Bevordering der Bouwkunst Bond van Nederlandsche Architecten, B.N.A.; 1073E, Netherlands Government Information Service/photo Hans Sibbelee; 1074A, B, Lucien Hervé: 1076A, Mies van der Rohe/Museum of Modern Art, New York; 1076B, Mies van der Rohe/Williams and Meyer; 1077A, Chevojon; 1077B, Stockholms Stadmuseum; 1078, Chevojon; 1081A, Staatliche Landbildstelle Hamburg; 1081B, Chevojon; 1081C, Austrian Embassy, London; 1081D, from P. Lavedan, *Architecture française*, Librairie Larousse, Paris 1944; 1082A, Mas; 1082B, C, Swedish Tourist Traffic Association/photos Heurlin; 1082D, Strüwing; 1083A, B, Chevojon; 1083C, Bernhard Moosbrugger; 1084A, Lucien Hervé; 1084B, Chevojon; 1084C, Josef Josuwek; 1087A, Bulloz; 1087B, \ iollet; 1088A, Chevojon; 1088F, C, from S. Giedion, *Space, Time and Architecture*, 3rd ed. Harvard 1954; 1089B, Chevojon; 1090A, copyright A.C.L. Brussels; 1090B, Rheinisches Bildarchiv, Cologne; 1091A, Netherlands Government Information Service/Aero-photo Nederland; 1091B, J. Allan Cash; 1092A, Alinari; 1092B, Bulloz; 1095A, Netherlands Government Information Service/photo E. M. van Ojen; 1095B, Kunstgewerbemuseum, Zurich; 1096A, Swedish Tourist Traffic Association/photo Wigfusson; 1096B, Swedish Tourist Traffic Association/photo Crispién; 1097A, The Architectural Association/F. R. Yerbury; 1097B, Dyckerhoff and Widmann; 1098A, C, Walter Gropius; 1098B, R. D. L. Felton; 1098D, Netherlands Government Information Service/photo Rousel; 1099A, Swedish Tourist Traffic Association/photo Pöppel; 1099B, Dyckerhoff and Widmann; 1099C, Finnish Embassy, London/photo G. Welin; 1100A, J. Allan Cash; 1100B, R. D. L. Felton; 1101A, G. E. Kidder Smith; 1101B, C, Chevojon; 1102A, C, Pier Luigi Nervi/photos Oscar Savio, Rome; 1102B, Pier Luigi Nervi/photo G. Gherhardi and A. Fiorelli, Rome; 1105A, Alinari; 1105B, from S. Giedion, *Space, Time and Architecture*, 3rd ed. Harvard 1954; 1105C, from *L'Architecte*, II, 1906, pl. x; 1105D, Chevojon; 1105E, Viollet; 1105F, 1106A, Chevojon; 1106B, Viollet; 1107A, from Pevsner (p. 1118); 1107B, Bildarchiv Stadt Stuttgart/Ludwig Windstrosser; 1108A, Swiss National Tourist Office/photo Mischol; 1108B, Junkers Luftbild; 1109A, Netherlands Government Information Service/photo E. M. van Ojen; 1109B, R. D. L. Felton; 1110A, Pirelli Ltd/Publifoto, Milan; 1110B, Fagus-Werk Karl Benscheidt/photo Renger-Patzsch; 1110C, Pier Luigi Nervi/photo Moisio, Turin; 1113A, Omniafoto, Turin;

1113B, J. Allan Cash; 1117, Strüwing; 1118, Netherlands Government Information Service.

ARCHITECTURE OF THE AMERICAS
1119, Hedrich-Blessing; 1129A, D, from Sanford (p. 1169, W. W. Norton); 1129B, F, American Museum of Natural History; 1129C, Grace Line Inc; 1129E, 1130A, Wayne Andrews; 1130B, Mrs. Hiram Bingham; 1133A–E, Wayne Andrews; 1134A, from Kelemen (p. 1169, Macmillan, New York); 1134B, G. E. Kidder Smith; 1134C, Sawders from Cushing; 1134D–F, from Sanford (p. 1169, W. W. Norton); 1137A, B, Wayne Andrews; 1137C, Library of Congress; 1137D, E, 1138A, Wayne Andrews; 1138B, City of Philadelphia; 1138C, Wayne Andrews; 1138D, photo by Abbie Rowe, courtesy National Park Service; 1141A, Colonial Williamsburg photograph; 1141B, 1142A–D, Wayne Andrews; 1142E, Chicago Architectural Photo Co.; 1145A, 1146A, Wayne Andrews; 1146B, City of Philadelphia; 1149A, B, Brown Brothers; 1149C, The J. Clarence Davies Collection, Museum of the City of New York; 1149D, courtesy Supreme Council 33°, Southern Jurisdiction; 1149E, Wayne Andrews; 1150A, courtesy City of Philadelphia; 1150B, Museum of Modern Art, New York; 1150C, Chicago Architectural Photo Co.; 1150D, E, Wayne Andrews; 1150F, Hedrich-Blessing; 1153A, U.S. Department of Interior; 1153B–D, Chicago Architectural Photo Co.; 1153E, Wayne Andrews; 1154A, Thomas Airviews; 1154B, Charles Phelps Cushing; 1154C, Empire State Building Corporation; 1157A, Hedrich-Blessing; 1157B, 1158, 1161A, B, Wayne Andrews; 1161C, Black Star/Armin Haab; 1162A, courtesy of Johnson's Wax; 1162B, Ezra Stoller; 1165A, C, Wayne Andrews; 1165B, Black Star/Carl Frank; 1170, Chicago Architectural Photo Co.; 1171, from F. Gutheim, *One Hundred Years of Architecture in America*, Reinhold Publishing Corporation, New York 1957/photo Moulin Studios.

ARCHITECTURE OF INDIA AND PAKISTAN
1182B, 1186A, B, Department of Archaeology, Government of India.

JAPANESE ARCHITECTURE
1220, reproduced by permission of the publishers of *Chambers's Encyclopaedia*; 1221, Ministry of Education and National Commission for Protection of Cultural Properties, Japan.

MUSLIM ARCHITECTURE
1227B, K. A. C. Creswell; 1236A, B, from Pope (p. 1252, Oxford University Press); 1243B, Radio Times Hulton Picture Library; 1251, A. F. Kersting.

GLOSSARY AND INDEX
1253, 1255, Wayne Andrews; 1275, Public Archives of Canada.

Stonehenge (*c.* 1500 B.C.). A photograph taken after
the reconstruction work in 1959. See p. 3

PREHISTORIC ARCHITECTURE

ARCHAEOLOGISTS recognize three main stages in the cultural evolution of mankind, respectively known as the 'Stone', 'Bronze' and 'Iron' Ages, according to the
use made of these materials for tools and weapons. The Stone Age was immensely
long, and so is broken down into 'Palaeolithic' (Old Stone), 'Mesolithic' (Middle
Stone) and 'Neolithic' (New Stone) periods. Except in a given locality, no absolute
dates can be generalized for these 'Ages', as the rate of progress varied enormously
in different parts of the world. Successively too, Man passed through phases in the
means of gaining subsistence. In the 'savage' state, livelihood came from hunting,
fishing and food gathering; in the 'barbarian', roughly according with the Neolithic
period, crop and cattle-rearing had been learnt and men could live a settled life.
True 'civilization' was only reached when economic and social development had
advanced sufficiently to allow the building of towns and cities, wherein a proportion of the populace could engage in trade, industry and professional pursuits.
These latter employments necessitate records and communication by means of
writing, and writing consequently is conclusive evidence of a community having
reached a civilized state. It is with the earliest civilizations that our History of
Architecture really begins, though account will nevertheless be taken of preceding
architectural developments plainly relating to them. For the rest, there are various
ancient structures or remains distributed throughout Europe which are intriguing,
often impressive and invariably of great interest to the prehistorian but which call
only for brief comment here.

Architecture had a simple origin in the primitive endeavours of mankind to
secure protection against the elements and from attack (p. 2). The 'savage' hunter
sought shelter in rock caves (p. 2H), the earliest form of dwelling, and learnt to

A   H.O.A.

A THE HUT

B MONOLITH: LOCMARIAKER: BRITTANY

C SHIELINGS: JURA: SCOTLAND

D BEEHIVE HUTS: LEWIS: SCOTLAND

E BEEHIVE HUT: IRELAND

F DOLMEN: NR. REGNIER: SAVOY

G STONEHENGE (AS RESTORED BY WALTIRE)

106' 0"

H THE CAVE

J THE TENT

build huts of reeds, rushes and wattle-and-daub or tents of saplings sheathed in bark, skins, turves or brushwood. The counterparts of these can still be found in use to-day (p. 2A, C, J). Some such types served the 'barbarian' too, with his flocks and herds, and crystallized into rectangular or round houses (p. 2D, E) of stone, clay or timber in the settlements which he established near his crops. Remains have been recovered of ancient timber-framed houses in compact 'Lake Villages', built on piles, in Switzerland and elsewhere, including Glastonbury and other places in England. When towns developed, houses had to be adapted to urban conditions; more solidly built, crowded together and rising to two or more storeys.

But it is remarkable that once the problem of shelter and subsistence had been effectively solved, communal effort was increasingly devoted to other than purely material ends. Taming the landscape, ensuring water supplies and building fortifications might be necessities of communal life, but after these, the greatest achievements of rising civilizations usually were works of a sacred character, places of worship or tombs. Thus the majority of the chief prehistoric building-remains in Europe have a religious connection. Many are 'megalithic', built of massive stones of astounding size when one considers that each was shaped with the most primitive of stone or bronze tools and hauled and raised with next to nothing in the way of mechanical tackle. Most of those belonging to tombs and now free-standing were once part of round or long 'barrows' (tumuli), earthen mounds containing upright and lintel stones forming chambers for consecutive burials of several to a couple of hundred persons. The surviving megaliths commonly are called 'dolmens' (p. 2F) or 'cromlechs'. Barrows vary greatly in size. Those with chambers, which were of different types, date from the late third or early second millennium B.C. In Britain, unchambered round barrows continued to be built until late Saxon times.

Isolated great upright stones, 'monoliths' or 'menhirs', such as those at Locmariaker (p. 2B) and Carnac, in Brittany (the latter is 63 ft high, 14 ft in diameter and weighs 260 tons), perhaps were religious monuments. The famous Bronze Age stone circles at Avebury (c. 1800 B.C.) and Stonehenge (c. 1500 B.C.), in Wiltshire, almost certainly were sacred structures. At Stonehenge, four concentric rings of upright stones surround a sandstone altar slab (pp. 1, 2G). The outer ring, 106 ft in diameter, comprises thirty massive sarsens (local stone), tenoned at the head into lintels dovetailed continuously together. The next ring is of much smaller 'blue stones' brought from the Prescelly Hills in Wales. The inner circuits are horseshoe-shaped, the one made up of five enormous sarsen trilithons of graduated height, and the innermost of small stones again of Prescelly origin. Another type of megalithic sacred monument is the 'Stone Row', well represented by the extensive remains at Carnac, Brittany, where some 3,000 stones stand spaced apart in ten to thirteen lines stretching for about three miles.

The above-mentioned prehistoric remains show little constructive development or sequence. Historic architecture, to which we now turn, while waxing and waning in virility, yet followed a continuous evolutionary course. The ancient styles of Egypt and Mesopotamia generated the succession in Western Asia, North Africa, Europe and the New World on the one hand (Part I), and on the other, contributed to the styles of the East (Part II). Muslim architecture bracketed West and East, but as its relationship with the East was the more persistent, it is included with the latter group.

REFERENCE BOOKS

CHILDE, V. GORDON. *The Dawn of European Civilisation*. London, 1950.

—. *Progress and Archaeology*. London, 1945.

—. *What Happened in History*. Pelican Books, Harmondsworth, 1942.

GARNIER, C. and AMMANN, A. *L'Habitation humaine—préhistorique et historique*. Paris, 1892.

GRINSELL, L. V. *The Ancient Burial Mounds of England*. London, 1936.

HAWKES, C. and J. *Prehistoric Britain*. Pelican Books, Harmondsworth, 1949.

PIGGOTT, S. *British Prehistory*. London, 1949.

le ROVZIC, Z. *Les Monuments megalithiques de Carnac et de Locmariaquer*. Paris, 1931.

VIOLLET-LE-DUC, E. E. *The Habitations of Man in all Ages*. Trans. B. Bucknall. London, 1876.

PART I

Ancient Architecture and the Western Succession

INTRODUCTION

THE History of Architecture is a record of continuous evolution, beginning with the simple and massive forms of Egypt and Mesopotamia, followed by the more highly developed temple-building of Greece; passing through the complex types of Imperial Rome, with her multitudinous public needs, and also through the ages of Christendom, when faith and fear reared cathedrals and castles, until the men of the Renaissance reverted to the Classic types for the varied buildings of this great period in human development. Architecture, striding down the ages, was evolved, moulded, and adapted to meet the changing needs of nations in their religious, political, and domestic development. A glance along the perspective of past ages reveals architecture as a lithic history of social conditions, progress, and religion, and of events which are landmarks in the history of mankind; for as architecture is in all periods intimately connected with national life, the genius of a nation is unmistakably stamped on its architectural monuments, whether they are Egyptian, Greek, Roman, Mediaeval, or Renaissance. Throughout the history of the human race, architecture, the mother of all arts, has supplied shrines for religion, homes for the living, and monuments for the dead.

The architecture of Egypt is characterized by massive walls and sturdy, close-spaced columns carrying stone lintels which, in their turn, support a flat roof. The Pyramids, which are amongst the oldest monuments in stone, were the outcome of that insistent belief in a future life which was the governing idea of the religion of the Egyptians, who also believed that the preservation of the body was essential to secure the immortality of the soul. The Pharaohs therefore reared, as royal fortresses for their mummified bodies, those stupendous mounds of masonry which, even in these days of engineering skill, remain a wonder to the world. Pyramids and mastabas reveal the Egyptian belief in a future state; while temples, with their courts guarded by enclosing walls, are the outward and material expression of the supremacy of a powerful priesthood, with its traditional and mystical religious rites. Temples, approached along imposing avenues of sphinxes, alike in their sombre, eerie interiors and forbidding aspect, tell of the exclusiveness of the Egyptian religion; for they were not places of worship for the people, but rather sanctuaries for kings and priests. These colossal monuments reveal not only the religious faith, but also the social and industrial conditions of the land of the Pharaohs in those far-off days; for such massive buildings would have been impossible without a despotic government commanding the labour of a teeming population of peasants and captives.

Great Temple of Ammon, Karnak: view across Hypostyle Hall,
showing clear-story lighting (1312–1301 B.C.). See p. 39

The architecture of Western Asia equally reflects national characteristics and indicates that the Babylonians were an industrious and superstitious agricultural people, while the Assyrians and Persians were warriors and huntsmen, more concerned with material than spiritual matters. The Babylonians laboured arduously in servile fear of awesome gods, erecting vast temple-terraces and artificial mountains in diminishing stages, from the summit of which astrologer-priests consulted the starry vault of heaven; for their aggressive leaders the Assyrians and Persians built lordly palaces on elevated platforms, decorated with mural sculptures of hunting, fighting and ceremonies of state, in preference to stupendous temples and tombs for guarding spiritual mysteries. The development of brick construction in Babylonia, due to the absence of stone, led to the evolution of arch, vault and dome instead of the simple trabeated systems adopted in Egypt and upland Persia, where stone was readily available. The influence of Egypt, Mesopotamia and Persia upon the architecture of Greece is readily traceable.

The architecture of Greece reflects each stage of Greek history with remarkable accuracy. Buildings of the 'Aegean' period indicate the adventurous and progressive character of the early inhabitants of Crete, the neighbouring islands and the mainland; but it was after a Dark Age of some five centuries that, with the Hellenic period, there was ushered in the most refined architecture and sculpture the world has ever seen, and this was concurrent with similar developments in literature and political institutions. Greece has, indeed, been the source of the highest artistic inspiration, and her architecture has influenced all styles almost down to our own day. The religion of the Greeks naturally engendered a desire to erect stately temples, and the national exultation at the final defeat of the Persians at Marathon and Salamis found expression in the building of many fine temples in the fifty years following the overthrow of their enemies. The world-famous buildings on the Acropolis were completed during the rule of Pericles (444–429 B.C.), a period which marked the climax of Athenian prosperity, art, and culture. Whereas Egyptian temples were royal monuments with high forbidding walls to hide the mysterious halls from the public gaze, Greek temples, on the other hand, were public monuments with only a small naos for the god, surrounded by open colonnades set out with all the beauty of column, entablature, and sculptured pediment in full view of the whole people. Egyptian temples were a royal prerogative; Greek temples were the peoples' patrimony. Greek national games and festivals encouraged literature, music, and the drama, and these were responsible for the erection of stadia, palaestra, and theatres. The record in architecture of historical events can also be traced beyond the confines of Greece and her colonies even to Northern India, where the influence of Hellenic art is manifest in the architecture, which in its turn influenced Muslim art. The Greek type of architecture is a development from a wooden structure of upright posts supporting beams and sloping rafters. This primitive timber architecture was reproduced in stone, and remained simple in character until the qualities inherent in stone resulted in further developments. The subtle artistic sense of the Greeks led them to make full use of the clear, shining atmosphere and fine-grained marble of their native country to produce delicacy of outline, while their technical skill is seen in the perfect proportions and refined treatment which are the distinguishing characteristics of that marvellous architecture which has never since been equalled. Two versions of the column and entablature were elaborated, the Doric of the western and the Ionic of the eastern Greek territories, and from the latter evolved a third, the Corinthian (p. 96). The three are known as 'Orders of Architecture'. In the Hellenistic period which followed, many fresh building-types were developed, and building procedure was simplified by the improvement of hoisting tackle and the invention of the roof truss, which made it possible to span large unimpeded spaces. Buildings became more complex, and new civic developments were formally planned. It was Hellenistic rather than Hellenic architecture that the Romans imitated, especially after 146 B.C., when Greece became a Roman province.

The architecture of Rome was influenced by the masoncraft of their forerunners, the Etruscans, and combined the use of the arch with that of the column. Though the Romans initiated the use of column and entablature as decorative facings to piers with semicircular arches, they still used columns constructively, as in the magnificent colonnades of forums, palaces, and temples. Social and political development among the Romans is displayed in the variety and monumental nature of their buildings, for, in addition to stately temples adorned with fine sculpture, there were public buildings of complicated construction designed for many purposes. Imperial palaces on an immense scale tell of the magnificence and luxury of the Roman court; while superbly decorated private houses, as at Pompeii, indicate the importance of the home under the *patria potestas*, which was the basis of Roman law. The Roman love of justice is also evident in the numerous basilicas or courts of law; while theatres indicate a different idea of the drama from that of the Greeks. Amphitheatres were a new departure built for contests between men and wild beasts, and they bear witness to that coarseness yet strength of character which enabled the Romans to bring the whole of the then-known world under their domination; while the great 'thermae' are evidences of the luxury which contributed to the decline and fall of the Empire. The great Roman roads and triumphal arches in various parts of Europe are permanent expressions of Roman power and dominion. Further, by the use of the newly-invented concrete and by the employment of arch, vault and dome, the Romans were largely independent of local building methods, and thus the architecture of Rome was reproduced in all parts of her Empire, and became the foundation of all European architecture. The decadence of Rome, faithfully portrayed in her later architecture, culminated in her final loss of world power; thus was closed a great chapter both in civilization and architecture.

A change was now gradually initiated by the introduction of Christianity, a new force in the world's history. The Christian faith was first spread throughout the Roman Empire by means of the military highways, and the Christian propaganda was carried from its birthplace in Judaea, first to Rome and then out from this centre to the extremities of the civilized world. The establishment of Christianity as the State religion resulted in the construction in Rome of over thirty churches of the basilican type. These churches, while retaining pagan architectural features, were gradually modified to meet the requirements of the new religion. A new direction was given to architecture by the transference of the capital from Rome to Byzantium, when a style was evolved known as Byzantine, which reached its culmination in S. Sophia, Constantinople (Istanbul), and became the official architecture of the Eastern or Greek Church. This style, like the Orthodox faith it serves, has remained strangely unchanged even to recent times.

There was a pause in architectural development in Western Europe from the break-up of the Roman Empire till Charlemagne revived the arts in the eighth century, and thus cathedrals, churches, monasteries, and castles were erected, especially during the tenth, eleventh, and twelfth centuries, by the new nations of Europe in a style which was an evolution from late Roman architecture, and is therefore called Romanesque.

The religious enthusiasm, manifested in the Crusades, gave an impetus to the marvellous architectural developments of the Mediaeval period, which were in their turn evolved from Romanesque architecture, and to which the name of Gothic has since been given. The wealth and power of the clergy and the monastic orders made the Church the one great avenue for advancement in the Middle Ages, and this, aided by popular religious fervour, was responsible for the outburst of church-building in the thirteenth century, when all classes of craftsmen worked continuously on these Gothic churches. A new method of construction was evolved in which small stones were held together in equilibrium, and the pointed arch is the outstanding feature of the style. The pointed 'rib and panel' vaults, over lofty church naves, were now held in position by surrounding buttresses and flying buttresses, weighted by pinnacles; these buttresses took the thrust of the roof, and the walls, no longer required to support it, could be replaced with huge windows of stained glass. The development of the style in England clearly shows the power of priests as exemplified in the plain and somewhat ascetic character of the Early English or thirteenth-century style; the dominance of the nobles in the more florid treatment of the Decorated style, and the rise of merchants in the matter-of-fact yet ornamental nature of the Perpendicular or fifteenth-century style, characteristics which were surprisingly similar in all countries of Europe, as each of these classes became the dominant power. Gothic cathedrals hold a unique place in the national life of the countries of Europe as faithful exponents of Mediaeval civilization; for they served as schools, free libraries, museums and picture-galleries, and in the absence of printed matter they formed the history books, sacred and profane, of the period. Sculpture and stained-glass windows not only presented incidents of Bible history from the Creation to the Redemption, but were also chronicles of the doings of kings and nobles, priests and people, knights and commoners. Periodical pilgrimages to the shrines of relics and saints, the veneration of the Virgin Mary, besides changes of ritual, influenced church plans by such additions as processional aisles and chapels. The magnificence of Mediaeval cathedrals was largely due to the concentration on them of the artistic energy of the period, instead of its being spread, as nowadays, over a variety of buildings. On the secular side, the fortified and frowning castles of the nobles form an eloquent, though silent, testimony to the power of the feudal system, as also to the unsettled condition of Europe. By the commencement of the sixteenth century, Gothic architecture, like the Mediaeval civilization which it accompanied, had run its course and was overthrown by a succession of events which altered the face of Europe.

European architecture up to this period may be divided into three main types, differentiated by important constructive principles, viz.: (1) the Greek or trabeated style, consisting of column and beam, (2) the Roman or composite style, combining column and semicircular arch, (3) the Gothic or arcuated style, in which the pointed arch prevailed.

There now came a break in the orderly evolution of architectural forms; but we can trace the influences which paved the way for the 'Renaissance,' that great revival of old Roman architecture, which naturally commenced in Italy. The new movement had its birth in the prosperous commercial city of Florence, where it was fostered by the Medici, and by the writings of Dante, Petrarch, and Boccaccio; while it was further strengthened by the newly discovered Greek and Latin authors, foremost among which were the writings of Vitruvius. Many important factors contributed to freedom of thought and action in an age ripe for change. The invention of printing aided the diffusion of knowledge; the use of gunpowder helped to change methods of warfare; the mariner's compass opened up the New World, and the immigration of Greeks into Europe after the fall of Constantinople in 1453 was also not without its influence. All this thought and activity affected artists, such as Della Robbia, Ghiberti, Brunelleschi, Alberti, Donatello, Bramante, Peruzzi, Sangallo, Raphael, Vignola, Michelangelo, Sansovino, Palladio and a host of others. The Renaissance at length entered upon a Baroque phase. The character of the architecture of the new churches and palaces faithfully reflects these changes in favour of Classic traditions by the use, in modified forms, of the Roman Orders of Architecture, hemispherical domes and other Classic features, instead of pointed arches, intersecting vaults, and vertical features of the Gothic period. This Renaissance movement spread from Italy through France, Germany, Spain, the Netherlands and England, though variously delayed by distance from the fountain-head.

In France the new style was grafted upon the native Gothic architecture, in a most delightful and picturesque fashion, in royal palaces, town halls and country houses, rather than in ecclesiastical buildings, for the churches built in the Middle Ages long sufficed for the religious needs of the people. The influence of Italy upon France was the more pronounced because, on the return of Charles VIII and Francis I from their campaigns in Italy, artists and craftsmen followed in their train.

In Germany and the Netherlands the Reformation accompanied or even preceded a fresh building era, but the existence of independent states prevented any such national effort as in France; although ecclesiastical, commercial and municipal buildings reflect the flourishing condition of some of the principal towns of this part of Europe.

In Spain, after the fall of Granada in 1492, and the expulsion of the Muslim Moors, the country was unified under Ferdinand and Isabella, and the new style took root, although the Moorish tradition added special richness and intricacy in architectural decoration.

In England the Renaissance synchronized with the Reformation, and was brought about by many historical events, such as the meeting of Henry VIII with the French king on the Field of the Cloth of Gold, and the subsequent introduction into England of Italian and French architects. The suppression of monasteries (1536–40) had brought about the distribution of vast revenues amongst the courtiers of Henry VIII, and had led to the erection of mansions, and also to the building of grammar schools and colleges. The Elizabethan period, when England had become Protestant, is marked by the influx, not only of Huguenot, but also of Flemish and German Protestant craftsmen, who influenced the design of numerous mansions. The Renaissance style, however, in accordance with traditional English methods, was only slowly adopted, and the new mansions retained many features of the castles and manor houses, such as the great hall, long gallery and mullioned windows. They were designed on generous lines illustrating the scale of hospitality which obtained in the spacious days of Queen Elizabeth. The later Renaissance period came more definitely under Classical influence, owing to the study of Italian art by Inigo Jones, and to the work of Sir Christopher Wren in the latter half of the seventeenth century. After the Great Fire of London, numerous Renaissance churches were erected for the Protestant religion, which demanded a great central preaching space, rather than processional aisles. Georgian or eighteenth century architecture is celebrated for its dignity, grace and charm, and for a unity of expression extending to buildings of whatever type or class; it progressed from Palladianism to a spare, light style, with slender components, which especially denotes the Regency, its concluding, early nineteenth-century, phase.

With the nineteenth century, the Industrial Revolution was set in its course. Population increased enormously, concentrated in the zones of industrial production, where buildings of a great variety of entirely new types were required—social, civic, industrial and commercial. Ease of transport virtually destroyed regional character in architecture, as formerly endowed by local building-materials, yet itself created fresh demands for unprecedented types of structure. In quality and in kind, so vast was the building programme that, for a while, utilitarian objectives prevailed, and function and external expression became almost completely divorced. For outward dress, old architectural styles were deliberately revived, often on no greater justification than the predilection of individual architects. Before 1914, almost every known style had had its vogue. Meanwhile, undercurrents had been at work. Engineer-architects, with little thought of display, solved their gigantic structural problems with spectacular success, in wood, brick, steel and, at length, reinforced concrete; these last and other new materials slowly proceeded to inform more commonplace structures and to produce their own genuine external character; enlightened designers progressively brought the new building-types into subjection and, using machine-age materials rationally, achieved harmonious wholes. From modest beginnings in the Arts and Crafts movement of the late nineteenth century, by way of *Art Nouveau* and a rabid Functionalism, architecture has achieved a new and cleanly expression in the present century. Steel and reinforced concrete are its bones, and concrete, brick, metal, glass and a host of other natural and synthetic materials its flesh. It is not yet mature, nor has it reached whole-hearted popular acceptance; there are many problems awaiting solution. This architecture of the machine-age is increasingly acquiring a common complexion throughout Europe and the New World.

The Sphinx, Gizeh, near Cairo, with the pyramid of Cheops in background
(*Before* 2600 B.C.). See p. 35

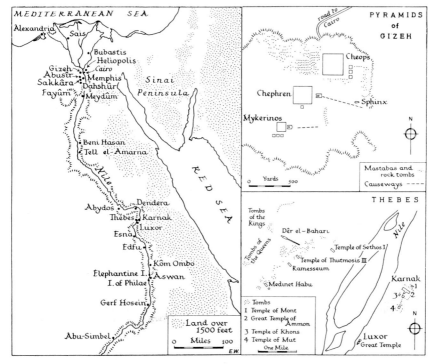

Ancient Egypt: the Great Pyramids: Thebes

I. EGYPTIAN ARCHITECTURE

(*Circa* 3000 B.C.–A.D. 1st cent.)

INFLUENCES

GEOGRAPHICAL. Egypt, the land of the Pharaohs, consists of a narrow strip of fertile, alluvial soil along both banks of the Nile, flanked by shelves of barren land and rugged cliffs, beyond which lie arid, desert plateaux. In its lower or northern part, the river divides to form a great delta of sluggish outlets to the Mediterranean Sea, while to the east, and roughly parallel with its course, extends the Red Sea. Egypt was the only country of the ancient world which, by means of these two seas, commanded outlets and inlets for both western and eastern foreign trade. The Nile itself was of untold value, not only as a trade route and unfailing means of communication but also because its overflowing and fertilizing waters made desert sands into fruitful fields, and it may truly be described as the rich life-blood which runs in the veins of Egypt. On its banks therefore, from time immemorial, the Egyptians sited their villages, cities and cemeteries, and here are the tombs of the nobles, the royal pyramids and the priest-dominated temples.

GEOLOGICAL. The natural products, such as timber, brick, clay and stone, largely determine the character of the architecture of a country. Stone is abundant in Egypt in quantity and variety, and was used not only for buildings and their embellishment, but also for vases, and even for personal ornaments, as the country was poor in metals, apart from copper, gained chiefly from the Sinai Peninsula. Tin was at length imported for the making of bronze. Iron, extremely rare, was of meteoric origin, and not mined. For building, the chief kinds of stone were lime-stone, sandstone and some alabaster; among the harder stones, granite, quartzite and basalt. Porphyry was little used before Roman times. Foremost in use in the earlier periods was a fine limestone from famous quarries at Tura and Ma'sara in the Mokattam Hills, a few miles south of modern Cairo, but as this was unsuitable for long beams it was supplemented by the red or grey granite (syenite) found at Aswan, much farther south. The limestone rocks extend up-river from the Mokat-tam Hills as far as Edfu, and there are other ancient quarries along the river valley. Beyond Edfu the formation changes, and at Silsila was quarried much of the sand-stone of which Ancient Egypt's finest temples were built. It is partly owing to the durable nature of these building materials that so many monuments still exist. The gigantic scale which distinguishes Egyptian architecture was made possible not only by the materials, but also by the methods of quarrying, transporting and raising enormous blocks of stone into position. Quarrying was done with copper tools and by the use of timber wedges which, when swollen by water, split the blocks away from the natural rock. Massive blocks of the harder stones were often obtained by laboriously pounding trenches around them with balls of dolerite, a very tough, greenish stone. Dolerite also was used for dressing the hard stones. Drilling and sawing were known from early times. Palaces, houses and most buildings other than tombs or temples were constructed of large, sun-dried bricks, which, when pro-tected against the weather on the external face were strong and lasting: burnt bricks were very rare before the coming of the Romans. There was very little building timber, but acacia served for boats and sycamore for mummy cases; while the indigenous date palm, whose fruit is a staple food of the people, was sometimes used, in logs, for roofing. Cedar and other woods were imported. Palm leaves, reeds and rushes and similar light materials, used to frame or reinforce mud-brick constructions, or as mats for such as panels, partitions and fences, had a great and permanent influence on the form and character of stone architecture.

CLIMATIC. Egypt has been said to have but two seasons, spring and summer. The climate is equable and warm; snow and frost are unknown, while, except in the Delta, storm and even rain are rare, and these conditions have contributed to the preservation of buildings. Such a climate, with its brilliant sunshine, conduced also to simplicity of design; for as sufficient light reached the interior of temples through doors and roof slits, there was no real need for windows, and thus unbroken massive walls not only protected the interior from the fierce heat of the sun, but also provided an uninterrupted surface for hieroglyphics or pictorial representations of religious ritual, historic events and daily pursuits. During the inundation (July to October) the ground could not be tilled, so the vast population was available for building work. In view of the rarity of rain, roof drainage was not an important consideration, and flat roofs of stone slabs sufficed to cover the buildings, and exclude the heat, while the roofs served also for religious ceremonies.

RELIGIOUS. The close connection between religion and architecture is every-where manifest; for the priesthood was powerful, invested with unlimited autho-rity and equipped with all the learning of the age. The religious rites of the Egyp-tians were traditional, virtually unchangeable, and mysterious, and these traits are reproduced in the architecture, both of tombs and temples. The religion was mono-theistic in theory, but polytheistic in practice through the cult of many gods repre-senting natural phenomena and the heavenly bodies, such as the sun, moon and stars, and by the worship of animals as personifications of gods. Egyptian mythology was further complicated by the multiplication of local gods for different centres. The keynote of the Egyptian religion was that of awe and submission to the great power represented by the sun, while the chief worship was for Osiris, the man-god, who died and rose again, the god of death, and through death of resurrection to life eternal. Judged by the elaborate preparations for the care of their bodies after death, one may say that the Egyptians pre-eminently realized the truth that 'in the midst of life we are in death', so the wealthy built themselves lordly tomb-houses against the time when they should enter the great land of silence. The deceased Pharaoh was transported across the Nile to the Western Bank where was the Domain of the Dead, and the religious ceremonies were conducted in a funerary temple or chapel (p. 24L).

In those dawning days of the world's history in Egypt there was no strict dividing line between gods and kings; no need for the doctrine of the divine right of kings; for kings were ranked, both by themselves and by their people, as actual divinities. Often they filled the double function as kings of their people and priests of their gods, and yet again were themselves gods, commanding priestly service. On the other hand the gods themselves were invested with superhuman and therefore with inventive powers, as when the awesome art of writing was regarded as the invention of the god Thoth. So gods, kings and priests kept sacred mysteries shrouded from the public vision, and the people groped in darkness and reached out vain hands to a world outside their own experience, which was only partially revealed to them through signs and symbols, and against the evil of which they sought to protect themselves by amulets and offerings. The gods they frequently associated in triads; thus Ammon the sun-god, Mut his wife, the mother of all things, and Khons their son, the moon-god, were the great Theban triad; while Ptah, a creator, Sekhmet, goddess of war, his female counterpart, and Nefertem, their son, formed the Memphis triad. Other gods were the powerful Osiris, god of the dead; Isis, his wife; Horus, the sky-god; Hathor, goddess of love; Set, dread god of evil, and Serapis, a bull-god, representing that strange cult of the sacred bulls. All these and many more, totalling many hundreds, occur in turn or in combination, and the unchanging, traditional architecture of ancient Egypt appears and reappears in all the jealously closed temples, erected for the use of kings and priests in the service of the gods. The outstanding feature of the religion of the Egyptians was their strong belief in a future state, hence the erection of such everlasting monuments as pyramids for the preservation of the dead. The dwelling-house was regarded as a temporary lodging, and the tomb as the permanent abode. This religious attitude is typified in the two predominant types of buildings, the solemn and mysterious temples of the gods and the enduring and tremendous tomb pyramids of the early kings. Here too is an epitome of the Egyptian outlook: hope of eternal life, the supremacy of the gods in the hidden world, the omnipotence of kings in the seen world, and the power of priests in touch with both worlds.

SOCIAL. The Egyptian civilization is among the most ancient of which we have any clear knowledge. Our information is derived from ancient literary sources, from records on papyri and tablets, but more particularly from Egyptian buildings and their inscriptions, through which it is traced back more than 3,000 years before the Christian era. It was the custom to record matters of history on temples, and of domestic and social interest on tombs and stelae.

Social and industrial conditions in Egypt were largely determined by the inflexible rule of an omnipotent government, which while employing large staffs of trained craftsmen continuously, levied vast armies of labourers for the erection of monumental buildings when the annual inundations made agriculture impossible. Prisoners of war were also turned on to the same work, and during the reign of

Rameses II there were so many captives and foreigners in the country employed in public works that, as recorded in Exodus (i. 9–11), the natives viewed with alarm the growing power of these strangers in their midst. The Bible story of the captivity of the Children of Israel in Egypt (perhaps c. 1360–1230 B.C.) throws a vivid light on the system of labour, on the tyranny of overseers, on the tasks imposed, and on the social conditions of the labourers employed by the Pharaohs to build these enduring monuments of Old Egypt. Forced labour is written over them all, and we can picture the gangs of slaves and impressed natives striving in the stone mines and quarries, toiling on the boats and rafts to drift the building materials down the Nile, and then strenuously hauling them into position. Social life is also graphically depicted in wall-sculptures of tombs, such as that of Thi, (p. 24F) a court official, which portray the Egyptians at war, at play, at the chase, on the farm and in the weaving shed and workshop, as well as at business. Craftsmanship was very highly developed, particularly in the royal workshops, and the Egyptians attained great skill in weaving, glass-blowing, pottery-turning, metal-working, and in making musical instruments, jewellery, and furniture. The pursuit of learning, astronomy, mathematics and philosophy was continuously carried on, especially by the priests, and much Egyptian literature has been preserved on papyri made from the pith of the once-abundant papyrus plant. New discoveries of such records, and of funeral stelae, from time to time, make increasing contributions to our knowledge of Egyptian life and customs.

The kings of Ancient Egypt are known as Pharaohs, a name given to them by the Hebrews and derived from the Egyptian Per-aa, the 'Great House'. The Pharaohs, like the Colossi of Memnon, are silhouetted against the mysterious desert background; sometimes they appear as gods or demi-gods, often as mystery priests, generally as builders, but rarely as fathers of their people. A study of the social system in Ancient Egypt conjures up a forbidding picture of an almighty Pharaoh, with his court, officials and priesthood at one end of the scale and the strenuously-toiling peasantry at the other. Of this system the royal pyramids and the frowning temples are the outward and material testimony to this day. The Pharaohs practised religious rites, stimulated the arts, protected their country, waged wars, fostered trading enterprise, and encouraged industries and handicrafts, but the welfare of the common people was of less account in all these ambitious undertakings than the aggrandizement of the great House of Pharaoh. All these conditions were as traditional and unchanging in their general aspect throughout successive dynasties as was Egyptian architecture, and both alike were the product of the Nile and the surrounding desert.

The Pharaohs have been divided into thirty dynasties by Manetho, an Egyptian priest who, about 300 B.C., compiled a history of Egypt in Greek. These dynasties are here, for convenience, grouped into three divisions, with dates which are quite approximate up to 1580 B.C., but progressively more firm thereafter. As is plain from the remains which archaeologists have uncovered, the Egyptian civilization was already well advanced when the first dynasty was inaugurated by Menes, who united Upper and Lower Egypt in a single kingdom.

1. Ancient Kingdom (Dynasties I–X), 3000–2130 B.C. Menes, the first dynastic king, is reputed to have founded Memphis, at the southern extremity of Lower Egypt, where it could command Upper Egypt too. Memphis was the capital throughout the great pyramid-building age, extending from the Third to the Sixth Dynasty; but from the dark period of anarchy which then ensued, in which the arts came to be so despised that, for a time, earlier masterpieces were defaced and monuments pillaged and even destroyed, it was Thebes that emerged, in the Eleventh Dynasty, as the chief city. During the First and Second Dynasties,

civilization progressed; the art of writing and the hieroglyphic system already were being developed. The tombs of the kings and nobles were of the 'mastaba' type, rectangular, with flat tops, and these, like the houses, were built of sun-dried bricks. In the Third Dynasty the royal mastaba evolved towards the true pyramid, as is shown by the 'Step' Pyramid of the Pharaoh Zoser at Sakkâra. This was of stone, as were also by this time many of the mastabas, which were to continue as the customary form of tomb for the less great personages. But it was in the Fourth Dynasty that, after further experiments at Meydûm and Dahshûr, the royal pyramid became fully evolved, and the culmination of achievement is represented by the famous three at Gizeh; the Great Pyramid, built by the Pharaoh Cheops; the Second, by Chephren; and the Third, by Mykerinos. Many other pyramids followed, chiefly at Abusîr and Sakkâra in the Fifth Dynasty, among which that of Sahura at the first place and that of Unas at the second are to be remarked. Sakkâra was again the favoured location for the pyramids of Sixth Dynasty kings, but in the latter part of the period pyramids give evidence of a decline, heralding the political and social upheavals of the Seventh and later Dynasties.

2. Middle Kingdom (Dynasties XI–XVII), 2130–1580 B.C. The Eleventh Dynasty saw a progressive recovery of political stability and of mastery of the arts. Under Mentuhetep II the country was unified again. He built an elaborate, terraced mortuary temple at Dêr el-Bahari, in which was combined a small, completely-solid pyramid, raised on a high base, with a rock-cut tomb driven deep into the base of the sheer cliffs behind. Thereafter pyramids usually were of crude brick, faced with masonry; and in the New Empire period royal tombs were without exception rock-cut, secreted in the Theban hills, their funerary temples being completely detached and standing on the rocky shelf westward of the cultivated land. Amenemhat I of the Twelfth Dynasty was energetic and enterprising. He consolidated the administrative system, made a survey of the country, set boundaries to the provinces, carried out irrigation, re-opened the quarries at Tura, restored the temples and founded the great temple at Karnak. Other kings there were, three more of the same name and three Senusrets, who fostered commerce and built temples and pyramids; the latter still grand in dimensions but inferior in construction to the stone-cored pyramids of the III–VI Dynasties. Senusret I erected at Heliopolis the earliest-known instance of a large obelisk. Amenemhat III, a man of many parts, fostered art and industry, irrigated the Fayûm, and probably built there the Labyrinth described by Herodotus. To the Eleventh and Twelfth Dynasties belongs a series of open-fronted tombs at Beni Hasan. Then followed five Dynasties of such confusion that even the succession of kings is uncertain. As a consequence of a great movement of peoples taking place in nearer Asia at this time, nomad tribes swept through Syria and Palestine and overran the Delta, and their leaders became the Hyksos or Shepherd Kings who, though they adopted the Egyptian language and religion, were so hated by the peoples that there was no rest in the land until the usurpers were finally driven out at the beginning of the Eighteenth Dynasty. It was the Hyksos peoples who introduced the horse and chariot to Egypt.

3. New Empire (Dynasties XVIII–XXX), 1580–332 B.C. In the two earlier Dynasties of this period, Egypt was glorious alike in the arts of peace and war. Her fortunes were varied thereafter, but never again reached the same peak. Amasis I, founder of the epoch, completed the expulsion of the Hyksos from the Delta and pursued them into Palestine, thus inaugurating Egypt's dominion over her Near-Eastern neighbours. Thebes was the capital, and many buildings were erected. Thothmes I (1530 B.C.) commenced those additions to the Temple of Ammon, Karnak, by which successive Pharaohs made it the most imposing building in

Egypt, and he was the first Pharaoh to be buried in the rock-cut 'corridor' Tombs of the Kings in the Theban mountains. Egypt prospered under the firm rule of kings who had now overcome the power of petty rulers at home, established a standing army, and were following a policy of aggression abroad. A remarkable figure was Hatshepsut, the 'Queen Elizabeth I' of Egypt, who patronized the arts of peace, re-established religious rites, and built below the mountain-side her fascinating terraced funerary temple at Dêr el-Bahari, adjacent to that of Mentu-hetep II of the early Middle Kingdom. This, covered with coloured reliefs of the pursuits she loved, gleams like a gem set in the living rock. Thothmes III was one of the greatest of the Pharaohs and is renowned alike for foreign wars and home reforms, while he rebuilt and decorated many temples. Thothmes IV (1425 B.C.) cleared away the sand from the famous Sphinx related to Chephren's pyramid at Gizeh, as recorded on the tablet between its paws. Amenophis III built the greater part of the temple at Luxor, dignified that at Karnak by pylons and sphinxes, and erected the renowned Colossi of Memnon. Amenophis IV, who in the fourth year of his reign changed his name to Akhnaten, daringly broke away from dynastic and religious traditions, deserted Thebes and founded his capital at Tell el-Amarna, laid out on formal lines and with a great palace and a temple to the sole god Aten, whose symbol was the 'solar disc'. A heretic Pharaoh is a striking anomaly in a country bound by such strong chains to tradition and orthodoxy. The Tomb of Tutankhamen, who was shortly to follow, was discovered in A.D. 1922 (p. 59). Rameses I (1314 B.C.), founder of the Nineteenth Dynasty, commenced the great Hypostyle Hall at Karnak. Seti I carried on wars without and temple-building within, continued his father's work at Karnak, restored many shattered monuments, built his great Temple at Abydos and his own sepulchre among the Tombs of the Kings. Rameses II (1301 B.C.) was called by early Egyptologists 'the Great', owing to the remarkable number of monuments labelled with his name. It is known now that he was given to usurping the achievements of his predecessors; yet undoubtedly he was a mighty builder. He finished and erected many temples, such as the Rock Temples at Abu-Simbel, the Hypostyle Hall at Karnak and the Rameseum at Thebes, but craftsmanship had begun to deteriorate in this and following reigns. Rameses III (1198 B.C.), second king of the Twentieth Dynasty (1200–1085 B.C.) was a religious devotee who made such offerings to the priests that about one-sixth of the land belonged to the temple revenues. The name of Rameses was borne by all succeeding kings of the dynasty, concluding with Rameses XI; their power waned as that of the priests of Ammon waxed strong. It is significant of the times that, while the temples of the gods were still respected, the tombs of the kings were desecrated and rifled of their treasure, and so the Twentieth Dynasty tottered to its end. Mediocrity, at best, marks the following dynasties of priestly and foreign rulers, until, with the Twenty-sixth (663–525 B.C.) a period of good government and trade prosperity ensued, and there was an attempt at revival of the art of the Ancient Kingdom. Psammetichus I, the first king, completed the rout of the invading Assyrians, and encouraged the immigration of Greeks, who brought in new ideas. Egypt again extended her Mediterranean trade, developed the arts and crafts of bronze-casting, pottery and portrait-painting, and attained a high standard in commercial and legal procedure. Necho (609 B.C.) attempted a canal between the Red Sea and the Nile, but the undertaking was only completed by Darius (522–486 B.C.). From 525 B.C. Egypt was a Persian province for about a hundred years under Cambyses the conqueror, Darius the administrator, Xerxes the tyrant, and other rulers.

4. The Ptolemaic Period (332–30 B.C.). Alexander the Great, who rescued the Egyptians from their hated oppressors, was hailed by the priests as the Son of

Ammon. He founded Alexandria as the capital, and it became the centre of Greek culture. On his death in 323 B.C., Egypt fell to his general Ptolemy, and for three centuries the lower valley of the Nile was the seat of a prosperous and powerful kingdom. Greek customs and methods of government crept in, but the Ptolemies upheld the gods, built temples of the native type at Alexandria, Dendera, Esna, Edfu and Philae, patronized native art, and married the daughters of Egypt. The reign of Ptolemy II is famous for the Pharos, or light-house, the history by Manetho, and the production of the Septuagint. Ptolemy III founded the Great Serapeum of Alexandria, which, after being re-built in the Roman period, was among the most magnificent buildings of the ancient world. Ptolemy V was so great a benefactor of the temples that the priests accorded honours to him and his ancestors in a decree which has proved the 'Open Sesame' to our knowledge of Ancient Egypt; for this threefold inscription in hieroglyphic, demotic, and Greek writing on the Rosetta stone, dug up in A.D. 1798 and now in the British Museum, provided a valuable key to those wonderful hieroglyphic records of Egyptian history. Struggles with Rome were continuous, and on the death of Cleopatra Egypt became a Roman province.

5. The Roman Period (30 B.C.–A.D. 395). Egypt under Caesar entered on another phase of prosperity, and many Roman emperors took Egyptian titles and even inscribed them, in the Egyptian manner, in cartouches. Thus did the Imperial masters of the world seek to find favour with this important grain-producing province. From this period dates the famous 'Pharaoh's Bed' at Philae. Hadrian twice included Egypt, as he did Britain, in his Imperial visits. Under Constantine, Roman control in Egypt extended even to religion, when in A.D. 324 Christianity was declared to be the recognized religion of the State; the Bible was translated into Coptic, but controversies and troubles soon overtook the Christians in Egypt. When Theodosius the Great issued his edict in A.D. 381, decreeing that the whole of the Roman Empire should be Christian, many temples were either diverted to Christian use or churches were built within their precincts—a curious mingling in architecture of the old and the new. Thus a change passed over the spirit of Old Egypt and dealt the death-blow to her indigenous and traditional architecture, which no longer served its original purpose and became merely a relic of the past.

6. Later Periods (A.D. 395 to the present day). The Byzantine Period (A.D. 395–640). Changes of Empire influenced politics and art even in the distant provinces, and when Egypt was ruled by the Eastern Roman emperors from Constantinople (now Istanbul), Christian churches were erected in the Byzantine style, another mingling of east and west, which has placed domed Byzantine churches side by side with trabeated Egyptian temples.

Egypt under the Arabs (A.D. 640–1517). The country fell under the influence of those social customs which are inextricably bound up with the Muslim religion; conditions which from 1517 onwards were further enforced under Ottoman rule (Ch. XXXIII).

Egypt then passed in the nineteenth century first under French influence and later, in 1881, it became virtually a British Protectorate. From 1914 her destinies were presided over by a Sultan under British protection, and at length in 1922 Egypt became an independent State.

HISTORICAL. Historical influences, as distinct from internal and social, are here considered as arising from military and commercial contact with other countries. It is interesting to observe that historical events are generally recorded on temples, and social matters on tombs. Under social influences we have sketched the successive dynasties and have indicated those kings whose personality left the greatest impression upon their country. It now therefore only remains to show the salient historical or external events and foreign wars which were factors in Egyptian development. The earliest historical incidents are naturally connected with the land nearest to the Egyptian borders, i.e. the Sudan, the country of the Nubians or Ethiopians. The Palermo Stele tells us that Seneferu, first king of the Fourth Dynasty, raided the Sudan and brought back prisoners and loot from that vast territory which is the Biblical Cush, and which, during the Middle Kingdom, was finally conquered and, with its gold, copper and turquoise mines, added to the realm of Egypt. Mentuhetep IV sent a force of ten thousand on a campaign in the eastern desert, and a few years later, the masterful Amenemhat I, founder of the Twelfth Dynasty, subjugated four tribes in the coveted Sudan. His son, Senusret I, exacted tribute there, worked the copper mines and built a fort and a temple at Wadi Halfa; while Senusret III finally conquered that country and built forts along the Nile to protect the transport of gold. The latter also made a determined sally into Palestine. Various kings sent expeditions to Sinai for copper, that territory having been exploited by Egypt from early dynastic times. Later, the incursions of nomadic tribes resulted in centuries of hated Hyksos rule and there were often two rival kings, till after years of strife the usurpers were finally expelled and pursued into Syria by Amasis I. He restored Nubia to Egypt and exacted more tribute, as did also the next three Pharaohs. Egyptian power penetrated too into Western Asia as far as the Euphrates. Queen Hatshepsut carried out a trade expedition to 'Punt' (perhaps in south-west Arabia) to secure ebony, ivory, gold and myrrh for temple service and for the embalming of the dead; the story of the expedition is recorded on the walls of her temple at Dêr el-Bahari. The mighty warrior Thothmes III waged victorious wars in Phoenicia, in the upper Euphrates valley and in the Sudan, and the treasure he secured was devoted to temple building, including a great Hall of Columns at Karnak, where his successes are proudly recorded. So wars went on against Syria and Nubia till Amenophis III, the Memnon of the Greeks, declared himself to be not only the conqueror, but also the god of Nubia. He carried on friendly intercourse with Asia, and through inter-marriage introduced a foreign element into Egypt, which largely found expression in the monotheistic tendencies of his son Amenophis IV, later to call himself Akhnaten, who forsook Ammon, King of Gods, and worshipped Aten as the sole god. Akhnaten's religious bigotry brought him into stern conflict with the priesthood, whose power it was part of his policy to check; but though tenacious in his religious opinions and gifted as a builder, his rule was disastrously weak, and he came to be execrated in later years if not already in his own time. He built a fine new capital at Tell el-Amarna in central Egypt, but while he was busy building it and a temple for the god of his choice, he lost hold over the Empire in Asia. Years later, Seti I reverted to raids on the Sudan for gold and expeditions to Sinai for copper, and successfully clashed with the Hittites, then dominant in Syria. His activities were emulated by his son, Rameses II, the Great, who after bitter struggles came to amicable terms with the Hittites over rights in Syria, and joined in a treaty which brought peace to nearer Asia for some fifty years, the residue of Rameses' long reign.

Meneptah, who succeeded him, quashed a revolt in Palestine, but found sterner work in resisting the inroads of the Libyans, on the west. Egypt then suffered internal dynastic and social troubles for a decade or two. Rameses III vigorously restored order again, but had to withstand the ferocious attacks upon Egypt by a confederation of 'Peoples of the Sea', displaced from the northern parts of the Mediterranean by pressure from still farther north. Both by land and sea, Rameses conquered these militant hosts. Nevertheless, Egypt thereafter gradually declined in vigour till the end of the Twentieth Dynasty. Government was poor or bad, and the populace went increasingly in need, so that in the reign of Rameses IX, tomb robbery and the desecration of temples were rife. Decadence and the disintegration of effective control were the keynotes too, of the Twenty-first Dynasty. Then in the Twenty-second, Shishak I, a chieftain of Libyan origin, ushered in a Libyan royal succession which, though split for a long period into two overlapping dynasties, endured for over two hundred years. Shishak I, a capable leader, had re-established Egyptian rule in Syria, Nubia and Palestine, and pillaged Jerusalem. The Nubians, constituting the Twenty-fifth Dynasty, next seized the succession; but the Assyrian Empire now threatened the peace of Egypt and Esarhaddon defeated the Egyptians and took Memphis (671 B.C.), while Ashurbanipal, his son, invaded the country and sacked Thebes (663 B.C.). The withdrawal of the Nubian rulers into their own lands left the kingdom to Psammetichus I, founder of the last notable independent Egyptian dynasty, the Twenty-sixth (663–525 B.C.). Psammetichus began his reign as a mere vassal of Assyria, but with the help of Greek and other mercenaries he threw off the foreign yoke and chased the Assyrians into Palestine. Prosperity was restored and, again with much Greek help, trade re-established. This commercial intercourse introduced new ideas, and once more the Delta, with Sais as the capital, became the centre of Egyptian power. Necho (609 B.C.) emulated his father in supporting trade and briefly re-conquered Syria, but retired after a disastrous encounter with Nebuchadnezzar. Prosperity attended the following reigns, and art flourished, emulating the characteristics of Ancient Kingdom masterpieces. Then, in 525 B.C., Egypt fell under Persian rule. Cambyses II dethroned Psammetichus III, who had reigned for scarcely a year, and for well over a hundred years, Egypt was a Persian province, prosperous under Darius, oppressed under Xerxes the Great, and in revolt under Artaxerxes I. Egyptian resistance secured eventual success by the opportunism of Amyrtis, the only Pharaoh of the Twenty-eighth Dynasty (404–398 B.C.). Two further dynasties of uneasy rule followed, with eight kings in less than sixty years, concluding with the defeat of the last native Pharaoh, Nectanebus II, and succeeded by a second, though brief, Persian domination (341–332 B.C.). In the latter year, Alexander the Great, having conquered Darius III, was invited to undertake the protection of Egypt and was hailed by the populace as saviour and as the son of Ammon. His capital, Alexandria, became the centre for Greek scholars and artists, and under the new impetus, architecture and the arts flourished again.

The first of the Ptolemies, the Greek general who succeeded Alexander, encouraged the influx of Jewish traders, and this increased the prosperity of the country. So the tale of the Ptolemies went on with occasional wars and expeditions, but it came about that Ptolemy XIII and his wife and sister Cleopatra were, in the will of their royal father, placed under the protection of Rome. Court intrigues and trouble with Rome followed, with the ultimate result that Egypt was declared a Roman province (30 B.C.). So Greek officials gave way to Roman, and Egypt was exploited as the granary of Rome, while Nubia was invaded for her mineral wealth. Nero even succeeded in diverting via Egypt the trade from India and Arabia. Under Nero too, it is said that Christianity first reached Egypt, where it soon entered on many conflicts and, as elsewhere, suffered many vicissitudes. At times, many Christian or Coptic churches were either erected or adapted, and by the time of Hadrian, architecture had assumed a Graeco-Roman style. During the reign of Constantine the Great (A.D. 324–337) the government of Egypt was reorganized, and on the division of the Roman Empire, Egypt came under the Eastern Emperor at Constantinople. Under Justinian (A.D. 527–565), a new and more stable administration was formed, but in A.D. 616 the country was captured by the Persians, and in A.D. 640 passed to the Muslims, whose architecture is described later (Ch. XXXIII). Art in Ancient Egypt continued strangely unchanged through the various phases of foreign influence from Assyria, Persia, Greece, and Rome; and, through all, the indigenous architecture maintained that solemn dignity so suited to the immense stretches of surrounding desert.

ARCHITECTURAL CHARACTER

Ancient Egyptian architecture was carried on, as far as the historical period is concerned, from about 3000 B.C. to the first century of the Christian Era.

The primitive architecture in the valley of the Nile consisted of readily-available tractable materials like reeds, papyrus (now practically extinct) and palm-branch ribs, plastered over with clay. With bundles of stems placed vertically side by side and lashed to a bundle placed horizontally near the top, walls or fences could be made. Alternatively, palm-leaf ribs were planted in the ground at short intervals, with others laced in a diagonal network across them and secured to a horizontal member near the top, the whole being daubed with mud afterwards. Buildings with circular plans could have domical coverings of similar construction, or, if rectangular, could have a tunnel-shaped covering or a flat roof. The pressure of the flat reed-and-mud roofs against the tops of the wall reeds may have produced the characteristic Egyptian 'gorge' cornice (p. 55J), while the 'kheker' cresting less frequently appearing in later architecture may have originated in the terminal tufts of a papyrus-stalk wall (p. 55B). The horizontal binders and angle bundles survived in the roll moulding of stone cornices and wall angles of the historic period (p. 55J). A type of pavilion or kiosk which came to have a special religious significance in connection with the 'Heb-sed' or jubilee festivals of the Pharaohs—though originally commonly used on Nile boats as well as on land—consisted of a light, rectangular structure, open-fronted and with a porch carried on two slender angle-shafts and having a slab-like roof arching from the back to the front. In the Heb-sed ceremony, held at definite intervals of years in the king's reign, the Pharaoh seated himself on a throne beneath such an awning, raised on a high podium and approached by a flight of steps at the front. Timber, once quite plentiful, also was used for the better buildings, in square, heavy vertical plates, lapping one in front of the other and producing an effect of composite buttresses joined at the head and enframing narrow panels, in the upper parts of which window-vents might occur. Palm logs, rounded on the underside, were sometimes used for roofs. All these various forms of construction produced their effects on matured art and architecture, and apart from timber, which had become scarce by dynastic times, never entirely went out of use. Stone was not much employed before the Third Dynasty, except as rubble and as a stiffening or foundation to mud solid walls. Sun-dried mud-brick walling never ceased to be employed, for it was only for the finest buildings of religious character that cut stone became normal. Even palaces remained always relatively frail, for it was the after-life and not the present which dominated Egyptian contemplation. Made of Nile mud and mixed with chopped straw or sand, and thoroughly matured by exposure to the sun, the mud bricks were very lasting. They were large, approximating to 14 ins long by 7 ins wide and 4 ins thick. For stability, walls diminished course by course towards the top, chiefly because of the alternate shrinkage and expansion of the soil caused by the annual inundation. As the inner face of the walls had to be vertical for ordinary convenience, it was the outer face only which showed this inward inclination, or 'batter', which remained throughout one of the principal characteristics of Egyptian architecture whether in brick or stone. Sometimes fibre or reed mats were placed between the brick courses at intervals up the walls, to reinforce them, particularly at a building's angles; and a late development was the use of sagging concave courses, for alternate lengths of a long wall, built in advance of the intervening stretches, to allow of the drying out of the inner brickwork, since walls such as those around the great temple enclosures were very thick, between thirty and eighty feet. Though the true arch was never used in monumental stonework, the principle was known very early on. There are brick vaults as early as the beginning of the Third Dynasty. Frequently, the arch rings were built in sloping courses, so that no 'centering' or temporary support was needed, and usually, there were two or more arched rings arranged concentrically, the one lying upon the other. The Romans adopted the method of building arches in concentric, superposed rings, though they did not slope them but used centering in the normal way. The surface decoration of the masonry walls is also held to have been derived from the practice of scratching pictures on the early mud-plaster walls, which manifestly did not lend themselves to modelled or projecting ornament, though their flat and windowless surfaces were eminently suitable for incised relief and explanatory hieroglyphs (pp. 54, 56)—a method of popular teaching which has its parallel in the sculptured façades and stained-glass windows of mediaeval cathedrals. Egyptian columns (p. 55) have a distinctive character, and a very large proportion of them plainly advertise their vegetable origin, their shafts indicative of bundles of plant stems, gathered in a little at the base, and with capitals seemingly derived from the lotus bud (p. 55G) or the papyrus flower (p. 55C), or representing the ubiquitous palm.

Egyptian monumental architecture, which is essentially a columnar and trabeated style, is expressed mainly in pyramids and other tombs and in temples, in contrast to the West Asiatic, its nearest in age, in which tombs are insignificant and spacious palaces assume an importance rivalling that of temple structure. Egyptian temples (p. 38), approached by impressive avenues of sphinxes—mythical monsters, each with the body of a lion and the head of a man, hawk, ram, or woman—possess in their massive pylons, great courts, hypostyle halls, inner sanctuaries and dim, secret rooms, a special character; for typically, temples grew by accretion or replacement according to the increasing requirements of a powerful priesthood, or to satisfy the pious ambition of successive kings. Greek temples were each planned as one homogeneous whole, to shelter the statue of a god, and the component parts were all essential to the complete design, while some of the greatest Egyptian temples were but a string of successive buildings diminishing in height behind their imposing pylons (p. 38E).

Egyptian architecture persistently maintained its traditions, and when necessity dictated a change in methods of construction or in the materials used, the traditional forms, hallowed by long use, were perpetuated in spite of novel conditions. It is impressive by its solemnity and gloom as well as by its ponderous solidity, which suggests that the buildings were intended to last eternally. The idea is not without foundation when we realize that the avowed purpose of the pyramids was not only to preserve the mummy of the Pharaoh for the return of the soul in the infinite hereafter, but also to be the centre of the cult of the royal dead, and, by consequence, the dominant element of the vast monumental complex.

EXAMPLES

TOMB ARCHITECTURE

The tombs were of three main types: (a) Mastabas, (b) Royal Pyramids, and (c) Rock-hewn tombs.

(a) *Mastabas.* Since the Ancient Egyptians believed so strongly in an after life,

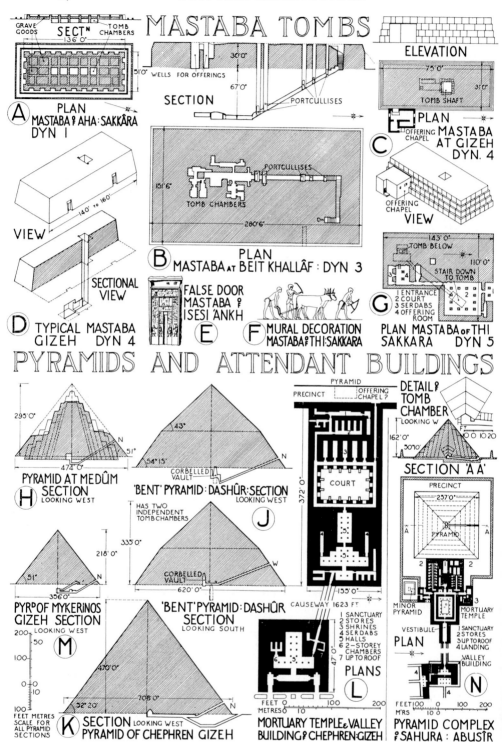

MASTABA TOMBS

SECTN GRAVE GOODS · TOMB CHAMBERS
136'0"
51'0"

A PLAN
MASTABA of AHA : SAKKÂRA
DYN I

WELLS FOR OFFERINGS
30'0"
67'0"
SECTION
PORTCULLISES

ELEVATION
75'0"
31'0"
TOMB SHAFT

PLAN MASTABA
AT GIZEH
DYN. 4
OFFERING CHAPEL

C

151'6"
PORTCULLISES
TOMB CHAMBERS
280'6"

B PLAN
MASTABA at BEIT KHALLÂF : DYN 3

OFFERING CHAPEL
VIEW

VIEW
140' to 160'

SECTIONAL VIEW

D TYPICAL MASTABA
GIZEH DYN 4

E FALSE DOOR
MASTABA of
ISESI 'ANKH

F MURAL DECORATION
MASTABA of THI : SAKKARA

TOMB BELOW
143'0"
110'0"
STAIR DOWN TO TOMB
1 ENTRANCE
2 COURT
3 SERDABS
4 OFFERING ROOM

G PLAN MASTABA of THI
SAKKARA DYN 5

PYRAMIDS AND ATTENDANT BUILDINGS

295'0"
N
51°
474'0"

H PYRAMID AT MEDÛM
SECTION
LOOKING WEST

143°
54°15'
CORBELLED VAULT
N

J 'BENT' PYRAMID : DASHÛR : SECTION
LOOKING WEST

HAS TWO INDEPENDENT TOMB CHAMBERS
335'0"
620'0"
CORBELLED VAULT
N

'BENT' PYRAMID : DASHÛR
SECTION
LOOKING SOUTH

PYRAMID
PRECINCT
OFFERING CHAPEL?
372'0"
COURT
155'0"

DETAIL of
TOMB CHAMBER
LOOKING W
162'0"
30'10"
FT 0 0 10 20

SECTION 'AA'

PRECINCT
257'0"
PYRAMID
A ————— A

218'0"
51°
356'0"
N

M PYRP OF MYKERINOS
GIZEH SECTION
LOOKING WEST

200
50
100
0 0
10
100
FEET METRES
SCALE FOR ALL PYRAMID SECTIONS

470'0"
32°20'
708'0"
N

K SECTION LOOKING WEST
PYRAMID OF CHEPHREN GIZEH

CAUSEWAY 1623 FT

47'0"
1 SANCTUARY
2 STORES
3 SHRINES
4 SERDABS
5 HALLS
6 2-STOREY CHAMBERS
7 UP TO ROOF

PLANS

L
FEET 0   100   200
METRES 0   10

**MORTUARY TEMPLE & VALLEY
BUILDING of CHEPHREN GIZEH**

MINOR PYRAMID
MORTUARY TEMPLE
VESTIBULE
1 SANCTUARY
2 STORES
3 UP TO ROOF
4 LANDING
PLAN
VALLEY BUILDING

N
FEET 100   0   100   200
M'RS   10   0

**PYRAMID COMPLEX
of SAHURA : ABUSÎR**

they did their utmost, each according to his means, to build lasting tombs, to preserve the body, and to bury with it the finest commodities that might be needed
for the sustenance and eternal enjoyment of the deceased. Embalming was initiated
during, if not before, the Third Dynasty and reached the highest perfection in the
Eighteenth. It seems that in the Ancient Kingdom, the king and other principal
personages might have two tombs, purporting to stand one in the Upper and one
in the Lower of the two kingdoms united by Menes, the first of the Pharaohs. Only
one tomb, of course, could take the real burial and the other would be the cenotaph. There is an important early necropolis at Sakkâra, and another at Abydos,
much higher up the Nile.

By the First Dynasty, the more elaborate graves had come to simulate house
plans of several small rooms, a central one containing the sarcophagus and others
surrounding it to receive the abundant funerary offerings (p. 24A). The whole was
constructed in a broad pit below ground, the wooden roof being supported by
timber posts or crude brick pillars and the entire area covered by a rectangular,
flat-topped mound of the spoil from the excavation, retained in place by very thick
brick walls. The outer faces were either serrated with alternate buttress-like projections and narrow recesses—the so-called 'palace façade' arrangement, derived
from timber panelling—or plain, and sloped backwards at an angle of about 75
degrees. Such tombs are nowadays known as mastabas, from their resemblance to
the low benches built outside the Egyptian modern house. Closely surrounding
them was an enclosure wall.

Typical of the Second and Third Dynasties is the 'stairway' mastaba, the tomb
chamber, with its attendant magazines, having been sunk much deeper and cut in
the rock below (p. 24B). Normally, the main axis of the tomb lay north and south,
and steps and ramps led from the north end of the top of the mastaba to connect
with a shaft which descended to the level of the tomb chamber. After the burial,
heavy stone portcullises were dropped across the approach from slots built to receive them, and this was then filled in and all surface traces removed. Externally,
the imitation of panelling was usually abandoned in favour of the plain battered
sides, except that there were two well-spaced recesses on the east long side. This
was the front towards the Nile. The southernmost of the two recesses was a false
door (p. 24E), allowing the spirit of the deceased to enter or leave at will, and in
front of it was a table for the daily offerings of fresh food.

It was here that about the Fourth Dynasty a small offering chapel developed,
tacked on to the mastaba, or an offering room was constructed within the mastaba
itself (p. 24C). Tomb chambers were sunk more deeply still, approached by a
short horizontal passage from a vertical shaft sunk from the north end of the top
of the superstructure. There are many such 'shaft' mastabas at Gizeh (p. 24D). By
this time the majority of the mastabas were of limestone, which had been used only
sparingly for floors and wall linings in the finest of the brick mastabas of early
dynastic times. With the Fifth and Sixth Dynasties the offering room or chapel at
ground level tended to become increasingly elaborate (p. 24F, G). In the most
sumptuous examples, there might be a group of rooms, within or adjacent to the
mastaba mound, including a columned hall, the walls lined with vividly-coloured
reliefs, depicting scenes from the daily life of the deceased. Important among the
rooms was the 'serdab'—sometimes there was more than one—completely enclosed except for a slot opposite the head of a statue of the deceased contained
within. In the offering room was a 'stele', an upright stone slab inscribed with the
name of the deceased, funerary texts and relief carvings intended to serve in the
event of failure in the supply of daily offerings. An offering-table stood at its foot.

The **Mastaba of Aha, Sakkâra** (p. 24A), second king of the First Dynasty, takes the form of a shallow pit, subdivided by crude-brick walls into five chambers, the centre one for the body of the king and the others for his intimate possessions. Above them, the brick superstructure covered a broader area and had twenty-seven compartments containing other grave goods, including jars for foodstuffs, ceiled with timber and covered with brick or débris. The exterior had the so-called 'panelled' or 'palace-façade' decoration of serrated vertical projections and recèses, and was closely surrounded by two girdle walls.

The **Mastaba K. 1 at Beit Khallaf** (p. 24B) is a massive 'stairway' tomb of crude brick, typical of the Third Dynasty. The stairs and ramp, guarded by five stone portcullises, lead to a rock-cut, stone-lined tomb chamber surrounded by a knot of magazines for the funerary offerings. Above ground, the mastaba is plain and virtually solid.

The **Mastabas at Gizeh,** mostly of the Fourth and Fifth Dynasties, number two or three hundred, arranged in orderly ranks, and adjoin the famous pyramids there (pp. 13, 24C, D, 31A). Fourth Dynasty examples illustrate, on the one hand, the development of the offering chapel (p. 24C), and on the other, the typical 'shaft' mastaba (p. 24D) with deep, underground tomb chambers and a sloping-sided superstructure having two widely spaced recesses on the long east side, the southern of which served as a false door (p. 24E) and for offerings.

The **Mastaba of Thi, Sakkâra** (p. 24G), a high dignitary of the Fifth Dynasty, has all the elaboration of its time. A large pillared court is attached to the north end of the east side, approached from the north by a portico which has a serdab along-side. A passage connects the court with a small chamber and an offering-room, with two pillars, lying inside the mastaba itself. This is equipped with two stelae and an offering-table against the west wall; and south of it is a second serdab, with three slots through the intervening wall corresponding with the three duplicate statues of Thi enclosed there. The low-relief sculptures of this tomb are among the finest and most interesting in Egypt (p. 24F). The actual tomb chamber is below the south end of the mastaba, behind the west wall of the offering-room but at a much lower level. It is reached from a passage slanting diagonally to connect with a stair-way emerging in the centre of the court.

(*b*) *Royal Pyramids.* The great pyramids of the Third to Sixth Dynasties are on sites distributed intermittently along the west side of the Nile for about fifty miles southward of the apex of the Delta, standing on the rocky shelf clear of the culti-vated land. Early royal tombs were of the mastaba type, from which the true pyramid evolved, the most important stages being demonstrated by the early Third Dynasty 'Step' pyramid of the Pharaoh Zoser at Sakkâra (pp. 27–30). Further stages of development are marked by one at Meydûm and by two at Dahshûr by Seneferu, first king of the Fourth Dynasty, including the so-called 'Bent' pyramid. The finest true pyramids are the famous three at Gizeh, built by the Fourth Dynasty succes-sors of Seneferu. Pyramids did not stand in solitary isolation but were the primary part of a complex of buildings. They were surrounded by a walled enclosure, had (i) an offering chapel, with a stele, usually abutting the east side of the pyramid but occasionally on the north; (ii) a mortuary temple for the worship of the dead and deified Pharaoh, on the north side in Zoser's complex but normally projecting from the enclosure on the east side; (iii) a raised and enclosed causeway leading to the nearer, western edge of the cultivation where stood (iv) a 'Valley Building' in which embalmment was carried out and interment rites performed. A canal was built to connect the Valley Building with the Nile, by which the funeral cortège magnificently arrived. Pyramids were built with immense outlay in labour and material, in the lifetime of the Pharaohs concerned, to secure the preservation of the body after death till that time should have passed when, according to their belief in immortality, the soul would once more return to the body. Infinite pains were taken to conceal and protect the tomb chamber and its contents, as well as the approach passages, but all precautions proved to be vain, for they were successively rifled first in the period of chaos which followed the Sixth Dynasty and again in the Persian, Roman and Arab periods. Pyramids were founded on the living rock, levelled to receive them, and were of limestone quarried in their locality, faced with the finer limestone coming from Tura on the opposite, eastern, side of the Nile. Granite, in limited use for such as the linings of the chambers and passages, was brought from up-river at Aswân. Tomb chambers and their approaches were either cut in the rock below the monument or were in its constructed core. Entrances normally were from the north side and the sides were scrupulously orientated with the cardinal points. In all known cases, pyramids were built in a series of concentric sloping slices or layers, around a steep pyramidal core, so that the whole mass first appeared in step-like tiers; until, in the case of the true pyramidal form, the steps had been filled in with packing blocks and brought with finely finished facings to their ultimate shape, at the chosen angle of inclination. Nevertheless, all the inner layers were built more or less at the same time, course by course, so that as it proceeded, the top was always approximately level. The final meticulous dressing of the finished faces was from top to bottom, and the apex stone probably was gilded. The Egyptians did not know of the pulley, and their principal tool for raising and turning stone blocks was the lever. To transport them overland, wooden sledges were used, with or without the aid of rollers dropped in turn in front of a sledge and picked up again behind. Blocks for the pyramids were hauled up great broad-topped, sloping ramps of sand or earth, reinforced with crude brick walls, such ramps being placed at right angles to the most convenient of the faces.

The **Step Pyramid of Zoser, Sakkâra** (2778 B.C., beginning of Third Dynasty) (pp. 28, 29) is remarkable as being the world's first large-scale monument in stone. King Zoser's architect, Imhotep, was greatly revered both in his own and later times, and in the Twenty-sixth Dynasty was deified. The pyramid itself shows no less than five changes of plan in the course of building. It began as a complete mastaba, 26 ft high, unusual in having a square plan, of 207 ft side. It was then twice extended, first by a regular addition of 14 ft to each of its sloping sides and next by an extension eastwards of 28 ft. At this stage the whole was used as a basis for a four-stepped pyramid, made up of layers inclined against a steep-sided core, and again enlarged at the same time so that its plan became a rectangle of about 272 ft by 244 ft. A further enormous addition on the north and west, followed by a quite slight one all round, brought it to its final dimensions of 411 ft from east to west by 358 ft wide and 200 ft high, and added two more steps to the height, making six in all. In this stepped form it remained. Usually, underground tomb chambers were finished before the superstructure had been begun, but there were here two stages owing to the successive enlargements above. A pit of 24 ft side and 28 ft deep was the counterpart of the first mastaba, approached by a horizontal tunnel emerging at the north side in an open ramp; but this pit was deepened to 92 ft at the pyramid stage of development, and had an Aswân granite tomb chamber at the bottom above which was a limestone-walled room containing a granite plug to stop a hole at the top of the tomb-chamber when the burial had been completed. The approach tunnel too was deepened and converted to a ramp entering the pit at a point some 70 ft above its base. From the bottom of the pit four corridors extend irregularly towards the four cardinal points, connecting to galleries running in approximate parallel with the four sides of the pyramid, and having spur galleries thrusting from them. Independent of the main subterranean system is a

A. Restored view of the pyramid and enclosure from the flooded Nile valley

B. Aerial view of the pyramid and enclosure (restored model)

C. Processional corridor (restored)   D. Angle of great court

Step Pyramid, Sakkâra (2778 B.C.). See p. 27

STEP PYRAMID OF ZOSER : SAKKARA

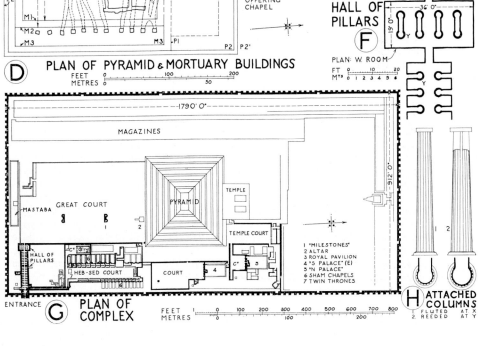

A ROYAL PAVILION (3) & S.W. END OF HEB·SED COURT

ROYAL PAVILION 3
COURT

DUMMY CHAPELS 6

FT MT'S

CASING

200' 0"

P1 & P2   P1

P2

P2'
P1&P2'   M1
M2

M1
M2

C SECTION LOOKING WEST

B 'KHEKER' & COBRA CRESTINGS

D PLAN OF PYRAMID & MORTUARY BUILDINGS

358' 0"

P2'
P2

P1

M2
M1

207' 0"

410' 0"

207' 0"

P1&2
P2'

M1

M2
M3

M3   P1

P2   P2'

MORTUARY TEMPLE

COURT

COURT

ENTᶜᴱ
OFFERING CHAPEL

FEET   100   200
METRES 0   50

E SOUTH PALACE PART PLAN

FEET 0   10
MT'S 0

ELEVATION

50' 0"

F HALL OF PILLARS

PLAN: W. ROOM

36' 0"

19' 0"

Y

Y

FT 0   10   20
MT'S 0 1 2 3 4 5 6

G PLAN OF COMPLEX

1790' 0"

MAGAZINES

GREAT COURT

MASTABA

PYRAMID

TEMPLE

912' 0"

HALL OF PILLARS

HEB·SED COURT

COURT

TEMPLE COURT

ENTRANCE

1 "MILESTONES"
2 ALTAR
3 ROYAL PAVILION
4 "S PALACE" (E)
5 "N PALACE"
6 SHAM CHAPELS
7 TWIN THRONES

FEET   0   100 200 300 400 500 600 700 800
METRES 0   100   200

H ATTACHED COLUMNS
1 FLUTED   AT X
2 REEDED   AT Y

1   2

series of eleven separate pits, 106 ft deep, on the east side of the original mastaba. These were tombs of members of the royal family. The tomb entrances were sealed by the third extension of the mastaba.

Surrounding the pyramid was a vast rectangular enclosure, 1790 ft from north to south and 912 ft wide, with a massive Tura limestone wall, 35 ft high, indented in the manner of the earlier mastaba façades (pp. 28, 29). Around the walls were bastions, fourteen in all, and each had stone false doors. The only entrance was in a broader bastion near the southern end of the eastern face. In the fact that there is a small offering chapel (with stelae, offering table and a statue of Zoser) and a well-developed mortuary temple, containing two courts, a maze of corridors and many rooms, the buildings inside the enclosure show some relation to earlier developments of the mastaba; but these two buildings abut the north face of the pyramid, instead of the east as was to be the common practice, and all the rest of the structures are quite exceptional and unique to this complex. They are dummy representations of the palace of Zoser and the buildings used in connection with the celebration of his jubilee in his lifetime. Most of them therefore are solid, or almost so, comprised of earth or débris faced with Tura limestone. They are grouped around courts. The entrance to the great enclosure leads to a long processional corridor lined with reeded columns—this site provides the only known instances of the type—which bore architraves and a roof of long stones shaped on the underside like timber logs (p. 28C). At the inner end of the corridor is a pillared hall, with reeded columns attached in pairs, beyond which is the Great Court (p. 29D), where there are two low B-shaped pedestals, used in the royal ceremonial, an altar near the pyramid south face and, on the south side of the court, a mastaba, unusually aligned east-west. Just inside the enclosure entrance a narrow corridor runs deviously northwards to the Heb-sed Court, the principal scene of this festival, lined with sham chapels, each with its small forecourt, those on the western side representing the provinces or 'nomes' of Upper Egypt and those on the eastern, of Lower Egypt. These virtually solid structures had segmental-arched roofs; as also had two similarly-solid large halls of unequal sizes farther north, each facing southwards into its own court and which might have symbolized the two kingdoms. The façades of all of them, chapels and halls, bore three slender, attached columns. Near to the Heb-sed Court, to the west, is the so-called 'Royal Pavilion', within which are three fluted, attached columns. In Zoser's complex as a whole, the masonry technique and the almost total absence of free-standing columns, together with the small spans of the stone beam roofs, indicates the novelty of stone as a building material at this time. The architectural forms show clearly their derivation variously from earlier structure in reeds, timber or sun-dried brick.

The **Pyramid at Meydûm** (p. 24H) is attributed to Huni, last king of the Third Dynasty. Though eventually completed as a true pyramid, it is definitely known that at one stage it was a seven-stepped structure, contrived by building six thick layers of masonry, each faced with Tura limestone, against a nucleus with sides sloping steeply at 75°; and that there was then an addition of a fresh layer all round, raising the number of steps to eight. These again were faced with Tura limestone, dressed only where the faces showed. Thus both the seven- and the eight-step pyramids had at the time been regarded as finished. But there was yet a further development, in which the steps were packed out and the sides made smooth with finely-dressed Tura stone. Of this ultimate true pyramid, 476 ft square on base and 298 ft high, with sides sloping at 51°, the lower portion still survives, but the upper part has been oddly denuded into a shouldered, tower-like structure. The simple, corbel-roofed tomb chamber was at ground-level in the heart of the

Pyramid of
Mykerinos

Pyramid of
Chephren

Pyramid of
Cheops

A. The Pyramids, Gizeh: aerial view from S.E., with the Sphinx and Valley Building of Chephren in the middle foreground (*c.* 2723–2563 B.C.). See pp. 32–35

B. Tombs at Beni Hasan (2130–1785 B.C.). See p. 35

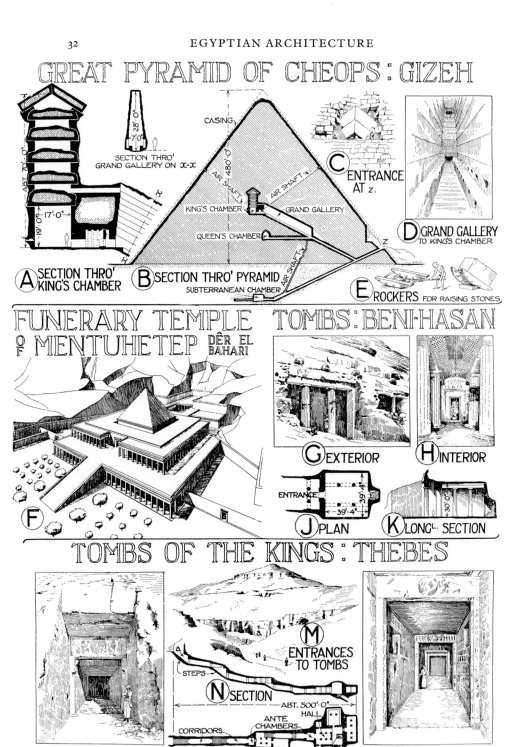

GREAT PYRAMID OF CHEOPS : GIZEH

SECTION THRO' GRAND GALLERY ON X-X

CASING

AIR SHAFT

KING'S CHAMBER

GRAND GALLERY

AIR SHAFT

QUEEN'S CHAMBER

AIR SHAFT

ABT 70' O"

480' O"

7'28' O"
7' O"

17' O"
19' O"

A SECTION THRO' KING'S CHAMBER

B SECTION THRO' PYRAMID
SUBTERRANEAN CHAMBER

C ENTRANCE AT z.

D GRAND GALLERY TO KING'S CHAMBER

E ROCKERS FOR RAISING STONES

FUNERARY TEMPLE OF MENTUHETEP DÊR EL BAHARI

F

TOMBS : BENI-HASAN

G EXTERIOR

H INTERIOR

J PLAN   ENTRANCE   39'·4"

K LONG.L SECTION   30' O"

TOMBS OF THE KINGS : THEBES

L ENTRANCE TO A TOMB : THEBES

M ENTRANCES TO TOMBS

N SECTION
STEPS
ABT. 500'· O"
HALL
CORRIDORS
ANTE CHAMBERS
TO MUMMY SHAFT

P PLAN : TOMB OF SETI · I

Q ENTRANCE TO TOMB OF RAMESES · IX

masonry. Around the pyramid was a stone enclosure wall, 764 ft from north to south, by 686 ft, within which were a small pyramid on the south side and a mastaba on the north. Also, in the normal position abutting the centre of the east face of the pyramid, was a small offering-chapel, with an offering-table, flanked by two stelae, in its inner small court. There was no mortuary temple, but a causeway from the eastern wall led to the Valley Building, now submerged.

The **Bent, or South Pyramid of Seneferu,** Dahshûr (2723 B.C.) (p. 24J) has the peculiarities, firstly, that the angle of inclination of the sides changes about half-way up from 54° 15′ in the lower part to 43° in the upper, where it shows hasty completion; and secondly that it has two entirely independent tomb chambers, reached one from the north side and one from the west. The change in slope had the object of lightening the weight of the upper masonry, as the walls of chambers and passages began to show fissures. The plan is square, 620 ft, and the height about 320 ft, the materials being the usual local stone with Tura limestone facing, well-preserved. The tomb-chambers are covered by corbelled roofs with gradually in-stepping courses from all four sides, that over the lower chamber concluding with a 1 ft span some 80 ft above the floor. Corbelling, as instanced here and at Meydûm, is thus one of the earliest experimental devices for constructing a stone vault. Around the pyramid there was a double-walled rectangular enclosure, an offering chapel and a mortuary temple on the east side and a causeway leading to the Valley Building. The subsidiary structures here probably provide the first instance of what was to be the customary complement and arrangement.

The **North Pyramid of Seneferu,** Dahshûr, made after the abandonment of the Bent Pyramid, was the actual place of burial of Seneferu, for nearby are tombs of the royal family and officiating priests; also, it was designed and completed as a true pyramid, the earliest known. The pitch of its sides, however, is unusually low; 43° 36′, instead of the usual 52° or so, and thus is very similar to that of the upper part of the Bent Pyramid. For the rest the pyramid is normal. The attendant buildings are being excavated.

The **Great Pyramid of Cheops** (Khufu), **near Cairo,** (pp. 13, 31A, 32). Cheops was the son of Seneferu, and the second king of the Fourth Dynasty. His pyramid, largest of the famous three on this site, was originally 480 ft high and 756 ft square on plan, with an area of about 13 acres, or more than twice that of S. Peter, Rome. The four sides, which, as in all periods with only a minor exception, face the cardinal points, are nearly equilateral triangles and make an angle of 51° 52′ with the ground. There are three separate internal chambers, due to changes of plan in the course of building. The subterranean chamber and the so-called 'Queen's Chamber' are discarded projects, abandoned in turn in favour of the 'King's Chamber' where the granite sarcophagus is located. The entrance is 24 ft off-centre on the north side, and 55 ft above ground level, measured vertically, leading to a corridor descending at about 26° to the original rock-cut chamber. In this descending corridor, after the first change of plan, an ascending corridor was cut in the ceiling, about 60 ft along, rising to some 70 ft above ground, at which level the Queen's Chamber was constructed. But before it was entirely completed, the approach was sealed off and the ascending corridor extended into what is now known as the Grand Gallery (p. 32D), a passage 7 ft wide and 7 ft 6 ins high, covered by a ramped, corbelled vault of seven great courses, rising to a height of 28 ft vertically from the floor, where the surviving span of 3 ft 6 ins is closed by stone slabs. At the top, the Grand Gallery gave on to the King's Chamber (17 ft 2 ins from north to south, 34 ft 4 ins long and 19 ft high) which like its vestibule, is lined in granite. In the vestibule there were originally three massive granite slabs, let down in slots in the side walls to seal the chamber after the burial. The covering

B

of the chamber is most elaborate. Five tiers of great stone beams, nine to a tier and together weighing about 400 tons, are ranged one above the other, with a void space between the layers. Above them all is an embryonic vault of pairs of great stones inclined against one another. This latter device occurs also over the Queen's Chamber and again over the pyramid entrance, where just within the former casing there are pairs of inclined stones superposed in two tiers (p. 32C). Two shafts (8 ins × 6 ins) which lead from the King's Chamber to the outer face of the pyramid may have been for ventilation or to allow the free passage of the Ka or spirit of the dead king. There are similar shafts from the Queen's Chamber, left incomplete like the chamber itself. Built solidly of local stone, the pyramid originally was cased in finely-dressed Tura limestone blocks and the apex stone perhaps gilded, but only a few stones at the base now survive. The average weight of blocks is 2½ tons; they are bedded in a thin lime-mortar, used as a lubricant during fixing rather than as an adhesive, laid with amazingly fine joints. Little trace of the pyramid enclosure wall now exists, nor does there much remain of the customary attendant buildings. The offering chapel abutted the centre of the pyramid east face, and the mortuary temple stood axially in front of it, joined by a causeway which led askew eastwards towards the Valley Building. Flanking the temple on east and west are two boat-shaped pits cut in the rock, and there is a third alongside the north flank of the causeway. Whether these actually contained wooden boats for the king's transport in his after life is not definitely known. In A.D. 1954 two more pits were discovered adjacent to the south side of the pyramid, covered with stone beams as originally the others had been, in which wooden boats, 115 ft long, were disclosed intact and in a remarkably fine state of preservation. At a little distance south-east of the east face of the pyramid are three subsidiary pyramids, with chapels on their own east sides, tombs of Cheops' queens.

The **Pyramid of Chephren** (Khafra) (Fourth Dynasty) (pp. 13, 24L, 31A) is the second of the three at Gizeh and only a little less large than the Great Pyramid (708 ft side and 471 ft high), but has a steeper slope (52° 20′). There is only one chamber at the core, partly in the rock and partly built-up, but two approaches to it from the north; one through the stonework and the other subterranean, these joining halfway. Near the apex of the pyramid much of the original limestone casing is preserved, and there are fragments to show that the two base courses of the facing were of granite. The remaining buildings of the complex too, are better preserved than in other cases. The offering chapel and the mortuary temple were in the normal positions axial on the east face. The latter, 370 ft from east to west and 160 ft wide, was of limestone, lined internally with granite. Flanking it were five boat-shaped pits, three on the south and two on the north. It was extremely solid and barren of features externally. To the west of a great open court, with twelve statues against the piers between the many openings leading to a surrounding corridor, were five deep chambers for statues of the Pharaoh, the central one wider than the rest, whilst behind them were corresponding stores, serdabs, and the only entrance to the pyramid enclosure. East of the court was a fore-temple, very similar in plan to the Valley Building, with twin pillared halls and long serdabs on the wings. From an entrance corridor there opened in the north-east corner of the block a series of four rooms in alabaster, where there were alabaster chests containing elements of the viscera, and in the south-east corner, two rooms in granite which received the two royal crowns. Despite the essential symmetry of the plan, the entrance was insignificant and off-centre, leading aslant to the causeway from the Valley Building, which survives substantially intact. The Valley Building (p. 24L) is 147 ft square and 43 ft high, of massive construction in local stone between granite facings, battered outside and vertical within. In this building and on its roof, various ceremonies of purification, mummification and 'opening of the mouth' were conducted. Dual entrances lead from a landing place to a transverse vestibule, and thence to a T-shaped granite-pillared hall, around which were ranged twenty-three statues of the king, the hall being lighted by slots in the angle of wall and ceiling (as p. 40E). Off the southern arm of the hall, there are three chambers in two tiers, while on the opposite flank, an alabaster stair turns through angles to the roof, cutting across the approach to the causeway in the process. A little to the north-west of the Valley Building is the **Great Sphinx of Chephren** (pp. 12, 13, 31A), the colossal enigmatic monster carved from a spur of rock left by Cheops' quarry-masons. It bears the head of Chephren, wearing the royal head-dress, false beard and cobra brow-ornament, and has the body of a recumbent lion. Thus does the Pharaoh himself take the guise of the occult protector of the complex. The sculpture is 240 ft long and 66 ft maximum height, the face being 13 ft 6 ins across. Deficiencies in the rock were made good in stonework. Between the forepaws is a large, inscribed granite stele, recording a restoration made by Thothmes IV (Eighteenth Dynasty).

The **Pyramid of Mykerinos** (Menkaura) (Fourth Dynasty) (pp. 24M, 31A) is much smaller than its two predecessors at Gizeh (356 ft square and 218 ft high, with sides sloping at 51°). Much of the casing is preserved, and is mainly Tura limestone but includes sixteen base courses in granite.

The principal pyramids of the Fifth and Sixth Dynasties (2563–2263 B.C.), all built at Abusîr and Sakkâra, were inferior in size and construction to those of the previous dynasty, and tomb chambers and their corridors were simpler and more stereotyped in arrangement.

The **Pyramid of Sahura, Abusîr** (Fifth Dynasty) (p. 24N), is remarkable for the triple series of enormous paired-stone false arches which cover its tomb chamber. It is representative of Fifth and Sixth Dynasty practice in several important particulars. Its complex still has the old elements of valley building, causeway and mortuary temple, but the offering-chapel is now incorporated in the temple. A subsidiary small pyramid is included in the south-east angle of the enclosure; this was not a burial place for a queen but had a ritual significance. Relative to the Fourth Dynasty, there is a considerable increase in the number of store-chambers, which tend to enlarge and complicate the plan of the mortuary temple. In decoration, wall reliefs are profuse—a circumstance which applies also to contemporary mastabas (e.g. the Mastaba of Thi, p. 24F). Particularly important architecturally was the use now of granite, free-standing columns, with reeded or plain shafts, and lotus, papyrus or palm capitals, replacing the wholly plain and square pillars of Fourth Dynasty buildings.

(c) *Rock-hewn tombs*. These are rare before the Middle Kingdom, and even so, are at that time a type serving for the nobility rather than royalty; pyramids, though of indifferent construction, remain the principal form of royal tomb.

The **Tombs, Beni Hasan**, numbering thirty-nine, are of the Eleventh and Twelfth Dynasties (2130–1785 B.C.) and belonged to a provincial great family. They are wholly rock-hewn and consist of a chamber behind a porticoed façade plainly imitating wooden construction in the character of the eight- or sixteen-sided, slightly-fluted and tapered columns, their trabeation and the rafter ends above (pp. 31B, 32G–K). Some of the tombs, like that of Khnemhetep, have slightly-vaulted rock ceilings, supported on fluted or reeded columns, and walls in general were lightly stuccoed and painted with pastoral, domestic and other scenes.

The **Tombs of the Kings, Thebes** (p. 32L–Q) are in the arid mountains on the west side of the Nile. They witness a complete abandonment of the royal pyramid tomb in the New Empire period in favour of a corridor type, in which stairs, passages and chambers extend as much as 690 ft into the mountain side and up to 315 ft below the valley floor. The sarcophagus usually lay in a concluding rock-columned hall, and the walls were elaborately painted with ceremonial funerary scenes and religious texts. The most important tombs are those of Seti I and Rameses III, IV and IX. The tombs served only for the sarcophagus and funerary deposits; the mortuary temples stood completely detached (e.g. the Ramesseum, that at Medînet-Habu and Queen Hatshepsut's temple at Dêr el-Bahari), sited in the necropolis adjacent to the western, cultivated land, where there were similar but smaller tombs of high-ranking persons. The temple of Mentuhetep II at Dêr el-Bahari (Middle Kingdom) is transitional, in that it is conjoined with the actual rock-cut tomb, whilst also having a small pyramid in its confines.

TEMPLES

Temples were of two main classes; the mortuary temples, for ministrations to deified Pharaohs; and the cult temples, for the popular worship of the ancient and mysterious gods. The mortuary temples developed from the offering-chapels of the royal mastabas and pyramids, assuming early permanence and ever greater importance. In the Middle Kingdom, when royal burials began to be made in the hillside, they became architecturally the more important of the two elements; and in the New Empire, stood entirely detached from the then-customary corridor tombs. Thereafter, their special character tended increasingly to merge into that of the cult temples, and distinction between the two types was eventually lost. Cult temples began in the worship of multifarious local deities. The original essentials were a rectangular palisaded court, entered from a narrow end flanked by pennon-poles and having centrally within them an emblem of the deity. Inside the further end of the court was a pavilion, comprising vestibule and sanctuary. Owing to successive rebuildings upon these ancient sites, the stages of development are difficult to trace. Apparently, little but the sanctuary and attendant apartments was being built in stone at the opening of the Eighteenth Dynasty, but somewhat later in the New Empire, the influx of wealth and the universal spread of favoured cults brought the cult temples into full flower. By this time, both mortuary and cult temples had most features in common, yet still bore a resemblance of arrangement to the most venerable shrines. Along a main axis, not specifically orientated, there was a walled open court, with colonnades around, leading to a covered structure, comprising a transverse columned vestibule or 'hypostyle hall' and a sanctuary beyond (or more than one if the temple had a multiple dedication) attended by chapels and other rooms needed by the priesthood. An impressive axial gateway to the court was traditional; it now was extended across the whole width of the court to form a towering, sloping-sided pair of pylons, with tall portal between, equipped with pennon-masts, gorge cornice and roll-moulded outer angles. Temple services were held thrice daily, but none but the priesthood was admitted to them, though privileged persons might sometimes be admitted to the court for certain ceremonies. In the cult temples, processions were a feature, particularly during the periodic festivals. So free circulation was required through or around the sanctuary. Numerous festivals were celebrated during the year, some of which might last for days; at times, shrines of the gods were carried by land or water, to other temples or sacred sites in the neighbourhood, and it was only on such occasions that the populace in general took any kind of part. The whole temple itself stood within a great enclosure, and about it were houses of the priests, official buildings, stores, granaries and a sacred pool or lake (p. 48A).

The **Temple of Khons, Karnak** (1198 B.C.) (pp. 13, 38E–H), a cult temple, may

TEMPLE PLANS: NEW EMPIRE | PTOLEMAIC AND ROMAN

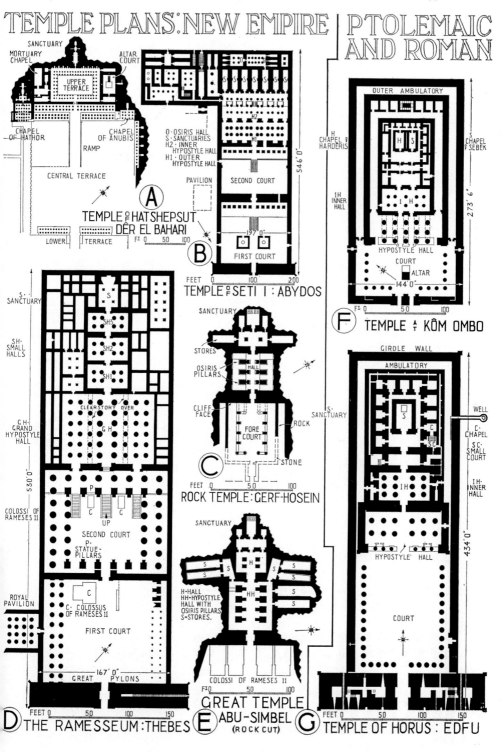

SANCTUARY
MORTUARY CHAPEL
UPPER TERRACE
ALTAR COURT
CHAPEL OF HATHOR
CHAPEL OF ANUBIS
RAMP
CENTRAL TERRACE
LOWER TERRACE

A TEMPLE OF HATSHEPSUT DÊR EL BAHARI

FT 0   50   100

O·OSIRIS HALL
S·SANCTUARIES
H2·INNER HYPOSTYLE HALL
H1·OUTER HYPOSTYLE HALL

PAVILION
SECOND COURT
546'0"
197'0"

B FIRST COURT

FEET 0   100   200

TEMPLE OF SETI I : ABYDOS

SANCTUARY
STORES
OSIRIS PILLARS
CLIFF FACE
HALL
FORE COURT
ROCK
STONE

C ROCK TEMPLE: GERF-HOSEIN

FEET 0   50   100

OUTER AMBULATORY
H CHAPEL OF HARDERIS
S CHAPEL OF SEBEK
H S
1 H
1H INNER HALL
HYPOSTYLE HALL
COURT
ALTAR
273'6"
144'0"

F TEMPLE OF KÔM OMBO

FT 0   50   100

S·SANCTUARY
SH·SMALL HALLS
S
SH2
SH2
SH1
G.H·GRAND HYPOSTYLE HALL
CLEARSTORY OVER
G H
COLOSSI OF RAMESES II
P
C   C
UP
SECOND COURT
P· STATUE-PILLARS
ROYAL PAVILION
C
C· COLOSSUS OF RAMESES II
FIRST COURT
530'0"
167'0"
GREAT PYLONS

D THE RAMESSEUM: THEBES

FEET 0   50   100   150

SANCTUARY
S
S   S
H
S   S
HH
S
S
H·HALL
HH·HYPOSTYLE HALL WITH OSIRIS PILLARS
S·STORES.
COLOSSI OF RAMESES II

E GREAT TEMPLE ABU-SIMBEL (ROCK CUT)

FT 0   50   100

GIRDLE WALL
AMBULATORY
S· SANCTUARY
S
C
SC
WELL
C· CHAPEL
S C· SMALL COURT
IH· INNER HALL
I H
HYPOSTYLE HALL
COURT
434'0"

G TEMPLE OF HORUS : EDFU

FEET 0   50   100   150

MAMMISI TEMPLE : ISLAND ⚭ ELEPHANTINE
(RESTORED)

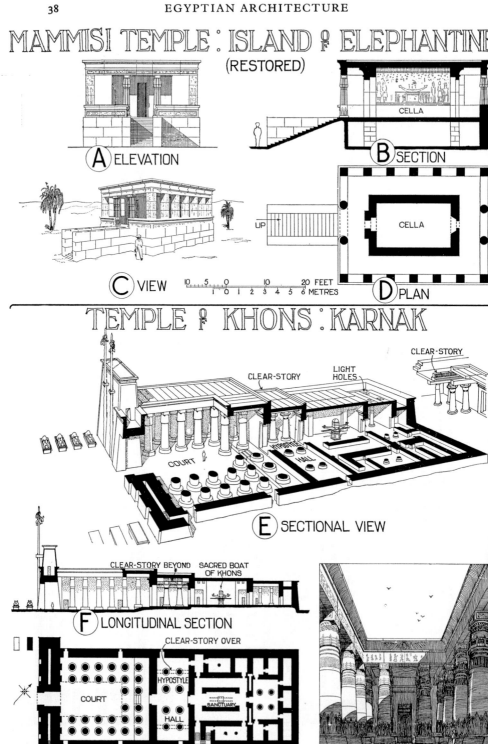

Ⓐ ELEVATION

Ⓑ SECTION

CELLA

Ⓒ VIEW

UP

CELLA

10 5 0   10   20 FEET
1 0 1 2 3 4 5 6 METRES

Ⓓ PLAN

TEMPLE ⚭ KHONS : KARNAK

CLEAR-STORY

CLEAR-STORY   LIGHT HOLES

COURT

HYPOSTYLE HALL

Ⓔ SECTIONAL VIEW

CLEAR-STORY BEYOND   SACRED BOAT OF KHONS

Ⓕ LONGITUDINAL SECTION

CLEAR-STORY OVER

HYPOSTYLE

COURT

SANCTUARY

HALL

Ⓖ PLAN

10 0 10 20 30 40 50 FEET
5 0 5   10   15 METRES

Ⓗ COURT FROM ENTRANCE

be taken as the usual type, characterized by entrance pylons, court, hypostyle hall, sanctuary, and various chapels, all enclosed by a high girdle wall. The entrance pylons, fronted by obelisks, were approached through an imposing avenue of sphinxes. The portal gave on to the open court, surrounded on three sides by a double colonnade and leading to the hypostyle hall, to which light was admitted by a clear-story, formed by the increased height of the columns of the central aisle. Beyond was the sanctuary, with openings front and rear and a circulating passage around, and beyond this again was a four-columned hall. The smaller rooms flanking the sanctuary and at its rear mostly were chapels or served for purposes of the ritual. The temple was protected by a great wall of the same height as the halls themselves, and like them therefore, decreased in height towards the sanctuary end.

The examples which follow are arranged in approximate chronological order.

1. Middle Kingdom (2130–1580 B.C.).

The **Temple of Mentuhetep, Dêr el-Bahari, Thebes** (2065 B.C.) (p. 32F) is exceptional in that it is a mortuary temple directly related to a corridor tomb. It is terraced in two main levels, at the base of steep cliffs. The upper terrace, faced with double colonnades, is approached from a tree-planted forecourt by an inclined way. On the upper terrace a small, completely solid pyramid, raised aloft on a high podium, is wholly surrounded by a walled, hypostyle hall which has further double colonnades outside it. The pyramid was really a cenotaph, for in the rock below it is a dummy burial chamber, approached by an irregular passage from the forecourt. In the rear of the temple is another pillared hall, recessed into the rock face, preceded by an open court from the centre of which a ramp leads down to Mentuhetep's 500 ft-long corridor tomb. Like the Ancient Kingdom pyramids, this temple had a causeway, shielded by walls, leading down to a Valley Building three-quarters of a mile away.

2. New Empire (1580–332 B.C.).

The **Temple of Hatshepsut, Dêr el-Bahari, Thebes** (1520 B.C.) (pp. 37A, 42A) was built by her architect, Senmut, alongside that of Mentuhetep, of 500 years previously. It is terraced similarly, but her place of burial lay far away in a corridor tomb in the mountains beyond, and this was solely a mortuary temple, dedicated to Ammon and other gods. A processional way of sphinxes connected the temple with the valley. The terraces, approached by ramps, are in three levels, mounting towards the base of the cliffs, their faces lined with double colonnades. The upper terrace is a walled court, lined with a further double colonnade, flanked on the left by the queen's mortuary chapel and on the right by a minor court containing an enormous altar to the sun god Ra. The chief sanctuary lies axially in the rear of the upper court, cut deep in the rock. To right and left of the face of the middle terrace are sanctuaries of Hathor and Anubis. The wall reliefs in this temple are exceptionally fine, and include representations of the queen's trade expedition sent to Punt, and of her allegedly divine birth. Many of the pillars are of the eight- or sixteen-sided types reminiscent of the Greek Doric.

The **Great Temple of Ammon, Karnak, Thebes** (1530–323 B.C.) (pp. 6, 13, 40, 41A), the grandest of all Egyptian temples, was not built upon one complete plan, but owes its size, disposition and magnificence to the work of many kings. Originally it consisted of a modest shrine constructed early in the Middle Kingdom, about 2000 B.C.; the first considerable enlargement was made by Thothmes I (1530 B.C.). It occupies a site of 1,200 ft by 360 ft, and is placed in an immense enclosure along with other temples and a sacred lake, surrounded by a girdle wall 20 ft to 30 ft thick, while it was connected by an avenue of sphinxes with the temple at

GREAT TEMPLE OF AMMON : KARNAK

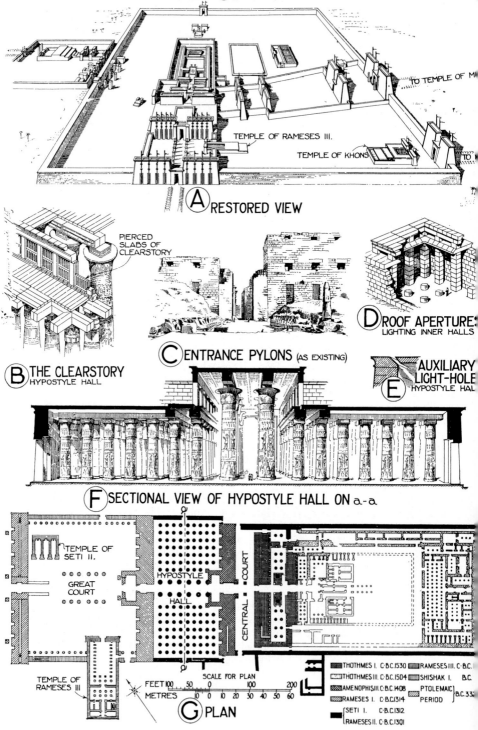

TO TEMPLE OF M

TEMPLE OF RAMESES III.

TEMPLE OF KHONS

TO

Ⓐ RESTORED VIEW

PIERCED SLABS OF CLEARSTORY

Ⓓ ROOF APERTURE: LIGHTING INNER HALLS

Ⓒ ENTRANCE PYLONS (AS EXISTING)

Ⓑ THE CLEARSTORY HYPOSTYLE HALL

Ⓔ AUXILIARY LIGHT-HOLE HYPOSTYLE HALL

Ⓕ SECTIONAL VIEW OF HYPOSTYLE HALL ON a-a

TEMPLE OF SETI II.

GREAT COURT

HYPOSTYLE

CENTRAL ▪ COURT

HALL

TEMPLE OF RAMESES III

SCALE FOR PLAN
FEET 100   50   0   100   200
METRES 0   0   10   20   30   40   50   60

Ⓖ PLAN

THOTHMES I. C·B.C.1530   RAMESES III. C·B.C.
THOTHMES III. C·B.C.1504   SHISHAK I.   B.C.
AMENOPHIS III. C·B.C.1408   PTOLEMAIC
RAMESES I. C·B.C.1314   PERIOD   B.C.33
SETI I.   C·B.C.1312
RAMESES II. C·B.C.1301

A. Great Temple of Ammon, Karnak: Hypostyle Hall (restored model)
(c. 1312–1301 B.C.). See p. 39

B. Temple of Seti I, Abydos: second Hypostyle Hall
(c. 1312 B.C.). See p. 43

A. Temple of Queen Hatshepsut, Dêr el-Bahari (*c.* 1520 B.C.). See p. 39

B. Temple of Ammon, Luxor (*c.* 1408–1300 B.C.). See p. 43

Luxor. The temple had six pairs of pylons, added by successive rulers, and consists of various courts and halls leading to the sanctuary, and a large ceremonial hall by Thothmes III in the rear. A great court, 338 ft by 275 ft deep, gives entrance to the vast hypostyle hall, by Seti I and Rameses II, some 338 ft by 170 ft internally. The roof of enormous slabs of stone is supported by 134 columns in sixteen rows; the central avenues are about 78 ft in height and have columns, 69 ft high and 11 ft 9 ins in diameter, with capitals of the papyrus-flower or bell type, while, in order to admit light through the clear-story, the side avenues are lower, with columns 42 ft 6 ins high and 8 ft 9 ins in diameter, with papyrus-bud capitals (pp. 40B–F, 55A)—a method of clear-story lighting more fully developed during the Gothic period in Europe. The effect produced by this forest of columns is most awe-inspiring; the eye is led from the smaller columns of the side avenues, which gradually vanish into semi-darkness and give an idea of unlimited extent, to the larger columns of the central avenues. Incised inscriptions and reliefs in colour, which cover the walls, column shafts and architraves, give the names and exploits of the royal personages who contributed to its grandeur, and praise the gods to whom it was dedicated. In these ancient carvings we find the germ of the idea which, centuries later, led in Christian churches to the employment of coloured mosaics and frescoes, stained-glass windows and mural statues to record the incidents of Bible history and the lives of saints and heroes. Thus have the exponents of successive and diverse religions had recourse to an appeal to the eye for manifesting their authority and for setting their religious tenets before the common people.

The **Temple at Luxor,** Thebes (1408–1300 B.C.) (pp. 13, 42B) though founded on an older sanctuary, and like most temples, altered and repaired subsequently, is substantially the work of Amenophis III, apart from a great forecourt, with pylons, added by Rameses II. It was dedicated to the Theban triad, Ammon, Mut and Khons. The illustration shows remains of the forecourt, with papyrus-bud capitals and a seated colossus of Rameses, connected by twin colonnades, 174 ft long, to a lesser court by Amenophis in the distance. The twin colonnades of bell-capital columns, 42 ft high, were the only part ever built of a grand hypostyle hall projected by Amenophis, or by the last king of his dynasty, Horemheb. Amenophis III also built a mortuary temple on the west bank at Thebes, but little survives except the twin seated statues of himself, originally 68 ft high, famous from ancient times as the **Colossi of Memnon.**

The **Temple, Island of Elephantine** (1408 B.C.) (p. 38), destroyed in A.D. 1922, was one of the small so-called Mammisi temples or Birth Houses which often stood in the outer enclosures of large temples and were subsidiary to them. They were sanctuaries perpetuating the tradition of the divine birth of a Pharaoh from a union of the god Horus and a mortal mother, and Hathor, the mother-goddess, or the god Bes, protector of the newly born, usually attended the event. The Birth Houses comprise a single room, or little more, surrounded by a portico of pillars or columns and sometimes stand on a raised podium, approached by a flight of steps from one end. Design for external effect is not typical of Egyptian buildings, but there are instances from the early Eighteenth Dynasty onwards, and the tendency increases in the Ptolemaic and Roman periods.

The **Temple of Seti I, Abydos** (1312 B.C.) (pp. 37B, 41B) has two pylons, two forecourts and two hypostyle halls, and is unique in that it has seven sanctuaries side by side, each roofed with stone, corbelled courses cut in the shape of a segmental arch on the underside. Another unusual feature of the temple is a wing of chambers projecting at right angles to the main structure, following the shape of the eminence on which the temple stands. The historical reliefs on the walls of close-grained limestone are among the finest in Egypt. Seti I built a second mortuary temple on the west bank at Thebes, his successor, Rameses II, adding the finishing touches to both.

The **Ramesseum, Thebes** (1301 B.C.) (pp. 37D, 54H) by Rameses II, is as typical of the New Empire mortuary temples as is that of Khons, Karnak, of the cult type, though the differences of principle are not very great. In such temples the Pharaoh was worshipped and offerings were made, while his tomb lay far in the mountains behind. The front pylons were 220 ft wide, and led to two columned courts, the second having Osiris pillars on the front and rear walls; and so to a grand hypostyle hall, succeeded by three smaller columned halls, which preceded the sanctuary at the far end of the building. There are no arrangements for processional circulation around the sanctuaries of mortuary temples. The hypostyle hall is much smaller than that at Karnak (98 ft by 196 ft), possessing only 48 columns, including 12 with bell capitals, but like it had an elevated roof over the three axial avenues and an equally well-developed clear-story. Around the temple, ruins of the temenos walls and the brick-built priests' houses, granaries, stores, etc., still survive. There are fragmentary remains of another mortuary temple by Rameses II at Abydos; and one by Rameses III (1198 B.C.) at Medînet-Habu which closely resembles the Ramesseum, and similarly still has evidences of its temenos and brick-built subsidiary buildings surviving (p. 48A).

The **Great Temple, Abu-Simbel** (c. 1301 B.C.) (pp. 37E, 45A, B) is one of two rock-hewn temples at this place commanded by the indefatigable Rameses II, and quite the most stupendous and impressive of its class. An entrance forecourt leads to the imposing façade, 119 ft wide and 105 ft high, formed as a pylon, immediately in front of which are four rock-cut seated colossal statues of Rameses, over 65 ft high. The hall beyond, 30 ft high, has eight Osiris pillars and vividly-coloured wall reliefs. Eight smaller chambers open off unsymmetrically to right and left, while on the main axis is a smaller hall with four pillars, leading to a vestibule serving three apartments, the central one being the sanctuary and containing four statues of gods (including Rameses) and a support for a sacred boat.

The **Small Temple, Abu-Simbel** (c. 1301 B.C.) (p. 45C), by Rameses II, close to the Great Temple, was dedicated to his deified Queen, Nefertari, and the goddess Hathor. The façade here is 90 ft wide and 40 ft high, and comprises six niches recessed in the face of the rock and containing six colossal statues, 33 ft high; two represent Rameses and one Nefertari on each side of the portal, which leads to a vestibule and a hall, 34 ft by 27 ft, with six pillars bearing the sculptured head of Hathor.

The **Rock-cut Temple at Gerf Hosein** (c. 1301 B.C.) (p. 37C), is still another example due to Rameses II. It is of interest in that it retains quite a little of its forecourt, the walls of which are in part rock-cut.

3. Ptolemaic and Roman Period (332 B.C.–A.D. 1st cent.).

The **Temple of Isis, on the island of Philae** (pp. 46, 47) marks a very ancient sacred site. Minor parts of the surviving buildings belong to the Thirtieth Dynasty (378–341 B.C.) but most are by the Ptolemies II–XIII (283–47 B.C.). The irregularities of the plan are due to piecemeal building. The principle of arrangement, however, remains much the same as at the height of the New Empire period, a thousand years earlier—a progressive concentration of effect from outer and inner courts and pylons to the ultimate sanctuary in the temple nucleus. Such changes as there are, largely concern details. Column capitals are coarser and more ornate, varied in design from column to column, and have very deep abacus blocks; colonnades appear more frequently on the exterior of buildings, their

A. Great Temple, Abu-Simbel (*c.* 1301 B.C.). See p. 44

B. Great Temple, Abu-Simbel.
See p. 44

C. Small Temple, Abu-Simbel
(*c.* 1301 B.C.). See p. 44

A. Island of Philae: aerial view from E. when not submerged: Kiosk in foreground (*c.* A.D. 96); Pylons, Temple of Isis and Mammisi Temple on farther side of island (283–47 B.C.). See p. 44

B. Temple of Isis, Philae: colonnade in forecourt

A. Temple of Isis, Philae (283–47 B.C.), with Kiosk (*c.* A.D. 96) partly submerged

B' Temple of Isis, Philae: entrance court, showing Pylons. See p. 44

A. Mortuary Temple of Rameses III, Medînet-Habu (1198 B.C.) showing surrounding brick-built buildings in temenos. See p. 44

B. Temple of Hathor, Dendera (110 B.C.–A.D. 68). See p. 49

columns linked by screen walls reaching some half-way up the height. Such characteristics are notable in the 'Birth House' or Mammisi temple on the west side of the inner court. Also, in a pavilion known as the 'Kiosk' or 'Pharaoh's Bed', standing on the east side of the island; though this is of Roman date (c. A.D. 96) (pp. 46, 47A). It is roofless, and has four columns on the ends and five on the flanks. The two portals axial on the short sides are designed without a central part to the lintels, so as to permit the passage of banners and effigies carried in procession. The whole island nowadays is submerged during a part of the year, leaving only the tops of the buildings visible.

The **Temple of Horus, Edfu** (237–57 B.C.) (pp. 37G, 51A, B), is a fine, well-preserved example of the period. It was built in three stages, with protracted intervals between; first the temple proper by Ptolemy III, then the outer hypostyle hall (140–124 B.C.), and finally the perimeter wall and pylons. It is plainly a processional cult temple. There is a passage surrounding the sanctuary, which serves also to give access to thirteen small chapels, and another completing the entire circuit of the enclosing wall. All the inner rooms were completely dark and windowless. The grand pylons are some 205 ft across and 100 ft high. Though in the main the temple demonstrates the tenacity of the ancient traditions, there are here again those distinguishing features of the period, particularly notable in the main hypostyle hall; the foliated or palm capitals, varying in design in pairs astride the axis, the deep abaci, the screen walls between the columns, and the 'broken' lintel of the central portal.

The **Mammisi Temple, Edfu** (116 B.C.) (p. 52A), in the outer enclosure of the Temple of Horus, is typical of all externally-colonnaded birth-houses, and similar to others at Elephantine, Philae (see above) and Dendera, where there are two, one Ptolemaic and the other Roman.

The **Temple of Hathor, Dendera** (110 B.C.–A.D. 68) (p. 48B) is most imposing, standing in a brick-walled temenos 951 ft by 918 ft wide. Except in lacking pylons, it closely resembles that at Edfu, and, as there, the hypostyle hall was added to the Ptolemaic nucleus in Roman times, along with the peripheral wall, which stands sufficiently clear of the temple to allow a complete processional circuit. The four-sided, Hathor-headed capitals of the hypostyle hall, carrying a conventional representation of the birth-house on the deep abaci above, are typical of the period. Many narrow chambers are concealed in the thickness of the massive outer walls, and stairs lead to the roof, where ceremonies took place.

The **Temple of Sebek and Haroeris at Kôm Ombo** (145 B.C.–A.D. 14) (p. 37F) is peculiar in having a double approach to its twin sanctuaries and two peripheral processional circuits.

OBELISKS

The Obelisks, originating in the sacred symbol of the sun god of Heliopolis, and which usually stood in pairs astride temple entrances, are huge monoliths, square on plan and tapering to an electrum-capped pyramidion at the summit, which was the sacred part. They have a height of nine or ten times the diameter at the base, and the four sides are cut with hieroglyphs. The granite for obelisks was quarried by the very laborious method of pounding trenches around the tremendous block with balls of dolerite, a very hard stone, as the more normal method of splitting from the parent rock by means of timber wedges, which expanded after soaking, was too hazardous for so long a unit. Mural reliefs show that obelisks were transported on sledges and river-barges, and erected on their foundations by hauling them up earthen ramps, and then tilting them into position. Many were removed from Egypt by the Roman Emperors, and there are at least twelve in Rome alone.

The **Obelisk** in the Piazza of S. Giovanni in Laterano (p. 664) was brought to Rome from the Temple of Ammon at Karnak (Thebes), where it was originally erected by Thothmes III, and is the largest known. It is a monolith of red granite from Aswân, 105 ft high without the added pedestal, 9 ft square at the base and 6 ft 2 ins at the top, and weighs about 230 tons.

'**Cleopatra's Needle**', the obelisk on the Thames Embankment, London, originally at Heliopolis, was brought to England from Alexandria in 1878. It bears inscriptions of Thothmes III and Rameses II. It is 68 ft 6 ins high, 8 ft by 7 ft 6 ins at the base, and weighs 180 tons.

DWELLINGS

Clay models deposited in tombs indicate that ordinary dwellings were of crude brick, one or two storeys high, with flat or arched ceilings and a parapeted roof partly occupied by a loggia. Rooms looked towards a north-facing court. Remains of barrack-like dwellings for workers exist at the pyramid sites of Chephren at Gizeh (Fourth Dynasty) and of Sesostris II at Kahun (Twelfth Dynasty) on the eastern edge of the Fayum; and again at Tell el-Amarna, where the Pharaoh Akhnaten (Eighteenth Dynasty) built his ephemeral new town, occupied only for about fifteen years (c. 1366–1351 B.C.). Each workers' establishment constituted a considerable village, laid out on rigidly formal lines. More freely planned was a village at Dêr el-Medina, constructed for those engaged upon the Theban royal corridor-tombs, and which endured for four centuries. Though in the towns even the better houses were on constricted plots and therefore might be three or four storeys high, where space allowed mansions stood in their own grounds, laid out formally with groves, gardens, pools and minor structures surrounding the rectangular, crude-brick dwelling, this having its door and window openings dressed around in stone (p. 52B). Columns and beams, doors and window frames were of precious timber. Typically, there was a central hall or living room, raised sufficiently high with the help of columns to allow clear-story light on one or more sides, for first floors were only partial. Regularly there were three fundamental parts; a reception suite, on the cooler, north side of the house; service; and private quarters. Archaic palaces were faced with overlapping vertical timbers, giving the so-called 'palace façade' effect which left its decorative impress upon funerary stone architecture for some time. Not much is known about later dynastic palaces, apart from the remains of Akhnaten's palace at Tell el-Amarna and of that of Meneptah at Memphis and from what can be gleaned from wall reliefs. Being largely of crude brick, they have left little trace. Except in size, they resembled the mansions.

COMPARATIVE ANALYSIS

PLANS. Royal pyramids of the Ancient Kingdom stood in a walled enclosure, normally containing a much smaller pyramid or mastaba at the south end, and an offering-chapel on the east side which eventually was embodied in the mortuary temple which also stood on the east side. A long, enclosed causeway connected the mortuary temple with a Valley Building where initial burial rites were conducted. The developed, independent temples of the New Empire and later periods were of two types, the mortuary type, descended from its predecessor in the pyramid complex, and the cult or processional type, which had its own unbroken history from the earliest times. The two types had very much in common, and they differed in many respects from the Greek temple. An imposing avenue of sphinxes led to the main entrance, flanked by slender obelisks which contrasted strongly with the

A. Temple of Horus, Edfu (237–57 B.C.). See p. 49

B. Temple of Horus, Edfu: portico with screen between columns

A. Mammisi Temple, Edfu (restored model)
(*c.* 116 B.C.). See p. 49

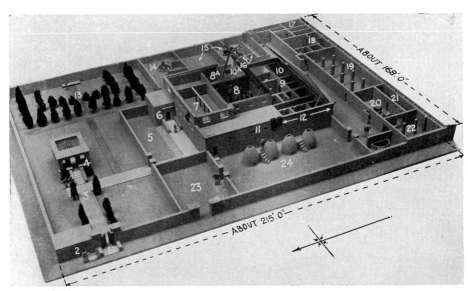

B. A typical Egyptian mansion, Tell el-Amarna (*c.* 1366 B.C.): restored model.
1. Main entrance. 2. Porter's lodge. 3. Avenue of small trees in outer court.
4. Private chapel. 5. Inner court. 6. Porch. 7. Room over North Hall. 8. Central
room (clear-story lighting). 8A. Staircase. 9. Women's quarters. 10. Master's
bedroom. 10A. Bath room and closet. 11. West Hall. 12. Guests' chambers.
13. Formal garden. 14 Well. 15. Byres. 16. Dog kennels. 17. Kitchen. 18.
Steward's quarters. 19. Servants' quarters. 20. Stables. 21. Store (harness, etc.).
22. Chariots. 23. Tradesmen's entrance. 24. Granary court, with conical grain
bins. See p. 50

massive pylons. Courts and halls alike were designed to produce an impressive internal effect, and the hypostyle hall, crowded with columns and lit mysteriously from above, was the grandest achievement of Egyptian planning (pp. 6, 41A). Temples frequently were rebuilt many times on ancient sites, or resulted from a series of additions over many centuries. In the latter respect they resemble the growth of English cathedrals. Symmetry about the main axis was most strongly marked, except in such cases as the temple on the Island of Philae, where the nature of the site and the process of accretion led to distortion of the customary arrangements (p. 46A). Temples had large outer enclosures, containing subsidiary temples and 'birth-houses' in the more important instances, and sacred lakes and groves; also—in crude brick—priests' houses, stables, granaries and many stores, all encompassed in a mighty brick wall.

WALLS. Temple walls were very thick, immense in the Ancient Kingdom, of limestone, sandstone, or more rarely of granite. Mortar, when employed, was used as a lubricant rather than as an adhesive. The walls sloped inwards towards the top, giving a massive appearance (p. 48B). This practice arose from the use of sun-dried brick for buildings on land liable to movement from the annual inundation, though stone buildings were in fact mostly constructed on rocky sites. Columns, which are the leading external features of Greek architecture, are not often used externally in Egyptian buildings, which normally have a massive blank wall crowned with the characteristic 'gorge' cornice of roll and hollow moulding (p. 55J). Walls, even when of granite, were generally carved in low relief, sometimes coated with a thin skin of stucco, about the thickness of a sheet of paper, to receive the colour (p. 57). Simplicity, solidity and grandeur, obtained by broad masses of unbroken walling, are the chief characteristics of Egyptian architecture.

OPENINGS. Colonnades (p. 46B) and doorways (pp. 47B, 54J) were spanned by massive lintels—not arches—in this essentially trabeated architecture of Ancient Egypt. Windows are seldom found in the outer walls of temples—there is a rare example at Medînet-Habu (p. 54K)—as such light as was needed was admitted through clear-story screens in New Empire architecture, or, in the Ptolemaic and Roman periods, over walls rising half-way up the façade columns, as at Philae, Edfu, Dendera and Kôm Ombo. Stone window-gratings of various patterns have been found (p. 40B) and small slit-openings were also used in walls and roofs to light rooms and staircases (p. 40D, E).

ROOFS. For religious buildings, heavy stone slabs were placed side by side, either spanning a narrow apartment directly, or resting upon paired architrave-beams passing from column to column in the case of pillared halls (pp. 28C, 40B). In the Ancient Kingdom, the limestones then employed were not capable of spans greater than about nine feet, and granite then had to be used, though corbelled or pent roofs could be put over pyramid corridors and chambers. It was only when sandstone from Silsila or higher up the Nile came to be quarried that the mighty temples of the New Empire became practicable. With this, clear spans could be much increased. South of the Delta, rain was infrequent, but even so, roof slabs were cut so as to guide rainwater away from roof joints and eject it from waterspouts. Temple roofs served for ceremonies and processions, and sometimes had pavilions and chapels upon them. The Egyptians knew of the true arched principle, but did not normally employ it in stone buildings, though they utilized arches frequently in crude-brick buildings from the Third Dynasty onwards. The arch rings were seldom single, but laid one on top of the other up to a number of nine; and the arches were sloped backwards so as to evade the need of temporary timberwork.

COLUMNS. The simplest form of support was (a) the square pillar, in regular use until the later New Empire. Pillars or columns seldom exceeded six times their

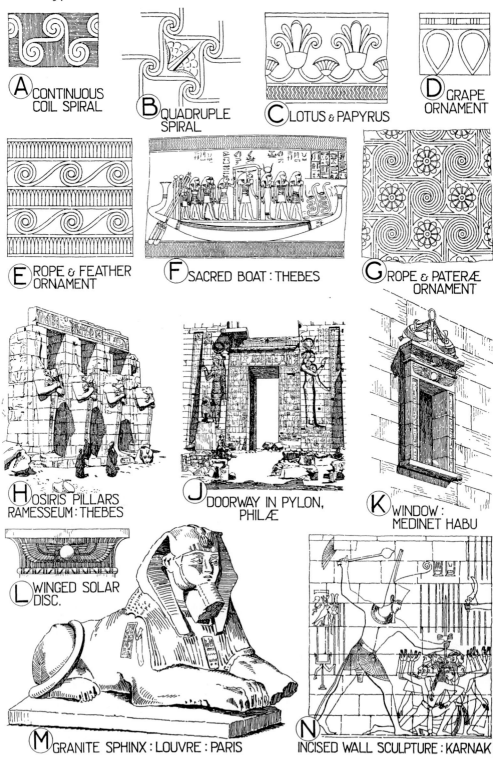

A CONTINUOUS COIL SPIRAL

B QUADRUPLE SPIRAL

C LOTUS & PAPYRUS

D GRAPE ORNAMENT

E ROPE & FEATHER ORNAMENT

F SACRED BOAT : THEBES

G ROPE & PATERÆ ORNAMENT

H OSIRIS PILLARS RAMESSEUM : THEBES

J DOORWAY IN PYLON, PHILÆ

K WINDOW : MEDINET HABU

L WINGED SOLAR DISC.

M GRANITE SPHINX : LOUVRE : PARIS

N INCISED WALL SCULPTURE : KARNAK

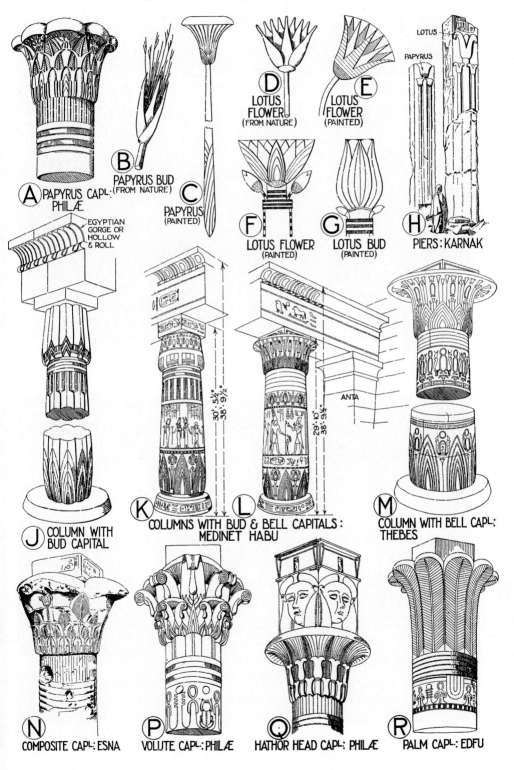

A PAPYRUS CAPL.: PHILÆ

B PAPYRUS BUD (FROM NATURE)

C PAPYRUS (PAINTED)

D LOTUS FLOWER (FROM NATURE)

E LOTUS FLOWER (PAINTED)

F LOTUS FLOWER (PAINTED)

G LOTUS BUD (PAINTED)

H PIERS: KARNAK

LOTUS
PAPYRUS

EGYPTIAN GORGE. OR HOLLOW & ROLL

J COLUMN WITH BUD CAPITAL

K L COLUMNS WITH BUD & BELL CAPITALS: MEDINET HABU

ANTA

M COLUMN WITH BELL CAPL.: THEBES

N COMPOSITE CAPL.: ESNA

P VOLUTE CAPL.: PHILÆ

Q HATHOR HEAD CAPL.: PHILÆ

R PALM CAPL.: EDFU

A. Wall sculptures, Dêr el-Bahari (*c.* 1520 B.C.). See p. 57

B. Wall sculptures, Temple of Seti I, Abydos (*c.* 1312 B.C.). See p. 57

own diameter in height, and commonly were elaborated with painting and low-relief carving. Columns had an abacus, tremendously high in Ptolemaic times, and a wide-spreading disc-shaped base with a rounded upper edge. Shafts tapered a little towards the top, but there was no 'entasis' or outward swelling of the profile. (b) Polygonal columns, used only in the Middle Kingdom and New Empire, had either eight or sixteen sides. There were also shallow-fluted columns, not used after the Eighteenth Dynasty, and solitary instances of reeded shafts in King Zoser's pyramid complex at Sakkâra (p. 28c). (c) The Palm type, in continuous use till Roman times, had a simple cylindrical shaft (p. 55R). The (d) Bud and (e) Bell columns derive from bundles of papyrus reeds, with lashings underneath the capitals; and the shafts are gathered in a little above the base. The bud type, first used in the Fifth Dynasty, shows eight papyrus stems, these reflected upwards into the capital (p. 55J); until, in the Eighteenth Dynasty, both capital and shaft were made smooth (p. 55K, L). Very occasionally, chiefly in the Ancient Kingdom, the lotus was used as a model for the bud capital instead of the papyrus. These plants, lotus and papyrus, were respectively the emblems of Upper and Lower Egypt (p. 55H). The bell type almost invariably has a plain circular capital and shaft (p. 55M), until the Ptolemaic period when the shaft acquired a reeded neck-ing. (f) Foliated capitals, of various ornate types (p. 55A, N, P), are typical of the Ptolemaic and Roman periods, different designs being used side by side, inter-spersed with the palm type. (g) Hathor-headed capitals, supporting models of the birth-house of Horus, are generally of similarly late date (p. 55Q). (h) The Osiris pillar (p. 54H), forerunner of the caryatid of the Greeks, occurs principally in the New Empire period. After the Ancient Kingdom, when monoliths were some-times employed, columns were invariably built-up in coursed stone blocks, many pieces being needed for the larger capitals (p. 42B).

MOULDINGS. Mouldings were few, and consisted of the torus or roll-moulding for the angles of buildings, and the hollow, generally used in conjunction with the roll of the 'gorge' moulding to crown the upper parts of pylons and walls (p. 55J). This is sometimes either capped or substituted by the 'cobra' or the 'kheker' crest-ing (p. 28D).

ORNAMENT (p. 54). This important element in the style was often symbolical, including such features as the solar disc and vulture with outspread wings as a symbol of protection; while diaper patterns, spirals (p. 54A, B, E, G) and the feather ornament were largely used. The scarab, or sacred beetle, obtained its mystical virtue as the symbol of resurrection probably because of its habit of allowing the sun to hatch its eggs in the desert sand. The decoration of temple walls consisted largely of representations of acts of adoration of the monarch to his gods, to whom he ascribed all his success in war. The Egyptians, masters in the use of colour, carried out their schemes of decoration chiefly in blue, red and yellow. The wall to be decorated was probably prepared as follows: (a) the surface was first chiselled smooth and rubbed down; (b) the figures or hieroglyphs were then drawn with a red line by an artist and corrected with a black line by the chief artist; (c) the sculptor made his carvings in low relief or incised the outline, slightly rounding the enclosed form towards its boundaries; (d) a thin coat of stucco was then applied to receive the colour, and the painter carried on his work in the strong hues of the primary colours. The hieroglyphs (p. 56B) were sometimes incised direct on the stone or granite and then coloured, as may be seen in the sculptures at the British Museum. They are instructive as well as decorative, and from them is learnt a great deal of what is known of Egyptian history and society (pp. 54N, 56). The Egyptians possessed great power of conventionalizing natural objects and they took the papyrus, lotus and palm as motifs for design. These were nature symbols of the fertility given to the country by the over-flowing Nile, and as such they continually appear both in construction and ornament.

REFERENCE BOOKS

BADAWY, A. *A History of Egyptian Architecture*, vol. i. Giza, 1954.
BLACKMAN, A. M. *Luxor and its Temples*. London, 1923.
BORCHARDT, L. *Das Grabdenkmal des Königs Sahu-Rē*. Leipzig, 1910–13.
—. *Die Entstehung der Pyramide an der Baugeschichte der Pyramide bei Mejdum nachgewiesen*. Berlin, 1928.
BREASTED, J. H. *A History of Egypt*. New York, 1905.
—. *Ancient Records of Egypt*. 4 vols. Chicago, 1906–7.
CAPART, J. *L'Art égyptien*. 2 vols. Bruxelles, 1909–11.
—. *Thebes*. London, 1926.
CARTER, H., and MACE, A. C. *The Tomb of Tut-ankh-Amen*. 3 vols. London, 1923–33.
CHOISY, A. *L'Art de bâtir chez les égyptiens*. Paris, 1904.
CLARKE, G. SOMERS, and ENGELBACH, R. *Ancient Egyptian Masonry*. London, 1930.
Description de l'Égypte (known as 'Napoleon's Egypt'). 23 vols. Paris, 1809–22.
DRIOTON, É., and LAUER, J. P. *Sakkarah. The Monuments of Zoser*. Cairo, 1939.
DRIOTON, É., and VANDIER, J. *Les Peuples de l'orient mediterranéen (l'Égypte)*. Paris, 1952.
EDWARDS, I. E. S. *The Pyramids of Egypt*. Penguin Books, Harmondsworth [1947].
EMERY, W. B. *The Tomb of Hor-Aha*. Cairo, 1939.
EMERY, W. B., and others. *Great Tombs of the First Dynasty*. 2 vols. 1949, 1954.
FAIRMAN, H. W. 'Town Planning in Pharaonic Egypt,' *Town Planning Review*, vol. xx, no. 1. 1949.
—. 'Worship and Festivals in an Egyptian Temple,' *Bulletin of the John Rylands Library*, vol. 37, no. 1. 1954.
FIRTH, C. M., QUIBELL, J. E., and LAUER, J. P. *The Step Pyramid*. Cairo, 1935.
GARDINER, A. H. *The Temple of King Sethos I at Abydos*, vols. i–iii. London and Chicago, 1933–8.
'Les grandes découvertes archéologiques de 1954,' *La Revue de Caire*, vol. xxxiii, no. 175, Numéro Spécial.
GARSTANG, J. *Mahasna and Bêt-Khallâf*. London, 1902.
HÖLSCHER, UVO. *Das Grabdenkmal des Königs Chrephren*. Leipzig, 1912.
—. *The Excavation of Medinet Habu*. Chicago, 1934.
JÉQUIER, G. *L'architecture et la décoration de l'ancienne Égypte*. 3 vols. Paris, 1919–24.
—. *Manuel d'archéologie égyptienne*. Paris, 1924.
LANGE, K., and HIRMER, M., trans. Boothroyd, R. H. *Egypt*. London, 1956.
LAUER, J.-P. *La pyramide à degrés*. Cairo, 1936–9.
—. *Sakkarah. Les Monuments de Zoser*. Cairo, 1939.
LEPSIUS, R. *Denkmaeler aus Aegypten und Aethiopien*. 12 vols. plates, and 1 vol. text. Berlin, 1849–59.
LUCAS, A. *Ancient Egyptian Materials and Industries*. London, 1948.
MASPERO, G. *Art in Egypt*. New York, 1912.
—. *Manual of Egyptian Archaeology*. New York and London, 1914.
MURRAY, M. A. *Egyptian Sculpture*. London, 1930.
—. *Egyptian Temples*. London, 1931.
NAVILLE, E., and CLARKE, SOMERS. *The XIth Dynasty Temple at Deir el-Bahari*, Parts I and II. London, 1907, 1910.
PERROT and CHIPIEZ. *History of Art in Ancient Egypt*. London, 1883.
PETRIE, W. M. FLINDERS. *Egyptian Architecture*. London, 1938.
—. *The Pyramids and Temples of Gizeh*. London, 1883.
—. *Social Life in Ancient Egypt*. London, 1923.
PORTER, B., and MOSS, R. L. B. *Topographical Bibliography of Ancient Egyptian Hieroglyphic Texts, Reliefs, and Paintings*. 7 vols. Oxford, 1927–51.

REISNER, G. A. *A History of the Giza Necropolis*. Cambridge, Mass., 1931.

—. *The development of the Egyptian Tomb down to the accession of Cheops*. Cambridge (Mass.), and London, 1935.

STEINDORFF, G., and SEELE, K. C. *When Egypt ruled the East*. Chicago, 1942.

SMITH, W. STEPHENSON. *The History of Egyptian Sculpture and Painting in the Old Kingdom*. London, 1946.

VYSE, H., and PERRING, J. S. *Operations carried on at the Pyramid of Gizeh*. 3 vols. London, 1840–2.

WHITE, MANCHIP J. C. *Ancient Egypt*. London, 1952.

Publications of: the Archaeological Survey of Egypt; Egypt Exploration Fund; Annales du Service des Antiquités de l'Égypte.

Tomb of Tutankhamen, Thebes: entrance to sepulchral hall showing the shrine (*c.* 1340 B.C.). See p. 18

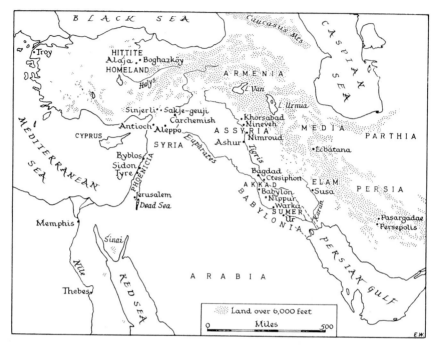

The Western Asiatic Empires

II. WEST ASIATIC ARCHITECTURE

(*Circa* 3000–331 B.C.)

IN West Asia, Mesopotamia was the primary centre and the following account is chiefly concerned with the architecture of the peoples successively dominant there prior to the time of Alexander in the late fourth century B.C.; but an outline is appended of the later architecture of the region up to the Muslim conquest, *c.* A.D. 642, and—to represent the rest of West Asia—of that of the ancient Hittites in Asia Minor (*c.* 1750–1200 B.C.) and of architecture in old Syria (*c.* 2000–700 B.C.).

INFLUENCES

GEOGRAPHICAL. The earliest civilization of Western Asia flourished in the fertile plains of the twin rivers, Tigris and Euphrates. To this district is given the name of Mesopotamia (Gk. *mesos* = middle + *potamos* = river). In ancient times the rivers entered the Persian Gulf separately, though now joined in a single mouth, and the Gulf extended some one hundred and thirty miles farther north than at present. The courses followed by the rivers in their lower reaches too have changed considerably. Unlike Egypt, Mesopotamia lacks natural defensive boundaries. On the west it shades gradually through downlands into the undulating steppes of the Arabian desert, and while on the east the Zagros mountain range turns in an arc to embrace it, the valleys and folds of the mountains were sufficiently fertile to nurture neighbouring peoples watchfully envious of the richer living offered by the lush Mesopotamian plains. Eastward again of the Zagros range is the vast Persian plateau. To the north-west, the river plains join with Syria, and Syria and Palestine, facing the Mediterranean, together afford a link with Egypt; the whole constituting the 'Fertile Crescent', containing the majority of worth-while land in the Near East. Syria and Palestine thus were liable to incursions of imperialists from either hand, offering the more tempting prey in that they commanded trade communications from all quarters, including those from the high table-lands of Anatolia (Asia Minor and Armenia). From beyond Anatolia came those successive hordes of northern invaders who were so often to disturb and disrupt the settled peoples, and it was in central Anatolia that one group of invaders, the Hittites, developed an important civilization in the second millennium B.C. The cultures of these western regions, from Anatolia in the north to Palestine in the south, though very old, were not so much indigenous as derived from one or more of the three main civilizations of the western world, Egypt, Mesopotamia and Crete. The last of these is reviewed in Chapter III (p. 89). The Mesopotamian twin rivers rise in the mountains of Armenia, reinforced in their courses by other rivers and streams. Their head waters rush down the mountain valleys and after the melting of the snows, rise to flood volume in May. To check the inundations and to irrigate the plains, the ancient Mesopotamian peoples constructed a network of canals, storage basins and ditches which besides conserving the rivers in their courses gave a marvellous fertility to the alluvial land. The abundant harvests of grain, fruit and vegetables, the fish and the fowl and the animal husbandry were a source of astonishment to visiting travellers and writers. The canals and the rivers served as waterways too, and made roads largely unnecessary.

GEOLOGICAL. The Mesopotamian plain is mostly alluvial, and before systematic control of the flood waters from the mountain sources, contained a very great deal of marshland. Reeds and rushes always could be had in profusion, but for building timber, although the ubiquitous palm could be made to serve, the ancients had to rely almost wholly on imports, either from the slopes of the eastern or northern mountains or, for the finest supplies, from Lebanon, on the Syrian coast, where grew the cedars so famous in early historical times. Apart from occasional boulders carried down by bygone floods, stone too was lacking, and the small amount of limestone and alabaster that was employed had to be transported laboriously from the uplands. So also had the minerals; iron, copper, tin and lead. The one building material universally available was the clay from the soil itself, well suited for the making of bricks, which were either sun-dried or, when intended for the facing of important structures, kiln-burnt and for decorative purposes glazed in different colours. Chopped straw was mixed with the sun-dried bricks to improve their cohesion. Burnt bricks sometimes were laid in lime mortar, but more often in bitumen, a natural material, readily available. On the Persian plateau, ample stone was forthcoming.

CLIMATIC. Mesopotamia suffers very considerable climatic extremes, a scorching sun in the summer, particularly in the southern half, and in the winter, cold, searching blasts from the northern mountains. There is little rainfall, except in the northern districts, and crops wither without ample moisture. Had it not been for the complex and efficient irrigation system, which while draining the marshes distributed the river waters and lent such high fertility to the alluvial soil, the ancient civilization would never have attained the high pitch that it did. In adjacent Persia, while the climate similarly ranges to extremes, the higher elevation gives a dry and exhilarating air and accounts for the frequency of light, columned halls and porticoes in the Persian royal buildings.

RELIGIOUS The polytheism of the ancient peoples of the plains was of much the same character throughout the entire region at any given time. Religion reflected the way of life, of which agriculture was the mainstay, precariously and painstakingly maintained under the ever-present threat of disastrous flood, drought or marsh fire. Thus the gods were conceived as awful beings of uncertain temper whom mortals existed to serve. The part played by the distant mountains in determining the fortunes of the plains was clearly seen, so the gods were thought to reside in the heights and to approach them, temples were built on great, elevated artificial platforms, often provided with 'ziggurats' or holy mountains, with a shrine at the apex. Religion dominated daily life; it produced a sombre outlook, for there was an ever-present apprehension that the will of the gods might have been imperfectly foreseen. Signs and portents were sought at every move and in whatever activity. Spells were woven and magic practised, and the need for the higher skills in medicine, divination, mystic interpretation and religious ritual produced a powerful class of astrologer priests, in whom reposed all the wisdom of the age. Each city had its chief presiding deity who was deemed to rule the city as its overlord. The chief gods were Anu, the sky god; Enlil (Bel), the earth god; and Ea, god of the waters. These formed a triad, such as was noted also in Egypt. Of them, Anu was the greatest, but he at length gave way in importance to Bel-Marduk, who came to usurp the place of Enlil in this primary triad. Marduk in his turn was supplanted by Ashur, the national god of the Assyrians. A second triad comprised Shamash, the sun god; Nannar (later, Sin), the moon god; and Ishtar, goddess of passion and war. Besides the gods there were heroes, born of a divine father and a human mother, and a host of genies or demons, some good but mostly monstrous, deformed and evil, representing the powers of darkness. Symbolism and superstition prevailed everywhere. Unlike the Egyptians, the Mesopotamians were not great tomb builders, as they had not the same strong belief in a future life. As to the Persians of the eastern plateau, their religion at first reflected that of the plains people, but some time prior to their ascendancy they adapted it to embrace the religion of Zoroaster, a system of ethical forces representing good and evil at war from the beginning of time. The two protagonists were Ahuramazda, the sky god and creator of good and, opposed to him, Ahriman, the destructive spirit, or power of evil. There was thus a strong tendency towards monotheism, Ahuramazda being supreme, but the popular religion if not the official continued to recognize lesser, supporting gods, among whom Mithras, the sun god, became the most famous. Others worshipped were those of the moon, earth, fire, water and wind. Temples were simple, one-roomed square towers, where the Magi, a priestly class, tended the sacred fire; there were no public ceremonies there, as these were carried on in the neighbouring open countryside, sacrifices being made before altars again carrying the sacred fire. Religion had little effect upon Persian architecture.

SOCIAL. In Ancient Mesopotamia it was the needs of agriculture that shaped the form of the social structure and conditioned the nature of labour, commerce, art, science and religion. The complexities of irrigation enforced communal effort; land had to be scrupulously divided, so surveying and mathematics arose; boundary disputes needed to be settled, so law developed; the seasons had to be predicted and a calendar established, so astronomy came into being. These several pursuits, conducted in the service of mysterious gods, produced astrology, medicine and the practice of divination and magic, besides exorcism and other defensive rites against evil powers. Though rich in agricultural produce the land was devoid of minerals and many other needful commodities, hence trading became a major activity. Great skills were developed in metal working, weaving, and pottery making; the potter's wheel was known as early as 3000 B.C. A host of minor vocations filled out the fundamental social structure. So high a social organization demanded records and a means of indirect communication, to which the art of writing, the mark of a civilized people, was the response. Cuneiform or wedge-shaped characters on clay tablets or cylinders have proved more lasting than the Egyptian records on perishable papyrus, and among them are accounts of all kinds of ecclesiastical, royal and legal enactments and transactions, and endless business documents. They gave employment to great numbers of scribes. The deciphering of the 'Code of Laws' on the stele of Hammurabi (c. 1792–1750 B.C.) has allowed us a wonderful insight into habits, customs and private life prior to his time. Well-drawn laws governed urban and country life, commerce and the rights of buyer and seller, land tenure, feudal service, taxation and the organization of labour. The vast undertakings in irrigation, aqueducts, military fortifications, temples and palaces largely were the work of the people themselves, in the off-seasons for agriculture, rather than of slaves.

In Assyria, a military autocracy with a conscript army was the dominating class, and the Assyrians were fighters rather than traders. Between bitter and cruel wars their leaders exercised their lethal skills by the trap-hunting of wild animals. From this epoch there are very many fine wall sculptures surviving which portray social conditions and form an illustrated history of the battles and exploits of monarchs; the emphasis of these delicately-incised reliefs is upon war and the chase; there is little reference to religion. Yet society in general continued much the same way of life as before, and in the towns were carpenters, sculptors, smiths, makers of musical instruments, engineers, scientists, mathematicians, poets, musicians and the like, each in the correct stratum of the complex economy.

The Persian domination was due to the military superiority of this hardy upland race, who imposed their rule over the countries of Western Asia through the agency of 'satraps', these being governors or viceroys of the twenty satrapies into which the empire was divided. The rule was not harsh, and the customs and religions of the various conquered peoples were respected. Craftsmen of many races, including Greeks and Egyptians, emigrated to the heart of this new world empire, ruled from Babylon at its foundation but afterwards from Susa, and other places more suitably located. The successive kings and their courts often resided at their summer palaces in nearer Persia; at Ecbatana, which had served as the capital of Cyrus the Great before his conquest of Babylon in 539 B.C.; at Pasargadae, the place of coronation of all the Persian monarchs; and Persepolis, which came to supplant Pasargadae in the royal favour. The erection of these and other splendid palaces gave ample opportunity for the development of Persian architecture and decorative art.

HISTORICAL. The historical period is taken to begin c. 3000 B.C. with the bringing to perfection of the art of writing and the full development of urban life; but as in the case of Egypt, the Mesopotamian civilization had been shaping many centuries previously. There are remains of important buildings that can be ascribed to an 'Archaic' stage, c. 3500–3000 B.C. There are four main historical periods.

(a) Babylonian period (c. 3000–1250 B.C.). This is a customary title for the phase, but is actually a misnomer, as Babylon did not rise to prominence until the time of its king Hammurabi (c. 1792–1750 B.C.). The civilization grew in the south, where we find the Sumerians, an 'Asianic' people, occupying city states ruled by dynasties of local kings who might for a time dominate their neighbours. Mingled with the Sumerians and exceeding them numerically in the central region and the north was a Semitic people, the Akkadians, organized in a corresponding fashion. The first comprehensive kingdom in Mesopotamia was established by Sargon I, of Akkad, c. 2340 B.C. Already by this time the influence of the civilization was being transmitted to surrounding countries, and its splendour attracting their envy. The kingdom of 'Sumer and Akkad' suffered invasions from the eastern mountains but they had not much permanent effect upon the character of the culture. Prominent among the cities was Ur, whose king Urnammu (2125 B.C.) again established a united realm which lasted for a hundred years. Babylon at length appeared as a dominant power under the great king Hammurabi (c. 1792–1750 B.C.). The dynasty he founded was brought to a close by the invasion of a foreign power, the Hittites, who, under their king Mursilis I captured Babylon in c. 1595 B.C. The Hittites were an important people centred in Anatolia, about whom some account will be given later (p. 81). They withdrew almost immediately, leaving the realm open to seizure by the Kassites, mountaineers from the central region of the Zagros range, whose very long but increasingly supine rule lasted until 1171 B.C.

(b) Assyrian period (c. 1250–612 B.C.). Meanwhile, the Assyrians, who were Semitic Akkadians, by incessant battles developed an independent state in the upper Tigris region. Tukulti-Ninurta I (c. 1250–1210 B.C.) overcame the Babylonians and ruled over the whole realm, but this was by no means the end of a bitter struggle for supremacy, which lasted for centuries. Both states declined greatly in the late second millennium, due to foreign incursions, and it was not until the reign of Tukulti-Ninurta II (890–884 B.C.) that the greatest period of Assyrian history really began. His son, Ashurnasirpal II (883–859 B.C.) waged war on every side, and removed the government from Ashur to Nimrod (Calah), where he built a palace and patronized art. His son, Shalmaneser III (859–824 B.C.) made himself master of western Asia from the Persian Gulf to the Anatolian mountains and from the Zagros range to the Mediterranean. Tiglath Pileser III (742–727 B.C.) extended the empire to the borders of Egypt. Sargon II (722–705 B.C.), most famous of Assyrian kings, warred against the Medes, occupying north-west Persia, and also against Elam, and was the first to defeat the Egyptians, in a battle near their own frontier. He was a great builder, as is testified by his new residential city and magnificent palace at Khorsabad (p. 73). Sennacherib (705–681 B.C.), the able son of Sargon, was chiefly occupied in putting down revolts and sustaining the frontiers of the Empire, but found time to build a mighty palace and other works at Nineveh. Esarhaddon, his son (681–669 B.C.), conquered Lower Egypt in 671 B.C. He too, undertook great palaces at Nimroud and Nineveh and built temples to the gods. Ashurbanipal (668–626 B.C.) fought three campaigns in Egypt and sacked Thebes (663 B.C.). He extended the boundaries of his kingdom on the north and east, and the records of his last campaign were sculptured on the wall slabs of his palace at Nineveh, which are now in the British Museum. The Empire was then at its zenith; but in 634 B.C., with the incursions of the Medes, decline set in, until in 612 B.C. Nineveh was captured and destroyed, and the Assyrian Empire divided. The northern part came under the sway of the Medes, while the southern part fell to the Babylonians, who for a century or two had been receiving strong infusions of Chaldeans, a Semitic people moving in from the south-west.

(c) Neo-Babylonian period (612–539 B.C.). The Babylonian leader was Nabopolassar, a Chaldean. He was succeeded by his son, Nebuchadnezzar II (605–563 B.C.), of Bible fame, despoiler of Jerusalem and responsible for the captivity of the Children of Israel (597–538 B.C.); he is lastingly associated with the wonders of Babylon, its palaces, hanging gardens and towered walls. The dynasty ended with Nabonidus, defeated by the Persian king, Cyrus, in 539 B.C.

(d) Persian period (539–331 B.C.). From a relatively small state in south-west Persia, Cyrus the Great, founder of the Achaemenian dynasty, achieved an enormous empire. Beginning with the establishment of his leadership over Media and

Assyria, Cyrus overcame Croesus, king of Lydia, and completed the subjugation of the Greek colonists of western Asia Minor with the capture of Sardis in 546 B.C. He then returned to secure his north-eastern frontier on the line of the river Jaxartes. Babylon was next in turn (539 B.C.), and with it fell the Babylonian possessions in Palestine. Cyrus gave the Jews in Babylonia their freedom and allowed them to return to the Promised Land. Cambyses II (529–521 B.C.), his son, extended the Persian conquests to Egypt (525 B.C.), and the impression produced by the marvellous buildings of Memphis and Thebes, no less than the sight of the wonders of the Greek cities of the western Asia Minor coast, popularized columnar architecture among the Persians. Next came Darius I (522–486 B.C.), a capable and enterprising administrator. He built a network of arterial roads. In Egypt he carried out a scheme for a canal between the Red Sea and the Nile originally projected by the Pharaoh Necho. With him, Persian arms were carried still farther eastwards to the river Indus, and in the west he pushed into Europe as far as the Danube. He also hankered after Greece, and his ambitions in that direction stirred up a revolt of the Asia Minor Greeks (499–494 B.C.) and led to his sack of Miletus, where he destroyed the famous Ionic temple (p. 131). He was, however, defeated by the Greeks at Marathon (490 B.C.). Xerxes I (486–465 B.C.), who pursued the same ambition, also met with defeat by the Greeks, not only in the sea battle of Salamis (480 B.C.) but also in the land battle of Plataea (479 B.C.). Several other Persian kings followed. With the battle of Gaugamela, in Assyria, in 331 B.C., Alexander the Great (336–323 B.C.) crushed Darius III, the last king of the Achaemenian dynasty, and all west Asia became a Greek province. After Alexander's death, Persia passed successively under the Seleucid (312–247 B.C.), Parthian (247 B.C.–A.D. 226) and Sassanian (A.D. 226–641) dynasties (p. 78), and towards the end of the latter period, was in process of defeat by the Muslims, who next assumed power (Ch. XXXIII).

ARCHITECTURAL CHARACTER

Ancient architecture in Mesopotamia and Persia was in course of historical development from about 3000 B.C. to the conquest of Alexander the Great in the late fourth century before Christ.

In the alluvial plains of the Tigris and Euphrates, stone and timber suitable for building were rare. There was, however, abundance of clay, which, compressed in moulds and either dried in the sun or kiln-burnt, provided bricks for every kind of structure. Besides massive, towered fortifications, temple-complexes and palaces were the outstanding constructions, temples being typical of Babylonian architecture and palaces of Assyrian. Buildings were raised on crude-brick platforms, each according to its importance, and the chief temples had sacred 'ziggurats,' artificial mountains made up of tiered, rectangular stages which rose in number from one to seven in the course of Mesopotamian history. Apart from the fortifications and the ziggurats, buildings of all types were arranged around large and small courts, the rooms narrow and thick-walled, carrying brick barrel vaults and sometimes domes. The roofs were usually flat outside, except where domes protruded. Alternatively, in early or commonplace buildings, palm logs supporting rushes and packed clay served for coverings, or, for the best work, cedar or other fine timber was drawn from the uplands or laboriously imported. Burnt brick was used sparingly for facings or where special stress was expected. Walls were whitewashed, or, as in the case of the developed ziggurat, painted in colour. Essentially, architecture was arcuated, the true arch with radiating voussoirs having been known by the third millennium B.C. For want of stone, columns were not used, except for a few

C

instances in late Assyrian and Neo-Babylonian work. Towers or flat buttress strips served to relieve the bare walls, which in Assyrian architecture commonly were vertically panelled and finished in stepped battlements above and stone plinths below, with colossal winged bulls guarding chief portals; in palaces the alabaster plinths or dadoes of state courts and chambers bore low-relief carving, the walls above them internally being painted with bands of continuous friezes on the thin-plaster coverings. Facing in polychrome glazed bricks, introduced by the Assyrians, was another mode of decoration for arches and walls, especially favoured by the Neo-Babylonians, in lieu of sculptured stone slabs, since in Babylonia stone was scarcer than in Assyria.

The architecture of the Persians was columnar, and thus vastly different from the massive arcuated architecture of the Mesopotamian peoples they conquered. Its light and airy character was due to the nomadic origin of the Persians and the climate of their native table-lands. Flat, timber roofs rather than vaults served for coverings, which allowed columns to be slender and graceful; while with their help, rooms could be large where necessary, and of square proportions rather than elongated as the Mesopotamian brick vaults demanded. For ceilings, wooden brackets and beams carried by the columns supported a covering of clay on a bedding of reeds on logs or planks (p. 76A). The use of double (crude-brick) walls for stability, as at Persepolis (p. 76c), may have allowed small windows just below ceiling level without their appearing on the severe external façades. Stone was plentiful on the upland sites, but was used sparingly for such as fire-temples and palace platforms, for door and window surrounds, richly-ornate columns and relief sculpture. The Persians were at first relatively inexperienced craftsmen, and drew upon the superior skills of the peoples of the empire; many of the usages and features evidence derivation from Egyptian, Mesopotamian, Syrian, Ionian Greek and other sources.

EXAMPLES

Ancient architecture in Mesopotamia and Persia is considered under three headings (brief accounts of three other cultures in the West Asiatic area follow thereafter):

Babylonian and Neo-Babylonian (c. 3000–1250 B.C. and 612–539 B.C.).
Assyrian (c. 1250–612 B.C.).
Persian (539–331 B.C.).

BABYLONIAN AND NEO-BABYLONIAN ARCHITECTURE

The earliest architectural remains belong to an 'archaic' stage preceding the true historical period; towns already were walled and were a maze of streets and crude-brick buildings elevated above threat of flood upon the spoils of the buildings of many bygone generations. The chief buildings of the Babylonians were temples, palaces at first being relatively unimportant; and as the social system was theocratic, the temple complexes provided for civic, commercial and even industrial activities as well as for religious needs. They were raised upon great platforms, usually near the centre of a town. The ancillary buildings formed forecourts to the temple court, wherein the temple stood as a climax, the courts rising in terraces towards it. Great cities acquired several prime temple groups, and in the most important of them, the mound supporting the temple-shrine reached such a height as to form a 'ziggurat' or holy mountain, its 'upper temple' then supplemented

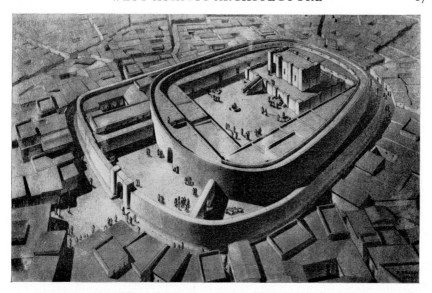

A. The Temple Oval at Khafaje. Third Millennium B.C. See p. 69

B. The Temple Complex at Ishchali. Early Second Millennium B.C. See p. 70

ZIGGURATS

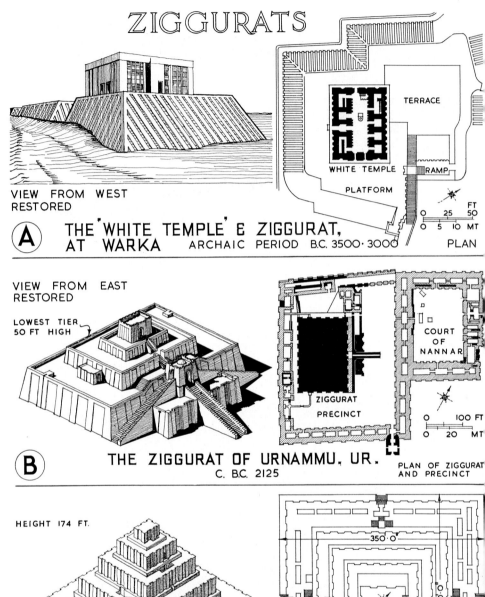

VIEW FROM WEST
RESTORED

TERRACE

WHITE TEMPLE   RAMP

PLATFORM

FT
0   25   50
0   5   10 MT

(A) THE 'WHITE TEMPLE' & ZIGGURAT, AT WARKA   ARCHAIC PERIOD B.C. 3500·3000   PLAN

VIEW FROM EAST
RESTORED

LOWEST TIER
50 FT HIGH

COURT
OF
NANNAR

ZIGGURAT
PRECINCT

0   100 FT
0   20 MT

(B) THE ZIGGURAT OF URNAMMU, UR.
C. B.C. 2125

PLAN OF ZIGGURAT
AND PRECINCT

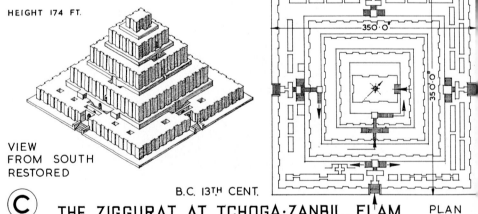

HEIGHT 174 FT.

350·0"

350·0"

VIEW
FROM SOUTH
RESTORED

B.C. 13TH CENT.

(C) THE ZIGGURAT AT TCHOGA·ZANBIL, ELAM   PLAN

by a 'lower temple' near the ziggurat base. Regularly, the corners of temple-complexes and ziggurats were orientated towards the cardinal points. The ordinary or terrace type of temple continued to be built throughout Babylonian history, as well as those with enormous ziggurats. The archaic ziggurat had only one flat-topped rectangular mound carrying the upper temple (p. 68A). In the late third millennium two or more stages had become usual, each tier strongly battered and ornamented with broad pilaster strips (p. 68B). The plan was rectangular, not square, and the ascent was made from one of the longer sides by three very steep single-flight stairways, two adjacent to the ziggurat and one on the axis, all meeting at a single landing. In the second millennium B.C. the plan became square and the number of tiers increased to four or five, now vertical but still carrying buttress strips, while the total proportions became less squat (p. 68C). These tendencies continued, and in Neo-Babylonian times there were as many as seven stages below the crowning temple. Meanwhile the Assyrians developed their own imitative version, a seven-staged square-based ziggurat of tall proportions, ascended by a continuous ramp, circulating the sides in turn (p. 72A). This reacted upon the southern type, producing instances with mixed characteristics.

The **White Temple, Warka** (Uruk; the Biblical Erech) (Archaic period, c. 3500–3000 B.C.) (p. 68A) was raised upon the earliest form of Babylonian ziggurat, flat-topped, of one stage only, 42 ft 6 ins high. The sloping sides, except the south-east, were decorated with flat buttresses. A subsidiary broad, square platform, of similar height, overlapped the north corner, served by a long flight of easy steps from which a circuitous ramp led off from an intermediate landing. The temple, originally white-washed, had an end-to-end hall of 15 ft span, flanked on both sides by a series of smaller rooms, three of which contained stairways leading to the roof. Of four entrances, the chief was placed asymmetrically on one long side, giving a 'bent-axis' approach to the sanctuary, marked by an altar platform, 4 ft high, in the north corner of the hall. Centrally nearby was a brick offering table, adjoined by a low, semicircular hearth. Shallow buttresses formed the principal decoration of the hall and of the external walls. That this temple was of a common type is indicated by several others of earlier or similar date, though standing on raised terraces, not ziggurats.

The **Temple Oval at Khafaje** (p. 67A) was one of a small number of temple complexes contained in an oval enclosure, all of the third millennium B.C. Here, there was one enclosure within another, 328 ft by 230 ft overall. Despite the un-orthodox shape, the group affords an excellent illustration of the parts of a temple complex of the terrace type normal in the early historical period. Within the ovals the lay-out was rectilinear, the corners orientated N.E.S.W. Of three ascending terrace levels, the lowest made a forecourt approached through an arched and towered gateway from the town and having a many-roomed building on one side which was either an administrative building or a dwelling for the arch-priest. The second terrace, wholly surrounded by rooms used as workshops and stores, had at its farther end the temple platform, about 12 ft high. Near its staircase, against the side of the temple terrace, was an external sacrificial altar, while elsewhere in the court were a well and two basins for ritual ablutions.

The **Ziggurat and Precinct, Ur** (p. 68B), already old, were extensively re-modelled by Urnammu and others of the third dynasty of its kings (c. 2125–2025 B.C.). Comprising the complex were the ziggurat and its court; a secondary court attached to it; and two great temples and a palace, all raised on a great rectangular platform at the heart of an oval-shaped, walled city of tight-packed houses, itself standing 20 ft above the plain. The ziggurat, 205 ft by 141 ft on base and about 70 ft high, carried the usual 'upper temple' and had the normal orientation. The restoration (p. 68B) serves to illustrate the features of the Babylonian type, of which there are substantial remains on numerous sites in southern Mesopotamia and in some of the more northerly cities too. The Ur ziggurat had a solid core of sun-dried brick, covered with a skin of burnt brickwork, 8 ft thick, laid in bitumen and with layers of matting at intervals to improve cohesion.

The **Temple Complex at Ishchali** (early second millennium B.C.) (p. 67B) was of the terrace type, without a ziggurat. It was rectangular in plan, but otherwise its arrangements were not unlike those of the Temple Oval in the neighbouring town of Khafaje. It had a large main terrace court and an upper one in which the temple lay at right angles to the chief axis. On the corresponding side of the main court there were two minor courts, and all were lined with rooms.

The **Ziggurat at Tchoga-Zanbil, near Susa, Elam** (13th cent. B.C.) (p. 68C), built by King Untash-Gal, stands in the rival state east of Babylonia. The remarkably complete remains, recently exposed, give fuller and more authentic particulars of the upper parts of a ziggurat than hitherto have been forthcoming. There were five tiers, the lowest shallower than the rest, each mounted on a plinth. The base is 350 ft square and the total height was about 174 ft. Flights of stairs, recessed in the mass, led to the top of the first tier on the centre of each front, but only that on the south-west led to the second tier, while the rest of the height had to be accomplished on the south-east, principal, side.

The **City of Babylon,** famous in history and legend, was rebuilt by Nebuchadnezzar II (605–563 B.C.), for it had been comprehensively destroyed by the Assyrian king, Sennacherib, in 689 B.C. It had an inner and outer part, each heavily fortified. The inner town was approximately square in plan, of about 1,450 yards side, containing the principal buildings, the Euphrates river forming the west side. The few main streets intersected starkly at right angles, terminating in tower-framed bronze gates where they met the walls. Between the main streets, tiered dwellings, business houses, temples, chapels and shrines jostled in lively disarray. The principal sites lined the river front, and behind them ran a grand, processional way, its vista closed on the north by the Ishtar Gate, glowing in coloured glazed bricks, patterned with yellow and white bulls and dragons in relief upon a blue ground (p. 71C). Hereabouts there were palace-citadels, and connected with Nebuchadnezzar's great palace complex on the waterside, 900 ft by 600 ft overall, was that marvel of the ancient world, the Hanging Gardens; among its maze of rooms was a vast throne room, 170 ft by 56 ft, its long façade decorated with polychrome glazed bricks. The central sites on the river front were occupied by the chief temple of the god of the city, Marduk, and, to the north of it, the expansive precinct where rose the associated ziggurat, the 'Tower of Babel'. Of these, the illustration on p. 88 gives an imaginative view, looking south-east. The celebrated ziggurat appears to have been one combining the triple stairway approach and massive lower tier customary in old Babylonia with upper stages arranged spirally according to Assyrian developed practice. The plan was square, of 295 ft side, and there were seven stages in all, the summit temple being faced with blue glazed bricks.

ASSYRIAN ARCHITECTURE

In the earlier part of the period, Babylonian practice was closely followed. There were temples both with and without ziggurats; but palaces were much more frequent and important. The Assyrians introduced polychrome ornamental brickwork —so popular with the Neo-Babylonians later on—and also high plinths or dadoes made of great stone slabs placed on edge, usually carved with low-relief sculpture.

A. Palaces of Esarhaddon (680–669 B.C.) and Ashurnasirpal II (883–859 B.C.),
Nimroud (imaginative view). See p. 73

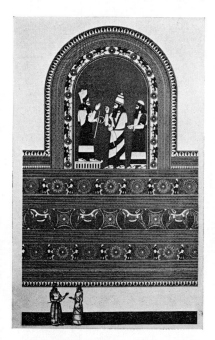

B. Wall painting, Palace of Sargon II,
Khorsabad (722–705 B.C.). See p. 73

C. The Ishtar Gate, Babylon. Nebuchadnezzar
II (605–563 B.C.). See p. 70

Ⓐ ASSYRIAN RAMPED TEMPLE

Ⓑ WALL SLAB: NINEVEH

Ⓒ DRAIN
UNDER PALACE PLATFORM
KHORSABAD

Ⓓ ELEVATION   PORTAL IN S.E. CITY
                   GATEWAY 3, KHORSABAD

14' 3"

21' 4"

12' 6"

Ⓔ SECTION

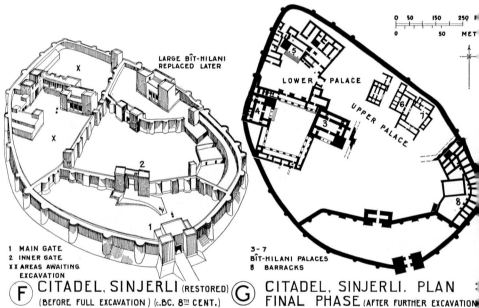

LARGE BÎT-HILANI
REPLACED LATER

X

X

2

1

1 MAIN GATE
2 INNER GATE
XX AREAS AWAITING
   EXCAVATION

Ⓕ CITADEL, SINJERLI (RESTORED)
   (BEFORE FULL EXCAVATION) (c.BC. 8ᵀᴴ CENT.)

0   50   150   250 F
├──┼──┼──┼──┼──┤
0   50   MET

LOWER PALACE

5

UPPER PALACE

4

3

6 7

8

3-7
BÎT-HILANI PALACES
8 BARRACKS

Ⓖ CITADEL, SINJERLI. PLAN
   FINAL PHASE (AFTER FURTHER EXCAVATION

Continuous decorative friezes of stone, polychrome brickwork or painted on the plastered walls (p. 71B), were a characteristic feature of their interior decoration.

The **City of Ashur** of *c*. 1000 B.C. had in its chief precinct two ziggurat temples, one to Ashur and another to the gods Anu-Adad, the latter having twin ziggurat-towers with the related temples spanning between them. There were also two further temples without ziggurats and two enormous palaces, one being primarily for administrative purposes. The increasing importance of palaces as demonstrated here is significant, for in the second half of the Assyrian period they became dominant, temples and their ziggurats taking a decidedly subsidiary place.

The **City of Nineveh** (Kouyunjik) first became a capital about 1100 B.C., succeeded in turn by Ashur, Nimroud (Calah) and Khorsabad. Sennacherib (705–681 B.C.) restored its status, encircled it with mighty walls and built palaces and other structures. More palaces were built there by his immediate successors, Esarhaddon and Ashurbanipal. Relief sculptures recovered from the site and now in the British Museum show not only warlike pursuits but also building operations (pp. 72B, 84J).

The **City of Nimroud** (Calah) had a rectangular raised temenos carrying the chief buildings. In one angle was an ancient ziggurat, and elsewhere on the platform were two or more temples and four or five palaces by kings from Ashurnasirpal II (883–859 B.C.) to Esarhaddon (680–669 B.C.). The restoration (p. 71A) gives an imaginative impression of the original appearance of the west side of the temenos. From Ashurnasirpal's palace came some remarkable wall slabs now in the British Museum (p. 84A, E, F, G, H).

The **City of Khorsabad**, built by Sargon II (722–705 B.C.), was abandoned at his death. It was square-planned, defensively-walled, and covered nearly a square mile (p. 74C). There were two gateways spaced on each tower-serrated wall, except that the place of one of the gates on the north-west wall was taken by an extensive citadel enclosure, containing all but one of the town's chief buildings. These comprised a palace for the king's brother, who was his vizier; a temple to Nabu; several official buildings; and, dominating all, the **Palace of Sargon** himself, a complex of large and small courts, corridors and rooms, covering twenty-three acres (p. 74). Each of the buildings was raised upon a terrace, that of the Palace of Sargon reaching to the level of the town walls, which the palace site bestrode. It was approached by broad ramps from the citadel court, which allowed access equally to pedestrians, horses and chariots. The main entrance to the palace grand court was flanked by great towers and guarded by man-headed winged bulls, 12 ft 6 ins high, supporting a bold, semicircular arch decorated with brilliantly-coloured glazed bricks. The palace had three main parts, each abutting the grand court. On the left on entering was a group of three large and three small temples; on the right, service quarters and administrative offices; and opposite, the private and residential apartments, with the state chambers behind. The state chambers had their own court, almost as large as the first, which could be approached from the grand court or from an independent gateway. Here, foreign and other dignitaries would be impressively received. All around the state court were dado slabs, over 7 ft high, bearing reliefs of the king and his courtiers, facing towards the throne room, a grand apartment flanking the inner long side of the court, with a main and two flank entrances guarded by sculptured, man-headed winged bulls. The lofty throne room, about 160 ft by 35 ft, was the outermost of a state suite planned around its own internal court. It probably was one of the few apartments to have a flat timber ceiling, for fine timber was rare and costly. The plastered walls bore a painted decoration of a triple band of friezes, framed in running ornament, about 18 ft high overall, circulating the room above a stone dado of reliefs (p. 71B). In general, walls were thick; on the average, about 20 ft. In the Grand

PALACE OF SARGON: KHORSABAD

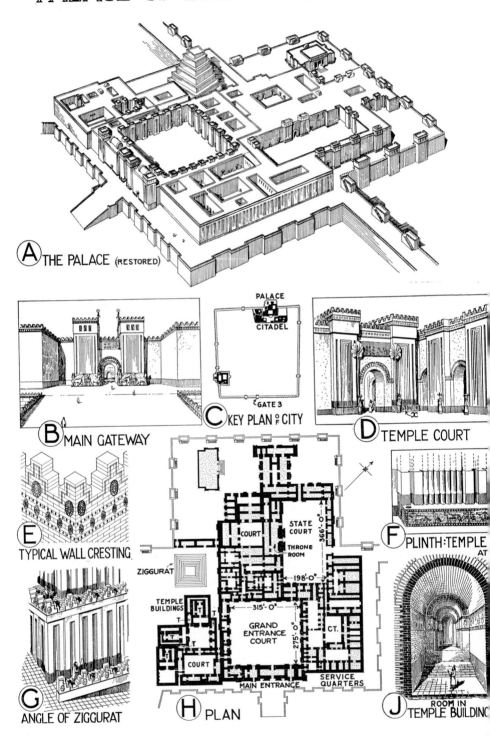

A THE PALACE (RESTORED)

B MAIN GATEWAY

C KEY PLAN OF CITY

PALACE
CITADEL
GATE 3

D TEMPLE COURT

E TYPICAL WALL CRESTING

F PLINTH: TEMPLE AT

G ANGLE OF ZIGGURAT

H PLAN

ZIGGURAT
TEMPLE BUILDINGS
COURT
STATE COURT
COURT
THRONE ROOM
GRAND ENTRANCE COURT
CT.
SERVICE QUARTERS
MAIN ENTRANCE
366'-0"
198'-0"
315'-0"
275'-0"

J ROOM IN TEMPLE BUILDING

and Temple Courts, decoration was contrived by sunken vertical panelling on the whitewashed walls and towers, finishing in stepped battlements above and stone plinths below, plain or carved (p. 74D). Within the mud-brick platforms of the palace there were jointed terra-cotta drains to carry away rainwater, joining larger drains of burnt brick covered with vaults which were slightly pointed and in which the brick courses were laid obliquely, so that wood centering might be avoided (p. 72C). This device was well-known to the Egyptians too. Only stone dadoes so far have been mentioned; at the approach to the three chief temples there were high plinths projecting from the wall, faced in polychrome glazed bricks portraying sacred motifs and serving as pedestals for high cedar masts ringed with ornamental bronze bands (p. 74F). The wall behind was panelled with a series of abutted half-columns, a revival of an ancient motif originating in the imitation of palm logs. It is remarkable to find that the only ziggurat of the city is associated with the palace temples and not with the large Nabu temple nearby. On a square base of 148 ft side, the seven-tiered ziggurat rose to the same height (148 ft—including the shrine at the top), ascended by a winding ramp, 6 ft wide. The successive tiers were panelled and battlemented and were painted in different colours on the plastered faces (p. 74A, G).

PERSIAN ARCHITECTURE

Palaces and tombs of the Persians show that many features of their remarkable columnar architecture were derived from the older civilizations; the gorge mould-ing from Egypt; the raised platforms, sculptured monsters, relief slabs and poly-chrome brickwork from Mesopotamia.

The **Palace of Cyrus the Great at Pasargadae** (*c.* 550 B.C.—before Cyrus came to full power), indicates that the Persians were still at this time more accustomed to nomadic than to urban life, for the few scattered buildings resembled pavilions, dispersed in a parkland enclosure, the latter serving for assembly on special occa-sions. Widely separated, a gatehouse, audience hall and residence were of quite new character, comprising many-columned rooms and external double porticoes. South-west of the palace was the **Tomb of Cyrus** (*d.* 529 B.C.), a simple box-like monument of limestone 10 ft 6 ins by 7 ft 6 ins, gabled and standing on a platform of six steps.

Susa, ancient city of Elam, became the Persian capital in succession to Babylon with the building there of a citadel and palace complex by Darius I (522–486 B.C.). A most illuminating building inscription tells how the resources and skills of the whole empire were utilized in the construction of the palace buildings. Cedar was brought from Lebanon, teak from the Zagros mountains and southern Persia, while the baked bricks were made by the Babylonian method. Most significant of all, craftsmen were drawn from the Assyrians, Babylonians, Egyptians and Ionian Greeks. The remarkable compound of features which constitute the unique and gracious architecture of Persia is thus explained. From this palace and a later one by Artaxerxes II (404–358 B.C.) come the famous glazed-brick decorations, por-traying processions of archers, lions, bulls or dragons (p. 76F, G).

The **Palace of Persepolis** (p. 76A–E), begun in 518 B.C. by Darius I, was mostly executed by Xerxes I (486–465 B.C.) and finished by Artaxerxes I about 460 B.C. The various buildings stood on a platform, partly built up and partly excavated, faced in well-laid local stone bound with iron cramps, about 1,500 ft by 900 ft in extent and rising 50 ft above the plain at the base of a rocky spur. The approach on the north-west was by a magnificent flight of steps, 22 ft wide, shallow enough for horses to ascend. A gatehouse by Xerxes had mud-brick walls, faced

A. Persepolis: Hall of the Hundred Columns (restored) (*c.* 518–460 B.C.). See p. 78.
Other details of the palaces at Persepolis are given below

B DOUBLE "BULL" CAP: APADANA OF XERXES

10'-5"

17'-10"

C PLAN OF PALACE PLATFORM.

1. STAIRWAY TO TERRACE
2. GATEHOUSE OF XERXES
3. APADANA OF DARIUS I
4. PALACE OF DARIUS I
5. PALACE OF XERXES
6. TRIPYLON
7. HAREM
8. TREASURY
9. HALL OF 100 COLUMNS
10. INNER GATEHOUSE

D DOUBLE "UNICORN" CAP: APADANA OF XERXES

17'-11½"

63'-7¼"

E BAS-RELIEF: PERSEPOLIS.

ABT. 7.10"

F LION FRIEZE: SUSA.

ABT. 4.0"

G ARCHER FRIEZE: SUSA

5'-0"

A. Stairway of the Tripylon, Persepolis (518–486 B.C.). See p. 78

B. Tomb of Darius, Naksh-i-Rustam (485 B.C.). See p. 78

c. Fire Temple, Naksh-i-Rustam. See p. 78

with polychrome bricks, and front and rear portals guarded by stone bulls. A third doorway on the south led towards the 'Apadana', a grand audience hall, 250 ft square and with thirty-six columns within its 20 ft-thick walls, begun by Darius but completed by his two successors. It stood on its own terrace, 10 ft high; had three porticoes, each with double colonnades; stately stairways on the north and east sides; and minor rooms across the south side and in the four angle towers. The Palace of Darius, small by comparison, lay immediately south of the Apadana, near the west terrace wall. This might have been finished in his lifetime, as also the terraced 'Tripylon', which lay centrally among the buildings and acted as a reception chamber and guard-room for the more private quarters of the palace group. Also by Darius was the 'Treasury', in the south-east angle of the site, a double-walled administrative and storehouse building with columned halls of different sizes and only a single doorway. The buildings of Darius were arranged in the loose fashion of earlier times. Xerxes added his in between. He built his own palace near the south-west angle, connected with an L-shaped building, identified as the women's quarters (harim) which completed the enclosure of a court south of the Tripylon. He also commenced the famous 'Hall of the Hundred Columns' (finished by Artaxerxes I), this a Throne Hall, 225 ft square, with columns 37 ft high, supporting a flat, cedar roof (p. 76A, C). The walls were double, except on the north side, where a portico faced a forecourt, with its own gate-house, separated from the Apadana forecourt by a stout wall. The Throne Hall had two doorways and seven windows on the entrance wall, matched on the other three sides except that niches substituted the windows. All were framed in stone surrounds in the 11-ft thick brick wall. From Persepolis have been recovered many wonderful architectural sculptures. All the monumental stairs were lined with reliefs, as also the Apadana terrace, where they were arranged in triple tiers or 'registers', separated by bands of rosettes. Nobles, courtiers, chieftains, tribute-bearers and guardsmen advanced in dignified procession, and traditional subjects filled the awkward angles of the stairways and the deep jambs of the doorways (p. 76E). Stepped battlements crowned the parapet walls. All these sculptures were originally in brilliant colour. Columns of the lesser apartments had wooden shafts, thickly plastered and decoratively painted, but those of the Halls were of stone throughout. They have a character all their own, with moulded bases, fluted shafts and curious, complex capitals with vertical Ionic-like volutes and twin bulls or dragons supporting the roof beams (p. 76B, D).

The **Tomb of Darius, Naksh-i-Rustam,** (485 B.C.) (p. 77B), eight miles north of Persepolis, is one of four rock-hewn sepulchres of the great Achaemenian kings. Its façade, 60 ft wide, appears to reproduce the south front of Darius' palace at Persepolis, with four columns of the double-bull type, central doorway with Egyptian-like cornice, and upper compartment in which an elaborate throne, 9 ft high, is supported by two rows of figures, above which the king stands before a fire altar, Ahuramazda floating overhead. A little distance in front of the tomb stands a **Fire Temple,** a stone, square tower containing a single room, approached by an outside stairway (p. 77C).

SELEUCID, PARTHIAN AND SASSANIAN ARCHITECTURE
(312 B.C.–A.D. 641)

The architecture which succeeded that of the Achaemenian Persian phase is interesting, though not of great importance.

The Seleucid Empire, founded in 312 B.C. after the death of Alexander, began to disintegrate about 247 B.C., and after 140 B.C. was confined to the region west of the Euphrates, finally giving way to the Romans in 64 B.C. Meanwhile there was a considerable influx of Macedonian and Greek settlers, who built many new towns, including Seleucia, near Babylon, and Antioch, in Syria. In Bactria, on the eastern border, they spread Greek civilization to India; but in general, their influence was uneven, and in art and architecture it was sometimes the Hellenistic and sometimes the local Persian character that prevailed. The Parthians, who wrested the eastern and Mesopotamian territories piecemeal from the Seleucids, respected the Hellenistic culture and institutions and under their long rule the new Greek cities flourished. Yet as integration proceeded, the arts profoundly declined. With the Sassanian dynasty (A.D. 226–642), when the principal city was Ctesiphon, near Babylon, vigour sprang anew and a number of fine buildings were erected which form a connecting link between the old Mesopotamian architecture on the one hand and Byzantine on the other. Palaces were the dominant type.

The **Palace, Feruz-abad** (south of Persepolis) (*c*. A.D. 250) (p. 80), built of stone rubble faced with plaster, has a deep, open-fronted arched entrance leading to three domed halls, forming a reception suite, beyond which is a court surrounded by private chambers. The domes are seated over the three square halls with the help of 'squinch' arches thrown across the angles (p. 80C), while the internal walls below them are ornamented with niches having plaster archivolts and enframements of a classical complexion but capped with cornices of the Egyptian 'gorge' type (p. 80C, F).

The **Palace of Shapur I, Bishapur,** (west of Persepolis) (*c*. A.D. 260), was a remarkable building built of plastered stone rubble, with a cruciform plan, dominated by a central dome of elliptical section springing from floor level. The coloured-plaster wall-decoration of modelled architectural features again had a classical character.

The **Palace, Sarvistan,** (vicinity of Persepolis) (*c*. A.D. 350) (p. 80) was fronted by the typical deep barrel-vaulted porches, behind which rose a bee-hive dome, carried on squinch arches (p. 80H), marking the principal apartment. The dome was pierced with openings for light and ventilation. Two long side chambers had barrel vaults supported on massive piers which themselves stood on pairs of stumpy columns (p. 80K), a most ingenious method of reducing the effective span and obtaining powerful abutment to the vaults.

At Feruz-abad and Bishapur there were towered fire-temples, used in connection with open-air ceremonies, similar to that at Naksh-i-Rustam, of the Achaemenian Persian period, mentioned opposite.

The **Palace, Ctesiphon** (p. 80) is usually attributed to Chosroes I (A.D. 531–579) but is probably of the fourth century A.D. As it is in the Mesopotamian plain, it is of brick. The principal part surviving is a vast banqueting hall, open-fronted like the reception tents of tribal sheiks in nomadic days, with flanking private wings screened by an enormous wall, 112 ft 6 ins high. The latter is ornamented with tiers of attached columns and arcades, an arrangement betraying Roman influence. One wing of the façade fell in 1909 after an exceptional Tigris flood. The elliptical barrel vault over the hall, 24 ft thick at the base and rising 120 ft from the floor to cover the 83 ft span, equalled if it did not surpass the mightiest structural achievements of Ancient Rome. The lower part of the vault is constructed in horizontal courses—Sassanian domes were usually constructed wholly in this manner—but substantially the vault is made up of arch rings sloped against an end wall, so as to avoid the necessity of temporary wood centering. This is a practice which we have seen to have been adopted for brick vaults equally in Ancient Egyptian and in Assyrian architecture.

An account of Muslim Architecture in Persia is given on pp. 1234–7.

PALACE ⚔ FERUZ-ABAD

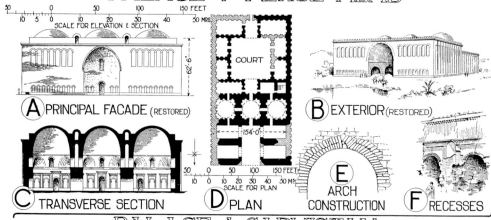

50   0   50   100   150 FEET
10 5 0   10   20   30   40   50 MRS
SCALE FOR ELEVATION & SECTION

62'-6"

(A) PRINCIPAL FACADE (RESTORED)

COURT

154'-0"

50   0   50   100   150 FEET
10   0   10   20   30   40   50 M³
SCALE FOR PLAN

(B) EXTERIOR (RESTORED)

(C) TRANSVERSE SECTION

(D) PLAN

(E) ARCH CONSTRUCTION

(F) RECESSES

PALACE ⚔ SARVISTAN

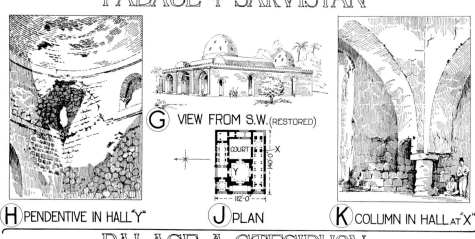

(G) VIEW FROM S.W. (RESTORED)

COURT
X
Y
140'-0"
112'-0"

(H) PENDENTIVE IN HALL "Y"

(J) PLAN

(K) COLUMN IN HALL AT "X"

PALACE ⚔ CTESIPHON

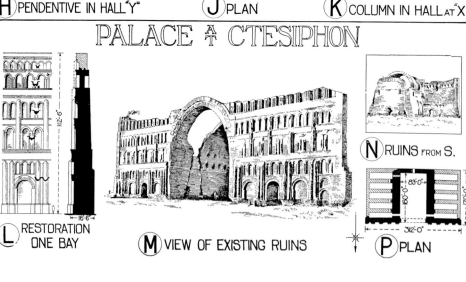

112'-6"

16'-6"

(L) RESTORATION ONE BAY

(M) VIEW OF EXISTING RUINS

(N) RUINS FROM S.

83'-0"
80'-0"
312'-0"
170'-0"

(P) PLAN

HITTITE ARCHITECTURE
(*Circa* 1750–1200 B.C.)

While the Mesopotamian civilization proceeded, numerous petty states grew up in Anatolia. One group coalesced in the central upland of Asia Minor to form the powerful kingdom of the Hittites, with its principal city at Boghazköy (ancient Hattusas). The 'Old Kingdom' gave way to 'The Empire' about 1460 B.C. In the former period, the redoubtable Mursilis I raided Syria and even captured Babylon (1595 B.C.), though he almost immediately withdrew; in the latter, the Hittites firmly established their supremacy over neighbouring states and in Syria clashed with their imperialist rivals, the Egyptians. A trial of strength with Rameses II (1301–1235 B.C.) led to a treaty between the two powers *c.* 1280 B.C. The Hittite Empire collapsed suddenly about 1200 B.C., due to the same overwhelming invasion that produced the prodigious onslaught of the 'Peoples of the Sea' upon Egypt, repelled by Rameses II (1198–1166 B.C.).

Mesopotamian influences were strong in Hittite architecture, but there was much in it that was individual. In important structures, massive stone masonry was a feature, though the upper parts of walls, even of highland town fortifications, were commonly of sun-dried bricks in timber-framing: wood is still used for building in the mountains of Anatolia, and in ancient times was undoubtedly more plentiful than now. The chief remains are of town walls, palaces and temples. There survive also many impressive rock sculptures of a sacred character, widely distributed in isolated highland sites.

The outer **Town Walls, Boghazköy** (Hattusas) (*c.* 1360 B.C.) (p. 83A, B) enclosed an area of some 300 acres. They were double, like those of Mesopotamia, connected by cross-walls, the compartments thus formed being packed with rubble. Square towers projected at frequent intervals, and some 20 ft in front was a lesser wall, with its own minor towers. The outer shell of the main wall was particularly strong, built of large, rock-faced, close-jointed stones up to 5 ft long, varying in shape from the rectangular to the polygonal. The upper parts of the walls were of brick, towers and walls finishing in crenellations similar to the Mesopotamian. Five gateways partially survive. These were flanked by great towers and had peculiar elliptical openings of which the corbelled upper parts stood on pairs of enormous monolithic stone jambs (p. 83A). Broad archivolts surrounded the portals, and ornamenting the jambs of three of the gates were boldly-projecting sculptures. On the 'King's Gate' was an armed warrior on the reveal; on the 'Lion Gate', foreparts of lions on the face of the jambs; and on the 'Sphinx Gate', sphinxes not only project forwards but show the full body-length on the reveals, thus anticipating the similar monsters of Assyrian times by some five centuries. At **Alaja**, 20 miles north-east of Boghazköy, is another Sphinx Gate, and from thereabouts also come some dado slabs in relief, which again are prototypes of the splendid mural sculptures of the Assyrians.

Temple 1, Boghazköy (Empire period) (p. 83E) is the largest and oldest of five identified there, which have no regular orientation but show other principal features in common. They consist of a number of rooms arranged around a central court, with cloister or corridor access on two or more sides. These rooms presumably were administrative offices for the control of the agricultural lands of the temples, for in the case of Temple 1, the building is girdled by a paved road beyond which are numerous magazines, many still filled with great earthenware jars and one containing cuneiform tablets constituting the temple records. Asymmetrically placed was a special unit of several rooms, the largest of all being a sanctuary, only to be reached circuitously through adjacent smaller rooms. The sanctuary projected at one end, so that windows might give side illumination to the cult-statue. Unlike Mesopotamian temples, light to most rooms came from deep windows on the external walls. The entrance also was asymmetrical, whether through a simple recessed porch on the flank, or, as in Temple I, on the front opposite the sanctuary unit. To one side of the court in Temple I stood a cell built of granite, as was the sanctuary unit, the building elsewhere being of limestone. At Alaja was a similar temple.

The **Open-air Sanctuary, Yazilikaya** (Empire period) (p. 83D), about two miles north-east of Boghazköy, is a deep re-entrant in an almost sheer limestone face, with processions of some seventy religious figures, about 3 ft high, carved at eye-level on the faces, converging on a rear panel. A minor grotto adjoined on the east. Screening the groves was a temple, comprising three buildings in series, linked by walls; a deep propylaeum (see Glossary); the temple proper, with rooms on three sides of a court in which stood a walled cell and from which a left-hand turn was made towards the sacred groves through a second, pillared propylaeum; and a large sanctuary, independently approached. The propylaeum unit, as twice encountered here, is frequent in the contemporary 'Aegean' architecture of mainland Greece (p. 99B, C).

ARCHITECTURE IN SYRIA
(*Circa* 2000–700 B.C.)

Syria, which in ancient times included the Palestine extension, was geographically poorly circumstanced to develop a homogeneous architecture, being elongated and extremely diverse physically, whilst constantly liable to interference or invasion from the great powers around it as well as to the incursion of migrant peoples in search of living space. Its history is scarcely less long than that of Egypt or Mesopotamia, but while it was almost continuously influenced by them, its culture was relatively retarded due to these conditions. Mostly it was politically subdivided into numerous small states, even when under foreign domination. Nevertheless it played a great part in history in transmitting or transmuting the cultures of its progressive neighbours. Already before the chariots of the Hyksos had swept into Egypt about 1750 B.C., the port of Byblos had become virtually an outpost of Egypt, whose requirements of timber led to the commercial hegemony which the latter held in the country. Egypt expelled the Hyksos and returned to Syria, and then battled with the Hittites, dividing the country with them by the treaty of *c.* 1280 B.C. Meanwhile the Phoenicians, occupying the central coastal strip, developed their Mediterranean trade apace. The further tremendous upheaval caused by the 'Peoples of the Sea' and other invaders about 1200 B.C., seriously preoccupied or, in the case of the Hittites, destroyed, the established neighbouring powers, and in the following centuries Syrian states were able to move towards independence. The Philistines, residue of the Peoples of the Sea, settled 'Palestine' in the south; Israel emerged; and Phoenicia, with its famous cities of Tyre and Sidon, nurtured seafarers who succeeded the 'Aegean' mariners as the supreme traders of the Mediterranean (see p. 89); among their many colonies and trading-stations was Carthage, founded *c.* 814 B.C., later to become the bitter enemy of Rome. After *c.* 700 B.C., Syria succumbed in turn to Assyria, Egypt, Neo-Babylonia, Persia and Alexander.

Architecturally, a phase of some importance was that in North Syria in the period *c.* 900–700 B.C., often known as the 'Syro-Hittite', for among the mixed peoples of that region strong elements of the Hittites still survived: we see from the

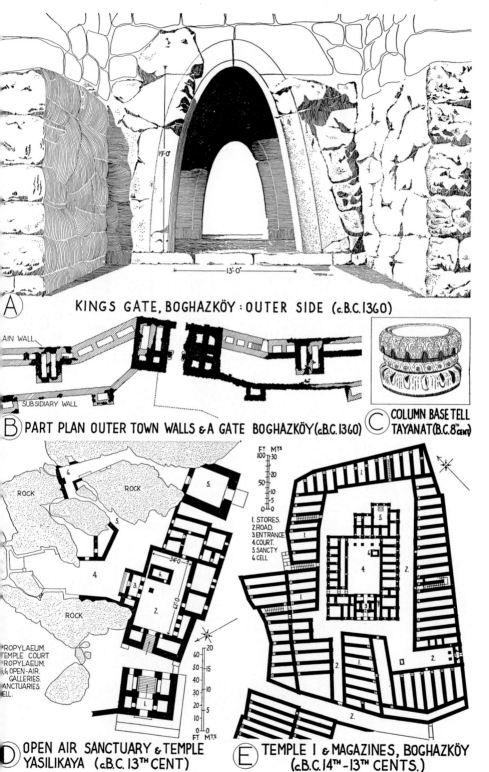

A KINGS GATE, BOGHAZKÖY: OUTER SIDE (c.B.C.1360)

19'-0"

13'-0"

AIN WALL

SUBSIDIARY WALL

B PART PLAN OUTER TOWN WALLS & A GATE BOGHAZKÖY(c.B.C.1360)

C COLUMN BASE TELL TAYANAT(B.C.8TH CENT)

FT MTS
100 30
50 20
10
5
0 0

I. STORES.
2.ROAD.
3.ENTRANCE
4.COURT.
5.SANCTY
6.CELL

ROCK   ROCK

4

5

4

34'-0"

42'-0"

ROCK

PROPYLAEUM.
TEMPLE COURT.
PROPYLAEUM.
5,6 OPEN-AIR.
GALLERIES.
SANCTUARIES.
CELL.

FT
60 20
50 15
40 10
30
20 5
10
0 0
FT MTS

D OPEN AIR SANCTUARY & TEMPLE YASILIKAYA (c.B.C. 13TH CENT)

E TEMPLE I & MAGAZINES, BOGHAZKÖY (c.B.C.14TH-13TH CENTS.)

A WALL SLAB : LION HUNT
FROM N.W. PALACE : NIMROUD

B WINGED GLOBE
WITH FIGURE

C MARBLE PAVEMENT SLAB
FROM NINEVEH

D CEILING DECORATION
LOTUS FLOWERS AND BUDS

E WINGED HUMAN HEADED LION
FROM PALACE OF ASHUR-NASIR-PAL : NIMROUD

F HEAD OF A LION
IN WHITE LIMESTONE

G WALL SLAB : KING ON THRONE AND ATTENDANTS : FROM PALACE OF ASHUR-NASIR-PAL : NIMROUD

H WINGED DEITY : NIMROUD   J TRANSPORT OF A BULL : NINEVEH   K EGYPTIAN KING IN IVORY

Bible that in their own time they gave their name to the populace there. A feature repeatedly appearing in the palaces of the local monarchs was the 'bît-hilâni' or porched house, a standard reception unit that already had been developing in north Syria at a much earlier time.

The **Citadel, Sinjerli,** (p. 72F, G) was of oval plan, standing centrally on a mound in a walled town which, like so many in ancient West Asia, was completely circular. The construction of the citadel walls was typical of the period in being of timber-framed, sun-dried brick, standing on a couple of courses of cut masonry on rubble foundations. Internally, the citadel was divided into defensive zones by cross walls, securing the approaches to an 'Upper' and a 'Lower' Palace (c. 8th cent. B.C.). Each comprised bît-hilâni units, two of which are particularly plain in the plan of the Lower Palace (p. 72G). They stood on opposite sides of a large, cloistered court. Each had a two-columned porch, with a stair on the right, leading to a transverse hall or throne room, beyond which was a range of smaller rooms including bedroom and bathroom. In front of the throne was a circular hearth (a hall in the Upper Palace had a movable iron hearth on bronze wheels). The porch columns were of wood, with stone bases shaped either as a pair of lions or monsters, or in triple, ornamented stone cushions having some likeness to the earliest versions of the base of the classical Greek Ionic Order (p. 125). Instances of both occur at **Tell Tayanat,** west of Antioch (p. 83C). Following the old Hittite tradition and contemporary Assyrian practice, gates were protected by stone monsters and had 'orthostates' (plinth or dado vertical slabs) carved in relief. Typically Syro-Hittite is the lavish use of timber in the reinforcement of upper, sun-dried brick walls, above the stone dadoes. Other notable Syro-Hittite towns were **Carchemish** and **Sakjegeuzi.**

COMPARATIVE ANALYSIS
(Mesopotamia and Persia, *circa* 3000–331 B.C.)

PLANS. The Mesopotamians, in which term are included Babylonians and Assyrians, erected terraced temples and palaces on high, artificial platforms in towns and cities which were themselves amply raised above the surrounding alluvial plains. Halls and rooms grouped around quadrangles and courts were long and narrow, so as to be easy to vault (p. 74H). The ziggurats (p. 68) associated with the chief temples, which rose tower-like in diminishing terraces to a crowning upper temple or shrine, had their angles towards the cardinal points, unlike Egyptian pyramids whose sides were so placed. Mesopotamian buildings were designed for both internal and external effect, contrasting with Egyptian temples which, apart from the frontal pylons were wholly plain outside. The Persians imitated the Mesopotamians in the use of platforms and terraces, but faced the former in stone ashlar and the latter with low-relief slabs (pp. 76E, 77A). Timber roofs, supported by numerous columns, allowed rooms to be large and of square proportions compared with the corridor-like vaulted apartments of the Babylonians and Assyrians.

WALLS. In the Mesopotamian plains, the sun-dried brick walls were very thick, sometimes with a deep facing of baked bricks in bitumen jointing, which contrast with the stone, massive walls of the Egyptians and the spare, fine-jointed ashlar constructions of the Greeks. External walls were plainly treated, apart from buttress strips or projecting towers (p. 74A, B, D), the mud-wall faces being protected by tinted washes. The Assyrians employed battlemented cresting and stone or alabaster dadoes or plinths, ornamented with reliefs portraying military and sporting events; they also introduced mural decoration in polychrome bricks and internal painting of continuous friezes on plaster (p. 71B). Persian palace walls similarly were of sun-dried brick, whitewashed or tinted externally, and had the same types of cresting, mural decoration in polychrome bricks (p. 476F, G) and dado relief slabs as the Assyrians, but they used massive stone surrounds to door and window openings and elaborate monumental stairways lined with relief sculptures (p. 77A).

OPENINGS. Mesopotamian doorways were spanned by double semicircular arches, sometimes ornamented with polychrome glazed bricks in developed Assyrian architecture (pp. 72D, E; 74B, D). Instances of the pointed arch occur at Susa and Khorsabad in aqueducts and gateways, and in drains under the palace platform at the latter place (p. 72C) (c. 722 B.C.). Windows were rare, square-headed and high up the walls; tall doorways normally sufficed to admit light. Ventilation was contrived by terracotta pipes carried through the vaults. Persian doorways and windows in the Persepolis Throne Hall were square-headed and of stone set in the sun-dried brick walls, the doorways having a cornice cresting resembling the Egyptian gorge. The Tomb of Darius shows a typical doorway (p. 77B).

ROOFS. Babylonian roofs were at first spanned by poles or logs carrying packed-clay coverings on reeds, but the typical Mesopotamian roof for the better buildings was the brick barrel vault, of two or more arch-rings, made flat on top, and doubtless protected by bitumen (p. 74J). Domes also became a frequent form of covering for square apartments of modest dimensions, as is shown by Assyrian wall slabs, and these sometimes were egg-shaped with an aperture at the top (p. 72B). Persian palace buildings were roofed in timber, with columns supporting brackets and beams and thus panels of plates or poles carrying a packed-clay covering on reeds (p. 76A).

COLUMNS. These are rare in earlier Mesopotamian architecture, but occasional instances are known in Assyrian and in Neo-Babylonian works. The Persians, on the contrary, used columns extensively, widely-spaced and comparatively slender as they had only to support the timber and clay roofs, instead of ponderous stone beams and slabs as in Egypt (p. 76A, B, D). The Persians invented a most distinctive type of column, with a high moulded base, fluted shaft and a capital of recurring vertical scrolls, echoing developments also taking place about the same time in the eastern Mediterranean, including Ionian Greece (p. 126A–N). The bracket form of the topmost part, with a socket for a supported beam, together with the column as a whole, may well have sprung from a forked pole such as still is used to support roof beams in Persian houses to-day. The brackets were fashioned variously as the foreparts of twin bulls (sometimes human-headed), or dragons. Column shafts in some of the lesser buildings at Persepolis were of wood, on stone bases, covered with a very thick coat of plaster and decoratively painted.

MOULDINGS. The buildings of Mesopotamia, like those of Egypt, were generally of too vast a scale to need mouldings; or, as in Assyrian architecture, broad areas of ornament served a corresponding function (p. 74E, G). It was the Greeks who developed mouldings so highly, in relation to their comparatively small but most refined buildings. The Persians, however, shared in the evolution, as is seen in the elements introduced into column bases and capitals (p. 76B, D), and above all, in the cornices carried by palace porticoes, as reproduced in the rock carving of the Tomb of Darius, Naksh-i-Rustam (p. 77B), which may be compared with the similar cornice of the Temple of Artemis, Ephesus (p. 130A). Also, a gorge moulding of the Egyptian type is found over Persian doorways as, again, at Naksh-i-Rustam.

ORNAMENT. The old Babylonians do not appear to have used architectural ornament extensively, though in their later wall-treatments we see the beginnings of the Assyrian systems. The Assyrians used as their chief form of mural decoration stone dado-slabs with relief carving which shows an extraordinary refinement of treatment (p. 84). These slabs, some of which are in the British Museum, form an illustrated record of Assyrian pursuits (p. 84A, G, J). Pavement slabs (p. 84C), with patterns derived from carpets, comprise bands of rosettes, palmettes and lotus buds, demonstrating the influence of Egypt, just as do similar patterns found in Greek art. The Assyrians were also skilled craftsmen in bronze. Flanking the entrances to palaces were guardian, sculptured monsters, partly built into the walls. The invention in Egypt of polychrome glazing was turned to account by the Assyrians in the eleventh cent. B.C. in the form of enamelled bricks, blue, white, yellow and green, used as a form of mural art. It became very popular with the Neo-Babylonians, but in Assyria, where stone could be obtained more readily, was later largely replaced by the dado reliefs. The Persians inherited all three types of ornament; the monsters flanking entrance portals, as in the Gate-House of Xerxes at Persepolis; mural decoration by polychrome bricks, as in the 'Archer' and 'Lion' panels from Susa, now in the Louvre, Paris (p. 76F, G); and low-relief slabs applied to stair-walls and parapets and terrace platforms (p. 77A). Persian, like Assyrian surface ornament, was concentrated around the lower portions of buildings, unlike the Egyptian, which was distributed uniformly over pylons, column shafts and inner walls.

REFERENCE BOOKS

ALBRIGHT, W. F. *The Archaeology of Palestine.* Pelican Books, Harmondsworth, 1949.
ARIK, R. O. *Les Fouilles d'Alaça-Hüyük.* Ankara, 1937.
BELL, E. *Early Architecture in Western Asia.* London, 1924.
BITTEL, K. Reports of excavations at Boghazköy, in *Mitteilungen der Deutschen Orient-gesellschaft,* lxx–lxxviii, 1932–9.
BOTTA, P. E. et FLANDIN, E. *Monuments de Ninive.* 5 vols., Paris, 1849–50.
CHILDE, V. G. *New Light on the Most Ancient East.* 4th Ed. New York, 1953.
CONTENAU, G. *Everyday Life in Babylon and Assyria,* trans. K. R. and A. R. Maxwell-Hyslop. London and New York, 1954.
—. *Manuel d'archéologie orientale.* 4 vols., Paris, 1947.
DIEULAFOY, M. *L'Art antique de la Perse.* 5 vols., Paris, 1884–9.
FERGUSSON, J. *The Palaces of Nineveh and Persepolis Restored.* London, 1851.
FRANKFORT, H. *The Art and Architecture of the Ancient Orient.* Harmondsworth, 1954.
—. *The Birth of Civilisation in the Near East.* London, 1954.
GHIRSHMAN, R. *Iran.* Pelican Books, Harmondsworth, 1954.
—. Report on the Ziggurat at Tchoga-Zanbil. *Illustrated London News,* Sept. 8, 1956.
GURNEY, O. R. *The Hittites.* Pelican Books, Harmondsworth, 1952.
KELLER, W. *The Bible as History.* London, 1956.
LAYARD, A. H. *Monuments of Nineveh.* 2 vols., London, 1849.
—. *Nineveh and its Palaces.* 2 vols., London, 1849.
LLOYD, SETON. *Early Anatolia.* Pelican Books, Harmondsworth, 1956.
—. *Ruined Cities of Iraq.* 3rd ed., London, 1946.
LOUD, GORDON. *Khorsabad.* 2 vols., Chicago, 1936–8.
LUSCHAN, F., and others. *Ausgrabungen in Sendschirli.* 5 vols., Berlin, 1893–1943.
MALLOWAN, M. E. L. *Twenty-five years of Mesopotamian Discovery.* Brochure. London, 1956.
OLMSTEAD, A. T. *History of Palestine and Syria to the Macedonian Conquest.* London and New York, 1931.
—. *History of the Persian Empire—Achaemenid Period.* Chicago, 1948.
PARROT, A. *Archéologie mésopotamienne.* Paris, 1946.
—. *Ziggurats et Tour de Babel.* Paris, 1949.
PERROT, G., and CHIPIEZ. *History of Art in Chaldaea and Assyria; Persia, Phrygia and Judaea.* 5 vols., London and New York, 1884–92.
PLACE, VICTOR. *Ninève et l'Assyrie.* 3 vols., Paris, 1867–70.
PUCHSTEIN, O. *Boghazköy. Die Bauwerke.* Leipzig, 1912.

SCHMIDT, E. F. *Persepolis I*. Chicago, 1953.
SMITH, S. *Alalakh and Chronology*. Brochure. London, 1940.
SPIERS, R. P. *Architecture East and West*. London, 1905.
TEXIER, C. *L'Arménie, la Perse, et la Mesopotamie*. 2 vols., Paris, 1842–52.
WOOLLEY, SIR L. *A Forgotten Kingdom*. Pelican Books, Harmondsworth, 1953.
—. *Ur of the Chaldees*. Pelican Books, Harmondsworth, 1954.
WRIGHT, G. E. *Biblical Archaeology*. Philadelphia and London, 1957.

Babylon (conjectural restoration) in the sixth century B.C. See p. 70

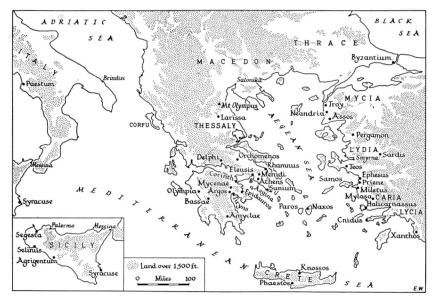

The Central Lands of the Greek World

III. GREEK ARCHITECTURE

(650–30 B.C.; preceded by Aegean, *circa* 3000–1100 B.C.)

INFLUENCES

GEOGRAPHICAL. It was upon the island of Crete that arose the first great sea-power of the Mediterranean, which flourished a thousand years before the Greek civilization reached its peak. This 'Aegean' culture extended to Greece and her islands, and was founded on trade around the whole eastern Mediterranean sea-board, with Asia Minor, Cyprus, Syria, Palestine, Egypt and Libya. Trading vessels also reached South Italy and Sicily. Routes were thus established which, when the Aegean civilization had crumbled, were followed by swarming colonists who were to help to found the Greece of classical times, which comprised not only the mother-land itself and the neighbouring islands, but settlements in South Italy and Sicily, western Asia Minor, Cyrenaica and others distributed sporadically elsewhere around the Mediterranean and the Black Sea. Geography determined the fortunes of both the Aegean and the Greek cultures, for the rugged nature of the Greek peninsula and its islands, with mountainous hinterlands which rendered internal communication difficult, made the sea the inevitable means of intercourse, fostering maritime activity and producing hardy and adventurous seamen. Also, the mountains of inland Greece separated the inhabitants into groups or clans, and thus arose that rivalry which characterized the Greek states, whether in peace or war. In the Greek period, two phases can be determined, for after the true 'Hellenic' civilization had flowered, the conquests of Alexander extended Greek culture thinly over vast territories in western Asia, Egypt and Libya, and to this latter phase the term 'Hellenistic' is applied.

GEOLOGICAL. Greece and her domains had ample supplies of good building-stone, but the mineral of greatest importance to her architecture was her unrivalled marble, the most beautiful and monumental of all building materials, and one which facilitates exactness of line and refinement of detail. This marble is found in abundance, notably in the mountains of Hymettus and Pentelicus near Athens, and in the islands of Paros and Naxos. The Greeks attached so much importance to the quality of fine-grained marble for producing exact outlines and smooth surfaces that, as in the Temples at Paestum, Italy, they even coated coarse-grained limestone with a layer of marble 'stucco' in order to secure this effect, which is the great characteristic of their architecture.

CLIMATIC. The climate was intermediate between rigorous cold and relaxing heat; hence the Greek character, combining the energy of the north with the lethargy of the south, produced a unique civilization. The clear atmosphere and intensity of light, largely resulting from the rocky nature of the country and the sparsity of forests, was conducive to the development of that love of precise and exact forms which are special attributes of Greek architecture. The climate favoured an outdoor life, and consequently the administration of justice, dramatic representations, and most public ceremonies took place in the open air, even in winter, and to this is largely due the limited variety of public buildings other than temples. The hot summer sun and sudden winter showers, together with the Greek love of conversation, were probably answerable for the porticoes and colonnades which were such important features.

RELIGIOUS. The religion of the 'Aegeans' was a nature worship which went through a series of primitive stages. Though eventually divinities were conceived in human form, and represented by small idols, rocks and stone pillars and all sorts of trees and animals continued to be venerated. Mysteries of masculine force were represented by the sacred bull, symbolized by the 'horns of consecration', and the shield and the sacrificial double axe also had mystical virtues. The supreme deity was the fertility- or mother-goddess, Rhea, later identified with Hera by the Greeks. Priestesses, rather than priests, conducted the religious rites. Worship centred on sacrificial altars, in open-air enclosures, caves, small chapels or household shrines. Temples were not needed until after the collapse of the Aegean civilization, when the Greeks began to represent their deities by large statues. The religious ceremonies and festivals of the Aegeans included sacred games and ritual dances, establishing traditions upon which the classical Greek athletic contests and arts of the theatre were founded.

The Greek religion also was in the main a worship of natural phenomena, but more highly developed. The gods were personifications of particular elements, or were deified heroes, and each town or district had its own local preferences, ceremonies and traditions. There was no regular priesthood. The priests and priestesses were not members of an exclusive class but led the normal community life.

The principal Greek deities with their attributes and Roman names are as follows:

GREEK (The twelve Olympians)		ROMAN
Zeus	The supreme god, and ruler of the sky	Jupiter (Jove)
Hera	Wife of Zeus, and goddess of marriage	Juno
Apollo	God of law and reason, art, music and poetry; founder of cities	Apollo
Athena	Goddess of wisdom and learning	Minerva
Poseidon	The sea god	Neptune
Dionysos	God of wine, feasting and revelry	Bacchus
Demeter	Goddess of earth and agriculture	Ceres

GREEK (The twelve Olympians)		ROMAN
Artemis	Goddess of the chase	Diana
Hermes	Messenger of the gods. God of commerce	Mercury
Aphrodite	Goddess of love and beauty	Venus
Hephaestus	God of fire, flame and forge. God of handicrafts	Vulcan
Ares	God of war	Mars

Also: Hestia (Vesta), goddess of the hearth (sacred fire); Helios (Sol), the sun god; Selene (Luna), the moon goddess; Pan (Pan), god of the flocks. Two mortals who became gods were Heracles (Hercules), god of strength and labour, and Asclepius (Aesculapius), god of healing.

SOCIAL. The high degree of civilization reached in Crete during the Bronze Age was due to the immensely long period of security the island enjoyed to pursue its thriving trade with the countries surrounding the eastern Mediterranean. This was a 'thalassocracy'—a naval empire. The Greek mainland, however, though participating in the Aegean culture, suffered repeated incursions of northern peoples. The racial stock there became increasingly different, and life centred in politically-independent, stronghold towns, such as Mycenae and Tiryns. In Crete there were ninety or more cities within its compass of 3,300 square miles. They early became politically united, first under Phaestos, on the south coast, then under Knossos, on the north. Complex palaces existed at both these populous places, as also in the lesser towns such as Gournia; whilst at Hagia Triada, near Phaestos, was a royal villa. Commerce was the mainstay, but Crete was also an originating centre in the decorative arts and minor crafts, and its pottery was widely exported. Chief diversions were music and dancing, wrestling, boxing, gymnastics and bull-leaping, often in a religious connection. Women took an important part in social life, and participated even in hunting and the more strenuous games, as well as in craftwork.

In the Hellenic civilization which next emerged, in Greece, centuries later, the various Greek states, despite political dissensions, were united by a similar devotion to their religion, and by religious festivals, as well as by their love of music, the drama, and the fine arts, and also by national games and by emulation in those manly sports and contests for which they were so distinguished. The Greeks were essentially democratic, despite the assumption of power in some instances by eminent families or by 'tyrants'. Normally, the citizens shared in all affairs of state in greater or less degree. Palaces, the dominant type of building in the Aegean age, scarcely appear in Greek architecture.

HISTORICAL. The Aegean civilization was initiated, about 3000 B.C., by a movement of peoples from Asia Minor to Crete, where they mingled with the original inhabitants, who were of ancient Mediterranean stock. The civilization grew and expanded, penetrating the mainland some five hundred years later; but about 2000 B.C. the mainland suffered an incursion of northern invaders. Recovery followed, and between 1600–1400 B.C. the whole Aegean culture reached its peak. Then came a further invasion of a northern Greek tribe, the Achaeans, who swept beyond the mainland to the islands and Crete itself, where they ravaged and burnt the unprotected cities. The blow was severe, but not fatal. The final catastrophe was due to yet another devastating northern incursion, this time of the Dorian Greeks, by whom the civilization was almost completely destroyed (c. 1100 B.C.). Great numbers of the Aegeans fled, settling chiefly upon the neighbouring coast of Asia Minor instead, where, as Ionians, they at length built prosperous cities anew. In course of time, about the eighth and seventh centuries B.C., subsistence proved too meagre for the Dorians themselves, and having learnt the arts of the sea they became ardent colonists too, though turning mainly to the West, to South Italy and Sicily.

Thus 'Hellenic' Greece was born and a new civilization arose from the ashes of the old. By 600 B.C., the cities of Greece had settled down to their several forms of government—tyrannic, aristocratic or democratic—and most of their colonies had been founded. The Ionians of Asia Minor were to find themselves involved politically with the Persian monarchy. Cyrus won a decisive victory at Sardis (546 B.C.) and the Persians eventually conquered the Greek cities in Asia Minor. These Ionian Greeks revolted (499–493 B.C.) but were reconquered by the Persians. Under Darius I, the Persians later invaded Greece itself, but were defeated at Marathon (490 B.C.). A second Persian invasion by Xerxes was terminated by the naval victory of Salamis (480 B.C.) and the land battle of Plataea (479 B.C.). The national exultation over these victories is largely responsible for the fact that the most important temples were built in the fifty years which followed the battles of Salamis and Plataea. The rule of Pericles (444–429 B.C.) marks the climax of Athenian prosperity, but the wonderfully rapid growth of Athens excited the jealousy of the slower Spartans, and this brought about the Peloponnesian war (431–404 B.C.), which ultimately established the supremacy of Sparta, but her arbitrary and high-handed conduct roused other states against her, and the leadership passed successively to Thebes and Macedonia. The latter had hitherto been considered a half-barbarian state; but thanks to the ability of Philip, king of Macedonia, and of his son Alexander the Great, it rose to a leading position in Greece. In 334 B.C. Alexander set out on his great expedition, and in six years he subdued the Persian Empire, having besieged and taken Tyre *en route* and received the submission of Egypt, where he founded the famous city of Alexandria, on a site to the east of the Egyptian town of Rhacotis. His conquests extended to northern India, and Greek art and civilization thus spread through western Asia.

On Alexander's death at Babylon (323 B.C.) the empire he had created was split up among his generals and Egypt fell to Ptolemy, who founded a dynasty (p. 19); while in Greece an unsuccessful attempt was made to start leagues between cities, such as the Achaean and Aetolian Leagues. The natural isolation and mutual animosity of the Greek communities afforded all too good an opportunity for the intrusion of the centralized and united power of Rome, and thus Roman interference gradually increased until Greece became a Roman province (146 B.C.). Already the Romans had entered Asia Minor, and between 190–133 B.C., the Greek states there came piecemeal within her control. Syria followed suit in 64 B.C. and Egypt in 30 B.C.

ARCHITECTURAL CHARACTER

AEGEAN ARCHITECTURE

(*Circa* 3000–1100 B.C.)

The architecture of Crete and the other islands differed from that of the mainland, although in the minor arts, practice was common. The island peoples were partly Asiatic in origin, and their buildings had the flat roofs typical of eastern countries. The flat roofs allowed buildings to be drawn together, when necessary, in large blocks, two, three or even four storeys high, light-wells being used to admit natural light to the inner parts of the blocks. Spacious stairways were developed, in return flights, and the flat roofs formed part of the serviceable accommodation. The mainland peoples, on the other hand, brought their northern practices with them, and used low-pitched roofs, so that, apart from exceptions due to Island influence, their buildings were single-storeyed, and allowance had to be made between the comparatively small units for the removal of rain-water. The characteristic mainland domestic unit was the megaron, which had a deep plan, comprising an entrance porch, the living-apartment or megaron proper (p. 99C, 6, 8), and normally, a thalamus or sleeping-room behind. The powerful Cretan navy made fortifications largely unnecessary on the islands, and gave freedom in the selection of town sites; on the mainland the liability to hostile irruption made it essential to choose elevated sites, encircled by massive defensive walls. As a whole, houses and palaces are the principal building-types representative of Aegean architecture, with, chiefly on the mainland, an important class of underground tomb. Buildings were constructed of rubble or cut stonework to dado height, the upper parts having a heavy, double frame of timber, the panels being infilled with sun-dried brick or stone rubble. The walls were coated with stucco outside, and either tinted, or, on the islands, painted with patterns inspired by the framed construction which lay behind. Gypsum, plentiful in Crete, also served to make hard, polished floors and roof-deckings carried on rounded logs, or was used in slabs for similar purposes. Masonry technique was well-developed, and particularly on the mainland, ranged from a 'cyclopean' type comprised of great boulder-like stones, used in fortifications, to coarse or fine ashlar of heavy blocks (p. 99G). No mortar was ever employed, though clay sometimes served for bedding in rubble or cyclopean work. Polygonal walling, an advanced technique, was not invented until Hellenic times. False arches of heavy blocks, or of corbels advanced course by course until a triangular head had been formed, covered the openings in stone walls (p. 100H), and the corbel method was normal too for vaults or pointed domes, as in the Treasury of Atreus, Mycenae (p. 100). Square, masonry pillars, with a bracket form of capital, sometimes gave intermediate support on lower floors, but the distinctive type of column was of cypress wood, with a downward-tapering, cylindrical shaft, a slight, disc-like base and a widely-projecting capital with two main parts, a square abacus above, and a circular, bulbous echinus below (p. 100D); not unlike the Doric capital of later times, except that there are here additional small mouldings above and below the echinus. This broad-topped form of column was necessary to collect the weight of the thick, supported walls (p. 99F).

GREEK ARCHITECTURE
(650–30 B.C.)

There are two principal phases, the Hellenic and the Hellenistic.

1. The Hellenic Period (650–323 B.C.). Greek culture naturally owed much to preceding civilizations, but the Hellenic Greeks, by reason of their innate artistic sense, so profoundly influenced the development of European art that Greece must be regarded as the veritable source of literary and artistic inspiration, and it has been said, 'Whate'er we hold of beauty, half is hers'.

The 'Dark Age' which followed the Aegean civilization broke the continuity of the arts and threw them back to their early beginnings; but because some of the causative factors were similar, early Hellenic architecture had features in common with its predecessor. Though temples were now the chief building type, the earliest resembled the Aegean megaron in plan and in having timber-laced, sun-dried brick walls, stucco-covered, on stone dadoes; timber-enframed portals (the origin of the door architrave), narrowing a little towards the top; timber antae or uprights protecting the free ends of the naos walls where they embraced the pronaos or porch; and a low-pitched roof showing pediments or gables over the narrow ends. Then too, temple enclosures had propylaea, also found in Aegean architecture (p. 99C). But the outstanding difference was that, almost from the first, colonnades appear, surrounding the temple and forming an essential part of it. Greek architecture was essentially columnar and trabeated (*trabs* =a beam), and this gave it that simple straightforward character in which the constructive system is self-evident, uncomplicated by such devices as are involved in arch, vault and dome. From first to last in this period, the wooden roofs were untrussed, the rafters being supported by longitudinal beams—wall-plates, purlins and ridge-piece—laid on the walls and colonnades themselves or propped on struts from cross-beams (p. 154B). As the principle of triangulation was unknown, spans could not be large, unless internal lines of columns were supplied, and these usually were in two superimposed tiers (pp. 116B; 154B). This contrast with the constructive genius of the Romans is most marked (p. 199), and a reminder that the two architectures have to be assessed quite differently. Greek columns and their entablatures were at first entirely of timber, with terra-cotta decorations in the upper trabeation, but were converted into stone quite early in the period, about 600 B.C. The translation was quite direct, timber forms being imitated in stone with remarkable exactness. For this reason Greek architecture sometimes has been called 'a carpentry in marble', though in fact comparatively few buildings were erected comprehensively in marble before the fifth century B.C., this material meantime being sparingly employed for the finer details and for sculpture. The walls, too, became wholly of stone about the same time (600 B.C.), yet the tradition of the dado always survived in the special way the stones were arranged at the base of the wall (p. 132C, E). Ceilings, sometimes omitted, leaving an open roof, were treated decoratively with timber-panelled coffers, or, within the colonnades around temples, were of flat, stone slabs, coffered to imitate the timber. Almost all kinds of stone walls were used, from coursed rubble to the finest ashlar, well-bonded but always without mortar, unless for the smallest quantity necessary to ensure that the stones were firmly bedded. In the best buildings, such as temples, ashlar was normal, and the greatest precautions were taken to minimize the joints, so that they might not impair the architectural effect. In such work, the stones were secured together by wrought-iron cramps and dowels, protected by molten lead.

Several important refinements were practised in Greek architecture, in order to correct optical illusions. At the peak of the period, some of these were of a most delicate nature, and testify to a most advanced sensitivity to form. The Parthenon is the supreme example. The long horizontal lines of such features as stylobates, architraves, and cornices, which, if straight in reality would have appeared to the Greek eye to sag or drop in the middle of their length, were formed with slightly convex outlines (p. 95E, F, G). In the Parthenon, the stylobate has an upward curvature towards its centre of $2\frac{3}{8}$ ins on the east and west façades, and of $4\frac{5}{16}$ ins on the lateral façades. Vertical features were also inclined inwards towards the top to correct the appearance of falling outwards; thus the axes of the angle columns lean inwards $2\frac{3}{8}$ ins and the axes of the columns, if produced, would meet at a distance of one and a half miles above the stylobate (p. 95C). Greek columns usually, though not invariably, have an entasis (see Glossary and p. 95H, J). The shafts of the Parthenon have this slight convexity of silhouette—as well as the usual upward taper, or diminution—the deviation amounting to $\frac{11}{16}$ in, in a height of 31 ft (p. 95D). Entasis is most pronounced in the Basilica at Paestum (p. 114E, H), where it amounts to $2\frac{1}{8}$ ins, and at its most delicate in the North Porch of the Erechtheion (p. 134), where it is less than $\frac{1}{4}$ in. Angle columns of temples were not only set closer to the adjacent columns, but were also stouter, as it was found that they appeared thinner against the open sky than those seen against the solid background of the 'naos' wall (p. 96B). In the case of the Parthenon, to heighten the perspective effect induced by the narrowed spacings of the angle columns, the large elements in the frieze, known as triglyphs (p. 110A), were spaced progressively more closely together from the centre outwards on the two short fronts, so that

OPTICAL CORRECTIONS IN ARCHITECTURE

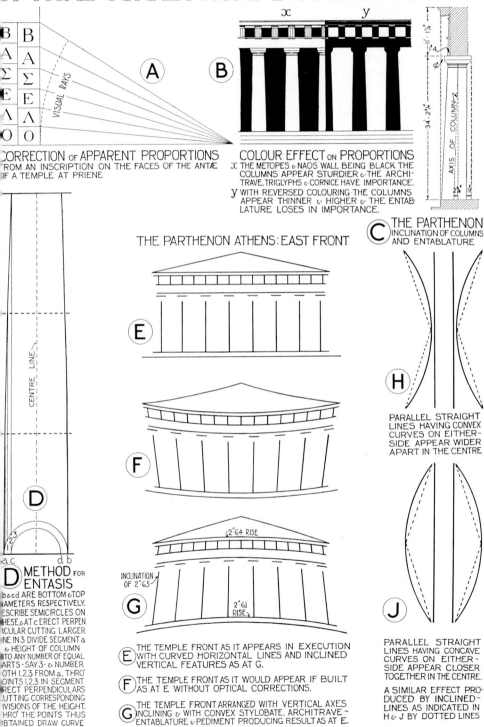

A CORRECTION of APPARENT PROPORTIONS
FROM AN INSCRIPTION ON THE FACES OF THE ANTÆ
OF A TEMPLE AT PRIENE

B COLOUR EFFECT on PROPORTIONS
𝑥 THE METOPES & NAOS WALL BEING BLACK THE
COLUMNS APPEAR STURDIER & THE ARCHI-
TRAVE, TRIGLYPHS & CORNICE HAVE IMPORTANCE.
𝑦 WITH REVERSED COLOURING THE COLUMNS
APPEAR THINNER & HIGHER & THE ENTAB-
LATURE LOSES IN IMPORTANCE.

C THE PARTHENON
INCLINATION OF COLUMNS
AND ENTABLATURE

THE PARTHENON ATHENS: EAST FRONT

D METHOD FOR
ENTASIS
b & d ARE BOTTOM & TOP
DIAMETERS RESPECTIVELY.
DESCRIBE SEMICIRCLES ON
THESE & AT c ERECT PERPEN
DICULAR CUTTING LARGER
ONE IN 3. DIVIDE SEGMENT a
& HEIGHT OF COLUMN
INTO ANY NUMBER OF EQUAL
PARTS - SAY 3 - & NUMBER
BOTH 1,2,3 FROM a. THRO'
POINTS 1,2,3 IN SEGMENT
ERECT PERPENDICULARS
CUTTING CORRESPONDING
DIVISIONS OF THE HEIGHT.
THRO' THE POINTS THUS
OBTAINED DRAW CURVE

E THE TEMPLE FRONT AS IT APPEARS IN EXECUTION
WITH CURVED HORIZONTAL LINES AND INCLINED
VERTICAL FEATURES AS AT G.

F THE TEMPLE FRONT AS IT WOULD APPEAR IF BUILT
AS AT E WITHOUT OPTICAL CORRECTIONS.

G THE TEMPLE FRONT ARRANGED WITH VERTICAL AXES
INCLINING & WITH CONVEX STYLOBATE, ARCHITRAVE
ENTABLATURE & PEDIMENT PRODUCING RESULT AS AT E.

H PARALLEL STRAIGHT
LINES HAVING CONVEX
CURVES ON EITHER-
SIDE APPEAR WIDER
APART IN THE CENTRE

J PARALLEL STRAIGHT
LINES HAVING CONCAVE
CURVES ON EITHER-
SIDE APPEAR CLOSER
TOGETHER IN THE CENTRE.

A SIMILAR EFFECT PRO-
DUCED BY INCLINED-
LINES AS INDICATED IN
H & J BY DOTTED LINES

none is precisely above a column. The intervals differ by a maximum of $4\frac{1}{8}$ ins. Another correction was to make the letters of inscriptions, when raised up on buildings, larger in the upper lines than in the lower, so that they might appear all of one size when viewed from below (p. 95A). The finest sculpture completed the most important buildings, and the delicate adjustment and refined treatment, alike of the architecture and sculpture, were made possible by the hard, fine grain of the marble. Early sculptures in stone usually were coloured all over, but when marble came to be employed, bright colours and gilding were applied only to selected parts, so as to emphasize the fine qualities of the material itself. Similarly, in the best buildings, colour was restricted to the architectural detail, the broader, flat surfaces being left plain. Most of the mouldings, particularly those with curved profiles, had their own kind of conventional running ornament painted on, or carved and painted. When marble-masonry was not forthcoming, a coating of hard stucco, made with powdered marble, gave the desired quality of finish to stone-built structures. Mural painting, as on the walls of temples and porticoes, was a highly developed art.

From the original two 'Orders of Architecture', Doric and Ionic, evolved simultaneously by the two main branches of the Greek race, there at length arose a third, the Corinthian, a purely decorative variant which although invented by the Hellenic Greeks was only to attain its full identity in the hands of the Romans. The Etruscans (p. 170) developed the Tuscan, inspired by the Doric and a simpler and cruder version of it; while the last to appear was the 'Composite', a Roman contribution which did not differ greatly from the Corinthian, and which, like it, was an off-shoot from the Ionic. These were the 'Five Orders of Architecture' of classical times. An 'Order' consists of the upright column or support, including the capital, and base, if any, and the horizontal entablature or part supported. The entablature is divided into architrave or lowest part, frieze or middle part, and cornice or upper part. The proportions of column and entablature vary in the different 'Orders', as do also mouldings and ornament (p. 160). The origin and evolution of the different parts of the three Greek Orders are considered under their respective headings in Examples (pp. 108, 125, 137).

The Doric style was practised chiefly in South Italy and Sicily and on the Greek Mainland; Asia Minor was the true home of the Ionic. Cyrenaica, in North Africa, was Doric too, but the surviving monuments there are not as fully recorded as they are elsewhere. Though there are some important remains in Greece of the earliest experiments in Doric Architecture, it was the western colonies that showed the greater vigour in the archaic stages of development. Examples to show the corresponding evolution in Ionic Asia Minor are decidedly fewer in number. The finest buildings of the Hellenic period, in either style, are found on the mainland; and the select few in Athens herself, where they mostly belong to the last sixty years of the fifth century B.C. The reasons for the apparently odd circumstance that Athens should bring to fruition the Ionic as well as the Doric style, have to do with her ancient history—Athens was a stronghold in Aegean times—as well as her political circumstances. In Greece proper, the Doric and Ionic influenced one another to some extent in the process of formative development, but in Asia Minor the Ionic, since it originated there, resisted the innovations introduced on the mainland until the fourth century B.C., by which time there was a general slight decline in Greek taste, compensated however by a progressive widening of the scope of architecture to new types of building and more ambitious and extensive arrangements.

2. The Hellenistic Period (323–30 B.C.). In this period, due to the conquests of Alexander, Greek culture was diffused over many Near-Eastern lands, and in newly-founded cities, no less than in the old strongholds in Asia Minor, made

fresh and brilliant advances. Athens, despite political vicissitudes, maintained much of her artistic prestige and renown. To this resplendent Grecian world the Romans came as comparative novices in the arts, deeply admiring and avidly assimilating whatever ideas and methods their practical minds deemed of value to their own evolving systems. Roman architecture was taking its own florid shape just at this time, and it was Greek Hellenistic architecture that provided much of the decorative inspiration as well as the embryos of quite a few of the Roman building-types. Even later, in the Roman Imperial age, Rome continued to draw from the art of the old Greek territories almost as much as it gave in the way of brilliant constructional theory and practical procedure.

Greek Hellenic architecture mostly had been of a religious character, but from the fourth century B.C. onwards, public buildings multiplied in type and number and passed into permanent form. Indeed, there were almost as many different kinds as there are to-day. They were dignified and gracious structures, and a quite new departure was that they now were related formally to one another, instead of being disposed irregularly on undulating natural sites. Civic design developed apace, and entire groups of buildings, themselves quite complex, were laid out on symmetrical lines in orderly schemes, often linked by colonnaded porticoes or 'stoas'. Town planning, an art which had originated as early as the fifth century B.C., became normal for new developments. Trabeated architecture still was usual, but arches began to appear over wall-openings, and large, niche-like recesses in building-plans. Such 'exedrae' previously had only been employed outdoors. Stone vaults, with radiating voussoirs, though used mostly for the coverings of tombs, were no longer uncommon. Of the highest importance was the advent, about the third century B.C., of the roof truss, which allowed large spaces to be covered without the aid of encumbering lines of intermediate pillars; though it was the Romans who were to secure the full advantage of this development. Due to the increased complexity of buildings, all kinds of new situations arose to be met by the Orders of Architecture, and they lost much of their original purity of form and simplicity of use. Taste declined, and the ornate Corinthian gained in popularity at the expense of the Doric, which at length, according to the Roman author Vitruvius, writing in the late first century B.C., came to be considered as unsuitable for sacred buildings. At times, novelty was deliberately sought. Parts were interchanged between Doric and Ionic, and two Orders commonly were used in the same building. They also were superimposed in tiers, sometimes of necessity, as when colonnaded buildings were two storeys high, but at other times solely as a decorative caprice. These departures from the strict canons of the Hellenic period were observed by the Romans and led to the practices which came to be characteristic of their use of the Orders.

EXAMPLES

AEGEAN ARCHITECTURE

In the whole epoch of Aegean art, from c. 3000–1100 B.C., followed by a 'Dark Age' up to c. 650 B.C., a climax of achievement was reached in the two centuries 1600–1400 B.C. The architecture of Crete—the originating centre—and the neighbouring Aegean islands, differed in important respects from that of the Greek mainland, which suffered successive northern invasions, and thus had a somewhat different racial complexion. Of the many towns in Crete, Knossos and Phaestos were the most important, and Tiryns and Mycenae represent the mainland. Athens and Orchomenos were other important mainland centres. The principal remains of the period are of palaces and tombs, though quite a little is known too, about lesser domestic buildings.

D   H.O.A.

PALACES

Island towns had few defences, as they early were politically unified, and were protected by the powerful mercantile navy of Crete. Mainland settlements, on the
other hand, needed fortified strongholds to protect the agricultural villages from
which livelihood was drawn, and to which the villagers could repair in times of
danger. The elaborate palaces of the kings or local chieftains and their retinues
were the main structures of the period.

The **Palace of King Minos, Knossos** (p. 99B), represents the Cretan type and
was the chief upon the island, as the other towns were subject to Knossos. It was
destroyed about 1400 B.C., and had grown by stages from a series of separate buildings into a continuous complex arranged around an open court, 170 ft by 90 ft
wide. The whole spanned roughly 400 ft each way, and covered about four acres.
Additionally, on the west side, there was a paved market-court, and to the north of
it, a theatral area, flanked by banks of broad, shallow steps, for public displays
and sports. The town proper lay still further to the west. The site of the palace is a
slight eminence, but the ground falls more steeply to the south and south-east.
The buildings mostly were of at least two storeys, the lower merely 8 ft high,
divided into long narrow storerooms on the west wing, stocked with enormous
earthenware oil jars (p. 99E) and with storage bins cut along the centre of their
floors. At the northern end were stored the archives, comprised of thousands of
inscribed clay tablets: and facing towards the central court in this wing was a
'Throne Room', which appears to have been a chapel for religious observance,
containing an alabaster throne for the priest-king (p. 99D) with benches on each
side for priestesses, all facing towards a colonnaded light-well or lustral tank.
Frescoed griffins on the wall behind face towards the throne. The throne room was
approached from an ante-room opening from the courtyard by four pairs of folding
doors. In general, the buildings were of cut stone or gypsum blocks in the lower
tier, but of sun-dried brick or rubble, laced with timber, in the upper. On the principal (first) floor of the western wing were spacious state-rooms, approached by a
circuitous ceremonial approach from the west market-court, via a grand staircase
near the south end of the block. On the north or coastward side was an entrance to
the central court, protected by a massive guardroom, one of the few evidences of
defence on the whole site. To the east of this entrance were the industrial quarters,
where pottery, jewellery and other crafts were practised and where oil was refined.
Centrally in the east wing at the upper level was a further hall of state. Near the
south-east corner of the courtyard the slope was cut away for the royal domestic
apartments, three storeys high, the upper at courtyard level and the two lower facing outwards to terraced gardens. They were connected by a stately staircase, in
return flights, lighted by a ramped colonnade of wooden columns from an adjacent
light-well (p. 99F). Each floor was similar, with the queen's suite secluded from
the rest and with no external windows, all the light proceeding from light-wells.
Most remarkable were the sanitary arrangements, the queen's rooms having bathroom and water closets (the latter with a flushing device), connected to a drainage
system of socketted earthenware pipes which served the royal quarters as a whole.
Stairways, light-wells and colonnades of downward-tapering cypress-wood columns
(p. 99F) are typical of Island palaces, as also are double-folding doors, arranged in
close series so that a whole length of wall could be thrown almost completely open.
Walls regularly were plastered, and decorated with splendid frescoes. The palace
at Phaestos had almost precisely similar features.

The **Palace, Tiryns** (c. 1300 B.C.) (p. 99C), is a hill-top citadel, surrounded by
enormous defensive walls, upwards of 24 ft thick. At points where there are storage

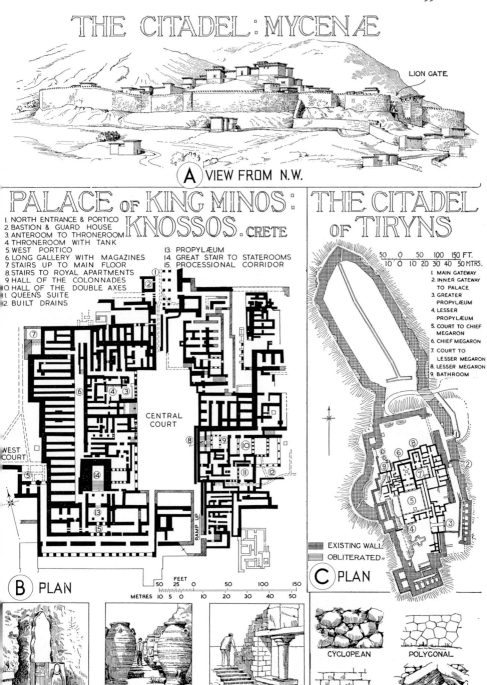

THE CITADEL: MYCENÆ

LION GATE

A VIEW FROM N.W.

PALACE of KING MINOS: KNOSSOS. CRETE

1. NORTH ENTRANCE & PORTICO
2. BASTION & GUARD HOUSE
3. ANTEROOM TO THRONEROOM
4. THRONEROOM WITH TANK
5. WEST PORTICO
6. LONG GALLERY WITH MAGAZINES
7. STAIRS UP TO MAIN FLOOR
8. STAIRS TO ROYAL APARTMENTS
9. HALL OF THE COLONNADES
10. HALL OF THE DOUBLE AXES
11. QUEEN'S SUITE
12. BUILT DRAINS
13. PROPYLÆUM
14. GREAT STAIR TO STATEROOMS
15. PROCESSIONAL CORRIDOR

CENTRAL COURT

WEST COURT

RAMP UP

B PLAN

FEET
50 25 0 50 100 150
METRES 10 5 0 10 20 30 40 50

THE CITADEL of TIRYNS

50 0 50 100 150 FT.
10 0 10 20 30 40 50 MTRS.

1. MAIN GATEWAY
2. INNER GATEWAY TO PALACE
3. GREATER PROPYLÆUM
4. LESSER PROPYLÆUM
5. COURT TO CHIEF MEGARON
6. CHIEF MEGARON
7. COURT TO LESSER MEGARON
8. LESSER MEGARON
9. BATHROOM

▓ EXISTING WALL
▤ OBLITERATED "

C PLAN

D ALABASTER THRONE

E STORAGE JARS

F STAIR IN ROYAL APARTMENTS

CYCLOPEAN   POLYGONAL

RECTANGULAR   INCLINED BLOCKS

G METHODS OF WALLING

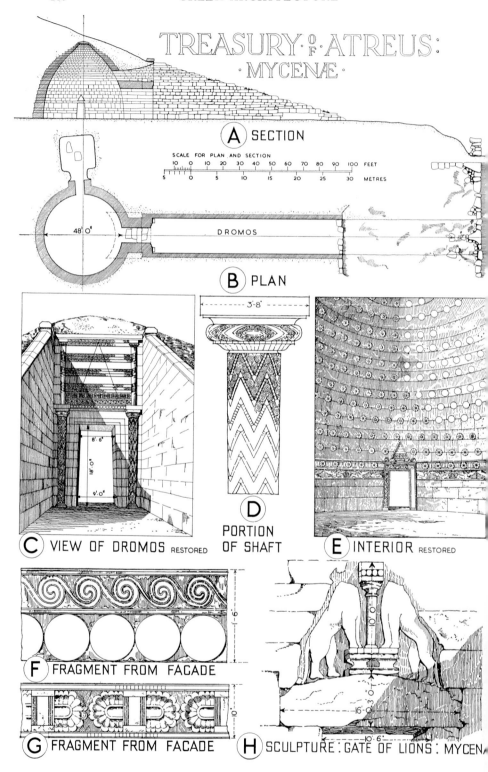

TREASURY·OF·ATREUS·
·MYCENÆ·

(A) SECTION

SCALE FOR PLAN AND SECTION
10 0 10 20 30 40 50 60 70 80 90 100 FEET
5 0 5 10 15 20 25 30 METRES

48'0"

DROMOS

(B) PLAN

8'6"
18'0"
9'0"

(C) VIEW OF DROMOS RESTORED

3'8"

(D) PORTION OF SHAFT

(E) INTERIOR RESTORED

(F) FRAGMENT FROM FACADE

(G) FRAGMENT FROM FACADE

16'0"
10'6"

(H) SCULPTURE: GATE OF LIONS: MYCEN

chambers embodied, the thickness is as much as 57 ft. The massive masonry is of the cyclopean type (p. 99G), except for short stretches of ashlar done at a later stage. The palace occupies the highest part of the elongated enclosure, and to the north of it were the dwellings of retainers, all these being divided by a defensive cross wall from a lower terrace, bare of buildings and intended as a place of refuge for the villagers and their flocks and herds in times of war; for here, there was no neighbouring town. The circuitous approach to the palace was devised so as to facilitate defence. It led through two gateways and two propylaea before reaching the second of two large, colonnaded courts. These propylaea, each comprising an inner and outer columned porch, sheltering a single portal in the dividing wall, anticipate the famous propylaea of classical Greece, such as that to the Acropolis at Athens (p. 143). Dominant in the plan, facing south into the inner large court, is a large megaron, 32 ft wide inside, the distinctive domestic unit of the mainland, though here serving a ceremonial purpose as well, for to one side of the main apartment is a throne, raised on steps, facing a fixed, central hearth. The megaron had a low-pitched roof, and in many other features of detail and construction resembled the early temples of Hellenic Greece. A second, smaller megaron, 20 ft wide inside, may have served as women's quarters. This and a third, still smaller, megaron were cut off from the inner large court and could only be approached by a tortuous route from the outer propylon. Though the palace was essentially one-storey, there were parts with upper floors, due to Island influences On the western side of the large megaron was a bathroom with a floor of a single black stone, measuring 13 ft by 11 ft. Of the corresponding palace at Mycenae, of about the same date, less evidence survives, but whatever is forthcoming confirms the principles already noted at Tiryns.

The **Lion Gate, Mycenae** (c. 1250 B.C.) (pp. 99A, 100H) is the principal and most famous feature of the above palace, standing in the circuit of its massive walls, which elsewhere are of the cyclopean type. The gateway, and the adjacent ashlar walls, represent a later modification. It has always stood above ground. Great, upright stone jambs support an immense lintel, spanning 10 ft 6 ins and measuring 16 ft long, by $3\frac{1}{2}$ ft high in the middle, by 8 ft deep. Above is a triangular relieving opening, formed by advancing stone courses, trimmed to shape and filled with a stone slab, 2 ins thick, bearing a relief carving of two rampant lions facing a central column. This device had a religious meaning. The sculpture records for us the nature of the typical downward-tapering timber column of the Aegeans. It is shown carrying a lintel made up of timber plates trapping rounded logs between them.

TOMBS

Of the several forms of tomb used by the Aegeans, two types offer architectural interest. They are found principally on the mainland. One is the rock-cut or chamber tomb, in which a rectangular chamber, about 12–20 ft cube, is cut within the slope of a convenient hillside and approached by a passage or 'dromos', open to the sky, leading to a doorway in the rock façade. Similar, but far more elaborate is the 'tholos' type of tomb, a subterranean stone-vaulted construction shaped like an old-fashioned skip beehive.

The **'Treasury of Atreus', Mycenae** (c. 1325 B.C.) (p. 100), also known as the 'Tomb of Agamemnon', is the finest of these. It is 48 ft in diameter and 44 ft high inside, made up of 34 rings of masonry, capped by a single stone, dressed after completion to the form of a pointed dome. The courses are laid on flat beds, so no centering was needed. There were three metal friezes decorating the lower courses, and metal rosettes studded the vault face elsewhere. The whole construction was built within a cylindrical pit, upon a rammed clay floor, the apex just reaching the ground level of a hillside. A lateral, rock-cut, chamber, 27 ft square and 19 ft high, probably lined with heavy marble slabs originally, was the actual place of burial. The approach to the tomb was by a dromos, open to the sky, 21 ft wide and 115 ft long, its masonry walls rising with the hillside to a maximum of 45 ft. These walls were up to 10 ft thick, and behind them were further very thick walls of sun-dried brick, to protect them from damp. The impressive façade stood 24 feet in front of the chamber, and its portal, 9 ft wide and 18 ft high, narrowing by 1 ft towards the top, required two enormous lintels in the depth, one of them weighing more than 100 tons. There were triangular relieving openings over this and the side-chamber portals. The façade was embellished with architectural dressings in green, red and white stones, including the relieving opening, and flanking the door were single, green alabaster attached columns, of typical Aegean form, 20 ft high, tapering downwards from 22 ins to 20½ ins, decorated with bands of chevron ornament in relief. One of these columns is now in the British Museum.

Of a number of other such tombs, showing progressive stages of advance, the finest are the 'Tomb of Clytemnestra', Mycenae, and the 'Treasury of Minyas' at Orchomenos, Boeotia. The flanking columns of the former had fluted shafts. Portals in most cases were walled-up between burials, but some had actual doors, turning in pivots in lintel and threshold.

GREEK ARCHITECTURE

In Greek cities there was a place apart, usually upon the highest part, for the 'temenos' or sacred enclosure, as at Delphi (p. 106A). Often, topography allowed this to be a citadel too, an Acropolis or upper city, where the principal sacred buildings might stand, both for dignity and safety. These were walled, like the city itself, and sometimes were very irregular in shape, due to the lie of the land.

The **Acropolis, Athens** (pp. 103B, 104), is the supreme example, foremost among world-famous building-sites. A general idea of the original appearance of the Acropolis can be obtained from the restoration (p. 103B).

Normally, a city temenos contained a principal temple and maybe one or two subsidiary temples or shrines, together with treasuries in which were stored the offerings and processional regalia of other cities that held the presiding deity in esteem. There were also stoas, or colonnaded shelters; altars; statues or votive columns set up in honour of heroes, benefactors or victors in the games; exedrae, i.e. semi-circular seats or walled recesses for rest and contemplation; and sacred groves of trees. **Olympia** (p. 105B), **Delphi** (p. 106A), **Epidauros** (p. 106B), **Corinth, Eleusis** and **Delos** were further towns having a temenos famous in Doric Greece. But temples and shrines were to be found too, adjacent to the Agora, the city square or market place, the focus of Greek political, social, business and economic life. About it were the Prytaneion or Civic Hall; the Bouleuterion or Council House, a covered place of assembly; market enclosures of various types and stoas facing towards the Agora and serving miscellaneous functions. Colonnades sheltered the public fountains, and the vital importance of clear, pure water gave the fountain building a high civic prestige. At first, the Agora also served for open-air public meetings, religious assemblies and as a theatral area for contests, games and spectacles, but by Hellenistic times a number of the former uses of the Agora had been relegated to specially designed buildings. There were very fine, formal civic squares at **Priene** (p. 132G), **Miletus** and **Ephesus**, all in Asia Minor.

A. The Parthenon, Athens (447–432 B.C.). See p. 119

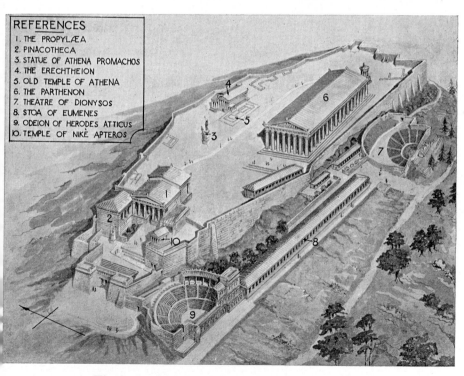

REFERENCES
1. THE PROPYLÆA
2. PINACOTHECA
3. STATUE OF ATHENA PROMACHOS
4. THE ERECHTHEION
5. OLD TEMPLE OF ATHENA
6. THE PARTHENON
7. THEATRE OF DIONYSOS
8. STOA OF EUMENES
9. ODEION OF HERODES ATTICUS
10. TEMPLE OF NIKÉ APTEROS

B. The Acropolis, Athens (restored): aerial view from S.W.
(c. A.D. 161). See p. 102

THE ACROPOLIS: ATHENS

THE ERECHTHEION   THE PARTHENON

WALL OF KIMON

THE OLD TEMPLE OF ATHENA

CAVE WITH SACRED SPRING

(A) SECTION FROM NORTH TO SOUTH

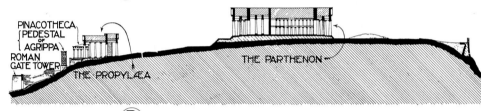

PINACOTHECA
PEDESTAL OF AGRIPPA
ROMAN GATE TOWER

THE PROPYLÆA

THE PARTHENON

(B) SECTION FROM EAST TO WEST

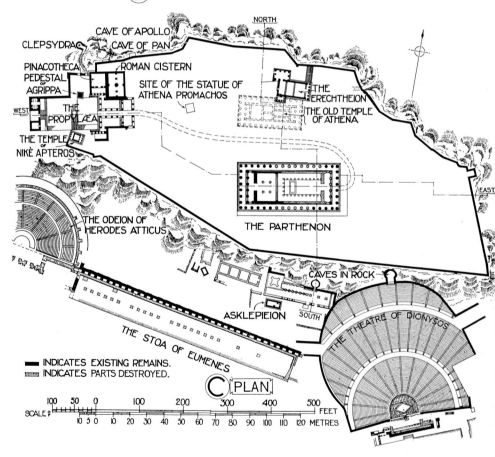

NORTH

CAVE OF APOLLO
CLEPSYDRA
CAVE OF PAN
PINACOTHECA
PEDESTAL OF AGRIPPA
ROMAN CISTERN
SITE OF THE STATUE OF ATHENA PROMACHOS

THE ERECHTHEION
THE OLD TEMPLE OF ATHENA

WEST
THE PROPYLÆA

THE TEMPLE OF NIKÈ APTEROS

EAST

THE ODEION OF HERODES ATTICUS

THE PARTHENON

CAVES IN ROCK

ASKLEPIEION   SOUTH

THE THEATRE OF DIONYSOS

THE STOA OF EUMENES

■ INDICATES EXISTING REMAINS.
▨ INDICATES PARTS DESTROYED.

(C) PLAN

SCALE?
100   50   0   100   200   300   400   500 FEET
10 5 0   10   20   30   40   50   60   70   80   90   100   110   120 METRES

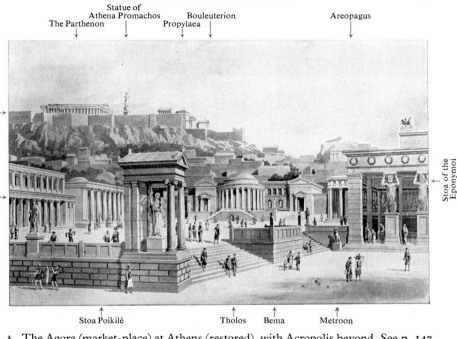

Statue of
The Parthenon | Athena Promachos | Bouleuterion | Areopagus
| | Propylaea | |

Stoa of the Eponymoi

Stoa Poikilè | Tholos | Bema | Metroon

A. The Agora (market-place) at Athens (restored), with Acropolis beyond. See p. 147

Valley of the Kladeos River | Arcadian Mountains | Kronos Hill | Me-troon | State Treasuries | Valley of the Alpheios River
| | Exedra | | | |

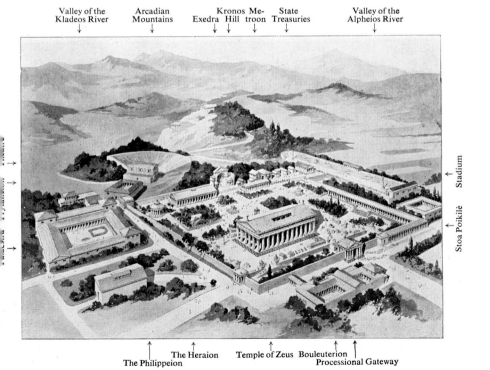

Stadium

Stoa Poikilè

The Philippeion | The Heraion | Temple of Zeus | Bouleuterion | Processional Gateway

B. The Altis, Olympia (restored). See p. 147

A. Delphi: sacred precinct (restored model). See pp. 102, 147
(*centre*) Temple of Apollo; (*top left*) Theatre; (*foreground*) Treasuries;
(*right*) Stoas

B. The Hieron, Epidauros, from S. (restored model). See pp. 102, 147
1. Tholos   3. Temple of Asclepius 5. Propylaea
2. Stoas for the sick 4. Temple of Artemis   6. Stadium

TEMPLES

Temples were the chief class of building in the Hellenic period, and we now describe their purpose and the different types in use. They were built with special regard to outward effect, since they were not intended for internal worship and the altar stood opposite the east front. They were adorned with fine sculpture in order to form fitting shrines to the deities to whom they were dedicated. They generally stood upon a crepidoma (see Glossary) of three or more steps. The 'naos', containing the statue of the god or goddess, was the kernel of the plan, and there was sometimes a treasury chamber, as well as front and rear porticoes, respectively known as the pronaos and opisthodomos (epinaos). Colonnades wholly surrounded all but the smallest buildings. It will thus be seen that Greek temples differ materially in purpose and design from the large temples of Egypt, though they somewhat resemble the relatively small 'Mammisi' temples of the Egyptians (p. 49).

With one or two exceptions, Greek temples were not large, but even so, as the principle of the roof truss was not understood before the Hellenistic period, internal double-tiered colonnades were often needed to help support the roof. On the two short ends of the temple, a triangular-shaped pediment, usually filled with sculpture, terminated the simple span roof (pp. 116A, 118A). These roofs were constructed of timber members, boarded and covered with terra-cotta or marble tiles, overlapping one another and finished off at the eaves with antefixes (p. 110H) or, in the case of Ionic temples, stopping behind a crowning moulding ornamented with lion-head sculptured masks which served to eject rainwater (p. 132J). The entrance doors normally were within the pronaos on the east front, and as they were tall, reaching about two-thirds the height of the lofty naos, when open they would allow ample light to illuminate the statue in the naos. Even when closed, metal grilles in the panels of the doors would admit sufficient light for ordinary purposes. Windows were rare in temple buildings, and consequently it was at one time thought that quite a few temples must have been 'hypaethral', i.e. partly open to the sky. One or two large ones were, such as the Temple of Apollo at Didyma, near Miletus (p. 131), but rarely, and due rather to incompletion than intention, as was, apparently, the case at the Heraeum, Samos (p. 128) and the Temples of Zeus Olympius at Agrigentum (pp. 109G, 115) and Athens (p. 140) at the time when the latter was seen by Vitruvius. Surviving fragments of marble roof tiles from a dozen sites show that light was quite often admitted to roof spaces through holes cut in specially large tiles.

The comparative plans (p. 109) show the different types of temple employed by the Greeks. Rectangular temples are described (a) according to the number of columns on the entrance front and (b) by the arrangement of the exterior columns of the temple in relation to the naos, as below:

(a) Henostyle—one column   Heptastyle—seven columns
    Distyle—two columns   Octastyle—eight columns
    Tristyle—three columns   Enneastyle—nine columns
    Tetrastyle—four columns   Decastyle—ten columns
    Pentastyle—five columns   Dodecastyle—twelve columns.
    Hexastyle —six columns

(b) 'In antis' temples have from one to four columns between antae at the front. Two is the usual number.

'Amphi-antis' temples have from one to four columns between antae at front and rear. Two is the usual number.

'Prostyle' temples have a portico of columns at the front.

'Amphi-prostyle' temples have a portico of columns at front and rear.
'Peripteral' temples have a single line of columns surrounding the naos.
'Pseudo-peripteral' temples have flank columns attached to the naos wall.
'Dipteral' temples have a double line of columns surrounding the naos.
'Pseudo-dipteral' temples are like the last, but the inner range of columns is
   omitted on the flanks of the naos.

Examples are:
   (i) Distyle in antis—The Temple of Nemesis, Rhamnus. Doric (p. 109A).
  (ii) Amphi-antis distyle—No surviving example, but the type is shown at p.
       109B.
 (iii) Prostyle tetrastyle—Temple 'B' at Selinus, Sicily. Doric (p. 109C).
  (iv) Amphi-prostyle tetrastyle—Temple on the Ilissus, Athens. Ionic (p. 109D).
   (v) Peripteral hexastyle—Theseion, Athens. Doric (pp. 109J, 120L).
  (vi) Pseudo-peripteral heptastyle—Temple of Zeus Olympius, Agrigentum.
       Doric (pp. 109G, 114K).
 (vii) Peripteral octastyle—Parthenon, Athens. Doric (pp. 109M, 122G).
(viii) Dipteral octastyle—Olympieion, Athens. Corinthian (p. 109H).
  (ix) Pseudo-dipteral octastyle—Temple 'G.T.', Selinus, Sicily. Doric (p. 109L).
   (x) Peripteral enneastyle—'Basilica', Paestum. Doric (pp. 109K, 114H).
  (xi) Dipteral decastyle—Temple of Apollo at Didyma, near Miletus. Ionic (p.
       109N).

Types (i) and (iii), above, often served too as treasuries. The larger temples in
the Doric style are usually hexastyle or octastyle. Pseudo-peripteral arrangements
are very rare before the Hellenistic period, but became the favourite with the
Romans. The more important Ionic temples of Asia Minor nearly always are
dipteral or pseudo-dipteral and of a more variable and ostentatious nature than the
Doric; they normally have a deep pronaos, and a shallow opisthodomos or none at
all. The use of the Corinthian Order for the whole of a temple is not common
until later Hellenistic times. The Erechtheion, Athens (p. 134F) is an exceptional
instance of irregular planning. Greek circular temples usually were peripteral, as
the Philippeion, Olympia (pp. 105B, 109F), and the Tholos, Epidauros (p. 106B,
109E).

THE DORIC ORDER

Though at one time the question was debated, there is now no doubt that the Order
had a timber origin (p. 110F). Whilst there are certain resemblances between the
Aegean megaron and the earliest temples (see p. 93), these do not concern the
peristyles, which are distinctively Greek, and in any case there is evidence that
between the Aegean and the Greek periods temple structure goes back to very
primitive beginnings and virtually begins anew. Simple structures like those illustrated on p. 110C, D, doubtless continued to be built even while those of a sacred
character were being progressively refined for their very special purpose, and
indeed close counterparts can still be found among rustic structures to-day.
Evidently, Greek columns began as tapered tree trunks, the function of the square
abacus and circular echinus comprising the capital being to gather and transmit
the load of the entablature to the column shaft. The architrave is readily identifi-
able as a lintel—in fact, pairs of lintels, plated together—spanning from column
to column and sustaining cross beams showing their ends as triglyphs in the frieze.
Cross beams were heavy and numerous for the reason already seen; roof trusses
were unknown and the beams had to support struts to prop up the sloping roofs.
The lowest member of the cornice represents a wooden plate across the tops of

COMPARATIVE PLANS ⁛ GREEK TEMPLES

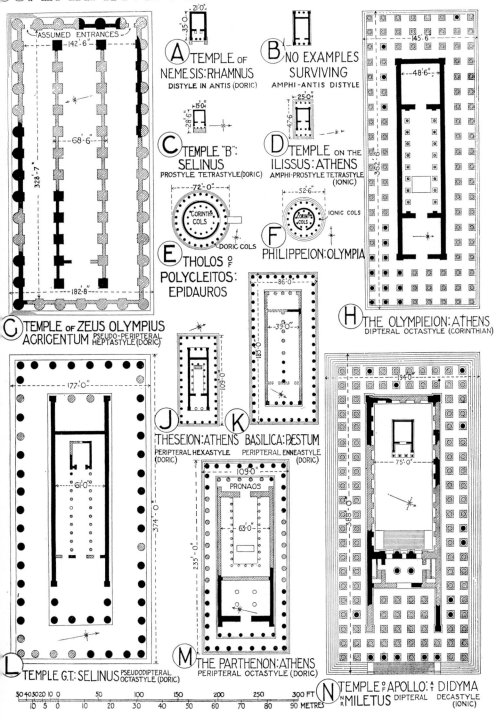

A TEMPLE OF NEMESIS: RHAMNUS
DISTYLE IN ANTIS (DORIC)

B NO EXAMPLES SURVIVING
AMPHI-ANTIS DISTYLE

C TEMPLE "B": SELINUS
PROSTYLE TETRASTYLE (DORIC)

D TEMPLE ON THE ILISSUS: ATHENS
AMPHI-PROSTYLE TETRASTYLE (IONIC)

E THOLOS ᵒF POLYCLEITOS: EPIDAUROS

F PHILIPPEION: OLYMPIA

G TEMPLE OF ZEUS OLYMPIUS ACRIGENTUM
PSEUDO-PERIPTERAL HEPTASTYLE (DORIC)

H THE OLYMPIEION: ATHENS
DIPTERAL OCTASTYLE (CORINTHIAN)

J THESEION: ATHENS
PERIPTERAL HEXASTYLE (DORIC)

K BASILICA: PÆSTUM
PERIPTERAL ENNEASTYLE (DORIC)

L TEMPLE G.T.: SELINUS
PSEUDODIPTERAL OCTASTYLE (DORIC)

M THE PARTHENON: ATHENS
PERIPTERAL OCTASTYLE (DORIC)

N TEMPLE ᵒF APOLLO: ⁛ DIDYMA ᴺᴿ MILETUS
DIPTERAL DECASTYLE (IONIC)

50 40 30 20 10 0   50   100   150   200   250   300 FT
10 5 0   10   20   30   40   50   60   70   80   90 METRES

EVOLUTION OF DORIC ORDER

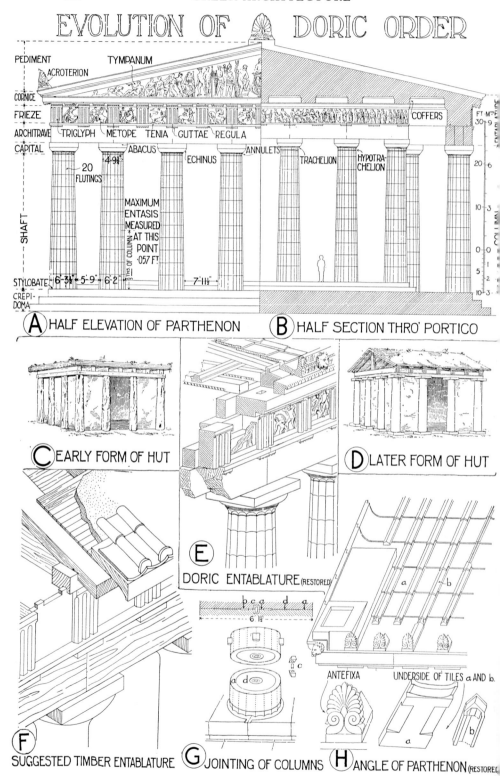

PEDIMENT
ACROTERION
TYMPANUM
CORNICE
FRIEZE
COFFERS
ARCHITRAVE TRIGLYPH METOPE TENIA GUTTAE REGULA
CAPITAL
ABACUS
ANNULETS
ECHINUS
TRACHELION
HYPOTRA-
CHELION
20
FLUTINGS
4·9½
SHAFT
MAXIMUM
ENTASIS
MEASURED
AT THIS
POINT
·057 FT
STYLOBATE 6·3½ 5·9 6·2
7·11½
CREPI-
DOMA

(A) HALF ELEVATION OF PARTHENON   (B) HALF SECTION THRO' PORTICO

(C) EARLY FORM OF HUT

(D) LATER FORM OF HUT

(E) DORIC ENTABLATURE (RESTORED)

(F) SUGGESTED TIMBER ENTABLATURE   (G) JOINTING OF COLUMNS   (H) ANGLE OF PARTHENON (RESTORED)

ANTEFIXA   UNDERSIDE OF TILES a AND b

the triglyphs to receive the wide, flat rafters, recognizable in stone architecture as mutules, which always retain a slope echoing the pitch of the roof. On their undersides are seen the guttae, stone replicas of wooden pins driven through the mutules to secure the roof boarding, on which were laid terra-cotta tiles bedded on mud or clay. The eaves tiles were specially made so that flanges could droop over the rafter ends to conceal them and present a continuous fascia which survives in stone architecture as the corona, the principal projecting member of the cornice. Just before wooden colonnades were converted into stone, the terra-cotta eaves crestings were very ornate and differed quite a little in design from place to place. There were also decorative terra-cotta plates slotted into the interspaces (metopes) between the triglyphs. These terra-cottas, of which quite a few survive, were richly painted in dark colours. The earliest stone colonnades, from about 600 B.C., had very clumsy proportions, as the capacities of stone were imperfectly known. The Temple of Apollo, Syracuse, Sicily (c. 565 B.C.) had columns little more than four times their own diameter in height and a ponderous stone entablature about half the height of the column. All the details were similarly crude. Afterwards, the Doric Order underwent a progressive lightening of parts which did not halt when the style had been perfected, but went on continuously throughout the two Greek periods. In the case of the Parthenon, the entablature is about one-third the height of the columns. Typical arrangements will now be described.

The **Doric Column** (pp. 110A, 113) stands without a base directly on a crepidoma, usually of three steps, and has a height, including the capital, of from 4 to 6 times the diameter at the base in the Hellenic period and up to $7\frac{1}{4}$ in the Hellenistic. The circular shaft, diminishing at the top from $\frac{3}{4}$ to $\frac{2}{3}$ of this diameter, is divided as a rule into 20 shallow flutes or channels separated by sharp 'arrises', but sometimes there are 12, 16, 18, or, as at Paestum, 24 (p. 113C). With the normal 20, a projection or arris came under the angles of the square abacus above, while a flute lay astride each of the main, rectangular axes. The shaft has normally a slightly convex profile called the entasis, discussed earlier (p. 94), to counteract the hollow appearance which results from straight-sided columns (p. 95D). The shaft terminates in the 'hypotrachelion', usually formed of three grooves in archaic examples and later of one groove, and immediately above it is the continuation of the fluted shaft known as the 'trachelion' or necking. The distinctive capital consists of abacus and echinus. Near the base of the echinus are 'annulets' or horizontal fillets, from three to five in number, which stop the vertical lines of the arrises and flutes of the shaft. The form of the echinus varies with the date of the building. In the earlier temples at Paestum (p. 113B, C) it has considerable projection, and is fuller in outline, approximating to a parabolic section; whereas in mature examples such as the Theseion (p. 113E) and the Parthenon (p. 113F) the projection is less and the profile more subtle, approximating to a hyperbolic curve. In Hellenistic work, when the column has become slender, the whole capital is shallower and the curve of the echinus approaches a straight line. The abacus, which forms the upper member of the capital, is a square slab, unmoulded until very late Greek times, when it begins to acquire a small moulding at the top.

The **Doric entablature** (p. 110A, E) which, in the case of the Parthenon, is $1\frac{3}{4}$ times the lower diameter of the column in height, varies between the earliest and latest examples from $2\frac{1}{4}$ to as little as $1\frac{1}{3}$, by the same kind of internal measure. An entablature has three main divisions: (a) The architrave or principal beam usually is made up of two or three slabs in the depth, the outermost showing a vertical face in one plane. Capping it is a flat projecting band called the taenia, and under this, at intervals corresponding to the triglyphs, are strips each known as a regula, with six guttae or small conical drops below. (b) The frieze is formed of triglyphs with three upright channels which alternate with metopes or square spaces, often ornamented with fine relief sculpture, as in the Parthenon (p. 123). A triglyph is aligned over each column and there is usually one over each inter-columniation. At the angles of the temple, however, two triglyphs meet with a bevelled edge, and the intercolumniation is less by about half a triglyph in width than that of the others. Where extra convenience was needed, as in the Propylaea, Athens (p. 142A), a central intercolumniation sometimes was made three metopes wide. Also, when in the Hellenistic period the proportions of the Order became very light, it was necessary regularly to increase the number of metopes in each intercolumniation. At Cora, Italy, a Roman temple built under Hellenistic influ-ence, four metopes were needed to each intercolumniation (p. 160B). (c) The cornice, the upper or crowning part, has at the top a cymatium or gutter moulding resting on a bird's beak moulding, and below this is the corona or vertical face. The soffit or underside of the cornice has an inclination approximating to the slope of the roof, and has flat blocks or mutules, which suggest the ends of sloping rafters. A mutule occurs over each triglyph and each metope, and is usually ornamented with eighteen guttae, in three rows of six each.

The principal Doric temples were in Greece, Sicily and South Italy, as set forth below.

Doric Temples in Greece

c. 590 B.C.	The Heraion, Olympia (below)
c. 540 B.C.	Temple of Apollo, Corinth
c. 510 B.C.	Temple of Apollo, Delphi (p. 106A)
c. 490 B.C.	Temple of Aphaia, Aegina (p. 115)
c. 460 B.C.	Temple of Zeus, Olympia (p. 119)
449–444 B.C.	The Theseion (Temple of Hephaestus), Athens (p. 119)
c. 450–425 B.C.	Temple of Apollo Epicurius, Bassae (p. 123)
447–432 B.C.	The Parthenon, Athens (p. 119)
444–440 B.C.	Temple of Poseidon, Sunium
c. 350 B.C.	The Tholos, Epidauros (p. 109E)
436–432 B.C.	Temple of Nemesis, Rhamnus (p. 109A)
c. 380 B.C.	Temple of Asclepius, Epidauros (p. 106B)
c. 300 B.C.	Temple of Apollo, Delos (p. 113G)

Doric Temples in Sicily and South Italy

c. 565 B.C.	Temple of Apollo, Syracuse (p. 111)
c. 550–530 B.C.	Temple 'C', Selinus
c. 530 B.C.	The 'Basilica', Paestum (p. 115)
c. 520–450 B.C.	The Great Temple of Apollo (G.T.), Selinus (p. 109L)
c. 510 B.C.	Temple of Demeter, Paestum (p. 115)
c. 510–409 B.C.	Temple of Zeus Olympius, Agrigentum (p. 115)
480 B.C.	Temple of Athena, Syracuse (p. 262)
c. 460 B.C.	Temple of Hera Lacinia, Agrigentum
c. 460 B.C.	Temple of Poseidon, Paestum (p. 115)
c. 430 B.C.	Temple of Concord, Agrigentum
c. 424–416 B.C.	Temple at Segesta, Sicily

The **Heraion, Olympia** (c. 590 B.C.) (p. 114C, F), dedicated to Hera, is most interesting as it illustrates the process of transition from timber construction to stone. It stands on a platform of two steps, measuring 168 ft by 64 ft 6 ins. As usual with early Doric temples, the plan has long proportions. The thick naos walls are of ashlar stone to a height of 3 ft 6 ins, but all the upper walls were of sun-dried brick, strengthened with wooden framing, a method of construction

THE DORIC ORDER

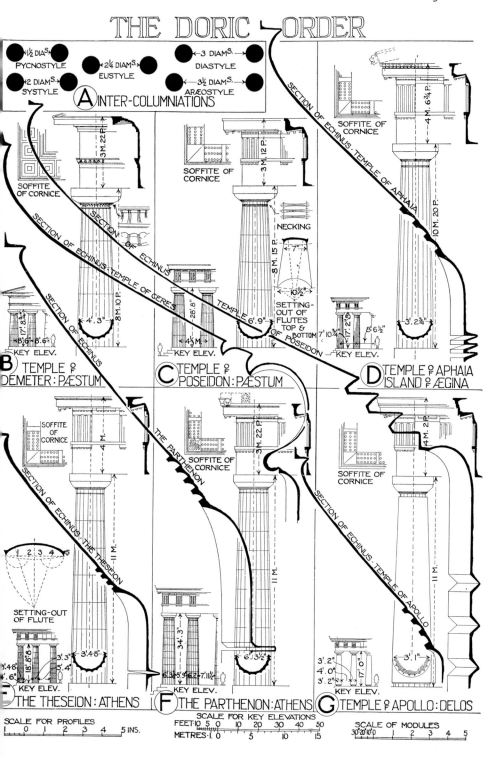

A INTER-COLUMNIATIONS

←1½ DIAS→ PYCNOSTYLE
←2 DIAMS→ SYSTYLE
←2¼ DIAMS→ EUSTYLE
←3 DIAMS→ DIASTYLE
←3½ DIAMS→ ARÆOSTYLE

SOFFITE OF CORNICE

SECTION OF ECHINUS · TEMPLE OF CERES

SECTION OF ECHINUS

B TEMPLE OF DEMETER : PÆSTUM

KEY ELEV.
17'.8¾"
8'.6'←8'.6"
8 M. 10 P.
4'.3"

C TEMPLE OF POSEIDON : PÆSTUM

SOFFITE OF CORNICE
3 M. 12 P.
8 M. 15 P.
26'.6"
4½ M.
6'.9"
KEY ELEV.
NECKING
SETTING-OUT OF FLUTES TOP & BOTTOM
10½"
7'.10¾"

SECTION OF ECHINUS · TEMPLE OF POSEIDON

D TEMPLE OF APHAIA ISLAND OF ÆGINA

SOFFITE OF CORNICE
4 M. 6¾ P.
10 M. 20 P.
3'.2¾"
KEY ELEV.
17'.2½"
8'.6½"

SECTION OF ECHINUS · TEMPLE OF APHAIA

3 M. 22 P.

SECTION OF ECHINUS · THE THESEION

E THE THESEION : ATHENS

SOFFITE OF CORNICE
4 M.
11 M.
SETTING-OUT OF FLUTE
1 2 3 4 5
KEY ELEV.
17'.8¾"
3'.3"
3'.4.8"
5'.4"
3'.4.8"
'.6"

THE PARTHENON

F THE PARTHENON : ATHENS

SOFFITE OF CORNICE
3 M. 22 P.
11 M.
34'.3"
6'.3½"
6'.3½'.5'.9"'.6'.2'-7'.11½"
KEY ELEV.

SECTION OF ECHINUS · TEMPLE OF APOLLO

G TEMPLE OF APOLLO : DELOS

SOFFITE OF CORNICE
4 M. 2 P.
11 M.
3'.1"
KEY ELEV.
17'.0"
3'.2"
4'.0"
3'.2"

SCALE FOR PROFILES
0 1 2 3 4 5 INS.

SCALE FOR KEY ELEVATIONS
FEET·10 5 0   10   20   30   40   50
METRES·1· 0   5   10   15

SCALE OF MODULES
30·20·10·0   1   2   3   4   5

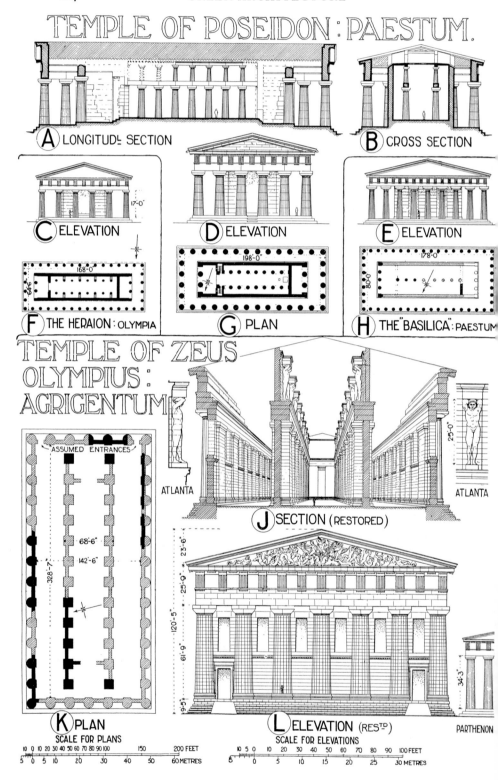

TEMPLE OF POSEIDON : PAESTUM.

Ⓐ LONGITUDL SECTION

Ⓑ CROSS SECTION

Ⓒ ELEVATION 17'-0"

Ⓓ ELEVATION

Ⓔ ELEVATION

Ⓕ THE HERAION : OLYMPIA — 168'-0" — 64'-6"

Ⓖ PLAN — 198'-0"

Ⓗ THE "BASILICA" : PAESTUM — 178'-0" — 80'-0"

TEMPLE OF ZEUS OLYMPIUS : AGRIGENTUM

ASSUMED ENTRANCES

Ⓚ PLAN — 328'-7" — 142'-6" — 68'-6"

SCALE FOR PLANS
10 0 10 20 30 40 50 60 70 80 90 100   150   200 FEET
5 0 5 10   20   30   40   50   60 METRES

ATLANTA

Ⓙ SECTION (RESTORED)

ATLANTA 25'-0"

Ⓛ ELEVATION (RESTD) — 120'-5" — 23'-6" — 25'-9" — 61'-9" — 19'-5"

PARTHENON 34'-3"

SCALE FOR ELEVATIONS
10 5 0 10 20 30 40 50 60 70 80 90 100 FEET
5 0 5 10 15 20 25 30 METRES

reminiscent of Aegean practice. Inside the temple, alternate columns of a range of eight on each side were attached by spur walls to the naos walls. The internal columns and all those in the colonnades outside were originally of wood, but were replaced with stone from time to time over a period of centuries. Thus they vary very much in their details, and are either monolithic or built-up in a varying number of courses or 'drums'. The entablature remained always of timber, and the antae and the door casings were also of wood.

The **'Basilica', Paestum** (*c.* 530 B.C.) (p. 114E, H), in reality a temple, is unusual in being enneastyle, the central line of eight columns in the naos assisting to divide the width of the temple into four parts, to allow easy support for the roof timbers. For this reason too, the ambulatory is very wide at the sides and the temple consequently almost pseudo-dipteral, while the pronaos is tristyle in antis. The columns have a pronounced diminution and entasis, and the capitals are heavy and wide-spreading. A peculiarity of this temple and the neighbouring **Temple of Demeter** (Ceres) (*c.* 510 B.C.) is the decorative treatment of the trachelion (p. 113B), showing Ionic influence.

The **Temple of Zeus Olympius, Agrigentum** (*c.* 510–409 B.C.) (pp. 109G, 114) also is of archaic, unusual design, with a heptastyle, pseudo-peripteral arrangement and a plan comprising a central naos and two slightly narrower flanking apartments. At the west a portion of the naos was cut off to form a sanctuary. The temple is now in a ruinous condition, but measured 173 ft by 361 ft over the stylobate, so large that its roofing appears never to have been completed. That there were pediments over the short ends is clear from an ancient description and from surviving fragments. The enormous attached, external columns, 13 ft 3 ins diameter and over 56 ft high, show traces of Ionic influence in having mouldings across the base. In the upper portion of the screen wall, between the outer columns, were giant 'Atlantes', sculptured figures, 25 ft high, giving intermediate support to the massive entablature. Some authorities place the Atlantes in the naos (p. 114J). Because of the great scale, the Order had to be made up of many stone pieces. The coarse stone was finished with a thin coating of fine marble stucco.

The **Temple of Poseidon, Paestum** (*c.* 460 B.C.) (pp. 113C; 114A, B ,D, G; 116), is one of the best preserved of all early Greek temples. Though more mature than the three last-named temples from Doric western territory—the two at Paestum and that at Agrigentum—and now approaching the perfected type, the plan is still rather long and the Order heavy. The columns are about 29 ft high and thus 4·3 times their lower diameter of 6 ft 9 ins. The temple is peripteral hexastyle, with fourteen columns on the flanks, and has the normal crepidoma of three steps, pronaos, naos and opisthodomos. Near the entrance, steps led to the roof space. The columns in the naos, preserved almost intact, are in a double tier, the upper separated from the lower solely by a stone architrave, and not a full entablature. The number of flutes varies; the columns of the outer colonnade have 24, the lower, inner Order the normal 20, and the upper range only 16.

The **Temple of Aphaia, Aegina** (*c.* 490 B.C.) (pp. 117, 154B), on an island about twenty-five miles from Athens, like the last example represents the almost perfected temple type, but its appreciably earlier date indicates that mainland Greece by this time was showing the greater initiative. It is hexastyle, with all the normal parts and arrangement, including a shortened plan, requiring only twelve flanking columns. The off-centre doorway to the opisthodomos, though contemporary, was an afterthought. This temple, like the last, possessed a double range of interior columns, separated simply by an architrave. It now seems unlikely that the temple was hypaethral, as sometimes had been thought. All the exterior columns had monolithic shafts, except three adjacent ones on the north side,

A. Temple of Poseidon, Paestum (*c.* 460 B.C.). See p. 115

B. Temple of Poseidon, Paestum, showing superimposed columns

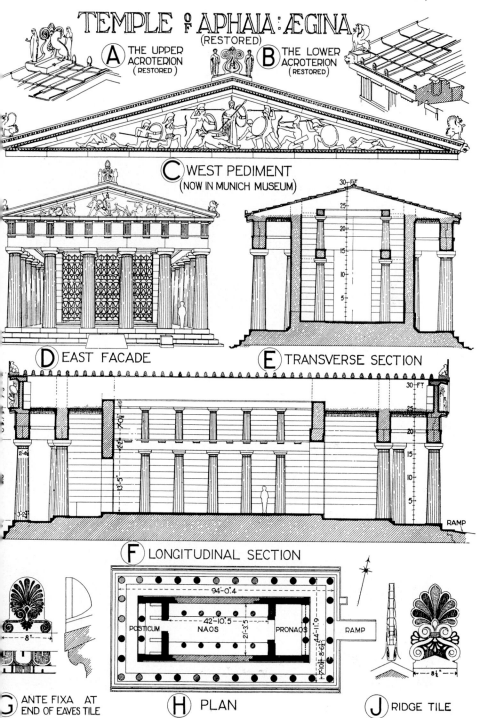

TEMPLE OF APHAIA : ÆGINA
(RESTORED)

Ⓐ THE UPPER ACROTERION (RESTORED)

Ⓑ THE LOWER ACROTERION (RESTORED)

Ⓒ WEST PEDIMENT
(NOW IN MUNICH MUSEUM)

Ⓓ EAST FACADE

Ⓔ TRANSVERSE SECTION

Ⓕ LONGITUDINAL SECTION

Ⓖ ANTE FIXA AT END OF EAVES TILE

Ⓗ PLAN

Ⓙ RIDGE TILE

A. Temple of Zeus, Olympia (restored) (*c.* 460 B.C.). See p. 119

B. The Theseion, Athens (*c.* 449–444 B.C.). See p. 119

which were built up in drums after the naos had been completed. The pediment sculptures, the elaborately-carved acroteria, the antefixae and the roof slabs over the pediments and eaves were in Parian marble, the rest of the roof tiles being in terra-cotta (p. 117A, B, C, G, J). The entablature was painted in glowing colours. The pediments contained remarkable sculptures belonging to the latest phase of archaic Greek art, dating from c. 490 B.C., like the temple itself. These sculptures, now in Munich, are shown as disposed in Cockerell's restorations, but later authorities have suggested different arrangements of the figures. The majority of the temple was of local limestone, treated usually with a coat of marble stucco.

The **Temple of Zeus, Olympia** (c. 460 B.C.) (pp. 105B, 118A), designed by Libon of Elis, belongs to the best phase of Greek architecture. It was normal in arrangement but grand in its dimensions, being 90 ft by 210 ft over the stylobate. Mostly, it was built of limestone, faced with marble stucco, but had Parian marble for the sculptured pediments, the carved metopes over the inner porches, the cymatium and all the roof slabs. The splendid architectural effect was heightened by picking out the mouldings and ornament in blue, red and gold, the main surfaces being left white. The acroteria were of bronze. About 448 B.C., the temple received the colossal gold-and-ivory statue, 40 ft high above its base, by Pheidias, most famous sculptor of all time. Inside the naos, once again, were double-tiered colonnades. Fragments of large, marble tiles, with elliptical holes cut within them, through which light was admitted to the roof space, were found on this site, so the temple does not appear to have been hypaethral.

The **Theseion, Athens** (449–444 B.C.) (pp. 118B, 120), is now thought to be a temple to Hephaestus. It is very well preserved externally, owing to its having been converted into a church by the Byzantine Greeks, who however, gutted the naos and constructed an apse at the east end. The plan is normal, except for a roomier arrangement within the east front and a crepidoma of only two steps; also, the double tier of inner columns, which hitherto ran the whole length of the naos, here returns across the west end. The building was almost wholly of marble. Relief sculptures once existed in the pediments, but otherwise were limited to friezes over the pronaos and opisthodomos porches, and to metopes across the east front and the neighbouring four on each flank. Much survives of the stone coffered ceilings over the ambulatory, with some traces of the original colouring.

The **Parthenon, Athens** (447–432 B.C.) (pp. 103, 104, 110, 113F, 122, 144B), erected on the Acropolis, south of the old Temple of Athena (p. 104), in the time of Pericles, was dedicated to Athena Parthenos, the virgin Athena. Ictinus and Callicrates were the architects, and Pheidias was the master sculptor. The temple is peripteral octastyle in plan, with seventeen columns on the flanks, and stands on a crepidoma of three steps, which measures 101 ft 4 ins by 228 ft along the top, i.e., a relation of breadth to length of about 4 to 9. Each of the steps is about 1 ft 8 ins high and 2 ft 4 ins wide, and as these were too steep to ascend with comfort, intermediate steps were provided at the centre of the east and west ends (p. 122A). The principal doorway on the east led into the naos, known as the 'Hecatompedon', after an archaic temple which had stood upon the site and was so named because its naos had measured 100 Attic feet long. This eastern chamber, 63 ft wide and 98 ft long, had Doric colonnades on three sides, forming an ambulatory. They were in two tiers, separated by an architrave, and gave support to the roof timbers. There were ten columns on each side, and five across the west end, counting the angle columns twice. Near the western end stood the famous statue of Athena Parthenos, one of the most marvellous works of Pheidias, representing Athena fully armed with spear, helmet, aegis and shield, supporting a winged Victory in her right hand (p. 122H). It was a 'chryselephantine' or gold and ivory statue,

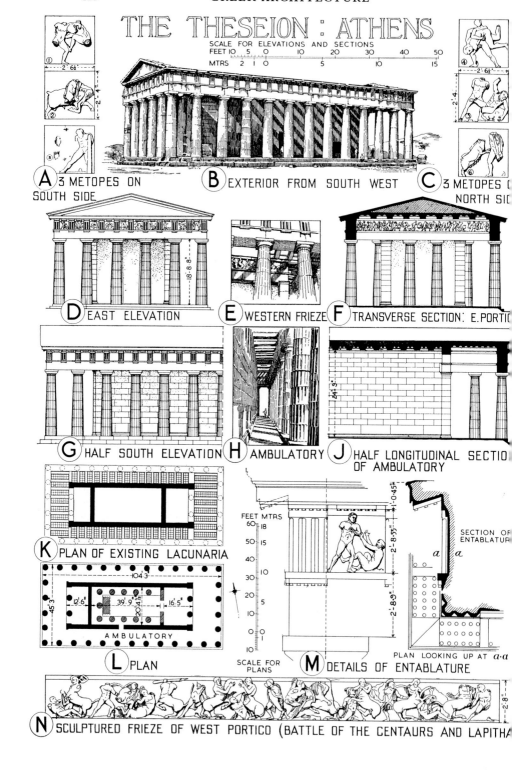

THE THESEION : ATHENS

SCALE FOR ELEVATIONS AND SECTIONS
FEET 10 5 0   10   20   30   40   50
MTRS 2 1 0   5   10   15

A 3 METOPES ON SOUTH SIDE

B EXTERIOR FROM SOUTH WEST

C 3 METOPES ON NORTH SIDE

D EAST ELEVATION

E WESTERN FRIEZE

F TRANSVERSE SECTION : E. PORTICO

G HALF SOUTH ELEVATION

H AMBULATORY

J HALF LONGITUDINAL SECTION OF AMBULATORY

K PLAN OF EXISTING LACUNARIA

L PLAN

FEET MTRS
60 — 18
50 — 15
40 — 10
30
20 — 5
10
0 — 0
10

SCALE FOR PLANS

M DETAILS OF ENTABLATURE

SECTION OF ENTABLATURE

PLAN LOOKING UP AT a·a

N SCULPTURED FRIEZE OF WEST PORTICO (BATTLE OF THE CENTAURS AND LAPITHAE)

about 42 ft high including pedestal, and the gold plates which formed the drapery, armour and accessories over the wooden core were detachable, so that they could be removed in case of danger. The face, hands and feet were of ivory, and the eyes of precious stones. The ceiling of the naos was of wood, decoratively painted, ornamented with sunken 'lacunaria' or coffers. Various suggestions have been made as to how the naos was lighted (p. 122J, K), but the very large double doors, when open, might have been the sole means of admitting natural light. To the west of the naos was the Parthenon or virgin's chamber, from which the temple took its name. This was entered from the opisthodomos by a large doorway corresponding to the eastern one, and its roof was supported by four Ionic columns (p. 122E, F). As this chamber was shallow and high, a double tier of Doric columns would have appeared exceptionally clumsy, while a single range would have encumbered the floor space unduly. So Ionic columns were used instead, and both Orders are found in the one building, a practice increasingly prevalent from this time onwards. Numerous other evidences of Ionic influence are found in this essentially Doric building. The naos and virgin's chamber were enclosed by walls about 4 ft thick, and the whole temple was encircled by an ambulatory 9 ft wide on the sides and 11 ft in the front and rear. The pronaos and opisthodomos, each about 60 ft by 12 ft, were arranged in a somewhat unusual manner with six columns about $5\frac{1}{2}$ ft in diameter and 33 ft high, forming a prostyle portico on an upper platform of two steps. Both pronaos and opisthodomos were used as treasuries, and, in order to render them secure, lofty metal grilles extending from top to bottom were fixed between the columns, with the entrance gates in the central intercolumniation.

Externally, the dominant feature is the stately peristyle of fluted marble columns (pp. 95C, 113F). The columns are about 6 ft 2 ins in diameter at the base and 34 ft 3 ins high: or, to express their proportions directly, they are nearly $5\frac{1}{2}$ times their own lower diameter in height. The angle columns are a little larger in diameter; 6 ft $3\frac{1}{2}$ ins. All diminish at the top of the shaft to a little more than three-quarters the lower diameter. The columns support an entablature about 11 ft high (p. 95C). which has the usual divisions of architrave, frieze and cornice (pp. 110A, 122C, 144B), The architrave was ornamented with bronze shields, probably presented by Alexander the Great in 334 B.C., and with dedicatory inscriptions in bronze letters. The joints of the marble roof-slabs above the cornice were masked by carved antefixae, which formed an ornamental cresting along the sides of the building (pp. 110H, 122C). The pediments, which have an inclination of $13\frac{1}{2}$ degrees, terminated the roof at each end of the temple, and had large floral acroteria, about 9 ft high, at the apex and lower angles (pp. 110A, 122B, D). The peristyle ceiling was enriched with lacunaria and marble beams. The optical refinements used in the different parts of the Parthenon have already been described (p. 94). The tympana in the pediments were filled with the finest sculpture of Pheidias. That of the eastern pediment represented the birth of Athena and of the west, the contest of Athena and Poseidon for the soil of Attica. The use of sculptured friezes, both inside and outside the temple, is another evidence of Ionic influence. The celebrated Panathenaic frieze was carved along the top of the naos wall just below the peristyle ceiling, and was taken across the east and west ends above the six columns of the pronaos and opisthodomos. It is 3 ft 4 ins high, in very slight relief of about $1\frac{1}{2}$ ins, and the sculpture is treated in such a way as to be seen effectively by the light reflected up from the white marble pavement below, the shadow being thrown upwards (p. 122A). It represents the Panathenaic procession (p. 163H), which went every fourth year to the Acropolis to present the 'peplos' to the goddess Athena, and it portrays the preparations of Athenian knights, and the great procession of

THE PARTHENON: ATHENS

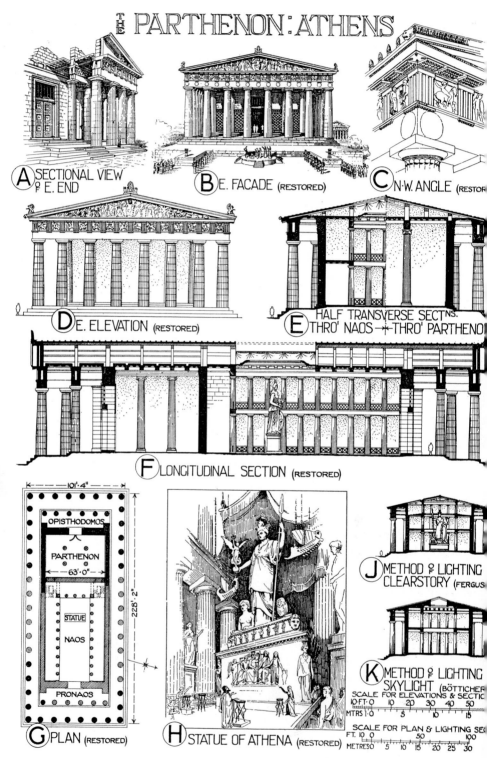

(A) SECTIONAL VIEW OF E. END

(B) E. FACADE (RESTORED)

(C) N·W. ANGLE (RESTOR..

(D) E. ELEVATION (RESTORED)

(E) HALF TRANSVERSE SECT.NS THRO' NAOS →← THRO' PARTHENO..

(F) LONGITUDINAL SECTION (RESTORED)

101'·4"

OPISTHODOMOS

PARTHENON

63'·0"

228'·2"

STATUE

NAOS

PRONAOS

(G) PLAN (RESTORED)

(H) STATUE OF ATHENA (RESTORED)

(J) METHOD OF LIGHTING CLEARSTORY (FERGUS..

(K) METHOD OF LIGHTING SKYLIGHT (BÖTTICHER

SCALE FOR ELEVATIONS & SECTIC..
10·FT·0   10   20   30   40   50
MTRS 1·0   5   10   15

SCALE FOR PLAN & LIGHTING SEC..
FT. 10 0   50   100
METRES 0   5   10   15   20   25   30

cavalry, chariots, men with olive branches, musicians, youths, sacrificial animals, maidens with sacrificial vessels, magistrates and gods, all culminating in a great central group at the eastern end over the principal entrance to the temple, while the imposing chryselephantine statue of Athena in the naos was seen through the open door (p. 122H). Out of the original length of 524 ft, only 335 ft are in existence. The western frieze, excepting the three central figures, is in its original position; the greater portion of that belonging to the northern, southern and eastern sides is in the British Museum, while the remainder, with the exception of eight fragments of the eastern frieze in the Louvre, is in the Athens Museum. The sculptured metopes (p. 163K, M), about 4 ft 5 ins square, numbering fourteen on each front and thirty-two on each side, are in high relief. Those on the eastern façade represent contests between gods and giants; on the western, between Greeks and Amazons; on the southern, between Centaurs and Lapiths; and on the northern, scenes from the siege of Troy. Traces of bright colours have been found on the sculptures in pediment, metope and frieze. This miracle of architecture, compact of glistening marble, marvellous sculpture and glowing colour, has thrown its glamour over men through all the ages, and more than justifies the poetic description of Emerson:

> Earth proudly wears the Parthenon
> As the best gem upon her zone.

In the fifth or sixth century the Parthenon was converted into a Byzantine Christian church, dedicated to the 'Divine Wisdom', and an apse was formed at its eastern end. From about A.D. 1204, under the Frankish dukes of Athens, it served as a Latin church, until, in A.D. 1458 it was converted into a Turkish mosque. Then, during the capture of Athens by the Venetians in A.D. 1687, it was much damaged by a shell which fell into the portion of the building used as a powder magazine. The Venetians withdrew in the following year. In A.D. 1801–3, through the instrumentality of Lord Elgin, many of the sculptures were removed to the British Museum. After some further damage from various causes, including that from an earthquake in A.D. 1894, and some trivial attempts at restoration, the north side was re-assembled from the scattered fragments between A.D. 1921–9. Little survives, however, of the interior.

The **Temple of Apollo Epicurius, Bassae**, in Arcadia (c. 450–425 B.C.) (p. 124) is a mainland temple contemporary with the Parthenon, and Ictinus was again the architect. The temple took a long time in building, owing to Ictinus' preoccupation with the Parthenon, begun a year or two later, though completed earlier. A most remarkable feature of this temple is the use in it of all three of the Greek Orders of Architecture—Doric outside and Ionic and Corinthian within; it seems evident that the practice of using different Orders in one building was introduced by Ictinus. The plan is hexastyle peripteral, with fifteen columns on the flanks, all built up in drums. Most of the building is of a hard, fine-grained grey limestone, but marble was used for the sculptures and the more decorative parts, including the ceilings over the pronaos, the opisthodomos and the short sides of the ambulatory, which otherwise were of stone. The temple has other peculiarities. It faces north, instead of east, and the statue of Apollo was placed in an adyton, or inner sanctuary, partially screened off from the naos proper and lighted from a large opening in the eastern, side wall. On both sides of the naos are Ionic half-columns, attached to spur walls, the recesses thus formed with the main naos wall having a stone, coffered ceiling. Between the adyton and the naos was a single, free-standing column, with a Corinthian capital (p. 138F). Until recently it was thought this was the

TEMPLE ᵒꜰ APOLLO EPICURIUS : BASSÆ

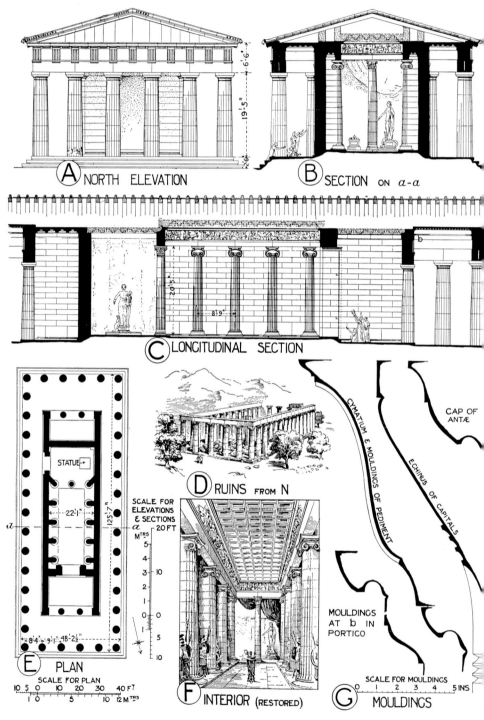

Ⓐ NORTH ELEVATION

Ⓑ SECTION ON *a-a*

Ⓒ LONGITUDINAL SECTION

Ⓓ RUINS FROM N

Ⓔ PLAN

SCALE FOR PLAN

SCALE FOR ELEVATIONS & SECTIONS

Ⓕ INTERIOR (RESTORED)

Ⓖ MOULDINGS

CYMATIUM & MOULDINGS OF PEDIMENT

CAP OF ANTÆ

ECHINUS OF CAPITALS

MOULDINGS AT b IN PORTICO

SCALE FOR MOULDINGS

STATUE

solitary instance in the temple, but Professor Dinsmoor now has disclosed that the adjacent spur walls, splayed diagonally from the main walls, also had partial Corinthian capitals. These three are the first instances known of the Corinthian Order. There is a possibility that Callimachus himself designed them (see p. 139). The entablature was Ionic and continuous with that over the four Ionic half-columns on each side. The capitals of the latter were of unique design, with diagonal volutes, and they had high wide-flaring bases (p. 127C). Professor Dinsmoor shows too, that the naos had a coffered timber ceiling and that there was no hypaethral lighting, although some light was undoubtedly admitted to the roof space through rectangular openings in many of the marble roof tiles. The celebrated sculptured marble frieze over the half-columns, portions of which are in the British Museum, must have been poorly illuminated. It is 2 ft high and ran 100 ft long, representing battles of Centaurs and Lapiths and Athenians and Amazons.

THE IONIC ORDER

The Ionic Order (p. 127) is specially remarkable for its volute or scroll capital, which, like so many other decorative motifs, may have been derived from the Egyptian lotus (p. 126B), which must have undergone sundry modifications on its way from Egypt through Assyria and divers other Near Eastern countries to Asia Minor (p. 126E). The spiral was also a common motif in Aegean art, and this could well account for its survival in those places which had inherited the Aegean tradition. The early Ionic capitals at Cyprus (p. 126A), Neandria (p. 126M), Lesbos and Larissa exhibit volutes of a distinctly vegetable type with a palmette interposed. Other Ionic capitals at the Greek colony of Naucratis in Egypt (p. 126K), or at Delos (p. 126J), Delphi (p. 126L) and Athens, where they had served as votive offerings, would seem to form a link between these and later types.

The nautilus shell (p. 126D) with its simple spiral and the ram's horns (p. 126G) are examples of nature's spirals which were at hand for the observant architect; and scrolls, quite obviously derived from nature, are seen on Egyptian wall paintings (p. 126F), Cypriote vases (p. 126H), and bronze armour plates (p. 126N). The bracket capital (p. 126C) shows a simple device for decreasing the bearing of an architrave, still frequently employed at the present day. The long and shallow form of many early capitals (p. 126J, L) indicates this kind of purpose and points unmistakably to a wooden origin. There is indeed no doubt that, as a whole, the Ionic Order of Asia Minor, like the Doric Order from further west, evolved from timber forms. Originally, the architrave spanning from column to column was made up of broad timber plates, laid one on top of the other. On the architrave were laid cross-beams, but these were smaller and more numerous than the Doric triglyph beams, and relatively to the architrave took up far less height. Even with the longitudinal timbers above them providing seating for the rafters and cover for their ends, the whole entablature was much shallower, and therefore lighter, than the Doric; so that after translation into stone, there was less need for sturdy column support. Thus Ionic columns were always comparatively slender, and needed a base at their lower end to spread the weight transmitted. In the entablature there were only two main parts; the architrave, with its fasciae, representing the original plates, and a cornice of which the 'dentils', derived from the closely-spaced cross-beams, formed an integral part. There was no frieze in the entablature of the true Ionic Order of Asia Minor, and none was acquired there until late fourth century B.C. The Ionians, whose architecture always tended towards excessive ornamentation, loved the sculptured frieze, but it was used on the body of the temple rather than as an essential part of the entablature.

Ionic columns, including capital and base, are usually about nine times their

THE IONIC VOLUTE

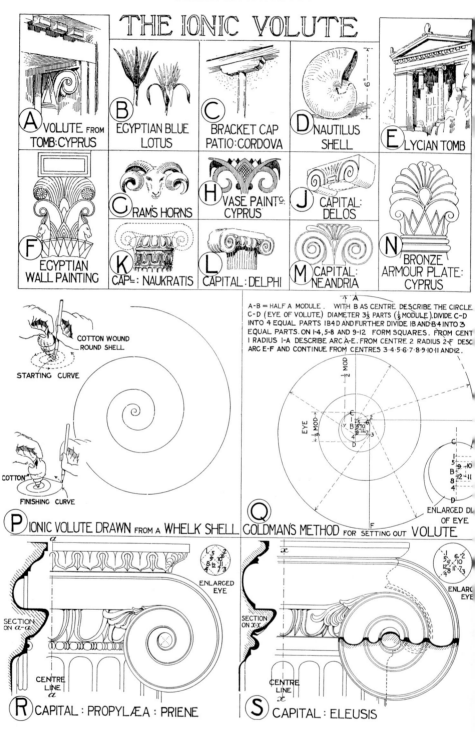

A — VOLUTE FROM TOMB: CYPRUS

B — EGYPTIAN BLUE LOTUS

C — BRACKET CAP PATIO: CORDOVA

D — NAUTILUS SHELL

E — LYCIAN TOMB

F — EGYPTIAN WALL PAINTING

G — RAM'S HORNS

H — VASE PAINTG. CYPRUS

J — CAPITAL: DELOS

K — CAPL: NAUKRATIS

L — CAPITAL: DELPHI

M — CAPITAL: NEANDRIA

N — BRONZE ARMOUR PLATE: CYPRUS

COTTON WOUND ROUND SHELL

STARTING CURVE

COTTON

FINISHING CURVE

P — IONIC VOLUTE DRAWN FROM A WHELK SHELL

A-B = HALF A MODULE. WITH B AS CENTRE DESCRIBE THE CIRCLE C-D (EYE OF VOLUTE) DIAMETER 3½ PARTS (⅛ MODULE). DIVIDE C-D INTO 4 EQUAL PARTS 1B4D AND FURTHER DIVIDE 1B AND B4 INTO 3 EQUAL PARTS. ON 1-4, 5-8 AND 9-12 FORM SQUARES. FROM CENT 1 RADIUS 1-A DESCRIBE ARC A-E. FROM CENTRE 2 RADIUS 2-F DESC ARC E-F AND CONTINUE FROM CENTRES 3·4·5·6·7·8·9·10·11 AND 12.

EYE

ENLARGED DI OF EYE

Q — GOLDMAN'S METHOD FOR SETTING OUT VOLUTE

SECTION ON a-a

ENLARGED EYE

CENTRE LINE a

R — CAPITAL: PROPYLÆA: PRIENE

SECTION ON x-x

ENLARG EYE

CENTRE LINE x

S — CAPITAL: ELEUSIS

THE IONIC ORDER

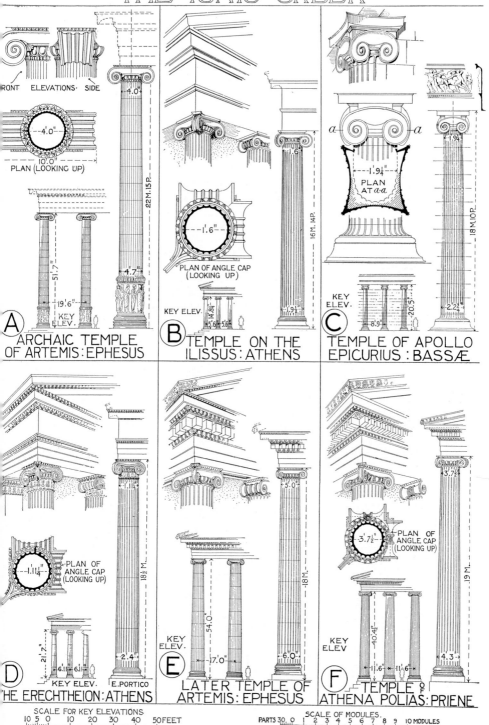

FRONT ELEVATIONS · SIDE

—4'.0"—

—4'.0"—

—10'.0"—
PLAN (LOOKING UP)

22 M. 15 P.

—4'.7"—

51'.7"

—19'.6"—
KEY
ELEV.

A ARCHAIC TEMPLE
OF ARTEMIS: EPHESUS

—1'.6"—

—1'.6"—
PLAN OF ANGLE CAP
(LOOKING UP)

16 M. 14 P.

KEY ELEV.

14'.8½"

5'.6" 5'.6"

1'.9¼"

B TEMPLE ON THE
ILISSUS: ATHENS

a   a

—1'.9¼"—
PLAN
AT a-a

—1'.9¼"—

KEY
ELEV.

18 M. 10 P.

—20'.5"—

8'.9"

2'.2½"

C TEMPLE OF APOLLO
EPICURIUS: BASSÆ

—1'.11¼"—
PLAN OF
ANGLE CAP
(LOOKING UP)

18½ M.

—2'.4"—

21'.7"

6'.1" 6'.1"
KEY ELEV. E.PORTICO

D THE ERECHTHEION: ATHENS

—5'.0"—

18 M.

54'.0"

KEY
ELEV.

—17'.0"—

—6'.0"—

E LATER TEMPLE OF
ARTEMIS: EPHESUS

—3'.7½"—

—3'.7½"—
PLAN OF
ANGLE CAP
(LOOKING UP)

19 M.

—4'.3"—

40'.4½"

KEY
ELEV

11'.6" 11'.6"

F TEMPLE OF
ATHENA POLIAS: PRIENE

SCALE FOR KEY ELEVATIONS
10 5 0   10   20   30   40   50 FEET

SCALE OF MODULES.
PARTS 30 0 1 2 3 4 5 6 7 8 9 10 MODULES

lower diameter in height and have twenty-four flutes separated by fillets and not by arrises or sharp edges as in the Doric column. Early examples, however, may have as many as forty (p. 127A), forty-four, or forty-eight flutes, which then are shallow and do meet on a sharp arris. The moulded base evolved by stages into that known as the 'Attic' base (p. 165H), having been brought to this perfected form in Attica. It consists of an upper and lower torus, divided by a scotia and fillets, but until late in the Hellenic period there is no square plinth. The capital has a pair of volutes or spirals, about two-thirds the diameter in height, showing to front and back and joined at the sides by a concave cushion, sometimes plain but usually ornamented with numerous flutes, fillets and beads. The volute scroll rests on an echinus, circular on plan, carved with egg-and-dart and resting on a bead moulding. Methods of setting out volutes are shown (p. 126P, Q, R, S). Above the volute scrolls was a shallow abacus, with moulded edge, which at first was elongated in the direction of the architrave it supported, but which eventually became square on plan. The Greek double-fronted capital represented difficulties at the outer angles of a rectangular building, and in such positions a canted angle volute was used (p. 127B, D, E, F). The four-fronted capital, like that indicated by the Order in the Temple at Bassae (p. 127C), is exceptional in Greek Hellenic architecture though it became increasingly common in the Hellenistic period.

The **Ionic entablature** (p. 127) passed through important stages of development during the Hellenic period. As evolved in Asia Minor, it had only two main parts, architrave and cornice, the latter containing large dentils in the bed-mould. It was therefore very light in relation to the columns, being as little as one-sixth of their height. The Order was soon used on the mainland too, at first only in treasuries, but afterwards importantly in temples, like the Erechtheion (p. 133) and the Temple of Nikè Apteros, Athens (p. 133), which are the finest examples of the style. On the mainland, the influence of the Doric caused a frieze to be inserted in the entablature, but with the consequence that, until late fourth century B.C., the bed-mould was omitted from the cornice except for a minor moulding under the widely-projecting corona. At about this time (late fourth century B.C.), Asia Minor adopted mainland practice and the three-part entablature became universal for the Order, but with the fresh development that henceforward the dentilled bed-mould type of cornice as well as the frieze became established parts of the entablature. Whenever the frieze was present, at whatever stage of the evolution, on the mainland or in Ionia, the entablature still was much lighter than the Doric—about one-quarter the height of the column, i.e. rather more than two diameters high. The Ionic architrave, normally with three fasciae, is capped by a small group of mouldings. The frieze, when present, sometimes is plain, but more often is ornamented with a continuous band of sculpture. Ionic temples do not show antefixae on the flanks; instead, the cymatium or gutter moulding of the inclined cornices at the ends of the temple is carried along the side cornices too, and carved lion heads at intervals serve to eject the rainwater from the roof (p. 163B).

The principal examples of the Ionic Order, found in Asia Minor and on the Greek mainland, are set forth below.

Ionic Temples in Asia Minor

c. 560 B.C.	Archaic Temple of Artemis, Ephesus (p. 129)
c. 540 B.C.	Temple of Hera, Samos
c. 356 B.C.	Later Temple of Artemis, Ephesus (p. 129)
c. 334 B.C.	Temple of Athena Polias, Priene (p. 131)
c. 325 B.C.	Temple of Artemis-Cybele, Sardis
313 B.C.–A.D. 41	Temple of Apollo Didymaeus, Miletus (p. 131)
193 B.C.	Temple of Dionysus, Teos

Ionic Temples in Greece

449 B.C.	Temple on the Ilissus, Athens (p. 131)
c. 450–425 B.C.	Temple of Apollo Epicurius, Bassae (internal Order only) (p. 123)
427 B.C.	Temple of Nikè Apteros, Athens (p. 133)
421–405 B.C.	The Erechtheion, Athens (p. 133)
339 B.C.	The Philippeion, Olympia (external colonnade) (pp. 105B, 109F)

The **Later Temple of Artemis, Ephesus** (c. 356 B.C.) (p. 130), was the fifth in succession to stand upon this very famous site. The three earliest had been relatively small; the immediate predecessor, known as the 'Archaic' temple (c. 550 B.C.), was burnt down in 356 B.C. and built anew in still more magnificent style, but on an identical plan. The only substantial differences between the old and the new were in the quality of the detail and the fact that the Later Temple stood on a platform of steps, about 9 ft high, instead of upon a two-step crepidoma, as formerly. Yet owing to the scanty remains, there are uncertainties about the arrangement of the plan, and several somewhat different restorations have been proposed. The temple was dipteral, octastyle at the front but perhaps enneastyle (nine columns) at the rear. The object of an extra rear column would be to evade the very serious difficulties of spanning the exceptionally wide central intercolumniation, which, although inescapable at the front, was not essential on the rear. The column spacings on the main front were progressively less wide from the centre outwards to the angles, and the central one was more than 28 ft, to be spanned by a marble architrave block about 4 ft high; for the temple was grand in dimensions, though not the largest in Ionia. Over the stylobate, it measured about 170 ft by 366 ft, with the flights of steps in addition. The columns were some 6 ft in diameter and almost 58 ft high. The entablature was relatively shallow, being of the usual Asiatic type, comprising architrave and dentilled cornice but no frieze. We have seen earlier that grandiose plans, dipteral as here, or pseudo-dipteral, are typical of the Ionic of Asia Minor. Equally characteristic are the deep pronaos, having several pairs of columns within it, and the shallow opisthodomos, which in some cases is absent altogether. About the internal arrangements of this temple, nothing is definitely known. The orientation is unusual, as for traditional reasons on this site, the temple faced west instead of east. The building was one of the most impressive of Greek temples and was celebrated for its sculptures. The pediment bore a sculptured tympanum representing Artemis mothering her devotees bringing their offerings, while the crowning acroteria portrayed the goddess enthroned. There were 117 columns altogether (interpretations differ), 36 of which bore sculptures on their lower parts. The preceding temple had similar sculptures, and fragments from both periods, along with elements of corresponding capitals and shafts, some of which are in the British Museum, allow us to compare the early and late work (pp. 127A, E; 130C, E). The volutes of the earlier capitals spread widely beyond the column shaft, and the abacus is nearly twice as long as it is wide; in the later examples the volutes are much more compact, and the abacus consequently is almost square. Flutes on the column shafts, numbering up to 48 in the earlier instances, in the later have settled to the normal 24, separated by fillets instead of sharp arrises. It is typical of Asia Minor practice that in neither temple were the columns identical in all respects. The designs varied a little between one column and the next. Thus in the older temple, rosettes might be substituted for the inner part of the conventional volute. Base mouldings in Asia Minor in the Hellenic period commonly had only two main elements, a large torus upon a deep, circular disc, both of them lavishly ornamented with horizontal flutes and reeds, separated by fillets or beads; but it was with the Archaic Temple at

E   H.O.A.

THE TEMPLE OF ARTEMIS:EPHESU

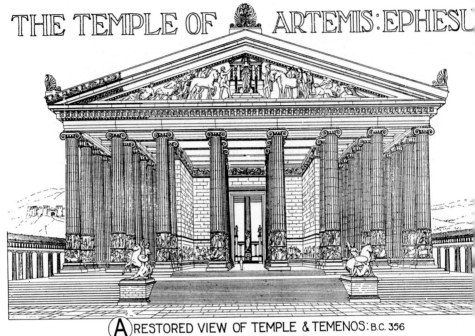

Ⓐ RESTORED VIEW OF TEMPLE & TEMENOS: B.C. 356

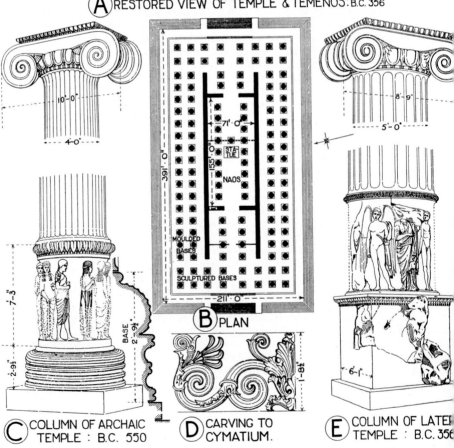

Ⓑ PLAN

Ⓒ COLUMN OF ARCHAIC TEMPLE : B.C. 550

Ⓓ CARVING TO CYMATIUM.

Ⓔ COLUMN OF LATER TEMPLE : B.C. 356

Ephesus that a square plinth first came to be associated with the Ionic base (p. 130C). Also, the site evidences early instances of the pedestal under the Order (p. 130E), which henceforward became accepted as an optional element in the classical decorative system. The building of the Later Temple is said to have extended well into the Hellenistic period. Like its predecessor, it ranked as one of the seven wonders of the Ancient World. The original designers were Demetrius and Paeonius of Ephesus, and probably Deinocrates. Famous sculptors, particularly Scopas, were employed in its decoration. The Temple of Artemis was the centre of the Pan-Ionian festival of the Asiatic colonies, as the Parthenon was of the Panathenaic festival in the motherland.

The **Temple of Athena Polias, Priene** (*c.* 334 B.C.) (pp. 127F, 132) is finely proportioned but more modest in plan and scale than other principal Asia Minor temples. Pythius, the architect, wrote a book about it. For once, the plan is peripteral, 64 ft × 122 ft over the stylobate, with a hexastyle front and eleven columns on the sides, exactly twice as long as broad. The deep pronaos and shallow opisthodomos are normal, while the column bases have the now usual plinth. The two-part entablature, still omitting the frieze, shows how deep-rooted in Asia Minor was this traditional arrangement (p. 127F). (Restorations showing a frieze, as p. 132, are no longer accepted as correct.) The columns are 4 ft 3 ins in diameter, and had a height of 37 ft 6 ins, supporting an entablature almost 6 ft 10 ins in height, including the cymatium. Fragments of the Order are in the British Museum.

The **Temple of Apollo Didymaeus, Miletus** (313 B.C.–A.D. 41) (pp. 109N, 141), was so long under construction as to be essentially a Hellenistic building, and even so, was never quite completed. It was designed by Paeonius of Ephesus and Daphnis of Miletus, and was of great size, 150 ft by 359 ft at the top of the seven-step crepidoma, so vast that the naos was never roofed over. The 120 columns were 6 ft 8 ins in diameter and 64 ft 8 ins high. The upper part of the cornice remained incomplete. The column bases (p. 141M) varied in design, in pairs astride the main axis of the temple. The general arrangement was dipteral decastyle (ten columns), and there was the customary deep pronaos, and no opisthodomos. There were peculiarities in the design of the naos. Two inclined ways led downwards from the pronaos, under staircases flanking a vestibule, to the hypaethral, paved courtyard, some 13 ft below peristyle level, where a roofed shrine sheltered the effigy of Apollo. High up on the inner face of the naos wall, their bases 4 ft 6 ins above the peristyle level, were great pilasters, 6 ft wide and 3 ft projection (p. 141J), ornamented in a way usual for anta capitals in Asia Minor. Leading back from the courtyard, an imposing flight of steps gave access to the vestibule, 6 ft above the pronaos, between doorways flanked by Corinthian attached columns (p. 141L, P), their capitals immature in design in lacking the minor pairs of volutes and in having sharply pointed angles to their abaci.

The **Temple on the Ilissus, Athens** (449 B.C.) (pp. 127B, 132), an amphiprostyle tetrastyle small temple, of Pentelic marble, measured about 20 ft by 42 ft over a three-step crepidoma. The architect was Callicrates, who, with Ictinus, was responsible for the Parthenon. It is a developed example of mainland Ionic, showing certain differences which occur there, due to the influence of the Doric. Even in the sixth century B.C., the archaic phase, treasuries built at sacred sites in Greece by Ionian cities represented at the festivals, possessed these differences from the native types; and in two cases, the Cnidian and Siphnian treasuries, both at Delphi, respectively of 565 B.C. and 530 B.C., the in-antis porches had pairs of 'caryatid' sculptured female figures instead of columns, foreshadowing the famous examples of the Erechtheion (pp. 134G, 136). The principal traits referred to however, concern the entablature, which in mainland Ionic possessed a frieze from the beginning,

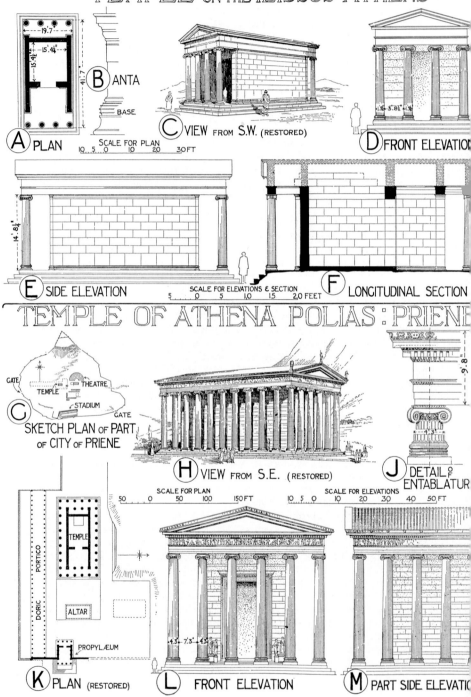

TEMPLE ON THE ILISSUS: ATHENS

A PLAN
19'.7"
15'.4½"
15'.4¼"
41'.7"

B ANTA
BASE

SCALE FOR PLAN
10 5 0 10 20 30 FT

C VIEW FROM S.W. (RESTORED)

D FRONT ELEVATION
3'.3⅞"

E SIDE ELEVATION
14'.8¼"

SCALE FOR ELEVATIONS & SECTION
5 0 5 10 15 20 FEET

F LONGITUDINAL SECTION

TEMPLE OF ATHENA POLIAS: PRIENE

G SKETCH PLAN OF PART OF CITY OF PRIENE
GATE
THEATRE
TEMPLE
STADIUM
GATE

H VIEW FROM S.E. (RESTORED)

J DETAIL OF ENTABLATURE
9'.8"
4'.3"

SCALE FOR PLAN
50 0 50 100 150 FT

SCALE FOR ELEVATIONS
10 5 0 10 20 30 40 50 FT

K PLAN (RESTORED)
DORIC PORTICO
TEMPLE
ALTAR
PROPYLÆUM

L FRONT ELEVATION
4'.3" 7'.3" 4'.3"

M PART SIDE ELEVATION

but with a resulting ejection of most of the bed-mould of the cornice, including the distinctive dentils, there remaining only a cyma-reversa moulding in this position. The architrave too, quite often is plain, like the Doric, without the bands or fasciae normal in Asia Minor. Such features are found in this temple; and the column bases are 'Attic', there being an extra small torus below the disc—now become a hollow scotia mould—and the upper large torus usual in Ionia at this time.

The **Temple of Nikè Apteros, Athens** (427 B.C.) (pp. 103B, 104C, 135B, 142B, H), is an exquisite amphi-prostyle tetrastyle small temple of marble, about 18 ft by 27 ft over the stylobate, dedicated to 'Wingless Victory', standing picturesquely on the south-western spur of the Acropolis. Callicrates was again the architect. The bastion which forms its site was surrounded on three sides by a marble balustrade, 3 ft 2 ins high, enriched with very fine sculpture. The temple is quite small, the columns being 1 ft 9 ins diameter and 13 ft 3 ins high, standing upon a crepidoma of three steps. The columns thus are unusually short in proportion, rather less than eight diameters. Apart from this circumstance and the fact that the architrave has fascia bands, the Ionic Order closely resembles that of the Temple on the Ilissus. The entablature has a frieze, which bore beautiful relief sculpture, of which there are examples in the British Museum. The temple was taken down by the Turks in 1687, and built into a battery on the Acropolis; but in 1836, the materials were recovered and the temple was reconstructed on the original site.

The **Erechtheion, Athens** (421–405 B.C.) (pp. 103B, 104, 127D, 134, 135A, 136, 157J), designed by Mnesicles, stands on the Acropolis north of the Parthenon, adjacent to the site of an older temple of Athena badly damaged in 480 B.C. by the Persians. It is unusual and irregular in plan (p. 134F), having three porches as well as an attached colonnade on the western end, and was constructed at two different levels, the western half of the naos and the ground to the north and west sides of the building being 10 ft 6 ins below the rest. A flight of steps north of the east portico joined the two levels. The temple was intended as a replacement of the old temple of Athena, on a similar plan; but it having been decided to retain the western half of the naos of the older building, which had suffered less than the remainder from the Persian depredations, the new structure was thrust further north on to an awkward, falling site, where too, there were several sacred spots, much venerated by the Athenians. These had to be preserved intact, and led to severe distortions of the original design. The eastern part of the main block, forming the shrine of Athena Polias, guardian of the city, is at the general Acropolis level, approached from a hexastyle porch, with columns 2 ft 3 ins in diameter and 21 ft 6 ins high, by a high doorway flanked by a window on each side. Windows are quite rare in Greek temple architecture. The western part of the naos, at the lower level, was divided into three chambers, together comprising the shrine of Erechtheus. The westernmost served as a vestibule to the other two, which were separated by a longitudinal wall. The walls sub-dividing the western part were about 13 ft high and did not reach the ceiling, which they all shared. In the western vestibule was the tank containing the salt sea of Poseidon. This vestibule also connected the North Portico and that roughly balancing it on the south side, the Caryatid Porch, which, being at the higher level, had the necessary flight of steps within it. The North Porch probably was a substitute for a western portico, for if there had been one in the latter position, it would have encroached upon the sanctuary of Pandrosus, an enclosure outside the west front and in which grew the sacred olive tree of Athens, and impinged upon the tomb of Cecrops which lay adjacent to the west wall. In fact, to escape the latter, the position of the west wall had to be altered after the building had started, withdrawn a little towards the east. On the

THE ERECHTHEION : ATHENS

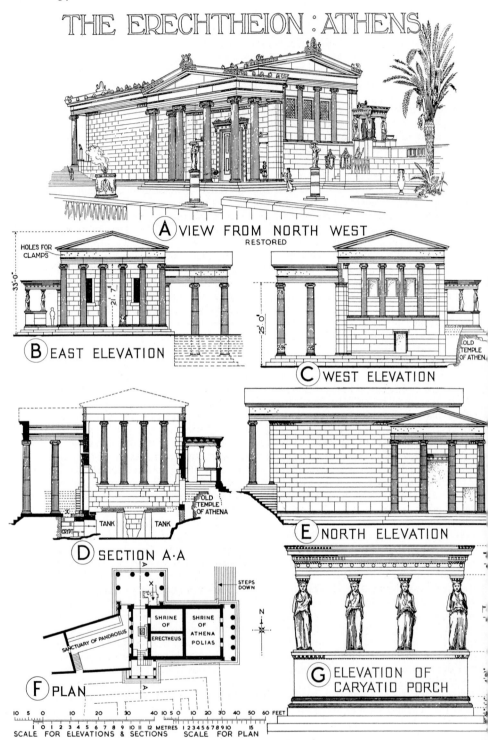

A VIEW FROM NORTH WEST
RESTORED

HOLES FOR CLAMPS

33'-0"

2'-7"

B EAST ELEVATION

25'-0"

23'

29'

28'

OLD TEMPLE OF ATHENA

C WEST ELEVATION

OLD TEMPLE OF ATHENA

CRYPT   TANK   TANK

D SECTION A·A

E NORTH ELEVATION

STEPS DOWN

X

SHRINE OF ERECTHEUS

SHRINE OF ATHENA POLIAS

SANCTUARY OF PANDROSUS

N

F PLAN

G ELEVATION OF CARYATID PORCH

10 5 0   10   20   30   40   10 5 0   10   20   30   40   50   60 FEET
1 0 1 2 3 4 5 6 7 8 9 10 11 12 METRES   1 2 3 4 5 6 7 8 9 10   15
SCALE FOR ELEVATIONS & SECTIONS   SCALE FOR PLAN

A. The Erechtheion, Athens (*c.* 421–405 B.C.). See p. 133

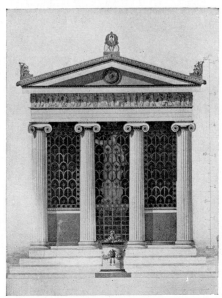

B. Temple of Nikè Apteros (Athena Nikè), Athens (restored) (*c.* 427 B.C.). See p. 133

C. Nereid Monument, Xanthos (restored) (*c.* 400 B.C.). See p. 148

The Erechtheion, Athens (*c.* 421–405 B.C.). Caryatid Porch. See opposite page

west wall there was only the semblance of a portico, for its upper part bore an attached colonnade of four columns in antis, while in the lower was a doorway leading from the western enclosed vestibule to the sanctuary of Pandrosus.

A general view of the former appearance of the building, built splendidly in Pentelic marble, is given in the restoration (p. 134A). The main block, measuring 38 ft by 75 ft, was roofed at a common level, and the east porch and the attached portico on the west shared the same entablature, of the Attic type, without dentils, which surrounded the whole building. The anta moulding too, continued along the flanks (p. 163L). As the bases of the western attached columns were raised about 3 ft above those of the east porch, the two Orders necessarily had different proportions. The tetrastyle North Porch, two bays deep, has columns 2 ft 8 ins in diameter and 25 ft high. The Porch stands at the lower level and its entablature fits just below the main one, resembling it in design and, like it, having a frieze of black Eleusinian limestone to which relief sculpture in white marble formerly was attached by cramps. Under the North Porch floor is a basement, and the marks on its rock floor where the trident of Poseidon had struck could be exposed to the sky through a trap in the basement ceiling and a marble shaft in the porch roof. The North Porch capitals are very fine (p. 135A). The spirals of the volutes are enriched with intermediate fillets, and below them is an ornamental band of anthemion ornament. At the outer angles of the Porch, as on the East front too (p. 127D), the volutes are canted at forty-five degrees to overcome the difficulty of expressing adjacent faces of the capitals. Within the Porch is a famous doorway, excellently preserved (p. 159D, E). The proportions of the columns of the three porches differ, being 9½ diameters on the east front, 9⅜ diameters in the North Porch and 9 diameters for the half columns on the west front. As originally arranged, the latter columns on the west were attached to piers, between which there were per-haps grilles in metal or wood, but these openings were walled up in Roman times except for windows in the three central intercolumniations (p. 134C). The southern or Caryatid Porch (pp. 134, 135A, 136, 157J) had six draped female figures or Caryatids, 7 ft 9 ins high, standing on a solid marble wall rising about 8 ft above the Acropolis level. All the figures face southwards; the three western lean on the right and the three eastern on the left leg, giving an effect of resistance to the weight of the entablature which, because of the special circumstances is of the shallow, Asiatic type of design, lacking the frieze and with dentils in the cornice, though the dentils are less large than the true Ionic type. The second caryatid from the west is in the British Museum, and is replaced by a terra-cotta copy (p. 134G, and opposite).

The Erechtheion has passed through various vicissitudes, having suffered con-version to other uses and much damage from time to time. Internally, very little survives of the former arrangements, but of the rest there are considerable remains, all of which in the present century have been skilfully restored to their former place.

THE CORINTHIAN ORDER

The Corinthian Order (p. 160E) did not evolve from a constructive basis like the Doric and Ionic, but made its first appearance in Greek architecture in the fifth century B.C. as a decorative variant of the Ionic, the difference lying almost entirely in the column capital. It came to acquire a more distinct identity as time progressed, though it was the Romans who brought it to full maturity in the late first century B.C. There are few Hellenic examples; its popularity increased greatly in the Hellen-istic period.

The **Corinthian column,** with base and shaft resembling the Ionic, tended to become more slender, and eventually a proportion of ten diameters was regarded

EVOLUTION OF THE CORINTHIAN CAPITAL

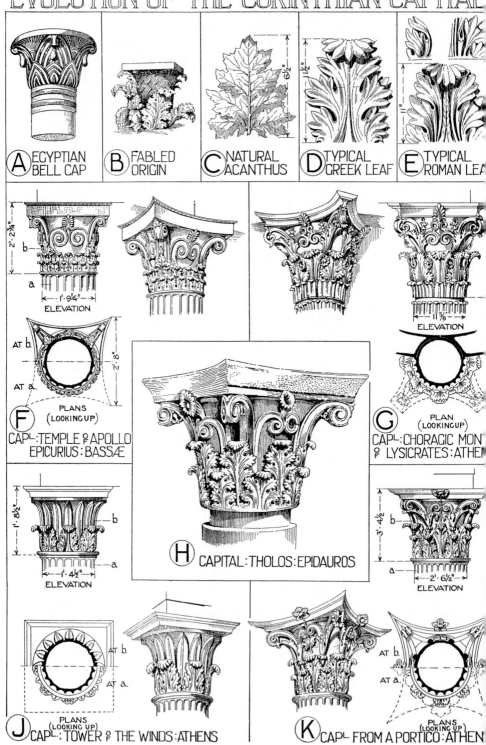

(A) EGYPTIAN BELL CAP

(B) FABLED ORIGIN

(C) NATURAL ACANTHUS

(D) TYPICAL GREEK LEAF

(E) TYPICAL ROMAN LEAF

(F) PLANS (LOOKING UP)
CAPL: TEMPLE OF APOLLO EPICURIUS: BASSÆ

(G) PLAN (LOOKING UP)
CAPL: CHORAGIC MON^T OF LYSICRATES: ATHEN

(H) CAPITAL: THOLOS: EPIDAUROS

(J) PLANS (LOOKING UP)
CAPL: TOWER OF THE WINDS: ATHENS

(K) PLANS (LOOKING UP)
CAPL: FROM A PORTICO: ATHEN

ELEVATION

as fitting. The distinctive feature is the capital, which is much deeper than the Ionic, and though of variable height at first, settled down to a proportion of about 1⅛ diameters high (p. 138). Vitruvius records the tradition (bk. IV, chap. i) that the invention of the capital was due to Callimachus, a worker in Corinthian bronze, who obtained the idea from observing a basket over the grave of a Corinthian maiden, covered with a tile to protect the offerings it contained. Accidentally, the basket was placed over the root of an acanthus plant, the stems and foliage of which grew and turned into volutes at the angle of the tile (p. 138B). The earlier examples appear to have been in bronze. The perfected type has a deep, inverted bell, the lower part of which is surrounded by two tiers of eight acanthus leaves (p. 138C, D), and from between the leaves of the upper row rise eight caulicoli (*caulis* = a stalk), each surmounted by a calyx from which emerge volutes or helices supporting the angles of the abacus and the central foliated ornaments. Each face of the moulded abacus is curved outwards to a point at the angles (pp. 141L, P; 138F, H, K; 162A), or the abacus is chamfered at each angle (p. 138G). Another and rarer type has one row of acanthus leaves with water leaves above and no volutes, and a moulded abacus, square on plan (p. 138J).

The **Corinthian entablature** is not distinguishable from the Ionic in Greek architecture; in the earliest known instance of the Order, in the Temple of Apollo Epicurius at Bassae (p. 124), Corinthian and Ionic internal columns share the same entablature. Throughout the Hellenic period the Order is used with either the Doric or the Ionic Order in the same building, the notable exception being the Monument of Lysicrates, Athens (below), where also it appears externally for the first time. Invariably there are three parts to the Corinthian entablature, architrave, frieze and cornice, and the latter normally is the developed type, with small dentils in the bed-mould. Eventually, in Roman hands, the Order is enriched by extra small mouldings, and an important 'modillion' band is added to the bed-mould, the modillions being consoles or brackets, giving support to the projecting corona of the cornice (compare E and F, p. 160).

Corinthian Examples

c. 450–425 B.C.	Temple of Apollo Epicurius, Bassae (internal) (p. 124)
c. 400 B.C.	The Tholos, Delphi (internal Order)
c. 350 B.C.	The Tholos, Epidauros (internal Order) (pp. 106B, 109E, 138H)
339 B.C.	The Tholos (Philippeion), Olympia (internal Order)(pp.105B,109F)
334 B.C.	Choragic Monument of Lysicrates, Athens (below)
313 B.C.–A.D. 41	Temple of Apollo Didymaeus, Miletus (internal) (p. 131)
174 B.C.–A.D. 132	The Olympieion, Athens (p. 140)
c. 48 B.C.	Tower of the Winds, Athens (p. 140)

The **Choragic Monument of Lysicrates**, Athens (334 B.C.) (pp. 138G, 141, 160E, 163E) is a type of monument erected to support a tripod, as a prize for athletic exercises, or musical competitions in Greek festivals. There were many of these in the Street of Tripods. Lysicrates had been the leader of a successful chorus, and this elaborate monument was built to commemorate the event. Of its two stages, the lower is a lofty podium of Piraeus stone, 9 ft 6 ins square on plan, decoratively treated with drafted margins to the masonry joints, with a high, stepped base and a simple, projecting capping. The upper part is a hollow cylinder of white Pentelic marble, 6 ft in diameter inside, standing upon a base of bluish Hymettian marble, around which are six Corinthian columns, appearing to be attached, though in reality complete, as the curving wall forms panels between them. Between the column capitals there are sculptured bas-reliefs. Above the entablature is a dome shaped from a single block of Pentelic marble, carved to imitate fish-scale tiling, and bearing three sculptured scrolls terminating in a floral

ornament, which formerly bore a bronze tripod, its base 34 ft above the ground
(p. 163E). Marble acroteria, linked together as a decorative cresting, served in place
of the usual cymatium to the cornice. This monument provides the first instance of
the Corinthian Order used externally, and of a building employing it as the sole
Order. For the first time too, an entablature, whether Corinthian or Ionic, appears
with both frieze and dentilled cornice, a type of design which henceforward was to
become universal (p. 141E). The columns are 11 ft 7 ins high and have capitals of
graceful if imperfect design which relatively are of unusual depth; 1 ft 7 ins, or
1½ diameters. The upper halves of the capitals fit awkwardly upon the lower, and
are too narrow-waisted at that point. The flutings of the shafts terminate as leaves,
and the channel above them may have had a bronze collar. Between the acanthus
leaves of the capitals, which have each only a single range, the place of a lower
being taken by water leaves, there are eight-petalled rosettes, which appear to
imitate bronze clips such as might have been used in earlier instances to secure
metal foliage (p. 141B). The architrave bears an inscription indicating the purpose
of the monument, and the frieze is sculptured to represent the myth of Dionysos
and the pirates of the Tyrrhenian Sea.

The **Temple of Zeus Olympius (Olympieion), Athens** (174 B.C.–A.D. 132)
(pp. 109H, 146A, 162A), stands on a site of an earlier Doric temple commenced in
515 B.C. It was built as the gift to Athens of Antiochus Epiphanes of Syria, from
designs by Cossutius, a Roman architect. Yet there was much that was Greek in its
conception and execution, so far as it was constructed at that time, and it demonstrates the growing fondness for the Corinthian Order in the Hellenistic period.
It remained incomplete, and Sulla in 86 B.C. transported some of the columns to
Rome for the Temple of Jupiter Capitolinus (p. 180), where they had an important
effect on Roman taste. Work was resumed under Augustus, but it was completed
and dedicated by Hadrian, in A.D. 132. It was dipteral octastyle (p. 109H) and
measured 145 ft 6 ins by 362 ft 6 ins, standing in a magnificent peribolus or enclosure of 424 ft by 680 ft. Vitruvius records that it was hypaethral, but it is probable
that it was covered in after his time. The fifteen columns remaining of the former
one hundred and four columns of the peristyle bear witness to its pristine grandeur.
They were 6 ft 4 ins in diameter and 56 ft high, a proportion of about one to nine.
The surviving capitals appear to date from all three periods of construction, though
the later maintain the character of the original design.

The **Tower of the Winds, Athens** (c. 48 B.C.) (pp. 138J, 141, 162B, C), another
Hellenistic building, is also known as the Horologium of Andronikos Cyrrhestes,
who erected it for measuring time by means of a clepsydra or water-clock internally
and by a sundial externally; while it was also provided with a weather-vane. The
building, on a crepidoma of three steps, is octagonal, and its eight sides face the
more important points of the compass. It is of marble, and measures 22 ft 4 ins
internally, and on the north-east and north-west sides are distyle porticoes with
fluted columns 13 ft 6 ins high, without bases and bearing capitals which vary from
the normal Corinthian design, having square abaci, no volutes and a range of water
leaves occupying the upper half of the bell, over a single row of acanthus leaves
(p. 138J). From the south side projected a circular water cistern, supplying the
water-clock. The interior is 40 ft 9 ins high, and the upper part is encircled by
small, fluted Doric columns, standing on a projecting band. The external wall of
the octagonal structure is plain for a height of 29 ft with the exception of incised
lines forming the sundial, and above this, boldly sculptured figures on each face
represent the eight principal winds (p. 162B, C). The roof, formed of twenty-four
radiating, wedge-shaped blocks of marble, was once surmounted by a bronze
Triton, pivoting to show with his rod the quarter in which the wind lay.

THE CHORAGIC MONUMENT OF LYSICRATES : ATHENS

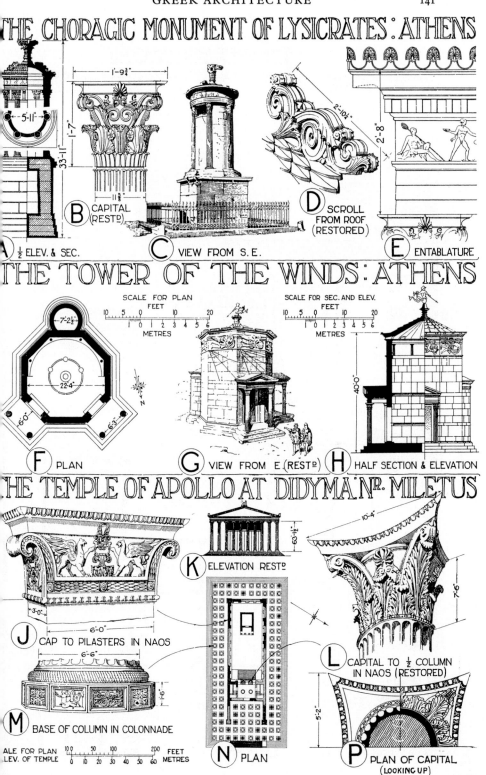

A ½ ELEV. & SEC.

B CAPITAL (RESTD.)

C VIEW FROM S.E.

D SCROLL FROM ROOF (RESTORED)

E ENTABLATURE

THE TOWER OF THE WINDS : ATHENS

SCALE FOR PLAN
FEET

METRES

SCALE FOR SEC. AND ELEV.
FEET

METRES

F PLAN

G VIEW FROM E. (RESTD.)

H HALF SECTION & ELEVATION

THE TEMPLE OF APOLLO AT DIDYMA. NR. MILETUS

J CAP TO PILASTERS IN NAOS

K ELEVATION RESTD.

L CAPITAL TO ½ COLUMN IN NAOS (RESTORED)

M BASE OF COLUMN IN COLONNADE

N PLAN

P PLAN OF CAPITAL (LOOKING UP)

SCALE FOR PLAN
& ELEV. OF TEMPLE
FEET
METRES

THE PROPYLÆA: ATHENS

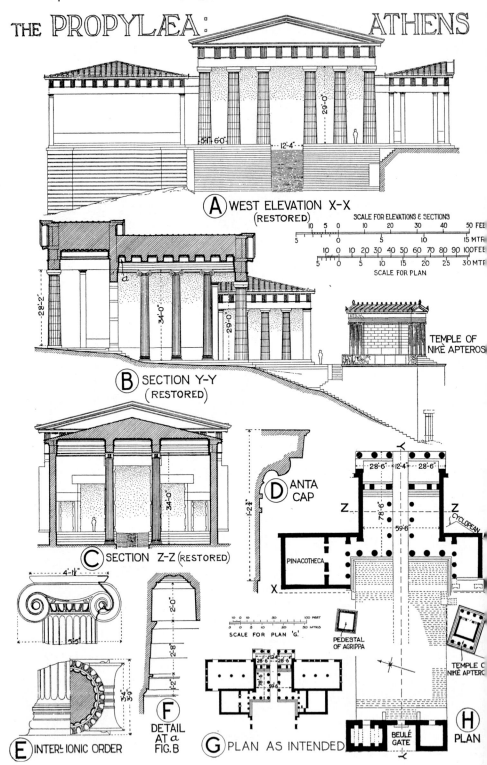

Ⓐ WEST ELEVATION X-X
(RESTORED)

SCALE FOR ELEVATIONS & SECTIONS

TEMPLE OF
NIKÈ APTEROS

Ⓑ SECTION Y-Y
(RESTORED)

Ⓓ ANTA
CAP

Ⓒ SECTION Z-Z (RESTORED)

PINACOTHECA

CYCLOPEAN

Ⓔ INTERⁿ IONIC ORDER

Ⓕ DETAIL AT a FIG. B

SCALE FOR PLAN 'G'

Ⓖ PLAN AS INTENDED

PEDESTAL
OF AGRIPPA

TEMPLE C
NIKÈ APTERO

BEULÉ
GATE

Ⓗ PLAN

PROPYLAEA

Propylaea, or entrance gateways, marked the approach to the sacred enclosures in many cities, such as Athens, Epidauros (p. 106B), Eleusis and Priene.

The **Propylaea, Athens** (437–432 B.C.) (pp. 103B, 104, 142), erected under Pericles by the architect Mnesicles, forms the imposing entrance to the Acropolis, approached by a steep ascent from the plain below. The front and rear hexastyle Doric porticoes are on different levels, and give access to a covered hall with a wide central passage flanked by Ionic columns and with an eastern wall with five doorways of different heights. The projecting wings on either side of the western front have three Doric columns, smaller than those of the main block. The northern wing, provided with windows, was used as a pinacotheca (p. 142H), but the southern wing was never completed, probably to avoid encroaching on the sacred precincts of the Temple of Nikè Apteros. The general appearance, showing the important position of the Propylaea as part of the world-famous group of Acropolis buildings, is shown in the view (p. 103B). The original design was never realized in full owing to the Peloponnesian war (p. 142G).

THEATRES

The Greek theatre, an open-air structure, which consisted of orchestra, auditorium or cavea and scene-building, was generally hollowed out of the slope of a hillside, in or near a city. The orchestra was a complete circle, usually with an altar to Dionysos at the centre, where the chorus chanted and danced. The orchestra was slightly raised and edged by a kerb, outside of which was a paved ambulatory, allowing spectators to reach their seats from the lower level. The cavea rose in tiers of stone seats, founded on natural rock, divided into wedge-shaped blocks or 'cunei' by radiating flights of steps. Above a horizontal pathway or 'diazoma', the number of cunei was doubled, because of the enlarged radius. The outer ends of the horseshoe-shaped cavea were buttressed by retaining walls, and alongside them were passages to the orchestra which completely separated the cavea from the scene-building except for a slight link afforded by a lintelled entrance portal on either side.

The theatre first acquired permanent form about the fifth century B.C., but still at the end of the Hellenic period, 323 B.C., the scene-building was only partially developed. This 'skene' or scene-building originally was merely a tent or booth in which the players prepared. It had become a permanent structure, serving also for the storage of properties, showing a plain wall towards the orchestra, with three large, square-headed recesses within it for the exhibition of conventional scenery. At its ends, wings or 'parascenia' projected forwards, marking the width of the orchestra. Early in the Hellenistic period, a 'proscenium', at first of wood and later (second century B.C.) of stone, came to be built in front of the scene-building, its roof serving as a stage or 'logeion' (speaking-place). The proscenium averaged 8 ft deep and 10–12 ft high, faced with colonnades infilled with panels. Parascenia projected slightly at the ends, following the old tradition. With the advent of the proscenium, the importance of the orchestra declined. The scene-building became two-storeyed, the upper providing a raised background or 'episcenium', with the three wide recesses for scenery, while sloping ramps or stairs at the ends of the block gave the necessary access to the stage. Though at first simple, the Greek episcenium was to lead to the rich and extravagantly-ornate permanent architectural settings of the Romans; the use of a low stage, typical of the Roman theatre, was a separate development arising in the Hellenistic period.

The **Theatre, Epidauros** (c. 350 B.C.) (pp. 144C, 145A, B), designed by Polycleitus,

A. Theatre of Dionysos, Athens
(*c.* 330 B.C.). A priest's throne.
See p. 147

B. The Parthenon, Athens (447–432 B.C.).
View of angle. See p. 121

C. Theatre, Epidauros (*c.* 350 B.C.). See p. 143

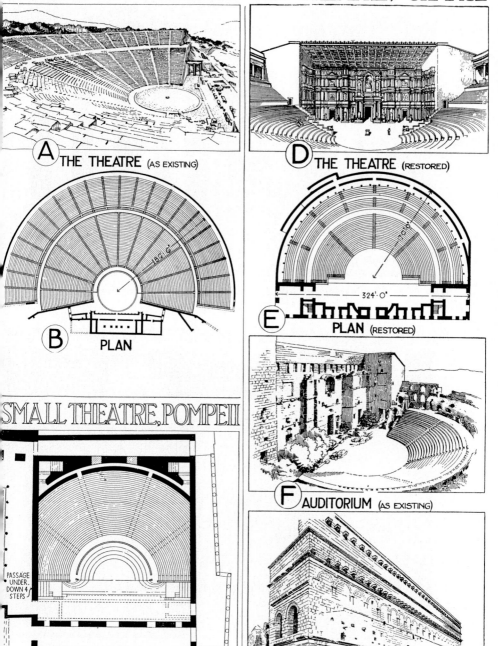

THE THEATRE, EPIDAUROS

Ⓐ THE THEATRE (AS EXISTING)

Ⓑ PLAN

SMALL THEATRE, POMPEII

PASSAGE UNDER. DOWN 4 STEPS

Ⓒ PLAN

SCALE

FEET 10 0 10 20 30 40 50 60 70 80

METRES 0 5 10 15 20 25

THE THEATRE, ORANGE

Ⓓ THE THEATRE (RESTORED)

324'.0"

Ⓔ PLAN (RESTORED)

Ⓕ AUDITORIUM (AS EXISTING)

Ⓖ EXTERIOR SHOWING STAGE WALL

A. The Olympieion, Athens (174 B.C.–A.D. 132) with the Acropolis in the distance. See p. 140

B. The Stadium, Athens, looking towards entrance (reconstructed c. A.D. 160 and restored in 1896). See p. 148

is a well-preserved and typical example. The orchestra, a complete circle, is 67 ft across and the total diameter of the theatre, 387 ft. The lower part of the cavea has 34 rows of seats, divided by a diazoma from the upper, containing 21 rows, which slope at a steeper angle. 'Parodoi', forming entrances at orchestra level, separate the cavea from the ruined stone scene-building, which was of later date and due to a Hellenistic reconstruction of about 200 B.C. Sloping ramps, starting from outside the simple stone gateways, led to a high proscenium, providing a stage or logeion about 10 ft deep, faced with an Ionic colonnade and having projecting wings or parascenia at the ends. The scene-building no doubt would have risen up behind the proscenium to form an episcenium background.

The **Theatre of Dionysos, Athens** (reconstructed *c.* 330 B.C.) (pp. 103B, 104C, 144A) accommodating eighteen thousand spectators, was founded about 500 B.C. and suffered successive modifications through the Greek and Roman times. It is scooped out of the Acropolis rock, and is tremendously deep, having three banks of seats and two diazomata. On the front row were sixty-seven marble thrones for city dignitaries, of individual design, added about the first century B.C. (p. 144A).

A theatre was usual in every Greek town of consequence, as at **Delphi** (p. 106A), **Ephesus, Syracuse, Delos** and **Priene,** but very many were altered by the Romans.

PUBLIC BUILDINGS

The restorations of Athens (p. 105A), Olympia (p. 105B), Delphi (p. 106A) and Epidauros (p. 106B), give an idea of the distribution of buildings on these famous sites.

The **Agora** (p. 105), or town square, was the centre of Greek social and business life, around or near which were stoas or colonnaded porticoes, temples, administrative and public buildings, markets, places of entertainment, monuments and shrines.

The **Stoa** (pp. 104C, 105, 132K), a long, colonnaded building, served many purposes, as until late times the Greeks could not easily erect complex structures. Stoas were used around public places and as shelters at religious shrines. Important instances are the Stoa Poikilè or Echo Colonnade, Olympia (p. 105B), about 330 ft by 30 ft, two at Epidauros (p. 106B), three at Delphi (p. 106A), and the Stoas of Eumenes, Athens (p. 103B) and Attalos II (pp. 105A, 158), Athens.

The **Prytaneion** served as senate house for the chief dignitaries of the city and as a place where distinguished visitors and citizens might be entertained. It contained the official banqueting room and also the symbolic communal hearth on which a fire burnt perpetually, associated with the cult of Hestia, goddess of the hearth. Instances occur at Olympia (p. 105B), Athens and Priene.

The **Bouleuterion,** or council house was a covered meeting place for the democratically-elected councils. Early examples necessarily were small and needed many columns to support the roof; Hellenistic examples might accommodate more than five hundred persons, but still needed some intermediate roof supports. They were usually rectangular buildings with banked seats facing inwards on three sides or arranged in a semi-circle. Those at Olympia (p. 105B) and Athens were repeatedly enlarged. That at Miletus (*c.* 170 B.C.) accommodated 1,200 people (p. 154A).

Assembly Halls, for citizens in general, were similar, but needed to be larger. Until constructive skill was sufficiently advanced, public assemblies met in the open air, in the case of Athens at the hill-side Pnyx. Covered assembly halls went by special names in different places, e.g. the Thersilion, Megalopolis (*c.* 370 B.C.) and, the Ecclesiasterion, Priene (*c.* 200 B.C.). The Telesterion, or Hall of the Mysteries, Eleusis, served a religious purpose.

The **Odeion,** a kindred type to the theatre, was a building in which musicians performed their works for the approval of the public and competed for prizes. The Odeion of Pericles, Athens (c. 435 B.C.), adjoined the theatre of Dionysus, and served too for rehearsals. It was a square building with eighty-one columns—nine by nine—so placed as to give clear sight lines. The Odeion of Herodes Atticus, Athens (c. A.D. 161) (pp. 103B, 104) was very much more ambitious. It resembled a theatre in plan and probably was not wholly roofed over.

The **Stadium** was the foot racecourse in cities where games were celebrated, and had a length of about 600 ft between banks of seats founded on convenient natural ground or on the spoil from excavation on flat sites. The starting end was straight, the other semi-circular. The oldest stadium in Greece is that at Olympia (p. 105B). There are others at Epidauros (p. 106B), Delphi, Ephesus and Athens. The latter (p. 146B), commenced 331 B.C. and reconstructed in A.D. 160 by Herodes Atticus, was restored from A.D. 1896 for the Olympic Games of 1906. It is said to accommodate 50,000 spectators.

The **Hippodrome** was a similar, though longer type of building for horse and chariot racing, and was the prototype of the Roman circus. Few traces now remain.

The **Palaestra** was a wrestling-school, but the term is usually used interchangeably with **Gymnasium**, a place for physical exercises of all kinds. Gymnasia, as at Olympia (p. 105B), Ephesus and Pergamon, were prototypes of the Roman thermae, and in the Hellenistic period were formal structures comprising courts for athletes, tanks for bathers, rooms for dressing and toilet, places for rest and conversation, exedrae and other seats for spectators, stores and an ephebeum or club-room which served too for lectures.

Naval buildings included ship-sheds and stores. The Arsenal at the Piraeus, built c. 340 B.C., a long narrow building for the storage of sailing tackle of the Athenian navy, is chiefly important in that the specification survives to show that still at that time the principle of the timber roof truss was not understood. The so-called **Sanctuary of the Bulls, Delos** (third century B.C.) (p. 157C, E, F, H) was similar in form, 220 ft long and 30 ft wide, and was a sacred, commemorative building housing a war galley in a shallow, dry tank. At the far end was a sanctuary approached through an entrance flanked by piers which were half Doric columns and half antae capped by recumbent sculptured bulls.

TOMBS

The **Nereid Monument, Xanthos** (c. 400 B.C.) (p. 135C) typifies Ionian sculptural luxuriance and the use in Greek Asia Minor of a temple form of tomb, elevated on a high podium. The entablature lacks a true frieze, but the architrave is sculptured and there are other bas-relief friezes on the podium. Between the columns stood nereids or marine nymphs. The remains of the monument are in the British Museum.

The **Mausoleum, Halicarnassos** (355–350 B.C.) (p. 149), the most famous of all tombs and one of the seven wonders of the world, was erected to King Mausolos by his widow, Artemisia, and from it is derived the term 'mausoleum', applied to monumental tombs. It had a lofty podium and a temple-like upper part surrounded by Ionic columns and surmounted by a pyramidal roof, with a marble quadriga and a group of statuary at its apex (p. 149C, L). The early restoration of Newton and Pullan is shown in detail (p. 149A–D, L), and some of the other restorations made of this monument (p. 149E–K). The achitects were Pythius and Satyrus, and Scopas was among the famous sculptors employed. Portions of three friezes, the statues of Mausolos and Artemisia, with the horses, quadriga, and other fragments, are grouped together in the British Museum.

The **Lion Tomb, Cnidos** (c. 350 B.C.) (p. 150A–F) is unusual for Asia Minor

THE MAUSOLEUM : HALICARNASSOS

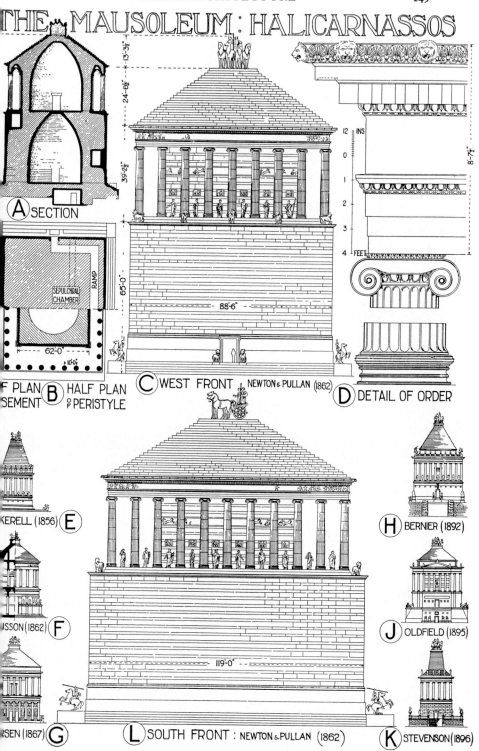

A SECTION

PLAN OF BASEMENT

SEPULCHRAL CHAMBER

RAMP

62'-0"

10'-0"

B HALF PLAN OF PERISTYLE

C WEST FRONT : NEWTON & PULLAN (1862)

88'-6"

65'-0"

39'-2½"

24'-0½"

13'-3½"

D DETAIL OF ORDER

8'-7½"

12 INS
0
1
2
3
4 FEET

E KERELL (1856)

F USSON (1862)

G RSEN (1867)

H BERNIER (1892)

J OLDFIELD (1895)

K STEVENSON (1896)

L SOUTH FRONT : NEWTON & PULLAN (1862)

119'-0"

LION TOMB AT CNIDOS
(RESTORED)

A SIDE ELEVATION

B SECTION

C FRONT ELEVATION

D PLAN & BASE

SCALE FOR PLANS

E KEY PLAN

WALL

101'-0"

SCALE FOR ELEVATIONS

F PLAN OF PERISTYLE

LID RAISED ON PROPS

5'-6"

G H THE "ALEXANDER" SARCOPHAGUS: SIDON

10'-4"

J TOMB AT CNIDOS

K TOMB OF THE WEEPERS: SIDON

ABT 9-5

in having Doric columns. Unusual too is their pseudo-peripteral arrangement. This was another early instance of the introduction of the Egyptian, stepped pyramidal crown, from which the terminal crouching lion, which gives the tomb its name, is in the British Museum. The circular interior was roofed with a corbelled dome (p. 150B).

The **Sarcophagus, Cnidos** (p. 150J), is an interesting and beautiful example, taken from a tomb chamber, of the ornamental treatment given to a stone coffin hewn out of one block of marble and with sculptures of a late period.

The **Tomb of the Weepers, Sidon** (350 B.C.) (p. 150K), now in the Museum at Istanbul, is a sarcophagus in the form of a miniature Ionic temple, with sculptured figures of mourners between the columns.

The **Alexander Sarcophagus** (330–320 B.C.) (p. 150G, H), also found near Sidon and now in the Istanbul Museum, is the most beautiful and best preserved surviving example of this class of monuments. It is so called because marble sculptures on its sides represent battles and hunting scenes of Alexander.

There are also important rock-cut tombs in Cyrenaica, North Africa, and in Asia Minor (p. 126E), including two from Lycia, now in the British Museum, which illustrate the genesis of the Ionic entablature from a wooden prototype.

The **Stele** (p. 157G) consisted of a slab of stone placed upright in the ground, like a modern headstone, carved in bas-relief and generally terminated with floriated ornament; many of these can be seen in the British Museum (pp. 162D, 163D), the Metropolitan Museum of Art, New York, and the Boston Museum.

The **Tomb, Mylasa** (p. 220A–D), in Asia Minor, though built in the Roman period, shows the strength of the Greek tradition there. It is of the temple-tomb class, and resembles the Halicarnassos Mausoleum; it has Corinthian tetrastyle colonnades raised on a high podium, and a pyramidal crown of stone slabs, of which the lowest course has diagonal beams across the angles. The angle pillars are square, and the intermediate columns elliptical, their bearing area being increased by the insertion of pilaster strips on each side. The tomb at **Dougga** (p. 220R), near Tunis, is somewhat similar, but has a walled-up colonnade.

DOMESTIC BUILDINGS

The Greeks lived much of their waking life in the public and sacred parts of the city, and their houses were at first modest in scope and materials. The rooms looked towards a small court, the chief apartments being on the north side, facing the winter sun, with others on the east and west sides. Two-storey arrangements were quite common. In Asia Minor, the Ionians long retained the Aegean megaron as a chief element in their houses (p. 234C, D), but the Dorian Greeks developed the 'pastas' house (p. 153), the pastas being a long, shallow room, crossing the house from side to side and partly open on the south towards the court, whilst serving too for access to the main inner rooms to the north. In old parts of towns, houses were irregular and crowded, and still were varied in design when towns came to be regularly planned. Second storeys sometimes were flats, and shops might occupy parts of the frontages. Knowledge of Greek house design comes principally from the planned lay-outs of Olynthos, Macedonia (between 432–348 B.C.) and Priene, Asia Minor (fourth and third centuries B.C.), and from Delos (second century B.C.) on the island of that name. Full colonnaded peristyles began to develop around the internal courts of the Greek house from the third century B.C.

'**House No. 33', Priene** (p. 234C, E), measuring about 98 ft by 57 ft overall, is one of the best examples in this planned town (p. 132G) of the survival of the megaron element, usually found in a block of four apartments, in which the megaron and its columned porch, facing south on to the inner court, give access to two further rooms ranged along one flank. All four apartments were as much as twenty feet high.

The **'Maison de la Colline', Delos** (p. 153) is an unusually regular house, nearly square, illustrating the pastas type which became general and influenced Roman arrangements. The court was fully colonnaded, with a water cistern centrally below it, its north side lighting the pastas which extended the full width of the house. From the latter opened a large room, occupying half the available width, and two other principal apartments of differing sizes. The entrance was on the west, with a kitchen adjoining, and in the south-west corner was a wooden staircase to bedrooms opening from a gallery on a second floor. Other Delian houses, usually with peristyles, were much less formal, and none was symmetrical, like the typical Roman house at Pompeii (p. 234B).

COMPARATIVE ANALYSIS
(for Aegean architecture see p. 92)

PLANS (p. 109). Temple plans normally were simple, rectangular and symmetrical, though occasionally asymmetrical, as at the Erechtheion (p. 134F), or circular, like the Tholos, Epidauros (pp. 106B, 109E). House plans were invariably asymmetrical. The plans of all roofed buildings were so arranged that the spans were nowhere too large for the untrussed timber roofs, and for this reason internal pillar supports had often to be used in temples, stoas and halls. Greek temples were, however, planned principally for external effect, the single naos being surrounded by those open colonnades which are their special charm; quite the reverse from the typical Egyptian temple with its courts and massive, stone-roofed, columned halls enclosed within a high girdle wall. In Greek architecture, the spacing of columns generally was regular, except where, for reasons of effect, they were more closely spaced at the angles of temples, or, where for practical purposes, the central intercolumniation was increased, as in the Propylaea at Athens (p. 142H) where the Panathenaic procession with its mounted knights had to pass. The Greeks employed the circular plan for open-air theatres, tumulus tombs and sometimes for monuments, such as that of Lysicrates at Athens (p. 141A), while the octagonal plan was adopted for the Tower of the Winds, Athens (p. 141F).

WALLS. For temples and the best buildings, walls were constructed solidly of fine, bonded masonry of stone or marble, bound together by cramps and dowels of wood or lead in the archaic period and iron, run with lead, in later times. Mortar was not used, except in small quantities to ensure even bedding. Coarse-grained masonry was sheathed over with an excellent marble stucco, polished on completion; the better quality stones and marbles were so carefully fitted that the joints could scarcely be seen, and the surface was made faultlessly smooth. Coloured marbles were not used, the only possible exception being the limited employment of blue-black Eleusinian limestone, as for the frieze of the Erechtheion (p 135A). Masonry courses were of even height, until Hellenistic times, when alternately high and narrow courses were often used instead. During the process of construction of temples, the masonry of crepidoma, walls and column bases and shafts was left in the rough until the fully-carved entablature had been fitted. Walls had entablatures or cornices even when the Order was not present; string courses were rare. At the base of temple walls externally, stones were fitted as vertical slabs, these 'orthostates' recalling primitive times when the upper walls were of timber-framed, sun-dried brick. In the sixth and fifth centuries B.C., terrace and retaining walls sometimes were faced with polygonal masonry of very large stones fitted together so precisely that the wall produced an effect like that of a picture-puzzle (p. 161).

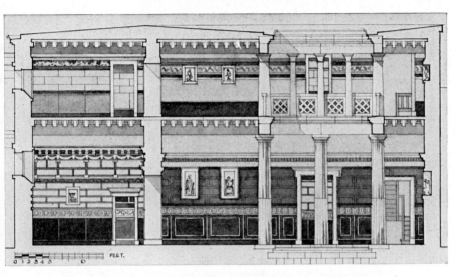

A. Section (restored)

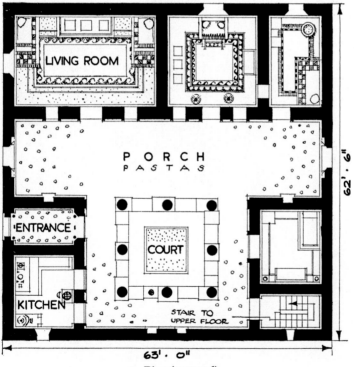

B. Plan (restored)

'Maison de la Colline', Delos (second century B.C.). See opposite page

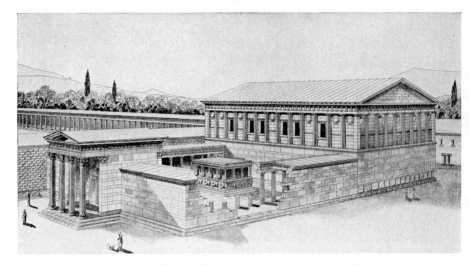

A. Bouleuterion (Council House), Miletus (*c.* 170 B.C.). See p. 147

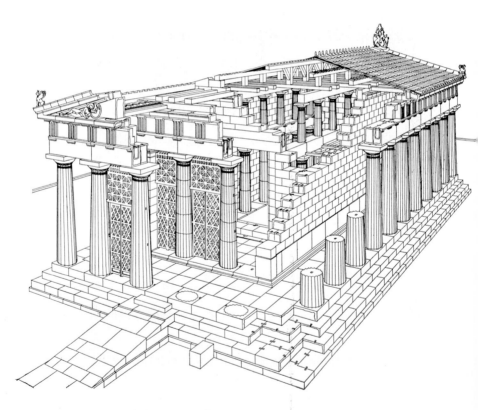

B. Temple of Aphaia, Aegina. Sectional view, restored (*c.* 490 B.C.). See p. 115

The masonry of defensive city walls, also mortarless, varied in quality from coursed rubble to the best ashlar, but usually was left rough-faced, giving it an appearance of rugged strength; the cores of such walls sometimes were of rough rubble or earth. Square or round towers were spaced at frequent intervals. House walls until late times had stonework only at the base, the upper parts being of stucco-covered sun-dried brick.

OPENINGS. Greek architecture was essentially trabeated, and openings were square-headed and spanned by a lintel. Columns had to be placed close together when carrying lintels or architraves of stone or marble, but internally, when carrying timber, could be spaced much farther apart. Façades of temples, which rarely had windows, would have appeared barren without the alternation of light and shade produced by the succession of free-standing columns and the shadows seen in the spaces between them. Door and window openings usually were narrowed towards the top, as in the doorway of the Erechtheion (p. 159D).

ROOFS. The inclination of temple pediments was governed by the slope of the roof, which was low-pitched, as the principle of roof-triangulation was not employed until very late times (p. 154B). For the latter reason, internal columns were sometimes needed in temples, as at Paestum (p. 116B). The timber rafters of the roof were boarded and buildings of all classes were covered externally with terra-cotta tiles, or, in the case of temple buildings, with specially-cut marble tiles (p. 110H). The flat, marble ceilings of temple porches and peristyles were enriched by lacunaria or sunken coffers (pp. 120K, 154B).

COLUMNS. Temples were one-storey high, and columns, with their entablature, comprised the entire height of the buildings externally. Internally, some temples had double tiers of columns to help support the roof, separated only by an architrave, and not a full entablature (pp. 116B, 122F). Hellenistic buildings, other than temples, were quite often of two tiers; the Stoa of Attalos, Athens (pp. 105A, 158), had Doric columns in the lower tier and Ionic in the upper.

The Orders (p. 160), which have been fully dealt with, may be summarized as follows:

The Doric (p. 108) is the sturdiest of the Orders, and its finest examples are in the Parthenon and the Theseion (p. 119).

The Ionic (p. 125) was more slender, and two typical examples are in the Erechtheion (p. 133) and the Temple of Athena Polias, Priene (p. 131).

The Corinthian (p. 137), which apart from its elaborate capital differed little from the Ionic, was a purely decorative invention of the Greeks and was not much used until late Hellenistic times. The best-known examples are the Monument of Lysicrates, Athens (p. 139) and the Olympieion (p. 140) upon which the Romans based their own version of the Order and brought it to full fruition.

Caryatids (pp. 136, 157J), Canephorae (p. 157D), which were draped female figures, and Atlantes or Telamones (p. 114J), carved male figures, were sometimes used in place of columns or as supports.

MOULDINGS. Mouldings are an architectural device whereby, with the help of the light and shade they produce, definition is given to the salient lines of a building (pp. 164, 165). Thus the delicacy of moulded contours is in proportion to the strength of sunlight in any given country, always making due allowance for national tendencies and the possibilities of the material used. Greek love of refinement found full opportunity for expression in graceful mouldings in the sunny climate of Greece; the Roman character, in a somewhat similar climate, displayed itself in more pronounced mouldings; while in grey and sombre England mouldings became coarse and full-bodied to secure sufficient shadow to throw up their lines. Greek mouldings were refined and delicate in contour, due first to the fine-grained marble in which often they were carved, and secondly to the clear atmosphere and continuous sunshine which produced strong shadows from slight projections. Though the sections of these mouldings were probably formed by hand, they approach very closely to various conic sections, such as parabolas, hyperbolas and ellipses. As a general rule the lines of the carved ornament on any Greek moulding correspond to the profile of that moulding and thus emphasize it by the expression of its own curvature in an enriched form. The examples given of mouldings taken from the Parthenon, Erechtheion, and elsewhere may be studied (pp. 164, 165).

The following is a classified list of the most important mouldings compared with the Roman (p. 164).

(a) The cyma recta (Hogarth's 'line of beauty') which is often carved with honeysuckle ornament, whose outline corresponds with the section (pp. 164G, 165Q).

(b) The cyma reversa (ogee) when enriched is carved with the water leaf and tongue (pp. 164H, 165N, Q).

(c) The ovolo (egg-like) when enriched is carved with the egg and dart, or egg and tongue ornament (pp. 164F, 165L, Q).

(d) The fillet, a small plain face to separate other mouldings (p. 164A), is usually without enrichment.

(e) The astragal or bead serves much the same purpose as the fillet, but approaches a circle in section. It is sometimes carved with the 'bead and reel' or with beads, which, in fact, gave the name to the moulding (p. 164B).

(f) The cavetto is a simple hollow (p. 164D).

(g) The scotia is a deep hollow which occurs in bases, and is generally not enriched (p. 164E).

(h) The torus is really a magnified bead moulding which, when enriched, is carved with the guilloche or plait ornament, or with bundles of leaves tied with bands (p. 164L).

(i) The bird's-beak moulding occurs frequently in the Doric Order, and gives a deep shadow (pp. 164K, 165A, E).

(j) The corona, or deep vertical face of the upper portion of the cornice, was frequently painted with a Greek 'fret' ornament (p. 165C).

ORNAMENT (pp. 157, 162, 163). Greek ornament is specially refined in character, and on it architectural ornament of all succeeding styles has been based. The acanthus leaf and scroll play an important part in Greek ornamentation (p. 138C). The leaf from which these were derived grows in the south of Europe in two varieties. The 'acanthus spinosus', preferred by the Greeks, has pointed, narrow lobes, V-shaped in section with deeply drilled eyes giving a sharp, crisp shadow (p. 138D). The 'acanthus mollis', preferred by the Romans, has broad, blunt tips, flat in section (p. 138E). The leaf was used principally in the Corinthian capital (p. 138), and is also found in the capital (pp. 138G, 141) and crowning finial of the Choragic Monument of Lysicrates (p. 163E). The scroll which accompanies the leaf and acts as a stalk is usually V-shaped in section with sharp edges. The anthemion, palmette, or honeysuckle ornament (p. 163A) was a favourite Greek decoration, and was largely used to ornament anta capitals (p. 163L), cyma recta mouldings (p. 164G), and neckings of columns as in the Erechtheion (p. 127D). It is also frequently employed on stele-heads and antefixae (pp. 157G, 162D, 163D).

Greek sculpture, which has never been excelled, may be classified as follows: (a) architectural sculpture, which includes friezes (pp. 120N, 163H), tympana of pediments (p. 117C), acroteria at the base and summit of pediments (p. 117A, B), sculptured metopes (pp. 120A, C, 163K, M), caryatids (pp. 136, 157J), and figure sculptures, as the 'Gigantomachy' of the Altar of Zeus at Pergamon in Asia Minor

A PEDESTAL: PRIENE

B AN ACROTERION

C DETAIL OF CAP AT a

SIDE   FRONT

D A CANEPHORA

E KEY PLAN

SANCTUARY

SUNKEN AREA

ABT. 210'-0"

F

G STELE

H SANCTUARY OF THE BULLS: DELOS: ELEV. AT a

J CARYATID: ERECHTHEION

(197–159 B.C.); (b) sculptured reliefs, as seen on the stele (p. 157G); (c) free-standing statuary, consisting of groups, single figures, bigas (two-horse chariots) or quadrigas (four-horse chariots) (p. 149C, L).

Colour, of which traces survive, was largely used, particularly on buildings of a religious character. In many instances stone and sun-dried brick were covered with carefully prepared stucco, to receive paintings or colour decoration, made with powdered marble dust, which was very thin in the best buildings but became much thicker in Hellenistic times. This marble stucco was capable of such high polish that Vitruvius mentions that it would reflect like a mirror.

The Stoa of Attalos II, Athens (reconstruction by the American School of Classical Studies, Athens). c. 150 B.C. See p. 147

REFERENCE BOOKS

BELL, E. *Hellenic Architecture*. London, 1920.
—. *Pre-Hellenic Architecture*. London, 1926.
CARY, M. *The Geographical Background of Greek and Roman History*. Oxford, 1949.
COCKERELL, C. R. *The Temples at Aegina and Bassae*. London, 1860.
COTTRELL, L. *The Bull of Minos*. London, 1953.
D'ESPOUY, H. *Fragments de l'architecture antique*. Paris, 1899.
D'ESPOUY et SEURE. *Monuments antiques*. 4 vols., Paris (19—).
DINSMOOR, W. B. *The Architecture of Ancient Greece*. 3rd ed., London, 1950.
DORPFELD, W. *Das griechische Theater*. Athens, 1896.
DURM, J. *Die Baukunst der Griechen*. Leipzig, 1910.
EVANS, SIR ARTHUR. *Palace of Minos at Knossos*. 4 vols., London, 1921–3.
FERGUSSON, J. *The Parthenon*. London, 1883.
FRAZER, J. G. *Pausanias's Description of Greece*. 6 vols., London, 1898.
FURTWÄNGLER, A. and others. *Aegina: das Heiligtum der Aphaia*. 2 vols., Munich, 1906.
FYFE, T. *Hellenistic Architecture*. Cambridge, 1936.
GLOTZ, G. *The Aegean Civilization*. New York, 1925.
GOODYEAR, W. H. *Greek Refinements*. Yale and London, 1912.
GROMORT, G. *Histoire abrégée de l'architecture en Grèce et à Rome*. Paris, 1947.
HAVERFIELD, F. *Ancient Town Planning*. Oxford, 1913.
HOMOLLE, T. and others. *Exploration archéologique de Délos*. Paris, 1902.
HULOT, J. *Selinonte*. Paris, 1910.
INWOOD, H. W. *The Erechtheion at Athens*. London, 1827.
The Antiquities of Ionia (Dilettanti Society). 5 vols., London, 1769–1915.
KOLDEWEY, R. and PUCHSTEIN, O. *Die Griechischen Tempel von Unteritalien und Sicilien*. 2 vols., Berlin, 1899.

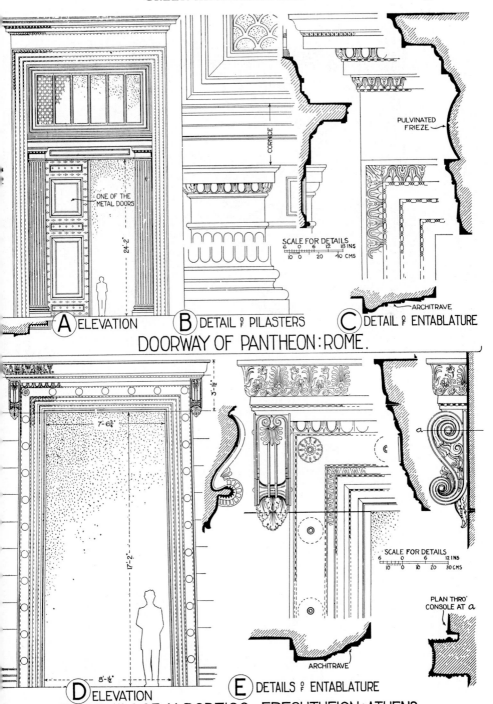

ONE OF THE
METAL DOORS

24'-2"

CORNICE

PULVINATED
FRIEZE

SCALE FOR DETAILS

ARCHITRAVE

(A) ELEVATION (B) DETAIL ᵒᶠ PILASTERS (C) DETAIL ᵒᶠ ENTABLATURE

DOORWAY OF PANTHEON: ROME.

3'-1½"

7'-6½"

17'-2"

a

SCALE FOR DETAILS

PLAN THRO'
CONSOLE AT a

8'-1½"

ARCHITRAVE

(D) ELEVATION (E) DETAILS ᵒᶠ ENTABLATURE

DOORWAY OF N. PORTICO: ERECHTHEION: ATHENS

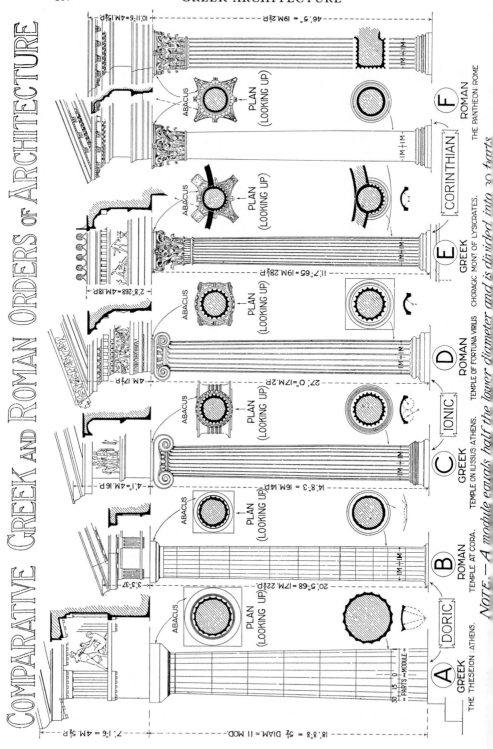

COMPARATIVE GREEK AND ROMAN ORDERS OF ARCHITECTURE

A DORIC — GREEK — THE THESEION : ATHENS.

B — ROMAN — TEMPLE AT CORA.

C IONIC — GREEK — TEMPLE ON ILISSUS: ATHENS.

D — ROMAN — TEMPLE OF FORTUNA VIRILIS

E CORINTHIAN — GREEK — CHORAGIC MONT OF LYSICRATES.

F — ROMAN — THE PANTHEON: ROME.

NOTE.—A module equals half the lower diameter and is divided into 30 parts

LALOUX, V. et MONCEAUX, P. *La restauration d'Olympie.* Paris, 1889.

LAWRENCE, A. W. *Greek Architecture.* Penguin Books, Harmondsworth, 1957.

LETHABY, W. R. *Greek Buildings.* London, 1908.

MARQUAND, A. *Handbook of Greek Architecture.* New York, 1909.

MAUCH, J. M. VON. *Die Architektonischen Ordnungen der Griechen und Römer.* Berlin, 1896.

MIDDLETON, J. H. *Plans and Drawings of Athenian Buildings.* 1900.

NEWTON, C. T. and PULLAN, R. P. *A History of Discoveries at Halicarnassus, Cnidus and Branchidae.* 3 vols., London, 1862–3.

PENNETHORNE, JOHN. *The Geometry and Optics of Ancient Architecture.* London and Edinburgh, 1878.

PENROSE, F. C. *The Principles of Athenian Architecture.* London, 1888.

PERROT, G. and CHIPIEZ, C. *Art in Primitive Greece.* 2 vols., London, 1894.

QUENNELL, M. and C. H. B. *Everyday Things in Greece.* 3 vols., London, 1929–32.

Restaurations des monuments antiques, publiées par l'Académie de la France à Rome. Paris, 1877–90.

ROBERTSON, D. S. *Handbook of Greek and Roman Architecture.* 2nd ed., Cambridge, 1943.

SELTMAN, C. *The Twelve Olympians.* Pan Books, London, 1952.

SPIERS, R. P. *The Orders of Architecture.* London, 1926.

STOBART, J. C. *The Glory that was Greece.* (Reprint) London, 1948.

STRATTON, A. *The Orders of Architecture.* London, 1931.

STUART, J. and REVETT, N. *Antiquities of Athens.* 5 vols., London, 1762–1832.

WATT, J. C. *Greek and Pompeian Decorative Work,* London, 1897.

WIEGAND, T. and others. *Milet: Die Ergebnisse der Ausgrabungen und Untersuchungen.* Berlin, 1906– (in progress).

WILKINS, W. *Antiquities of Magna Graecia.* Cambridge, 1807.

WYCHERLEY, R. E. *How the Greeks built Cities.* London, 1949.

Delphi. Polygonal masonry of the sixth century B.C.
See p. 152

8'-6"

BROKEN AWAY

(A) CAPITAL: THE OLYMPIEION ATHENS.

ΑΓΗΛΩΤΗΣ

5'-5"

(B) SCULPTURE REPRESENTING E. WIND
TOWER OF THE WINDS: ATHENS

ΒΟΡΕΑΣ

5'-5"

(C) SCULPTURE REPRESENTING N. WIND
TOWER OF THE WINDS: ATHENS

(D) STELE HEAD WITH ANTHEMION

A ANTHEMION ORNAMENT· ERECHTHEION

B RAIN WATER SPOUT

C ANTEFIXA ORNAMENT

D STELE HEAD

E ROOF OF LYSICRATES MONUMENT

F FRET ORNAMENT

G PATERA

H PORTION OF PANATHENAIC FRIEZE : THE PARTHENON

J PATERA

K METOPE : PARTHENON

L ANTA CAP : ERECHTHEION

M METOPE : PARTHENON

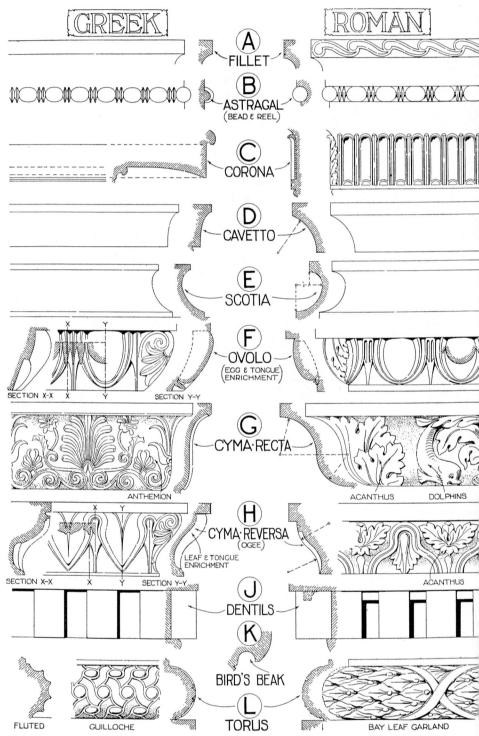

GREEK

ROMAN

A FILLET

B ASTRAGAL (BEAD & REEL)

C CORONA

D CAVETTO

E SCOTIA

F OVOLO (EGG & TONGUE ENRICHMENT)

SECTION X-X   SECTION Y-Y

G CYMA·RECTA

ANTHEMION   ACANTHUS   DOLPHINS

H CYMA·REVERSA (OGEE)

LEAF & TONGUE ENRICHMENT

SECTION X-X   SECTION Y-Y   ACANTHUS

J DENTILS

K BIRD'S BEAK

L TORUS

FLUTED   GUILLOCHE   BAY LEAF GARLAND

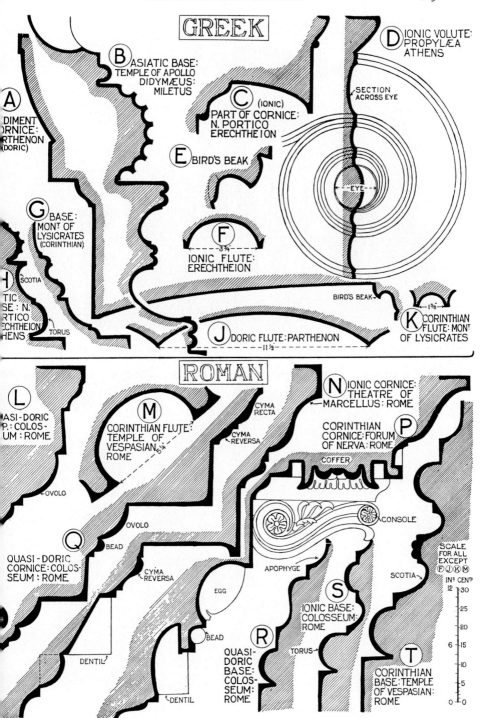

GREEK

A PEDIMENT CORNICE: PARTHENON (DORIC)

B ASIATIC BASE: TEMPLE OF APOLLO DIDYMÆUS: MILETUS

C (IONIC) PART OF CORNICE: N. PORTICO ERECHTHEION

D IONIC VOLUTE: PROPYLÆA ATHENS

SECTION ACROSS EYE

EYE

E BIRD'S BEAK

F IONIC FLUTE: ERECHTHEION
3¾

G BASE: MONᵀ OF LYSICRATES (CORINTHIAN)

H ATTIC BASE: N. PORTICO ERECHTHEION ATHENS
SCOTIA
TORUS

BIRD'S BEAK

J DORIC FLUTE: PARTHENON
11½

K CORINTHIAN FLUTE: MONᵀ OF LYSICRATES
1⅜

ROMAN

L QUASI-DORIC CAP.: COLOSSEUM: ROME
OVOLO

M CORINTHIAN FLUTE: TEMPLE OF VESPASIAN: ROME

CYMA RECTA

CYMA REVERSA

N IONIC CORNICE: THEATRE OF MARCELLUS: ROME

COFFER

P CORINTHIAN CORNICE: FORUM OF NERVA: ROME

CONSOLE

Q QUASI-DORIC CORNICE: COLOSSEUM: ROME
OVOLO
BEAD
CYMA REVERSA
DENTIL

APOPHYGE

EGG

BEAD

R QUASI-DORIC BASE: COLOSSEUM: ROME

S IONIC BASE: COLOSSEUM: ROME
TORUS

SCOTIA

DENTIL

T CORINTHIAN BASE: TEMPLE OF VESPASIAN: ROME

SCALE FOR ALL EXCEPT F J K M

INˢ CENᵀˢ
12 — 30
25
20
6 — 15
10
5
0 — 0

A. The Colosseum, Rome (A.D. 70–82; upper storey added 222–224). See p. 210

B. The Colosseum, Rome: the arena and auditorium

The Roman Empire

IV. ROMAN ARCHITECTURE

(300 B.C.–A.D. 365; preceded by Etruscan, 750–100 B.C.)

INFLUENCES

GEOGRAPHICAL. The Etruscans, an immigrant people, whose civilization the Romans arrested and absorbed, occupied only the west-central portion of Italy, and not the whole, as did the Romans, later on.

The comparative simplicity of the long coast-line of the Italian peninsula forms a strong contrast to the complexity of the indented coast-lines of Greece and the innumerable islands of the Archipelago. Italy has few natural harbours and few islands along her shores. The great chain of the Apennines runs like a spine down the centre of Italy and much of the country is very mountainous, but it is not broken up into isolated little valleys to the same extent as is Greece. These clearly marked geographical differences between the countries of the Greeks and the Romans have their counterpart in equally clearly defined differences of national character. The central and commanding position of Italy in the Mediterranean Sea enabled Rome to act as an intermediary in spreading art and civilization over Europe, Western Asia, and North Africa. In their empire-building the Romans proceeded logically: they conquered first by war, dominated by force of character, and then ruled by laws and civilized by arts and letters. It was also natural that, under different geographical conditions, the methods adopted by Rome for extending her influence should have differed from those of Greece. The Romans were not a seafaring people like the Greeks, and did not send out colonists in the same way to all parts of the then-known world: they depended for the extension of their power, not on colonization, but on conquest. The Roman power was built up, first of all in Italy itself, by a gradual absorption of little states, at a time when there were few rival cities and when small towns were not over tenacious of their separate independence; whereas neither Athens nor Sparta was able to carry out a similar process of absorption, owing to the fierce independence of the small Greek cities, protected as they were in their isolated and well-nigh impregnable valleys. The Roman Empire was ultimately not confined geographically to Italy, but, as shown in the map (p. 167), included all those parts of Europe, North Africa and Western Asia which constituted the then-known world.

GEOLOGICAL. The mineral wealth of early Italy was concentrated in Etruria, and it was to the iron of the island of Elba, and the copper and tin of the adjacent mainland that the rise of the Etruscan civilization was due. These provided the means of economic exchange and were the principal materials of its manufactures, crafts and arts. For building, there was ample good stone and, at that time, adequate timber.

The Romans, in their turn, took very great pains to exploit natural resources to the full. The geological formation of Italy differs from that of Greece, where the chief and almost the only building materials are stone and marble; whereas in addition to these, the Romans could procure suitable earths for the making of terra-cotta and brick, the latter very extensively used, even for important buildings. In the neighbourhood of Rome building stones included tufa, of varying degrees of hardness, from calcareous deposits in Rome itself and immediate vicinity; peperino, a stone of volcanic origin from Mount Albano; travertine, a hard limestone of fine quality from Tivoli; lava from volcanic eruptions; besides excellent sand and gravel. The building material, however, which led to great structural innovations was concrete, which rendered possible some of the finest examples of Roman architecture. Not only vaults and domes but also walls were frequently made of this concrete. It was formed of stone or brick rubble and a mortar of which the important ingredient was pozzolana, a volcanic earth, found in thick strata in and around Rome and in the region of Naples. Pozzolana is a much superior substitute for sand, and when mixed with lime and wetted, produces mortar of very great strength and tenacity. The mortar will set under water; the proportions of the ingredients were varied according to the nature of the work for which it was intended, and crushed tiles or potsherds were sometimes added. Roman concrete consisted of alternate layers of mortar and rubble firmly compressed, and not, as to-day, of a mixture made before being placed in position. The facings of the ponderous walls were much more carefully laid than their cores, and presented a neat appearance of cut stonework of various types or of brickwork. Nevertheless, except in the case of utilitarian buildings, these fine constructive facings often were covered over with plaster, or sheathed with alabaster, porphyry and other marbles, hewn from countless quarries by armies of slaves. Pliny records that enormous quantities of white and coloured marbles were imported from all parts of the Empire to special wharves on the Tiber, and were then worked up by gangs of slaves and convicts. Roman architecture, as it spread over almost the whole of the then-known world, was naturally variously influenced by the materials found in the widely differing localities where it planted itself; but concrete, which in conjunction with its brick or stone facings was the favourite material, helped to give uniformity of style throughout the Empire, and thus local geological influences were to a certain extent at a discount. Yet in the countries around the eastern Mediterranean, where already there were deep-rooted traditions, and where stone was so abundant that it might, at times, be used in enormous blocks, as at Baalbek in Syria, or Philae in Egypt, concrete was but little favoured and the customary usage of those countries for the most part prevailed.

CLIMATIC. North Italy has the climate of the temperate region of Europe, Central Italy is genial and sunny, while the south is almost tropical. This variety of climatic conditions is sufficient to account for diversity of architectural features and treatment in the peninsula itself, while the differing climates of the various Roman provinces from Britain to North Africa, and from Syria to Spain, produced local modifications in details, though Roman architectural character was so pronounced and assertive as to leave little choice in general design.

RELIGIOUS. Since the Romans were originally a mixed people, their polytheistic religion was a fusion of several cults, but owed most to the Etruscans. In course of time, many of the chief Roman gods acquired similar attributes to those of the Greeks, but retained their Latin names and rites. The religion of Ancient Rome soon became part of the constitution of the state, and even the worship of the gods was eventually kept up only as a matter of state policy. The Emperor ultimately received divine honours and may almost be described as the head of the pantheon of deities of the various provinces which came under the tolerant and widespread Roman rule. Religious feeling had not so strong a hold on the Romans as on the Greeks, and did not enter in the same degree into the life of the people; nor do we find that it formed the bond of union among the different provinces of the Empire. Dissatisfaction with state religion showed itself from time to time in the introduction to Rome of alien cults from Egypt and the Near East. The position of the Emperor as Pontifex Maximus is rather indicative of the glorification of the Empire than of religion, and officialism stamped its character even on temple architecture. The principal buildings are not only temples, as in Hellenic Greece, but also public buildings, which were the material expression of Roman rule and imperial power. Sacerdotalism had no place in Roman religion, and the priests were not, as in Egypt, a powerful and privileged class, but only performed the sacrifices, while augurs ascertained from omens the will of the gods. Every house, whether palace, villa, or 'domus' had an altar to the Lares or family gods, and ancestor worship was a recognized part of religious rites; so it came about that Vesta, goddess of the hearth, was exalted to a high position in the Roman pantheon of gods, and vestal virgins, attached to the temples of Vesta, were of greater importance than the ordinary priests of sacrifice.

SOCIAL. In early historical times, Etruria, in west-central Italy, was occupied by the Etruscans. Their antecedents are uncertain, but they most probably were Asiatic immigrants, who about 750 B.C. had come deviously by sea from Lydia in Asia Minor. They subjugated the local inhabitants. Italy was not inhabited by one race alone but by several. North of the Etruscans were the Ligurians; to the east were the Picenes, and to the south the Samnites and Latins. Newcomers, in addition to the Etruscans, were the Greeks, who from mid-eighth century B.C. onwards planted their colonies in South Italy and Sicily, these territories being collectively known in ancient times as 'Magna Graecia'. The early form of government in Italy resembled that of Greece, and towns or districts intermittently were joined together in leagues. Etruria had twelve great cities, loosely linked together for religious practices and occasionally for political or military objects. The Etruscans were great builders, redoubtable sailors and skilled craftsmen in metalwork and pottery. The government of Rome was at an early period carried on by chosen kings (753–509 B.C.) aided by popular assembly, but at the latter date Rome became a republic. On Pompey's defeat at Pharsalus, Julius Caesar remained without a rival, but was murdered in 44 B.C., when there followed a period of great confusion. Then came the Triumvirate, consisting of Marcus Antonius, Caius Octavius (great-nephew of Julius Caesar), and Marcus Æmilius Lepidus, who were opposed to Brutus and Cassius and eventually defeated them. On the defeat of Marcus

Antonius at Actium (31 B.C.) Caius Octavius commenced to rule, and when the need for centralized government of distant provinces resulted in the formation of the Empire he received the title of 'Imperator' and in 27 B.C. that of 'Augustus', afterwards used as a surname by all Roman Emperors. The Augustan Age was one of the great eras in the world's history, like the Periclean Age in Greece, the Elizabethan Age in England, and the nineteenth century throughout Europe. At such epochs a new spring seems to well up in national and individual life, vitalizing art and literature. It was indeed the boast of Augustus that he found Rome a city of brick and left it of marble; though this colourful claim should not be taken too literally, as the use of marble was restricted to exceptional buildings, and stone and concrete were more representative of his day. The poets Virgil (70–19 B.C.), Horace (65–8 B.C.), Ovid (43 B.C.–A.D. 17), and Livy the historian (59 B.C.–A.D. 17), all flourished during this great period. The poems of Virgil and Horace show that the population flocked into the cities and disliked rural life, so that the land gradually went out of cultivation and the people depended on imported corn. Following Augustus, who died A.D. 14, came a line of famous Emperors, of whom Nero (A.D. 54–68), Vespasian (A.D. 69–79), Trajan (A.D. 98–117), Hadrian (A.D. 117–38), Septimius Severus (A.D. 193–211), Caracalla (A.D. 211–17), and Diocletian (A.D. 284–305) were the greatest patrons of architecture. The 'Building Acts' of Augustus and of his successors, Nero and Trajan, show the controlling influence of the state on architecture. Then ensued a period when a turbulent populace within the Imperial City, and the huge armies required to keep in check the barbarian tribes on every frontier, dominated the government. Emperors were no sooner chosen than they were murdered, and social chaos weakened the political power of the Empire. The social life of the Romans is clearly revealed in their architecture—there were thermae for games and bathing, circuses for races, amphitheatres for gladiatorial contests, theatres for dramas, basilicas for lawsuits, state temples for religion, and the apartment house or the 'domus' for the family life, while the forum was everywhere the centre of public life and national commerce. Amidst all this diversity of pursuits there is one consistent trait running through all Roman life, and this is that capacity for obedience which was the basis alike of society and the state. The *patria potestas*, or supreme power of the father, was the foundation-stone of family life, and out of their obedience to authority, whether to the head of the household, or to censors in the state, tne Romans developed their capacity as law-makers, and through this one characteristic they have left a special mark on the world's history. Based on slavery and aristocratic in origin, the Roman social system lacked a strong middle class. Roman women were held in high respect, family life was protected, and the Temple of Vesta, the most sacred spot in Rome, has recorded for all time the sacredness attached by the Romans to their family hearth.

HISTORICAL. From about the eighth century B.C. when they first came to historical notice, the power of the Etruscans waxed until it was the mightiest in Italy and its western seas. Their territories expanded; down the west coast beyond the Bay of Naples and Pompeii; northwards into the valley of the Po; and eastwards towards the Adriatic sea (p. 167). Through the sixth century B.C., Rome itself was under Etruscan domination and was ruled by Etruscan kings. The turn in fortune came with the fall of the monarchy and the collapse of Etruscan power in Rome in 509 B.C., cutting off Etruria from her southern domains; followed in 474 B.C. by the further disaster of the defeat of the Etruscans in sea-battle by the Syracusans, allies of Cumae, the oldest of the Greek colonies in South Italy. The initiative then passed to Rome. The traditional date for the foundation of the city is 753 B.C. The Republic established in Rome after the expulsion of Tarquinius Superbus, the last

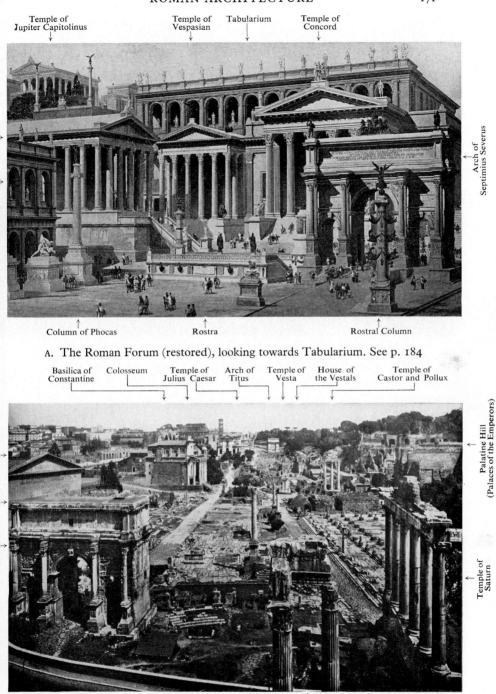

Temple of Jupiter Capitolinus | Temple of Vespasian | Tabularium | Temple of Concord | Arch of Septimius Severus

Column of Phocas | Rostra | Rostral Column

A. The Roman Forum (restored), looking towards Tabularium. See p. 184

Basilica of Constantine | Colosseum | Temple of Julius Caesar | Arch of Titus | Temple of Vesta | House of the Vestals | Temple of Castor and Pollux

Palatine Hill (Palaces of the Emperors)

Temple of Saturn

Forum | Rostra | Column of Phocas | Temple of Vespasian | Basilica Julia

B. Remains of the Roman Forum, looking towards the Colosseum. See p. 184

A. Forum Boarium, Rome (restored) in the time of Constantine. See p. 184
(*Left*) Temple of Fortuna Virilis; (*left centre*) Arch of Janus
Quadrifrons; (*right centre*) Ara Maxima; (*right*) Temple of Portunus

B. Temple of Jupiter Capitolinus, Rome (restored)
(Dedicated 509 B.C., and as rebuilt in A.D. 82 by Domitian). See p. 180

of the Etruscan kings, engaged in many wars, extending her power among her neighbours and conquering Veii, the nearest of the great Etruscan cities; but was defeated in 390 B.C. by the Gauls, who continued for some time afterwards to hold the northern part of Italy. The Gauls also weakened the resistance of the surviving Etruscan towns, though they only fell to the revived aggression of Rome by slow stages. Meanwhile, the force of Roman arms had prevailed in the south, and the conquest of lower Italy was concluded by c. 273 B.C. Then came the wars with peoples outside Italy. The first Punic war (264–241 B.C.) against Carthage brought about the annexation of Sicily as the first Roman province. The second Punic war (218–201 B.C.) was the most severe struggle in which the Romans had engaged; for Hannibal, the great Carthaginian general, entered Italy from the north, defeated the Roman armies, and maintained himself in Italy until recalled to meet a counter-attack of the Romans, under Scipio, upon Carthage itself. The third Punic war (149–146 B.C.) ended in the destruction of Carthage, which with its territory became a Roman province in Africa. The conquest of Macedonia (168 B.C.) and of Greece (from 146 B.C.) added two more provinces to the Roman Empire, and also stimulated the importation of Greek artists and art into Italy. Greece, in its turn, formed a stepping-stone to Asia Minor, of which a chief part became the Roman province of Asia in 133 B.C., the rest being gradually subdued over the ensuing century and a half. With the conquests of Spain (133 B.C.) and Syria (64 B.C.), the Roman Empire extended from the Euphrates to the Atlantic, while Caesar's campaign (58–49 B.C.) made the Rhine and the English Channel its northern boundaries. In 30 B.C. Egypt was added to the Empire, and in A.D. 43 Britain became a Roman province. Then later, when the Empire had reached its greatest extent, discontent at the centre and barbarian attacks on the frontiers led to that weakening of authority which resulted in its decline and final fall. Constantine (A.D. 306–337) removed his capital to Byzantium in A.D. 330 as a more convenient centre for the extended Empire, but in A.D. 365 the Roman Empire was divided into East and West with two Emperors, and the year A.D. 476 marks the end of the Western Roman Empire by the election of Odoacer as the first king of Italy.

ARCHITECTURAL CHARACTER
ETRUSCAN ARCHITECTURE
(750–100 B.C.)

The Etruscans, who were the early inhabitants of west-central Italy, were great builders, and their methods were taken over by the Romans. They made remarkable advances in the organization of large-scale undertakings, such as the construction of city walls and sewers, the draining of marshes and the control of rivers, and the cutting of channels to regulate the water-level of lakes. They are credited with the earliest use in Italy, if not in Europe, of the true or radiating arch, and with the invention of a new Order of Architecture, called the Tuscan, an addition to the three, Doric, Ionic and Corinthian, originated by the Greeks. Etruscan towns were fortified with powerful stone walls, several feet thick, which were alternatively of the Cyclopean type, like that of the Aegeans; of polygonal work, as occasionally used by the Greeks (pp. 99G, 161); or, when the available stone was easily worked, of fine squared and bonded masonry laid in alternate courses of header and stretcher blocks sometimes more than two feet high. No mortar was used. Exceptionally, city walls were of very large, partly-burnt bricks, as at Arezzo, where the bricks were approximately $1\frac{1}{2} \times 1 \times \frac{1}{2}$ ft, laid in clay mortar through the thickness of the 14 ft 6 ins wall. A stone city gateway at Volterra, the Porta all'Arco, bears the remains of the earliest known arch above ground, dating from about

300 B.C. Tombs, which exist in great numbers, were located outside the city walls on special necropolis sites, the earliest often taking the form of great, conical tumuli, with stone burial chambers concealed within their earthen mounds. The majority were underground, cut in the soft tufa rock and simulating the interior of the contemporary house. The 'atrium' type of house, characteristic of Roman times, is believed to have originated with the Etruscans, though there is little to show now, for dwellings were of sun-dried brick, covered with terracotta-tiled wooden roofs. Temples too were at first of sun-dried brick, but had timber frames and columns to sustain the wide-eaved, low pitched roofs, lavishly ornamented with brilliantly-coloured terra-cotta slabs and crestings along the pediments, cornices and ridge. Columns themselves sometimes were sheathed in terra-cotta. From the fourth century B.C., walls and columns were of stone throughout, as at all times were the high platforms, or 'podiums', on which the temples stood. Temples were invariably frontal, and usually faced south. Despite the eventual Roman occupation, Etruria retained much of its own architectural character until the first century B.C.

ROMAN ARCHITECTURE
(300 B.C.–A.D. 365)

Roman building work retained its Etruscan character for some time after the Republic had been founded in 509 B.C., but in the third century B.C. began to derive much of its external complexion from Greek sources, whilst at the same time developing the constructive traits that were to make it the most stupendous architecture in the history of the western world. By about 200 B.C., its own identity was well established, though experiments with technique and building method, and the exploitation of building materials, were to progress continuously until well into the Christian era. The mightiest achievements, for which Roman architecture is justly famed, belong to the period of the Roman Empire, growing increasingly daring as time progressed.

The Romans adopted the columnar and trabeated style of the Greeks, and developed also the arch and the vault from the beginnings made by the Etruscans. This combined use of column, beam, and arch is the keynote of the Roman style in its earliest stages. The Colosseum, Rome (p. 210), everywhere throughout its structure, displays these two features in combination, for piers strengthened and faced by attached half-columns support arches, which in their turn carry the entablature. In works of an engineering character, such as aqueducts, the arch was supported on piers without the facing column. Thus the Orders of architecture which, as used by the Greeks, were essentially constructive were frequently employed by the Romans as decorative features which could be omitted and even at times lost their original use, although the Romans also used them constructively in temple colonnades and basilicas (p. 200A).

The Doric, Ionic, and Corinthian Orders of architecture were used by the Greeks (p. 96), and the Etruscans and Romans added respectively the Tuscan and Composite (p. 244), making five in all. The Tuscan Order (p. 181J, K) is a simplified version of the Doric Order, about 7 diameters high, with base, unfluted shaft, and simply-moulded capital, and with a plain entablature. Actually, in ancient times it was used only with the wooden entablatures of the Etruscans, and there is no certain Roman example. Vitruvius, the Roman authority on architecture in the late first century B.C., recorded it, and it was revived with a stone entablature in Renaissance days. An example is that of S. Paul, Covent Garden, London (p. 898). Vitruvius also gives the proportions of the Doric, Ionic and

Corinthian Orders, but not of the Composite, which was not evolved until the first century A.D. The proportions of the various Orders were studied in the Renaissance period by famous architects, such as Palladio, Vignola, and Sir William Chambers (p. 972).

Temples were the predominating buildings of the Hellenic Greeks and were of one storey, but the complex civilization and varied needs of the Romans introduced other types and necessitated the use of several storeys, which were frequently ornamented, as in the Colosseum, by attached half-columns superimposed one above the other. The architectural aims of the Romans were essentially utilitarian, and thermae, amphitheatres, basilicas, aqueducts and bridges all testify to the great constructive ability they possessed; their majestic buildings are in accord with the grandeur of Roman Imperial power.

The Romans continued and developed the Etruscan method of using large blocks of stone without mortar during the Republic, but their practical mind eventually hit upon greater economy of materials by the use of concrete, a hard composition which consists of small fragments of stone, such as tufa of its various kinds, peperino or travertine, or again, broken bricks, laid in an excellent mortar of lime and well-selected sand. The 'sand' was, in fact, usually pozzolana, a special earth which abounds in all the volcanic regions of Italy: in places where it was not forthcoming equivalents were painstakingly sought. The important parts of the work were done by skilled craftsmen, who built up the outer carcase of the ponderous walls and saw to the erection of the temporary wooden centerings for arches and vaults. Under their direction, the purely mechanical tasks of dumping alternate layers of mortar and broken stones or brick, which would solidify into concrete, were performed by local slaves liable to statute labour on public buildings or, in the case of military works, by soldiers of the Roman legions. This extended use of concrete originated a new constructive system which was adapted with rare sagacity to diverse types of important buildings.

Roman walls, both of stone and concrete, are of special character and must be described in detail. Walls of 'opus quadratum', i.e. rectangular blocks of stone, with or without mortar joints but frequently secured with dowels or cramps, still continued in use. In the best work, the stones were very regular, $4 \times 2 \times 2$ Roman feet in dimensions (the Roman foot is $\frac{1}{2}$ inch less than the English), laid in the usual alternate courses of headers and stretchers. Sometimes, such walls were solid throughout, at others, used as a facing to the concrete core, as in the case of temple podiums. Roman concrete walls presented a succession of face effects. Good mortar of lime and sand first began to be used extensively in the third century B.C., and when its virtues had been realized, stones became quite small, and on the wall faces appeared in a loose pattern roughly resembling the polygonal work from which the techniques derived. This pattern is known as 'opus incertum' (p. 177B). Gradually, it became more regular, until by the time of Augustus it had assumed the net-like effect of 'opus reticulatum' (p. 177C), with fine joints running diagonally, so that each stone unit was precisely square, though set lozenge fashion. In both the incertum and the reticulate work, the stones were only 4 ins or so across the face, and tailed into the wall pyramidally for about 8–10 ins. Specially cut stones were used at outer vertical angles. Reticulate work in its turn was superseded by brick facing, or 'opus testaceum' (p. 177D), which became the hall-mark of the Imperial period in Italy and elsewhere. Wall cores then sometimes were of broken brick too, but generally, stone fragments still continued to be used. The 'bricks' were in fact old roofing tiles, upwards of $1\frac{1}{2}$ ins thick and of considerable but irregular length, raggedly broken to tail back into the wall: only in the second half of the first century A.D. were triangular bricks specially made for facing the walls. Except in the case of opus incertum, the wall faces were necessarily laid a little in advance of the core of a wall, in better mortar, and they consequently tended to come adrift. Hence bonding courses of large square tiles or 'bipedales', two Roman feet square were soon introduced to pass back into or even right through the wall, distributed at frequent intervals up the height. A variant kind of facing appeared for a while about the time of Hadrian, in which panels of reticulate work were enframed in horizontal and vertical strips of brickwork. A final type, 'opus mixtum', an alternation of courses of brickwork and small, squared stone blocks, began to be used towards the end of the Empire period. These several kinds of facing to concrete walls were not used everywhere; in many of the Roman provinces, Britain included, a coursed-rubble facing of squared units only a few inches high was usual. No special facings could, of course, be employed when the concrete was laid against earth or boarding in foundations or vaults (p. 177A, E).

Concrete was a manufactured material, and as such not being special to any country could be used in every part of the Empire; thus throughout the Roman dominions it gave uniformity and similarity to the buildings, whose character was thus largely independent of local conditions.

It was upon the capacity to span over enormous spaces that the character of Roman architecture largely depended. The Greeks of Hellenic times had been limited to what could be achieved by simple beams of wood, and so had had to introduce double lines of superimposed columns inside even their temples, to support the roof timbers, whenever extra space was needed. It was not till about the third century B.C. that the Greeks began timidly to employ the principle of triangulation of the elements of wooden roof trusses. The Romans seized upon the idea, and developed it apace: Vitruvius, the Augustan architect, tells us of the wooden-roofed basilica he built at Fano, in North Italy, where the central unimpeded space was sixty feet wide and one hundred and twenty feet long. Similarly, the Romans developed the stone arch of the Etruscans; and already before the end of the Republic could bridge a span of 80 ft, as in the Pons Fabricius at Rome (pp. 238C, 241E). But it was, above all, concrete which allowed the Romans to build vaults of a magnitude never equalled till the introduction of steel for buildings in the nineteenth century. How puny seem the naves of English vaulted cathedrals, rarely as much as 40 ft wide, against the great Roman halls, 80 or 90 ft across. Concrete vaults had the advantage over stone in that they could be accommodated to complicated plan forms without involving difficult and laborious stone cutting. The vaults were supported on 'centering' or temporary wooden framework until the concrete had set. In important cases, such vaults were constructed of brick ribs, with concrete filling, the object being to lighten the load imposed on the centering and to guard against cracks (p. 177E). The various vaults used in Roman buildings were as follows (p. 177): (a) The semicircular or waggon-headed vault, otherwise known as the 'barrel' or 'tunnel' vault, was borne throughout its length on the two parallel walls of a rectangular apartment (p. 370A). (b) The cross-vault (pp. 370B, 373A), which was formed by the intersection of two semicircular vaults of equal span, was used over a square apartment and the pressure was taken by the four angles. When cross-vaults were used over long halls or corridors, the hall was divided by piers into square bays, each of which was covered with a cross-vault, which allowed of the insertion of windows in the upper part of the walls, as in the central hall of the Thermae of Caracalla (p. 177L) and the Thermae of Diocletian, Rome (p. 207A). The lines of intersection of these cross-vaults are known as 'groins'. (c) Hemispherical domes or cupolas (cupa = a cup) (p. 196) were used over circular structures, and semi-domes for exedrae or semicircular recesses (p. 177H, K).

CONSTRUCTION OF WALLS AND ARCHES

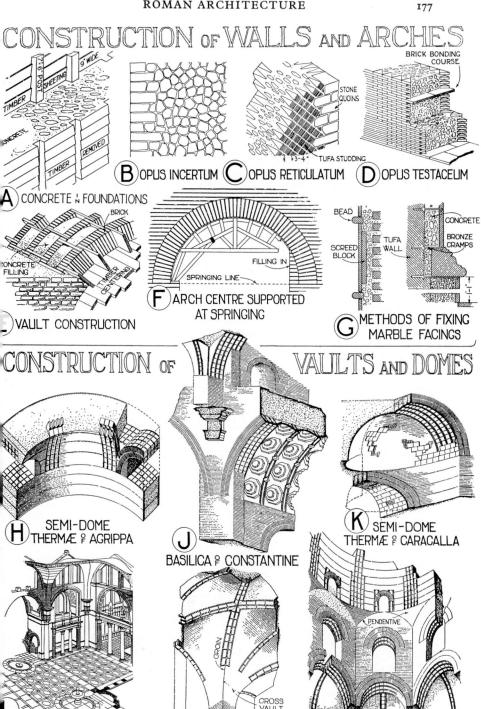

A CONCRETE IN FOUNDATIONS

B OPUS INCERTUM **C** OPUS RETICULATUM **D** OPUS TESTACEUM

E VAULT CONSTRUCTION

F ARCH CENTRE SUPPORTED AT SPRINGING

G METHODS OF FIXING MARBLE FACINGS

CONSTRUCTION OF VAULTS AND DOMES

H SEMI-DOME THERMÆ OF AGRIPPA

J BASILICA OF CONSTANTINE

K SEMI-DOME THERMÆ OF CARACALLA

L VAULT OF CENTRAL HALL THERMÆ OF CARACALLA: ROME

M THERMÆ OF DIOCLETIAN

N VAULT: MINERVA MEDICA: ROME

In all these vaulting forms, concrete was the important factor, for it was economical of skilled labour and had much greater cohesion than vaults made up of
separate stone units. Yet it remained necessary to buttress the oblique sideways
thrusts exerted against the walls by the enormously heavy concrete vaults, which
even at the crown, were several feet thick. The barrel vaults over the side aisles or
recesses of the Basilica of Constantine, Rome, for instance, each of which spans
76 ft, were 8 ft thick at the top (p. 177J), and the dome of the famous Pantheon,
142 ft across, is more than 4 ft thick in its upper part (p. 199A). To a certain extent
the ponderous walls absorbed these stresses, but the Romans took no chances and
devised an elaborate buttressing system. The fact is not always apparent, for in
complex buildings the thrusts of one vault were balanced against those of another,
as in the Thermae of Diocletian (p. 207D), where the enormous central hall was
surrounded by lesser apartments with their walls aligned against the points where
the stresses of the groined triple vault were received. Also, the Romans usually
concealed their buttresses with a masking wall. The art of buttressing was developed in the course of early engineering works, which frequently required the
retaining of masses of earth. Three principal types of buttress were used. (i) The
hemicycle or niche, which is the best of all buttresses for retaining earth. This type
was used on an enormous scale in the Forum of Trajan, north-east side, where the
hemicycle cuts into the foot of the Quirinal (p. 185B). Galleries of shops and offices
in three tiers conceal its utilitarian purpose. (ii) The ordinary 'Gothic' type of
'spur' buttress, familiar in countless Mediaeval buildings. The niche type was not
very suitable for buildings where large openings for windows and doors were
needed—though a pair can be seen flanking the portal between the central hall
and the frigidarium of the Thermae of Diocletian (p. 207D)—so for convenience
in normal buildings it was squared-off into spur buttresses and a linking wall in
which windows could be placed. The connecting wall, however, was put across the
outer edge of the buttresses so that the space between them could be covered over
with a vault and included in the useful interior accommodation. The aisles of the
Basilica of Constantine utilize the space between the great buttresses in this way
(p. 200D, E, F), and the latter can be seen, with their sloping tops, rising above the
vaults of the aisles to catch the thrusts of the main vaults where they are concentrated in the pockets above the columned pillars (p. 200D). Instances of flying buttresses are known (p. 185E, F). (iii) The principle of the pinnacle too, was
extensively used. Pinnacles were placed on the tops of spur buttresses to help by
their weight to drive the oblique thrusts more steeply down to earth. They are of
very great size at the Thermae of Diocletian (p. 207B), but, as is almost invariably
the case in Roman architecture, their mundane purpose is disguised by architectural ornament; in this instance by canopied sculptures. In buildings of which the
walls were not too much broken up by window or other openings, the same principle was applied, but the extra load then ran continuously along the top of the
wall outside the base of the vault, as an abutment, to reduce the danger of its
collapsing outwards.

The Pantheon at Rome, the finest of all illustrations of Roman construction,
embodies every form of Roman buttress. It will be noted there (p. 199A) that the
building is two tiers high to the springing of the hemispherical dome inside, but
there is an extra tier on the outside, providing rigid and weighty haunches to prevent the dome from splitting outwards; and, as an extra precaution, a further series
of steps of concrete rises two-thirds the height of the dome. It is for this constructional reason that Roman domes are always saucer-shaped outside, though hemispherical within. Very adroitly in this building, the weight of the vault is reduced
by omitting a portion at the crown—the most difficult part to construct—to provide

an 'eye' which is the sole source of natural light. The twenty-feet thick walls are not by any means solid; the decorative recesses inside are contrived within spur buttresses linking inner and outer shells, and between these recesses are constructional niches which run the full three-tier height and are crowned with semi-domes at the top of each tier; in the upper tiers they are split in half by spur buttresses (p. 199A, B). Thus all the forms of buttress used later in developed Mediaeval architecture were anticipated by Roman architects, but with the difference that the Roman were far less light and compact, and were not usually plainly exposed to view.

Concrete vaults often were lightened by recesses or 'coffers' on the underside, but concrete does not lend itself to carved enrichment, like stonework, and walls and vaults normally received a decorative sheathing of plaster, stucco, marble or mosaic. Various plasters of lime and sand were used outside, and plaster or stucco within. The latter was of marble dust and lime, and frequently was modelled into shallow, geometrical patterns, the panels thus created being ornamented with low-relief figures and foliage, and painted in attractive colours. In such cases the stucco was as much as 3 ins in thickness. When bold mouldings or entire columns were required in this material, as in the peristyles of houses, they would have a concrete or brick core. Alternatively for walls, especially in domestic work, the stucco was carefully prepared, in as many as five successive coats, to receive elaborate and brilliant paintings in fresco, tempera or encaustic. A special mixture, 'opus signi-num', of ground terra-cotta and lime, with or without sand, was used for the lining of water-channels, aqueducts and reservoirs and in damp situations.

Marble was rarely used solidly throughout a wall; and only the white was so employed, never the coloured. Normally it was just a facing, up to a foot or so thick when the marble was the native 'Luna' from Carrara, but in mere veneers down to $\frac{1}{2}$ inch thick in the case of coloured marbles. Marble, porphyry, jasper or granite veneers were laid against a stucco backing and secured to the walls by iron or bronze cramps (p. 177G); they were arranged in geometrical patterns of different varieties ('opus sectile'), and were used in this manner too for floors. Coloured marbles were too expensive for universal use, and on walls, the pattern was frequently simulated in paint instead. When the Orders of Architecture were constructed in marble as a whole, as in the case of temple porches, it was only the column shafts that might be of the coloured varieties; and to show their veinings or textures to best advantage, they were unfluted monoliths, shaped at the quarry before shipping. The omission of fluting in such instances affected usage in general, and as often as not the flutes were omitted even when the shafts were built up in stone, whatever the Order employed.

Marble mosaics were employed to some extent for walls and vaults, but above all, for floors—as an alternative to the opus sectile—in an infinite variety of geometrical and pictorial patterns (pp. 241F, 249H, K–M). A humbler type of paving was 'opus spicatum', made of small bricks set in herring-bone pattern. Glass mosaics were not suitable for floors, but made a brilliant decoration for vaults and were excellent for structures and situations liable to damp, such as garden ornaments and pavilions, fountains and semi-subterranean porticoes and grottoes. Gilding was sometimes applied to wood ornaments and to bronze-covered roofs of important buildings, such as the Pantheon (p. 198).

The abundance of statues brought from Greece led to the formation of wall niches for their reception, and these were either semicircular or rectangular, and were occasionally flanked by columns supporting a pediment, to form a frame for the statue, or were fronted by a screen of columns, as in the Pantheon (pp. 196B, 199B).

EXAMPLES

ETRUSCAN ARCHITECTURE

The character of Etruscan architecture has been referred to (p. 173). The remains consist chiefly of tombs, city walls, gateways, bridges, and culverts.

The **Cloaca Maxima, Rome,** was first constructed in the late Regal period as an open drain for the valleys between the hills of Rome; which is its only title to be included as an Etruscan example, as nothing of the present remains is so old. The drain was subsequently covered in, and underwent many repairs in ancient times. At its outlet to the river Tiber (p. 181A), it shows a semicircular (Roman) vault of peperino stone, of *c.* 78 B.C., 11 ft in span, of three concentric rings of voussoirs, each 2 ft 6 ins high. The oldest known true arch in Rome is that over a similar drain in front of the Temple of Saturn, dating from about the fourth century B.C. In Etruria, voussoir barrel vaults occur in numerous underground tombs of the third and fourth centuries B.C., in the region of Chiusi and Perugia.

The **Arch of Augustus, Perugia** (late second century B.C.) (p. 181B) is so called because of the inscription 'Augusta Perusia', carved on the arch after 27 B.C. Although Perugia fell to the Romans in 310 B.C., the arch still retains a strong Etruscan character, as do the contemporary city walls, about two miles long, surrounding the ancient city. Both are built of large blocks of travertine stone, without mortar. An earlier arch, partially surviving, is the Porta all'Arco, Volterra, of the fourth or third century B.C., in walls of roughly-squared, large blocks of sandstone of the sixth century B.C. Volterra did not succumb to the Romans until the first century B.C.

The **Temple of Jupiter Capitolinus, Rome** (509 B.C.) (pp. 172B, 182A), the principal example of this type of building, had its cella divided into three chambers for statues of Jupiter, Minerva, and Juno, and was nearly square on plan, with widely spaced columns to support timber architraves. It was burnt in 83 B.C., and rebuilt by Sulla, who here made use of some of the marble Corinthian columns taken from the Olympieion, Athens (p. 140), but afterwards destroyed.

The **Temple of Juno Sospita, Lanuvium** (fifth century B.C.) (p. 181H, J) is restored from the description by Vitruvius (Bk. IV, chap. vii). The plan has three cells for three deities, and a front portico with two rows of four columns, widely spaced and approached by walled-in steps—a type of temple plan afterwards adopted by the Romans, and in contrast to the Greek type. The restored elevation (p. 181J) shows the steps between flanking walls and the portico columns supporting a terracotta-covered timber entablature and pediment. The roof carpentry of an Etruscan temple is included in this reconstruction (p. 181K) and the terra-cotta roof covering of this Temple has been set up in the British Museum (p. 181H), while an interesting Renaissance version of the portico is seen in S. Paul, Covent Garden, London (pp. 898, 902G–J).

The **Temple, Alatri** (third century B.C.) (p. 181L), remains of which were found in A.D. 1882, has been re-erected in the court of the Villa of Pope Julius, Rome. This small Etruscan temple rests on a podium, and a sloping ramp gives access to a portico of two columns from which the central doorway opens into the cella. It is now known that there was no rear porch. The typical entablature of enriched terra-cotta, pediment with acroteria, and eaves with antefixae, resemble those from Lanuvium. Greek influence is probably responsible for the return to the single cella. Alatri is not in Etruria, but in the centre of Latium.

Etruscan Tomb, Corneto-Tarquinia. Of many rock-cut tombs at Etruscan Tarquinia, near the present Corneto, some twenty-three are especially renowned

A CLOACA MAXIMA: ROME

B ARCH OF AUGUSTUS PERUGIA

C ETRUSCAN SARCOPHAGUS

D CAPITAL ETRUSCAN TOMB: VULCI (BRITISH MUS.)

E ETRUSCAN SARCOPHAGUS (BRITISH MUS)

ETRUSCAN TOMB: CORNETO: INTERIOR

ETRUSCAN TEMPLE OF JUNO SOSPITA: LANUVIUM

PLAN

ANTEFIXA

RUSCAN TOMB: CORNETO LONGITUDINAL SECTION

½ SECTION

H TERRA-COTTA ROOFING RECONSTRUCTED AT BRITISH MUSEUM

J CONJECTURAL RESTORATION

PLAN

K ROOF CONSTRUCTION OF ETRUSCAN TEMPLE (RESTORED)

ETRUSCAN TEMPLE CONSTRUCTED IN THE COURT VILLA POPE JULIUS: ROME

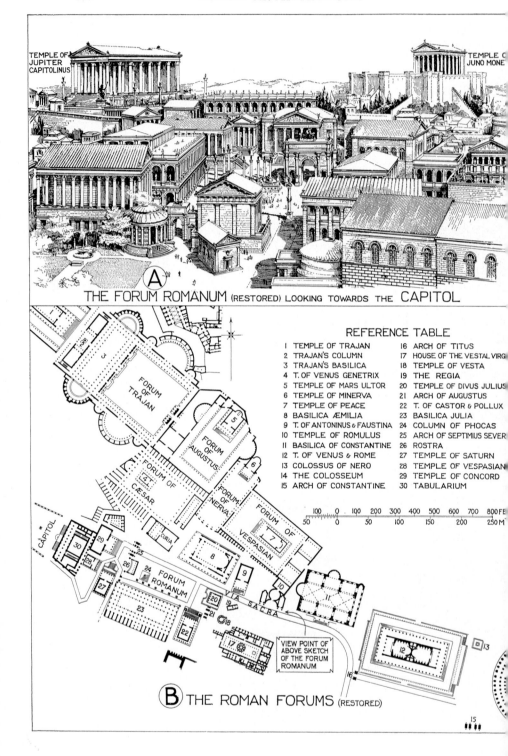

TEMPLE OF JUPITER CAPITOLINUS

TEMPLE OF JUNO MONETA

THE FORUM ROMANUM (RESTORED) LOOKING TOWARDS THE CAPITOL

FORUM OF TRAJAN

FORUM OF AUGUSTUS

FORUM OF CÆSAR

FORUM OF NERVA

FORUM OF VESPASIAN

CAPITOL

CURIA

FORUM ROMANUM

VIA SACRA

REFERENCE TABLE

1	TEMPLE OF TRAJAN	16	ARCH OF TITUS
2	TRAJAN'S COLUMN	17	HOUSE OF THE VESTAL VIRGINS
3	TRAJAN'S BASILICA	18	TEMPLE OF VESTA
4	T. OF VENUS GENETRIX	19	THE REGIA
5	TEMPLE OF MARS ULTOR	20	TEMPLE OF DIVUS JULIUS
6	TEMPLE OF MINERVA	21	ARCH OF AUGUSTUS
7	TEMPLE OF PEACE	22	T. OF CASTOR & POLLUX
8	BASILICA ÆMILIA	23	BASILICA JULIA
9	T. OF ANTONINUS & FAUSTINA	24	COLUMN OF PHOCAS
10	TEMPLE OF ROMULUS	25	ARCH OF SEPTIMIUS SEVERUS
11	BASILICA OF CONSTANTINE	26	ROSTRA
12	T. OF VENUS & ROME	27	TEMPLE OF SATURN
13	COLOSSUS OF NERO	28	TEMPLE OF VESPASIAN
14	THE COLOSSEUM	29	TEMPLE OF CONCORD
15	ARCH OF CONSTANTINE	30	TABULARIUM

100   0   100   200   300   400   500   600   700   800 FEET
50   0   50   100   150   200   250 M

VIEW POINT OF ABOVE SKETCH OF THE FORUM ROMANUM

Ⓑ THE ROMAN FORUMS (RESTORED)

for their vivid wall paintings, which retain a remarkable freshness. One tomb shows architectural importance as well (p. 181F, G). The entrance leads to an outer chamber, somewhat resembling the atrium of an Etruscan house as described by Vitruvius, with a rock roof carved in imitation of rafters sloping up to a central opening which admitted light through a vertical shaft. A doorway leads to a smaller, inner chamber at a lower level.

The **Necropolis, Cerveteri,** is one of the most remarkable of Etruscan burial sites. The tombs are laid out systematically along paved streets, like a town for the living. The oldest tombs, which include the seventh century B.C. Regolini-Galassi example, where rich treasures were found in A.D. 1836, are distributed irregularly in the neighbourhood, whereas the great tumulus mounds and the underground rock-cut chamber-tombs, chiefly of the sixth and fifth centuries B.C., are grouped compactly together to save space. Most famous among the latter are the late-seventh century Tomb of the Shields and Stools and the fifth century Tomb of the Alcove, which reproduce in rock the interior features of houses; and the Tomb of the Stucco Reliefs, third century B.C., where the personal and household possessions of the deceased noble and his wife are modelled in stucco on the walls.

The **Necropolis, Vulci.** The ancient city site has long been deserted, but the tombs of its necropolis were discovered and despoiled of their priceless store of jewellery and painted vases in the nineteenth century. But there, as elsewhere, tombs were often adorned with architectural features, as well as wall paintings. A tomb from Vulci, discovered in A.D. 1833, has been reconstructed in the British Museum. It includes a short, sturdy column with a capital (p. 181D) which is distinctively Etruscan, with upspringing volutes at the corners, and carved human heads between. It derives from a primitive type from the Near East, but the heads are an Etruscan addition; used quite frequently too, for the decoration of the keystones of arches. The acanthus leaves show the influence of the Greek Corinthian Order. We have seen that the Etruscans imitated the Greek Doric Order and produced from it their own 'Tuscan' variant. They also had their versions of the Greek Ionic, as seen in the Arch of Augustus, Perugia (p. 181B).

Etruscan Sarcophagi. Both ordinary burial and cremation were practised in Etruria. The receptacles grew increasingly large, until in the fourth century B.C., sarcophagi of stone, alabaster and terra-cotta were used in very large numbers. The deceased were normally represented as reclining on a couch. The sarcophagus from the British Museum (p. 181E) has marine monsters on the side, and the reclining figure holds the plate for the coin to be paid to Charon for ferrying the departed across the Styx. The example from Cerveteri, now in the Villa of Pope Julius Etruscan Museum, Rome (p. 181C) is in terra-cotta, and in portraying man and wife together, shows the high status which women enjoyed in Etruscan society.

ROMAN ARCHITECTURE

Examples of Roman architecture are found not in Italy only, but wherever Roman government extended, as at Nîmes and Arles in France; Tarragona and Segovia in Spain; Trèves and Aix-la-Chapelle in Germany; Constantine, Leptis Magna, and Timgad in North Africa; Baalbek and Palmyra in Syria, besides Silchester, Dover, Verulamium and Bath in England (p. 383).

FORUMS

The forum, corresponding to the agora in a Greek city, was a central open space used as a meeting-place, market, or rendezvous for political demonstrations, like the French 'place', the Italian 'piazza' and the English market-place. For small towns a single forum might suffice, but in the larger several were needed, though there was always one of principal importance. In towns which had grown from small beginnings, forums underwent piecemeal changes and were often somewhat irregular in shape, but when towns were newly founded or for some reason partially rebuilt, the forums were laid out systematically, on formal lines. All were designed to meet the requirements of Roman citizens, and with the surrounding buildings they reflect not only the religion, law, and commerce, but also the busy corporate life of the city, which was much the same whatever the form of government, whether of elected kings, Republic, or Empire (p. 169).

The **Forum Romanum, Rome,** the oldest and most important in the city, was sited in the valley between Rome's famous hills. It is not strictly rectangular; it was originally an all-purpose forum, but as the city grew its shops were removed elsewhere and the contests and displays which once had taken place there were relegated to the theatre, amphitheatre and circus. Only the chief public buildings then were grouped around it, and its appearance in the heyday of ancient Rome, adorned with pillars of victory and statues and surrounded by porticoes, colonnades, temples, basilicas, and state buildings, must indeed have been imposing (pp. 171A, 182), as viewed from the arcaded Tabularium (78 B.C.), where the public archives were preserved. Rome, with its great Empire, required more civic space than the Forum Romanum allowed, and successive Emperors laid out imposing new symmetrical forums which were at the same time monuments to themselves. Julius Caesar added the first; then the Emperors Augustus, Vespasian, Nerva and Trajan in turn (p. 182B).

The **Forum of Trajan, Rome** (A.D. 98–113) (pp. 182B, 185, 186), was the largest. It comprised four parts: (i) the forum proper, with large hemicycles on either side, screened off by colonnades, containing tiers of shops; (ii) a marketing area comprising shops and a two-storey vaulted hall on the slopes of the Quirinal Hill beyond the N.E. hemicycle (pp. 185E, F, 186); (iii) the Basilica of Trajan and two adjoining libraries separated by a court from which rose Trajan's commemorative column; and (iv) a peristyled enclosure containing the Temple of Trajan.

Besides these forums, others, such as the **'Forum Boarium'** (p. 172A), served as markets for special purposes. Pompeii, as all towns of importance, had a forum as a centre of civic life, which was crowded on festival days when sacrifices took place before the temples (p. 226B). The forums of Rome and the provinces provide many instances of well-considered town-planning, and there were fine examples even in the outskirts of the Empire, as at Palmyra, Samaria, Damascus, Antioch and Bosra in Syria; Pergamon in Asia Minor; Timgad and Tebessa in North Africa; and at Silchester and elsewhere in England; in all of which there were colonnaded streets to give shelter from the sun.

RECTANGULAR TEMPLES

Roman temples are an amalgamation of Etruscan and Greek types; for while in many respects they resembled the Greek, the typical prostyle portico and podium were derived from Etruscan temples (p. 180). There are several types, of which the most characteristic is pseudo-peripteral (p. 189H), which, instead of side colonnades, has half-columns attached to the walls with a prostyle portico in front. The steps to the principal entrance were flanked by massive, low walls which were an extension of the lateral podium, and they frequently supported groups of statuary (p. 189G). Greek peripteral temples were normally twice as long as their width, but Roman temples were much shorter in proportion, while the cella itself, used as a treasure house and as a museum for Greek statuary, frequently occupied the whole width of the building. The intercolumniation was sometimes wider than in Greek

A. Northern hemicycle of Forum of
Trajan, from below

B. Northern hemicycle of Forum of
Trajan, from above

C. East end of northern hemicycle of
Forum, containing a buttressing apse

D. Shops with balcony over, to the right
of the façade shown in 185 C

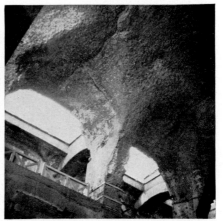

E. Flying buttresses over clear-story
passage of Great Hall in Markets of Trajan

F. Flying buttresses to vault of Great
Hall in Markets of Trajan

Forum and Markets of Trajan (A.D. 98–113). See opposite page

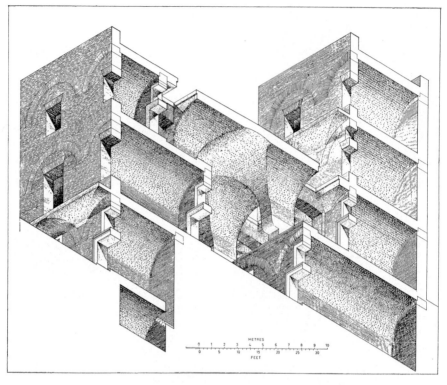

Cross section, showing vaults

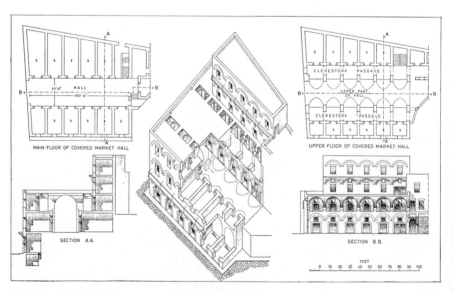

Great Hall of the Markets of Trajan, N.E. of the Forum of Trajan (A.D. 98–113).
See p. 184

temples, and then the architrave and frieze were built in voussoirs as flat arches, but this treatment was unnecessary where walls supported the entablature. Most rectangular temples were simple structures compared with buildings erected for public relaxation, like theatres, amphitheatres and thermae, and the latter types are more truly representative of Roman architectural taste and constructional skill. Nevertheless, temples quite clearly evidence Roman ability to cover large spaces without the aid of intermediate supports. Spans of fifty or sixty feet were common. Normally, the roofs were of trussed timbers, like the basilicas, and probably were elaborately coffered with wooden panelling on the underside. Some few temples were vaulted, as the Temple of Venus and Rome at Rome (p. 192C, E). Roman temples sometimes were partially or wholly isolated in precincts, like those in the Imperial Forums at Rome (p. 182B), though most were intended to be seen from the forum which they faced, and the entrance was emphasized by the deep portico and steps. There was no attempt at orientation, as in the Greek temples, which regularly faced east, or the Etruscan, which usually faced south.

The **Temple of Fortuna Virilis, Rome** (c. 40 B.C.) (pp. 189A, B, C, 251) is pseudo-peripteral tetrastyle with the deep portico common in Roman temples and which illustrates the retention of Etruscan practice. The Ionic Order used, however, shows Hellenistic Greek influence in almost all its details. The capitals are two-faced, so there had to be a canted volute on those at the angles, as in the East Portico of the Erechtheion, Athens (p. 127D), but the front wall of the cella raised a special difficulty, as the two attached columns which mark its position had to have canted volutes too. The temple demonstrates Roman selective use of materials according to their respective properties, for whilst the majority of the building is faced in tough travertine, the shafts of the intermediate attached columns on the side and rear walls, the cella itself and the portion of entablature above it are of tufa stone, and the podium core is concrete.

The **Temple of Mars Ultor, Rome** (14–2 B.C.) (pp. 182B, 190), in the Forum of Augustus, was dedicated to Mars the Avenger by Augustus in fulfilment of his vow to avenge the death of Caesar. It was one of the largest and finest of temples; from the artistic point of view, Roman architecture reached its climax in Augustan times, though the great constructional achievements had then barely commenced. Quite a little of the temple survives. Apart from its being attached to the forum wall, it was peripteral and had Corinthian columns 58 ft high (p. 246D). The walls were of peperino stone, faced with thin slabs of Luna marble, tied back at intervals up the height by solid marble bonding courses, whilst for the podium there were upright large facing slabs of marble about a foot thick. The cella, nearly square, had internal columns and pilasters (p. 246C), and an apsidal recess—one of the earliest instances of a feature afterwards adopted in Early Christian churches. It stood in front of the Quirinal Hill in a peribolus surrounded by a wall some 100 ft high, of peperino stone and ornamented with niches for statues (p. 190A).

The **Temple of Concord, Rome** (7 B.C.–A.D. 10) (pp. 182B, 171A), had a very large cella, unusual in being wider than deep—148 ft × 82 ft—due to its cramped position against the base of the Capitol Hill. Its deep hexastyle prostyle porch occupied the centre of one of the longer sides, and the whole stood on a platform about 20 ft above the roadway. The cornice of this temple affords one of the earliest instances in Rome of the use of 'modillions' or scrolled consoles, which under the Empire became an orthodox part of the Corinthian entablature (cf. p. 191).

The **Temple of Castor and Pollux, Rome** (7 B.C.–A.D. 6) (pp. 182B, 191) had been dedicated in 482 B.C. to the twin gods in gratitude for their aid at the battle of Lake Regillus in 496 B.C. This peripteral temple had an octastyle portico on a raised podium, 22 ft high, faced with Pentelic marble and filled in solid except for vaulted small chambers below the side intercolumniations which served as strong-rooms for storing the temple treasure and for testing weights and measures. The three existing columns of Pentelic marble are 48 ft 5 ins high and have unique Corinthian capitals in which the central volutes intertwine, and between these and the angle volutes rises a tendril from which foliage is carried along the abacus (p. 191D). The entablature, 12 ft 6½ ins high, has an architrave with carved mouldings, a plain frieze, and a cornice enriched with modillions, dentils and cymatium, and lion heads throw off rain-water. The angle (p. 191C) shows a clever arrangement of ornamental features.

The **Maison Carrée, Nîmes** (16 B.C.) (p. 190E–G) is the best-preserved Roman temple in existence. It is raised on a podium 12 ft high, with steps only on the entrance façade, and it is pseudo-peripteral prostyle hexastyle, with Corinthian columns supporting a rich entablature, affording a further early instance of a modillioned cornice.

The **Temple of Diana, Nîmes** (c. A.D. 130) (p. 192), is a misnomer for a grand staircase hall which dignified the approach to a baths establishment at a higher level. The walls of the hall have internal columns, enframing niches, with capitals that can be interpreted either as Corinthian or Composite, and an entablature from which springs a stone-ribbed barrel vault, the thrust of which is counteracted by continuous vaults over the side aisles. Above the vaults was a solid, pitched roof covered with stone slates (p. 192J). In these arrangements, the building was prob-ably a prototype of the vaulting of many southern French Romanesque churches (p. 340).

The **Temple of Vespasian, Rome** (A.D. 94) (pp. 165M, T, 171A, 182B), erected by Domitian, beside the Temple of Concord, had a prostyle hexastyle Corinthian portico, of which only three columns remain, and portion of an ornate entablature with a heavily sculptured frieze.

The **Temple of Venus and Rome, Rome** (A.D. 123–35) (pp. 182B, 192), of which little remains, was designed for Hadrian by Apollodorus of Damascus, and was raised on a platform about 540 ft by 340 ft, which was entered through gateways in a surrounding colonnade of nearly 200 columns of Egyptian granite and porphyry, which formed a magnificent frame to this imposing temple (p. 192B). The plan was pseudo-dipteral decastyle, and was still more unusual in that it had two cellas with apses placed back to back, and there was a pronaos at each front. The cella walls, which internally had monolithic columns framing niches for statues, were of extra thickness to take the thrust of the semicircular coffered vault, and the two apses for the statues of Venus and Rome had semi-domes which still exist. The plan (p. 192A) gives the usually accepted arrangement of this building. The restoration (p. 192B) shows the peribolus of columns surrounding the temenos, and the temple centrally within, with its Pentelic columns, sculptured pediments, and a great roof, covered with gold-plated bronze tiles, which were stripped off by Pope Honorius (A.D. 625) to cover the basilican church of S. Peter.

The **Temple of Antoninus and Faustina, Rome** (A.D. 141) (pp. 182B, 189D, E, F) is prostyle hexastyle, and has a deep portico, reached by steps between the podium walls, leading into a spacious cella, 57 ft 2 ins wide, with plain external walling without attached columns. The pediment was destroyed and the upper part altered when it was converted into the Church of S. Lorenzo in Miranda in A.D. 1602.

The **Temple of Saturn, Rome** (A.D. 284) (pp. 182B, 189G, H, J) is a pseudo-peripteral prostyle hexastyle example of a debased type, in a commanding position close to the Capitol. The temple is raised on a podium 12 ft 3 ins high and steps lead to the portico of granite columns, 39 ft 4½ ins high, of which only eight remain,

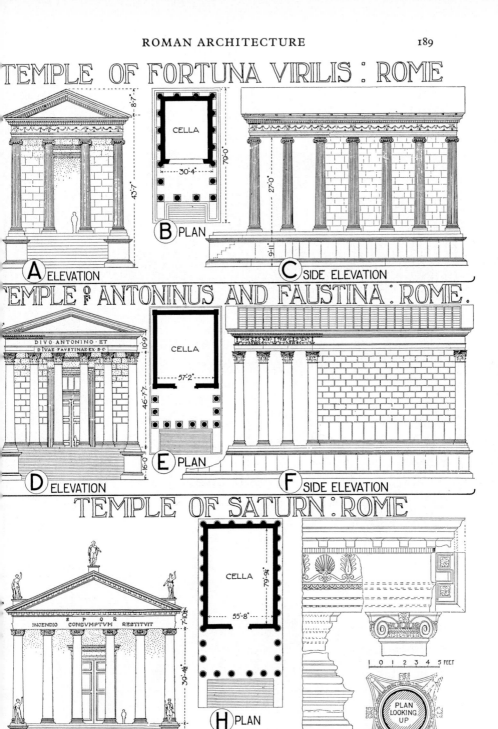

TEMPLE OF FORTUNA VIRILIS : ROME

A ELEVATION

B PLAN
CELLA
30'-4"
79'-0"
8'-7"
43'-7"

C SIDE ELEVATION
27'-0"
9'-11"

TEMPLE OF ANTONINUS AND FAUSTINA : ROME.

DIVO ANTONINO · ET
DIVAE FAVSTINAE EX · S·C·

D ELEVATION
10'-9"
46'-7"
6'-0"

E PLAN
CELLA
57'-2"

F SIDE ELEVATION

TEMPLE OF SATURN : ROME

G ELEVATION
S · P · Q · R
INCENDIO CONSVMPTVM RESTITVIT
7'-10½"
39'-4½"
12'-3"

H PLAN
CELLA
79'-9"
55'-8"

J DETAILS OF ORDER
0 1 2 3 4 5 FEET
PLAN
LOOKING
UP

TEMPLE OF MARS ULTOR : ROME

A TEMPLE AND FORUM OF AUGUSTUS (RESTORED)

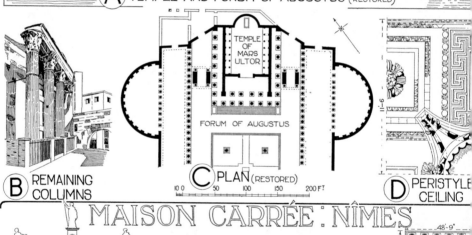

B REMAINING COLUMNS

TEMPLE OF MARS ULTOR

FORUM OF AUGUSTUS

C PLAN (RESTORED)

10 0   50   100   150   200 F!

D PERISTYLE CEILING

MAISON CARRÉE : NÎMES

E ELEVATION

F EXTERIOR FROM S.W.

CELLA

G PLAN

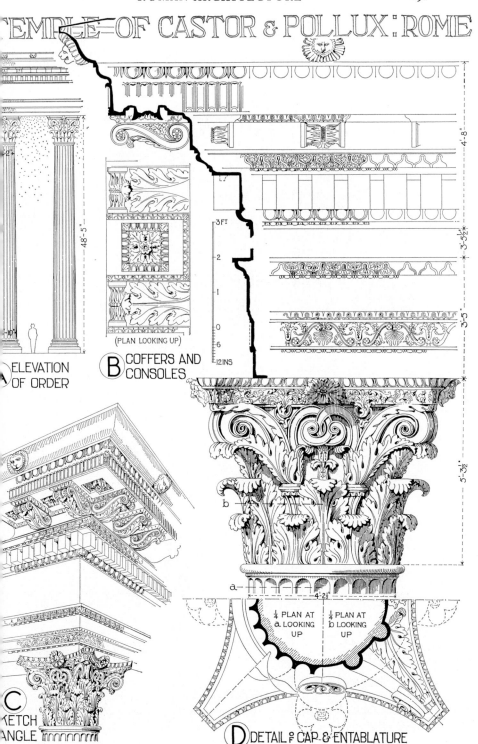

TEMPLE—OF CASTOR & POLLUX: ROME

(A) ELEVATION OF ORDER

(B) COFFERS AND CONSOLES

(PLAN LOOKING UP)

3FT

2

1

0

6

12INS

b

a

4'.2¹⁄₂"

¹⁄₄ PLAN AT
a LOOKING
UP

¹⁄₄ PLAN AT
b LOOKING
UP

(C) SKETCH ANGLE

(D) DETAIL OF CAP & ENTABLATURE

48'.5"

4'.8"

3'.5¹⁄₂"

3'.5

5'.3¹⁄₂"

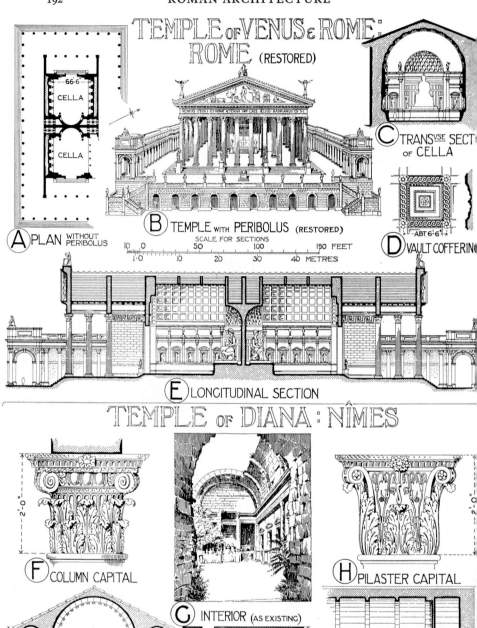

TEMPLE of VENUS & ROME:
ROME (RESTORED)

66·6

CELLA

CELLA

Ⓐ PLAN WITHOUT PERIBOLUS

Ⓑ TEMPLE with PERIBOLUS (RESTORED)

VENERI · FELICI · ET · ROMÆ · ÆTERNÆ · IMP · CÆS · ÆLIUS · HADRIANUS · EX · S · C

SCALE FOR SECTIONS

10   0   50   100   150 FEET

1·0   10   20   30   40 METRES

Ⓒ TRANSᵛˢᵉ SECT of CELLA

ABT 6·6

Ⓓ VAULT COFFERIN

Ⓔ LONGITUDINAL SECTION

TEMPLE of DIANA: NÎMES

2'-0"

Ⓕ COLUMN CAPITAL

Ⓖ INTERIOR (AS EXISTING)

2'-0"

Ⓗ PILASTER CAPITAL

34'-6"

Ⓙ TRANSVERSE SECTION

CELLA

68'-0"

94'-0"

Ⓚ PLAN

Ⓛ LONGITUDINAL SECTION

TEMPLES AT BAALBEK : LEBANON

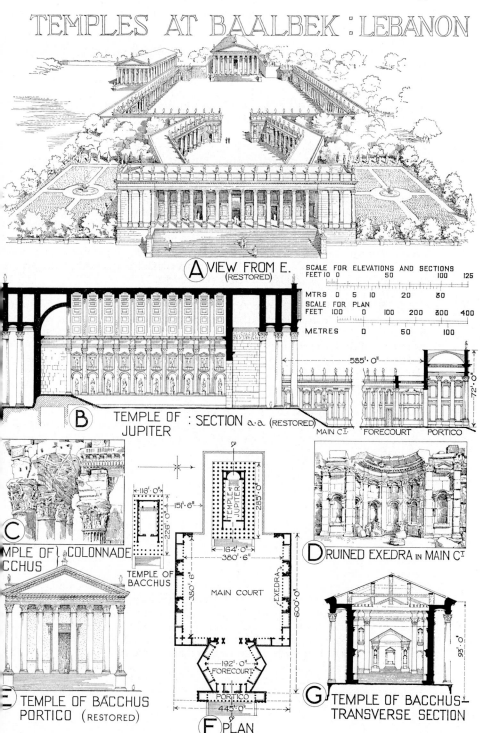

A VIEW FROM E. (RESTORED)

SCALE FOR ELEVATIONS AND SECTIONS
FEET 10 0   50   100   125
MTRS 0   5   10   20   30
SCALE FOR PLAN
FEET 100   0   100   200   300   400
METRES   0   50   100

585'·0"
72'·0"

B TEMPLE OF JUPITER : SECTION a·a (RESTORED)

MAIN CT   FORECOURT   PORTICO

C TEMPLE OF BACCHUS COLONNADE

116'·0"
226'·0"
151'·6"
TEMPLE OF BACCHUS

TEMPLE OF JUPITER
285'·0"
164'·0"
380'·6"

D RUINED EXEDRA IN MAIN CT

380'·6"
MAIN COURT
EXEDRA
600'·0"

192'·0"
FORECOURT
PORTICO
445'·0"

E TEMPLE OF BACCHUS PORTICO (RESTORED)

F PLAN

95'·0"

G TEMPLE OF BACCHUS— TRANSVERSE SECTION

with Ionic capitals having typical angle volutes, but the pediment no longer exists. The architrave mouldings were omitted along the front to admit of the inscription (p. 189G).

The **Temple of Jupiter, Baalbek** (p. 193), was commenced about A.D. 10, the forepart undertaken by Antoninus Pius (A.D. 138–61) and the entrance portico not completed till *c.* A.D. 249. The whole structure, built of hard limestone, forms part of the magnificent temple group which rears its massive form high above the plain, below the hills of Lebanon. It was raised on a high platform, approached by steps which led to a dodecastyle Corinthian portico 'in antis'. Three doorways opened into a hexastyle forecourt with rectangular exedrae on either side, each fronted with four columns. Another three-fold portal led into the main court, 380 ft 6 ins square, with rectangular and semicircular exedrae on three sides, all fronted with columns. The wall enclosing the main court rises 70 ft above the plain, and the substructure of the actual temple is formed of gigantic blocks of stone on the western side. Three of these are known as the Trilithon, and are about 64 ft long, 11 ft 3 ins thick, and 14 ft 9 ins high, and 725 tons in weight. The temple itself, also constructed of large blocks without mortar, faced the main court, and stood on a podium 17 ft above it. It was dipteral decastyle, and the unfluted Corinthian columns, of which only six remain, are about 65 ft high and 7 ft in diameter, carrying an entablature 13 ft 3 ins high. The temple was much damaged by Theodosius the Great (A.D. 379–95), and later by Arabs and Turks.

The so-called **'Temple of Bacchus', Baalbek** (second century A.D.) (p. 193), which stands beside the Temple of Jupiter, is peripteral octastyle, with fifteen columns on each side, and is approached on the east by steps between wing walls. The interior has fluted Corinthian half-columns, supporting a returned entablature, with two tiers of niches between the half-columns. The cella, once thought to have had a coffered stone vault, is now known to have been timber-ceiled, though there was a vaulted sanctuary approached by steps from the cella. Some stone coffering with medallions and busts of gods and emperors still remains in position in the peristyle ceiling.

The **Great Temple of the Sun, Palmyra** (first century A.D.), with its single peristyle of giant Corinthian columns, stood on a raised platform in the centre of a colonnaded court, and was approached from the town through a long street of columns, which ended in a triumphal arch.

The **Temple of Jupiter, Spalato** (A.D. 300), is a small prostyle tetrastyle temple within the palace of Diocletian (p. 231).

CIRCULAR AND POLYGONAL TEMPLES

The Romans sometimes employed the circular form, which was probably derived from the similar temples of the Greeks.

The **Temple of Vesta, Rome** (A.D. 205) (pp. 182B, 195), in the Forum Romanum, was the most sacred shrine in the Imperial city, and here under the custody of the Vestal Virgins the sacred fire was kept alight which signified the home hearth as the centre and source of Roman life and power (p. 170). It was founded in 715 B.C., but was frequently destroyed by fire and repeatedly rebuilt, finally by Septimius Severus in A.D. 205 (p. 195C). According to recent excavations, it seems to have had a podium 10 ft high supporting a circular cella, 30 ft in diameter, surrounded by eighteen Corinthian columns, 17 ft 6 ins high, and fragments of columns have been found with fillets for the insertion of metal screens.

The **Temple of Vesta, Tivoli** (*c.* 80 B.C.) (p. 195) is circular peripteral with a podium supporting a cella 24 ft in diameter, surrounded by a peristyle of eighteen corinthian columns 23 ft 6 ins high. The cella has two windows and a doorway

TEMPLE OF VESTA: ROME (RESTORED)

Ⓐ PLAN

Ⓑ THE ORDER

Ⓒ ELEVATION

18'·6"

21'·6"

TEMPLE OF VESTA : TIVOLI.

LAN

Ⓔ CAPITAL

Ⓕ ELEVATION (RESTORED)

24'·0"

2'·5"

23'·6"

10'·0"

4'·3"

TEMPLE OF VENUS : BAALBEK
(RESTORED)

Ⓖ PLAN

Ⓗ EXTERIOR FROM N.W.

Ⓙ ½ SECTION   ½ ELEVATᴺ

32'·0"

A. Exterior (A.D. 120-24: portico reconstructed from an earlier temple of 25 B.C.)

B. Drawing of interior by Piranesi
The Pantheon, Rome (A.D. 120-24). See opposite page

approached by steps. The columns are nearly 9¾ diameters high, and the capitals, with large and unusual central flower and foliage derived from a crinkly variety of the 'acanthus mollis', are one diameter in height. This early temple, like that of Portunus, Rome, shows Hellenistic influence very strongly.

The **Temple of Portunus, Rome** (pp. 172A, 181A, 251), formerly known as the Temple of Vesta, now S.M. del Sole, is not later than the time of Augustus. It is situated in the Forum Boarium on a circular platform of eight marble steps. It is of Parian marble and is circular peripteral with twenty Corinthian columns, 34 ft 7 ins high and 3 ft 2 ins in diameter and therefore nearly eleven diameters high, which surround a cella 28 ft in diameter. The capitals have acanthus leaves V-shaped in section and with sharp-pointed lobes which generally indicate Greek craftsmanship. The roof was probably of timber rafters covered with bronze tiles.

The **Pantheon, Rome** (pp. 196, 199, 246A, F) is in the most perfect preservation of all ancient buildings in Rome; much has been removed, much has been restored, but the walls and vaulting of this great circular structure with its magnificent colonnaded portico still remain. It belongs to two different periods. Its site was previously a large open place, 8 ft below the present level, on to which faced the south front of the predecessor of the Pantheon, a temple completed in 25 B.C. by Agrippa, son-in-law of Augustus. Agrippa's temple was broad and shallow, 143 ft 6 ins wide × 65 ft deep, and probably of the three-celled Etruscan type. It was severely damaged by fire late in the first century A.D. The Rotunda was erected (A.D. 120–4) by the Emperor Hadrian on the forecourt to the older temple, but at the higher level and in such a manner that the podium of the latter could serve for the foundations of a boldly projecting porch, now facing north instead of south. The portico of Agrippa's temple too was re-used, but made octastyle instead of decastyle, the pediment consequently having a steeper pitch than before. Agrippa's original inscription still appears on the frieze, along with an addition made by Severus and Caracalla, recording a restoration of A.D. 202. The Corinthian octastyle portico, 110 ft wide by 60 ft deep in the centre, forms an imposing entrance to this grandest of all circular temples. The unfluted monolithic columns of Egyptian granite, with Corinthian capitals of white Pentelic marble, are 46 ft 5 ins high, 4 ft 11½ ins in diameter at the base, and 4 ft 3½ ins at the top (p. 199C, D, E). They support an entablature 11 ft high, and a pediment which originally had a bronze relief, as is indicated by the holes for fixing it which still remain (p. 199A). The eight front columns with the others form a triple colonnade, as in Etruscan temples (p. 199B). At the back of this portico are niches in which stood colossal statues of Augustus and Agrippa, and in the thickness of the wall behind these niches stairs lead to the upper parts of the building (p. 199B). The ancient bronze doors which, with the fanlight, were originally plated with gold (p. 159A), still remain, but the bronze plates of the original segmental vaulting were removed in 1626 and recast for the baldachino in S. Peter's (p. 720B) and for the cannon of the Castle of S. Angelo.

The Rotunda is circular, with an internal diameter and height each of 142 ft 6 ins. A massive circular foundation, 14 ft 9 ins deep, supports the wall of brick-faced concrete, which, as we have seen (p. 178), was not solid but comprised an elaborate constructive system, carefully devised to meet every kind of stress and strain to which it was likely to be subjected. Internally, the wall was lined with marble and porphyry. There are eight great recesses, one of which forms the entrance, while the others—three of which are semicircular and four rectangular exedrae, probably contained statues of the gods of the seven planets. Each of the exedrae, except that opposite the entrance, which has a semi-dome, has two monolithic marble columns in antis, 34 ft 10 ins high, with their lower third reeded and their upper portion fluted, and Corinthian capitals supporting an entablature (pp. 196B, 199A). Above these columns are hidden relieving arches. The eight piers have three tiers of constructive niches concealed within them. The marble facings to these piers, as well as the pedimented altars projecting from them, are later additions. The pavement of granite, porphyry and marble was restored in the nineteenth century. The attic, or upper part of the circular wall, was originally faced with marble pilasters (six of the capitals of which are in the British Museum) and panelling of giallo antico, serpentine, and pavonazetto, but in 1747 this was replaced by stucco decoration.

In effect, the Rotunda is a cylinder, three tiers high; the hemispherical dome, fitted inside, springs from the top of the second tier, so that the third stage forms an abutment to its base. The inner surface of the dome is coffered in five ranges, in each of which the mouldings are adjusted or foreshortened with regard to their appearance from below and were originally embellished with central ornaments of stucco. The coffers not only ornament the surface of the dome, but also serve to reduce its weight. The Pantheon is an instance of the Roman skilful variation of the composition of concrete according to the function it has to serve. Researches carried out for the Italian government under the superintendence of Sig. Alberto Terenzio from 1929–34, have shown that the hand-laid courses of the brick-faced walls are alternately of travertine and tufa stone lumps in the lowest tier, and of tufa and brick in the second and third, there being large bonding tiles at intervals. The tufa and brick alternation continues in the lower part of the dome, but turns to a lighter alternation of tufa and pumice above the top of the third range of coffers. The courses everywhere are horizontal. The lighting of the building is effected by one circular unglazed opening, 27 ft in diameter, in the crown of the dome, and it still retains its original bronze cornice (pp. 196B, 199A). This method of lighting produces the most solemn and impressive effect. It is a matter of no small surprise that from this one single source ample light should be thrown round all parts of the building, even when the great bronze doors are not open to admit the Italian sunlight.

Originally, the lower storey of the Pantheon was faced externally with large slabs of gleaming white Pentelic marble and its two upper storeys were coated with stucco. The dome, the lower portion of which is formed in steps, was covered with gilded bronze plates, till they were removed to Constantinople in A.D. 655 and replaced by lead. The octastyle portico contained in its pediment a magnificent bronze relief representing a 'gigantomachy' or battle of the Titans and various deities, while the massive attic behind supported imposing groups of bronze statuary as restored in the Metropolitan Museum of Art, New York.

The Pantheon has survived centuries of change, both temporal and spiritual, and is still devoted to the service of religion, but it is the religion of the one God of Christianity instead of the pantheon of heathen deities. In A.D. 608 it was dedicated by Pope Boniface IV to S. Maria ad Martyres, when many loads of martyrs' bones were brought here from the Catacombs. It is now known as S. Maria Rotonda and is shorn of statuary, marble sheathing, iridescent bronze, and glittering gold which rendered it magnificent in the days of Imperial Rome, but it still compels world-wide admiration by reason of the severe simplicity and unity of the design (p. 196A).

The **Temple of Venus, Baalbek** (A.D. 273) (p. 195) has a cella, 32 ft in diameter, raised on a podium and approached by steps. It is surrounded by Corinthian columns 33 ft 8 ins high, some having five-sided capitals, six of which are well advanced from the cella wall and occupy positions resulting from the division of the circle into seven equal parts (p. 195G). The line of the entablature supported by these six columns is curved inwards between the columns towards the cella wall, forming a decoratively-treated buttressing system to a stone dome, which,

THE PANTHEON : ROME

EYE (UNGLAZED)

4'·0" THICK

2'·6"

BRONZE MOULDING
TO EYE OF DOME

43'·1"

Ⓐ SECTION THRO' PORTICO AND ROTUNDA

24'·11½"

4'·1"

85'·7"

24'·10⅜"

142'·6"

14

Ⓑ PLAN

a

5'·3½"

b

c

4'·3½"

CENTRAL
VOLUTES

1'·9"

ANGLE
VOLUTES

1'·4¼"

CAULICOLUS
AND
ACANTHUS
LEAVES

3'·1½"

a b

b c

PLANS OF CAPITAL
(LOOKING UP) AT a·b & c.

4'·11½"

2'·7½"

4'·11½"

PORTICO ORDER Ⓓ DETAILS OF CAPITAL Ⓔ DETAILS OF PORTICO COLUMNS

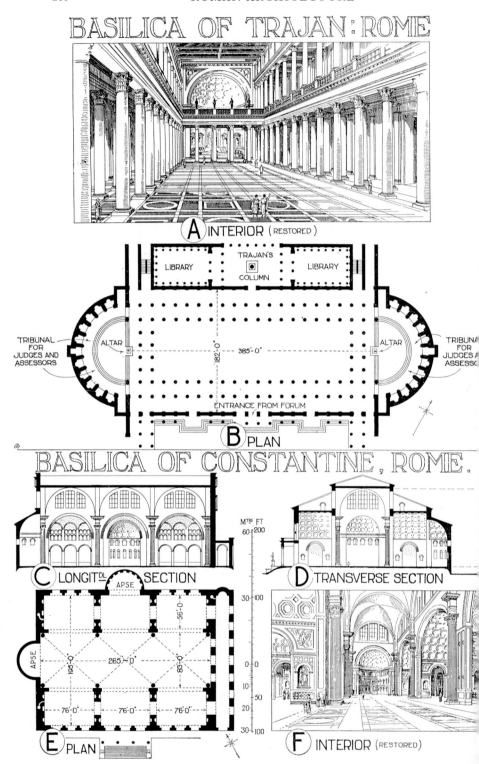

BASILICA OF TRAJAN : ROME

Ⓐ INTERIOR (RESTORED)

PLAN LABELS:
LIBRARY — TRAJAN'S COLUMN — LIBRARY
TRIBUNAL FOR JUDGES AND ASSESSORS — ALTAR — 182'-0" — 385'-0" — ALTAR — TRIBUNAL FOR JUDGES AND ASSESSORS
ENTRANCE FROM FORUM

Ⓑ PLAN

BASILICA OF CONSTANTINE, ROME.

Ⓒ LONGIT^DL SECTION

APSE

Ⓓ TRANSVERSE SECTION

M^TRS FT
60 — 200
30 — 100
0 — 0
10 — 50
20 —
30 — 100

PLAN LABELS:
APSE — 56'-0" — 265'-0" — 83'-0" — 195'-0" — APSE — 76'-0" — 76'-0" — 76'-0"

Ⓔ PLAN

Ⓕ INTERIOR (RESTORED)

however, has fallen. The entrance is placed centrally between two divisions of the circle, and has a column on either side. The external wall of the cella has Corinthian pilasters behind the columns, with semicircular niches for statuary between them; while internally it has superimposed Ionic and Corinthian Orders.

Christian baptisteries were evolved from such little circular buildings (see also the Mausoleum of Diocletian, p. 218), which therefore hold an extremely interesting position in architectural evolution (p. 293).

BASILICAS

Basilicas, which were halls of justice and commercial exchanges, indicate clearly, by their central position, the importance of law and business in Old Rome. These buildings, which are of a pronounced type, are a link between Classic and Christian architecture (p. 258). The usual plan of a basilica was a rectangle twice as long as its width. Either two or four rows of columns forming a 'nave' and two or four aisles ran the whole length, and there were sometimes galleries over the aisles. The nave roof was raised above that of the aisles, so that the windows might be placed in the upper walls between the two levels. The entrance was either at the side or at one end. The tribunal, opposite the entrance, was on a raised dais, generally in a semicircular apse, and sometimes separated from the main building by a screen of columns or by a low balustrade. Ranged round the apse were seats for the assessors, with a raised seat in the centre for the praetor, and in front was the altar where sacrifice was offered before transacting business. The roof was generally of wood, which the Roman knowledge of the principles of the roof truss permitted them to use over very large spaces, when required. Basilicas usually presented a simple and unadorned exterior in comparison with the interior: they were sometimes without walls at the sides.

Trajan's Basilica, Rome (A.D. 98–112) (pp. 182B, 200), by Apollodorus of Damascus, was entered through a portico from Trajan's Forum (p. 200B). Adjoining the Basilica were the Greek and Latin libraries with Trajan's famous Column in an open court between them (p. 200B). It had a central nave (p. 200A), 385 ft long and 87 ft wide, with double aisles, each 23 ft 9 ins wide, and the total internal height was about 120 ft. The columns separating nave and aisles were of red granite from Syene, with white marble Corinthian capitals, and they supported galleries over the side aisles, above which came the clear-story and simple timber roof. At each end were raised tribunals with semicircular apses and sacrificial altars in front.

The **Basilica of Constantine, Rome** (A.D. 310–13) (pp. 182B, 200, 241A), also known as the Basilica of Maxentius or Basilica Nova, adjoins the Forum Romanum. It consists of a central nave, 265 ft long by 83 ft wide, and was crowned at a height of 120 ft by an immense groined vault in three compartments. North and south are aisles also in three compartments, each roofed with a great semicircular vault, 76 ft in span, springing from walls which are at right angles to the nave and pierced by openings, and these walls, steadied by the pressure of the aisle vaults, supported the nave vault. Monolithic columns stood in front of these transverse walls and supported entablatures from which sprang the nave cross-vaults (p. 200F). There were two apses, that on the north being an addition made by the Emperor Constantine, who finished the building, brought almost to completion by his predecessor, Maxentius. Light was introduced in the upper part of the nave over the aisle vaults by lunettes in the wall formed under the intersecting vaulting. The building is similar to the central halls of the thermae (p. 202) and with them, manifestly foreshadows the planning and structural organization of the greatest of Byzantine buildings, S. Sophia, Constantinople (p. 280). It is too, in many respects a prototype of a Gothic structure, in which the thrust and weight of intersecting vaults are collected and brought down on to piers built to receive them. The vaults to the northern aisle remain with their deep coffering, and show a series of embedded brick arches, spanning the vaults from side to side (p. 177J). These were intended to localize cracks which might arise in the concrete. The main vault had similar 'box' ribs of brickwork, and other ribs following the groins, which greatly eased construction. Such ribs were a feature of many vaults of the later Imperial period, but they were reserved for the best work. A portion of the main vault still overhangs in mid-air, showing the extraordinary cohesive quality of concrete.

Other basilicas at Rome were the **Basilica Porcia** (184 B.C.), the first to be built in the city; the **Basilica Julia** (46 B.C.) (p. 182B); and the **Basilica Æmilia** (p. 182B). The Basilica, Pompeii, and those at Trèves, Timgad, and Silchester in England, are other examples, and there can be no doubt that wherever Rome established her power a basilica for the administration of justice formed an important feature in her town-planning.

THERMAE

The Thermae (Gk. *thermos* = hot) or palatial public baths of Imperial Rome, which were probably derived from the Greek gymnasia, portray, even in their ruin, the manners and customs of the pleasure-loving populace, and are as characteristic of Roman civilization as are the amphitheatres. The principal ruins of thermae in Italy are at Rome and Pompeii. The thermae were not only designed for luxurious bathing, but were resorted to for news and gossip, and served, like a modern club, as a rendezvous of social life besides being used for lectures and athletic sports, and indeed entered largely into the daily life of the Imperial City. A small entrance charge of a quadrans ($\frac{1}{2}$ farthing) was sometimes made, but in later times they were opened free to the populace by emperors in search of popularity. The thermae were under the management of the 'aediles'; there were also 'balneatores' to take the entrance money, and janitors to guard the doors, with a staff of attendants, including anointers, manicurists, barbers, shampooers, besides stokers, lamplighters, and hundreds of slaves to make the process of bathing a luxurious relaxation.

The thermae were generally raised on a high platform within an enclosing wall, and underneath were the furnaces and rooms connected with the service of the establishment, which usually consisted of three main parts, as shown in the Thermae of Caracalla (p. 203B) and Diocletian (p. 207D).

(*a*) A main building. In this was a dominant central hall, about which all other rooms were symmetrically arranged, having on its cross axis the three chief apartments of the whole thermae—the 'tepidarium', or warm room, through which was reached the 'calidarium' or hot room, each with heated-water baths; and, on the other side of the central hall, the 'frigidarium', containing an unheated swimming bath. The rest of the rooms were duplicated. On each side there might be a 'laconicum' ('sudatorium'), or dry sweating room; and invariably there were 'apodyteria', or dressing rooms, and 'unctuaria' for oils and ungents, where the 'aliptor' shampooed, oiled, sanded and anointed the bathers and scraped the skin with the 'strigil'. Invariably also, there was a palaestra, for physical exercise, comprising an open peristyle court and attendant surrounding rooms including, sometimes, a bath for athletes. Large heated rooms usually needed a vault, and glass or translucent marble windows, to contain the heat.

(*b*) A large open space. This was a park-like enclosure surrounding the central structure, planted with trees and ornamented with statues and fountains. Part of it was used as a stadium, for foot-racing, with raised seats at the side for spectators.

THERMÆ ੦f CARACALLA ⁚ ROME

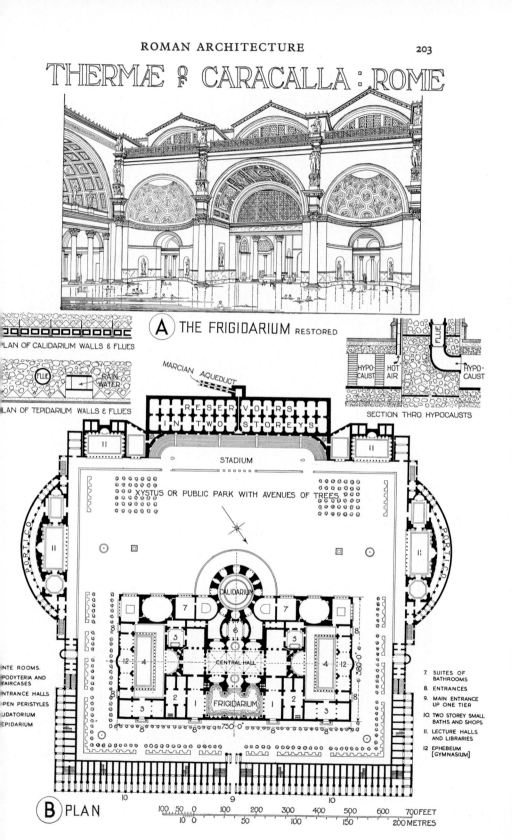

Ⓐ THE FRIGIDARIUM RESTORED

PLAN OF CALIDARIUM WALLS & FLUES

FLUE   RAIN WATER

PLAN OF TEPIDARIUM WALLS & FLUES

MARCIAN AQUEDUCT

HYPO-CAUST   HOT AIR   FLUE   HYPO-CAUST

SECTION THRO HYPOCAUSTS

RESERVOIRS IN TWO STOREYS

STADIUM

XYSTUS OR PUBLIC PARK WITH AVENUES OF TREES

PORTICO   PORTICO

CALIDARIUM

CENTRAL HALL

FRIGIDARIUM

750'.0"

7   SUITES OF BATHROOMS

8   ENTRANCES

9   MAIN ENTRANCE UP ONE TIER

IO. TWO STOREY SMALL BATHS AND SHOPS

II. LECTURE HALLS AND LIBRARIES

I2 EPHEBEUM [GYMNASIUM]

WAITE ROOMS.
APODYTERIA AND STAIRCASES
ENTRANCE HALLS
OPEN PERISTYLES
SUDATORIUM
TEPIDARIUM

Ⓑ PLAN

100 50 0   100   200   300   400   500   600   700 FEET
    10 0   50   100   150   200 METRES

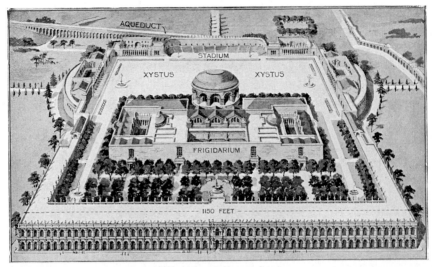

A. View from the north-east

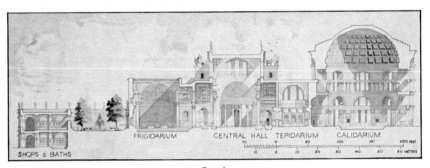

B. Section

c. The Frigidarium   D. The Central Hall

The Thermae of Caracalla, Rome (A.D. 211–217), restored. See opposite page

(c) An outer ring of apartments. These included lecture rooms and exedrae for philosophers, poets, and statesmen; while colonnades, a feature of all open spaces in Rome, served as a protection from the sun. A large reservoir fed by a special aqueduct supplied all the water needed for the bath apartments, fountains, and miscellaneous purposes. Other apartments were let off as shops or accommodated the numerous slaves of the establishment.

The **Thermae of Caracalla, Rome** (A.D. 211–17) (pp. 177K, L, 203, 204), with accommodation for 1,600 bathers, give a splendid idea of the size and magnificence of these establishments; for although now in ruins, the relative positions of tepidarium, calidarium, frigidarium, apodyteria, and other apartments can still be traced. The thermae stood on a platform 20 ft high, measuring over one-fifth of a mile each way, and underneath were the vaulted store-chambers, corridors, furnaces, hypocausts and hot-air ducts for heating the buildings (p. 203). A colonnade on the entrance side screened two storeys forming shops on the ground level and 'slipper' baths on the platform level. The main entrance led to the park-like enclosure, laid out for wrestling and games, around which were grouped halls for dramatic representations and lectures. On the opposite side of the platform and beyond the stadium was the great vaulted reservoir of water supplied by the Marcian aqueduct, carried through leaden pipes to the places needed, and for the hot baths, heated by furnaces in the substructure nearby. The main building block measured 750 ft by 380 ft, thus covering an area of 285,000 sq. ft, i.e. about equal to Westminster Palace, and larger than either the British Museum or the Royal Courts of Justice, London. There were only four doorways on the north-east side, which was exposed to cold winds; but large columned openings to the gardens were a feature of the south-west side. The symmetrical planning of this building on axial lines gave vistas through the various halls and saloons, while exedrae and screens of columns prevented any loss of scale and emphasized the vastness of the building.

The great central hall was the controlling feature of the plan and around it subsidiary halls were grouped (pp. 203B, 204D). It was 183 ft by 79 ft, roofed with an immense semicircular, intersecting vault of concrete, in three compartments 108 ft high, which rested on eight massive piers of masonry, fronted with granite columns 38 ft high and 5 ft 4 ins in diameter, supporting short pieces of entablature (p. 177L). This great hall was lighted by clear-story windows under the intersecting vaults, which rose above the roofs of adjoining halls, as in the Thermae of Diocletian (p. 207A), and the Basilica of Constantine (p. 200C, D, F). The calidarium had a dome similar to that of the Pantheon, and special attention was given to heating this apartment by wall flues (p. 203). The frigidarium was probably open to the sky, and this open-air swimming-bath formed a welcome retreat during the hot and sultry months in the Imperial City (pp. 203A, 204C). The interior, unlike the exterior, was evidently elaborately decorated, in marked contrast to Greek methods. Pavements were formed of bright-coloured mosaics in geometrical patterns or with figures of athletes; the lower parts of the concrete walls were sheathed with many-coloured marbles, and the upper parts with painted and modelled stucco; the great columns under the vault springers were of granite, porphyry, giallo antico, alabaster or other rare marbles. Various coloured marble columns were used constructively to support the upper balconies and peristyle roofs, and decoratively to form frames for the superimposed niches in the walls. The great vaults were also richly ornamented with coffering, modelled and painted stucco, or coloured glass mosaic.

These magnificent halls sheltered some of the finest sculpture of antiquity, which was brought from Greece or executed by Greek artists in Rome. During the excavation of the thermae in the Renaissance period many of these masterpieces of art were removed to the Vatican and other museums in Rome, whence later some were carried off to the museums of Europe. Additional interest was given to interiors by the perpetual streams of running water which, issuing from the mouths of lions sculptured in marble or wrought in brightly polished silver, fell into marble basins and produced a delicious coolness in hot, sultry weather. The exteriors of these great thermae appear to have been treated very plainly in stucco, except on the side open to the main gardens, where they were more elaborate.

The **Thermae of Agrippa, Rome** (c. 20 B.C.), which were the earliest, have disappeared, and such fragments as remain belong to later restorations. The **Thermae of Trajan** were still partly standing till A.D. 1795.

The **Thermae of Titus, Rome** (A.D. 80), stood on a great platform, partly over the foundations of Nero's Golden House on the Esquiline Hill, and when excavated about A.D. 1500 many remarkable frescoes (p. 249B) were discovered, which had considerable influence on the painting of that period; and some of the finest statues of antiquity, such as the Laocoon group, found their way into the art galleries of Europe.

The **Thermae of Diocletian, Rome** (A.D. 302) (p. 207), which accommodated over 3,000 bathers, resembled the Baths of Caracalla in their general distribution (p. 207D). The great central hall, 200 ft by 80 ft and 90 ft high, has the original cross vaulting of concrete (p. 177M), springing from eight monolithic columns of Egyptian granite, 50 ft high and 5 ft in diameter, with Composite capitals of white marble, supporting an ornamental entablature (p. 207A). This building is of special interest, first because it gives the general appearance of these great halls, and secondly because Michelangelo converted it in 1563 into the Church of S.Maria degli Angeli (pp. 207A, D, 714). A choir was added on one side by Vanvitelli (A.D. 1749), which converted the nave into a transept. The restorations of the frigidarium (p. 207B) and the ephebeum (p. 207H) give a good idea of the sumptuous character of the building.

The unbounded licence of the public baths, which were resorted to for all sorts of dissipation, brought them under the ban of the Early Christians, who held that bathing might be practised for cleanliness, but not for pleasure. Then in the fifth century the thermae fell further into disuse and decay, owing to the destruction of aqueducts by the Huns, and also to the decrease of the population. Later they served as quarries for Mediaeval and Renaissance builders.

The **Balneum** or small private bath was very usual in Roman palaces (p. 231D) and houses, and under the Republic gave its name to public baths, which were simpler in character than the later thermae of the Empire, in which bathing became secondary to luxury and entertainment. The **Stabian Baths, Pompeii** (c. 120 B.C.) and the **Forum Baths, Pompeii** (c. 80 B.C.), are on the lines of these small public baths.

Wherever the Romans settled they built thermae for the people, and thus at that notable Roman city of Timgad, North Africa, there are the ruins of no less than eleven of these sumptuous thermal establishments. The **Roman Thermae, Bath** (England), the 'Aquae Solis' of the Romans, are the most remarkable in existence, where the hot water still gushes up and flows through the massive leaden conduit into the great swimming-bath. The Romans also used slipper baths, many of which were beautifully carved (p. 250E, G).

The **Minerva Medica, Rome** (c. A.D. 260) (p. 285A, B), is now generally regarded as having been a nymphaeum in the sumptuous Licinian gardens, since numerous other remains of important garden buildings have been found in the neighbourhood. The absence of a hypocaust and of flue tiles precludes it having

THERMÆ OF DIOCLETIAN : ROME

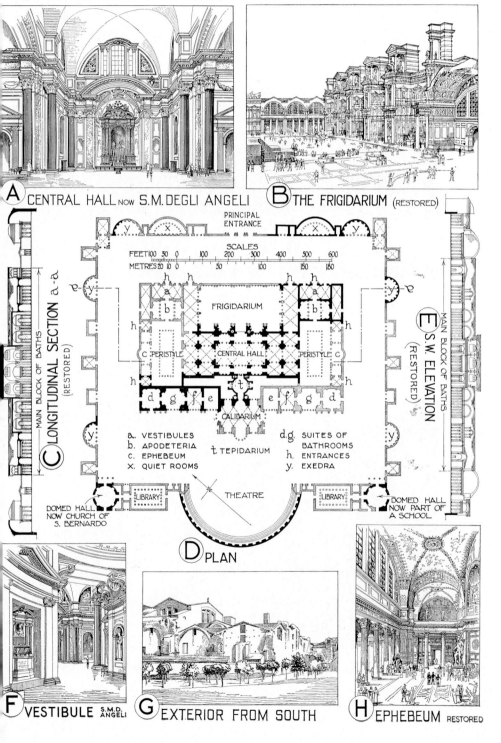

A CENTRAL HALL NOW S.M. DEGLI ANGELI

B THE FRIGIDARIUM (RESTORED)

C LONGITUDINAL SECTION a-a (RESTORED)

MAIN BLOCK OF BATHS

E S.W. ELEVATION (RESTORED)

MAIN BLOCK OF BATHS

PRINCIPAL ENTRANCE

SCALES

FEET 100 50 0 100 200 300 400 500 600
METRES 20 10 0 50 100 150 180

FRIGIDARIUM

PERISTYLE   CENTRAL HALL   PERISTYLE

CALIDARIUM

a. VESTIBULES
b. APODETERIA
c. EPHEBEUM
x. QUIET ROOMS

t. TEPIDARIUM

d.g. SUITES OF BATHROOMS
h. ENTRANCES
y. EXEDRA

LIBRARY   THEATRE   LIBRARY

DOMED HALL NOW CHURCH OF S. BERNARDO

DOMED HALL NOW PART OF A SCHOOL

D PLAN

F VESTIBULE S.M.D. ANGELI

G EXTERIOR FROM SOUTH

H EPHEBEUM RESTORED

A. Portico of Octavia (re-erected by Augustus, 27 B.C.–A.D. 14) and
Theatre of Marcellus (23–13 B.C.), Rome (restored).
See pp. 209, 225

B. Roman Theatre, Ostia, near Rome (restored).
(c. A.D. 10: enlarged c. 193–217). See p. 210

served for heated baths of any kind. It is decagonal on plan, 80 ft in diameter, with semicircular niches on nine sides and the entrance on the tenth. The niches are both decorative and constructional. They are reversed compared with those in the walls of the Pantheon (p. 199B), yet they serve, as there, to give stability to the structure. In the angles between them there are spur buttresses which rise up the angles of the building to stiffen an upper tier, in which there is a range of large windows to give light and air to the growing plants, assisted by other windows at the back of a pair of niches on either side. The buttresses proved too weak to retain the concrete dome, despite the aid given by a heavy, stepped haunch rising around the base of the dome in the usual Roman fashion, and almost at once, the building was strengthened on the rear with two tremendous buttresses. These again proved insufficient, and in the fourth century, exedrae were added on both flanks, decorative in appearance but really to give added strength to the too-frail supports. The dome, which bears a remarkable resemblance to S. Vitale, Ravenna (p. 280), is particularly interesting because here roughly formed 'pendentives' are employed to set its circular rim upon the decagonal base (p. 177N), a device further developed by the Byzantines. In the dome are embedded box ribs, laced together by tile horizontal courses, running upwards towards the crown. Such box ribs have been noted at the Basilica of Constantine (p. 201): they first appear in Roman work in barrel vaults at the Colosseum (A.D. 70–82), in groined vaults by the end of the first century and in domes in early second century A.D. Tile ribs made vaults tougher, lighter, and easier to build. Although this garden building would be unimportant to the Romans, it marks a definite stage towards the more lightly poised constructional system of the Byzantines, and the evolution of the dome.

THEATRES

Roman theatres were often adapted from the Greek to suit the Roman drama, and for this the auditorium, with its tiers of seats one above the other, was restricted to a semicircle (p. 145). The central area at the ground level, which in Greek theatres was occupied by the chorus, became part of the auditorium and was assigned to senators and other dignitaries. The stage increased in importance and was raised and brought into immediate connection with the auditorium. Roman theatres were not only hollowed out of a hill-side, but they were also built up by means of concrete vaulting, supporting tiers of seats, under which were the connecting corridors used for retreat in case of sudden showers.

The **Theatre, Orange** (*c.* A.D. 50) (p. 145D, E, F, G), in the south of France, is in an unusual state of preservation, and here the auditorium, which holds 7,000 spectators, is partly constructed and partly hollowed out of the hill-side. It is 340 ft in diameter between the enclosing walls, and has stairways on either side of the various levels. The stage was 203 ft wide by 45 ft deep, and is enclosed by return walls at right angles to the wall at the back of the stage. The great wall of the outer façade, 324 ft long by 116 ft high, is ornamented with wall arcading, and there still remain the two tiers of corbel stones pierced with holes for the seating of towering masts, from the top of which, chains extended to support the front of a wooden sloping awning over the stage. An enormous portico, which once extended across the full width of the façade, has entirely disappeared.

The **Theatre of Marcellus, Rome** (23–13 B.C.) (p. 208A), was built up on a level site, and therefore the seats of the auditorium were supported not on a hill-side, but, like those of the Colosseum, on radiating walls and concrete vaulting. It is the only ancient theatre now in Rome, and, though in a ruinous condition, portions of its auditorium still remain, consisting of two tiers of arcading, with superimposed Doric and Ionic Orders. The third tier has disappeared.

The **Odeion of Herodes Atticus, Athens** (A.D. 161) (pp. 103B, 104C), connected by an arcade with the Theatre of Dionysus (p. 147), is Roman in plan, partly hewn out of the Acropolis rock and partly constructed, and its marble seats accommodated 6,000 people; while cedar wood, found buried on the site, would suggest that there may have been a roof to the stage. The **'Small Theatre',** **Pompeii** (80 B.C.) (p. 145C) was definitely a roofed building, for an audience of about 1,500.

The **Theatre, Ostia** (p. 208B), the large theatre at Pompeii, as well as those at Taormina and Syracuse in Sicily, at Fiesole near Florence, at Timgad and Sabratha in North Africa, and Aspendus in Asia Minor, are other Roman examples.

The **Roman Theatre, Verulamium** (second century A.D.), near S. Albans, is the only known Roman theatre in England.

AMPHITHEATRES

Amphitheatres, unknown to the Greeks, are characteristically Roman buildings found in every important settlement and are good exponents of the character and life of the Romans, who preferred displays of mortal combats, considered to be a good training for a nation of warriors, to the tame mimicry of the stage. Gladiatorial combats had their origin in funeral religious rites connected with human sacrifices to the *manes* of the dead. The elliptical amphitheatre, with its rising tiers of seats, may be regarded as a compound of two theatres, stage to stage, thus making a continuous auditorium round a central arena. In addition to their normal purposes, they were also used for naval exhibitions, and water-pipes for flooding some of the arenas still exist. Spanish bull-rings of to-day give some idea of the arrangement and uses of Roman amphitheatres. The arena, a Latin word meaning sand or beach, was so called because of the sand with which it was strewn to absorb the blood of the combatants.

The **Colosseum, Rome** (pp. 166, 211, 212), also known as the Flavian Amphitheatre, was commenced by Vespasian (A.D. 70) and completed by Domitian (A.D. 82). It is situated in the level valley between the Esquiline and Caelian Hills, and in plan it is a vast ellipse, 620 ft by 513 ft, with eighty external arcaded openings on each storey, those on the ground floor forming entrances from which the various tiers of seats were reached (p. 212). The arena proper is an oval 287 ft by 180 ft surrounded by a wall 15 ft high, behind which was the podium, with the Imperial throne and seats for the Pontifex Maximus, Vestal Virgins, Senators, Praetors and other officers of state. Behind the podium rose the auditorium seats for some 50,000 spectators, with corridors and stairs beneath, while dens for the wild beasts were under the lowest tier, on a level with the arena (pp. 166B, 211B). The seats, which have been removed, were in four main divisions, the two lower or grand tiers for those of equestrian rank and for Roman citizens, separated from the third tier by a high encircling wall, above which was the top range and colonnade, all of which were reached by stairs from the surrounding corridors placed at intervals between radiating walls (p. 166B). The construction is notable for the skilful combination of materials, according to the purpose to which they were applied. The component parts of the concrete vary thus: (i) lava was used for solid foundations, (ii) tufa and brick for the supporting walls, (iii) pumice stone for the vaults to reduce their weight (p. 212B). Travertine blocks, set without mortar and held together with metal cramps, were used in the façade, while marble was employed for the columns, seats, and ornament. The supporting mass has been calculated to occupy as much as one-sixth of the whole area of the building, and consists of wedge-shaped piers, radiating inwards and supporting concrete vaults sloping downwards towards the centre, all producing a structure of great

A. The Colosseum, Rome: exterior (restored). See opposite page

B. The Colosseum, Rome: interior (restored)

THE COLOSSEUM : ROME

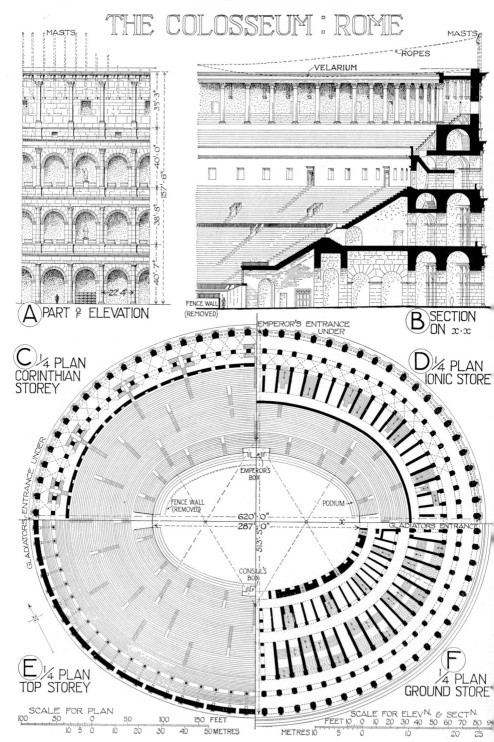

MASTS

MASTS

ROPES

VELARIUM

38' 3"

40' 0"

157' 6"

38' 8"

40' 7"

22' 4"

FENCE WALL
(REMOVED)

Ⓐ PART OF ELEVATION

Ⓑ SECTION
ON x·x

EMPEROR'S ENTRANCE
UNDER

Ⓒ ¼ PLAN
CORINTHIAN
STOREY

Ⓓ ¼ PLAN
IONIC STOREY

GLADIATORS ENTRANCE UNDER

EMPEROR'S
BOX

FENCE WALL
(REMOVED)

PODIUM

620' 0"

287' 0"

513' 5"

x

GLADIATORS ENTRANCE

CONSUL'S
BOX

Ⓔ ¼ PLAN
TOP STOREY

Ⓕ ¼ PLAN
GROUND STOREY

SCALE FOR PLAN
100   50   0   50   100   150 FEET
10 5 0   10   20   30   40   50 METRES

SCALE FOR ELEVN. & SECTN.
FEET 10 0 10 20 30 40 50 60 70 80 90
METRES 10   5   0   10   20   25

inherent strength and consequently difficult to destroy—a fact well expressed by the line:

> When falls the Colosseum, Rome shall fall.

The external façade, 157 ft 6 ins high, is divided into four storeys, the lower of which are pierced with arches, and have attached three-quarter-columns of quasi-Doric, Ionic, and Corinthian Orders, while the top storey has Corinthian pilasters, with corbels between to support the masts of the velarium which was drawn across the auditorium (pp. 211, 212A, B).

Some of the special architectural features of this wonderful building are: (i) the massive piers which support the three tiers of apparently countless arcades which encircle the exterior and form covered ambulatories; (ii) the decorative use of the Classic Orders of architecture, which are superimposed and are thus in strong contrast to the Greek use of single Orders; (iii) the grand sweeping lines of the unbroken entablatures round the building (p. 211A). The proportions of the attached columns, which all have the same diameter, are unusual, for the Doric columns are about $9\frac{1}{3}$ diameters high, and the Ionic and Corinthian about $8\frac{3}{4}$ diameters.

The Colosseum is of a type unique among ancient buildings. The structural problems involved were engineering in character, and all the more so because the Romans built up the whole gigantic edifice without that extraneous support which the Greeks secured in theatre building, by scooping the auditorium out of the earth. Here, then, is an entirely new departure made possible by the invention and use of concrete, employed not only in corridors and cells, even in chambers under the arena itself, but also in multitudes of raking vaults, which formed the almost indestructible foundations of each of the four tiers of seats reared one above the other in a great ellipse, to the crowning colonnade. Greek architecture had been simple in appearance and self-evident in design, with columns standing on a crepidoma below and supporting an entablature above. Roman architecture, especially as carried out first in the Theatre of Marcellus and afterwards in numerous amphitheatres, became complex in appearance and hidden in design; for not only were columns placed in front of piers, but there were columns above columns, entablatures above entablatures, and arches above arches, while radiating vaults round the whole building were hidden supports to the auditorium seats. In the Greek theatres the steps which radiated at regular intervals to the various ranges of seats were slabs of marble between the seats; in a Roman amphitheatre the stairs emerged at intervals from the vaulted supporting corridors which swept round the building. Stupendous in proportions, complex in structure, and yet consistent in the constant repetition of the external design, the Colosseum compels alike awe and admiration of a nation who conceived and carried to completion such an immense undertaking to serve popular amusements. The Colosseum is still magnificent, even in its ruin, and recalls the gladiatorial contests, the naval displays, and the martyrdom of Christians which took place within its giant walls before it became a Mediaeval fortress or was plundered to provide building materials for Renaissance palaces and churches.

The **Amphitheatre, Verona** (A.D. 290) (p. 214), is in unusually good preservation, and nearly all the stone seats are intact, although only four complete bays of the upper part of the external wall are standing.

The **Amphitheatre, Pompeii** (70 B.C.), the earliest to be built, and those at Pozzuoli, Capua, Syracuse, Pola, Nîmes, Arles, and El Djem (near Carthage), are other examples, besides the remains known as the 'Maumbury Rings' at Dorchester, and the Amphitheatre at Caerleon (Monmouth).

A. The Amphitheatre, Verona
(The surviving four bays of the external façade are seen on the left)

B. The Amphitheatre, Verona: the arena and auditorium
(c. A.D. 290). See p. 213

CIRCUSES

The Roman circus, for horse and chariot racing, was derived from the Greek hippodrome, and attained great magnificence. (For foot-racing and athletic games there was the stadium, based upon the Greek stadium, usually included with the amenities of the thermae rather than appearing as a separate building.) Chariot racing was enormously popular, and vast sums were spent upon the training and selection of men and horses. Famous charioteers were the idols of the day, and though risking life and limb, reaped rich rewards. Four-horsed chariots were usual, but races were varied by using two, three, or sometimes six, eight or ten horses, and by equestrian displays and acrobatic riding. The teams of the four factions or 'stables' of Rome competed against one another. Heavy betting gave intensity to the popular interest, and brought its attendant evils. Until a permanent amphitheatre had been provided in Rome, in the late first century B.C., the hippodrome was used too for the brutal contests of man and beast which then were relegated there.

The **Circus Maximus, Rome** (p. 216B, C, D), so called from its great size, was sited in the valley between the Aventine and Palatine Hills, but has long since disappeared. It was the oldest in Rome and underwent many improvements and restorations. Julius Caesar, from 46 B.C., followed by Augustus, first gave it the monumental proportions for which it is so famous, and later emperors, Claudius, Nero, Titus and Trajan, added their enrichments of costly marbles, columns and statues. From Heliopolis, Egypt, came the obelisk of Rameses II, now standing in the Piazza del Popolo, brought by Augustus to occupy the centre of the spina or dividing wall, which ran down the middle of the arena in a slightly oblique direction, so that the chariots might have more room at the starting end. The restored view (p. 216D), shows its probable appearance in the fourth century A.D. It measured 2,000 ft long and 650 ft wide, and seated 255,000 spectators. The twelve 'carceres' held the contestant chariots and horses, and each race required seven laps of the spina, equal to a distance of about 2¼ miles. In the time of Caligula, the number of races held in one day of the games was doubled, from twelve to twenty-four. When a race was in progress, the laps were signalled by moving seven large wooden eggs on the spina. Despite the twelve carceres, it seems that not more than four chariot teams raced at a time. The bas-relief gives a good idea of a racing quadriga (p. 216C) and the relief on a lamp shows the triumphant victor in a race (p. 216B). Around the track rose the triple banks of seats, supported on concrete vaults: outside, the circus showed three ranges of marble arcades like those of the Colosseum, under which thronged the excited crowds, importuned by wine-sellers, caterers, tipsters and cheap-jacks who plied their trades there. The last race to take place in the Circus was in A.D. 549.

The **Circus of Maxentius, Rome** (A.D. 311) (p. 216A), of which vestiges still remain, consisted of a long, open, circular-ended arena with a 'spina' on its longer axis, and was surrounded by tiers of marble seats, supported on raking vaults. At one end of the arena were the 'carceres' or stalls for horses and chariots, with a central processional entrance and two side entrances, and at the opposite end was the 'Porta Triumphalis', and the whole was enclosed by a concrete wall.

The circuses of Flaminius and Nero were other examples in the Imperial City.

TOMBS

The Romans practised both forms of burial, cremation and interment, and thus sarcophagi for the body and urns for the ashes are sometimes found in the same tomb chamber. During the first three centuries of the Christian era, the body of

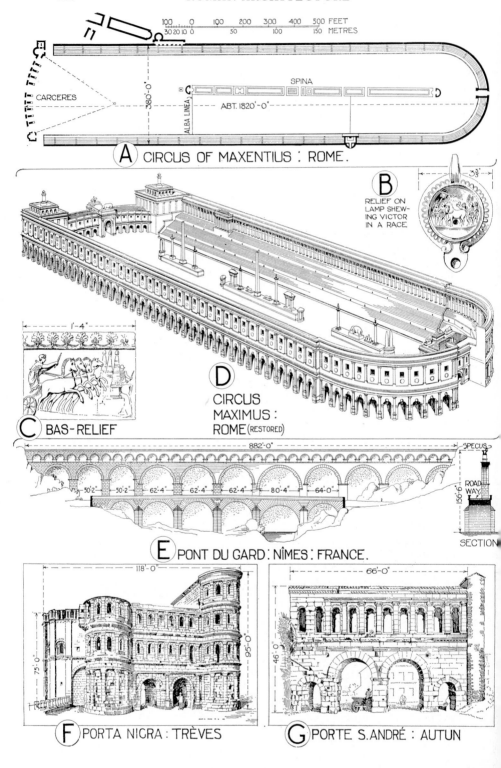

100 0   100   200   300   400   500 FEET
30 20 10 0   50   100   150 METRES

CARCERES

380'-0"

SPINA

ALBA LINEA

ABT. 1820'-0"

C   D

A CIRCUS OF MAXENTIUS : ROME.

B RELIEF ON LAMP SHEW-ING VICTOR IN A RACE

1'-4"

D CIRCUS MAXIMUS : ROME (RESTORED)

C BAS-RELIEF

882'-0"

5PECUS

50'2" 50'2" 62'4" 62'4" 62'4" 80'4" 64'0"

ROAD WAY

156'-6"

SECTION

E PONT DU GARD : NÎMES : FRANCE.

118'-0"

75'-0"

95'-0"

F PORTA NIGRA : TRÈVES

66'-0"

46'-0"

G PORTE S.ANDRÉ : AUTUN

nearly every Emperor was burnt on a magnificent pyre, from which an eagle was released to symbolize his escaping soul. In the second century, when cremation became less usual, wealthy citizens were embalmed on their death and placed in massive and costly sarcophagi. Roman law forbade burial inside city confines, and tombs lined the main roads radiating from the town gates, as along the Via Appia, Rome, or the Street of the Tombs, Pompeii, with its fine Gate of Herculaneum or again, at Ostia.

The Romans had five classes of burial places: Coemeteria, Monumental tombs, Pyramidal tombs, Temple-shaped tombs, and Sculptured memorials of miscellaneous kinds.

1. *Coemeteria* or subterranean vaults contained both columbaria and loculi. 'Columbaria' (p. 220Q), so named because of their resemblance to pigeon-holes, were niches formed in the rock to receive a vase containing the ashes of the deceased, and with the name inscribed thereon. 'Loculi' or recesses for corpses were sealed with a front slab inscribed with the name, as in the tomb of the Gens Cornelia, Rome. Sarcophagi, often beautifully carved with figures and festoons, and surmounted by lids like roofs terminating in scrolls, were also placed in the vaults (p. 220P). Later these vaults were called Catacombs from 'ad Catacumbas', the place-name of a district in Rome, where many are found.

2. *Monumental tombs* are the most typical Roman class, descended from the Etruscan tumuli, with their embracing ring of stones or rock. They consisted of large cylindrical blocks, often on a quadrangular podium, topped with a conical crown of earth or stone.

The **Tomb of Caecilia Metella, Rome** (*c.* 20 B.C.) (p. 220J), is a landmark on the Via Appia. It has a podium, 100 ft square, supporting a circular mass, 94 ft in diameter, at the core of which was the tomb chamber containing the sarcophagus, now in the cortile of the Farnese Palace, Rome. The exterior, faced with travertine, was crowned by an entablature, the frieze of which is carved with ox-skulls and festoons, above which there was probably a conical earthen mound.

The **Mausoleum of Augustus, Rome** (*c.* 25 B.C.) (p. 237B), erected for himself and his heirs, was a huge cylinder, 290 ft in diameter, faced in travertine, supporting a mound of earth, 145 ft high from the ground, planted with evergreen trees and surmounted by a bronze effigy of Augustus. The interior was subdivided into tiers of compartments, some of them vaulted, by a complex system of ring and radial concrete walls, all of them finely finished with opus reticulatum facings although all the compartments were filled with earth, except for the sepulchral chamber and the passages leading to it. Behind the façade wall, a series of hemicycle buttresses completed the precautions for retaining and dividing the pressures of the great load of earth. A central pillar cored the system and supported the crowning statue. In the twelfth century the monument was converted into a fortress by the Colonna family; in its later history its collapsed ruins served in turn for a formal garden, a bull ring, a theatre, and a concert hall, the latter removed in 1934

The **Mausoleum of Hadrian, Rome** (*c.* A.D. 135) (pp. 220E, F, G, 237C), one of the most important of these tombs, is now the Castle of S. Angelo. It originally consisted, as shown in the conjectural restoration, of a square podium 285 ft each way and 42 ft high, below a drum-shaped mass, 230 ft in diameter and rising to over 100 ft. There was then a mound of earth, planted with funerary trees, capped by a massive, cylindrical tower, providing a platform, 180 ft from the ground, for a sculptured quadriga. The facing of the structure was Parian marble, and there were marble or gilded bronze equestrian groups at the angles of the podium as well as marble statues around the drum. The monument was surrounded by a bronze railing, adorned with gilt-bronze peacocks. In lateral dimension (300 Roman feet) it accords with the Mausoleum of Augustus, but was in every way a superior design. The barrel-vaulted tomb chamber, in which was the porphyry sarcophagus of Hadrian, was right at the heart of the building, its floor 44 ft above the entrance level and reached by a rising corridor which made a complete circuit of the drum before turning inwards, over the entrance passage, to reach the tomb chamber. There is evidence here again in this monument of structural compartmentation to divide the loads and stresses; the podium portion is entirely made up of narrow, structural chambers, radiating from the drum. The monument has been much despoiled by the Goths and later Vandals, and also much altered, for during the Middle Ages it was converted by the Popes into a fortress, was afterwards used as barracks, and is now a museum.

3. *Pyramidal tombs* were probably due to the introduction of Egyptian ideas after the conquest of Egypt (p. 19). The **Pyramid of Caestius, Rome** (12 B.C.) (p. 220K), is formed of concrete faced externally with white marble, and has a tomb chamber, the vaults and walls of which are decorated with figure paintings.

4. *Temple-shaped tombs* usually consisted of a mortuary chapel, often having a colonnaded portico or peristyle, standing on a podium in which was the sepulchral vault. In the chapel were niches containing statues of deities and portraits or busts of deceased members of the family. When there was no podium, the niches served for the cinerary urns too. Rock-cut tombs, which are numerous in the East, as around Palmyra, Jerusalem, Petra (Syria) and Cyrene (North Africa), often had temple-like façades in one or two storeys, with the sepulchral chamber cut in the rock behind.

The **Tomb of Annia Regilla, Rome** (*c.* A.D. 143) (p. 219A), 26 ft square on plan, had a broad flight of steps on its north side, leading to a mortuary chapel, standing over a podium containing the sepulchral chamber. Both chambers had groined vaults. Externally, it is a fine and well-preserved example of Roman polychrome brickwork, with russet-red bricks for the pilastered order and yellow ochre for the walls between. There are four Corinthian pilasters on the west and south sides, but on the east, the inner two are expressed as hexagonal columns, sunk into wall recesses. Centrally below them is the entrance to the vault. Originally, the podium was covered with a thin coating of stucco, painted brilliant plum-red and with white lines to imitate the very brickwork which lay underneath.

The **Tomb of the Caetennii, Rome,** is the richest among a score or so of chamber tombs recently excavated below the nave floor of the great church of S. Peter, where they had first been sealed from the light of day by its predecessor, Constantine's basilican church of A.D. 330 (p. 261). They date from the second century A.D. up to that time, and many wonderful art treasures have been disclosed, including a very early, Christian mosaic vault. They were closely ranged along a narrow street-way, their walls painted and white-lined to simulate with greater pungency the true brickwork behind. The Caetennii tomb, 17 ft wide and 18 ft deep, had a marble-faced dado below a continuous range of alternating square and semicircular niches, framed with stucco dressings, which held the cinerary urns. Frescoes decorated the lunettes of the groined vault, itself richly ornamented with low-relief stucco panelling, as were the similar vaults of the **Tombs of the Valerii** and **Pancratii** on the Via Latina, Rome (p. 219B, C).

The **Mausoleum of Diocletian, Spalato** (*c.* A.D. 300) (p. 231C, D), standing in Diocletian's palace, is elaborate, as befits an Emperor's tomb. It is octagonal externally, and is raised upon a podium containing the sepulchral chamber. Around it, there is a low peristyle of Corinthian columns. Internally, it is circular, 43 ft 8 ins diameter, with four semicircular and four rectangular recesses, including with the

A. The Tomb of Annia Regilla, near Rome (*c.* A.D. 143). See opposite page

B. Tomb of the Valerii, Via Latina, Rome: stuccoed vault (A.D. first century). See opposite page

C. Tomb of the Pancratii, Via Latina, Rome: stuccoed vault (A.D. second century). See opposite page

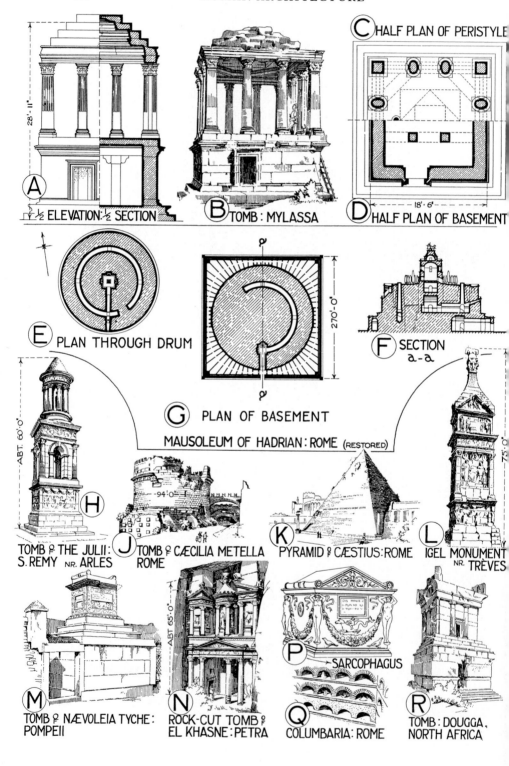

28'-11"

Ⓐ ½ ELEVATION: ½ SECTION

Ⓑ TOMB: MYLASSA

ⒸHALF PLAN OF PERISTYLE

18'-6'

Ⓓ HALF PLAN OF BASEMENT

Ⓔ PLAN THROUGH DRUM

270'-0'

Ⓕ SECTION a-a

Ⓖ PLAN OF BASEMENT

MAUSOLEUM OF HADRIAN: ROME (RESTORED)

ABT. 60'-0'

Ⓗ TOMB OF THE JULII: S. REMY NR. ARLES

-94'-0'

Ⓙ TOMB OF CÆCILIA METELLA ROME

Ⓚ PYRAMID OF CÆSTIUS: ROME

75'-0'

Ⓛ IGEL MONUMENT NR. TRÈVES

Ⓜ TOMB OF NÆVOLEIA TYCHE: POMPEII

ABT. 65'-0'

Ⓝ ROCK-CUT TOMB OF EL KHASNE: PETRA

DIS MANIS

SARCOPHAGUS

Ⓟ

Ⓠ COLUMBARIA: ROME

Ⓡ TOMB: DOUGGA, NORTH AFRICA

latter the one containing the entrance. Between the recesses stand eight granite Corinthian columns, carrying an entablature broken back around them. Above them are eight more columns, much smaller and alternately Corinthian and Composite. But the remarkable feature is the hemispherical dome, which is of two contiguous shells of brickwork, each about one foot thick, the inner one being made up entirely of brick arches, arranged fishscale fashion. This dome represents the ultimate achievement in Roman vaulting, presaging Byzantine construction, massive concrete having given way to compact, wide-jointed brickwork, systematically laid through the whole thickness of the vault. Above the brick shells however, light concrete was used to sustain an octagonal, pyramidal roof (p. 231c).

The **Tomb of 'El Khasne', Petra** (*c.* A.D. 120) (p. 220N) is one of the most interesting of all the rock-cut tombs in that district, which number over 750. The façade, 65 ft high, is of a debased type of architecture; the lower storey has a hexastyle Corinthian portico from which central and side doors lead into tomb chambers, while the upper storey also has columns supporting a broken pediment and a central circular structure surmounted by a conical roof and urn.

5. *Sculptured Memorials.* Minor tombs were extremely varied in their forms, but though comparatively small, might be richly ornate outside. Many represented an altar, with a sepulchral chamber contained in a high base; others appeared as semi-domed niches, commemorative arches, pillars or as semicircular benches or walled and paved enclosures.

The **Tomb of Naevoleia Tyche, Pompeii** (p. 220M) is of the altar type, the sepulchral chamber in the base having a large niche opposite the doorway and others elsewhere in the walls. In them, cinerary urns were discovered, as well as upon stone benches at the foot of the side walls. Three of the urns were of glass, protected by lead containers. The marble-faced altar above was raised upon a flight of three marble steps, its front and sides decorated with reliefs, surrounded by borders of acanthus scrolls.

Cenotaphs or memorial monuments to persons buried elsewhere were also occasionally erected, as in the following instances:

The **Tomb of the Julii, S. Rémy** (*c.* 40 B.C.) (p. 220H), in Provence, is a cenotaph, and consists of a high pedestal ornamented with bas-reliefs and supporting engaged Corinthian angle columns with arched openings between. Above is a circular storey with fluted Corinthian columns and entablature, crowned with a conical stone roof.

The **Igel Monument, near Trèves** (A.D. 250) (p. 220L), is of similar design, erected by the Secundini family. It consists of a sculptured podium about 16 ft square, supporting an intermediate stage with an Order of Corinthian pilasters, enclosing a large sculptured panel above which comes an attic surmounted by a sculptured pediment and crowned by a curved pyramidal roof, terminating at a height of 75 ft above the ground.

TRIUMPHAL ARCHES

Monumental arches first occur about 200 B.C., but few now surviving are much earlier than the reign of Augustus. Chief among them are the triumphal arches erected to emperors and generals, commemorating victorious campaigns. Such arches were adorned with appropriate bas-reliefs and usually carried gilt-bronze statuary on an attic storey, the latter having a dedicatory inscription on its face. They had either one or three openings, two of the latter being footways, and the piers were ornamented with Corinthian or Composite pilasters or columns: slightly detached, full columns often were used after the early second century A.D.

The **Arch of Tiberius, Orange** (*c.* 30 B.C.) (p. 226A). In A.D. 25, Tiberius added his inscription to this monument, built before his reign. Triple openings, which appear here, are rare before the second century A.D. The arch is very ornate, with a double attic, and has Corinthian three-quarter columns flanking the central opening and at the outer angles. There also are attached columns at the side, and, remarkably for its early date, the inner pair carries a false arch above an entablature broken back sympathetically to receive it.

The **Arch of Titus, Rome** (A.D. 82) (p. 223), of the single-opening type, commemorates the capture of Jerusalem. On each main face there are attached columns flanking the opening and at the outer angles, and these are the earliest known examples of the fully-developed Roman Composite Order (p. 223G). The soffit of the archway is ornamented with deeply recessed coffers, and a relief in the centre represents the apotheosis of Titus. On one side of the opening is a carved relief of the Emperor in a triumphal car, and on the other is a representation of the spoils taken from the Temple at Jerusalem. The keystones, which project considerably to support the main architrave, are also richly carved and are faced with figures of Roma and Fortuna (p. 223A). The attic storey, with the dedication, was originally surmounted by a bronze quadriga (p. 223F).

The **Arch of Trajan, Ancona** (A.D. 113) (p. 224J) was erected astride a causeway in honour of that emperor, who had made the harbour. It is of marble and is well preserved, although its bronze enrichments have disappeared. It is approached by a flight of steps and has a high podium with an archway 10 ft wide, flanked on both sides by pairs of fluted Corinthian columns on pedestals, supporting an entablature and attic stage for inscriptions. The total height is 61 ft.

The **Arch of Trajan, Beneventum** (A.D. 114) (p. 377D) is one of the best-preserved Roman structures in South Italy; in arrangement it is similar to the arch of Titus, Rome, and like it, has Composite column-capitals. It is of Greek marble; and the profuse bas-reliefs commemorate Trajan's Dacian wars and triumphs.

There are other single arches at Pola (c. 30 B.C.), Rimini (27 B.C.), Aosta (25 B.C.), S. Rémy (c. 25 B.C.) and Susa (7 B.C.). The archways in London at Hyde Park Corner and Constitution Hill are modern examples of the type.

The **Arch of the Goldsmiths, Rome** (A.D. 204) (p. 223H, J, K), erected in honour of Septimius Severus, is not a triumphal arch, nor is it of arched construction, for the opening is spanned by a horizontal entablature; while the workmanship is poor and over-elaborated. It adjoins the Campanile of the Church of S. Giorgio in Velabro.

The **Arch of Septimius Severus, Rome** (A.D. 203) (pp. 171A, 182, 224A–G, 377E), of the triple-arch type, was dedicated to the Emperor and his two sons to commemorate their Parthian victories. It is of white marble, and the three archways rest on piers, in front of which are detached Composite columns on pedestals. The central archway, with a richly coffered semicircular vault, has lateral openings to the side archways. On the summit, all in bronze, were statues of the Emperor and his two sons, Caracalla and Geta, in a six-horse chariot, with soldiers on either side.

The **Arch of Constantine, Rome** (A.D. 312) (p. 224H), built in honour of Constantine's victory over Maxentius, is of fine proportions. It has eight monolithic detached Corinthian columns supporting an entablature returned back to the wall, and on the attic storey was a quadriga. Much of the decorative sculpture was brought from earlier monuments of the time of Trajan, and represents incidents of his reign.

Commemorative arches sometimes were erected on bridges, as at Saintes (A.D. 17), where there were twin passageways, or the Roman bridge at Alcantara (A.D. 105–16) (p. 239).

THE ARCH OF TITUS : ROME

A KEYSTONE

B ELEVATION

SENATVS
POPVLVS QVE ROMANVS
DIVO TITO DIVI VESPASIANI F
VESPASIANO AVGVSTO

3'.6½"

47'.4"

17'.9"

43'.8"
PLAN

C SECTION

15'.6"

FT 50   15 MTS
40
30   10
20
5
10
10
5
0   0

D FIGURE IN SPANDREL

E FIGURE IN SPANDREL

F ARCH (RESTORED)

SENATVS
POPVLVS QVE ROMANVS
DIVO TITO DIVIVESPASIANI
VESPASIANO   AVGVSTO

G DETAIL OF ORDER

2'.1"
1'.7"
1'.7"
2'.6"

RCH OF GOLDSMITHS : ROME

ARCH OF JANUS : ROME

H EXTERIOR FROM S.W.

J ELEVATION (RESTORED)

21'.3"

10'.5"

K PLAN

6'.10"

L THE CROSS VAULT

M EXTERIOR

ARCH OF SEPTIMIUS SEVERUS : ROME

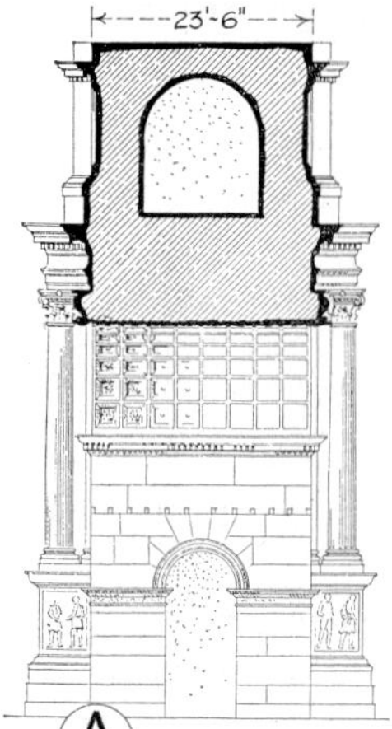
23'-6"

(A) SECTION

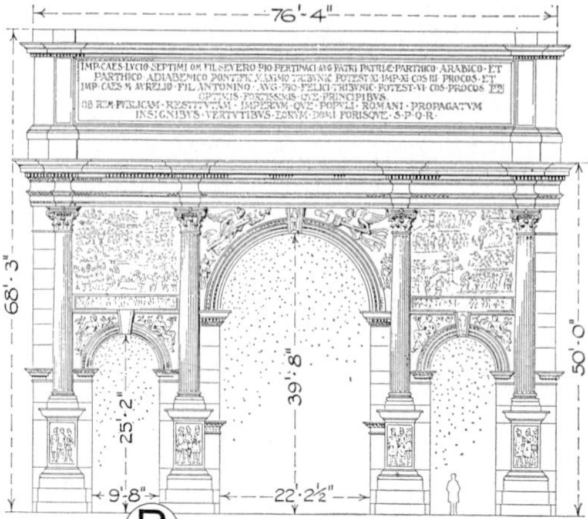
76'-4"
68'-3"
39'-8"
25'-2"
50'-0"
9'-8"
22'-2½"

(B) ELEVATION TO CAPITOL

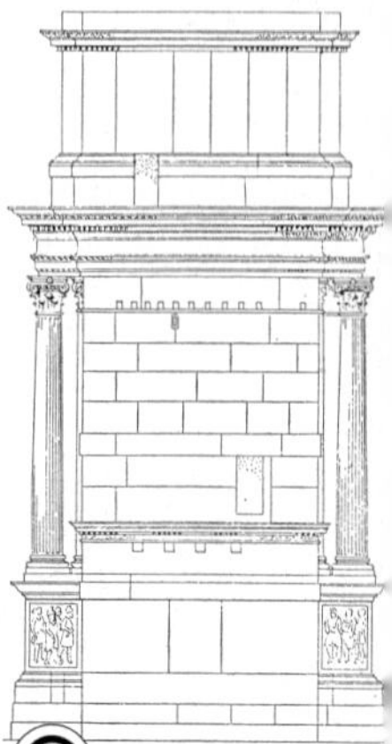

(C) S. ELEVATION

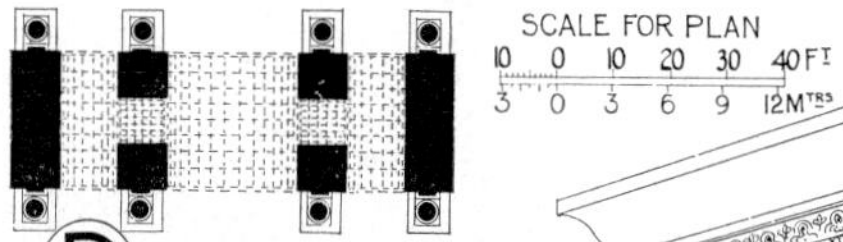
SCALE FOR PLAN
10 0 10 20 30 40 FT
3 0 3 6 9 12 MTRS

(D) PLAN

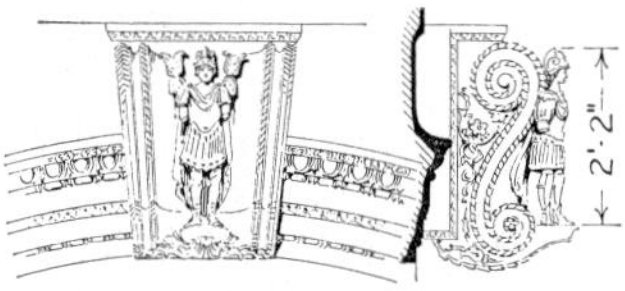
2'-2"

FRONT AND SIDE ELEVATIONS OF KEYSTONE

SCALE FOR ELEVATIONS & SECTION
10 5 0 10 20 30 40 FT

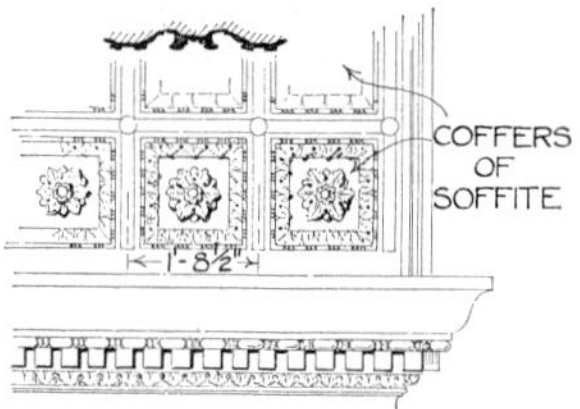
COFFERS OF SOFFITE
1'-8½"

(E) DETAILS OF CENTRAL ARCH

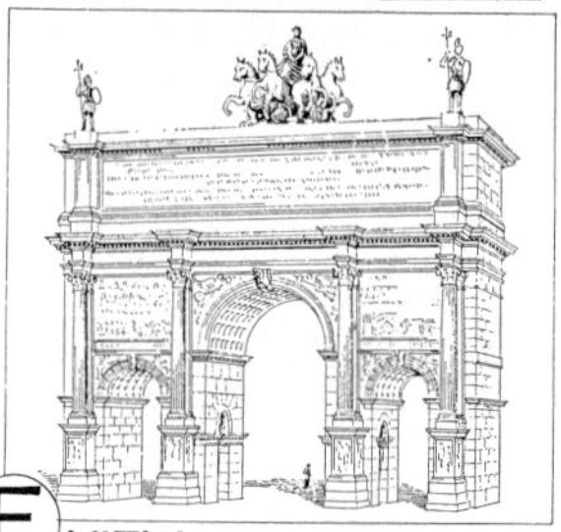

(F) VIEW (RESTORED)

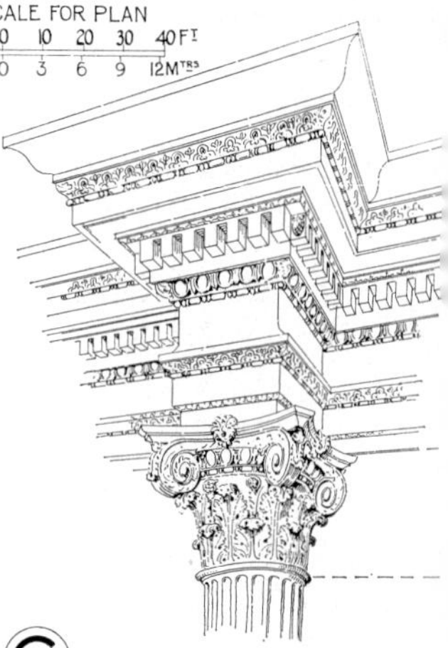

(G) CAPITAL & ENTABLATURE

OTHER TRIUMPHAL ARCHES

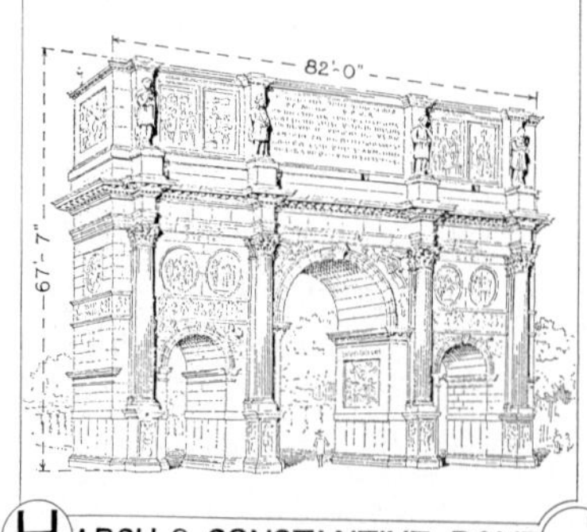
82'-0"
67'-7"

(H) ARCH OF CONSTANTINE : ROME

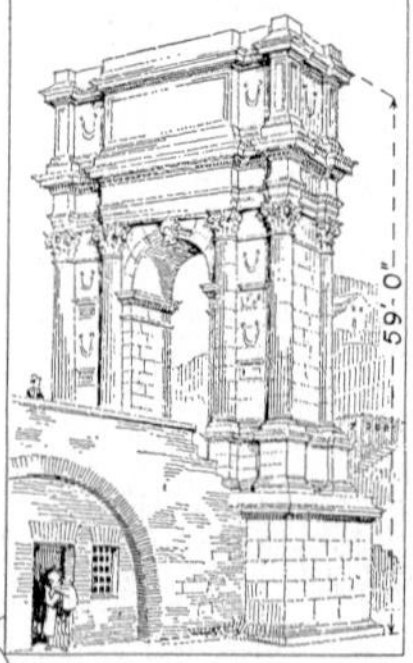
59'-0"

(J) ARCH OF TRAJAN : ANCONA

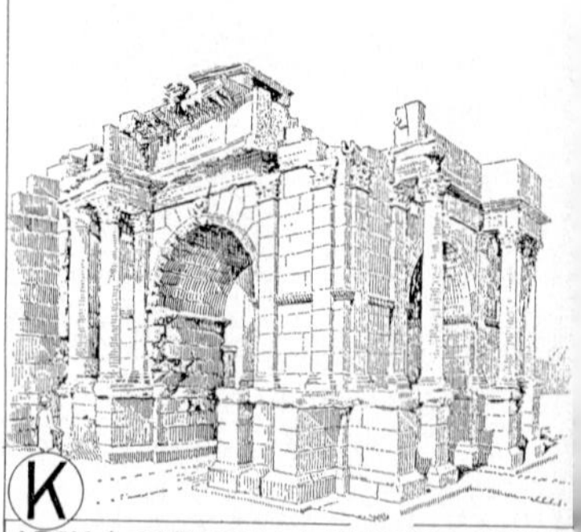

(K) ARCH OF CARACALLA : TEBESSA : N. AFRICA

Town Gateways and Archways

Town gateways were of three main types: (1) those forming part of the protective wall circuit, usually simple, but sometimes elaborated into commemorative monuments; (2) ornamental portals to forums, market places or other large enclosures; (3) arches built at main street intersections, particularly when the main streets were colonnaded, as in many towns in North Africa and Syria. Gateways of the first type, in town walls, might have one main archway and a footway on each side, or, more often, two main archways, with or without a pair of side footways.

1. The **Porte S. André** (p. 216G) and the **Porte d'Arroux, Autun,** probably of the time of Augustus, have four archways, two for vehicles and two for pedestrians. Above the openings are arcaded galleries, connecting the ramparts on either side, decorated with pilasters of the Ionic Order in the case of the Porte S. André, and of the Corinthian in the other.

The **Porte de Mars, Rheims** (first century A.D.), which now lacks its entablature and upper parts, is of grand dimensions, about 108 ft wide. It has three openings, those on the flanks almost as large as that in the centre. The piers are decorated with pairs of Corinthian attached columns on both back and front, and as too there is a pair of attached columns on the sides, the arch must always have been free-standing and is not an ordinary gateway.

Little survives of the gateways of the walled towns of Roman Britain, such as London, York, Chester, Colchester and Lincoln.

The **Porta Nigra, Trèves** (c. A.D. 300) (p. 216F), though heavily ornamented with tiers of crudely-carved Tuscan attached columns, enframing arcades above the lowest stage, is truly a defensive gateway, with a double archway equipped with portcullises and leading to an unroofed court which could be defended against besiegers. Flanking semicircular towers form part of the structure, which is 115 ft wide and reaches 95 ft at its highest part.

2. The **Portico of Octavia, Rome** (p. 208A), erected by Augustus as a reconstruction of an older arrangement, had a fine double colonnade, but only five columns are still standing. The portico formed part of a rectangular peribolus comprising 300 smaller columns, surrounding an enclosure in which stood temples of Jupiter and Juno.

The **Arch of Tiberius, Pompeii** (p. 226B), one of several entrances to the forum, is now divested of its former marbles.

3. The **Arch of Caracalla, Tebessa** (A.D. 214) (p. 224K), formerly stood at the meeting of four roads in the centre of this ancient town in Algeria, but is now attached to the city walls built by Justinian in A.D. 535. It occupies a square of 36 ft with archways 16 ft wide on each front, flanked by detached Corinthian columns surmounted by an entablature having a frieze of unusual depth in order to receive the inscription.

There was a similar four-sided arch at Palmyra, famous for its colonnaded streets, as were Gerasa, also in Syria, and Timgad, in North Africa.

The **Arch of Janus Quadrifrons, Rome** (c. A.D. 315) (pp. 172A, 223M), in the Forum Boarium, is another example of a four-way arch, but is of poor design. It has a simple cross-vault (p. 223L) with embedded brick box-ribs at the groins, affording a further instance of the progressive character of Roman constructive techniques: such ribs are possibly the prototypes of Gothic ribbed vaults.

Pillars of Victory

Pillars of Victory or memorial columns were erected to record triumphs of victorious generals.

H   H.O.A.

A. Arch of Tiberius, Orange, France (c. 30 B.C.). See p. 221

B. Pompeii, the Forum, with the remains of the temple of Jupiter (left), the covered market (right), and the Arch of Tiberius. See pp. 184, 225

Trajan's Column, Rome (A.D. 113) (pp. 182B, 228), was adjacent to his Basilica and stood in an open colonnaded court carrying galleries at different levels, from which the bas-reliefs on its shaft could be viewed (p. 228B). It is a Roman Doric column, entirely of marble, with a total height of 115 ft 7 ins. In the pedestal, ornamented with sculptured trophies, is an entrance to the tomb chamber of Trajan. The shaft, 12 ft 2 ins in diameter, contains a spiral staircase lighted by small openings and was originally surmounted by a bronze eagle, replaced by a bronze statue of Trajan after his death. This in turn was removed at some time unknown, and the present statue of S. Peter has crowned the column since 1588. The bas-reliefs illustrating incidents of Trajan's war with the Dacians were probably intended to represent the unwinding of a parchment scroll (p. 228E, F). There were 2,500 human figures, full of dramatic vigour, and many incidents of military campaigning by land and water, all carved on a spiral band over 800 ft long and about 3 ft 10 ins wide. There is a full-sized plaster reproduction in the Victoria and Albert Museum.

The **Column of Antoninus Pius, Rome** (A.D. 161), of which the pedestal now stands in the great hemicycle of the Giardino della Pigna of the Vatican (pp. 720A, 721B) was founded on the design of Trajan's column.

The **Column of Marcus Aurelius, Rome** (A.D. 174) (p. 228), which stands in the Piazza Colonna, commemorates the Emperor's victory on the Danube. It resembles Trajan's column and formerly stood in front of a temple dedicated to the Emperor. The marble pedestal is surmounted by a shaft 97 ft 3 ins high and 13 ft 2 ins in diameter, carved with remarkable spiral reliefs. The top is reached by 197 steps and was crowned by the statue of Marcus Aurelius till it was replaced (A.D. 1589) in the time of Pope Sixtus V by the existing statue of S. Paul. The spiral band winds round the column in twenty tiers, and represents the campaigns of Marcus Aurelius against the German tribes north of the Danube. One relief (p. 228H) shows Marcus Aurelius, and another (p. 228J) represents a pontoon bridge over which Roman troops with baggage are passing.

Rostral columns (pp. 171A, 228G) were frequently erected in the time of the Emperors to celebrate naval victories, and took their name from the rostra, or prows of captured ships, with which they were embellished, while an inscription recorded the deeds which led to their erection.

PALACES

The **Palaces of the Emperors, Rome** (p. 232), are impressive even as ruins, of which enough remain to show their vast extent and imposing character. Excavations on the Palatine Hill have revealed remains of a group of magnificent palaces to which successive emperors, notably Augustus, Tiberius, Caligula, Domitian and Septimius Severus, made their contribution. The palaces, which crowned the Palatine and looked down on the centre of civic life in the valley below, were approached from the Forum Romanum by sloping ways of which the chief was the Clivus Palatinus, which branched off from the Via Sacra, west of the Arch of Titus.

Quite a little still survives of the modest house of the second half of the first century B.C. which Augustus purchased for his own occupation (p. 232E 16) and extended; but a substantial part of the remains on the Palatine are due to new buildings and drastic reconstructions carried out for Domitian by his architect, Rabirius. The main elements of Domitian's palace (p. 232E) were the State Suite (21); the private apartments (the so-called 'Palace of Augustus') (10), which at a lower level had a grand segmental portico and stepped terraces overlooking the Circus Maximus lying below the south-west slope of the hill; and a large walled

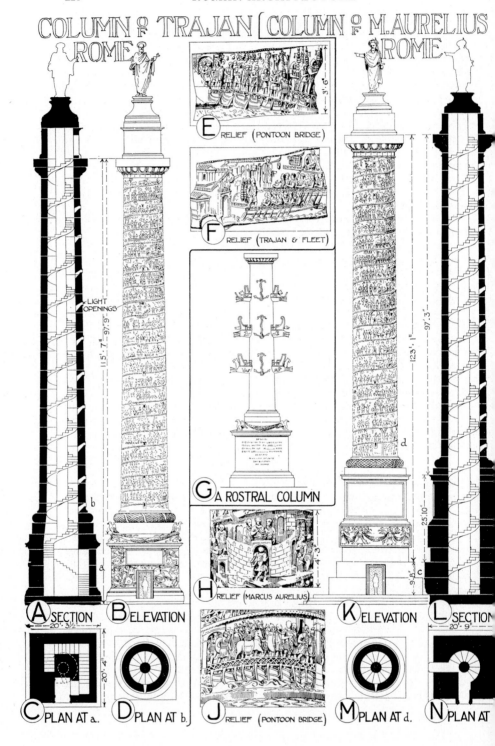

COLUMN OF TRAJAN ROME   COLUMN OF M. AURELIUS ROME

E RELIEF (PONTOON BRIDGE)

F RELIEF (TRAJAN & FLEET)

G A ROSTRAL COLUMN

H RELIEF (MARCUS AURELIUS)

LIGHT OPENINGS

A SECTION

B ELEVATION

C PLAN AT a.

D PLAN AT b.

J RELIEF (PONTOON BRIDGE)

K ELEVATION

L SECTION

M PLAN AT d.

N PLAN AT

garden (8), with a great hemicycle (7) on one long side, behind which were baths buildings. The latter were partly rebuilt by Septimius Severus, who also made massive additions in this locality (9).

Domitian's palace affords a splendid instance of Roman axial planning, with the magnificent vistas it allowed, and of the devices used to mask awkward changes of alignment. The grandest part of the palace was the State Suite. The north-eastern portico (p. 232A; E 21 H), of cippolino columns, led into the public halls, the Tablinum or throne-room (21 F), flanked on one side by the Temple of the Lares or Imperial household gods (21 E), and on the other by the Basilica or Hall of Justice (21 G). Thus, according to tradition, the Imperial power was firmly planted, in architectural planning at any rate, between religion and justice. Directly beyond the throne-room was the Peristyle (21 D), a rectangular garden surrounded by marble colonnades designed for court life and pageantry. This, in its turn, opened into the Triclinium or Banqueting Hall (21 B), with its three couches for reclining guests. This social sanctum of time-honoured hospitality was remote from the distraction of the public courts and looked out into the peristyle and two nymphaea or open gardens with flowering plants, playing fountains, and running water. Not only were the Imperial palaces on the Palatine imposing in extent, plan, and proportions, but both within and without they were decorated on the grand scale and in a manner made familiar to us by the revelations of the buried city of Pompeii. The floors were worked in conventional and pictorial mosaics for which the craftsmen of Italy are still famous; the walls were relieved by marble columns and painted with frescoes, and the ceiling vaults were modelled in low-relief stucco picked out with bright colours, while everywhere there were niches for the splendid statues brought from conquered Greece.

The **Golden House of Nero, Rome** (A.D. 65), built after the great fire in the city, has become a synonym for all that is magnificent in royal palaces, but it was destroyed by the Flavian Emperors and made room for the Colosseum and Imperial Thermae. Pliny describes the lavish ornamentation and fittings, and Raphael drew inspiration from its buried frescoes.

The **Palace of Diocletian, Spalato** (Split) (A.D. 300) (p. 231) forms the greater part of the Mediaeval town of Spalato in Dalmatia, which has therefore been called a city in a house. This magnificent palace, with its imposing arcade, stretches along the sea-front of the Adriatic and may be described as a royal country house, or a château by the sea. Its original appearance can be well understood from the restored view (p. 231C). The plan of the palace was approximately rectangular, occupying 8 acres, almost equal in extent to the Escorial in Spain (p. 853). There was a square tower at each angle, and in the centre of the north, east, and west sides were the 'golden', 'silver', and 'iron' gateways, flanked by octagonal towers with sub-entrances to broad, colonnaded avenues, 36 ft wide, which met in the centre and gave the palace the character of a Roman camp. The two northern portions were probably for guests and principal officers of the household; while across the southern portion there were the Imperial apartments, flanked by two courts in one of which stood Diocletian's Mausoleum, described earlier (p. 218), and in the other, a temple dedicated to Jupiter. A vestibule, circular inside and preceded by a porch of four columns in antis led to a suite of spacious rooms fronting south on to a grand arcaded gallery, 524 ft long and 24 ft wide, overlooking the sea, which probably contained works of art besides serving for leisurely promenades (cf. Elizabethan gallery, p. 882). Centrally below the gallery was a watergate, the Porta Aenea or Brazen Gate. Elsewhere, the outer walls of the palace were lined internally on three sides with cells for slaves and soldiers of the Imperial retinue. Besides the novel construction of the vault of the mausoleum (p. 218) there are other features of this fortress-like building which give it a transitional character and foreshadow future developments. Its architecture is still classical, but is debased and hints strongly of the Byzantine, especially in the flattened profile of the mouldings and the fretted running ornament (cf. p. 300). Also, the arch form appears here in a connection for which there are few precedents in earlier Roman work. Above the northern gateway there are decorative arches springing directly from the capitals of columns (p. 231A), and the portal itself has a decorative archivolt above a flat lintel made up of joggled voussoirs. Similarly, the Corinthian columns flanking the approach to the vestibule of the Imperial apartments carry arches from their capitals, and over the central intercolumniation of the porch the whole entablature is turned into an arch (p. 231B). Thus here are early instances of a principle which was carried to its logical conclusion in the Romanesque and Gothic styles.

ROMAN HOUSES

Roman dwelling-houses are of three types: (*a*) The domus or private house; (*b*) the villa or country house; and (*c*) the insula or many-storeyed tenement.

(*a*) The *domus* or private house combined the features of the old Italic or Etruscan dwelling with other elements derived, about the second century B.C., from the Greek house. An atrium formed the more public portion of the building and beyond was the peristyle of Greek origin, the centre of the family apartments.

The **'Atrium Vestae', Rome** (*c.* A.D. 66) (pp. 171B, 182B) or House of the Vestals, much modified in the late second century A.D., was a special kind of dwelling near the Forum where lived the six Vestal Virgins who tended the sacred fire in the adjacent Temple of Vesta. Rooms were arranged in two storeys alongside a great colonnaded court, 180 ft by 48 ft, with a large, vaulted hall and other principal apartments across the rear short end.

The **House of Livia, Rome** (*c.* 55 B.C.) (p. 232E 16), on the Palatine, which the Emperor Augustus purchased for his own use, is the most interesting of the remains of a domus in the Imperial city.

Pompeii and Herculaneum were provincial towns buried by deposits of volcanic ash at the devastating eruption of Vesuvius in A.D. 79. Pompeian houses were thus remarkably preserved. Excavations show how the lay-out of the town was greatly enlarged, *c.* fifth century B.C., either by the Etruscans or the Samnites, who secured power in turn, from a small and irregular settlement of the Oscans, the earliest inhabitants, into an extensive but still modest market town of some 160 acres. The new part had a regular 'grid-iron' street arrangement, cutting the building sites into rectangular blocks. The streets were very narrow, 8, 12 or 15 ft wide, while the widest were 23 ft 6 ins with a roadway 13 ft 6 ins and paths 5 ft wide. Houses were spaciously laid out at first, but as the town became congested, small houses and shops grew up around them and lined the street frontages, while second storeys became increasingly common. The Romans had become masters in 80 B.C. By Imperial times Pompeii had become thoroughly Latinized, and Greek influences, which had been important throughout, gave place to the Roman. In the last phases before the eruption, commerce and industry were encroaching upon the dwellings of the patricians, and they and the wealthy citizens had begun to move out beyond the obsolete defensive walls to nearby suburbs and villas.

The rooms of a Pompeian mansion were lighted by openings on to internal courts, as in Mediaeval times in England and France, and as in Eastern houses to this day; some of the courts were small, but the light is strong in sunny Italy. Braziers were used for heating. The domestic water supply was drawn from wells or was rain-water collected from roofs until in the first century B.C. a branch aqueduct was

PALACE OF DIOCLETIAN : SPALATO

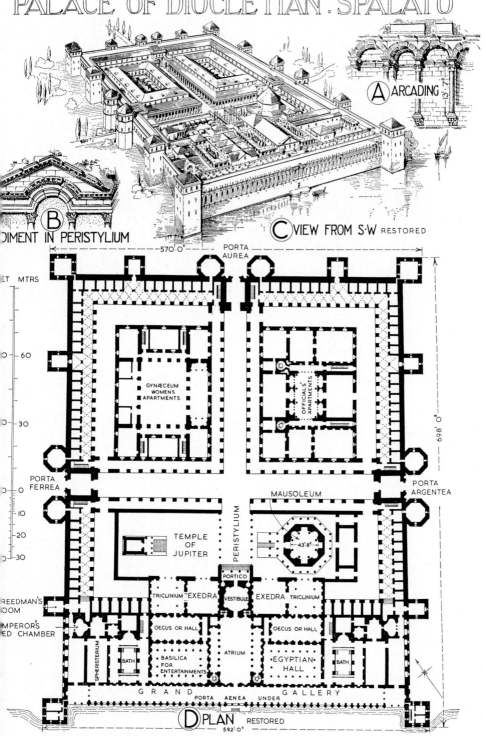

Ⓐ ARCADING

Ⓑ ...DIMENT IN PERISTYLIUM

Ⓒ VIEW FROM S·W RESTORED

570'·0"

PORTA AUREA

...ET MTRS

60

30

GYNÆCEUM
WOMENS
APARTMENTS

OFFICIALS APARTMENTS

698'·0"

PORTA
FERREA

PORTA
ARGENTEA

0

10

20

30

MAUSOLEUM

PERISTYLIUM

TEMPLE
OF
JUPITER

43'·8"

...REEDMAN'S
...OOM

...MPEROR'S
...ED CHAMBER

PORTICO

TRICLINIUM EXEDRA

VESTIBULE

EXEDRA TRICLINIUM

OECUS OR HALL

OECUS OR HALL

SPHERISTERIUM

BATH

BASILICA
FOR
ENTERTAINMENTS

ATRIUM

EGYPTIAN
HALL

BATH

G R A N D   G A L L E R Y

PORTA AENEA UNDER

Ⓓ PLAN RESTORED

592'·0"

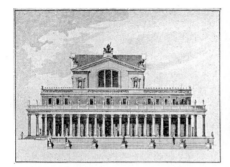

A. Palace of Domitian, N. façade

B. The Tablinium

C. The Basilica

D. The Triclinium

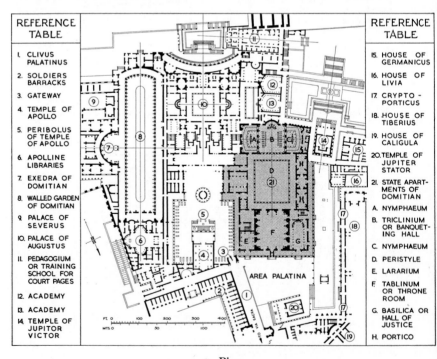

REFERENCE TABLE	REFERENCE TABLE
1. CLIVUS PALATINUS	15. HOUSE OF GERMANICUS
2. SOLDIERS BARRACKS	16. HOUSE OF LIVIA
3. GATEWAY	17. CRYPTO-PORTICUS
4. TEMPLE OF APOLLO	18. HOUSE OF TIBERIUS
5. PERIBOLUS OF TEMPLE OF APOLLO	19. HOUSE OF CALIGULA
6. APOLLINE LIBRARIES	20. TEMPLE OF JUPITER STATOR
7. EXEDRA OF DOMITIAN	21. STATE APARTMENTS OF DOMITIAN
8. WALLED GARDEN OF DOMITIAN	A. NYMPHAEUM
9. PALACE OF SEVERUS	B. TRICLINIUM OR BANQUETING HALL
10. PALACE OF AUGUSTUS	C. NYMPHAEUM
11. PEDAGOGIUM OR TRAINING SCHOOL FOR COURT PAGES	D. PERISTYLE
	E. LARARIUM
12. ACADEMY	F. TABLINUM OR THRONE ROOM
13. ACADEMY	G. BASILICA OR HALL OF JUSTICE
14. TEMPLE OF JUPITOR VICTOR	H. PORTICO

E. Plan

The Palaces of the Emperors on the Palatine Hill, Rome (restored)
(Commenced A.D. 3 and continued by the Emperors till A.D. 212). See p. 227

made; profuse supplies then were carried in leaden pipes to domestic taps in all but the smallest dwellings, and to street and garden fountains and basins. Despite the three public baths in the town, most of the larger houses had their own bath-room suites.

The **House of the Surgeon, Pompeii** (fourth century B.C.) (p. 249F), represents the oldest type of house, as yet unaffected by Greek influence. All its chief rooms were arranged around an 'atrium', a covered court of which only a small central portion was open to the sky.

The **House of Pansa, Pompeii** (second century B.C.) (pp. 234, 238A), illustrates the typical domus or family mansion, fully developed. It comprises two main portions; the atrium, or forepart, which served for formal occasions as well as normal use; and a rear or 'peristyle' portion, which was the more intimate, private part. The first of these, the atrium, is the traditional Italic house, which in the House of the Surgeon represents the entire dwelling; the second, the colonnaded peristyle, is an additional chief element derived from the Greek house, becoming common from the early second century B.C. From this latter time too, Greek influ-ence caused columns sometimes to be used to support the margins of the roof opening or 'compluvium' of an enlarged atrium, which in the original lacked columns. Privacy was assured for the whole house since all the rooms, with rare exceptions, faced inwards towards atrium or peristyle, light being gained for them through tall doorways with metal grilles within their doors or hung with curtains. Window glass was rare, even in Pompeii's last days. Encircling the House of Pansa on three sides were shops, bakeries and three smaller dwellings. A 'prothyrum' or entrance passage led from the street to the atrium, where a central, shallow rect-angular basin or 'impluvium' was sunk in the pavement directly below the com-pluvium opening in the 'lean-to' roof above, which sloped down four ways towards it. The atrium also contained the shrine of the family gods, and near to the im-pluvium there stood a marble table, a traditional survival of the ancient banqueting board (p. 249J). An open living-room or 'tablinum' was curtained off between the atrium and the peristyle, and at the side was a passage, the 'fauces'. The peristyle, enframed by sixteen Ionic columns, was laid out with flower beds and graced with statuary, fountains and water-basins. 'Cubicula' or bedrooms, 'triclinia' or dining-rooms with different aspects for summer and winter, the 'oecus' or reception-room, and 'alae' or recesses for conversation surrounded the peristyle. Dining-rooms were fitted with three couches for nine people, the recognized number for a Roman feast. Floors were decorated with mosaics and walls with fresco paintings. The kitchen and pantry were at the side of the peristyle, farthest from the entrance, but convenient for the side street. There was a series of small upper rooms round the atrium and peristyle.

The **House of the Vettii, Pompeii** (A.D. first century) (p. 234D, F) differs from others in that the atrium, owing to the restricted site, adjoins the peristyle. The kitchen, with its cooking apparatus still *in situ*, and the triclinium, with its wall frescoes representing Classical myths, are typical of many other houses.

The **Houses** of **the Faun, Diomede, Sallust, and the Tragic Poet** are typical residences, with floors, walls, and vaulted ceilings decorated in the char-acteristic Pompeian style, and furnished with candelabra, lamps, vases, statues, and fountains, many of which are in the Naples and Pompeii Museums (pp. 249, 250). The floors were of patterned mosaic, in black and white (p. 249H, K) or coloured marbles. The walls were painted, unpretentiously at first, but from *c.* 200 B.C. in fresco decorations in a series of 'styles': the *first* imitated coloured marble veneering, in paint and modelled stucco (second century to 80 B.C.); the *second* shows either architecturally-enframed panels of large paintings or the realistic and

HOUSE OF PANSA : POMPEII

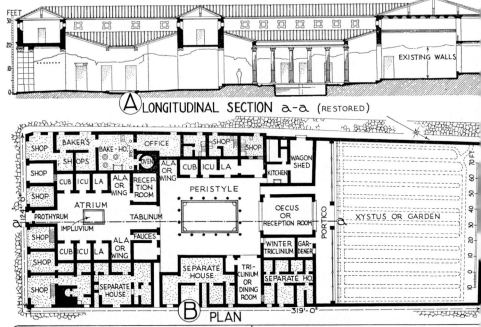

A LONGITUDINAL SECTION a-a (RESTORED)

B PLAN

HOUSE XXXIII : PRIENE (GREEK)

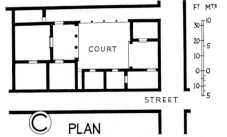

C PLAN

HOUSE OF THE VETII POMPEII · (ROMAN)

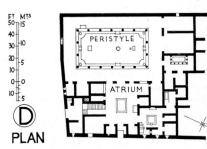

D PLAN

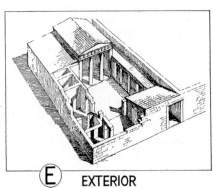

E EXTERIOR

F EXTERIOR FROM N.

robust representation of architectural elements, in the shape of arcades, colonnades and other spatial scenes (80 B.C.–A.D. 14); in the *third*, wall panels have architectural frames but of unrealistic, slender and often grotesque 'Egyptian' elements surrounding small, isolated pictures of Greek character, though vistas still appear, especially in the frieze (A.D. 14–63) (p. 249G); and in the *fourth*, vistas of fantastically-slender and fragile shrines, porticoes and similar structures occupy the whole body of the wall (overlaps with third style—A.D. 50–79) (cf. p. 249B). Ceilings and vaults, covered with stucco, had frescoed decoration related to that of the walls. Roofs were covered externally with tiles. The remains of these houses, as excavated in such cities as Pompeii and Timgad, reveal in the details of their arrangement the everyday life of Roman citizens.

(*b*) The *villa* or country house. **Hadrian's Villa, Tivoli** (A.D. 124) resembled a city, for, with its surroundings and gardens (p. 241D), it occupied about seven square miles. Besides the Imperial apartments there were terraces, colonnades, palaestrae, theatres, and thermae. Apart from this exceptional palatial example, villas abounded in the more attractive parts of the Empire, once peaceful conditions had been securely established. In type they ranged from luxurious country retreats, replete with every urban innovation, to modest farmsteads with a minimum of residential refinement. Few villas were erected in Britain primarily for pleasure. The average villa, however, combined comfort with utility, the elegant suite of rooms of the well-to-do owner being segregated from the working parts, operated by slaves in the charge of an overseer. Buildings were arranged around a court or a peristyle, or, after the first century A.D., were often of the 'corridor' type in which a single bank of rooms was connected by open or closed porticoes running externally. Adaptations were made for climatic conditions; a bath house was regularly present in the later villas of Roman Britain (Ch. XII).

(*c*) The *insula* or apartment block was far more common than the domus in Rome, where space was very precious; and also in Ostia, the port of Rome, where large numbers of workers had to be adjacent to the docks (pp. 237A, 241C). Flat blocks rose four, five and even more storeys high, and Augustus and Nero in turn vainly placed restrictions of 68 ft and 58 ft upon them. Built economically of brick-faced concrete, with architectural dressings in a deeper colour, their appearance was surprisingly modern. Continuous balconies in concrete or timber, sometimes enclosed, were a frequent feature (p. 237A). Rooms of each flat were reached one through the other from common stairs (p. 237A), and numerous large windows faced both ways to surrounding streets and alleys and on to large internal, garden courts. Window glass was rare, and folding shutters or hanging cloths must largely have been used. Ground floor flats sometimes were occupied by the wealthy, but otherwise served, as at Pompeii, for workshops and bakeries or for 'tabernae', shops or miniature dwellings of one open-fronted room, with a wooden-floored loft over, reached by a few stone steps and a ladder (pp. 185D, 186). Well water sufficed until the aqueducts came, but even then, water did not reach upper floors and their tenants had to use street fountains and public baths and latrines. Fire risk was very high. Heating and cooking were by brazier and stove.

AQUEDUCTS

Ruined aqueducts throughout the Empire show the importance attached by the Romans to an adequate water supply. Immense quantities of water were required for the great thermae and for public fountains, to say nothing of the domestic supply for the large population, and it has been computed that 350,000,000 gallons were daily poured into Rome through the eleven great aqueducts. The Romans were acquainted with the simple hydrostatic law that water rises to its own level in closed pipes, and in towns, water was distributed to public buildings, street fountains, workshops and the ground floor of dwellings by lead pipes (or sometimes of terra-cotta or wood) from large reservoirs and cisterns located in suitable positions for the regulation of supplies. Occasionally too, the trunk supply was siphoned across deep valleys, the water being divided for the purpose into nine or ten small-bore (c. 1½ ins) lead pipes between reservoirs at each side; for the Romans were unable to make cast-iron pipes or to devise other trustworthy means of withstanding the great pressures occasioned in the process. Usually, since labour was abundant, it was more practicable to build tiers of stone or concrete arches, sometimes 100 ft high, over ravines and low-lying places, to make tunnels through obstructions of earth or rock, and otherwise by the most direct means to maintain a slight but consistent fall for the water-conveying duct or 'specus' from the springs or rivers at the source to the reservoir where distribution began. Circuitous routes were often necessary. Across plains, particularly outside towns, an aqueduct had to be raised high enough to give a sufficient 'head' to the supply, and the use of arches obviated obstruction to traffic. The ducts varied in dimension according to need—from 1½ ft to 4 ft wide and from 2 ft to 8 ft high—and were lined with a very hard hydraulic cement.

The **Aqua Marcia, Rome** (144 B.C.), forms part of a triple aqueduct which, by the Porta S. Lorenzo, carried the Aqua Marcia, the Aqua Tepula (127 B.C.), and the Aqua Julia (33 B.C.)—an economical arrangement by which several channels, one above the other, are carried by one series of arches.

The **Aqua Claudia, Rome** (A.D. 38) (p. 242A), built by the Emperors Caligula and Claudius, brought water to Rome from Subiaco, 45 miles distant; part of its length is on solid masonry, and for 9½ miles it is borne on lofty arches, great lengths of which remain in the Campagna. It is probably the finest of all Roman aqueducts, and some of the arches are over 100 ft high. Three miles from Rome it is joined by the Anio Novus (A.D. 38), 62 miles in length.

The **Pont du Gard, Nîmes,** France (c. A.D. 14) (pp. 216E, 242B), forms part of a magnificent aqueduct, 25 miles long, constructed to bring water to Nîmes from the neighbourhood of Uzes. It is well preserved, 882 ft long, and formed of three tiers of arches, crossing the valley 155 ft above the river Gard. In the two lower tiers the arch above the river is the widest and the others vary in width, while in the uppermost tier there are thirty-five arches of 14 ft span, supporting the 'specus' or water channel. Except for the top tier, the masonry is laid dry, without mortar, and some of the arch voussoirs of the intermediate tier were made to project to carry the temporary wooden framing or centering on which the arch was formed (p. 242B).

Aqueducts at Tarragona, **Segovia** (c. A.D. 10) (p. 241B), Spalato, and elsewhere testify to the importance attached to a good water supply, and the regulations throw a light on Roman administrative methods in the Imperial City and Roman Provinces.

BRIDGES

Roman bridges were simple, solid, and practical in construction and designed to offer a well-calculated resistance to the rush of water. The roadway usually sloped upwards a little at the approaches, but otherwise was level. Early bridges were of timber, which was used too for the lesser constructions at all times, though often with stone piers. The finest were of stone. Very great spans were achieved when necessary; the arch of an Augustan bridge near Aosta, in north-west Italy, was 117 ft across.

The **Pons Sublicius, Rome** (p. 245A), was for long the only bridge across the

A. Block of flats at Ostia (restored). See p. 235

B. Mausoleum of Augustus, Rome (restored) (*c.* 25 B.C.). See p. 217

C. Mausoleum of Hadrian, Rome (restored) (*c.* A.D. 135). See p. 217

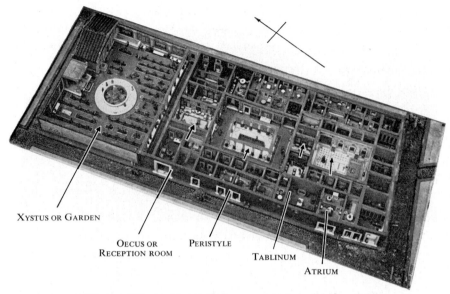

XYSTUS OR GARDEN

OECUS OR
RECEPTION ROOM

PERISTYLE

TABLINUM

ATRIUM

A. House of Pansa, Pompeii: from restored model. See p. 233

B. Roman bridge over the Tagus, Alcantara, Spain (A.D. 105–16) See opposite page

C. (*Right*) Pons Fabricius, Rome (62–21 B.C.). See opposite page
(*Left*) Pons Cestius

Tiber, and Livy records its destruction by the Roman garrison when the Etruscans were advancing upon Rome; while Macaulay has immortalized the incident of its defence by Horatius Cocles.

The **Pons Mulvius, Rome** (109 B.C.) (p. 245B), now known as the Ponte Molle, has semicircular arches over massive piers with protecting 'starlings' or cut-waters and extra arches above them to allow the flood waters to pass through. It was here that Cicero arrested the Gaulish ambassadors and Maxentius met death and defeat at the hands of Constantine (A.D. 312).

The **Pons Fabricius, Rome** (62–21 B.C.) (pp. 238, 241E), with its flood water aperture and starlings, is one of the best preserved Roman bridges. Each of its twin arches spans about 80 ft.

The **Bridge of Augustus, Rimini** (A.D. 14–20) (p. 245C), is the best preserved and one of the finest ancient structures in Italy, with its stretch of five arches over the river Marecchia.

The **Roman Bridge, Alcantara** (A.D. 105–16) (pp. 222, 238B), the larger arches of which are nearly 90 ft wide, exemplifies one of two impressive types found in Spain, viz. (*a*) the many-arched type, of which that at Salamanca (p. 634A), of extreme length, is an example; (*b*) the single-arched type, such as the later Moorish and Gothic bridge at Toledo which, with the romantic sweep of its gigantic arch, spans the rocky valley of the Tagus (p. 645B).

FOUNTAINS

Fountains (Ch. xx) are striking features of ancient and modern Rome, on account of their graceful design and the splashing of clear water in a hot and crowded city. Public fountains, which were numerous, amounting to many hundreds in the various Roman cities, were designed either as a large basin of water ('lacus'), or as spouting jets ('salientes'), or the two were combined with marble columns and statues. Private fountains existed in great numbers, mainly in the courts and gardens of houses, with great variety of design in coloured marbles and porphyries, and were often decorated with bronze statuettes. The water sometimes issued from fishes, shells, or other objects supported by a figure of a nymph and sometimes from lions' heads in wall niches lined with mosaics, as at Pompeii.

The ancient Roman regard for running waters, which almost amounted to adoration, found expression not only in triumphant aqueducts and monumental thermae, but also in these numberless fountains in the cities which made up that great Empire. Water, ever fresh and ever changing, was used to commemorate great men and noble deeds. Water-shrines as sculptured fountains honoured the dead and served the living. This cult of water in Classic times became a continuous tradition, and we have only to look on the fountains of Mediaeval and Renaissance Rome to realize how much the city owes of charm to this universal display of gushing and falling waters. Great is the mystery of water and its courses and there are other waters in this city of many centuries, which, buried under much building, are now only known as the hidden waters of Rome (pp. 730B, 754F, H).

COMPARATIVE ANALYSIS

GREEK

PLANS. Plans display simplicity, beauty, and perfection of proportions which give dignity and grandeur in spite of smallness of scale. Unity and symmetry resulted from the self-contained character of the temples, while varied and unsymmetrical planning occurs only in certain buildings like the Erechtheion (pp. 109, 134F). The Greek ideal of life lent much more importance to religious than to utilitarian buildings, for which there was only a restricted need, due to the independence of the numerous city-states.

The post and beam or trabeated form of construction made for simplicity and did not allow such variety and boldness of plan as did the arcuated Roman style. There is no mingling of constructive principles in Greek buildings, and the structural limitations of the trabeated style prevented the novel developments to which the arcuated style gave rise.

The true arch with voussoirs was rarely used before 300 B.C., though the principle was known by 5th cent. B.C. if not before; while 'false' or corbelled arches were quite frequent in Aegean architecture. The Treasury of Atreus, Mycenae, has a domical, pointed vault of diminishing rings of stones laid on horizontal beds (p. 100A).

Greek temples were usually orientated, so that the rising sun might light up the statue (p. 122G).

WALLS. As walls were built without mortar, there was a tendency to employ large stones, so as to reduce the number of joints and thus minimize the weakness they might cause. Aegean defensive walls were of massive, 'Cyclopean', uncut boulders; the Greeks perfected 'Polygonal' masonry, an advanced type with extremely fine joints. For the best work, large, rectangular blocks of stone or marble were carefully bonded and secured together by metal cramps and dowels. Coarse stone frequently was covered with polished stucco; marble blocks were fitted so exactly together that the joints were almost invisible.

The Anta was employed to emphasize and strengthen the angles of naos walls (pp. 132C, 135A).

ROMAN

PLANS. Plans convey an impression of vastness and magnificence, and are characteristic of a powerful and energetic race. The Romans were pre-eminently great constructors, and by their concentration on practical problems were able to erect public buildings of enormous size, like the thermae and basilicas (pp. 200B, E, 203B), besides temples (pp. 189B, E, H, 199B) and many types of utilitarian structures, such as aqueducts and bridges required by the expanding civilization of the Roman Empire (pp. 238B, C, 242).

The arch, vault, dome and roof-truss were the keynotes to the system of construction. The arch and the timber roof-truss made it possible to span wide openings; vaults and domes could be thrown over large and complicated plans in which square and semicircular recesses (p. 203B) gave boldness and variety, while the combination of trabeated and arcuated styles permitted novel types of plans.

The true arch with wedge-shaped blocks was continued from Etruscan times. Intersecting vaults concentrated the weight of the superstructure on piers (p. 200C–F), instead of distributing it along a continuous wall as in the 'Temple of Diana', Nîmes (p. 192) (a step towards Gothic methods of construction).

Roman temples, regardless of orientation, faced the adjacent forum so as to be easy of access.

WALLS. The Romans revolutionized wall construction by the use of concrete. This novel and durable building material was not special to any country, as suitable ingredients could be had almost anywhere. Walls were very thick and their outer casings might be of regular coursed rubble or of brick, whilst fragments of these materials served for cores, laid in a lavish mortar of lime and 'pozzolana' or sand (p. 168). These walls were composite in character, and thus differed essentially from those of the Greeks. Ashlar masonry still was used for the finest structures, following methods similar to the Greek.

The Pilaster, which corresponded to the Anta, was used decoratively on walls instead of half-columns (pp. 189F, 196B).

A. Basilica of Constantine, Rome (A.D. 310–13) (c. A.D. 66). See p. 201

B. Aqueduct at Segovia, Spain, (c. A.D. 10). See p. 236

C. West side of the 'Casa di Diana', a block of flats at Ostia. See p. 235

D. 'Teatro Marittimo', in the Villa of Hadrian, Tivoli (A.D. 124). See p. 235

E. Pons Fabricius, Rome (62–21 B.C.). See p. 239

F. Marine mosaic in the Baths of Neptune, Ostia. See p. 179

A. The Aqua Claudia, Rome (A.D. 38–52). See p. 136

B. The Pont du Gard, Nîmes (c. A.D. 14). See p. 236

GREEK

OPENINGS. Colonnades, by providing variety in the play of light and shade, rendered openings in walls of minor importance in the design of the exterior, and indeed colonnades are the outstanding features of Greek Architecture (p. 103A), and were sometimes superimposed. Doorways were square-headed and often crowned with a cornice supported by consoles, as in the fine north doorway of the Erechtheion, Athens (p. 159D).

Windows, except on rare occasions (p. 107), were not often used in temples, as light was obtained from the tall doorways, or from metal grilles within the double doors when the latter were closed. Sometimes the naos was too large to be roofed (p. 107).

ROOFS. These were always of timber framing (p. 154B) covered with terra-cotta or marble tiling, finished at the eaves with antefixae (pp. 110H, 117G)—or, in Ionic temples, with a gutter-moulding or cymatium (p. 127D, E, F)—and at the angles of the pediments with acroteria (pp. 117A, B, C, 122D). As the principle of the roof-truss was unknown before c. 3rd cent. B.C., interior columns had often to be introduced to support the roof timbers of temples, usually arranged in two tiers, divided by an architrave, not a full entablature.

Ceilings of peristyles were coffered in square or rectangular panels of carved stone or marble, as in the Theseion (p. 120H, J), the Parthenon (p. 122E, F), and Temple of Apollo Epicurius (p. 124B, C). Coffered timbered ceilings were probably employed over the naos.

COLUMNS. Primitive columns were of timber, like the Aegean, but were comparatively stumpy when first converted into stone. Their proportions became progressively lighter. The column with its entablature is the essence of Greek trabeated architecture (p. 160). Columns were usually constructed in 'drums', the flutes being cut after erection.

Orders were never superimposed in the Hellenic period, unless for constructional reasons, as in the interior of temples, to support the roof timbers (pp. 114A, B, 116B, 117E, F, 122E, F, 154B), or in stoas of two storeys. They stood on stepped crepidomas and instances of

ROMAN

OPENINGS. Colonnades and the new system of arcades were both in use internally and externally, and the latter occur in storeys one above the other as in the Colosseum (pp. 166A, 211A). Thus colonnades were largely superseded by arches and column-faced piers. Doorways were both square and semicircular-headed and became decorative features of importance in the external design of large public buildings, as in the Pantheon, Rome (p. 159A).

Windows, generally semicircular-headed, were frequently divided vertically by two mullions; but sometimes they were segmental, a shape produced after the removal of the wooden centering, by filling in the side space vertically above the springing line (p. 177F).

ROOFS. With vault, dome and roof-truss great spaces could be covered without intermediate supports, and this represented a tremendous architectural change. The concrete vaults demanded the development of methods of buttressing which in certain respects resembled those employed in western Gothic architecture of later times; spans achieved by Roman vaults were two to three times greater than those of English cathedrals. Roof coverings normally were terra-cotta tiles, but occasionally marble, or bronze, as in the Pantheon.

Ceilings of temple peristyles had stone or marble coffers, at times elaborated into geometrical patterns (p. 193C). Coffering was usual too on the underside of vaults, domes and half-domes, or for timber ceilings, which alternatively might be flatly covered with low-relief, painted stucco.

COLUMNS. The Orders (p. 160) were often used in conjunction with the pier and arch, and then lost their structural importance and became chiefly decorative, as in the Colosseum and Triumphal Arches. Columns were frequently unfluted monoliths, fluting being unsuitable to granite and veined marble.

Orders were often superimposed, as in the Colosseum (p. 212A). The Romans introduced pedestals on which they placed the column to secure greater height. Canons of proportions, as formulated by Vitruvius, were gradually standardized for all the Orders, which the Romans increased

GREEK

pedestals supporting columns are rare (e.g. the Temple of Artemis, Ephesus, p. 130). There were only three Greek Orders.

The Tuscan Order, an even simpler form than the Doric, was not used by the Greeks.

The Doric Order (pp. 113, 160A), sturdy and dignified, was, with the Ionic, an original Order from which the others developed later. It is without a base but stands on a crepidoma, and the capital has a plain, square abacus, beneath which is the echinus, which has a varying outline (p. 113). Columns are usually fluted, and from being extremely sturdy became more slender in their proportions. The vertical plane of the architrave projects in advance of the face of the column, and the triglyphs are over the central axes of the columns except at the angles, where the triglyph is at the extremity of the frieze (p. 144B).

The channels in triglyphs are rounded at the top.

The mutules, over triglyphs and metopes, slope downwards with the soffit and project beneath it.

The *Ionic Order* (pp. 127, 160C) was used with great refinement of line by the Greeks. The distinctive capital has the scrolls showing on two sides only, although angle volutes are found at Bassae (p. 127C).

The *Corinthian Order* (pp. 138, 160E) was a development out of the Ionic Order, introduced late in the Hellenic period, although the earliest known example in the Temple of Apollo Epicurius, Bassae, dates from *c.* 450–425 B.C. The Order appears to have been used principally in small buildings, such as the Monument of Lysicrates, Athens (334 B.C.) (p. 141A–E). This is the first known instance of the Order used externally, complete with its own entablature, which nevertheless is Ionic in character. In the Greek Corinthian the acanthus leaves surrounding the 'bell' of the capital were of the prickly acanthus type (*Acanthus spinosus*) having pointed leaves of V-shaped section (p. 138D). Shafts of columns were fluted, as described at the commencement of this section.

The *Composite Order* was unknown to the Hellenic Greeks, but a somewhat similar

ROMAN

to five by adding the Tuscan and Composite.

The Tuscan Order (p. 174) is a simplified version of the Greek Doric, due to the Etruscans (p. 181J, K).

The Doric Order (p. 160B), little used by the Romans, was too severely simple for the buildings they required. The Temple of Hercules, Cora (p. 160B), is the only Roman temple in this style, but quasi-Doric columns occur in the Theatre of Marcellus (p. 208A). The Romans added a base, varied the abacus and echinus, and sometimes used dentils instead of mutules in the cornice. The columns were usually unfluted. The architrave does not project beyond the face of the column, but is in the same plane with it, and the triglyphs in the frieze were over the central axes of the columns, even at the angles.

The channels in triglyphs are rectangular at the top.

The mutules, when present, usually occur over triglyphs only and are but slightly inclined, not projecting below the soffit.

The *Ionic Order* (p. 160D) of the Romans was less refined. Some late examples, such as those at Pompeii and the Temple of Saturn, have angle volutes, thus showing the scroll on all four sides (p. 189G, J).

The *Corinthian Order* (p. 160F) was the favourite of the Romans, and was used in the largest temples, as those of Castor and Pollux (p. 191) and Vespasian, Rome. The capital is very ornate and the leaves surrounding the 'bell' are often naturalistic and derived from the leaves of the *Acanthus mollis*, which are blunt-ended and flat in section (p. 138E), or from the olive leaf, as in the Temple of Castor and Pollux. The entablature is rich in carved ornament (p. 191); in the cornice there are 'modillions' (consoles or brackets), first introduced in Rome in the late 1st cent. B.C., which serve to distinguish it from the Ionic cornice. Between the modillions, on the soffit of the corona, are sculptured coffers. Shafts of columns were fluted or plain, whether in stone or marble.

The *Composite Order* (pp. 174, 223G, 224G), invented by the Romans, first appears in

A. Pons Sublicius, Rome (restored). See p. 236

B. The Pons Mulvius (Ponte Molle), Rome (109 B.C.). See p. 239

C. Bridge of Augustus, Rimini (A.D. 14–20). See p. 239

A · A PILASTER CAP^L· PANTHEON : ROME

B · CORNICE FORUM OF NERVA · ROME

SCALE   INCHES   3 0 3 6 9

PLAN (LOOKING UP)

C · HALF CAPITAL · MARS ULTOR : ROME

3'·0"

D · CAPITAL TEMPLE OF MARS ULTOR : ROME

6'·6½"

MARBLE

E · PILASTER · VILLA MEDICI : ROME

2'·8"

F · PANEL · PANTHEON : ROME

4'·11½"

2'·2"

G · PILASTER · VILLA MEDICI · ROME

H · CAPITAL : POMPEII

1'·2½"

J · PORTION OF FRIEZE TEMPLE OF ANTONINUS AND FAUSTINA

3'·3"

K · CAPITAL · POMPEII

1'·9¼"

L · PILASTER CAP^L·

M · ACANTHUS FRIEZE · FORUM OF TRAJAN

3'·2"

N · PILASTER CAP^L·

GREEK

treatment is seen in the carved anthemion ornament on the necking of the capitals in the Erechtheion.

MOULDINGS (pp. 164, 165). The Greeks relied for effect on the graceful contour of their mouldings, which approach conic sections in profile and are often decorated with carving of so delicate a character as not to obscure but enhance the grace of the outlines, as clearly shown in the illustrations. Executed in fine marble, mouldings were often undercut so as to produce a fretted effect.

Greek dentils are large, far apart and occupy the whole depth of the moulding.

Greek consoles were used only as vertical brackets to door cornices, as in the Erechtheion (p. 159E).

ORNAMENT (pp. 157, 162, 163). The sculpture of the Greeks has never been equalled, whether executed in isolated groups of statuary or within the boundaries of an architectural framing, as in the pediments, metopes, and friezes of the Parthenon. It is generally held that exteriors of temples were coloured, at least in part, and this must have added greatly to the general effect. Polygnotos and other great artists were employed for decorative painting upon temples and other buildings, and part of the Propylaea was known as the 'pinacotheca' (see Glossary). The early frescoes were probably in the style of the vase paintings of that period, while the later, if judged from the provincial imitations at Pompeii, must have been grand and decorative. See 'Comparative Analysis' under Greek Architecture (p. 156). Mosaic decoration for floors and walls was well-developed by Hellenistic times.

The Anthemion or Honeysuckle was the characteristic motif of Greek surface ornament and also of cyma recta mouldings (pp. 162D, 165A).

The Greeks, consciously or unconsciously, practised extreme simplicity in art, and the fine-grained marble in which much of their work was done encouraged the tendency to leave purity of outline to speak for itself. Thus, whether on the grand scale of a temple building like the Parthenon or in the single human figure as the Hermes of Olympia, they were content with beauty unadorned by distracting ornament.

The perfection of Greek art lies in its

ROMAN

the Arch of Titus, Rome (A.D. 82). The entablature resembles the Corinthian; neither Order followed any strict rule.

MOULDINGS (pp. 164, 165). The Romans on the contrary relied for effect on the abundant carving on their mouldings rather than on the contours, which are usually parts of circles in profile. Ostentation replaces refinement. Workmanship frequently was coarse, due in part to the vast extent of Roman undertakings and sometimes to the quality of the stone employed.

Roman dentils are small, close together, and finished with a fillet below (p. 223G).

Roman consoles were used also horizontally as modillions in cornices (p. 191C) and vertically as keystones (p. 223A).

ORNAMENT (pp. 246, 249, 250). The Romans recognized the pre-eminence of the Greeks in sculpture or painting, and so Greek artists were employed and Greek sculpture was much prized and copied. Both vaults and floors were often covered with mosaic (p. 241F). In the marble wall-facings and floors good effects were produced, as the Romans were connoisseurs in the use of marble. The ox-heads connected by garlands, so frequently carved in Roman friezes, originated in the actual skulls and garlands hung on the altars after the beasts themselves had been slain. A fine marble cement was frequently used as a covering to walls and stone columns, to form a ground on which paintings could be executed, as at Pompeii. The modelled plasterwork and frescoes on the walls and vaults of the Roman Thermae largely influenced the mural decorations of the Renaissance period (p. 249B).

The Acanthus scroll, boldly carved with continuous stem and spirals, is specially characteristic of Roman ornament and friezes (p. 246E, G, M).

The Romans never seem to have been satisfied till they had loaded their monumental buildings with every possible ornamental addition. Here too again the influence of material is apparent; for concrete demanded a disguise, and coarse limestone did not permit of delicate purity of line and thus called for extraneous ornament, so the Romans completed the magnificence of their monuments by a wealth of decoration.

The characteristic of Roman art lies in its

GREEK

simplicity. The Greeks were artists by nature, and Greek art was the outward expression of the national love of beauty.

ROMAN

forcefulness. The Romans were rulers by nature, and Roman art was the outward expression of the national love of power.

REFERENCE BOOKS

ADAM, R. *Ruins of the Palace of Diocletian at Spalato.* London, 1764.

ANDERSON, W. J., SPIERS, R. P. and ASHBY, T. *The Architecture of Ancient Rome.* London, 1927.

Baalbek. 2 vols. 4to, Berlin and Leipzig, 1921–3.

BLAKE, M. E. *Ancient Roman Construction in Italy from the Prehistoric Period to Augustus.* Washington, 1947.

BIEBER, M. *The History of the Greek and Roman Theatre.* Princeton, N.J., 1939.

BLOUET, G. A. *Restauration des Thermes d'Antonin Caracalla à Rome.* Paris, 1828.

BROGAN, O. *Roman Gaul.* London, 1953.

CAMERON, C. *Description of the Baths of the Romans.* London, 1772.

CARCOPINO, J. *Daily Life in Ancient Rome,* trans. Lorimer, E. O. London, 1946.

CARRINGTON, R. C. *Pompeii.* Oxford, 1936.

CARY, M. *Geographic Background of Greek and Roman History.* Oxford, 1949.

CHOISY, A. *L'Art de bâtir chez les romains.* Paris, 1856.

CORDINGLEY, R.A. and RICHMOND, I. A. 'The Mausoleum of Augustus'. *Journal of the British School at Rome,* vol. x., 1927.

COURTOIS, C. *Timgad.* Algiers, 1951.

COZZO, G. *Ingegneria romana.* Rome, 1928.

D'ESPOUY, H. *Fragments de l'architecture antique.* 2 vols., folio. Paris, 1899.

D'ESPOUY et SEURE. *Monuments antiques* 4 vols., Paris (19—).

DURM, J. *Die Baukunst der Etrusker und Römer.* Leipzig, 1905.

—. *Handbuch der Architektur.* Vol 2., Leipzig, 1905.

DUTERT, F. *Le Forum romain et les forums de Jules Caesar, d'Auguste, de Vespasian, de Nerva, et de Trajan.* Paris, 1876.

FYFE, T. *Hellenistic Architecture.* Cambridge, 1936.

GIOVANNONI, G. *La Tecnica della costruzione presso i Romani.* Rome, 1925.

HAYNES, D. E. L. *The Antiquities of Tripolitania.* Rome, 1924. 1955.

HÉBRARD, E. et ZEILLER, J. *Spalato: Le palais de Dioclétien, relevés et restaurations.* Paris, 1912.

LANCIANI, R. *Ruins and Excavations pf Ancient Rome.* London, 1897.

MAU, A. *Pompeii: Its Life and Art,* trans. Kelsey, F. W. New York, 1902.

MEIGGS, R. *Roman Ostia.* Oxford, 1960.

MIDDLETON, J. H. *The Remains of Ancient Rome.* 2 vols., London, 1892.

MINOPRIO, A. 'A Restoration of the Basilica of Constantine, Rome'. *Journal of the British School at Rome,* vol. xii, 1933.

OVERBECK, J. *Pompeii,* revised Mau, A. Leipzig, 1884.

PALLADIO, ANDREA. *I Quattro libri dell'architettura.* Venice, 1570, and other editions.

PALLOTTINO, M. *The Etruscans,* trans. Cremona, J. Penguin Books, Harmondsworth, 1955.

PAULIN, E. *Thermes de Dioclétien.* Paris, 1877.

PIERCE, S. R. 'The Mausoleum of Hadrian and the Pons Aelius', *Journal of Roman Studies,* vol. xv, part 1. 1925.

PLINY. *Historia naturalis* (A.D. 23–79).

RANDALL-MACIVER, D. *The Etruscans.* Oxford, 1927.

RICHMOND, I. A. *Roman Britain.* Penguin Books, Harmondsworth, 1955.

RIVOIRA, G. T. *Roman Architecture.* Oxford, 1925.

ROBERTSON, D. S. *A Handbook of Greek and Roman Architecture.* Cambridge, 1943.

STRONG, MRS. A. *Roman Sculpture from Augustus to Constantine.* London and New York, 1907.

A · A WRESTLER HERCULANEUM

B · FRESCO: THERMÆ OF TITUS: ROME

C · A WRESTLER HERCULANEUM

D · WALL SHRINE: POMPEII

E · AN ALTAR: ARLES

F · PLAN: HOUSE OF THE SURGEON POMPEII.

1. FAUCES
2. ATRIUM
3. ALAE
4. TABLINUM

0 2 4 6 8 10

G · WALL FRESCO: POMPEII

H · MOSAIC PAVING: POMPEII

CAVE CANEM

J · TABLE SUPPORTS: POMPEII

K · POMPEIAN MOSAIC PAVING

L · POMPEIAN MOSAIC: NAPLES MUSEUM

M · POMPEIAN MOSAIC

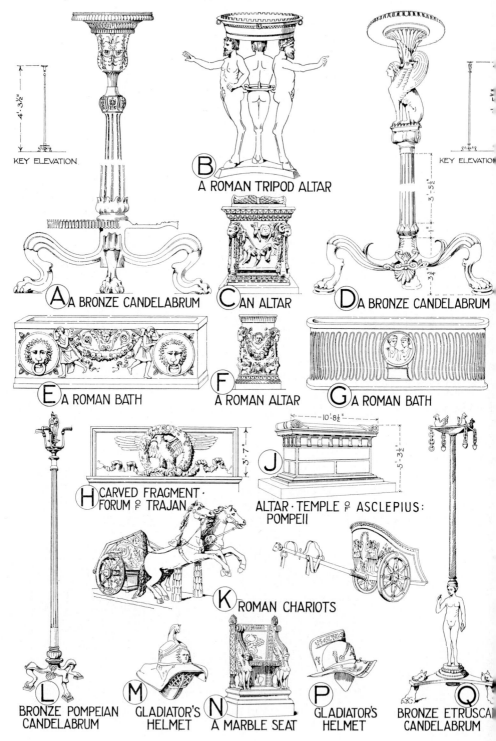

KEY ELEVATION

4'-3½"

A A BRONZE CANDELABRUM

B A ROMAN TRIPOD ALTAR

C AN ALTAR

D A BRONZE CANDELABRUM

KEY ELEVATION

3'-5½"

E A ROMAN BATH

F A ROMAN ALTAR

G A ROMAN BATH

H CARVED FRAGMENT· FORUM OF TRAJAN

3'-7"

J ALTAR·TEMPLE OF ASCLEPIUS: POMPEII

10'-8½"

5'-3½"

K ROMAN CHARIOTS

L BRONZE POMPEIAN CANDELABRUM

M GLADIATOR'S HELMET

N A MARBLE SEAT

P GLADIATOR'S HELMET

Q BRONZE ETRUSCAN CANDELABRUM

TAYLOR, G. L. and CRESY, E. *The Architectural Antiquities of Rome*. London, 1821–2.

TOYNBEE, J. and PERKINS, J. W. *The Shrine of St. Peter*. London and New York, 1956.

VITRUVIUS. *De Architectura*. First printed (in Latin), Rome, *c.* 1486. Various English translations.

WHEELER, SIR M. *Rome Beyond the Imperial Frontiers*. Penguin Books, Harmondsworth, 1954.

WISEMAN, F. J. *Roman Spain*. London, 1956.

WOOD, R. *The Ruins of Palmyra; and the Ruins of Baalbec*. 2 vols., London, 1753–7.

For *Classic Orders*, see:

NORMAND, C. *A New Parallel of the Orders of Architecture*. First printed London, 1829. Various editions.

SPIERS, R. P. *The Orders of Architecture*. 5th ed., London, 1926.

STRATTON, A. *The Orders of Architecture*. London, 1931.

Temples of Portunus (left) (*c.* 31 B.C.) (p. 197) and Fortuna Virilis (*c.* 40 B.C.) (p. 187), in the Forum Boarium, Rome

A. The basilican church of S. Apollinare in Classe, Ravenna (534-9). See p. 262

B. The basilican church of S. Apollinare in Classe, Ravenna. Nave looking E.

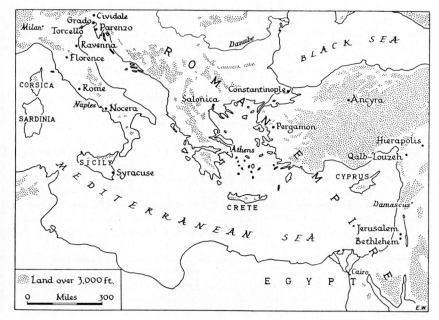

The Early Christian World

V. EARLY CHRISTIAN
ARCHITECTURE

(313–800)

INFLUENCES

GEOGRAPHICAL. Christianity had its birth in Judaea, an eastern province of the Roman Empire, but directly it became a living organism it was naturally carried by S. Peter, S. Paul, and other missionaries to Rome, as the centre of the World-Empire. There at the fountain-head of power and influence, and in spite of opposition and persecution, the new religion took root and grew, till it was strong enough to become the recognized universal religion of the whole Roman Empire. Early Christian architecture in Rome was influenced by, and was the logical outcome of, existing Roman art, and it was modified in other parts of the Empire according to the type already recognized as suitable for the geographical situation of those countries, such as Syria, Asia Minor, North Africa, and Egypt.

GEOLOGICAL. Geological influences may be said to have acted indirectly rather than directly on Early Christian architecture, for the ruins of Roman buildings often provided the quarry whence materials were obtained. This influenced the style, both as regards construction and decoration; for columns and other architectural features, as well as fine sculptures and mosaics from older buildings, were worked into basilican churches of the new faith.

CLIMATIC. The climate of Italy, the most important centre of building activity in this epoch, has been dealt with in the chapter on Roman architecture (p. 169). The climatic conditions of such Roman provinces as Egypt, Syria, and North Africa where Christianity was established naturally modified the style. The fiercer sun and hotter climate necessitated small windows and other eastern features.

RELIGIOUS. In all human history there is no record so striking as that of the rise of Christianity, and no phenomenon so outstanding as the rapidity with which it was diffused throughout the civilized world. Not only in this period but also in all subsequent ages, Christianity has inspired the building of some of the greatest architectural monuments. The number of Christian communities established by the Apostle Paul in his missionary journeys round the Eastern Mediterranean, in Syria, Asia Minor, Greece, and Italy, might lead us to expect many more ruins of Early Christian basilican churches throughout these districts. In this connection, however, it must be remembered that the god preached by S. Paul was 'not like unto gold or silver or stone graven by art and device of man,' nor a god dwelling 'in temples made with hands' like those of the old Greeks and Romans which were built to shelter the statues of the gods. The purpose of the Christian church was to shelter worshippers who met for prayer and praise to an unseen deity, and, during the unsettled conditions at the beginning of Christianity, various places were adapted for this worship. Thus the building of pagan temples ceased before any attempt was made to build Christian churches. In 313 Constantine and Licinus issued their celebrated Edict of Milan, giving Christianity equal rights with other religions, and in 326 Constantine made it the official religion of the Roman Empire. Fortified by its official position and thus freed from the need for unity within, which had been engendered by persecution from without, the Church was soon divided by doctrinal differences and the Council of Nicaea (325), called by Constantine, was the first of several such councils for the settlement of disputes about heresies. The steady progress of Christianity was temporarily arrested by a reaction (361–3) under Julian the Apostate, and then for several generations religion suffered an eclipse as a power in European civilization, and the whole continent was given over to war and anarchy. Pope Gregory the Great (590–604) employed the Imperial army of Constantinople to defend Rome against the Lombards, and thus, by making common cause with the people, early laid the foundations of the temporal power of the Papacy, which steadily increased, especially under Popes Adrian I and Leo III. Throughout the whole Early Christian period the power of the eastern, or Byzantine, half of the Empire, with Constantinople as its centre, had been growing, and rivalry between East and West led to a schism in the Church which culminated in the coronation of Charlemagne in 800, under the title of Emperor of the Romans.

SOCIAL. Constantine changed the capital of the Empire from Rome to Byzantium in 330, when the old Roman political system came to an end, and this royal convert reigned as an absolute monarch till his death in 337. Besides the troubles caused by Julian the Apostate, Christianity suffered further disabilities during the unsettled conditions consequent upon the division of the Roman Empire, which first took place in 364 when Valentinian became Emperor of the West and his brother Valens of the East. Theodosius the Great (379–95) reunited, for a time, the Eastern and Western Empires, and in 438 Theodosius II published his legal code, an important work on the constitutions of the Emperors from the time of Constantine. The series of Emperors in the West came to an end in A.D. 476, and the Eastern and Western Empires were nominally reunited by Zeno, who reigned at Constantinople. Then again the seat of power was changed, and Theodoric the Goth reigned in Italy (493–526) during a period of peace and prosperity. In the

S. CLEMENTE : ROME

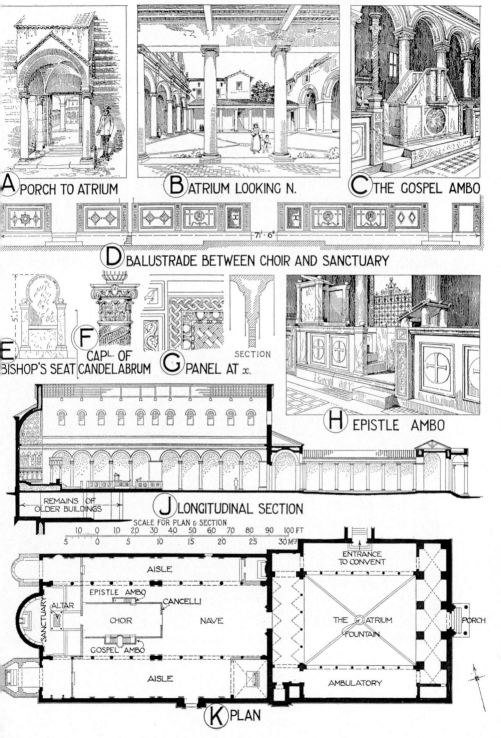

A PORCH TO ATRIUM

B ATRIUM LOOKING N.

C THE GOSPEL AMBO

D BALUSTRADE BETWEEN CHOIR AND SANCTUARY

7'·6"

E BISHOP'S SEAT

F CAPL· OF CANDELABRUM

G PANEL AT x.

SECTION

H EPISTLE AMBO

5'·1"

J LONGITUDINAL SECTION

REMAINS OF OLDER BUILDINGS

SCALE FOR PLAN & SECTION
10 0 10 20 30 40 50 60 70 80 90 100 FT
5 0 5 10 15 20 25 30 MTS

K PLAN

AISLE
EPISTLE AMBO
CANCELLI
ALTAR
SANCTUARY
CHOIR
NAVE
GOSPEL AMBO
AISLE
PORCH
ENTRANCE TO CONVENT
THE ATRIUM
FOUNTAIN
AMBULATORY

A. The basilican church of S. Clemente, Rome
(rebuilt 1084–1108 over a sixth century church). See p. 258

B. The basilican church of S. Maria Maggiore, Rome
(432, with later alterations). See p. 261

wake of this change, Byzantine art influenced Early Christian art by way of Ravenna, which rivalled Rome in importance and was the capital of the Gothic rulers, 493–553, with the exception of a short period when it was subdued by Justinian (537). Kings were now elected for the separate states of Spain, Gaul, Northern Africa, and Italy. The emancipation of Western Europe from direct Imperial control resulted in the development of Romano-Teutonic civilization, which facilitated the growth of new states and nationalities, gave a fresh impulse to Christianity, and eventually strengthened the power of the bishops of Rome. The formation of these new states resulted also in the growth and development of Romance and Teutonic languages, which, for general use, largely replaced Latin. It is clear that these many social changes and political disturbances could not fail to be reflected in the architecture of a period in which great formative forces were at work.

HISTORICAL. The Early Christian period is generally taken as lasting from Constantine to the coronation of Charlemagne (800). The incursions of the Huns into Europe about 376 eventually brought about invasions from the north into Italy, and in 410 Rome itself was sacked by the Goths under Alaric. So many conflicting forces were at work in Europe that the spread of the new religion was arrested during this period of change and upheaval, till 451, when the defeat of Attila, king of the Huns, at the battle of Châlons aided in the consolidation of Christianity in Europe. In 568 the Lombards penetrated into Italy and held the northern part for 200 years. Then in 800 Charlemagne was crowned by the Pope in Rome, and from this date the Empire was styled the Holy Roman Empire, a title which survived until 1806. From 800 to 1000, the dominant architectural influence was no longer Rome but Lombardy, and the style which developed there was Romanesque (pp. 303 ff.).

ARCHITECTURAL CHARACTER

The character of Early Christian architecture is chiefly to be seen in buildings of the fourth to the ninth century, though the style persisted in Rome up to the Renaissance.

Each age of human development inevitably modifies the art it has inherited, in its effort, sometimes conscious and sometimes unconscious, to adapt the art of the past to express the outlook of the present. Thus in architecture one style is generally evolved from that preceding by a series of gradual changes. The early Christians, as Roman craftsmen, continued old Roman traditions, but prosperity was declining and it was natural that for their new buildings they should utilize as far as possible the materials from Roman temples which had become useless for their original purpose. Further, in their churches, modelled on Roman basilicas, they used old columns which by various devices were brought to a uniform height (p. 256A). On this account, although extremely interesting from an archaeological point of view, Early Christian buildings hardly have the architectural value of a style produced by the solution of constructive problems. Basilican churches had either closely spaced columns carrying the entablature (p. 256B), or more widely spaced columns carrying semicircular arches (p. 256A). The basilican church with three or five aisles, covered by a simple timber roof, is typical of the Early Christian style (p. 269B) as opposed to the vaulted Byzantine church with its central circular dome placed over a square by means of pendentives (p. 276).

The architectural character of the basilican churches is rendered impressive and dignified by the long perspective of columns which carry the eye along to the sanctuary; a treatment which, combined with the comparatively low height of

I

interiors, makes these churches appear longer than they really are, as is seen in S. Paolo fuori le Mura (p. 259F), and S. Maria Maggiore (p. 256B). An 'arch of triumph', figurative of the transition through death to life eternal, gave entrance to the sanctuary with the high altar in the centre standing free under its balda-chino upheld by marble columns. The vista was rounded off by an apse lined with marble slabs and crowned with a semi-dome encrusted with glittering golden mosaics in which Christ appears surrounded by prophets, saints, and martyrs (pp. 252B, 256A).

EXAMPLES

BASILICAN CHURCHES

Basilicas or Roman halls of justice probably served the early Christians as models for their churches, which thus form a connecting link between buildings of pagan Classic times and those of the Romanesque period which followed. The term 'basilica' (Gk. *basilikos* =kingly), which was applied to a Christian church as early as the fourth century, was a peculiarly appropriate designation for buildings dedi-cated to the service of the King of Kings. Some authorities, however, believe Early Christian churches to have been evolved from Roman dwelling-houses, where the community had been in the habit of assembling, from the 'scholae' or lecture-rooms of the philosophers, or even from pagan temples (p. 190C). Others trace the general plan and arrangement to the catacombs outside Rome, where some of the earliest Christian services were held. A basilican church was usually erected over the burial-place of the saint to whom the church was dedicated, and immedi-ately over this burial-place, crypt, or 'confessio' was the high altar covered by a ciborium, also known as a tabernacle or baldachino (p. 256B). There were thirty-one basilican churches in Rome alone.

S. Clemente, Rome (1099–1108) (pp. 255, 256A), was rebuilt over a much earlier church, some of the foundations of which still survive in the crypt. The present church retains the original arrangement and fittings and shows the suit-ability of the basilican plan for Christian ritual and for sheltering a number of worshippers. An atrium or open rectangular forecourt (p. 255B), surrounded by arcades, forms an imposing approach to the church, and in the centre is a fountain of water for ablutions—a custom which is still symbolized amongst Roman Catholics by the use of the stoup of holy water at the entrance to the church. Next came the covered narthex, between the atrium and the church, which was assigned to penitents. The narthex opened into the nave, lighted by a clear-story of small windows, with an aisle on either side, usually half the width of the nave. Occasion-ally there are two aisles on each side of the nave, as in the basilicas of Old S. Peter (p. 259B, C), S. Paolo (p. 259E, F), and S. Giovanni in Laterano. Galleries for women were sometimes placed over the aisles, as at S. Agnese (p. 264A, C, D, E) and S. Lorenzo, Rome (p. 263A), but otherwise the sexes sat on opposite sides of the nave. There is no 'bema' (Gk. platform) in S. Clemente, but this feature is found in other basilicas such as S. Peter's, Rome (p. 261), and may have been the germ of the Mediaeval transept which later converted the plan into a Latin cross. Some con-sider, however, that this cruciform plan was derived from buildings which had been erected for sepulchral purposes, as, for example, the Tomb of Galla Placidia (p. 297). A choir, which became necessary owing to the growth of ritual, was enclosed by low screen walls or 'cancelli' (hence 'chancel') and was provided with an 'ambo' or pulpit on either side, dating from the first church, from which the Gospel and Epistle were read (pp. 255H, K, 256A). In the apse or sanctuary the bishop took the central place, which had been that of the 'praetor' in the Roman basilica, and the

BASILICAN CHURCH OF S. PETER : ROME

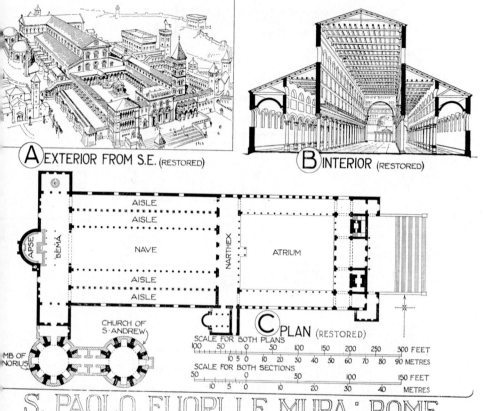

Ⓐ EXTERIOR FROM S.E. (RESTORED)

Ⓑ INTERIOR (RESTORED)

AISLE
AISLE
NAVE
AISLE
AISLE
APSE
BEMA
NARTHEX
ATRIUM
CHURCH OF S·ANDREW
MB OF NORIUS

Ⓒ PLAN (RESTORED)

SCALE FOR BOTH PLANS
100 50 0 50 100 150 200 250 300 FEET
10 5 0 10 20 30 40 50 60 70 80 90 METRES

SCALE FOR BOTH SECTIONS
50 0 50 100 150 FEET
10 5 0 10 20 30 40 METRES

S. PAOLO FUORI LE MURA : ROME

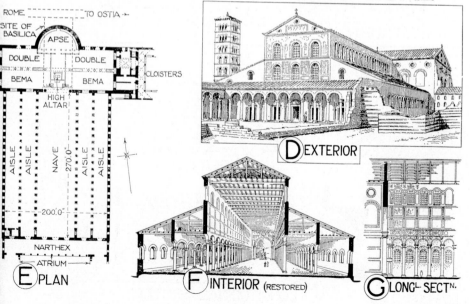

ROME - - - - TO OSTIA →
SITE OF BASILICA
APSE
DOUBLE
DOUBLE
BEMA
BEMA
CLOISTERS
HIGH ALTAR
AISLE
AISLE
NAVE 270'.0"
AISLE
AISLE
200'.0"
NARTHEX
ATRIUM

Ⓔ PLAN

Ⓓ EXTERIOR

Ⓕ INTERIOR (RESTORED)

Ⓖ LONGL SECTN.

CHURCH OF THE NATIVITY: BETHLEHEM

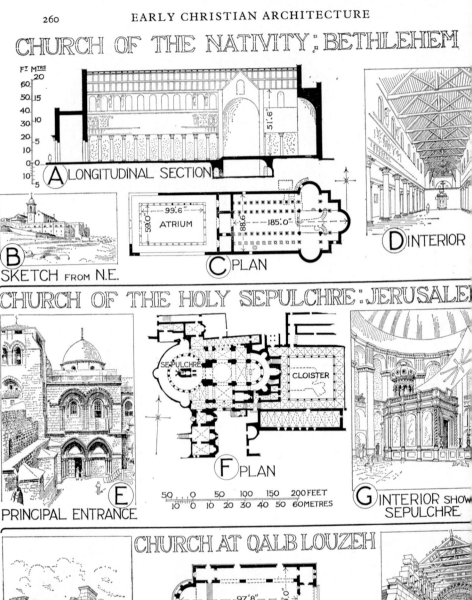

A LONGITUDINAL SECTION

B SKETCH FROM N.E.

C PLAN

D INTERIOR

CHURCH OF THE HOLY SEPULCHRE: JERUSALEM

E PRINCIPAL ENTRANCE

F PLAN

50   0   50   100   150   200 FEET
10 0 10 20 30 40 50 60 METRES

G INTERIOR SHOW SEPULCHRE

CHURCH AT QALB LOUZEH

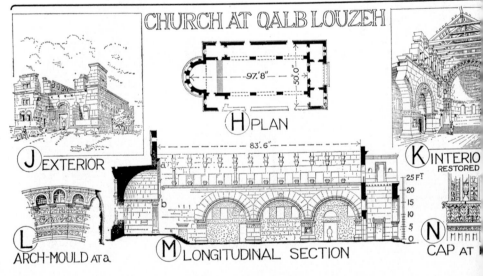

H PLAN

J EXTERIOR

K INTERIO RESTORED

L ARCH-MOULD AT a

M LONGITUDINAL SECTION

N CAP AT

presbyters, or members of the church council, occupied seats on either side corresponding to those used by the Roman 'assessors'. The altar, in front of the apse,
which in the basilica had been used for libations or sacrifices to the gods, was now
adapted for the celebration of Christian rites, and a baldachino or canopy, supported on marble columns, was erected over it. The interiors of S. Clemente and
other churches owe much of their rich effect to the use of glass mosaic ('opus
Grecanicum') in the semi-dome of the apse (p. 256A), with figures of saints in glory
against a golden background, as at S. Agnese (p. 267A) or S. Maria Maggiore
(p. 267B).

The timber roofs were plainly treated with visible rafters (pp. 264A, 269B) often
cased, in Renaissance times, with richly gilded coffers (pp. 256A, B, 269A). The
pavement was formed from the abundant store of old marbles in Rome, and slices
of columns were laid as centres to surrounding bands of inlay in intricate geometric
patterns (p. 256A) as at S. Lorenzo (p. 267Q) and SS. Giovanni e Paolo (p. 267T).

The **Basilican Church of S. Peter, Rome** (330) (p. 259A–C), erected by Constantine near the site of the martyrdom of S. Peter in the circus of Nero, was pulled
down to make way for the present cathedral (p. 714). The atrium led
through the narthex to the great nave with double aisles terminating in five arches,
the central of which was called the arch of triumph (p. 259B, C). Beyond was the
bema (see Glossary) and the sanctuary or semicircular apse with the Pope's seat
against the centre of the wall. The priest, as in all Early Christian basilican
churches, stood behind the altar and faced east, as the chancel was in this case at
the west end (p. 259C).

S. **Giovanni in Laterano, Rome** (330) is also a double-aisled basilica, but has been
so much altered at various times as to have lost its original Early Christian character.

S. **Paolo fuori le Mura, Rome** (pp. 259D–G, 267G), founded in 380, was
destroyed in 1823, but was rebuilt on the original design, and is the largest
and most impressive of all basilican churches. The nave has eighty great columns
of Simplon granite, with mosaic mural medallions of the Popes above. The arch
of triumph with fifth-century mosaics, the double bema, the apse with mosaics of
the thirteenth century, and the remarkable high altar with its double baldachino
over the confessio of S. Paul, all contribute to the grandeur of the interior.

S. **Maria Maggiore, Rome** (432) (pp. 256B, 267B), was built by Pope Sixtus III
and is the only church of which there is evidence that it was originally a pagan
basilica. It is one of the most typical of basilican churches. The interior (p. 256B)
is the most beautiful of the single-aisled basilicas, with its ranges of Ionic columns
of Hymettian marble and entablature surmounted by the original mosaics of Sixtus
III dealing with Old Testament history, culminating in the arch of triumph, high
altar, and baldachino, beneath which is the confessio.

S. **Lorenzo fuori le Mura, Rome** (p. 263A), is the product of two churches
with their apses placed back to back, as in the temple of Venus and Rome, Rome
(p. 188). The two churches, of which one was founded in 432 and the other rebuilt
in 578, were joined in 1216 by the removal of the apses and insertion of columns.
Because of differences in level of the two churches, the eastern half was provided
with a gallery.

S. **Sabina, Rome** (425) (p. 269B), although often altered, retains its original
character. The basilican plan has nave and aisles separated by twenty-four Corinthian columns of Hymettian marble supporting semicircular arches, plain clear-
story walls, and a simple open timber roof. The bareness of the interior is relieved
by the eleventh-century chancel screen and high altar, and the mosaics of the apse,
which date from 822.

S. **Agnese fuori le Mura, Rome** (625–38) (pp. 264A–E, 267A), was founded by

Constantine in 324 over the tomb of S. Agnese. It shares with S. Lorenzo fuori le Mura the peculiarity of having aisles in two storeys. Between nave and aisles are sixteen ancient columns supporting arches, with smaller gallery columns above. The apse with altar and baldachino is at the western end, and mosaics in the semi-dome (1525) represent S. Agnese between two popes (p. 267A). The exterior, with simple clear-story windows, is plain and the apse is flanked by a campanile (776) (p. 264B).

S. Stefano Rotondo, Rome (468) (p. 295A–D), is exceptional in that it has a circular plan. This is the largest circular church in existence, having a diameter of 210 ft, and there is reason to believe that it may be a rebuilding of a Roman market hall of the first century. Its high central and lower aisle roofs are supported by two rings of columns from older buildings; the outer range supports arches and the inner a horizontal architrave. Two central columns and a cross wall give additional support to the main roof timbers. The suggested restoration (p. 295B) shows a possible original arrangement.

S. Apollinare Nuovo, Ravenna (493–525) (p. 269A), was erected by Theodoric the Great and has many points of resemblance to its neighbour, S. Apollinare in Classe, especially in the remarkable campanile and world-famous band of mosaics above the nave arcade.

S. Apollinare in Classe, Ravenna (534–9) (pp. 252, 264F–K, 267E, H, J), was erected by the Emperor Justinian on the site of a temple of Apollo and, like the sister church S. Apollinare Nuovo, was probably built by Byzantine craftsmen, for here the influence of Constantinople was strong. The simple plan forms a single-aisled basilican church, 150 ft long and 98 ft wide. The atrium has disappeared, but a narthex leads into the church. The eastern apse, which is circular internally and polygonal externally, is raised above the crypt and contains the high altar with ciborium. On the north is one of the earliest circular campanili, of the same date. The interior is impressive with nave arcade of cipollino columns, Byzantine capitals, and dosseret blocks (pp. 252B, 267E, J) supporting arches, above which is the band, 5 ft high, of portraits of bishops of Ravenna, while the apse retains its original mosaics showing the saint preaching to his flock.

Torcello Cathedral (rebuilt 1008) (pp. 268A, B, 270), still has the foundations of the original bishop's throne flanked by six rising tiers of seats in the apse, which give a good idea of Early Christian arrangements. This church, with the towering mass of the campanile and the Byzantine church of S. Fosca (pp. 270, 290), compose an historic group.

Syracuse Cathedral, Sicily (p. 268C), still clearly shows how a pagan temple of Athena (p. 112) was converted in 640 into a Christian church, by the construction of a wall between its peristyle columns and the formation of openings in its cella walls.

The Church of the Nativity, Bethlehem (330) (p. 260A–D), founded by Constantine over the traditional birthplace of Christ and rebuilt 527–65, is one of a number of basilican churches in Palestine and Syria erected between the third and seventh centuries, before the Muslim hordes overran the country. It is surrounded by a high wall which encloses the precincts of the Latins, Greeks, and Armenians, who jointly own the church. This historic building, with the monolithic Corinthian columns, 19 ft high, of the nave and double aisles, and the three apses of the sanctuary, is still, in spite of restorations, grand in its simplicity of plan and must have been peculiarly suitable to receive the immense number of worshippers at the birth-shrine of the founder of Christianity.

The Church of the Holy Sepulchre, Jerusalem (p. 260E–G), erected by Constantine over the reputed tomb of Christ, defaced and damaged by the Persians and Muslims, rebuilt by Crusaders and often restored, appears to date from the twelfth century, for its architecture resembles that of Sicily in that period. The

A. S. Lorenzo fuori le Mura, Rome. Interior looking towards sanctuary. (Two churches dating from 432 and 578 respectively, joined together in 1216). See p. 261

B. S. Francesco, Ravenna (560). See p. 265

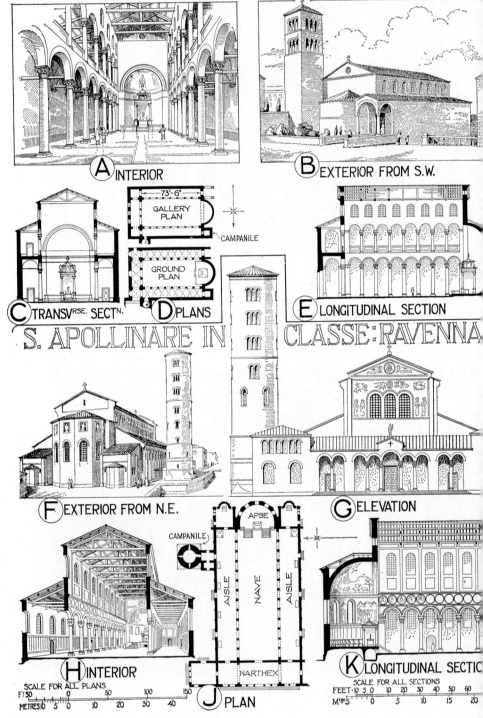

S. AGNESE FUORI LE MURA : ROME

A INTERIOR

B EXTERIOR FROM S.W.

C TRANSVᴿˢᴱ· SECTᴺ·

73'-6"

GALLERY PLAN

CAMPANILE

GROUND PLAN

D PLANS

E LONGITUDINAL SECTION

S. APOLLINARE IN CLASSE : RAVENNA

F EXTERIOR FROM N.E.

CAMPANILE

G ELEVATION

H INTERIOR

APSE

AISLE NAVE AISLE

NARTHEX

J PLAN

K LONGITUDINAL SECTIC

SCALE FOR ALL PLANS
FT·50   0   50   100   150
METRES 10   5   0   10   20   30   40

SCALE FOR ALL SECTIONS
FEET·10   5   0   10   20   30   40   50   60
Mᵀᴿˢ 5   0   5   10   15   20

entrance (1140) (p. 260E) leads into the transept, to the left of which is the rotunda, rebuilt by the Crusaders 1099, with the Holy Sepulchre itself, reconstructed in recent times; while on the right is the church of the Crusaders. This circular type was copied at S. Gereon, Cologne (p. 587); Little Maplestead, Essex; S. Sepulchre, Cambridge; Northampton; Ludlow Castle Chapel, and the Temple Church, London (pp. 305, 388).

The **Church at Qalb Louzeh** (sixth century) (p. 260H–N), in Syria, has a basilican plan with entrance flanked by two towers, and nave separated by piers carrying semicircular arches. Above are corbels supporting short columns to carry the roof trusses. The church exhibits many points common to all Syrian churches, which broke away from the Roman type owing to distance from the capital.

S. Francesco, Ravenna (560) (p. 263B) was erected by Bishop Neone, and is divided by two rows of columns of Greek marble. In 1261 it was granted to conventual friars, who gave it its present name.

S. Demetrius, Salonica (500–50) (damaged 1917, and since completely restored) is a five-aisled basilican church with transepts and galleries, and shows the variety of treatment during this period.

In Asia Minor, as at Ancyra, Pergamon, and Hierapolis; in North Africa as at Algiers; and also in Egypt, where the early Christians were known as Copts, there are a number of basilican churches of the period, but in all the style died out owing to the Muslim conquest in the seventh century.

COMPARATIVE ANALYSIS

PLANS. The Early Christians followed the basilican model for their new churches (pp. 255, 259), and may also have used old Roman halls, baths, dwelling-houses, and even pagan temples as places of worship. The basis was a long nave with either single or double aisles on either side, culminating in an apse and preceded by an atrium or forecourt.

WALLS. These were still constructed according to Roman methods of using hand-laid rubble-concrete of brick or stone, sometimes faced with plaster (p. 252A). Mosaic decoration was added internally (p. 269A), and sometimes also externally on west façades; though little regard was paid to external architectural effect (p. 264G).

OPENINGS. Arcades, doors, and windows were spanned either by a semi-circular arch which, in nave arcades, often rested directly on the capitals without any entablatures (pp. 267E, 269B), or by a lintel, as in the doorway of the Tomb of Theodoric, Ravenna (p. 267R). The marble doors at Cividale, near Udine, in north-east Italy, show the ornate character sometimes attempted (p. 267M). Windows, filled in with pierced slabs of marble, alabaster, or plaster, were small (p. 267L, P); those of the nave were in the walls above the aisle roofs (pp. 252A, 264B). This system was developed in the wonderful clear-storeys of Gothic architecture (p. 372).

ROOFS. Timber roofs (pp. 264A, H, 269B) covered the central nave, and only simple forms of construction, such as king and queen post trusses, were employed. It is believed that the decoration of the visible framework was of later date, as at S. Miniato, Florence pp. 320, 321A, B). The narrower side aisles were occasionally vaulted and the apse was usually domed and lined with beautiful glass mosaics, which formed a fitting background to the sanctuary (pp. 252B, 256A, 267A, B).

COLUMNS. These differ both in design and size, as they were often taken from earlier Roman buildings, which had either fallen into ruin or been purposely destroyed (pp. 256A, 263, 269). It was natural that early Christian builders should use materials and ornament of the pagan Romans, and, as these belonged to the later period of Roman art, a grand effect was obtained though the details of the design were not necessarily homogeneous. It is possible that all the fine marble columns, whether Doric, Ionic, or Corinthian, in the churches of Rome were taken from ancient Roman buildings, except those in S. Paolo fuori le Mura.

The carved capitals are governed by Roman pagan precedent (p. 267G) and sometimes by Byzantine (pp. 252B, 267J), and in both the acanthus leaf forms an important part (p. 267C, D).

MOULDINGS. These are coarse variations of old Roman types, and the carving, though rich in general effect, is crude; for the technique of the craftsman had gradually declined (p. 267R). Enrichments were incised on mouldings in low relief, and the acanthus ornament, although still copied from the antique, became more conventional in form.

ORNAMENT. The introduction of colour gave richness and glimmering mystery to interiors. The mosaics which lined the domed apses generally represented Christ, the Virgin, apostles or saints with all those symbolic emblems which now entered largely into decoration (pp. 252B, 267A, B). The arch of triumph, separating the nave from the bema, was ornamented with appropriate subjects (p. 256); long friezes of figures lined the wall above nave arcades (p. 269A), and the wall spaces between the clear-story windows often had mosaics illustrating Christian history or doctrine. The figures were treated in strong colours on a gold background in a bold and simple design, and an earnest and solemn expression, fitting well the position they occupy, characterized the groups. The method of execution was coarse and bold, and no attempt was made at neatness of joint or regularity of bedding of the mosaic cubes. The mosaic work is comparable with that in Byzantine churches (p. 292B) and was usually executed by Greek workmen. The coloured pavements were largely formed of slices from old Roman porphyry or marble columns, worked into designs by connecting bands of geometrical inlay on a field of white marble (p. 267Q, S, T), and were highly decorative. The glass mosaics of the high altar, ambones, screens, Easter candlesticks, and episcopal chairs, as in the fittings of the church of S. Clemente, Rome (p. 255C–H), were of a more delicate description. Fonts, as in the Venice Museum (p. 267K), and well-heads, as that from the cloisters of S. Giovanni in Laterano, Rome (p. 267N), were subjects upon which much skilful carving was expended. The sculptured sarcophagi of the Early Christians belonging to the great families of Rome, though of small artistic merit, had carved bas-reliefs in the quaint and crude craftsmanship of the period (p. 267H), and it is not unusual to find, crowded together on one and the same sarcophagus, such various incidents as Adam and Eve in the Garden, Moses striking the rock, Daniel in the lions' den, the Virgin and Child worshipped by the Magi, and the denial of Peter. Sometimes, as in S. Apollinare in Classe, Ravenna, the Cross, the symbol of Christianity, was accompanied by other Christian symbols (p. 252B) such as the emblems of evangelists and saints, which now replaced the attributes of heathen deities, and became usual features in the decorative scheme (p. 267D, E, K, N). The Angel of S. Matthew, the Lion of S. Mark, the Ox of S. Luke, and the Eagle of S. John, as well as the dove, peacock, anchor, olive branch, and monogram of Christ (the Chi-rho), are woven into the scheme of symbolism of the new religion. Pictures, emblems and symbols are all used miscellaneously to represent the various aspects of the Christian faith. Besides all this sumptuous decoration of church apses, roofs, walls, piers, and floors, there was the more delicate ornamental work in ivory and precious metals for diptychs, croziers, pyxes, chalices, and patens, and all the small appurtenances of Christian ritual, of which many beautiful specimens are to be seen in museums.

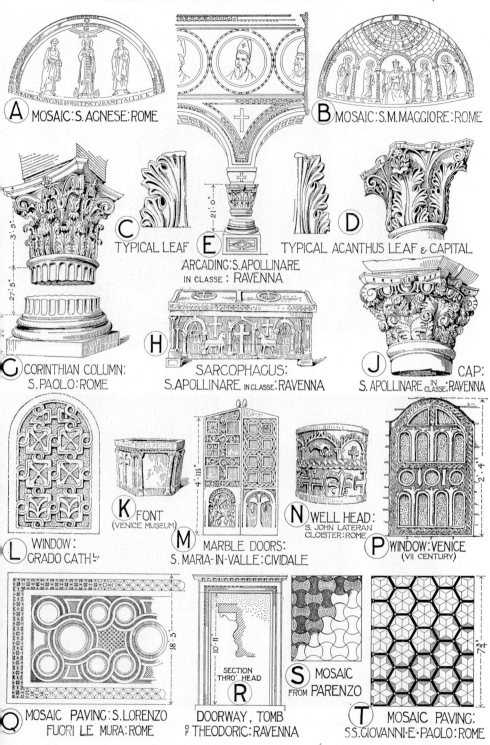

A MOSAIC: S. AGNESE: ROME

B MOSAIC: S.M. MAGGIORE: ROME

C TYPICAL LEAF

D TYPICAL ACANTHUS LEAF & CAPITAL

E ARCADING: S. APOLLINARE IN CLASSE: RAVENNA

G CORINTHIAN COLUMN: S. PAOLO: ROME

H SARCOPHAGUS: S. APOLLINARE IN CLASSE: RAVENNA

J CAP: S. APOLLINARE IN CLASSE: RAVENNA

K FONT (VENICE MUSEUM)

L WINDOW: GRADO CATH.

M MARBLE DOORS: S. MARIA-IN-VALLE: CIVIDALE

N WELL HEAD: S. JOHN LATERAN CLOISTER: ROME

P WINDOW: VENICE (VII CENTURY)

Q MOSAIC PAVING: S. LORENZO FUORI LE MURA: ROME

R DOORWAY, TOMB OF THEODORIC: RAVENNA
SECTION THRO' HEAD

S MOSAIC FROM PARENZO

T MOSAIC PAVING: SS. GIOVANNI · E · PAOLO: ROME

A. Torcello Cathedral, near Venice (rebuilt 1008). Apsidal end. See p. 262

B. Torcello Cathedral: interior showing screen and sanctuary

C. Syracuse Cathedral. Converted (640) from Greek Doric Temple of Athena (c. 480 B.C.). See p. 262

A. The basilican church of S. Apollinare Nuovo, Ravenna (493–525). See p. 262

B. The basilican church of S. Sabina, Rome (425). See p. 261

REFERENCE BOOKS

BROWN, G. BALDWIN. *From Schola to Cathedral.* Edinburgh, 1886.

BUNSEN, C. C. J. *Die Basiliken des christlichen Roms.* Munich, 1843.

BUTLER, A. J. *The Ancient Coptic Churches of Egypt.* 2 vols., Oxford, 1884.

BUTLER, H. C. *Ancient Architecture in Syria: Expedition 1904–5.* 2 vols., Leyden, 1907–20.

CLAUSSE, G. *Les monuments du christianisme au Moyen Age.* 2 vols., Paris, 1893.

CUMMINGS, C. A. *A History of Architecture in Italy.* 2 vols., New York, 1901; London, 1928.

DAVIES, J. G. *The Origin and Development of Early Christian Architecture.* London, 1952.

FROTHINGHAM, A. L. *Monuments of Christian Rome.* New York, 1908.

HARVEY, W. *Church of the Nativity, Bethlehem.* Oxford and London, 1935.

—. *Church of the Holy Sepulchre, Jerusalem.* Oxford and London, 1935.

HUBSCH, H. *Monuments de l'architecture chrétienne depuis Constantin jusqu'à Charlemagne.* Paris, 1866.

LEROUX, G. *Les origines de l'édifice hypostyle.* Paris, 1913.

MARUCCHI, O. *Basiliques et églises de Rome.* Paris, 1902.

MEER, F. VAN DER and MOHRMANN, CHRISTINE. *Atlas of the Early Christian World.* English translation by Mary F. Hedlund and H. H. Rowley. London, 1958.

MICHEL, A. *Histoire de l'art*, vol. i, pt. i. Paris, 1905.

RIVOIRA, G. T. *Lombardic Architecture.* English translation by G. McN. Rushforth. 2 vols., London, 1910.

STEWART, CECIL. *Early Christian, Byzantine and Romanesque Architecture* (vol. ii of Simpson, F. M., *History of Architectural Development*). London, 1954.

STRZYGOWSKI, J. *Orient oder Rom.* Leipzig, 1901; *Kleinasien.* Leipzig, 1903. *Byzantinische Denkmäler.* 3 vols., Vienna, 1891–1903; and *Early Church Art in Northern Europe.* London, 1928.

VOGÜÉ, MARQUIS DE. *Les églises de la Terre-Sainte.* Paris, 1860.

—. *Syrie centrale.* 2 vols., Paris, 1865–7.

WULFF, O. *Altchristliche Kunst.* Berlin and Potsdam, 1914.

S. Fosca, Torcello (see p. 290).
The basilican cathedral and campanile on the left (see p. 262)

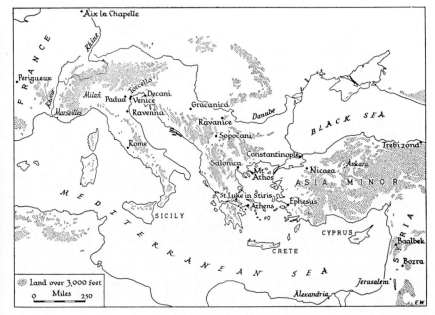

The Byzantine Empire

VI. BYZANTINE ARCHITECTURE

(330 to 1453 and later)

INFLUENCES

GEOGRAPHICAL. Byzantium, renamed Constantinople* after Constantine the Great, its Imperial founder, and also called 'New Rome', was inaugurated as capital of the Roman Empire in 330. It stood at the junction of the Bosphorus and the Sea of Marmora, where Europe and Asia are divided by only a narrow strip of water. This gave it a commanding and central position for the government of the eastern and most valuable part of the Roman Empire. It was also at the intersection of two great highways of commerce, the water highway between the Black Sea and Mediterranean, and the trade route between Europe and Asia; and thus it controlled the corn trade from the northern shores of the Euxine. The natural harbour of the Golden Horn possesses unusual advantages for commerce; for it is four miles in length, unaffected by tides, and of sufficient depth to render its quays accessible to ships of deep draught. Byzantine art pervaded all parts of the Eastern Roman Empire and was carried by traders to Greece, Serbia, Russia, Asia Minor, North Africa and further west, where it is found in Venice, Ravenna, and Périgueux, and it had considerable influence on the architecture of these districts. Venice, by her situation, was a connecting link between the Byzantine and Frankish Empires, and a depot for merchandise from both East and West.

GEOLOGICAL. Constantinople had no good building stone, and local materials

* The name Constantinople is retained in the text of this chapter, but the city has been renamed Istanbul.

such as clay for bricks and rubble for concrete were employed. Other materials more monumental in character had therefore to be imported; marble was brought from the quarries in the islands and along the shores of the Eastern Mediterranean to Constantinople, which was the chief marble-working centre and supplied all parts of the Roman Empire. Byzantine architecture was further considerably influenced by the multitude of monolithic columns of such sizes as were obtainable from the different quarries. These were even introduced into the underground cisterns for the water storage of this Imperial city.

CLIMATIC. The Romans adapted their methods of building to suit the needs of the new eastern capital and to those conditions of life which had there already created traditional forms of art: thus flat roofs for summer resort were combined with oriental domes, and these, with small windows often high up in otherwise unbroken walls, formed the chief features of the style, and sheltering arcades surrounded the open courts.

RELIGIOUS. In the year 313 the Edict of Milan was issued, which granted toleration to Christians, and in 330 Constantinople became the capital of the first Christian Empire. It follows that the chief buildings erected in the new capital were churches for the new religion. At first they were of the basilican Early Christian type, but later the domical Byzantine style was developed. Disputes and differences soon sprang up in the Church and became so rife that the Council of Nicaea (325) was only the first of a series called to suppress heresies. The political division, too, between East and West was followed by a division of the Churches, due in part to the 'Filioque controversy' which developed in the ninth century and eventually culminated in the 'Great Schism' in 1054. The Western Church held that the Spirit proceeded from the Father and Son, while the Eastern Church maintained that the Spirit proceeded from the Father only. The Eastern and Western Churches had been further divided by the 'Iconoclastic movement,' which resulted from the decree of the Eastern Emperor, Leo III (717–41), who, fearing that idolatry would be fostered by the use of sculpture, forbade all representations of human or animal forms. Many Greek artists thereupon left Constantinople for Italy, where, under Pope Gregory II, they could carry on their art unmolested by Imperial decrees. This movement resulted in the admission of painted figures in the decoration of Eastern churches, but all statues were still excluded. These controversies and other differences in ritual have vitally affected Byzantine church architecture up to the present day. Byzantine architecture, devoid of statues, has always been and still remains the official style of the Greek or Orthodox Church of eastern Europe which has conserved unchanged its doctrines and ritual. Therefore the architecture also became stereotyped in form through all periods, in sharp contrast with the changes and additions which characterize the developments of mediaeval architecture to suit it to the varying requirements of church economy and ritual in western Europe.

SOCIAL. Constantine reviewed the attempt initiated by Diocletian (284–305) to provide adequate civil government and military protection throughout the widespread Roman Empire and showed his statesmanship in his manner of dealing with this political problem, just as he did in securing support for himself from the growing power of Christianity by establishing it as the state religion. Diocletian's attempt, however, to solve the difficulty of managing the Eastern Empire from the west of Italy by instituting three seats of government, in addition to that of Rome, had proved ineffectual and open to abuse, and therefore when Constantine in his turn was confronted with the same difficulty he took the bold course of transplanting his capital from Rome to Byzantium (330) because he recognized the political value of its central position in the Empire. Byzantium was an old Greek city,

S. Sophia, Constantinople, from S.W. (532–7). See pp. 280 ff.
The minarets are a Turkish addition

S. Sophia, Constantinople: interior looking towards apse (532–7). See pp. 280 ff.

and so the new Imperial buildings were executed by Greek craftsmen untrammelled by Roman traditions. Within the fortifications of Constantine, the new city was laid out on Roman lines, so far as the hills and site allowed. There was the central dividing street running through a succession of six forums of which the original Augusteum was adjoined, not only by S. Sophia, the greatest glory of early Christendom, but also by the Imperial palace, senate house, and law courts. The Forum of Constantine, with its great porphyry column, was the centre of commercial life, while, in the Hippodrome hard by, the chariot races took place which were the chief amusement of New Rome, as gladiatorial combat had been of Old Rome. The Hippodrome held the same position in the social life of New Rome as the Colosseum and thermae did in Old Rome, and was indeed used for all purposes and on all occasions—for the election of emperors, burning of martyrs, execution of criminals, and for triumphal processions—and so was truly termed the axis of the Byzantine world. The emperors paid the same attention to the water supply of their new as of their old capital, for water was brought by aqueducts and stored in enormous underground cisterns with roofs upheld by many hundreds of columns. As time went on and the population increased the city of Constantine was extended, and the Great Wall with its famous military gates and many towers was built by Theodosius II (413) to set a circle of land and water fortifications against the attacks of Huns and Goths. Constantine, the strong man and despotic ruler, was followed by emperors too weak to assert their authority, and thus the Empire was divided in 364. After Theodosius, the first emperor to emerge into prominence was Justinian (A.D. 527–65), who codified the Roman laws, was a great patron of architecture, and was responsible not only for the rebuilding of S. Sophia, but also for many other churches in the city and in Syria and Palestine. During the Macedonian dynasty (867–1057) and the Comnenian dynasty (1081–1185) there was a remarkable outburst of building activity. In spite of its culture, commercial prosperity and industrial activity, the Byzantine Empire's increasingly isolated situation as a bulwark of Christian civilisation, and its exposure to attacks by barbarians from the north and Muslims from the east, led in the end to its destruction. Decay from within facilitated defeat from without. The final crash came when the capital was captured by the Ottoman Turks in 1453.

HISTORICAL. Byzantium was founded as a Greek colony c. 660 B.C., and in A.D. 330 became the capital of the Roman Empire. On the death of the Emperor Theodosius I (395) the Empire was finally divided, and Byzantium continued to be the capital of the Eastern Empire, and throughout the Middle Ages was the bulwark of Christianity against the attacks of Slav barbarians on the west, and of Muslims on the east. Honorius (395–423), the first Western Emperor of the newly divided Empire, removed his residence from Rome to Ravenna on the east coast of Italy (404), and consequently there was great building activity in that city, which, from its position, was peculiarly susceptible to Byzantine influence. A further impetus was given to building when Ravenna became an archiepiscopal see in 438. During the reign of Justinian (527–565) Sicily and Italy were recovered to the Eastern Empire, and this new connection promoted a revival of building in Italy; here again Byzantine influence came into play, and from before 584 to 752 Ravenna was the seat of the exarch or representative of the Byzantine Emperors, and its buildings of this period became of a still more pronounced Byzantine type. The history of the Byzantine Empire from the fifth to the eleventh century is one of fluctuating and gradually declining fortunes. It first lost its western provinces in the fifth century, some of which, including Italy and Sicily, were regained in the sixth century under Justinian; while again in the following century its strength was greatly reduced by conflict with the Persians, but yet once more in the eighth century the

Empire somewhat recovered itself, till in the ninth century it was again strong enough to carry on fierce contests against the Muslims, who were long kept at bay on the eastern side. In the eleventh century the decline was accelerated because, besides having enemies on the east and north, the Empire was now attacked by Normans and Venetians, till the 'Latin occupation' of Constantinople was accomplished in 1204 and lasted to 1261. The old Empire still staggered on for nearly two hundred years, but its vitality had been sapped by internal dissensions and continuous warfare against the Persians and Turks, and it was finally captured by Ottoman Turks in 1453. Nevertheless, the spirit of the Byzantine Empire persisted even after the Empire had fallen, especially in Russia and in the Balkans. Constantinople has continued up to the present day as the seat of a Patriarch of the Orthodox Church.

ARCHITECTURAL CHARACTER

The character of Byzantine architecture, which dates from the fifth century to the present day, is determined by the novel development of the dome to cover polygonal and square plans for churches, tombs, and baptisteries. The practice of using a domical system of roof construction is in strong contrast to the Early Christian timber trusses and the Romanesque system of stone vaults. It may be broadly stated that the basilican type of plan belongs to Early Christian architecture (Chapter V) and the domed, centralized type of plan to the Byzantine. At the same time, during the first few centuries of the Byzantine Empire one may find domical constructions in Italy and basilican plans in the Eastern Empire. The system of construction in hand-laid concrete, introduced by the Romans, progressively had become more like regular brickwork, and in this form was adopted by the Byzantines. The carcase of brickwork was first completed and allowed to settle before the interior surface sheathing of unyielding marble slabs was added, and this independence of the component parts is characteristic of Byzantine construction (p. 277G, M). Brickwork, moreover, lent itself externally to decorative caprices in patterns and banding, and internally it was suitable for covering with marble, mosaic, and fresco decoration. The Byzantines therefore took great pains in the manufacture of bricks, which were employed alike in military, ecclesiastical, and domestic architecture. The ordinary bricks were like the Roman, about an inch and a half in depth, and were laid on thick beds of mortar. This general use of brickwork necessitated special care in making mortar, which was composed of lime and sand with crushed pottery, tiles, or bricks, and much of it remains as hard as that in the best buildings of Rome. The decorative character of external façades depended largely on the arrangement of the facing bricks, which were not always laid horizontally, but sometimes obliquely, sometimes in the form of the meander fret, sometimes in the chevron or herring-bone pattern, and in many other similar designs, giving great variety to the façades. An attempt was also made to ornament the rough brick exteriors by the use of stone bands and decorative arches. Walls were sheeted internally with marble (p. 277L), and vaults and domes with coloured glass mosaics on a golden background. The churches of Constantinople, Nicaea, and Salonica show the perfection to which this scheme of decoration was carried.

The dome, which had always been a traditional feature in the East, became the prevailing motif of Byzantine architecture, which was a fusion of the domical construction with the Classical columnar style. Domes of various types (p. 277) were now placed over square compartments by means of 'pendentives' (pp. 274, 277, 281, 288), whereas in Roman architecture domes were only used over circular or polygonal structures. These domes were usually constructed of bricks or of some light porous stone, such as pumice, or even of pottery, as at S. Vitale, Ravenna

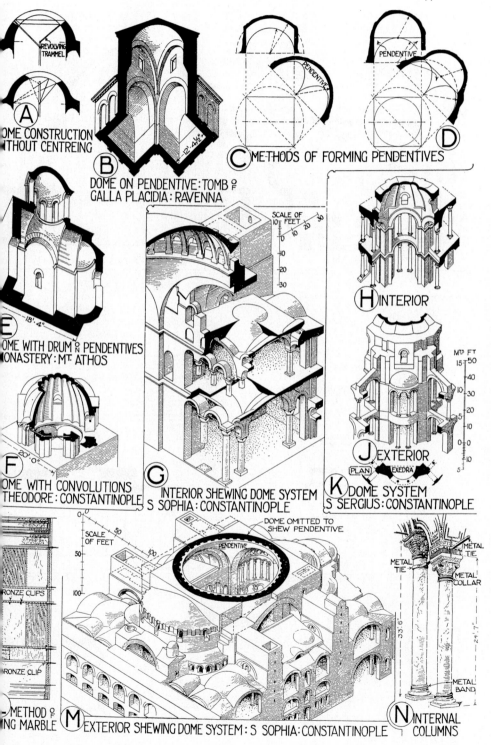

A DOME CONSTRUCTION WITHOUT CENTREING

REVOLVING TRAMMEL

B DOME ON PENDENTIVE: TOMB OF GALLA PLACIDIA: RAVENNA

C METHODS OF FORMING PENDENTIVES

PENDENTIVE

D

PENDENTIVE

E DOME WITH DRUM ON PENDENTIVES MONASTERY: MT. ATHOS

F DOME WITH CONVOLUTIONS THEODORE: CONSTANTINOPLE

G INTERIOR SHEWING DOME SYSTEM S SOPHIA: CONSTANTINOPLE

SCALE OF FEET

H INTERIOR

J EXTERIOR

PLAN EXEDRA

K DOME SYSTEM S SERGIUS: CONSTANTINOPLE

BRONZE CLIPS

BRONZE CLIP

L METHOD OF FIXING MARBLE

DOME OMITTED TO SHEW PENDENTIVE

PENDENTIVE

SCALE OF FEET

M EXTERIOR SHEWING DOME SYSTEM: S SOPHIA: CONSTANTINOPLE

METAL TIE

METAL TIE

METAL COLLAR

METAL BAND

N INTERNAL COLUMNS

SS. SERGIUS & BACCHUS : CONSTANTINOPLE

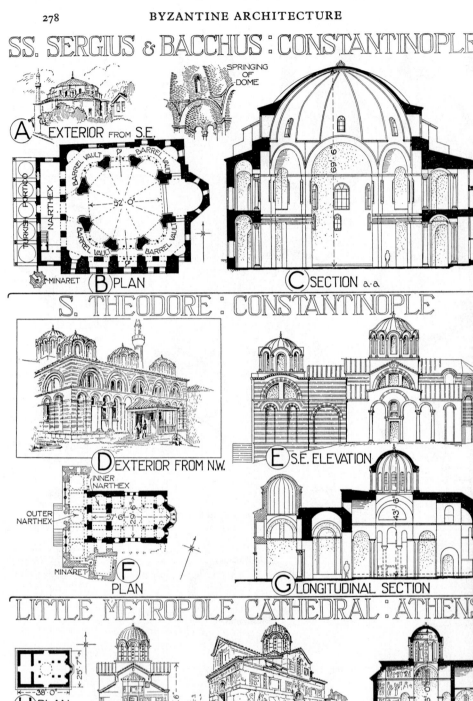

A. EXTERIOR FROM S.E.

SPRINGING OF DOME

TURKISH PORTICO

NARTHEX

BARREL VAULT

BARREL VAULT

BARREL VAULT

BARREL VAULT

52' 0"

MINARET

B. PLAN

C. SECTION a·a

S. THEODORE : CONSTANTINOPLE

D. EXTERIOR FROM N.W.

E. S.E. ELEVATION

INNER NARTHEX

OUTER NARTHEX

57' 6"

29' 6"

MINARET

F. PLAN

G. LONGITUDINAL SECTION

43' 6"

LITTLE METROPOLE CATHEDRAL : ATHENS

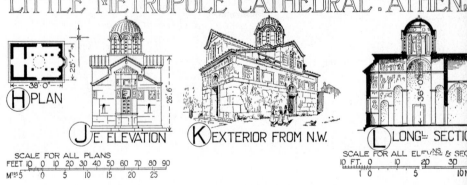

25' 7"

38' 0"

26' 6"

H. PLAN

J. E. ELEVATION

K. EXTERIOR FROM N.W.

L. LONGᴸ SECTIᴼ

36' 0"

SCALE FOR ALL PLANS
FEET 10 0 10 20 30 40 50 60 70 80 90
Mᵀᴿˢ 5 0 5 10 15 20 25

SCALE FOR ALL ELEVᴺˢ & SEC
10 FT. 0 10 20 30
1 0 5 10 M

(p. 285D). Byzantine domes and vaults were, it is believed, constructed without temporary support or 'centering' by the simple use of large flat bricks, and this is a quite distinct system probably derived from Eastern methods. Windows were formed in the lower portion of the dome which, in the later period, was hoisted upon a high 'drum'—a feature which was still further developed in western Renaissance architecture by the addition of an external peristyle. At S. Sophia the haunches were strengthened by a ring of small buttresses to compensate for the weakening effect of the window openings (pp. 273, 281A). The grouping of small domes or semi-domes round the large central dome was effective (pp. 273, 277M), and one of the characteristic features of Byzantine churches was that the forms of the vaults and domes were visible externally, undisguised by any timbered roof (p. 281A, D); thus in the Byzantine style the exterior closely corresponds with the interior. In S. Sophia is seen the perfect expression of the Byzantine style: for the columns are not merely ornamental, but really support the galleries, and semicircular arches rest directly on columns with capitals suitable for supporting the springers of arches of which the voussoirs were rectangular blocks, not set in receding moulded planes as in Mediaeval architecture (p. 330A, B). The Byzantine capital was shaped to form a simple transition from the square abacus to the circular shaft. The numerous columns in S. Sophia exhibit the remarkable and beautiful structural expedient of surrounding the shafts, both under the capital and above the base, by bronze annulets (pp. 277N, 282A, B). Monolithic shafts which, owing to the height required, had to be set up contrary to the stratification of the quarry, were therefore liable to split, and these bronze annulets not only overcame this danger, but also prevented the lead 'seating' from being forced out by the superincumbent weight. Although marble columns from old buildings were utilized, the importation of newly-quarried columns and rare marbles for decorative purposes continued, and the Theodosian code encouraged and regulated this industry, so that coloured marbles were employed to a greater extent than in preceding styles. The interiors were beautified by pavements in 'opus sectile' or 'opus Alexandrinum' (p. 332K), and in domes and apses by coloured mosaics, which were of glass rendered opaque by oxide of tin, an invention which had also been employed in the Early Christian architecture. This use of rich marbles and mosaics resulted in the rounding of angles and in an absence of mouldings and cornices, so that the mosaic designs and pictures might continue uninterrupted over wall surfaces, piers, arches, domes, and apses. Marble and mosaic were used broadly to make a complete lining for a rough carcase, and mouldings were replaced by decorative bands formed in the mosaic. One surface melts into another as the mosaic is continued from arch and pendentive upwards to the dome, while the gold of the background was even introduced into the figures, and thus unity of treatment was always maintained. In late examples fresco painting was often used instead of mosaic. Invariably the pictures were arranged in a special order: the head and shoulders of Christ usually occupied the dome and the four Evangelists were set in the pendentives; the Virgin and Child were customarily located in the apse, and all round the walls were representations of the saints and pictures of incidents in the life of Christ.

The character of Byzantine architecture shows development in its three main periods: (1) 330–850, including the reign of Justinian; (2) 850–1200, including the Macedonian and Comnenian dynasties; (3) 1200 to recent times. The character was also affected by local influences, as seen in examples found in Turkey, Italy, Greece, Macedonia, Armenia, Syria, Russia, Serbia, and France.

The Greek church in Moscow Road, London, designed by Oldrid Scott, and the Roman Catholic Cathedral, Westminster, by John F. Bentley, are modern examples of Byzantine treatment in England.

EXAMPLES

CHURCHES

Byzantine churches are distinguished by the centralized type of plan, having a dome over the nave which, in early examples, is sometimes supported by semi-domes. In later examples the churches are much smaller and the dome is raised upon a high drum with, occasionally, additional smaller domes rising at a lower level. There is usually a narthex, or entrance porch, at the west end, and the east end is cut off from the nave by an 'iconostas', or screen of pictures.

SS. Sergius and Bacchus, Constantinople (527) (pp. 278, 286c), erected by Justinian, is nearly square on plan, 109 ft by 92 ft, and the arrangement of the interior is similar to that of S. Vitale (p. 285c), but it has only four colonnaded exedrae to the central octagon. The church would resemble S. Sophia in plan if it were cut in two, and a dome on pendentives placed over an intervening square and the whole doubled in size. The dome over the central space, 52 ft in diameter and 69 ft 6 ins high, is visible externally, for there is no outer timber roof, and has a peculiar, melon-like form with ridges and furrows from base to summit (p. 277H, J, K).

S. Vitale, Ravenna (526–47) (pp. 285, 299B), was founded by Justinian to commemorate his recovery of Ravenna and was designed on the model of the 'Minerva Medica,' Rome (pp. 206, 285A, B); but Byzantine influence is everywhere evident. An inner octagon of 54 ft 9 ins is enclosed by an outer octagon of 115 ft. The apsidal chancel is successfully designed to open direct from one side of the inner octagon, while the other seven arches enclose columns placed on a half-circle carrying the gallery usual in Eastern churches. The dome is curious, as it rests on pendentives formed of small arches (p. 285D) and is constructed of earthen pots fitted into each other, those in the upper part being laid horizontally, thus producing a lightness of structure which did not require the arches and buttresses found necessary in SS. Sergius and Bacchus and S. Sophia, Constantinople. This remarkable construction in pottery is protected by a timber roof, thus differing from Roman usage and approximating to the practice which prevailed among Mediaeval architects (p. 285D). It is also worthy of notice that the walls, being carried up to support the timber roof, act as haunches and assist in directing the thrust of the dome downwards. The interior is remarkable for the beauty of its carved capitals with dosseret blocks (pp. 299B, 300C), while the mosaics which line the vaults of the sanctuary are unique in this form of Christian art inasmuch as they are a most valuable record of the costumes of the period. Here are life-size figures of Justinian and the Empress Theodora at the consecration of the church in all the glittering array of state panoply and surrounded by the ladies of the Court. Prominent in the centre of the apse is the commanding figure of Christ seated on an azure globe and holding the Crown of Life and the seven-sealed book. The exterior in large thin bricks with thick mortar joints is characteristic of the simple external treatment of so many Byzantine buildings. The fine cathedral of Aix-la-Chapelle (Aachen) (p. 285E, F, G), which was built by Charlemagne as a mausoleum, much resembles S. Vitale, and in all probability was derived from it (p. 357), while SS. Sergius and Bacchus is also similar in plan, but consists of an octagon enclosed in a square p. 278B).

S. Sophia, Constantinople (*Hagia Sophia* = divine wisdom) (532–7) (pp. 273, 274, 281, 282A, B), was built for Justinian by the architects Anthemius of Tralles and Isodorus of Miletus, on the site of two successive basilican churches of the same name, erected respectively by Constantine (*c.* 335) and Theodosius II (415). It was the most important church in Constantinople. The noble atrium forming the

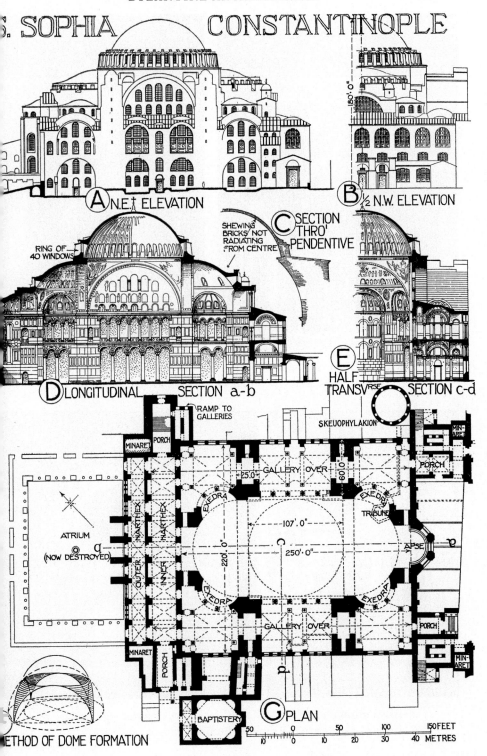

S. SOPHIA CONSTANTINOPLE

A. N.E. ELEVATION

B. ½ N.W. ELEVATION

180'.0"

C. SECTION THRO' PENDENTIVE

SHEWING BRICKS NOT RADIATING FROM CENTRE

RING OF 40 WINDOWS

D. LONGITUDINAL SECTION a-b

E. HALF TRANSVᴿˢᴱ SECTION c-d

RAMP TO GALLERIES

SKEUOPHYLAKION

MINARET
PORCH
MINARET
PORCH
MIN-ARET

GALLERY OVER
25'.0"
60'.0"

OUTER NARTHEX
INNER NARTHEX

EXEDRA
EXEDRA
TRIBUNE

ATRIUM
(NOW DESTROYED)

107'.0"
220'.0"
250'.0"

APSE

EXEDRA
EXEDRA

GALLERY OVER

PORCH

MINARET
PORCH

MIN-ARET

BAPTISTERY

G. PLAN

METHOD OF DOME FORMATION

50   0   50   100   150 FEET
10 0 10 20 30 40 METRES

A. North aisle, looking east

B. Interior from an exedra

S. Sophia, Constantinople (532–7). See pp. 280 ff.

C. Exterior from S.E.

D. Interior looking E.

S. Irene, Constantinople. Rebuilt by Justinian 527–65, and again rebuilt 740.
See p. 284

approach to the church led through the great triple portal to the outer narthex; beyond is the imposing main narthex, 200 ft by 30 ft, which is in two storeys, the lower of which was used by catechumens and penitents, while the upper forms part of the gallery to the church. The plan consists of a central space 107 ft square, with four massive stone piers 25 ft by 60 ft, pierced by arches for aisles and gallery, supporting four semicircular arches upon which rests the dome, 107 ft in diameter and 180 ft above the ground. East and west of this central area are great hemicycles, crowned with semi-domes, the space thus enclosed forming a great oval nave, 225 ft by 107 ft, being about 28 ft wider than the huge vaulted tepidarium of the Thermae of Caracalla. The great hemicycles are flanked by exedrae with semi-domes, and at the extreme east is the apse. North and south of the nave are two-storeyed aisles over 50 ft wide, the upper storey being the 'gynaeceum' or women's gallery, reached from the outside by ramps at each corner and by stone steps in the exterior. These aisles bring the main building approximately to a square which, excluding the eastern apse and the narthex, measures 250 ft by 220 ft. North and south, forming continuations of the four great piers already mentioned, are massive buttresses 25 ft wide by 60 ft long, which take the thrust of the main arches and central dome on the two sides where there are no semi-domes (p. 277M). The two principal semi-domes, east and west, abut against the great supporting arches and thus act as buttresses to the central dome.

The monumental interior (p. 274) gives the impression of one vast domed space, but the detailed effect, with the great hemicycles and smaller exedrae, is one of extreme intricacy, in spite of the simplicity of the general scheme. Scale is obtained by the gradation of the various parts, from the two-storeyed arcades of the aisles to the lofty dome which rests, with little apparent support, like a canopy over the centre, or, as Procopius described it, 'as if suspended by a chain from heaven.' Gigantic pendentives to the central dome overhang about 25 ft and are themselves over 60 ft high (p. 281C), above which the dome itself rises only 50 ft. The dome is constructed of bricks about 27 ins square in the lower part and 24 ins square at the crown, and 2 ins thick, with mortar joints of nearly the same thickness. The joints do not radiate from the centre of the dome, but have a flatter inclination, in order to diminish the thrust. Walls and piers are sheeted with marbles of Phrygian white, Laconian green, Libyan blue, Celtic black, besides Thessalian and Bosphorus marbles, all fixed by metal clips (p. 277L). Floors are laid with coloured mosaics in various patterns, and vaults and domes are enriched with glass mosaics representing apostles, angels, and saints on a glittering golden ground. When the church was used as a mosque most of these were covered with plaster, which is now being removed. The Muslims did, however, leave the representations in the four pendentives of the six-winged seraphim, whom they acknowledged under the names of the Archangels Gabriel, Michael, Raphael and Israfil.

107 columns of marbles are used constructively to support the groined vaults under the galleries, and moulded bronze rings encircle the column shafts at their junction with capitals and bases, while the outward pressure of the arches is counteracted by tie-rods (pp. 277N, 282A, B). The lower storeys of the aisles north and south of the central space are supported by four columns of dark-green marble from the Temple of Artemis, Ephesus (pp. 129, 282B), while the upper storeys have six columns of the same marble. Each of the four exedrae (p. 282B) has two large columns of dark-red porphyry from the Temple of Jupiter, Baalbek (p. 194), and six smaller columns in the gallery (p. 281D). The capitals are mostly of the cubiform type, with small Ionic angle volutes and delicately incised carving, in which is sometimes woven the monogram of Justinian, while a variation of the dosseret block on the lines of the Classical abacus is generally used above the capital. The

lighting is partly effected by forty small windows in the lower part of the dome (pp. 273, 274) and by twelve windows grouped in the spandrel walls north and south under the great arches (p. 274) which support the dome, while there are windows in the lower part of the domes of the exedrae and of the apse. Many of the windows are small and spanned by semicircular arches; others are more elaborate, as in the 'gynaeceum' in which large semicircular-headed openings are divided into six by columns in two heights, between which marble lattice screens admit light through glazed openings about 7 ins square (p. 300K). The building is now a museum.

The exterior (p. 273) is less impressive than the interior, for the brick walls are plastered over and distempered conveying a drab effect at close quarters. The actual shape of the domes and semi-domes is visible, as there is only a covering of lead, ¼ inch thick, resting on wooden battens placed immediately on the outer surface of the brick domes. The immense buttresses and the deeply recessed spandrel wall between them are imposing features in an exterior which depends for effect entirely on the massiveness and general symmetry of its proportions. The lofty minarets were not part of the original design, but were added by the Turks after the capture of Constantinople (1453), and they frame in the subsidiary buildings of the Turkish period. S. Sophia is the supreme monument of Byzantine architecture, and provided the model for many of the great mosques which were built after the Turkish capture. It is the masterpiece of Byzantine architecture, as the Parthenon is the masterpiece of Greek architecture and the Pantheon of Roman.

S. Irene, Constantinople (740) (p. 282C, D) was originally erected by Constantine, but was several times destroyed and finally rebuilt. It is one of the twenty-one Christian churches which still remain in Constantinople, though diverted to other uses. It preserves the basilican plan of nave and aisles with eastern apse and western atrium, and the dome is believed to be the earliest example raised on a high drum pierced with windows. This was found to give dignity to the church, and so became the usual treatment.

S. Theodore, Constantinople (*c.* 1100) (p. 278D, E, F, G), is a perfect specimen of a typical small Byzantine church, although now a mosque. It has a double narthex crowned with domes leading into a nave 29 ft 6 ins square, with central dome formed with curved flutings and set on a drum 13 ft in diameter (p. 277F), and with an apse semicircular internally and polygonal externally. The plan is what is commonly known as the 'cross-in-square' and is characteristic of the later development of the style. The basis of the design is a dome and drum raised upon pendentives over a square space which is usually defined by four columns. From this square project four arms, which are usually barrel-vaulted. At each internal angle is a smaller area, roofed at a lower level, so that the building has a square ground plan but is cruciform above. Sometimes, as at S. Theodore, there is an additional bay at the east end, and usually a narthex at the west end. The exterior is one of the most elaborate of all Byzantine churches in Constantinople, built of brick and stone in bands, with columns supporting semicircular arches surmounted by windows within a second tier of similar arches recessed in rings, while over the outer narthex are the three octagonal tile-covered domes on high drums.

S. Saviour in the Chora, Constantinople (*c.* 1050) (p. 299A), was founded in the fourth century. The central area has a dome on a high drum, 17 ft 6 ins in diameter, pierced by windows, and the nave has semicircular windows on three sides and an apse at the sanctuary end. The inner and outer narthex, with their domes, are richly ornamented with fine early mosaics, and hence it is known as the 'Mosaic Mosque.'

The **Church of the Apostles, Constantinople,** founded by Constantine

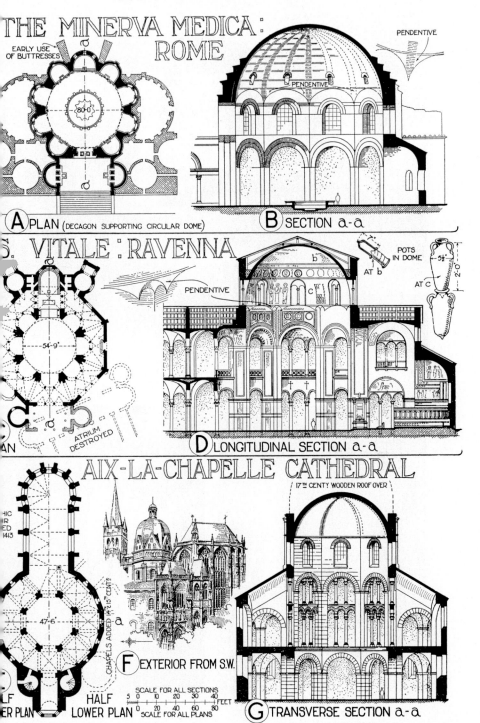

THE MINERVA MEDICA : ROME

EARLY USE OF BUTTRESSES

PENDENTIVE

PENDENTIVE

80·0

Ⓐ PLAN (DECAGON SUPPORTING CIRCULAR DOME)

Ⓑ SECTION a-a

S. VITALE : RAVENNA

54·9

PENDENTIVE

POTS IN DOME

AT b

AT c

ATRIUM DESTROYED

Ⓓ LONGITUDINAL SECTION a-a

AIX-LA-CHAPELLE CATHEDRAL

17ᵀᴴ CENTY WOODEN ROOF OVER

CHAPELS ADDED 14ᵀᴴ&15ᵀᴴ CENTS

47·6

Ⓕ EXTERIOR FROM S.W.

SCALE FOR ALL SECTIONS

HALF LOWER PLAN

SCALE FOR ALL PLANS

Ⓖ TRANSVERSE SECTION a-a

A. S. Theodore, Athens (1049). See p. 290

B. Monastery of S. Luke of Stiris:
interior of small church looking E.
(11th century). See p. 290

c. SS. Sergius and Bacchus,
Constantinople (527).
See p. 280

A. S. Mary Pammakaristos, Constantinople (13th century). South side. See p. 290

B. Church of the Apostles, Athens. See p. 290

S. MARK: VENICE & S. FRONT: PERIGUEUX

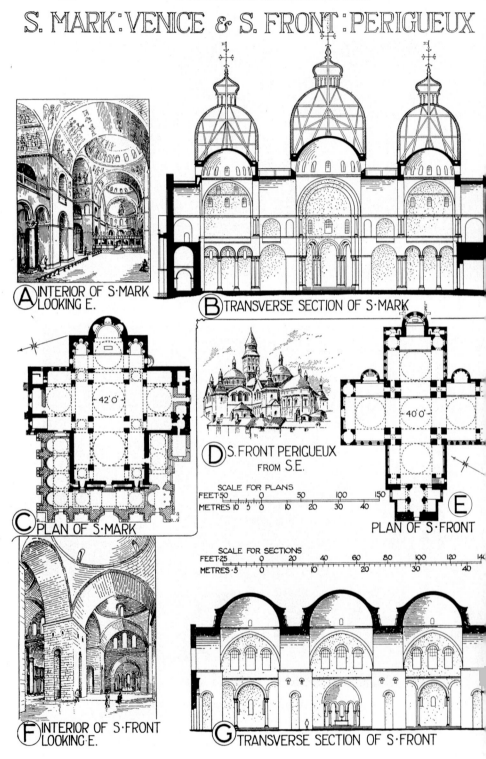

Ⓐ INTERIOR OF S·MARK LOOKING E.

Ⓑ TRANSVERSE SECTION OF S·MARK

Ⓒ PLAN OF S·MARK

42'0"

Ⓓ S·FRONT PERIGUEUX FROM S.E.

SCALE FOR PLANS
FEET·50   0   50   100   150
METRES 10 5 0   10   20   30   40

Ⓔ PLAN OF S·FRONT

40'0"

SCALE FOR SECTIONS
FEET·25   0   20   40   60   80   100   120   140
METRES·5   0   10   20   30   40

Ⓕ INTERIOR OF S·FRONT LOOKING·E.

Ⓖ TRANSVERSE SECTION OF S·FRONT

the Great, was rebuilt by Justinian and destroyed in 1463 to make way for the mosque of Sultan Mohammad II, and had a special interest, as with its cruciform plan and five domes it is said to have been the prototype of S. Mark, Venice and S. Front, Périgueux (p. 290).

S. Mark, Venice (1042–85) (pp. 288, 291, 292), reflects the art of Byzantium which so largely influenced the architecture of Venice, situated midway between East and West. The glittering, resplendent façade of the narthex faces the great Piazza of San Marco, which was, like the Forum in ancient Rome, the centre of city life, with the soaring campanile and the Palace of the Doge, all surrounded by stately arcades. This vast open space, paved in marble, forms, in fact, a great public atrium to the church dedicated to the sea-city's patron saint. The history of this city planning, which swept away the waters of an intruding canal and pushed back the buildings to give space to the church, reveals the pride of the prosperous Republic in her glorious religious monument, which was, in its architectural style, an assertion of the independent spirit of a freedom-loving people who were always intolerant of the domination of the Popes of Rome. This world-famous edifice stands on the site of the original basilican church, which was founded in 864 to receive the body of S. Mark, and partially burnt down in 976. Between 1042 and 1085 the plan was completely transformed to resemble that of the Church of the Apostles, Constantinople (p. 284): transepts were added, the sanctuary was extended, the narthex was continued round the sides, and the interior altered from the basilican to the Byzantine plan of a Greek cross surmounted by domes. The plan (p. 288c) has a central dome, 42 ft in diameter, and a dome over each arm of the cross. The great square piers, 28 ft by 21 ft, which carry the dome are pierced on both the ground and gallery levels, and arcades support passages connecting the central piers to the extremities of the nave and transepts. The addition of the narthex and bapistery (p. 292A) makes the church approximately square on plan.

The interior (p. 291B) is gorgeous in coloured marbles and brilliant glass mosaics which, extending in one continuous surface over vault and dome, picture the story of the Creation, the fall of man and the Redemption, the miracles of Christ and the legends of the saints, all enshrined in a glowing golden background. Mosaic is here, as also in the vaulted narthex (p. 292B), the real and essential decoration, to which all architectural detail is subordinated, and it is used like the stained glass of Mediaeval churches to produce a popular representation of incidents from the Old and New Testaments.

The exterior, dating partly from the twelfth century, with its five entrance portals (p. 291A), was much enriched by mosaic and marble decoration during the Renaissance. The exterior has indeed a character peculiarly its own; for it is a marvellous blending into one homogeneous whole of a variety of features from many foreign lands. Bronze horses from the triumphal arch of Nero, columns of porphyry, alabaster, and verde-antico from Constantinople and Alexandria, coloured marble facing from Eastern cities, all form part of the world-wide contribution which, in the twelfth century, commanders of warships and captains of trading vessels were alike bidden to levy and bring in as votive offerings for success in commerce and victory in war. In the thirteenth century a crown of gold was given to the building by the unique timber domes (p. 288B), and finally, in the fifteenth century, the façade was further embellished by Gothic canopied niches, ogee arches, and crocketed pinnacles, all of which form a delicate stone framework to the glittering mosaics below. S. Mark depends for beauty externally not only on delicate sculpture, but also on subtle, variable, and indescribable colour, produced by transparent alabaster, polished marble, and lustrous gold mosaic, all set against the azure blue of the Venetian sky and bathed in the sunshine reflected from the shimmering waters of the Adriatic.

S. Front, Périgueux (1120) (p. 288D–G), is an interesting product of Byzantine influence carried west along trade routes by Venetian merchants, and is an almost identical copy in plan of S. Mark, Venice. The entire absence of mosaic, however, shows by contrast how much Byzantine interiors owe to that art, for this French version, appears bare and plain in comparison with the pure Byzantine original.

S. Fosca, Torcello (1108), forming, with the old cathedral (p. 270) and campanile, a picturesque group rising from this island in the lagoons of Venice, is based on the Byzantine plan, with central dome supported by eight columns, while externally an arcade on five sides forms a semi-octagon. The details indicate that this simple building was constructed by Byzantine Greeks who also worked on the rebuilding of S. Mark, Venice.

S. Mary Pammakaristos (Church of the Theotokos) (eighth century) (p. 287A), S. Theodosia (ninth century), and the triple church of **S. Saviour Pantokrator** (founded by the Empress Irene early in the twelfth century), are some of the Byzantine churches erected in Constantinople which have been well preserved considering their conversion into mosques, and are excellent examples of the smaller structures on the typical Byzantine plan of a Greek cross with a central dome, the influence of which spread to Italy, e.g. S. Antonio, Padua (p. 604).

The **Little Metropole Cathedral, Athens** (c. 1250) (p. 278H–L), is the smallest building in the world dignified by the name of cathedral, for it measures only 38 ft by about 25 ft, and the dome, supported on a high octagonal drum, is only 9 ft in diameter, pierced by tiny windows, and its façades are largely made up of miscellaneous marbles from old Greek buildings.

The **Kapnikarea Church, Athens** (875), and **S. Theodore, Athens** (1049) (p. 286A), are similar churches with small central domes raised on octagonal drums, while the **Churches of the Monastery of S. Luke of Stiris** in Phocis (eleventh century) (pp. 286B, 294A), have domes with remarkable mosaics and screens to bema (pp. 286B, 300L, 302). The diminutive proportions of these churches are due to the simple ritual of the Greek Orthodox Church and to the absence of instrumental music and of chairs for the worshippers—an influence which did not apply to churches in the Byzantine style erected, like S. Mark, Venice, for Catholic ritual.

S. Sophia, Salonica (495), one of the earliest Byzantine domed churches, altered by the Turks, has some fine ninth-century mosaics, while the **Church of the Holy Apostles, Salonica** (14th century), has a central and four smaller domes, typical of later Byzantine architecture. Also in Salonica there is a very early domed church, **S. George** (400), which it is believed may have been built on a Roman temple of the pattern of the Pantheon, Rome.

The **Church of the Apostles, Athens** (p. 287B) is an eleventh-century cross-in-square church which has recently been restored. It is situated in a corner of the classical Agora in Athens, and has characteristic Byzantine brick and stone wall construction.

The **Churches** at **Bozra** and **Ezra** in Syria follow a favourite plan of a circle or octagon within a square with niches in the angles. They are considered to be prototypes of Byzantine churches like SS. Sergius and Bacchus, Constantinople (p. 278B), and S. Vitale, Ravenna (p. 285C).

The **Church** at **Gračanica** (1321), in Serbia, with its characteristic exterior of brick and stone and its domes on high drums grouped around the dominating central dome, is probably the most remarkable of all the churches in that country, where the architecture was midway between two influences, arising respectively from Constantinople on the east and Rome on the west, the former prevailing. The churches at Sopoćani (1190), Hilandar (1196), Dečani (1330), Ravanica (1387), and the Lazarica church at Kruševac are other Serbian examples of note.

A. S. Mark, Venice: west façade
(12th century, 13th century gilded domes and 15th century additions).
See p. 289

B. S. Mark, Venice: interior looking E.
(1042–85; cancelli erected 1393). See p. 289

A. S. Mark, Venice: interior of baptistery (1042–85). See p. 289

B. S. Mark, Venice: detail of mosaic in narthex. See p. 289

The churches in Russia are a development of Byzantine architecture. S. Sophia at **Kiev** (1036) is distinguished by having twelve supplementary domes. At S. **Sophia, Novgorod** (1052), the top surface of the dome is steepened, partly to throw off snow and partly for aesthetic reasons (p. 294B); later, considerable emphasis seems to have been laid on the skyline, for the domes have a curious bulbous shape and are raised on tall, cylindrical drums. The most striking example of the style is **S. Basil** in the Red Square at **Moscow** (1554), where there are eight bulb-like domes, each different and all painted in the most brilliant colours.

<h2 style="text-align:center">BAPTISTERIES</h2>

Separate buildings used only for the sacrament of baptism were a feature of Early Christianity. For this rite, Roman circular temples and tombs were occasionally used. As the rite was administered only on three great Christian festivals—Easter, Pentecost, and Epiphany—these buildings had to be of considerable size, and until the end of the sixth century of our era they sometimes adjoined the atrium or forecourt of the church; but after this period, and especially with the introduction of infant baptism, the baptistery was replaced by a font in the church, close to the entrance. When circular Roman temples or tombs were modified to meet the new requirements, these sometimes had to be enlarged. It was difficult to cover the enclosed area with one roof supported only by outside walls, and therefore, whereas the Romans had used internal columns attached to the walls in a decorative way, the Byzantines used columns constructively to support the central roof, and surrounded the whole with a one-storeyed aisle enclosed by an outer wall, which supported a lower roof (p. 295E–J).

The **Baptistery, Nocera** (350) (p. 295H, J), 80 ft in diameter, with a ring of thirty antique columns in pairs, appears to be the first instance of the combination of an internal dome covered by a wooden roof externally; for Roman architects had previously allowed the vault to show externally, as in the Pantheon. This treatment is similar to the practice of Gothic architects, who covered the thin stone vaults of their churches with protecting timber roofs (p. 369C, F).

The **Baptistery of Constantine, Rome** (430–40) (pp. 295E, F, G), built near the Lateran church by Sixtus III, and not by Constantine to whom it is generally attributed, is among the oldest of Italian baptisteries, of which it was probably the model. It is octagonal and the roof is supported by a two-storeyed ring of eight porphyry and marble columns taken from old pagan buildings, while in the centre is an old Roman bath of green basalt converted into a font.

The **Baptistery, Ravenna,** erected 449–52 for the Orthodox community, is octagonal with two internal wall arcades one above the other, similarly placed to the superimposed columns in the Mausoleum of Diocletian, now the Cathedral, at Spalato (Split) (p. 218). The upper arcade is subdivided into triple arches under each main arch, the earliest example of a treatment which became so usual in the Romanesque period (p. 330D). The dome, constructed of hollow tiles, has fine fifth-century mosaics representing the baptism of Christ.

<h2 style="text-align:center">TOMBS</h2>

Up to the fourth century, burial within city boundaries was usually prohibited by law, but the Christian objection to cremation and insistence on burial in consecrated ground, together with the desire to provide monumental tombs which were at once an expression of the Christian faith in immortality and a memorial to the dead, led to the erection of imposing structures, which were usually domed and often enriched with lavish mosaic decorations.

S. Costanza, Rome (330) (p. 296A, B, C, D, E), erected by Constantine for his

A. Monastery of S. Luke of Stiris: the two churches from E.
(11th century). See p. 290

B. S. Sophia, Novgorod (1052). See p. 293

S. STEFANO ROTONDO : ROME

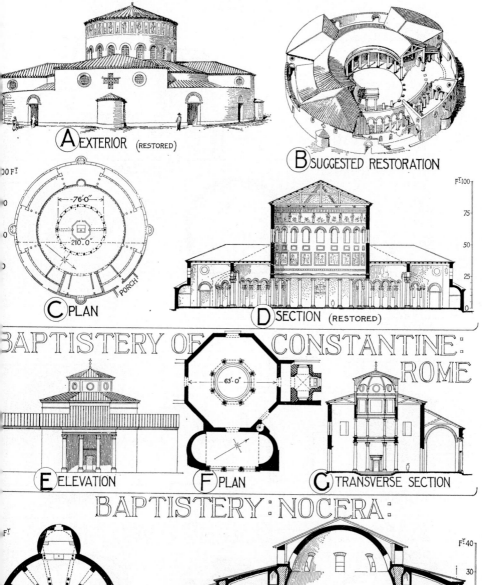

A EXTERIOR (RESTORED)

B SUGGESTED RESTORATION

C PLAN

D SECTION (RESTORED)

BAPTISTERY OF CONSTANTINE : ROME

E ELEVATION

F PLAN

G TRANSVERSE SECTION

BAPTISTERY : NOCERA :

H PLAN

J SECTION

S. COSTANZA : ROME

20 MTRS

FT 60

50 — 15

40 —

30 — 10

20 — 5

10 —

0 — 0

(A) ELEVATION

(B) SECTION ON a·a

40'-0"

(C) SECTIONAL VIEW

FT 100 — 30 MTRS

80 — 25

60 — 20

15

40 —

10

20 — 5

0 — 0

74'-0"
40'-0"

(D) PLAN (RESTORED)

(E) INTERIOR

TOMB OF GALLA PLACIDIA : RAVENNA

(F) EXTERIOR

33'-0"
39'-0"

(G) PLAN

KEY DIAGRAM OF DOME.

(H) TRANSVERSE SECTN.

(J) INTERIOR

TOMB OF THEODORIC : RAVENNA

(K) EXTERIOR

UPPER
CHAMBER
LOWER
CHAMBER

(L) PLAN

(M) SECTION

daughter Constantia, was converted into a church in 1256. The entrance leads to the central space, 40 ft in diameter, encircled by twelve pairs of coupled granite columns which support the dome, and it has a surrounding aisle covered with a barrel vault, ornamented with mosaics of the fourth century representing the vintage.

The **Tomb of Galla Placidia, Ravenna** (420) (pp. 277B, 296F, G, H, J,), appears to be the earliest building which is cruciform in plan, and is extremely interesting as the sarcophagi still remain in their original positions in the arms of the cross. It is 39 ft by 33 ft internally, and the crossing is covered by an unusual dome in which both dome and pendentives are portions of the same hemisphere (p. 277B, C)· The walls are lined with marble slabs, and the dome and vaults still retain the ancient coloured mosaics.

The **Tomb of Theodoric, Ravenna** (530) (pp. 296K, L, M, 299C), is in two storeys, of which the lower, a decagon externally 45 ft in diameter, encloses a cruciform crypt, while the upper storey is circular internally and has traces of an external arcade. The extraordinary roof is formed of one huge slab of stone weighing 470 tons and hollowed into a flattish dome, 35 ft in diameter, on which stone handles are formed for hoisting it into position. The ashes of the founder were deposited in an urn above the dome.

COMPARATIVE ANALYSIS

PLANS. The domical method of construction governs the plan of Byzantine churches, which are all distinguished by a central square, covered with a dome on pendentives (pp. 277, 281). Short arms on each side form a Greek cross, and the filling in of the angles brings the plan nearly to a square (p. 278B). Opposite the entrance was the apse for the altar in the sanctuary, which was screened off by the characteristic 'iconostas' with its three doors, and there were also lateral ritual chapels. The narthex formed an entrance vestibule and was frequently crowned with domes. The essential difference in plan between a Byzantine and an Early Christian church may be summed up as follows: Byzantine churches, unlike Early Christian churches with their campanili, had no bell-towers. The Byzantine church, because of the grouping of subsidiary domes round a central dome, gives a vertical impression; for the eye is gradually drawn upwards towards the central culminating dome (p. 273). The Early Christian church, because of the vista of columns, entablatures, and simple timber roof, gives a horizontal impression; for the eye is led along these horizontal lines to the apsidal sanctuary which is the important feature (p. 256B).

WALLS. The walls were usually constructed of brick and internally encrusted with rich coloured marbles and shining glass mosaics, which swept from wall to arch and arch to vault almost to the exclusion of mouldings and sculptured ornament. In this lavish application of colour to a flat surface all the oriental love of magnificence found full expression. In later examples, fresco painting is more common, and the technique of the Byzantines preceded and equalled the achievements of the early Italian Renaissance artists, Giotto and Duccio. Externally the walls were comparatively plain and depended largely for effect on the brilliant oriental sunshine which clothed them with a garment of glowing colour. The façades were often thrown into prominence by alternate layers or bands of brick and stone, reminiscent of the strata of a quarry (pp. 278D, E, 294A). This simple device further accentuated the connection of the building with the ground in which it had its foundations.

OPENINGS. Arcades or semicircular arches were employed in churches to support the galleries (p. 282B). Doors were usually spanned by semicircular arches (p. 291A), but flat and stilted arches were also used. Pointed arches had been employed in Mesopotamia since the eighth century B.C.; the earliest Byzantine instances, 561–4, built in the reign of Justinian, appear in Syria at Qasr ibn Wardān. In some examples, windows were arranged in tiers (p. 282B). The encircling ring of windows at the base of the dome, or in the drum upon which the dome was raised, was often the chief source of light in the church (p. 274). Windows were also occasionally formed of a thin frame, 3 ins thick, of translucent marble, filled in with glass (p. 300K) and creamy, golden-hued alabaster which the brilliant sunshine wrought into colour like stained glass. The Gothic architects of Northern Europe, where large windows were necessary owing to dullness of the climate, adopted a translucent scheme of decoration by means of painted glass pictures in the large traceried windows instead of sheathing their walls with mosaics.

ROOFS. The method of roofing was by domes of brick, stone, or concrete, often with no further covering (pp. 273, 277, 278). In S. Sophia the vaults are covered with sheets of lead, a quarter of an inch thick, fastened to timber laths resting on the vaults. Hollow earthenware jars were used in order to reduce the thrust on the supporting walls at S. Vitale, Ravenna (p. 285D). The Byzantines practised the system of placing the dome over a square or octagon by means of pendentives (p. 277M), which had only been employed tentatively by the Romans, as in the Minerva Medica, Rome (pp. 177N, 209, 285A, B). Examples of an even earlier date have been discovered in Asia Minor and elsewhere in the East, but wherever the pendentive may have originated, it was the Byzantines who were the first to develop its use on a grand scale.

Domes are of three types: (i) simple, (ii) compound, (iii) melon-shaped (p. 277). In the simple type of dome, pendentives and dome were part of the same sphere. A good idea of this type is obtained by halving an orange, cutting off four slices, each at right angles to the last, to represent the four arches and then scooping out the interior; the portion above the crown of these semicircles is the dome and the intervening triangles are the pendentives. Such a form of dome is, however, rare, and perhaps the only example in Europe before the Renaissance is that over the Tomb of Galla Placidia (p. 277B, C). The compound type of dome gives greater height and was of two varieties, in the first of which the dome ceased to be part of the same sphere as the pendentives, but rose independently above them (p. 277D), and in the second the dome was raised on a high drum pierced with windows (p. 277E). In Russia a further development took place. The dome, instead of having a simple hemispherical outline, was transformed, partly to throw off snow and partly to provide a more attractive silhouette, into a bulbous onion shape (p. 294B). The melon-shaped type of dome was an alternative which involved the treatment of the inner surface, and consisted of curved flutings, as at S. Theodore, Constantinople, and SS. Sergius and Bacchus (p. 277 F, H–K).

COLUMNS. Columns were used constructively, but were always subordinate features and generally introduced to support galleries, as massive piers and walls supported the superstructure (p. 277). In the first instance, columns were taken from ancient buildings, but these were not so numerous in the East as in the neighbourhood of Rome, and therefore the supply was sooner exhausted. This provided an opportunity for designing monolithic shafts. For capitals, the Roman Ionic (p. 300E) and Corinthian and Composite types (p. 300B, D) were sometimes used, but from these was derived a new cubiform type with convex sides (p 300C), suited to carry a rising arch, which took the place of the horizontal entablature, and this resulted in the gradual disuse of the Roman 'Orders' of architecture. Over each type was frequently placed a deep abacus or 'dosseret block,' reminiscent of the

A. S. Saviour in the Chora, Constantinople, with Turkish minaret
(founded 4th century, but rebuilt *c.* 1050). See p. 284

B. S. Vitale, Ravenna (526–47).
See p. 280

C. Mausoleum of Theodoric, Ravenna
(530). See p. 297

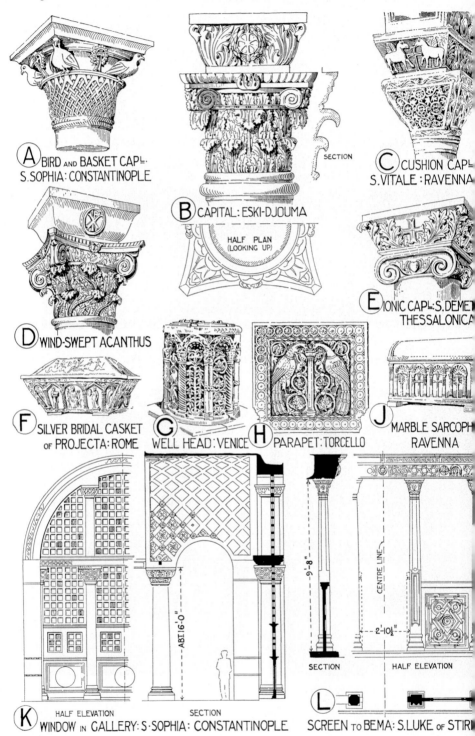

A   BIRD AND BASKET CAP^{L.} S.SOPHIA: CONSTANTINOPLE

B   CAPITAL: ESKI-DJOUMA

SECTION

HALF PLAN (LOOKING UP)

C   CUSHION CAP^{L.} S.VITALE: RAVENNA

D   WIND-SWEPT ACANTHUS

E   IONIC CAP^{L.}: S.DEME^T THESSALONICA

F   SILVER BRIDAL CASKET OF PROJECTA: ROME

G   WELL HEAD: VENICE

H   PARAPET: TORCELLO

J   MARBLE SARCOPH RAVENNA

K   HALF ELEVATION   SECTION WINDOW IN GALLERY: S·SOPHIA: CONSTANTINOPLE

ABT16·1·0"

L   SCREEN TO BEMA: S.LUKE OF STIR

SECTION   HALF ELEVATION

9'-8"   CENTRE LINE   2'-10½"

Classic entablature, or a new invention which performed the function of enlarging the surface of the capital to support the wide voussoirs of the arch or a thick wall (p. 300C, D, E). These capitals were carved with incised foliage of sharp outline with drilled eyes between the leaves, all contained within the general outline of the capital (p. 300C). An effective type is the bird-and-basket capital (p. 300A) from S. Sophia, Constantinople.

MOULDINGS. Mouldings were little used because the marble and mosaic wall linings ran continuously over the surface of walls and arches. Internally, decorative panels of marble and mosaic were sometimes framed in billet mouldings, probably derived from the Classic dentil course, and flat splayed mouldings, with incised ornament, were also used (p. 277L). Externally the simple treatment of walls in flat expanses of brickwork, with occasional stone banded courses, did not leave the same scope for mouldings as in other styles. Flat stone bandings flush with the wall surface were used instead of string courses and cornices (p. 278D, E).

ORNAMENT. The scheme of ornamentation was elaborate in the extreme, for internal walls were lined with costly marbles with veining carefully arranged to form patterns, while vaults and upper walls were sheathed with glass mosaic pictures of symbolic figures, groups of saints, the peacock as the emblem of immortal life, the endless knot as the emblem of eternity, and the sacred monogram of Christ. Byzantine pavements of many-coloured marbles and mosaics were carried out in great variety of patterns, such as 'opus sectile' and 'opus Alexandrinum,' and thus the general colour-scheme was carried throughout the church over floor, walls, arches, and vaults. Mosaic in small cubes was used broadly as a complete lining to brick structures, and mouldings were replaced by decorative bands in the mosaic. One surface melts into another as the mosaics creep from wall, arch, and pendentive to the dome, while one universal golden background gives unity of effect to the whole surface. Greek rather than Roman technique was followed in the carving, on account of the Greek origin of Byzantine craftsmen. A special character of the carving was due to the use of the drill instead of the chisel. The acanthus leaf, deeply channelled and of V-shaped section, was adopted from the Greek variety, but became more conventional in treatment with acute-pointed leaves drilled with deep holes at the springings (p. 300D, E). The great characteristic of Byzantine ornament as compared with Classical is that the pattern is incised instead of raised and was cut into the surface without breaking the general outline. The bridal casket of Projecta (p. 300F), the marble sarcophagus (p. 300J), the wellhead from Venice (p. 300G), and the parapet panel (p. 300H) are all typical examples of Byzantine art and show the close alliance between architecture and subsidiary arts. The screen to the bema of S. Luke of Stiris (p. 300L), with its cubiform capitals and unending knot ornamentation, is an example of church fittings. Figure sculpture was not allowed by the Greek Church, as it was held to savour of idolatry, and so this was an additional reason for the Byzantine type of decoration which expressed itself in flat-coloured pictures and not in raised sculptured figures. Where mosaic was not used, fresco painting was substituted. In their own special way these Byzantine artists, with their miracles of colour effects, rivalled even the artists of Old Greece, whose sculpture stands unchallenged through all ages.

It was as well for the fame of Byzantine art that it had no chance of entering into rivalry with the art of Greece. It was compelled to seek another form of expression, and this necessity gave rise to the wonderful pictures which clothe Byzantine churches in the glowing beauty of surface decoration.

Mosaic in S. Luke of Stiris. See pp. 290, 301

REFERENCE BOOKS

BEYLIÉ, L. DE. *L'Habitation byzantine.* Grenoble and Paris, 1902–3.

CHOISY, A. *L'Art de bâtir chez les Byzantins.* Paris, 1883.

COLASANTI, A. *L'arte bisantina in Italia.* Milan [1912].

DALTON, O. M. *Byzantine Art and Archaeology.* Oxford, 1911.

DIDRON, A. N. *Christian Iconography.* 2 vols., London, 1886.

DIEHL, C. *Manuel d'art byzantin.* Paris, 1910.

EBERSOLT, J. *Monuments d'architecture byzantine.* Paris, 1934.

ERRARD, C. et GAYET. *L'art byzantin.* 4 vols., Paris [1901–11].

FOORD, E. *The Byzantine Empire.* London, 1911.

FOSSATI, G. *Aya Sofia, Constantinople.* London, 1852.

GEORGE, WALTER S. *The Church of S. Eirene at Constantinople.* London, 1912.

GURLITT, C. *Die Baukunst Konstantinopels.* 2 vols., Berlin, 1907–12.

HAMILTON, J. ARNOTT. *Byzantine Architecture and Decoration.* London, 1933.

HARVEY, W. *Church of the Nativity, Bethlehem.* London, 1910.

JACKSON, SIR T. G. *Byzantine and Romanesque Architecture.* Cambridge, 1920.

KNIGHT, H. G. *Ecclesiastical Architecture of Italy.* 2 vols., London, 1842–4.

LETHABY, W. R. *Church of Sancta Sophia, Constantinople.* London and New York, 1894.

MICHEL, A. *Histoire de l'art.* Vol. i, pt. i. Paris, 1905.

MILLINGEN, A. VAN. *Byzantine Constantinople.* London, 1899.

—. *Byzantine Churches in Constantinople.* London, 1912.

ONGANIA, F. *Saint Mark's, Venice.* A large and beautiful monograph in several vols. Venice, 1881.

PORTER, A. K. *Mediaeval Architecture.* 2 vols., New York and London, 1909.

RICE, D. TALBOT. *Byzantine Art.* Pelican Books, London, 1954.

SALZENBURG, W. *Alt-christliche Baudenkmäler von Constantinopel.* 2 vols., Berlin, 1854–55.

SCHULTZ, R. W. and BARNSLEY, S. H. *The Monastery of St. Luke of Stiris in Phocis.* Folio. London, 1901.

SOTIRION, G. A. *The Byzantine Monuments of Cyprus.* Vol. i. Athens, 1935. (In Greek).

SPIERS, R. *Architecture East and West.* London, 1905.

STEWART, CECIL. *Early Christian, Byzantine and Romanesque Architecture.* (Vol. ii of Simpson, F. M., *History of Architectural Development*). London, 1954.

STRZYGOWSKI, J. *Kleinasien.* 4to., 1903; *Byzantinische Denkmäler.* 2 vols., Vienna, 1891–1903.

TEXIER, C. and PULLAN, R. P. *Byzantine Architecture.* London, 1864.

Europe about 1100

VII. ROMANESQUE ARCHITECTURE IN EUROPE

(ninth–twelfth century)

INFLUENCES

GEOGRAPHICAL. On the decline of the Roman Empire, the Romanesque style grew up in those countries of Western Europe which had been under the rule of Rome, and geographical position determined many of the peculiarities of the style in each country. Apart from its Roman origin, from which it took its name, the Romanesque style owed something to Byzantine art, which was carried westwards along the great trade routes, by way of such centres as Venice, Ravenna, and Marseilles, and thus exercised a formative influence, especially in certain districts, as will be seen in later chapters.

GEOLOGICAL. The use of local materials, whether stone or brick, marble or terra-cotta, as well as of ready-made columns and other features from old Roman buildings, accounts for many of the varying characteristics in each country over this wide area, with its different geological formations.

CLIMATIC. Climatic conditions also contributed to differences of treatment north and south of the Alps and Pyrenees. In the duller climates of the north, window openings were enlarged to admit sufficient light, while in the south they were kept small to exclude the dazzling sunshine. The slope of roofs was also largely determined by climate; and it will be seen that the flat roofs of the south gave way to the high-pitched roofs in the north to throw off rain and snow.

RELIGIOUS. Christianity, the chief source of education and culture, was gradually spreading throughout northern Europe, and the erection of a church often resulted in the foundation of a city; for the Papacy had been rising to great power and influence, and rivalled, or even controlled, such civil government as existed. Justinian's Pragmatic Sanction of 554 had already conferred authority on bishops over provincial and municipal governments, and this had increased the power of the Church, which now often nominated public officials. Bishops and abbots were also, by reason of their feudal rank, military chiefs who sometimes took the field in person, and thus the Church was everywhere predominant. Religious enthusiasm and zeal found their material expression in the magnificent cathedral churches and monastic buildings, which were an even more characteristic outcome of this period than were the castles of feudal chiefs. This same religious fervour led to the Crusades against the 'Saracens' who had overrun Palestine and taken the Holy Places, and this long-continued warfare (1095–1270) between Christians of the West and Muslims of the East was not without its effect on Western art. Monastic communities had come into existence as early as the sixth century, and were fostered by Charlemagne, but the eleventh century was remarkable for that great development of the monastic system which gave an impulse to civilization, promoted new methods in agriculture, and exercised its influence on architecture; indeed, until the middle of the twelfth century, science, letters, art, and culture were the monopoly of the religious Orders. The schools attached to monasteries trained youths for the service of religion; monks and their pupils were often the designers of cathedrals, and up to the thirteenth century architecture was almost regarded as a sacred science. (For a description of a typical monastery plan see p. 308).

The chief religious Orders were as follows:

(1) The Benedictine Order was founded during the sixth century in South Italy by S. Benedict, who decreed that architecture, painting, and all branches of art were to be taught. All the pre-conquest monasteries in England, including those of Canterbury (p. 405) and Westminster (p. 423), belonged to this Order.

(2) The Cluniac Order was founded in 910 with the celebrated Abbey of Cluny in central France as its headquarters. Cluniac houses were introduced into England by William the Conqueror at Barnstaple and Lewes.

(3) The Cistercian Order was founded in 1098 at Cîteaux, Burgundy, in protest against the extravagance of the Benedictine system of life and architecture. The Cistercian influence extended to England, and the Abbeys of Furness, Fountains (p. 429) and Kirkstall were built by this Order.

(4) The Order of Augustinian Canons differed little from the Benedictine and was introduced into England in 1108. Carlisle cathedral (p. 406), the abbey churches at Bristol (p. 405) and Oxford (p. 421) which became cathedrals at the Reformation, and S. Bartholomew the Great, London (p. 390), were founded by this Order.

(5) The Order of Premonstratensian Canons was instituted at Prémontré, Picardy (1120). Easby Abbey, Yorks (1152), and Bayham Abbey are examples of its monastic buildings in England.

(6) The Carthusian Order was founded by S. Bruno in 1084. The Grande Chartreuse, near Grenoble, is the French headquarters, and other monasteries of this Order were at Vauvert, Clermont (Auvergne), the Certosa near Florence, the Certosa near Pavia (p. 604), and the Charterhouse, London (p. 885). By the rules of the Order the Carthusians had to work, eat, and drink in solitude. Such a regime explains the original severity of their architecture.

(7) The Military Orders included the Knights Hospitallers or Knights of S. John (1113) and the Knights Templars (1118). The Temple Church, London (p. 390), and the round churches at Cambridge, Little Maplestead, and Northampton were founded by these Orders.

(8) The Friars (*Fratres, Frères*, hence Friars), of which there were several Orders, were of later origin, and their churches, such as S. Andrew's Hall, Norwich, were designed for preaching. (*a*) The Dominicans (preaching or Black Friars) were founded by S. Dominic in 1216, and came to England in 1221. Fra Angelico was one of the best-known members of this Order, which held a high place in Christian art. (*b*) The Franciscans (mendicant or Grey Friars) were founded by S. Francis of Assisi in 1209, and came to England in 1224. Roger Bacon was one of the most distinguished members of this Order, which came to be noted for intellectual attainments. (*c*) The Carmelites (White Friars) received papal recognition in 1226 and came to England in 1240-1. (*d*) The Austin Friars (or Hermits). (*e*) The Friars or more properly Canons of the Holy Trinity, instituted in 1198. (*f*) The Friars of the Holy Cross (Crutched or Crouched Friars), instituted in Bologna in 1169.

(9) The Jesuits belonged to a much later epoch; the Society of Jesus was established in 1540 by S. Ignatius Loyola as a counterforce to the Reformation, and did not reach England until 1580.

SOCIAL. The introduction of the system of feudal tenure, or the holding of land on condition of military service, caused important changes in the social and political organization of states; for through its operation the class of actual slaves died out, but at the same time the poorer freemen degenerated into serfs, bound to the land and passing with it on a change of ownership. As civilization advanced the towns grew in importance, but constant warfare rendered the condition of the people unsettled and craftsmanship was consequently at a low ebb. Each country, as will be seen later, had its special social conditions which affected architecture, while in the days of its greatest prosperity the monastic system played an important part in the life of the people of all countries, especially in rural districts before the establishment of hospitals, and when all learning, even medical, was monopolized by the Church. Guilds of masons, by reason of privileges gradually acquired, did much to facilitate the building of churches.

HISTORICAL. The break-up of the Roman Empire in the West led to the rise of the independent states and nations of Europe. The coronation by the Pope of the Frankish king Charlemagne (800) as Holy Roman Emperor marks the beginning of a new era. From the fall of the Roman Empire till the time of Charlemagne few buildings had been erected, but he gathered artists and craftsmen around him, and before his death (814) he had, in a great measure, restored the arts and civilization to Western Europe. For the next two hundred years little progress was made. After this period buildings sprang up which, with their local peculiarities, will be noticed under each country; but change was slow, as traditional forms were first modified in design and detail, and new features were only added later. Nearly all the nations of Europe had by this time struggled into existence. France, Germany, and Spain were becoming powerful enough to begin to set aside the rule of the Holy Roman Empire, which was afterwards little more than a title. Denmark,

Sweden, and Norway were distinct kingdoms, and at the end of the eleventh century England had been welded into one by William the Norman.

ARCHITECTURAL CHARACTER

The term Romanesque includes those phases of European architecture which were based on Roman art from the beginning of the ninth to the end of the twelfth century, when the Gothic style, combining the pointed arch, flying buttress, traceried window and ribbed vault, was generally adopted. This survey of the Romanesque style is given before treating of the development in each country, viz. in Italy (p. 311), France (p. 335), Germany (p. 353), and England (p. 379). After the Imperial rule of Rome had passed away, her genius still asserted itself in the architecture of the new states and gave it all a certain similarity, until each country developed its own style. Certain districts of Europe fell specially under the influence of Byzantine art, which was itself partly derived from Rome, but which, as East and West drifted apart, had assumed a special character. Western European architecture exhibiting Eastern influence in a paramount degree is classified as Byzantine. To appreciate the character of Romanesque architecture, we must form a mental picture of the conditions of Europe during the period known as the Dark Ages. We must imagine the remains of an ancient civilization, vast in extent and uniform in character, no longer regulated by Roman law and no longer protected by Roman power. Its former glory was now recognizable only by the multitude of its monuments; some were still intact, others were injured or partially destroyed, most were unused, and all were alike unguarded and neglected. This is the Rip Van Winkle period of European architecture. We next see Europe rising like a strong man from the lethargy of a long sleep. He yawns, rubs his eyes, stretches his giant limbs, shakes off his slumber, and stumbles to his feet to look out again upon the work-a-day world and the treasures scattered around. He finds himself surrounded by the achievements of a proud past, and as he becomes conscious of his own needs he realizes the possibilities of the present. Then with dazed eyes and groping hands he collects these treasures of art and applies them to his daily needs. From the ruins of mighty edifices, he gathers fragments of hewn stone, carved capital and sculptured frieze, and places them together, with monoliths of porphyry and marble, upon old foundations to construct some building of service to himself. Thus, by a gradual discovery and understanding of the uses of these old fragments, did he succeed in adapting them to new needs, and thus was a new art founded on the old. Here we have indeed 'new lamps for old.' In this way the birth of Romanesque architecture may be explained, for the ruins of ancient buildings served as the quarry for the new, and necessarily determined the character, both of construction and decoration, in proportion to the extent to which old features were employed.

The later Romanesque style of the tenth to the twelfth centuries was remarkable for the tentative use of a new constructive principle. This was the deliberate articulation of structure, in which each constructive part played a designed rôle in establishing equilibrium. This was in contrast to Roman construction, which had depended upon opposing unco-ordinated masses. This new system, which was accompanied by the use of dressedstones of comparatively small size connected by thick beds of mortar, led in the thirteenth century, after many experiments, to the full development of the Gothic system of architecture, in which elasticity and equilibrium were jointly employed in the erection of the magnificent series of Gothic cathedrals. The general architectural character of the Romanesque style is sober and dignified, while picturesqueness depends on the grouping of towers and the projection of transepts and choir. It will be seen that in Italy, France, England,

and Germany exceptional tendencies were brought about by local conditions; but in all these countries the character depends on the employment of vaulting, based on Roman methods.

Roman cross-vaults (pp. 370, 373) were used throughout Europe till the beginning of the twelfth century, but they were heavy and difficult to construct and were gradually superseded by 'rib and panel' vaulting, in which a framework of ribs supported thin stone panels. The new method consisted in designing the profile of the ribs to which the form of the panels was adapted; whereas in Roman architecture the shape of the vault itself determined the groin, which was formed by the intersection of the vaults. Romanesque architects therefore first decided the profile of the transverse, longitudinal, and diagonal ribs, which last, as groins, had previously been settled naturally by the intersection of the vault surfaces; this arrangement produced the quadripartite (four-part) vault. If the cross-vaults were semi-cylindrical the diagonal groin would be a semi-ellipse (p. 370D), but Romanesque architects did not resort to the use of ordinates as was afterwards done in the Renaissance period; instead, they surmounted the difficulty arising from the different spans of diagonal and transverse ribs in various ways. In France and Germany the vaulting ribs of a square vaulting compartment were usually semicircular curves starting from the same level; therefore the diagonal rib, having the longest span, rose to a greater height than the transverse and longitudinal ribs, and when the panelling was filled in on the top of these ribs each vault was domical (p. 370G). In England vaults were generally constructed with continuous level ridges, instead of in this domical form, and the difference in height between diagonal and transverse ribs in a square vaulting compartment was equalized by 'stilting' the latter or by making the diagonal rib a segment of a larger circle than that of the longitudinal and transverse ribs, which were semicircular, as shown on p. 370G. In vaulting an oblong compartment the difference between the heights of diagonal and transverse ribs was still greater than in a square compartment and produced an awkward waving line of the ribs on plan (p. 373B), but little attempt was made to vault any but square compartments. At Worms (p. 356J), Mainz, and Speyer the difficulty of vaulting oblong nave compartments was partially surmounted by including two of them to make one square bay of vaulting, each corresponding with two square compartments of the side aisles. In some instances, as in the Abbaye-aux-Hommes (p. 342F) and Abbaye-aux-Dames at Caen (p. 338B), Notre Dame, Paris (pp. 531F, G, 532B), and Canterbury (p. 411B), the intermediate pier was carried up as a vaulting shaft to support a rib which altered the quadripartite vaulting compartment into six parts, known as 'sexpartite' vaulting (p. 370E). The main piers were usually more massive than the intermediate because they supported the chief weight of the vaulting. The difficulty of equalizing the height of ribs of different spans, especially in oblong compartments, was finally surmounted by the introduction of the pointed arch in the Gothic period (p. 370G), when the system of 'rib and panel' vaulting was further elaborated by the addition of various supplementary ribs (p. 371).

EXAMPLES

Examples of various buildings, such as cathedrals, churches, and castles, are given under their respective countries. Churches were places of congregation for the people in contrast to pagan temples which sheltered the statue of a deity. The monastic system was necessitated by the requirements of monkish communities which sprang up during the period in different European countries. R. L. Palmer, in *English Monasteries in the Middle Ages*, gives a vivid description of the life and varied pursuits of the monks, which not only helps us to realize the disposition, uses, and extent of the various buildings in a conventual establishment, but also shows the important rôle played by monasteries in the social system of the Middle Ages. They formed indeed the connecting link between the ecclesiastical hierarchy on the one hand and the secular life of the people on the other. These monastic settlements were factors in the development of Mediaeval architecture.

The monks followed different pursuits according to the Order to which they belonged (p. 304). The Benedictine was the chronicler and most learned of all monks; the Augustinian was the preacher and given to disputations; the Cistercian was the recluse and interested in agricultural pursuits; the Cluniac was the student and artist; and the Carthusian was the ascetic. The Friars were the missionary preachers of a later period (p. 305).

A plan has been preserved of the Benedictine monastery of S. Gall, Switzerland (p. 358), which shows that a complete monastic establishment, like Westminster Abbey (p. 425H) or Fountains Abbey (p. 432), consisted of a group of buildings designed for all occupations, both spiritual and temporal, of the monks, and resembled a village with the monastic church as the centre. The monastic group was planned to include the following essential departments: (a) The Monastic Church, situated in a court or Close open to the public. (b) A Cloister Court off which were the chapter house, sacristy, and dormitory with its staircase into the church, while the cellarage for beer, wine, and oil was often under the dormitory. The refectory and kitchens, with their noise and smell, were on the side of the cloister away from the church. The lavatory was usually in the south cloister walk, as at Westminster, Wells, Chester, Peterborough, and Gloucester. (c) An Inner Court with infirmary, guest house, kitchen, servants' hall, library, and the scriptorium for writing and illuminating. (d) A Common Court, approached through a gateway for carts, and surrounded by granaries, bakehouses, stables, store-rooms, servants' rooms, tribunal, prison, abbot's lodging, and barn. (e) Mills, workshops, gardens, orchards, and fish ponds, which completed the monastic settlement. Monasteries served the purpose of inns in little-frequented places, as is the case to this day in some districts on the continent. The plans of some monastic establishments differed in certain details from this description of a Benedictine monastery.

The plans of the churches of the Cluniac Order had double transepts, a feature which was adopted at Castle Acre Priory and in some English cathedrals, as Lincoln (p. 410F) and Salisbury (p. 410E).

The churches of the Cistercian Order were divided transversely into three parts by screens, walls or steps, and there were often no aisles, while the transepts and eastern arm of the cross were short, so that the choir extended westward of the transepts. There was an absence of towers and painted glass.

The Carthusians usually provided two churches, one for the monks and another for the people. A typical feature was the great rectangular cloister, surrounded by an arcade on to which opened the monks' cells, which were self-contained and had their own gardens.

Another variation is found in the churches of the Military Orders, and especially of the Knights Templars. Their churches were circular, in imitation of the Rotunda of the Holy Sepulchre, Jerusalem (p. 262)

COMPARATIVE ANALYSIS

PLANS. The Roman basilica had been the model for Early Christian churches, the plan of which was subject to new developments during the Romanesque period. The addition of transepts and the prolongation of the sanctuary or chancel made the church a well-defined cross on plan, as at S. Michele, Pavia (p. 322E). Transepts were generally the same breadth as the nave, which was usually twice the width of the aisles. The choir was often raised on piers above the level of the nave and over a vaulted crypt, in which saint or martyr had been buried, as at S. Miniato, Florence (p. 321B) and S. Michele, Pavia (p. 322A). In later churches aisles were sometimes carried round the chancel to form an ambulatory. Cloisters in connection with monastic churches are often very elaborately treated with twisted columns, carved capitals, and sculptured arches. Towers, square, octagonal, or circular, are prominent features of most Romanesque churches. They may occur over the crossing, at the west end centrally with the nave, or at the east end. Sometimes they are arranged in pairs at the west end and at the ends of the transepts or at the eastern ends of the aisles, and they often rise to a great height in well-marked stages pierced with windows.

WALLS. Roman methods of craftsmanship still influenced constructive art in Europe, but technical skill in general was at a low ebb. Walls were roughly built, and were relieved externally by shallow buttresses or pilaster strips, connected at the top by bands of horizontal mouldings or by a series of semicircular arches on corbels (pp. 350C, 355C). Attached columns, with rough capitals supporting semicircular arches, formed wall arcading, which was a frequent decorative feature (p. 350G).

OPENINGS. Arcades consisted of massive circular columns or piers which supported semicircular arches, as in the naves of Norman cathedrals (p. 392B). Door and window openings are very characteristic, with jambs or sides formed in a series of receding moulded planes known as 'orders,' in which are set circular shafts surmounted by a continuous abacus. The semicircular arch above was also constructed in receding concentric rings (p. 330B), which followed the lines of the recesses below. A rose or wheel window was often placed over the principal west door, as at S. Zeno Maggiore, Verona (p. 325A), and in South Italian churches, as at Palermo. Glass does not appear to have come into general use till the ninth century.

ROOFS. The general employment of vaulting in the eleventh century, especially over side aisles, may have been due to the desire to fire-proof the building, although the central nave often had only a simple wooden roof. The form of arch employed in vaulting as elsewhere was semicircular, often raised or 'stilted' (p. 370C). Unmoulded ribs were first used about 1100, and later on they were moulded quite simply. Intersecting barrel or cross-vaults (p. 399A) were usual over a square plan, but the difficulty in constructing these over oblong bays finally led to the use of pointed arches in the Gothic period (p. 370G). When the crossing of nave and transepts was crowned by an octagonal dome, four of its sides were carried on 'squinch' arches (p. 322A, D). Romanesque architects began to use flying buttresses under the aisle roofs to counteract the thrust of a vaulted nave roof (p. 342C); but it was left for Gothic architects to place these flying buttresses outside the aisle roof and to weight them with pinnacles.

COLUMNS. In Italy, the traditional monolithic column, often of Roman origin, was usual, but in the West, and especially in France and England, the columns were generally cylindrical and of massive proportions, built up with ashlar masonry and having a rubble core. These were treated with flutings or with spiral, trellis or chevron patterns (p. 392B). Variations of Corinthian or Ionic capitals were used, as in S. John's Chapel, Tower of London (p. 504A), and elsewhere (pp. 332E, F, 351C, G), and in later times the capital was often of a cushion (cubiform) shape, as also in S. John's Chapel, Tower of London (p. 436C), and Winchester (p. 503C), and was sometimes richly carved and scalloped (pp. 503B, D, E, 504 A–C).

MOULDINGS. These were often elaborately carved, as will be seen in English Romanesque (Norman) architecture (p. 508). The base of the column was generally an adaptation of the old Attic form, but the circular moulding often projected over the square plinth below, at the angles of which flowers or animals were occasionally carved to fill up the triangular part (p. 503H). The abacus above the capital (p. 503E) was distinctive in form; it was higher, but projected less than in the Classical column and was moulded with alternate fillets and hollows.

ORNAMENT. Ornament, into which entered vegetable and animal forms, was treated conventionally, and carving and sculpture were often rough (pp. 332, 351, 362, 508). For interiors, frescoes were more usual than mosaics, which had been such a feature of Early Christian churches, while stained glass was as yet little used. Ornament, like all other features, was affected by various influences which are referred to in the chapters special to each country.

REFERENCE BOOKS

CLAPHAM, A. W. *Romanesque Architecture in Western Europe.* Oxford, 1936.

JACKSON, T. G. *Byzantine and Romanesque Architecture.* 2 vols., Cambridge, 1920.

LETHABY, W. R. *Mediaeval Art.* 1904. Revised and edited by D. Talbot Rice. London, 1949.

PALMER, R. L. *English Monasteries in the Middle Ages.* London, 1930.

STEWART, CECIL. *Early Christian, Byzantine and Romanesque Architecture.* (Vol. ii of Simpson, F. M., *History of Architectural Development*). London, 1954.

See also list under each country: Italy (p. 331), France (p. 352), Germany (p. 364), and England (p. 513).

A. S. Denis, Paris: vaulting in narthex.
See p. 344

B. Autun Cathedral: interior looking towards sanctuary (1090–1132).
See p. 343

Italy in the Tenth Century

VIII. ITALIAN ROMANESQUE

(ninth–twelfth century)

INFLUENCES

GEOGRAPHICAL. The long, narrow peninsula of Italy stretches from the snowy Alps on the north, right down through the waters of the Mediterranean, almost to sultry Africa on the south. These geographical variations were accompanied by other differences which influenced the architecture in such varying degrees that it may be most conveniently considered under (a) Central Italy, within the inner zone of Roman influence; (b) Northern Italy, in contact with Western Europe; (c) South Italy and Sicily, open to influences from the East.

(a) *Central Italy.*—The central region lies between Florence, commanding the passage of the Arno, on the north; Pisa, the maritime power on the west; and Naples, the naval port on the south; Rome, the Imperial City, rich in ancient pagan monuments and Early Christian churches, here exercised a paramount influence on architecture. (*b*) *North Italy.*—Milan, the capital of Lombardy, enjoyed great prosperity on account of its proximity to several Alpine passes and its situation in the fertile plains of Lombardy, where the cultivation of the vine and mulberry was then, as now, a staple industry. Venice and Ravenna, which were connecting trade links between East and West, fell geographically under the influences of Byzantine art. (*c*) *South Italy and Sicily.*—South Italy, including Calabria, was by position specially susceptible to influence from the East, and, after passing under Greek and Roman rule, it formed part of the Byzantine Empire under Justinian. Sicily, an island which is triangular in form, is situated in the Mediterranean sea, and, facing Greece on one side, Italy on another, and North Africa on the third, was exposed to influences from all three countries.

GEOLOGICAL. (*a*) *Central Italy.*—Tuscany possessed great mineral wealth and an abundance of stone. Various building materials were used in Rome, including bricks, volcanic tufa or peperino, travertine stone from Tivoli, and marble from Carrara and from Paros and other Greek islands. Much material was also obtained from the ruins of Classic buildings. (*b*) *North Italy.*—The low-lying plains of Lombardy supplied clay for making bricks, which, used with marble from the hills, gave a special character to the architecture. Venice on the Adriatic imported marbles in her merchant vessels. (*c*) *South Italy and Sicily.*—The mountains of South Italy and Sicily supplied calcareous and shelly limestone as well as many kinds of marble, while the sulphur mines, especially of Sicily, largely contributed to that prosperity which was conducive to building enterprise.

CLIMATIC. (*a*) *Central Italy.*—The brilliant sunshine demanded, as in the Roman period, small windows and thick walls, both in cities of the plain and in cities built on the hill-tops. The climate varies not only from north to south, but also from east to west according to the proximity to the Apennines, which are often snow-clad, or to the sea-board. (*b*) *North Italy.*—The climate resembles that of Central Europe, and varies between extremes of heat and cold. The towns from Milan on the west to Venice on the east lie below the Alps, and thus in the winter they are swept by the ice-winds from the mountains; while in the summer these same mountains protect them from the north winds, when the heat in the plains is often excessive. (*c*) *South Italy and Sicily.*—The climate is almost sub-tropical; palms grow in the open air and the orange and lemon groves of Palermo are famous. On the southern coasts of Italy buildings have the flat roofs and other characteristics of Oriental cities.

RELIGIOUS. (*a*) *Central Italy.*—During this period the Popes, although they had only small temporal dominions, began to be a power in civil government, and thus started opposing policies and rival factions. Pepin, king of the Franks, sided with Pope Stephen II against the Lombards and restored to him Ravenna, the chief city of the Exarchate. In 755 Central Italy became independent under the Pope, and so inaugurated the temporal power of the papacy. Then Charlemagne, invited by Pope Adrian I (772–95), advanced into Italy in 773, defeated the Lombards and entered Rome for the first time, in 774. He bestowed the dukedom of Spoleto on Pope Adrian, and thus added to his temporal power, while the wealth of the Church rapidly increased, and from this period the papal connection with Byzantium was broken off. The decisions of Gregory VII (1073–85) that the clergy should not marry, and that no temporal prince should bestow any ecclesiastical benefice, resulted in the long struggles between Guelphs and Ghibellines (pp. 315, 603). (*b*) *North Italy.*—The Emperor Theodosius had, in Early Christian times, been forced to do penance for the massacre in Thessalonica, and S. Ambrose, bishop of

PISA CATHEDRAL

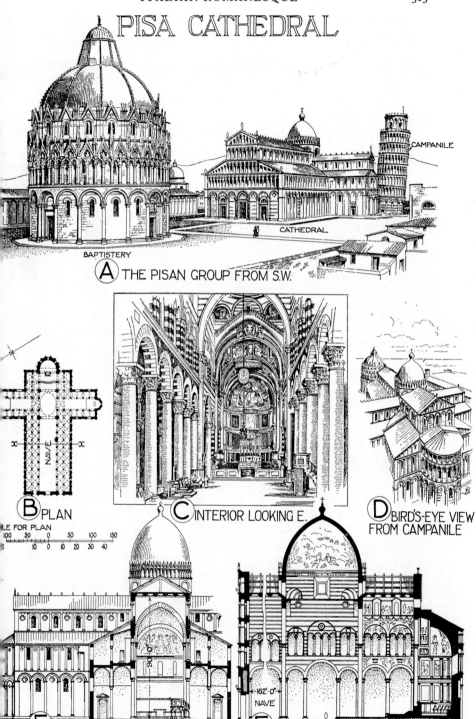

A THE PISAN GROUP FROM S.W.

BAPTISTERY

CATHEDRAL

CAMPANILE

B PLAN

NAVE

SCALE FOR PLAN
100 50 0   50   100   150
      10 0 10 20 30 40

C INTERIOR LOOKING E.

D BIRD'S-EYE VIEW FROM CAMPANILE

E TRANSVERSE SECTION x·x

F LONGITUDINAL SECTION

NAVE 162'·0"

APSE

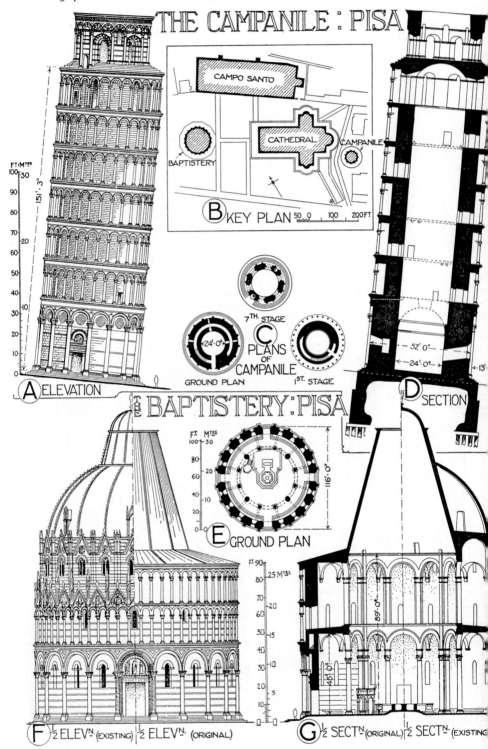

THE CAMPANILE : PISA

B KEY PLAN

CAMPO SANTO

CATHEDRAL

BAPTISTERY

CAMPANILE

50   0   100   200 FT

C PLANS OF CAMPANILE

7TH. STAGE

GROUND PLAN   1ST. STAGE

24'·0"

A ELEVATION

151'·3"

D SECTION

52' 0"

24'·0"

13'

THE BAPTISTERY : PISA

E GROUND PLAN

116' 0"

F ½ ELEVN. (EXISTING) | ½ ELEVN. (ORIGINAL)

G ½ SECTN. (ORIGINAL) | ½ SECTN. (EXISTING)

89' 0"

45' 0"

Milan (374–98), closed the church doors against him. This is significant of the great power the Church had acquired. The influence of S. Ambrose had been sufficient to establish the Ambrosian ritual, which introduced more metrical chanting into the service, and, owing to his fame, it was long maintained in Milan instead of the Roman liturgy. The power, both spiritual and temporal, of the archbishops of Milan, especially under Aribert (1018–45), was firmly established by their espousal of the people's cause and their stand for popular rights against the Lombard kings. (c) *South Italy and Sicily.*—Under Muslim rule (827–1061), which reached Sicily from North Africa, even church façades were ornamented with geometrical patterns, because the Muslim religion forbade representations of the human figure (Ch. XXXIII). The Muslim and the earlier Byzantine influence persisted even after the Norman conquest of the region in 1061.

SOCIAL. (a) *Central Italy.*—The artistic activity of Tuscany in the eleventh century showed itself chiefly in architecture, which provided a suitable setting for the daughter arts of painting and sculpture. The growth of an industrial population, the increase of commerce, and the rise of ruling families promoted the foundation of independent and fortified cities, such as Pisa, Lucca, and Pistoia, which were all competitors in architectural achievements. (b) *North Italy.*—The devastating inroads by the Goths into the North Italian plains led to the gradual rise of the powerful Venetian state; for the hardy northern traders planted their new colony on the islands of the lagoons. There, safe from serious attacks, they settled on a republican form of government, which afterwards became an oligarchy under a Doge, who was invested with supreme authority. Commerce and art were the special care of the Venetians. They raised glorious buildings in the sea and brought precious freights from the East, even including relics from the Holy Land. Thus did the East triumph in the West through its influence on the buildings of the Queen of the Adriatic. All the free cities, or independent commonwealths of Italy, such as Milan, Pavia, Verona, and Genoa, vied with one another in the beauty of their public buildings, and this spirit of rivalry encouraged the most remarkable structural advances in all Italy. (c) *South Italy and Sicily.*—The Muslims stimulated commercial enterprise in Sicily. Civilization there had been, however, considerably aided by earlier Byzantine influences. The traditional use of mosaic in decoration was fostered by the Norman kings who established a school of mosaic at Palermo. Southern Italy, which always maintained a close connection with Sicily, has yet to be fully explored for traces of its architectural development.

HISTORICAL. (a) *Central Italy.*—Pisa, like Genoa in the north and Amalfi in the south, sent merchant fleets to the Holy Land for the Eastern Fair at Jerusalem, and thus were the Pisans brought into contact with Eastern art. At the commencement of the eleventh century Pisa was the rival of Venice and Genoa as a great commercial and naval power, and took the lead in the wars against the infidels, defeating the Muslims in 1025, 1030, and 1089. The Pisans also captured Palermo in 1062, and this contact with the Muslims probably accounts for the characteristic Pisan use of striped marbles. The Pisans were defeated by the Genoese in 1284, and this was the beginning of their decline. The rise of Florence dates from 1125, when the inhabitants of Fiesole moved there, owing to the destruction of their city, and in the following century Florence rivalled Pisa in commerce. Lucca, another important city during this period, was rent by the feuds of the Guelphs, supporters of the Popes, and the Ghibellines, who sided with the Emperors. This dual influence is traceable in architectural features of the city, such as battlements of castles and fortifications. (b) *North Italy.*—The close alliance which Venice kept up with Constantinople increased the commercial and naval importance of the sea-state so that, by the end of the eleventh century, her trade extended beyond Dalmatia,

Croatia, and Istria to the Black Sea and the Mediterranean coasts. In spite of the intervening Alps, the invaders who had occupied the valley of the Po kept up commercial communications with those on the Rhine, by means of the Alpine passes; so that Milan in the plains of Lombardy was subject, then as afterwards, to German influence in art, but the old Roman influence reasserted itself in the eleventh and twelfth centuries which witnessed great building activities in Lombardy. (*c*) *South Italy and Sicily.*—In 827 the Muslims landed in Sicily and gradually overran the island, which had formed part of the Byzantine Empire. The latter part of the tenth century was the most prosperous period of their sway, but sanguinary religious struggles ended in the downfall of the Muslim dynasty. From 1061 to 1090 the Normans, under Robert and Roger Guiscard, were engaged in the conquest of the island, and in 1130 a descendant of the latter was crowned at Palermo. During the succeeding years Sicily was again prosperous, as may be judged by the number and beauty of the buildings of this period, and her fleet was powerful enough to defeat the Arabs and Greeks.

ARCHITECTURAL CHARACTER

The Romanesque Period in Italy may be taken to date approximately from the ninth to the twelfth century.

(*a*) *Central Italy.*—The basilican type of church was closely adhered to during this period; for Italians were slow to adopt a new system of construction and preferred to concentrate on beauty and delicacy of ornamental detail, while the architectural character was much governed by Classic traditions. The most pronounced features of façades were the ornamental arcades which rose one above the other, sometimes even into the gables (pp. 313A, 314). This decorative use of arcaded galleries is one instance of the employment of an architectural feature having a constructive origin. When a wooden roof was placed over a vault there was no need to continue the solid external walls above the springing of the vault, as wooden rafters exerted little thrust (p. 295J); hence this upper portion of the wall could be pierced or arcaded (p. 330E, G), and this arcading came to be employed, especially by the Pisans, as a decorative feature, and sometimes even entirely covered the western façade (p. 313A). In a similar way the battlemented parapet, primarily designed for defence, was used as a purely decorative feature. It must also be understood that by carrying the external walls above the springing of the vault, an additional load was provided which usefully deflected the vault thrust. The use of marble for facing walls distinguishes Romanesque architecture in Italy from that of the rest of Europe (p. 321A). The churches had, for the most part, simple open timber roofs ornamented with bright colouring. Byzantine influence was strong in Ravenna and Pisa, which developed their own individual styles. Campanili or bell-towers, which seem to have originated in the sixth century, for carrying the bells which summoned Christians to prayer, now became an integral part of the church group, and henceforward gave special character to ecclesiastical architecture (p. 325A).

(*b*) *North Italy.*—Romanesque art in this district shows influence from north of the Alps, where the principal innovation was the development of the ribbed vault which brought about the adoption of many new constructive features. The churches are basilican in type, but naves as well as side aisles are vaulted and have external wooden roofs. Aisles are often two storeys in height, while thick walls between the side chapels act as buttresses to resist the pressure of the vaults. The flat, severe entrance façades stretch across the whole church, thus masking externally the division of nave and aisles. There is often a central projecting porch, with

A. Pistoia Cathedral (*c.* 1150). See p. 320

B. S. Antonino, Piacenza (1104). See p. 320

C. Torre Asinelli, Bologna (1109). See p. 323

A. S. Ambrogio, Milan, showing atrium (1088–1128). See p. 320

B. S. Ambrogio, Milan: nave looking E.

columns standing on the backs of crouching beasts and a wheel window above to light the nave (p. 330J). The gable is characteristically outlined with raking arcades and there are also arcades round the apse under the eaves. The general character becomes less refined, owing to the increased use of stone and brick instead of marble, and ornament shows a departure from Classic precedent, and portrays, with an element of the grotesque, the rough outdoor life of the invaders from the north. The Comacine masters, a privileged guild of architects and sculptors originating in Como, carried out church building and characteristic decoration during the eleventh century, not only in the north, but also in other parts of Italy.

(c) *South Italy and Sicily.*—The changing architectural character can be traced through Byzantine, Muslim, and Norman rule, and each successive period carried with it something from the past. Byzantine influence is evident in the mosaic decoration of interiors and predominates in the plans of such buildings as the church of the Martorana at Palermo, where the dome, supported on four columns, covers the square central space. Muslim influence is especially seen in the application of stripes of coloured marbles and in the use of stilted pointed arches. The Norman character is displayed in the planning and construction of the cathedral of Monreale, which has a cruciform plan, is decorated with mosaics and has a nave arcade of stilted pointed arches.

EXAMPLES

CENTRAL ITALY

Pisa Cathedral (1063–92) (pp. 313, 314B) with Baptistery, Campanile, and Campo Santo, together form one of the most famous building groups of the world (p. 313A). The cathedral is one of the finest of the Romanesque period and has a strongly marked individuality. It resembles other early basilican churches in plan, with long rows of columns connected by arches, double aisles, and a nave which has the usual timber roof (p. 313C). The exterior has bands of red and white marble, and the ground storey is faced with wall arcading, while the entrance façade is thrown into relief by tiers of open arcades which rise one above another right into the gable end. The transepts, with a segmental apse at each end, were an advance on the simple basilican plan. The elliptical dome over the crossing, or intersection of nave and transepts, is of later date (p. 313D). The building depends for its interest on its general proportions and on the beauty and delicacy of its ornamental features, rather than on any new structural development, such as may be seen in Northern Italy.

The **Campanile, Pisa** (1174) (pp. 313, 314), is a circular tower, 52 ft in diameter, rising in eight storeys of encircling arcades. This world-famous leaning tower, which is the most arresting feature of this marvellous group, has been the subject of much discussion, but there is little doubt that its inclination, which recent measurements proved to be on the increase, is due to subsidence in the foundations. The upper part of the tower now overhangs its base as much as 13 ft 10 ins, and it thus has a very unstable appearance. The belfry was not added till 1350.

The **Baptistery, Pisa** (1153–1278) (pp. 313A, D, 314, 377F), was designed by Dioti Salvi, on a circular plan, with a central space or nave, 60 ft in diameter, separated by four piers and eight columns from the surrounding two-storeyed aisle, which makes the building 129 ft in diameter. Externally it is surrounded on the lower storey by half-columns, connected by semicircular arches, under one of which is the door (p. 330K), with, above, an open arcade of small detached shafts.

This arcade is surmounted by Gothic additions of the fourteenth century, which disguise the original design. The structure is crowned by an outer hemispherical roof, through which penetrates a truncated cone capped by a small dome, covering the central space (p. 314F, G). This Baptistery resembles the church of S. Donato (ninth century) at Zadar, Dalmatia, in which, however, the central space is only 30 ft in diameter.

S. Martino, Lucca (1060, façade 1204) and **S. Michele, Lucca** (1188), with a façade (1288) of which the gables are mere screens, are very similar in style to the buildings of the Pisan group, because at the time of their erection Lucca had fallen under the power of Pisa.

Pistoia Cathedral (*c.* 1150) was also built under the influence of the Pisan school, and with its porch and arcaded façade in black and white marble formed the model for other churches in the city (p. 317A).

The **Cloisters of S. Giovanni in Laterano, Rome** (1234) and of **S. Paolo fuori le Mura, Rome** (1241) (p. 330H) are of special interest, since they are virtually the only instances of Romanesque art in Rome which show any progressive character, owing to the survival of the Classical tradition; besides which, the use of Roman architectural fragments still gave the churches a basilican character. The delicate twisted twin columns, inlaid with patterned glass mosaics, are the special features of these cloisters, and are a triumph of craftsmanship which has given to these coils of stone the subtlety of living forms. The coupled columns carry semicircular arches in groups of five or more openings between the recurrent piers, and form an arcade round the four sides of the cloister.

S. Miniato, Florence (1013–) (p. 321A, B) is important as showing some innovations; for the length of the church is divided by piers and transverse diaphragm arches into three main compartments, of which the raised eastern portion has a crypt open to the nave and containing the tomb of the saint. This division seems a prelude to the idea of vaulting in compartments, and is a departure from the basilican type of long, unbroken ranges of columns and arches. The novel panelling and banding in black and white marble, both of exterior and interior, were carried further in the Gothic period in Italy. The sanctuary has translucent marble, instead of glass, in the window openings. The open timber roof, with its bright colour decoration recently restored, gives an excellent idea of the effect produced by the use of simple colour on these basilican roofs.

NORTH ITALY

S. Antonino, Piacenza (1104) (p. 317B), rebuilt on the site of an earlier cathedral, is noted for its later Gothic porch, Il Paradiso (1350).

S. Ambrogio, Milan (1088–1128) (p. 318), founded by the great S. Ambrose in the fourth century, raised on its present plan (*c.* 850) and partly rebuilt with vault and dome in the twelfth century, has a proud history, and set a type for Lombard churches, as did its founder for Lombard ritual, which included the metrical chanting of the Mass. Here S. Augustine was baptized, the Emperor Theodosius was excommunicated, and Lombard kings and Germanic emperors were crowned. The plan includes the only existing atrium among Lombard churches, a narthex flanked by towers, vaulted nave and aisles with an octagon over the crossing, triforium gallery, raised choir over the crypt, and an apse. The interior (p. 318B) is severely plain and impressive. The pulpit (p. 332B), which is built over a sixth-century sarcophagus, consists of an arcade with characteristic Lombard ornamentation of carved birds and animals.

S. Michele, Pavia (*c.* 1117) (p. 322), is a notable instance of a treatment which

A. S. Miniato, Florence (1013–). See opposite page

B. S. Miniato, Florence
(1013–)

C. The Baptistery, Cremona (1167).
See p. 323

H.O. A.

S. MICHELE : PAVIA

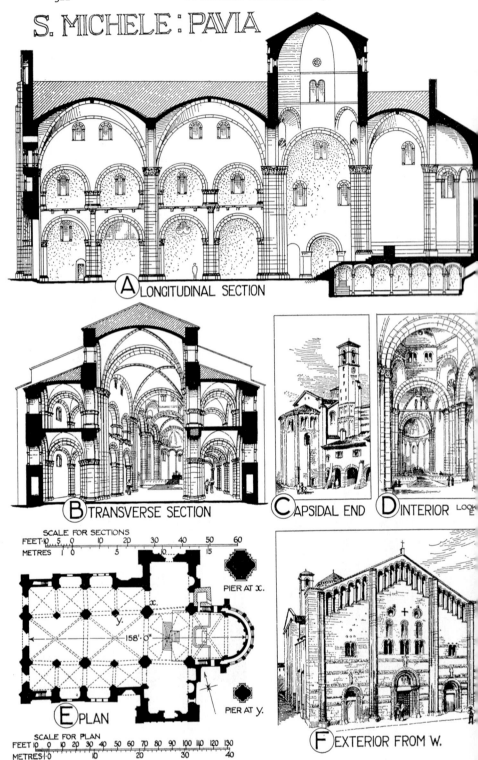

A. LONGITUDINAL SECTION

B. TRANSVERSE SECTION

C. APSIDAL END

D. INTERIOR LOOKING E.

SCALE FOR SECTIONS
FEET·10 5 0 10 20 30 40 50 60
METRES 1 0 5 10 15

PIER AT x.

158'·0"

PIER AT y.

E. PLAN

SCALE FOR PLAN
FEET 10 0 10 20 30 40 50 60 70 80 90 100 110 120 130
METRES 1·0 10 20 30 40

F. EXTERIOR FROM W.

is an advance on the divisions, marked only by piers, in S. Miniato; for here not only is the nave divided into square bays by transverse arches but the dividing piers are of a clustered character, shaped to receive the vaulting ribs. This church is cruciform in plan with well-defined transepts and a raised choir, under which is a vaulted crypt. The side aisles, which are two storeys in height, are also vaulted in square compartments, two of which correspond to one vaulting bay of the nave. The flat façade shows little play of light and shade, with its three simple, recessed portals and four vertical pilaster strips from ground to gable, almost akin to buttresses. The wide-spreading gable stretches across nave and aisles and is emphasized by a characteristic raking arcaded gallery which is the only prominent feature of this simple design (p. 322F).

S. Zeno Maggiore, Verona (1138–) (p. 325), has a façade which is stern in its simplicity. The fine projecting porch has two free-standing columns, which rest on the backs of crouching beasts and support a semicircular vault, over which is a gabled roof (p. 326C). Above is the great wheel window which lights the nave, one of the earliest in Italy, and the whole façade is relieved by pilaster strips connected by corbel tables under the slopes of the centre gable and side roofs. The interior (p. 325B) has a nave arcade of compound piers with uncarved capitals, and the nave shaft is carried up as if to support a vault. Intermediate columns with carved capitals support semicircular arches, surmounted by a wall banded in red brick and stone. There is no triforium, but a clear-story, and above this is a wooden ceiling of trefoil form. The choir, 7 ft above the nave floor, has a high pointed fourteenth-century vault and an apse, and beneath is the crypt, in seven aisles, with the shrine of S. Zeno. The campanile (p. 325A) is detached, as usual in Italy, has no buttresses, and is of alternate courses of marble and brick, terminating in open arcades to the bell-chamber, angle pinnacles, and a high-pitched roof. The sturdy tower formerly belonged to a residence of the Mediaeval German emperors and is finished with Ghibelline battlements.

Baptisteries are a special feature of Italian architecture and represent a period of Christianity when the baptismal rite was carried out only three times a year—Easter, Pentecost, and the Epiphany—and therefore required a large and separate building. The **Baptistery, Cremona** (1167) (p. 321C), is octagonal, and has a projecting porch and the usual pilaster strips, corbel tables, and arcading. The **Baptistery, Asti** (1050), and the **Baptistery, Parma** (1196–1270) (p. 327A, B), are octagonal, modelled on that of Constantine, Rome.

The *Campanili* or bell-towers are a product of the period, and, unlike the church towers of England, France, and Germany, generally stand alone, though they were sometimes connected by cloisters with the church. Campanili of North Italian towns are often civic monuments rather than integral parts of churches, and, like the civic towers of Belgium (p. 577), were symbols of power, and served also as watch-towers. They are square in plan, without the projecting buttresses which are usual north of the Alps, and their design is generally simple, broken only by windows which light the internal staircase or sloping way. The window openings increase in number with the height of the tower and often form an open loggia at the top, through which may be seen the swinging of the bells, and the whole is often surmounted by a pyramidal roof, as in the rebuilt campanile of S. Mark, Venice (pp. 608, 611A), originally built 888, and also in that of S. Zeno Maggiore, Verona (p. 325A), which dates originally from 1172.

The **Torre Asinelli, Bologna** (1109) (p. 317C), 225 ft high, and the **Torre Garisenda, Bologna** (1100), 130 ft high, date from the time when the town was prominent in the struggles of the period, and are the leaning towers referred to by Dante, while **San Gimignano** (p. 625C), with its thirteen towers, built for defence and ostentation, has the appearance of a Romanesque city so often pictured by Raphael in later times.

The **Fondaco dei Turchi, Venice** (p. 326A), a twelfth-century mercantile palace (since rebuilt) on the Grand Canal, is an example of the high level which domestic architecture reached in Venice as the outcome of her prosperous trade with the East. The **Palazzo Farsetti** and the **Palazzo Loredan** (twelfth century) are in the same style, with cubiform capitals carrying semicircular arches which are sometimes stilted.

SOUTH ITALY AND SICILY

Monreale Cathedral (1176–82) (pp. 326, 328) stands on the heights south-west of Palermo, and is the most splendid of all the monuments erected under Norman rule in Sicily. The plan is basilican in its western part and quasi-Byzantine in its eastern part, with a choir raised above the nave and with eastern apses. The nave columns have capitals of Byzantine form with 'dosseret-blocks' encrusted with mosaic, to support pointed arches, which are not in recessed planes as in northern Romanesque buildings, and in the aisles there are pointed windows without tracery. The walls are covered with mosaics in gold and colour, representing scenes from Biblical history with a figure of Christ in the apse, framed in arabesques; while a high dado of white marble slabs is bordered by inlaid patterns in coloured porphyries. The open timber roofs, intricate in design, are brightly painted in the Muslim style. The interior is solemn and grand, an effect produced by the severity of the design, enhanced by the coloured decoration. The low, oblong central lantern and the antique bronze doors add to the beauty and distinction of this famous church. The cloisters (p. 328B), the only remaining portion of the Benedictine monastery, are the finest of the style. They consist of coupled columns, in some cases inlaid with glass mosaics, supporting pointed arches, and have beautiful Corinthianesque capitals (p. 332E, F), one of which represents William I of Sicily offering the Church to the Virgin.

The **Capella Palatina, Palermo** (1132–40) (p. 327C), the chapel in the Royal Palace, has gilt and coloured mosaics in the interior, and a dome, 18 ft in diameter, indicative of Byzantine influence, while the carved stalactite ceiling, pulpit, candelabrum, and organ gallery show Muslim craftsmanship.

S. Giovanni degli Eremiti, Palermo (1132–), **La Martorana, Palermo** (1129–1143), and **S. Cataldo, Palermo** (1161–) are other churches which, in the arrangement of their domes and ornamentation, show the blending of Muslim and Byzantine art.

S. Nicola, Bari (1087–1139) and the **Cathedral Bitonto** (p. 333), of about the same date, like other churches of Southern Italy, are small in comparison with those of the same period in the north. The feature in the main façade of these southern churches is the projecting porch with columns standing on lions' backs, supporting a roof, and above this is usually the characteristic wheel window. The decorative detail is refined and graceful, largely due to the Greek descent of the craftsmen of this part of Italy.

Crypts are a special feature in the south and there is a crypt at Otranto Cathedral (eleventh century) which is remarkable for the unusual number of columns which support the choir.

La Zisa, Palermo (Arabic, *El Aziza* =Palace of Delights) (1154–66) (p. 327D), is a three-storeyed Norman castle with battlemented parapet, and shows the influence of Muslim art. The vestibule is rich in marble columns and coloured tiles, while the stalactite vaults over the alcoves recall the glories of the Alhambra, Granada.

A. S. Zeno Maggiore, Verona (1138–). See p. 323

B. S. Zeno Maggiore, Verona

A. Fondaco dei Turchi, Venice (twelfth century, but largely rebuilt). See p. 324

B. Monreale Cathedral (1176–82):
apses at east end. See p. 324

C. S. Zeno Maggiore, Verona (1138–):
porch. See p. 323

A. Exterior   B. Interior

The Baptistery, Parma (1196–1270). See p. 323

C. The Capella Palatina, Palermo: D. La Zisa, Palermo (1154–66).
interior (1132–40). See p. 324   See p. 324

A. Monreale Cathedral: interior looking E. (1176–82). See p. 324

B. Monreale Cathedral: the cloisters

COMPARATIVE ANALYSIS

PLANS. In Central Italy church plans adhered substantially to those of basilicas, and naves were divided from aisles by antique columns (p. 313B). The choir was occasionally raised above a crypt reached by steps from the nave. In the North, the most important architectural developments took place. Churches were mostly vaulted and occasionally had transepts, as at S. Michele, Pavia (p. 322). There were many baptisteries, usually octagonal or circular, such as the one at Novara, which is connected to the Cathedral by an atrium similar to the famous atrium at S. Ambrogio, Milan. Open arcades round the apses, with the arcaded octagonal lantern at the crossing, give great charm to the buildings externally (p. 330E, G). Projecting porches, which were preferred to recessed doorways, are bold arched structures often of two storeys, flanked by isolated columns on huge semi-grotesque beasts, as at Verona (p. 330J). Towers are straight shafts, often detached, as at Verona (p. 325A), without buttresses or spires (pp. 317B, 318A, 330F). In the South the low lanterns at the crossing of nave and transepts are marked features, as at Monreale Cathedral.

WALLS. In Central Italy the Pisan school elaborated wall arcades into many storeys of galleries, which decorated alike façades, apses, and towers (p. 313A). In North Italy the façades have less play of light and shade, and they usually rely upon simple pilaster strip decoration, running from the ground and ending in small arches under the eaves, as at S. Abbondio, Como (p. 330F). Sometimes there is a large circular window over the entrance, and usually this front extends the whole width of nave and aisles and terminates in one wide-spreading gable filled in with open arcaded galleries which spring either from horizontal or from stepped bases, as at Pavia (p. 322F). In South Italy the lateral walls are occasionally decorated with flat pilaster strips connected horizontally by small arches springing from corbels.

OPENINGS. In consequence of the brilliant climate, while arcades are universal, doors and windows, whether in Central, North, or South Italy, are small and unimportant, with 'jambs' in rectangular recesses or 'orders' filled in with small shafts, crowned with semicircular arches (p. 330B, C, K) in contrast with the classic architrave. Window tracery, which was a later invention of the Gothic period, was at no time employed to any great extent in Italy, and even wheel windows are only rudimentary in pattern (p. 325A); but in South Italy, as in the churches of Palermo, these windows are often made of sheets of pierced marble and highly elaborate.

ROOFS. In Central Italy timber roofs over naves are of the simple, open basilican type with rafters and tie-beams often effectively decorated in colour; while aisles occasionally have groined vaults of small span, divided into compartments by transverse arches (p. 321B). In North Italy not only aisles but also naves began to be vaulted (p. 322B). In South Italy domes rather than vaults were adopted, but timber roofs were the rule in Sicily under Muslim influence and had stalactite ceilings, rich in design and colour.

COLUMNS. In Central Italy during this period a vast number of columns from ancient Roman temples were utilized in the new churches, and this retarded the development of the novel types which were introduced in districts more remote from Rome (pp. 313C, 321B). In some places, as at Tuscania, rudely carved Corinthianesque columns carry round-arched arcades instead of entablatures. The finely carved and slender twisted columns in the cloisters of S. Giovanni in Laterano and S. Paolo fuori le Mura, Rome, are delicate variations of the Classic type (p. 330H). In North Italy sturdy piers faced with attached half-columns took the place of the Classic column, as supports to the heavy stone vaulting (p. 322B, D). The half-columns on the side towards the nave were carried up as vaulting

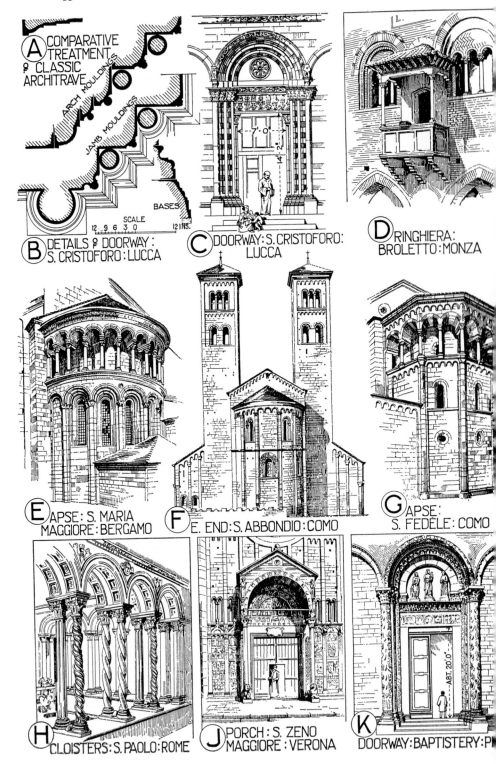

A. COMPARATIVE TREATMENT OF CLASSIC ARCHITRAVE

ARCH MOULDINGS

JAMB MOULDINGS

BASES

SCALE
12 9 6 3 0   12 INS.

B. DETAILS OF DOORWAY: S. CRISTOFORO: LUCCA

C. DOORWAY: S. CRISTOFORO: LUCCA

D. RINGHIERA: BROLETTO: MONZA

E. APSE: S. MARIA MAGGIORE: BERGAMO

F. E. END: S. ABBONDIO: COMO

G. APSE: S. FEDELE: COMO

H. CLOISTERS: S. PAOLO: ROME

J. PORCH: S. ZENO MAGGIORE: VERONA

K. DOORWAY: BAPTISTERY: P

shafts, and this was the beginning of a system which was destined in the Gothic period to transform the shape of piers. In South Italy, and especially in Sicily, greater variety in columns and capitals was brought about by changes which resulted from the successive introduction of Byzantine, Muslim, and Norman art, of which the nave arcade columns (p. 328A) and the coupled columns in the cloisters at Monreale (pp. 328B, 332E, F) are good examples.

MOULDINGS. In Central Italy there are rough imitations of old Classic mouldings, but elaborate variations of a more pronounced Romanesque type in recessed planes were used in doorways and windows (p. 330B, C, D, E, K). In North Italy flat moulded bands or strings on the exterior are varied by a series of small arches connecting the pilaster strips (pp. 330F, G, 332H). In South Italy mouldings are specially characterized by grace of contour and intricacy of carving (p. 332E, F).

ORNAMENT (p. 332). In Central Italy Classic models were followed so as to suit the old fragments incorporated in the new buildings, and rough variations of the old Roman acanthus scroll are frequent (p. 332D, J). The rows of Apostles on doorway lintels, as at Pistoia, are similar in style to Byzantine ivories. In all parts of Italy Christian symbolism now entered into decorative carving and mosaics. The monogram of Christ, the emblems of evangelists and saints, and the whole system of symbolism, represented by trees, birds, fishes, and animals, are all worked into the decorative scheme. The High Altar (p. 332C) and the mosaic paving (p. 332K) are characteristic examples of the period. In North Italy roughly carved grotesques of men and beasts occur, along with vigorous hunting scenes and incidents of daily life. Crouching beasts support columns of projecting porches and of bishops' thrones (p. 332A). The font (p. 332L), similarly supported, and the corbel tables (p. 332H) are typical. In South Italy elaborately modelled bronze doors are characteristic externally, while coloured mosaics add to the beauty of the interiors of Palermo churches. Colour, in spreading masses of geometric design, was the predominant note of internal decoration of South Italian and more especially of Sicilian churches, while the bronze pilasters (p. 332D, G) clearly indicate the influence of the Classic tradition.

REFERENCE BOOKS

ARATA, G. U. *L'architettura arabo-normanna in Sicilia.* Milan, 1914.

AVENA, A. *Monumente dell' Italia meridionale.* Rome, 1911.

CATTANEO, R. *Architecture in Italy from the VIth to the XIth Centuries.* Translated from the Italian. London, 1896.

CLAPHAM, A. W. *Romanesque Architecture in Western Europe.* Oxford, 1936.

CRESY, E. and TAYLOR, G. L. *Pisa.* London, 1829.

CUMMINGS, C. A. *A History of Architecture in Italy.* 2 vols., 2nd ed., New York and London, 1928.

DARTEIN, F. DE. *Etude sur l'architecture lombarde.* 2 vols., Paris, 1865–82.

DELHI, A. J. and CHAMBERLIN, G. H. *Norman Antiquities of Palermo and Environs.* Boston, 1892.

GRAVINA, D. D. B. *Il Duomo di Monreale.* 2 vols., Palermo, 1859.

GRÜNER, L. *Terra-Cotta Architecture of North Italy.* London, 1867.

GURLITT, C. *Denkmäler der Kunst in Dalmatien.* 2 vols., Berlin, 1910.

HITTORFF, J. I. et ZANTH, C. L. W. *Architecture antique de la Sicile.* Paris, 1827.

JACKSON, SIR T. G. *Byzantine and Romanesque Architecture.* 2 vols., Cambridge, 1920.

KNIGHT, H. G. *Normans in Sicily.* London, 1838.

—. *Saracenic and Norman Remains to illustrate the Normans in Sicily.* London, 1830.

LETHABY, W. R. *Mediaeval Art.* London, 1912.

MARTIN, C. *L'art roman en Italie.* Paris, [1912].

OSTEN, F. *Die Bauwerke in der Lombardei vom 7 bis 14 Jahrhunderts.* Folio. Darmstadt, 1846–54.

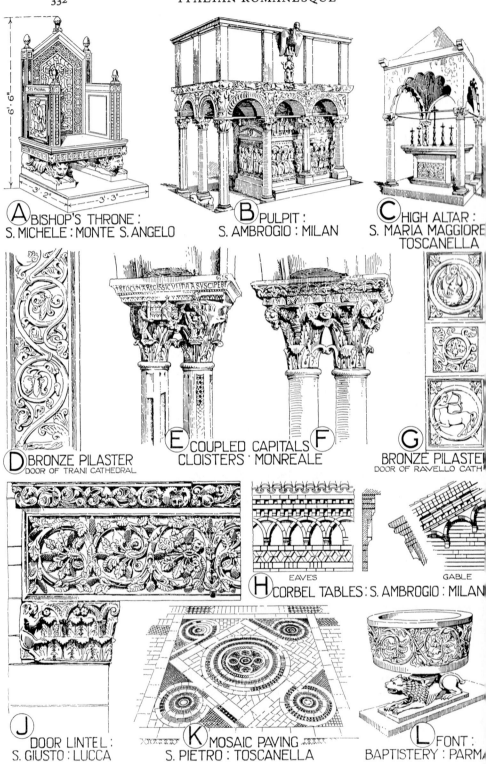

A BISHOP'S THRONE :
S. MICHELE : MONTE S. ANGELO

B PULPIT :
S. AMBROGIO : MILAN

C HIGH ALTAR :
S. MARIA MAGGIORE
TOSCANELLA

D BRONZE PILASTER
DOOR OF TRANI CATHEDRAL

E COUPLED CAPITALS
CLOISTERS · MONREALE

F

G BRONZE PILASTER
DOOR OF RAVELLO CATH.

EAVES

GABLE

H CORBEL TABLES : S. AMBROGIO : MILAN

J DOOR LINTEL :
S. GIUSTO : LUCCA

K MOSAIC PAVING
S. PIETRO : TOSCANELLA

L FONT :
BAPTISTERY : PARMA

PORTER, A. K. *Mediaeval Architecture*. 2 vols., New York and London, 1909.
—. *The Construction of Lombard and Gothic Vaults*. New Haven and London, 1911.
RICCI, C. *Romanesque Architecture in Italy*. London, 1925.
RIVOIRA, G. T. *Le origini della architettura lombarda*. Milan, 1908. English translation by Rushforth. 2 vols., London, 1910.
ROHAULT DE FLEURY. *Monuments de Pise au moyen age*. 2 vols., Paris, 1866.
SALAZARO, D. *Studi sui monumenti dell' Italia Meridionale dal IVe al XIIIe Secolo*. 2 vols., Naples, 1871–7.
SCHULZ, H. W. *Denkmaeler der Kunst des Mittelalters in Unteritalien*. 3 vols., Dresden, 1860.
STREET, G. E. *Brick and Marble Architecture of North Italy*. London, 1874.
VENTURI, A. *Storia dell' arte italiana*. Vols. ii and iii. Milan, 1902–4.

Bitonto Cathedral (11th and 12th centuries). See p. 324

ANGOULÊME CATHEDRAL

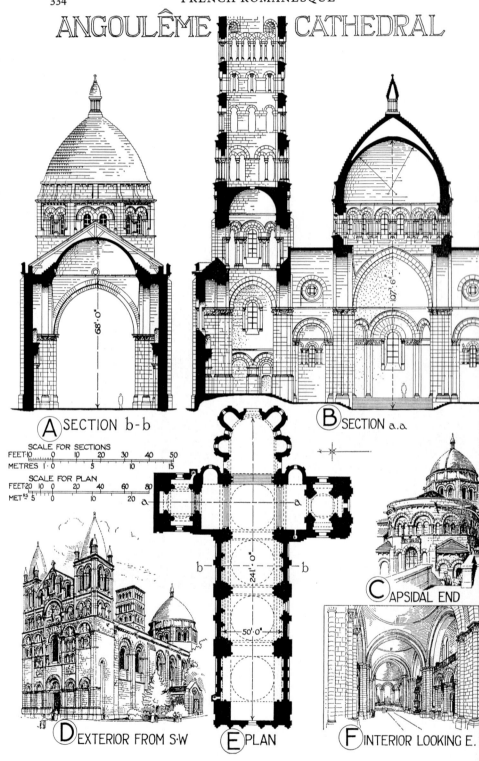

Ⓐ SECTION b-b

Ⓑ SECTION a.a

SCALE FOR SECTIONS
FEET·10   0   10   20   30   40   50
METRES 1·0   5   10   15

SCALE FOR PLAN
FEET·20 10 0   20   40   60   80
MET.RS 5   0   10   20

68'·0"

107'·6"

241'·0"

50'·0"

Ⓒ APSIDAL END

Ⓓ EXTERIOR FROM S·W

Ⓔ PLAN

Ⓕ INTERIOR LOOKING E.

France about the year 1000

IX. FRENCH ROMANESQUE

(ninth–twelfth century)

INFLUENCES

GEOGRAPHICAL. France holds a central position between north and south on the western confines of Europe, and has great natural highways along the valleys of the Rhône, Saône, Seine, and Garonne which connect the Mediterranean with the Atlantic Ocean and the English Channel. The different territories into which the country was divided at this period had strongly marked characteristics in architecture, as in all else, partly due to the difference in geographical position. Roman civilization had spread through France along the historic highway of the fertile Rhône valley, where the influence of Roman architecture is everywhere evident. Somewhat later, the trade route from the Mediterranean along the Garonne valley carried Venetian and Eastern influence across the south-west of France to the district around Périgueux, where we find a version in stone of Byzantine architecture. North of the River Loire is seen the influence of the Northmen who came by sea, and of the Franks who stretched across the country from the Rhine to Brittany.

GEOLOGICAL. France has an abundance of good stone, easily quarried and freely used for all types of buildings. In the north the fine-grained Caen stone was not only available throughout Normandy, but was so plentiful that it was shipped to England, both for ecclesiastical and secular buildings. In the volcanic district of Auvergne a special character was given to architecture by the coloured pumice and tufa, which were not only used for walls and inlaid decoration, but were so light in weight that they were also employed in large blocks for the solid stone vaulted roofs peculiar to the district.

CLIMATIC. The climate of the north resembles that of the south of England; in the west on the Atlantic coast it is warmer, owing to the Gulf Stream; while in the south, on the Mediterranean, it is sub-tropical. These climatic variations regulate door and window openings, which decrease in size towards the south. The climate also determines the pitch of roofs which, from being steep in the north to throw off snow, become almost flat in the south, and these features largely control the general architectural style.

RELIGIOUS. Christianity, like Roman civilization, was carried along the natural highways of France, and was first established in the Rhône valley, where Lyons contributed martyrs to the cause. There is a tradition that in A.D. 55 there arrived in Gaul the Apostle-bishops who founded churches at Arles, Narbonne, Limoges, Clermont, Tours, and Toulouse, while later S. Denis (c. 250) became bishop and martyr of Paris. In 910 the Cluniac Order was founded at Cluny, Burgundy, and was followed in 1098 by the Cistercian Order at Cîteaux, Burgundy, the severity of whose rules as to simplicity in church buildings caused a reaction from the decorative treatment found at S. Gilles and S. Trophime, Arles (p. 343). Attention was then concentrated upon producing grand and severe rather than ornate buildings. The eleventh century was marked by a desire to follow the monastic life apart from the world; this resulted in the foundation of monasteries, which gave an impulse to architecture and also fostered art and learning. Religious zeal was, however, not confined within monastic walls, but was also evident in that more active spirit which found vent in the Crusades, which began in 1096 under Geoffrey de Bouillon and were continued under Louis VII (1147). This intercourse with the East reacted in its turn on the art of the West. This crusading king, through his minister, the Abbé Suger, also extended his religious zeal to the building of churches.

SOCIAL. Caesar's conquest of Gaul (58–49 B.C.) was followed by the systematic Romanization of the country, which had begun with the making of roads, with Lyons as the centre, and the development of thriving commercial colonies which adopted the Roman social system in their independent municipalities. The 'Pax Romana' was established, and by the early third century, when Caracalla extended Roman citizenship to the whole Empire, social conditions had become stable; but thereafter Roman administration and industrial and commercial development were progressively undermined by barbarian incursions and the growth of the power of great individual landowners. In 496 Clovis united all the Franks, expelled the Romans from Northern Gaul, and by embracing Christianity secured the allegiance of the powerful leaders of the Church, and so established himself in the place of the Roman Emperor. After two and a half centuries of civil war and conflicts between kings and nobles, King Pepin (752–68) united the four kingdoms of the 'Ile de France.' His successor, Charlemagne (768–814), brought Western Europe under his sway, promoted education and learning, but only succeeded in establishing the unity of France and the power of the feudal system for his lifetime, so that within a century of his death France again became a series of small states. In 911, owing to the inroads of the Northmen (Normans) the duchy of Normandy was established.

A. The façade   B. The interior

S. Madeleine, Vézelay (1089–1206). See p. 343

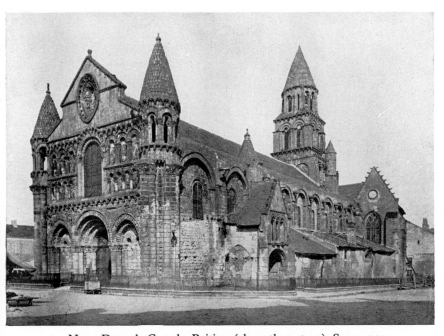

C. Notre Dame la Grande, Poitiers (eleventh century). See p. 343

A. Notre Dame la Grande, Poitiers
(eleventh century). See p. 343

B. The Abbaye-aux-Dames, Caen
(vault 1100–10)

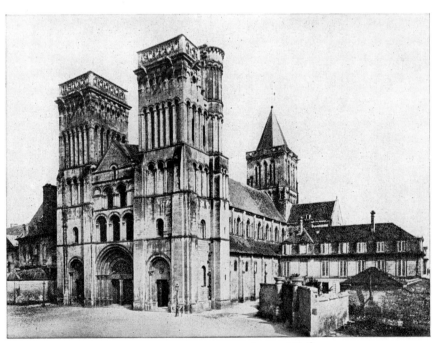

c. The Abbaye-aux-Dames, Caen (1062–1140). See p. 344

Hugh Capet (987–96) ascended the Frankish throne, and Paris became the capital of his kingdom, but his authority extended little beyond Paris and Orleans, as the greater part of France was held by the independent lords of Aquitaine, Auvergne, Provence, Anjou, Burgundy, Normandy, and Brittany. In 1066 Duke William conquered England, and numerous churches and castles in Normandy are a material expression of the prosperity of his duchy. Throughout the period the feudal system was developing, the basis of which was land and protection, the lord promising protection and land to the tenants in return for service. To check the power of the feudal lords, Louis VI (1108–37) encouraged the growth of independent communes and towns which, through the guild system, improved standards of craftsmanship and fostered artistic development.

HISTORICAL. Gaul is introduced by Caesar with the statement: 'Gallia in tres partes divisa est,' and it was occupied by different races, whose quarrels enabled Caesar (49 B.C.) to complete the Roman conquest of Gaul; for five centuries she remained a Roman province and absorbed Roman ideas. In A.D. 250 Frankish barbarians began their attacks, and strife continued till Goths, Franks, and Romans united to defeat Attila, king of the Huns (451). Then Clovis, king of the Salian Franks, defeated the Romans (486) at Soissons, absorbed the kingdom of Burgundy, drove Alaric II, king of the Visigoths, out of Aquitaine (507), united the Frankish tribes and established the Merovingian dynasty, and thus achieved the Frankish conquest of Gaul. The Muslims overran southern France (719–732). Charles Martel, by his conquest of them at Poitiers (732), changed the future of Western Europe. The Carolingian dynasty followed, and Pepin was crowned as the first Carolingian king by Pope Stephen II (754), to whom he presented the exarchate of Ravenna, and thus first established the temporal power of the papacy. The old Roman monarchical idea was now supplanted by the feudal system in France. Charlemagne, Pepin's son, king of a united France (768–814), also arrogated to himself all Western Europe as the Holy Roman Empire, and then learning, culture, and architecture all took a step forward. On his death France was ravaged by the Northmen from overseas, and also again divided into many small states; for Louis the Pious (814–840) left it to his three sons, and the Treaty of Verdun (843) divided the Eastern and Western Franks into Germany and France, with Charles the Bald as king of France (843–77). The Northmen insistently penetrated up the rivers, the monarchy grew weaker, and feudal lords grew strong enough to elect the king. Charles III ceded Normandy to Duke Rollo (911), and this foreign influence reacted on the architecture of Northern France. Hugh Capet brought in the Capetian dynasty (987), which, with its centre in the Ile de France, was hemmed in by powerful enemies, but under Philip I (1060–1105) the king's power was increased, because the conquest of England by the Normans withdrew their attacks from his kingdom. Louis VI (1108–37) began an unsuccessful struggle against Henry I, king of England and duke of Normandy, championed the towns, and kindled national sentiment. But Louis VII (1137–80) weakened his kingdom by divorcing Eleanor of Aquitaine (1152), who married Henry of Anjou, king of England, and so the English king now owned more than half of France. The country again rallied under Philip Augustus (1180–1223), who was strong enough to subdue the feudal lords and attack Henry II of England. Such were the forces at this period, external and internal, which went to the making of the French people; while the influence of Roman civilization is specially noticeable during the period when monasticism produced that grand series of Romanesque buildings in France.

ARCHITECTURAL CHARACTER

Romanesque architecture in France dates from the ninth to the twelfth century. The character differs in the north and south, which are approximately divided by the Loire valley. Further modifications crept in according to the various territories into which France was divided at this period.

The south is remarkable for richly decorated church façades and graceful cloisters, and for the use of old Roman architectural features which seem to have acquired a fresh significance. Roman buildings at Arles, Nîmes, Orange, and other places in the Rhône valley naturally exerted considerable influence throughout Provence. In Aquitaine and Anjou the aisleless naves, covered with domes on pendentives (p. 334), or vaulting supported only by the massive walls of the recessed chapels, recall the great halls of Roman thermae. The development of vaulting (p. 307) progressed, and naves were often covered with barrel vaults (p. 338A), whose thrust was resisted by half-barrel vaults over two-storeyed aisles, thus suppressing the clear-story, as at Notre Dame du Port, Clermont-Ferrand. The pointed arch, early used in the south of France, has been held to be due to contact with the Muslims who overran this part of the country from 719 to 732.

In the north, where Roman remains were less abundant, there was greater freedom in developing a new style, and western façades of churches, especially in Normandy, are distinguished by the introduction of two flanking towers, while plain, massive side walls with flat buttresses emphasize the richness of the façades. The interiors, close set with pier and pillar and roofed with ponderous arching, form a link with the light and graceful structures of the Gothic period. Naves are covered by ribbed vaults which are often sexpartite and in square compartments or 'severies,' the ribs being constructed independently and supporting the panels (pp. 338B, 342D, F). The gradual change to the Gothic system was promoted by repeated attempts to cover oblong compartments with 'rib and panel' vaults, a problem which was eventually solved by the introduction of the pointed arch, first used in the south of France and introduced into the north in the twelfth century. The solution to the many problems which had faced the Romanesque designers was found in the building of the choir of the Abbey of S. Denis (1137–44), near Paris, where the ribbed vault, pointed arch and flying buttress are successfully combined.

EXAMPLES

ECCLESIASTICAL ARCHITECTURE

Southern France includes Aquitaine, Auvergne, Provence, Anjou, and Burgundy, each with its special architectural peculiarities, the extent of which can be traced in the examples which follow.

S. Sernin, Toulouse (1080–96) (p. 341A, B), in Aquitaine, is cruciform with nave, double aisles, and transepts. The nave has a round-arched barrel vault, with plain square ribs, supporting the roofing slabs direct, and the high triforium chamber has external windows which light the nave, for there is no clear-story. The central octagonal tower (1250) with a spire (1478), 215 ft high, belongs to the Gothic period (p. 549). Santiago de Compostela, Spain (p. 640) a pilgrimage centre of importance, is similar in many respects to the church of S. Sernin, Toulouse.

Angoulême Cathedral (1105–30) (p. 334), in Aquitaine, has a long aisleless nave, 50 ft wide, transepts with lateral chapels, and an apsidal choir with four chapels, forming a Latin cross on plan. The nave is covered with three stone domes

A. S. Sernin, Toulouse from S.W. (1080–96). See opposite page

B. S. Sernin, Toulouse: nave
looking E.

C. S. Denis, near Paris: nave looking E,
(1137–44). See p. 344

ABBAYE-AUX-HOMMES (S. ETIENNE): CAE

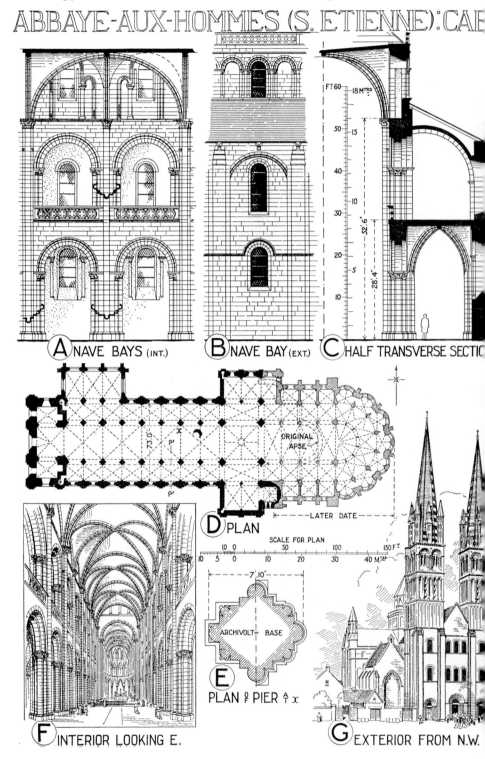

A NAVE BAYS (INT.)

B NAVE BAY (EXT.)

C HALF TRANSVERSE SECTIO

D PLAN

ORIGINAL APSE

LATER DATE

73.0

SCALE FOR PLAN
10 0   50   100   150 FT
10 5 0   10   20   30   40 MTRS

E PLAN OF PIER AT x

7' 10"

ARCHIVOLT   BASE

F INTERIOR LOOKING E.

G EXTERIOR FROM N.W.

on pendentives and a double dome over the crossing raised on a drum with sixteen windows and crowned by a finial. Both transepts originally had towers, but the southern one was destroyed in 1568. The western façade (p. 334D) is exceptionally rich with tiers of arcades divided into five bays by lofty shafts. Over the entrance is a high window framed in sculpture, and there are two flanking western towers.

Cahors Cathedral (1119), also in Aquitaine, is an aisleless church crowned by two domes on pendentives, and somewhat resembles S. Irene, Constantinople (p. 284).

Notre Dame du Port, Clermont-Ferrand, S. Austremoine, Issoire, and **Le Puy Cathedral,** all in Auvergne and of the twelfth century, have local character imparted to them by the light stone vaults, and inlaid decoration of different-coloured lavas of the Puy de Dôme district.

Notre Dame, Avignon, in Provence, is one of the numerous churches of the eleventh and twelfth centuries in which pointed barrel vaults were used, and which show Classical influence.

S. Trophîme, Arles (1150), has beautiful cloisters with coupled carved capitals (p. 350F) and a fine porch (p. 350K), based on a Roman triumphal arch, but with modifications, such as deeply recessed jambs and columns resting on lions, behind which are sculptured saints; the entablature carries a row of figures and the sculptured tympanum represents Christ as Judge of the World.

The **Church of S. Gilles** (c. 1150), near Arles, has probably the most elaborate sculptured façade in Provence (pp. 349A, 351L), with three porches connected by colonnades which may have suggested the façade of S. Mark, Venice (p. 289).

Notre Dame la Grande, Poitiers (eleventh century) (pp. 337C, 338A), in Anjou, has a fine sculptured west front and imposing conical dome over the crossing, while the interior (p. 338A) has neither triforium nor clear-story, but is covered by a barrel vault with prominent unmoulded transverse ribs.

Fontevrault Abbey (1101–19) (p. 346A) also in Anjou, resembles Angoulême Cathedral in its nave and general arrangement, and is interesting to Englishmen as the burial-place of the English kings, Henry II and Richard I.

The **Abbey Church, Cluny** (1089–1131), formed part of the most famous monastic establishment in Burgundy, which influenced the design of the churches, many of which, like Cluny itself, have been destroyed. It was the longest in France (443 ft), with nave and choir, each with double aisles, double transepts, and a chevet of five apsidal chapels. The pointed arch, possibly the earliest in Europe, was employed in the nave arcades, and the nave was covered with a great barrel vault, while the aisles probably had groined vaulting, but little now remains.

Autun Cathedral (1090–1132) (p. 310B), another Burgundian church, has a nave covered with a pointed barrel vault on transverse arches which spring so low down as almost to squeeze out the clear-story windows. At the east end there are three apses, and the portals of the west front are rich in the Burgundian style of sculpture.

S. Madeleine, Vézelay (1089–1206) (pp. 337A, 349B), in Burgundy, has a most remarkable narthex (1130) with nave and aisles crowned, it is believed, by the earliest pointed cross-vault in France; this leads into the church, which also has nave and aisles, the transepts, choir, and chevet being completed in 1206. The nave has no triforium, but a clear-story with small windows between the immense transverse arches of the highly domical, groined intersecting vault (p. 337B). The central portal (p. 337A), with two square-headed doorways, separated by a Corinthianesque column, is spanned by a large semicircular arch containing a relief of the Last Judgment. Left and right are side portals, and in the upper part of the façade is a large five-light window richly sculptured and flanked by towers, that on the left rising only to the height of the nave.

S. Philibert, Tournus (*c.* 1009), in Burgundy, once the Abbey Church of the Benedictine monastery, has arches which span the nave from pier to pier, and support barrel vaults under which windows were formed.

Northern France includes Normandy, the Ile de France and Brittany.

The **Abbey of Bernay** (1050) was probably the first important Norman church. It had a nave of seven bays, of which five are still intact, divided into arcade, triforium and clear-story. The choir and side aisles terminated in apses and there were transepts, and over the crossing a tower.

The **Abbaye-aux-Hommes, Caen** (1066–86) (pp. 342, 345), known as S. Etienne, is one of the many fine churches in Normandy of this period, which were the product of the prosperity and power of the Norman dukes. It was commenced by William the Conqueror, and is of the vaulted, basilican type which was developed into the complete Gothic in the thirteenth century, and may have been modelled on the Romanesque cathedral of Speyer (p. 358). Its original eastern apse was superseded in 1166 by the characteristic chevet (pp. 342D, 345). The western façade, flanked by two square towers, crowned by octagonal spires which with angle pinnacles were added in the thirteenth century, was the prototype of later Gothic façades. The nave provides an interesting example of 'sexpartite' vaulting (pp. 307, 342F). Here, over the large square bays, intermediate transverse ribs are introduced which cut the diagonal ribs at their intersections and thus support them. This method was superseded on the introduction of the pointed arch, when each compartment, whatever its shape, could be vaulted without reference to the neighbouring one, because the difference between the width of the nave and the distance longitudinally between the piers could easily be surmounted by pointed arches of different radii manipulated so as to equalize the height of the ribs. The thrust of this nave vault, one of the earliest, was counteracted by a semi-barrel vault over the triforium gallery, protected externally by a timber roof, and forming, as it were, a concealed flying buttress, which later in the thirteenth century was emphasized externally as a feature of the design. The Abbaye-aux-Hommes is a remarkable instance of the use of spires as architectural features; for there are no less than nine spires, giving the vertical expression which became characteristic of Gothic architecture (p. 368).

The **Abbaye-aux-Dames ('La Trinité'), Caen** (1062–1140) (p. 338B, C), founded by Matilda, wife of William the Conqueror, has a fine western façade with two square towers in arcaded stages, strengthened at the angles by flat buttresses and formerly crowned by spires. The massive walls of nave and aisles with slightly projecting buttresses and the square tower over the crossing complete this homogeneous design. The interior (p. 338B) has a remarkable intersecting sexpartite ribbed vault, as in the Abbaye-aux-Hommes, in which two bays are included in each vaulting compartment, with semicircular diagonal and transverse ribs and intermediate ribs which support a vertical piece of walling.

In addition to the abbeys mentioned above there are a number of smaller churches, of which the most important are **Bernières, Ouistreham** and **S. Georges, Boscherville**, all of which are vaulted, and have interesting towers built in stages and culminating in pyramidal stone roofs.

The **Abbey of S. Denis** (1137–44) (p. 310A), near Paris, erected by the builder Abbé Suger, is one of the few buildings in this style in the royal domain of the Ile de France, which during this period comprised only a small territory, and it was not until the Gothic period that the great outburst of building activity occurred in this district. The Abbey Church is of great interest as the burial-place of the French kings. The original choir and two internal bays still remain, and a Gothic nave and transept (*c.* A.D. 1231) have been wedged between them (p. 341C). The west front,

The Abbaye-aux-Hommes, Caen, from E. (1066–77). See opposite page

A. Abbey of Fontevrault, from N.E. (1101–19). See p. 343

B. Church of Jumièges (1050). View of nave, showing alternation
of clustered piers and columns. See p. 348

with its mingling of round and pointed arches, is an early instance of the use of the pointed arch, while the eastern end, though still retaining many Romanesque features, is probably the earliest truly Gothic structure.

SECULAR ARCHITECTURE

Buildings other than ecclesiastical have not been well preserved, because they were not sacred against attack, because they were generally built for military purposes and so were liable to destruction, and because of the risk of injury by fire and adaptation to changed requirements. **Fortified towns,** like Carcassonne (p. 549), which dates from Roman times; **Bridges,** like the Pont d'Avignon (1177–85) (p. 549), built by the *frères-pontifes* or sacred guild of bridge builders; **Castles,** such as the Château de Chateaudun (p. 555) and the fortified Abbey of Mont S. Michel (p. 549), and the stone **Houses** of the twelfth century still found at Cluny and elsewhere, are types of buildings which started in the Romanesque style, but were much altered or extended in the Gothic period. The Monastic Kitchen, Fontevrault (1115) (p. 350D), with its fine roof, and the fireplace and chimney from S. Gilles (p. 350B), are remnants which show the character of the secular work of this period.

COMPARATIVE ANALYSIS

PLANS. In the south, churches were cruciform in plan and frequently had naves covered with barrel vaults whose thrust was taken by half-barrel vaults over aisles in two storeys (pp. 334E, 342D). Buttresses are internal and form the divisions between the chapels which flank the nave, as at Vienne Cathedral. Towers are sometimes detached, like Italian campanili. Cloisters are treated with the utmost elaboration, as at S. Trophîme, Arles (p. 350F), and form a special feature in the plan of many churches of the period. Circular churches are rarely found, but the development of the semicircular east end as an ambulatory, with radiating chapels, is common in southern France. In the north, plans were of the basilican type with nave and aisles. The use of high nave vaults changed the setting-out of the bays, which were brought to a square by making one nave vaulting compartment equal to the length of two bays of the aisles (p. 342D), until the introduction of the pointed arch overcame the difficulty of vaulting oblong compartments with ribbed vaults.

WALLS. The massive walls characteristic of this period were, in both south and north, of rubble faced with squared stone. Sculptured and moulded ornament was concentrated on wall arcades, especially on western façades, which thus stand out in contrast to the general simplicity of the external wall treatment (p. 337C). Façades were often divided by string courses or horizontal mouldings into storeys relieved by single, coupled, or grouped windows, and frequently had arcading as at Echillais (p. 350C). Buttresses were wide strips of slight projection (p. 338C) or half-round shafts (p. 350G); while flying buttresses, admitting of high clear-story windows to light the nave, were introduced in the latter half of the twelfth century (p. 345). Towers were generally square with pyramidal or conical roofs (p. 350A), and by their grouping and number gave a vertical character to the style, as at the Abbaye-aux-Hommes, Caen (p. 345).

OPENINGS. In the south, nave wall arcades of aisleless churches are semicircular, with mouldings in recesses or 'orders' (p. 337B), while arcades of cloisters are elaborated with coupled columns in the depth of the walls, and with carved capitals which support the semicircular arches of the narrow bays, which were left unglazed as in Italy (p. 350F). The western portals of such churches as S. Trophîme,

Arles (p. 350K), and S. Gilles (p. 349A) recall the columns and horizontal entablatures of the Romans, but in other cases doorways have recessed jambs as usual in this period (p. 350J, L). Narrow windows with semicircular heads and wide splays inwards suffice to admit light, especially in the south (p. 350G). In the north, nave arcades are spanned by semicircular arches which are repeated in the deep triforiums, as at the Abbaye-aux-Hommes. Imposing western doorways (pp. 337A, C, 338C) with sculptured tympana were the forerunners of the magnificent sculptured entrances of the Gothic period. Windows with semicircular heads are sometimes grouped together and enclosed in a larger arch, as in the nave wall or clear-story immediately beneath the vault (p. 338B).

ROOFS. In the south, naves were first covered by barrel vaults (p. 338A) buttressed by half-barrel vaults over aisles, which were sometimes two storeys high and thus left no space for a clear-story. The vault was sometimes pointed (p. 310B), and this had the advantage of lessening the superincumbent thrust of the stone roofing slabs which, especially in Auvergne, were frequently laid direct upon the vaults and were given the low pitch suitable to the south. The narthex or antechapel of S. Madeleine, Vézelay (1130) (p. 349B), is believed to have the earliest pointed cross-vaults in France. As to the external treatment of roofs in southern France, while climatic conditions decided that they need only be low in pitch, other factors entered into the nature of their construction; for in the volcanic district of Auvergne the light nature of the stone resulted in stone-covered vaults; while in Aquitaine, the trade route from the East occasioned the use of domical construction, as at Angoulême. In the north, the height of clear-storeys was increased by means of intersecting ribbed vaults whose thrust was taken by buttress arches under the aisle roofs (p. 342C)—a step towards the later external flying buttresses. In the north, also, the most important developments in stone vaulting technique took place, with the introduction of the rib and panel system. The vaults were usually covered by wooden framed roofs, finished with slates and of steep pitch, as the need to throw off snow and water was a determining factor in their construction (p. 345).

COLUMNS. In the south, the piers were derived from the Roman square pier, with attached columns to which were added nook shafts, and on the nave side the half-round shafts were carried up to the springing of the vaults (p. 337B). These piers, as at Lessay (p. 350H), were the prototypes of the richly clustered Gothic piers. Capitals, as at Aix, clearly show the influence of Classic buildings (p. 351K). In the north, similar piers were in use, while cylindrical piers, as at Notre Dame, Paris (p. 532B), were also frequent, surmounted with carved capitals of Corinthianesque type and square abacus, from which the vaulting shafts start awkwardly (p. 350M, N, P, Q, R). In Normandy, the system of alternating clustered pier and column along the nave was introduced, as at Jumièges (p. 346B).

MOULDINGS. Mouldings executed in stone are coarser than those in the marble of Italy. In the south, Classic tradition is reflected in the graceful moulding contours. Capitals and bases are either rough imitations of the old Roman Corinthian type (p. 351C, H) or have considerable variations, due to the introduction of animal figures. In the north, the jambs are formed in receding planes, with recesses filled with nook shafts fluted or carved with zigzag ornament. Capitals are frequently cubiform blocks, sometimes carved with animal subjects (p. 351). Corbel tables of great richness, supported by grotesquely carved heads, often form the wall cornices (p. 351E).

ORNAMENT. In the south, painted glass was not favoured, and small clear-glazed openings were employed to set off the opaque colour decoration of the walls. Figure sculpture is at its best in Provence, as in the portals of S. Trophîme, Arles

A. S. Gilles: west façade (*c.* 1150). See p. 343

B. S. Madeleine, Vézelay: the narthex (1130). See p. 343

A S.ESTÈPHE

B FIREPLACE & CHIMNEY:
ABBEY of SENANQUE:
S.GILLES

C WEST FAÇADE:
E.CHILLAIS

D MONASTIC KITCHEN
FONTEVRAULT

F CLOISTERS: S.TROPHÎME: ARLES

G APSE: S·PIERRE: AULNAY

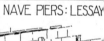

H

NAVE PIERS: LESSAY

J DOORWAY: SERQUIGNY

JAMB

K PORCH: S·TROPHÎME: ARLES

L DOORWAY: FONTGOMBA

M
EARLY NAVE PIER

N
CERISY-LA-FORET

5'-6"

P
S.GILLES

7'-3½"

Q
ABBAYE AUX DAMES
CAEN

5'-2½"

R
BERNIERES-SUR-

4'-9"

NAVE PIERS

A CAPITAL: FLEAC

B TYMPANUM: LA CHARITÉ·Sʀ·LOIRE

C CAPITAL: S. AIGNAN·Sʀ·CHER

D TWIN CAPITALS: S. SERNIN: TOULOUSE

E APSIDAL END: SELLES-SUR-CHER

F CARVING: VENCE

G TWIN CAPˢ CLOISTER S. TROPHÎME: ARLES

H BASES: AIX CATHˡ

J SCULPᴰ·FRIEZE: ANGOULÊME CATHˡ

K PIER ᴀɴᴅ COLUMNS: CLOISTER: AIX CATHˡ

L DOORWAY: S. GILLES

M SCULPᴰ SPANDREL. BAYEUX CATHEDRAL

(p.350K) and S. Gilles (p. 351L), where we can see the early promise of the remarkable sculpture of the French Gothic period; while in Aquitaine sculpture is confined to the capitals, which are sometimes carved with figures, animals, and Bible subjects, and are frequently derived from Roman Corinthian prototypes (p. 351A, C, D, G). Façades of churches of the Charente district in Aquitaine have this elaborate carved ornament representing foliage, or figures of men and animals (p. 351J), and capitals of columns on the ground storey are often continued as a rich, broad frieze across the building (p. 351L). In the north, stained glass, which was more suitable to large openings, was only gradually developed. The diaper work in the spandrels of arches is supposed to be an imitation in carving of the colour-pattern work or stuff draperies that originally occupied the same position, while the period is rich in carving of zigzags, rosettes, and billets (p. 351F, M). The carved tympana, dealing with Biblical subjects, are frequently of great interest (pp. 349B, 351B). Owing, however, to the comparative absence of antique Roman models in the north, figure sculpture is rare in this period and never approached the beauty of the sculpture at Arles in the south.

REFERENCE BOOKS

BAUM, J. *Romanesque Architecture in France.* London, 1928.

ENLART, C. *L'architecture réligieuse en France.* Paris, 1902.

EVANS, JOAN. *The Romanesque Architecture of the Order of Cluny.* Cambridge, 1938.

LAVEDAN, P. *French Architecture.* London, 1956.

MCGIBBON, D. *The Architecture of Provence and the Riviera.* Edinburgh, 1888.

MARTIN, C. *L'art roman en France.* Paris, [1912].

MICHEL, A. *Histoire de l'art.* Vol. i, pt. i (for article by C. Enlart on Romanesque). Paris, 1905.

PORTER, A. K. *Mediaeval Architecture.* 2 vols., New York and London, 1909.

PUGIN, A. and LE KEUX. *Architectural Antiquities of Normandy.* London, 1828. New ed., 1874.

RAMÉE, D. *Histoire de l'Architecture.* 2 vols., Paris, 1870.

RÉVOIL, H. *Architecture Romane du Midi de la France.* 3 vols., Paris, 1864–73.

RUPRICH-ROBERT, V. *L'Architecture Normande aux XIᵉ et XIIᵉ siècles.* 2 vols., Paris, 1885–7.

SHARPE, EDMUND. *The Domed Churches of Charente.* London, 1882.

SPIERS, R. PHENÉ. Saint Front of Périgueux and the Domed Churches of Perigord and La Charente. *RIBA Journal,* 20 Feb. 1896.

THIOLLER, N. and F. *L'architecture religieuse à l'époque romane dans l'ancien diocèse du Puy.* Le Puy, 1900.

VERNEILH, F. DE. *L'Architecture Byzantin en France.* Paris, 1851.

VIOLLET-LE-DUC. *Dictionnaire de l'Architecture.* 10 vols., Paris, 1859. [A translation of the article 'Construction', by G. M. Huss, was published under the title of *Rationale Building.* New York, 1895.]

WARD, C. *Mediaeval Church Vaulting.* Princeton, 1915.

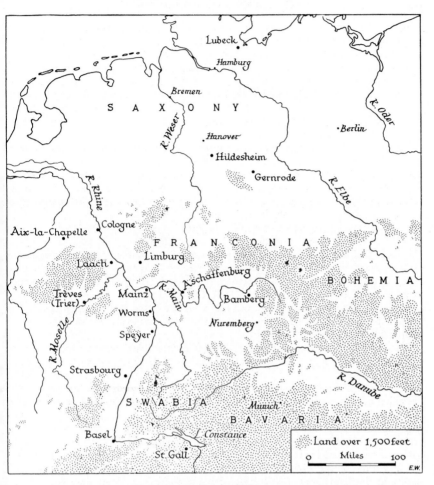

Germany in the twelfth century

X. GERMAN ROMANESQUE
(ninth–thirteenth century)

INFLUENCES

GEOGRAPHICAL. Germany was through many centuries a conglomeration, first of various tribes fighting amongst themselves, and then of various independent states, principalities, and powers occupying the great central district of Europe. This country north of the Alps was not geographically so generally accessible to Roman influence as was Gaul, with her sea-ports and great trade routes, but here the Rhine played the same part in civilization as the Rhône did in Gaul, and Roman civilization spread north-west along the fertile Rhineland and into Saxony, while the region to the east was untouched. The 'Peutinger Tabula,' a Mediaeval copy of a Roman map, now at Vienna, shows the principal Roman towns on the Rhine, with their thermae and other public buildings.

GEOLOGICAL. Stone from the mountains along the Rhine Valley was the material used for buildings in this district, and the churches were rendered more permanent and fireproof by the early introduction of vaulting. Along the Baltic shores and in central and southern Germany there was an ample supply of timber. As there was no stone or timber in the plains of the north, brick was there employed, almost exclusively in the district east of the Elbe, and the style consequently differs from that of other districts.

CLIMATIC. The average temperature of central Germany is much the same as in southern England, but the heat in summer is ten degrees higher and in winter correspondingly lower. Roman influence on architecture of this period was so insistent that even the northern climate did not exert its full influence in building. Nevertheless there was a distinct tendency to large windows, suitable for the north, and to steep roofs to throw off snow.

RELIGIOUS. Christianity naturally followed along much the same lines as Roman civilization, and under the influence of Rome it took root in southern Germany and in the Rhineland, while the rest of the country remained pagan. As early as the sixth century the bishops of Trier and Cologne were conspicuous in promoting church building, of which evidences can still be traced. Charlemagne, in furtherance of his desire to extend the Christian religion, forced the people of Saxony to embrace Christianity, and this resulted in the erection of a number of circular baptisteries, as the conversion of the tribes made a great demand for the baptismal rite.

SOCIAL. The social development of these central districts was much the same as in Europe generally: a few strong kings emerged from among weak ones, while feudal lords were constantly intolerant of kingly authority and oppressive towards the people, who became freemen or fell back as serfs, according as kings and cities prevailed against feudal tyranny, and at this period churches were only churches of monks and not of the common people. Germany, united under Charlemagne, afterwards split up into small principalities. This naturally fostered differences in architectural style. The feudal system made great strides, as it appealed to the desire of the feudal lords to become dukes of independent states, who could defy the authority of the king and tyrannize over freemen. Cities, which first grew strong in the Rhineland, found more consideration from kings than from feudal lords, so that the country was distracted by constant strife, till in 919 Henry the Fowler made himself king of a united Germany and there was peace in his time, during which many towns sprang up and freemen found it possible to carry on their industries.

HISTORICAL. Charlemagne (768–814), the first Frankish king who became Roman Emperor, was crowned in 800 at Rome by the Pope, and ruled over the land of the Franks, which included central Germany and northern France, and he also established the Frankish dominion over southern France and northern Italy (p. 312). He restored civilization in a great measure to Western Europe, and was a patron of architecture and the allied arts. Charlemagne died in 814, and before the death of his son and successor Louis the Pious in 840 the empire had already begun to crumble to pieces. The German princes demanded the right to elect their own sovereign, and Conrad I (911–19) reigned as king of Germany. Henry the Fowler (919–36) drove the Magyars out of Saxony, subjugated Bohemia and the tribes between the Elbe and the Oder, thus again establishing a united Germany. Otto the Great (936–73) was crowned king at Aix-la-Chapelle. His wars, including his conquest of Lombardy (951), made him the greatest sovereign in Europe, and in

CHURCH OF THE APOSTLES: COLOGNE

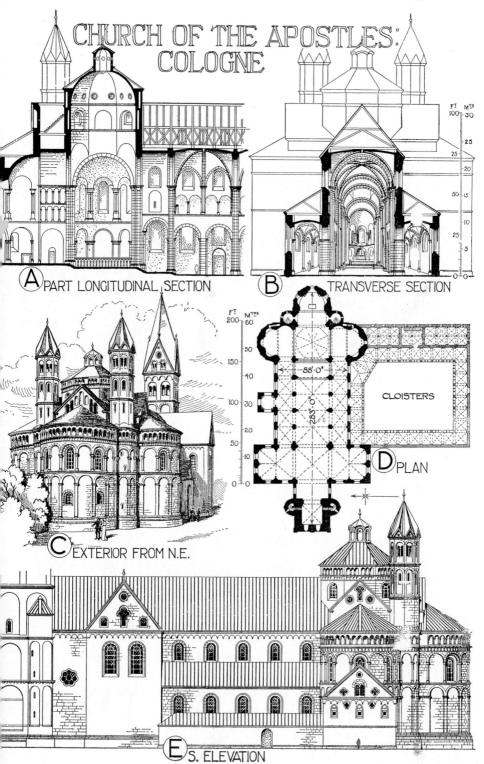

(A) PART LONGITUDINAL SECTION

(B) TRANSVERSE SECTION

(C) EXTERIOR FROM N.E.

(D) PLAN

CLOISTERS

88'·0"

283'·0"

(E) S. ELEVATION

WORMS CATHEDRAL

SCALE FOR SECTIONS &c.

(A) WESTERN APSE

(B) NAVE BAY (INT.)

(C) TRANSVERSE SECTION x·x

(D) CORNICE (E

(E) NAVE PIER
ELEVATION
PLAN
6'·5"
WESTERN APSE

(F) EXTERIOR FROM N.E.

(G) EXTERNAL ANGLE ọ CHOI

(H) JAMB ọ N. DOORW
ELEVATI

(J) PLAN
353
84·0"
EASTERN APSE

SCALE FOR PLAN

961 he received the Imperial crown at Rome; but for two centuries after his death the royal authority remained weak. His power is reflected not only in the extent of his empire, but also in the number of important buildings erected in his dominions. When Conrad II in 1024 became king of Germany. Denmark, under Canute the Great, threatened his power on the north, and Poland and Hungary on the east, but he inaugurated the great Imperial age, by restricting the power of both secular and ecclesiastical princes. After wars between rival claimants, Conrad III in 1138 became the first of the Hohenstaufen dynasty and was followed by Frederick Barbarossa (1152–90), who was also crowned Emperor at Rome. He defeated Denmark and Poland, secured the alliance of Hungary and negotiated with France and England, but his interference in papal schisms brought disaster, till emperor and pope were reconciled under Gregory VIII. The position of Germany was again reasserted in Europe by the brilliant Frederick II (1218–50), who united in himself the crowns of the Holy Roman Empire, Germany, Sicily, Lombardy, Burgundy, and Jerusalem. The political connection of the Hohenstaufen (or Swabian) emperors (1138–1254) with Lombardy is evidenced in the similarity of the architecture of the two countries during the Romanesque period.

ARCHITECTURAL CHARACTER

German Romanesque architecture dates from the ninth to the thirteenth century The style, owing to historical influences (as mentioned above), bears a striking similarity to that of Lombardy, and in some instances lasted as late as the middle of the thirteenth century, more especially in the Rhineland and Saxony, where it is found in its most highly developed form.

Church plans are peculiar in having both western and eastern apses (p. 356J), and thus there are no great western entrances as in France. The reason for these double apses has never been thoroughly explained; some think that the eastern apse may have been used for the abbot and monks and the western apse for the bishop and laity, or that the western apse may be the survival of the detached baptistery which had been usual in earlier churches. The general character is picturesque by reason of numerous circular and octagonal turrets, polygonal cupolas, and arcaded galleries under the eaves (p. 356F). Doorways were placed laterally in the aisles and are the most richly ornamented features of the churches, with shafts and capitals boldly and effectively carved. Vaulting appears not to have come into use in the Rhenish churches until some fifty years after its general adoption in France.

EXAMPLES

Aix-la-Chapelle (Aachen) Cathedral (796–804) (pp. 280, 285E–G), built by the Emperor Charlemagne as his royal tomb-house, resembles S. Vitale, Ravenna (p. 285C, D). The entrance, flanked by staircase turrets, leads into a polygon of sixteen sides, 105 ft in diameter. Every two angles of this polygon converge on to one pier, and thus form an internal octagon, the eight piers of which support a dome 47 ft 6 ins in diameter, rising above the two-storeyed surrounding aisles. The building has been much altered since the time of Charlemagne, for the Gothic choir was added (1353–1413), the gables date from the thirteenth century and the lofty outer roof of the octagon from the seventeenth century. The surrounding chapels are of the fourteenth and fifteenth centuries and the western steeple has been added in recent years (p. 285F). The building is of historic interest as the prototype of other similar churches in Germany, but more especially as the place of coronation of the Holy Roman Emperors.

Gernrode Abbey (958–1050) has a nave, covered by a wooden roof, aisles, and a fine triforium, and is probably the earliest instance of a church with an apse at both ends, a feature peculiar to Germany.

The **Monastery of S. Gall** (*c.* 820) (p. 308), in modern Switzerland, is a typical German Benedictine monastery of the period. A complete plan found in the seventeenth century appears to have been prepared by Eginhardt, Charlemagne's architect, and shows a double-apse church with cloisters, abbot's lodging, school, refectory, dormitory, guest-house, dispensary, infirmary, granaries, bakehouses, orchard, and cemetery—thus showing the thoroughness with which every need was provided for in the planning of a monastic colony.

S. Godehard, Hildesheim (1133–70), and **S. Michael, Hildesheim** (*c.* 1015–1186), have nave arcades in which square piers and columns are used to support semicircular arches.

The **Church of the Apostles, Cologne** (1035–1220) (p. 355), is one of the series of triapsal churches in that city. The plan consists of a broad nave, aisles half its width, western transepts, and a triapsal choir, while over the crossing a low octagonal tower gives dignity to the effective external grouping (p. 355C). The entrance is by a northern porch, and there is no great western portal as in France, the west end being occupied by a tower flanked by stair turrets, crowned with a typical Rhenish roof, consisting of a steep gable on each face from which ride the ridges of a pyramidal roof. An Anglo-Saxon example can be seen at Sompting, Sussex (p. 387E). The triapsal end has wall arcading in two storeys crowned with the characteristic eaves arcade, and on the south side are the cloisters. This church was severely damaged during the 1939–45 war.

S. Maria im Capitol, Cologne (rebuilt 1047), **S. Martin, Cologne** (1150–70) (p. 359A, B), and **S. Cunibert, Cologne,** are other triapsal churches which have suffered from war damage.

Worms Cathedral (A.D. 1110–81) (p. 356) vies with the **Cathedrals of Speyer** (1030) (p. 359C, D) and **Mainz** (1036) (p. 360B) as a typical church of this period. The plan is apsidal at both ends, with eastern and western octagons, while one vaulting bay of the nave corresponds with two of the aisles, and cross-vaults are employed in both cases (p. 356C, J). Twin circular towers containing stairs flank the eastern and western apses, and the crossing of the nave and transept is covered with a low octagonal tower, crowned with a pointed roof. The entrances are in the aisles, a position which found favour both in Germany and England. The lateral façades have circular-headed windows, between the characteristic flat pilaster strips.

Laach Abbey (1093–1156) (p. 361B) is a Benedictine church. The plan differs from most others because on either side of the western apse, which is used as a tomb-house, are entrances from the cloistered atrium which still exists, and there are also three eastern apses. The vaulting bays of nave and aisles are of the same width, which shows an advance towards the Gothic system. The church is built chiefly of local lava and the exterior is a fine grouping of six towers, double transepts, and east and west apses.

Lübeck Cathedral (1173) is an example of the brick architecture of north Germany; but the Gothic choir and aisles were not added till 1335 (p. 588), thus converting it into a 'hall' church (p. 587).

Trier Cathedral (1016–47) (pp. 361A, 364) is reminiscent of the importance of this ancient city which, in the fourth century, was one of the residences of Roman Emperors, and for nearly 1,500 years remained the seat of bishops, archbishops, and electors. The cathedral succeeded a basilican church several times destroyed by Franks and Normans, but rebuilt and enlarged in the eleventh

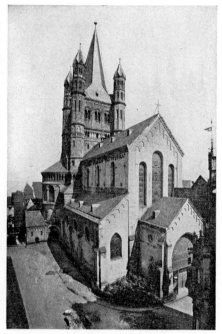

A. Nave looking E.   B. Exterior from N.W.

S. Martin, Cologne (1150–70). See opposite page

C. Towers and external gallery   D. Detail of doorway

Speyer Cathedral (1030). See opposite page

A. S. Gereon, Cologne, from E. (1160)
See pp. 265, 587

B. Mainz Cathedral from S.W. (1036).
See p. 358

C. S. Gereon, Cologne, from S. (straight-sided choir 1075; towers and apse 1160;
oval nave 1219–27). See pp. 265, 587

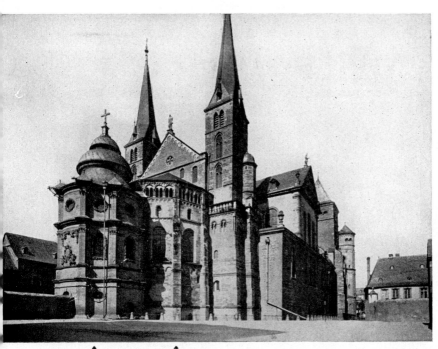

(Added 18th century)   (1152–69)

A. Trier Cathedral from N.E. (1016–47 and later). See p. 358

B. Laach Abbey Church from N. (1093–1156). See p. 358

A B CAPITALS
ABBEY-CHURCH, CONRADSBURG.

C CAPITALS D
ILSENBURG   :   CONRADSBU

E CAPITALS: LIMBURG

F

G ORNAMENT: LIMBURG

H WINDOW: GERNRODE.

J COLUMN
HECKLINGEN

K W. TOWERS: LIMBURG CATH.

M WINDOW: LAAC

L COLUMN
ILSENBURG.

N PORTAL: BÂLE.

P CLOISTERS: ASCHAFFENBURG.

Q TOWER: S.COLUMBA, COLOC

JAMB

5'.8"

R DOORWAY
S.MARTIN, WORMS.

S DOORWAY: STRASSBURG CATH.

T N.E. PORTAL: BAMBER

century. It has an eastern apse and also a western apse flanked by entrances, and forms an important group with the Liebfrauenkirche, which is described in Chapter XVI (pp. 587, 589A, B).

Germany is remarkable for two-storeyed churches, generally attached to castles, as at Nuremberg, Landsberg, and Steinfurt in Westphalia. It is supposed that the upper church was used by the prince and his retinue, and the lower by his retainers.

COMPARATIVE ANALYSIS

PLANS. Naves and aisles of churches are vaulted in square bays, one vaulting bay of the nave being equal to two of the aisles, as in Worms Cathedral (p. 356J), and the Church of the Apostles, Cologne (p. 355D). The plans of churches are complicated by the multiplication of towers, transepts, and apses at either end, while the choir is always apsidal and often raised, as in Lombardy, to admit of a crypt beneath. Apses also frequently terminate the western end of the nave, as at Worms (p. 356J) and Laach, and churches are sometimes triapsal, as the Church of the Apostles, Cologne (p. 355D), while in others there are also western transepts with towers over the crossing. Towers, square, circular, or polygonal, numbering often as many as six, two at the east end flanking the apse, and two similarly at the west end, give a varied skyline to churches (p. 362K).

WALLS. The plain wall surface is relieved by pilaster strips, connected horizontally at different stages by ranges of arches on corbels which, owing to the smallness of scale, have the appearance of moulded string courses (pp. 355C, 356F, 362K). Arcaded galleries, the origin of which has already been considered, are frequent under the eaves of roofs, especially round apses (p. 355C). All these features are derived from Lombardy. Churches usually have a triforium and always a clear-story (p. 355A).

OPENINGS. Nave arcades are frequently unmoulded and the semicircular arches spring from piers (pp. 355, 356) or cylinders, while alternate piers are sometimes carried up to support the vault ribs (pp. 355A, 356B). Cloisters frequently have small columns supporting arches in groups of three (p. 362P). The eaves galleries (p. 355C), borrowed from Lombardy, are special features, sometimes carried entirely round the church, as at Speyer (p. 359C). Doorways are frequently in the side aisles instead of in the west front or transepts, and have recesses with nook shafts (p. 362R, S, T). Windows are usually single, but occasionally grouped (p. 362M), and sometimes have a mid-wall shaft (p. 362H, Q), the germ of Gothic tracery windows.

ROOFS. In the Rhine district the semicircular cross-vault of the nave is of a domical nature, owing to the use of semicircular ribs, which rise to a greater height over the diagonal of the compartment. The system of including two bays of the aisle in one nave vaulting compartment was generally adopted (pp. 355A, B, 356B, C). Timber roofs were also employed for naves with large spans, as at Gernrode. Square towers, divided into storeys by moulded courses, frequently terminate in four gables with hipped rafters rising from the apex of each, and the roofing planes intersect at these rafters and thus form a pyramidal or 'helm' roof with four diamond-shaped sides meeting at the apex (pp. 355C, 362K). Polygonal towers have similar roofs, but with valleys between the gables (p. 355C), and all show the commencement of the evolution of spires which became the feature of the Gothic period.

COLUMNS. In nave arcades square piers with attached half-columns were usual, though sometimes varied by the alternation of compound piers and cylinders crowned by capitals bold in execution and well designed (p. 362A, B, C, D). The shafts and capitals in doorways were frequently elaborately carved with figures of men, birds, and animals (p. 362E, J, L, N).

MOULDINGS (p. 359D). There is a general absence of mouldings in nave arcades, which gives a bold appearance to interiors. When they occur, mouldings are as a rule of indifferent design, and those of capitals and bases take a distinctive form intermediate between Roman and Gothic.

ORNAMENT. Internally the flat wall surfaces may have been painted originally, but the general effect to-day is extremely bare. Characteristic carving in bands was employed (p. 362G), and in the north, lines of coloured bricks were used externally. The sculpture is often well executed (p. 362N), and the craftsmanship of this period is seen in the bronze doors of Hildesheim Cathedral (A.D. 1015), which are wrought in wonderful detail to represent the Creation, the Fall, and the Redemption, as seen in a reproduction in the Victoria and Albert Museum, London.

REFERENCE BOOKS

BOISSERÉE, S. *Denkmäler der Baukunst am Nieder-Rhein.* Munich, 1844.

HAUPT, A. VON. *Die Baukunst der Germanen von der Völkerwanderung bis zu Karl dem Grossen.* Leipzig, 1909.

MOLLER, G. *Denkmäler der Deutschen Baukunst.* Leipzig, 1852.

OTTE, H. *Geschichte der romanischen Baukunst.* Leipzig, 1874.

Trier Cathedral (1016–47) and the Liebfrauenkirche (1227–43) from W.
See pp. 358, 587

Europe in the fourteenth century

XI. GOTHIC ARCHITECTURE IN EUROPE

(twelfth–sixteenth century)

INFLUENCES

GEOGRAPHICAL. The various peoples of Western Europe, who had once been under the dominion and civilization of Rome, had by the end of the twelfth century formed into separate nations, with a consequent new territorial distribution of the map of Europe. The Latin races of France, Italy, and Spain developed into independent kingdoms; Germany was the centre of the Holy Roman Empire; England, under her Norman kings, possessed large domains in France and was thus linked up with Western Europe. Poland, the north-eastern Baltic lands and Scandinavia— apart from Norway, influenced by England—were less affected by this movement and reflected German art. Russia played little part. The Gothic style originated in France, and until the beginning of the thirteenth century French influence was paramount.

GEOLOGICAL. Geological conditions vary so much in Europe that they contribute a definite influence in differentiating the style according to countries; thus the white and coloured marbles of Italy, the coarse-grained stone of France and England, the brick of northern Germany and of Lombardy are all factors, as will be seen, in determining the character of the architecture of these countries.

CLIMATIC. Climatic conditions, which, even in Europe, vary from north to south and east to west, have in all ages and countries had considerable influence in deciding the style of the architecture in any given district. Thus in the slanting rays of the northern sun the most effective shadows are cast by vertical features, such as the buttresses and pinnacles which surround northern Gothic churches. The southern sun moves higher in the firmament and thus the deepest shadows are cast from horizontal cornices, and these are therefore frequently retained in Italian Gothic. Although this did not wholly determine the difference in treatment, it is interesting to observe that the highest development of Gothic architecture was achieved in northern latitudes. Climate, as will be seen, more especially affected the use of arcades and the size of door and window openings; while heavy snow-falls necessitated steep Gothic roofs in the north.

RELIGIOUS. The conditions of the Christian Church and the rise of monastic communities precedent to the Gothic period have been dealt with under Romanesque architecture (p. 304). The immense power of the popes in the thirteenth century can be judged from the way they made and unmade emperors and kings and disposed of their dominions. The clergy, by reason of their learning, were prominent not only in spiritual but also in temporal affairs, and thus attracted wealth and power to the church. In Germany many of the abbots and bishops were princes of the Empire, and the archbishops of Cologne, Trier (Trèves), and Mainz were among the Electors of the Holy Roman Empire. The periodical pilgrimages to shrines of local saints and holy relics, and the various forms of an increasingly ornate ritual, influenced the plans of cathedrals. In England homage paid to the Virgin Mary led to the building of Lady chapels, either as a prolongation of the eastern end, as at Salisbury (p. 410E), or as a lateral addition, as at Ely (p. 410A). The extension of the sanctuary to provide for the increase in the numbers of the clergy, chapels dedicated to special saints, processional ambulatories, chantry chapels for masses for the dead, all in turn modified and extended the original plan in the different countries.

SOCIAL. The rapid growth of towns and the development of commercial activity, with the consequent increase of wealth, inspired a rivalry between neighbouring cities which was expressed in the erection of magnificent buildings both municipal and ecclesiastical. The countries of Europe developed along different lines according to the genius of the people, as set forth in the following chapters—English (p. 382), French (p. 529), Belgian and Dutch (p. 569), German (p.583), Italian (p.599), and Spanish (p.635) Gothic architecture. In Germany towns formed associations for mutual defence, the Hanseatic League being a famous example. France and England were much under the heel of the feudal system, which retarded municipal activity but gave opportunity for domestic architecture. Italy was divided into republics and dukedoms, in which smaller cities were subject to the more powerful, and here city life developed with greater freedom owing to disputes between the Papacy and the Holy Roman Empire and to the comparative freedom of Italy from the feudal system.

HISTORICAL. The principal historical events which influenced the architecture of the different countries are referred to in subsequent chapters; but, briefly, they were the loss of the English possessions in France, the gradual subjugation of the various provinces of France under one king, the disintegration of Germany into a number of independent states, the contests between the Muslim Moors and the Christians in Spain, and the Latin conquest of Constantinople (Istanbul) in 1204, which transferred the commerce of the East to the cities of Italy. The historical influences affecting English Gothic architecture were of a varying nature and are referred to in detail on p. 385.

ARCHITECTURAL CHARACTER

The following diagram emphasizes the broad lines of the evolution of styles leading up to the Gothic architecture of Western Europe:

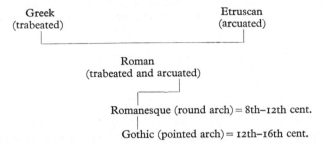

Greek
(trabeated)

Etruscan
(arcuated)

Roman
(trabeated and arcuated)

Romanesque (round arch) = 8th–12th cent.

Gothic (pointed arch) = 12th–16th cent.

The term 'Gothic' was used by Vasari (1511–74) and also by Sir Christopher Wren in the seventeenth century as a term of reproach for this style, which had departed from those Classic lines which he was instrumental in establishing in this country. This term is now, by common consent, given to the Mediaeval architecture of the twelfth to the early sixteenth century in Europe. The Gothic of the thirteenth century throughout Europe was slowly evolved from Romanesque architecture and is mainly distinguished by the introduction and general use of the pointed arch, whose original home was Mesopotamia; from Assyria (p. 86) it passed to Sassanian Persia; when the Muslims conquered Persia (c. 641) it became part of their stock-in-trade. The adventurous Normans found it well established when they wrested Sicily from the Muslims (1061–90) and in Syria it was in frequent use at the opening of the Crusades (1096). This feature, in conjunction with buttresses and lofty pinnacles, gives to the style the aspiring tendency which has been regarded as symbolic of the religious aspirations of the period. Romanesque architects (p. 306) had begun to recognize the differing functions performed by the respective parts of vaulted buildings and to provide for them more economically than the Romans had done. Gothic architects further extended the application of the principles of counter-poise, and by employing small stones laid in shallow courses with thick mortar joints, endeavoured to secure the greatest amount of elasticity compatible with stability. The Gothic masons, throwing the rein on the neck of experiment, utilized stone to its utmost capacity. They heaped up stone in towers that, rising above the lofty roofs of nave and transepts, tapered upwards in slender spires embroidered with lace-like tracery. They suspended it overhead in ponderous vaults, ornamented so as to seem mere gossamer webs pierced by cunning pendants, which pleased the fancy of the fifteenth century, and which in reality sustain the very vaults from which they appear to hang. Finally, emboldened by success, they even ventured to cut granular stone as thin as fibrous wood. The stability of a Gothic cathedral depends upon the proper adjustment of thrust and counter-thrust. The collected pressures of the nave vaulting, which are downward owing to their weight and oblique owing to the arched form of the vault, are counteracted partially by the dead weight of the outer roof loaded upon the upward extension of the clear-story walls, and for the rest by arches carried above the aisle roofs to press against the nave wall, these arches being retained by an outer line of massive buttresses weighted by pinnacles. Whereas in Roman buildings the buttressing system is often an integral part of the enormously thick walls (pp. 199A, 369A), which rise up to weight the haunches of barrel vaults or domes, in a Gothic building (p. 369B) the wall system consists of pieces of wall, or buttresses, at right angles to the building, to take the collected pressures of the ribbed vault. This structural contrivance of transmitting the accumulated pressures to the ground is known as a 'flying buttress'. The entire structure consists of a skeleton of piers, buttresses, arches, and ribbed vaulting, all held in equilibrium by the combination of oblique and vertical forces neutralizing each other, as is clearly shown by the illustrations which explain the constructive principles (p. 369). The walls were thus merely required to enclose and not to support the structure, and indeed they principally consisted of glazed windows with vertical mullions and traceried heads. It is evident that the development of this complicated system of construction would have been impossible apart from the use of such material as could be laid in the small stones with thick mortar joints, which were necessary to give elasticity to the structure. These principles led to much novelty in the treatment of capitals and piers; for the vaulting ribs, collected at intervals, were supported on capitals shaped to fit them, and shafts, when continued to the ground, modified the form of the nave piers of which they formed a part. The difficulties in the quarrying and transport of stone, which resulted from the social and industrial conditions of the age, taught the Gothic architects economy in the use of materials, and there was consequently less waste in the working of stone in Mediaeval than in Classic times. Gothic architecture, in common with Greek, relies on the evident truthfulness of its structural features, which in both styles are component parts of the artistic scheme. The self-contained Greek temple, however, is reposeful in the repetition of its columns and the severity of its horizontal entablatures, whereas the Gothic cathedral is a complex, virile structure composed of many vertical features, to which unity was given by a due observance of relative proportions. Thus in Gothic architecture the features were not left to mere artistic caprice, but were in the main determined by stern structural utility, as exemplified in the novel shape of a capital specially designed to support a novel superstructure, and in the ribs of vaults which accurately express their function as sinews to support the vaulting panels. Although most of the forms were founded primarily on structural necessity, others were the expression of artistic invention; thus the spire fulfilled no structural requirement, but it served as a symbol and formed an outward and visible expression of the religious aspirations of the time and directed the thoughts of men heavenwards. Compared with Greek or Roman monumental construction in masonry, the Gothic was an architecture of small stones, for easy transport; for fine material was not usually so immediate to the sites as in Greece, nor was there such a well-developed road system as the Roman. Indeed roads were very poor, and if practicable, water-carriage by boat or barge on sea, river or stream was preferable, however circuitous, and decidedly cheaper than overland haulage by pack-horse or waggon. There are frequent instances of stone being brought from Caen, Normandy, to south-eastern England, or being brought long distances around the coast rather than overland from quarries much nearer to hand.

The evolution of stone vaulting from Roman to late Gothic times is an interesting subject which can be clearly explained by diagrams (pp. 369, 370, 373, 399). The Roman system of stone vaulting, comprising the waggon and the intersecting vault (p. 370A, B), was continued in the Romanesque period (p. 370D), but an innovation was that of placing a vault over an oblong compartment of a church nave (p. 370C), when difficulties occurred owing to the differences in height between semicircular arches over spans of varying width. The illustrations (p. 370G) give the several means of overcoming the difficulty, which was only entirely surmounted when the pointed arch was introduced (p. 370F, H). A careful study of the illustrations (pp. 370, 373) will clearly demonstrate the various problems encountered in the evolution

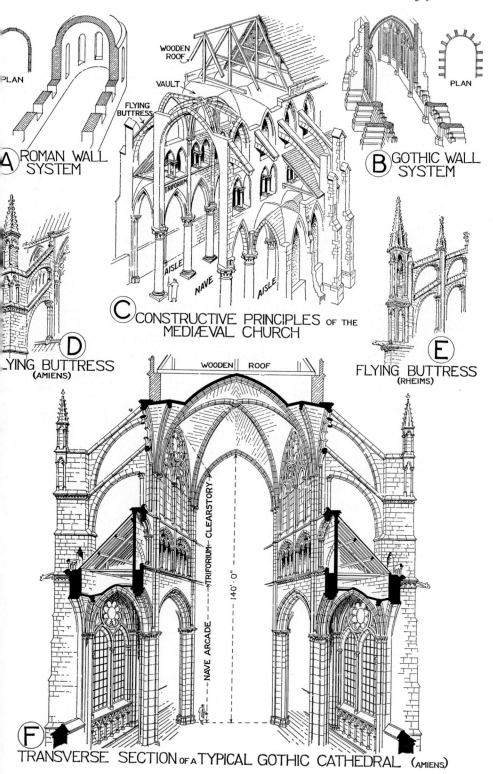

PLAN

WOODEN ROOF

VAULT

FLYING BUTTRESS

TRIFORIUM

AISLE NAVE AISLE

Ⓐ ROMAN WALL SYSTEM

Ⓑ GOTHIC WALL SYSTEM

Ⓒ CONSTRUCTIVE PRINCIPLES of the MEDIÆVAL CHURCH

Ⓓ FLYING BUTTRESS (AMIENS)

Ⓔ FLYING BUTTRESS (RHEIMS)

WOODEN ROOF

NAVE ARCADE — TRIFORIUM — CLEARSTORY

140'-0"

Ⓕ TRANSVERSE SECTION of a TYPICAL GOTHIC CATHEDRAL (AMIENS)

EVOLUTION OF GOTHIC VAULTING

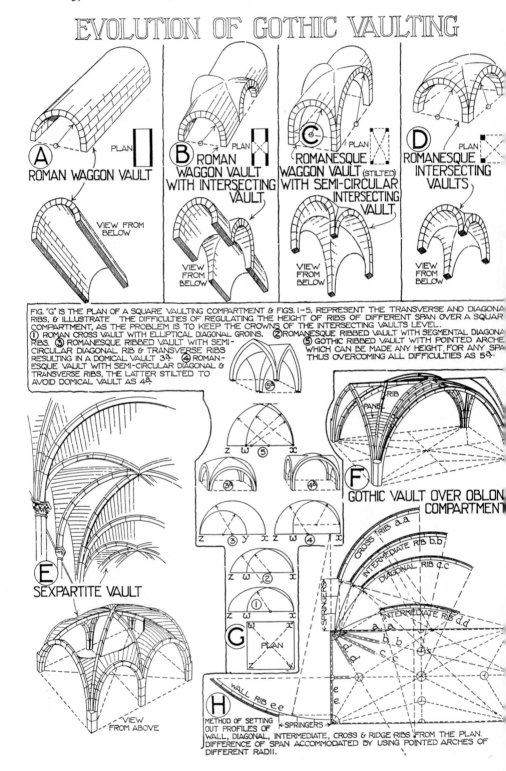

A ROMAN WAGGON VAULT

PLAN

VIEW FROM BELOW

B ROMAN WAGGON VAULT WITH INTERSECTING VAULT

PLAN

VIEW FROM BELOW

C ROMANESQUE WAGGON VAULT (STILTED) WITH SEMI-CIRCULAR INTERSECTING VAULT

PLAN

VIEW FROM BELOW

D ROMANESQUE INTERSECTING VAULTS

PLAN

VIEW FROM BELOW

FIG. "G" IS THE PLAN OF A SQUARE VAULTING COMPARTMENT & FIGS. 1–5. REPRESENT THE TRANSVERSE AND DIAGONAL RIBS, & ILLUSTRATE THE DIFFICULTIES OF REGULATING THE HEIGHT OF RIBS OF DIFFERENT SPAN OVER A SQUARE COMPARTMENT, AS THE PROBLEM IS TO KEEP THE CROWNS OF THE INTERSECTING VAULTS LEVEL.
① ROMAN CROSS VAULT WITH ELLIPTICAL DIAGONAL GROINS. ② ROMANESQUE RIBBED VAULT WITH SEGMENTAL DIAGONAL RIBS. ③ ROMANESQUE RIBBED VAULT WITH SEMI-CIRCULAR DIAGONAL RIB & TRANSVERSE RIBS RESULTING IN A DOMICAL VAULT 3ª. ④ ROMANESQUE VAULT WITH SEMI-CIRCULAR DIAGONAL & TRANSVERSE RIBS, THE LATTER STILTED TO AVOID DOMICAL VAULT AS 4ª. ⑤ GOTHIC RIBBED VAULT WITH POINTED ARCHES WHICH CAN BE MADE ANY HEIGHT, FOR ANY SPAN, THUS OVERCOMING ALL DIFFICULTIES AS 5ª.

RIB
PANEL

F GOTHIC VAULT OVER OBLONG COMPARTMENT

E SEXPARTITE VAULT

VIEW FROM ABOVE

G PLAN

CROSS RIB a.a
INTERMEDIATE RIB b.b
DIAGONAL RIB c.c
INTERMEDIATE RIB d.d
WALL RIB e.e
SPRINGERS

H METHOD OF SETTING OUT PROFILES OF WALL, DIAGONAL, INTERMEDIATE, CROSS & RIDGE RIBS FROM THE PLAN. DIFFERENCE OF SPAN ACCOMMODATED BY USING POINTED ARCHES OF DIFFERENT RADII.

from the Roman stone vault to the ribbed Gothic vault over an oblong compartment. The setting-out of one compartment of a Gothic vault is given, with plans at different levels of the springers (p. 373C), and the method of obtaining the outline of the various ribs is also shown (p. 370H). This flexibility allowed in vaulting by the use of the pointed arch—always regarded as the chief visible characteristic of Gothic architecture—is a virtue which might seem to explain the readiness with which it was adopted from Muslim art, were it not for the fact that the pointed arch appears to have been used over wall-openings (soon after 1100 at Cluny, France; p. 343) before it was employed in vaults (over Durham Cathedral nave, 1128–33; p. 392B).

Gothic vaulting consists of a framework of stone ribs, which support thin stone panels, known as 'rib and panel' vaulting, which was an extension of the Romanesque method which had been evolved from the Roman. The ribs were constructed as permanent supports and on them the thin stone panels were laid, being supported temporarily on a movable centre sometimes known as a 'circe' (p. 373E). The difficulty of vaulting oblong compartments was overcome by the use of the pointed arch over the shorter spans, while the semicircular arch was for some time retained for the diagonal or longer spans. The licence which Gothic masons allowed themselves in the treatment and disposition of ribs, with which they spun an intricate web of many strands, makes the evolution of Gothic vaulting a most fascinating study. Vault thrusts are considered in the chapter on English Mediaeval architecture (p. 394), and it is sufficient to say here that the vault pressures were both downwards by the weight of the stone, through the action of the law of gravitation, and outwards by the pressure of the arch voussoirs; both pressures were collected by the meeting of the ribs at the angles of vaulting compartments, and the resultant oblique pressure was then counteracted and transmitted to the ground by buttresses and flying buttresses weighted by pinnacles (pp. 369, 497, 532C, 539A, 564A). The weight of the roof, transmitted by the nave arcade walls, also played its part in driving thrusts to earth. The evolution of Gothic vaulting in England is referred to later (p. 394).

As a result of the development of the Gothic system of buttresses, walls became less necessary as supports; but were naturally retained to enclose the building and protect it against the elements. Another step in the evolution of the style was made possible by the invention of painted glass, which was forthwith used to form brilliant transparent pictures in the ever-recurring windows which were enclosed under the pointed vaults, which had, as already explained, been originally adopted for constructive reasons. The stonework of traceried windows in churches was merely a frame for pictures of incidents in Bible history. The brilliant translucent windowed walls of a Gothic cathedral rival in beauty the painted wall-reliefs and hieroglyphics of Egyptian temples, the sculptured slabs of Assyrian palaces, the paintings and sculpture of Greek temples, the stuccoes and frescoes of Roman thermae, and the mosaics of Byzantine and Romanesque churches. In the north of Europe the windows stretched from buttress to buttress, and thus provided full scope for the use of glowing painted glass as the chief internal decoration, and it followed that walls were kept uniformly flat internally so that the coloured windows might be seen by all; while structural features, such as buttresses and pinnacles, were placed externally (p. 369).

The question as to the real designers or architects of Mediaeval buildings and the methods of organization of building works has been undergoing investigation in recent years. The conception, or design, of new projects was the province of the master of the appropriate craft; thus usually a mason in works for the church, royal house or a civic authority. Master-masons acquired varying degrees of renown, and the greater the recognition of their prowess as architects and the more they concentrated on this function and the direction of subordinates, the less they worked at their craft with their own hands. Some became very famous indeed; their services were widely sought by great personages, so that they proceeded from one project to another or even controlled several at the same time. In general, as time elapsed, the masters of the respective crafts became progressively more firmly grouped into guilds or lodges, these being associations concerned to uphold the status and well-being of the crafts and to nourish craft secrets, as well as to assure the integrity of the members and the quality of the work produced in return for a fair price. In later times at least, representative masters of chapters or groups of lodges met at intervals to concert regulations and to advance their art. Great distances sometimes were covered. In these and other ways, fresh ideas were constantly disseminated. From time to time great masters were called from widely afield into consultative council on projects of particular importance or difficulty. Travels also were undertaken by masters in search of suitable building materials. The names of some five hundred European—including British—leading architect-craftsmen are known. Among these are such as Villard de Honnecourt of thirteenth-century France; Arnolfo di Cambio (1232–1301) of Italy; Peter Parler (1333–99) of Germany; Henry Yevele (c. 1320-1400) and Hugh Herland (fl. 1360–1405) of England, the last being a master-carpenter. Ordinary craftsmen necessarily left a completed project for another, which in church or domestic work might be quite far away. For royal works, craftsmen as well as workmen could be impressed. Contrary to popular belief, monks or clerics took no part in actual building operations, though they might discharge duties of collecting or disbursing funds or controlling accounts. Until the later Middle Ages, when trading in building materials had made some progress, the organization of a large building project included the drawing together of all the necessary materials from their respective sources, shaping them when requisite and obtaining the necessary plant and gear. Building processes much resembled those of to-day; but comprehensive 'working drawings' for an entire scheme were not made; only for the part as work proceeded, and much was done by direct setting-out at full scale in temporary booths or lodges constructed on the site. The core of the church mason's knowledge was that of the geometrical mysteries of bay structure, which the more progressive masters were constantly concerned to refine and improve. Templates, patterns, diagrams and other devices for setting-out were treasured possessions of building-craftsmen and their guilds.

EXAMPLES

CATHEDRALS

Cathedrals and churches in Mediaeval times occupied an important place in national life, and their construction was continued from one generation to another. The term 'cathedral' (Gk. seat or throne) was applied to the episcopal church of the diocese. They were the history books of the period when few people could read, and thus were a medium of popular education, taking the place of such modern institutions as free schools, libraries, museums, picture galleries, and concert halls. Sculpture and painted glass reflected incidents of Bible history from the Creation to the Redemption of mankind, and this pictorial presentment was peculiarly adapted for people to whom the written word was a sealed book. The virtues and vices, surrounded by all the imagery of Mediaeval symbolism, were depicted in sculptured figure and coloured glass before the gaze of the passing people, and the moral was pointed for the encouragement or warning of all by representations, often crude and realistic, of the rewards or punishments that might be expected to result from the practice of the particular virtue or vice. Saints with devout mien

COMPARATIVE DIAGRAMS OF VAULTS

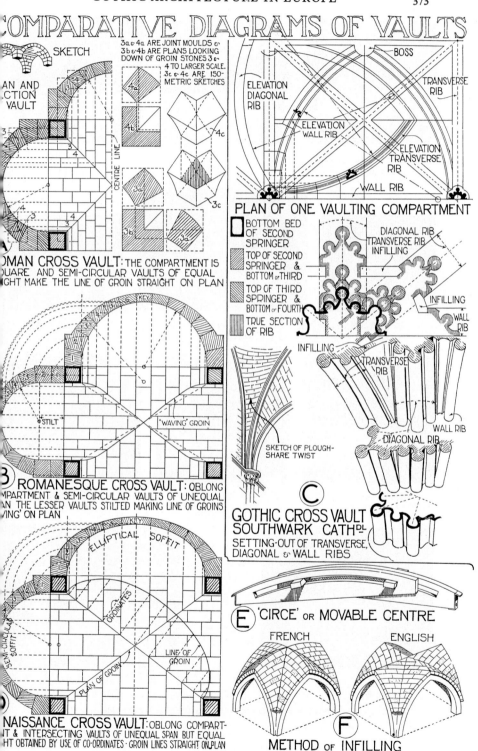

SKETCH

3a & 4a ARE JOINT MOULDS & 3b & 4b ARE PLANS LOOKING DOWN OF GROIN STONES 3 & 4 TO LARGER SCALE. 3c & 4c ARE ISO-METRIC SKETCHES

AN AND
CTION
VAULT

4a
4b
4c
3c
3b
3a

CENTRE LINE

ELEVATION
DIAGONAL
RIB

BOSS

TRANSVERSE
RIB

ELEVATION
WALL RIB

ELEVATION
TRANSVERSE
RIB

WALL RIB

PLAN OF ONE VAULTING COMPARTMENT

A) ROMAN CROSS VAULT: THE COMPARTMENT IS SQUARE AND SEMI-CIRCULAR VAULTS OF EQUAL HEIGHT MAKE THE LINE OF GROIN STRAIGHT ON PLAN

☐ BOTTOM BED
OF SECOND
SPRINGER

TOP OF SECOND
SPRINGER &
BOTTOM of THIRD

TOP OF THIRD
SPRINGER &
BOTTOM of FOURTH

TRUE SECTION
OF RIB

DIAGONAL RIB
TRANSVERSE RIB
INFILLING

INFILLING

WALL
RIB

KEY

STILT

'WAVING' GROIN

INFILLING

TRANSVERSE
RIB

WALL RIB

DIAGONAL RIB

SKETCH OF PLOUGH-
SHARE TWIST

B) ROMANESQUE CROSS VAULT: OBLONG COMPARTMENT & SEMI-CIRCULAR VAULTS OF UNEQUAL SPAN THE LESSER VAULTS STILTED MAKING LINE OF GROINS 'WAVING' ON PLAN

C) GOTHIC CROSS VAULT SOUTHWARK CATH.DL

SETTING-OUT OF TRANSVERSE, DIAGONAL & WALL RIBS

KEY

ELLIPTICAL SOFFIT

ORDINATES

SEMI-CIRCULAR SOFFIT

LINE OF GROIN

PLAN OF GROIN

E) 'CIRCE' OR MOVABLE CENTRE

FRENCH

ENGLISH

D) RENAISSANCE CROSS VAULT: OBLONG COMPART-MENT & INTERSECTING VAULTS OF UNEQUAL SPAN BUT EQUAL HEIGHT OBTAINED BY USE OF CO-ORDINATES · GROIN LINES STRAIGHT ON PLAN

F) METHOD OF INFILLING

A. Nôtre Dame, Paris
see p. 534

B. Rouen
see p. 541

C. Amiens
see p. 541

D. Evreux
see p. 541

E. Chartres
see p. 538

F. Beauvais
see p. 542

G. Strasbourg
see p. 542

H. Antwerp
see p. 574

J. Vienna
see p. 588

K. Cologne
see p. 587

L. Milan
see p. 604

Comparative Models of Continental Cathedrals

and angels of joyful aspect carried the thoughts of men to a future and higher life; while all the manifold energies of mankind, as expressed in the various handicrafts of peace and war, were represented in cathedral wall and window to stimulate energy and action in daily life. Thus we see that Mediaeval architecture is a grand chronicler also of secular history in which kings, nobles, knights, and people were represented as playing their part. The plans of cathedrals differ in every country in Europe, and Continental cathedrals (p. 374) form an interesting comparison with English cathedrals (pp. 407, 408, 409).

Church plans in England (pp. 410, 411, 412, 413), France (p. 561), Belgium (p. 571F), Germany (p. 590H), and Italy (p. 602C) are generally in the form of a Latin cross of which the short arms form the north and south transepts. The derivation of this cruciform plan is conjectural, and has been the subject of various theories of origin. It may have been formed from the Early Christian basilican churches (p. 258), such as old S. Peter, Rome (p. 259C), and S. Paolo fuori le Mura (p. 259E), by the extension of the 'bema' into well-marked transepts; or it may have been suggested by the cruciform tombs of the period of Constantine (p. 296G). Its complicated development during the Mediaeval period was due to the require- ments of an increasingly ornate and ceremonial ritual of which it forms a material expression in stone. The main body of the church generally stretches westward and the choir and sanctuary eastward from the 'crossing' of nave and transepts, which is often marked externally, especially in England, by a tower, sometimes tapering into a spire. These main divisions east and west, and the transepts north and south, are often further divided into central nave with side aisles, separated by columns or piers. The principal entrance is generally either at the west, as in France, where it is flanked by towers (p. 543), or on the south or north side, as in England, where it is protected by a porch (p. 412B). The columns or piers which separate nave and aisles support the nave arcades and the walls which rise above the aisle roofs (p. 369C, F). Above is the triforium or 'blind-story', which is the space beneath the sloping roof over the aisle vault and enclosed on the nave side by a series of arches. Above the triforium is a range of windows to light the nave, called the 'clear-story', probably from the French word 'clair'. By means of cross vaults these clear-story windows generally rise to the level of the ridge of the nave vault, which is covered by a high-pitched wooden roof.

The eastern arm, or the choir, reached by steps from the nave level, is generally the most ornate part of the church.

The general form of a church may also be explained in practical terms. Whereas developing ritual prescribed the mason-architect's objective, structure and materials set limitations, as did the need for adequate natural light. Wooden roof-trusses and stone vaults could not economically span naves much wider than about 40 ft (50 ft in France), but the use of either one or two aisles on each side, with clear-story lighting for the nave, doubled or trebled the accommodation. Transepts, organized on the same principle, added further to the useful space but left a dark intersection or 'crossing', which for this reason was usually elevated into a clear-story central tower, often called a 'lantern' in the past, because of this function. In France, the great height of the transepts allowed light to reach the crossing from the transept end walls, and obviated the need for a central tower (p. 545E). Weighty towers, turrets or massive buttresses were needed to counter the cumulative thrusts at the outer ends of the nave and transept arcades (e.g. Durham Cathedral, pp. 392, 408C, 411E).

In England, although the general preference was for a square end to the sanc- tuary, many cathedrals when rebuilt in Norman times were given a circular end, which was sometimes partially developed into a chevet (see Glossary). This may still be distinguished in the plans of Peterborough, Norwich, Canterbury, Gloucester, Lichfield, Ely, Winchester, Durham, S. Albans, and Chester (pp. 410,411,412,413). Many cathedrals were enlarged in later years and were then given a square termination, thus reverting to the Anglo-Saxon usage. Westminster Abbey, built under French influence, is unique in England in having a chevet with complete ring of chapels (pp. 424D, 426A), and French cathedrals are generally finished with a distinctive semicircular chevet (pp. 531, 545, 561). The Lady chapel was added at the extreme east end, as at Norwich (p. 411), Exeter (p. 412), York (p. 410), Salisbury (p. 410), Gloucester (p. 411), and elsewhere; or on one side as at Ely (p. 410).

The cloisters attached to many English cathedrals formed a part of the original monastic buildings and are generally in the most sheltered position, south of the nave and west of the transept, and served as a means of communication between different parts of the abbey and as a general meeting-place for members of the monastic community (pp. 410, 411, 412, 413). This is the general distribution of the various parts of a conventual cathedral church, from which there are many deviations, such as the number of transepts and aisles, the position of entrances, chapels, choir, and presbytery, cloisters and chapter house.

English cathedrals are conspicuous for great length in comparison to their width, and for central towers over the crossing, as at Gloucester, Canterbury, and elsewhere. Some English cathedrals, as Canterbury, York, and Ripon, also have western towers, which are usual in France, as at Paris, Rheims, and Amiens. The long, low, and clearly marked outlines of English cathedrals, accentuated by the central tower, are in strong contrast with the short, lofty, and less strongly defined outlines of Continental cathedrals, with their intricacy of flying buttresses and profusion of encircling chapels (p. 532C). English cathedrals owe much of their imposing appearance externally to their comparative detachment from surrounding buildings, as they often stand in an open space or Close, as at Canterbury, Lincoln (p. 416A), and Salisbury (p. 395A), or are picturesquely situated on a river, as at Worcester and Durham (p. 392A), described by Scott as 'Grand and vast that stands above the Wear'; or as at Winchester, Chichester, and Lichfield, which, as Milton so descriptively writes, are 'bosom'd high 'mid tufted trees'.

French cathedrals, on the other hand, are often surrounded by houses and shops, which, if not actually built against the church itself, are crowded so close to it as to detract from the dignity of the building, as at Chartres, S. Lô, and S. Omer. French cathedrals were popular rather than monastic in origin, and this accounts for the general absence of cloisters. Thus we see that there are some essential differences between English and French cathedrals (p. 559).

MONASTERIES

A general description of monastic establishments has already been given under Romanesque Architecture in Europe (p. 307).

PARISH CHURCHES

The parish churches both in town and country, erected throughout this period, were of a much less ambitious character than the cathedrals and monastic churches, but the origin and development of these smaller churches in England are of equal significance (p. 430), and the single western tower of the parish church is often the most striking landmark of the country-side.

SECULAR ARCHITECTURE

Castles and mansions of the nobles, manor houses of the gentry, dwellings of the people, hospitals, and other civil and domestic buildings are referred to under each

PRINCIPLES OF PROPORTIONS

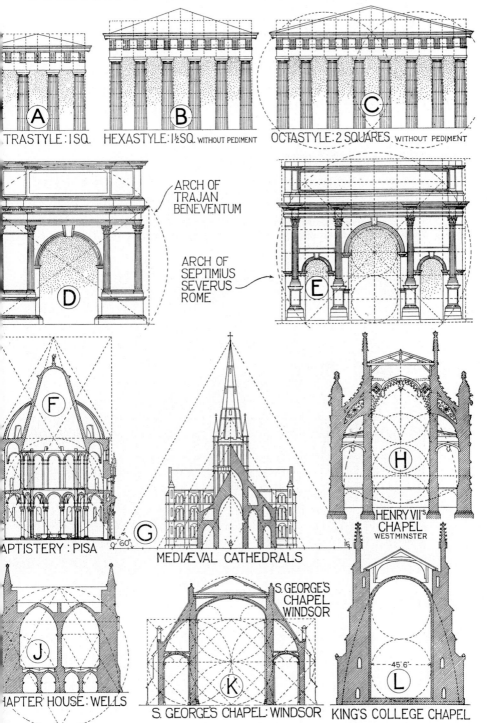

A — TRASTYLE : 1 SQ.

B — HEXASTYLE : 1½ SQ. WITHOUT PEDIMENT

C — OCTASTYLE : 2 SQUARES. WITHOUT PEDIMENT

ARCH OF TRAJAN BENEVENTUM

ARCH OF SEPTIMIUS SEVERUS ROME

D

E

F — BAPTISTERY : PISA

G — MEDIÆVAL CATHEDRALS

9' 60'   8'   16'

H — HENRY VII'S CHAPEL WESTMINSTER

J — CHAPTER HOUSE : WELLS

K — S. GEORGE'S CHAPEL : WINDSOR

S. GEORGE'S CHAPEL WINDSOR

L — KING'S COLLEGE CHAPEL

45' 6"

country as follows: England (p. 437 ff.), France (p. 549 ff.), Belgium (p. 577), Germany (p. 588 ff.), Spain (p. 644 ff.).

COMPARATIVE ANALYSIS

A comparative analysis of Gothic architecture in each country is given as follows: England (p. 489 ff.), France (p. 559 ff.), Belgium (p. 577 ff.), Germany (p. 593 ff.), Italy (p. 624 ff.), and Spain (p. 647 ff.).

A comparative table of the underlying differences between the Gothic and Renaissance styles is given on p. 660 ff.

REFERENCE BOOKS

BUNT, C. G. E. *Gothic Painting*. London, 1947.
HARVEY, J. M. *The Gothic World*. London, 1950.
JACKSON, SIR T. G. *Gothic Architecture in France, England and Italy*. London, 1915.
KARLINGER, H. *Die Kunst der Gotik*. 2nd ed. Berlin, 1934.
LETHABY, W. R., and TALBOT RICE, D. *Medieval Art*. 3rd ed. London, 1949.

Reference books relating to Gothic architecture in the different countries of Europe are given as follows: England (p. 513), France (p. 568), Belgium (p. 582), Germany (p. 597), Italy (p. 633), and Spain (p. 653).

Hampton Court: the west gatehouse. See p. 459

Mediaeval England

XII. ENGLISH MEDIAEVAL ARCHITECTURE

ANGLO-SAXON, ROMANESQUE (NORMAN), AND GOTHIC
(fifth–sixteenth century)

INFLUENCES

GEOGRAPHICAL. England, remote from Rome, on the outskirts of civilization and an island in the North Sea, opposite the rich and populous continent of Europe, owed her national development both to her insular position and to her maritime intercourse with other countries. Her geographical position has thus given rise to a dual influence in the formation of national characteristics, the operation of which has varied at different periods. Thus, isolation by the sea continuously promoted the development of definite national characteristics, while intercourse with the Continent across the sea resulted from time to time in a marked importation of foreign ideas in architecture. England's former splendid isolation cannot be described more trenchantly than in the verses of England's greatest poet:

> This royal throne of kings, this scepter'd isle,
> This earth of majesty, this seat of Mars,
> This other Eden, demi-paradise;
> This fortress built by nature for herself
> Against infection and the hand of war ;
> This happy breed of men, this little world;
> This precious stone set in the silver sea,
> Which serves it in the office of a wall,
> Or as a moat defensive to a house,
> Against the envy of less happier lands.
>
> SHAKESPEARE, *Richard II*, II, i, 40–9.

GEOLOGICAL. The varied geological formation of Great Britain was responsible for the variety of materials employed in building (p. 379). A band of oolitic freestone, including the well-known Bath stone, stretches diagonally across the island from Somersetshire to Lincolnshire, and supplies such excellent natural materials for all types of buildings in its vicinity that this geological influence is seen in the cathedrals along its course and in the fine manor houses of Wiltshire and Northamptonshire. The granites of Cornwall and Devonshire, and the sandstone of Yorkshire in the north were both so hard in texture as to admit of little sculptured ornament, and this gives severity to the architecture of these districts. It is natural that in early times the material at hand should have been employed, and this in itself gave local character, but as methods of transport improved there has been a tendency for local distinctions to disappear. In the Middle Ages transport by road was a difficult, slow, and costly undertaking when, in the absence of good roads and of wheeled vehicles, stone had to be carried on pack-horses, so water-carriage, by sea or river, was often preferred for economy; thus our island stone was easily supplemented by Caen stone from Normandy, as at Canterbury Cathedral and the Tower of London. A limited supply of marble from the Isle of Purbeck and elsewhere was also used, chiefly for clustered piers in churches, during the Early English period. The flint work of Norfolk, Suffolk, and part of the south coast gives pronounced local character to the churches of these districts, especially when, as in the Tudor period, the flints were 'knapped' or split and shaped to form chequer work and traceried panels in walls The fine oak forests of old England, especially in Lancashire, Cheshire, Shropshire, and Sussex, provided another building material. Timber was specially serviceable for posts, beams, and braces of roofs, and for the fretted barge boards of gables, and it gives an intimate and attractive character to the half-timber houses which were such a marked development in the domestic architecture of later English Gothic (p. 469). Brickwork, which was an inevitable product of the clay in river valleys, had been made use of by the eminently practical Romans in their settlements in Britain; but this material fell into disuse till it was again requisitioned in the latter part of the thirteenth century, chiefly in low-lying districts around London and in the eastern counties. Little Wenham Hall, Suffolk (1270–80) (p. 448), is probably the earliest domestic brick building in England, and Hampton Court is a world-famous pile of sixteenth-century brickwork. Terra-cotta, introduced by Italian craftsmen in the reign of Henry VIII, was employed by Giovanni da Majano for the medallion bas-reliefs at Hampton Court (p. 459) and by Torrigiani for the celebrated tomb in the Rolls Chapel, London; it also was largely used in such houses as Layer Marney Towers, Essex (*c.* 1500–25), and Sutton Place, Guildford (1523–5) (pp. 457C, 462A, 463).

CLIMATIC. The temperate and humid English climate, with its searching winds and driving rain, has had its effect upon the plan and certain features of buildings. Thus, whereas great western portals, opening direct into nave and aisles, are marked features of French cathedrals, porches in England are generally planned in the side aisles and are deep and narrow, so as to act as screens against the direct blast of the wind. The general dullness of the climate and the absence of strong sunlight contributed to the increased size of traceried windows, which in late Gothic often stretch, as in S. George's Chapel, Windsor, across the whole width of the nave. The high-pitched roof to throw off snow and rain was another result of climatic conditions, and gave full scope internally for these elaborate timber roofs which are essentially English, while externally it accentuated the aspiring character of Gothic design.

RELIGIOUS. Christianity had first made its way into Britain during the Roman occupation, and henceforth religion ranks as a paramount influence in the development of the architecture of this country. The following events indicate the status and development of Christianity in Britain which influenced architecture along ecclesiastical lines.

305. The martyrdom of S. Alban, the first British martyr.

314. The bishops of York, London, and Lincoln are recorded as attending the Council of Arles.

449–607. Christianity was blotted out and churches destroyed during these years of the Anglo-Saxon settlements.

597. S. Augustine landed in England, converted the Kentish King Ethelbert and other kings of the Heptarchy and their people, and introduced the Benedictine Order of monks into England.

601. The see of London was revived and the see of Rochester founded.

655. The Benedictine monastery of Peterborough was founded.

668–90. Theodore, Archbishop of Canterbury, divided England into bishoprics.

669–91. Wilfred, Bishop of York, repaired the Minster there, rebuilt that at Ripon on a fresh site (670) and built a fine church at Hexham (674).

674, 682. Benedict Biscop founded monasteries at Wearmouth and Jarrow, of which remains still exist.

673–709. Aldhelm of Sherborne built churches in the south, as at Bradford-on-Avon (re-modelled in the tenth century).

735. The see of York acquired metropolitan rank.

793. The Benedictine monastery of S. Albans was founded by Offa.

871–99. King Alfred rebuilt monasteries destroyed during the Danish incursions.

960–88. Dunstan, archbishop of Canterbury, after directing the secular affairs of the kingdom, devoted himself to church government and the monastic revival.

1020. King Canute founded the monastery of Bury S. Edmunds.

1061. Harold's collegiate church at Waltham consecrated.

1042–66. Edward the Confessor's religious enthusiasm resulted in the building of Westminster Abbey.

1070. William the Conqueror appointed Lanfranc archbishop of Canterbury, and the newly imported bishops built magnificent cathedrals on the Norman model, though most English cathedrals formed part of monastic foundations (p. 304).

1096. The First Crusade, preached by Urban II and Peter the Hermit, followed by others, marked an era of religious zeal (p. 304).

1113, 1118. The Knights of S. John and the Knights Templars were founded as military religious orders—set up as a result of the Crusades—and they built a special type of round church (p. 390).

1128.   The Cistercians built their first English monastery at Waverley, Surrey, afterwards followed by Rievaulx (1131), Fountains (1132), and Kirkstall (1152), all three in Yorkshire.

1174–9.   William of Sens built the choir of Canterbury Cathedral.

1175–6.   The Carthusians built their first English monastery at Witham (Somerset).

1221.   The Dominicans (Black Friars) came to England and were followed in 1224 by the Franciscans (Grey Friars) and in 1240–1 by the Carmelites (White Friars) and all built spacious churches for preaching.

1376.   Wyclif asserted the freedom of religious thought, protested against the dogmas of the Papacy, and translated the Bible into English, so that ordinary people might read it for themselves.

1367–1404.   William of Wykeham built at Winchester, New College, Oxford, and elsewhere, in the Perpendicular style which had originated in the south transept of Gloucester Cathedral (1329–37) (pp. 394, 406).

1536–40. Dissolution of the Monasteries, after which Henry VIII handed over many monastic estates to nobles and merchant princes, and this resulted in the erection of mansions and manor houses throughout England.

SOCIAL

Pre-Roman period (to 55 B.C.). The earliest traces of man in Britain, in the shape of rudely-fashioned flint implements, date back very far, long before the country was severed from the European mainland in the floods of the last Ice Age. In the Palaeolithic (Old Stone) Age, upland caves provided him with shelter; in the Mesolithic (Middle Stone) Age, antler and bone tools supplemented those in flint. Newcomers to Britain in the Neolithic (New Stone) Age, about 2500 B.C., introduced farming and stock-breeding, and of them, the 'Windmill Hill' group, coming from northern France, built great ditch-surrounded camps of which there are considerable remains in the south, as well as 'long', unchambered barrows. Another group, hailing from Spain and France, passed to the west and to Wales, north and west Scotland and Ireland, making their burials in both long and round barrows, earthen mounds containing the megalithic 'dolmen', 'passage' and 'gallery' graves constructed of upright and lintel great stones (p. 2F). Then, about 1800 B.C., came the bronze-using 'Beaker Folk' from Brittany, who produced the megalithic sacred monuments such as the Avebury and Stonehenge circles and the stone rows and 'menhirs' (p. 3). Next came the 'Food Vessel' people into Wessex (*c.* 1700 B.C.) followed by a blending of all the stocks which after *c.* 1400 B.C. produced the 'Urn' people, whose culture became uniform over the country. Megalithic building and the use of the 'long' variety of barrow ceased about 1500 B.C., but round unchambered barrows of changing types continued sporadically even until late Saxon times. Meanwhile, fresh continental immigrations by people speaking Celtic languages occurred in the later Bronze Age (to *c.* 500 B.C.) and in the Iron Age, passing via southern and eastern England to the remoter parts of the British Isles. Thus by repeated contacts and its own resources British culture became well advanced.

*Roman period (*55 B.C.—A.D. 410). 55 and 54 B.C. Julius Caesar landed in Britain, and his expeditions were introductory to the subsequent Roman occupation.

A.D. 43.   The definitive Roman conquest of Britain began, and progress was made in developing her natural resources such as tin, iron, and lead mines, and the mineral waters of Bath and elsewhere were exploited. Agriculture received an impetus, due to improved methods and to the settled government maintained by the Roman legions, while Roman dress and language were adopted by those in contact with the new rulers. Where the Romans planted their standards, there they erected buildings to maintain their system of civil administration and social life; and in Britain, as in other Roman colonies, their building enterprise has been demonstrated by the excavation of forums, basilicas, baths, temples, and villas, as at Bignor (Sussex), Darenth (Kent), Corstopitum (Northumberland), Fifehead-Neville (Dorset), Silchester (Hants), Chedworth (Gloucester), and Bath (p. 206). There are ruins of a Roman lighthouse at Dover and of fortifications in the city walls of London, York, Lincoln, and Colchester, and the affix 'chester' (Latin, *castra* = camp) signifies a Roman military settlement, as Winchester, Leicester, Gloucester, and Exeter. Roman roads were important not only for military purposes, but also for promoting civilization by opening communications between different parts of the country. The four great roads in England were: (*a*) Watling Street from Dover to London and Wroxeter; (*b*) Ermine Street from London to Lincoln and York; (*c*) Fosse Way from Exeter, via Bath to Lincoln; (*d*) Icknield Street from Wallingford to Caister-by-Norwich.

A.D. 77–83. Agricola, Governor of Britain, built forts from the Clyde to the Forth.

A.D. 122–128. Hadrian built his stone wall, 80 miles long, from the Tyne to the Solway Firth.

A.D. 143. The wall of Antoninus Pius, of turves and clay, 36 miles long, was built across the Forth-Clyde isthmus.

A.D. 198–211. In the time of the Emperor Septimius Severus, after the occurrence of devastating incursions of north British tribes in which the two walls were wrecked, the Antonine wall was abandoned and Hadrian's wall rebuilt, together with the forts both before and behind it. The Emperor spent the last three years of his life in Britain campaigning against the northern raiders, and died at York in A.D. 211.

A.D. 410. After the departure of the Romans, much of their work was destroyed by the invading barbarians, and the chief record of the period is in the writings of Gildas and Nennius.

Anglo-Saxon period (A.D. 449–1066). 449–*c.* 600. The Jutes settled in Kent, and Saxon kingdoms were formed in Sussex, Wessex, Essex and Middlesex, while the Angles established themselves in East Anglia, Mercia and Northumbria. The legends attaching to the name of King Arthur tell us that the Britons offered strenuous resistance to the advance of these heathen invaders, but by the end of the sixth century the latter had subdued the country as far west as the Severn and the Mersey and there were two Anglian kingdoms north of the Humber.

c. 608–800. England became more settled under the 'Heptarchy', of which Wessex, Mercia and Northumbria were the chief kingdoms. The conversion to Christianity of Saxon kings and their people (p. 381) is evidenced by the numerous churches, towers and crosses of this period, many of which remain.

802–39. Egbert, king of the West Saxons, strongly advanced the cause of Wessex against the other English kingdoms and the Britons of Cornwall.

865–71. Danish raids, suffered from the opening of the century, turned to full-scale invasion, and the Danes occupied much of the north-eastern half of England.

871–99. Alfred the Great, king of Wessex, resisted the Danes, and after the Treaty of Wedmore (878) held the southern and south-western parts of the country. He founded schools, encouraged trade, made laws, established a navy and started the 'Anglo-Saxon Chronicle'.

899–924. Edward the Elder, son of Alfred, adopted a militant policy, and utilizing a system of 'burhs' or fortified towns to hold his territory, made himself master of England south of the Humber.

991–1016.   The people were impoverished by the raising of the 'Danegeld' to buy off fresh Danish onslaughts. However, Cnut (Canute), a Dane, became the acknowledged king of England at the latter date.

1042–66.   Edward the Confessor, who was Norman by association and education, consolidated the kingdom, introduced Norman architecture and appointed the Abbot of Jumièges to be Archbishop of Canterbury, and thus Norman influence began before the Conquest.

Norman period (1066–1154).   The Norman Conquest linked England to the Continent and introduced the feudal system, and feudal castles were built to strengthen the position of the Normans. Towns, which grew up round abbeys and castles, became trading centres, and through their merchant guilds laid the foundations of local government; but villages continued to be mere collections of rudimentary huts. Settled government promoted the pursuit of learning which later resulted in organized schools and universities, like that of Oxford in the thirteenth century. French was the language of the Court till the thirteenth century, when, owing to the resentment created by the introduction of strangers by the Angevin kings, English began to supplant it, and the final fusion of the English and Normans took place. The Magna Carta (1215) limited the king's power, and safeguarded the liberties of his subjects.

Plantagenet period (1154–1399).   1154–1216.   The fusion of the native English and Norman settlers was reflected in the architecture.

The framework of government by representatives of nobles, clergy, and commons was evolved, and the King's Council developed, and in 1264 burgesses were summoned to Simon de Montfort's Parliament.

1277–83.   The conquest of Wales led to further development in the planning and design of border castles.

1272–1307.   Edward I, though he continued the struggle to retain his French possessions, was able to consolidate his position at home. Law was codified and administered by the Courts of King's Bench, Common Pleas, Exchequer, and Chancery; while lawyers and schools of law rose in importance.

1326.   To encourage the wool industry, the wearing of foreign cloth was severely restricted, and foreign skilled textile workers, weavers and dyers, were welcomed as settlers in England. Flemish and other immigrants came to the chief centres of the industry, particularly to East Anglia. There was a consequent increase in the prosperity of the country, as seen in the development of manor houses.

The Universities of Oxford and Cambridge were more fully organized under different faculties. Matthew Paris, a monk of S. Albans Abbey, wrote a Latin history of England up to 1259. Froissart (1333–1404), the Frenchman at the English Court, chronicled incidents of the 'Hundred Years' War'; while Chaucer (1344–1400) in his 'Canterbury Tales' supplies by far the most valuable materials possessed by any European country elucidating the manners, customs, and modes of life and thought of people during the Middle Ages. The English Bible translated by Wyclif (1320–84) and his disciples, which was largely circulated as the spiritual authority for the laity, also aided in standardizing the English language.

c. 1350–1400.   During this period the English language came to be used instead of French in parliamentary proceedings and in the law courts.

1349–81.   The rise of the farmer class and of the free labourer after the 'Black Death' (1348–9), which had swept away one-third of the population, resulted in the Peasant's Revolt (1381), and social unrest. The towns continued to increase in importance.

About 1200 armoured warriors began to wear linen surcoats. These bore heraldic devices, as did their shields and horse-trappings. There thus came into being the new science of heraldry, which was to influence ornament in architecture. During the fourteenth century a transition was made from chain mail towards plate armour, and the surcoat gave place to the short, tight-fitting jupon, itself abandoned shortly after 1400, leaving the plate armour fully exposed. Gunpowder appears first to have been used in Britain in 1327 by Edward III against the Scots.

Lancastrian and Yorkist period (1399–1485). Development in national life was continued, and even during the 'Wars of the Roses' (1454–85) Englishmen cultivated the land and lived the free life described in the contemporary 'Paston letters'. The demand for wool in the Netherlands encouraged sheep-farming in England, and the consequent prosperity led to the erection of large parish churches in sheep-rearing counties. Increase in home trade, development of foreign commerce, and the change from villeinage to free labour gave importance to the guilds which controlled craftsmanship. All this industrial activity promoted the building of moot halls, market halls, guildhalls, inns, and bridges, besides houses for successful yeomen and traders. The adoption of printing after its introduction into England by Caxton in 1477 gave new facilities for study and an impetus to the building of schools of the type of Winchester (1382) and Eton (1440), and of colleges in the universities.

Tudor period (1485–1558). The marriage of Henry VII united the Houses of York and Lancaster and gave a great impulse to the development of political institutions. A notable social feature was the decline of the clergy, as the one great Mediaeval profession, and the rise of successful lawyers, medical men, wealthy merchants, and yeomen, who were gradually absorbed into the landed gentry. This was accompanied by the employment of Justices of the Peace who administered the law from their country houses and in Quarter Sessions. This upward movement, which was aided not only by the suppression of the monasteries and the distribution of their wealth amongst the new classes, but also by the spread of education and facilities for foreign travel, produced a national type of domestic architecture for houses of country squires which now display a new standard of comfort. The old nobility declined in importance, and thus the position of the monarchy was strengthened, especially through the Privy Council, which, with its offshoot, the 'Star Chamber', exercised wide judicial authority; while the House of Commons was strengthened by representatives from new boroughs—changes which indicate a movement towards modern methods of life and government. Henry VIII took much interest in building schemes, and introduced foreign artists, such as Da Trevigi, who was appointed Court architect; Torrigiani, the sculptor, and Holbein, the painter and designer in wood and metal.

1515–30. Cardinal Wolsey, who was also Lord Chancellor, built palaces, founded colleges, and patronized art. The writings of Colet and More reflect that breaking away from Mediaeval ideals which coincided with the last yet brilliant phase of English Gothic, known as Tudor architecture.

HISTORICAL. The varying history which influenced English architecture is here traced by salient dates and events which, though they may not be directly connected with architectural changes, help us to keep our touch on the pulse of that living art which is the outcome and expression of national fortunes.

55 B.C. Julius Caesar's first expedition into Britain opened the way for that Roman influence which was to exercise such power in moulding English civil, judicial, literary, and artistic life.

A.D. 43–7. The Emperor Claudius invaded Britain, and the lowland zone was made into a Roman province.

71–83. The Roman governors Cerealis, Frontinus and Agricola completed the conquest of northern England and lowland Scotland.

410.   The Roman troops withdrew from Britain.

449–*c*. 600.   The English (Angles, Saxons, and Jutes) conquered the greater part of Britain amidst much internal strife.

800–900.   The Danish invasions mark a lapse into barbarism, when the country was a prey to constant invasion and ruthless pillage by hordes of heathen Danes, who plundered and destroyed churches and monasteries till repelled by Alfred the Great (871–99), who laid the foundation of English unity.

965–1042.   Further Danish invasions resulted in the election (1016) of Canute the Dane, as King, and his line lasted till 1042.

1042.   The accession of Edward the Confessor, son of the English King Ethelred, paved the way for the introduction of Norman architecture.

1066.   The Norman Conquest not only brought England into contact with Continental civilization, but also inaugurated a great new era for England; for whereas the Romans came and went, the Normans came and stayed, and their ultimate fusion with the old inhabitants produced a hardy, enterprising race which was no longer Anglo-Saxon or Norman, but English, and the same process took place in architectural development.

1154–89.   Henry II of England had married in 1152 Eleanor of Aquitaine, divorced wife of Louis VII of France—a union which led to far-reaching results, because by this marriage Henry became possessed of more than half of France, resulting in rivalry between the two countries which developed during the succeeding centuries, and led to the 'Hundred Years' War' (1337–1453) (p. 533).

1096–1291.   The nine Crusades, which brought about intercourse between East and West, involved England in international movements, especially in the reign of Richard I, 'Coeur de Lion' (1189–99), who spent two years on the third Crusade, two more imprisoned in Germany afterwards and five defending his royal inheritance in France. The Crusades influenced the fortification of castles; gave rise to the use of the pointed arch in Western Mediaeval architecture; and gave an impetus to learning and to the universities, and in the foundation of the militant-religious orders.

1337–1453.   The war with France, known as the 'Hundred Years' War' (p. 533), was signalized by the campaigns of Crecy, Poitiers, Agincourt, and the siege of Orleans, and finally resulted in the loss of the English possessions with the exception of Calais (1453).

1500.   By the beginning of the sixteenth century new social conditions had already rendered the old feudal castle obsolete as an institution in national life, even before the general use of gunpowder, and new military methods made it useless as a defensive fortress. Houses were now built as residences, such as Sutton Place, near Guildford (1523–5), one of the earliest examples of a non-castellated domestic residence (p. 463).

1520.   Henry VIII and his courtiers visited the French King Francis I on the 'Field of the Cloth of Gold', and on their return to England introduced the Renaissance style, recently imported into France from Italy.

ARCHITECTURAL CHARACTER

The character of Romanesque and Gothic architecture in Europe has already been considered (pp. 306, 367). The development of Mediaeval architecture in England from the departure of the Romans till the sixteenth century shows a more complete sequence of styles than in other countries. It is usually divided into periods roughly corresponding with the centuries and having their own special characteristics; these are known as Anglo-Saxon, Norman, Early English, Decorated, Perpendicular, and

ANGLO-SAXON STYLE

STORED

A PLAN AT BELFRY STAGE — 15'.0"

B EARLS BARTON: TOWER WINDOW

C EARLS BARTON: TOWER

D SOMPTING: TOWER ARCH

E SOMPTING: TOWER

F S. BENET: CAMBRIDGE: IMPOST

G S. MARY THE YOUNGER: YORK: TOWER WINDOW

H WINDOW: WORTH CH. SUSSEX — PLAN — 4'.11" GLASS · GLASS

J DEERHURST: GLO'STERSHIRE: TOWER WINDOW

K BOARHUNT CH: HANTS

L WORTH CHURCH: SUSSEX

M BRADFORD-ON-AVON CH: WILTS

N PLAN — 59'.6" 18'.6"

P S. BENET: CAMBR^{GE}: TOWER

Q PLAN — PORCH — 14'.0" 42'.0"

A. Temple Church, London, from S.

B. Temple Church, London: interior looking E.
Rotunda 1185, see p. 390; Choir 1240, see p. 393

Tudor. The table given below of the nomenclature of the periods is based on the classification made by Rickman to coincide with the reigns of English sovereigns, and that of Sharpe, whose periods are determined by evolution of window tracery. These somewhat arbitrary style-names cannot be considered scientific, as they are based partly on historical periods and partly on architectural character; but, as they have held the field for so long in all descriptions of English architecture, they have become, as it were, an integral part of architectural phraseology. They refer approximately to the type of architecture prevalent during the centuries with which they are identified, and can best be understood by study at first hand of buildings belonging to the different periods, and of architectural details in the various museums. The periods subsequent to the departure of the Romans in 410 are classified alternatively as follows:

Dates	Periods	Style names	
449–1066	(5th to 11th century)	Anglo-Saxon	
1066–1189	(part of 11th and 12th cent.)	Norman (Transition, 1154–89)	
1189–1307	(13th century)	Early English ⎫	⎧ Lancet
1307–1377	(14th century)	Decorated ⎬ ⋯	⎨ Geometrical
		⎭	⎩ Curvilinear
1377–1485	(15th century)	Perpendicular ...... Rectilinear	
1485–1558	(first half of 16th century)	Tudor	

Although each period is thus defined, it must be remembered that the transition (the Norman Transition is specially named) from one style to another was slow and gradual and is often difficult to trace. The architectural character of each period is treated separately, and may be read in conjunction with the Comparative Analysis (p. 489) which demonstrates the gradual evolution through the different periods of plans, walls, openings, roofs, columns, mouldings, and ornament.

Pre-Roman period. The few traces that have been found of building in England before the Roman occupation indicate that it was so primitive in character as hardly to allow of its classification as architecture. Evidences of its type may be seen in such as the remarkable stone circles of Avebury and Stonehenge, in the stone rows, and the 'long' and 'round' barrows or the 'dolmen' remains of them in cases where the earthen mounds which once covered them have disappeared (pp. 2F, G, 3).

Roman period (55 B.C.—A.D. 410). The architecture of the Romans in England was of the same character as in other parts of Europe, and a considerable amount still remains, like Hadrian's Wall (A.D. 122–8); also of buildings in towns, such as Silchester, Bath, Chester, Corstopitum (Corbridge), Viriconium (Wroxeter) and Verulamium. Forums, basilicas, baths (p. 206), a theatre (p. 210), amphitheatres, temples, and villas have been uncovered; while in museums throughout England mosaic floors, pottery, and sculptures indicate the care which the Romans bestowed on dwelling-houses and on public buildings in this country. The standardized architecture of the Romans, which is dealt with in the chapter on Roman architecture (p. 174), was of such a virile character that it inevitably influenced the subsequent Anglo-Saxon and Romanesque (Norman) architecture.

Anglo-Saxon period (449–1066). It is difficult to arrive at a conclusive estimate of the architectural character of a period when buildings were sometimes composed either of fragments or of rough copies of Roman architectural details (p. 387). Timber was presumably largely employed in domestic building, but, because of its perishable nature, little evidence remains as to the way in which it was introduced. The great development which took place in the use of that material in later times is another instance of the natural tendency in England to turn to timber for house building, as for shipbuilding. Some even assert that the masonry of the early stone churches, which appear to have been first built about 650, is due to the influence of timber prototypes, as in the 'long and short work' (p. 387C), the triangular-headed openings (p. 387J), the pilaster strips (p. 387C, E, M) and the baluster mullions (p. 387B, G, H, P); but these features may equally well be derived from the Romanesque architecture of Italy. The few vaults of this period that have come down to us were founded on Roman, as the simple cross-vaults of a few church crypts. For Anglo-Saxon vaulting see p. 397. Churches of this period include those at Worth (pp. 387L, 491C), Barnack, Brixworth (c. 680), Earls Barton (c. 1000) (p. 387C), Boarhunt (p. 387K, N), Sompting (p. 387E), Wickham, Deerhurst (early tenth century) (p. 387J), Greensted (c. 1013), and in Dover Castle, while S. Lawrence, Bradford-on-Avon (c. eighth century, remodelled tenth century) (p. 387M, Q), and the church at Escomb, Durham (early eighth century) (p. 491B), are two beautiful examples on a small scale. S. Martin, Canterbury (seventh century), is a rebuilding of the church where King Ethelbert (560–616) was baptized by S. Augustine.

Norman period (1066–1189). The English Romanesque or Norman style comprises the reigns of William I (1066–87), William II (1087–1100), Henry I (1100–1135), Stephen (1135–54), and Henry II (1154–89). Norman architecture is bold and massive, and the distinguishing features are semicircular arches, ponderous cylindrical piers, and flat buttresses, similar to the architecture of Normandy, whence it was first introduced by Edward the Confessor, and it was subsequently established by William the Conqueror.

In Norman vaulting a new system was introduced in which groins or meeting surfaces of cross-vaults were replaced by specially constructed semicircular ribs thrown across the sides and diagonals of vaulting compartments, and these ribs support panels of stone. This novel system gave a new character to Norman architecture and eventually led, by the gradual introduction of additional ribs, to the complicated and characteristic 'rib and panel' vaults of the Gothic period. For Norman vaulting see p. 397.

In London the principal Norman buildings are the Keep and Chapel of the Tower of London (p. 438); the Rotunda of the Temple Church (1185) (p. 388) (Transitional); S. Bartholomew, Smithfield (p. 391A); and the crypts of S. Mary-le-Bow, Cheapside and S. John, Clerkenwell.

In the provinces the principal examples are found in the Cathedrals of Norwich (p. 421), Durham (p. 406), Oxford (p. 421), Gloucester (p. 406), Exeter (p. 406), Ely (p. 406), Hereford (p. 406), Peterborough (pp. 414, 421), Winchester (p. 421), S. Albans (p. 421), and Chichester (p. 406), and in Waltham and Tewkesbury Abbeys, while Barfreston Church, Kent, and Iffley Church, Oxford, are among the smaller churches. There are also circular churches (p. 305) at Cambridge, Northampton, Little Maplestead, and Ludlow (ruined), making with the Temple Church, London (p. 388), a total of five in England. Some manor houses date from this period (p. 447), and very many castles were established in their pristine form (p. 437).

Early English period (1189–1307). The thirteenth-century style, also known as Lancet, comprises the reigns of Richard I (1189–99), John (1199–1216), Henry III (1216–72), and Edward I (1272–1307). This style, less massive than the Norman, depends for effect on pleasing proportions, well-defined outlines, and simplicity in ornament. Tall and narrow lancet openings give height to the design, and exteriors are marked by projecting buttresses, pinnacles, and steep-pitched roofs. Internally, groups of slender shafts, connected to the piers by bands, replace the massive Norman pillars. Lines of dog-tooth ornament in the deeply channelled arch-mouldings, foliated capitals and bosses, and knots of pierced and hanging leaves, almost impart life to the stone framework of door and window openings. The rib and panel vaults of pointed form with transverse and diagonal ribs, which are both

A. S. Bartholomew the Great, Smithfield, London: the choir looking E.
(1123–50; and later additions.) See opposite page

B. S. Helen, Bishopsgate, London: interior looking E. (Nuns' choir 13th cent.
with 15th cent. arcade and later additions.) See p. 393

A. Durham Cathedral from the Wear (1093 onwards). See p. 406

B. Durham Cathedral: nave (1110–33) looking E.

bold and graceful, now generally spanned the wide naves of churches and cathedrals, as at Westminster and Lincoln (p. 417B). For Early English vaulting see p. 397.

In London the principal examples are the eastern portion of the Temple Church (1240), with nave and aisles of equal height, i.e. an English 'hall' church (p. 889A); the eastern arm, transepts, five bays of the nave, chapter house and part of the cloisters of Westminster Abbey (1245–69) (p. 423); the chapel of Lambeth Palace, and the choir, Lady chapel, and nave (restored) of Southwark Cathedral.

In the provinces the principal examples are Salisbury Cathedral (p. 421), York (transepts) (p. 423), Lincoln (nave and chapter house) (pp. 396B, 406), Rochester (choir and transepts) (p. 421), Wells (nave and west front) (p. 421), Lichfield (p. 406), Ely (choir, transepts, and 'Galilee Porch') (1198–1218) (p. 406), Worcester (choir) (p. 423), Bristol (Elder Lady Chapel) (p. 405), besides castles (p. 438), manor houses (p. 447), and other secular buildings, discussed later in the chapter (pp. 463, 473–89).

Decorated period (1307–77). The fourteenth-century style, also known as Geometrical and Curvilinear, comprises the reigns of Edward II (1307–27) and Edward III (1327–77). This style is much more ornate than the Early English and has an elaboration of decoration from which its name is derived. It is made all the more magnificent by the geometrical and flowing tracery, sometimes crowned with the ogee arch, which frames the glowing coloured-glass windows. Clear-storeys were enlarged at the expense of the triforium. Vaulting ribs became so numerous and complex by the addition of intermediate and lierne ribs that the vault with many ribs, often forming star-shaped patterns or stellar vaulting, was a main feature in the decoration of church interiors, as in Ely choir. For Decorated vaulting see p. 398.

In London the principal examples are Westminster Abbey (three bays of the east cloister), the Chapel of S. Etheldreda, Holborn (lately restored) and the Dutch Church, Austin Friars, destroyed in the Second World War.

In the provinces the principal examples are the cathedrals of Lincoln (east end, i.e. 'Angel Choir') (1256–80) (p. 406), Ely (three bays east of octagon) (p. 406), York (nave, west front, and chapter house) (p. 423), Exeter (p. 406) and Lichfield (naves) (p. 406), S. Albans (choir) (p. 421); octagonal chapter houses at Salisbury (p. 405), Wells (p. 405), and Southwell (p. 421); Stone Church, Kent, the Eleanor Crosses (pp. 486B, 509), besides castles (p. 443), manor houses (p. 448), and other secular buildings (pp. 463, 473–89).

Perpendicular period (1377–1485). The fifteenth-century style, also known as Rectilinear, comprises the reigns of Richard II (1377–99), Henry IV (1399–1413), Henry V (1413–22), Henry VI (1422–61), Edward IV (1461–83), Edward V (1483), and Richard III (1483–5). The general appearance is indicated by its name, which is derived from the vertical lines of the window tracery and of the panelling which covered both internal and external walls, and extended even over buttresses. Windows, now often crowned with four-centred arches, were, owing to their immense size, strengthened by horizontal transoms, by primary and secondary mullions (p. 499M), and sometimes by an inner gallery across the window, as at York. The triforium practically disappeared, owing to the greater height of nave arcades and the flatness of aisle roofs, while clear-storey and aisle windows were increased in height. Fan vaults too are characteristic, with their numerous ribs and panels, as in the cloisters of Gloucester Cathedral (1377) (p. 399H) and the complicated 'fan and pendant' vaults, as at Oxford Cathedral. This peculiarly English feature is seen in its loveliest form in the Chapel of Henry VII, Westminster (p. 428), which properly belongs to the Tudor period. For Perpendicular vaulting see p. 398.

In London the principal examples are the south and west cloisters of Westminster Abbey (p. 423); S. Margaret, Westminster; the arcade of S. Helen, Bishopsgate

(p. 391B); porch of S. Sepulchre, Holborn; Savoy Chapel, Strand; Westminster Hall, as remodelled by Henry Yevele and Hugh Herland (pp. 437, 502); Crosby Hall (now at Chelsea), the Guildhall Porch and the Great Hall, Lambeth Palace.

In the provinces the principal examples are the west fronts of Winchester (p. 420A), Gloucester (p. 406), and Beverley; S. George's Chapel, Windsor (pp. 469, 471); Sherborne Abbey; King's College Chapel, Cambridge (pp. 468, 469, 470A); the cathedrals of Canterbury (nave) (p. 405), York (choir) (p. 423), Gloucester (transepts—the earliest example of the Perpendicular style—choir and cloisters) (pp. 382, 406), and Winchester (nave) (pp. 420, 421, 495M); the Beauchamp Chapel, Warwick (pp. 469, 470B); towers at Gloucester (p. 406) and Canterbury (pp. 405, 418A); many colleges at Oxford and Cambridge (pp. 473, 476), besides castles (p. 443), manor houses (p. 451), and other secular buildings (pp. 463, 473–89).

Tudor period (1485–1558). The first half of the sixteenth century comprises the reigns of Henry VII (1485–1509), Henry VIII (1509–47), Edward VI (1547–53) and Mary (1553–8). The character of the style, which, in ecclesiastical architecture, was similar to Perpendicular in general treatment, was modified because it was now called into use for domestic rather than for ecclesiastical buildings. The revived Roman style, which originated in Italy in the fifteenth century, was gradually spreading through France to England, where, grafted on the late Gothic or Perpendicular, it produced a picturesque combination, as the product of craftsmen trained in Gothic traditions, but working under architects imbued with the Renaissance spirit and familiar with Classical details. Notable features in domestic buildings of this period were square-headed mullioned windows, reminiscent of the Perpendicular style; ornamental fireplaces with wide four-centred arch and lavish heraldic carving (p. 461A) sometimes provided with iron fire-backs (p. 461L); gables with lofty carved pinnacles which group up with high moulded chimneys (p. 461F) and carved finials (p. 461D), as seen in manor houses throughout the country. For Tudor vaulting see p. 401.

In London the principal examples are the beautiful Chapel of Henry VII, Westminster (pp. 426, 427), the gateway of S. James's Palace (p. 462B), and Morton's Tower, Lambeth Palace, and portions of some city churches.

In the provinces the principal examples are Compton Wynyates, Warwickshire (pp. 455B, 458, 459), Layer Marney (*c.* 1500–25) (pp. 462A, 463), Sutton Place, Guildford (1523–5) (pp. 457C, 458, 463), parts of Hampton Court Palace (pp. 459, 460A, G), the famous vaulted stairway, Christ Church, Oxford (1640) (p. 400A), besides many country mansions (p. 452) and other secular buildings (pp. 463, 473–89).

Tudor was followed by Elizabethan and Jacobean architecture (p. 868) in which may be traced increased Classical influence, until this early Renaissance architecture developed into the Stuart period of the late Renaissance. The process, however, was slow, and native Gothic survived in outlying districts till the end of the sixteenth century and even later, as in the extraordinary church of S. Mary, Warwick, rebuilt as a 'hall' church (1694–1704) (p. 482A), with a remarkable tower, in the Perpendicular style with Renaissance features, and the famous Beauchamp Chapel (1443–64) (p. 470B).

THE EVOLUTION OF ENGLISH GOTHIC VAULTING

The various problems which, by their solution, determined the evolution of Mediaeval vaulting exercised such an important influence on the general character of the architecture that it is desirable to give a consecutive description of vaulting evolution through the successive centuries in order to secure an uninterrupted view of such an integral part of Mediaeval architectural design. In the chapters on Romanesque and Gothic architecture in Europe (pp. 303, 365) we have dealt

A. Salisbury Cathedral (1220–65): aerial view from S.E. See p. 421

B. Salisbury Cathedral: the choir

A. Salisbury Cathedral: chapter house (1263–84). See pp. 405, 421

B. Lincoln Cathedral: chapter house (12: See p. 406

C. S. Mary the Virgin, Oxford, from S.W. (14th and 15th cents.; Porch 1637). See p. 490

D. Canterbury Cathedral Norman tower (c. 1100–1125). See p. 490

generally with the various aspects of these problems, and we here follow the evolution as it took place in England. The problem for the Mediaeval architect was to construct a stone vault over the lofty nave of a church of the basilican type, while leaving clear-story windows in the nave walls above the aisle roofs. While Roman vaulting consisted in the design either of semicircular vaults or of semicircular cross-vaults, of which the meeting lines or intersections are known as groins, Mediaeval vaulting was of quite a different type; for the simple groins were now replaced by specially constructed ribs on which the thin vaulting panels were placed. This was an economical form of building; for it dispensed with the large amount of 'centering' required for the temporary support of the heavy Roman vaults, as each rib, when constructed, itself became the support of the vault panel. The weight of the stone vault, high above the ground, exerted considerable thrust and so involved the solution of structural problems and resulted in the employment of responsive features, such as buttresses and pinnacles, to counteract the thrust of this nave vault, while the numerous ribs meeting on the pier capitals had to be supported, and so required novel types of piers, thus determining, in a remarkable degree, the character of English Mediaeval architecture.

Anglo-Saxon Vaulting. The vaulting that was carried out during this period was based on Roman, like that in the porch at Monkwearmouth, which is perhaps the only Saxon vault remaining above ground in England; while the vaulting in the Chapel of the Pyx, Westminster Abbey, though dating from the time of Edward the Confessor, is of Norman character.

Norman Vaulting (p. 399A, B). The Roman system of stone vaulting was in vogue till the introduction of transverse and diagonal ribs. Norman vaulting, originally similar to Roman, was either (*a*) cylindrical or barrel vaulting, as in S. John's Chapel, Tower of London (p. 436C); (*b*) groined cross-vaulting in square bays, as in the aisle of S. John's Chapel, Tower of London, and the crypt of Canterbury Cathedral (1096–1107) (p. 399A), and it is interesting to note that the earliest cross-vaults are found over low crypts of churches where they were easier to construct, and had only to support the floor of the church; (*c*) oblong bays in which the vaulting ribs or arches across the shorter span were either stilted (p. 370C, G) or in the later period slightly pointed; or (*d*) sexpartite (six-part) vaulting (p. 370E), as in the choir at Canterbury Cathedral (p. 418B), which has the same type of vaulting as at the Abbaye-aux-Hommes, Caen (p. 342F). In England the system, so frequent on the Continent, of raising the diagonal rib to produce the domical vault seems to have been little used, and the method was either to make diagonal ribs segmental, as in the aisles at Peterborough Cathedral (p. 399B), or to make the diagonal ribs semicircular and stilt or raise the springing of the transverse and longitudinal ribs. A great advance was made by the pointed arch, which was first used for the transverse and wall ribs only, the diagonal ribs (i.e. those with the longest span) remaining semicircular. The vault over the nave of Durham Cathedral (1128–33) has pointed transverse ribs which are believed to be the earliest examples of a pointed arch to a high vault in England (p. 392B).

Early English Vaulting (p. 399C, D). The pointed arch came into general use in the thirteenth century, and, without the aid of stilting or other contrivances, surmounted the difficulties created by the intersection of semicircular vaults of different spans (p. 370). The plain four-part (quadripartite) ribbed vault, primarily constructed as a skeleton framework of diagonal and transverse ribs, was chiefly used in this period, as in the naves of Durham, Salisbury (p. 415H) and Gloucester, and the aisles of Peterborough. Intermediate uprising ribs, known as 'tiercerons', were inserted later between the transverse and diagonal ribs to give additional support to the panels, as in the nave of Westminster Abbey (p. 399D). Ridge ribs were then introduced to resist the thrust of the opposing 'tiercerons' and keep them in position. In Continental examples the ridge rib is often not continuous and is only used for those ribs which abut obliquely at the summit. Ridge ribs are generally horizontal in England, but on the Continent are arched between the bosses. The courses of the vault panels meet at the ridge in zigzag lines, as in the nave of Westminster Abbey (p. 373F), Lincoln, Exeter, and Lichfield Cathedrals, as well as in the churches of south-west France. Wall ribs or 'formerets' enclosing the lateral wall space of the vaulting compartment came into use during this period. The 'ploughshare twist', which sometimes occurs in the panels between diagonal and wall ribs, as in Westminster Abbey and Southwark Cathedral (p. 373C), is produced by raising the springing of the wall rib above that of the diagonal rib in order to increase the size of clear-story windows, whose shape was thus influenced by the vault.

Decorated Vaulting (p. 399E, F). A general elaboration of vaulting is characteristic of this period, and is due not only to the greater use of intermediate and ridge ribs, as in the nave vault of Exeter Cathedral, but also to the addition of 'lierne' ribs (French, *lien* = tie or bond)—a term applied to any rib other than a ridge rib which does not start from the springing of the vaulting compartment. Previously each rib marked a change in the direction of the vaulting surface, but 'lierne' ribs merely follow the curved surface of the panel and, by their number and disposition, often give an intricate appearance to an otherwise simple vault (p. 399F). The star-shaped pattern thus produced is called 'stellar' vaulting (p. 399G) and there are examples in Gloucester (1337-77), Canterbury (1379-1400), Wells, Ely (choir) (p. 495K), Bristol and Winchester Cathedrals (p. 420H), and Tewkesbury Abbey. Vaulting during this period comprised transverse, diagonal, tierceron, ridge, and lierne ribs, and this increased number of ribs so decreased the size of the panels they supported that the space from rib to rib was frequently spanned by a single stone. Carved bosses (French, *bosse* = lump or knob) or keystones, which had already come into use in the thirteenth century, had their origin in a constructive use as keystones against which the ribs abutted and also in the need for disguising the awkward mitres made by the meeting of moulded ribs. In the fourteenth century the increase in the number of ribs led to a corresponding increase in the number of bosses which, as part of the general scheme, gave to these Gothic vaults an extremely ornamental and web-like appearance.

Perpendicular Vaulting (p. 399G, H). The intricate 'stellar' vaulting of the late fourteenth and early fifteenth centuries led, by experimental stages, to the type known as fan, palm, or conoidal vaulting, first used in the cloisters at Gloucester (1351-77) (p. 399H), in which the rising ribs are formed at equal angles on inverted concave cones and are thus of the same curve, and these are connected at different heights by horizontal lierne ribs. The development was somewhat as follows: In the thirteenth century the vault followed the outline of inverted, four-sided concave pyramids; in the fourteenth century the introduction of more ribs resulted in polygonal pyramids with ribs of different curves, while in the fifteenth century the design was simplified by the introduction of 'fan' vaulting in which all ribs are of similar curve (p. 399H). The reduction of the size of panels, consequent on the increase in the number of ribs, brought about a return to the Roman method of construction; for in fan vaulting the ribs and panels were often formed in the same piece of stone instead of the panels resting as separate stones on the ribs, and thus the ribs lost their structural use. This method seems to have been first adopted in vaults where ribs were most numerous, and in Tudor times both systems are found, as at King's College Chapel, Cambridge (1512-15) (p. 468); while in others, as in Henry the Seventh's Chapel, Westminster, the whole vault has ribs and panels

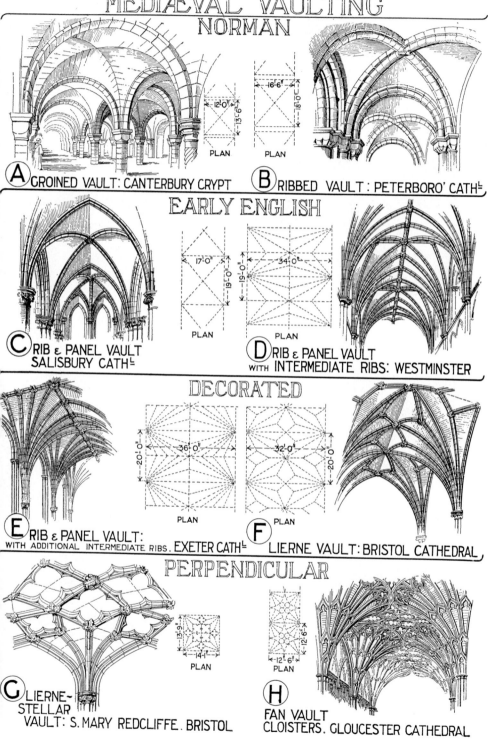

MEDIÆVAL VAULTING
NORMAN

A GROINED VAULT: CANTERBURY CRYPT

B RIBBED VAULT: PETERBORO' CATH^L

EARLY ENGLISH

C RIB & PANEL VAULT SALISBURY CATH^L

D RIB & PANEL VAULT WITH INTERMEDIATE RIBS: WESTMINSTER

DECORATED

E RIB & PANEL VAULT: WITH ADDITIONAL INTERMEDIATE RIBS. EXETER CATH^L

F LIERNE VAULT: BRISTOL CATHEDRAL

PERPENDICULAR

G LIERNE-STELLAR VAULT: S. MARY REDCLIFFE. BRISTOL

H FAN VAULT CLOISTERS. GLOUCESTER CATHEDRAL

A. Christ Church, Oxford: vaulted staircase (1640). See opposite page

B. Oxford Cathedral (Christ Church): interior looking E. (1158–80) (choir vault c. 1480–1500). See opposite page

C. Divinity School, Oxford: interior (1430–55; vault 1480–3). See opposite page

formed out of the same piece of stone. The problem of supporting the flat, lozenge-shaped space in the crown of the vault was comparatively easy in cloisters, where the vaulting compartments were approximately square, but difficulties arose in adapting fan vaulting to the bays of naves which generally measured twice as much transversely as longitudinally. In King's College Chapel the conoids are incomplete for the sides had to be cut off, forming awkward transverse junctions (p. 468). Henry the Seventh's Chapel (1503–19) has hidden transverse arches which penetrate above the vaulting and, at a distance from the walls, support pendants or elongated voussoirs, from which spring the conoids, thus reducing the central vaulting space from an oblong to a square (p. 426). At Oxford Cathedral, by a similar method, the pendants, supported by an upper arch, are placed at some distance from the walls, and from them spring the rib and panel vault (1480–1500) (p. 400B). Fan vaulting is confined to England, as at Sherborne Abbey (1475); the Divinity School, Oxford (1480–3) (p. 400C); Trinity Church, Ely; Gloucester Cathedral (p. 399H); S. George's Chapel, Windsor (1501–8) (p. 471H), and the retro-choir, Peterborough, and the tradition was maintained in the vault over the staircase at Christ Church, Oxford (1640) (p. 400A). Pendant vaulting without fan treatment is frequent in the Flamboyant period in France, as at Caudebec, Normandy (p. 564D).

Tudor Vaulting. The Tudor or four-centred arch (p. 1256, No. 17), so typical of the period, seems to have had its origin in the difficulty of making the various ribs in the oblong vaulting compartments of naves reach the same height. In an oblong Mediaeval vaulting compartment which had a lancet-shaped window in the nave wall, the diagonal ribs are either semicircular or pointed, i.e. struck from two centres in which each side of the arch must be less than the quadrant of a circle; and because the transverse and wall ribs are shorter than the diagonal ribs, they are still smaller segments of a circle. In oblong vaulting compartments of late Gothic vaults, which often had windows in the nave wall crowned with pointed arches of equilateral or, in early Tudor times, even of the 'drop' arch form (p. 1256, No. 13), the diagonal and transverse ribs had to be struck from four centres in order to accommodate their height to that of the window arch. These of necessity were low four-centred arches which started with the same curve as the window arch, but after a certain height the remainder of each rib was struck from another centre in order to bring the apex of all ribs to the same height as that of the window arch. The four-centred arches which were used in late Gothic vaults and conspicuously in fan vaulting were afterwards introduced over doors (p. 460A), windows (p. 445K, M), fireplaces (p. 445G, J), and wall tombs, as well as in traceried panels, possibly with a desire to harmonize with the vaulted superstructure.

The special forms of vault used in chapter houses are referred to later (p. 405).

EXAMPLES

The different types of buildings erected during the Middle Ages have been given in the chapter on Gothic architecture in Europe (pp. 365–78). In England all classes of buildings, whether ecclesiastical, such as cathedrals, churches, and monasteries, or secular, as castles, houses, and market-crosses, are generally classified according to their period, as Anglo-Saxon, Norman, Early English, Decorated, Perpendicular, or Tudor, of which the approximate dates have been given (p. 389).

CATHEDRALS

The important place which the Mediaeval cathedral occupied in national life has already been indicated (p. 372). English cathedrals, with the single exception of

Salisbury, were constantly in process of construction and alteration, and this characteristic invests them with a special fascination, both architectural and historical, for by combining successive stages in architectural style in a single building they one and all reflect national history and development during successive centuries and also form in themselves a complete record of the evolution of Gothic architecture. The special constitution and foundation of many English cathedrals made them monastic in character and were largely responsible for their general arrangement (pp. 410, 411, 412, 413), from which we can judge of their original purpose.

The cathedrals may be divided into (a) cathedrals of the old foundation, (b) cathedrals of the monastic foundation, and (c) cathedrals of the new foundation.

(a) The thirteen cathedrals of the old foundation which were served by secular clergy were not affected by the reforms of Henry VIII. They are the cathedrals of York, Lichfield, Wells, Exeter, Salisbury, Chichester, Lincoln, Hereford, London, and the Welsh Cathedrals of Llandaff, Bangor, S. David's, and S. Asaph.

(b) The thirteen cathedrals of the monastic foundation were originally served by regular clergy or monks, and were reconstituted at the Dissolution of the Monasteries as chapters of secular canons. They are the cathedrals of Canterbury, Durham, Rochester, Winchester, Worcester, Norwich, Ely, Carlisle, Peterborough, Gloucester, Chester, Oxford, and Bristol. The last five only became cathedrals at the Dissolution. Westminster Abbey was a cathedral church only from 1540 to 1545. When the change in these monastic establishments was made, the abbot became the bishop, the prior the dean, and the monks became canons and choristers, while the personnel generally remained the same.

(c) The cathedrals of the new foundation are those to which bishops have been more recently appointed, viz. Ripon and Southwell, which are old collegiate churches, as well as the parochial churches of Newcastle, Wakefield, Manchester, Birmingham, Truro, Chelmsford and Southwark, the abbey church of S. Albans, Bury S. Edmunds, Coventry, Liverpool, Guildford and others.

Before describing individual examples of cathedral churches it will be helpful to take a general survey of the features they have in common in this country and in which they offer a striking contrast to Continental and especially French cathedrals. Monastic cathedrals are indeed almost peculiar to England and Germany, where a large proportion of the present cathedral churches once formed part of monastic establishments with cloisters, refectories, dormitories, chapter houses, scriptorium, library, guest hall, infirmary, prison, wine cellar, mills, workshops, and gardens (cf. Monastery of S. Gall, p. 358). The cloisters round which the various buildings were grouped formed a covered way for the use of monks, but were also planned, as at Salisbury and Wells, as ornamental adjuncts to cathedrals which were not part of monastic establishments. The collegiate churches of Lichfield, Ripon, Southwell, York, and Manchester, and the Irish, Scottish, and Welsh cathedrals (S. David's excepted), have no cloisters. Much of this difference in treatment is occasioned by difference in purpose. In England these churches often served a two-fold purpose and provided services for monks at one end and for laymen at the other; while in France the cathedrals were largely built and paid for by laymen themselves and were designed for their use. In England, owing to this conventual origin, the choir or eastern arm had to be large enough to accommodate the monks, and it was often nearly as long as the nave or western arm.

English cathedrals, which often formed part of a monastic group with cloisters (p. 415J), refectory, and other buildings, are now set in a quiet 'close' and not among the houses of the town, as is so usual in France (p. 534). They are long and

A. Peterborough Cathedral: west façade (*c.* 1193–1230). See p. 421

B. Wells Cathedral: west façade (*c.* 1206–42). See p. 421

A. Worcester Cathedral from S.W. See p. 423

Worcester Cathedral: the choir (1224–60)
looking W. See p. 423

c. Gloucester Cathedral: Choir
looking W. See p. 406

narrow as compared with French; for whereas in France the length is seldom more than four times the width, due largely to the double aisles and side chapels, in England it is often as much as six times the width. This extreme length of vista, further emphasized by the comparatively low nave vault, gives English cathedrals much of their stately solemnity. There are fewer side chapels in England than in France, and this indicates the more general character of the services held for the laity. Many English cathedrals, such as Norwich and Canterbury, which were founded or remodelled after the Conquest by Norman prelates, had an apsidal east end which was sometimes developed into a chevet, but the English type reverted, as in Durham and Lincoln, to the square eastern termination of the Saxon proto-type (p. 491A, B). The transepts project considerably and secondary transepts occur, as at Salisbury, Canterbury, Lincoln, Wells, and Worcester, but in France the transepts are single and have little projection. The entrance was generally by a projecting south-western porch which acted as a screen against the wind, and is in contrast to the large recessed western portals which open directly into the nave in French cathedrals. The high central tower, as at Lincoln, York, Ely, Gloucester, Canterbury, and Durham, is effective by contrast with the low nave; its height is sometimes further increased by a tapering spire, as at Salisbury and Norwich. Occasionally there are two western towers, while at Lichfield all three towers are crowned with spires (p. 419B). Flying buttresses are not nearly so common as in France, owing to the comparative lowness of the nave vault. In France the flying buttresses to the chevet produce a complex, restless effect (p. 532C) which is absent from the simple square east ends of English churches. A description of English cathedrals would be incomplete without a reference to the sculptured west fronts of Wells (p. 403B) and Exeter, and to those internal fittings such as rood lofts, choir screens, carved stalls, misericords, bishops' thrones, sculptured reredoses, fonts, tombs, sedilia, pulpits, lecterns, brasses, triptychs, wall tablets, alms boxes, credences, oak chests, and other fittings which with the tiled floor not only give a rich and furnished appearance to the interiors of cathedrals and churches, but are also of importance as historical records (pp. 512, 515–19).

Chapter houses for the transaction of ecclesiastical business were originally rectangular in plan, as at Canterbury (p. 411B) and Bristol (1142–70) (p. 413K), but that at Durham (1133–40) (p. 411E) was apsidal, and that at Worcester (1084–1400) (p. 411A) is circular. The normal type is octagonal with a centre pillar to support the vaulting, as Westminster (1250) (pp. 422C, 424D), Salisbury (1263–84) (pp. 396A, 410E, 415G), and Wells (c. 1319) (pp. 377J, 412J), but Lincoln (1235) (pp. 396B, 410F, 416A) is decagonal. York chapter house (1280–1330) (p. 410B) is octagonal, 57 ft in diameter, with no central pillar, as the vault is of wood instead of stone.

The **comparative plans** (pp. 410–13) will clearly indicate the work of successive periods in each building, and the views of models (pp. 407–9) show the special features of a number of cathedrals.

In the short notices which follow, Early English, Decorated, and Perpendicular are abbreviated respectively as E.E., Dec., and Perp., and an asterisk * denotes those which were churches of Benedictine monasteries (p. 304).

1. **Bangor** (p. 412D). Repeatedly destroyed. Present church, which suffered much in the civil wars, is Dec. and Perp. Thoroughly restored by Sir George Gilbert Scott (1866).

2. **Bristol** (pp. 409A, 413K). Augustinian monastery. Rectangular Norman chapter house. E.E. 'Elder Lady Chapel'. Dec. choir (1306–32); modern nave by Street to match choir. Peculiar in having nave and aisles of nearly equal height, with lofty aisle windows, as in German 'hall' churches, without triforium and clear-story (p. 590D). Remarkable canopied wall recesses.

3. ***Canterbury** (pp. 408G, 411B, 418). First Norman church 1071–7. Choir replaced

and enlarged 1096–1126; choir rebuilt on the remains after fire and extended eastwards 1174–85 by master-mason William of Sens and his successor. Original Norman work of singular interest (p. 396D). Contraction in width of choir, to preserve two earlier Norman chapels. At extreme east is 'Becket's Crown' and Patriarchal Chair (p. 519C). Extensive crypts of 1100–25 under eastern portion. Double transepts. Splendid late Perp. central tower (1490–1503). Perp. nave begun 1379 by Henry Yevele. West front and towers unimportant. A treasure house of thirteenth-century glass. Oblong chapter house (1400) with fine wooden ceiling. Perp. cloisters on north of great beauty. Numerous side chapels.

4. **Carlisle** (pp. 409C, 413B). Augustinian abbey. Only two bays of Norman nave remain. East end of beautiful design with fine tracery windows.

5. **Chester** (pp. 409E, 413F). Originally the convent of S. Werburgh, became Benedictine abbey 1093. Built of red sandstone. Dec. nave: northern arcade has triforium and clearstory combined. Perp. central tower. Cloisters on north. Lady chapel at east end.

6. **Chichester** (pp. 407F, 412G). Chief example of double aisles, resulting from former lateral chapels. Fine central spire. Norman nave. Transitional retro-choir. Bell-tower (fifteenth century) is the only detached example to an English cathedral.

7. *****Durham** (pp. 392, 408C, 411E). Norman work (1093–1133). Massive E.E. eastern transept called the 'Chapel of the Nine Altars' (1242–80) and central Perp. tower (1465–90). A group of great dignity which has few rivals. Norman nave (1110–33) is finest in England with pillars about the same width as openings and quaintly channelled with chevrons, diapers and flutes. Norman north transept vault (c. 1110) said to be earliest surviving high vault in England, and Norman nave vaults (1128–33) first to incorporate pointed ribs.

8. *****Ely** (pp. 408A, 410A, 494E, F, 495J, K). Norman nave and transepts with timber roof (modern painting). Choir remarkable for carving. Unique central octagon (1322–40) 70 ft in diameter with unequal sides, by John Attegrene, master-mason, has rich wooden vault with octagonal lantern by William Hurley, master-carpenter. This plan influenced that of S. Paul, London (p. 906). Exceptional Lady chapel, 100 ft by 46 ft (1321–49) (cf. chapter house, Canterbury). Imposing west front (180 ft wide) with high tower, the same width as nave, flanked originally both north and south by transepts with octagonal turrets. In front of the tower projects the E.E. vaulted Galilee porch (1198–1215).

9. **Exeter** (pp. 407D, 412E). Unique twin towers over north and south transepts. The finest specimen of the Dec. style and rich in varied tracery and carved stonework. Unusual Perp. sculptured screen to W. façade.

10. *****Gloucester** (pp. 404C, 408D, 411C). Early Perp. south transept (1329–37) (pp. 382, 394) Norman choir cased with Perp. (cf. Winchester). Perp. fan-vaulted cloisters of singular completeness (pp. 399H, 401). Choir has largest Perp. windows in England. Elaborate Lady chapel. Central tower (225 ft high) with internal flying buttress.

11. **Hereford** (pp. 409F, 413H). Norman nave and choir. E.E. Lady chapel and Dec. central tower. Famous 'Mappa Mundi' in south choir aisle.

12. **Lichfield** (pp. 407E, 413J, 419, 495G, H). Built of reddish stone on sloping ground. Nave, transepts, chapter house, and west front in E.E. style. Graceful central and western spires in Dec. style form the only triple group of spires in England. Bow-sided triangular clear-story windows. No cloisters.

13. **Lincoln** (pp. 396B, 408H, 410F, 416, 417). Stands on steep hill dominating town. Some Norman work of 1073 and later at west end. Rebuilt 1192–1320. Choir and lesser transepts 1192–1200, the earliest example of E.E. work of known date. E.E. main transepts, nave, central tower, Galilee porch and chapter house (1209–53). Dec. 'Angel Choir' (retro-choir) also of remarkably advanced design for its date (1256–80). Central tower heightened (1307–11, from the designs of Richard of Stow), the highest (271 ft) in England. Cloisters on the north (1296). E.E. decagonal chapter house, vaulted to central pillar and surmounted by flying buttresses. Unusual west front consists of screen wall behind which rise two western towers.

14. **Llandaff** (p. 413C). Begun 1120. A long low building situated at foot of hill, without transepts or side chapels. E.E. west front. Two western towers. Nave much restored. Square chapter house with central pillar. No triforium or cloisters.

15. **Manchester** (p. 412B). Perp. (1422–1520). Remarkable for double aisles obtained, as at Chichester, by inclusion of side chapels. Fine stalls.

16. **Newcastle.** Late Dec. in style. Perp. tower (1474) with spire on crown of arches,

A. Wells

B. Ripon

C. Worcester

D. Exeter

E. Lichfield

F. Chichester

G. Salisbury

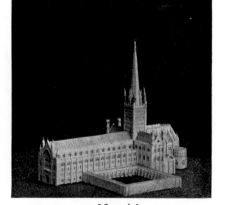

H. Norwich

Comparative models of English Cathedrals. See pp. 401 ff.

A. Ely

B. York

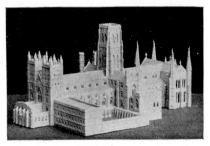

C. Durham

D. Gloucester

E. Winchester

F. Peterborough

G. Canterbury

H. Lincoln

Comparative models of English Cathedrals. See pp. 401 ff.

A. Bristol
(before addition of modern nave)

B. Oxford

C. Carlisle

D. Rochester
(before restoration of spire to
central tower)

E. Chester

F. Hereford

Comparative models of English Cathedrals. See pp. 401 ff.

COMPARATIVE PLANS OF ENGLISH CATHEDRALS

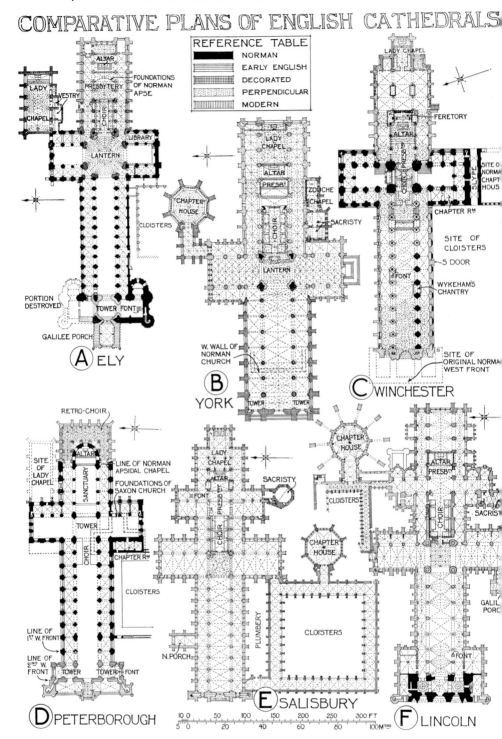

REFERENCE TABLE

■■■	NORMAN
≡≡≡	EARLY ENGLISH
▦▦▦	DECORATED
▨▨▨	PERPENDICULAR
▥▥▥	MODERN

(A) ELY

(B) YORK

(C) WINCHESTER

(D) PETERBOROUGH

(E) SALISBURY

(F) LINCOLN

COMPARATIVE PLANS OF ENGLISH CATHEDRALS

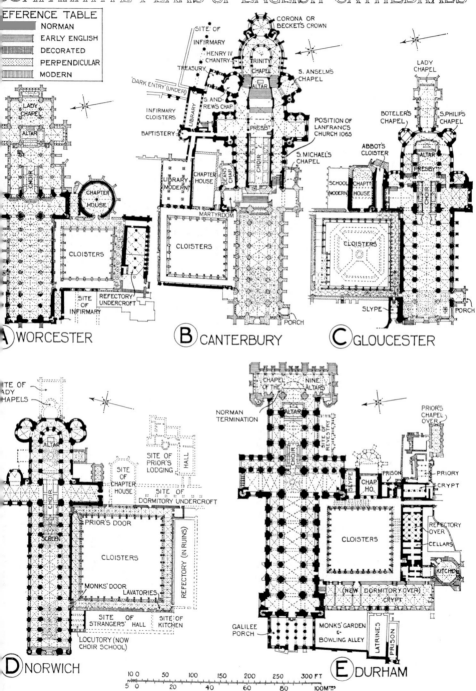

REFERENCE TABLE
- NORMAN
- EARLY ENGLISH
- DECORATED
- PERPENDICULAR
- MODERN

A WORCESTER

LADY CHAPEL
ALTAR
CHOIR
CHAPTER HOUSE
CLOISTERS
SITE OF INFIRMARY
REFECTORY UNDERCROFT

B CANTERBURY

SITE OF INFIRMARY
HENRY IV CHANTRY
TREASURY
DARK ENTRY (UNDER)
INFIRMARY CLOISTERS
BAPTISTERY
LIBRARY
S. ANDREW'S CHAP
LIBRARY (MODERN)
CHAPTER HOUSE
CHAP
MARTYRDOM
CLOISTERS
CORONA OR BECKET'S CROWN
TRINITY CHAPEL
ALTAR
S. ANSELM'S CHAPEL
PRESBY
POSITION OF LANFRANC'S CHURCH 1065
S. MICHAEL'S CHAPEL
CHOIR
PORCH

C GLOUCESTER

LADY CHAPEL
BOTELER'S CHAPEL
S. PHILIP'S CHAPEL
ABBOT'S CLOISTER
ALTAR
PRESBY
CHOIR
SCHOOL MODERN
CHAPTER HOUSE
CLOISTERS
SLYPE
PORCH

D NORWICH

SITE OF LADY CHAPELS
ALTAR
CHOIR
SCREEN
SITE OF CHAPTER HOUSE
SITE OF PRIOR'S LODGING
HALL
SITE OF DORMITORY UNDERCROFT
PRIOR'S DOOR
CLOISTERS
MONKS' DOOR
LAVATORIES
REFECTORY (IN RUINS)
SITE OF STRANGERS' HALL
SITE OF KITCHEN
LOCUTORY (NOW CHOIR SCHOOL)

E DURHAM

CHAPEL OF THE NINE ALTARS
NORMAN TERMINATION
ALTAR
CHOIR
REVESTRY
PRIOR'S CHAPEL OVER
SLYPE
CHAP HO.
PRISON
CHAP.
PRIORY CRYPT
CLOISTERS
REFECTORY OVER
CELLARS
KITCHEN
(NEW DORMITORY OVER)
CRYPT
GALILEE PORCH
MONKS' GARDEN & BOWLING ALLEY
LATRINES
PRISON

10 0   50   100   150   200   250   300 FT
5 0   20   40   60   80   100 M

COMPARATIVE PLANS OF ENGLISH CATHEDRAL

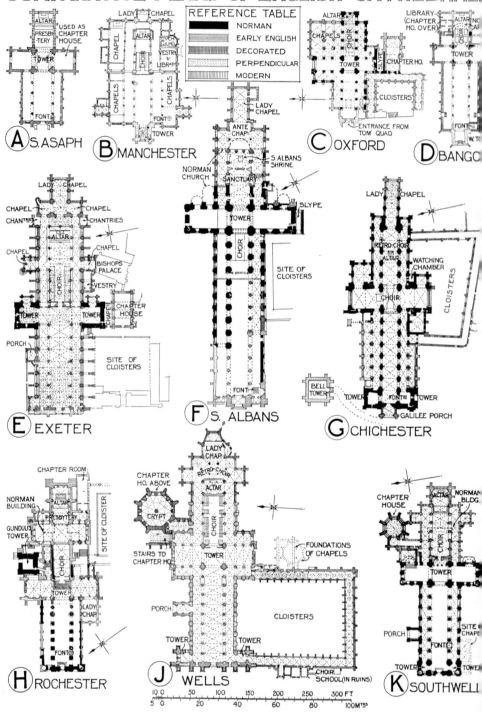

REFERENCE TABLE

▮	NORMAN
▨	EARLY ENGLISH
▨	DECORATED
▨	PERPENDICULAR
▨	MODERN

A. S. ASAPH

B. MANCHESTER

C. OXFORD

D. BANGOR

E. EXETER

F. S. ALBANS

G. CHICHESTER

H. ROCHESTER

J. WELLS

K. SOUTHWELL

OMPARATIVE PLANS OF ENGLISH CATHEDRALS

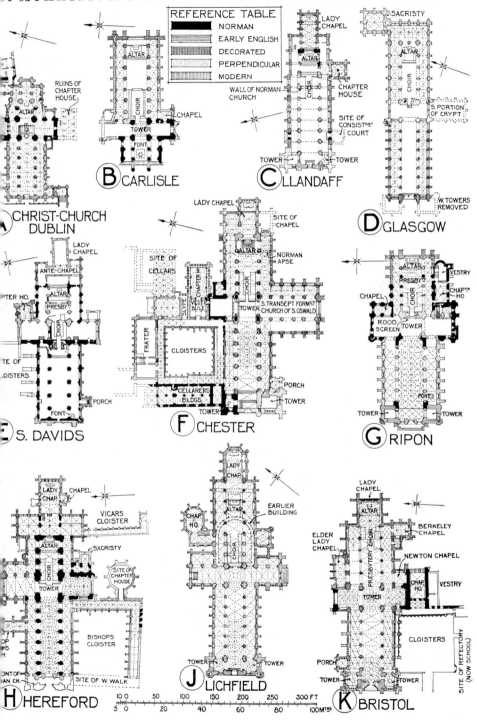

REFERENCE TABLE
- NORMAN
- EARLY ENGLISH
- DECORATED
- PERPENDICULAR
- MODERN

A. CHRIST-CHURCH DUBLIN

B. CARLISLE

C. LLANDAFF

D. GLASGOW

E. S. DAVIDS

F. CHESTER

G. RIPON

H. HEREFORD

J. LICHFIELD

K. BRISTOL

PETERBOROUGH CATHEDRAL

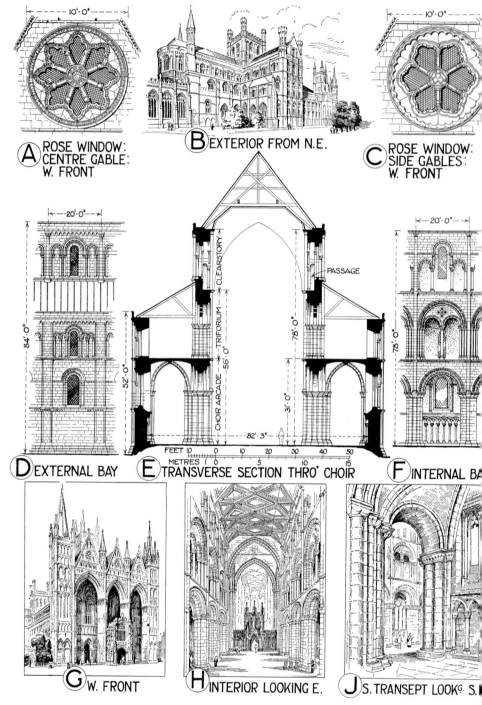

(A) ROSE WINDOW: CENTRE GABLE: W. FRONT

(B) EXTERIOR FROM N.E.

(C) ROSE WINDOW: SIDE GABLES: W. FRONT

10'.0"

10'.0"

20'.0"

84'.0"

52'.0"

CLEARSTORY

TRIFORIUM

56'.0"

CHOIR ARCADE

PASSAGE

78'.0"

31'.0"

82'.3"

20'.0"

78'.0"

FEET 10   0   10   20   30   40   50

METRES 1   0   5   10   15

(D) EXTERNAL BAY

(E) TRANSVERSE SECTION THRO' CHOIR

(F) INTERNAL BA[Y]

(G) W. FRONT

(H) INTERIOR LOOKING E.

(J) S. TRANSEPT LOOK^G. S.

SALISBURY CATHEDRAL

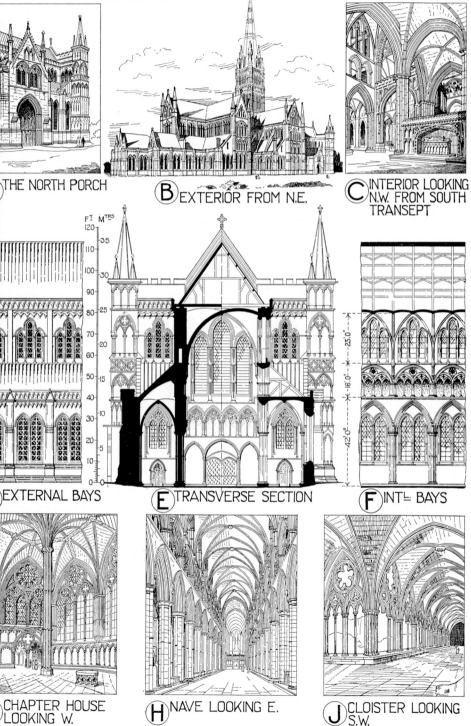

A THE NORTH PORCH

B EXTERIOR FROM N.E.

C INTERIOR LOOKING N.W. FROM SOUTH TRANSEPT

D EXTERNAL BAYS

E TRANSVERSE SECTION

F INTL BAYS

G CHAPTER HOUSE LOOKING W.

H NAVE LOOKING E.

J CLOISTER LOOKING S.W.

LINCOLN CATHEDRAL

87' 6"

Ⓑ NAVE BAY (EXT.)

Ⓐ EXTERIOR FROM S.E

Ⓒ NAVE BAY (INT)

FEET
80
70
60
50
40
30
20
10

Ⓓ SPANDREL : ANGEL CHOIR

PRESBYTERY
(ANGEL CHOIR)   CHOIR   Ⓔ LONGITUDINAL SECTION   NAVE

Ⓕ NAVE FROM S. TRANSEPT

Ⓖ ANGEL CHOIR LOOKING N.E

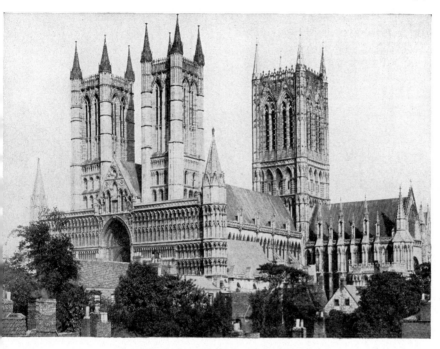

A. Lincoln Cathedral from S.W. See p. 406

B. Lincoln Cathedral: choir (1192–1200) looking W.

A. Canterbury Cathedral from S.W. See p. 405

B. Canterbury Cathedral: choir (1174–85) looking E.

LICHFIELD CATHEDRAL

LADY CHAPEL   B EXTERIOR FROM S.E.   C VESTIBULE LADY CHAPEL

BRACKETS: LADY CHAPEL   BRACKETS: LADY CHAPEL

EXT^L BAY   F TRANSVERSE SECTION THRO' NAVE   G INT^L BAY

AISLE   NAVE   AISLE

NAVE ARCADE — TRIFORIUM — CLEARSTORY

DOORWAY: CHAPTER H^{O.}   J INT^R: NAVE LOOKING E.   K WEST DOORWAY

WINCHESTER CATHEDRAL

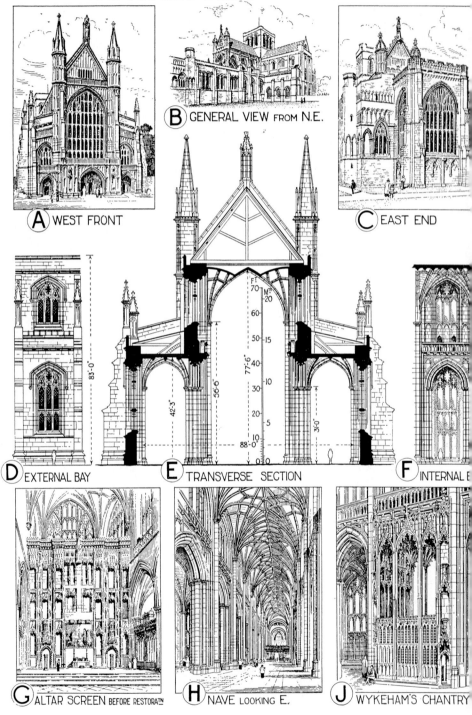

(A) WEST FRONT

(B) GENERAL VIEW FROM N.E.

(C) EAST END

(D) EXTERNAL BAY

(E) TRANSVERSE SECTION

(F) INTERNAL B

(G) ALTAR SCREEN BEFORE RESTORAT.N

(H) NAVE LOOKING E.

(J) WYKEHAM'S CHANTRY

similar to S. Giles, Edinburgh (p. 522), King's College, Aberdeen, and S. Dunstan in the East, London. No triforium in nave or choir. Fine modern stalls.

17. *Norwich (pp. 407H, 411D). Long narrow Norman nave (1096–1145), aisleless transepts, and choir with apsidal chapels. Bold central spire, choir, clear-story, some windows on south of nave and vaulting throughout are Perp. Remains of original bishop's throne behind High Altar. Eastern apsidal chapel replaced by Lady chapel, since destroyed. Chapter house, resembling Durham, also destroyed.

18. Oxford (pp. 400B, 409B, 412C). Augustinian Priory. Norman nave and choir (1158–1180). E.E. chapter house and Lady chapel. Nave pillars, alternately circular and polygonal, support lofty Norman arches beneath which is triforium gallery—an unusual arrangement in order to give height. Norman central tower with E.E. upper part and short spire. Nave, shortened by Cardinal Wolsey when building his college of Christ Church, forms a vestibule to choir, which has fine vaulting with pendants.

19. *Peterborough (pp. 403A, 408F, 410D, 414, 494A, B). A Norman church (1117–1193) with finest interior after Durham. Nave timber roof is probably oldest in England, with painted wooden ceiling of lozenge-shaped compartments. Nave aisles vaulted (cf. Ely). Apsidal choir enclosed on the east by rectangular Perp. retro-choir, fan-vaulted, as at King's College, Cambridge. Grand E.E. western façade (c. 1193–1230), 158 ft wide, has a portico of three gigantic arches, the full height of cathedral. A gable crowns each arch, and angle abutments are carried up as small towers with spires. Other towers rise immediately behind, over western bays of the aisles. Central archway encloses two-storeyed Perp. porch.

20. Ripon (pp. 407B, 413G, 494C, D). Begun c. 1179, but nave and much of choir rebuilt later. Central and two western towers. Saxon crypt. Rich choir stalls with tabernacle work. Perfect E.E. western façade (c. 1233) (restored by Sir George Gilbert Scott).

21. *Rochester (pp. 409D, 412H). Norman and E.E. crypt, Norman nave, Norman west doorway. E.E. walled-in choir and transepts. Perp. clear-story and wooden roof.

22. *S. Albans (p. 412F). Much destroyed and altered in modern times. Norman nave (longest in England, 284 ft), transepts, and choir. Western portion of nave is E.E. Dec. marble shrine of S. Alban discovered and re-erected by Sir George Gilbert Scott.

23. S. Asaph (p. 412A). Rebuilt in Dec. style. Central tower, formerly with timber spire. No triforium. Perp. roof and choir stalls. Restored by Sir George Gilbert Scott.

24. S. David's (p. 413E). Situated in valley of the Alan (Pembrokeshire) close to the sea. Central tower. Two-storeyed south porch. Transitional nave arches support a carved oak roof of Perp. design (1508). Dec. rood-screen. West front 1789. Restored by Sir G. G. Scott.

25. Salisbury (pp. 395, 407G, 410E, 415). On a level site, surrounded by the greensward of a wide 'close', broken only by elm trees. Almost entirely in the E.E. style (1220–58). Is characteristic of English Gothic, as Amiens is of French (p. 541). Double transepts, central tower, Dec. spire, 404 ft high, the loftiest in England. West façade (1258–65) is unimpressive, but a fine vaulted north porch projects boldly. Dec. cloisters. Restorations by Sir George Gilbert Scott. Vaulted octagonal chapter house (1263–84) (p. 396A).

26. Southwark (S. Saviour, or S. Mary Overie) (pp. 373C, 393). Restored nave. E.E. choir and retro-choir or Lady chapel.

27. Southwell (p. 412K). Norman nave, transepts and towers. E.E. choir. Dec. octagonal chapter house without central pillar, the chief glory of the cathedral, probably the model for York. Rich and well-preserved carving. No cloisters.

28. Wells (pp. 403B, 407A, 412J) (c. 1180–c. 1425). E.E. nave, double transepts, and western bays of choir. The E.E. west front (150 ft wide, including buttresses) is flanked by towers arcaded and enriched with sculpture—the highest development in English Gothic of this type of façade. Central tower, eastern Lady chapel and octagonal chapter house. Unique triforium of close-set openings. As illustrating the comparative height to width of English and French cathedrals, Wells is 32 ft wide and 67 ft high (two to one) and Amiens is 46 ft wide and 140 ft high (three to one).

29. *Winchester (pp. 408E, 410C, 420, 495L, M). Has greatest total length (560 ft) of any Mediaeval cathedral in Europe. Norman transepts and tower (1079–93). Norman nave and choir (1079–93) transformed by veneer of Perp. on Norman core and a vaulted roof. Largest E.E. retro-choir (1202–c. 1235) in England with Dec. stalls (cf. Gloucester). Tombs and chantries. Timber vault (1510–28) to choir.

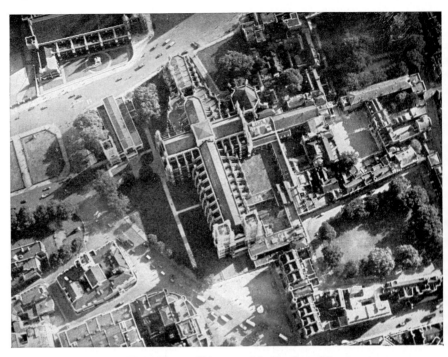

A. Westminster Abbey: aerial view from W.

B. North transept (1245–60)   C. Chapter house vault (1250)

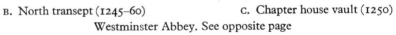

Westminster Abbey. See opposite page

30. *Worcester (pp. 404A, B, 407C, 411A). Level site on banks of Severn. Norman crypt, transepts, and circular chapter house (the only one in England). E.E. choir. Dec. and Perp. nave, cloisters, and central tower (196 ft high). Interesting monuments, including royal chantries of King John and Prince Arthur (p. 473).

31. York (pp. 408B, 410B). Largest in area and width, 106 ft within the walls, of any English Mediaeval cathedral. E.E. transepts remarkable for beauty of mouldings and the 'Five Sisters'—a name given to lancet windows of north transept, each 50 ft high and 5 ft wide. Unique fourteenth-century stained glass. Nave and octagonal chapter house, with wooden roof and without central column, of Edwardian Gothic (1261–1324). Perp. tower. No cloisters. Nave—second in height to Westminster Abbey—and choir have wooden imitation of stone vault. West front of French type. In spite of size the cathedral is less impressive than Durham in outline and grouping.

S. Paul, London. See p. 906.

Note. A comparative table which contrasts characteristics of English and French Gothic cathedrals is given (pp. 559 ff.), and will be found of interest.

MONASTERIES

The importance of the monastic system during the Mediaeval period throughout Europe and the general plan and purpose of monastic establishments are fully dealt with elsewhere (pp. 304, 307–8).

Westminster Abbey (pp. 422, 424–6, 428) stands on what was Thorney Island, opposite an ancient ford across the Thames. Traditionally said to occupy the site of a church built by Sebert in 616, the Benedictine monastery was founded by S. Dunstan in 960, and partly rebuilt (1055–65) by Edward the Confessor just before the Norman Conquest and dedicated to S. Peter. From the Confessor onward, kings were pulling down, rebuilding, adding to and repairing the abbey church, and so its character changed from Norman to Gothic; and the successive and merging phases of Early English, Decorated, Perpendicular, and Tudor, with their own peculiarly English features, find a place in various parts of the abbey church; while the Early Renaissance has also left its imprint on magnificent monuments, and even the more ponderous art of Queen Anne and the Georges is faithfully reproduced in the memorials to England's dead. Originally the church formed part of that great triple group—monastery, church, and royal palace—the last of which was superseded by the Houses of Parliament, thus keeping pace with the growth and changes of the English Constitution as it passed from absolute to constitutional monarchy and representative government.

The monastery was one of the largest Benedictine foundations, with a typical lay-out (p. 425H), which comprised the abbey church and a square cloister court, surrounded by open arcades of various dates (pp. 424D, 425A), with refectory, dormitory, and octagonal chapter house (1250) (p. 424D), with a fine vault (p. 422C) whose thrusts are balanced internally on a slender clustered pier, and met externally by bold flying buttresses (p. 426A). There was also a common court (now Dean's Yard), an inner court (now Little Dean's Yard), and the infirmary, besides mills, workshops, orchards, gardens, and the usual trout stream which, from the heights of Hampstead, here joined the Thames, and still runs under Great College Street. The precincts covered a large area, and formed a self-contained community, the germ of the later City of Westminster. Most of the existing monastic buildings date from the time of Abbot Litlington (mid-fourteenth century), and include the abbot's residence (now the deanery), with Jerusalem Chamber and dining-hall; but the Chapel of the Pyx and monks' day-room, forming the dormitory under-croft, come down from Edward the Confessor's time. The greater part of the abbey church was rebuilt on a grander scale by Henry III (his master-mason being Henry of Westminster), and to him are due the present eastern arm, north and south

WESTMINSTER ABBEY

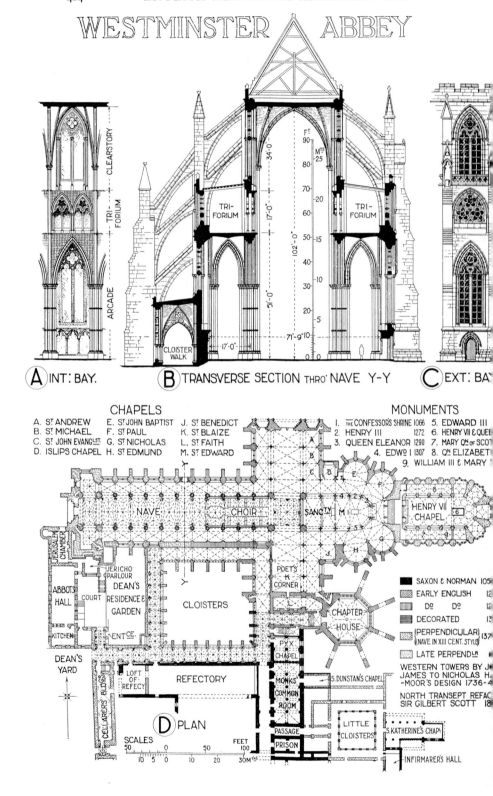

A INT: BAY.

B TRANSVERSE SECTION THRO' NAVE Y-Y

C EXT: BA

CHAPELS

MONUMENTS

A. ST ANDREW	E. ST JOHN BAPTIST	J. ST BENEDICT
B. ST MICHAEL	F. ST PAUL	K. ST BLAIZE
C. ST JOHN EVANGLST.	G. ST NICHOLAS	L. ST FAITH
D. ISLIPS CHAPEL	H. ST EDMUND	M. ST EDWARD

1. THE CONFESSOR'S SHRINE 1066   5. EDWARD III
2. HENRY III   1272   6. HENRY VII & QUEE
3. QUEEN ELEANOR 1290   7. MARY QN OF SCOT
4. EDWD I 1307   8. QN ELIZABET
                                   9. WILLIAM III & MARY

NAVE   CHOIR   SANCTY   M   HENRY VII CHAPEL   6

JERUSALEM CHAMBER

JERICHO PARLOUR

ABBOTS HALL   COURT   DEAN'S RESIDENCE & GARDEN

DEAN'S   CLOISTERS

KITCHEN   ENTCE.

POET'S CORNER

CHAPTER HOUSE

DEAN'S YARD

LOFT OF REFECY

REFECTORY

PYX CHAPEL

MONKS COMMON ROOM

S. DUNSTAN'S CHAPEL

D PLAN

SCALES   50   0   50   100
10 5 0   10   20   30 MYRS

PASSAGE

PRISON

LITTLE CLOISTERS

S. KATHERINE'S CHAPL

INFIRMARER'S HALL

■	SAXON & NORMAN 105
▨	EARLY ENGLISH 12
▥	DO DO 12
▧	DECORATED 13
▨	(PERPENDICULAR) (NAVE IN XIII CENT. STYLE) 137
▨	LATE PERPENDLR

WESTERN TOWERS BY J
JAMES TO NICHOLAS H.
-MOOR'S DESIGN 1736-4

NORTH TRANSEPT REFAC
SIR GILBERT SCOTT 18

WESTMINSTER ABBEY

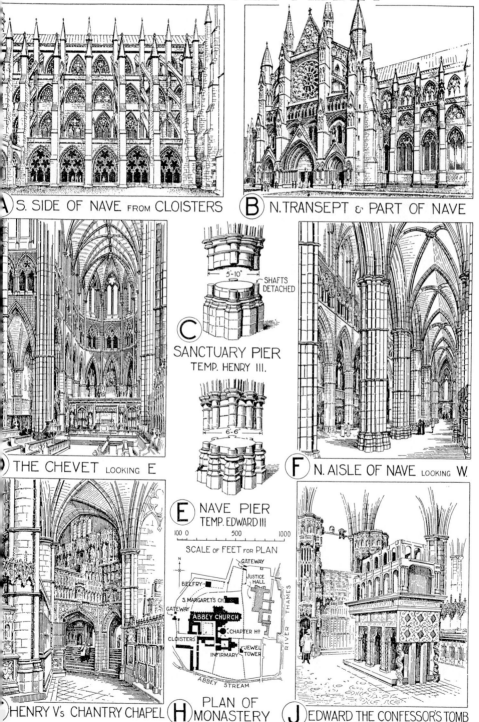

A) S. SIDE OF NAVE FROM CLOISTERS

B) N. TRANSEPT & PART OF NAVE

C) SANCTUARY PIER
TEMP. HENRY III.

5'-10"   SHAFTS DETACHED

D) THE CHEVET LOOKING E

E) NAVE PIER
TEMP. EDWARD III

6'-6"

F) N. AISLE OF NAVE LOOKING W.

100 0   500   1000
SCALE OF FEET FOR PLAN

GATEWAY
JUSTICE HALL
BELFRY
S. MARGARET'S CH.
GATEWAY
ABBEY CHURCH
CHAPTER H?
CLOISTERS
JEWEL TOWER
INFIRMARY
RIVER THAMES
ABBEY STREAM

HENRY V's CHANTRY CHAPEL

H) PLAN OF MONASTERY

J) EDWARD THE CONFESSOR'S TOMB

WESTMINSTER · ABBEY · HENRY · VII's · CHAPEL.

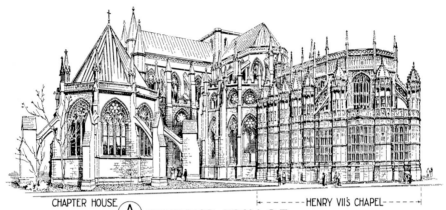

CHAPTER HOUSE   ⊢------ HENRY VII's CHAPEL -----⊣
(A) EXTERIOR FROM S.E.

(B) VAULT FROM ABOVE

(C) VAULT FROM BELOW

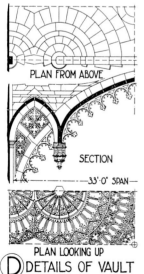

PLAN FROM ABOVE

SECTION

-- 33'·0" SPAN --

PLAN LOOKING UP

(D) DETAILS OF VAULT

(E) INTERIOR LOOKING W.

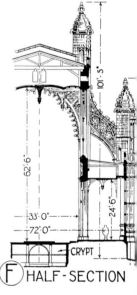

101'·5"

62'·6"

33'·0"
72'·0"

24'·6"

CRYPT

(F) HALF-SECTION

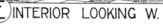

transepts, one bay of the western arm, all erected between 1245 and 1260, and four more bays of the western arm, built between 1260 and 1269. For nearly a century building was suspended, and the old Norman nave still remained standing, but was pulled down and the nave continued westward as set forth below. The church is in the main French in character, and is largely based on Rheims (the French coronation church) (p. 538). It is an early example in England of the Geometric style, while the pinnacles and bar-tracery windows are among the first in this country. The eastern arm of the church, terminating in a polygonal apse, with ambulatory and cluster of surrounding chapels (pp. 424D, 426A), which form the only complete 'chevet' in England, contains the much-venerated shrine of the Confessor, and the Coronation chair (p. 519A). The Confessor's shrine (p. 425J) stands in the centre of his chapel, and to this hallowed spot pilgrims have come from all parts of the world. Originally buried under the central tower of the Norman church, the body was translated to this shrine by Henry III in 1269. The monument, which was much damaged at the Reformation in 1538, is of Purbeck marble, and on each side of the pedestal are three trefoiled recesses in which sick people were placed in the hope of miraculous cures. Twisted columns at the angles, filled with glass mosaics, supported the reredos of the former altar, surmounted by a frieze of porphyry and serpentine; the tomb is covered by an oak superstructure, added by Abbot Feckenham (1554).

The interior of the Abbey betrays the French influence in loftiness and verticality produced by lancet arches and tall clear-story (pp. 422B, 424A). The north transept façade is emphatically French with cavernous porches and rose window (p. 425B). The nave (p. 425F), continued westward by Edward III and others (1375–1506), adhered to the thirteenth-century general design, but the Perpendicular date is revealed in such details as piers and mouldings. The periods of the building of the church are clearly seen in the piers themselves; in the sanctuary and transepts a cylindrical pier is surrounded by four detached shafts of Purbeck marble, as was usual in the Early English period (pp. 425C, 503K, L); in the first five bays west of the crossing four attached shafts are added to these four, and in the western part of the nave, designed by Master Henry Yevele, all eight shafts are attached, i.e. formed on the pier itself (p. 425E). The western towers were added (1736–45) by John James from designs made in 1734 by Nicholas Hawksmoor. The church, with an extreme internal length of 511 ft 6 ins, is notable for an unusually spacious triforium used for coronation ceremonies. Its nave vault, 102 ft high (p. 399D), the highest Gothic vault in England, has a complex system of strutting by flying buttresses across aisle and north cloister (pp. 425A, 497T). The church abounds with chapels and monuments, including—besides the Confessor's shrine—that of Henry III (p. 472M) and other kings, and these with many others (p. 472C, K, L) form a unique museum of sculpture of all periods, while over the east end of the ambulatory stands the richly sculptured fifteenth-century Chantry of Henry V (p. 425G). At the extreme east end is the celebrated Chapel of Henry VII (1503–19), built by the brothers Robert and William Vertue as a magnificent mausoleum of the king, on the site of a Lady chapel of 1220, and forming the culminating triumph of English Mediaeval architecture (pp. 424D, 426, 428). This is the chapel of the Knights of the Bath, and the low seats of the Esquires are backed by the richly carved canopied stalls of the Knights, embellished, as is the rest of the chapel, with elaborate heraldic devices (p. 517F). The tomb of Henry VII and of Elizabeth of York (p. 881) is enclosed by a metal screen of Gothic design, forming a chantry chapel (pp. 426E, 428). The famous fan vault of lace-like tracery (pp. 426, 428), with pendants hanging apparently unsupported, is really constructed on half-concealed transverse arches of which the pendants are merely elongated voussoirs, and around these pendants the conoidal web is built up. Instead

Westminster Abbey: Henry VII's chapel (1503–19) looking west and on right the bronze
screen (1509) enclosing the Chantry Chapel and tomb of Henry VII and his Queen.
See p. 427

of being attached to the clear-story wall, as in previous experiments of the kind, the main conoids are advanced upon these arches so as not to interfere with the broad clear-story windows, and are supported on pendants, and connected to the clear-story by other conoids above the level of the springing of the windows—a master-piece of English masonry. The buttresses are in the form of octagonal piers, between which the windows form a mere screen, and are many-sided on plan, while the flying arches are filled with tracery (pp. 426F, 497P).

The Abbey is impressive as a triumph of English Gothic architecture, as an outward and visible sign of English religious devotion, and as a record in stone of English history. It has grown with the national growth, and has woven itself into the fabric of the nation's life. At once the most sacred and most famous shrine in England, this venerable abbey represents the growth of centuries, both in its own building and in national history. From even before the time of the Confessor and onwards, it was slowly built, altered, adorned, and repaired. It has passed under the direction of divers master-masons and architects, from Henry of Westminster down to Wren and others of our own time. The Abbey and the nation have always been closely associated; for not only did the abbey church serve the monks of the Benedictine monastery, but it was also the centre of popular pilgrimages to the Confessor's shrine. It has also, through the centuries, been the scene of the gorgeous coronation pageants down to that for the present Queen, Elizabeth II; as well as of those memorial services for many of England's greatest sons, who have achieved distinction in every field of human endeavour. This association of 'the Abbey' with the nation's recognition of those who have greatly dared is enshrined in the words of Nelson when, in the battle off Cape S. Vincent, he exclaimed: 'Victory or Westminster Abbey!'

In its structure it is an epitome of architectural art; in its monuments and statues, tombs and tablets it is a record of the success of many men and women in many pur-suits in many parts of the world: Roman Catholic, Anglican, and Nonconformist; poet, priest, and king; warrior, writer, and play-actor; scientist and artist—all are commemorated within its walls. A royal foundation, associated with the memory of an English king, the burial-place of kings in the past, the coronation-place of kings to-day, the Abbey is, in very truth, the national shrine for the honoured dead, not of England only, but of the whole British Commonwealth.

Fountains Abbey, Yorkshire (p. 432), appears to have been founded (1135) soon after Rievaulx, the first Cistercian establishment in that county (1132), and before Kirkstall (1152). It is thought to have been named from the springs in the valley of the Skell. Although in ruins, owing to the care with which the place has been uncovered, it is easy here to make a mental picture of a great monastery (p. 432A, C). The gatehouse (p. 432B) led into the outer court; south of this were the guest house and the infirmary of the conversi, or lay brethren, and east of it was the cellarium, no less than 300 ft long, comprising storehouses and refectory of these conversi on the lower floor, with their dormitory above. Opposite the gatehouse is the conventual church, of which the nave and transepts date from about 1147, but the choir appears to have been enlarged between 1203 and 1247, and at the same time the transept known as the 'Chapel of the Nine Altars' was built. The tower, by Abbot Huby (1494–1526), is still the dominating feature in this beautiful valley. The door in the south-east angle of the nave leads into the cloister court, round which were ranged the chapter house, the monks' dormitory and its undercroft, the calefactory or warming house, the monks' refectory, the kitchen with two great fireplaces, and alongside was a washing lavatory, part of which still remains. Still farther east were the cells for refractory monks and the abbot's lodge, north of which a corridor led to the infirmary hall, with adjacent chapel, cellar, and kitchen.

The chapter house, of which the vaulting is now destroyed, was rectangular, and against the walls were stone benches rising one above another on which the monks were wont to sit. The complete monastic establishment must have existed till the time of Abbot William Thirsk (1526–36), after which the estate was sold (1540) to Sir Richard Gresham, whose successor pulled down the infirmary and the stone wall, and built Fountains Hall (p. 432B) on the site in 1611 (p. 894B).

PARISH CHURCHES

The building of churches in England progressed on distinctly national lines, and the 9,000 parish churches of the Mediaeval period indicate the evolution of the style, while the enlargement through the centuries of the parish church can be traced in the plans (p. 491).

S. Andrew, Heckington (1345–80) (p. 431) is a fine type of English parish church. It has (p. 431C) a western tower, nave with aisles, south entrance porch, transepts, aisleless chancel with priest's door, square east end due to Anglo-Saxon influence, and a sacristy. The interior is on the lines of many parish churches, with close-boarded roof to the chancel and open timber roof to the nave (p. 431B) which has no triforium. The exterior is simple and straightforward, with its single western tower and spire, 175 ft high, long roof over the nave and lower roof to the chancel (p. 431A).

Some larger parish churches which are cruciform on plan have the tower over the 'crossing' of nave and transepts. A spire, usually octagonal, often crowns the tower, and the change from the square to the octagon was effected in the thirteenth century by means of a 'broach' resting on angle squinch arches (p. 431D, E); while in the following centuries parapets with elaborate pinnacles and flying buttresses connected the tower to the base of the spire. The principal entrance was either through a south porch near the west end or by a door under the tower in the west façade, which gives dignity to the entrance. English village churches form in themselves a miniature history of ecclesiastical architecture in this country. Nearly every church has its own peculiar attraction, and with accessories and fittings is a mine of information for student and antiquary (pp. 405, 506, 509, 510, 515).

There is no feature of these churches more typically English than the timber roof, with all its manifold variations of structure and design, as gradually developed out of the combinations of rafters and beams. These were manipulated by English carpenters to form varieties of roofing, much as the same simple timber material was skilfully woven together by the shipwrights to form the wooden walls of Old England. These timber roofs form such an integral part of multitudes of parish churches that a description of their construction is here given, which can be applied, according to the type, to analyse any given timber roof. For chapels see p. 469.

TIMBER ROOFS

The English developed as did no other nation the construction of various types of open timber roofs, which culminated in the elaborate hammer-beam variety of the fifteenth century, often gaily painted in gold and colours. The French, on the contrary, favoured the stone vault, which generally necessitated external flying buttresses, and this makes a marked contrast, both internal and external, between the churches of the two countries.

Timber roofs were beautiful features of English Mediaeval churches, and their intricate construction was an important part of parish churches. Owing to the rich variety allowed by their highly decorative nature, the interaction of local styles and the fact that many of the earlier examples were subsequently replaced—

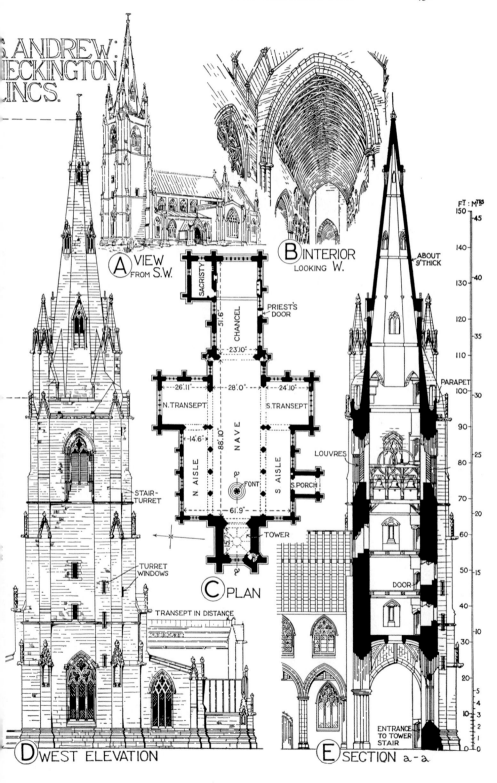

S. ANDREW:
ECKINGTON
LINCS.

Ⓐ VIEW FROM S.W.

Ⓑ INTERIOR LOOKING W.

Ⓒ PLAN

SACRISTY

51.6"

CHANCEL

PRIEST'S DOOR

23.10"

26.11"   28.0"   24.10"

N.TRANSEPT   S.TRANSEPT

14.6"   88.10"   NAVE

N. AISLE   S. AISLE   S.PORCH

FONT

61.9"

STAIR-TURRET

TURRET WINDOWS

15.7"   TOWER

TRANSEPT IN DISTANCE

Ⓓ WEST ELEVATION

Ⓔ SECTION a-a

ABOUT 9" THICK

PARAPET

LOUVRES

DOOR

ENTRANCE TO TOWER STAIR

FT: MTRS
150 — 45
140
130 — 40
120
      35
110
100 — 30
90
      25
80
70 — 20
60
50 — 15
40
      10
30
20
      5
      4
10 — 3
      2
      1
      0

FOUNTAINS ABBEY: YORKSHIRE

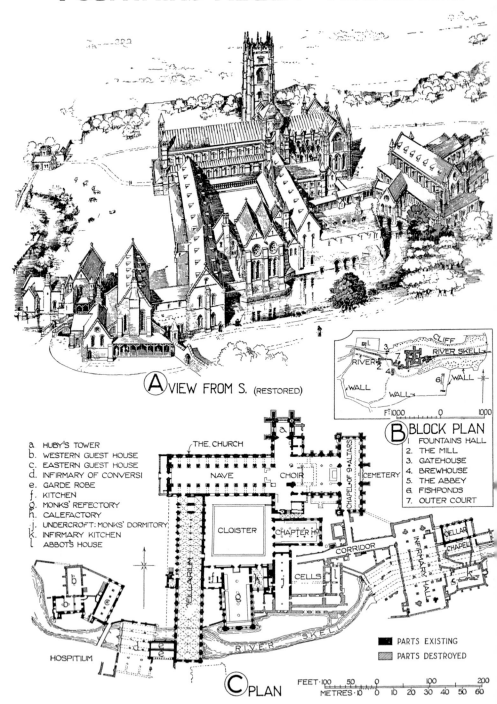

A VIEW FROM S. (RESTORED)

B BLOCK PLAN

CLIFF
RIVER SKELL
RIVER
WALL
WALL
WALL
FT 1000   0   1000

1. FOUNTAINS HALL
2. THE MILL
3. GATEHOUSE
4. BREWHOUSE
5. THE ABBEY
6. FISHPONDS
7. OUTER COURT

a. HUBY'S TOWER
b. WESTERN GUEST HOUSE
c. EASTERN GUEST HOUSE
d. INFIRMARY OF CONVERSI
e. GARDE ROBE
f. KITCHEN
g. MONKS' REFECTORY
h. CALEFACTORY
j. UNDERCROFT: MONKS' DORMITORY
k. INFIRMARY KITCHEN
l. ABBOT'S HOUSE

THE CHURCH
NAVE
CHOIR
CHAPEL OF 9 ALTARS
CEMETERY
CLOISTER
CHAPTER H⁵
CORRIDOR
CELLARIUM
CELLS
INFIRMARY HALL
CELLAR
CHAPEL
HOSPITIUM
RIVER SKELL

■ PARTS EXISTING
▨ PARTS DESTROYED

C PLAN

FEET·100   50   0   100   200
METRES·10   0   10   20   30   40   50   60

especially after the mid-fourteenth century, when roof pitches often were lowered, lead having become a popular substitute for less permanent coverings—evolution is by no means so clearly apparent as in the case of vaults. Few surviving roofs are earlier than the thirteenth century, and the majority are later Mediaeval. Constructional evolution is more readily demonstrated by the roofs of manor houses (p. 444) or barns (p. 483). 'Single' roofs (lacking principals), 'trussed-rafter' (p. 435A), 'hammer-beam' roofs (p. 435F, H, L), and those having a 'crown-post' (known also as a 'king-post') standing on a tie-beam to support a 'collar-purlin' (p. 446E), almost invariably belong to the south-eastern half of the country; the dividing line running approximately along the oolitic limestone belt shown in the inset map, p. 379. In the south-east too, the 'principal rafter' of roof trusses serves as a common rafter as well as to support side purlins, tenoned into them. The ridge-piece, if any, runs under the common rafters rather than between them as is modern practice. In the north-western half of the country and in Wales, roofs were almost invariably 'framed', there being well-defined principals supporting purlins and a ridge-piece upon their backs (p. 485C). Frequently, there were 'wind-braces' arching from the purlins to the principal rafters (p. 500B). 'Arch-braced' roofs, common from the fourteenth century, are found in both halves of the country. In general, roofs tended to become more elaborate and ornate as time elapsed. There was very much overlap in the types developing in succession.

The English open timber roofs of the Middle Ages (pp. 435, 500) may be classified as: (1) Trussed-rafter roofs. (2) Tie beam roofs. (3) Collar-braced roofs. (4) Hammer-beam roofs. (5) Aisle roofs.

(1) *Trussed-rafter roofs* (p. 435A) are nearly always steeply pitched, averaging fifty-five degrees; they are rare in churches after *c.* 1400. The fundamental form of roof in the south-east was that composed of 'couples' of rafters, each pair separate, without a ridge-piece; but as the rafters exercised outward thrust they were usually joined together by a collar, or pair of collars, or were stiffened further by braces from collar to rafters, as at Stow Bardolph Church, Norfolk. Sometimes the braces were extended past the collar, scissor-wise, as at Lympenhoe Church, Norfolk, or the scissor braces were themselves considered sufficient. The rafters rested on the outer portion of the wall, and thus left an unsightly ledge on the inside, covered by upright struts, which also added to the stability of the roof. The triangle thus formed is held to be the origin of the hammer-beam arrangement (p. 435K), when principals had been developed. The arched trussed-rafter roof was obtained by the use of curved timbers connecting the rafters and collars, as at Solihull Church, Warwickshire, and it was sometimes lined with boards to form a pentagonal 'barrel' ceiling, ornamented with ribs and bosses (p. 435C).

(2) *The Tie-Beam roof* (p. 435B, E) is found in connection both with steeply-pitched and low-pitched roofs. In early use the tie-beam represents a 'baulk-tie' which joined the wall-posts of timber buildings (p. 478F), and in stone buildings was often haphazardly placed to prevent the wall plates from spreading. It came to serve, usually cambered upwards, to carry an ornamental or plain crown-post, which in its turn and with the aid of struts sustained a collar-purlin, linking the collars and giving rigidity to a roof otherwise of the trussed-rafter class (pp. 446E, 500A). Even so, the type was rather frail, and many elementary or naïve devices were tried for the purpose of propping-up side purlins from the tie-beam (p. 486H) before true roof principals were evolved. So long as roofs were steeply pitched, the tie-beam obstructed the upper space; when from the thirteenth century roofs were progressively lowered it came into its own again, but then as a part of a truss, with principal rafters supporting purlins and ridge-piece, the triangle thus formed having various arrangements of vertical struts and tracery (p. 435B, E). Curved

braces often connected the underside of the tie-beam with vertical wall-pieces, and thus the whole was framed together in the form of a depressed arch, as at S. Martin, Leicester (p. 435E). A final phase for this class of roof (fifteenth and sixteenth century) was to depress the roof-pitch to such an extent, even less than ten degrees, that the roof could be carried on a cambered tie-beam with only a modicum of firring (pp. 446K, 480K).

(3) *The Collar-braced roof*, which may be said to originate about 1300, is a natural descendant of the 'cruck-truss' roof of the western half of the country (p. 467B), in which principals of the cruck type—spaced down the length of a building to carry purlins and a ridge, and these the rafters—are raised upon walls instead of starting from the ground, as formerly. In the process, the curved 'blades' or principal rafters of the crucks tend to be straightened out, and the former tie-beams appear as a collar connecting them together. When, as is usually the case in prime examples, braces are added below the collar to link it with the principal rafters, the outcome is what is known as an 'arch-braced' truss. Among domestic buildings, Stokesay Castle hall (p. 442B) affords a straightforward and very early example (thirteenth century). The roof pitch usually is steep—about fifty-two degrees, descending to below fifty degrees in the fifteenth century. In south-west England, where the 'framed' principle of roof construction was not so strongly traditional as in the north-west, arch-braced church roofs often lacked a ridge-piece; and in south-eastern England (including East Anglia), where it was quite alien, it was nevertheless soon adopted but very frequently to produce hybrid forms in which the 'single' and the 'framed' methods of construction of the roof members were confused (p. 435D). This mixture of practice is very marked in such secular examples as Sutton Courtenay, Berks (fourteenth century) (p. 500C) and Cobham, Kent (sixteenth century) (p. 480C). In the same region in the fifteenth century, as well as in Somerset and Devon, arch-braces sometimes swept to the roof apex without the intervention of a collar (p. 471C), or were omitted altogether. In all the variants of the type, there normally were arch-braces too at the feet of the principal rafters, connecting with wall-posts to carry the roof load down the inner wall faces and giving a pointed-arch profile to the lower edge of the roof trusses.

(4) The *Hammer-beam roof*, found principally in the south-eastern half of the country, was evolved during the fourteenth century, perhaps from the triangle at the foot of the trussed rafter roof (p. 435F, H, L). It consists of a series of trusses, repeated at intervals, to support the intermediate purlins and rafters, and its object is to transmit the weight and thrust of the roof as low down as possible in the supporting wall. The component parts of each truss are the two principal rafters and hammer-beams with struts, curved braces, and collars which vary in number and design. The hammer-beam itself is merely a lengthened sole piece (p. 435K), of which the projecting part is supported by a curved brace from the wall piece, and in its turn it supports a vertical strut to the principal rafter. This rigid system of timbers, all tenoned and pinned together, is designed to resist the outward pressure of the rafters, and is supplemented in the Gothic period by external buttresses. It has been suggested that the hammer-beam was the result of cutting away the centre of the tie-beam after the introduction of the curved brace, but there is little in common between a hammer-beam and a tie-beam roof, except that, in both, the trusses are at intervals. Moreover the tie-beam was used even in conjunction with the hammer-beam, as at Outwell, where the alternate trusses have hammer-beams. The chief varieties of the hammer-beam roof are: (*a*) those with hammer-beams, struts, collars, and curved braces, as at Little Welnetham, Suffolk; (*b*) those in which the collar-beam is omitted and curved braces are carried up to a wedge-shaped strut at the ridge, as at Wymondham, Norfolk (p. 435H), and Trunch,

TYPES OF TIMBER CHURCH ROOFS

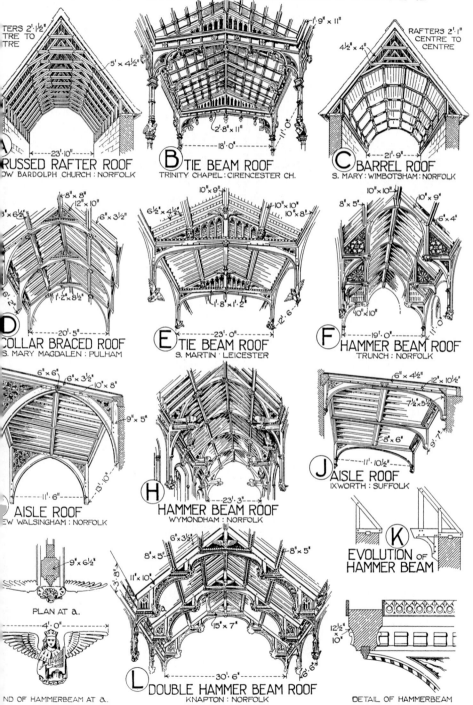

A TRUSSED RAFTER ROOF
OW BARDOLPH · CHURCH : NORFOLK

B TIE BEAM ROOF
TRINITY CHAPEL : CIRENCESTER CH.

C BARREL ROOF
S. MARY : WIMBOTSHAM : NORFOLK

D COLLAR BRACED ROOF
S. MARY MAGDALEN : PULHAM

E TIE BEAM ROOF
S. MARTIN · LEICESTER

F HAMMER BEAM ROOF
TRUNCH : NORFOLK

G AISLE ROOF
EW WALSINGHAM : NORFOLK

H HAMMER BEAM ROOF
WYMONDHAM : NORFOLK

J AISLE ROOF
IXWORTH : SUFFOLK

K EVOLUTION OF HAMMER BEAM

PLAN AT a.

ND OF HAMMERBEAM AT a.

L DOUBLE HAMMER BEAM ROOF
KNAPTON : NORFOLK

DETAIL OF HAMMERBEAM

THE TOWER OF LONDON

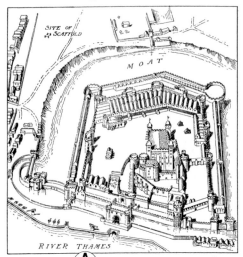

(A) A·D 1597   BIRD'S EYE VIEWS   (B) A·D 1918.

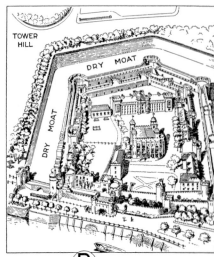

(C) INTERIOR OF S. JOHN'S CHAPEL LOOKING E.

(D) WHITE TOWER FROM S.E.

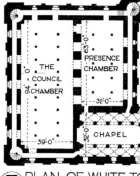

(E) PLAN OF WHITE TO... AT THIRD FLOOR LE...

(F) INTERIOR OF BYWARD TOWER

I MIDDLE TOWER·9 BRICK TOWER·17 BROAD ARROW Tr.
2 BYWARD " 10 MARTIN " 18 BELL TOWER
3 LEGGE'S MOUNT·11 S. PETER'S Ch·19 GUARD HOUSE
4 N. BASTION 12 WATERLOO Bks 20 WAKEFIELD Tr.
5 BRASS MOUNT·13 BEAUCHAMP Tr.·21 S. THOMAS'S
6 DEVEREUX Tr.·14 WHITE TOWER 22 TRAITOR'S GATE
7 FLINT TOWER·15 BARRACKS 23 LANTHORN Tr.
8 BOWYER TOWr.·16 CONSTABLE Tr.·24 SALT TOWER.
8a BLOODY Tr.·16a CRADLE Tr.·25 WELL TOWER

SCALE 100 0 100 200 300 400 500 600 700 FEET
0 50 100 150 200 METRES

(G) BLOCK PLAN

(H) BLOODY TOWER GATE... TRAITOR'S GATE BEY...

Norfolk (p. 435F); (c) those in which short hammer-beams support curved braces instead of struts, with collar-beams above, as at Capel S. Mary, Suffolk, and Hampton Court Palace (p. 463); (d) those in which curved braces rise from hammer-beam to ridge, as at Palgrave, Suffolk; (e) those with an arched rib which, springing from wall piece to collar, gives additional rigidity, as at Eltham Palace (1481) (p. 500G), and in that most magnificent of all timber roofs at Westminster Hall, by the distinguished master-carpenter, Hugh Herland, which dates from 1397–9 (p. 500D–F). (f) Double hammer-beam roofs, as at S. Margaret, Ipswich, Knapton (p. 435L) and Middle Temple Hall (1572) (p. 500H), have a second range of hammer-beams further to stiffen the principals and transmit the weight through the first range to the wall: they appear from the fifteenth century onwards.

(5) *Aisle Roofs* (p. 435G, J) usually reflected the design of the main roofs. Roof pitches changed in concert with those of the high roofs, except that they quite frequently were at a less angle in order to facilitate clear-story lighting of naves.

CASTLES

Just as the parish church is an indication of the religious life of the people, so is the English home, whether feudal castle or manor house, an index of social life under the feudal system, when every castle was not only a fortified stronghold, but also, like the manor house, a centre for administering justice and dispensing hospitality. Castles were built with little regard for domestic comfort and often retained their fortified character till the fifteenth century (pp. 436, 442, 445).

Anglo-Saxon period. There were no castles, as the forts or 'burhs' built at this time were for community use; properly speaking, castles were private strongholds for king or lord, and were an outcome of the feudal system, which did not apply in England until the Conquest, though one or two earthworks were built under Norman influence before that event.

Norman period. Of some fifteen hundred castles in England, more than twelve hundred were founded during the eleventh and twelfth centuries. Only a few of the most important had stone keeps from the outset; the majority began as 'motte and bailey' earthworks. The motte or mound usually was partly natural, partly artificial, its sides steepened by a ditch dug around its base. The flat-topped crest sometimes was broad enough to accommodate a timber dwelling. In other cases it served solely as a citadel, carrying a wooden defence tower, raised on angle posts. The dwelling and ancillary buildings then were sited in the bailey, this being a zone which looped from the foot of the motte, defined by ditches and earthen ramparts, and which was spacious enough also to provide refuge for dependants, peasantry and stock in times of need. An inclined wooden bridge connected the bailey with the motte. The fringe of the motte crest and the summits of the earth ramparts were lined by palisades of close-set timber baulks, or occasionally by rough stone walls.

Thetford, Norfolk, affords a fine instance, 80 ft high, of the hundreds of surviving mottes, and there are very many others with later stone buildings upon them, as at **Berkhamsted, Herts; Windsor** (p. 439A); and **Lewes, Sussex,** each constructed before *c.* 1125. Particularly early examples are those at **Cambridge** (1068) and **York,** where there are two (1069, 1069). **Dromore Castle, N. Ireland** (*c.* 1180) (p. 441A) has its motte and bailey almost in pristine condition, and is a relic of the Norman overlordship of Ireland after 1171.

Stone 'curtain' walls soon began to replace the perishable timber palisades, and in the twelfth century, particularly the latter half, mottes then assumed that form known as the 'shell-keep', because of the empty-looking crowning ring of high walls; though actually there usually were timber or stone buildings abutting the inner wall face. The bailey stone walls rode up the mound to join those of the shell-keep.

Windsor Castle (p. 439A) has a shell-keep of about 1170 (the upper half and the windows are nineteenth century), with an elongated bailey on each side. Other twelfth-century examples are **Conisborough, Yorkshire** (1185–90); **Carisbrooke, Isle of Wight** (*c.* 1140–50); **Launceston**, within which a round keep was built about 1240; **Restormel** (p. 441B); and **Trematon**. The last three are in Cornwall.

The greatest castles of the period had stone 'donjons' (nowadays known as keeps) rather than mottes, and similarly had baileys related to them. The earliest type was the rectangular 'hall-keep', in which the great hall and the private chamber were laid side by side, above a storage floor at ground level; sometimes there was an additional, entrance, floor between the two levels. About 1125 the 'tower-keep' became a frequent variant, the private chamber then being above the hall; and by 1150 practice was turning in favour of the polygonal or circular plan, since the square-angled keep was vulnerable to mining.

The **Tower of London** (*c.* 1086–97) (p. 436), a hall-keep, only assumed after several reigns its complete form as a 'concentric' castle, with successive lines of fortification—a plan probably based on Muslim models. Here, the rectangular keep of three storeys—the upper was divided into two, later on—92 ft in height, stands in the centre of an inner bailey, surrounded by a wall with thirteen towers (*c.* 1250), which is, in its turn, enclosed by an outer bailey and wall with eight towers and an encircling moat (*c.* 1280). Other examples, numbering about fifty, include **Colchester** (*c.* 1090), **Corfe, Dorset** (*c.* 1125), and **Castle Rising, Norfolk** (*c.* 1140), also hall-keeps; **Rochester** (1126–39), with wall fireplace (p. 519L) and **Hedingham, Essex** (*c.* 1140) (p. 440A), which are tower-keeps; and **Chilham, Kent** (*c.* 1160), **Orford, Suffolk** (1166–72) (p. 440B) and **Conisborough, Yorkshire** (1185–90) with octagonal or circular plans, each having protruding spurs. Keeps tended to become less magnificent as the strength of the outer defences advanced.

Early English period. During the thirteenth century, castles acquired really high curtain walls, with lofty towers projecting at intervals to give command of their whole length. Thus defence passed from passive to active. Occasionally rectangular (e.g. **Framlingham, Suffolk**, *c.* 1200), the mural towers mostly were polygonal or circular, against the danger of mining. 'Crenellation', or the indentation of parapets by 'embrasures', leaving upstanding 'merlons', with a rampart walk or 'alure' behind the parapets, was practised almost with the first high walls; from about John's reign (1199–1216), a 'license to crenellate' became necessary for all who wished to fortify a residence. 'Machicolations', floor apertures over gateways or between corbels of parapets, through which beseigers might be assailed with missiles, came progressively into use during the century. Castle gateways assumed an ever-increasing importance, and after mid-century, virtually supplanted the keep as the primary stronghold, though keeps with round or quatrefoil plans continued to be built for a time, chiefly in Wales and in the north. The grandest of all castles, representing the peak of mediaeval achievement, are those of Edward I (1272–1307), built after the conquest of Wales in 1282, together with one, **Caerphilly**, built a score of years earlier (1267–77).

Beaumaris, Anglesey (1283–1323) (p. 441C), with its concentric plan, is typical and perhaps the most perfect among them. It has inner and outer baileys, massive curtains and mural towers and two great gateways, all enclosed by a moat. Another concentric Welsh castle is **Harlech** (1283–90) (p. 441D). **Caernarvon** (1283–1323) and **Conway** (1283–9) are less regular in plan and have only single—yet mighty—defences. The main gateways of such castles, powerful though they are, were further protected by outworks or 'barbicans'.

A. Windsor Castle: aerial view from W. See opposite page

B. Bodiam Castle, Sussex (1386). See p. 443

A. Castle Hedingham, Essex:
Keep (*c*. 1140). See p. 438

B. Orford Castle, Suffolk:
Keep (1166–72). See p. 438

C. Tattershall Castle, Lincs: Keep (1436–46). See p. 444

A. Dromore Castle, N. Ireland
(c. 1180). See p. 437

B. Restormel Castle, Cornwall
(12th cent. and later). See p. 438

C. Beaumaris Castle, Anglesey
(1283–1323). See p. 438

D. Harlech Castle, Merionethshire
(1283-90). See p. 438

E. Bolton Castle, Yorkshire
(c. 1380). See p. 443

F. Deal Castle, Kent
(c. 1540). See p. 444

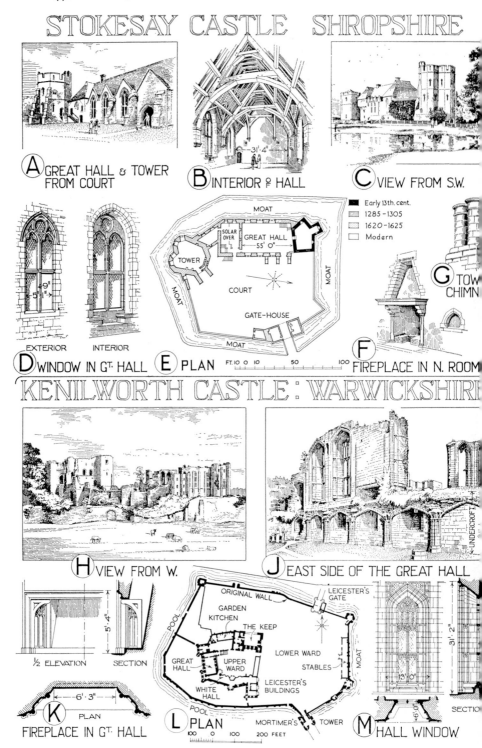

STOKESAY CASTLE SHROPSHIRE

(A) GREAT HALL & TOWER FROM COURT

(B) INTERIOR OF HALL
31'·4"

(C) VIEW FROM S.W.

■ Early 13th. cent.
▨ 1285-1305
▤ 1620-1625
□ Modern

MOAT
SOLAR OVER
GREAT HALL 55' 0"
TOWER
MOAT
COURT
MOAT
GATE-HOUSE
MOAT

(G) TOW CHIMN

EXTERIOR   INTERIOR
4'·9"
5'·1"

(D) WINDOW IN GT. HALL   **(E)** PLAN   FT. 10 0 10   50   100   **(F)** FIREPLACE IN N. ROOM

KENILWORTH CASTLE : WARWICKSHIRE

(H) VIEW FROM W.

(J) EAST SIDE OF THE GREAT HALL
UNDERCROFT

5'·4"
½ ELEVATION   SECTION

ORIGINAL WALL
LEICESTER'S GATE
GARDEN
KITCHEN
THE KEEP
POOL
GREAT HALL
UPPER WARD
LOWER WARD
STABLES
WHITE HALL
LEICESTER'S BUILDINGS
POOL
MORTIMER'S TOWER
MOAT

31'·2"
13'·0"
SECTIO
6'·

6'·3"
(K) PLAN
FIREPLACE IN GT. HALL

(L) PLAN   100 0 100   200 FEET

(M) HALL WINDOW

Castles in general now were often located on low-lying sites, with moats or other water defences, rather than on inconvenient eminences. In the quieter regions there was a growing tendency to risk safety for comfort, and from about 1250, fortified manor houses were in process of becoming a popular alternative to full-scale castles.

Stokesay Castle, Shropshire (c. 1285–1305) (p. 442) is an instance. It has an essentially domestic plan, of a kind rapidly becoming typical, and only the modest protection afforded by a crenellated polygonal tower, moat, curtain wall and gateway (the latter rebuilt c. 1620–5). The northern tower, erected in the early thirteenth century, has a jettied, half-timber third storey of the 1285–1305 period.

Decorated period. During the fourteenth century, the great gateway remained a chief feature of castles, though becoming more domestic and less military in purpose as time passed; increasingly, its accommodation was associated with that of other domestic and ancillary buildings ranged round the castle walls. By mid-century, the great day of mediaeval strongholds may be said to have passed, and by its end, the typical castle of central and southern England was a rectangle of buildings arranged around a court, the surviving military function being recognized by thickened outer walls, towers at the angles and sometimes at the centre of each side too, except where the gatehouse lay. Around the whole was usually the moat.

Bodiam Castle, Sussex (1386) (p. 439B), though built for coastal defence, is on this plan, while **Maxstoke, Warwickshire** (1346), a defended manor, is similar except in its thin, low walls and the fact that its domestic buildings line only a portion of the circuit. Even in the more unsettled parts of the country, castles were of similar, courtyard type—the windows looking inward—but more formidably strong, high and compact; as **Bolton, Yorkshire** (c. 1380) (p. 441E), another fortified manor, with five-storey angle towers.

Kenilworth Castle, Warwickshire (p. 442), particularly interesting in representing many periods of construction, was brought approximately to the courtyard form in this century by buildings erected (1392) by John of Gaunt, which included a magnificent banqueting-hall, with dais, screens, kitchen and other offices. The Norman keep (1160–80) formed part of the circuit, and between 1200–60, a large outer bailey had been added, with various towers on its walls, the moat reconstructed and a large lake formed to protect the whole. This concentric castle had withstood a stern siege in 1266. Subsequently, Henry VIII made his contribution to the buildings, and during the reign of Elizabeth the Earl of Leicester built the great northern gatehouse and erected the portion known as Leicester's buildings in 1571.

Raby Castle, Durham, a manor for which a licence to crenellate was received in 1378, has a fine vaulted kitchen, which as was quite usual in mediaeval great dwellings stood detached as a precaution against fire.

Perpendicular period. During the fifteenth century, such few further great castles as were constructed still more insistently followed the rectangular plan, the precursor of the wholly residential Tudor mansion. **Herstmonceux, Sussex** (1441), although built for coastal defence, is no exception. It is a spectacular, moated structure of red brick with stone dressings, with a charming gatehouse bearing quite unmilitary windows. Due to the development of fire artillery, defences on the old lines were obsolescent; gun ports now supplemented arrow slits. Fortified manors, sufficient against local disorders, were far more frequent than castles.

Raglan 'Castle', Monmouthshire (c. 1430–69) is an exceptionally elaborate instance of a fortified manor, as it occupied a strategic location. Its apartments are arranged informally around twin courtyards, the hall, with its attendant private and service rooms, dividing the courts. Nearby is a massive, moated tower, linked to the private apartments by a light bridge. Others among the many fortified manors are **Wingfield, Derbyshire** (1441–55) and **Ashby-de-la-Zouch, Leicestershire,** (1474). In the north of England, where conditions were for long unsettled, 'tower-houses' and their smaller versions, the 'pele-towers', were the appropriate response.

Warkworth Castle, Northumberland (p. 445), has a remarkable tower-house keep built at this time (*c*. 1400) upon an old Norman motte. The plan is rectangular, with a cruciform internal subdivision which occasions bold projections on each of the four sides. Spacious apartments are arranged around a small central air-shaft or 'lantern', the entrance and stores being on the ground floor, the hall and ancillary rooms and the chapel on the first floor, and the chambers on the second. The hall is 41 ft long, 25 ft wide and rises through two floors. Buildings of many periods (twelfth–sixteenth century) lay in the shovel-shaped bailey to the south of the tower; these already included splendid domestic accommodation, of which the very full suite in the tower was a duplication. The church in the bailey, commenced in the fifteenth century, apparently was never completed.

Tattershall, Lincolnshire (1436–46) (pp. 440C, 445), a five-storey tower-house about 112 ft high, built of excellent brickwork, is rectangular in plan, with angle turrets. Its commodious apartments are compressed into a solid block reminiscent of the old keeps. It stands on the edge of a moated inner bailey of a thirteenth-century castle.

Tudor period. Castle building now was drawing to a close, and some of the older structures already falling into ruin. There were few new constructions of first rank, save for a fine series of artillery forts along the south coast, numbering about twenty, built after 1540, in the time of Henry VIII. These, however, were purely military, not also dwellings. **Deal,** (p. 441F) and **Walmer,** both in Kent, are examples. Occasional fortified manors were built in the south, such as **Thornbury, Gloucestershire** (1511–21); and in the north a number of tower-houses and many pele-towers, the latter well-suited to provide havens in sudden border forays. Yet even these steadily acquired accretions at their bases, for pleasanter living.

MANOR HOUSES

One of the earliest types of dwelling in England was the aisled hall, known well before Roman times. Originally the chief form of tribal building, its social status declined temporarily in the Romano-British period, when it might be used in relation to a villa as servants' quarters, as an outbuilding or barn. In Anglo-Saxon times it could be on the one hand a palace or mansion or on the other a husbandman's steading, accommodating corn and fodder in the 'nave', oxen and horses in the 'aisles' and living quarters in the end opposite the entrance. In the Norman period the aisled timber building definitely emerged as a manorial type of residential hall, in each case forming almost the sole accommodation for living, eating and sleeping, privacy not being considered important. Supplementary accommodation, for cooking, stabling and the like was separate and relatively lightly built. The manor was a Norman feudal institution serving for local rural governance, and carrying rights over an extent of land and its tenants. Though the manor house was non-military in purpose, it for long needed defences against forays, disturbances and robbers, and thus was often moated and lightly protected. As time elapsed, standards of convenience and comfort developed, and certain of the original functions of the common hall were dispersed to separate rooms, so that the hall became less important, and building plans more elaborate. Norman castle building led to the use of a second type of manor house, placed on a first floor and thus usually in stone; eventually it merged with the first, during and after the late

WARKWORTH CASTLE : NORTHUMBERLAND

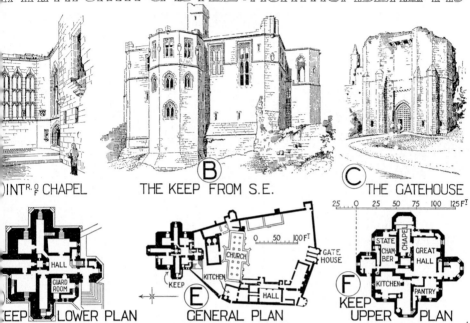

INT^{R.} ^OF CHAPEL   **B** THE KEEP FROM S.E.   **C** THE GATEHOUSE

25 0 25 50 75 100 125 F^T

HALL

GUARD ROOM

KEEP LOWER PLAN   CHURCH KITCHEN KEEP HALL GATE HOUSE

0 50 100 F^T

E GENERAL PLAN

STATE CHAMBER CHAPEL GREAT HALL KITCHEN PANTRY

F KEEP UPPER PLAN

TATTERSHALL CASTLE : LINCS.

HALL CHIMNEY-PIECE   **J** CHIMNEY-PIECE: SECOND FLOOR

AUDIENCE CHAMBER ON FIRST FLOOR

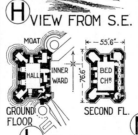

H VIEW FROM S.E.

MOAT

HALL INNER WARD

GROUND FLOOR

55'6"

76'6"

BED CHR

SECOND FL.

L PLANS

M WINDOW-RECESS IN HALL

N VAULTED CORRIDOR

MEDIÆVAL MANOR HOUSES

HOUSE AT CHRISTCHURCH (NORMAN)

Ⓐ

S. MARY'S GUILD, LINCOLN (NORMAN)

Ⓑ

BOOTHBY PAGNELL (NORMAN)

Ⓒ

CHARNEY-BASSET : BERKS (EARLY ENGLISH)

Ⓔ THE SOLAR

Ⓓ VIEW FROM S.E.

CHAPEL OVER

HALL

SOLAR OVER

Ⓕ GROUND PLAN

Ⓖ THE CHAPEL

LITTLE WENHAM HALL : SUFFOLK (EARLY ENGLISH)

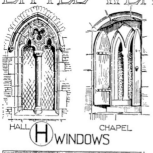

HALL   CHAPEL

Ⓗ WINDOWS

Ⓙ VIEW FROM N.W.

Ⓚ THE HALL

Ⓛ ENTRANCE & CHAPEL

CHAPEL

HALL

ENTRANCE

Ⓜ FIRST FL. PLAN

Ⓝ CHAPEL & TOWER STAIRS

thirteenth century. Because of the building material, this class has tended to survive more often than the timber ground-floor type. It is also to be noted that there were important differences in methods of structure—particularly of timber roofs —between south-eastern and north-western England, the dividing line being approximately the oolitic limestone belt (see inset map, p. 379), where hybrid types developed, as also in general in the Midlands.

Norman period. Such few examples as remain are mostly in the south-east. They have suffered variously drastic modifications. In the majority, stone-built, the domestic accommodation is raised on a first floor, over an 'undercroft' or storage 'cellar', this type probably reflecting contemporary castle-keep arrangements. **Boothby Pagnell, Lincs.** (p. 446C), **S. Mary's Guild, Lincoln** (p. 446B) and the **Norman House, Christchurch, Hants.** (p. 446A), are instances. On the first floor there might be little more than the one room, the hall, or additionally a smaller private chamber or 'solar', at the opposite end to the entrance. Cooking was probably done outdoors, and supplementary accommodation provided in frail shelters elsewhere in the enclosure. The second type, often wholly in timber, was a 'nave-and-aisles' single-storey structure, like a very simple church, all ancillary needs being provided for separately, as before. Roofs in general were of the 'trussed-rafter' kind typical in the south-east, lacking a ridge-piece; in the north-west, there normally were principals spaced down the length of the building, carrying purlins and a heavy ridge.

Early English. In the thirteenth century it was still necessary to retain some defensive character, and many licences to 'crenellate' or fortify manor houses were granted by Henry III. Most of the known examples, numbering about thirty-six, are again in the south-east or in central England, the ground-floor type of hall now being the more frequent and plainly gaining in favour. Plans varied quite a little, and had not yet settled down to what was to be the orthodox disposition in the later Middle Ages. Houses with the first floor hall might yet have only the single upper room, be sub-divided to provide a solar, or have the solar as a conjoined room whether on the same axis or placed crosswise; sometimes a chapel is the sole adjunct or there is a latrine chamber too. There are other variants; but the most significant development is the alliance of the two-storey block with a ground-floor hall of stone or timber, in which case the upper room becomes a solar, and its undercroft provides 'service' rooms (for food preparation and storage and domestic utensils) to the great common hall. The more pretentious, though not all, of the ground floor halls remained aisled, and in some cases one end was partitioned to form a service room or rooms, with perhaps a solar above them, reached by stairs from the hall or externally, the whole being under one roof. Thus the two types of manor-house plan tended to merge. Kitchens normally were separate, outdoors at the inferior or 'lower' end of the hall. Late in the century, as illustrated again at Stokesay (p. 442E), by the 1285–1305 additions, there was a new and important move towards establishing the solar at the superior or 'upper' end of the hall, raised over a storage basement or 'cellar', leaving the service rooms at the lower end intact, along with what then became an extra private or sleeping chamber over. This scheme, double tier at either end of the hall, the whole under one roof, became very popular for the smaller mansions in the south-east after the middle of the next century. As in the Norman period, ground floor halls had a central hearth for an open fire or brazier—actually slightly nearer the upper end—the smoke escaping by a louvre in the roof timbers above, or through small gablets at the two ends of the roof apex in the case of hipped roofs. In the case of the two-floored manor houses, wall fireplaces had been in use since late Norman times (as at Boothby Pagnell, see above); when they are not present, braziers would have served. Windows, often transomed, grew larger, and there was some use of glass, though wooden shutters still were normal. Main floors were of stone or tiles, upper floors of wood (or stone, if over vaults), inferior apartments of rammed earth.

Little Wenham Hall, Suffolk (*c.* 1270–80) (pp. 380, 446), the best-preserved manor-house of the period, is of brick, with stone and flint dressings. The plan (p. 446M) is L-shaped, comprising a small chapel adjoining a first-floor hall, both standing over stone-floored storage undercrofts having quadripartite brick vaults carried on stone ribs. The hall has fine, two-light foliated 'sitting-windows' on each wall (p. 446H, K); its tiled floor and chestnut beamed ceiling are sixteenth century. The entrance to the vaulted chapel is flanked by traceried openings (p. 446L), and from it opens a turret-stair in the re-entrant angle (p. 446N) leading down to the undercrofts and up to a room over the chapel which was probably a solar.

Charney Basset Manor House, Berkshire (*c.* 1280) (p. 446), can only be definitely ascribed to the thirteenth century as regards the two-storey south wing, but it is clear that this has always been a solar block, originally built in relation to a ground-floor hall, perhaps aisled, occupying a position similar to that shown on the plan (p. 446F). Such a combination of hall and first floor solar represents an important development. The undercroft to the solar probably afforded the service accommodation to the hall; the kitchen, however, would be external, reached by a passage running across the nearer part of the hall. Solar and chapel are timber floored; the roof timbers of the chapel (p. 446G) are not original; those over the solar (p. 455C) are genuine, and interesting in that they demonstrate the fundaments of south-eastern roof structure. There is no true principal; a cambered tie-beam supports a 'crown-post' (or 'king-post'—the first term is preferable for the type) which, with the aid of struts, carries a 'collar-purlin' running longitudinally to stiffen the ridgeless pairs of trussed rafters. The system is quite different from that at Stokesay Hall (p. 442B), which shows a north-western method by which arch-braced principals carry a ridge and side purlins on their backs.

Other examples are **Little Chesterford, Essex** (*c.* 1225), a stone, two-floor solar block, crosswise to an aisled, ground floor timber hall; and **Warnford, Hampshire** ('King John's House') (early thirteenth century), a flint-walled ground-floor hall, with columned aisles, from which one end is divided by a wall to form a service room.

Decorated period. The larger manor houses of the fourteenth century were generally castellated, and the greatest assumed a quadrangular plan, as did the castles of the period (p. 443), and had a central courtyard entered through a gate-house, protected by a portcullis and drawbridge over a moat around the whole group of buildings. The typical manor was smaller, and much more compact, nevertheless normally standing in its walled or moated enclosure. In all, however, the essentials were much the same, for a common type had now been established, centred on a ground-floor hall, and only the lesser manor houses maintained the former immature types of disposition. Typically, a porched entrance led to a passage which crossed the lower end of the hall to a second doorway in the opposite wall, the passage being separated from the hall by a screen with two doors or openings, while on its other side there were three doors into the service rooms. The term 'screens' is applied to the whole of this passage, which sometimes was ceiled, and allowed a minstrels' gallery above. Such galleries, popular from the fifteenth century, were often added to older buildings. The screens originated in projecting timber spurs or 'speres', giving protection against draughts from the doors; they were often connected to a roof principal which defined the passage, and which consequently is known as the 'spere-truss'. The hall was the whole height of the house, and at its further end was a shallow platform or dais, a feature which had

PENSHURST PLACE, KENT.

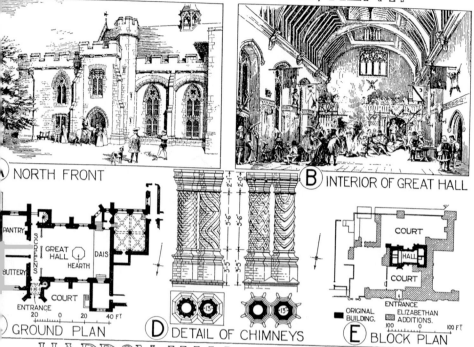

A NORTH FRONT

B INTERIOR OF GREAT HALL

C GROUND PLAN

PANTRY / SCREENS / GREAT HALL / DAIS / HEARTH / BUTTERY / COURT / ENTRANCE
20 0 20 40 FT

D DETAIL OF CHIMNEYS

E BLOCK PLAN

COURT / HALL / COURT / ENTRANCE
ORIGINAL BUILDING. ELIZABETHAN ADDITIONS.
100 0 100 FT

HADDON HALL, DERBYSHIRE.

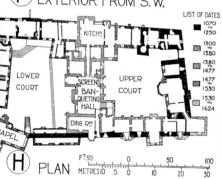

F EXTERIOR FROM S.W.

G INTERIOR OF CHAPEL

H PLAN

KITCHN / LOWER COURT / SCREENS / BAN-QUETING HALL / UPPER COURT / DINING RM / CHAPEL

LIST OF DATES
1070 TO 1250
1300 TO 1380
1380 TO 1477
1477 TO 1530
1530 TO 1624

FT 50   0   50   100
METRES 10 5 0   10   20   30

J BANQUETING HALL

P

GREAT CHALFIELD: WILTSHIRE

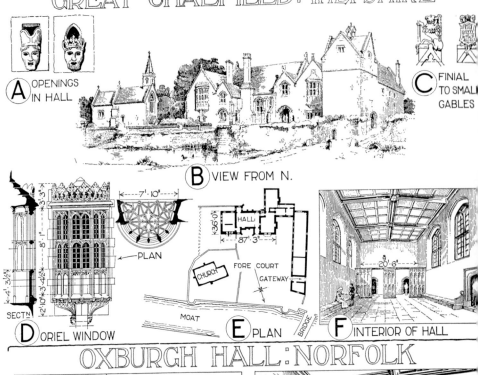

A OPENINGS IN HALL

B VIEW FROM N.

C FINIAL TO SMALL GABLES

D ORIEL WINDOW

E PLAN

F INTERIOR OF HALL

OXBURGH HALL: NORFOLK

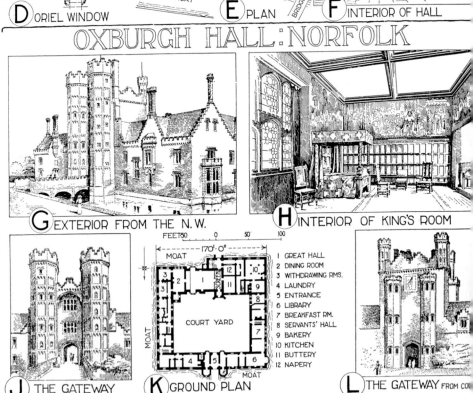

G EXTERIOR FROM THE N.W.

H INTERIOR OF KING'S ROOM

J THE GATEWAY WITH BRIDGE ACROSS MOAT

K GROUND PLAN

1 GREAT HALL
2 DINING ROOM
3 WITHDRAWING RMS.
4 LAUNDRY
5 ENTRANCE
6 LIBRARY
7 BREAKFAST RM.
8 SERVANTS' HALL
9 BAKERY
10 KITCHEN
11 BUTTERY
12 NAPERY

L THE GATEWAY FROM COURT

made its appearance in earlier times. The solar block now regularly stood at the upper end of the hall, but the solar itself now became known as the withdrawing-room; from its still usual position on the upper floor, a spyhole could allow the master to survey the hall below (p. 450A, F). In important houses, a lady's bower and additional rooms indicate an increased desire for privacy, and a chapel in this wing would have a gallery for the master and his family, while the retainers were below. The hall, which attained its greatest development in this century, was still a sleeping room for the retainers and had its floor strewn with rushes and its walls hung with tapestries and trophies of the chase. Glazed windows were as yet rare. Though wall fireplaces with hooded canopies were increasingly common, the hall sometimes still had a central hearth for an open fire or brazier burning turf, wood or charcoal, and a smoke louvre in the roof, as at **Penshurst** (p. 449) (1341–8). In this great hall the Lord of the Manor held his court and administered justice, and here too, on the dais, the family dined at the high table, while at long tables in the body of the hall his vassals took their meals. The dais sometimes had a lofty bay window which gave additional dignity to this part of the hall. Of the three doorways in the 'screens' on the side away from the hall, the central one led by a passage to the kitchen, still often detached from the main building, in case of fire, and in such case connected by a covered way. Another door gave on to the buttery (Fr. *bouteille* = bottle, from which the word butler, i.e. bottler, is derived) and the third on to the pantry (Fr. *pain* = bread), where butter, cheese, and bread, as well as platters and salt-cellars, were kept. In a large house, the larder (*lardarium*), in which the meats were larded or preserved, was an important adjunct and formed a store room.

Other examples are **Ightham Mote, Kent,** (p. 453B); **Baguley, Cheshire; Smithills, near Bolton, Lancs;** and **Sutton Courtenay, Berks,** which illustrates a type of development of the south-eastern trussed-rafter roof (p. 500C), having an arch-braced part principal. Other south-eastern experiments with roof principals led to the hammer-beam roof (p. 434), of which that of the **Hall of Westminster Palace** (1397–9) (pp. 437, 500) rivals in magnificence any ecclesiastical work of the kind.

Perpendicular period. In spite of the Wars of the Roses, the fifteenth century witnessed an improvement in social conditions and commercial prosperity. This was duly reflected in the architecture of manor houses by further provision for domestic comfort. The hall, with fine bay-window, canopied fireplace, and open timber roof, continued to be the principal feature; furniture was still scanty, trestle tables were in use, and the floor was only covered with rushes or matting. The withdrawing-room and lady's bower were now used only as sitting-rooms, while bedrooms increased in number, and the hall ceased to be the general dormitory. The kitchens at Stanton Harcourt, Oxon., and New College, Oxford, show the importance frequently given to this department, to which, besides buttery, pantry, and larder, were now added a scullery, bakehouse, brewhouse, and dairy, while corn mills, granaries, and stables became more numerous. **East Barsham Manor House, Norfolk** (*c.* 1500–15), with a fine detached gatehouse, has turrets and ornate chimneys showing the early use of brick in England.

Great Chalfield Manor House, Wilts. (*c.* 1450) (p. 450), is a singularly picturesque example, though much restored. It is almost surrounded by a moat and forms part of a group of church, house, and stables, approached across the bridge and under the gateway which leads into the forecourt. It had no fortifications, as it stood in the peaceful county of Wiltshire. The groined two-storeyed porch leads through the screens to a typical hall (about 36 ft by 20 ft 6 in and 20 ft high) with bay-window and panelled ceiling of wood and plaster (p. 450F). There are also curious masked openings (p. 450A, B) through which those in the upper chambers at either end could look down into the hall; and west of the screens are the kitchen and offices. The façade has two oriel windows (p. 450B, D), and gables with fine carved finials (p. 450C). This delightful group, somewhat resembling that at South Wraxall (p. 456C), is typical of the homeliness of English manor houses.

Oxburgh Hall, Norfolk (1482) (p. 450), is a fine specimen of brickwork, but it has been partly restored. The plan is quadrangular, with buildings round a court surrounded by a moat. The magnificent brick gatehouse is flanked by towers, seven storeys high, and is reached across a bridge which spans the moat, and leads to a courtyard and on to the great hall through the usual screens (destroyed 1778). The King's Room (p. 450H) in the gateway tower is said to have been occupied by Henry VII in 1487.

Haddon Hall, Derbyshire (p. 449), nestling on a hill-side amidst pastoral scenery, is famous both from historical associations and architectural interest. Dating from the Norman period onwards, its plan (p. 449H) somewhat resembles an Oxford or Cambridge college (p. 476), for the banqueting-hall, of the fourteenth century, is between the two courts, while the long gallery, south of the upper court, is Elizabethan (p. 881). The stepped entrance in the north-west angle is in an unusual position, with no driving way, and reminds us that in the Mediaeval period riding on horseback was a usual mode of travelling, but a carriage entrance leads into the upper court. The banqueting-hall, with its fine windows, great fireplace, and open timber roof, together with the long gallery (pp. 882, 884A) and the severe and simple chapel, give one a good idea of this stately, semi-fortified manor house amid its balustraded terraces and raised gardens.

Hever Castle, Kent (rebuilt 1462) (p. 454A), with moat and drawbridge, and **South Wraxall Manor House, Wiltshire** (1440) (p. 456C), show the change from the fortified type to the later dwelling-house. **Rufford Hall, Lancs.** (fifteenth century), of which little survives except the wonderfully fine hall, is a rare instance in which a movable screen, shielding the approach to kitchen, still survives (p. 457A), and at its upper end has a canopied tester (p. 457B) which lent extra dignity to the high table. **The Bishop's Palace, Wells,** though a semi-ecclesiastical building, has a fortified wall with gatehouse and moat, while the old **Archbishop's Palace, Croydon,** still retains its fine timber roof. **Cothay Manor House, Somerset** (1480) (p. 454C), is a gem of the period.

Tudor period. Manor houses of the first half of the sixteenth century were principally erected by new and wealthy trading families, who were taking the place of the old nobility, while the suppression of monasteries by Henry VIII provided him with both money and lands with which to enrich his favourites, who vied with one another in the building of fine houses. The Tudor house, with its increased number and variety of rooms, was usually still built round a quadrangular court from which many rooms were entered direct. Under the changed conditions such features as battlemented parapets and fortified gateways were retained for ornament rather than defence, while the addition of numerous ornamented chimneys is evidence of the increased comfort within (p. 458A). The entrance to the quadrangle was under a gatehouse, opposite which on the other side of the court was the porch leading to the 'screens' of the great hall, which now definitely declined in importance, owing to the addition of other rooms, and also to the reduction by legal enactments of military retainers. The hall, however, still remained a feature on which much artistic skill was lavished, and this is seen especially in the richly carved wall fireplace, oak-panelled walls, and timber roof, while the furniture, which became more plentiful, followed, as in previous periods, the architectural style (p. 519D, E, F, M). We now first hear of such additional rooms as the study, summer and winter parlours, and private dining-rooms; while bedrooms, though often only 'thoroughfare'

A. Ightham Mote, Kent: hall (14th century). From a 19th century lithograph by Joseph Nash. See p. 451

B. Ightham Mote: chapel (c. 1520–7). See pp. 451, 469

A. Hever Castle, Kent (rebuilt 1462). See p. 452

B. Hengrave Hall, Suffolk (1538). See p. 459

C. Cothay Manor House, Somerset (1480). See p. 452

A. Athelhampton Hall, Dorset (c. 1485–1509): the courtyard. From a 19th century lithograph by Joseph Nash. See p. 459

B. Compton Wynyates: hall with screens and minstrels' gallery (1520). See p. 459

C. Charney Bassett Manor House, Berks (c. 1280): the solar. See p. 448

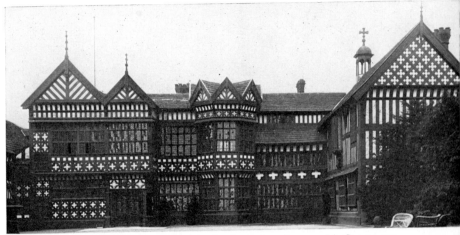

A. Bramhall Hall, Cheshire (15th cent. and onwards). See p. 459

B. Speke Hall, Lancs: garden front (15th and 16th cents.). See p. 459

C. South Wraxall Manor House, Wilts: S.W. front (1440). See p. 452

A. Lower end, with movable screen   B. Upper end, with canopied tester

Rufford Hall, Lancs: interior (15th cent.). See p. 452

C. Sutton Place, Guildford: entrance to hall (1523). See p. 463

COMPTON WYNYATES
WARWICKSHIRE

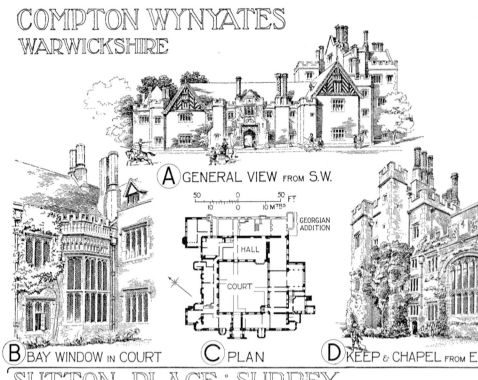

(A) GENERAL VIEW FROM S.W.

(B) BAY WINDOW IN COURT   (C) PLAN   (D) KEEP & CHAPEL FROM E.

HALL

COURT

GEORGIAN ADDITION

SUTTON PLACE : SURREY

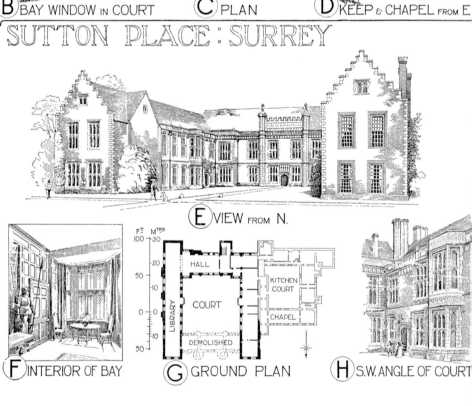

(E) VIEW FROM N.

(F) INTERIOR OF BAY   (G) GROUND PLAN   (H) S.W. ANGLE OF COURT

HALL

LIBRARY

COURT

KITCHEN COURT

CHAPEL

DEMOLISHED

rooms, were increased. **Hengrave Hall, Suffolk** (1538) (p. 454B), had no fewer than forty bedrooms, and an inventory includes, besides kitchen offices, pastry-room, laundry, linen-room, and still-rooms, in addition to those of the previous period. Gardens were now laid out on definite architectural plans to form fitting frames for the houses, with paved alleys, yew hedges, stone steps, and balustraded terraces.

Athelhampton Hall, Dorset (p. 455A), is a very fine Tudor structure, dating from the reign of Henry VII, and its notable features are the gatehouse (with oriel window), since destroyed, the beautiful octagonal bay-window of the hall, and the projecting porch, with its pointed archway. The hall, which measures about 38 ft by 22 ft, is of the usual type, with bay-window, panelled walls, and open timber roof.

Bramhall Hall, Cheshire (p. 456A), dating from the fifteenth century and later, is one of the many half-timber houses of Cheshire. Its bay-window is characteristic, but the hall (36 ft by 26 ft) is somewhat peculiar in being only 12 ft high. It has some beautiful leaded glass, but the pendant plaster ceiling no longer exists.

Speke Hall, Lancashire (p. 456B), is one of the best-preserved half-timber houses so characteristic of this part of England, and owes its charm to the disposition of the timbers, the quatrefoil filling, and the carved barge-boards and finials, which are in marked contrast to the style of brick and stone buildings.

Compton Wynyates, Warwickshire (1520) (pp. 455B, 458), one of the finest of Tudor mansions, was completed by Sir William Compton, a London merchant and favourite of Henry VIII. The entrance, under a low square battlemented tower, has a four-centred archway, surmounted by a three-light mullioned window. Opposite the entrance, on the other side of the court, are the screens, with the minstrels' gallery over (p. 455B), and these give access to the buttery and kitchens, and to the hall with its bay-window (p. 458B). South of the court are the drawing-room and chapel, while numerous turret stairs communicate with upper rooms. East of the hall are the eighteenth-century additions. The exterior shows a charming mingling of red brick, stone, and half-timber work, to which time has given beautiful and varied tints.

Hampton Court Palace (pp. 460, 461E, 923A) is one of the most remarkable domestic buildings in this country, and much of it (p. 460G) remains as built from *c.* 1520 for Cardinal Wolsey (1472–1530) from the designs of the chief mason, Henry Redman. Fitted with gorgeous furniture and tapestries, the palace seems to have excited so much royal envy that in 1526 the Cardinal made it over to Henry VIII, who between 1531–6 added north and south wings to the west front and the Great Hall and the Chapel, the designer then being John Molton, royal mason and successor of Redman at Hampton Court, who died in 1528. The eastern portion however, was pulled down by Sir Christopher Wren and rebuilt in the Renaissance style (pp. 914, 923). The palace has a delightful position on Thames-side (p. 460H), with the grand avenue through Bushey Park intended by Wren as an approach to the Great Hall, while on the east are the radiating avenues and Long Water. The original part of the palace is of mellow red brickwork, in diaper pattern, with battlemented parapets. The smaller courts and the Tudor chimneys (p. 460C) well exemplify the beauty of brick architecture in the time of Wolsey. Its ancient walls are invested with the glamour of kings and queens, poets and scholars, courtiers and ecclesiastics; they testify to the vanished pomp and glory of bygone ages. Entering by the Trophy Gates on the west, we pass through an outer court on to the bridge, over the ancient moat which surrounded the palace, and on through the great gatehouse (p. 378), with angle turrets, oriel window, and terra-cotta medallions of Roman emperors obtained by Wolsey from the sculptor Majano (p. 380). Underneath

HAMPTON COURT PALACE

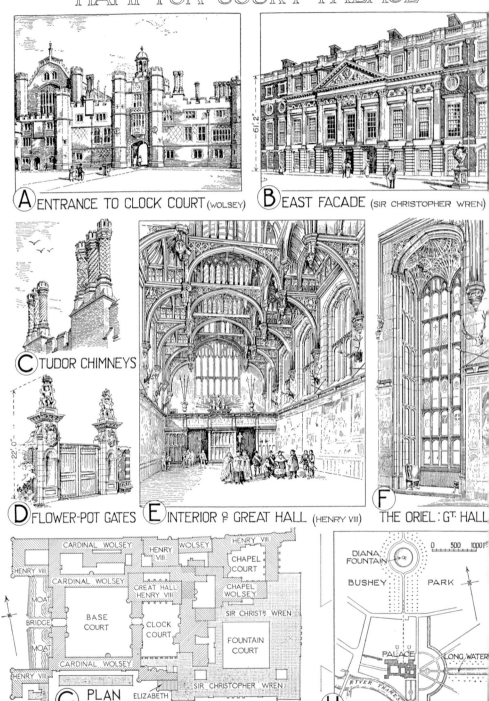

A ENTRANCE TO CLOCK COURT (WOLSEY)

B EAST FACADE (SIR CHRISTOPHER WREN)

C TUDOR CHIMNEYS

D FLOWER-POT GATES

E INTERIOR OF GREAT HALL (HENRY VIII)

F THE ORIEL: G^T. HALL

G PLAN

H KEY PLAN {SHOWING WREN'S PROPOSED LAY-OUT

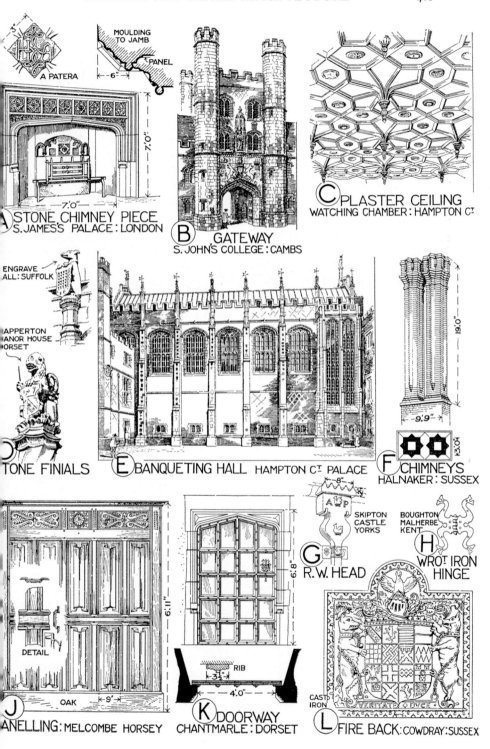

A PATERA

MOULDING TO JAMB
PANEL
6"

7'.0"

7'.0"

A STONE CHIMNEY PIECE
S. JAMES'S PALACE : LONDON

B GATEWAY
S. JOHN'S COLLEGE : CAMBS

C PLASTER CEILING
WATCHING CHAMBER : HAMPTON C.T

ENGRAVE
ALL : SUFFOLK

APPERTON
MANOR HOUSE
DORSET

STONE FINIALS

E BANQUETING HALL HAMPTON C.T PALACE

19'.0"

9'.9"

13'.0"

F CHIMNEYS
HALNAKER : SUSSEX

DETAIL

OAK 9'

6'.11"

J PANELLING : MELCOMBE HORSEY

6'.8"

RIB
3'
4'.0"

K DOORWAY
CHANTMARLE : DORSET

8"
A P
SKIPTON
CASTLE
YORKS

G R. W. HEAD

BOUGHTON
MALHERBE
KENT

H WROT IRON
HINGE

CAST
IRON

VERITATE DVCE

L FIRE BACK : COWDRAY : SUSSEX

A. Layer Marney Towers, Essex: entrance tower (*c.* 1520). See p. 463

B. S. James's Palace: Tudor gateway. See p. 394

C. Little Moreton Hall, Cheshire: courtyard (1550–9). See p. 463

the gateway to the Clock Court (p. 460A) steps lead to the Great Hall of Henry VIII (106 ft by 40 ft, and 60 ft high) (p. 460E), entered as usual through screens. Its walls are hung with tapestry, and the hammer-beam roof, by James Nedeham, is one of the richest of its type. This hall still retains its dais, and an oriel window (p. 460F) which forms a great feature of the exterior of the hall seen from the Clock Court (p. 461E), so called from a curious astronomical clock over one of its gateways. To the east of the Great Hall is the so-called Watching Chamber, with its plaster ceiling (p. 461C), and still farther east is the Tudor chapel with linen-fold panelling, Renaissance altar-piece, and coloured pendant roof. The famous Fountain Court, surrounded by cloisters, and the Ionic colonnade (1690) in the Clock Court are striking and restrained examples of the art of Sir Christopher Wren, and near the latter a grand staircase leads to the state rooms (now the picture galleries) in the east façade (p. 460B). On the south of the palace, extending to the river, are the Privy Garden, with its handsome iron gates by Tijou, and the Pond Garden, and to the north is the wilderness and Flower Pot Gates (p. 460D). Since the time of George II, Hampton Court has ceased to be a royal residence, but comprises suites of rooms for fortunate pensioners of the Crown.

Sutton Place, Guildford (1523–5) (pp. 457C, 458), was built by Sir Richard Weston, a trusted counsellor of Henry VIII. The plan was quadrangular, formerly entered through a central gateway which has been demolished. The entrance to the great hall, placed centrally on the axis of the former gateway, is an early instance of a desire for symmetry as opposed to convenience, and is flanked by bay windows in the corner of the façade. The terra-cotta work shows the influence of Italian Renaissance, as in the delicate flowering in the hollows of the mullions (p. 457B).

Other typical examples are **Layer Marney Towers, Essex** (c. 1500–25) (pp. 380, 462A), **Horham Hall, Essex** (1502–20), **Barrington Court, Somerset** (1514–48), and **Little Moreton Hall, Cheshire** (1550–9) (p. 462C), with its long gallery, 75 ft by 12 ft 6 in, sometimes regarded as an early Renaissance building.

Elizabethan mansions of the latter half of the sixteenth century, though incorporating new features, are based on Tudor models (pp. 868, 881).

SMALLER HOMES

The feudal system provided quarters for vassals and retainers within the castle walls, and in a similar manner monastic communities lodged their dependents and labourers in various conventual buildings, and both these great mediaeval institutions not only housed their dependents, but also protected them against marauders and outlaws. As population increased and conditions changed, more accommodation was required, and, nestling close under the protecting walls of the castles, primitive dwellings were erected to meet the simple requirements of an unexacting age, and as commerce expanded these tenements increased in number and were formed into thriving trading towns. Townships also grew up round the wealthy monasteries which formed refuges in case of danger, and these rising communities waxed strong enough to enter into conflict with the monastic authorities under whose protection they had developed. In some of these new towns the interests of the feudal lord conflicted with those of the mitred abbot, and this resulted in divided allegiance, as in Rochester, which is an instance of a town which grew up under both castle and monastery. The origin of these towns, with their consequent lack of municipal freedom, is accountable for the absence of town halls which are such characteristic buildings of the period in the free towns of Belgium, Italy and Germany. A typical house of the town tradesman consisted of a shop with arched openings on to the street, closed at night with hinged wooden shutters; there he plied his craft or sold his wares, and above were his sleeping-rooms. The character of the buildings

THE SMALLER HOMES

Ⓐ THE JEWS' HOUSE: LINCOLN

Ⓑ CHIDDINGSTONE: KENT

Ⓒ TONBRIDGE

Ⓕ BUTCHERS' ROW: SHREWSBURY

Ⓓ COGGESHALL: ESSE

Ⓖ BLETCHINGLEY: SURR

Ⓔ FINCHINGFIELD: ESSEX

Ⓗ COLSTON'S HOUSE: BRISTOL: GLOS.

Ⓙ THE MIDDLE HOUSE: MAYFIELD: SUSS

A. Farm at Abbey Dore, Herefordshire (14th cent. and later). See p. 469

B. Farm at Bishop's Frome, Herefordshire. See p. 469.
(Timber wing *c.* 1400, centre *c.* 1575, further wing *c.* 1625)

A. House at Colchester, Essex (late 15th century). See p. 469

B. Farm at Maiden Newton, Dorset (16th cent.). See p. 469

A. House and shop at Lavenham, Suffolk (Tudor). See p. 469

B. Small house with crucks, Putley, Herefordshire. See p. 469

C. Small house at Normanton-on-Soar, Nottinghamshire. See p. 469

King's College chapel, Cambridge (1446–1515).
Choir looking W. See p. 398

depended on local conditions and the materials at hand. Thus in stone districts town houses were solid and substantial, and the **Jew's House, Lincoln** (early twelfth century) (p. 464A), is a splendid relic which has come down from Norman times. In the clay lowlands of East Anglia the local brick gives colour and warmth to many a Mediaeval building. In districts where timber was plentiful, half-timber houses were common, and the interesting group of **Tudor Houses, Chiddingstone, Kent** (p. 464B); the **Abbot's House, Butcher's Row, Shrewsbury** (c. 1450) (p. 464F) and a **House at Tonbridge, Kent** (p. 464C), give a good idea of the black and white blending of beam and plaster, while **Colston's House, Bristol** (p. 464H) illustrates another interesting type. There are also many other houses of scarcely less social importance such as the **'Paycocke's', Coggeshall, Essex** (c. 1500) (p. 464D), and those at **Finchingfield, Bletchingley** (p. 464E, G) and **Mayfield** (p. 464J), the latter somewhat after our period (1575).

In the country, besides castles and manor houses of the nobility and gentry, there were the homesteads of small free-holders or yeomen of the Middle Ages, which were based upon the manor-house model, having a centrally-placed hall or 'house-part', usually combining the function of kitchen in later days, flanked at one end by service rooms and at the other by private rooms. A through passage crossed the house at the 'lower' or service end of the hall. Wall fireplaces did not become usual in yeomens' houses until Tudor times, which then gave complete freedom to add an upper floor. Up and down the country there still remain many picturesque Mediaeval smaller houses as at **Abbey Dore** (p. 465A), **Maiden Newton** (p. 466B), **Colchester** (p. 466A), **Bishop's Frome** (p. 465B), **Lavenham** (p. 467A) and **Normanton-on-Soar** (p. 467C), and that with crucks—a form of construction limited to the north-western half of England—at **Putley, Herefordshire** (p. 467B). Such houses were of much greater social importance in their time than would appear to-day. The homes of the peasants were quite primitive and might have only one room.

CHAPELS

Chapels varied in treatment according to the type of building to which they were attached and the special purpose for which they were erected, but a nave, to which aisles were sometimes added, was common to all. Some were attached to royal castles, as **S. John's Chapel** (Tower of London) (p. 436C, D, E); to royal palaces, as **S. Stephen's Chapel, Westminster** (1349–64) (p. 560C); to manor houses, as **Compton Wynyates** (p. 458D) and **Ightham Mote** (p. 453B); to colleges, such as **Merton College, Oxford** (1274) (p. 482B), **King's College, Cambridge** (1446–1515) (pp. 468, 470A, 475B), and **S. John's College, Cambridge** (p. 476); to schools, as **Eton College** (pp. 471, 477A); to ecclesiastical palaces, as **Lambeth Palace** (1250); or to bridges, as at **Wakefield** (fourteenth century); while others were designed as royal mortuary chapels, such as **S. George's Chapel, Windsor** (1473–1516) (p. 471) and **Henry VII's Chapel, Westminster** (1503–19) (pp. 424D, 426), or mortuary chapels of noble families, such as the **Beauchamp Chapel, Warwick** (1443–64) (p. 470B), which suggests Henry VII's Chapel. The **Pilgrim's Chapel. Houghton-le-Dale, Norfolk** (1350) (p. 471), is a complete example.

Lady chapels in most of our English cathedrals form a church within a church, as at York, Winchester, Salisbury (p. 410B, C, E), Worcester, Gloucester (p. 411A, C), Exeter, S. Albans, Chichester (p. 412E, F, G), Chester, Lichfield, and Bristol (p. 413F, J, K). The Chapels of the Nine Altars at Durham (p. 411E) and Fountains Abbey (p. 432C), and the Trinity Chapel and 'Becket's Crown', Canterbury (p. 411B), are unusual eastern terminations, due to special circumstances.

Chantry chapels were frequently endowed, previous to the Reformation, for the saying of masses for the souls of the pious founders and their families. These

A. King's College chapel, Cambridge (1446–1515) from S. See p. 469

B. S. Mary, Warwick: Beauchamp chapel, interior looking E. (1443–64). See p. 469

CHAPEL: HOUGHTON-LE-DALE NORFOLK

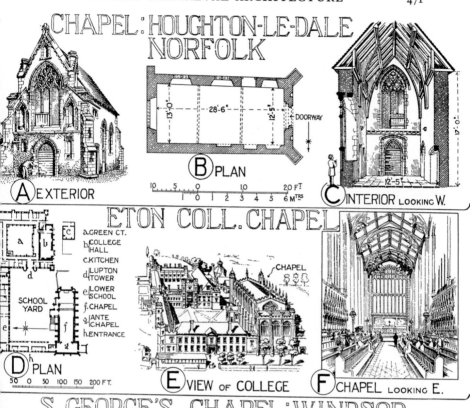

A EXTERIOR

B PLAN

28'-6" 13'-0" 12'-5"

DOORWAY

10 5 0 10 20 FT
0 1 2 3 4 5 6 M™S

C INTERIOR LOOKING W.

17'-0"

12'-5"

ETON COLL. CHAPEL

D PLAN

a. GREEN CT.
b. COLLEGE HALL
c. KITCHEN
d. LUPTON TOWER
e. LOWER SCHOOL
f. CHAPEL
g. ANTE CHAPEL
h. ENTRANCE

SCHOOL YARD

50 0 50 100 150 200 FT.

E VIEW OF COLLEGE

CHAPEL

F CHAPEL LOOKING E.

S. GEORGE'S CHAPEL: WINDSOR

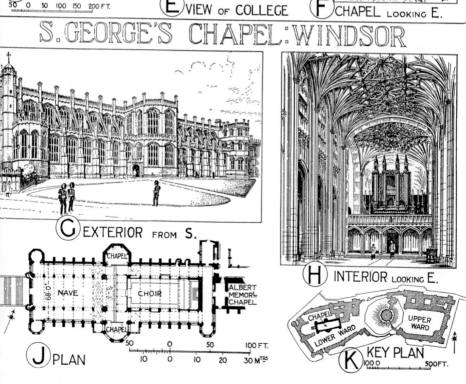

G EXTERIOR FROM S.

H INTERIOR LOOKING E.

J PLAN

CHAPEL
NAVE CHOIR
CHAPEL
ALBERT MEMORL CHAPEL
68'-0"

50 0 50 100 FT.
10 0 10 20 30 M™S

K KEY PLAN

CHAPEL
LOWER WARD
UPPER WARD
100.0 500FT.

CHANTRIES SHRINES & TOMBS

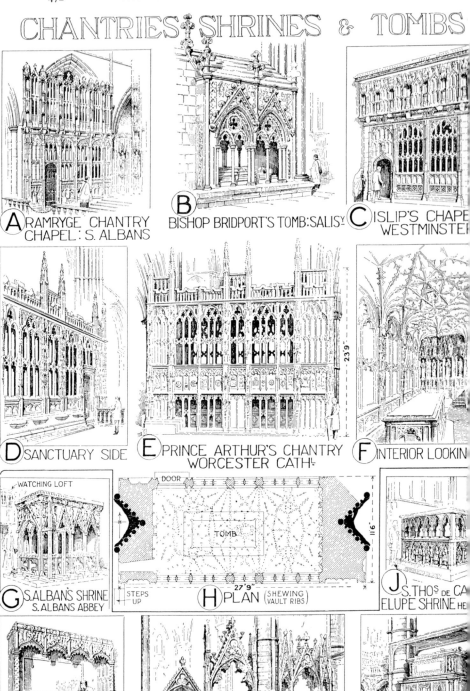

A RAMRYGE CHANTRY CHAPEL: S. ALBANS

B BISHOP BRIDPORT'S TOMB:SALIS.

C ISLIP'S CHAPEL WESTMINSTER

D SANCTUARY SIDE

E PRINCE ARTHUR'S CHANTRY WORCESTER CATHL.

F INTERIOR LOOKING

WATCHING LOFT

G S.ALBAN'S SHRINE S.ALBANS ABBEY

DOOR

TOMB

23'9"

11'6"

STEPS UP

H PLAN (SHEWING VAULT RIBS) 27'9"

J S.THOs DE CA ELUPE SHRINE HE

K CHAUCER'S TOMB WESTMINSTER ABBEY

L TOMBS IN SANCTUARY: WESTMSTR

M HENRY III'S TO WESTMINSTER AB

chapels were most numerous in abbeys and cathedrals where the privilege of burial could only be obtained by some beneficent offering. In English cathedrals, chantry chapels often occupied one or more bays in an aisle, and were enclosed by open screens, or were external additions to the original building, while others were independent structures within the edifice. The **Chantry Chapel, Worcester** (1504) (p. 472D–F, H), erected to Arthur, son of Henry VII, is a remarkably fine internal structure, of which the whole surface is covered, both externally and internally, with tracery, and sculptured; while the roof is a fine specimen of fan vaulting in miniature. This chapel never received the recumbent figure for which it was designed. The **Chantry Chapels, Tewkesbury Abbey,** are famous for their number and richness. Among many others elsewhere are the **Ramryge Chantry Chapel, S. Albans** (c. 1520) (p. 472A), and **Abbot Islip's Chapel, Westminster** (p. 472C); and **Chaucer's Tomb, Westminster** (p. 472K), with its prayer place and fine traceried canopy, seems to be a rudimentary chantry.

Shrines also figured largely in English cathedrals, such as **S. Alban's Shrine, S. Albans** (p. 472G), and the **Shrine of S. Thomas de Cantelupe, Hereford** (p. 472J), but many were destroyed at the Reformation.

COLLEGES

The University of Oxford appears to have been formed by English scholars from the University at Paris, and it dates from about 1167, while that of Cambridge (1209) arose through a migration from Oxford. Colleges were similar in general equipment to monastic establishments, and were based on the plan of the Mediaeval house, with hall and rooms grouped round a quadrangle; so that the colleges of Oxford and Cambridge and the Inns of Court, London, still give a good idea of the arrangement of hall, screens, and dais, with the bay-window and timber roof, of a Mediaeval manor house.

Halls of residence, or colleges, for communities of teachers and students to promote discipline and common interests date from the thirteenth century, and approximate dates of the foundation of some Colleges are appended:

Oxford (p. 475A): University College, 1249; Balliol, 1263; Merton, 1264; Exeter, 1314; Oriel, 1326; Queen's, 1340 (rebuilt 1692–1716) (p. 963); New, 1379; Lincoln, 1427; All Souls', 1438; Magdalen, 1458; Brasenose, 1509; Corpus Christi, 1517; Christ Church, 1546; Trinity, 1555; S. John's, 1555; and Jesus, 1571.

Cambridge (p. 475B): Peterhouse, 1284; Clare, 1326; Pembroke, 1347; Gonville and Caius, 1348; Trinity Hall, 1350; Corpus Christi, 1352; King's, 1441; Queens', 1448; S. Catharine's, 1473; Jesus, 1496; Christ's, 1505; S. John's, 1511; Magdalene, 1542; and Trinity, 1546.

S. John's College, Cambridge (1511) (pp. 461B, 476), may be taken as typical of the plan of Oxford and Cambridge Colleges, though they vary in size and lay-out. The typical entrance gateway bears the arms of the founder, Lady Margaret Beaufort (mother of Henry VII), and a statue of S. John, and, with its four angle turrets, forms a fine outstanding feature of the College, which is of patterned brickwork. To the left, on the upper floor, is the library, with its pointed windows, while to the right is the chapel, since rebuilt by Sir George Gilbert Scott, and forming the north side of the first court. Immediately opposite the entrance are (on the left) the kitchen and butteries, and on the right the hall, with its pointed traceried windows, buttresses, and large bay-windows. The second court, with its time-worn plum-red bricks, and containing the Master's Lodge, was added in 1598, and from this, through a second gateway tower, is reached the third court, on the north side of which is the second library, built in 1623, and on the west side is the Renaissance loggia (1669). The remainder of the buildings round the three courts are students' rooms, while from the third court the 'Bridge of Sighs' (1826) crosses the river to the New Court and college grounds.

SCHOOLS

There were, according to Bede, schools in England in the seventh century, as early as there were churches, but it appears that they were not monastic in origin, though often associated with cathedrals and collegiate churches. The first were probably at Canterbury (598), Dunwich, Rochester, and York (630), where Alcuin (Charlemagne's educational expert), a secular clerk and not a monk, was master in the eighth century, and where later the 'song' school was divided from the original 'grammar' (i.e. for Latin classics) school. Then came the grammar school at Winchester, which, we are told, was attended by one of the sons of King Alfred 'with other boys of gentle birth'. From his time onwards there were many grammar schools attached to cathedrals, churches, hospitals, and guilds. After his conquest of the Danes (897) more schools were founded, as at Bedford, Derby, Stafford, Bridgenorth, and Warwick, and even in 1123 the last appears to have been in continuous existence for 400 years. Even King Canute is credited with establishing schools, as at Bury S. Edmunds, while King Harold founded one at Waltham Cross. These were pre-Conquest schools. After the Conquest the secular schoolmaster or chancellor held a clearly defined position, and we find that in 1138 Henry the Schoolmaster gave teaching licences for the City of London. There were also grammar schools in towns founded by guilds—that at Louth is mentioned in 1276, that at Stratford-on-Avon in 1295, and that at Boston in 1326, and it is recorded that Thomas à Becket attended S. Paul's School in 1127. Further schools followed the increase of colleges at the Universities; and when William of Wykeham founded New College, Oxford, he also started **Winchester College** (1382) (p. 477B) to feed it, and this, the standard type of English public school, was followed by Henry VI when he founded **Eton** (1440–1) (p. 477A). In addition to public grammar schools and monastic schools for novices, a new type of charity schools sprang up in the fourteenth century for choristers, as at Durham, Reading, Coventry, and Westminster (1364), and the present Westminster public school was founded (1560) on the model of other grammar schools, of which there were at least 200 before Edward VI, while there were between 300 and 400 grammar schools, free and open to all classes, in most towns by 1535. During the fourteenth and fifteenth centuries other schools were kept by priests of newly endowed chantries, as at Oswestry (1406), Middleton (1412), Durham (1414), Sevenoaks (1432), City of London (1442), Alnwick (1448), Hull (1482), Chipping Campden (1487), Macclesfield (1502), and S. Paul's (1509). There were also schools of hospitals, as of Ewelme (p. 480), and of S. John's Hospital, Coventry (1545). With the reaction against the secular clergy, some schools had fallen under monastic rule, and these suffered severely at the Dissolution of the Monasteries (1536–40), so that it became necessary to start further schools, as at Sutton Coldfield (1544) and Tonbridge (1553). The Chantries Act (1548), which abolished guilds and chantries, was also disastrous for schools, while 'song' schools too were mostly suppressed as superstitious. Some schools, however, survived; some were re-established by Edward VI, others owed their rise to Reformation influences in his reign, and all these were called 'Free Grammar Schools of King Edward VI', such as Berkhamsted (1549) and Sherborne (1550). Shrewsbury (1551), Bedford (1552), and Christ's Hospital (1553) are conspicuous among many schools that were started after the Reformation.

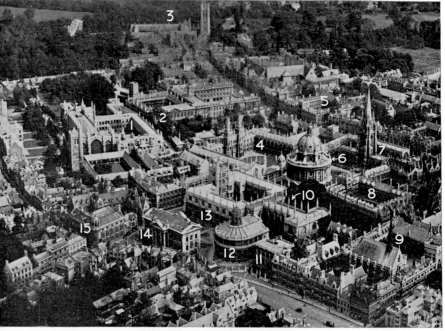

A. Oxford: arieal view from N.W.

1, New College. 2, Queen's College. 3, Magdalen College. 4, All Souls' College. 5, University College. 6, Radcliffe Library. 7, S. Mary. 8, Brasenose College. 9, Exeter College. 10, Divinity School. 11, Old Ashmolean Museum. 12, Sheldonian Theatre. 13, Bodleian Library. 14, Clarendon Building. 15, Indian Institute.

B. Cambridge: aerial view from S.

1, Senate House. 2, S. Mary. 3, King's College. 4, Clare College. 5, Trinity Hall. 6, Trinity College. 7, Gonville and Caius College. 8, S. John's College. 9, Magdalene College.

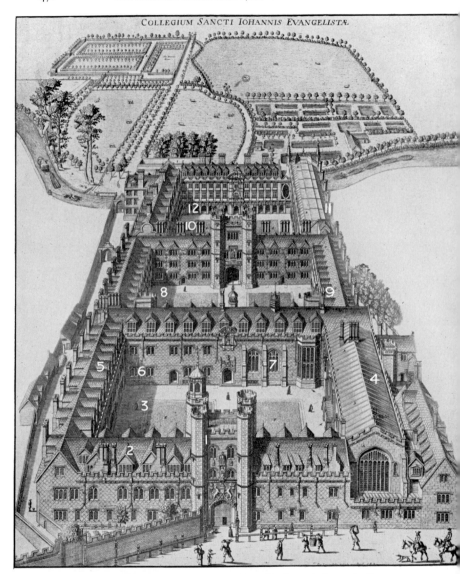

COLLEGIUM SANCTI IOHANNIS EVANGELISTÆ

S. John's College, Cambridge, from E. (founded 1511). See p. 473
1, Entrance gateway. 2, Library. 3, First court. 4, Chapel. 5, Chambers. 6, Kitchen. 7, H
8, Second court. 9, Masters' lodge. 10, Third court. 11, Library. 12, Loggia.

A. Eton College: aerial view. See p. 474

1, Entrance. 2, Chapel. 3, College Hall. 4, Upper School. 5, Weston's Yard.
6, Provost's Lodge. 7, Headmaster's House.

B. Winchester College: aerial view. See p. 474

1, Entrance tower. 2, Outer Court. 3, Chamber Court. 4, Chapel. 5, Hall.
6, Cloisters. 7, Fromont's Chantry. 8, Old School. 9, Classrooms. 10, Headmaster's
House. 11, Moberley Library. 12, Warden's Lodging.

HOSPITAL of S. CROSS: WINCHESTER

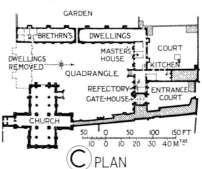

Ⓐ QUADRANGLE LOOKING N.

Ⓑ CHURCH FROM N.E.

Ⓒ PLAN

Ⓓ SECTⁿ THRO⁰ REFECTOᴿ

S. MARY'S HOSPᴸ. CHICHESTER

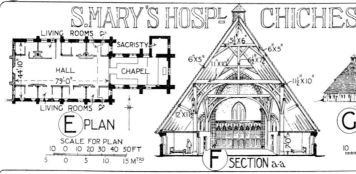

Ⓔ PLAN

SCALE FOR PLAN
10 0 10 20 30 40 50 FT
5 0 5 10 15 Mᵀᴿˢ

Ⓕ SECTION a-a

Ⓖ VIEW FROM S.E.

SCALE FOR SECTION
10 5 0   10   20
1   0   3   6

FORD'S HOSPITAL: COVENTRY

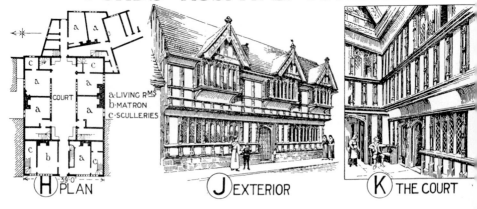

Ⓗ PLAN

Ⓙ EXTERIOR

Ⓚ THE COURT

HOSPITALS, ALMSHOUSES, AND BEDE HOUSES

Hospitals, Almshouses, and Bede Houses increased in number on the decline of the monasteries, some of whose lost service they were designed to meet, and thus there was much similarity between them in purpose and design. These buildings were founded in the main by persons charitably inclined, as refuges for the infirm and destitute, and were endowed with revenues for their support.

The **Hospital of S. Cross, Winchester** (1136) (p. 478), believed to be the oldest almshouse in England, was founded by Bishop Henry of Blois for thirteen poor and aged men. A second foundation was added by Cardinal Beaufort in 1445. It is a remarkable group of massive gatehouse, fine cruciform late Norman church (completed in 1225), and quadrangle around which are the master's house, refectory, and dwellings.

S. Mary's Hospital, Chichester, founded as a nunnery but after 1562 used for eight poor persons, dates from the end of the thirteenth century. The doorway leads into the hall (p. 478E) flanked by dwelling-rooms and covered by a wide-spreading timber roof (p. 478F), while behind the screen of the hall is a chapel, with ancient seating.

Ford's Hospital, Coventry (1529) (p. 478), much damaged in 1941, was a fascinating old refuge in the traditional half-timber style, founded for five poor men and one woman. The living-rooms range round an inner half-timber court and the exterior had fine carved barge-boards.

The **Almshouses, Cobham** (1598) (p. 480), also called the Priests' College, form a most attractive group close to the parish church with its famous brasses (p. 509). They were founded by Lord Cobham on the site of a chantry, and consist of a quadrangle round which are the dwelling-rooms, while there is a large hall with canopied fireplace and arched timber roof (p. 480C).

The **Hospital, Ewelme** (1436) (p. 480), founded by the Duke of Suffolk, consists of rooms round a quadrangle with cloister walk, above which rise dormers with carved barge-boards. Steps lead at the upper end to the church, in which are the tombs of the founders, while to the south are the school buildings in fine patterned brickwork. The triple group of hospital, school, and church on rising ground is one of the most picturesque in England.

The **Bede House, Stamford** (1490) (p. 480), was founded by Alderman Browne, for ten poor men and two nurses. The dignified entrance porch (p. 480J) leads into a quadrangle, south of which is the dormitory, arranged, like that of S. Mary's, Chichester, as a long hall with cubicles on either side and a chapel at the end, with large transomed windows; while to the north are nurses' and wardens' quarters.

Other examples are to be found in many English towns, such as **S. John's Hospital, Northampton** (1140), the **Great Hospital, Norwich** (1246), **S. John's Hospital, Sherborne** (1437), **Christ's Hospital, Abingdon** (1446), and **Leycester's Hospital, Warwick** (1571) (p. 481), with its fine half-timber work and galleried Court.

INNS

Inns of the Middle Ages, as well as monasteries, provided accommodation for travellers, whether the king and his retainers, merchants, wandering scholars, or pilgrims, while many inns were used as posting houses.

The **Guesten Hall, Worcester** (1320) (p. 485), south of the cathedral, must have been a most beautiful building, but it is now a picturesque ruin. It appears to have been set apart for strangers, because the monastic rules did not allow guests to sit with monks at the table. The fine timber roof (p. 485C) now covers Trinity Church, Worcester.

ALMSHOUSES (PRIESTS' COLL.): COBHAM: KEN

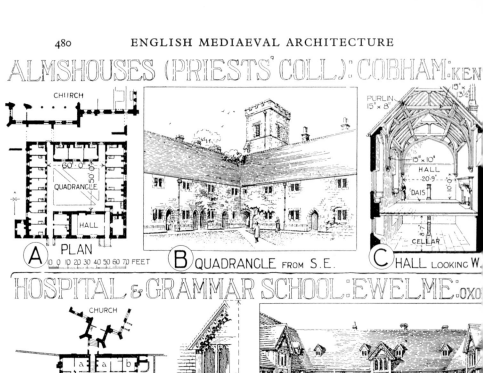

CHURCH

QUADRANGLE

60' 0"

50'

HALL

Ⓐ PLAN

10 0 10 20 30 40 50 60 70 FEET

Ⓑ QUADRANGLE FROM S.E.

PURLIN
15" × 8"

15"
3½"

15" × 10"

HALL
20·9"

DAIS

10·0"

8·7"

CELLAR

Ⓒ HALL LOOKING W.

HOSPITAL & GRAMMAR SCHOOL: EWELME: OXON

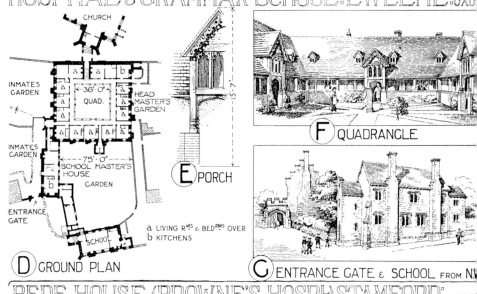

CHURCH

INMATES
GARDEN

36' 0"

QUAD.

HEAD
MASTER'S
GARDEN

INMATES
GARDEN

75' 0"

SCHOOL MASTER'S
HOUSE

GARDEN

ENTRANCE
GATE

SCHOOL

a LIVING R^{MS} & BED^{RMS} OVER
b KITCHENS

Ⓓ GROUND PLAN

15·7"

Ⓔ PORCH

Ⓕ QUADRANGLE

Ⓖ ENTRANCE GATE & SCHOOL FROM N.W.

BEDE HOUSE (BROWNE'S HOSP.): STAMFORD: LINC.

a HALL
b NURSES' KITCHEN
c WARDEN'S HOUSE
d CHAPEL
e CUBICLES

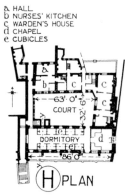

63' 0"

32' 6"

COURT

DORMITORY

86' 0"

Ⓗ PLAN

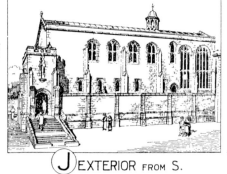

Ⓙ EXTERIOR FROM S.

AUDIT ROOM

18·3"

10·9"

Ⓚ SECTION y·y

A. Leycester's Hospital, Warwick (1571). See p. 479

B. Leycester's Hospital: courtyard

A. S. Mary, Warwick: nave looking E.
Rebuilt as a 'hall' church, 1694–1704.
See p. 394

B. Merton College chapel, Oxford
from S.W. (1274). See p. 469

c. The Guildhall, London: Great Hall, before damage in 1940, looking E. (1411–46).
See opposite page

The **George Inn, Glastonbury** (fifteenth century) (p. 484J), is a substantially built structure with mullioned and traceried windows.

The **Feathers Inn, Ludlow** (p. 484N), built as a private mansion, is a delightful half-timber building and, although dating from 1603, is a reminder of local Mediaeval art.

Among the Smaller Inns, which still exist (p. 484) may be mentioned the **Fighting Cocks, S. Albans**; the **George, Norton S. Philip**; the **Bell Inn, Woodbridge**; the **Anchor Inn, Ripley**; the **Six Bells, Hollingbourne**; the **King's Head, Sissinghurst**; the **Eagle and Child, Alderley Edge**; the **Star, Alfriston**; the **Fox and Hounds, Barley**; the **Falstaff Inn, Canterbury**, with its fine wrought-iron sign, and the **Dolphin Inn, Norwich**.

GUILDHALLS

The **Guildhall, London**, dating from 1411–46 (p. 482C), is the most important hall erected by the Guilds in the Middle Ages, but was partly burnt down in the Great Fire of 1666. It was altered by Wren, and has a Gothic-like façade (1789) by George Dance, Junior; but it was not until the nineteenth century that Sir Horace Jones restored the Great Hall to its original appearance and supplied a Gothic style open roof (1864–70), destroyed by enemy action in 1940 and again replaced in 1954 as a panelled flat ceiling on stone arches. It has been the stage upon which some of the most important events in English history have been enacted. The **Guildhall, York** (1448–80), severely damaged by bombing in 1942, was of unusual design, with a handsome, low-pitched roof carried on tall oak columns. The **Guildhall, Exeter** (1464), with an Elizabethan frontispiece, the **Guildhall, Cirencester** (c. 1500) (p. 485D) and the **Guildhall, Lavenham** (c. 1529) (p. 485G) are other examples. The **Hall of the Butchers Guild, Hereford** (1621) (p. 485E) though after the period maintains Mediaeval characteristics.

MARKET HALLS AND CROSSES

Markets were established in most provincial towns where the farmers could bring their produce for sale, and Domesday Book records about fifty such markets, while annual fairs provided other facilities for commerce, and sometimes, like the markets, were held in churchyards. The **Market Hall, Ledbury** (1633) (p. 485F), has a covered market with sixteen oak pillars, over which is the Town Hall. The beautiful **Market Crosses, Salisbury** (fourteenth century) (p. 486A) and **Chichester** (1500, restored 1724) (p. 486C), still serve their original purpose, which was akin to that of the market halls, and show the similarity in type of the commercial and ecclesiastical architecture of the period.

TITHE BARNS

Many old tithe barns throughout the country are fascinating in the simplicity of the rough but honest craftsmanship which went to the making of their walls and primitive timber roofs. The **Abbot's Barn, Glastonbury** (fourteenth century) (p. 486D–F), and the **Old Barn, Fullstone**, near Sittingbourne (p. 486G–J), show the sturdy character of this type of building and the carpenter's skill in framing up the timbers, both in wall and roof, while the barns at **Bradford-on-Avon** (1350), 170 ft long (p. 488A, B), Frocester, Gloucestershire, and Preston Plucknett display similar directness in construction.

CITY WALLS AND GATEWAYS

Towns which date from the Roman period and earlier were surrounded by defensive walls upon which Mediaeval walls were afterwards constructed, but much has been destroyed to allow for expansion. London, Canterbury, Colchester, Lincoln,

MEDIÆVAL INNS

Ⓐ THE FIGHTING COCKS:
S. ALBANS : HERTS

Ⓑ THE GEORGE :
NORTON Sᵀ PHILIP : SOMERSET

Ⓒ THE BELL INN :
WOODBRIDGE : SU

Ⓓ THE ANCHOR INN,
RIPLEY : SURREY

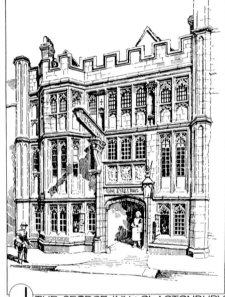

Ⓔ THE EAGLE & C
ALDERLEY EDG

Ⓕ THE SIX BELLS :
HOLLINGBOURNE

Ⓖ THE STAR IN
ALFRISTON : SUS

Ⓗ THE KING'S HEAD :
SISSINGHURST

Ⓙ THE GEORGE INN : GLASTONBURY

Ⓚ THE FOX & HOU
BARLEY : HEʀ

Ⓛ THE FALSTAFF INN :
CANTERBURY

Ⓜ THE DOLPHIN INN : NORWICH

Ⓝ THE FEATHERS
LUDLOW : SHR

THE GUESTEN HALL : WORCESTER

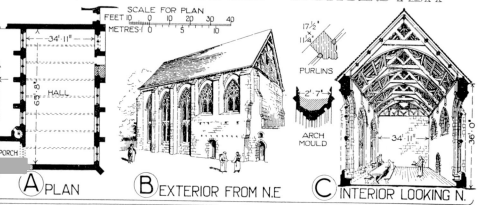

SCALE FOR PLAN
FEET 10 0 10 20 30 40
METRES 0 5 10

34'·11"

65'·8"

HALL

PORCH

(A) PLAN

(B) EXTERIOR FROM N.E

17½'
×
11¼'

PURLINS

2'·7"

ARCH
MOULD

34'·11"

36'·0"

(C) INTERIOR LOOKING N.

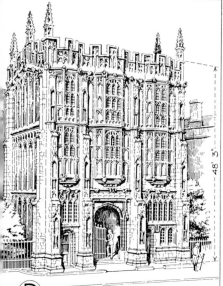

48'·3"

(D) GUILDHALL : CIRENCESTER

35'·8"

(E) HALL OF THE BUTCHERS' GUILD : HEREFORD

12'·6"

MARKET HALL : LEDBURY : HEREFORD

29'·9"

(G) GUILDHALL : LAVENHAM : SUFFOLK

MEDIÆVAL CROSSES & TITHE BARNS

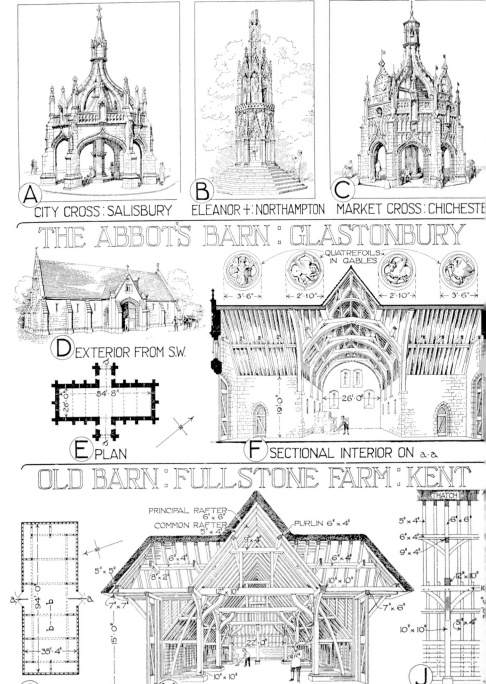

A CITY CROSS : SALISBURY

B ELEANOR + : NORTHAMPTON

C MARKET CROSS : CHICHESTER

THE ABBOT'S BARN : GLASTONBURY

D EXTERIOR FROM S.W.

E PLAN

QUATREFOILS IN GABLES

3'.6" 2'.10" 2'.10" 3'.6"

84'.8" 26'.0"

19'.0" 26'.0"

F SECTIONAL INTERIOR ON a·a

OLD BARN : FULLSTONE FARM : KENT

G PLAN

94'.0" 35'.4"

PRINCIPAL RAFTER 6" x 6"
COMMON RAFTER 5" x 4"
PURLIN 6" x 4"
9' x 4"
6" x 4" 6" x 4"
5" x 5" 8" x 2" 10" x 10"
12" x 10" 7" x 6"
7" x 7"
15'.0" 22'.0"
10" x 10"

H SECTIONAL INTERIOR ON a·a

THATCH
5" x 4" 6" x 6"
6" x 4"
9" x 4"
12" x 10"
10" x 10" 5" x 4"

J DETAIL AT b

CITY WALLS & GATEWAYS

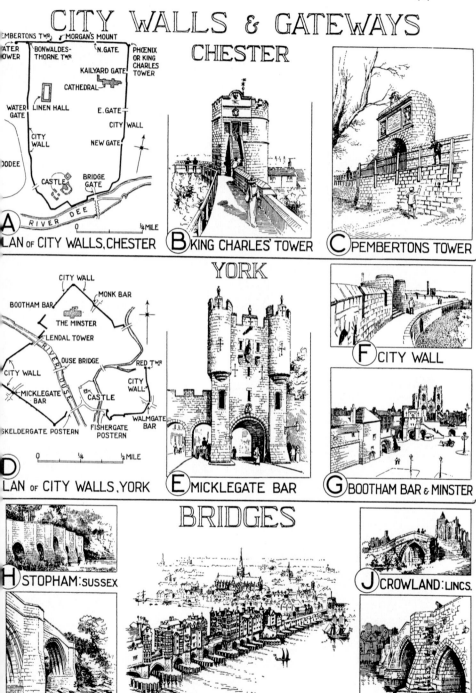

CHESTER

A PLAN of CITY WALLS, CHESTER

B KING CHARLES' TOWER

C PEMBERTONS TOWER

YORK

D PLAN of CITY WALLS, YORK

E MICKLEGATE BAR

F CITY WALL

G BOOTHAM BAR & MINSTER

BRIDGES

H STOPHAM : SUSSEX

J CROWLAND : LINCS.

K KIRKBY LONSDALE

L OLD LONDON BRIDGE (CIRCA A.D. 1647) FROM S.

M AYLESFORD : KENT

A. Old Tithe Barn, Bradford-on-Avon (1350). See p. 483

C. Pack-horse bridge, Coombe Bissett, Wilts. See p. 489

B. Tithe Barn, Bradford-on-Avon, interior

D. East Farleigh bridge, Kent (14th cent.). See p. 489

Gloucester, Chichester, Southampton, Chepstow, and Winchester among others, most with fragments of Roman origin, still retain portions more or less perfect of their Mediaeval walls and gateways.

The **City of Chester** (p. 487) still possesses its walls in fine preservation to a height of about 12 ft. They are about two miles in length and surround the city, and are strengthened at intervals by towers, of which King Charles' Tower is an example; both this and the Pemberton Tower show the walking way behind the parapet on which the defenders could keep watch.

The **City of York** (p. 487) still retains about two and a half miles of its Mediaeval wall on both sides of the River Ouse, principally dating from the reign of Edward III. The ramparts (p. 487F) are protected and strengthened by battlemented towers. Micklegate Bar (p. 487E), Bootham Bar (p. 487G), and Walmgate Bar, dating from the time of Edward I, are among the six imposing defensive gateways, each of which has portcullis, turrets or bartizans, and cross loopholes crowned by battlements.

BRIDGES

Bridges, which were important means of communication, were often semi-religious in character, and their maintenance was imposed on various authorities. **Old London Bridge** (1176–1209) (p. 487L), commenced by the religious fraternity of 'Fratres Pontis', and designed by Peter, priest of S. Mary Colechurch, was one of the most famous of all Mediaeval bridges, and must have presented a strangely picturesque appearance. It rested on eighteen solid stone piers, strengthened by 'starlings' to protect them against the scour of the tide. These piers, connected by arches, supported the roadway with its houses and shops which paid for the upkeep of the bridge, while on a pier near the centre was the chapel of S. Thomas of Canterbury. The bridge lasted over 600 years and was pulled down in 1832 when the present structure, designed by John Rennie, was completed 200 ft farther west. **Stopham Bridge** (p. 487H), **Kirkby Lonsdale Bridge** (p. 487K), **Aylesford Bridge** (p. 487M), **Wakefield Bridge**, with a chapel, and **Warkworth Bridge**, Northumberland, are in good preservation. **East Farleigh Bridge** (fourteenth century) (p. 488D) is an excellent example, while the **Pack-horse Bridge, Coombe Bissett** (p. 488C) is a survival of Mediaeval times. The **Bridge, Crowland** (p. 487J), is a peculiar triangular structure with three pointed arches, carrying three roads over three waterways.

COMPARATIVE ANALYSIS

The evolution of English architecture is here traced by comparison of plans, walls, openings, roofs, columns, mouldings, and ornament through the Anglo-Saxon, Norman, Early English, Decorated, Perpendicular, and Tudor periods, as set forth in Architectural Character on pp. 386 and 389.

PLANS

Anglo-Saxon (p. 491). A church was frequently planned as a simple rectangle (p. 491A) or as two unequal oblongs, of which the larger was the nave and the smaller the sanctuary, and the distinction was clearly marked, both internally and externally (pp. 387N, Q, 491B, C). These were joined by a chancel arch, under which steps usually led to a sanctuary (sometimes on a lower level). The latter was generally square-ended, following the Celtic type, as at Bradford-on-Avon (p. 387Q); but another type, derived from the Roman basilican church, had an apsidal end, as at Worth (p. 491C) and Brixworth. Towers are without buttresses, as at Earls Barton, Northants (p. 387C), S. Benet, Cambridge (p. 387P), and Sompting (p. 387E).

Norman (p. 491). The nave was lengthened, with aisles usually half its width, transepts were developed, and there was sometimes a tower over the crossing, and the sanctuary became apsidal in cathedrals and some churches (p. 491D, E). Many cathedrals were rebuilt in this period, and in those of Norwich, Durham, Ely, S. Albans, and Winchester the naves are conspicuous for their length. S. John's Chapel, Tower of London (p. 436C, E), is a Norman church in miniature. Towers are square and massive, as at S. Albans and Iffley, and a timber spire occurs at Canterbury (p. 396D). Churches in East Anglia have round towers, due to Scandinavian influence or the absence of stone suitable for square angles, as they are built of knapped or unknapped flints. Plans of English cathedrals are given on pp. 410, 411, 412, 413. For plans of castles and manor houses of this period see pp. 437, 444.

Early English (p. 491). Church plans were very similar to the Norman, and the difference was chiefly brought about by the introduction of the pointed arch, which made it possible to construct oblong instead of square vaulting compartments, each complete in itself; while many Norman apses were lengthened into square-ended sanctuaries of Anglo-Saxon type (p. 491H–N). The 'broach' spire rising from the square tower without a parapet was introduced (p. 492A), and the steeple of S. Mary, Oxford (pp. 396C, 475A, 492E), is an early example of a tower surmounted by clustered pinnacles behind which rises the low pyramidal spire. Plans of English cathedrals are given on pp. 410, 411, 412, 413. For plans of castles and manor houses of this period see pp. 438, 447.

Decorated (p. 491). Nave bays of new cathedrals and churches were given a wider spacing than in earlier periods; and in proportion as piers became more slender, the floor space was increased, thus the interiors were more spacious (p. 491P–S). Several great central towers were now carried up, as Salisbury (pp. 395A, 407G, 415B), and Lichfield (pp. 407E, 419B). The 'broach' spire gradually gave way to the lofty spire with parapets, angle pinnacles, and spire-lights, while moulded ribs, ornamented with crockets, accentuate the angles of these tapering spires (p. 492); sometimes the spire is raised on an octagonal basement, as at Bloxham (p. 492H). Plans of English cathedrals are given on pp. 410, 411, 412, 413. For plans of castles and manor houses of this period see pp. 443, 448.

Perpendicular (p. 491). Owing to the building activity of preceding centuries, few ecclesiastical buildings of first importance were planned, though many were altered or enlarged. Many parish churches indicate the tendency to reduce the size of piers and to throw the roof weight externally on projecting buttresses, which were rendered more necessary by the increased size of windows (p. 491T, U). Towers were erected without spires, as the Bell Tower, Evesham (1533), and elsewhere (p. 492D, F, G, J), but when a spire occurs it rises behind a parapet, as at S. Peter, Kettering (p. 492K). A novel type is at Newcastle, where open flying buttresses support a central pinnacle (p. 492B). Plans of English cathedrals are given (on pp. 410–13). For plans of castles and manor houses of this period see pp. 443, 451.

Tudor. Few churches were built and they were similar in plan to those of the last period. King's College Chapel, Cambridge, and the magnificent royal tomb-house of Henry VII at Westminster Abbey are the last ecclesiastical edifices of importance in the Gothic style. The most characteristic buildings of this period are the numerous manor houses for which a distinctly domestic plan and type of architecture were developed (p. 452).

WALLS

Anglo-Saxon. Walls were generally of rough rubble with ashlar masonry at the angles in 'long and short' courses, as at Earls Barton (p. 387C). Pilaster strips are also frequent, but no instance of buttresses occurs.

EVOLUTION OF CHURCH PLANS

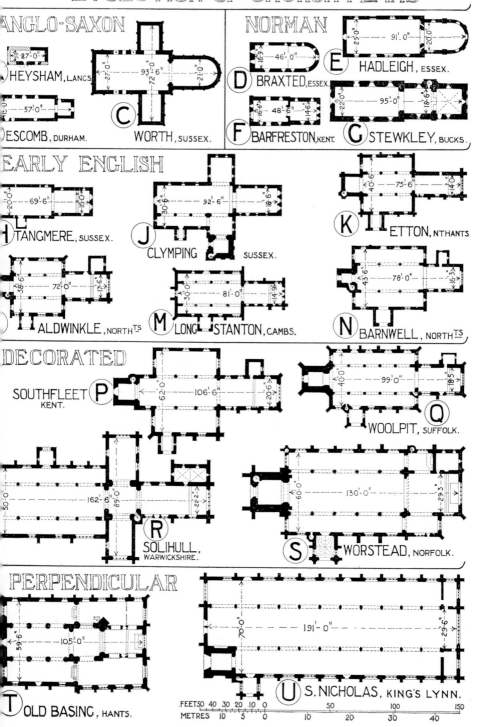

ANGLO-SAXON

87'·0"
HEYSHAM, LANCS.

57'·0"
ESCOMB, DURHAM.

27'·0"   93'·6"   21'·0"
72'·6"
C
WORTH, SUSSEX.

NORMAN

25'·0"   91'·0"   20'·0"
E HADLEIGH, ESSEX.

16'·9"   46'·0"
D BRAXTED, ESSEX.

16'·6"   48'·6"   14'·6"
F BARFRESTON, KENT.

22'·0"   95'·0"   18'·6"
G STEWKLEY, BUCKS.

EARLY ENGLISH

20'·0"   69'·6"   16'·0"
H TANGMERE, SUSSEX.

30'·6"   92'·6"   18'·6"
J CLYMPING   SUSSEX.

40'·6"   75'·6"   14'·0"
K ETTON, N'THANTS

38'·6"   72'·0"   17'·6"
L ALDWINKLE, NORTH'TS

30'·0"   81'·0"   14'·9"
M LONG STANTON, CAMBS.

43'·6"   78'·0"   16'·3"
N BARNWELL, NORTH'TS

DECORATED

P SOUTHFLEET KENT.
62'·0"   106'·6"   20'·6"

40'·0"   99'·0"   18'·5"
Q WOOLPIT, SUFFOLK.

50'·0"   162'·6"   89'·0"   22'·2"
R SOLIHULL, WARWICKSHIRE.

60'·0"   130'·0"   29'·3"
S WORSTEAD, NORFOLK.

PERPENDICULAR

59'·6"   105'·0"
T OLD BASING, HANTS.

70'·0"   191'·0"   29'·6"
U S. NICHOLAS, KING'S LYNN.

FEET 50 40 30 20 10 0   50   100   150
METRES 10   5   0   10   20   30   40

TOWERS & SPIRES

B S. NICHOLAS: NEWCASTLE (201 F.T.)

A S. PETER: RAUNDS (150 F.T.)

C S. MICHAEL: COVENTRY (300 F.T.)

D S. BOTOLPH: BOSTON (288 F.T.)

E S. MARY: OXFO (150

F S. MARY: S. NEOTS (128 F.T.)

G S. MARY: MANCHESTER (139 F.T.)

H S. MARY: BLOXHAM (198 F.T.)

J MAGDALEN COLL: OXFORD (145 F.T.)

K S. PETER: KETTERIN

Norman. Walls are thick but often defective in construction, as the core was imperfectly bonded with the facing, which, in the later period, was frequently ornamented with arcading. The height of interiors is nearly equally divided between nave arcade, triforium, and clear-story (pp. 414E, 494B), and, as in the churches at Caen, a passage occurs between the clear-story windows and the arches carrying the inner part of the wall, useful for window repairs (p. 391A). Broad, flat buttresses succeed the Anglo-Saxon pilaster strips and are often flush with the corbel table, which often supports a plain parapet (pp. 494A, C, 497A, B, 511A), useful for roof repairs.

Early English. Walls retain the massive character of Norman work, but more cut stone and less rubble core was employed. The concentration on buttresses of the weight of roof and vaulting began the process carried out in succeeding periods of reducing the walls to a mere enclosing screen of stained-glass windows. The excellent proportions between openings and piers give a light and graceful appearance, as in the transepts of Salisbury Cathedral. Buttresses gradually became more pronounced than in the Norman period till they were generally equal in projection to their width, in order to resist the outward pressure of the pointed vaults. They were formed in receding stages by weathered offsets which were often gabled, and their angles were sometimes chamfered (pp. 494E, 497C–F). Flying buttresses (p. 497Q, T) were first utilized as external features in this period, but were not common till later. In church interiors the nave arcade usually occupies half the height, and the upper half is equally divided between triforium and clear-story, as in the choirs of Ripon (p. 494D) and Ely (p. 495K), and the nave of Lincoln (p. 416C); but sometimes the triforium was reduced in order to allow of a greater display of glass above, as at Westminster (p. 424A) and Salisbury (p. 415F). Parapets have moulded copings and ornamental patternwork (p. 511B).

Decorated. Walls were gradually transformed, owing to the increased size of traceried windows. Tracery was sometimes extended as panelling even over walls (p. 495J). Buttresses of great projection were still in stages, and were sometimes ornamented with niches, crocketed canopies, and finials (p. 497H, J), while angle buttresses, set diagonally, were introduced (p. 497G) and flying buttresses were sometimes pierced (p. 497R). The internal division of nave arcade, triforium, and clear-story shows, in the latter part of the period, the tendency to reduce still further the height of the triforium in order to secure larger clear-story windows (p. 416), while in other examples there is extreme ornamentation (p. 495H, K). Parapets were occasionally pierced with flowing tracery (p. 511C), but this was a French feature, and the English generally preferred the battlemented form.

Perpendicular. Walls were profusely ornamented with panelling, resembling window tracery, as in the late Perpendicular or early Tudor Chapel of Henry VII, which is most elaborate in detail, and a miracle of beauty (p. 426A). Knapped flint was used as wall facing for panels, in conjunction with stone tracery in Norfolk and Suffolk. Parapets, embattled, panelled, or pierced (p. 511D, E, F), were ornate, as at Merton College, Oxford (p. 482B). Buttresses project boldly (p. 497K, L, M) and chapels were sometimes formed between them, as at King's College, Cambridge (pp. 468, 470A), and elsewhere. Flying buttresses span the aisle roofs and are moulded or pierced and sustained by pinnacles (p. 497N, S). Interiors frequently consist of two stages, viz. nave arcade and clear-storey. In place of the triforium there is often a mere line of panelling as at Winchester (p. 495M) and S. George's Chapel, Windsor (p. 471H), or of niches for statuary as in the Chapel of Henry VII, Westminster (pp. 426E, 428). Parish churches frequently have no triforium, owing to flat aisle roof.

Tudor. Walls followed on the same lines as the last period, as the Chapel of

THE COMPARATIVE TREATMENT O

NORMAN   TRANSITIONAL   EARLY ENGLIS
(LANCET)

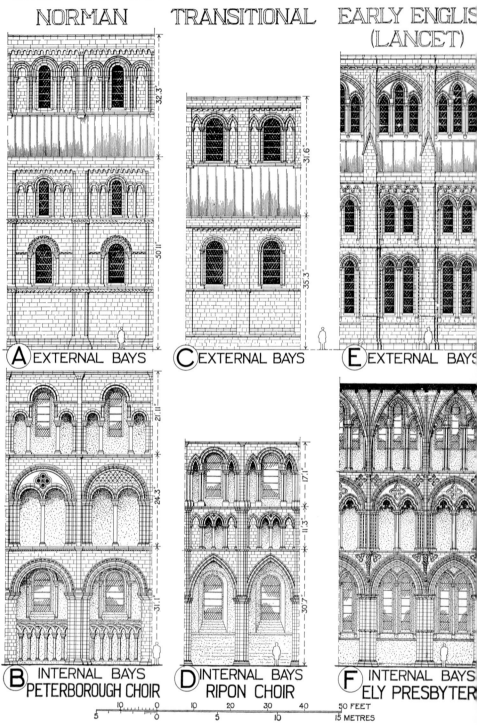

Ⓐ EXTERNAL BAYS   Ⓒ EXTERNAL BAYS   Ⓔ EXTERNAL BAYS

Ⓑ INTERNAL BAYS   Ⓓ INTERNAL BAYS   Ⓕ INTERNAL BAYS
PETERBOROUGH CHOIR   RIPON CHOIR   ELY PRESBYTER

10   0   10   20   30   40   50 FEET
5   0   5   10   15 METRES

ENGLISH GOTHIC CATHEDRALS

DECORATED (GEOMETRIC) DECORATED (CURVILINEAR) PERPENDICULAR (RECTILINEAR)

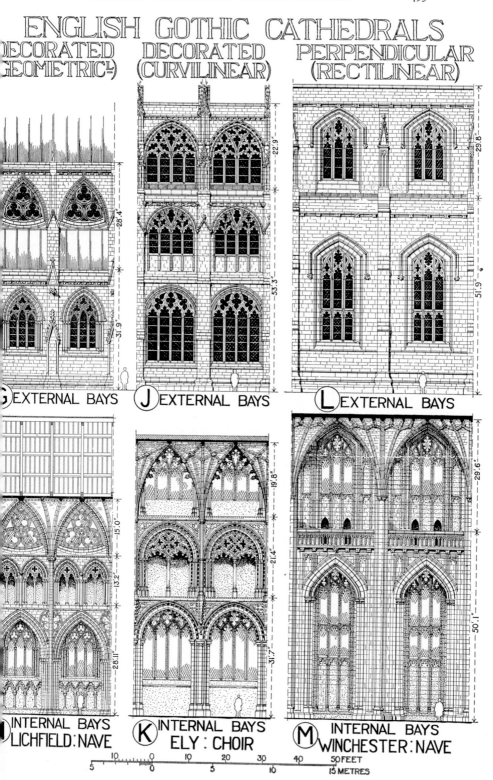

G EXTERNAL BAYS   J EXTERNAL BAYS   L EXTERNAL BAYS

INTERNAL BAYS
LICHFIELD : NAVE   K INTERNAL BAYS
ELY : CHOIR   M INTERNAL BAYS
WINCHESTER : NAVE

10   0   10   20   30   40   50 FEET
5   0   5   10   15 METRES

Henry VII (p. 426A), but in domestic buildings there is some novelty, as in the extended use of red brickwork with thick mortar joints, in which patterns were formed by darker 'headers', as at Hampton Court Palace, Compton Wynyates, and other manor houses. Buttresses have traceried panels, as in the Chapel of Henry VII, and are crowned with finials, often ornamented with crockets, while flying buttresses are often pierced (pp. 426A, F, 497P). Interiors have much panelling.

OPENINGS

Anglo-Saxon. Arches, as in the chancel arch, Escomb, and the tower arch, Sompting, are semicircular (p. 387D) and often unmoulded, and the sides or jambs frequently have 'long and short work'. Doorways are plainly framed with square, unmoulded jambs, and semicircular arches (p. 387C, D). Windows have square jambs and either round or triangular heads, as at Deerhurst (p. 387J), with the occasional addition of a central baluster, as at Worth (p. 387H) and S. Mary the Younger, York (p. 387G), and another treatment is that at Earls Barton (p. 387A, B, C).

Norman. Arcades invariably consist of semicircular arches (p. 494B), unmoulded in the early part of the period, as in S. John's Chapel, Tower of London (p. 436C), and in the later period they are enriched with mouldings, as S. Bartholomew, London (p. 391A), and Waltham Abbey. Doorways and windows have jambs in square recesses or 'orders' enclosing nook-shafts. These 'orders' are frequently carved with zigzag and beak-head ornament, as at Etton (p. 498A, B), or elaborately sculptured, as at Barfreston, Kent. Windows are small and the internal jambs are deeply splayed (pp. 388B, 499A). They are in single lights, often flanked by blind arcading (p. 494A), although double windows with central shaft occur (often in towers), while three openings, the middle being the largest, are grouped together, as in S. Bartholomew, London (p. 391A), and elsewhere (p. 494).

Early English. Arcades are of more slender proportions, and pointed lancet arches come into general use (p. 494D, F), at first side by side with round arches (p. 494C, D) and in connection with vaulting, and then in arches, as at Westminster Abbey and the Temple Church (p. 388B). Doorways (p. 498C, D, E) have jambs enriched with mouldings, detached shafts, and carved ornaments, crowned with lancet arches and hood moulds. Windows (p. 499B–E) of lancet shape are grouped in two, three, or even five lights, as in the 'Five Sisters' in York Minster (p. 423). The glass is often near the face of the wall, thus making deep internal jambs. The early form of 'plate' tracery (p. 499D) cut through a plate of stone was developed into 'bar' tracery, an innovation which led to extraordinary developments in design. The two-light windows of Westminster Abbey, with geometrical tracery (1245) are among the earliest bar traceried windows in England (p. 425D). Cusps let into the soffit of tracery arches in separate pieces, were introduced, as at Raunds, Northants, especially in circular lights, but in later window-heads the cusps are an integral part of the traceried mouldings. The spaces between the cusps are known as trefoil (p. 442D), quatrefoil, or cinquefoil according to whether they are composed of three, four, or five openings.

Decorated. Arcades became wider in proportion to their height and were crowned with equilateral arches (p. 495H, K), i.e. struck from the points of equilateral triangles, as at York and Lichfield, and the ogee arch came into use. Doorways (p. 498F–L) have jambs of less depth than in the Early English style, and are ornamented with engaged instead of detached shafts. Windows (p. 499H, J, K) are large and divided by mullions into two or more lights, and the enlargement of clear-story windows proceeded *pari passu* with the diminution in height of the triforium. Tracery at first consisted of geometric forms, as at Westminster Abbey, the cloisters of Salisbury (p. 415J), the choir clear-stories of Lincoln (p. 416G) and

COMPARATIVE BUTTRESSES

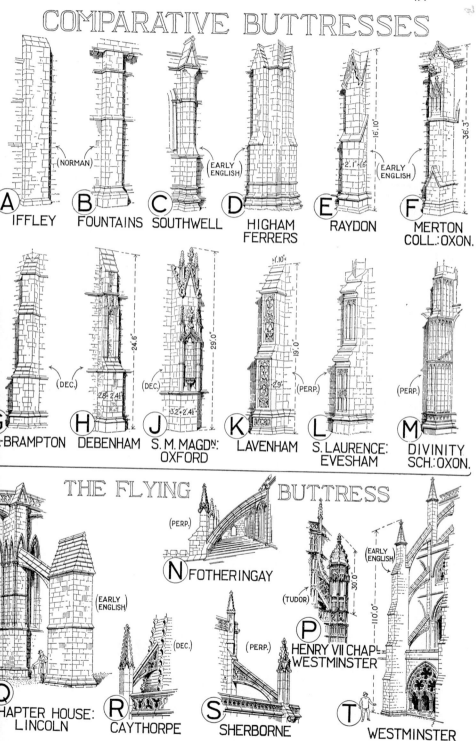

A IFFLEY (NORMAN)

B FOUNTAINS

C SOUTHWELL

D HIGHAM FERRERS (EARLY ENGLISH)

E RAYDON — 16.'10" — 2.'1"×1.'6"

F MERTON COLL.: OXON. (EARLY ENGLISH) — 36.'3"

G BRAMPTON (DEC.)

H DEBENHAM — 24.'6" — 2.'8"×2.'4" (DEC.)

J S. M. MAGDN: OXFORD — 29.'0" — 3.'2"×2.'4" (DEC.)

K LAVENHAM — 1.'10" — 19.'0" (PERP.)

L S. LAURENCE: EVESHAM — 2.'9" (PERP.)

M DIVINITY SCH.: OXON. (PERP.)

THE FLYING BUTTRESS

Q CHAPTER HOUSE: LINCOLN (EARLY ENGLISH)

N FOTHERINGAY (PERP.)

P HENRY VII CHAPL WESTMINSTER (TUDOR) — 30.'0"

R CAYTHORPE (DEC.)

S SHERBORNE (PERP.)

T WESTMINSTER (EARLY ENGLISH) — 110.'0"

COMPARATIVE DOORWAYS

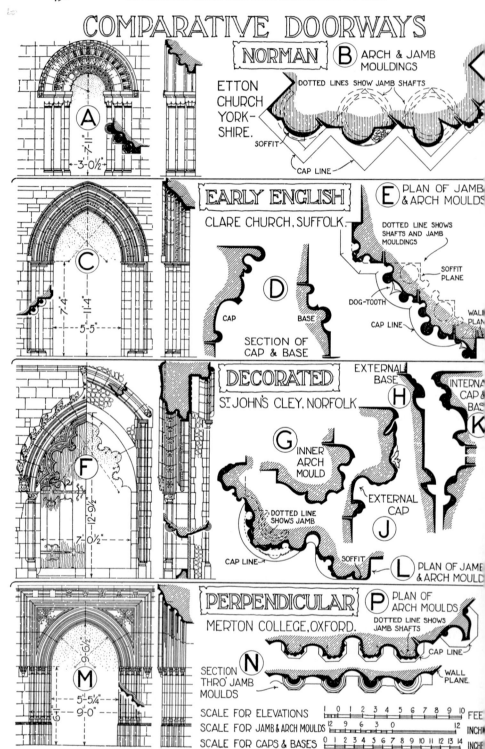

NORMAN (B) ARCH & JAMB MOULDINGS

ETTON CHURCH YORKSHIRE.

DOTTED LINES SHOW JAMB SHAFTS

SOFFIT

CAP LINE

A

3'-0½"

7'-11"

EARLY ENGLISH (E) PLAN OF JAMB & ARCH MOULDS

CLARE CHURCH, SUFFOLK.

DOTTED LINE SHOWS SHAFTS AND JAMB MOULDINGS

SOFFIT PLANE

DOG-TOOTH

CAP LINE

WALL PLAN

C

7'-4" 11'-4"

5'-5"

D

CAP   BASE

SECTION OF CAP & BASE

DECORATED

ST JOHN'S CLEY, NORFOLK.

EXTERNAL BASE

H

INTERNAL CAP & BASE

K

G INNER ARCH MOULD

EXTERNAL CAP

J

DOTTED LINE SHOWS JAMB

CAP LINE   SOFFIT

L PLAN OF JAMB & ARCH MOULD

F

12'-9½"

7'-0½"

PERPENDICULAR (P) PLAN OF ARCH MOULDS

MERTON COLLEGE, OXFORD.

DOTTED LINE SHOWS JAMB SHAFTS

CAP LINE

WALL PLANE

SECTION THRO' JAMB MOULDS

N

M

5'-5¼"

9'-0"

9'-6½"

SCALE FOR ELEVATIONS   0 1 2 3 4 5 6 7 8 9 10 FEET

SCALE FOR JAMB & ARCH MOULDS   12 9 6 3 0   12 INCHES

SCALE FOR CAPS & BASES   0 1 2 3 4 5 6 7 8 9 10 11 12 13 14 INCHES

COMPARATIVE WINDOWS

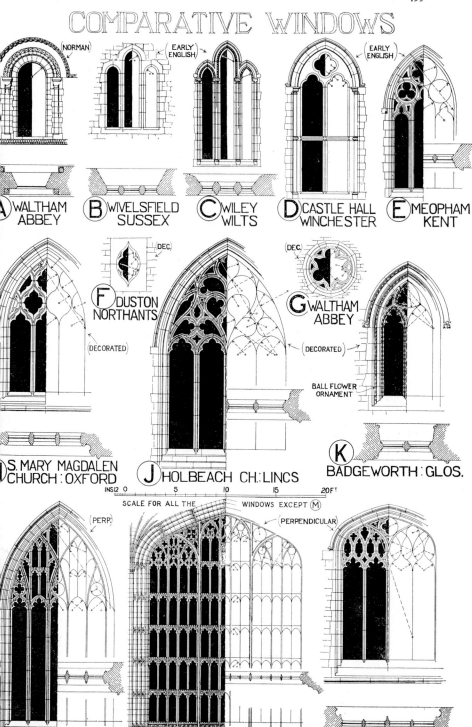

(NORMAN)

(EARLY ENGLISH)

(EARLY ENGLISH)

Ⓐ WALTHAM ABBEY

Ⓑ WIVELSFIELD SUSSEX

Ⓒ WILEY WILTS

Ⓓ CASTLE HALL WINCHESTER

Ⓔ MEOPHAM KENT

(DEC.)

Ⓕ DUSTON NORTHANTS

(DECORATED)

(DEC.)

Ⓖ WALTHAM ABBEY

(DECORATED)

BALL FLOWER ORNAMENT

Ⓗ S. MARY MAGDALEN CHURCH : OXFORD

Ⓙ HOLBEACH CH.: LINCS

Ⓚ BADGEWORTH : GLOS.

INS 12 0   5   10   15   20 FT
SCALE FOR ALL THE   WINDOWS EXCEPT Ⓜ

(PERP.)

(PERPENDICULAR)

Ⓛ WAWNE : YORKS

5 0 5 10 FT

Ⓜ S. GEORGE'S CHAPEL : WINDSOR

Ⓝ S. MICHAEL : BASINGSTOKE

TYPES OF SECULAR TIMBER ROOFS

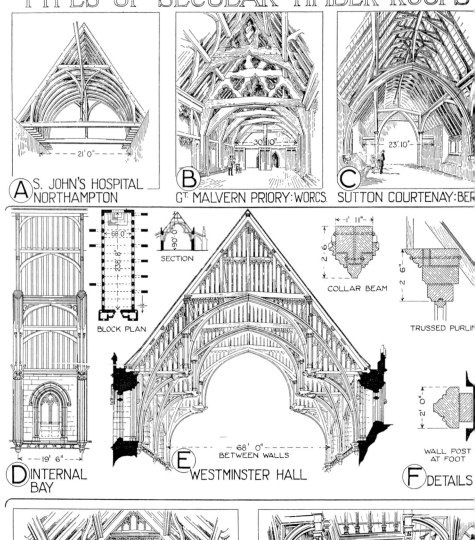

A · S. JOHN'S HOSPITAL NORTHAMPTON — 21' 0"

B · G^t MALVERN PRIORY : WORCS. — 30' 10"

C · SUTTON COURTENAY : BER — 23' 10"

D · INTERNAL BAY — 19' 6"

68' 0" · 38' 8" · SECTION 90' 0" · BLOCK PLAN

E · WESTMINSTER HALL — 68' 0" BETWEEN WALLS

COLLAR BEAM — 1' 11" · 2' 6"

TRUSSED PURLIN — 2' 6"

WALL POST AT FOOT — 2' 0"

F · DETAILS

G · ELTHAM PALACE : KENT — 36' 3"

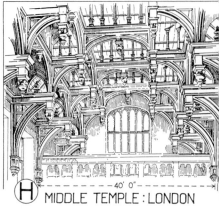

H · MIDDLE TEMPLE : LONDON — 40' 0"

the naves of Lichfield (p. 495G), and York. In the latter part of the period it consisted of curvilinear or flowing lines, as in the choirs of Ely (p. 495J) and Wells. Cusps which, in the Early English style, had often been let into the stone tracery now formed part of it. Smaller types of windows still occur (p. 499F, G).

Perpendicular. Arcades now usually consist either of 'drop' arches (p. 391B) or in the later period of four-centred arches (p. 495L), of which the spandrels are sometimes filled with tracery or carving (p. 495M). Doorways are generally finished with a square hood-moulding over the arch, and the spandrels are orna-mented, as in the doorway of Merton College, Oxford (p. 498M). Windows, of which the earliest in the style are probably those at Winchester (p. 420), have mullions continued vertically through their whole height up to the main arch, an arrangement which produces a perpendicular effect and gives the name to the style (p. 499L, M). In many cases they are of enormous size, strengthened by hori-zontal transoms, and even form a wall of glass, as at S. George's Chapel, Windsor (pp. 471, 499M), the east window at Gloucester (38 ft wide by 72 ft high, an area approximating to that of a tennis court), King's College Chapel, Cambridge (p. 468), and Henry VII Chapel, Westminster (p. 428).

Tudor. Arcades are of wider span and are generally crowned by typical four-centred Tudor arches with spandrels filled with either tracery or carving. Doorways are based on the Perpendicular type with four-centred arches (p. 461K), often enclosed in a square hood-moulding, and the spandrels are often carved with heraldic devices (p. 461B). Large windows with perpendicular mullions and hori-zontal transoms were now chiefly used for domestic architecture (p. 461E), and the pointed arch was frequently replaced by a square head, to suit the flat ceilings of living-rooms, and its place externally taken by a hood-moulding terminating laterally in carved bosses (p. 458A). Projecting bay and oriel windows give variety and picturesqueness to manor houses, as at Compton Wynyates (p 458B), Great Chalfield (p. 450D), and Athelhampton (p. 455A), and also of the numerous colleges of a quasi-religious nature, as at Oxford and Cambridge.

Roofs*

Anglo-Saxon. Saxon vaults, based on Roman masonry vaults, were plain and simple. There is no exact knowledge of roofs of this period, as none exist, but they were probably either of simple timber construction covered with slate (p. 387K, L, M), or of stone slabs in horizontal layers approaching each other till they met at the apex, as in early Irish churches. In some illuminated manuscripts buildings are represen-ted as covered with slates or shingles. The well-known and unique tower roof at Sompting (p. 387E), formed by four planes lying on the gables and meeting in ridges above the apex in each case is a peculiar form shown in some Rhenish churches.

Norman. Norman roofs have an inclination of about forty-five degrees finished with dripping eaves or parapet. The simple framing is either left exposed or there is a flat ceiling, boarded and painted, as at Ely and Peterborough (p. 414H). Some cathedrals and abbeys of this period originally had wooden ceilings, but were vaulted later, as Gloucester, Exeter, and the south transept of Durham. The introduction of rib and panel vaulting (p. 399B) eventually supplanted the Roman method of cross-vaults in which the meeting lines were simple groins, as in the crypt of Canterbury Cathedral (1096–1107) (p. 399A) and the aisles of S. John's Chapel, Tower of London. Early rib and panel vaulting is seen in the ambulatory, Canterbury Cathedral, and the choir aisles of Durham Cathedral (1093–6). There is sexpartite vaulting in the choir of Canterbury (p. 418B), erected by William of Sens

* For the evolution of English vaulting see p. 394, and for a description of English Mediaeval roofs see p. 430.

(1195), while the nave vault at Durham has, it is believed, the earliest pointed arches over a high vault in England (1128–33) (p. 392B).

Early English. Roofs became steeper externally with an inclination of about fifty-five degrees. Where there was no stone vaulting the framing was left exposed internally, and in the south-eastern part of the country, a characteristic was that the braces or ribs, together with the close-set rafters, produced the effect of a barrel-shaped vault (pp. 435C, 500A). Vaults (p. 399C, D) are marked by the general use of the pointed arch as in Westminster Abbey, which surmounted all difficulties of vaulting the oblong nave compartment, which had ribs of such varying span. The main ribs consisted of transverse, diagonal, and wall ribs, to which were added later intermediate ribs or 'tiercerons' and ridge ribs, as in Lincoln and Westminster (p. 399D).

Decorated. Roofs are of more moderate pitch, about fifty degrees, and sometimes have open framing internally, of which Great Malvern Priory (p. 500B), Heckington Church (p. 431B), and S. Etheldreda, Holborn, are good specimens. Arch-braced and the simpler types of hammer-beam roof come into favour in parish churches. Vaults (p. 399E, F) have an increased number of intermediate ribs which tend to reduce the size of panels, and the 'lierne' rib led to complicated star-shaped patterns known as 'stellar' vaulting, as in the choir of Ely (1322) and the nave of Canterbury (1379), while the number of bosses occasioned by the numerous ribs adds richness to the vaulting surface.

Perpendicular. Besides arch-braced varieties, timber roofs of the hammer-beam type are numerous, as at Eltham (p. 500G), especially in East Anglia, and were often richly ornamented with carved figures of angels and pierced tracery (pp. 435, 500), while the later roofs in the style became nearly flat and resembled a floor in construction (pp. 435G, J, 446K, 480K). The roof of Westminster Hall (p. 500), erected 1397–9 to the designs of Hugh Herland, master-carpenter, covers an area of nearly half an acre, and is one of the largest timber roofs, unsupported by pillars, in the world. Fan, palm, or conoidal vaulting (pp. 399H, 468) was evolved from the 'stellar' vaults of the period and consists of inverted concave cones, with ribs of similar radius, as in the Gloucester cloisters, but the lierne and fan vaults are sometimes combined, as at Sherborne Abbey (1475). Pendant vaulting was introduced, in which strong transverse arches support elongated voussoirs forming pendants, from which spring the vault ribs, as in the Divinity Schools, Oxford (1480–3) (p. 400C), and Oxford Cathedral (1480–1500) (p. 400B).

Tudor. Hammer-beam roofs and other roofs with exposed horizontal rafters were thrown across the halls of many lordly manor houses giving a distinctive charm, as in Compton Wynyates and Wolsey's palace at Hampton Court (p. 460E), and these continued in use up to the Elizabethan period, as in the Middle Temple Hall (p. 500H). Vaulting continued on the same lines as in the fan vault of King's College Chapel, Cambridge, and culminated in the magnificent fan and pendant vault of the Chapel of Henry VII (p. 428), while the vault of S. George's Chapel, Windsor (1501–8) (p. 471H) is an unusual example of side lierne vaults connected to a central barrel vault. Many plaster ceilings of geometrical and pendant type date from this period (p. 461C). For examples of timber roofs in English parish churches of all periods see p. 435.

COLUMNS

Anglo-Saxon. Piers were short, stumpy cylinders crowned with square blocks of stone instead of moulded capitals, and the roughly formed balusters in belfry windows appear to have been turned by a lathe and have projecting capitals to support the thick wall (p. 387B, D, F, G, H, J).

COMPARATIVE PIERS, CAPS & BASES.

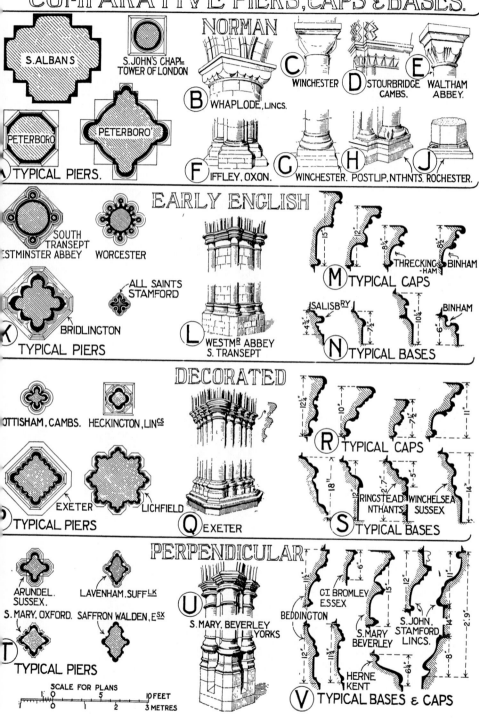

NORMAN

S. ALBANS

S. JOHN'S CHAP.L TOWER OF LONDON

PETERBORO'

PETERBORO'

A TYPICAL PIERS.

B WHAPLODE, LINCS.

WINCHESTER

C

D STOURBRIDGE CAMBS.

E WALTHAM ABBEY.

F IFFLEY, OXON.

G WINCHESTER.

H POSTLIP, NTHNTS.

J ROCHESTER.

EARLY ENGLISH

SOUTH TRANSEPT
WESTMINSTER ABBEY

WORCESTER

ALL SAINTS STAMFORD

K BRIDLINGTON
TYPICAL PIERS

L WESTM.R ABBEY S. TRANSEPT

M TYPICAL CAPS

THRECKING-HAM

BINHAM

SALISB.RY

N TYPICAL BASES

BINHAM

DECORATED

OTTISHAM, CAMBS.

HECKINGTON, LINC.S

EXETER

LICHFIELD

P TYPICAL PIERS

Q EXETER

R TYPICAL CAPS

RINGSTEAD NTHANTS

WINCHELSEA SUSSEX

S TYPICAL BASES

PERPENDICULAR

ARUNDEL. SUSSEX.

LAVENHAM. SUFF.LK

S. MARY, OXFORD.

SAFFRON WALDEN, E.SX

T TYPICAL PIERS

U S. MARY. BEVERLEY YORKS

GT BROMLEY ESSEX

BEDDINGTON

S.MARY BEVERLEY

S. JOHN, STAMFORD LINCS.

HERNE KENT

V TYPICAL BASES & CAPS

SCALE FOR PLANS
10 FEET
3 METRES

COMPARATIVE CARVED CAPITALS

NORMAN

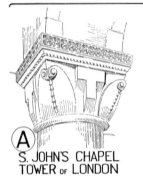

A S. JOHN'S CHAPEL TOWER OF LONDON

B S. PETER : NORTHAMPTON

C GALILEE : DURHAM CATH.

EARLY ENGLISH

D GALILEE PORCH ELY CATHEDRAL ⊢ 4¾ ⊣

E BRIDLINGTON PRIORY : YORKS

F CHAPTER HOUSE SALISBURY CATHL ⊢ 4⅜″ ⊣

DECORATED

G BEVERLEY MINSTER : YORKS

H CHAPTER HOUSE SOUTHWELL MINSTER

J LADY CHAPEL ELY CATHEDRAL

PERPENDICULAR

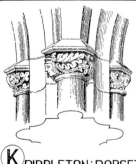

K PIDDLETON : DORSET

L WOLBOROUGH : DEVON

M KENTON : DEVON

Norman. Piers (p. 503), short and massive, are cylindrical or polygonal, as at Gloucester, Hereford, Southwell, and S. John's Chapel, Tower of London (p. 436C), while at Durham lozenge, chevron and vertical channellings were worked on the cylindrical piers (p. 392B). Compound piers, with rectangular recesses containing shafts, as at Peterborough (p. 414J) and Durham (p. 392B), were often used alternately with cylindrical piers, as at Norwich, Durham, and Waltham. The shape of piers during the Mediaeval period was influenced by the vaulting shafts which they supported. The small shafts in the recessed 'orders' of doorways and windows were sometimes richly carved. Capitals (pp. 503, 504) are usually cubiform or cushion type, sometimes carved and scalloped, but some, such as the Ionic capital in the Tower of London, are reminiscent of Roman architecture, though the Corinthian type, which occurs in Canterbury (p. 418B), is more frequently seen in France.

Early English. Piers (p. 503) are either compound, cylindrical, or octagonal, and often surrounded by detached shafts of Purbeck marble (p. 425C) held together by bands of stone or metal at intervals, as at Salisbury (p. 415H), the Temple Church (p. 388B), and Westminster Abbey (p. 422B). Capitals were frequently boldly moulded so as to produce deep shadows, or carved with conventional foliage (p. 504), and the normal abacus is circular on plan, and thus differs from the square abacus of France. Capitals were also of the 'crocket' and 'water-leaf' types. The water table base was common (pp. 498D, 503N).

Decorated. Piers (p. 503), which are sometimes diamond-shaped on plan, are surrounded by engaged shafts, a development from detached Early English shafts. Capitals are usually circular on plan; and when moulded are similar to Early English, but not so deeply undercut, and the carved foliage of oak, ivy, maple, or vine is more naturalistic (pp. 419D, 504).

Perpendicular. Piers (p. 503) frequently have four semicircular shafts connected by hollows and side fillets, which are also sometimes carried round the arch (p. 391B). Piers became more slender and were often oblong on plan with the greater dimension north and south, regulated by the carrying up of the vaulting shafts from the ground. Capitals, now often polygonal on plan, have less pronounced mouldings and the abacus and bell are not so clearly defined (p. 425E). Capitals when carved have conventional foliage, shallow and square in outline (p. 504). Bases to piers are often polygonal on plan and the 'bracket' moulding was in constant use (p. 503V).

Tudor. Piers adhered to the slender Perpendicular type with octagonal moulded base and capital, and are seen in chantry chapels, sepulchral monuments, choir stalls, and domestic fittings.

Mouldings

Anglo-Saxon. Mouldings were few, and consisted of simple rounds and hollows in capitals (p. 387D, F) and bases (p. 387D) formed by the axe, which appears to have been the chief tool employed, but turned balusters in tower windows indicate greater technical skill (p. 387B).

Norman. The development of mouldings was a marked feature of this period (p. 507) and are an index of date in all periods. The jambs of door and window openings were formed in recesses or 'orders' and the outer edges were rounded off in bowtell mouldings (see Glossary), and from this simple beginning the complicated mouldings of subsequent periods were evolved. The mouldings themselves were elaborately carved with chevron or zigzag, billet, beak-head, nail-head, cable, embattled, and double cone, and form an important decorative element in the style (p. 508).

Early English. Mouldings are bold and deeply undercut, but still follow and accentuate the outline of the rectangular recesses by being arranged on the 'wall' and 'soffit planes' (p. 507G, H, J, K). The bowtell moulding is occasionally accompanied by a side or front fillet, and is sometimes so developed with hollows on either side as to be pear-shaped in section, while sometimes it is pointed and formed as a 'keel' moulding (p. 507G, see Glossary). The chiselled dog-tooth (see Glossary) succeeded the axed nail-head of the Norman period and gives a play of light and shade to deeply cut hollow mouldings (p. 508).

Decorated. Mouldings depart from precedent, as they are sometimes formed on the diagonal or 'chamfer plane' instead of on planes parallel either with the wall face or jamb face (p. 507). There is a tendency to disregard the recesses or 'orders', which are now sometimes disguised by hollow mouldings at their junction. New varieties are the wave and the ogee mouldings, while the scroll moulding is used in capitals (see Glossary for these terms). Hollow mouldings are ornamented with the characteristic ball-flower and the tablet-flower (p. 508). Base mouldings to walls are strongly marked, as in the exterior of Lincoln (p. 416B) and Exeter (p. 497Q). Cornices and strings often have their deep hollows filled with carved foliage (p. 508), while hood-moulds or dripstones are ornamented with crockets terminated with carved heads or grotesques, as at Cley, Norfolk (p. 498F).

Perpendicular. Mouldings were set on the diagonal plane, being wide and shallow, and often large and coarse (p. 507). The wide flat hollow known as the 'casement' and also the bracket or 'brace' moulding (see Glossary) are common. Pier mouldings are often continued up from the base round the arch without the intervention of capitals. One set of mouldings, especially in bases, often interpenetrates (i.e. passes behind or in front of) another, and this gives a complicated and intricate appearance. Carved mouldings are enriched with tablet-flowers and flowing vine and rose, and crestings frequently surmount the cornice mouldings (pp. 508, 511J, K), and diminutive battlements occur along the transoms of windows, while the hollows are enriched with successive cornice flowers.

Tudor. Mouldings are similar to those of the last period, but owing to their use in fittings of domestic buildings, such as chimney-pieces, wall panels, doors, and ceilings, they are generally smaller and more refined. The lofty moulded and twisted brick chimney-stacks are prominent features in this period (pp. 449D, 460C). Mouldings begin to indicate the influence of the great Renaissance movement which was gradually being felt in England.

ORNAMENT

Anglo-Saxon. Sculpture was roughly executed, probably by the mason's axe, and betrays the influence of Roman art; but in the absence of technical skill little carved ornament was incorporated in the fabric of the buildings, which, it is believed, depended on tapestry hangings for internal decoration (p. 387F).

Norman. Carved ornament was now often applied to mouldings. Carved foliage, especially the acanthus scroll, is clearly due to Roman art, though executed in a bolder and less refined manner. The tympana over many Norman doorways, such as the Priest's door at Ely, are sculptured with effective though rough representations of Scriptural subjects. Arcading of intersecting arches (p. 414J) along aisle walls are frequent, and are often piled up in storeys to ornament the whole wall. Stained glass now began to be used, though sparingly, in small pieces, leaded together in mosaic-like patterns. The glass panels in the choir at Canterbury (1174) represent Biblical subjects, set in a blue or ruby ground, and framed in brilliantly-coloured scroll-work. Timber roofs were coloured, sometimes with lozenge-shaped panels, as at Peterborough (p. 414H), and the restored roof in Waltham Abbey gives an idea of the original colour treatment. Hanging tapestries gave warmth and interest to interiors, as the famous Bayeux tapestry testifies. The font (p. 515A), piscina

COMPARATIVE MOULDINGS

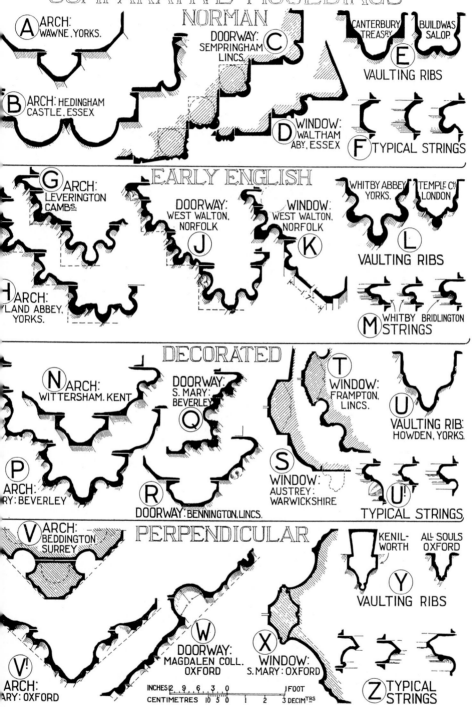

NORMAN

A — ARCH: WAWNE, YORKS.

B — ARCH: HEDINGHAM CASTLE, ESSEX

C — DOORWAY: SEMPRINGHAM LINCS.

D — WINDOW: WALTHAM ABY, ESSEX

E — VAULTING RIBS — CANTERBURY TREASRY — BUILDWAS SALOP.

F — TYPICAL STRINGS

EARLY ENGLISH

G — ARCH: LEVERINGTON CAMBS.

H — ARCH: LAND ABBEY, YORKS.

J — DOORWAY: WEST WALTON, NORFOLK

K — WINDOW: WEST WALTON, NORFOLK

L — VAULTING RIBS — WHITBY ABBEY YORKS. — TEMPLE CH LONDON

M — STRINGS — WHITBY BRIDLINGTON

DECORATED

N — ARCH: WITTERSHAM, KENT

P — ARCH: RY: BEVERLEY

Q — DOORWAY: S. MARY: BEVERLEY

R — DOORWAY: BENNINGTON, LINCS.

S — WINDOW: AUSTREY: WARWICKSHIRE

T — WINDOW: FRAMPTON, LINCS.

U — VAULTING RIB: HOWDEN, YORKS.

U¹

TYPICAL STRINGS

PERPENDICULAR

V — ARCH: BEDDINGTON SURREY

V¹ — ARCH: RY: OXFORD

W — DOORWAY: MAGDALEN COLL. OXFORD

X — WINDOW: S. MARY: OXFORD

Y — VAULTING RIBS — KENILWORTH — ALL SOULS OXFORD

Z — TYPICAL STRINGS

INCHES 12 9 6 3 0 | 1 FOOT
CENTIMETRES 10 5 0 | 1 | 2 | 3 DECIMTRS

COMPARATIVE ORNAMENTED MOULDINGS

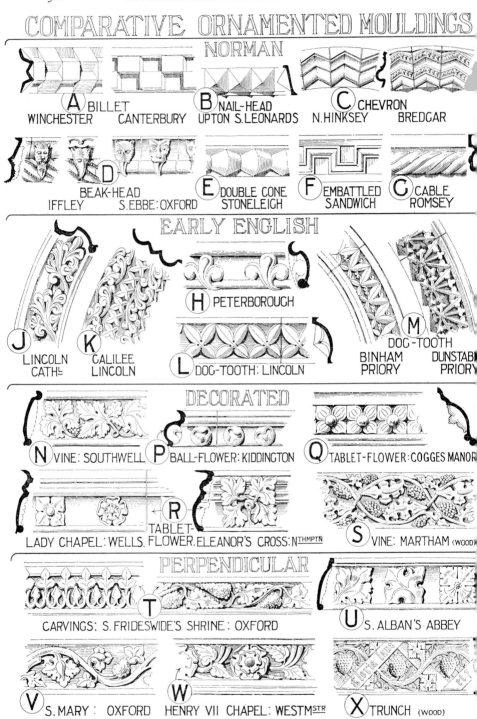

NORMAL

- A BILLET WINCHESTER — CANTERBURY
- B NAIL-HEAD UPTON S.LEONARDS
- C CHEVRON N.HINKSEY — BREDGAR
- D BEAK-HEAD IFFLEY — S.EBBE: OXFORD
- E DOUBLE CONE STONELEIGH
- F EMBATTLED SANDWICH
- G CABLE ROMSEY

EARLY ENGLISH

- H PETERBOROUGH
- J LINCOLN CATH.
- K GALILEE LINCOLN
- L DOG-TOOTH: LINCOLN
- M DOG-TOOTH BINHAM PRIORY — DUNSTABLE PRIORY

DECORATED

- N VINE: SOUTHWELL
- P BALL-FLOWER: KIDDINGTON
- Q TABLET-FLOWER: COGGES MANOR
- R TABLET-FLOWER. ELEANOR'S CROSS: N.THMPTN LADY CHAPEL: WELLS.
- S VINE: MARTHAM (WOOD)

PERPENDICULAR

- T CARVINGS: S. FRIDESWIDE'S SHRINE: OXFORD
- U S. ALBAN'S ABBEY
- V S. MARY: OXFORD
- W HENRY VII CHAPEL: WESTM.STR
- X TRUNCH (WOOD)

(p. 515E), sedilia (p. 515K), gable cross (p. 512A), boss (p. 512J), and corbel (p. 512N) show the craftsmanship expended on carving, fittings, and furniture in many a country church.

Early English. The dog-tooth ornament in hollow mouldings was used in great profusion (p. 508L, M) and the chisel replaced the axe of the early Norman period. Carved foliage is conventional in treatment, and consists of crisp, curling masses of 'stiff leaf foliage' (pp. 504D, E, F, 508J, 512P). Flat surfaces, as in Westminster Abbey (p. 422B), are often carved with delicate 'diaper' patterns (see Glossary), sometimes painted, and doubtless copied from tapestry hangings or painted panels. Large sculptured figures were often placed in canopied niches, and the west front of Wells (1230–60), with 300 statues, is a design on the grand scale in which sculpture is combined with architecture (p. 403B). Arcading of pointed arches often ornamented the lower part of walls, as at Salisbury. Stained-glass windows increased in number and small pieces of glass were still leaded in mosaic-like patterns, in which a violet-blue was a favourite colour, as in Becket's Crown, Canterbury, the 'Five Sisters', York, and the rose window, Lincoln. Many fine monuments now added to the beauty of interiors, and Bishop Bridport's monument (p. 472B) in Salisbury Cathedral and the Cantelupe shrine, Hereford Cathedral (p. 472J), are beautiful examples of the fine decorative stonework of this period, while the Early English font (p. 515B), piscina (p. 515F), sedilia (p. 515M) and tabernacle (p. 515J), gable cross (p. 512B), finial (p. 512E), boss (p. 512K), gargoyle (p. 511H), crocket (p. 511N, P), and bracket (p. 512P) show that much careful craftsmanship was lavished on these features. The Psalters, Missals, Books of Hours, and Chronicles are a valuable record of contemporary life in which huntsman, shepherd, fisherman, labourer, scribe, monk, king, knight, and saint all bear their part. The British Museum and the Victoria and Albert Museum contain armour, caskets, pyxes, and triptychs wrought in metals, ivory, and wood, with architectural features freely used in the designs.

Decorated. The ball-flower (see Glossary) and tablet-flower often enrich mouldings. Carving generally became more naturalistic and reproduced the actual forms of ivy, oak, vine-leaves, and even of seaweed (pp. 508, 512L, Q). Figures in canopied niches were frequently added to exteriors, as at Exeter, and arcading, resembling window tracery, lined the wall surfaces. Stained glass, losing its primitive mosaic character, became translucent in tone and more free in design, and the large windows glowed with luminous coloured pictures of figures in architectural canopies with borders of vine and ivy, such as are seen in York Minster, Tewkesbury Abbey, and Merton College, Oxford.

Shrines and tombs in cathedrals and churches (p. 472G, K, L) are miniature buildings in themselves, with beautiful detail of canopy, crocket (p. 511Q, R), and pinnacle. Fittings, especially in woodwork, such as pierced screens, bishops' thrones (p. 517E), carved choir stalls (p. 517D), pews (p. 517A), and pulpits, under the influence of sacerdotalism, acquired importance in decoration (pp. 417B, 418B). The font (p. 515C), piscina (p. 515G), tabernacle (p. 515L), gargoyles (p. 511L, M), sedilia (p. 515N), corbel (p. 512Q), eagle lecterns (p. 518E), gable cross (p. 512C), finial (p. 512F), boss (p. 512L), and the Eleanor Crosses (p. 486B), well show the decorative treatment of the period, while brasses at Cobham (p. 518M) and Stoke d'Abernon—the earliest in England—are examples of commemorative monuments.

Perpendicular. Vine leaves and grapes often enrich the mouldings, which also have cornice flowers at intervals (p. 508U). Carved foliage is both conventional and naturalistic (pp. 507, 508, 511), while the special ornaments of the period are the Tudor rose, the portcullis, and the fleur-de-lis, all of which were used abundantly as in Henry VII's Chapel. Fine figure sculpture takes the form of angels and heraldic figures supporting emblems, such as the portcullis, rose, and crown, as in Henry VII's Chapel (p. 428), and the carved angels on the 'Jacob's ladder' at Bath Abbey. Wall arcading was replaced by panelling, which, resembling window tracery, overlaid the wall surfaces and buttresses from floor to vault, as at Gloucester, while miniature battlements decorated window transoms and cornices (pp. 495M, 499M, 516A). Architectural canopies in stained glass have a mellow golden tinge, produced by silver stain, which sets off the large single figures in ruby and blue, which are often ranged one above the other. Window design became more pictorial, as the use of perspective overcame the difficulties inherent in transparent glass. Heraldic devices of shields with armorial bearings and scroll inscriptions were frequent, as at King's College Chapel, Cambridge, Fairford Church, Gloucestershire, and Canterbury Cathedral. Shrines and chantry chapels, as at Winchester (p. 420J) and Canterbury, and reredoses, as at Winchester (p. 420G), were often delicately modelled miniatures of the design of the larger building, which they adorn. Chancel screens, often supporting rood lofts (many of which have been destroyed since 1561), were formed of mullions, open tracery and sculptured statues under crocketed canopies, the whole crowned with Tudor flower cresting (p. 511J). Colour was frequently applied to fittings and timber roofs, as in the churches of East Anglia. Choir stalls (p. 517F) were elaborate and misericords under choir seats were carved with grotesques and delicate foliage (p. 517), while bench-ends were terminated with carved poppy-heads (p. 517B, C, G). Examples of a Perpendicular font (p. 515D), piscina (p. 515H), sedilia (p. 515P), chancel and rood screens (p. 516), a bench-end (p. 517C), pulpits (p. 517), rood loft (p. 516C), parclose screen (p. 516A), chantry chapels (p. 472A, C), a gable cross (p. 512D), crockets (p. 511S, T), finial (p. 512G, H), pendant (p. 512R), and boss (p. 512M) are given. Metalwork in door fittings, grilles, and in fine brasses was used in profusion with much variety and beauty of design and execution (p. 518).

Tudor. Tudor ornament began to appear during the late Perpendicular period in church monuments, and also in domestic architecture. The Tudor rose (p. 508W) enriches mouldings and, with curling vine-leaf and tendril, is frequent in the spandrels of four-centred door-heads. Chantry chapels, as at Worcester (p. 472), were striking features in some of the cathedrals. Sculpture generally betrays Renaissance influence, and the roundels at Hampton Court Palace were actually brought from Italy. Chimney-pieces offered a fine field for the decorative display of carving with heraldic devices, as in the famous chimney-pieces of Tattershall Keep (p. 445G, J). Woodwork is finely carved, as in the linenfold panels of walls (p. 461J) and doors, and also of furniture, which now became more plentiful. Modelled plaster ceilings with moulded ribs give finish to interiors, as at Loseley Park (p. 887A), Levens Hall, and Hampton Court (p. 461C). Timber buildings sometimes are covered externally with ornamental plaster 'pargetting' (see Glossary). Leadwork also received ornamental treatment, as in the turrets at Hampton Court, and rain-water heads (p. 461G). Wrought-iron door fittings (p. 461H) and metal work as the screen to Henry VII's Chantry Chapel (p. 428) are architectural in character. Glass, coloured with heraldic devices, was now more largely used in domestic architecture in patterned lead 'cames', as in the windows at Ockwells Manor, Berkshire. Castles of the feudal type, designed for military operations and for defensive purposes, and often as bare of ornament as of comfort, were passing away. The manor houses which sprang up were developed on domestic rather than on military lines, as the fortified stronghold gave way before the dwelling-house. With this change of purpose came a desire for comfort and decoration, and so ornament, which had been the faithful handmaid of ecclesiastical architecture, had a fresh chance of development in the service of domestic architecture. Thus, the tendency of Tudor ornament was

PARAPETS, GARGOYLES, CRESTINGS & CROCKETS

PARAPETS

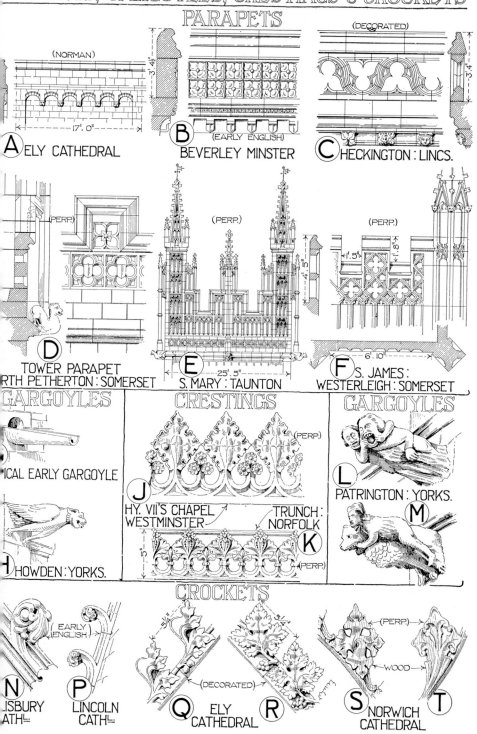

A — (NORMAN) — 17'. 0" — ELY CATHEDRAL

B — (EARLY ENGLISH) — BEVERLEY MINSTER

C — (DECORATED) — HECKINGTON : LINCS.

D — (PERP.) — TOWER PARAPET
NORTH PETHERTON : SOMERSET

E — (PERP.) — 25'. 5" — S. MARY : TAUNTON

F — (PERP.) — 6'. 10" — S. JAMES :
WESTERLEIGH : SOMERSET

GARGOYLES

H — TYPICAL EARLY GARGOYLE

H — HOWDEN : YORKS.

CRESTINGS

J — (PERP.) — HY. VII'S CHAPEL WESTMINSTER

K — TRUNCH : NORFOLK — (PERP.)

GARGOYLES

L — PATRINGTON : YORKS.

M

CROCKETS

N — (EARLY ENGLISH) — SALISBURY CATH^L.

P — LINCOLN CATH^L.

Q — (DECORATED) — ELY CATHEDRAL

R

S — (PERP.) — NORWICH CATHEDRAL

T — WOOD

CROSSES, FINIALS, BOSSES, CORBELS, ETC

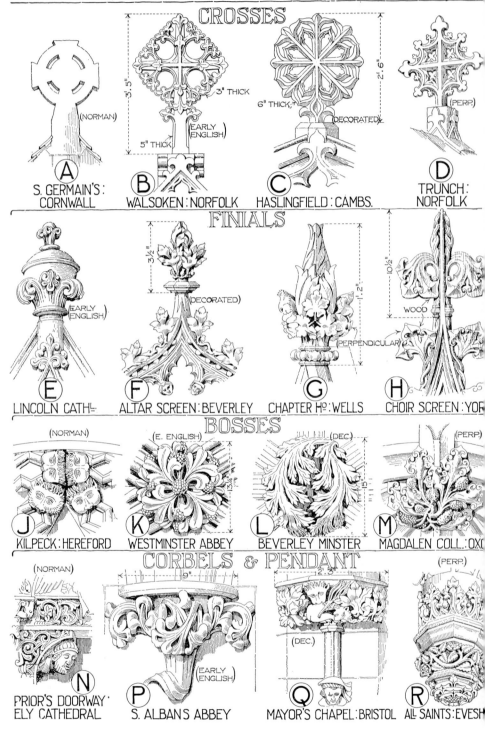

CROSSES

A — S. GERMAIN'S: CORNWALL (NORMAN)

B — WALSOKEN: NORFOLK — 3'.5", 5" THICK, 3" THICK (EARLY ENGLISH)

C — HASLINGFIELD: CAMBS. — 2'.6", 6" THICK (DECORATED)

D — TRUNCH: NORFOLK (PERP.)

FINIALS

E — LINCOLN CATHL. (EARLY ENGLISH)

F — ALTAR SCREEN: BEVERLEY — 3½" (DECORATED)

G — CHAPTER HO: WELLS — 1'.2" (PERPENDICULAR)

H — CHOIR SCREEN: YORK — 10½", WOOD

BOSSES

J — KILPECK: HEREFORD (NORMAN)

K — WESTMINSTER ABBEY (E. ENGLISH) — 13¼"

L — BEVERLEY MINSTER (DEC.) — 15"

M — MAGDALEN COLL.: OXON (PERP.)

CORBELS & PENDANT

N — PRIOR'S DOORWAY ELY CATHEDRAL (NORMAN)

P — S. ALBAN'S ABBEY — 9" (EARLY ENGLISH)

Q — MAYOR'S CHAPEL: BRISTOL — 2'.3" (DEC.)

R — ALL SAINTS: EVESHAM (PERP.)

largely governed by its incorporation in domestic building. This, together with the influence of the incoming Renaissance, gives it a special character and associates it intimately with the new English homes, which were then rising throughout the country in place of old monastic establishments. Here then, again, we see that ornament adds its peculiar attribute to each period.

REFERENCE BOOKS

ADDY, S. O. *The Evolution of the English House.* London, 1933.

BATSFORD, H., and FRY, C. *The Cathedrals of England.* London, 1936.

—. *The Greater English Church.* London, 1940.

BOND, F. *Gothic Architecture in England.* London, 1905.

—. *Introduction to English Church Architecture.* 2 vols. London, 1913.

—. *Westminster Abbey.* London, 1909.

BRANDON, R., and J. A. *Analysis of Gothic Architecture.* 1847. New ed., 2 vols. Edinburgh 1903.

—. *Open Timber Roofs of the Middle Ages.* London, 1849.

—. *Parish Churches.* 2 vols. London, 1851.

BRAUN, H. *The English Castle.* 3rd ed., London, 1947–8.

BRITTON, J. *Cathedral Antiquities.* 13 vols. London, 1817–35.

—. *Architectural Antiquities.* 5 vols. London, 1807–26.

BROWN, G. BALDWIN. *The Arts in Early England.* 2 vols. London, 1903.

BROWN, R. ALLEN. *English Medieval Castles.* London, 1954.

CLAPHAM, A. W. *English Romanesque Architecture.* 2 vols. Oxford, 1930–4.

CLARK, G. T. *Mediaeval Military Architecture in England.* 2 vols. London, 1884.

CLARK, GRAHAME. *Prehistoric England.* 4th ed. London, 1948.

COOK, G. H. *Mediaeval Chantries and Chantry Chapels.* London, 1947.

COX, J. C. *The Parish Churches of England.* London, 1937.

—. (Editor) *The English County Church Series.* 12 vols. 1910–13.

—. *English Church Fittings, etc.* London, 1933.

CROSSLEY, F. H. *English Church Monuments. A.D. 1150–1550.* London, 1921.

—. *The English Abbey.* London, 1935.

—. *English Church Craftsmanship.* London, 1941.

—. *Timber Building in England.* London, 1951.

GARDNER, S. *A Guide to English Gothic Architecture.* Cambridge, 1922.

GARNER, T., and STRATTON, A. *The Domestic Architecture of England during the Tudor Period.* 2 vols. London, 1929.

GODFREY, W. H. *Story of Architecture in England.* London, 1928.

GOTCH, J. A. *The Growth of the English House.* London, 1928.

GREEN, J. R. *Short History of the English People.* London, 1907.

HARVEY, J. H. 'Education of Mediaeval Architects', *Journal R.I.B.A.*, June, 1945.

—. *English Cathedrals.* 2nd ed. London, 1956.

—. *Gothic England.* 2nd ed. London, 1948.

—. *Henry Yevele.* 2nd ed. London, 1946.

HAWKES, J., and C. *Prehistoric Britain.* Pelican books, 1949.

HOWARD, F. E., and CROSSLEY, F. H. *English Church Woodwork.* 2nd ed. London, 1927.

HOWARD, F. E. *The Mediaeval Styles of the English Parish Church.* London, 1936.

JACKSON, SIR T. G. *Gothic Architecture in France, England and Italy.* 2 vols. London, 1915.

JONES, S. R. *English Village Homes.* London, 1936.

KNOOP, D., and JONES, G. P. *The Mediaeval Mason.* Manchester, 1933.

LETHABY, W. R. *Westminster Abbey and the King's Craftsmen.* London, 1906.

MOORMAN, J. P. *Church Life in England in the 13th Century.* Cambridge, 1945.

O'NEIL, B. H. ST. J. *Castles.* H.M.S.O., 1953.

PALMER, R. L. *English Monasteries in the Middle Ages.* London, 1930.

PARKER, J. H. *Glossary of Terms in Grecian, Roman, Italian and Gothic Architecture.* 3 vols. 11th ed. London, 1905.

R

POWER, C. E. *English Mediaeval Architecture*. 2nd ed., 3 vols. London, 1923.

PRIOR, E. S. *A History of Gothic Art in England*. London, 1900.

PUGIN, A., and A. W. *Examples of Gothic Architecture*. London, 1838.

PUGIN, A. *Specimens of Gothic Architecture*. 2 vols. London, 1821.

QUENNELL, M., and C. H. B. *A History of Everyday Things in England, 1066–1499.* London, 1931.

—. *Everyday Life in Anglo-Saxon, Viking, and Norman Times*. London, 1926.

RICHMOND, I. A. *Roman Britain*. Pelican books, 1955.

RICKMAN, T. *Gothic Architecture*. Oxford and London, 1881.

ROSENBERG, G. 'The Functional Aspect of the Gothic Style', *R.I.B.A. Journal*, Jan. and Feb., 1936.

SALZMAN, L. F. *Building in England down to 1540*. Oxford, 1952.

—. *English Life in the Middle Ages*. Oxford, 1927.

—. *England in Tudor Times*. London, 1926.

SCOTT, SIR G. GILBERT. *Lectures on Mediaeval Architecture*. 2 vols. London, 1879.

—. *History of English Church Architecture*. London, 1881.

SHARPE, E. *Seven Periods of English Architecture*. London, 1888.

—. *Architectural Parallels*. London, 1848.

—. *Mouldings of the Six Periods of British Architecture*. London, 1871–4.

—. *Rise and Progress of decorated Window Tracery in England*. 2 vols. London, 1849.

—. *Churches of the Nene Valley, Northants.* 1880.

SMITH, J. T. 'Medieval Aisled Halls and their Derivatives', *Archaeological Journal*, vol. cxii, 1956.

STATHAM, H. H. (Editor). *Cathedrals of England and Wales* (The 'Builder' Series.) 1898, with series of plans to a large scale.

SWARTWOUT, R. E. *The Monastic Craftsman*. Cambridge, 1932.

THOMPSON, A. HAMILTON. *Military Architecture in England*. London, 1912.

—. *The Ground Plan of the English Parish Church*. Cambridge, 1911.

—. *Historical Growth of the English Parish Church*. Cambridge, 1913.

—. *English Monasteries*. Cambridge, 1913.

TIPPING, H. A. *English Homes*. Period I, 1066–1485; Period II, 1485–1558. 3 vols. London, 1921–37.

TOY, SYDNEY. *Castles of Great Britain*. 2nd ed. London, 1954.

TURNER, T. H., and PARKER, J. H. *Some Account of the Domestic Architecture in England during the Middle Ages*. 3 vols. Oxford, 1859–77.

VALLANCE, AYMER. *The Old Colleges of Oxford*. London, 1912.

—. *English Church Screens*. London, 1936.

—. *Old Crosses and Lychgates*. London, 1933.

WEBB, GEOFFREY. *Architecture in Britain—The Middle Ages*. Pelican History of Art, 1956.

WICKES, C. *Spires and Towers of the Mediaeval Churches of England*. 3 vols. London 1853–9.

WILLIS, R. 'Vaults of the Middle Ages', *Trans. R.I.B.A.*, 1842.

—. *Architectural History of Canterbury Cathedral*. London, 1845.

WONNACOTT, E. W. M. *History and Development of Vaulting in England*. London, 1891.

WOOD, MARGARET E. 'Thirteenth Century Domestic Architecture in England', *Archaeological Journal*, vol. cx, Supplement, 1950.

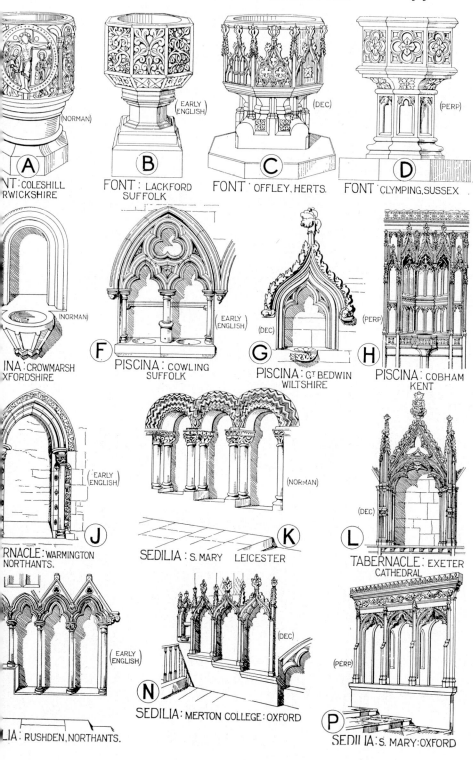

A — FONT: COLESHILL WARWICKSHIRE (NORMAN)

B — FONT: LACKFORD SUFFOLK (EARLY ENGLISH)

C — FONT: OFFLEY, HERTS. (DEC)

D — FONT: CLYMPING, SUSSEX (PERP)

E — PISCINA: CROWMARSH OXFORDSHIRE (NORMAN)

F — PISCINA: COWLING SUFFOLK (EARLY ENGLISH)

G — PISCINA: GT BEDWIN WILTSHIRE (DEC)

H — PISCINA: COBHAM KENT (PERP)

J — TABERNACLE: WARMINGTON NORTHANTS. (EARLY ENGLISH)

K — SEDILIA: S. MARY LEICESTER (NORMAN)

L — TABERNACLE: EXETER CATHEDRAL (DEC)

M — SEDILIA: RUSHDEN, NORTHANTS. (EARLY ENGLISH)

N — SEDILIA: MERTON COLLEGE: OXFORD (DEC)

P — SEDILIA: S. MARY: OXFORD (PERP)

SCREENS & ROOD LOFTS

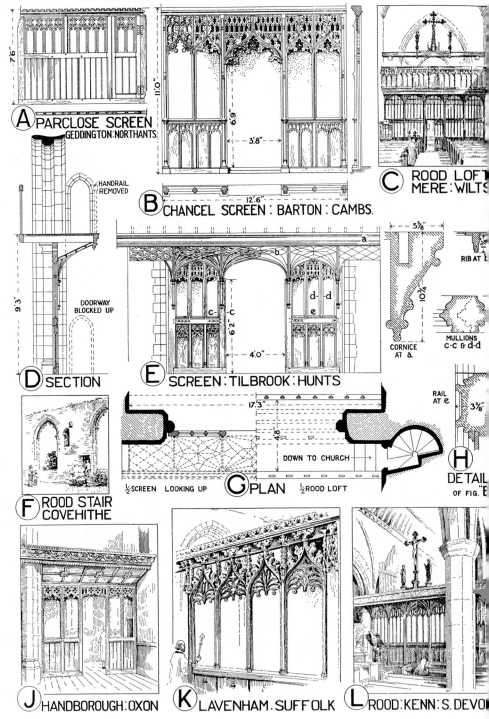

A PARCLOSE SCREEN
GEDDINGTON : NORTHANTS.

7'6"

B CHANCEL SCREEN : BARTON : CAMBS.
11'0"
6'9"
3'8"
12'6"

C ROOD LOFT
MERE : WILTS

D SECTION
9'3"
HANDRAIL REMOVED
DOORWAY BLOCKED UP

E SCREEN : TILBROOK : HUNTS
a
b
c—c
d—d
e
6'2"
4'0"

CORNICE AT a
5⅜"
10¾"

RIB AT
MULLIONS c—c & d—d

RAIL AT e
3⅜"

F ROOD STAIR
COVEHITHE

G PLAN ½ ROOD LOFT
½ SCREEN LOOKING UP
17'3"
4'8"
DOWN TO CHURCH

H DETAIL
OF FIG. "E"

J HANDBOROUGH : OXON

K LAVENHAM . SUFFOLK

L ROOD : KENN : S. DEVON

MEDIÆVAL CHURCH FITTINGS

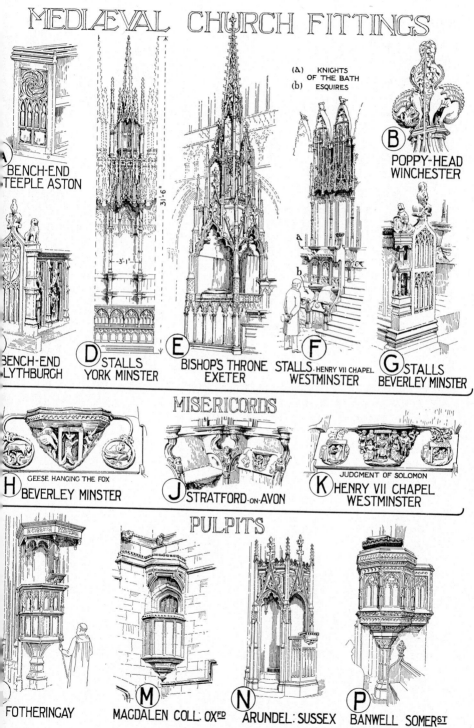

A BENCH-END TEEPLE ASTON

B POPPY-HEAD WINCHESTER

(a) KNIGHTS OF THE BATH
(b) ESQUIRES

31'-6"

3'-1"

BENCH-END LYTHBURGH

D STALLS YORK MINSTER

E BISHOP'S THRONE EXETER

F STALLS HENRY VII CHAPEL WESTMINSTER

G STALLS BEVERLEY MINSTER

MISERICORDS

H BEVERLEY MINSTER
GEESE HANGING THE FOX

J STRATFORD-ON-AVON

K HENRY VII CHAPEL WESTMINSTER
JUDGMENT OF SOLOMON

PULPITS

FOTHERINGAY

M MAGDALEN COLL: OXFD

N ARUNDEL: SUSSEX

P BANWELL SOMERST

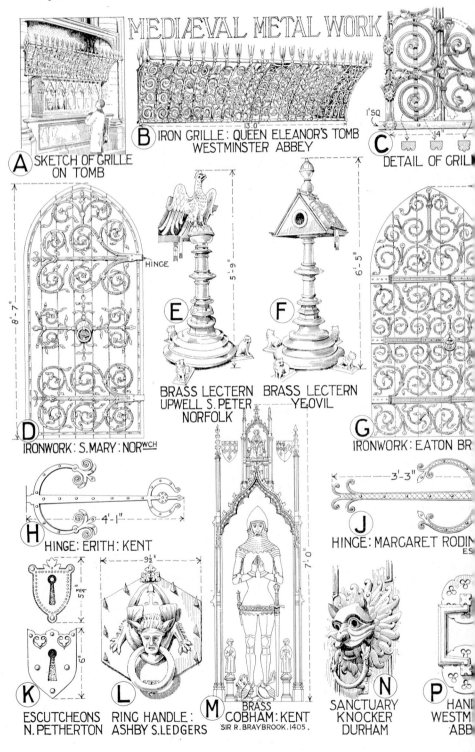

MEDIÆVAL METAL WORK

A SKETCH OF GRILLE ON TOMB

B IRON GRILLE: QUEEN ELEANOR'S TOMB WESTMINSTER ABBEY

13.0

C DETAIL OF GRILL

1"SQ   3/4"

D IRONWORK: S. MARY: NOR^{WCH}

8'-7"

HINGE

E BRASS LECTERN UPWELL S. PETER NORFOLK

5'-9"

F BRASS LECTERN YEOVIL

G IRONWORK: EATON BR

6'-5"

H HINGE: ERITH: KENT

4'-1"

J HINGE: MARGARET RODIN
ES

3'-3"

K ESCUTCHEONS N. PETHERTON

5 3/4"

6"

L RING HANDLE: ASHBY S. LEDGERS

9 1/2"

M BRASS COBHAM: KENT
SIR R. BRAYBROOK. 1405.

7'-0"

N SANCTUARY KNOCKER DURHAM

P HAN
WESTM
ABB

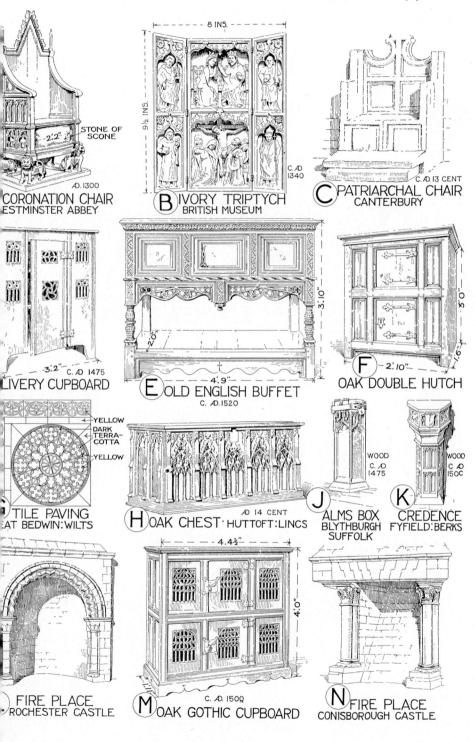

A CORONATION CHAIR
ESTMINSTER ABBEY

STONE OF SCONE

2'2"

AD. 1300

B IVORY TRIPTYCH
BRITISH MUSEUM

8 INS.

9½ INS.

C. AD 1340

C PATRIARCHAL CHAIR
CANTERBURY

C. AD. 13 CENT

D LIVERY CUPBOARD

3'2" C. AD 1475

E OLD ENGLISH BUFFET
C. AD. 1520

3'10"

2'6"

4'9"

F OAK DOUBLE HUTCH

5'0"

2'10"

1'6"

G TILE PAVING
AT BEDWIN: WILTS

YELLOW
DARK TERRA-COTTA
YELLOW

H OAK CHEST · HUTTOFT: LINCS

AD 14 CENT

J ALMS BOX
BLYTHBURGH SUFFOLK

WOOD
C. AD 1475

K CREDENCE
FYFIELD: BERKS

WOOD
C AD 150C

L FIRE PLACE
ROCHESTER CASTLE

M OAK GOTHIC CUPBOARD

4'4½"

4'0"

C. AD 1500

N FIRE PLACE
CONISBOROUGH CASTLE

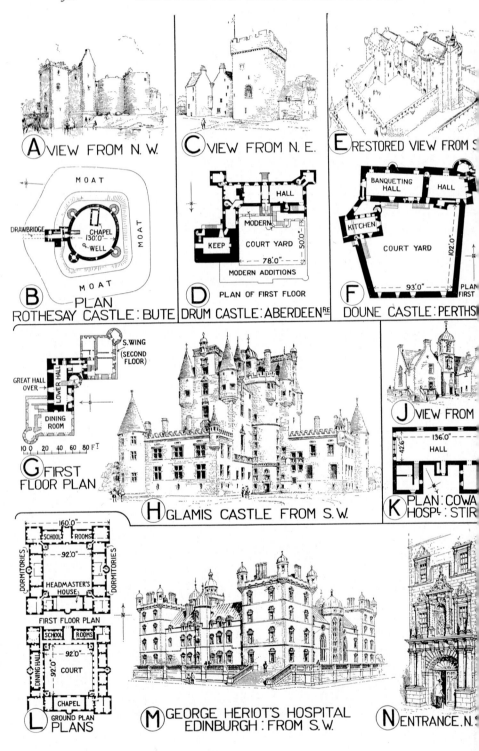

(A) VIEW FROM N. W.

(C) VIEW FROM N. E.

(E) RESTORED VIEW FROM S

MOAT

DRAWBRIDGE

CHAPEL 130'.0"
WELL

MOAT

MOAT

MOAT

(B) PLAN
ROTHESAY CASTLE : BUTE

HALL

MODERN

KEEP

COURT YARD

78'.0"

50'.0"

MODERN ADDITIONS

(D) PLAN OF FIRST FLOOR
DRUM CASTLE : ABERDEEN RE

BANQUETING HALL

HALL

KITCHEN

COURT YARD

93'.0"

102'.0"

(F) PLAN FIRST
DOUNE CASTLE : PERTHS

S. WING
(SECOND FLOOR)

GREAT HALL OVER

LOWER HALL

DINING ROOM

10 0 20 40 60 80 FT

(G) FIRST FLOOR PLAN

(H) GLAMIS CASTLE FROM S. W.

(J) VIEW FROM

136'.0"

HALL

42'.6

(K) PLAN : COWA
HOSPL : STIR

160'.0"

SCHOOL ROOMS

92'.0"

DORMITORIES

DORMITORIES

HEADMASTER'S HOUSE

FIRST FLOOR PLAN

SCHOOL ROOMS

92'.0"

92'.0"

DINING HALL

COURT

CHAPEL

(L) GROUND PLAN
PLANS

(M) GEORGE HERIOT'S HOSPITAL
EDINBURGH : FROM S. W.

(N) ENTRANCE. N.

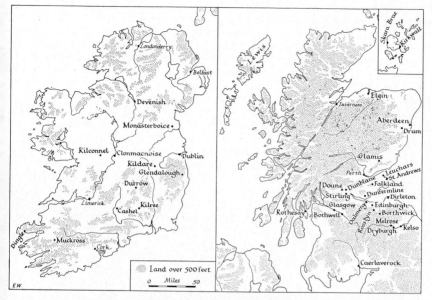

Ireland and Scotland, sixth–seventeenth centuries

XIII. SCOTTISH AND IRISH ARCHITECTURE

SCOTTISH ARCHITECTURE
(twelfth–seventeenth century)

ANTECEDENTS of Scottish architecture include: mesolithic cave-dwellings; neolithic 'long' barrows ('horned cairns') and round barrows of successive epochs; late neolithic houses, of which there are substantial remains at Skara Brae, in the Orkneys, comprising eight rectangular, round-cornered beach-cobble dwellings of *c.* 1800 B.C., linked by stone-slate-covered passages and fitted with a central square stone hearth and two stone-enclosed box beds on opposite walls; Celtic 'beehive' huts such as those of Lewis in the Outer Hebrides (p. 2D); lake dwellings of the later type, not raised on piles but built upon artificial islands or 'crannogs', which in Scotland are not earlier than Roman times and which in some cases continued in use until the seventeenth century; forts or 'duns' of which a lofty, circular special type known as 'brochs', of dry-stone walling and between 40–70 ft diameter, were built in the two centuries following 100 B.C. From about the eighth century A.D. to 1150, when Scottish Mediaeval architecture began to follow English lines, some oratories, small churches and round towers were built showing an affinity with Irish Celtic architecture.

Mediaeval architecture in Scotland followed on much the same lines as in England until the fifteenth century, when it assumed a more definitely national character. Inspiration was largely drawn from France, with which country there was close political connection. This resulted in a picturesque and interesting development on French lines, especially after Robert Bruce (1306–29) secured the independence of Scotland. In **Melrose Abbey** (1450–1505) (p. 524C) are seen French influences, while **Rosslyn Chapel** (1447) (p. 524A, B) bears a strong resemblance to the Portuguese church of Belem, near Lisbon (p. 644), though the latter is some fifty years later. Lancet windows either singly or in groups were used long after they had been discontinued in England; while the Flamboyant tracery of French Gothic was preferred to the Perpendicular style of English Gothic.

Glasgow Cathedral (1181–1508) (p. 413D) is the best preserved Gothic edifice in Scotland, and, although of different dates, is very uniform in appearance. It has an internal length of 283 ft, with nave and aisles, choir and aisles, eastern aisle with chapels beyond, and chapter house and sacristy. The fine vaulted crypt (1233–58) (p. 523B), fashioned in the fall of the ground, encloses the shrine of S. Mungo.

Other important cathedrals are those of Edinburgh, S. Andrews (1160–1318), Kirkwall (1138–1550), Dunblane (1238–60, with Romanesque tower), one of the finest Mediaeval buildings in Scotland, Aberdeen (c. 1357–1522) and Elgin. **S. Giles, Edinburgh** (mainly 1385–1416) (p. 523A) has a crown-like spire (–1495), while the abbeys of Kelso (1128–), Melrose, Dunfermline (nave, 1125–30), Holyrood (late thirteenth century) and Dryburgh are well known. **Dalmeny Church** (c. 1175) and **Leuchars Church** (p. 523C) are amongst the most notable of many parish churches.

Castles and mansions in Scotland from the twelfth to the seventeenth century have a national character. Of about eight hundred instances of the castle or private stronghold, the Anglo-Norman type of earthwork of the twelfth century was some fifty years later than in England. While the orthodox motte-and-bailey arrangement was common, more frequently the motte and bailey were undivided by a ditch and together stood elevated on a great mound. On the motte was a wooden tower within a palisade; in the bailey, itself surrounded by palisaded ramparts, were other timber buildings forming chapel, kitchen, bakehouse, stables and storehouses and the like.

In the thirteenth century, the bailey type of defended residence took firmer shape, yet still in 1300 most castles were wholly of timber, and the smaller ones in diminishing numbers afterwards; only the most important had acquired stone walls. These major exceptions, of the latter part of the period, included Dirleton Castle, East Lothian, Bothwell, Lanarkshire and Caerlaverock, Lanarkshire, in their initial form.

Of fourteenth century instances, **Rothesay Castle, Bute** (1312–34) (p. 520A, B) is less advanced than the castles last named but representative in its girdle of high, towered walls (the gatehouse and chapel are later), though baileys were not usually so regular and variously were triangular, rectangular or polygonal, according to site circumstances. Sometimes there was nothing but a stone-walled enclosure; ordinarily, there were projecting round towers, and one, occasionally rectangular, was larger than the rest and thus reminiscent of the original motte with its special tower. The towers served for residential chambers and other uses, but most of the living and ancillary accommodation was still provided in separate buildings, irregularly dispersed in the bailey, the more important, such as the chapel and hall, increasingly tending to appear as stone structures as the century proceeded. The hall then almost invariably was raised on an undercroft, often vaulted. The defended homes of the lesser gentry, sporadically changing to stone late in the period, were more compact, a single tower or 'fortalice' sufficing, this having a restricted court or 'barmkin' at its foot, demarcated by a wall about 9–12 ft high, and a ditch beyond. The first modest stone 'peles' of the border country belong to the same time and class.

Fifteenth century prosperity produced a spate of building. Military traditions

A. S. Giles' Cathedral, Edinburgh, from W. (1385–1416: spire 1495). See p. 522

в. Glasgow Cathedral: crypt (1233–58).
See p. 522

c. Leuchars Church from N.E.
(1172–85). See p. 522

A. Exterior from S.W.   B. Interior: Master's pillar

Rosslyn Chapel (*c.* 1447). See p. 522

C. Melrose Abbey from E. (1450–1505). See p. 522

weakened. In the great houses the first-storey hall block, as much as 100 ft long, now assumed higher importance than the great tower, and the two were often conjoined to form a frontispiece to the bailey or court behind. In this block the 'long gallery' made its appearance under direct French influence, as at Falkland Castle, Fife, in 1461, long before such a feature appeared in England (p. 882). Crenellated and corbelled parapets already were normal, but machicolated parapets, with apertures between the corbels, are limited almost precisely to this century in the Scottish castle. The angle turret or 'bartizan' was another French borrowing which contributes to the special character of the national style. **Doune Castle, Perthshire** (early fifteenth century) (p. 520E, F) illustrates these points and the equally typical pitched roofs with their 'corbie' or 'crow-stepped' gables. Quite often, such roofs were carried on pointed barrel vaults; and the lowest floor of castles, under the main floor, too was usually vaulted, as well as intermediate floors in some cases. Of numerous tower houses (fortalices), **Borthwick Castle, Midlothian** (1430–) is a simple rectangular block with two shallow wings on one flank.

Sixteenth and seventeenth century major castles and mansions tended to become more elaborate; the number of storeys increased at times and wings thrown out behind the frontal block might enclose the entire court to form such a regular plan as that of **George Heriot's Hospital, Edinburgh** (*c*. early seventeenth century) (p. 520L, M, N), a fine building in the early Renaissance style of which the quality of detail is especially marked in the entrance gateway. **Drum Castle, Aberdeen** (p. 520O, D), shows a partial step in the same direction. The dwellings of simpler fashion persisted in their Mediaeval form with little consistent change, save that barmkins and parapets often were dispensed with, and angle turrets or bartizans, round or square, were roofed over. In general in the lesser dwellings, fortalice or border pele, the first-floor hall was a principal element just as in the mansions, and to provide minor rooms without impeding natural light, wings were often thrown out from the angles of the main block, giving plans approximating to L, Z, T or E forms, as at **Cowane's Hospital** or **Guildhall, Stirling** (1639) (p. 520J, K), or **Glamis Castle, Angus** (*c*. 1606) (p. 520G, H), which has a Z plan produced from an original L arrangement by low-wing extensions made later in the century.

The plans and sketches of these different types of building given on p. 520 illustrate the national character of Scottish secular architecture.

IRISH ARCHITECTURE*
(sixth–sixteenth century)

THE architecture of Ireland can be divided into three main periods—Celtic, Mediaeval, and Renaissance—and in each there are a number of interesting buildings of distinctive character.

Celtic Architecture. Early Christian buildings in Ireland are archaic, and existing remains indicate that the building monks largely followed types of pre-Christian times. The chief interest lies in Celtic architecture from the sixth century to the English Conquest, 1169–72. The Celtic or 'Runic' cross is a modification of the Latin cross and is often capped with a sloping roof to throw off the rain, as in the crosses of Durrow and Monasterboice (923). They are divided into panels containing carved representations of Biblical episodes, the unending knot, and much other symbolism. The majority of the earliest churches were of timber, thatched with reeds, and have disappeared. The surviving stone churches are extremely small and appear to have been principally used as oratories for priests, with small

* See 'Prehistoric Architecture,' p. 1.

A. Oratory of Gallerus, Dingle, County Kerry (6th or 7th century). See p. 527

B. 'S. Kevin's Kitchen', Glendalough; church with adjoining house
and bell-tower (c. 850). See p. 527

square chancels attached. The naves have barrel vaults surmounted by an 'over-croft' covered by a steep roof of stone, as at **Cormac's Chapel, Cashel** (1127–34) (p. 528), probably the finest in Ireland, and the much earlier **S. Kevin's Kitchen, Glendalough** (c. 850) (p. 526B). Windows appear to have been unglazed in these primitive churches. There were also monastic establishments, and there is a group of seven small churches at Clonmacnoise similar to some in Asia Minor. The monastic cells at the Skelligs are of beehive form, with domed stone roofs in horizontal courses, as in the Treasury of Atreus, Mycenae (p. 100A). Of similar dry-stone technique is the remarkable **Oratory of Gallerus, Dingle** (sixth or seventh century) (p. 526A). It is rectangular, 22 ft × 18 ft 6 in externally, with a pointed section contrived by corbelled courses. Round towers, which are generally detached from the churches, were built between 890 and 1238. They were used as treasure-houses, refuges, or bell towers, and for displaying lamps at night. The entrance doorway was several feet from the ground, and the towers, which taper slightly towards the summit, are crowned, as in the **Tower, Devenish** (p. 528G), with a conical roof, or, as at the **Tower, Kilree** (p. 528J), with a battlemented parapet.

Mediaeval Architecture. Within the English domain in Ireland the influence of Continental art was felt during the Middle Ages, but few monuments of importance were erected. The cathedrals of **Dublin** (p. 413A), **Kildare,** and **Cashel** are the most important. The absence of parish churches is remarkable, while those of monasteries and friaries (principally Franciscan) are small and usually have a nave and choir—probably once divided by a wooden screen—transept and southern aisle, cloisters, and a tower, often added in the fifteenth century. The best known are those at Cashel, Kilconnel, and Muckross.

The earlier castles of the Irish chieftains are an interesting study, and the Anglo-Norman overlordship after 1171 has left its military traces (p. 441A); but owing to the disturbances in Elizabethan times there is little domestic architecture left of this period. Irish architecture of the Renaissance period is included with English architecture of that period.

REFERENCE BOOKS

BILLINGS, R. W. *Baronial and Ecclesiastical Antiquities of Scotland.* 4 vols. Edinburgh and London, 1848.
CHAMPNEYS, A. C. *Irish Ecclesiastical Architecture.* London, 1910.
CHILDE, V. G. *Prehistory of Scotland.* London, 1935.
DUNRAVEN, EARL OF. *Notes on Irish Architecture.* 2 vols. London, 1875–7.
Edinburgh Architectural Association, Sketch Book. 1878–94.
GILLESPIE, J. *Details of Scottish Domestic Architecture.* 1922.
Glasgow Architectural Association, Sketch Book. 3 vols. 1885.
HENRY, F. *Irish Art.* 1940.
HILL, A. *Ardfert Cathedral, Co. Kerry.* Cork, 1870.
LEASK, H. G. *Irish Castles and Castellated Houses.* 1942.
LINDSAY, I. G. *The Cathedrals of Scotland.* 1926.
MACGIBBON, D., and ROSS, T. *Castellated and Domestic Architecture of Scotland.* 5 vols. Edinburgh, 1887.
—. *Ecclesiastical Architecture of Scotland.* 3 vols. Edinburgh, 1896.
MACKENZIE, H. G. *The Mediaeval Castle in Scotland.* 1927.
MUNRO, R. *Ancient Scottish Lake Dwellings.* 1882.
National Art Survey of Scotland. Scottish Architecture, 12th–17th Cents. 4 vols. 1921–33.
PETRIE, G. *Ecclesiastical Architecture of Ireland.* Dublin, 1845.
PINCHES, F. *The Abbey Church of Melrose.* London, 1879.
PLUNKETT, COUNT. *Early Christian Churches in Ireland.*
SCOTT-MONCRIEFF, G. (ed.) *The Stones of Scotland.* 1938.
STOKES, M. *Early Christian Architecture in Ireland.* London, 1878.

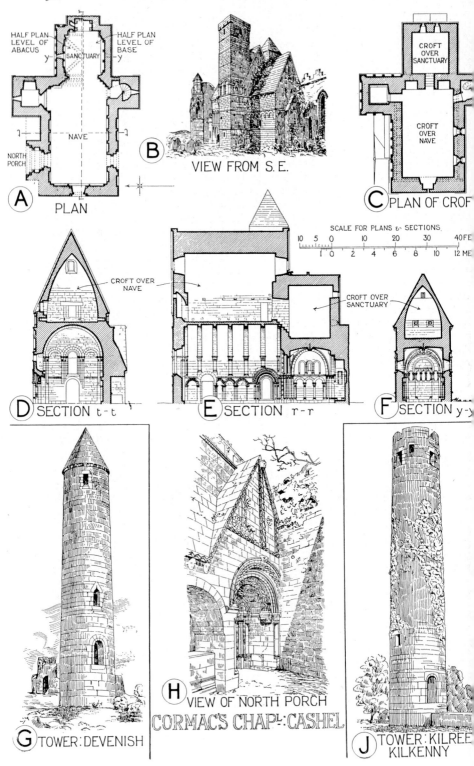

HALF PLAN LEVEL OF ABACUS

HALF PLAN LEVEL OF BASE

SANCTUARY

NAVE

NORTH PORCH

(A) PLAN

(B) VIEW FROM S.E.

CROFT OVER SANCTUARY

CROFT OVER NAVE

(C) PLAN OF CROF

CROFT OVER NAVE

(D) SECTION t-t

SCALE FOR PLANS & SECTIONS
10 5 0   10   20   30   40 FE
1 0   2   4   6   8   10   12 ME

CROFT OVER SANCTUARY

(E) SECTION r-r

(F) SECTION y-y

(G) TOWER: DEVENISH

(H) VIEW OF NORTH PORCH

CORMAC'S CHAPL: CASHEL

(J) TOWER: KILREE KILKENNY

France in the fourteenth century

XIV. FRENCH GOTHIC

(twelfth–sixteenth century)

INFLUENCES

GEOGRAPHICAL. France, on the western confines of Europe, may be considered, from an architectural standpoint, as divided into two parts by the River Loire. With the Franks on the north and the Romance races on the south, architecture was influenced not only by geographical position, but also by racial differences. The buildings of old Roman settlers in Provence and along the fertile Rhône valley not only determined the character of Romanesque in this district (p. 335), but also exercised an influence over the Gothic which followed. In the well-defined valley of the Garonne, which had been a trade-route from Marseilles to Bordeaux for merchants from the East, it is natural that there should be traces of Byzantine traditions, even as late as the Gothic period. Moorish Spain made its contribution too. The north of France, on the other hand, had been exposed to incursions of

Northmen, and this element left an impression on Gothic architecture there. The 'Ile de France' or Royal Domain—an old district forming a kind of island bounded by the Seine, the Marne, and other rivers, with Paris as its capital, became, as the headquarters of the kings of France, the district where, after the introduction of the pointed arch through the Muslims during the early Crusades, the great French Gothic cathedrals were first built in rapid succession, as at Paris and Bourges and in neighbouring provinces at Chartres, Laon, Le Mans, Amiens, and Rheims.

GEOLOGICAL. The excellent building stone of France continued as abundant as in the Romanesque period (p. 336), and that found near Caen aided in the development of the northern Gothic style. In the mountainous districts of Auvergne the use of volcanic stone gave a rich chromatic appearance to the buildings; while in the extreme south good local stone helped to continue the Classical traditions handed down through the Romanesque period (p. 340), but are in contrast with the fine marble of Italy.

CLIMATIC. This influence remained the same as during the previous period (p. 336), and all that it is necessary to note here is that the comparatively dull climate of the north permitted, and even invited, the extension of large traceried windows to light the vast interiors.

RELIGIOUS. The religious zeal of the thirteenth century, when Christianity was united against the Muslims, was especially manifested in France in the Third Crusade (1189) under Philip Augustus, and the Eighth and Ninth Crusades (1249, 1270) under S. Louis, and was marked by the erection of many grand cathedrals which were the work of the laity and the free communes, in contrast with the monastic church-building of the Romanesque period, such as that of Abbé Suger, minister of Louis VII (1137–80). The clergy, as a corporate body, had reached the summit of their power, largely due to their championship of justice and their adhesion to the royal cause. The papacy, in spite of vicissitudes, was undoubtedly powerful in France during the seventy years (1307–77) of the residence of the Popes in their fortress-palace at Avignon. The religious spirit of the age found an outlet in the inauguration of cults of special saints in different localities, and this brought fame to certain shrines which thus acquired wealth and importance as pilgrimage centres, and this is reflected in the beautiful architecture and decoration of the churches. The active zeal with which urban populations set about building cathedrals produced almost miraculously rapid results, and so much did this outburst of building activity transform the face of France, that it has been compared by Viollet-le-Duc to the commercial movement which, in later times, covered Europe with railways. A crusade against the heretical Albigenses (see below) of Albi, Toulouse, and Carcassonne was preached by the Cistercians in 1204, and relentless war was waged during the thirteenth century, under papal orders, by the king of France and the nobles of the north against the south, and ended in the destruction of the famous culture of Provence, the humiliation of the princes of the south, and the ultimate extermination of the heresy.

SOCIAL. Before the establishment of the kingdom of France, when Hugh Capet became 'King of the French' (987), the country had been peopled by races differing in origin who were at war with one another and who perpetuated differences in government, customs, and language. The consequent diversity of influences was not without its effect both on Romanesque (p. 336) and on Gothic architecture. The period during which Gothic architecture in France had its growth was marked by all the restlessness that characterizes the style, which is instinct with the intellectual and spiritual aspirations of that age. The feudal system was the root from which sprang the tyranny of the lords over the common people as well as the revolt of the same lords against the kingly power; when kings were strong, the nobles were kept

NOTRE DAME : PARIS

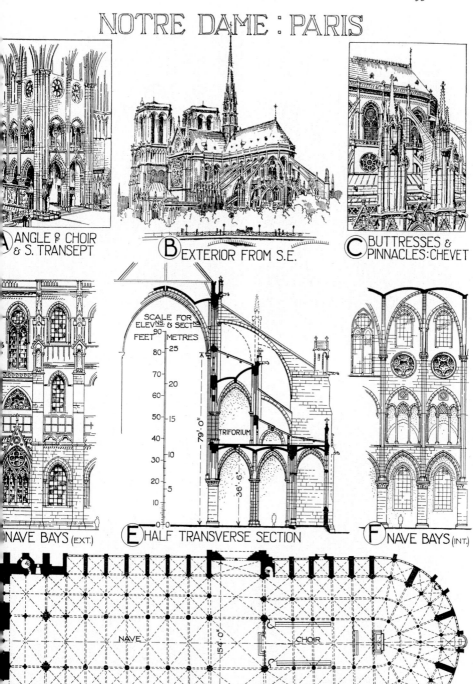

A ANGLE OF CHOIR & S. TRANSEPT

B EXTERIOR FROM S.E.

C BUTTRESSES & PINNACLES : CHEVET

SCALE FOR ELEVNS. & SECTNS

FEET   METRES

90
80 ─ 25
70 ─ 20
60 ─
50 ─ 15
40 ─ 10
30 ─
20 ─ 5
10 ─
0 ─ 0

79'·0"

36'·6"

TRIFORIUM

E HALF TRANSVERSE SECTION

D NAVE BAYS (EXT.)

F NAVE BAYS (INT.)

NAVE   CHOIR

154'·0"

0 25 50 75 100 FEET   G PLAN   METRES 10 0   10   20   30

A. West façade   B. Nave looking E.

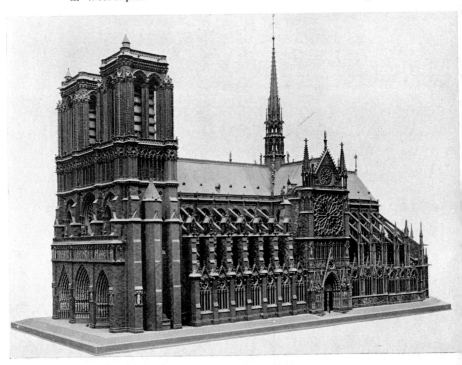

c. Exterior (model) from S.W.
(transept façade 1250–70: chapels between buttresses 1296–1325).

Notre Dame, Paris (1163–c. 1250). See p. 534

in check and the people prospered, and thus kings and people naturally fostered the communes against the nobles. The twelfth century was remarkable for the continuous struggle of the communes to assert their freedom. During the reign of Philip IV (1285–1314) the Parlement de Paris became the principal law court, and the constitutional power of the central authority grew at the expense of feudal and ecclesiastical powers. Vast stretches of fertile country were brought under cultivation for corn, vine, and olive, and these and other industries were carried on by a thrifty, sturdy population which worked, much as in England, for the feudal lord of château or manoir. Though the Black Death (1347–49) swept off a large part of the population and inevitably retarded progress in architecture, the richness of the soil still continued to supply the prosperity which, on the secular side, built the world-famous châteaux of France and the hôtels de ville of the manufacturing towns, such as Arras and Rouen, while on the ecclesiastical side a powerful and religious laity erected, with their own funds, and often with their own hands, that wonderful series of cathedrals which are at once the marvel and the glory of France.

HISTORICAL. Philip Augustus (1180–1223), after declaring King John of England to have forfeited all the fiefs he held of the French crown, proceeded to conquer Normandy and the other English possessions, with the exception of Aquitaine. Philip next defeated the combined English, German, and Flemish forces at Bovines (1214), and it was in the reign of this strong monarch that a number of French cathedrals were commenced. The power of France was so predominant that the English barons were induced to offer the crown of England to Philip's eldest son, Louis. Louis IX (S. Louis) (1226–70) further increased the power of the crown, but died at Tunis, when setting out on the ninth or last Crusade. The overthrow of the independent counts of Toulouse by Louis IX, during the religious wars against the Albigenses, so extended the kingdom of France that it obtained a triple sea-board on the Mediterranean, the Atlantic, and the English Channel, and this consolidation of the French Kingdom, by which the different nationalities were gradually absorbed under one king, corresponds with the great cathedral-building epoch of the thirteenth century.

Philip VI (1328–50) defeated the Flemings at Cassel, in 1328. In 1337, the Hundred Years' War with England (p. 386), began because of claims which arose from the marriage of Isabella of France with Edward II of England, and in 1346 the Battle of Crecy was won by the English. The French were again defeated by the English at Poitiers in 1356. Henry V of England defeated the French at Agincourt (1415) and entered Paris (1420). During the reign of Charles VII (1422–61) there was a great outburst of national sentiment when Joan of Arc raised the siege of Orleans (1429) and was burnt at Rouen as a witch by the English. In 1453 the English were expelled from the whole of France except Calais. So ended the Hundred Years' War. Louis XI (1461–83) inaugurated reforms, strengthened the central power, and worked for the unity of France by annexing Burgundy, Artois, and Provence. Charles VIII (1483–98), by his marriage with Anne of Brittany, united that province to the French crown. Thus the close of the Mediaeval period marks a united France, free from foreign invasion.

ARCHITECTURAL CHARACTER

The character and principles of Gothic architecture generally must be borne in mind in considering its developments in any particular country (p. 367). The main idea or prevailing principle of Gothic architecture in northern France was the same as in other parts of Europe, while in the south the strong Roman traditions influenced the new style, which in fact had not the same scope as in the north, owing to the great building activity of the previous Romanesque period. The vertical and aspiring tendency was accentuated in the north by lofty vaults with high-pitched roofs, western towers, tapering spires, pinnacles, flying buttresses, and tall traceried windows, and all these features show the experimental treatment of thrust and counterthrust described in detail in Chapter XI, Gothic architecture in Europe (pp. 368–71). It should be noted that the style started some half-century earlier in France than in England.

The Gothic style or 'Style ogivale', as it is called in France, lasted approximately from 1150 to 1500, and is divided by M. de Caumont into: (1) *Primaire* (twelfth century) or 'Gothique à Lancettes', a period distinguished by pointed arches and geometric traceried windows, and the transition from the Romanesque began first in the Ile de France at S. Denis (1137–44) (p. 344), Sens (1143), Senlis (1150), and Noyon (1145) (p. 541). (2) *Secondaire* (thirteenth century) or 'Rayonnant', a period characterized by circular windows with wheel tracery, as at Rheims, Amiens, and Bourges. (3) *Tertiaire* (fourteenth, fifteenth, and part sixteenth century) or 'Flamboyant', from the flame-like or free-flowing window tracery, as at S. Ouen, Rouen, S. Jacques, Dieppe, Albi, and Caudebec (p. 564D).

EXAMPLES

CATHEDRALS AND CHURCHES

The unique position occupied by cathedrals in the general social and civic life of Mediaeval times, which is nowhere more pronounced than in France, has been described in the chapter on Gothic architecture in Europe (p. 372). It is important here to remember that the original use and intention of these national monuments was so different from their modern function, which has become purely religious and ecclesiastical, that it is impossible for the reader to appreciate their meaning and value without bearing in mind this wider aspect of old French cathedrals at the time of their building, when there were practically no other public meeting-places. French cathedrals, about one hundred and fifty in number, were erected in the first half of the thirteenth century out of funds provided chiefly by the laity, and since commonly they did not originate as part of monastic establishments they differ considerably from most English cathedrals in purpose and consequently in plan and design (p. 559). The situation and surroundings of the cathedrals of France also form a marked contrast with those of England; for French cathedrals were a part of the life of the townspeople and jostled their houses shoulder to shoulder, and were not, as they generally were in England, set apart in a secluded close (p. 376).

Furthermore, these national churches, by means of the painted glass of the interior and the statuary of the exterior, served the citizens as an illustrated Bible when few could read, as has been already described in Chapter XI, Gothic architecture in Europe (p. 372).

Notre Dame, Paris (1163–*c.* 1250) (pp. 374A, 531, 532, 563C, E, F), one of the oldest of French Gothic cathedrals, was begun by Bishop Maurice de Sully. The plan, which either by accident or intention is on a bent axial line, is typical, with wide nave and double aisles, transepts of small projection practically in line with the aisles, and a notable chevet, with double aisles and surrounding chapels (of later date) between the buttresses. The choir, transepts, and all but two bays of the nave were completed by 1196; the latter bays and the main part of the western front by 1220; the upper stage of the west front, containing the rose window, by 1225 and the western towers by about 1250. Considerable modifications then were made to the fully completed building. Between 1250–70 the transepts were extended by the

A. West façade   B. Exterior from S.E.

C. Interior looking E.   D. South choir aisle, looking west

Amiens Cathedral (1220–88). See p. 541

A. Interior looking E.   B. West façade

Laon Cathedral (1160–1225). See opposite page

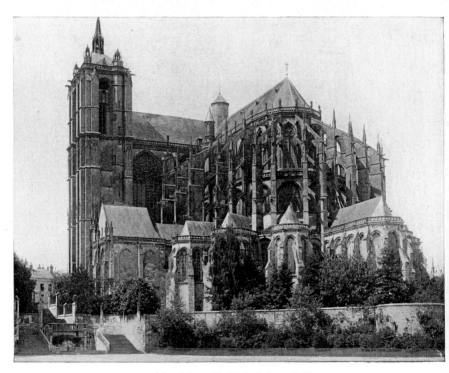

C. Le Mans Cathedral from S.E.

(Nave 12th cent.; S. transept 14th cent.; choir 1217–). See opposite page

depth of their original buttresses, and chapels afterwards thrown out between the buttresses of the nave, while the former circular upper triforium windows and the clear-story windows were together replaced by taller clear-story windows: those nearest the crossing were reinstated by Viollet-le-Duc (p. 531A). The radiating chapels between the buttresses of the choir were constructed from 1296–1325. The impressive but sombre interior has a nave arcade with cylindrical columns and Corinthianesque capitals carrying pointed arches and shafts to support the ribs of the lofty sexpartite vaulting. The wide-spreading western façade (p. 532A) is probably the finest and most characteristic in France, and served as a model for many later churches. It has three deeply recessed portals with successive encircling tiers of statued niches, and the central doorway is divided by a pillar with a statue of Christ, while above and across this stretches a band of statues of the kings of France. This is surmounted by a central wheel window of great beauty, 42 ft in diameter, flanked by high coupled windows, over which again a pierced arcaded screen stretches across the façade in front of the nave roof and connecting the two western towers, which have high pointed louvred openings. It is a façade of distinctly harmonious composition and peculiarly suitable to the flat island site from which it rises alone in its impressiveness, without aid from surroundings and position; although it has lost some dignity by the removal of the flight of steps which formed a base. The lateral façades (p. 532C) are unimposing, as chapels are wedged in between the buttresses (1296), which obscure the original design. The east end, however, presents a fairylike appearance with slender flying buttresses and chevet chapels which, with the gabled transepts and delicate flèche soaring 300 ft above the ground, backed by the western towers, form one of the most striking of cathedral groups (p. 531B).

Laon 'Cathedral' (1160–1225) (p. 536A, B)—still so-called, though not actually the seat of a bishop since 1789—a Latin cross in plan, is in the early French Gothic style. The nave has an arcade of circular columns with varied Corinthianesque capitals and square abaci to carry pointed arches and shafts to support the ribs of the sexpartite vaulting. The triforium gallery has a high, slightly pointed enclosing arch over two smaller pointed arches resting on a central column; above this and under the clear-story windows is a second triforium gallery, as at Noyon, thus dividing the nave into four storeys instead of the usual three. The boldly projecting transepts have later two-storeyed chapels, outside the original plan (p. 563G). The sanctuary is unusual in having a square end as in England, instead of apsidal, due to the influence of an English bishop who held the see in the twelfth century. The west façade (p. 536B), imitated later at Rheims and certain German cathedrals, is an architectural masterpiece, with three boldly projecting porches, emphasized by gables and turrets and a central rose window surmounted by blind arcading. Two open traceried towers, square below and octagonal above, are adorned with figures of the so-called miraculous oxen, said to have carted the building stone up the rocky rampart on which stands the great cathedral, which reflects in its style the independent spirit of the citizens. If completed, it would have been a still more striking composition, with two western towers, two towers over each transept, and a central tower—a seven-towered building.

Soissons Cathedral (1180–1225), the church of a royal abbey of monks and nuns, is fully-developed early Gothic. The south transept, with clustered columns, narrow pointed arches and shafts which support the vaulting ribs, is unusual in that it is apsidal. The choir, completed in 1212, imitates Chartres, and the interior has the four-storey arrangement with additional triforium.

Le Mans Cathedral is remarkable for an austere nave in the Romanesque style (twelfth century), and for the vast choir (1217–54), which is said to be larger than the whole Cathedral of Soissons. It has nave, double aisles, and a notable chevet, with thirteen chapels of unusual projection, of which there is an excellent view from a neighbouring open space (p. 536C).

Bourges Cathedral (1192–1275) (pp. 539, 548A, 561A), ultra-French in type, is remarkable for absence of transepts and shortness in proportion to width, and it has a general resemblance in plan to Notre Dame, Paris; while the nave has triforium, clear-story, and sexpartite vault, 125 ft high (p. 539C). The double aisles, in different heights, are unique in France, resembling Milan Cathedral (pp. 601B, 602D). The exterior presents an imposing appearance owing to its uniform width, unbroken by transeptal projections, while the west façade, 180 ft wide, flanked by towers, has five portals approached by a fine flight of steps. The principal portal (p. 539B) nas double semicircular-headed doorways, with deeply recessed jambs and trefoil wall arcading, surmounted by richly canopied niches, and those on the right side still contain statues. A wide-spreading pointed arch spans the whole, in six rings, each filled with saints in canopied niches, and the tympanum has an elaborately sculptured Last Judgment—all surmounted by a steep gable enclosing a wheel window and niches. The exterior from the east end reveals a picturesque confusion of innumerable double flying buttresses over the aisles, with pinnacles and other features (p. 539A); while the thirteenth-century stained-glass windows are amongst the finest in France.

Chartres Cathedral (rebuilt 1194–1260) (pp. 374E, 540, 561E, 563B, 564B, G, 566D, E, 567A, D, E, G), dominating the town, has an extensive crypt, a remnant of the Romanesque earlier church, still used for pilgrimages to the shrine of the Vièrge Noire. The plan has a short nave, strongly marked aisled transepts, each provided with two towers, which, with the two western and two contemplated eastern towers and a central tower, would have made a magnificent pile of nine important towers. The unusual chevet is built above the crypt of the older church, while the spire (1507–14) of the north tower is one of the most beautiful in Europe, and forms a contrast with the earlier one on the south (1145–70). The interior (p. 540B, C) has a fine nave arcade of circular piers with four shafts, low arcaded triforium surmounted by a clear-story of two-light pointed windows, all crowned with a quadripartite vault, 120 ft high, in oblong bays—probably the first example in which the square bay was abandoned. The cathedral is remarkable, even in France, for the wonderful thirteenth-century stained glass of its one hundred and sixty windows, and for the profusion of fine sculptured figures in the doorways of the west front and in the triple porches of the north (p. 566D, E) and south transepts. These famous figures, though somewhat archaic and stiff, are more ambitious than any previous French statuary. The flying buttresses are in three arches one above another, the two lower of which are connected by radiating balusters resembling the spokes of a wheel (p. 564B).

Rheims Cathedral (1211–90) (pp. 543, 544) owes its arrangement to its purpose as the coronation church of the kings of France; for the nave and aisles of the western arm are broadened out in the eastern arm (finished 1241) into a nave and double aisles, so as to include the projecting transepts and thus give space for coronation ceremonies; while the chevet has a ring of five chapels (p. 544A, C, G), similar to Westminster Abbey, the design of which was largely inspired by this building (p. 424D). The names of successive mason-architects are known. The western façade (c. 1255–90), by Bernard de Soissons, more ornate than that of Notre Dame, Paris, has the usual recessed portals exquisitely carved with some five hundred statues; the tympana are occupied by rose windows instead of sculpture, and each is framed in by five rings of statues and enclosed by richly ornamented gables, of which the central one contains the group of the Coronation of the

A. Cathedral from S.E.

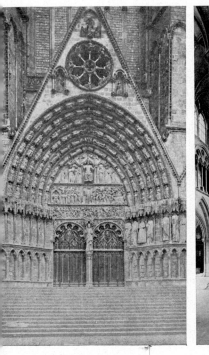

B. West doorway   C. Interior looking E.

Bourges Cathedral (1192–1275). See opposite page

A. Cathedral from N.W.

B. Interior looking E.   C. Interior looking W.

Chartres Cathedral (1194–1260 and later North Spire). See p. 538

Virgin (p. 543). Above the central portal is the magnificent rose window, 40 ft in diameter, flanked by high traceried openings; while in the upper stage, instead of the open arcade of Notre Dame, is a band of tabernacled statues of the kings of France, above which rise the two western towers (1305–1427), 267 ft high, with angle turrets and incomplete spires. The interior (p. 544B) gives one an impression of vast space, and is grand in the extreme, with its nave arcade of clustered piers (p. 544J) supporting pointed arches, surmounted by shallow triforium, lofty clear-story (p. 544D), and fine intersecting vault, 125 ft above the floor, while in the distance is seen the chevet with its columns. Flying buttresses, over single aisles in the nave (p. 544E) and over double aisles at the east end (p. 369E), show how the thrust of the vault is transmitted by arches to piers weighted by pinnacles and statuary. This great cathedral, which was the shrine of religion, the pride of France and a treasure house of art, was much damaged in the 1914–18 war, but has been skilfully restored.

Amiens Cathedral (1220–88) (pp. 374C, 535, 560B, 563A, 564C, H, 566H) was begun with the nave, an unusual procedure, designed by Robert de Luzarches and completed in 1236. The choir was next (1236–70), in the charge successively of Thomas and Regnault de Cormont, father and son, and afterwards the transepts. The upper part of the west front and the western towers followed after an interval (1366–1420). The cathedral is typically French, 450 ft long and 150 ft wide, with transepts only slightly projecting, and a sweeping chevet of seven chapels. The buttress chapels are later additions. The noble interior, spacious in its soaring height, seems but to enclose and not exclude the sky above, and the stone vault, 140 ft high, is upheld by cylindrical columns with four attached smaller columns (p. 369F). The great glory of this cathedral—the 'Bible of Amiens'—is the wonder of its carved woodwork in the choir stalls, which breaks away from studied lines and soars above like the branches of living trees. Other cathedrals are glorious without in sculptured stone, but Amiens is also lovely within, in carved wood. The western façade is one of the noblest among the wonderful façades in France (p. 535A), and with its serried ranks of statues resembles Notre Dame and Rheims. The central western doors are separated by one of the noblest of sculptured figures in the world, the 'Beau Dieu d'Amiens'. The ridge of the external wooden roof is over 200 ft above the ground. The upper flying buttresses have only one aisle to span (p. 369D). The slender timber flèche (p. 564C, H), rising 180 ft above the roof, forms the crowning feature of this beautiful church (p. 535B).

Bayeux Cathedral (thirteenth–fifteenth century) (p. 548B), built on to the remains of a church of c. 1077, had its Romanesque nave transformed in the early thirteenth century, a new choir constructed after 1230 and a central tower added in the fifteenth century. It is remarkable for its twenty-two chapels and immense Romanesque crypt under the sanctuary.

Noyon Cathedral (1145–1228), an early Gothic building combining the German triapsal plan and the French chevet, has a large vaulted triforium.

Coutances Cathedral (1218–91) (p. 548D), on its dominating hill site, is famous for the two western towers and spires, and the beautiful octagonal lantern over the crossing of nave and transepts.

Rouen Cathedral (1202–30 and later) (pp. 374B, 561C) has a double-storeyed nave arcade and three beautiful towers: the spire of that over the crossing was rebuilt in cast-iron, 1823–76. The building was seriously war-damaged in 1944.

Evreux Cathedral (1119–1531) (pp. 374D, 561B), **Troyes Cathedral** (1208–1429) (p. 548C), grand and wide, with five aisles, ancient choir, chevet and decorated west façade, and **Dol Cathedral** (1204–sixteenth century), a massive pile with square east end, are other interesting examples. **S. Urbain, Troyes** (1262) (p. 564E), exquisite with triple porches; **S. Pierre, Caen**, (1308–1521) (p. 794) with its bold turreted tower, of which the spire was destroyed in 1944; and **S. Pierre, Lisieux** (1170–1235), raised high on its approaching steps, are some among the crowd of wonderful churches which make the church fame of Normandy.

La Sainte Chapelle, Paris (1243–8) (p. 546A, B), built by Pierre de Montreuil, one of the greatest architects of the thirteenth century, with the space between the buttresses occupied by windows, 15 ft wide and 50 ft high, is often quoted as a typical Gothic structure. The plan (p. 560D) was in size similar to that of S. Stephen, Westminster (p. 560C), which was ruined by fire, and demolished for the rebuilding of Westminster Palace. It has a richly vaulted crypt, and such characteristic French features as the apsidal termination and high stone-vaulted roof.

Beauvais Cathedral (1247–1568) (pp. 374F, 545) was never completed westward of the choir and transepts (p. 545G), and the site of the proposed nave is partly occupied by the Romanesque church of *c.* 997 known as the 'Basse Œuvre'. The roof fell (1284), and the choir was reconstructed and strengthened by additional piers (1337–47), and in the sixteenth century the transepts were built. There was an open-work spire, 500 ft high, over the crossing, which collapsed in 1573, partly because there was no nave to buttress it on the west. The building is of extreme height, 157 ft 6 in to the vault—the loftiest in Europe—and about three and a half times its span. This soaring pile is perhaps the most daring achievement in Gothic architecture, and has been regarded as one of the wonders of Mediaeval France. The structure is held together internally only by a network of iron tie-rods, which suggests that these ambitious builders had attempted more than they could properly achieve, while flying buttresses (p. 545B, D), in three tiers and of immense thickness, take the vault thrust. The polygonal chevet has seven encircling chapels (p. 545A, C), and the rich stained-glass windows (p. 545E) are of the thirteenth, fourteenth, and sixteenth centuries. The south transept façade (p. 545B), now denuded of statues, is an ornate design in the Flamboyant style, even excelling the western fronts of many cathedrals, and the carved wooden doors are masterpieces of Gothic and Renaissance workmanship.

S. Ouen, Rouen (1318–1515) (pp. 546D, 561D, 563H), of which the choir (1318–1339) is contemporary with Cologne; **S. Maclou, Rouen** (1432–1500), probably the richest Flamboyant example in France with a fine pentagonal porch (badly damaged, 1944); **S. Jacques, Dieppe** (1350–1440), and **S. Vulfran, Abbeville** (1488–1534) (p. 546C), are later examples in the north of France, mostly in the Flamboyant style.

Strasbourg Cathedral (1230–1365) (pp. 374G, 547) has a Gothic nave which was added to the Romanesque choir and transepts (1179). The beautiful western façade of 1276–1365 has a recessed portal (p. 547C), richly carved, as is usual in France, surmounted by an open-work gable and tracery in two planes, above which is a rose window, 42 ft in diameter, flanked with double traceried windows and two western towers, one of which terminates in an open-work octagon and spire, 466 ft high, erected 1399–1439. The north doorway (p. 547D) has a crown of triple gables, and pierced parapets with intersecting mouldings. Like many an English cathedral it is the outcome of centuries of work, and one generation succeeded another in adding its part to this triumphal expression of devotional art, which ranks amongst the finest religious monuments of France.

In the south of France there are fewer churches of the Middle Ages, partly because of the number erected in the Romanesque period, and they differ from northern churches in plan and design, owing to the proximity and influence of Roman buildings.

Rheims Cathedral from W. (1211–90; towers *c.* 1305–1427). See p. 538

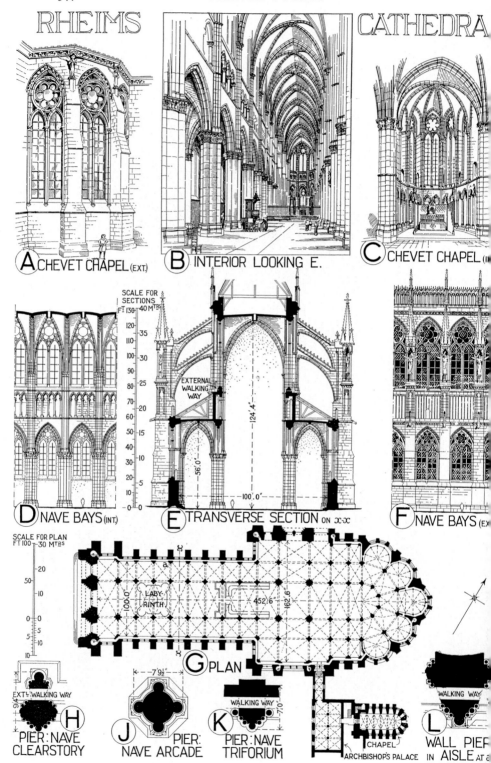

RHEIMS CATHEDRAL

A CHEVET CHAPEL (EXT.)

B INTERIOR LOOKING E.

C CHEVET CHAPEL (INT.)

D NAVE BAYS (INT.)

SCALE FOR SECTIONS
FT 130 — 40 MTRS

EXTERNAL WALKING WAY

E TRANSVERSE SECTION ON x-x

F NAVE BAYS (EXT.)

SCALE FOR PLAN
FT 100 — 30 MTRS

LABY-RINTH

G PLAN

EXT'L WALKING WAY

H PIER: NAVE CLEARSTORY

J PIER: NAVE ARCADE

K PIER: NAVE TRIFORIUM

WALKING WAY

CHAPEL

ARCHBISHOP'S PALACE

WALKING WAY

L WALL PIER IN AISLE AT a

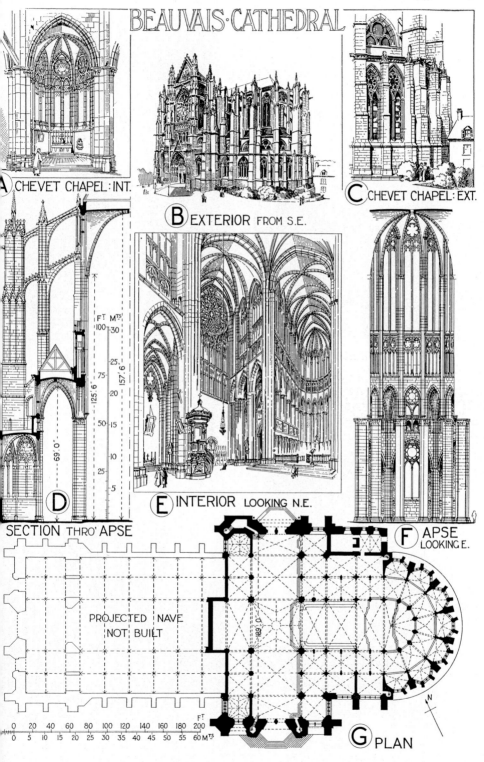

BEAUVAIS·CATHEDRAL

A CHEVET CHAPEL: INT.

B EXTERIOR FROM S.E.

C CHEVET CHAPEL: EXT.

D SECTION THRO' APSE

E INTERIOR LOOKING N.E.

F APSE LOOKING E.

PROJECTED NAVE NOT BUILT

G PLAN

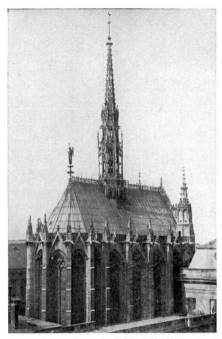

A. Exterior from N.E. B. Upper chapel looking E.
La Sainte Chapelle, Paris (1243–8). See p. 542

C. S. Vulfran, Abbeville D. S. Ouen, Rouen, from S.E.
(1488–1534). See p. 542 (1318–1515). See p. 542

A. West façade (1276–1439)

B. Nave, looking E. (1230–75)

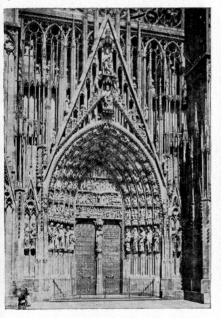

C. West doorway

D. North doorway

Strasbourg Cathedral (1230–1318; spire 1439). See p. 542

A. Bourges Cathedral: west façade
(1192–1275). See p. 538

B. Bayeux Cathedral from E.
(13th–15th cents.; choir 1230–). See p. 541

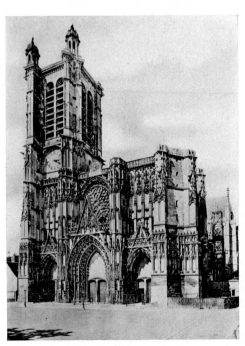

C. Troyes Cathedral: west façade
(1208–1429). See p. 541

D. Coutances Cathedral: west façade
(1218–91). See p. 541

S. Sernin, Toulouse (1080–96), a five-aisled Romanesque church (p. 340), has a Gothic tower and spire (p. 341A).

Albi Cathedral (1282–1390) (pp. 550B, C, 561F), a fortress-church, consists of a large impressive vaulted hall (59 ft wide), which is the widest in France, with an apsidal end, a series of flanking chapels separated by internal buttresses, and an unrivalled rood screen of *c.* 1500. The richly ornate south porch of 1520–35 contrasts vigorously with the sheer mass of the church brickwork.

The **Church of the Cordeliers, Toulouse** (1350), partially destroyed in 1871, was of this type, and has some similarity in plan with King's College Chapel, Cambridge (pp. 468, 470). **Angers Cathedral** (1149–1274) and **Poitiers Cathedral** (1162–1379), with its square east end, are notable churches.

FORTIFIED TOWNS

France is rich in many types of secular Gothic buildings. There is a tendency to think that Gothic architecture was confined to churches, but the style was employed for all buildings alike, whether domestic, military, civil, or ecclesiastical, although the purpose naturally influenced the design.

Carcassonne (p. 551A, B) and **Aigues Mortes** are notable thirteenth century fortified towns. The former has a double wall, of which the inner circuit is partly sixth century; these, with their fifty towers and moat still give an idea of a Mediaeval fortress-town, entered through two fortified gateways guarded by machicolations, drawbridge, and portcullis.

Avignon (1349–68) (p. 551C), although without its moat, is still encircled by machicolated walls and towers (p. 552B). The town contains the imposing palace with its cliff-like walls (1316–64), which was the headquarters of the popes from 1309–77. The famous Pont d'Avignon, with its midway chapel (1177–85), was thrown across the river by the *Frères Pontifes,* or guild of bridge-builders, to connect the town with Villeneuve.

Mont S. Michel (thirteenth century and later, restored by Viollet-le-Duc) (p. 550A) was a fortified monastery rather than a town, but containing within its walls secular buildings. The main element of the world-famous monastery is the storeyed 'Merveille' (1203–28), with its cloisters and 'Salle des Chevaliers'.

CASTLES

Castles were generally built on mounds above rivers to command valleys and had thick walls and small windows to resist attack, thus presenting a very different appearance from Gothic cathedrals, with their large traceried windows and forests of flying buttresses. Many castles were adapted to make more convenient residences in the Renaissance period, and there are many such castles along the historic River Loire.

The **Château Gaillard, Les Andelys** (1196–8), built by Richard Cœur-de-Lion, was a fine castle with a 'donjon', or keep, protected by three lines of outworks and many towers, but little now remains.

The **Château de Pierrefonds** (1390–1400) (p. 552C), restored by Viollet-le-Duc, gives an admirable idea of other castles of this period. It stands on a rocky height above the village, and its cliff-like walls, 20 ft thick, rise sheer from the ground, and, like the eight massive round towers, have machicolations and battlemented parapets surrounding an irregular courtyard, while the entrance is guarded by a drawbridge over the moat.

The **Château d'Amboise** (1434 and later) (p. 553A, B), like many other castles, is picturesquely perched above the Loire to command the surrounding valleys and has early Renaissance additions.

A. Mont S. Michel from S. Crowning church; Romanesque nave 1122–35;
Gothic choir 1450–1521. See p. 549

B. Exterior from E.   C. Interior looking W.

Albi Cathedral (1282–1390; S. porch 1520–35). See p. 549

A. Carcassonne: entrance to Château with bridge over moat

B. Carcassonne: aerial view of old walled town from W.
13th cent. Restored by Viollet-le-Duc. See p. 549

Pont d'Avignon
↓

C. Avignon: aerial view from S. showing the Palace of the Popes
(1349–68). See p. 549

A. House of Jacques Cœur, Bourges: the courtyard (1442–53). See p. 559

B. Avignon: town walls, showing machicolations (1349–68). See p. 549

C. Château de Pierrefonds (1390–1400). See p. 549

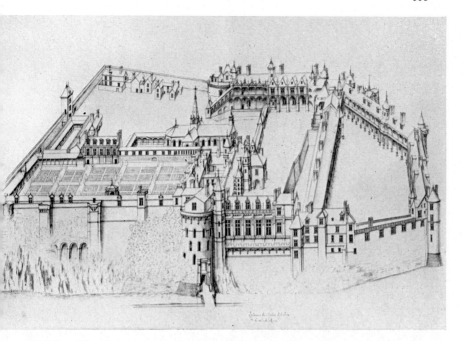

A. Château d'Amboise from N. Drawing by J. A. du Cerceau in the 16th century.
(1434 and later). See p. 549

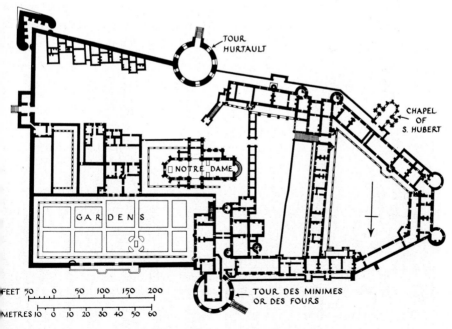

B. Château d'Amboise: plan in 1575

A. Hôtel du Bourgtheroulde, Rouen
(c. 1475; wing on left 1501–37).
See p. 559

B. Hôtel de Ville, Arras (1510; rebuilt
after 1919). See p. 555

C. Hôtel de Ville, Compiègne
(15th cent.). See p. 555

D. Hôtel de Ville, Dreux
(1502–37). See p. 555

Hôtels de Ville

These are few, as there was little municipal life under the feudal system, and in this France differed from Flanders and Italy. Communal business was probably carried on in the market-place or in churches and cloisters.

The **Hôtel de Ville, Arras** (1510) (p. 554B), has an arcade under a large hall with traceried windows, and a steep roof, containing three storeys of dormer windows; while the giant belfry reached 250 ft above the ground; but all has been rebuilt since the Great War of 1914–18.

The **Hôtel de Ville, Bourges** (fifteenth century), is notable for a Flamboyant tower (p. 558C) with tracery, crockets, sculptured figures, and windows, while internally the chimney-piece is unusually fine, even for this period (p. 558F).

The **Hôtel de Ville, Dreux** (1502–37) (p. 554D), resembles a square donjon with pyramidal roof, and the **Hôtel de Ville, Compiègne** (early fifteenth century) (p. 554C), is a beautiful example of civic architecture, with mullioned windows, traceried parapet, and central tower, which was also subjected to German bombardment in the war of 1914–18.

Palais de Justice

These were originally the great halls in which kings and nobles dispensed justice to their vassals, while ecclesiastical courts dealt with matrimonial cases and laws of inheritance; but towns with charters eventually obtained their own magistrates. The **Palais de Justice, Rouen** (1493–1508) (pp. 556B, 558B), severely damaged in 1944, was an exceedingly rich specimen of French municipal architecture and eloquent of the importance of this old city of the Norman kings. The magnificent hall (135 ft by 57 ft) (destroyed), rivalling the Guildhall, London, in size, occupied one side of the building, and had a fine pointed timber roof; while from the centre of the group rose the tower with traceried windows. The late Gothic façades were crowned with a steep roof and dormer windows.

Hospitals

The 'Maisons-Dieu' were attached to monasteries or provided in cities for the treatment of the sick, and for distribution of alms to travellers and pilgrims. The **Hôtel Dieu, Beaune** (1443–51), still in use, has a spacious hall with beds along the walls. There are old timber galleries round a courtyard for open-air treatment, thus forecasting modern sanatoria. The gabled roofs, in coloured tiles, have dormer windows with barge-boards and tall finials, while a stair-turret in the angle of the court completes the quaint setting of this quiet enclosed space.

Country Houses

On the introduction of gunpowder, and with the development of the new social order in the fifteenth century, country houses took the place of fortified castles, though they were still called 'châteaux'. The **Château d'O, Mortrée** (p. 558A), and the **Château de Chateaudun** (rebuilt 1441) are both stately mansions rather than castles. The **Château de Blois** (east wing) (1498–1504) has a thirteenth century Salle des Etats and gateway to the court, around which later buildings were added (p. 770). The Gothic spiral staircase of Louis XII (p. 558E) was probably the model for the marvellous staircase of Francis I of the early Renaissance period (p. 771A, C). The **Château de Josselin, Brittany** (p. 556A), although dating from the twelfth century, was rebuilt in the early sixteenth century, and with its circular towers,

A. Château de Josselin, Brittany (16th cent.). See p. 555

B. Palais de Justice, Rouen (1493–1508). See p. 555

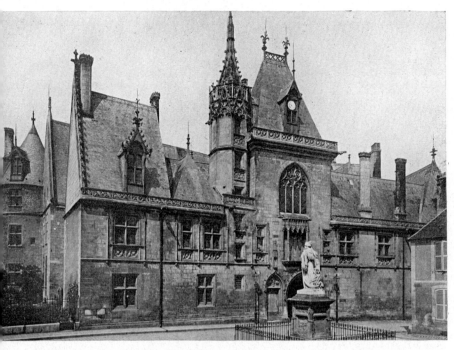

A. House of Jacques Cœur, Bourges: entrance façade (1443–50). See p. 559

B. Hôtel de Cluny, Paris (1485). See p. 559

A LE CHATEAU D'O
MORTREE

B PALAIS DE JUSTICE: ROUEN

C HOTEL DE VILLE
BOURGES

E LOUIS XII STAIR: CHAT. DE BLOIS

F STONE CHIMNEY-PIEC
HOTEL DE VILLE: BOURGE

D TIMBER HOUSE
CAEN

G TIMBER HOUSE: BEAUVAIS

H HOTEL DE CLUNY: PARIS

J HALF-TIMBER HOUSE: S.L

ogee door-heads, mullioned windows, traceried parapet, and steep roof with dormer windows, forms a picturesque group typical of so many others scattered throughout France.

TOWN HOUSES

The 'maisons nobles' began to rise in the fifteenth century when French nobles ceased to be feudal lords in fortified castles, and erected houses, known to this day as 'hôtels', planned, as in the country, round a court and with an elaborate façade to the street. The **House of Jacques Cœur, Bourges** (1442–53) (pp. 552A, 557A), is undoubtedly the finest Mediaeval town residence in France. It was built by a merchant prince, partly on the town ramparts, round a central court and has seven turret stairs. The **Hôtel du Bourgtheroulde, Rouen** (c. 1475) (p. 554A), exemplifies this type of house, with its enclosed court surrounded by façades somewhat resembling the Palais de Justice in the same city. Juxtaposed in the court is an early Renaissance building of 1501–37, on which the lower bas-relief panels depict the meeting of Francis I and Henry VII of England on the 'Field of the Cloth of Gold' in 1520. The façades were severely damaged in 1944. The **Hôtel Chambellan, Dijon** (fifteenth century), was one of the great town houses of this period. The central court contains an angle turret stair with newel branching into a richly carved head; while the street façade has some fine figures carved in wood. The **Hôtel de Cluny, Paris** (1485–98) (p. 557B)—now a museum—retains its Mediaeval character, and is a fine specimen of late Gothic. The chapel (p. 558H), as seen from the court behind the museum, stands above an arcade which supports on its central pier an oriel window of pleasing proportions with Flamboyant tracery, crockets, and finials.

Smaller domestic buildings still exist, as in Cluny, where doors and windows are of the later Romanesque type; while in S. Lô (p. 558J), Lisieux, Caen (p. 558D), Chartres, Beauvais (p. 558G), and Rouen there are timber houses with carved barge-boards and overhanging storeys; but a large number have succumbed to the ravages of time and fire. They are not generally earlier than the fifteenth century.

Market halls, fortified farmhouses, and great timber barns all reveal the development of country life in Old France.

COMPARATIVE ANALYSIS

This comparative table contrasts the differences in the development of the Gothic style in France and England.

FRENCH GOTHIC	ENGLISH GOTHIC
PLANS. (pp. 560B, 561). Cathedrals are short, wide, and lofty.	PLANS. (p. 560A). Cathedrals are long, narrow, and low.
Length about four times the width.	Length about six times the width.
Cloisters rare, except in the south, owing to the lay origin of French cathedrals.	Cloisters usual, owing to monastic origin of many English cathedrals.
Transepts have slight projection, as at Paris (p. 531G) and Amiens (p. 560B), or they are absent, as at Bourges (p. 561A).	Transepts have bold projection and secondary transepts are found, as at Salisbury (p. 560A), Lincoln (p. 410F), Canterbury (p. 411B), and Rochester (p. 412H).
Lateral chapels numerous for the popular worship of saints and the saying of masses (p. 563J).	Lateral chapels rare in those cathedrals which were designed for monks and not for laity.
The apsidal east end developed into the 'chevet' by addition of processional aisle and chapels (p. 560B). Laon, Dol, and Poitiers are exceptions.	The square east end replaced the apse, while the 'Chapel of the Nine Altars', Durham, forms an eastern transept. Westminster has the French 'chevet'.
Aisles are sometimes double, as at Notre	Aisles are single, both in sanctuary and

TYPICAL ENGLISH & FRENCH GOTHIC PLAN

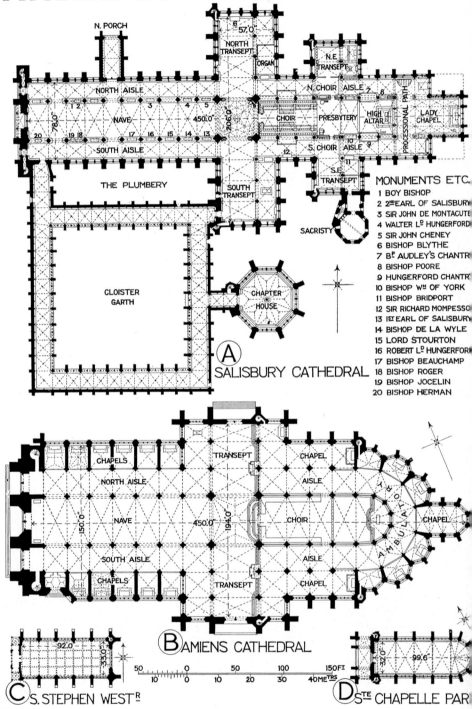

A SALISBURY CATHEDRAL

N. PORCH

NORTH TRANSEPT
57'.0"
ORGAN

N.E. TRANSEPT

NORTH AISLE

NAVE — 450'.0"

SOUTH AISLE

THE PLUMBERY

SOUTH TRANSEPT

N. CHOIR AISLE

CHOIR   PRESBYTERY   HIGH ALTAR   LADY CHAPEL

S. CHOIR AISLE

PROCESSIONAL PATH

S.E. TRANSEPT

SACRISTY

CLOISTER GARTH

CHAPTER HOUSE

MONUMENTS ETC.

1 BOY BISHOP
2 2ᴺᴰ EARL OF SALISBURY
3 SIR JOHN DE MONTACUTE
4 WALTER Lᴰ HUNGERFORD
5 SIR JOHN CHENEY
6 BISHOP BLYTHE
7 Bᴾ AUDLEY'S CHANTR
8 BISHOP POORE
9 HUNGERFORD CHANTR
10 BISHOP Wᴹ OF YORK
11 BISHOP BRIDPORT
12 SIR RICHARD MOMPESSO
13 1ˢᵀ EARL OF SALISBURY
14 BISHOP DE LA WYLE
15 LORD STOURTON
16 ROBERT Lᴰ HUNGERFORD
17 BISHOP BEAUCHAMP
18 BISHOP ROGER
19 BISHOP JOCELIN
20 BISHOP HERMAN

B AMIENS CATHEDRAL

CHAPELS

NORTH AISLE

NAVE — 450'.0" — 150'.0" — 194'.0"

SOUTH AISLE

CHAPELS

TRANSEPT

CHAPEL

AISLE

CHOIR

AISLE

CHAPEL

TRANSEPT

CHAPEL

AMBULATORY

CHAPEL

50   0   50   100   150 FT
10   0   10   20   30   40 METRES

C S. STEPHEN WESTR
92'.0"

D Sᵀᴱ CHAPELLE PARᴵ
99'.6"

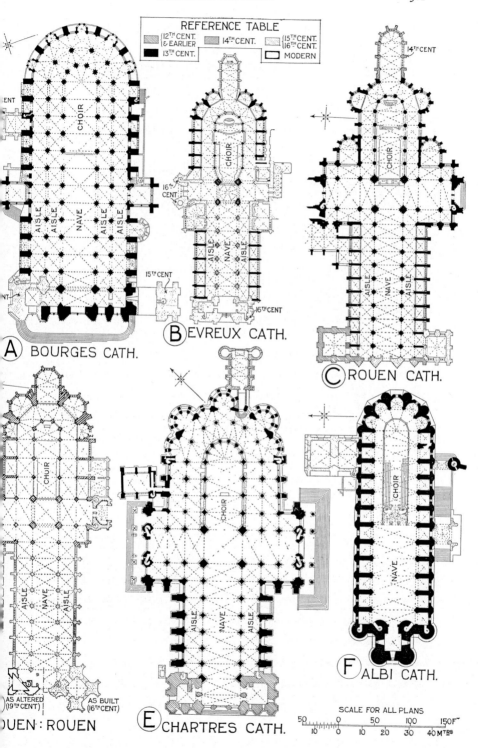

REFERENCE TABLE

12TH CENT. & EARLIER
13TH CENT.
14TH CENT.
15TH CENT. 16TH CENT.
MODERN

A BOURGES CATH.

B EVREUX CATH.

C ROUEN CATH.

ROUEN : ROUEN

AS ALTERED (19TH CENT)

AS BUILT (16TH CENT)

E CHARTRES CATH.

F ALBI CATH.

SCALE FOR ALL PLANS

Dame, Paris (p. 531G), Bourges (p. 561A), and the choirs of Rheims (p. 544G), and Chartres (p. 561E). Albi (p. 561F) has no aisles.

Two western towers characteristic, as at Paris (p. 532A), Rheims (p. 543), and Amiens (p. 535A), and owing to the great height of the nave a flèche, as at Amiens (p. 564C, H) and Paris (p. 532C), was often substituted for the central tower, which was usual in England.

Central spires are common in Normandy, as at Rouen (p. 374B) and Caen (p. 794B).

Towers are sometimes designed in groups; there were to have been seven at Laon (p. 537) and nine at Chartres (p. 538).

Piers of nave arcades widely spaced.

Chapter houses rectangular.

WALLS. Early buttresses were a development from Romanesque pilaster strips or were semicircular, especially in apses. Later buttresses of deep projection have chapels between them (p. 531G), and are weighted by statuary niches and pinnacles.

Buttresses often vertical without offsets (p. 545D). Weatherings to offsets of buttresses are flatter the higher they occur.

Flying buttresses largely employed on account of height of naves and width of double aisles (pp. 369D, E, F, 564A, B). They were used with special effect round the chevet (pp. 531B, C, 532C, 539A, 545B), and are often in two or more tiers.

Interiors owe their effect largely to great height, otherwise they are less ornate than English interiors.

Parapets have open tracery (pp. 563H, 564F).

The characteristic west front is that of Notre Dame, Paris (p. 532A).

OPENINGS. Arcades developed through high pointed to three-centred arches in the late period.

Doorways are elaborate (p. 564E, F), large, and deeply recessed in the west façades and framed in with statues of saints round the arches in serried rows, as at Paris, Bourges (p. 539B), Rheims (p. 543), Grand Andely (p. 567B), Chartres (p. 566D, E), and Troyes (p. 548C).

Windows have 'plate' tracery which developed, through geometric 'bar' tracery, into 'flamboyant', probably derived from English curvilinear (p. 563D).

There is an absence of cusps in late French tracery.

Circular windows occur in west fronts, as at Rheims (p. 543), Paris (p. 563E), Troyes (p. 548C), and in transepts as at Chartres (p. 540A) and S. Ouen, Rouen (p. 563H).

nave, with the exception of Chichester (p. 412G) and Manchester (p. 412B), where double aisles result from the inclusion of former lateral chapels.

A central tower the predominant feature, as at Gloucester (p. 408D), Hereford (p. 409F), Rochester (p. 409D), Salisbury (with spire) (p. 407G), or combined with western towers as at Canterbury (p.408G), Durham (p. 408C), and York (p. 408B). Lichfield with three spires is unique (p. 407E).

A single western steeple is usual in churches, as at Heckington (p. 431A).

Towers never exceeded three, two western and one central, as at Canterbury (p. 418A), Lincoln (p. 417A), Durham (p. 392A), and York (p. 408B).

Piers of nave arcades closely spaced.

Chapter houses often polygonal.

WALLS. Early buttresses project more than Norman and have gabled heads, as at Salisbury, Westminster, and Southwell (p. 497C). Later buttresses are strongly marked with offsets and pinnacles ornamented with niches and panelling (p. 497J, K).

Buttresses usually in stages with offsets (p. 497). Weatherings to offsets of buttresses are steeper the higher they occur.

Flying buttresses are not so frequent, because the nave with its clear-story is comparatively low and there are no double aisles or chevet; none were required for the square east end.

Interiors owe much to the elaboration of complex piers, triforium, variety of clear-stories, and ribbed vaulting.

Parapets are battlemented (p. 511D, E, F).

The characteristic west front is that of Wells Cathedral (p. 403B).

OPENINGS. Arcades developed through high pointed to four-centred arches in the late period.

Doorways are usually placed laterally within a protecting porch encrusted with statuary in canopied niches, and are either on the south, as at Canterbury (p. 418A) and Gloucester (p. 408D), or on the north as at Salisbury (p. 415A, B) and Wells.

Windows developed through 'plate' tracery to geometrical and curvilinear and the final English treatment, known as perpendicular tracery (p. 499).

Cusping became very elaborate in late English tracery.

Circular windows are not used for west fronts, but form special features in transepts, as at Westminster (p. 425B), Durham, Lincoln (p. 408H), and elsewhere.

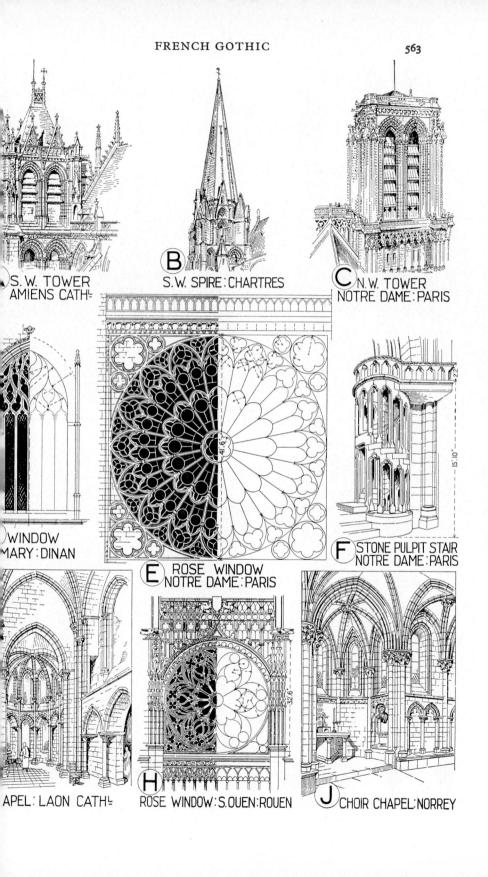

S.W. TOWER
AMIENS CATH^L

B S.W. SPIRE : CHARTRES

C N.W. TOWER
NOTRE DAME : PARIS

WINDOW
MARY : DINAN

E ROSE WINDOW
NOTRE DAME : PARIS

F STONE PULPIT STAIR
NOTRE DAME : PARIS

APEL : LAON CATH^L

ROSE WINDOW : S. OUEN : ROUEN

J CHOIR CHAPEL : NORREY

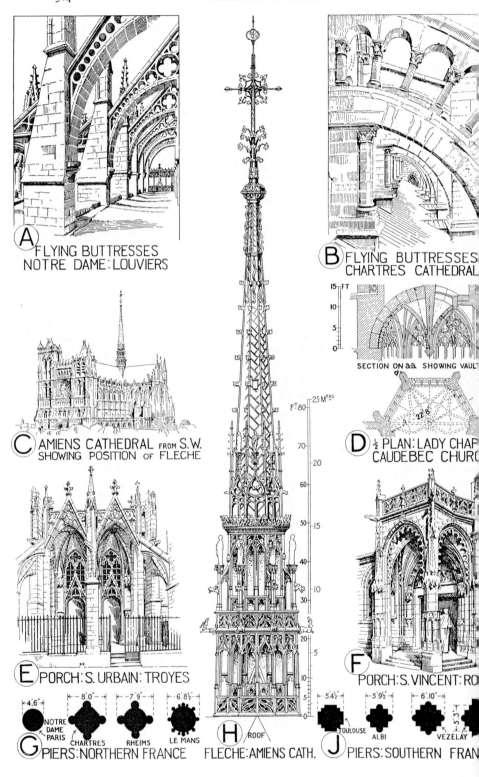

A FLYING BUTTRESSES
NOTRE DAME: LOUVIERS

B FLYING BUTTRESSES
CHARTRES CATHEDRAL

C AMIENS CATHEDRAL FROM S.W.
SHOWING POSITION OF FLECHE

15 FT
10
5
0

SECTION ON aa SHOWING VAUL

D ½ PLAN: LADY CHAP
CAUDEBEC CHURC

E PORCH: S. URBAIN: TROYES

25 MTRS
FT 80
70   20
60
50   15
40
30   10
20
10   5
5   0

F PORCH: S. VINCENT: RO

G PIERS: NORTHERN FRANCE
4.6" NOTRE DAME PARIS
8.0" CHARTRES
7.9" RHEIMS
6.8½" LE MANS

H FLECHE: AMIENS CATH.
ROOF

J PIERS: SOUTHERN FRAN
5.4½" TOULOUSE
5.9½" ALBI
6.10" VEZELAY
5.3"

FRENCH GOTHIC	ENGLISH GOTHIC

ROOFS. Always steep and finished with metal ridges and finials (p. 531B).

Usually constructed with double timbers of a special type to surmount high vaults, as at Rheims and Amiens.

Ornamental wooden roofs not much developed as part of internal design, because of preference for vaults.

Slates were used as roof coverings.

Vaults were in general use both for cathedrals and churches. Usually of great height and domical, and provided with transverse and diagonal ribs and bosses (p. 566A, C), they show little evolution in design and treatment. Ridge, intermediate and lierne ribs were rare (pp. 532B, 539C).

The joints of the panels are laid in courses, parallel to the ridge lines (p. 373F).

Pendant vaulting is frequent in the 'Flamboyant' period (p. 564D).

COLUMNS. Plain cylindrical piers are characteristic, as at Paris (pp. 531F, 532B, 564G), where the vaulting shafts start awkwardly above the square abaci of the arcade columns (p. 567A, C). Square piers, with attached threequarter columns, owing to Roman tradition (p. 564J), are found in the south. Piers are sometimes without capitals, as at Lisieux, when the arch mouldings die into the cylindrical piers, and the vaulting shafts rest on corbels.

Capitals with foliage of the Corinthianesque type lasted well into the style, and 'stiff-leaf' foliage and the 'crocket' capital (p. 566J) were characteristic, crowned with a square abacus. Moulded 'bell' capitals without foliage are found in Normandy with circular abaci, as in England.

MOULDINGS. Large, less varied (p. 566F), and not so ornate as in England and often at some distance from window openings. In the late or Flamboyant period mouldings were almost as deeply undercut in stone as in wood and only limited by the granular nature of the material.

ORNAMENT. Decorative figure sculpture reached its greatest perfection in the cavernous doorways of the west fronts of Paris (p. 532A), Amiens, Rheims (p. 543), and in the north and south porches of Chartres (p. 566D, E), where numerous tiers of statues in niches surround the arches (pp. 539B, 567).

Carved tombs (p. 567F), fonts (p. 566G), gargoyles (p. 566B), finials, crockets, and corbels are of fine workmanship, and animals, birds, and grotesques were introduced, especially in the south.

Stained glass was much developed, and at

ROOFS. Moderate in pitch, approaching flatness in later periods (p. 435).

Carpentry was more advanced, and so single-framed timbers were used over vaults.

Ornamental wooden roofs, such as 'hammer-beam', are elaborated as part of internal design.

Lead was the usual roof covering.

Vaults were used in cathedrals and timber roofs in parish churches. Level ridge ribs, longitudinal, transverse, diagonal, tierceron, and lierne ribs resulted in complicated stellar vaulting (p. 399). Vaults sometimes of wood, as at York (p. 423). See Evolution of Vaulting (p. 394).

The joints of panels are at right angles to line bisecting the panels (p. 373F).

Fan tracery vaulting (p. 399H), sometimes with pendants (p. 426B–F), was peculiar to England.

COLUMNS. Clustered piers are special features, as in Salisbury and Exeter (p. 503P, Q), and were preferred to cylindrical piers. The adoption of attenuated shafts to continue the lines of the vaulting ribs largely determined the form of piers and avoided the difficulty met with in France, and the characteristic evolution of moulded piers in each period was controlled by the increasing number of vaulting shafts (p. 503).

Capitals of a Classic type were employed in the Norman period, as in S. John's Chapel, Tower of London, while Early English carved capitals have 'stiff-leaf' foliage (p. 504D–F). Moulded 'bell' capitals are common to all periods and are crowned by round, octagonal, or polygonal abaci (p. 503L, Q, U).

MOULDINGS. Bold, rich, and of great variety and applied to bases, capitals, and pier arches, as well as door and window openings (pp. 503, 507). Mouldings show gradual development from the pronounced bowtells and deep hollows of the early period to the flat bracket moulding of the late period.

ORNAMENT. Decorative figure sculpture was not so freely used, and of such high quality as in France, and was not confined to portals, but was spread over whole façades, as at Wells, Lichfield, and Exeter. The 'dog-tooth', ball-flower, and Tudor rose enriched the hollow mouldings (p. 508).

Carving varies considerably in each period, conventional in Early English, naturalistic in Decorated, and again partly conventional in Perpendicular (pp. 504, 508, 511, 512).

Stained glass was developed on similar

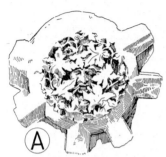

VAULTING BOSS: DIJON MUS^M

GARGOYLE : ILE DE FRANCE

GARGOYLE: S.CHAPELLE:PARIS

BOSS: MONT. S. MICHEL

D NORTH PORCH:CHARTRES CATHEDRAL

E NORTH PORCH: CHARTRES FROM N.

F BASES
S.MICHAEL'S
CHAPEL.MONTREALE

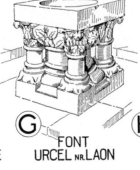

G FONT
URCEL NR.LAON

H DIAPER ON PEDESTAL
AMIENS CATHEDRAL

DETAIL O
CROCKET
AT a

J CROCKET
CAPITAL : SEMU

A CAPITAL: N. PORCH CHARTRES CATHEDRAL

B JAMB: W. DOORWAY: GRAND ANDELY

C CAPITAL: NOTRE DAME CHALONS-SUR-MARNE

PLAN

8'10¼"

SECTION THROUGH PILASTER

2'3"

SECTION THROUGH PILASTER

2'3"

SCALE F: 10 — 3 M^{TRS}

D TYMPANUM LEFT DOORWAY of WEST PORTAL: CHARTRES

14'8"   14'8"

PILASTER PORCH: CHARTRES

F TOMB of PHILIBERT LE BEAU: BROU

G PILASTER S. PORCH: CHARTRES

FRENCH GOTHIC

FRENCH GOTHIC

Chartres a prevailing blue merging into violet gives an idea of the general effect which artists intended to produce in church interiors. Much of the best stained glass has, however, been destroyed, notably at Rheims.

Colour decoration in frescoes and applied to sculpture seems to have been much used, and hangings were imitated in diaper work (p. 566H) and wall decorations.

ENGLISH GOTHIC

lines as in France—earlier examples, as at Canterbury, were in small heavily leaded pieces; whereas later windows consist of large figures in simulated niches with crocketed canopies and other architectural features.

Colour decoration of walls and sculpture was much employed. Painted timber roofs and rood screens are characteristic in the Perpendicular period.

REFERENCE BOOKS

AUBERT, M. *L'Architecture française à l'époque gothique*. Paris, 1943.

—. *Archives de la Commission des Monuments Historiques*. 5 vols., Paris, 1898.

BAUDOT, A. DE, and PERRAULT-DABOT, A. *Les cathédrales de France*. 2 vols., Paris, 1905.

BURGES, W. *Architectural Drawings*. London, 1870.

DURAND, P. *Monographie de Notre Dame de Chartres*. 2 vols., fo. and 4to, Paris, 1881.

—. *La Cathédrale d'Amiens*. Paris, 1901.

ENLART, C. *Manuel d'archéologie française*. 2 vols., Paris, 1902–4.

GAILHABAUD, J. *L'Architecture du Ve au XVIe siècle*. 1 vol. fo. and 4 vols. 4to. Paris, 1869–72.

GARDNER, A. *Introduction to French Church Architecture*. Cambridge, 1938.

GONSE, L. *L'Art gothique*. Paris, 1890.

JACKSON, SIR T. G. *Gothic Architecture in France, England and Italy*. 2 vols., London, 1915.

JOHNSON, R. J. *Early French Architecture*. Large fo. Newcastle, 1864.

LANDRIEUX, M. *The Cathedral of Reims*. Trans. E. E. Williams. 1920.

LASSUS, J. B. A. *La Cathédrale de Chartres*. Fo., and 4to. Paris, 1867–81.

—. et VIOLLET-LE-DUC, E. E. *Monographie de Notre Dame de Paris*. Folio. Paris, 186–?

LASTEYRIE, R. DE. *L'Architecture religieuse en France à l'époque gothique*. Paris, 1926–7.

LAVEDAN, P. *L'Architecture française*. Paris, 1944. (English translation, *French Architecture*, Penguin Books, Harmondsworth, 1956).

LENOIR, A. A. *Architecture monastique*. 2 vols. Paris, 1852–6.

MÂLE, E. *L'Art religieux du XIIIe siècle en France*. Paris, 1902. English trans. by Dora Nussey, 1913.

MARTIN, C. *L'Art gothique en France*. Fo. Paris [19—].

MICHEL, A. *Histoire de l'art*. Vol. 2 and Vol. 3 pt. 1. Paris, 1907–29.

MOORE, C. H. *Gothic Architecture*. New York, 1899.

MOREAU-NELATON, E. *Les églises chez nous*. 3 vols., Paris, 1914.

NESFIELD, E. *Specimens of Mediaeval Architecture*. London, 1862.

PORTER, A. K. *Mediaeval Architecture*. 2 vols., New York and London, 1909.

PUGIN, A. *Architectural Antiquities of Normandy*. London, 1828.

ROSE, E. W. *Cathedrals and Cloisters of Midland France*. 2 vols., New York and London, 1907.

RUPRICH-ROBERT, V. M. C. *L'Architecture normande aux XIe et XIIe siècles*. 2 vols., fo., Paris, 1889.

SHAW, R. NORMAN. *Architectural Sketches from the Continent*. London, 1858.

VERDIER, A., and CATTOIS, F. P. *Architecture civile et domestique au Moyen Age, et de la Renaissance*. 2 vols., Paris, 1858.

VERRIER, A. and G. *L'Architecture française*. 1941.

VIOLLET-LE-DUC, E. E. *Dictionnaire raisonné de l'architecture française*. 10 vols., Paris, 1859. A translation of the article 'Construction' was issued under the title of 'Rational Building' by G. M. Huss, New York, 1895.

VITRY, P. *La Cathédrale de Reims*. 2 vols., fo., Paris [19—].

WEST, G. H. *Gothic Architecture in England and France*. London, 1927.

WILLIS, R. *Facsimile of the Sketch-Book of Wilars de Honecourt* (eighteenth-century architect). London, 1859.

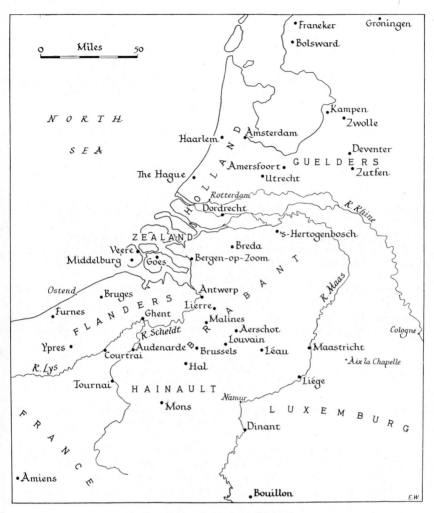

The Netherlands in the Middle Ages

XV. BELGIAN AND DUTCH GOTHIC

(twelfth–sixteenth century)

INFLUENCES

GEOGRAPHICAL. The Netherlands consists of the basins and delta lands of the Rhine, Meuse (Maas) and Scheldt, the flat, low-lying coastal areas and the hills of the Ardennes. The fertile land and the great navigable rivers created and maintained a number of Mediaeval states and prosperous cities, dependent culturally on either France or Germany. To-day, the area is divided between the kingdoms of Belgium and the Netherlands, the latter popularly called Holland.

GEOLOGICAL. Belgium has marbles, limestone, sandstone and granite, and these were employed on the great churches of Brussels, Antwerp, Ghent, Liége and Tournai, and in the later Middle Ages, for palaces, houses and town halls in the prosperous cities. In Flanders, where clay is abundant, a characteristic and beautiful brick architecture developed; from the forests of the Ardennes and Fagnes came timber, not only for building, but also for wood-carving for which Belgium is famous.

Holland being wholly without stone except around Maastricht, and without forests too, had to import tufa, limestone and sandstone from Germany and Belgium. This deficiency early caused the Dutch to make bricks from her clay soil, and from them their buildings obtained a characteristic simplicity, texture and soft colouring which is enhanced by the reflected light of the seldom-distant water.

CLIMATIC. The climate of the Netherlands is similar to that of south-eastern England, but there are greater degrees of heat and cold. An often grey and rainy climate gave rise to many and large windows in houses and to great traceried windows in churches and town halls. Window-shutters against driving rain and belts of trees as wind screens are common in Holland and Flanders, while in the north-east, windows are fewer and smaller and buildings plainer, to withstand the winds which sweep across the sea and the level land.

RELIGIOUS. Until the year 1558, the bishoprics of Utrecht and Liége came under the jurisdiction of Cologne, and there were further connections with Münster; while Arras, Cambrai, Tournai and Thérouanne owed allegiance to Rheims: through these affiliations came both German and French influences on the architecture. Later, the Spanish rule left its mark on Belgian architecture in the form of exuberant and florid decoration. Through the Benedictine, Cistercian and Premonstratensian Orders, the early styles of Italy, France and Germany were brought to the Netherlands and moulded to the local idiom. The Brabantine style, of mainly French origin, became the major national style; the architecture of Holland, while depending largely on Brabant and Flanders, developed other regional styles by assimilation of Westphalian and Rhineland characteristics.

SOCIAL. Mediaeval architecture followed closely on the social progress of these sturdy, brave and industrious peoples, and the independent towns rivalled each other for power and in the arts, much as they did in Italy. Guild houses and town halls of great magnificence, large in conception and rich in detail, reflect the prosperity and civic pride of such towns as Bruges, Antwerp, Louvain, Ghent, Ypres and Courtrai in the south, and Middelburg, Veere and Gouda in the north. The fame of these and many other cities is a record of the industry, of unending struggle against the waters, of ventures on land and sea, of commercial acumen and manufacturing enterprise which made the Netherlands among the first in commerce and sea power. The glory of Flemish weaving was immortalized by the establishment at Bruges in 1430, by Philip the Good, of the 'Order of the Golden Fleece'.

HISTORICAL. Celt and Roman, Frisian, Saxon and Frank made up the pattern of ruler and ruled until, in the Middle Ages, the Netherlands comprised many feudal states, such as the counties of Flanders, Holland and Guelders, the principality of Liége, the duchy of Brabant and the bishopric of Utrecht, all owing some sort of allegiance to France or the Empire. Though not united politically, these formed a growing cultural unity by the thirteenth century, dependent on the common interests and ambitions of the towns rather than on their rulers.

Flanders passed to Burgundy in 1369, and under Charles the Bold (1433–77) formed, with most of the rest of the Netherlands, an almost national state. In 1482, through the marriage of Maximilian of Austria with Mary of Burgundy, the Netherlands became a Hapsburg domain. Charles V (1500–58), born at Ghent and

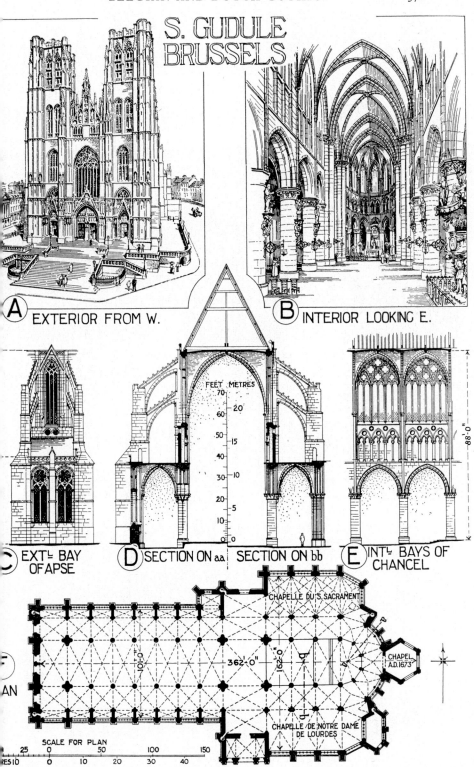

S. GUDULE BRUSSELS

A EXTERIOR FROM W.

B INTERIOR LOOKING E.

C EXTL BAY OF APSE

D SECTION ON aa   SECTION ON bb

E INTL BAYS OF CHANCEL

FEET METRES
70
60   20
50   15
40
30   10
20   5
10
0   0

88'-0"

F PLAN

CHAPELLE DU S. SACRAMENT

362'-0"

162'-0"

CHAPEL A.D.1673

CHAPELLE DE NOTRE DAME DE LOURDES

SCALE FOR PLAN
25   0   50   100   150
RES10   0   10   20   30   40

ANTWERP CATHEDRAL

Ⓐ PLAN

AISLES · NAVE · AISLES

172' 0"

388' 0"

TOWER

Ⓒ SECTION a-a

96' 0"

50   0   50   100   150 FT
10   0   10   20   30   40 MTS

Ⓑ INTERIOR LOOKING E.

Ⓓ EXTERIOR FROM N. W.

a prince of the Netherlands, became king of Spain in 1516. Against the Spanish rule and against Philip II (1555–98), a movement of revolt began in which William, Prince of Orange and Count of Nassau, took a leading part; the outcome was partition in 1581 with Holland and Protestantism supreme in the north, and Spain and Catholicism retaining the south.

ARCHITECTURAL CHARACTER

The Carolingian chapels of the Valkhof at Nijmegen, the eleventh and twelfth-century churches at Nivelles, Soignies and Liége in Belgium, and Utrecht and Maastricht in Holland and, above all, the great triapsal and five-towered cathedral at Tournai, established the Romanesque in the Netherlands. The best surviving examples of this period are the nave and towers of Tournai Cathedral (p. 580B), the westblocks (see Glossary) of S. Denis and of S. Barthélémy at Liège, the churches of Our Lady and S. Servaas at Maastricht and S. Peter at Utrecht.

Gothic architecture of the Netherlands was governed by the same principles as applied to the rest of Europe (p. 367), but owing to Rhenish conservatism, reached there only after 1220 through Hainault, Brabant and Flanders. Thus French cathedral Gothic of Sens, Senlis, Noyon, and Laon formed its basis, and from this grew the Brabantine style which spread north in its pure form as far as 's-Hertogen-bosch and Utrecht. From another direction, through Cologne, the Gothic of Rheims and Amiens was the inspiration for the cathedral of Utrecht in the mid-thirteenth century, while the older traditions and the manners of Westphalia and the Rhineland were continued in the eastern and northern parts of Belgium and Holland. These latter include the long, narrow and low-set sanctuary windows and, later, the 'hall' churches, in which nave and aisles were approximately of equal height. In Flanders, a national variant adapted to brick, developed and spread northward along the coast of Zealand, Holland and Friesland, and far beyond to Scandinavia and the Baltic. Adaptation to brick entailed simplification of detail and ornament, most evident in the Dutch churches; many of these lack vaults or the vaults are of timber, though sometimes the reason is instability of the ground. Nonetheless, few Dutch or Flemish churches are without an immense, high and ornate tower, the product of civic rivalry in wealth and splendour.

Not only did the rich towns build vast churches and elaborate town halls, guildhalls and trade halls, but also, merchants built houses and warehouses, with stepped gables and many regular windows. Compared with the intricate elaboration of the town halls at Louvain, Audenarde and Alost, those of Gouda, Kuilenburg and Haarlem are simple.

EXAMPLES

Ecclesiastical Architecture

S. Gudule, Brussels (1220–1475) (p. 571), has a choir which is the earliest example of Gothic in the Netherlands, deriving from the north-eastern French style but with a triforium arcade still suggesting Romanesque. It expresses a mixture of influences which include those from Tournai, Valenciennes, Burgundy and Champagne, all of which go to create the Gothic of Brabant. Typical of the Netherlands is the plan, which lacks aisles to the transepts and a full chevet of chapels but includes wide chapels flanking the choir. The nave was added in 1425–75, still with the cylindrical piers and Brabantine foliage capitals, but with a blind tri-forium united to the clear-story windows by tracery panelling. The western façade seems strangely English, flat and with a central window, though it is probably of German derivation.

Tournai Cathedral (1066–1340) is of three periods, and is built largely of black Tournai marble. The nave is Romanesque, the apsidal transepts (p. 580B) and the five towers Transitional (mid-twelfth century), while the choir, with a complete chevet, is of French Gothic design (1242–). The influence of Tournai was widely felt in Flanders and beyond. The Chapel of S. Piat (p. 581G) is in the florid fifteenth-century style.

Notre-Dame de Pamele, Audenarde (1235 and after), of blue-black Tournai limestone, is partly in the local Scheldt Gothic, the style which soon afterwards established itself in Zealand.

Notre-Dame, Bruges (1239–97) with its tall plain tower, and **S. Bavon, Ghent** (choir, 1274–1300), are characteristic of early Flemish Gothic adapting itself to brickwork.

Antwerp Cathedral (1352–1411) (pp. 374H, 572), by Jean Amel de Boulogne, is in the mature Belgian style, with further outside influences. It is remarkable for its great width—a nave flanked by triple aisles—yet the transepts are aisleless and the spread of chapels each side of the choir is typical of the Netherlands. Tracery wall panelling, many slender pier shafts, often without capitals, and huge clear-story windows mark the period. The west front was undertaken between 1422–74, but only the dominating north-west tower by R. Keldermans and D. van Waghemakere was completed (1519); it is 400 ft high and capped by a three-stage lantern with pinnacle buttresses.

Malines Cathedral (begun 1341) has an unfinished tower (1461–1533) designed by Andries Keldermans, the finest in Belgium—324 ft high—with strongly stressed verticals and stone detailing like lace.

The **Chapelle du Saint-Sang, Bruges,** is a reliquary shrine, its lower parts mid-twelfth century and the upper, fifteenth century, with a Flamboyant doorway and brick spiral-staircase.

S. Jacques, Liége (1513–38) (p. 580C), represents the extreme Brabantine Flamboyant; it was perhaps influenced by Spain.

Utrecht Cathedral (1254–fourteenth century and later) (p. 575A) is the major example of French cathedral-Gothic in Holland, deriving from Amiens through Cologne; changing detail from the apse westward through the choir to the transepts is noticeable, especially in the omission of capitals. The nave collapsed in the seventeenth century and the western axial tower is isolated. Built between 1321–82 by Jan van Henegouwen (i.e. Hainault), it was an important Dutch prototype.

S. John, 's-Hertogenbosch (1370–1559) (pp. 575B, 582) is a rare example of pure and rich Brabantine in Holland, comparable with S. Peter, Louvain, and S. Waldru, Mons. The rectilinear wall-panelling resembles English Perpendicular; it is profusely decorated, with much sculpture by Alard van Hameel (1478–1529). The Great Churches of **Dordrecht** (1339–sixteenth century) and **Haarlem** (1400–90) are more typically Dutch, being of brick and stone, spacious and plain. Both are simplified Brabantine, with Haarlem belonging to the local style of Aerschot, called Demer Gothic. Dordrecht has brick vaulting, but that of Haarlem nave is timber. In Zealand the churches of **Middelburg, Goes, Hulst, Veere** and others followed the Scheldt and coastal Flemish-Brabantine traditions. **S. Michael, Zwolle** (c. 1350–1450) is a hall church deriving from Germany; these are common in east and central Holland but rare in Belgium—**Damme,** in west Flanders, is an exception.

The ruined **Abbey Church of Villers** (Belgian Luxemburg) (1216–67) and the **Dominican Church, Maastricht** (after 1260), represent early Maas (Meuse) Gothic with blind triforium arcades and typical leaf capitals, while **Meersen** (fourteenth century) is later and richer. This Maas style includes tall, narrow apse windows reaching to within a few feet of the ground.

Utrecht Cathedral: choir (1254–67).
See opposite page

B. S. John, 's-Hertogenbosch: choir
(1370–1415). See opposite page

C. Castle of Muiden, near Amsterdam (13th century). See p. 577

Renaissance, 1595–1622)   (Gothic, 1515–28)

A. Town Hall, Ghent. See opposite page

(1202–1304)   Hôtel de Ville (1575–1621)

B. Cloth Hall, Ypres (rebuilt since the 1914–18 war). See opposite page

In the north-east of Holland at **Bolsward, Franeker** and **Groningen** there are churches in provincial variants of the main styles. Here the parish churches in villages are of brick and very simple, with high domed vaults and much wall arcading—very different from those of other parts; examples are **Stedum** and **Zuidbroek.**

SECULAR ARCHITECTURE

At **Kampen,** three fifteenth-century gateways, white and capped by steep conical roofs, give an idea of a Dutch Mediaeval walled town, and at **Ghent,** the **Rabot Fort** (1488) remains of the fortifications together with the **Chateau des Comtes** (twelfth century); while at **Bouillon** is a castle more typical of the countryside. In Holland the **Castle of Muiden** (thirteenth century) (p. 575C), near Amsterdam, relied largely on water for its defence, and the **Binnenhof,** seat of the Counts of Holland at The Hague, has a knight's hall of 1250 with a typical large arch-braced roof.

The **Hospital, the Byloke, Ghent** (thirteenth century and later) and the **Béguinage** there, are examples of precinct planning and grouping. A Béguinage (Dutch Begijnhof) is an open Order for women, founded in Brabant in the thirteenth century, and peculiar to the Netherlands; the work of the Sisters is amongst the poor, and they live in houses grouped around a court containing a chapel. The establishments at **Bruges, Courtrai** and **Breda** are still in use, but not that at **Amsterdam**—few have much Mediaeval building left.

Belgium, and to a lesser extent Holland, are rich in Mediaeval town halls symptomatic of the wealth of her cities. **Bruges** (1376–) (p. 579F), **Louvain** (1448–1463) (p. 579G) by Mathieu de Layens, **Ghent** (1515–28 and later) (p. 576A) by D. de Waghemakere, **Audenarde** (1525–30) (p. 579A) by Jan van Pede and **Brussels** (1402–) (p. 579E) by Jakob van Thienen, with a tower (1448–63) by Jan van Ruysbroeck (1448–63), are magnificent and ornate; simpler is **Damme** (sixteenth century), near Bruges. Dutch examples in the Flemish-Brabantine style are **Middelburg** (1412–1599), by the Keldermans of Malines (rebuilt after 1945), and **Veere** (1474–1599). Weighhouses are also typical of Holland; the one at **Deventer,** of brick and stone, is late Gothic.

The greatest of the Cloth Halls was at **Ypres** (1202–1304) (p. 576B), outstanding not only because of its size (440 ft long), but also because of its majestic simplicity. It was destroyed in 1915, and the present one is a replica. That at **Bruges** (Halles, p. 579C) has a tower 400 ft high (1280 with later lantern), and is typical of Flemish brick and stone civic architecture. The Guild Houses in the Grand' Place, **Antwerp,** (p. 829A) though sixteenth century, have only a little classical ornament, but those of **Brussels** (p. 829B) belong to the early Renaissance. The **Skipper's House, Ghent** (1531) (p. 579B) and the **Vieille Boucherie, Antwerp** (1501) are further examples of Guild Houses.

The **Maison Havart, Liége** (1594) and S. **Peter's House, Middelburg** (sixteenth century) are among the few surviving timber-framed houses; patrician and merchants' houses in stone such as some at Malines (p. 579D) and others in brick are more numerous. The **Zoudenbalch House, Utrecht** (1467) and **Het Lammetje, Veere** (House of the Scottish Merchants) (mid-sixteenth century) are stone houses of very different types. Typical brick houses are found at **Furnes** and **Goes** in the Flemish style, and in eastern Holland at **Zutfen** in another style.

COMPARATIVE ANALYSIS

PLANS. Church plans were generally short, in proportion to their width, a feature most marked in Antwerp Cathedral, where the seven aisles give an extraordinary width (p. 572A). The French ritual choir with full chevet of chapels is sometimes found, but often, and especially in Holland, the radiating chapels are partly or even wholly omitted. Large chapels sometimes flank the choir aisles, as at S. Gudule, Brussels (p. 571F) and Dordrecht (one only)—the north-east chapel was usually the Lady chapel. A flèche is used over the crossing, though lantern towers occur too, for example at 's-Hertogenbosch (p. 582). Both twin western towers and a single axial tower are found in Belgium, but in Holland the latter is ubiquitous, probably through German influence.

WALLS. Blind arcading was a feature of both early Maas and Scheldt Gothic, and became an important feature of brick Gothic, especially in Friesland and Groningen, where walls depend almost wholly on arcading for decoration. Flying buttresses, later with cusping and even figures on their copings, are more common in Belgium, but are found also in Holland; it is however characteristic of Dutch churches to do without flying buttresses and even to have very slight wall-buttresses. By the fifteenth century, particularly in the south and in secular buildings, a very regular rhythm of bays and windows is noticeable (p. 579G), usually decorated with thin, wirelike tracery, pinnacles and statuary (p. 579F).

OPENINGS. Arches developed from the lancet type to the three- and four-centred types, or occasionally even to the Moorish cusped arch, and in the Flamboyant period cusping was generally popular (pp. 580C, 581G). Where single western towers occur, the entrance may be through the tower or by a further projecting porch; other entrances often have marked importance, one of the best instances being the south transept portal at 's-Hertogenbosch. Whereas window tracery became rich and intricate in Belgium, due to the use of brick in Holland it tended there to remain comparatively simple, yet the tall nave and transept end windows, such as those at Leiden and Alkmaar, have a dramatic effect of their own.

ROOFS. As in most northern countries the steep roof is common, its gable end stepped or with pinnacles and tracery being the chief national characteristic. Vaulting is usually of the simple quadripartite type (p. 571B), but 'net' vaulting was common in late Gothic and where German influences prevailed. On later secular buildings in Belgium, numerous turrets, gabled dormers and ornate chimneys appear.

COLUMNS. The cylindrical pier remained normal until the mid-thirteenth century (p. 571B), and was used until the end in several parts of Holland, but the shafted pier, later without capitals, generally replaced it (p. 572B). The crocket capital was succeeded by a foliage capital in Brabant, with two rows of staggered and spaced foliage.

MOULDINGS. In Belgium a profusion of mouldings was used, often heavier and coarser than in France, perhaps due to the evolution of brick detailing in Flanders. The more general use of brick in Holland led to considerable simplification of mouldings, which in turn influenced those in stone.

ORNAMENT. From the end of the fourteenth century the Netherlands, particularly Flanders, rose to be a leading art centre in northern Europe, a position held for over two centuries. The Burgundian court—which patronized the sculptor Claus Sluter (working at Dijon 1380–1400)—the Emperor Maximilian and, above all, the citizens and the great cities—none outside Italy was richer than Antwerp—promoted and encouraged the interests of the artists. Hence Belgium is especially well favoured with paintings and sculpture in wood and stone, with which her architecture is richly adorned, as well as with altars (p. 581C), shrines (p. 581D), triptychs, screens, tombs (p. 581G), stalls and chimney pieces. The position of Holland was, by comparison, less fortunate and many Dutch artists were attracted to the great opportunities available in the south, so it was not until after the Mediaeval

N HALL: AUDENARDE

B THE SKIPPER'S HO. GHENT

C CLOTH HALL & BELFRY: BRUGES

D OLD HOUSES MALINES

TOWN HALL: BRUSSELS

F TOWN HALL: BRUGES

G TOWN HALL: LOUVAIN

A. WINDOWS TOWN HALL: LOUVAIN

B. S. APSE: TOURNAI

C. ARCHWAY S. JACQUES: LIE

D. CHIMNEY-PIECE. TOWN HALL: COURTRAI

E. CHIMNEY-PIECE: TOWN HALL: AUDENA

F. ARCADE & VAULTING: THE BOURSE: ANTWERP

G. SCREEN: AERSCHOT

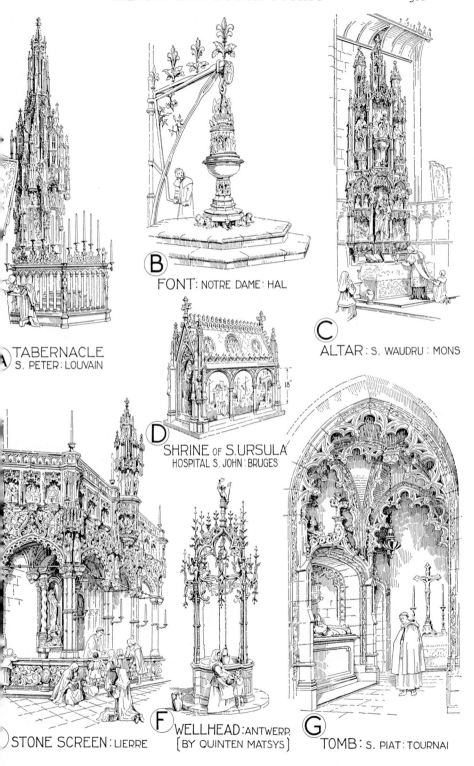

TABERNACLE
S. PETER: LOUVAIN

B FONT: NOTRE DAME: HAL

C ALTAR: S. WAUDRU: MONS

D SHRINE OF S. URSULA
HOSPITAL S. JOHN: BRUGES

STONE SCREEN: LIERRE

F WELLHEAD: ANTWERP.
[BY QUINTEN MATSYS]

G TOMB: S. PIAT: TOURNAI

S. John's, 's-Hertogenbosch (1370–1415). See p. 574

period that the tide turned in her favour. The rood screens at Lierre (1535) (p. 581E), Dixmude (1540) and Aerschot (p. 580G) are among the richest; in Holland the stone screen at Amersfoort and the brick screen at Franeker are among the best. Sacrament houses, where the consecrated Host was kept, great towering and pinnacled structures in stone, were a feature of the Netherlands as they were of Germany; they survive at S. Peter, Louvain (1450) (p. 581A), which is 50 ft high, and at Meersen (c. 1500). The choir stalls of Notre-Dame, Bruges, of Breda and 's-Hertogenbosch are good examples. The tomb of Mary of Burgundy (1495) in Notre-Dame, Bruges, is typical of late sepulchral work, with a fine recumbent figure in chased and gilded copper on a marble sarcophagus with armorial bearings. The shrine of S. Ursula at the Hospital, Bruges (1489) (p. 581D), is a reliquary formed as a miniature Gothic chapel combining the arts of the architect and sculptor, and painted by Memlinc. Good chimney pieces are found in the town halls at Audenarde, Courtrai (p. 580D, E) and Bergen-op-Zoom, the latter by R. Keldermans (1512). In addition to paintings and altar pieces, the most famous is the van Eycks' polyptych at S. Bavon, Ghent. The walls and vaults of the churches were painted too. These frescoes survived best in Holland where, due to Puritanism, they were covered in whitewash; many are now visible again, for example at the church of Our Lady, Breda, at the cathedral and S. Peter, Utrecht and especially at S. Martin, Groningen; also in Belgium at S. Jacques, Liége. The font, Hal (p. 581B), is an elaborate piece of craftsmanship, while the well-head, Antwerp (p. 581F), by Quinten Matsys, show Flemish excellence in ironwork. The art of the Flemish weavers created tapestries which enriched the interiors of town halls, guild houses and the houses of the nobility and patricians.

REFERENCE BOOKS

DESSART, CHAS. Editor. *Images de Belgique.* 7 vols.
Edition des Deux Mondes. *Pierres flamandes.* Paris.
FOKEMA, ANDREAE, TER KUILE and OZINGA. *Duizend Jaar Bouwen in Nederland.* Vol. 1, Amsterdam, 1948.
LAURENT, M. *L'Architecture et la sculpture en Belgique.* Paris and Brussels, 1928.
LUYKX, THEO. *Atlas culturel et historique de Belgique.* 1954.
Ministry of Education, Arts and Science, The Hague. *Guide to Dutch Art.* 1953.
VRIEND, J. J. *De Bouwkunst van ons Land.* 3 vols. Amsterdam, 1942.
YSENDYCK, J. J. VAN. *Documents classés de l'art dans les Pays-Bas.* 5 vols. Antwerp, 1880–9.

Germany in the fifteenth century

XVI. GERMAN GOTHIC
(thirteenth–sixteenth century)

INFLUENCES

GEOGRAPHICAL. The country in Central Europe, formerly a collection of states which became the German Empire, was, by its geographical position, in contact with the architecture of neighbouring countries. The chief influence on German Gothic architecture came from France and is conspicuous in the Rhine Provinces and Westphalia, notably in Cologne Cathedral and other churches, castles, town halls, and domestic buildings along the Rhine, which was always an important highway of commerce. Elsewhere in Germany geographical influence was of less consequence in the Gothic period.

GEOLOGICAL. We have dealt with geological influence under Romanesque architecture (p. 354), and this influence obviously remains fairly constant in this period. The northern plains of Germany provide little building material but brick, which gives a special character to the architecture of the north, particularly in the districts of the Oder and Elbe. In the centre and south and along the Rhine, excellent stone was found; while timber from the great forests in these regions gives an individuality to domestic buildings, as in wooded districts of England.

CLIMATIC. The climate, referred to in considering Romanesque architecture (p. 354), is without the fierce sun of the south, and therefore admitted of large traceried windows, as in England and France, but the snows of severe winters rendered steep roofs a necessary and special characteristic.

RELIGIOUS. The most salient feature, apart from monastic establishments, in the religious life of Mediaeval Germany before the Reformation, was the exercise of civil power by prince-bishops, who included in their ranks Electors of the Holy Roman Empire, and whose principalities were only finally swept away by the European upheaval during the French Revolution. The activities of these powerful prelates are evidenced in numerous churches, and costly tombs erected by them or in their honour. Papal abuses and disputes led inevitably to the revolt against the authority of Rome, until in 1517 Luther nailed to the church door at Wittenberg his famous theses against indulgences. The Reformation divided Germany into the Protestant north and Catholic south, but churches were not damaged, as in Puritan times in England.

SOCIAL. For a right understanding of the types of architecture peculiar to different districts it must be remembered that Germany was not one, but many states, among which were the provinces under the Houses of Luxemburg, Wittelsbach, and Hapsburg; ecclesiastical states, such as Münster; Imperial cities like Strasbourg and Ulm, while the 'Hanseatic League', an alliance of the great commercial towns of north Germany, such as Lübeck and Hamburg, exercised considerable influence on the peaceful arts, and in the fourteenth century the power of the League secured to the larger towns comparative independence, which necessitated the erection of municipal buildings. Then there was the Rhineland on the French frontier, across which came the Gothic architecture which in castle, convent, and church played its part in the folklore of the Rhine. Thus the style of architecture varies with the locality, just as does the constitution of the various states and cities. Trade guilds during this period acquired great importance and built elaborate halls, while Freemasons have been credited with much influence in the design and working out of the Gothic style (p. 305). The feudal system in Germany was so complicated by the existence of the many principalities of differing degrees of importance and independence that by the beginning of the sixteenth century any real relation between nobles and vassals had become merely nominal.

HISTORICAL. The tangled skein of German history in the Mediaeval period is complicated by the successive rise and fall of imperial and royal dynasties, by the intrigues of princely and ducal houses of the various states to secure kingly power, and by the secular ambition of prince-bishops who combined the intolerance of ecclesiastical with the arrogance of secular tyrants. In the twelfth and thirteenth centuries Germany was the centre of the Western Empire, and under the Hohenstaufen emperors long wars were carried on with the Lombard league of the north Italian towns (p. 316). After the fall of the Hohenstaufen dynasty on the death of Conrad IV, the following years (1254–73), known as the 'Great Interregnum', were times of confusion and lawlessness, not conducive to progress in architecture. The house of Hapsburg came into power in 1273, and the general adoption of Gothic architecture from France coincides with that event and lasted till the reign of Maximilian I (1486–1519), which marks the end of the Middle Ages and the commencement of the Renaissance movement (p. 807).

ARCHITECTURAL CHARACTER

Gothic architecture in Germany was similar in general character to that in other parts of Europe (p. 367), and may be considered to have lasted from 1250–1550. The style, however, came direct from France and was not evolved from German Romanesque, and this method of its introduction may be due to the extent to which Romanesque building had been developed in Germany, where a preference for the ponderous Romanesque style had resulted in the adaptation of vaulting to new

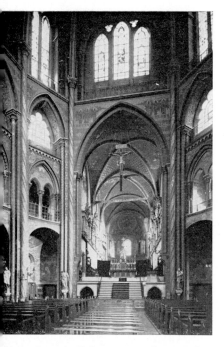

A. S. Gereon, Cologne: nave (1219–27),
looking E. See p. 587

B. Freiburg Cathedral from S.
(1250–1360). See p. 588

C. Regensburg Cathedral: nave
(1275–1534). See p. 588

D. S. Ulrich, Augsburg: nave (1467).
See p. 594

A. Façade   B. Nave

Cologne Cathedral (1284 onwards; completed 1824–80). See opposite page

C. Regensburg Cathedral   D. Ulm Cathedral (1377–1492; upper part
(1275–1534). See p. 588   of tower 19th cent.). See p. 588

See opposite page   See p. 588   See p. 588

needs without resorting to the pointed arch and other Gothic features. The Gothic style was therefore only reluctantly adopted in the middle of the thirteenth century when it was near its zenith in France, but Romanesque precedents were long followed, and although the pointed arch appears in 1140 in Paderborn Cathedral, it was long before it supplanted the round arch of the Romanesque. In northern Germany and in the valley of the Elbe the architecture was carried out in brick, and at Lübeck even window mullions and tracery were of brick, and this brick architecture, although more meagre in design than that of Lombardy, has the character due to the material.

The 'hall' churches (*dreischiffige Kirche*) are a special characteristic of German Gothic, more particularly in the north, and in these the nave and aisles are approximately the same height, with the consequent absence of triforium and clear-story (p. 590A). The only English cathedral of this unusual type is Bristol, although it occurs in the Temple Church, London (p. 393), and in some parish churches (p. 394). Another marked feature is a single western tower or western apse in place of the wide, sculptured doorways of French cathedrals, thus giving a totally different external appearance (p. 586D). It has been suggested (p. 357) that this apse at the west end may have been derived from a detached baptistery; or it may have been for the use of the laity in cases where the eastern apse was devoted to conventual use.

EXAMPLES

ECCLESIASTICAL ARCHITECTURE

S. Gereon, Cologne (pp. 265, 360A, C, 585A), on the site of a tomb, 126 ft in diameter, possibly erected by Helena, mother of Constantine, has an unusual grouping, recalling the tomb at Aix-la-Chapelle. The straight-sided choir with its sacristy dates from the Romanesque period (1075–). The eastern apse and towers were added in 1160, while the ten-sided nave, 66 ft by 55 ft, oval on plan, was built (1219–27) in the Gothic style with pointed windows, eaves gallery, and a pyramidal roof. The church was partly ruined in the 1939–45 war.

Limburg Cathedral (1213–42) (p. 362 E–G, K), is a fine Transitional church, and with its seven towers forms an imposing group above the River Lahn.

The **Liebfrauenkirche, Trèves (Trier)** (1242–53) (pp. 364, 589A, B), severely damaged in the 1939–45 war, forms part of the cathedral group (p. 358), and is a copy of Braisne Abbey Church, near Soissons. It is a Transitional building with both round and pointed arches; the cruciform upper part has clear-story windows and a fine vault, and there is an elaborately sculptured western doorway.

S. Elizabeth, Marburg (*c*. 1257–83) (p. 590), is the typical 'hall' church in which nave and aisles are of equal height, and thus there is no triforium or clear-story. The plan has nave and aisles, western entrance between two towers, and apses at the ends of the transepts and sanctuary. The exterior is peculiar in having a continuous external walking way at the level of each stage of windows, carried right through the buttresses. Flying buttresses were unnecessary, and the interior has the appearance of a large columned hall (p. 590A).

Cologne Cathedral (1248 onwards) (pp. 374K, 586A, B), the largest Gothic church of Northern Europe, covering about 91,000 square ft, is a conspicuous instance of the adoption of the details of a style, without having assimilated the spirit that created it. The huge plan has a width out of all proportion to its length, 468 ft long by 275 ft wide, and the nave (1388), with a clear width of 41 ft 6 in, is 150 ft high, almost as high as Beauvais; while the double aisles are equal in width to the nave and there are two enormous towers at the west end. The aisled transepts, with entrances, project one bay more than at Amiens, and the eastern half of the church, which is a reproduction of Amiens in plan and dimensions, has an apsidal end and processional aisle and chevet of seven chapels. The building, which was only finished, according to the original design, between the years 1824–80, displays a lack of proportion and an absence of judicious disposition of parts; for the nave with its double aisles is disproportionately short for the width, the aisles are low in proportion to the height of the nave, while the twin western towers, overpowering in bulk at the base and monotonous in repetition of lace-like detail above, altogether dwarf the main building. In matters of the delicate adjustment of proportions, which test the greatness of a creation, German architects fall short of French masters. Cologne Cathedral nevertheless makes an imposing monument, as, with its great twin-towers 500 ft high, it stands on the level plain of the wide Rhine valley.

The **Frauenkirche, Nuremberg** (1354–61) (p. 589C, D), completely ruined in the 1939–45 war, was a 'hall' church in the market-place. Its immense roof covered nave and aisles, while its two-storeyed western porch was surmounted by a curious old clock with central figure of Charles IV and moving figures of the seven Electors, which appeared at noon. The interior (p. 589D) showed the equal heights of nave and aisles, separated by cylindrical piers with foliated capitals, encircled with figures, behind which sprang the vaulting ribs.

S. Lambert, Hildesheim, S. Stephen, Mainz (1257–1328), and S. Quentin, Mainz (1450), are also 'hall' churches, while Munich Cathedral (1468–88), S. Barbara, Kuttenberg, and S. Martin, Landshut (1404), with a fine tower, 436 ft high, are further instances of similar type.

Freiburg Cathedral (c. 1250–1360) (p. 585B) has Romanesque transepts and side towers and a remarkable single western tower and spire 385 ft high, dating from 1310–50, similar to those of Cologne. The tower is square at the base, which contains the porch, octagonal in its second stage, and terminates in a lace-like spire (p. 585B), which completes a pleasing group.

Regensburg (Ratisbon) Cathedral (1275–1534) (pp. 585C, 586C) is regular in plan with three eastern apses without ambulatory, in the German manner. The west front flanked by towers and open-work crocketed spires, added in 1859–69, has a beautiful little triangular porch in the centre (1482). The cloisters (p. 597) show a mingling of Gothic and Renaissance details.

Ulm Cathedral (1377–1492) (p. 586D), spacious and lofty, is an instance, not uncommon in Germany, of excellence in masonry and poverty in design, for the smallness of the ratio of the supports to the area produces an unpleasing interior. The polygonal eastern apse is without ambulatory. The exterior has an arcaded eaves gallery, due to Romanesque traditions, and a great western tower and spire, 529 ft in height, the upper part of which was completed only in the nineteenth century, though to the original designs.

S. Stephen, Vienna (c. 1300–1510) (pp. 374J, 591), is a characteristic 'hall' church in Austria, without clear-story or triforium, for the three aisles are nearly equal in width and height, and the great roof covers the church in one span. The transepts serve as entrance porches, one of which is carried up as a tower terminated by a splendid spire, less open than usual in Germany. The vaults are traceried and the windows still contain some original stained glass.

Lübeck Cathedral (1173–1335) (p. 358) and the **Marienkirche, Lübeck** (1251–1310), much damaged in the 1939–45 war, express the possibilities of design in brickwork, so usual in north Germany.

SECULAR ARCHITECTURE

Castles were erected in goodly numbers, as at Marienburg (1280–), and Meissen, Saxony (1471–), and the old fortified town of Rothenburg still retains its Mediaeval walls, with defensive towers (p. 592B).

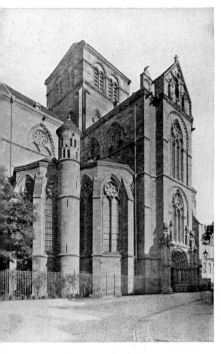

A. Exterior from S.E.   B. Interior

Liebfrauenkirche, Trèves (Trier) (1242–53). See p. 587

c. Exterior from S.W.   D. Interior looking E.

Frauenkirche, Nuremberg (1354–61). See p. 588

S. ELIZABETH : MARBURG

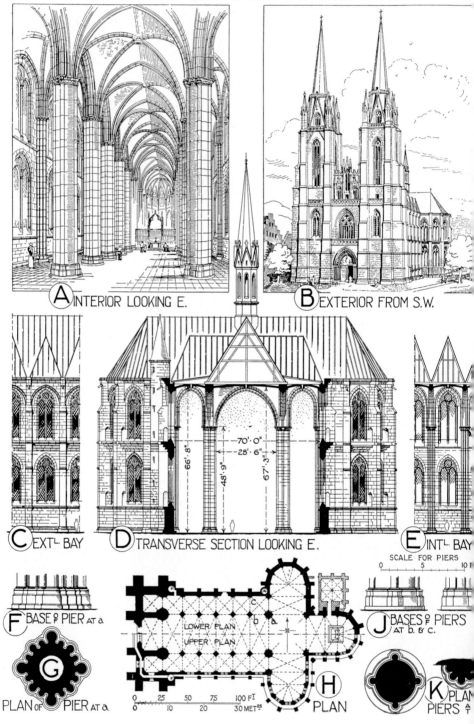

A. INTERIOR LOOKING E.

B. EXTERIOR FROM S.W.

C. EXT'L BAY

D. TRANSVERSE SECTION LOOKING E.

70' 0"
28' 6"
66' 8"
48' 9"
67' 3"

E. INT'L BAY

SCALE FOR PIERS
0   5   10 F

F. BASE OF PIER AT a

G. PLAN OF PIER AT a

LOWER PLAN
UPPER PLAN

c
b a

0   25   50   75   100 F'
0   10   20   30 MET'S

H. PLAN

J. BASES OF PIERS AT b. & c.

K. PLAN PIERS

S. STEPHEN : VIENNA

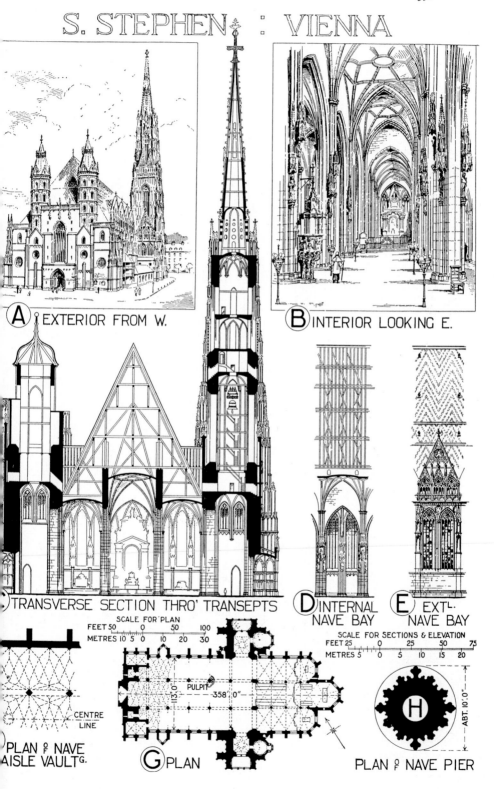

Ⓐ EXTERIOR FROM W.

Ⓑ INTERIOR LOOKING E.

Ⓒ TRANSVERSE SECTION THRO' TRANSEPTS

Ⓓ INTERNAL NAVE BAY

Ⓔ EXTL. NAVE BAY

SCALE FOR PLAN
FEET 50   0   50   100
METRES 10 5 0   10   20   30

SCALE FOR SECTIONS & ELEVATION
FEET 25   0   25   50   75
METRES 5   0   5   10   15   20

PULPIT
-358' 0"-
113' 0"

CENTRE LINE

Ⓕ PLAN OF NAVE AISLE VAULT ᴳ·

Ⓖ PLAN

Ⓗ

ABT. 10' 0"

PLAN OF NAVE PIER

A. OLD HOUSE : BRUNSWICK

B. KLINGENTOR ROTHENBURG

C. THE KAISERWORTH : GOSLA

D. OLD HOUSES : NUREMBERG

E. THE CUSTOM HOUSE : NUREMBERG

F. WINDOW : FURSTENBURG PALACE : INNSBRUCK

G. RATHHAUS REGENSBURG

H. CHAPEL OLD RATHHAUS : PRAGUE

The **Town Halls** (Rathaus) at Brunswick, Hildesheim, Cologne, Halberstadt, Münster, Regensburg (Ratisbon) (p. 592G), Ulm, and Lübeck, are prominent and impressive buildings in these semi-independent German towns, and, with the town gates in the Baltic provinces, are evidences of the prosperity of those times.

The **Custom House, Nuremberg** (1498) (p. 592E), used as a warehouse, is remarkable, with three storeys in the walls and no less than six storeys in its high roof, finished with a fine traceried gable.

The **Old Houses, Brunswick** (p. 592A) and **Nuremberg** (p. 592D), and the **Kaiserworth, Goslar** (p. 592C), are characteristic examples of the secular architecture of the period, while timber houses, in which a lower storey of masonry supports a timber upper part, were frequent, as at **Erfurt** (p. 595A), **Hildesheim** (p. 595C), and elsewhere.

Domestic Architecture was marked by lofty roofs which frequently had more storeys than the walls, and were provided with dormer windows to make a through current of air for their use as a 'drying ground' for the large monthly wash. The planning of the roof-ridge, either parallel with or at right angles to the street, considerably influenced design; thus in Nuremberg, where the ridge is generally parallel with the street, dormer windows are plentiful and party walls are finished off at the roof level with artistic treatment, while at Landshut and elsewhere the ridge at right angles to the street results in gables of great variety of design, often with a hoist in the top gable to raise goods from the ground level.

COMPARATIVE ANALYSIS

PLANS. Church plans are of varied types, and the larger number were derived from German Romanesque churches with apsidal ends, usually semi-octagonal. Apses are found both east and west, as at Naumburg, and also at ends of transepts, when they are known as triapsal plans, as in S. Elizabeth, Marburg (p. 590H). Another type of plan is the result of French influence, and has the chevet, as at Cologne, Magdeburg, Lübeck, Freiburg, and Prague. Twin western towers, as at Regensburg Cathedral (p. 586C), and single western towers, as at Ulm, are found (p. 586D); while in later buildings a central tower crowns the crossing, as in some English cathedrals. Entrances are often small and insignificant, and are on the north and south instead of at the west, and are formed in transepts and dignified with towers, as in S. Stephen, Vienna (p. 591A, G).

WALLS. Apsidal galleries of the Romanesque style were reproduced over wall surfaces without reference to their origin and purpose. Tracery was employed on both outer and inner wall surfaces, and wall tracery was often carried up in front of inner traceried windows and across gables, as seen in many churches. Towers with spires were much used, but the junction of spire and tower was often so little marked as to render the outline, though ornamented, somewhat confused and unsatisfactory (p. 586C). Open tracery spires (p. 586D), complicated alike in design and construction, are favourite features and were probably suggested by the numerous turrets with many openings used in Romanesque buildings. The typical examples are Freiburg (p. 585B), Regensburg (p. 586C), Cologne (p. 586A), and Vienna Cathedrals (p. 591A).

OPENINGS. Nave arcades in 'hall' churches were necessarily lofty, owing to the height of the aisles, such as those in S. Stephen and S. Quentin, Mainz, the Frauenkirche, Nuremberg (p. 589D), S. Elizabeth, Marburg (p. 590A, E), and S. Stephen, Vienna (p. 591B, D). Doorways, though often unimportant, as at Marburg (p. 595H), are sometimes elaborated with sculpture (p. 595F), especially under French influence, as at Cologne (p. 586A) and Erfurt (p. 595G).

Traceried windows, like the nave arcading in 'hall' churches, are of excessive height, as in the choir, Erfurt (p. 595J), but sometimes in the lofty aisles they are in two tiers, as at Marburg (p. 590C, D). Clear-story windows, when employed, start almost immediately above the nave arcade so as to provide a great expanse of stained glass. Tracery was much elaborated and double-traceried windows are not uncommon. Rose windows of intricate design were popular, as in the Lorenzkirche, Nuremberg; while oriel windows to give an additional outlook are much used in domestic architecture, as in the Kaiserworth, Goslar (p. 592C), S. Sebald's Parsonage, Nuremberg, and the Rathaus Chapel, Prague (p. 592H).

ROOFS. Vaulting, which was usually employed for churches, was excellent both in proportion and construction. One square nave vaulting bay frequently corresponds with two in the aisle, but vaulting in oblong bays afterwards became general, as at Freiburg, Regensburg (p. 585C), Cologne (p. 586B), Oppenheim, and elsewhere. The special German feature is the immense roof of the 'hall' church which, in one span, covers the nave and lofty aisles (pp. 589C, 591C). The retention of the quaint tower roofs of the Romanesque period was often another distinctive feature in an otherwise Gothic exterior, and as at Innsbruck (p. 592F).

COLUMNS. Nave piers, with or without caps, as at Augsburg (p. 585D), were used in preference to columns of French Gothic type, and owing to the height of the aisles they assumed the appearance of lofty posts (pp. 589B, D, 590A) supporting the spreading vault. Capitals are frequently carved (p. 596A, B, D, E) and exhibit skill in technique rather than design.

MOULDINGS. The mouldings, particularly of the later period, indicate a desire for intricacy rather than simplicity, and this found expression, as also to some extent in England and France, in the complicated system of 'interpenetration' of different sets of mouldings, which, appearing and disappearing in the same stone, required great skill in stone-cutting for their effective execution (p. 596). The search after effect further led to exaggerating the size of distant features, such as the roof pinnacles at Cologne: thus scale was sacrificed to detail, whereas in England and France the size of features was subordinated to the general proportions of the building.

ORNAMENT (pp. 595, 596). Sculpture was carried out much as in France, and the triangular porch of Regensburg Cathedral, with its saints on columns beneath traceried canopies, is an instance of the richness of detail occasionally lavished on church porches (p. 586C). The carving is better in execution than design, and there was a tendency towards the exact reproduction of natural foliage, such as interlaced boughs and branches of trees, which appealed to the craftsmen, who were adepts at executing interpenetrating mouldings. This idea was even carried into the 'branch-tracery' of later Gothic windows, where, again, technical skill is more evident than artistic creation and grace of outline. The enforced use of brick in the north eliminated sculpture, and moulded and coloured brick took its place in decoration. Tabernacles or sacrament houses, dating from the time when the placing of the consecrated Host above the altar was discontinued in Germany, gave ample scope for German decorative art. They are lofty, spire-like structures, tapering up in many stages of carved wood or stone with traceried openings, pinnacles, statues, and canopies, to contain the eucharistic pyx. Some are very lofty, as at Regensburg (52 ft), the Lorenzkirche, Nuremberg (1493) (64 ft) and Ulm (90 ft). Stained glass is often excellent, as in S. Sebald, Nuremberg, while the delicate and intricate ironwork of Germany, as seen in the fountains of Nuremberg, is famous throughout the world. The choir stalls at Halberstadt (p. 595E) and Lübeck (p. 596H), the screens at Oberwesel (p. 595B), the pulpit, Nuremberg (p. 596J), the altar and canopy, Regensburg (p. 596L), the stall-end, Erfurt (p. 596F), the tomb at

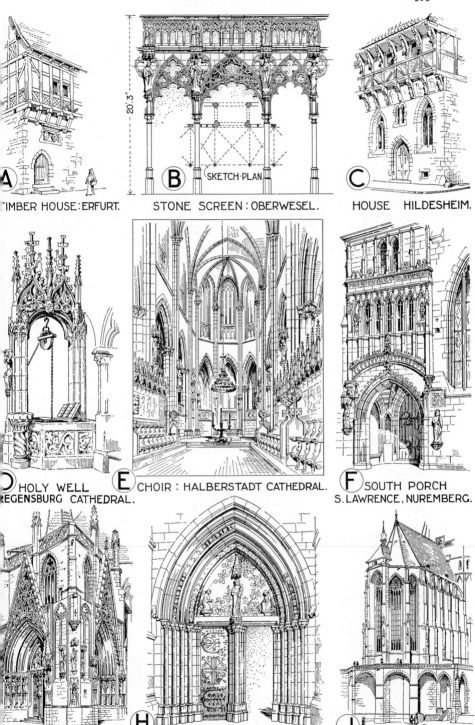

20.3"

A TIMBER HOUSE : ERFURT.

B STONE SCREEN : OBERWESEL.

SKETCH·PLAN

C HOUSE HILDESHEIM.

D HOLY WELL REGENSBURG CATHEDRAL.

E CHOIR : HALBERSTADT CATHEDRAL.

F SOUTH PORCH S. LAWRENCE, NUREMBERG.

PORCH : ERFURT CATH.

H W. PORTAL : S. ELIZABETH, MARBURG.

J CHOIR : ERFURT CATH.

A CAPITALS: S. PAUL . WORMS

B CAPITAL : MARBURG

C TRIPTYCH: NUREMBERG

D E CAPITALS W. DOORWAY FREIBURG

F STALL END: ERFURT

G S. SEBALD'S SHRINE: NUREMBERG

H STALLS MARIENKIRCHE: LUBECK

J PULPIT: NUREMBERG

K TOMB OF LANDGRAVE HENRI: MARBURG

PLANS

L ALTAR & CANOPY: REGENSE

Marburg (p. 596K), the holy well at Regensburg (p. 595D), and the triptych, Nuremberg (p. 596C), are representative specimens of the Mediaeval art of Germany. S. Sebald's shrine, Nuremberg (1508–19) (p. 596G), by Peter Vischer, exemplifies the craze for over-elaboration which characterized German craftsmen. Here twelve snails support the columns and bronze statues of the twelve Apostles who stand under their intricate fretwork canopies, guarding and enclosing the silver sarcophagus of the saint.

REFERENCE BOOKS

BERGNER, H. *Kirchliche Kunstaltertümer in Deutschland.* 1905.

BOISSERÉE, S. *Histoire et description de la cathedrale de Cologne.* 4to and folio. Munich, 1843.

DEHIO, G., and BEZOLD, G. V. *Die kirchliche Baukunst des Abendlandes.* Folio. Stuttgart, 1884, etc.

HARTEL, A. *Architektonische Detaile und Ornamente der kirchlichen Baukunst.* 2 vols., folio. Berlin, 1891.

KING, T. H. *Study-book of Mediaeval Architecture and Art.* 4 vols. London, 1858–68.

LÜBKE, W. *Ecclesiastical Art in Germany during the Middle Ages.* Edinburgh, 1873.

—. *Geschichte der deutschen Kunst.* 1880.

MOLLER, G. *Denkmäler der deutschen Baukunst.* Folio. Leipzig, 1852.

PUTTRICH, L. *Denkmäler der Baukunst des Mittelalters in Sachsen.* 4 vols., folio. Leipzig, 1836–50.

SCHAEFER, C., and STIEHL, O. *Die Kirchbauten des Mittelalters in Deutschland.* Folio. 1901.

STURGIS, R., and FROTHINGHAM, A. L. *A History of Architecture.* Vols. III, IV. New York, 1915.

WHEWELL, W. *Architectural Notes on German Churches.* Cambridge, 1842.

Regensburg Cathedral: cloisters (*c.* 1534). See p. 588

A. Milan Cathedral from S. (*c*. 1385–1485). See p. 604

B. Milan Cathedral: east end   C. Milan Cathedral: flèche

Italy in the Mediaeval Period

XVII. ITALIAN GOTHIC

(twelfth–sixteenth century)

INFLUENCES

GEOGRAPHICAL. Geographical influence in Italy varied considerably in the north, centre, and south of this long, narrow peninsula. North Italy includes the great Lombard plains and the islands of the Venetian Republic, and was brought into intercourse with Germany through Milan and Verona by the S. Gothard and Brenner Passes across the natural barrier of the Alps; while the Venetian state on the coast of the Adriatic was, through her overseas trade, in constant contact with the Byzantine sphere and the East. Thus seas and mountains, often regarded as nature's barriers, were turned, by an expanding civilization, into high-roads of art and commerce, especially on that coast 'where Venice sat in state, throned on her hundred isles'. Central Italy, although dominated by the enduring tradition of Old Rome, yet produced, in the districts to the north and farther from Rome, magnificent Gothic churches of a type peculiar to this district, as at Florence, Siena, and Assisi. South Italy and Sicily, exposed in the past to Greek and Byzantine influences on the east, Roman on the north, and Muslim on the south, was a veritable battlefield of art, and these conflicting influences produced a peculiar blend of Mediaeval architecture, further emphasized by Norman rule.

GEOLOGICAL. North Italy is especially remarkable for the abundance of clay in the alluvial Lombard plains, from which were made the beautiful red bricks and terra-cotta used for many buildings, both ecclesiastical and secular, such as the Frari Church, Venice, the Certosa, Pavia, and the Ospedale Maggiore, Milan; while lustrous white and coloured marbles from the mountains to the north were also employed, as at Milan, Genoa, and Verona. Central Italy is characterized by the extensive use of coloured marbles, frequently in zebra stripes or framed panels, which are wrought into the fabric as colour decoration, as at Florence, Siena (p. 619C), Orvieto, and Lucca. South Italy and Sicily are so rich in coloured marbles that the term 'Sicilian marble' has become a household word, and the architectural decoration of Palermo Cathedral is achieved by the deft mingling of marble in two colours. Thus did the geological formation supply materials for the development of unusually pronounced styles.

CLIMATIC. North Italy has a climate similar to the temperate region of Central Europe, and this contributed to the development of those essentially Gothic features, such as large traceried windows, with the consequent necessity for buttresses instead of walls, as seen in Milan Cathedral and to a less extent in the buildings of Padua, Verona, and Venice. In central and south Italy, the sunny climate and brilliant atmosphere naturally demanded small windows and thick walls to exclude the glare and heat of the sun. The preference, moreover, for opaque wall decoration, whether in mosaic, fresco, or marble, handed down from the ancient Romans through the Romanesque period, counteracted any tendency to supersede opaque walls of stone by transparent walls of glass, and thus there was little chance for the development of window tracery.

RELIGIOUS. The power of the pope, as head of the Western Church, waned after the death of Boniface VIII (1303), for succeeding popes were under the influence of the kings of France, and for almost seventy years (1309–77), a period known as the 'Babylonish captivity', they resided at Avignon, losing authority and influence during their absence from Rome, in which city it is significant that there should be only one Gothic church. After the return of Gregory XI to Rome and his death in 1378, Western Christendom was plunged by rival popes into the religious turmoil of the 'Great Schism of the West' (1378–1417), which was only terminated by the Council of Constance and the accession of Martin V. It is not surprising that this period of confusion was unfavourable to the building of churches in Italy. S. Francis of Assisi (1182–1226) founded the Order of Franciscans or Grey Friars, which fired the religious imagination of the time and revolutionized religious life; for, as Dante says, 'he rose like a sun and illumined everything with his rays'. The movement he had started gained strength, so that by the eighteenth century there were 9,000 convents of this Order in Europe.

SOCIAL. Italy had no national unity at this period, but was cut up into principalities and commonwealths, such as the republics of Venice, Florence, and Genoa, the duchy of Milan, the kingdom of Naples, and the Papal States. This absence of national unity is mirrored in the varied architectural treatment in different parts of the peninsula. Political life was full of rivalry and activity, and small

MILAN CATHEDRAL

Ⓐ EXTERIOR FROM S.W.

Ⓑ INTERIOR LOOKING E.

MILAN CATHEDRAL

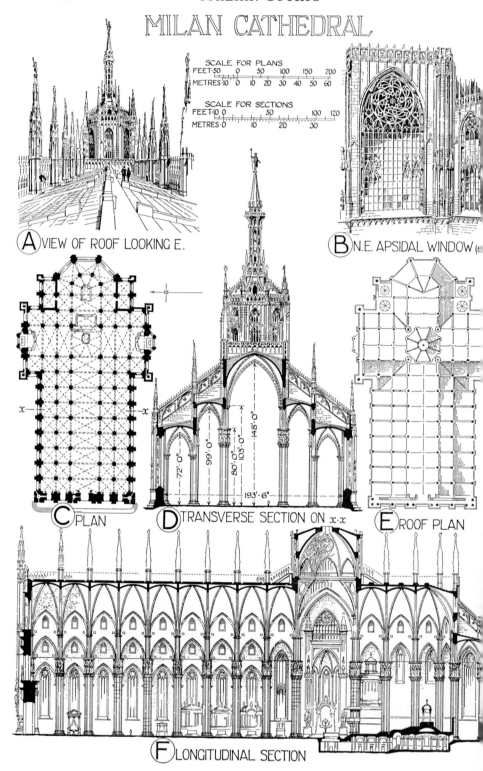

SCALE FOR PLANS
FEET·50 0 50 100 150 200
METRES·10 0 10 20 30 40 50 60

SCALE FOR SECTIONS
FEET·10 0 50 100 120
METRES·0 10 20 30

(A) VIEW OF ROOF LOOKING E.

(B) N.E. APSIDAL WINDOW (E

(C) PLAN

(D) TRANSVERSE SECTION ON $x \cdot x$

148'·0"
99'·0"
72'·0"
103'·0"
80'·0"
193'·6"

(E) ROOF PLAN

(F) LONGITUDINAL SECTION

wars were of constant occurrence. The erection of the cathedrals of Siena, Orvieto, Florence, Milan, and Lucca was largely due to the vigorous civic pride of rival cities; while during the struggles between popes and emperors and their respective factions, the Guelphs and Ghibellines, both sides had to reckon with the increasing power of the townsmen who erected those numerous town halls which attest the growth of municipal institutions. Thus architecture was used more freely in the service of the people. The unsettled condition of the times may be gathered both from the contemporary chronicles of Giovanni Villani and from the later poet Tasso, who says that the citizens on each holiday blew trumpets and proceeded to sack the neighbouring town. Italian was tentatively used as a written language about 1200. Dante (1265–1321) presents a vivid picture of the age in his *Divina Commedia*, and this poem, which standardized the Italian language in literature, also coincided with the development of Italian Gothic architecture.

HISTORICAL. In spite of internal turmoil, Italy led the way in Europe in arts, learning, and commerce, and the revival of learning, known as the Renaissance, took place there nearly a century in advance of northern Europe, and effectually arrested the further evolution of the Gothic style in Italy. The Latin conquest of Constantinople (Istanbul) (1204) during the fourth crusade, in which the republic of Venice played such a prominent part, and the subsequent years of the Latin occupation of the city (1204–61), were partly responsible for the immigration, in the thirteenth century, of Graeco-Byzantine artists into Italy. These skilled craftsmen, trained in Classical traditions, settled in Genoa, Venice, Pisa, Florence, Siena, and many another town, and gave an impetus to the creative arts which enriched Italy, and then spread their influence throughout Europe. The rise of Venice was marked by the defeat of the Genoese off the Sardinian coast in 1353, and of the Turkish fleet in 1416. These victories fired the Venetians with a desire to make the Doge's Palace a fit symbol of their success, and it was completed when Venice reached the zenith of her power and prosperity.

ARCHITECTURAL CHARACTER

The general character of Gothic architecture in Europe has already been dealt with (p. 367). The style in Italy dates approximately from the twelfth to the sixteenth century, but the influence of Roman tradition remained so strong that the conspicuous verticality of northern Gothic is generally neutralized in Italy by horizontal cornices and string courses. Churches are marked externally by the following features: flatness of roofs (pp. 598, 615A), the screen wall of the west façade which masks the aisle roofs (pp. 601A, 617A), the circular window of the west front (p. 628A, G), an absence of pinnacles and of flying buttresses (p. 615A), stripes of coloured marbles instead of mouldings, occasional frescoes and mosaics in panels, and small windows without tracery (p. 615A). The projecting entrance porches with columns, often resting on the backs of lion-like beasts (p. 629E), are in striking contrast to the cavernous porches of Northern Europe.

The sculpture and carving (pp. 630, 631), executed in the fine-grained marble of Italy, continued to be as refined as in the Classical period, and the influence of Old Rome is seen in modified Corinthian capitals with their acanthus leaves. The sculpture, although superior in technique to that of Northern Europe, is not such an essential part of a style which, as we shall see, never developed, as in France and England, into the highest form of Gothic. The brickwork and plastic terra-cotta of the Lombard plains resulted in a smallness of detail and intricacy of ornament natural to this material, as in the Frari Church, Venice (p. 628G), the Certosa, Pavia (p. 617F), and Chiaravalle (p. 629D), and many civic buildings. Colour effect and delicate detail were relied on, rather than depth of shadow and boldness of design; thus was the material allowed to give full expression to its own capabilities without forcing it beyond its limitations. The variety of influences in south Italy, and more especially in Sicily, produced a type of architecture which owes its beauty to the combination of Greek inspiration, Roman construction, and Byzantine decoration (p. 301).

EXAMPLES

NORTH ITALY

Milan Cathedral (c. 1385–1485) (pp. 374L, 598, 601, 602), initiated by the populace and clergy of the city and sponsored by Giovanni Galeazzo Visconti, duke of Milan, is, with the exception of Seville, the largest Mediaeval cathedral, and is somewhat German in character, as among the fifty or so architects who had a part in it were consultants from north of the Alps. The choir and transepts were finished about 1450, and the nave and aisles were commenced in 1452. In plan (p. 602C) it consists of a nave, 55 ft wide between the piers, lofty double aisles and transepts terminated with a circlet of columns in the French manner, but enclosed in a German polygonal apse, while there is an absence of lateral chapels. The interior (pp. 601B, 602D) is vast, lofty, and imposing, with fine perspective views, rendered all the more impressive by the dimness and mystery which result from lack of light. It has huge piers, 60 ft high, surrounded by engaged shafts and surmounted by enormous capitals, 20 ft in height, containing canopied niches with statues, from which spring the nave arches supporting the vault 148 ft above the ground. It resembles S. Petronio, Bologna, and owing to the excessive height of the aisles there is no triforium and the clear-story is small, in striking contrast with French and English Gothic cathedrals. The exterior is a gleaming mass of white marble with lofty traceried windows, panelled buttresses, flying buttresses, and pinnacles crowned with statues (pp. 598, 601A), all wrought into a soaring design of lace-like intricacy. The three magnificent traceried windows of the apse, 68 ft by 28 ft, are the finest of their type in Italy (p. 598B). The flat-pitched roofs are constructed of massive marble slabs laid on the vaulting (p. 598C), and over the crossing is a domical vault, 215 ft above the ground, designed by Amadeo and Dolcebuono in a competition in 1490, finishing in a lantern to which in 1750 an open-work spire was added, rising 350 ft above the ground (pp. 598C, 602A). The later façade (p. 601A), which has the widespreading gable lines of Romanesque churches, such as S. Michele, Pavia (p. 322F), remained long unfinished, and was partly built from the designs of Carlo Buzzi after 1653, but only completed by Napoleon at the beginning of the nineteenth century.

The **Certosa, Pavia** (1396–1497) (p. 617D–F), a famous Carthusian monastery, was commenced by Giovanni Galeazzo Visconti, and forms a splendid memorial of the Milan dynasties. The monastic buildings were nearly completed at his death in 1492. The church was in progress by 1453. In plan (p. 617D) it is a Latin cross and similar to many German churches in the triapsal terminations to sanctuary and transepts, but the nave is in square, and the aisles in oblong bays, in the Italian manner. On the south are the two cloisters, richly wrought in terra-cotta. The exterior (p. 617F) is a fascinating instance of Lombard transitional Gothic-Renaissance style with arcading and terra-cotta ornament; while the monumental façade (1473–c. 1501) is wholly of Renaissance character (pp. 684, 686A).

S. Antonio, Padua (1232–1307) (p. 605), is a seven-domed pilgrimage church resembling S. Mark, Venice (p. 289), in general conception. The nave is in square bays covered with domes on pendentives, which are also placed over the crossing, transepts, and choir, beyond which is an apse and chevet with nine radiating

A. S. Antonio, Padua, from N.W. (1232–1307; domes heightened 1424). See p. 604

B. S. Antonio, Padua: nave

A. SS. Giovanni e Paolo, Venice, from W. (1260–1385; façade 1430—unfinished;
dome of later date). See opposite page

B. S. Francesco, Assisi: upper church   C. SS. Giovanni e Paolo, Venice:
    (1228–53). See p. 623   interior

chapels similar to contemporary churches in France. The interior also was obviously influenced by the Venetian church, but falls far short of the original, as it lacks the glamour of coloured mosaic decoration. The exterior has an arcade of pointed arches and an upper arcaded gallery, like the Romanesque churches of Lombardy, while the domes, heightened in 1424, and minaret-like turrets give it a curious Byzantine aspect.

SS. Giovanni e Paolo, Venice (1260–1385) (p. 606), a Dominican church of imposing proportions and of historic importance, contains the tombs of the Doges. The Latin cross of the plan is elaborated by pronounced transepts with eastern chapels, and by a polygonal apse to the choir. The interior is essentially Italian in the wide spacing of piers, the square bays of the nave vaulting, and the oblong bays of the aisles, and internal wooden ties take the place of external flying buttresses. The exterior is of beautiful brickwork with pointed windows and moulded cornices, and the clear-story is loftier than usual in Italy, while a dome of later date crowns the crossing.

S. Maria Gloriosa dei Frari, Venice (1250–1338) (p. 628E, F, G), is a Franciscan church, designed by Niccolo Pisano, in which there are six eastern transept chapels. The interior (p. 628F) has lofty stone cylindrical piers tied together by wooden beams, supporting an arcade of pointed arches and brick vaulting in square bays with massive ribs resting on shafts rising from the pier capitals. The exterior (p. 628G) is in fine coloured brickwork, the plain west façade is set off by the sculptured central doorway and circular window above, and by small lateral windows, while along the aisles are pointed windows. The square campanile has vertical panels and a belfry of open arches, and is crowned with an octagonal lantern. The apse (p. 628E), with its double tiers of pointed tracery windows, flanked by the eastern transept chapels, is the great glory of the church.

S. Anastasia, Verona (1261–) (p. 610A), with its delightful portal and brick campanile, is a beautiful expression of Italian Gothic, and S. Andrea, Vercelli (1219–), has a character of its own derived from its two western towers and English type of plan.

S. Petronio, Bologna (1390–1437) (p. 609A, B), was designed for this famous university city by Antonio di Vincenzo to eclipse the cathedral at Florence. It was to have consisted of nave, aisles, outer chapels, transepts, chancel, and chevet, and if completed would have been one of the largest churches in Italy, but the eastern part was never built. The interior resembles Milan in having nave and aisles in diminishing heights, and the nave, with little ornamental detail, has widely spaced piers, resembling those of Florence. The chief feature of the entrance façade is the great doorway with its sculptured ornament designed in 1425 by Jacopo della Quercia. The exterior was never finished, although a competition was held about 1535 in which Palladio, Vignola, and others took part, and fifty designs are still preserved.

There are churches at Bologna, Vicenza, Padua, Cremona, and Venice which are examples of the influence of brick and terra-cotta material on architectural treatment.

The Doge's Palace, Venice (pp. 611, 731), the façades of which date from 1309–1424, and are from designs by Giov. and Bart. Buon, is the grandest effort in civic architecture of the period, and is material evidence of the proud position of Venice as a great trading community, whose commerce was protected by the supremacy of her navy. The palace, started in the ninth century, several times rebuilt, and completed in the Renaissance period (p. 731), forms part of that great scheme of town-planning which was carried out through successive centuries (p. 611D). The façades, with a total length of nearly 500 ft, have open arcades in the two lower storeys, and the third storey was rebuilt after a fire in the sixteenth century, so as to extend over the arcades (p. 611B). This upper storey is faced with white and rose-coloured marble walls, resembling patterned brickwork, pierced by a few large and ornate windows (p. 628B) and finished with a lace-like parapet of oriental cresting. The arcade columns (p. 611E), which originally stood on a stylobate of three steps, now rise from the ground without bases, and the sturdy continuous tracery of the second tier of arcades lends an appearance of strength to the open arches, so heavily loaded by the solid walls above. The capitals of the columns, particularly the angle capital (p. 631J) eulogized by Ruskin in *The Stones of Venice*, are celebrated for the delicate carving in low relief, which was made possible by the use of fine-grained marble. The whole scheme of columned and pointed arcades, with its combination of carved capitals and long horizontal lines of open tracery, is of that unique design which can only be termed Venetian Gothic. The 'Porta della Carta' gives entrance to the Cortile (p. 731).

The **Palazzo Pubblico, Cremona** (1206-45), the **Palazzo Pubblico, Piacenza** (1281-), and the **Mercanzia, Bologna** (1382-4) (p. 629G), are similar with pointed arcades and an upper storey, often with a projecting *ringhiera* or tribune, and there are the familiar forked battlements.

The **Broletto, Monza** (thirteenth century), possesses, like many another town hall, a *ringhiera* or balcony (p. 330D) on a level with the floor of the great hall, from which the magistrates were wont to address the citizens.

The **Ca d'Oro, Venice** (1424-36) (p. 612C), is another fine design by the architects of the Doge's Palace for one of those palatial homes of merchant princes with which the sea-city abounds. The windows are grouped together in the usual Venetian manner to form a centre for the façade which, however, in this instance seems to lack one wing. The arcaded entrance of five arches, lighting the deep central hall, is surmounted by an arcade divided into six openings, filled with characteristically Venetian tracery, and flanked by wider arches with projecting balconies, above which is another storey lighter in treatment, and there is a curious roof cresting of Saracenic design. The finished wing of the façade is of solid masonry, which sets off the intricate tracery of the centre.

The **Palazzi Foscari** (fifteenth century), **Contarini-Fasan** (fourteenth century), **Cavalli** (fifteenth century), and **Pisani** (fifteenth century) (p. 612B) are famous Gothic palaces on the Grand Canal. They display the concentration of traceried openings in the centre to light the hall, and have solid unbroken wings, which produce a reposeful reflection in the water below.

The **Ponte di Castel Vecchio** or **Scaligero, Verona** (1335), wholly destroyed in the 1939-45 war, was one of many bridges which were of such importance as means of intercommunication that they were considered sacred. It was a fortified bridge across the Adige, with a tower on either bank, and had segmental arches, a low octagonal tower at every pier, and forked Ghibelline battlements along its whole length (p. 632B).

The **Torre del Commune, Verona** (1172) (p. 628D), is one of those communal towers which sprang up as a result of Mediaeval civic life; for they served as bell towers to summon the citizens and as watch towers against fire and enemies. The square shaft of striped stone and brickwork has a belfry of three lights on each face; the crowning octagonal turret, in two stages, rises to a height of 272 ft, and was added after 1404, when the city lost its independence to Venice.

The **Torrazzo, Cremona** (1261-84), the highest (nearly 400 ft) in Italy, and the celebrated **Campanile of S. Mark, Venice** (pp. 323, 611A), rebuilt since its collapse in 1902 in the form it had possessed since the early sixteenth century, add to the world-fame of Italian towers.

The **Ospedale Maggiore, Milan** (1457-*c*. 1624) (p. 698F-H), is unusual in that

A. S. Petronio, Bologna, from N. (1390–1437). See p. 607

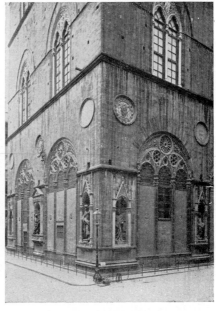

B. S. Petronio, Bologna: nave looking E.

C. Or San Michele, Florence (1337–1404). See p. 614

u

A. S. Anastasia, Verona (1261–).   B. Arena Chapel, Padua
        See p. 607   (c. 1300–1305). See p. 633

C. Palazzo Vecchio (1298–1314) and Piazza della Signoria, Florence
    with the Loggia dei Lanzi (right) (1376–82). See p. 623

THE DOGE'S PALACE
VENICE

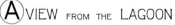

Ⓐ VIEW FROM THE LAGOON

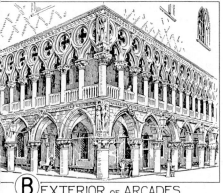

Ⓑ EXTERIOR OF ARCADES

Ⓒ THE UPPER ARCADE

Ⓓ PLAN OF PIAZZA

Ⓔ THE LOWER ARCADE

A THE BIGALLO : FLORENCE

B PALAZZO PISANI : VENICE

← PROJECTED EXTENSION

C PALAZZO CA D'ORO : VENICE

D PALAZZO PUBBLICO : SIENA

E BALCONY : VENICE

F PAL. DEI PRIORI : VOLTERRA

G MEDIÆVAL Hᵒ : VITERBO

H PAᴸ PUBBLICO : MONTEPULCIA

it was begun in transitional Renaissance style by Antonio Filarete of Florence (p. 684), but continued from 1465 in late Gothic. It is built of brick and terra-cotta, the use of which has resulted in delicacy of modelling in the broad frieze between the storeys and in the ornamental bands round the windows. It was the first lay hospital. The interior was severely damaged in the 1939–45 war.

CENTRAL ITALY

Florence Cathedral (1296–1462) (pp. 615A, B, 616), also known as S. Maria del Fiore, was designed by Arnolfo di Cambio, and is essentially Italian in character without the vertical features of northern Gothic. It was built around the old church of S. Reparata when, in 1296, the city council decided to erect a new cathedral worthy of the prosperity of the citizens. If forms the centre of the group which emphasizes the importance of Florence and the ambition of her sons during the Middle Ages. On Arnolfo's death either in 1302 or 1310 the building was stopped till 1334, when Giotto was appointed master of the works, and he was followed by Andrea Pisano and Francesco Talenti, who in 1357 enlarged Arnolfo's scheme, while in 1365 a commission of architects laid out the choir and transepts. The three apses were completed in 1421, the dome was added by Brunelleschi (1420–34) as the result of a competition (p. 677), and the lantern was placed over it in 1462 by Giuliano da Maiano, after Brunelleschi's death in 1446. The plan (p. 616F) is a peculiar type of Latin cross, and remarkable for the large central nave, 270 ft long, and wide spacing of nave arcades, for there are only four square bays of 60 ft (p. 615B). This vast nave forms an impressive though sombre approach to the majestic octagon (p. 616G), 138 ft 6 in in diameter, off which are the three immense apses with fifteen radiating chapels. The piers have attached pilasters and unmoulded pointed arches; there is no triforium, but a small clear-story of circular windows below the vaulted roof. The exterior (pp. 615A, 616A) is notable for its coloured marble panelling, small traceried windows, absence of buttresses and pinnacles, and for the horizontal lines of the design, the unique semi-octagonal apses, and the pointed dome. The marble facing of the west façade, partially completed under Arnolfo di Cambio (p. 616E) but destroyed in 1588, was recommenced in 1875 (p. 616A), with its panels of coloured marble, sculptures, and mosaics, and finished in 1887.

The **Campanile, Florence** (1334–59) (pp. 615A, 616A), on the site of an earlier tower (888), is 45 ft square and 275 ft high, and was designed by Giotto on traditional Italian lines. Only the lowest stage was finished in Giotto's time, and the design was twice changed as it proceeded, first by Andrea Pisano and finally by Francesco Talenti. It rises sheer from the pavement without supporting buttresses, and all its four sides are panelled in coloured marble and embellished with sculptured friezes and marble inlay. It is divided into four principal stages, of which the topmost is the belfry, crowned by an arched corbel table, instead of the spire intended by Giotto.

The **Baptistery, Florence** (p. 615A), thought to have started as a fifth-century church, converted into a baptistery in the middle of the eleventh century, received various minor adornments during the thirteenth century and, standing to the west of the Cathedral, forms part of this world-famous group. The octagon is 90 ft in diameter, covered with an internal dome, 103 ft high, probably modelled on that of the Pantheon. The façades are in three stages of dark green and white marble, crowned with a low roof and lantern. The Baptistery is noted for the marvellous workmanship of its famous bronze doors, which were added in the fourteenth (1330–6) and fifteenth (1403–24 and 1425–52) centuries by Andrea Pisano and Lorenzo Ghiberti (p. 672). In 1514, in view of threatened collapse, Michelangelo introduced an iron chain around the base of the dome.

Siena Cathedral (*c.* 1226–1380) (pp. 617A–C, 619A, C), one of the most stupendous undertakings since the building of Pisa Cathedral, was largely the outcome of civic pride, and all the artists of Siena contributed their works to its building and adornment. The plan is cruciform, with an unusual irregular hexagon at the crossing, 58 ft in diameter (p. 617C), covered by a dome and lantern of 1259–64; while the sanctuary, owing to the slope of the ground, is built over the Baptistery of S. Giovanni, which thus forms a crypt, and is entered from the lower level. The interior is striking in its combination of unusual features (pp. 617B, 619C). The zebra marble striping on wall and pier, the squinch-arches of the strange hexagon, and the incised marble floor (fourteenth–fifteenth century), by the famous pavement-artists of Siena, form suitable surroundings for the famous sculptured pulpit by Niccolo Pisano (1265–9). Between 1339–48 a grandiose project for adding a new nave, to which the existing church would have formed transepts, was begun and abandoned. The building stands on a stepped platform (p. 619A) which gives dignity to the composition, and it has an elaborately sculptured western façade (lower part 1284–1300, upper, 1377–80) which is merely a frontispiece faced with white marble relieved with pieces of Siena red and Prato green marble and with three highly ornate recessed doorways (p. 619A). The shaft-like campanile, (thirteenth century) in striped marble, has six stages of windows which increase in size, and, rising from the south transept, it forms the central feature of the group.

The **Campo Santo, Pisa** (1278–83) (pp. 313A, 314B, 618A), by Giov. Pisano, consists of an open rectangle surrounded by a cloister with round-arched openings, filled with beautiful open tracery in 1463.

S. Maria della Spina, Pisa (1323) (p. 618B), is a miniature church on the banks of the Arno with shrine-like façade of crocketed gables and pinnacled canopies.

Orvieto Cathedral (1290–1330) (pp. 619B, 628C), of which the first architect was probably Arnolfo di Cambio, stands on an eminence in this isolated hill-city. Its plan is basilican with nave, aisles, and projecting semicircular chapels. The interior (p. 619B) shows basilican influence, with its lofty cylindrical pillars in grey and white marble, which support semicircular arches surmounted by a striped clear-story and pointed windows, all crowned by a timber roof of basilican type. The exterior also is of striped marble (basalt and travertine) carried round the aisle chapels, the windows of which are partly filled with alabaster. The façade (1310–30, not fully completed until 1580) resembles Siena with its three porches, gables, and rose window, and is a glowing mass of symbolism carried out in coloured mosaic, carving, and sculpture of great beauty, but is a mere frontispiece.

S. Maria Novella, Florence (1278–1350) (p. 632A), was designed by two Dominican friars as a Latin cross of great size with transepts, chapels, and beautiful cloisters. The nave has no triforium, but a low clear-story with circular windows and a ribbed vault. The original design of the unfinished exterior is indicated by some blind arcading on the entrance façade, which was completed from designs by Alberti in the Renaissance period (p. 683).

S. Croce, Florence (1294–1442) (p. 622A), one of the largest churches in Europe, was by Arnolfo di Cambio, and contains many monuments to celebrated Italians; hence it has been called the Westminster Abbey of Italy. It is a Gothic version of a basilican church, with widely spaced columns and open timber roof. The western façade, left unfinished, was completed 1857–63, and is similar in character to that of Siena Cathedral.

Or San Michele, Florence (1337–1404) (p. 609C), designed by Francesco Talenti and others, was originally called 'S. Michele in Orto', from its orchard site. It has a rectangular ground storey originally serving as a church of the trade guilds, which has fine three-light windows with slender columns and elaborate tracery

Campanile (1334–59)

A. Florence Cathedral from S.E. (1296–1462). See p. 613

B. Florence Cathedral: nave looking E.

C. Loggia dei Lanzi, Florence (1376–82). See p. 623

S. MARIA DEL FIORE : ✝FLORENCE

SCALE FOR Ⓑ
FT 200

A EXTERIOR FROM N.W.

B LONGITUDINAL SECTION

LANTERN HERE

STEPS

LANTERN

C CONSTRUCTION OF DOME

PLAN d PLAN e

PLAN c

PLAN b

PLAN a

COUNTERFORTS

SECTION ON X-X

SECTIONAL PLAN

D OF DOME

E UNCOMPLETED FACADE

138'6"

130'0"

FT MTRS
200 60

F PLAN

G INTERIOR LOOKING E.

SIENA CATH.

(A) EXTERIOR FROM W.

(B) INTERIOR SHOWING HEXAGON

(C) PLAN OF SIENA CATHEDRAL

DOWN 50 0 50 100 150 F.T
10 5 0 10 20 30 40 M.T.RS

HEXAGON
320.0

PROPOSED NEW NAVE
NEVER COMPLETED

NAVE

FT 250 M.T.RS
70
200 60
150 50
40
100 30
20
50 10
0 0
5
50 10

LA CERTOSA : PAVIA

(D) PLAN OF LA CERTOSA

270.0

SMALL
CLOISTER

GREAT
CLOISTER

(E) INTERIOR LOOKING E.

(F) EXTERIOR FROM N.

A. Campo Santo, Pisa (1278–1463). See p. 614

B. S. Maria della Spina, Pisa (1323). See p. 614

A. Siena Cathedral: exterior.
See p. 614

B. Orvieto Cathedral (1290–1330): nave
looking E. See p. 614

C. Siena Cathedral: interior (1226–1380). See p. 614

A. S. Francesco, Assisi: aerial view from W. showing Monastery
and Church (1228–53). See p. 623

B. S. Francesco, Assisi: lower church

A. S. Francesco, Assisi, from lower terrace on E. (1228–53). See p. 623

B. S. Francesco, Assisi: Great Cloister showing W. end

A. S. Croce, Florence: nave (1294–1442). See p. 614

B. S. Maria Sopra Minerva, Rome: nave (1285). See opposite page enclosed in semicircular arches. These arcade infillings were an afterthought, dating from 1366–81. Externally, between the windows, are niches filled with statues by celebrated sculptors, such as Donatello and Ghiberti, as offerings from the twelve great trade guilds of Florence between 1428 and 1550. In the interior is a beautiful tabernacle and high altar by Andrea Orcagna (1349–59). There are two upper storeys over the church which have two-light windows; down to 1569 they formed granaries and are now used for State archives.

S. Francesco, Assisi (1228–53) (pp. 606B, 620, 621), the great pilgrimage church on the hill above the historic plain, owes much of its imposing character to its lofty position, while the hill-slope facilitated the erection of an upper and lower church. The vast monastic buildings on their massive masonry substructures testify to the magnetic influence of the great Italian saint and founder. Both churches are vaulted, and the dim mystery of the aisleless interiors, terminated by a polygonal apse, gives a sense of solemnity to the brilliant frescoes of Cimabue and Giotto, representing scenes from the life of S. Francis and incidents in the history of the Franciscan Order. These frescoes form a complete and consistent scheme of decoration, thoroughly in harmony with Italian tradition; they make one of the most glowing church interiors in all Italy, and are a fitting memorial-shrine of one who trod the path of self-abnegation. The pulpit (p. 630K) and the monuments (p. 631G) are of great interest. The doorways of both upper and lower church, the circular window of the nave, and the turret-shaped buttresses, with low flying arches, are the main features of the exterior. A sturdy campanile, which retains the Lombard Romanesque character, crowns this famous group.

S. Maria sopra Minerva, Rome (c. 1285) (p. 622B), designed by Fra Sisto and Fra Ristoro, the two friars who were also the architects of S. Maria Novella, Florence (p. 632A), is the only Gothic church in Rome—an evidence of the impregnable fortress which the citadel of Classic Rome presented to the advance of Gothic art—besides which the city had been supplied with many churches during the early Christian period.

The **Palazzo del Podesta** or **Bargello, Florence** (1255–), the **Palazzo Vecchio, Florence** (1298–1314) (p. 610C), the **Palazzo Pubblico, Siena** (1289–1309) (p. 612D), the **Palazzo del Municipio, Perugia** (1281–), and the **Palazzo Pubblico, Montepulciano** (late fourteenth century) (p. 612H), represent the municipal life and enterprise of these Mediaeval cities, and stand, grave and severe, amidst the bustle of modern life, with their lofty watch towers and fortified façades, often finished with machicolations and battlements.

The **Palazzo dei Priori, Volterra** (1208–57) (p. 612F), is in four storeys with two-light windows, now irregularly placed. It is crowned with heavy battlements and the square tower rising above the front wall is capped with a belfry.

The **Castle, Volterra** (1343), high on its rocky site, is a typical Mediaeval stronghold of imposing outline with massive walls, small windows, central circular keep, round towers, and machicolations (p. 625A).

The **Bigallo, Florence** (1352–58) (p. 612A), is a delicately arcaded little loggia, designed to shelter foundlings who were there displayed by the Capitane of S. Maria to appeal to the charity of the public.

The **Loggia dei Lanzi, Florence** (1376–82) (p. 615C), with its bold semicircular arches and compound piers, forms a part only of a great town-planning scheme to surround the piazza which would have made it the most magnificent arcaded square in Italy.

The **Mediaeval House, Viterbo** (p. 612G), with its arcaded ground storey and traceried windows, is interesting among many such houses as evidence of a phase of civilization which has passed away.

San Gimignano (pp. 323, 625C) on its hill-top still retains thirteen towers built by rival local families—adherents of the Ghibellines and Guelphs—which vividly suggest the condition of the times when, as we are told, the municipality had to make building regulations to limit the height of the towers of these fortress-houses, mainly of the tenth and eleventh centuries, which still give a strangely mediaeval aspect to this picturesque hill-city.

The **Ponte Vecchio, Florence** (1345) (p. 625B), by Taddeo Gaddi, the oldest bridge in Florence, has a quaint character, with its three segmental arches springing boldly from massive piers to withstand the waters of the Arno when swollen with the melting snows of the Appenines, while along both sides of its roadway are the small shops of the goldsmiths' quarter. The corridor above the shops is by Vasari (1564).

SOUTHERN ITALY AND SICILY

Messina Cathedral (1092–1197), frequently altered after damage by fire and earthquakes until it was practically destroyed by the earthquake of 1908, was basilican in plan with timber roof in Muslim honeycomb work.

Palermo Cathedral (1170–85) (p. 626A) repeatedly altered, built on the site of an earlier Muslim mosque, is also basilican in plan and was commenced by King William the Good of Sicily. The open porch (c. 1480), with slender columns supporting stilted pointed arches of Muslim type, is reminiscent of the Alhambra, Granada; while the roof battlements recall those of the Doge's Palace. At the west end the Cathedral, which is Muslim in character, is connected across the street by two pointed arches to the tower of the Archbishop's Palace. Two slender minaret towers on either side resemble those at the east end, and in its vigour of skyline the whole group suggests Northern Gothic. The external decoration is in stone of two colours, and the apses are particularly fine in treatment with polychrome interlaced blind arcading. The dome is an addition of 1781–1801.

The **Castello Nuovo, Naples** (1279–83), built by Charles I of Anjou, is a lofty, rectangular structure, with three machicolated round towers and curtain walls, now pierced with Renaissance windows.

The **Palazzo Stefano, Taormina** (1330) (p. 626B)—one of many palaces in that ancient precipice-city which have pointed two-light windows with trefoil heads and crowning machicolated cornices—and the **Archbishop's Palace, Palermo,** designed with flamboyant tracery windows (15th cent.) (p. 626C)—now mostly blocked up to keep out the southern sun—are typical secular buildings of the Mediaeval period.

COMPARATIVE ANALYSIS

PLANS. The desire for a great central space, as at Florence (p. 616F) and Siena (p. 617C), shows the influence of Roman models. Nave arcades are widely spaced, the triforium usually omitted, as at Florence (p. 616G) and Milan (p. 602D), and the clear-story reduced to vault spandrels pierced by small and generally circular windows (p. 602F, 616B). These lofty arcades practically include the aisles and nave in one composition and give the effect of a single hall (p. 601B). Nave vaulting is frequently set out in square compartments, as in Florence Cathedral (p. 616F) and the Certosa, Pavia (p. 617D); while the aisles have oblong compartments (p. 616F), thus reversing the northern Gothic practice. Towers, usually isolated, are square shafts without buttresses, continuing the Romanesque tradition, but often have beautiful surface ornament, and they, unlike northern examples, develop no spire growth. The best known are at Florence (p. 615A), Siena (p. 617A), Lucca, Verona (p. 628D), Mantua, and Pistoia. The dome was the most imposing external feature, as at Siena (p. 617A) and Florence (p. 615A). The central towers in diminishing

A. The Castle, Volterra (1343). See p. 623

B. The Ponte Vecchio, Florence (1345). See opposite page

C. San Gimignano: view of the Towers (13th–14th cent.).
See pp. 323, 624

Open porch (*c.* 1480)   A. Palermo Cathedral from S.
(1170–85 : dome 1781–1801). See p. 624

B. Palazzo S. Stefano,
Taormina (1330). See p. 624

C. Window in Palazzo Archivescovile,
Palermo (15th cent.). See p. 624

stages, as at Chiaravalle (p. 629D), and Milan (pp. 598C, 601A), are an advance on the Romanesque lanterns at the crossing and may be compared with English examples, especially the octagon at Ely.

WALLS. The absence of large windows obviated the necessity for projecting buttresses, as the high walls were comparatively solid throughout their length and were thus able to withstand the vault pressure (p. 615A). Use also was made of tie-bars of wood or metal, particularly to stabilize arcades (pp. 601B, 615B, 622B). Owing to the absence of vertical features with their shadows, flatness is the predominant characteristic of the walls. Façades are treated independently as decorative compositions, and often have no relation to the structure or roofs behind (p. 617A), while the marble facing was often left unfinished on the score of expense. Marble was used in bands of two colours at Siena (pp. 617A, B, 619A, C) and Orvieto (p. 619B), and in decorative panels at Florence (p. 615A), while some façades of extraordinary richness have three high gables (pp. 617A, 619A). This treatment, probably borrowed from the Byzantines and Muslims, contrasts with northern methods, where the effect is obtained by string courses, projecting buttresses, and soaring pinnacles.

OPENINGS. Arcades, as a protection from the sun, were as necessary as in previous periods and generally consisted of slender columns with Corinthianesque capitals, supporting slightly pointed arches held together by iron ties (p. 611). Nave arcades have, for the most part, widely spaced and lofty columns (pp. 617E, 628C, F) or piers faced with pilasters, as at Florence (p. 615B). Doorways, although sometimes richly moulded and flanked by half-columns in Orders, have not the cavernous character of French Gothic; while the projecting portico of the Romanesque period was often retained in North Italy, as at Parma, Verona, and the three-storeyed portico at Bergamo (p. 629E). Windows, which are comparatively small, except occasionally in the north as at the interesting church of S. Agostino, Bergamo (1444) (p. 629H), have semicircular or pointed arches and shafts with square capitals of Corinthian type (p. 626C), instead of moulded mullions as in northern Gothic. These slender shafts are sometimes twisted and even inlaid with glass mosaic known as 'cosmato' work from craftsmen of that name; while the capitals are richly sculptured (pp. 628B, 629F). The tracery of Venetian windows is a special form of geometric combinations (p. 611B), finishing in a horizontal line suitable to flat ceilings of secular buildings, and is often of great beauty (pp. 612B, C, 629C). Many of the circular traceried windows are of extreme delicacy, as at Carrara (p. 628A). A moulded keystone is often provided to pointed arches, which are also sometimes enclosed in a square frame; but circular-headed windows continued in use throughout the Gothic period. At Venice many houses overlooking the canals have beautiful window balconies (p. 612E), usually with tiny columns serving as balusters, as the true baluster was not developed until the early Renaissance period: alternatively the balustrades were carved panels, based on Byzantine models.

ROOFS. The roofs are of low pitch, being scarcely visible from below (pp. 612, 615A, 621A, 628G). Sometimes a single gable covers the whole façade and indicates the influence of the Roman temple pediment. The steep gables of the elaborate façades were sometimes adopted from Northern Europe and hide the flat Italian roofs (p. 617A). Iron or timber tie-beams were often used, in the place of buttresses, to prevent the spread of the roof timbers, arcades, or vaults (usually quadripartite) (pp. 616G, 628F), and it is believed that there are only seven buildings in Italy with flying buttresses.

COLUMNS. The piers of arcades in churches are at times surprisingly clumsy, four pilasters combined, back to back, being a common plan (p. 616B). Columns with capitals and bases, recalling Roman work, were also used (p. 628C, F), but the gradual evolution of pier design, so noticeable in England, where it was due to the

A WHEEL WINDOW: CARRARA CATH.

B WINDOW: DOGES' PALACE: VE

C ORVIETO CATHEDRAL INTERIOR LOOKING E

D CAMPANILE: PAL. DEL COMUNE: VERONA

E S. M. GLORIOSA DEI FRA VENICE: THE APSE

F INTERIOR LOOKING E. S. M. GLORIOSA DEI FRARI: VENICE

G EXTERIOR FROM

A THE FONTE GATTESCHI VITERBO

B A TOMB OF THE SCALIGERS VERONA

C GLE WINDOW VENICE

D LA CERTOSA: CHIARAVALLE

E PORCH: S.M. MAGGIORE BERGAMO

F PORCH: THE DUOMO FERRARA

G LOGGIA DEI MERCANTI BOLOGNA

H FACADE: S. AGOSTINO BERGAMO

Ⓐ DOORHEAD:
ORATORIO DEGLI
AVVOCATI: VITERBO

Ⓑ RELIQUARY
S.M. NOVELLA: FLORENCE

Ⓒ TOMB:
S. ANTONIO: PADUA

Ⓕ SCULPTURE: PULP
CATHEDRAL: PISA

Ⓓ PULPIT CAP.ᴸ AT a.

Ⓔ PULPIT: BAPTISTERY: PISA

Ⓖ BASE: PULPIT: CATH.ᴸ

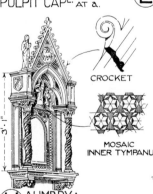

CROCKET

MOSAIC
INNER TYMPANUM

Ⓗ AUMBRY:
S. CLEMENTE: ROME

Ⓙ CANTORIA:
MONZA CATHEDRAL

Ⓚ PULPIT:
S. FRANCESCO: ASSIS

Ⓐ TOMB of S. PETER RTYR: S. EUSTORGIO: MILAN

Ⓑ MONUMENT of ALIOTTI: S.M. NOVELLA: FLORENCE

Ⓓ WOOD BENCH·END S. CORATO MOLFETTA

Ⓕ WOOD BENCH·END S. CORATO MOLFETTA

MONᴹᵀ ᴛᴏ HADRIAN V. S. FRANCESCO: VITERBO

Ⓔ MARBLE CANDELABRUM BAPTISTERY: FLORENCE

Ⓖ MONᴹᵀ ᴛᴏ NICCOLO SPECCHI S. FRANCESCO: ASSISI

Ⓝ PAINTED REREDOS S. CROCE: FLORENCE

Ⓙ CAP JUDGMENT ᴼᶠ SOLOMON DUCAL PALACE: VENICE

Ⓚ SCULPTURED REREDOS S. EUSTORGIO: MILAN

A. S. Maria Novella, Florence (1278–1350; façade 1456–70). See pp. 614, 683

B. The Ponte di Castel Vecchio, or Ponte Scaligero, Veaona (1335). See p. 608

exigencies of vaulting, is not observable. The lofty circular piers in Milan Cathedral, with engaged shafts and high tabernacle capitals, produce the effect of a columnar interior (p. 601B).

MOULDINGS. Mouldings are subordinated to surface decoration, and the most interesting are those in the brickwork of north Italy. They are little changed from the Roman style and the arch moulding is often identical with the jamb, although there may be capitals at the impost (p. 630A).

ORNAMENT (pp. 630, 631). Opaque wall decoration in fresco and mosaic was preferred to translucent stained glass, and the painting schools were developed. The Arena Chapel, Padua (p. 610B), is a mere shell for internal frescoes (1300–05) which take the place of architectural features. Giotto's work here forms a mediaeval anticipation of the Renaissance paintings of Raphael and Michelangelo in the Sistine Chapel, Rome. Carving and sculpture (p. 630) inherited the refinement of Classical times and contrast markedly with the grotesque element of northern art. The carving, painting, and mosaics of sumptuous altars, canopy tombs (p. 631B, C, G), pavements, choir stalls (p. 631D, F), and aumbries (p. 630H), in addition to the coloured marble façades, well display the decorative side of the style. The Tomb of Mastino II of the Scaligers, Verona (1351) (p. 629B), is an instance of this rich decoration, and many churches also at Rome have elaborate mosaic work of 'cosmato' design on twisted column and arch. No country in Europe is as rich as Italy in architectural accessories, including pulpits as at Pisa and Assisi (p. 630E, K), reredoses as at Florence and Milan (p. 631H, K), carved screens as at the Frari Church, Venice (p. 628F), cantoria as at Monza (p. 630J), tombs as at Padua (p. 630C), shrines as at S. Eustorgio, Milan (p. 631A), fountains as at Viterbo (p. 629A), candelabra as at Florence (p. 631E), and reliquaries as at S. Maria Novella, Florence (p. 630B).

REFERENCE BOOKS

BERTAUX, E. L'art dans l'Italie méridionale. 1904.

BROWNING, OSCAR. A Short History of Mediaeval Italy, 1250–1409. 1893.

CUMMINGS, C. A. A History of Architecture in Italy from the Time of Constantine to the Dawn of the Renaissance. 2 vols., new ed. 1928.

ENLART, C. Origines françaises de l'architecture gothique en Italie. Paris, 1894.

FRANKLIN, J. W. The Cathedrals of Italy. 1958.

GRÜNER, L. Terra-Cotta Architecture of North Italy. 1867.

HUBBARD, G. 'The Cathedral Church of Cefalu, Sicily', R.I.B.A. Journal, April 4, 1908.

JACKSON, SIR T. G. Gothic Architecture in France, England and Italy. 2 vols. London, 1915.

KNIGHT, H. G. Ecclesiastical Architecture of Italy. 2 vols. London, 1842–4.

NESFIELD, E. Specimens of Mediaeval Architecture. London, 1862.

PORTER, A. K. Mediaeval Architecture. 2 vols. New York and London, 1909.

ROHAULT DE FLEURY, G. La Toscane au moyen age. 2 vols., folio. Paris, 1874.

RUSKIN, J. Stones of Venice. 3 vols. 1886.

SCHULZ, H. W. Denkmaeler der Kunst des Mittelalters in Unter-Italien. 2 vols., folio and 4to. Dresden, 1860.

STRACK, H. Ziegelbauwerke des Mittelalters und der Renaissance in Italien. Folio. Berlin, 1889.

STREET, G. E. Brick and Marble in the Middle Ages. London, 1874.

TOESCA, P. Storia dell' Arte Italiana: Il Medioevo. Vol. 2. Turin, 1927.

—. Storia dell' Arte Italiana: Il Trecento. Turin, 1951.

WARING, J. B., and MACQUOID, T. R. Examples of Architectural Art in Italy and Spain. London, 1850.

A. Salamanca: the Old Cathedral (1120–78) backed by the New Cathedral (1512–1733) (see p. 640), with the Roman bridge (see p. 239)

Tower (17th cent.)

B. Toledo Cathedral from S.W. (1227–1493). See p. 643

C. The Monastery, Batalha: Capellas Imperfeitas (14th cent.). See p. 644

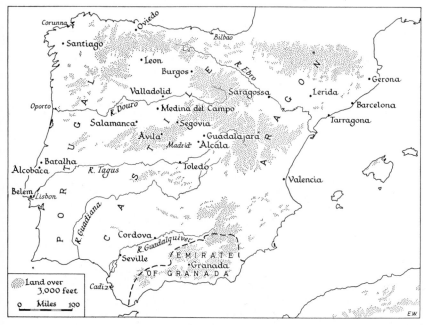

Spain in the Mediaeval Period

XVIII. SPANISH MEDIAEVAL ARCHITECTURE

(twelfth–sixteenth century)

INFLUENCES

GEOGRAPHICAL. Spain and Portugal occupy a peninsula, which is cut off from rather than united to the rest of Europe to the north by the mountainous barrier of the Pyrenees; from Africa to the south, however, access is easy across the narrow Straits of Gibraltar. The peninsula is broken into distinct natural regions by mountain ranges that cross it from east to west, enclosing high and bare tablelands and forming in the Mediaeval period natural boundaries for rival races and kingdoms; Portugal is separated from Spain by the barren western limits of these tablelands and by the steep gorges of four great rivers. There was French influence in the north and Moorish influence in the south. The emirate of Granada, where the Moors held out until 1492, centred on a very fertile plain encircled by high mountains.

GEOLOGICAL. 'Rocky Spain' is a short and graphic description of the geological conditions which prevail throughout the Peninsula, which is itself a great massif of rock, including the Sierras of Castile in the north, the mountains of Toledo in the middle, and the Sierra Morena in the south. Thus there is granite, especially in the north; limestone in the south and the basin of the Ebro; red sandstone in the Pyrenees and Andalusia, and eruptive rock everywhere, while semi-marbles are scattered throughout the country. Architecture is therefore naturally carried out in these various sorts of stone, while eruptive rock served for the rubble walling with brick bonding courses and quoins which was used under Moorish influence with much success, as in the towers and gates of the city of Toledo; while in Valladolid bricks of Roman character are laid in thick mortar beds. There are few forests in Spain, and the conspicuous absence of timber suitable for building accentuates still further the predominance of stone in architecture.

CLIMATIC. The climatic variations are as marked as geographical and as different as geological conditions; but there are four chief varieties of climate. In the provinces along the north and north-west sea-coast, the climate is mild, equable, and rainy, with the greatest rainfall at Santiago de Compostela in the west. The most marked variety of climate is that of the great central table-land and the basin of the Ebro, with great extremes of temperature, as in Madrid and Burgos; while the plains of Castile are swept by winds in winter and torrid in summer. The middle climate along the Mediterranean is moderate and the southern in Andalusia is sub-tropical like Africa, with the greatest heat in Cordova. The term 'sun-burnt Spain' indicates the nature of the climate which influenced the architecture of the Peninsula with its small windows and thick walls. Many large Gothic church windows, derived from France, were indeed often blocked up with stone in after years to keep out the scorching sun.

RELIGIOUS. The constant warfare waged against the Moors, which was religious even more than racial, gave a certain unity to the Christian states in the Peninsula. It has also always been characteristic of Spain to be united in allegiance to the papacy, and the great church of Santiago de Compostela (p. 640) in western Spain was a pilgrimage centre of national importance. Spain is one of the predominantly Catholic countries of the world. Throughout the Mediaeval period the Catholic Church was the strongest and most constant unifying force in the struggle against the Moors, and it thus obtained great temporal power and possessions. This fact, and the Spanish taste for dramatic ceremonial and ritual, determined the planning of cathedrals and churches with their great sanctuaries and enormous chapels of the Spanish grandees. The Muslim religion, introduced by the Moors in the Peninsula, forbade the human figure in sculpture and decoration and encouraged geometrical ornament, and the result of this ordinance is seen in the extreme richness and intricacy of surface decoration, even in Christian churches, on which craftsmen trained in Moorish traditions were employed. The establishment of the Spanish Inquisition (1477) in Castile and later in other provinces was designed to bring about national unity by first securing religious unity. This inquisitorial scheme resulted in the expulsion from Spain both of Jews and Muslims, who were valuable assets in commercial and industrial life, and Spain was thus materially weakened by their departure.

SOCIAL. The Christian states of Castile, Leon, Navarre, Aragon, and Portugal were growing up simultaneously, and gradually driving the Muslims into Andalusia. After many intermittent successes, such as the capture of Toledo (1085), Tarragona (probably in 1091), Saragossa (1118), and Lerida (1149), the battle of Tolosa (1212) was the final turning-point of the decline of Muslim influence. Ferdinand III (1217–52) united Castile and Leon, and won back Seville and Cordova from the Moors. As a result of the exultation over the conquest of the Muslims, Gothic art in this district, aided too by the plunder taken from the infidel, received a great impetus. James I (1213–76), king of Aragon, advanced in the east of Spain until the kingdom of Granada was the only portion left to the Muslims. As to general social conditions in Spain there was a great gulf fixed between the grandee and the common people, and an equally strongly marked dividing line between town folk and country folk. In the eastern districts, where the feudal system was strong, class distinctions were further accentuated, and only a small proportion of the population,

BURGOS CATH^{L.}

Ⓐ CAPILLA DEL CONDESTABLE

Ⓑ TRANSEPTS & CIMBORIO

Ⓒ EXTERIOR FROM S.E.

Ⓓ PLAN

Ⓔ EXTERIOR FROM W.

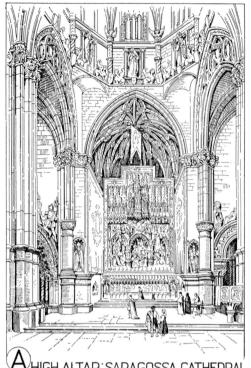

A HIGH ALTAR: SARAGOSSA CATHEDRAL

B CHAPEL OF SANTIAGO : TOLED

C CLOISTER: S. JUAN DE LOS REYES: TOLEDO

D DOORWAY TO CAPILLA DE LOS REYES: GRANADA CATHED

including citizens of chartered towns, were free; while under the system of land tenure the peasants were oppressed throughout the Middle Ages, a condition which produced the peasants' revolt of the fifteenth and sixteenth centuries. During the whole of the Mediaeval period, till 1492, Spain was cut up into different kingdoms under the independent rule of Christian kings and Muslim caliphs and emirs. From some of the internal dangers the country was delivered by Ferdinand (1479–1516) and Isabella (1474–1504), the Catholic sovereigns, who arrogated to themselves supreme power. They made use of Church, nobles, and cities as instruments of their government, established police against brigandage, annexed the power and money of the military Orders, and enforced military service from the nobles. They even reduced the Cortes to a money-granting machine and gradually crippled commerce and industry through the control of officials and the imposition of excise duties, and thus established an inquisition in commerce as well as in religion. Social life in Spain was dominated by the grandees and the Catholic clergy, and indeed churches and monasteries are the chief architectural monuments, while in domestic architecture there is little of importance except the houses of the nobility.

HISTORICAL. The outstanding feature of Spanish history during this period is the astonishing connection of Spain, not only with France, her near neighbour, but also with England through royal marriages; with Italy through papal supervision and the quarrels with the Angevins in Naples and Sicily, and with the Moors from Africa; and all this, as we shall see, affected in varying degrees the architecture of the Peninsula. After the Romans left Spain the Vandals and Visigoths took possession, and in 711–13 the country was invaded by the Moors from North Africa, whose influence was continuous for 800 years (p. 1225). The evidence of this is seen in the south in curious construction and exuberant detail, and occasionally also in the north owing to the demand there for Moorish craftsmen with their superior ability, for although Toledo was captured by the Christians in 1085, the Spanish conquests were only gradual. King Peter II of Aragon (1196–1213) came in contact with Italy, for he was crowned in Rome and as a prince of France died there in the defence of the Albigenses, and these connections were not without influence on Spanish architecture. From the death of James the Conqueror in 1276 to the death of Martin I in 1410, the kings of Aragon were at war with the Angevin party in Naples and Sicily, and this may have contributed to the introduction of certain Muslim and other architectural features from those countries. The final expulsion of the Moors did not take place till the fall of Granada in 1492, and so great was the interest which this decisive event roused in all Christendom that a thanksgiving service was held by order of Henry VII in old S. Paul's Cathedral, London. Thus were laid the foundations of a united Spain which then prepared to expand abroad.

ARCHITECTURAL CHARACTER

The character of Gothic architecture in Europe, which gives the general principles common to all countries, has already been given (p. 367). The salient aspect of Spanish Mediaeval architecture, which in this chapter includes the Romanesque and Gothic periods, dating from the twelfth to the sixteenth century, is the evident influence of Moorish art, which spread from the south and more especially from the Moorish capital, Toledo. The Gothic style followed the Romanesque, approximately c. 1210, and was most highly developed in Catalonia where, though mainly on French lines, the grand scale of the single-span vaulted interiors gives it, as at Gerona (p. 649C), a specifically Spanish character, and the same may be said of Leon Cathedral, which surpasses its French prototype at Amiens both in the expanse of window openings and the tenuity of the piers (p. 652C). Moorish influence made itself felt in such Muslim features as the horseshoe arch and pierced stone tracery, and notably in rich surface decoration of intricate geometrical and flowing patterns (pp. 650, 651), for which Muslim art is remarkable, as in the Sinagoga del Transito, Toledo (1360–6), while the early Spanish churches seem to have been the work of Moorish craftsmen. Church exteriors are flat in appearance, owing to the chapels which are so frequently inserted between the buttresses (p. 649). Unlike French Gothic, large wall surfaces and horizontal lines are conspicuous, and generally there is excessive ornament, due to Moorish influence, without regard to its constructive character (p. 641B). The cloisters of many cathedrals, as Barcelona (p. 652A), Toledo, Segovia (pp. 638C, 650A), and Lerida, are very characteristic. In the later period the grafting of Classical detail on Gothic forms produced most picturesque features, transitional in style, but they come under Renaissance (p. 845) rather than Gothic architecture. The Spanish Civil War (1936–9) resulted in the destruction of many buildings here described.

EXAMPLES

ECCLESIASTICAL ARCHITECTURE

Santiago de Compostela Cathedral (1075–1128) is Romanesque and one of the most remarkable Mediaeval buildings in Spain; it owes its size and character to having been a great pilgrimage centre. The plan resembles S. Sernin, Toulouse, but with three instead of five aisles, and with similar transepts and chevet due to French influence. The nave has a barrel vault and the aisles cross-vaults. The Portico de la Gloria (1168–1211) extends across the whole width of the church and is undoubtedly 'one of the greatest glories of Christian art', with its statues of the apostles, major prophets, twenty-four elders, and tympanum with the Last Judgment.

Avila Cathedral (1160–1211 and later), with its chevet built astride the city walls, is one of the most interesting in the Peninsula. The chevet has double aisles and semicircular chapels in the thickness of the walls, whose slit windows indicate that it was part of the city fortifications. The 'coro' or choir west of the transepts, the fine cloisters, the widely spaced nave bays, twin western towers, and two unique hammered-iron pulpits (pp. 651A, 653) are well-known features of this church.

Salamanca Old Cathedral (1120–78) forms, with the New Cathedral (1512–1733) (pp. 634A, 652D), a fine group above the River Tormes. The Romanesque building, apparently influenced by the churches of Aquitaine and Anjou, is specially famous for its dome, which is treated internally (p. 650D) with great originality. It has plain pendentives, supporting a high drum pierced with two storeys of windows and crowned with a stone ribbed cupola. The exterior (p. 650F) is effective, with high drum, semicircular windows, angle turrets, and octagonal spire with an unusual entasis.

S. Isidoro, Leon (1054–1149), only the narthex surviving of the original building of 1054–67, is a cruciform church and bears some resemblance to Santiago de Compostela Cathedral, with a barrel-vaulted nave and apsidal chapels (p. 650C) on the eastern side of the transepts.

Burgos Cathedral (1221–1457) (pp. 637, 641A, 652B, 852) is irregular in plan and the most poetic of all Spanish cathedrals. The two western towers, with open-work spires (p. 637E), recall Cologne, and a richly treated central lantern or 'cimborio' (p. 852) is a feature of the exterior (p. 637C). The interior has elaborate triforium tracery, massive piers rebuilt to support the high 'cimborio' which was added in 1539–67, and fine transeptal circular windows (p. 637B). The 'coro' is in the usual Spanish position west of the crossing, which reduces the nave to a vestibule (p. 637D). Among the side chapels, which are of extraordinary size, the octagonal Capilla del

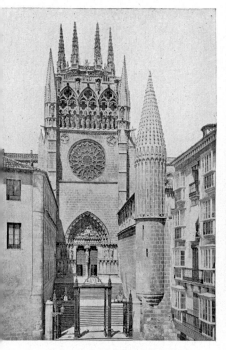

A. Burgos Cathedral: S. transept
(1243–60). See p. 640

B. College of S. Gregorio,
Valladolid (façade, 1492–6). See p. 643

C. Seville Cathedral: nave
looking E. (1402–1520). See p. 643

D. S. Juan de los Reyes, Toledo:
nave looking E. (1478–92). See p. 644

A. S. Vicente, Avila: principal doorway (12th cent.). See p. 648

B. Toledo Cathedral: interior looking E. (1227–1493). See p. 643

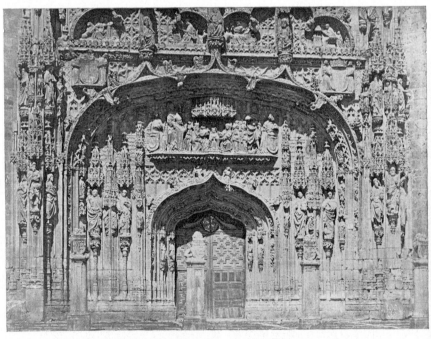

c. S. Pablo, Valladolid: principal doorway (1486–92). See p. 643

Condestable (1482–), over 50 ft in diameter, is specially remarkable for the beauty and magnificence of its late Gothic detail (p. 637A), and the altar of S. Ana has an altar-piece which is a miracle of richness (p. 651B).

Toledo Cathedral (1227–1493) (pp. 634B, 649D), with five aisles and a range of side chapels, resembles Bourges Cathedral in general plan. It is about the same length, but nearly 50 ft wider, with the choir enclosure, as usual in Spain, west of the crossing (p. 642B). A singularly shallow sanctuary, with immense wooden 'retablo', flanked by tiers of arcaded statuary, is terminated by a chevet of double aisles and chapels completing a most impressive interior. The exterior has a low roof, usual in most Spanish churches, and has a fine ornamental north-west steeple. The Chapel of Santiago (1435) (p. 638B), in the chevet, erected by Count de Luna as a mortuary chapel on the site of a chapel dedicated to S. Thomas of Canterbury, has doorways with elaborate screenwork and great frilled arches, supporting the octagonal vault, all contributing their wealth of detail to this grandiose composition. There are fine stained-glass windows, beautiful carved choir stalls, and a treasury, rich even for Spain, containing the famous silver-gilt 'Custodia'—the flower of Spanish Gothic miniature art.

The **College of S. Gregorio, Valladolid** (1488–96) (p. 641B), now the town hall, has a sculptured façade (1492–6) embellished with statues, heraldic devices, and a genealogical tree of Ferdinand and Isabella, all framed round with canopied niches and pinnacles, which show the influence of Moorish art in church ornament. The court (p. 650H) has arcades of the later period, with three-centred arches, twisted columns, and intricate Moorish-like carving (p. 650G).

S. Pablo, Valladolid (1276–1492), has a façade (1486–92) (p. 642C) and internal doorways which, in intricacy of detail, also show Moorish influence.

Barcelona Cathedral (1298–1448) (pp. 649B, 652A) is remarkably fine, with nave vaulted in square and aisles in oblong bays, in the Italian method, and with characteristic 'coro' west of the crossing (p. 647). There is a fine western lantern on pendentives (c. 1420–48), slightly projecting transepts surmounted by towers, as at Exeter (p. 407D), and chevet of nine chapels. The thrust of the vault is counteracted by the deep internal buttresses which enclose chapels along the aisles, as at Albi in France (p. 549). The vault, as is usual in Spain, is exposed externally and roofed by tiles (p. 652A). The fine cloisters were completed about 1448, with twenty-two chapels.

Gerona Cathedral (1312–1598) (p. 649C) is another instance where buttresses have internal chapels between them. There are no aisles, and the nave (1417–1598), 73 ft wide, in four compartments, has the widest Gothic vault in Europe, and this, together with the length of 275 ft, produces a fine effect with the enclosed choir and chevet (1312–1346) at the sanctuary end. The central hall of the Royal Courts of Justice, London, although only 48 ft wide, gives an idea of this interior, which resembles Albi (p. 549).

S. Maria del Mar, Barcelona (1328–83) (p. 649A), is a splendid town church, characterized both internally and externally by severe simplicity, and the front to the street is flanked by two octagonal pinnacles. The roof vaulting rests upon widely spaced octagonal granite piers. The nave and aisles are of great height; there is no triforium and only small clear-story windows in the vault spandrels.

SS. Justo y Pastor, Barcelona (1345), has an aisleless nave 45 ft wide, with chapels between internal buttresses. The altar stands in an unusual position in front of stalls ranged round the apse.

S. Maria del Pino, Barcelona (1453), similar in plan, has a fine heptagonal apse and western circular window.

Seville Cathedral (1402–1520) (pp. 641C, 645A), the largest Mediaeval cathedral in Europe, is, with the exception of S. Peter's, Rome, the largest church in the world.

It owes its plan and size, with nave, double aisles and side chapels, to its erection on the site of a mosque. This also controlled its rectangular outline, about 400 ft by 250 ft, and its square east end, unusual in Continental churches, to which is added a small apse. The Cathedral is indeed enormous, as may be realized by comparison with Westminster Abbey. The nave, about 45 ft wide in the clear, is nearly half as wide again as Westminster nave; each of the four aisles is approximately equal in width to the Abbey nave, and in addition there are surrounding chapels as wide as the aisles, so that with the chapels, Seville Cathedral is about eight times the width of Westminster nave. It has a total area, including the patio, of about 22,000 square yds as against Milan Cathedral with 13,984 square yds, and S. Paul's, London, with 9,336 square yds. The interior is impressive, owing to its great size and height, although the nave vault (130 ft high) has ribs which are somewhat confused in design and overloaded with bosses. The thirty-two immense clustered piers and numerous stained-glass windows produce an imposing effect, in spite of the absence of a triforium. The richness of the interior is enhanced by the sculptured stalls of the 'coro' occupying two nave bays, the fine 'reja' or grille (1518), the 'retablo', choir stalls, and archbishop's throne. The exterior, owing to many additions, has a certain shapelessness and absence of skyline, but bears a general resemblance to Milan Cathedral, although of a simpler Gothic type and less fanciful in detail. The slender 'Giralda' (1184–96, upper part 1568–), originally the minaret of the mosque, gives this massive group a curiously Oriental aspect (p. 1233).

S. Juan de los Reyes, Toledo (1478–92) (pp. 638C, 641D), is a royal sepulchral chapel erected by Ferdinand and Isabella for a purpose similar to that of Henry VII's Chapel, Westminster. This late Gothic building, with traces of the incoming Renaissance, has a sculptured façade and 'cimborio' with lofty pinnacles. The interior (p. 641D) is chiefly notable for the raised galleries for the use of kings and nobles, surmounted by the characteristic octagonal 'cimborio' with its beautiful squinch arches. The two-storeyed cloisters (p. 638C), with their traceried windows and canopied statues, are held to be the most beautiful Gothic creations in Spain.

Valencia Cathedral (1262–c. 1356) and **Leon Cathedral** (1255–1303) (p. 652C) show French influence.

Lerida Cathedral (1203–78) (p. 649E), long used as barracks but now cleared, is an impressive early building with octagonal 'cimborio', three eastern apses, and adjacent cloisters, and the roofing slabs rest directly on the stone vaults.

The **Monastery, Belem, near Lisbon** (1499–1522), is a fine ecclesiastical monument in Portugal, the western part of the Iberian peninsula. The cloisters have a two-storeyed arcade covered with delicate sculpture, and the church is a richly ornamented late Gothic structure.

The **Monastery, Batalha, Portugal** (1387–1415), with its unique fourteenth-century church and octagonal tomb chapel (p. 634C), forms a fine architectural group.

The **Cistercian Church, Alcobaça, Portugal** (1158–1223) is severe and simple in style, and in its interior resembles a German 'hall' church.

SECULAR ARCHITECTURE

The finest secular architecture is found in Catalonia, as seen in the much altered **Palacio de la Audiencia, Barcelona**, with its remarkable court containing a picturesque external stairway (p. 646B); the **Casa del Ayuntamiento, Barcelona** (1373–); the **Alcazar, Segovia** (1410–55), an old Castilian castle with massive towers; the **Torre del Clavero, Salamanca** (1480); the **Gateway of S. Maria, Burgos**, and the remarkable **Puente de Alcantara, Toledo** (1258), which spans the Tagus and is protected by a defensive tower (pp. 239, 645B).

The Giralda

A. Seville Cathedral from S.E. (1402–1520). See pp. 643–4

B. The Puente de Alcantara, Toledo (1258). See pp. 239, 644

Ⓐ COURT: DUCAL PALACE
GUADALAJARA

Ⓑ COURT: THE AUDIENCIA
BARCELONA

Ⓒ DOORWAY: FOUNDL
HOSPITAL: CORDO

Ⓓ LA LONJA: VALENCIA

Ⓔ CASTLE: MEDINA DEL CAMPO

Ⓕ PUERTA DE SERRANOS
VALENCIA

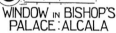

Ⓖ WINDOW IN BISHOP'S
PALACE: ALCALA

Ⓗ PUERTA DEL SOL: TOLE

The **Ducal Palace, Guadalajara** (1480–92) (pp. 646A, 843A), had a picturesque court, surrounded by two storeys of ornately sculptured arcades, with twisted columns and multifoil arches.

La Lonja de la Seda, Valencia (1482–98) (p. 646D), used as a silk exchange, has an unbalanced façade of nearly 200 ft, with central tower, an east wing with large gateway and two pointed windows, and a west wing with two rows of square-headed Gothic windows surmounted by open galleries.

The **Castillo de la Mota, Medina del Campo** (1440–) (p. 646E), is stern in aspect, with circular towers, battlemented parapets, and windowless curtain walls, and a high tower commands the surrounding country.

The **Puerta del Sol, Toledo** (p. 646H), much repaired at various times, forms part of the town walls of the ancient city, and with its horseshoe arches, intersecting arcades, and Moorish battlements indicates that the Mediaeval Spaniard, with craftsman-like skill, applied the art of the time to all secular buildings.

The **Puerta de Serranos, Valencia** (1349) (p. 646F), with its Mediaeval fortifications, has two polygonal towers flanking the gateway, above which is traceried wall panelling and a gallery on enormous corbels.

These and many more similar buildings are eloquent of the power and position of the Catholic Church and of the Spanish grandee, while the well-preserved town walls of such old-world cities as **Avila** and **Leon** indicate the unsettled conditions of those times.

COMPARATIVE ANALYSIS

PLANS. Cathedral plans are of great width and comparative shortness, and the 'coro' or choir, like that in Westminster Abbey (p. 424D), is generally in the nave, west of the crossing, but with a low screened passage between choir and sanctuary, as in Burgos (p. 637D), Toledo (p. 649D), and Barcelona (p. 649B). This central enclosure follows the Early Christian basilican plan (p. 255K), and supplied extra space for the clergy as necessity arose; it avoided the extension eastwards of the sanctuary usual in England, and sometimes it was enclosed by high walls forming a church within a church. Chapels are numerous and large, often surrounding the whole cathedral, and the 'parroquia' or parish church is sometimes included in the cathedral area, as at Seville. The 'cimborio' (pp. 637B, 641D) at the crossing of nave and transepts is similar in treatment to those of France; thus S. Sernin, Toulouse, and Burgos Cathedral resemble each other in arrangement, as do Valencia Cathedral and S. Ouen, Rouen, in design. The characteristic octagonal vaults over the crossing and chapels, intricate in design and ingenious in construction, were probably inspired by Moorish art.

WALLS. French wall treatment was largely followed, but characterized in the later period, owing to Moorish influence, by extreme and even fantastic surface ornament. There is an absence of skyline, and Burgos has effective horizontal arcades instead of gables, on the lines of the façade of Notre Dame, Paris. Many façades, as that of the College of S. Gregorio, Valladolid (p. 641B), have a bewildering number of niches containing statues, while figures supporting heraldic emblems combine to leave no vacant space, thus rivalling the elaboration of a 'retablo'. Traceried open-work spires, like those at Burgos, were frequent (p. 637E).

OPENINGS. Arcades were of special service in sunny Spain to form effective screens against the sun, and are numerous; those surrounding the 'patio' or court of the Ducal Palace, Guadalajara (p. 646A), La Audiencia, Barcelona (p. 646B), and the cloisters of Segovia Cathedral (p. 650A) are typical examples. The early use of the pointed arch in nave arcades is another feature probably due to Moorish influence. Doorways as at S. Vicente, Avila (p. 642A), and La Cartuja, Burgos (p. 650E), are French in design with sculptured figures and luxuriant capitals, while later doorways, as at Cordova (p. 646C), Granada (p. 638D), and Segovia (p. 650B), have elaborate features enclosed in intricate framework, due to Moorish craftsman-ship. Windows were often carried to excess, as in Leon Cathedral, where most of the wall surface of the clear-story is devoted to great traceried windows, some being 40 ft high. In the centre, and even in the south, as at Segovia (p. 650A) and Seville, openings are large, and stained glass was much used, owing to French influence, but many windows, as at Avila and Barcelona (p. 652A), have been partially blocked up as unsuitable to the sunny climate. The window in the Bishop's Palace, Alcalá (p. 646G), shows a novel tracery design, obviously due to Moorish influence.

ROOFS. Vaulting was freely used, but owes its character to tracery, bosses, and ribs, which produce a good effect, although the lines are not always good, and nothing comparable to English vaulting was produced (pp. 637A, 638A, C). The vaults were often without external wooden roofs found in other countries, and, as at Seville and Barcelona (p. 652A), bricks and tiles rest directly on the vaults, and form a fireproof roof. In Catalonia wide interiors were successfully vaulted in one span, that at Gerona being no less than 73 ft wide (p. 649C). The boldest and most original vaults are those that support galleries across the western ends of churches, extending through nave and aisles in three spans or in one span across the nave, and their decorated soffits frame in the view of the interior from the entrance. The 'cimborio' over the crossing is frequently octagonal, and is supported on ornate squinch arches, thrown across the angles of the square below, thus bringing it to an octagon (pp. 637B, 638A, 641D).

COLUMNS. The massive piers supporting the lantern over the crossing, as at Burgos (p. 637B), are circular in plan and contrast with the great octagonal piers of S. Sernin, Toulouse. In Seville Cathedral great column-like piers are employed for arcades (p. 641C), similar to Milan (p. 601B), but without tabernacle capitals. The circular piers so often used, with their fine shaft articulation, resemble those at Beauvais Cathedral, and there are capitals in Saragossa Museum (p. 650J) which indicate the prevailing Romanesque influence.

MOULDINGS. Refinement is not the usual characteristic of Spanish mouldings, but original and capricious forms were mingled with others borrowed from France (p. 650). In Catalonia the best and most artistic result was produced in a restrained manner, as in S. Maria del Mar, Barcelona, where every moulding has its purpose and expression, but this is far from being usual in Spain.

ORNAMENT (p. 651). The most decorative feature in Spanish churches is the vast 'retablo' (reredos), which, as at Saragossa and Oviedo, is often as wide as the nave and as high as the vault (p. 638A). It is of wood, stone, or alabaster, and crowded with niches, figures, canopies, and panelling. The 'retablos' at Toledo and Seville, resembling the great English altar reredoses, as at Winchester (p. 420G), are the richest specimens of Mediaeval woodwork in existence, and painting and gilding were used to heighten the effect. Sculpture in stone and marble is often life-size, naturalistic, and expressive (p. 651B, E, J), and, however deficient in other qualities, it helps to produce the impressive, if sensational, interiors of Spanish churches. Classic tradition led to refinement of detail, which contrasts with the often grotesque features of northern Gothic, but the general design frequently suffers from the multiplication of accessories. Stained glass, as used at Seville, Oviedo, and else-where, was Flemish in style, heavy in outline, and strong to gaudiness in colouring. 'Rejas' or lofty grilles (p. 637B) in hammered and chiselled iron are also characteris-tic, especially in the later period, the long vertical bars being relieved by figures in repoussé work, either single, or in duplicate back to back, and by freely employed

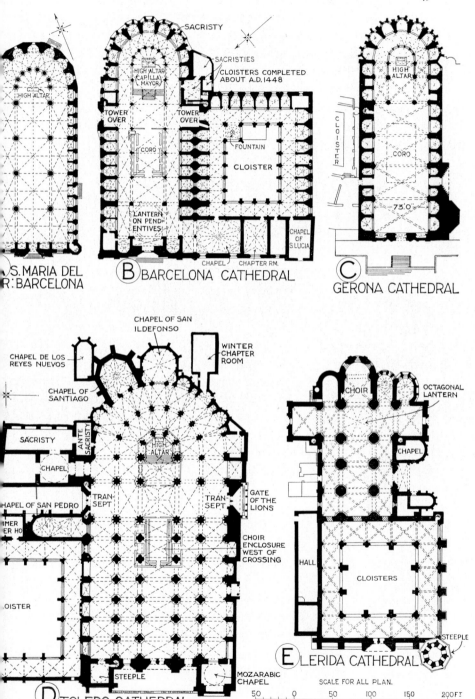

S.MARIA DEL R:BARCELONA

B BARCELONA CATHEDRAL

SACRISTY
SACRISTIES
CLOISTERS COMPLETED ABOUT A.D.1448
HIGH ALTAR CAPILLA MAYOR
TOWER OVER
TOWER OVER
CORO
FOUNTAIN
CLOISTER
LANTERN ON PENDENTIVES
CHAPEL OF S.LUCIA
CHAPEL CHAPTER RM.

C GERONA CATHEDRAL

HIGH ALTAR
CLOISTER
CORO
73.0

D TOLEDO CATHEDRAL

CHAPEL OF SAN ILDEFONSO
WINTER CHAPTER ROOM
CHAPEL DE LOS REYES NUEVOS
CHAPEL OF SANTIAGO
SACRISTY
ANTE SACRISTY
CHAPEL
HIGH ALTAR
HAPEL OF SAN PEDRO
MER ER HO
TRAN-SEPT
TRAN-SEPT
GATE OF THE LIONS
CHOIR ENCLOSURE WEST OF CROSSING
OISTER
STEEPLE
MOZARABIC CHAPEL

E LERIDA CATHEDRAL

CHOIR
OCTAGONAL LANTERN
CHAPEL
HALL
CLOISTERS
STEEPLE

SCALE FOR ALL PLAN.
50   0   50   100   150   200 FT
10   0   10   20   40   50   60 M.

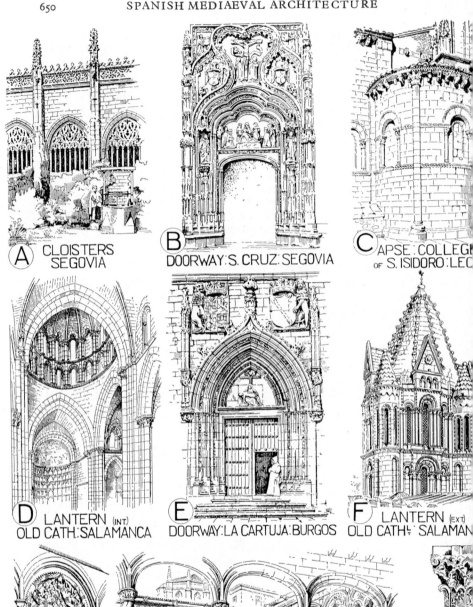

(A) CLOISTERS SEGOVIA

(B) DOORWAY: S. CRUZ: SEGOVIA

(C) APSE: COLLEG! OF S. ISIDORO: LEO

(D) LANTERN (INT.) OLD CATH: SALAMANCA

(E) DOORWAY: LA CARTUJA: BURGOS

(F) LANTERN (EXT.) OLD CATH!: SALAMAN

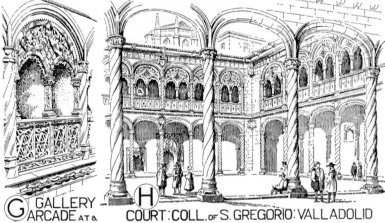

(G) GALLERY ARCADE AT a

(H) COURT: COLL. OF S. GREGORIO: VALLADOLID

(J) CAPS. IN SARAGO

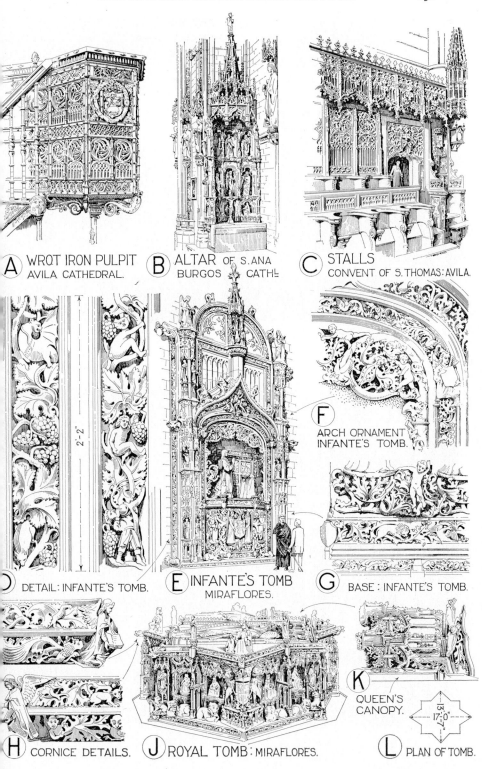

A WROT IRON PULPIT
AVILA CATHEDRAL.

B ALTAR OF S.ANA
BURGOS CATHL

C STALLS
CONVENT OF S.THOMAS:AVILA.

D DETAIL: INFANTE'S TOMB.

E INFANTE'S TOMB
MIRAFLORES.

F ARCH ORNAMENT
INFANTE'S TOMB.

G BASE: INFANTE'S TOMB.

H CORNICE DETAILS.

J ROYAL TOMB: MIRAFLORES.

K QUEEN'S CANOPY.

L PLAN OF TOMB.

A. Barcelona Cathedral: nave and towers
(1365–89); cloisters (1382–1448).
See p. 643

B. Burgos Cathedral: west front
(1442–57); central tower (1539–67).
See p. 640

C. Leon Cathedral: interior (1255–1303).
See p. 644

D. Salamanca New Cathedral: nave (1512
See p. 640

crestings and traceries, and there are few productions of the period in Spain which are more original and artistic. Magnificent stalls provided with separate canopies and tall spires, as at Avila (p. 651C), are common, and Barcelona Cathedral has some resembling those at Chester, while altars (p. 651B), bishops' thrones, lecterns, and choir desks were also very elaborate, and the unusual pulpit of hammered iron at Avila Cathedral is a remarkable specimen of the smith's craft (p. 651A). The Royal Tomb, Miraflores, near Burgos (p. 651J), is perhaps the most elaborate Mediaeval monument in Spain; it is star-shaped and meticulously carved, with angels, flowers (p. 651H), and canopied statuettes, all supporting the recumbent effigies of King John II and his queen. The Infante's Tomb, Miraflores (1470) (p. 651E), is elaborate in heraldic devices, kneeling figures, and tabernacle work (p. 651D–G). The cathedrals are veritable treasure-houses of beautiful Christian craftsmanship, displayed in holy crosses, reliquaries, monstrances, gold and silver images and candelabra, and as they have never been despoiled of their treasure, the cathedrals form the chief museums of art in Spain.

REFERENCE BOOKS

BEVAN, B. *History of Spanish Architecture.* 1938.

CALVERT, A. F. *Spain.* 2 vols. London, 1924.

CAPPER, S. H. *Masterpieces of Spanish Architecture.* 1909.

FORD, R. *Handbook for Travellers in Spain.* London, 1845, reprinted 1904.

HARVEY, J. *The Cathedrals of Spain.* London, 1957.

LAMPÉREZ Y ROMEA, V. *Historia de la arquitectura Cristiana española.* 2 vols. Madrid, 1908–9.

Monumentos Arquitectonicos de España (a magnificent work issued by the Spanish Government). 89 parts, atlas folio (not completed). Madrid, 1859–79.

STREET, G. E. *Account of Gothic Architecture in Spain.* 1874. Revised edition, with notes, by G. G. King. London, 1914.

STURGIS, R., and FROTHINGHAM, A. L. *A History of Architecture.* Vol. III. New York, 1915.

VILLA-AMIL, G. P. DE. *España artistica y monumental.* 3 vols., folio. Paris, 1842–50.

WARING, J. B. *Architectural Studies in Burgos.* London, 1852.

WARING, J. B., and MACQUOID, T. R. *Architectural Art in Italy and Spain.* London, 1850.

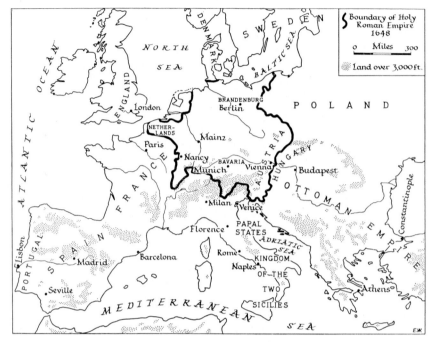

Europe in the seventeenth century

XIX. RENAISSANCE ARCHITECTURE IN EUROPE

(fifteenth–nineteenth century)

INFLUENCES

GEOGRAPHICAL. The Renaissance of Classic architecture, which started in Italy in the early fifteenth century, spread westwards throughout all those countries of Europe which had formed the Western Roman Empire. This general survey of the geographical extent of the insidious new development indicates broadly the lines along which it travelled; while the modifications it underwent, owing to geographical position, are explained in detail under each country. The Eastern Empire, with its capital at Constantinople, was gradually falling before the Turk, and therefore these districts did not come under the influence of the new movement. The countries of Italy (p. 665), France (p. 761), Germany (p. 806), Belgium and Holland (p. 827), Spain (p. 841), and England (p. 863) were subject to special geographical influences which affected the character of the architecture.

GEOLOGICAL. Geological formation varies so widely in different parts of Europe that its influence cannot here be taken into account with regard to the whole of Western Europe, but must be considered under each country. Geological conditions, however, are practically continuous in any given country, and they have already been described under the sections on Romanesque and Gothic architecture.

The countries of Italy (p. 666), France (p. 761), Germany (p. 806), Belgium and Holland (p. 828), Spain (p. 841), and England (p. 864) were subject to special geological influences which affected the character of the architecture.

CLIMATIC. The climate, which differs vastly over such an extensive area, is constant throughout the different periods, and has also been productive of widely different architectural treatment in each country to meet the weather conditions, as has been seen in the Romanesque and Gothic periods. The countries of Italy (p. 667), France (p. 762), Germany (p. 806), Belgium and Holland (p. 828), Spain (p. 842), and England (p. 864) were subject to special climatic influences which affected the character of the architecture.

RELIGIOUS. The whole trend of religious activities in Europe was affected by the invention of printing, and the consequent spread of knowledge engendered a spirit of inquiry and freedom of thought which, under Wyclif (1320–84) in England and Luther (1483–1546) in Germany, had produced a certain desire to break away from Romish influence. This renewed vigour in intellectual life led to Reformation in religion, and Renaissance in literature and architecture, with a consequent outbreak of building activity. In England this took the form of domestic architecture, which had also received a special impulse from the diffusion among laymen of the wealth and lands of monasteries dissolved by Henry VIII. In Italy, on the other hand, where the Reformation took no hold, and where, moreover, comparatively few churches were built during the Middle Ages, there was a revival of ecclesiastical as well as of domestic architecture, and Renaissance churches were erected on a great scale. France, Spain, and the Netherlands were all influenced in different degrees by the new movement, and, as we shall see, this was expressed architecturally in varying ways. The Jesuits, who headed the counter-Reformation, carried the later Renaissance style through all parts of Europe, while at the same time they gave a special character to the churches they erected (p. 659). The countries of Italy (p. 667), France (p. 762), Germany (p. 807), Belgium and Holland (p. 828), Spain (p. 842), and England (p. 865) were subject to special religious influences which affected the character of the architecture.

SOCIAL. The new intellectual movement manifested itself earlier in literature than in architecture, and thus had influenced public taste. Dante (1265–1321), Petrarch (1304–74), and Boccaccio (1313–75), by their writings, aided the spread of the newly discovered Classic literature which prepared the ground for a revolt against Mediaeval art, in favour of a revival of ancient Roman architecture, while the capture of the old Classic city of Constantinople by the Turks (1453) increased the influx of Greek scholars into Italy, and their learning further influenced an age already ripe for change. Amongst the Greek and Roman literature brought to light about this time was the *Treatise on Architecture* by Vitruvius, written in the time of Augustus, which, first issued in Latin at Rome (1486), was translated into Italian in 1521. Erasmus (1467–1536), one of the Greek scholars of the period, directed public attention to the original text of the New Testament and to the Greek Classics, as a corrective to the writings of mystical Mediaeval philosophers, whose authority had so long been in the ascendant. A return to Roman architectural style naturally came about first in Italy, where Mediaeval feudalism had never been firmly established, and where, moreover, city-states had developed municipal freedom and enterprise. The countries of Italy (p. 668), France (p. 762), Germany (p. 807), Belgium and Holland (p. 830), Spain (p. 842), and England (p. 865) were subject to special social influences which affected the character of the architecture.

HISTORICAL. At the beginning of the sixteenth century in Europe the smaller states were gradually grouped into kingdoms under powerful rulers, who maintained authority by means of large standing armies. Three great inventions contributed to the general upheaval of these changing times. Gunpowder changed the method of warfare. The mariner's compass led to the discovery of the Cape of Good Hope by Diaz (1487), and of America by Christopher Columbus (1492). When the Turks took Constantinople (Istanbul) (1453), and conquered Syria and Egypt, the old trade routes between East and West were blocked, but a new route was opened up when Vasco da Gama sailed round the Cape to India (1497), and thus started the foundation of colonies by European states. Printing by movable types, which was first made practicable by John Gutenberg and John Fust at Mainz about 1450, promoted that spirit of inquiry which brought about reformation in religion and revival of learning. Copperplate engraving also came into use towards the end of the fifteenth century, and helped to spread a knowledge of architectural forms. Galileo (1564–1642), by astronomical research and scientific discoveries, changed the intellectual perspective of the times, especially by his championing Copernicus's theory that the earth was not the centre of the universe, but merely a small planet in the solar system.   Italy (p. 670), France (p. 765), Germany (p. 807), Belgium and Holland (p. 830), Spain (p. 842), and England (p. 867) were subject to special historical influences which affected the architecture.

ARCHITECTURAL CHARACTER

The Renaissance movement, which began in Italy early in the fifteenth century, created a break in the continuous evolution of European architecture which, springing from Roman and proceeding through Early Christian and Romanesque, had, during the Middle Ages, developed into Gothic in each country on national lines. Italy, which was still rich in her ancient Roman monuments, was naturally the pioneer in the Renaissance movement, especially as the Gothic style had never taken firm root in a country which had always clung to her old traditions. Though there was a ready reversion to Classic architectural forms, Gothic methods of construction necessarily prevailed, since Roman methods of building massively in concrete had been superseded by more refined and compact systems. Fresh structural devices had been developed, to which Byzantine architecture as well as western Gothic had contributed. The mode of living had changed too, and with it many of the types of building in common use. Thus Renaissance architecture, in spite of the zeal with which architects sought to recover Classic ideals, remained fundamentally different, Classic only in external expression. The salient characteristic of this new departure was the employment of the Classic Roman 'Orders' of architecture, which were now reintroduced after having been in abeyance for nearly a thousand years. These Orders—Tuscan, Doric, Ionic, Corinthian, and Composite—which were standardized by Renaissance architects, such as Palladio, Vignola, Scamozzi and Chambers (p. 972), were used, as by the Romans, both rationally and decoratively; sometimes the Orders actually performed structural work and at other times were merely ornamental. Yet even in superficial terms the imitation of antiquity was not slavish; Roman precedent was followed, closely while the new style was being developed, but new combinations of Classic elements were progressively evolved, and in the Baroque period the need for Roman sanction was often totally disregarded. Since the Renaissance was not a natural outcome of structural method, and largely a decorative system derived from an ancient source, it was open to personal interpretations which, when made by accomplished masters, might be taken up by pupils and followers and institute 'schools' of design. This was particularly the case in the early days of the style. The biographies of architects, as given in the works of Vasari and Milizia, are instructive as revealing the surroundings and incidents of their lives. Italy was ripe, as we have seen, for this new phase; for the arts were in the hands of skilled craftsmen, goldsmiths, and workers in metals, such as Benvenuto Cellini, Ghiberti, Donatello, and Brunelleschi, who looked upon architecture as an art of form rather than of construction, and indeed were often, at the same time, painters and sculptors as well as architects. The various schools of painting likewise had their influence, so that buildings came to be treated very much as pictures, largely independent of structural necessity, which had been the controlling element in Mediaeval times. Thus, by a reversal of the Mediaeval process, architecture became an art of free expression, with beauty of design as the predominant idea. To the Roman stock-in-trade of elevational motifs the Renaissance made several important new contributions. Rusticated masonry, among these, was a principal class, exploited strongly in the Early Renaissance in Florence, as instanced by the Riccardi (p. 681), the Strozzi (p. 685) and the Rucellai (p. 680G) palaces, and by various others in north Italy; and thence extended throughout western Europe, rustications sometimes even being applied to the Orders themselves. The baluster, not known to the Romans, which was developed from candelabra, became an inseparable part of the Renaissance decorative system. Among the features contributed to Italian Mediaeval architecture by the Byzantines was the pendentived dome, allowing domical vaults to be erected over square or polygonal compartments. This was retained, and used in a variety of new as well as the old ways (p. 658), and a particular development was that of raising a high 'drum' above pendentives to accommodate not only windows but a decoration with the now inevitable columns, allowing the dome to appear as a grand dominating feature externally (pp. 663B, 704, 720). To provide for the foreshortened view, domes were made with a double or triple shell, that on the outside being pointed, and crowned with a lantern (pp. 663B, 722A, C, 800C, E). The pointed arch, which may be regarded as the sign-manual of Gothic architecture, was now ousted by the semicircular Roman arch. Gothic ribbed vaulting too, which was such a striking feature of Mediaeval buildings, now gave place to the ancient Roman semicircular vaults and cross-vaults (p. 373A). Cross-vaults of unequal span but equal height had the larger vault formed as an ellipse by means of 'ordinates', so that the groins followed straight lines on plan (p. 373D) instead of wavy lines as in the Romanesque period (p. 373B). The same principle allowed the development of many interesting types of vault in which series of minor vaults appear as lunette 'penetrations', as over the sanctuary of S. M. delle Grazie, Milan (p. 698E). Vaults of these various types, developed from Byzantine as well as Roman architecture, were often formed of timber framing plastered and richly painted, and were much used in the halls, apartments, corridors and grand staircases of Renaissance buildings.

The Renaissance passed through a series of stages in its development. Here it is considered as lasting until about 1830. In Italy, as in other countries where it came to be adopted, the first phase was that of learning, designers being intent upon accurate transcription of the Roman architectural elements and their use in contemporary buildings. As Italy had not travelled so far from Classic character as had countries where the Gothic had reached its highest development, the return was fairly readily accomplished, and by 1500 the average building was thoroughly classical in appearance. The next stage was the most important to the future of the style. In the first half of the sixteenth century architects had become thoroughly imbued with the classical spirit, and need not, if they so wished, any longer scrupulously pay regard to Roman precedent. The Renaissance became an individual style in its own right; about 1530. By this time the grasp of classical principles had expanded beyond the concept merely of individual buildings to buildings in their relationship one to another, to civic design, the setting of buildings and to gardens and garden art. But there then emerged a conflict of practice between those designers

COMPARATIVE DOMES

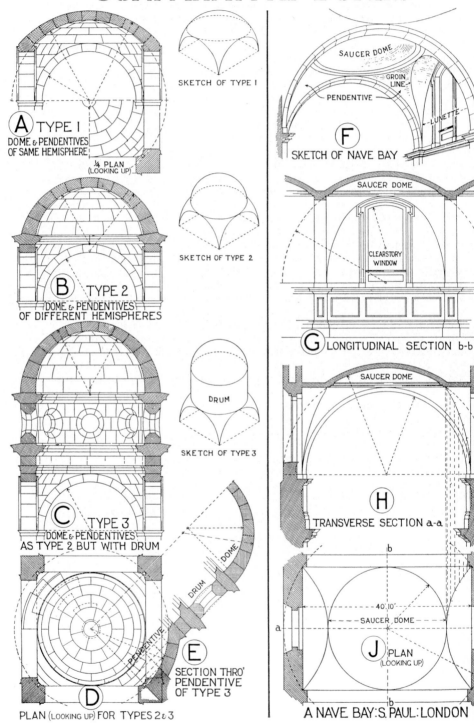

A TYPE 1
DOME & PENDENTIVES
OF SAME HEMISPHERE

¼ PLAN
(LOOKING UP)

SKETCH OF TYPE 1

B TYPE 2
DOME & PENDENTIVES
OF DIFFERENT HEMISPHERES

SKETCH OF TYPE 2

C TYPE 3
DOME & PENDENTIVES
AS TYPE 2 BUT WITH DRUM

DRUM

SKETCH OF TYPE 3

D PLAN (LOOKING UP) FOR TYPES 2 & 3

DOME

DRUM

PENDENTIVE

E SECTION THRO'
PENDENTIVE
OF TYPE 3

F SKETCH OF NAVE BAY

SAUCER DOME

GROIN
LINE

PENDENTIVE

LUNETTE

G LONGITUDINAL SECTION b-b

SAUCER DOME

CLEARSTORY
WINDOW

H TRANSVERSE SECTION a-a

SAUCER DOME

J PLAN
(LOOKING UP)

40.10"

SAUCER DOME

A NAVE BAY: S. PAUL: LONDON

who still held Roman precedent in high respect—though they might not always follow it meticulously—and others who were confident in their power to use the acquired classical vocabulary freely, to express their own ideas of form. This division of opinion and practice continued for a very long time, and indeed was never completely repaired. The 'purist' school may be said to be represented by Palladio (p. 738) and his followers, while on the other hand, Michelangelo (p. 713) was the leader of the 'Proto-Baroque' secessionists from the strict rule. Proto-Baroque freedom was encouraged by the rediscovery and exploitation of stucco as a plastic medium, and by the love of ornamentation in certain areas where the traditional use of brickwork already had endowed architecture with the attributes of intricacy and small scale, as, for example, the Lombard region and, outside Italy, the Low Countries. Proto-Baroque architecture is not, however, always profuse of ornament, though even when relatively plain it has a sculpturesque quality, and tends to exhibit an irrational and unsanctified use of the classical elements in greater or less degree. Compared with 'Palladian' architecture (using the term to denote a type rather than the actual output of this particular master), which is logical, staid and serene, Proto-Baroque architecture, also known as 'Mannerist', is vivid, virile and intense, sometimes disturbingly restless and confused. The Proto-Baroque version, as the term implies, leads directly to Baroque architecture, in which the previous unrestrained exuberance has been brought to subjection and effects contrived which are at once dramatic, rich, grand and alive, architecture, sculpture, painting and the minor arts all being used in harmony to produce the unified whole. The Baroque period in Italy has its beginning about 1600, and reached its best in the fifty years 1625–75. Ecclesiastical buildings rather than secular provided the most fruitful field for the display of its qualities, and Jesuit churches, in whatever country the style took hold, afford some of the finest and most spectacular examples. Baroque architecture normally is bold, opulent and impressive. Typically, forms and colours are manipulated to induce visual concentration upon local and dominant foci rather than being organized in dispersed consistent rhythms, as in the High Renaissance and 'Palladian' expressions. The devices employed have the main object of providing highly enriched play and flow of form, and to this end, the elements usually are multiform rather than single: the Orders are overlaid one upon the other, used in clusters, variously in pilastered, attached or freestanding condition and at irregular spacings; entablatures are heavily ornate and advance or recede in response to columnar arrangements below them; pediments, segmental or triangular, are whole or broken and the free ends turned into volute scrolls, or pediments are placed one within the other; attic mounts over attic; balustrades, with reiterated dies, bear balusters of various exotic types; while panelling, with 'ears' at the corners, cartouches, heraldic emblems and a great variety of other ornament as well as sculpture, painting and craftwork are used freely to produce the calculated effect. Above all, there is the index of the curved or sinuous line, frequently contrived by arranging concavities or convexities of the wall or by employing circular, elliptical or other curvilinear plans. As a whole, buildings were contrived for dramatic effect, and internally, great care was taken to control the incidence of natural light. Frequently, concealed windows directed the flow of light to specific points or areas. Interiors were conceived in terms of spatial volume rather than as a complex of individual surfaces, and the volume contained might be treated alternatively as a single geometrical complexity or as a series of lesser volumes of diversified character. Baroque architecture is grand, vigorous and robust, very decisive in its effects, and strongly modelled. It became progressively more refined and subtle as time passed, though the unity of architecture with all the subordinate arts became still more strongly marked. Exteriors became plainer than interiors.

This subsequent phase is recognized as the 'Rococo', reached in Italy about 1700. It endured for some fifty years, and was succeeded in its turn by the 'Antiquarian' phase, when designers looked back once more to ancient models. Renaissance architecture then acquired an austere aspect, to the extent that one version aspired to reproduce the stately simplicity of Grecian architecture. On the other hand, the old Gothic architecture too was romantically imitated.

In due course Renaissance architecture was adopted in all the European countries, delay depending upon distance from Italy and a variety of other factors. Below is a table showing, comparatively, its incidence in three important countries, Italy, France and England, and the phases through which it passed in each.

ITALY

1420 EARLY	HIGH RENAISSANCE & PROTO-BAROQUE	BAROQUE	ANTIQUARIAN
1500	1600	1760	1830

FRANCE

EARLY	CLASSICAL	LATE
1495 1589	1715	1830

ENGLAND

ELIZABETHAN JACOBEAN STUART	GEORGIAN
1558 1603 1625 1702	1830

Necessarily, the Renaissance had common characteristics in all the various countries, but the versions produced nevertheless were nationally quite distinct. France and England particularly, had first to counter Gothic architecture, so much more deeply rooted than in Italy, and in each country, national traits as well as contemporary events operated to determine the complexion which Renaissance architecture was to assume. The early Renaissance in each country was inevitably individual, being a compound of the Classical with the style or styles hitherto practised. The Baroque, as understood in Italy, never found great favour either in France, Holland or England, but blossomed extravagantly in Spain and delightfully in Central Europe, while finding congenial soil in Belgium too. Holland, England, and to some extent, France, inclined to reject the Baroque in favour of the 'Palladian' expression. All countries, however, were in unison from about 1750 in turning back again for inspiration to bygone styles; Roman, Greek and Gothic.

The variation in characteristics, with examples, will be shown for each country, Italy (p. 671), France (p. 765), Germany (p. 808), Belgium and Holland (p. 831), Spain (p. 845), and England (p. 868).

COMPARATIVE ANALYSIS

The following table gives the main differences between the Gothic and Renaissance styles in Europe:

GOTHIC	RENAISSANCE
PLANS. Plans were largely the fortuitous result of the various necessary parts arranged for convenience rather than for symmetry (p. 442E, L).	PLANS. Plans were arranged with special regard to symmetry, produced by similarity of parts on either side of central axial lines (pp. 680c, 690c).

GOTHIC

Church interiors were planned in oblong bays covered with rib and panel vaulting (p. 418B) or with open timber roofs (p. 435).

Naves are divided into numerous bays, and this repetition gives an appearance of length, as in Winchester Cathedral, which with a length of 270 ft has 12 divisions (p. 410C). Grandeur was thus produced by the large number of parts into which the building was divided.

Towers, often crowned with spires, are freely used and are predominant features which accentuate the verticality of the design. They occur as single western towers, towers over the crossing, twin western towers, and even in groups of nine, as intended at Chartres (p. 540).

WALLS. Walls are often constructed of rubble masonry (p. 490) not laid in horizontal courses, or of brick and rough flint in patterns. In accordance with Mediaeval usage materials were in small pieces, even when of squared stones or ashlar, fitted together to meet the requirements of a style in which church walls were practically replaced by glass windows and projecting buttresses.

Wall angles are often of squared ashlar masonry, while the rest of the walling is of rubble, flint, or brick.

Gables are steep, pierced with windows and finished either with stone parapets (p. 418A) or ornamented timber barge-boards (p. 456B).

Skylines are characterized by rising towers and the intricacy resulting from numerous pinnacles (pp. 345, 601).

OPENINGS. Arcades of pointed arches are characteristic, as in Westminster Abbey (p. 422B), and in cloisters are frequently filled with tracery, as in Westminster Abbey (p. 425A).

Door (pp. 498, 539B) and window openings (p. 499) have their sides or jambs in recessed planes, richly moulded and often provided with small nook-shafts (p. 330B). Openings were placed with regard to convenience rather than to symmetry or position one over another, and were usually spanned by pointed arches (pp. 449A, 558H).

Windows are divided by vertical mullions and horizontal transoms, and are often of enormous size for the display of

RENAISSANCE

Church interiors were planned in square bays covered with barrel or cross vaults and with a central dome (p. 723G).

Naves are divided into few bays, and thus an appearance of spaciousness is obtained, as in S. Paul, London, which with a length of 160 ft has only 4 divisions (p. 910). Grandeur was here obtained by the small number of large divisions or parts employed (pp. 908C, 909B).

Towers are sparingly used, and when they occur are symmetrically placed, whether in pairs, as at S. Paul, London (frontis.), or as a single western tower, as at S. Bride, where it is crowned by a spire (p. 919). The dome is a predominant feature externally (p. 739A).

WALLS. Walls are constructed of ashlar masonry, accurately laid in horizontal courses, or of brick lined up with bonding courses. In accordance with Roman practice, materials were in large blocks, which give dignity, often accentuated by rusticating the blocks in the lower part of walls, which were only pierced at intervals with windows (p. 681).

Wall angles are often rusticated to give an additional appearance of strength (p. 756).

Pediments are of low pitch (p. 742A), due to Classic influence, or semicircular (p. 735A), sometimes filled with sculpture.

Skylines are characterized by horizontal cornices and balustrades, which give simplicity of outline (pp. 699A, 705B).

OPENINGS. Arcades of semicircular arches appear in courtyards and street architecture, especially in Italy (p. 699B).

Door and window openings have their sides or jambs unrecessed and finished with a moulded architrave of Classic type (p. 330A). Openings were placed with regard to symmetry and to grouping one above the other, and were spanned by semicircular arches (p. 682B) or lintels (p. 756).

Windows, except under transition conditions, followed Classic lines and remained small as determined by the climate of

GOTHIC

painted glass—a translucent form of decoration which influenced the number and size of the windows (p. 499) as at S. George's Chapel, Windsor.

ROOFS. Vaulting is developed by means of the pointed arch and depends for effect on the beauty of curve of the numerous ribs which support the panels and which are frequently enriched at their junctions by carved 'bosses' (p. 399).

Open timber roofs are beautiful features of the style, especially in England, both in royal palaces, such as Westminster Hall (p. 500), and in parish churches (p. 435), and manor houses (p. 449B).

The external treatment of roofs varies in ecclesiastical and domestic buildings, but is characterized in general by towers and spires (p. 531B), high gables, elaborate chimneys (p. 455A), ornamental parapets (p. 511), lofty pinnacles, and slender flèches (p. 564), which give a jagged and spiky skyline.

COLUMNS. Columns were used structurally; the Classical proportions between height and diameter were not observed; capitals and bases were moulded and carved according to the fancy of the craftsman. Piers combined with shafts were frequently used instead of cylindrical piers, and their plan was determined by the moulded arches and vaulting ribs they had to support (pp. 503, 547B, 535C).

MOULDINGS. The contours of mouldings consist of curves forming parts of circles or combinations of these curves joined by fillets, which enriched the sides of openings and were contained within rectangular recesses or on a 'chamfer plane' (p. 507) at an angle of 45 degrees with the wall-face.

Mouldings, when used as horizontal string courses, are sometimes enriched with carved ornament varying in character according to the period (p. 508).

Projecting vertical buttresses, emphasized by their deep shadows, lofty moulded pinnacles, together with steep roofs, towers, and spires, all produce an effect of verticality (pp. 532C, 543, 663A), while parapets, battlemented or pierced with tracery, take the place of boldly projecting Classic cornices (pp. 511, 556, 563).

ORNAMENT. Ornament generally was

RENAISSANCE

Italy, and were unbroken by mullions and transoms (p. 692F) and not used as frames for painted glass pictures.

ROOFS. Vaulting is characterized by semicircular vaults without ribs (p. 705E), and depends for effect on coloured frescoes; the dome (pp. 658, 676A), whether of the flat saucer type or raised on a drum, is also frescoed (p. 679G).

Timber roofs are no longer left open, but are frequently lined internally with plaster ceilings, horizontal or arched, and enriched with plastic decoration (pp. 884, 904C, E, 939C, 977A, B).

The external treatment of roofs varies in each country; in Italy they are flat and hidden behind balustrades (p. 734D), while in England, Germany, and especially France they are high; the dome is the dominating feature and gives a smooth and rounded outline (p. 663B).

COLUMNS. The Classic 'Orders' were again used and their proportions standardized (p. 972), and they appear either decoratively in façades (pp. 690A, 699A) or structurally, as in porticoes (p. 703B). Shafts were varied by rustication, fluting, and carved foliage. In the Baroque period the Orders often were used in clustered form and in many other unorthodox ways (pp. 724E, 728B).

MOULDINGS. The contours of mouldings consist of curves formed of parts of circles joined by fillets, as in Roman entablatures (pp. 164, 165, 191), but were now used in novel combinations; while the sides of openings have simple architrave mouldings formed on the wall surface (pp. 699E, 749, 753C).

Mouldings, when used in intermediate cornices, are Roman in character and, when carved, the ornament is derived from the same source (pp. 750, 757, 758).

Projecting horizontal cornices casting deep shadows, with balconies and moulded string bands, all combine to produce an effect of horizontality. Above the crowning cornices there were often balustrades, the baluster being an important Renaissance invention, much exploited decoratively (pp. 686B, 689D, 718A, 740A, 756).

ORNAMENT. Ornament generally was

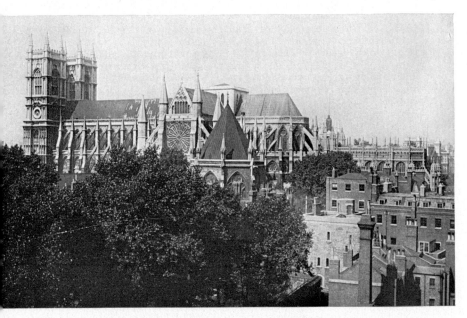

A. Westminster Abbey from S. (1055–c. 1740). See p. 423

B. S. Paul's Cathedral, London from S.W. (1675–1710). See p. 906

GOTHIC	RENAISSANCE
founded on Mediaeval mysticism and Christian subjects.	founded on Classical mythology and pagan subjects.
Carving, often boldly executed and grotesque, possesses a decorative character in harmony with the architecture, and enriches doorways, windows, buttresses, pinnacles, and gargoyles (pp. 512, 566). Sturdy craftsmanship characterizes the style, not only in stone, but also in metal and woodwork, and was determined by structural forms rather than by individual taste (pp. 517, 518).	Carving is generally carefully executed and has a character in harmony with Classic ideals and precedent, whether in cornices, consoles, capitals, friezes, pilaster shafts, or pediments (pp. 749, 750, 754, 757). Fine craftsmanship is distinctive of the Early Renaissance period, as seen in the metalwork of individual artists, such as Ghiberti, and in the glazed faïence of the Della Robbia family (p. 672).
The human figure determined the scale, both for statues and for doorways. The statues spring from and form part of the structural features of the buildings and are thus architectonic in character (pp. 543, 566), and are an integral part of the structure.	The human figure was not the unit of scale, either for statues or for doorways, both of which increased with the size of the building. Statues, anatomically correct, are not an integral part of the structure (pp. 663B, 686A, 720B, 721A, 724D–F, 736, 739A, C, 741, and frontispiece.
Stained glass is the coloured glory of the style and was largely the *raison d'être* of the immense traceried windows which framed the glowing pictures of Bible incident and church history (p. 371), and it culminated in the translucent coloured windows of Rheims.	Fresco painting gives the coloured mural decoration of the style in which windows were subordinate, and it was handed down from the Roman period and attained the height of elaboration on the walls and ceilings of Baroque interiors.
External colour schemes were usually the result of the combination of the materials used, as in Florence (p. 615A) and Siena Cathedrals (p. 617A).	External colour effects were usually produced by 'sgraffito' decoration on coloured plaster, as in the Palazzo del Consiglio, Verona (p. 744H).

The Palazzo del Laterano, Rome (1586; see p. 725),
with S. Giovanni in Laterano (*right*; see p. 729),
and the obelisk from Karnak (see p. 50)

Italy in the sixteenth century

XX. ITALIAN RENAISSANCE

(fifteenth–nineteenth century)

INFLUENCES

GEOGRAPHICAL. The Renaissance in Italy is best considered geographically under
the three great distinctive cities of its activity, Florence, Rome and Venice, which,
however, will be taken as centres of influence rather than localized schools. Each
had its own regional traits, though these became less marked as time progressed,
and gave way almost completely to universal characteristics during the Baroque
period. At no time did South Italy and Sicily play more than a minor or subservient
rôle.

Florence. The city-state of Florence, centrally situated, was one of the chief powers of Italy. Though its expanding dominions never included more than a small part of the peninsula, the Florentines not only exerted considerable influence over the whole of Tuscany but carried Renaissance architecture, which originated with them, much farther afield. Under Florence are included Genoa, a maritime republic, which was little affected by the new style until mid-sixteenth century, and Milan, centre of yet another powerful state and in which Florentine architects were the first to build in Renaissance style: Turin comes into the picture in later times.

Rome. The shrunken and distressed Mediaeval city began to recover its prestige and unique influence while the Renaissance was taking root in Florence, and soon popes and cardinals were reviving its glories in fine architecture. The ruins of ancient Rome, then better preserved than now, supplied the models for new buildings which, in their turn, became models for all Europe. The Popes claimed temporal rights over the Papal States, extending from the region of Rome northwards along the east-coast to link with the Republics of Florence and Venice. In the more remote of the States papal authority was negligible until the early sixteenth century, and they were in fact in the hands of despots, who created their own individual artistic environments.

Venice. The greatness of Venice was founded during the Mediaeval period (pp. 312, 599) on her Oriental commerce, and this prosperity continued well into Renaissance times. By 1500 her territories in Italy extended westward almost to Milan, thus embracing Padua, Vicenza, Verona, Brescia, Bergamo and other cities along the valley of the River Po, while across the Adriatic she retained Dalmatia and enlarged her holding in Istria. The history of the Venetian State was always influenced by her impregnable location in the Venetian lagoon, protected by a belt of islands, and by her sea-power which secured her maritime trade with the East; until geographical discoveries opened up new routes and she gradually sank into decline.

GEOLOGICAL

Florence. As shown previously (pp. 312, 600), the quarries of Tuscany yielded ample fine stone, obtainable, when needed, in large blocks. Siena, a rival republic until 1555, had her own local supplies, as well too of white and yellow marble. From Carrara and vicinity in the north-west of the modern province of Tuscany came the famed white marble—the Luna marble of Roman times—and also coloured, and from quarries at Fiesole, the Florentines won the 'pietra serena', a blue-grey stone of fine quality much employed in Early Renaissance buildings in the city, as well as the 'pietra forte', a brown stone more suitable for outside work. The Genoa district was equally well favoured, having ready access to the northward extension of the same massif as includes Carrara, and to the green- and vari-coloured marbles of Liguria and Piedmont. In the Milan region, where brick and terra-cotta were normal, coloured marbles could be obtained, though with some difficulty and therefore tended to be used in sparing, precious fashion.

Rome. Good building stone of many varieties was available within ready reach of the city (pp. 168, 253, 312), the finest being travertine, won from quarries around Tivoli, a stone much used by the Romans. But as in previous periods, Renaissance builders often found the decaying pagan buildings a much more handy source, as well too for the coloured marbles which the Romans had brought at such great pains from various parts of their mighty empire. Apart from the enlightened policies of Popes Leo X (1513–22) and Pius IV (1559–65), little respect was paid to the ancient monuments, and they long continued to be despoiled of their material, recovered sculptures and carvings being used for the adornment of Renaissance buildings and their stones for new constructions; or, in the case of suitable marbles and travertine, burnt for lime. The northerly Papal States also mostly lay in stone-producing districts, except around Bologna and the neighbouring lower Po valley, where brick was the natural material.

Venice. The site of the city was devoid of suitable materials, but brick-earths were accessible on the nearby mainland, and by easy water-carriage, stones, timber and marbles could be obtained according to need, as in the Mediaeval period (pp. 312, 600). Istrian cream-coloured stone continued to be used extensively in Venice, and red- and orange-coloured marbles were available near Verona. Westward, the cities under Venetian rule lay in the brick-producing zone, but stone from the neighbouring foothills of the Alps was never too far distant for the best work.

CLIMATIC

Florence. As elsewhere in Italy, the bright and sunny climate rendered large windows not only unnecessary but also unsuitable. The open 'cortile' or court, normal to palaces, and the sheltering colonnade or arcade are arrangements perpetuated from ancient times; while the low-pitched roof, natural in a country where snow was rare, lent itself to cornice and parapet or balustrade.

Rome. The effects of climate were much as in previous times (pp. 169, 312, 600). The narrow streets of Italian towns gave protection not alone against the blaze of summer sun but also against winter cold, severely felt in the indifferently-heated buildings. The cramped, bustling streets in their turn, along with the risks of faction fights, brawls and nocturnal depredations, led to living on upper floors of palaces, the first floor being the principal or 'piano nobile', while the ground floor was devoted to general service purposes.

Venice. As shown earlier (pp. 312, 600), the extreme heat of summer was here tempered by sea breezes, and to enjoy them, belvederes and balconies were usual, these all the more necessary in that the restricted island sites gave little room for gardens. On the other hand, the northern latitude and the winds that swept down from the snow-topped mountains, made fire-places almost essential, and the funnel-topped chimneys are a distinctive Venetian feature.

RELIGIOUS

Florence. The Dominican friar, Savonarola (1452–98), by his ardent piety and reforming zeal, changed the habits of the citizens, swayed the policy of the State and even menaced the authority of the Pope, Alexander VI. His impassioned denunciations of corruption in Church and State, his eloquent exhortations to purity of life and his personal devotion and singleness of purpose, spread consternation in the gay city of Florence; he roused the citizens to opposition to the oppressive tyranny of the Medici and called upon the rulers of Christendom to summon a general council to reform Church abuses. At one time banished from Florence by a Medici, at another excommunicated by a pope, and yet again forsaken by his own people, Savonarola, in spite of all, became the saviour, law-giver and dictator of the Florentine Republic. His influence lived on after his death.

Rome. The return of the Popes (1377) from Avignon to Rome had helped to reestablish her former position of importance and prosperity. From the time of the Council of Constance (1417), the Popes, notably Nicholas V (1447–55), Julius II (1503–13) and Leo X (1513–22), took a prominent position as Italian princes and patrons of art; Sixtus V (1585–90) is often credited with the comprehensive change to Renaissance character of the city. Directly or indirectly, certain of the Popes were concerned in attempts to consolidate Italian unity, endeavours by no means restricted to the objective of giving reality to papal authority over their legitimate temporal domains. Caesar Borgia (1475–1507), natural son of Alexander VI (1492–

1503), went his wilful way towards accomplishing the overthrow of the northern Italian States piecemeal, and after the death of his father, clashed with Julius II, member of a rival family, who pursued with considerable success the same militant aim directly on the papal account, bringing all the States of the Church to heel with the exception of Ferrara. Thus do we see the impossibility of unravelling into separate threads the warp of religious and social conditions of this restless period. Great wealth accrued to the Popes, and they were concerned in turn to benefit their families, or to mark their pontificate by the erection of costly buildings. The greater part of the famous palaces of Renaissance Rome, and the splendid villas fringing the ancient city, are associated with the name of one or other of these great papal families. Yet meantime the authority of the papacy had been undergoing challenge. The Reformation and the growth of nationalism in countries which formerly had submitted unquestioningly to the spiritual leadership of Rome, spurred the Church to put its own house in order, and one most important outcome was the appearance in the sixteenth century of fresh religious Orders, the Theatines (1524), the Capuchins (1536; a branch of the Franciscans, becoming a separate Order in 1619) and the Jesuits, founded by the Spaniard, Ignatius Loyola, in 1540. The latter proved by far the most important Order of the three, and strengthened Spanish influence in Italy. The Jesuits' purpose was to combat the effects of the Reformation by renewing the ideals of the Church, while buttressing the papal power. They built preaching churches and religious colleges, and were not only religious enthusiasts but also a building confraternity.

Venice. No part of Italy remained unaffected by the recovery of Rome and the papacy, but the Venetians were unsympathetic to spiritual control, and maintained a semi-independence of the Popes, specially manifested during the attempted Interdict (1607) of Paul V, when the learned theologian, Paolo Sarpi (1552–1623) was the adviser of the Venetian State.

SOCIAL

Florence. The rediscovery of classical literature produced a wave of enthusiasm throughout Italy for old Roman architecture. This new movement began in Florence about 1420, and was developed with enormous zeal. It was stimulated by the Medici family, founded in 1424 by Giovanni de' Medici (d. 1429), which acquired great wealth in the upsurge of commercial prosperity, and gradually assumed supreme authority in the State. Giovanni's son, Cosimo (d. 1464), founded the Medici Library and the Platonic Academy, and was a most generous patron of artists, such as Brunelleschi, Michelozzi, Donatello, Masaccio and Lippi. He in turn was succeeded by his son, Piero (d. 1469), followed by his grandson, Lorenzo 'the Magnificent', whose brilliant personal gifts and devotion to the Arts marked the most glorious phase in Florentine history. Through banking activities, from which their riches sprang, the Medici family had considerable repute in other Italian cities and even abroad; it produced two Popes, Leo X (1513–22) and Clement VII (1523–34), and its fortunes long remained interwoven with those of Florence. For at least a century after the inception of the Renaissance in architecture, Florentine social life exhibited intense vitality at every level, never quite paralleled elsewhere at this or any other time in Renaissance Italy. The welfare of the State was the deep concern of almost every citizen—the semi-fortified character of the palaces is witness to the feuds of rival political parties—and the arts and crafts were pursued with the utmost fervour, evidenced no less in the rivalries and petty jealousies which constantly arose, than in the admiration and delight ungrudgingly shown for the works and persons of the accomplished masters. For artists to be distinguished in several rather than a single art was almost a commonplace, and social distinctions rested far more upon ability in commerce, craftsmanship, literature and the arts than upon class. All the records of Florence of the time indicate a city of vital, pulsating energy, its streets a bustle of purposeful activity. The powerful and well-organized craft guilds, which had religious and not merely lay connotations, had a considerable share in directing the activities of studio and workshop which, inspired by the Renaissance movement, sprang up in every Florentine street. Florentines soon began to carry the Renaissance to other fields, and their ardent spirit rapidly inspired rivalry in other Tuscan cities. The earliest architects to work in Renaissance style in both Rome and Milan were Florentines. Genoa was more tardy, and scarcely began to show architectural evidences of the movement before the sixteenth century.

Rome. The ancient city took time to recover from its Mediaeval poverty, and it was the patronage of the Church, with its renewed temporal power, and of the great papal families, that drew flocking to it aspirants of every description. Population increased enormously, and building proceeded apace; splendid new palaces and churches were erected and embellished by eminent craftsmen and artists. The Renaissance took hold, and the movement was furthered by the setting-up of printing presses about 1465, which opened up to wider access the study of ancient writers. Because of the special circumstances, the social structure in Rome was substantially different from that of Florence. Rome had no commercial importance, and therefore no close-knit burgher community, and subsisted largely upon its metropolitan functions, exercised by an aristocracy that, through papal favours, now became extremely rich and powerful, while the former meagre populace received a tremendous infusion of newcomers whose common bond was little more than that of ambition. Though as in ancient times in Rome their dwellings might be intermingled, there was here a much greater distance between the social classes and between patron and client. Artists and architects stood out more strongly on their own personal count, rather than pursuing the Renaissance collectively, while airs and graces, and wealth lavishly expended in display, strongly distinguished lordly patrician from earnest artisan and homespun commoner. With interludes of comparative austerity, as after the sack of Rome by Spanish and German forces in 1537, or that due to the impact of the Counter-Reformation over the middle of the sixteenth century, the great families held almost regal court in their palaces, vying one with the other in cultivated extravagance. The Popes, avaricious of their revenues outside the city, spent them prodigally within, and even ran up enormous debts. Yet the eventual outcome was a grand and resplendent city, replete with fine buildings and civic embellishments, while outside the city were luxurious villas in the delectable neighbouring hills. Until brought under effective papal authority in the time of Julius II or later, certain of the more northerly of the States of the Church held their own petty but brilliant courts of the leaders of the tyrant families which governed them, such as the Malatesta family of Rimini, the Montefeltri of Urbino or the Este of Ferrara; and thus for a while, architecture in these centres was more responsive to local factors than to developments in Rome.

Venice. During the whole of the fifteenth century, Venice was engaged in conquering neighbouring towns, over which Venetian nobles were appointed as governors. The Republican government of Venice gave special care to the regulations for the development of trade, both in home and overseas markets. Her prosperity was due to a State commercial system, and was not the result of mere accident or of the enterprise of individuals. This successful trading community produced many kings of commerce, whose rivalry in display led to the erection of numerous fine palaces on the Grand Canal, which from their situation on the broad waterfront needed less protection against civic turmoil than was necessary in Florence and other inland cities, and so could be more splendid and open externally. John of Speyer established (1469) the first of those printing presses for which Venice became so famous when, at a later time, the Aldine Press issued its editions of the Greek classics. Thus, though her prosperity was fading as the Renaissance advanced, due to her receding Eastern trade, Venice was far-famed for her artistry, her theatre and her joyous, luxurious life. These survived even into the eighteenth century when her political importance had almost gone.

HISTORICAL

Florence. The grouping together of independent commonwealths in Italy is a feature of this period when, as in ancient Greece, one city bore rule over another. In 1406 Florence conquered Pisa and thus obtained a seaport, and in 1421 she took Leghorn from the Genoese and was strong enough to challenge Milan and Lucca in war, and so became the chief power in Italy and the art centre of Europe. The feuds between nobles were aggravated by the warfare between the Guelphs and Ghibellines (pp. 315, 603). In 1494 Charles VIII of France occupied Florence during his brief invasion of Italy to enforce his claims to the Kingdom of Naples. The short-lived Republic of Savonarola followed, but the Medici, in spite of successive banishments, were reinstated by the Emperor Charles V when he took the town in 1530, after a siege of eleven months, during which Michelangelo acted as engineer to the Republic. Political liberty was subsequently curtailed, especially under Cosimo I (1537–74), who, however, greatly extended the Florentine dominions and took Siena in 1555. The Grand Dukes of Tuscany passed through varying fortunes until, in 1737, the House of Medici became extinct and the Duchy passed to Austria. In 1801 Florence again attained political freedom as a republic and afterwards as the Kingdom of Etruria. Between 1807 and 1814 she was incorporated with France, and in 1860 she was united to the Kingdom of Italy.

Rome. The Council of Constance, which followed the return of the Popes after their long sojourn in Avignon, put an end not only to the scandal of rival Popes, but also to the factions of the barons within the papal city; so that times of more stable government and greater security resulted in an increase of wealth and prestige and a revival of building in Rome. That ambitious Pope, Julius II, besides extending the temporal power of the papacy, sought to aggrandize himself in the popular imagination, and thus his original intension of erecting a monumental tomb house for himself developed into the gigantic scheme for the rebuilding of S. Peter's, as the greatest cathedral in Christendom (p. 717). For the seventh and last time Rome was taken and plundered by the Emperor Charles V (1527). One external power after another then exercised authority in Italy, and so modified the natural tendency of Italian architecture. First came Charles V and the influence of Spain which, with her dignified state ceremonials, was responsible for the introduction of extravagant ornament. This was followed by the French ideas of the magnificent times of Louis XIV. Then the Italian peninsula passed largely under the yoke of Austria, until the Napoleonic interlude of 1796–1815.

Venice. In the middle of the fifteenth century, when Constantinople was taken by the Turks (1453), the supremacy of Venice, which had been her commercial ally, was undermined; while the discovery by Vasco da Gama in 1498 of the new route round the Cape to India diverted her commerce to the Portuguese. The League of Cambrai (1508–29) against Venice indicates the strength of the Republic. During the sixteenth and seventeenth centuries the Venetians were at constant war with the Turks, and eventually in 1718 Venice lost the whole of her possessions, except those in north Italy; but even when her territorial power was reduced and her commerce diverted, the mighty sea-republic still cherished the arts.

ARCHITECTURAL CHARACTER

The Renaissance in Italy may be divided broadly into three main periods, viz.:

Early Renaissance—fifteenth century
High Renaissance and Proto-Baroque—sixteenth century
Baroque—seventeenth and early eighteenth centuries.

Thereafter, from *c*. 1750–1830, the Renaissance follows an 'Antiquarian' trend.

It has been shown earlier (p. 603ff.) that the welter of influences upon Italian Gothic, including the ancient Roman, exerted by the still-numerous monumental remains, produced differing regional types, these mostly quite unlike the Gothic architecture of Western Europe. The round arch was never completely abandoned, and Byzantine structural and decorative practices, even more than the Western Gothic, were interwoven with those developed from the direct Roman and Romanesque succession. The Renaissance reversion to Ancient Roman architectural character was in fact more superficial than might at first appear, and indeed neither in their manner of construction nor in their building types nor purpose in planning did the Renaissance enthusiasts make the least attempt to turn back the hands of the clock. Roman mass construction had long been conclusively superseded by the more compact and scientific Mediaeval systems, and if there was some attempt to emulate the Roman grand manner of formal planning, it was for visual effect and not for the improvement of physical comfort and convenience. In all fundamental respects, from a threshold of its Gothic and Byzantine inheritance the Renaissance pursued its own individual and characteristic course. Thus for instance, in tracing its development we see a protracted struggle for favour between the Gothic longitudinal and the Byzantine centralized church plans, resolved in a happy marriage in the Baroque period when the Byzantine ordonnance was commonly adopted for the eastern half of a Latin-cross scheme, while without the aid of the Byzantine pendentive and the tie-bar system—which generated the hoop-tie principle (pp. 722C, 912)—we probably never should have known the glories of the domes of S. Peter's, Rome (p. 723) or S. Paul's, London (p. 663B).

In the Early Renaissance, regional character importantly survived; in the High Renaissance and Proto-Baroque period it was partially eradicated, owing to a widening dissemination of ideas fostered by travel and the convergence on Rome of so many architects for their training, while with the Baroque it almost wholly disappeared. By the High Renaissance, the stage of elementary learning of Roman decorative systems had been passed, and architects worked in the freedom of firmly acquired knowledge. The true nature of the Renaissance as a distinctive style then began to emerge. These relatively untrammelled adventures exposed the personal style of individual designers, and hard on the heels of the High Renaissance came the phase known in art history as 'Mannerist', wherein practices which had no ancient Roman precedent were interspersed among those fully sanctioned, or whole buildings were conceived in a non-Roman way. Such exuberance in design was in many cases strongly marked by the mid-sixteenth century, and was encouraged by the rediscovery of hard-plaster stucco as an artistic medium, long ago exploited in ancient Roman art. Here, the term 'Proto-Baroque' is used for these non-conforming manifestations—though 'Mannerism' is convenient for the less obvious departures from Roman precedent—since they represent a genuine stage towards that ultimate fulfilment of the entire Renaissance movement in the Baroque, on the threshold of the seventeenth century. The High Renaissance and Proto-Baroque phases, together covering the sixteenth century, cannot readily be separated, as the latter is at first spasmodic in its incidence. Further, it is a phenomenon of the Renaissance movement that even in the 'High' Baroque phase (*c.* 1625–75), ancient Roman canons retained their prestige, and from time to time monuments were produced which were almost wholly Classical in character; and about 1750, architecture as a whole returned to a profound regard for the Roman and Greek antique, in what is known alternatively as the 'Neo-Classical' or 'Antiquarian' phase.

Below, the course of development is considered in the three main regions under the headings of the great distinctive cities which represent them, to the point where regional differences almost wholly disappear in favour of the universal Baroque characteristics, explained on p. 659.

FLORENCE

The Renaissance of the fifteenth century in Italy had its birth in Florence, where, under unique conditions and influences, a type of palace-building was evolved, to which huge blocks of rusticated masonry give an unusually massive and rugged appearance. The typical palace was built round an internal court, similar to a Mediaeval cloister, surrounded by an arcade supporting the walls of the upper stories (pp. 681C, 690D). There is a general absence of pilasters as decorative features in the façades, which are therefore called 'astylar'; while sparing use of detail, together with concentration on pronounced features, produces boldness and simplicity of style. The imposing appearance of these massive palaces fronting on narrow streets is emphasized by boldly projecting roof cornices, which crown the walls and are proportioned to the height of the buildings, as in the Palazzo Riccardi (p. 681A, B). The columnar arcade is a favourite feature, not only in courtyards, but also in streets, as in the Foundling Hospital (p. 675A). Early Renaissance churches are conspicuous for refinement, in strong contrast to the rugged, fortress-like character of the palaces. The architectural character owes much of its interest to the individual fancy of sculptors and painters. Among others there were Luca della Robbia (1400–82), famous for his coloured glazed reliefs in terra-cotta, Lorenzo Ghiberti (1378–1455), who designed the Baptistery doors (p. 677), and also Donatello (1386–1466), Mino da Fiesole (1430–84), and Benedetto da Majano (1442–97), renowned for their bas-reliefs, carvings, and statues. Thus, with this wealth of genius, it is natural that altars and monuments, fonts and pulpits should be richly decorated with sculptured ornament. Florentine craftsmanship, whether displayed in capitals, consoles, corbels, arabesques, fountains, niches, or torch brackets, shows highly developed artistic perception and technical skill (pp. 749. 750). Not only does ornament depend upon the personality of the artist, but architectural design also now becomes the product of the individual architect rather than of a school of craftsmen working on traditional lines. The examples which follow will therefore be classified and considered under the names of the different architects.

Florence contains very many examples of Early Renaissance architecture, but fewer of the High Renaissance and Proto-Baroque period and almost none of the Baroque. In the second quarter of the sixteenth century Michelangelo led the Proto-Baroque breakaway from academic formalism in design with his New Sacristy of S. Lorenzo (p. 716A) and the Laurentian Library (p. 716B), and was soon emulated by local architects such as Ammanati and others in Rome and Genoa. About this same time Florentine garden art was approaching its zenith. The earliest Renaissance villas (from *c.* 1450) in the neighbouring beautifully-diversified, undulating countryside, had retained something of Mediaeval character; progressively they developed towards an intimate charm of formally related garden compartments of differing types, centred on a summer dwelling or 'casino', growing more natural as they merged at the fringe with the surrounding landscape. The Villa Gamberaia, Settignano (*c.* 1550–) (p. 712B) is a fine instance, while in the city itself are the Proto-Baroque Boboli Gardens (*c.* 1550–) (p. 712A), related to the rear façade of the famous Palazzo Pitti.

In Milan, the Early Renaissance at first secured only a precarious hold, but there then appeared a very distinctive small-scale diversified architecture, in the local brick and terra-cotta, of a character often associated with the name of Bramante, who worked hereabouts before his great High Renaissance achievements in Rome. In Genoa, almost the first appearance of the Renaissance was at the Proto-Baroque stage, its palaces distinguished by the remarkable treatment of their airy, axial staircases, and there, as in Milan and Turin, the Baroque reached full flower.

ROME

The Early Renaissance in Rome is comparatively unimportant, though some gracious buildings were completed in the various Papal States. The High Renaissance and later phases are splendidly represented. Roman palaces nearly always have a 'four-square' majesty and dignity (pp. 699A, 705B). At first the Classic Orders often were used in simple, direct arrangements in superimposed tiers on façades and in cortili (pp. 699, 705E, 710F, 753E), but afterwards in a giant arrangement extending the whole height of a building (pp. 710J, 718). Bramante was the chief figure of the High Renaissance, of which his Tempietto at S. Pietro in Montorio (p. 700B) is a notable example, but other great architects, scarcely a generation younger than he, began to show Mannerism in their buildings, using architectural elements in a free, decorative, and sometimes illogical way unsanctified by antique precedent, particularly around wall-openings and in novel treatments of rustication (p. 710B, E, G), while large and small Orders were employed in juxtaposition (p. 710F). Michelangelo's Roman work is of this Proto-Baroque class (p. 718). Peruzzi, an architect of great discernment and taste, showed scholarly appreciation of ancient architecture and at the same time manifested individuality in such as the use of the coupled Order and jewel-like enframements to windows of the façade of his Palazzo Massimi (p. 703). He, like Romano and Vignola, carried Proto-Baroque traits afield (pp. 709A, 711). Domestic planning evidences great skill and ingenuity together with a Roman formalism (pp. 703H, 705G, J, 710A, D, 711), and in churches the Byzantine-type centralized plan retained much of its popularity (pp. 704A, 722F). Civic design and the adornment of street and public open places made great strides, the pace increasing in the Baroque period (pp. 718, 721, 730A), and many splendid villas were created in the vicinity of the city. The Baroque flourished greatly in Rome. Carlo Maderna was its first successful exponent, and Bernini its most brilliant and versatile figure: among Bernini's several very able contemporaries was the eccentric Borromini, and together they mark the climax of the movement (*c.* 1625–75). Palaces maintained their cliff-like character, and generally were astylar, their planning now extremely adept and incorporating grand axial staircases and dignified ceremonial apartments, often of circular, elliptical or other regular geometrical shapes. Stylar treatment mostly was reserved for church façades, which are richly ornate with reiterated clusters of pilasters and columns, and have great vigour of expression, the fronts often being convex or concave on plan, to afford forceful contrasts of light and shade (pp. 727C, 728A, B). Unity is strongly marked, usually resolved in the entrance portal (p. 697B). Church plans were either centralized and compact, building up to a circular or elliptical dome (p. 728C), or the centralized plan served for the eastern half of a longitudinal scheme. The latter solution, originated with Vignola's Gesù church (1568–84) (p. 704D), became universally popular (p. 743H) and was eventually adopted for S. Peter's (p. 723G). The output of Rome diminished in quality, virility and bulk in the eighteenth century, and about 1750 the true Baroque gave place to a renewed and academic Classicism. As a whole, Roman Renaissance ornament displays great technical skill and fine crafts-manship (pp. 753, 754), and though exceptionally rich and even excessively exuberant in the Baroque period, shows a brilliant unity of all the Arts.

VENICE

The Renaissance style in Venice is distinguished from that of the rest of Europe by features peculiarly Venetian, and it is coloured by the history and unique character of the sea-city, with its own beautiful type of Mediaeval architecture, impressed more by Near-Eastern Byzantine trends than by the normal current of Gothic or by Rome and her Classic traditions. So strongly marked an individuality responded grudgingly to the new movement, and the Early Renaissance was delayed and at first hybrid in character, manifested in buildings which retained intermingled Gothic features, as in the courtyard of the Doge's Palace (p. 733B). The architecture of Venice is, in general, lighter and more graceful than that of Florence. Its special character is in some part due to the fact that its gleaming buildings are built upon a hundred islets on a multitude of wooden and stone piles, the mundane brickwork of their walls often concealed by sparkling marble sheathing; the ubiquitous waterways, spanned by charming bridges (p.757E), carry colourful reflections and throw back the brilliant light to expose every detail in crystal clarity. To such imponderous effects, rustication, though frequently practised, seems far less appropriate than to the massively-founded masonry of Florence. Marble sheathing is typical of the Early Renaissance, used in panels decorated centrally (or intermittently, in the case of friezes and architraves) with coloured marbles in ribboned medallions or jewel-like devices (pp. 733, 734, 739C). A notable Venetian feature is the central grouping of windows, marking deep rooms behind the comparatively flat palace façades which outline the waterways (p. 734). Orders are used freely on exteriors at most times, and are usually confined to the main storeys of palaces, these being crowned by entablatures often containing a deep, windowed frieze (pp. 734C, 740A). Balconies (pp. 734B, D, 757B) are graceful and important features, their projections adding materially to the play of light and shade. Palace plans normally were compact, owing to the cramped and precious sites, while early churches were simple and mostly aisleless, resplendent with marble encrustation within and without (p. 735). The Lombardi family, particularly Pietro, contributed greatly in the early period; Sansovino, with his rich, sculpturesque style (pp. 740, 757H) heralded the High Renaissance and Proto-Baroque period. The latter phase is denoted by the use of large and small Orders together, coupled columns and 'tabernacle' windows (as p. 757D). Sanmichele and the famous Palladio, working mostly in the inland towns of the Venetian State, used rustication more legitimately and effectively (p. 744B, J), and Palladio made great play with the giant Order in his many palaces and villas (p. 742). The Venetian sixteenth-century churches are mostly longitudinal, but with the Byzantine-type centralized arrangement toward the eastern end (p. 743D, H) in a kind of plan now popular everywhere. For church west fronts a giant Order masking the nave was combined with a threaded lesser Order extending to the aisle ends, a treatment not wholly successful (pp. 736A, 743C, G). Venetian orna-ment, whether in doorways, capitals, entablatures, panels or candelabra, is charac-terized by refinement and freedom of line, the sculptured carvings naturally having various maritime allusions.

Baroque architecture was adapted to the strict Venetian conditions, and there

A. The Foundling Hospital (Ospedale degli Innocenti), Florence: loggia (1421–4). See p. 677

B. The Ducal Palace, Urbino (1444–82): cortile. See p. 695

C. Palazzo Piccolomini, Siena (1469–). See p. 684

PAZZI CHAPEL: FLORENCE

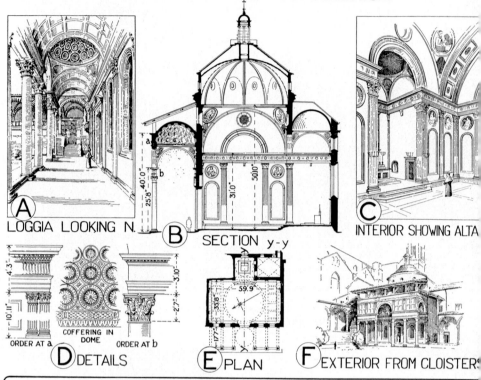

A. LOGGIA LOOKING N.

B. SECTION y-y

C. INTERIOR SHOWING ALTA[R]

ORDER AT a — COFFERING IN DOME — ORDER AT b

D. DETAILS

E. PLAN

F. EXTERIOR FROM CLOISTER[S]

S. LORENZO: FLORENCE

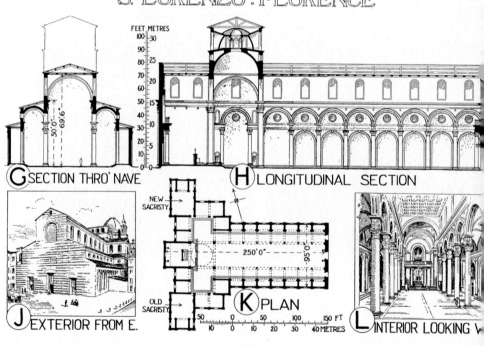

G. SECTION THRO' NAVE

H. LONGITUDINAL SECTION

J. EXTERIOR FROM E.

NEW SACRISTY

OLD SACRISTY

K. PLAN

L. INTERIOR LOOKING W

were few attempts to model frontages in curved plan advances and recessions. S. Maria della Salute (p. 739A), the masterpiece of Longhena, was a rare exception with a free site, and this spectacular church, rising gloriously from her water-steps, crowned by a great dome upheld by scrolled buttresses, is the finest monument of the Venetian Renaissance.

EXAMPLES
FLORENCE
EARLY RENAISSANCE

FILIPPO BRUNELLESCHI (1377–1446), one of the most famous sons of Florence, entered the competition among sculptors in 1401 for the bronze doors of the Baptistery, Florence—this competition marking the introduction of the Renaissance Lorenzo Ghiberti, however, was successful, and the doors were executed between 1403–24. Brunelleschi set out for Rome after the competition, to study Classic architecture at the fountain head. Returning to Florence, his career as an architect began in 1418. Most of his works were completed by others after his death.

The **Foundling Hospital, Florence** (1421–45) (p. 675A), the first of the kind in Europe and one of the first buildings undertaken by Brunelleschi, has a famous arcaded loggia (1421–4) of Corinthian columns supporting broad semicircular arches, with glazed terra-cotta medallions in the spandrils. In many respects the arcade maintains old Florentine traditions, as may be seen by comparing the west front of the Romanesque church of S. Miniato (p. 321A).

The **Dome of Florence Cathedral** (1420–34) (pp. 615A, 616A, B, C, D, F), which was entrusted to Brunelleschi as a result of a competition, is a miracle of design which triumphantly blended a Renaissance dome with a Gothic building and set the crown on that masterpiece of Mediaeval Florence. The dome covers an octagonal apartment, 138 ft 6 ins in diameter, and is raised on a drum, with circular windows to light the interior. This unique dome, pointed in form, consists of inner and outer shells constructed on the Gothic principle, with eight main and sixteen intermediate ribs supporting panels of brickwork with horizontal joints. It is said that it was erected without centering, but this may have been used to a limited extent. An entirely new departure in the history of building is the introduction of a hoop, made up of lengths of timber, secured with iron at the junctions, binding-in the base of the dome (p. 616D—plan C) to prevent its splitting outwards, thus obviating the need for buttresses and making it practicable to raise the dome on a drum. Tie-bars, a Byzantine invention, had long been used in Italian architecture, and indeed appear in the Mediaeval nave of the same building (p. 616G), but this is the first known example of the application of the tensional principle to domes. The other great historical domes, S. Peter's, Rome, and S. Paul's, London, are bound with iron chains (pp. 722C, 911E, 912).

S. **Lorenzo, Florence** (1421–60) (p. 676) is of the basilican type, with nave and aisles separated by Corinthian columns supporting entablature blocks, the earliest instance of such features in the Renaissance. The aisles have simple domes over each compartment, and the side-chapel openings are enframed with continuous mouldings, without imposts at the springing of the arches. At the crossing is a dome with pendentives, carried out by Antonio Manetti, who took over the work after Brunelleschi's death. The sanctuary is flanked by the Old Sacristy (1421–8), the earliest part of Brunelleschi's building, and the famous New Sacristy (1521–34) added by Michelangelo as described on p. 713 and illustrated on p. 716A. The west façade of the church was never built, and remains in rough brick.

S. Spirito, Florence (1445–82) (p. 679), barely begun in Brunelleschi's lifetime, is also of the basilican type, which Italians preferred through the Middle Ages, but has wide transepts making a Latin cross, and there are domical-vaulted aisles round nave, transepts and choir. The nave has arcades forming another early instance of columns supporting pieces of entablature interposed between them and the arches, while a flat timber ceiling covers the nave, and there is a dome over the crossing. The charming campanile (p. 679A) (c. 1506) is by Baccio d'Agnolo.

The **Pazzi Chapel, Florence** (1429–46) (p. 676) is an architectural gem which inspired many later buildings, such as the church of S. Maria delle Carceri, Prato (1485–91), by Giuliano da Sangallo, and is itself a developed version of the San Lorenzo Old Sacristy dispositions. It faces into the cloisters of S. Croce, and has a centralized plan covered in part by short barrel vaults but chiefly by a rib-vaulted dome on pendentives, capped by a lantern. The dome ribs support small barrel vaults diminishing towards the lantern; at their base, the lunettes allow circular windows in an upstanding drum, which, with its tiled conical roof, conceals the dome externally. A smaller pendentived dome covers the altar recess, and there is another of similar size, ornamented with coloured terra-cotta coffering, placed centrally in the stone barrel vault which spans the six-column portico. The stone-panelled front recalls the marble encrustations of the great Mediaeval monuments of the city. Indeed this miniature building may well be described as Byzantine in conception, Gothic in construction and Classical in decorative detail.

The **Palazzo Pitti, Florence** (1458–) (p. 680), designed for Luca Pitti, a friend of Cosimo de' Medici, is the largest palace in Italy except the Vatican. It was, however, erected piecemeal, and commenced only after Brunelleschi's death from his designs. The original design comprised solely the central portion, and this had proceeded up to the top of the second tier (1458–65) in the charge of Luca Fancelli when the palace was left unfinished; until brought to initial completion under Ammanati, who added the great cortile, and gave the present character to the rear façade (1558–70). Extensions to the length, which included the small lateral cortili, were made (1620–40) under G. and A. Parigi, and the outer projecting wings were added (1764–83) by Ruggeri. Minor alterations and internal remodellings followed later. The grand façade, with three-storeyed centre 119 ft high, is 660 ft in length. It is of astylar treatment, bearing in its rugged simplicity a curious resemblance to the bold Claudian Aqueduct, with its massive blocks of masonry and arches of the ground storey (p. 749F). The windows within these arches are by Ammanati, and the lions' heads below the sills are relatively modern (p. 749F). The cortile (p. 680D), facing the Boboli Gardens (p. 712A), is unique in its rusticated treatment of Doric, Ionic, and Corinthian attached columns. The palace became the grand-ducal residence and is partly occupied by the famous picture gallery.

The **Palazzo Quaratesi, Florence** (1462–72) (p. 680E), formerly Pazzi, is believed to have been designed by Brunelleschi but its execution was mainly due to Giuliano da Majano. The Pazzi arms survive on the angle of the façade, which has channelled masonry and characteristic windows, each with a central shaft supporting sub-arches, perpetuating Mediaeval practice (p. 749D). There is an overhanging roof in place of the usual cornice. The cortile is especially fine.

MICHELOZZO MICHELOZZI (1396–1472) was a friend of Cosimo de' Medici, whom he accompanied in exile to Venice. He also at one time visited Milan, where he built the Portinari Chapel (1462–6) in S. Eustorgio, domed like Brunelleschi's Old Sacristy in S. Lorenzo, Florence.

The **Palazzo Riccardi, Florence** (1444–60) (p. 681), is Michelozzi's best known building. It was built as the Medici home, and here Lorenzo the Magnificent kept his brilliant court. The palace was sold in 1659 to the Riccardi family, and in 1680

S. SPIRITO : FLORENCE

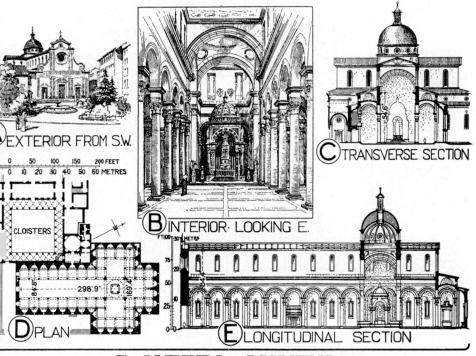

A EXTERIOR FROM S.W.

B INTERIOR · LOOKING · E.

C TRANSVERSE SECTION

D PLAN

CLOISTERS

E LONGITUDINAL SECTION

S. ANDREA : MANTUA

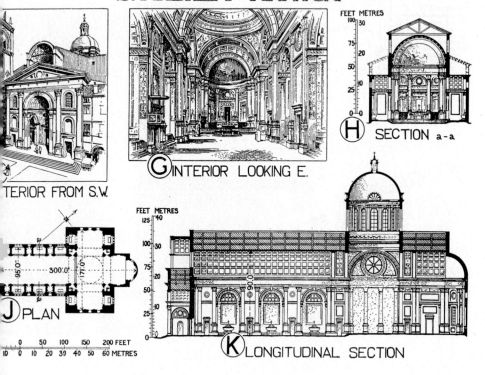

EXTERIOR FROM S.W.

G INTERIOR LOOKING E.

H SECTION a-a

J PLAN

K LONGITUDINAL SECTION

PALAZZO PITTI : FLORENCE

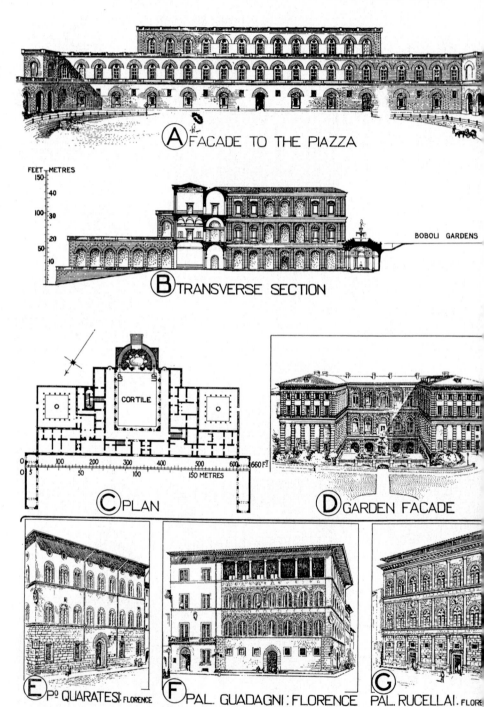

(A) FACADE TO THE PIAZZA

(B) TRANSVERSE SECTION

BOBOLI GARDENS

CORTILE

(C) PLAN

(D) GARDEN FACADE

(E) Pº QUARATESI. FLORENCE

(F) PAL. GUADAGNI : FLORENCE

(G) PAL. RUCELLAI. FLORE

PALAZZO RICCARDI : FLORENCE

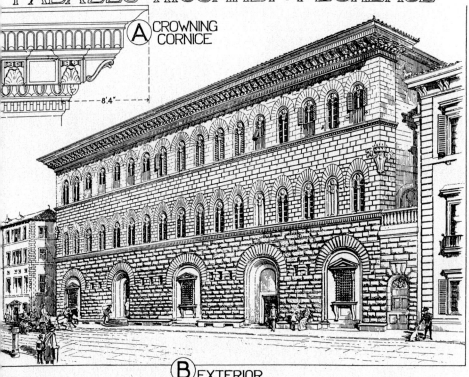

Ⓐ CROWNING CORNICE

8'.4"

Ⓑ EXTERIOR

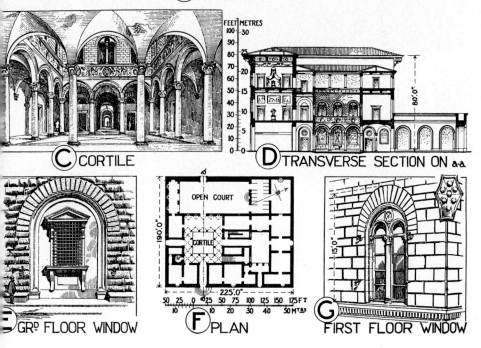

Ⓒ CORTILE

FEET METRES
100 — 30
90
80 — 25
70 — 20
60
50 — 15
40
30 — 10
20 — 5
10
0 — 0

80'.0"

Ⓓ TRANSVERSE SECTION ON a-a

Ⓔ GRᴰ FLOOR WINDOW

190'.0"

OPEN COURT

CORTILE

225'.0"

50 25 0 25 50 75 100 125 150 175 FT
10 0 10 20 30 40 50 MTRS

Ⓕ PLAN

15'.0"

Ⓖ FIRST FLOOR WINDOW

A. S. Francesco, Rimini (1446–50).
See opposite page

B. Palazzo Piccolomini, Pienza (c. 146
See p. 684

c. Ponte S. Trinità, Florence (1567–70). See p. 687

D. S. Maria in Carignano, Genoa
(1552–1603). See p. 688

E. Palazzo di Venezia, Rome (1455–64).
See p. 696

it was extended to the north, adding seven new windows to the original ten of the first floor on the main front. The older portion of the plan (p. 681F) shows a typical arrangement of the period, the rooms arranged around an open cortile (p. 681C), the main apartments being those on the 'piano nobile', approached by an unpretentious but generous staircase, not symmetrically placed. The more intimate of the family rooms were on the second floor. The exterior is an admirable astylar example and shows the effect of graduated rustication. The ground storey has heavily rusticated masonry, with semicircular arches enclosing windows added from the designs of Michelangelo (p. 681E); the intermediate storey has channelled masonry, with bifurcated windows not very different in appearance from the type usual in Florentine Gothic palaces (p. 681G); and the upper storey, in plain ashlar masonry, has similar windows. The whole façade is crowned by a bold cornice, about one-eighth the height of the building and projecting 8 ft 4 ins (p. 681A).

LEON BATTISTA ALBERTI (1404–72) was a student of classical literature, and his book on architecture, De Re Aedificatoria—the first architectural book published with movable type (1485)—helped the revival of the old Roman style. His academic attitude is reflected in the buildings he designed.

The **Palazzo Rucellai, Florence** (1446–51) (p. 680G), ornamented externally with superimposed pilasters, is thus the first 'stylar' building of the Renaissance. The presence of the tiers of pilasters brought the difficulty that the crowning cornice could not be in scale with the whole height of the building as well as with the order immediately below it, a problem which did not arise in 'astylar' palaces. The quality of the detail is refined, and set standards for future buildings of the type. Alberti was the designer, but the work was carried out by Rossellino (see below), an able architect in his own right.

S. Francesco, Rimini (1446–50) (p. 682A), a Gothic church, was remodelled for Sigismondo Malatesta, as a monument to himself and his wife, from the designs of Alberti externally but internally mainly by Agostino di Duccio (1418–81), a Florentine by birth, in charming and varied but somewhat naïve Renaissance details. The entrance façade, which was never completed, bears some resemblance to the Arch of Augustus in the same city; on the flank are arcaded recesses containing sarcophagi of scholars and poets who had figured at the Ducal court.

S. Maria Novella, Florence, a Gothic church (p. 614), has a Renaissance façade (1456–70) (p. 632A) designed by Alberti, and was one of the first churches in which flanking scrolls were used to connect aisles and nave into one composition.

S. Sebastiano, Mantua (1459) has suffered various misfortunes in the course of time and is ill preserved. It was the first church of the Renaissance to be designed on the Greek-cross plan, though chapels like Brunelleschi's Pazzi at Florence had already shown a development towards the Byzantine idea of 'centralized space'.

S. Andrea, Mantua (1472–94) (p. 679F–K), designed by Alberti, was begun only in the year of his death. The grand entrance portico, looking rather like a Roman triumphal arch (p. 679F), leads into an imposing and finely-proportioned barrel-vaulted aisleless nave, flanked by side-chapels between chambered piers which are faced by pairs of Corinthian columns on pedestals. This arrangement of the chapels allows a stronger and more unified building than is possible with the columned basilican plan. Eastwards, the crossing, transepts and apsidal sanctuary reflect the wide and narrow alternations of the nave, and yet give the spaciousness of Byzantine 'centralized space', the whole church establishing a Latin-cross type of plan which was to be followed in very many later churches. The eastern portions, including the transepts and crossing, were built in 1597–1600 and later, and the dome added by Juvarra (p. 695) in 1732–82; but the general conception is due to Alberti.

BERNARDO ROSSELLINO (1409–64), Florentine architect and sculptor, was the creator of the Bruni tomb (1445) in S. Croce, Florence, which established a type for this class of mural monument (p. 754L) .He was even more distinguished as an architect. From 1450 he, with Alberti, was employed for the reconstruction of the old S. Peter's at Rome. His work on the Palazzo Rucellai has been described above.

The **Palazzo Piccolomini, Pienza** (*c.* 1460) (p. 682B) closely follows the design of the Rucellai, having three tiers of regularly-spaced pilasters enframing round-headed windows on its channel-rusticated walls, crowned with a bold cornice. The palace faces the principal square of this tiny hill-town, twenty-four miles south-east of Siena, renamed Pienza after Pope Pius II, who was born here in 1405. Also facing the square are the Cathedral, again by Rossellino, the Palazzo Pubblico and the Episcopio (episcopal palace), attributed to him, all of about the same date.

The **Palazzo Piccolomini, Siena** (1469–) (p. 675C) shows a reversion to astylar design and to round-headed, bifurcated windows similar to those of the Riccardi at Florence, but the heights of the three storeys are less well graded and there is no differentiation of the rusticated stonework, which is channel-jointed throughout. Nevertheless, the palace has a fine, massive quality, the ground storey being especially forceful, and the cornice is quite novel in having a plain frieze below it, this affording an effective liaison with the façade and permitting a less ponderous cornice than would otherwise be necessary: small windows are inserted there.

IL CRONACA (1454–1508), properly Simone Pollaiuolo, had studied ancient architecture in Rome. Architect of the delightful Sacristy of S. Spirito (1489–92), conjointly with Giuliano da San Gallo, he is better known for the works below.

The **Palazzo Strozzi, Florence** (1489–1539) (p. 685), begun by Benedetto da Majano, was continued by Cronaca. It is the representative Florentine palace of the period. The chief features are a large central cortile with arcades on the three storeys, off which are the stairs and surrounding rooms. The astylar tripartite façade (p. 685B, D) is rusticated uniformly in bolster-like units which give the building a somewhat hard and mechanical appearance, and is capped by a grand cornice, projecting over 7 ft and occupying about one-thirteenth of the height of the building, with a plain astragal frieze like that of Rossellino's Palazzo Piccolomini at Siena, though here not containing windows (p. 685F). The main windows (p. 685H), angle-lanterns and link-holders (p. 685A, C) are attractive features of this famous building.

The **Palazzo Guadagni, Florence** (1490–1506) (p. 680F) has the two main storeys faced with 'sgraffito' of black plaster overlaid with white, cut away to show patterns, and an open loggia crowned with a widely-overhanging roof serving as a fourth storey.

ANTONIO FILARETE (1396–1465), a famous Florentine sculptor, was also an architect of note and is best known for his work in Milan, where he was among the first to introduce the Renaissance style, preceding Michelozzi there (p. 678).

The **Ospedale Maggiore, Milan** (1457–*c.* 1624) (p. 698F, G, H), the earliest municipal hospital (p. 608), has façades towards the grand cortili with delicate transitional detail, suitable to the plastic terra-cotta. These are the work of Filarete; but the style reverted to Late Gothic in 1465 under his successor, Solari, and the building was completed about 1624 by Ricchini. It was very badly damaged by bombing in 1943.

GIOVANNI AMADEO (1447–1522), Lombard sculptor and architect, was a notable figure in the early Lombard Renaissance, and took part with other famous masters in the work proceeding in his day at the cathedrals of Milan and Pavia and at the Certosa di Pavia.

The **Certosa di Pavia** (p. 617D, E, F) was begun in 1396 with the monastic portions, and the body of the church probably was not seriously undertaken before *c.* 1453 (p. 604). The church is transitional from the Gothic in its main features, and

PALAZZO STROZZI: FLORENCE

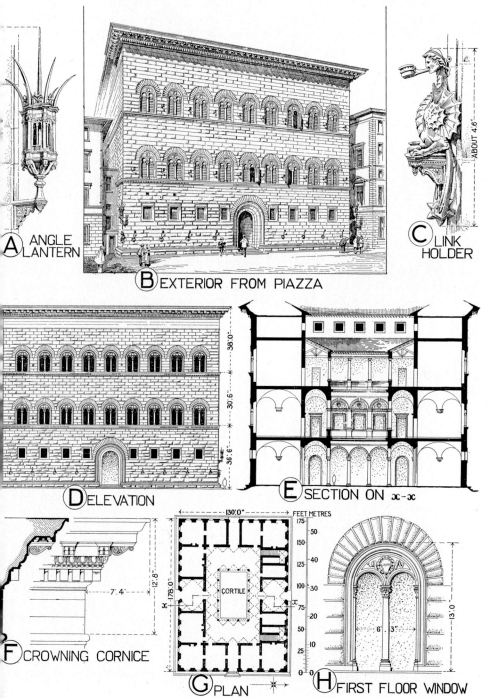

(A) ANGLE LANTERN

(B) EXTERIOR FROM PIAZZA

(C) LINK HOLDER

ABOUT 4'.6"

(D) ELEVATION

38'.0"   30'.6"   36'.6"

(E) SECTION ON x-x

(F) CROWNING CORNICE

12'.8"   7'.4"

(G) PLAN

130'.0"   178'.0"   CORTILE

FEET METRES

(H) FIRST FLOOR WINDOW

13'.0"   6'.3"

A. The Certosa, Pavia, from N.W.
(*c.* 1453–97; façade 1473–*c.* 1540). See pp. 604, 684

B. Palazzo Sauli, Genoa (*c.* 1555). See p. 688

except at the east end, the external expression is almost everywhere round-arched and bears little likeness to the western, pointed style. It is a brick and terra-cotta architecture, characteristically small in scale, and marble is used sparingly at important decorative points, while the crossing has the galleried cupola traditional in the Lombard region; the 'lanterns' at Chiaravalle (p. 629D) and Milan Cathedral (p. 598C) are versions rising to a spire. The church was finished by c. 1497 except for the west façade (p. 686A), constructed wholly in marble between 1473–1540. In this Amadeo contributed both as a sculptor and in the design, having been given charge of the work in 1491, at which time certain of the prepared marbles were ready for assembly in position. Several other sculptors took part. The upper half is simpler, owing to a halt in the progress of the work. The framework of the façade, with its canopied and pinnacled buttresses, still is partly Gothic, but filled in with Renaissance features, such as profusely ornamented windows, arcaded galleries and statues in niches, which, together with carved ornament and medallions, make it one of the most elaborate combinations of architecture and sculpture in Western history.

The **Colleoni Chapel, Bergamo** (1470–6) (p. 689A) is less sculptural externally than the Certosa di Pavia façade, but is extremely richly encrusted with white- and rose-coloured marbles, displayed in surface patterns, and profuse ornament. Lombard canopied pinnacles appear again, along with arcaded open galleries, medallions and many versions of the candelabrum motif. Indeed it is in this building that we find what are probably the earliest instances of the use of the true baluster, here occurring as alternating supports in the continuous arcade below the main cornice. The type came quickly into general use; in Rome, the first example is probably that of the Singing Gallery of the famous Sistine Chapel (c. 1480) (p. 754G). Hitherto, parapets had been made up of miniature columns (p. 750F, pulpit from design by Brunelleschi) or with low-relief or pierced panels (p. 758E, H) based on Byzantine precedents. The baluster thus is a Renaissance invention, derived from the candelabra ornament, and the subsequent development of baluster forms affords clues to the dating of monuments.

HIGH RENAISSANCE AND PROTO-BAROQUE

BARTOLOMEO AMMANATI (1511–92), sculptor and architect, worked in Lucca Montepulciano, Rome and his native Florence. He had considerable ability, and was responsible for a large number of buildings, one of the most important being the Collegio Romano, Rome (1582–4). In Florence or Tuscany in general, there was virtually no High Renaissance interlude following the vigorous early developments, and Ammanati's work shows most strongly that individualism or 'Mannerism' which is a first-found freedom from Classical restraints that presages the Baroque. He was thus a follower of Michelangelo, who, with Raphael, first evidenced in his architecture the new trend. Notable in much of Ammanati's work is the exploitation of rustication, and it is likely that the façades to his extensions of the Palazzo Pitti, referred to earlier (p. 678), influenced the design of the Luxembourg Palace, Paris, built for Marie de' Medici by de Brosse (p. 780).

The **Palazzo Micheletti, Lucca** (c. 1550) (p. 689C) is representative of Ammanati's earlier style, orthodox in most respects but showing Mannerist devices in the lower portion of the façade, especially in the use of rustication; the vertically-tooled cushion-like units are characteristic of his personal style.

The **Ponte S. Trinità, Florence** (1567–70) (p. 682C), by Ammanati, is of brilliant design, profoundly Renaissance in spirit but quite un-Roman in its flat-elliptical arches, panelled spandrels and gay keystones and cartouches. The bridge was blown up in 1944 and rebuilt to the original design in 1957–8.

GALEAZZO ALESSI (1512–72), born in Perugia and trained in Rome, came under the influence of Michelangelo. Nearly all his buildings are in Genoa, where he settled about 1549. Up to that time the Renaissance had had little important effect there. The work of Alessi and the small band of architects that gathered about him is still more strongly inclined towards Mannerist freedom of expression than that of Ammanati, for the local traditions, like those of Lombardy, favoured elaborate ornamentation; and also, as in Rome at this time, hard stucco had been rediscovered as a plastic medium admirable for the architectural adornment of brick-carcassed buildings. In essentials, the ancient Classical principles are reasonably observed, but the lesser features commonly are brilliantly ornate, and superficial decoration sometimes is modelled in extremely high relief, externally as well as indoors. Panelling, strip-rustication, masks, cartouches and scrolled foliations repeatedly occur, and great decorative emphasis often is placed on focal features, such as entrance doorways. Alessi was an architect of great originality and distinction and had a prodigious output of palaces and villas; such as the **Palazzo Sauli** (*c.* 1555) (p. 686B), of which little remains. Mostly of brick faced with stucco, they are famous for their entrance vestibules, courtyards, and flights of steps, and the sloping sites were utilized to form beautiful vistas of terraces and hanging gardens. The façades frequently have rusticated basements surmounted by pilasters and a bold crowning cornice over attic windows between supporting consoles.

S. Maria in Carignano, Genoa (1552, completed 1603) (p. 682D) resembles Bramante's church of SS. Celso and Guiliano, Rome (destroyed) and his more elaborate scheme for S. Peter's, maintained in essentials by Peruzzi (p. 722F), in being of Greek-cross type filled out with angle bays so as to form a square plan, with no significant projection except at the sanctuary apse. The arms of this large church are barrel-vaulted and the crossing domed. Tall, staged campanili rise on the wings of the entrance front, and the central doorway, with its columned enframement following a recessed curve and the rich ornamentation above, is clearly Proto-Baroque.

The **Palazzo Marino, Milan** (1558–60) (p. 724D) is a sumptuous example of Alessi's style, in which the influence of plastic stucco ornamentation is plainly demonstrated. The lavish enrichments include garlands, cartouches, masks, enframed sculptured panels, niches with statues, scroll-ended 'broken' pediments and downward-tapering pilasters, either with double Ionic capitals or these replaced with human-headed grotesque figures. Especially noteworthy are the graceful arcades, one of the first instances of the arrangement, with wide-spaced paired columns carrying the arches, in place of the single columns usual in early Florentine arcades.

ROCCO LURAGO (d. 1590), a Lombard working in Genoa, was one of the more important and talented of the contemporaries of Alessi. In his palace designs he showed great appreciation of the potentialities of falling sites.

The **Palazzo Municipale, Genoa** (1564) (p. 690) has a magnificent plan (p. 690C) on axial lines, with central entrance leading to a large vestibule and cortile, beyond which stairs lead to the 'piano nobile' and terraced gardens. The cortile (p. 690C, D) established a type followed by many others in this city of opulent palaces. The façade (p. 690A), a dignified composition about 200 ft long by 80 ft high, has Tuscan and Doric pilasters, each framing two storeys of windows, the lower Order being flanked by arcaded loggias giving breadth to the design.

BAROQUE

BARTOLOMMEO BIANCO (*c.* 1589–1657) made important contributions to the magnificent series of Genoese palaces. He followed Alessi's lead at some distance of time, and he is accounted Genoa's best Baroque architect. His palace work is

A. The Colleoni Chapel, Bergamo
(1470–6). See p. 687

B. S. Maria dei Miracoli, Brescia
(1488–, 1522–). See p. 732

C. Palazzo Micheletti. Lucca,
(c. 1550–). See p. 687

D. Palazzo Durazzo-Pallavicini, Genoa
(1619–). See p. 691

PALAZZO MUNICIPIO : GENOA

Ⓐ ENTRANCE FACADE

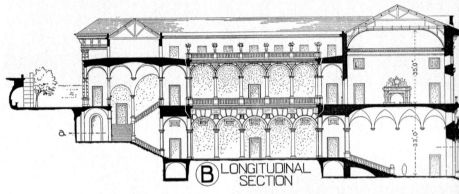

Ⓑ LONGITUDINAL SECTION

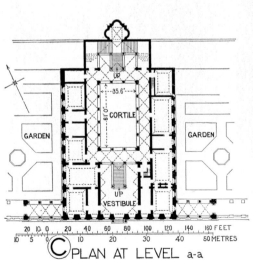

Ⓒ PLAN AT LEVEL a-a

Ⓓ CORTILE & GRAND STAIRCASE

much more pure and gracious than that of his predecessors, and freed of excessive sculptural ornamentation.

The **Palazzo Durazzo-Pallavicini, Genoa** (1619–) (p. 689D) follows the scheme used by Lurago for the Palazzo Municipio, the front being arranged in two double-tiered stages rising to a massive cornice over the centre block, with flanking shallow wings finishing in open loggias, though this time the loggias are on the level of the upper stage rather than on the lower. Comparatively, the treatment is grand and austere, though it is possible that the front was intended to be painted or frescoed in accordance with old local traditions.

The **Palazzo dell' Università, Genoa** (1634–6) (p. 692B, D), built as a Jesuit college and created a university in 1812, is Bianco's finest building. It improves upon the plan principle inaugurated by Lurago in the Palazzo Municipio; the cortile again is utilized in the stately stair approach to the 'piano nobile', but now the stairway beyond the cortile is duplicated to lead also to terraces above the arcades, while the lower tier of the latter is continued towards the street to form an airy enframement to the lofty vestibule (p. 692B). The light and gracious arcades stand upon columns more closely paired than in Alessi's Sauli and Marino palaces, surpassing in their airy simplicity those of the court of the Palazzo Borghese, Rome (1590–) (p. 724F), which otherwise they closely resemble.

The **Porta Pila, Genoa** (1633) (p. 693C), attributed to Bianco, a gateway now re-erected away from its original position, has the full power and vigour of the true Baroque, though its qualities are the less easy to appreciate in the lack of the contrasting plain walls within which it formerly stood. The massive entablature and heavily rusticated columns have precedents in gateways built for the defensive walls of Verona by Sanmichele more than a hundred years earlier; their impressive scale is emphasized by the relative delicacy of the shrine which stands aloft.

GIOVANNI BATTISTA ALEOTTI (1546–1636) is best known for his **Teatro Farnese, Parma** (1618–28) (p. 693D, F)—largely destroyed in the Second World War—showing an advance on the theatre at Vicenza (p. 693B) by Palladio and Scamozzi in having an elaborately-enframed proscenium spaced apart from a deep U-shaped auditorium by archways on each side. The superposed arcades surrounding the auditorium resemble those around Palladio's Basilica at Vicenza (p. 741). Both this theatre and that at Vicenza are fitted within rooms independently roofed.

FRANCESCO RICCHINI (1583–1658), studied in Rome and returned in 1603 to Milan, where such of his important Baroque work as has survived is to be found.

S. Giuseppe, Milan (1607–30) (p. 697A), the earliest Baroque building in the city, has a simple octagonal plan, 50 ft across, covered by a pendentived dome. The façade is skilfully integrated with the staged octagonal cupola, and the whole makes a strongly unified composition comparable with Carlo Maderna's S. Susanna, the earliest Baroque church in Rome (p. 697B).

GUARINO GUARINI (1624–83), an extraordinary genius whose remarkable buildings show some influence of Borromini (p. 726), was born in Modena and became a Theatine monk. He was at various times in Messina, Paris and elsewhere, and a church from his designs was erected in Lisbon (Portugal); from 1666 he worked mainly in Turin. The vaulting of his centralized churches there, such as **S. Lorenzo** (1668–) and the **S. Sindone Chapel** of the Cathedral (1667–90) (p. 693E) is an astonishing and unique complication of interlaced or imbricated ribs, usually carrying vertical windows instead of solid webs, the whole fabric rising externally in a series of stages perpetuating the cupola form of covering to the crossing which so long had been a tradition in Lombardy and Piedmont. Schematically, his church planning is based upon overlapping circles or ovals, usually of

A. Tempietto in S. Pietro in
Montorio, Rome: detail (1502–10).
See p. 701

B. Palazzo dell' Università, Genoa (1634–6):
vestibule. See p. 691

C. Hemicycle, Giardino della
Pigna, Vatican, Rome
(c. 1503–13). See p. 701

D. Palazzo dell' Università, Genoa: cortile (1634–6)
See p. 691

E. SS. Annunziata, Genoa (church,
1587; portico, c. 1800). See p. 695

F. Casa Pollini, Siena, (c. 1527). See p. 702

A. Villa d'Este, Tivoli
(16th cent.). Water organ.
See p. 713

B. Teatro Olimpico, Vicenza: interior (1580–4).
Scenery at back of stage. See p. 738

The Porta Pila, Genoa
(1633). See p. 691

D. Teatro Farnese, Parma: auditorium (1618–28).
See p. 691

E. S. Sindone Chapel, Turin:
dome (1667–90). See p. 691

F. Teatro Farnese, Parma: proscenium (1618–28).
See p. 691

A. The Superga, Turin (1717–31). See opposite page

B. Palazzo Carignano, Turin (1679). See opposite page

minor curvilinear shapes intruding into larger ones, and from these there proceeds in the internal structure a spatial illusion of interrelated volumes; while externally, walls follow sinuous or undulating lines, ornamented superficially with thin and scratchy architectural detail or locally by clustered pilasters and detached columns. His buildings, in particular the longitudinal churches, had a considerable influence on Late Baroque architecture in Southern Germany (p. 808).

The **Palazzo Carignano, Turin** (1679) (p. 694B), is the best known of Guarini's domestic buildings. The undulating central part, masking paired grand staircases alongside a spacious oval hall, relieves this majestic mass from any danger of monotony that might arise from the regular fenestration, much more effectively than could be contrived by any other means. The façades are almost wholly in brick and terra-cotta.

FILIPPO JUVARRA (1678–1736) is another outstanding personality in Piedmontese Baroque architecture, which flourished in the hundred years from about 1660, when initiative in Rome had begun to decline. A brilliant and prolific designer, Juvarra achieved great fame. Born in Messina, he studied in Rome under Carlo Fontana (p. 726), and thereafter was in demand in several countries abroad, working chiefly in and around Turin after 1714. There, he built many major structures; royal palaces, town residences and churches.

The **Superga, Turin** (1717–31) (p. 694A), a church and convent, is Juvarra's masterpiece. It stands on a hill overlooking the city; the domed church, with its columned portico and flanking campanile, precedes the monastic establishment of which the modest, window-studded façades lend emphasis to the majestic climax in the frontispiece. This building is as simple, forceful and straightforward as the work of Guarini is complex, and is one of the greatest monuments of the whole Renaissance.

SS. Annunziata, Genoa (p. 692E) has a fine portico (c. 1800) by Carlo Barabini (1768–1835), added to Giacomo della Porta's incomplete brick-faced façade (1587), which brings into contrast the strict Classical proprieties of the Antiquarian Phase and the free individualism of the Proto-Baroque.

ROME

EARLY RENAISSANCE

LUCIANO LAURANA (c. 1420/5–1480). Before the Renaissance reached Rome importantly, it had spread to the more northerly of the Papal States, and some charming, delicate work had been done at the Ducal Palaces of Urbino and Gubbio. With the first of these at least, the name of Laurana is associated. He came from Dalmatia, was perhaps trained in Venice, and worked mainly at Urbino, where Bramante was one of his pupils, for both Bramante and Raphael were born in that neighbourhood.

The **Ducal Palace, Urbino** (c. 1444–82), built for Federigo Montefeltro, is transitional in certain respects, but after Laurana took charge c. 1465 it took on Early Renaissance character. It is celebrated for the beauty and charm of its apartments, with their doorways, simple plaster vaults, marble-hooded chimneypieces and gracious windows. The cortile (p. 675B) shows Classic principles to have been well imbibed; the arcades stand on single columns like so many at Florence, though the arrangements for turning the angles on clustered piers are individual. The pilastered upper tier contains wooden, two-light transomed windows, with simple architrave surrounds and cap-moulds. The **Ducal Palace, Gubbio** (1474–80), also built for Federigo Montefeltro, is so similar in all respects that it safely may be ascribed to the same architect.

MEO DEL CAPRINO (1430–1501) was one of several Florentines who first brought the Renaissance to Rome, working there between 1462–89.

The **Palazzo di Venezia, Rome** (*c.* 1455–64) (p. 682E), built with stones from the Colosseum, was not designed by Caprino—it has been conjectured that Alberti was the designer—but he took part in the supervision of its erection, along with Francesco di Borgo di San Sepolcro. It is a transitional building, as the machicolations show, the Renaissance elements appearing mainly in the windows, those with transomes being distinctively Roman, and in the fine entrance doorway. There are several other Early Renaissance palaces or houses in Rome, and a few churches.

DONATO BRAMANTE (1444–1514) was Rome's first outstanding architect of the Renaissance, but he did not work there until 1499, and by then he had undertaken a number of important commissions in the Milan area. He was born near Urbino, and began as a painter. From 1467–72 he worked under Laurana at Urbino, settling in Milan *c.* 1477, practising still as a painter for a while. He was destined to have great influence on the development of Renaissance architecture, not in Italy only but also in Europe. It was he who made the first designs for the new S. Peter's at Rome, and inaugurated the rebuilding of the Vatican.

S. Satiro, Milan (1482–94) (p. 697C, D) was built alongside the old ninth-century small church—with campanile—of that name, which is now approached from the north transept of Bramante's church. The latter has aisled barrel-vaulted and coffered transepts and nave, but owing to the proximity of the street there was no room for a sanctuary arm, so Bramante rendered this in extremely shallow, modelled perspective, an art which was very much engrossing painters and architects at that time. The lunettes at the ends of the transept arms have each five 'wheel' windows forming a half circle around another semicircular shape, placed centrally; this was a favourite device with Bramante. The arcades are of the so-called 'Roman Order', here expressed as arches between pilasters. Above the crossing is a coffered dome carried on a deep entablature above pendentives, the exterior being concealed by a drum with conical tiled roof and a lantern, like Brunelleschi's Pazzi Chapel at Florence. Off the nave is a splendid octagonal sacristy (1488) (p. 697D), one of the most original of Bramante's designs.

S. Maria delle Grazie, Milan, is a fifteenth-century abbey-church to which in 1492–7 Bramante added the choir, transepts and crossing (p. 698). The crossing gives a Byzantine spaciousness, for it is a square the full width of the old church, covered by a dome, 65 ft across, concealed externally by a sixteen-sided galleried cupola, with sloping roof and lantern, all in the tradition of this northern region. Light is cleverly admitted through circular windows in the dome and from a range of windows in the shallow drum on which it stands, while the lunettes of the crossing have circular decorative panels in lieu of the wheel windows used in S. Satiro in this position. The choir arm is covered by a 'cloister' vault (square dome) penetrated by minor vaults which allow light from circular windows at the east end, over an apsidal termination. Two other apses serve in lieu of transepts. The exterior all is in brick and terra-cotta, except the column shafts in the cupola, which are of marble. The panelled pilasters, candelabra, medallion and wheel ornaments are normal to Lombard practice of the day. Other works by Bramante in this area are the Canonry of S. Ambrogio, Milan (1492), recently restored after war damage; the west façade to the abbey-church at Abbiategrasso (1497); and additions to the Castle of Vigevano (*c.* 1494).

HIGH RENAISSANCE AND PROTO-BAROQUE

The **Palazzo della Cancelleria, Rome** (1486–98) (p. 699) has for long been considered a work of Bramante, and indeed in certain respects it recalls his Milanese

A. S. Giuseppe, Milan: façade (1607–30).
See p. 691

B. S. Susanna, Rome: façade (1597–1603).
See p. 725

Old Church (restored externally in 1478) and
old campanile in foreground

D. Sacristy: interior (1488)

S. Satiro, Milan (1482–94). See opposite page

S. MARIA DELLE GRAZIE: MILAN

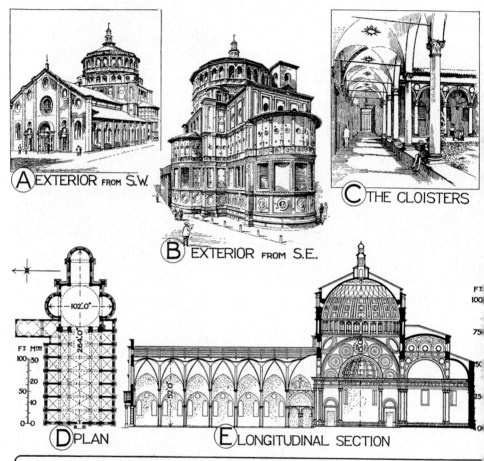

A EXTERIOR FROM S.W.

B EXTERIOR FROM S.E.

C THE CLOISTERS

D PLAN

E LONGITUDINAL SECTION

THE OSPEDALE MAGGIORE: MILAN

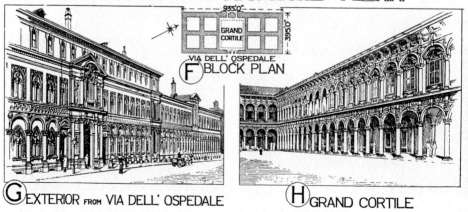

F BLOCK PLAN

G EXTERIOR FROM VIA DELL' OSPEDALE

H GRAND CORTILE

PAL. DELLA CANCELLERIA : ROME

Ⓐ FACADE TO THE PIAZZA

Ⓑ THE CORTILE FROM UPPER STOREY

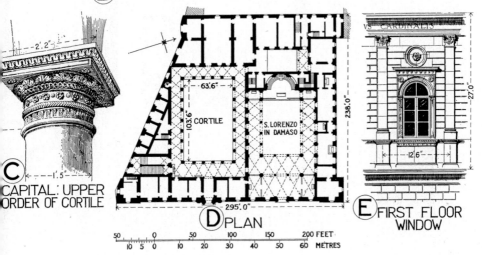

Ⓒ CAPITAL: UPPER ORDER OF CORTILE

Ⓓ PLAN

Ⓔ FIRST FLOOR WINDOW

TEMPIETTO ᴵᴺ CLOISTER: S. PIETRO IN MONTORIO ROME

A PLAN

5 . 0 5 10 15 20 25 FT
1 0 1 2 3 4 5 6 7 METS

B EXTERIOR FROM CLOISTER .

C SECTION ON LINE y-ẏ

S. ANDREA : ROME

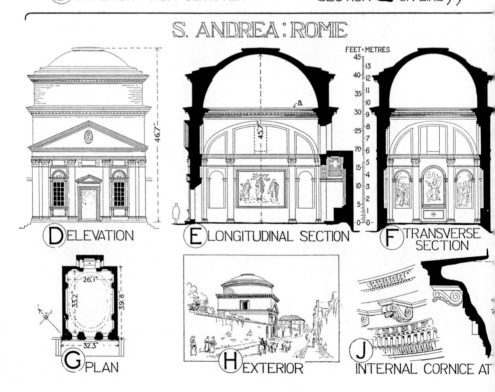

FEET·METRES

D ELEVATION

E LONGITUDINAL SECTION

F TRANSVERSE SECTION

G PLAN

H EXTERIOR

J INTERNAL CORNICE AT

style, but it was substantially complete before his arrival in Rome and the architect is unknown. Still slightly immature, it is the first really important Renaissance building in Rome, and was a rebuilt residence for Cardinal Riario, incorporating S. Lorenzo in Damaso, an ancient basilica which previously had been on another site (p. 699D). The façades are of travertine stone robbed from the Colosseum; they rise in three main tiers, the lowest in channelled masonry and the two upper each ornamented with plain Corinthian pilasters arranged in alternating spacings instead of the regular spacings of earlier stylar palaces. The intermediate full entablature is subdued, while that at the top has vertical modillions across the frieze, giving it all the vigour of the crowning cornice of the Colosseum. The shallow pilasters stand upon simulated pedestals, the corresponding 'blind' parapets serving as aprons to the main windows, which latter have arched openings on the first floor, fitted within square, corniced heads (p. 699E). The main doorway is an addition by Domenico Fontana (1589). The wings of the principal façades are advanced slightly, and round the corner to the left of the entrance front (p. 699A) is a first floor balcony with extremely delicate decoration (p. 753C). The imposing cortile, 103 ft 6 ins by 63 ft 6 ins, is surrounded by two stories of arcades (p. 699B) of Doric columns (p. 699C) carrying a third, solid, storey ornamented with pilasters spanning two tiers of small windows in height and carrying a bold cornice similar to that used on the fronts.

S. Maria della Pace, Rome has a beautiful cloister (1500–4) (p. 753E) surrounded by a two-storeyed arcade designed by Bramante, in which, as in examples by him in the Milan area, the upper storey has twice as many openings as the lower. The church itself was reconstructed by Pietro da Cortona in 1656–7, to whom is due the skilfully designed plan and semicircular portico (p. 729).

The Tempietto at S. Pietro in Montorio, Rome (1502–10) (pp. 692A, 700), erected to mark the spot where S. Peter was martyred, is a perfect architectural gem by Bramante, in full High Renaissance style, resembling in design a small Roman circular temple. It is only 15 ft in diameter internally and is surrounded by a Doric peristyle, behind which rises the drum, pierced with windows alternating with shell-headed niches and carrying a dome. The crypt was superficially redesigned internally in 1628.

Cortili of S. Damaso and Belvedere, Vatican (pp. 720A, 721A, B). The home of the Popes contains the Court of S. Damaso, of which the lower arcades are by Bramante (p. 721A), and the much larger Belvedere Court which also he undertook for Julius II (1503–13). The latter court (pp. 720A, 721), extremely long and narrow, was later subdivided into two by other buildings on the line of a series of terraces, which had formed part of Bramante's scheme, and the one half, called the Giardino della Pigna (Garden of the Pine Cone), contains at its northern end a great, three-storeyed, half-domed hemicycle, with a terrace and pavilions over (p. 692C). The buildings flanking this feature are two-storeyed and ornamented with pilasters in alternating spacings; on the lower storey the wider spacings contain arches, and thus give an effect of a series of 'triumphal arch' motifs.

BALDASSARE PERUZZI (1481–1536) designed many buildings in Rome and his work shows great versatility and skill as well as a refinement often approaching the Greek. Born in Siena, he settled in Rome in 1503, studying ancient architecture and travelling extensively in Italy. A design by him in 1523 for the west front of S. Petronio, Bologna (p. 607), was not carried out.

The Villa Farnesina, Rome (1509–11) (p. 710H), built for Agostino Chigi, a Sienese banker, has two stories of superimposed Orders and a central arcaded loggia between projecting wings on the rear side, and is famous for frescoes by Peruzzi, Raphael and others. The topmost storey has a deep ornamental frieze, in which windows are inserted, an idea originated by Rossellino in his astylar Palazzo

Piccolomini at Siena (p. 684) and afterwards adopted by Sansovino in the Library of S. Mark, Venice (p. 740A).

The **Palazzo Pietro Massimi, Rome** (1532–6) (p. 703), refined both in design and detail, is especially interesting for the clever treatment of a convex façade to follow the line of the street. The plan (p. 703H) shows remarkable skill in arranging two separate palaces on an irregular site. The entrance to the right-hand palace is a recessed vestibule (p. 703C) which leads into a cortile (p. 703G) with portico (p. 703J) and steps to an upper loggia (p. 703F), whence the grand salon (p. 703E) is reached. The façade (p. 703B) relies for effect on the Doric Order of columns and pilasters stretching from end to end of the ground storey, contrasted with the severe astylar treatment of the upper storeys, with architrave-enframed windows, unadorned balconies and a vigorous crowning cornice. In several particulars the Massimi shows 'Mannerist' departures from strict Classical precedent, as do several other of the buildings of Peruzzi's later life. The chaste **Casa Pollini, Siena** (*c.* 1527) (p. 692F), and the **Palazzo Albergati, Bologna** (1519–40), the latter only partially completed in his lifetime, are other well-known buildings attributed to him.

S. Maria della Consolazione, Todi (1508–1604) (p. 704), designed by Cola da Caprarola, with Peruzzi as adviser, was a long time in building. It is another of the churches based on the popular Greek-cross plan, here with apses forming the four arms (p. 704A) of a square crossing 50 ft in diameter. The exterior (p. 704B) has superimposed pilasters, surmounted by a low attic, above which semi-domes abut the dome on its high, windowed drum, the whole rising to a height of 180 ft. The interior (p. 704C) has a similar pilaster treatment, and the line of these is carried up in dome ribs. Giant pilasters mark the angles of the crossing, and carry arches between which span the dome pendentives.

The **Madonna di S. Biagio, Monthepulciano** (1518–29) (p. 706A), built by Antonio da Sangallo the Elder (1455–1534), is another splendid Greek-cross church of confident High Renaissance design, here with four rectangular arms, that at the east end being extended to form an apse. Twin, free-standing campanili towers were intended to flank the west front, but only one was fully completed. The arms are barrel-vaulted, and the dome over the crossing is sustained on a high, windowed drum over pendentives. The one completed campanile has superimposed Doric, Ionic and Corinthian Orders paired at the angles of the square-planned tower, the inner shafts being in the round, and above them is a squat, staged octagonal spire. Also at Montepulciano is the **Palazzo Contucci**, begun by Sangallo and finished by Peruzzi about 1535 in thorough-paced Mannerist style.

ANTONIO DA SANGALLO the Younger (1485–1546) worked in Rome most of his life, and for a time after 1506 was an assistant of Bramante.

The **Palazzo Farnese, Rome** (1530–) (p. 705), the grandest palace of this period, was designed by Sangallo. The plan (p. 705G) is rectangular and symmetrically arranged on axial lines with main entrance, vestibule (p. 705H) and side colonnades. The cortile, 81 ft square, is surrounded by arcades off which are the apartments and a fine staircase, not itself symmetrically aligned, leading to the 'piano nobile'. The ground floor loggia in the centre of the rear façade opens on to the garden. The façade to the piazza (p. 705B) is an imposing astylar composition without any break, 185 ft long by 96 ft 6 ins high, of three storeys of nearly equal height, of brick covered with stucco and stone dressings of travertine from the Colosseum. The ground storey has a fine central entrance (p. 705C), flanked by windows; the first floor has pedimented windows (p. 753A), alternately triangular and segmental, carried by a full Order, a regular and characteristic practice at this period. The top storey, added by Michelangelo (1546–), has windows definitely of Proto-Baroque design (p. 753B), with columns on brackets, surmounted by triangular pediments,

PALAZZO PIETRO MASSIMI : ROME

Ⓐ ENTRANCE CORRIDOR

Ⓑ EXTERIOR FROM CORSO V. EMANUELE

Ⓒ VESTIBULE

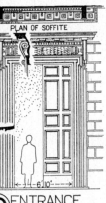

PLAN OF SOFFITE

6' 10"

Ⓓ ENTRANCE DOORWAY

Ⓔ INTERIOR OF GRAND SALON PIANO NOBILE

Ⓕ UPPER LOGGIA

Ⓖ CORTILE

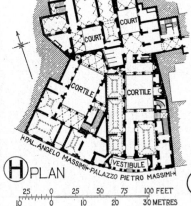

COURT COURT
CORTILE CORTILE
K PAL. ANGELO MASSIMI · PALAZZO PIETRO MASSIMI
VESTIBULE

Ⓗ PLAN

25   0   25   50   75   100 FEET
10   0   10   20   30 METRES

Ⓙ PORTICO TO CORTILE

S. MARIA·DELLA CONSOLAZIONE·: TODI

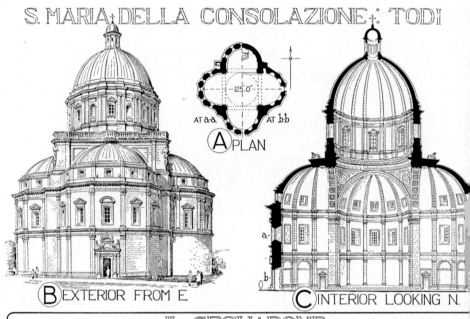

(A) PLAN

(B) EXTERIOR FROM E.

(C) INTERIOR LOOKING N.

IL GESU : ROME

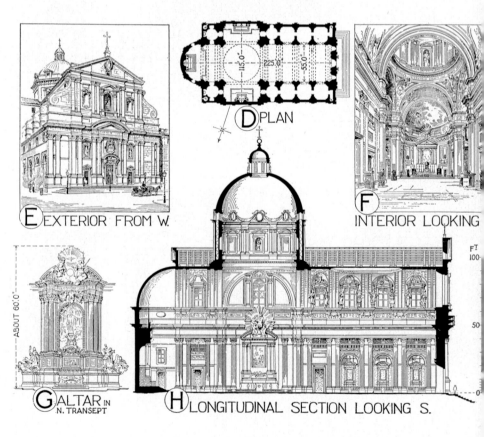

(D) PLAN

(E) EXTERIOR FROM W.

(F) INTERIOR LOOKING

(G) ALTAR IN N. TRANSEPT

(H) LONGITUDINAL SECTION LOOKING S.

PALAZZO FARNESE : ROME

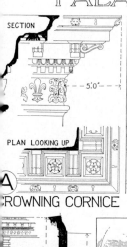

SECTION

5'.0"

PLAN LOOKING UP

30.8

28.8

(A) CROWNING CORNICE

(B) FACADE TO PIAZZA

(C) ENTRANCE

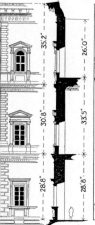

35.2

26.0"

30.8

33.5

28.8

28.8

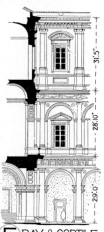

31.5

28.10

29.0

(D) BAY OF FACADE

(E) THE CORTILE FROM ARCADE

(F) BAY OF CORTILE

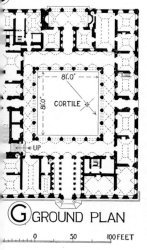

81'.0"

81'.0"

CORTILE

UP

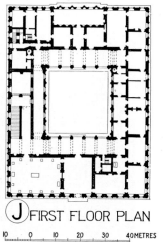

(G) GROUND PLAN

0   50   100 FEET

(H) ENTRANCE VESTIBULE

(J) FIRST FLOOR PLAN

10   0   10   20   30   40 METRES

Z

H.O.A.

A. Madonna di S. Biagio, Montepulciano (1518–29). See p. 702

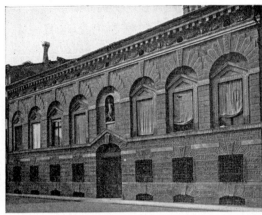

B. Giulio Romano's house, Mantua (c. 1544).
See p. 708

C. Garden Pavilion, Caprarola
(c. 1549). See p. 713

D. Palazzo Odescalchi, Rome (1664–).
See p. 726

E. Villa Medici, Rome (1574–80).
See p. 713

F. Palazzo del Laterano, Rome:
cortile (1586). See p. 725

the window arch encroaching on the entablature. The great crowning cornice (p. 705A) is allied to the wall by an ornamental frieze, which allows it to be lighter than that of the Strozzi at Florence (p. 685F)—here about one-eighteenth of the height of the façade, or one-eleventh if the frieze is included. The façade was taken by Sir Charles Barry as the model for the Reform Club, London (p. 1019). In the cortile the storeys are marked by superimposed attached Orders, arcaded in the two lower tiers, while in the upper the overlying pilasters and the window enframements again evidence Michelangelo's Proto-Baroque style.

RAPHAEL SANTI (1483–1520) of Urbino, one of the world's greatest painters and an architect of distinction, was active in Urbino, Perugia and Florence before being invited by Julius II to Rome in 1508, where his reputation as a painter had preceded him. Pope Leo X in turn employed him extensively, and it was he who called Raphael to advise as to the design of S. Peter's (p. 717) though Raphael does not appear to have taken any actual part in carrying it out. The exploration of such half-buried ruins as the Baths of Titus, Nero's Golden House and the other mouldering ancient buildings gave artists the opportunity of studying Roman mural decorations and frescoes, in which flowers and foliage, men and monsters, birds, vessels and trophies were all blended together in delicate colour schemes, and on these Raphael based his decoration of the world-famous Vatican Loggie. As Cellini tells in his fascinating *Memoirs*, the term 'grotesque' was coined to describe the Roman arabesques through their 'being found in certain subterranean caverns in Rome by students of antiquity; which caverns were formerly chambers, hot-baths, cabinets for study, halls and apartments of like nature', buried in the processes of time. Other architect-decorators were similarly inspired by these ancient mural decorations, and modelled stucco was enthusiastically exploited for the next few decades, sometimes to extravagant extremes (p. 715B), invading architecture externally as well as indoors.

The **Villa Madama, Rome** (1516–) (p. 710J), designed by Raphael and continued after his death by his assistant, Guilio Romano, was never completed, but the part executed became the model for nearly all the formal gardens of Italy. The charming loggia, which is virtually all now to be seen of the ambitious residence or 'casino' intended, was brilliantly decorated with stuccoes and frescoes by Romano and Giovanni da Udine.

The **Palazzo Pandolfini, Florence** (c. 1520–7) (p. 756), one of Raphael's most famous designs, was carried out jointly by two local architects. It inspired the design of the Traveller's Club, London (p. 987). The stuccoed walls are set off with angle rustications, while the windows are the High Renaissance 'tabernacle' type, with flanking pilasters or attached columns carrying entablatures with alternating triangular and segmental pediments. The effective cornice, above an astragal frieze, is of wood. A low, one-storey wing gives asymmetry to the composition, and the portal giving access to the garden approach has the extremely deep voussoirs to the arched head favoured by Raphael in other palace designs.

GIULIO ROMANO (1492–1546), a pupil of Raphael, approached architecture through painting, and acquired great skill in combining stucco decoration with frescoes in panels, an art learnt from Roman remains. He assisted Raphael at the Villa Madama and at the Loggie and Stanze of the Vatican. In 1524 he left Rome for Mantua, where he was employed as painter, decorator, garden-designer and architect. At Mantua he had as a pupil Francesco Primaticcio (1504–70), who in 1532 joined Il Rosso in Fontainebleau, and thus spread the stuccoist art to France (pp. 762, 774).

The **Palazzo del Tè, Mantua** (1525–35) (p. 709A), a one-storey summer pleasure house for Duke Federico Gonzaga II, has a grim exterior for this class of building, but originally was only the chief feature in vast grounds, including sub-sidiary buildings, groves and avenues, mazes, fishponds and delightful formal gardens, furnished with pavilions, terraces, statues, fountains and pools. Primarily a decorator, Romano regularly shows himself impatient of Classical rules; here evidenced by the structurally-illogical distribution of the Doric pilasters on the façades, and the casual omission of triglyphs from the frieze to provide small windows. The palace is quadrangular on plan, with grand saloons and an arcaded garden vestibule around a central garden court, the rooms having splendid paintings and ornament by Romano and his pupils.

Giulio Romano's house, Mantua (*c.* 1544) (p. 706B) is among his latest and most accomplished architectural works, with rustications on two floors, pedimented, marble-enframed upper windows and marble and terra-cotta decorations. De-partures from Classical principles are again notable; in the stressed and rusticated voussoired arches duplicating the window-enframements, the elliptical-arched doorway and its rusticated pediment breaking through the string-moulding line, and the location of the ornaments within the arches. A niched statue of Mercury crowns the entrance doorway.

The **Villa Lante, Bagnaia,** near Viterbo, has one of the most delightfully inti-mate formal gardens of the Renaissance, laid out on axial principles on a gently sloping site, from designs by Romano and Vignola but only completed about 1580. With its terraces, fountains and other delectable features (p. 709B, C) it is an ex-ample of the many beautiful villas of the period, particularly abundant in the hills around Rome.

GIACOMO BAROZZI DA VIGNOLA (1507–73), born in Bologna, worked princi-pally there and in and around Rome, apart from two years in the service of Francis I of France (1541–3). Author of *The Five Orders of Architecture* (published 1562), he was destined to have great influence upon the course of the Renaissance and especially in France, where his precepts were followed in preference to those of Palladio, favoured in England. He was more academic in his writings than in his architecture, which shows great versatility, elegance and originality of design.

The **Villa of Pope Julius III, Rome** (1550–5) (p. 710), as it now survives is the nucleus of what formerly was a much more extensive scheme. Even so, it is an architectural gem. Other famous architects had a hand in it, including Michelangelo and Vasari, but essentially it is by Vignola and is his best-known work. Nowadays, it serves as the Etruscan Museum. The plan (p. 710A) shows a straight front with entrance leading to the semicircular portico; grand cortile with formal garden; sunken court embraced by summer rooms, approached by sweeping flights of steps and having a central fountain grotto with caryatid figures, rippling water and tiny cascades; and a further flower garden beyond. The whole forms a delightful piece of garden architecture. The façade (p. 710B) is a most pleasing composition and in-fluenced later buildings. It has rusticated ground-floor windows (p. 710E) and crested first-floor windows (p. 710G) which together with the central feature show some Proto-Baroque departures from Classical precedent. The semicircular façade to the grand cortile (p. 710F) instances a clever and attractive interweaving of large-scale and small-scale Orders of architecture.

The **Palazzo Farnese, Caprarola** (1547–9) (p. 711), a semi-fortress of pentagonal form situated on a mountain spur, is one of the most magnificent of all Renaissance buildings, and incorporates many brilliant features which have inspired later de-signs. The plan (p. 711D) is a great pentagon, each side being 150 ft long. Paired steps and staircases of varied patterns, interspersed with terraces and axial pavilions and grottoes, ascend on the main axis to the Gran Sala, beyond which is a circular cortile, 65 ft in diameter, with façades of two arcaded storeys, rusticated below and

A. Palazzo del Tè, Mantua (1525–35). See p. 707

B. Villa Lante, Bagnaia (sixteenth century): water garden and casino.
See opposite page

C. Villa Lante, Bagnaia: Fountain of the Giants

VILLA OF POPE JULIUS : ROME

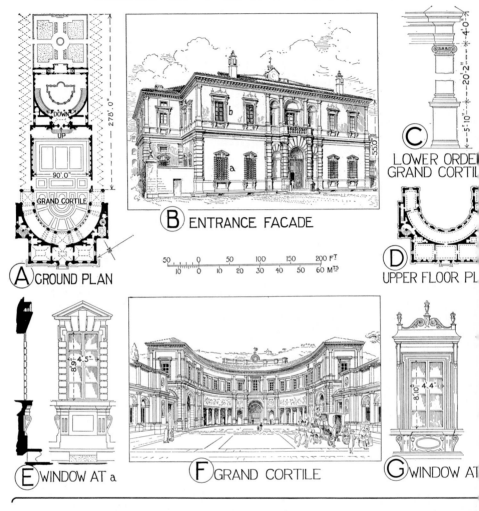

Ⓐ GROUND PLAN

Ⓑ ENTRANCE FACADE

Ⓒ LOWER ORDER GRAND CORTILE

Ⓓ UPPER FLOOR PLAN

Ⓔ WINDOW AT a

Ⓕ GRAND CORTILE

Ⓖ WINDOW AT

Ⓗ VILLA FARNESINA : ROME

Ⓙ VILLA MADAMA : ROME

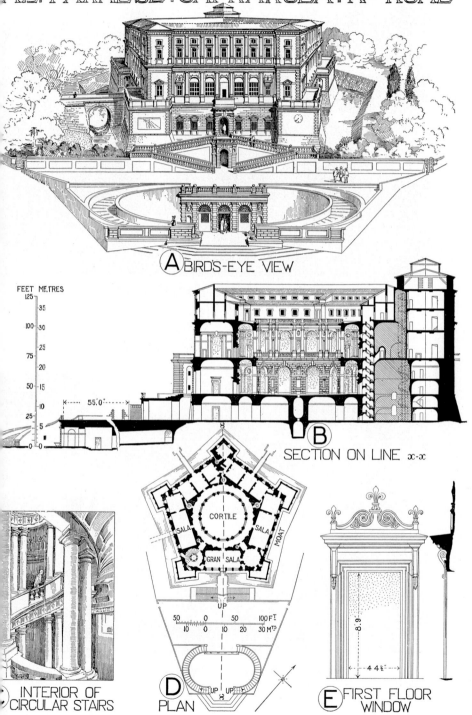

PAL. FARNESE: CAPRAROLA: N.ᴿ ROME

Ⓐ BIRD'S-EYE VIEW

FEET METRES
125
100
75
50
25
0

35
30
25
20
15
10
5
0

55.0

Ⓑ SECTION ON LINE x-x

CORTILE

SALA

SALA

MOAT

GRAN SALA

UP

50   0   50   100 Fᵀ
10   0   10   20   30 Mᵀᴿˢ

UP   UP

Ⓒ INTERIOR OF
CIRCULAR STAIRS

Ⓓ PLAN

8.9

4.4½

Ⓔ FIRST FLOOR
WINDOW

A. Boboli Gardens, Florence (sixteenth century). See pp. 673, 678

B. Villa Gamberaia, Settignano (*c.* 1550–). See p. 673

above ornamented with attached columns in a 'triumphal arch' arrangement. In one angle of the plan is the famous circular open staircase (p. 711C) (cf. Château de Chambord, p. 773). The general lay-out (p. 711A), with entrance portal, circular ramps, stairs and moat, makes a fine symmetrical and monumental group. Connected with the palace but a little distant from it there survives another famous formal garden, where a series of charming elements, including several kinds of water display, is arranged along a falling axis. Commanding them all, astride the axis, is a delightful garden house, single-storeyed on the upper side and double on the other, which is among Vignola's most original creations (p. 706C).

S. Andrea, Rome (c. 1550) (p. 700), on the Via Flaminia, is one of Vignola's smaller works, the very simple plan (p. 700G) being covered by an elliptical dome, borne on a normal Corinthian cornice (p. 700J) over pendentives, thus showing a new departure in Renaissance adventure. The method of buttressing the dome by a quasi-drum is the same as in the Pantheon, Rome (p. 199A). On the entrance front (p. 700D), a portico, with pediment, is simulated with pilasters.

The **Gesù Church, Rome** (1568–84) (p. 704), completed by Giacomo della Porta, who modified the scheme for the façade, is one of Vignola's best-known works. The interior was redecorated in 1668–83 and the walls lined with marble in 1860; the altar in the north transept (p. 704G), a superlative Baroque masterpiece by a great number of craftsmen, was designed in 1695–9 by Andrea Pozzo. Vignola's plan (p. 704D) is an improved version of that of Alberti for S. Andrea at Mantua (p. 679J), and became the type for very many later churches. It is the Byzantine centralized type, domed over the crossing, with short barrel-vaulted transept and sanctuary arms but an extended nave, where there are close-spaced chapels in lieu of aisles, and lunette windows over them in the base of the barrel-vault (p. 704H). The lunettes afford a much better lighted church than Alberti's. The Proto-Baroque façade has a centre-piece of two superimposed Orders, while the aisle roofs stop against large scroll brackets, as used by Alberti at S. Maria Novella, Florence (pp. 632A, 683).

The two small cupolas at S. Peter's (p. 717), and the Portico de' Banchi, Bologna (1562), were also from the designs of this master.

PIRRO LIGORIO (c. 1520–80) is remembered principally for his spectacular **Villa d'Este, Tivoli** (1549–) (pp. 693A, 715A), with its remarkable formal gardens containing endless natural and artificial delights; and his charming **Villa Pia, Rome** (1561) (pp. 715B, 721), embodying ornate pavilions around a decoratively-walled oval court in the Vatican gardens. In the garden features of both of these, stucco is used extensively: the passion for modelled stucco at this time extends freely to the encrustation of building exteriors, where too, antique panels were often embedded, and is illustrated by several well-known palaces and villas, including the **Villa Medici, Rome** (1574–80) (p. 706E) by Annibale Lippi. Stucco was a cheap and tractable medium eminently suited to the modelling of garden ornament, but used sculpturally on buildings tended to produce a restlessness conflicting with the architectural lines.

MICHELANGELO (1475–1564), the long-lived and world-famous Florentine sculptor and the painter of the vaulted ceiling of the Sistine Chapel (1508–), was no less distinguished in his later years as an architect, and is a most striking instance of the wonderful versatility of artists of this period.

The **Medici Chapel, Florence** (1521–34) (p. 716A) constitutes the New Sacristy (p. 676K) in S. Lorenzo, and was added by Michelangelo to correspond with the Old Sacristy built (1421–8) by Brunelleschi. The interior, 40 ft square, approximates in design to its counterpart; pilasters of black Istrian stone carry the main entablature, which is surmounted by an attic with pilaster-enframed windows and niches. A deep, dome-crowned recess contains the altar. Yet in the architectural settings for the funerary elements of the ducal tombs which give the building its special renown, there are very significant differences of style, manifesting the first important Proto-Baroque departures from ancient Classical precedent. The white marble mural tombs are those of Giuliano de' Medici and, directly opposite, Lorenzo (II) de' Medici, each with a commanding sculptured figure of the deceased against a background of pilaster-enframed niches, over a marble sarcophagus bearing recumbent allegorical figures, representing in the first case Night and Day, and in the other, Evening and Dawn. The architectural settings are treated sculpturally, and in quite a few respects are illogical in structural implication, both within themselves and in relation to the fundamental architectural theme of the Chapel.

The **Laurentian Library, Florence** (1525–) (p. 716B), adjoining S. Lorenzo, was well advanced by 1534 but continued afterwards by Giorgio Vasari (1511–74), best known for his *Lives of the Painters*, who, with Ammanati, carried out the vestibule and staircase from 1559 (p. 716B), with some modifications of Michelangelo's plans. Proto-Baroque features are again notable, in the triple staircase itself and on the flanking walls, where coupled columns, supported on consoles, are set within recesses between protruding sections of wall ornamented by panels and pedimented niches flanked by downward-tapering pilasters. The library, designed to contain the books and manuscripts collected by the Medici, has walls bearing pilasters and a fine timber ceiling; it probably was the model for Wren's Trinity College Library, Cambridge (p. 921F).

The **Capitol, Rome** (p. 718), the reconstruction of which was planned by Michelangelo about 1546, was his most successful civic work and a fine town-planning achievement. He not only remodelled on symmetrical lines the approaches to the piazza, but also designed the great palace façades on the three sides. He superintended the erection only of the approach stairway, the monumental double flight of steps of the palace opposite and, at an earlier time (1538), of the statue of Marcus Aurelius (p. 718C) in the centre of the piazza, the remainder being executed from his designs by his successors. The **Palazzo dei Conservatori** (1564–8) (p. 718A, D, E) has a façade 66 ft high. The **Palazzo del Senatore** (1592–), completed by Girolamo Rainaldi (1570–1655) with slight modifications of Michelangelo's designs, rises 90 ft high and has a rusticated basement behind the imposing staircases, and giant Corinthian pilasters carried through two storeys, while above the façade peers a campanile (1579), standing over the ancient Tabularium (pp. 182, 171A), overlooking the Forum Romanum. The 'Capitoline Museum' (1644–55) (p. 718A, B, E, F), again carried out by Girolamo Rainaldi, illustrates Michelangelo's method of securing unity by carrying up a giant Order, a feature of all three façades. The planning scheme is complemented by the fine flights of steps leading right and left to the triple-arched loggias designed (c. 1550–5) by Vignola.

S. Maria degli Angeli, Rome (p. 207A, D, F), was a daring experiment by which in 1563 Michelangelo converted the tepidarium of the Baths of Diocletian into a Christian church (p. 206). This hall (200 ft by 80 ft) became the nave of the church, but in 1749 Vanvitelli transformed the nave into a huge transept, placed the entrance on the west side, and formed a deep chancel on the east. The actual bases of the ancient monolithic granite columns are 7 ft below the new floor constructed by Michelangelo.

This great master was also responsible for many important features in the planning and final treatment of S. Peter, Rome, which is therefore dealt with under his name.

S. Peter, Rome (1506–1626) (pp. 720, 721, 722, 723), the most important building of this period, was the outcome of the work of many architects under the

B. Villa Pia, Rome (1561): garden pavilion.
See p. 713

A. Villa d'Este, Tivoli (1549–).
See p. 713

C. Scala Regia, Rome (Vatican) (1663–6).
See p. 726

A. The Medici Chapel (New Sacristy) S. Lorenzo, Florence (1521–34).
See p. 713

B. The Biblioteca Laurenziana, Florence: entrance (1525–; staircase 1559–).
See p. 714

direction of many popes during a period of 120 years. The present Cathedral had its origin in the intention of Pope Julius II to erect a tomb house for himself (1505) (p. 670). This Pope was an outstanding personality as pontiff, statesman, and patriot, with great ambitions for the papacy, the Church, and Italy; so his initial personal project finally took the form of ruthlessly pulling down the old basilican church (p. 259) in order to erect such a monument as should enshrine all the magnificence which he wished to stand as associated with the papal power, the Christian religion, and the Latin race. A competition produced a number of designs—still preserved in the Uffizi Gallery, Florence—and that of Bramante was selected. In 1506 the foundation stone was laid of Bramante's church, planned as a Greek cross, and his proposed dome (p. 722B) was founded on that of the Pantheon, with the addition of a peristyle and lantern. In 1513, on the death of Julius II, Bramante was superseded by Giuliano da Sangallo, Fra Giocondo, and Raphael, but the two former died in 1515. Raphael proposed a plan (p. 722E) in the shape of a Latin cross, but he died in 1520, and Baldassare Peruzzi, who was then appointed architect, reverted to the Greek-cross plan (p. 722F). Ecclesiastical funds were now running short, there were troubles both in Church and State, and finally the sack of Rome (1527) disorganized all artistic projects. In 1536, on the death of Peruzzi, Antonio da Sangallo the Younger submitted a slightly altered plan, with an extended vestibule (p. 722G), lofty campanile, and elaborated central dome (p. 722D). On his death, ten years later, Michelangelo, then in his seventy-second year, succeeded him, and the present building owes most of its outstanding features to his genius. He reverted to a Greek-cross plan, strengthened the piers of the dome, and redesigned the surrounding chapels and apses. He planned and indeed commenced the construction of the great dome, the drum of which was completed before his death, in 1564, and he left models for dome and lantern. From these models the dome was completed (1585–90) by Giacomo della Porta and Domenico Fontana. In 1564 Vignola had added side cupolas (pp. 721A, 723C), but these became ineffective when Carlo Maderna lengthened the nave to form a Latin cross (p. 723G), and added the gigantic façade (1606–12). Finally Bernini erected (1655–67) the noble entrance piazza, 650 ft wide, surrounded by 284 columns forming the imposing fourfold Tuscan colonnades (pp. 720, 721).

Cathedral, Piazza, and Vatican (p. 701) form a world-famous group (p. 721A, B). The completed plan (p. 723G), of vast proportions, is a Latin cross with an internal length of 600 ft, and an internal width across the transepts of 450 ft, while the total external length, including portico, is 700 ft, or about half as much again as that of Salisbury Cathedral. The nave, 84 ft wide, consists of four immense bays, and is about the same width as the Basilica of Constantine (p. 200E), but considerably longer. The crossing is covered by the majestic dome, 137 ft 6 ins internal diameter, while the short transepts and the sanctuary are terminated by semicircular apses. The magnificent entrance portico, 234 ft by 43 ft 6 ins, extends the whole width of the church (p. 723F, G), and leads to the interior (p. 720B), the walls of which are of brick faced with plaster coloured to imitate marble. It is almost impossible to gauge its vast proportions, and this difficulty is further increased by the false idea of scale given by such features as the colossal cherubs, about 7 ft high, which support the holy water stoups, and an idea of the actual size can only be estimated by comparison with the groups of moving people. The mighty nave is flanked by great piers faced by a gigantic Order of Corinthian pilasters, 83 ft 6 ins high, and entablature 20 ft high, or nearly double the height of the Pantheon portico (p. 199), surmounted by a semicircular barrel vault, coffered, gilded, and frescoed, 150 ft above the marble pavement. The four stupendous piers (60 ft square) which uphold the dome have colossal statues 16 ft high, and the impression on gazing into the vast internal

THE CAPITOL AT ROME

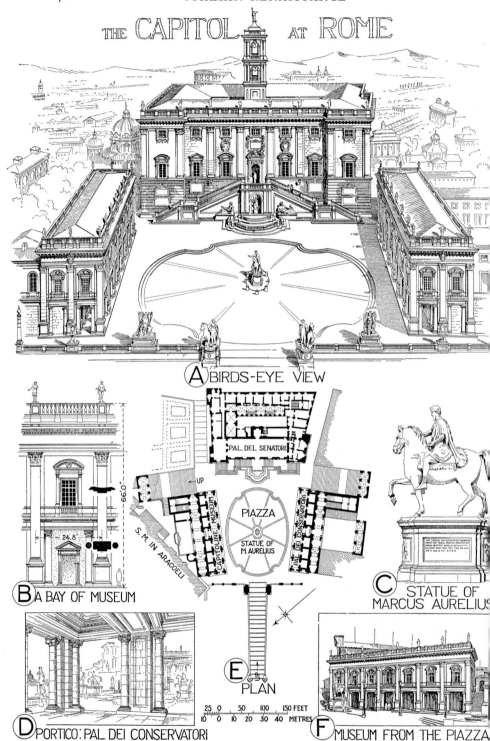

A BIRDS-EYE VIEW

B A BAY OF MUSEUM

66.0

24.8

C STATUE OF MARCUS AURELIUS

PAL. DEL SENATORE

UP

S. M. IN ARACOELI

CAPITOLINE MUSEUM

PIAZZA

STATUE OF M. AURELIUS

PAL. DEI CONSERVATORI

E PLAN

25 0   50   100   150 FEET
10 0 10 20 30 40 METRES

D PORTICO: PAL. DEI CONSERVATORI

F MUSEUM FROM THE PIAZZA

cupola, 335 ft high, with its coloured frescoes and mosaics, is awe-inspiring and sublime. The planning of the supports of the dome and its four pendentives is in marked contrast with that of S. Paul's, London (p. 912), with its eight piers. The Throne of S. Peter, in the western apse, is a Baroque work of Bernini, as is also the magnificent Baldachino (p. 720B), 100 ft high, covering the High Altar, which stands over the alleged tomb of S. Peter in the crypt, beneath the dome.

The exterior (pp. 720A, 721A, 723C), roughly executed in travertine stone, has a giant Order of Corinthian pilasters carried round the entire building, giving unity to the design, with podium 18 ft, Corinthian columns and pilasters 90 ft 9 ins (diameter 9 ft), entablature 20 ft, attic and balustrade 38 ft 6 ins, which, excluding the statues, 20 ft high, gives a total height of 167 ft 3 ins, or more than half as high again as the façade of S. Paul's Cathedral (p. 912). The gigantic scale of this building can best be realized by comparison with Trajan's Column, Rome (p. 228), which is 97 ft 7 ins high, with a diameter of 12 ft 2 ins, and is placed on a pedestal 18 ft high. Thus the countless half-columns and pilasters which encircle the great Cathedral are actually only about 7 ft less in height than the single column of Trajan. In no other building has an Order of such immense size been used. If Michelangelo's design for a portico of free-standing columns had been carried out, it would have been one of the most impressive features in all Christendom.

The great dome (pp. 721, 722A, C, 723), 9 ft thick at base and upper part, formed of two shells of brickwork, with stone ribs supporting the crowning lantern, nearly equals that of the Pantheon in diameter, but Michelangelo set himself a very difficult problem, inasmuch as the base of his dome is nearly 250 ft from the pavement, and depends for support only on four massive piers instead of on a continuous circular wall. No less than ten iron chains at the base have been inserted at different times to prevent the dome from spreading. Although the dome with the lantern is 452 ft in height—more than twice that of the towers of Westminster Abbey—its domi-nating effect is impaired externally, except from a distance, by Maderna's lengthened nave and additional portico, which latter is not only over 167 ft high, but is also as much as 450 ft from the centre of the crossing, and consequently hides the lower part of the dome from the near spectator. The Order round the drum, 50 ft high, might well have been on a larger scale, and it might have gained in impressiveness, had it been connected by scrolls with the attic above, as designed by Michelangelo. It is in effect far less pleasing than the colonnaded treatment of the dome of S. Paul's (pp. 663B, 909A). In spite of these conflicting elements in the design, the dome of S. Peter's is the greatest creation of the Renaissance, and a dominating feature in all views of Rome.

Lantern, dome, drum, balustrades, and statues, all in turn piled above the gigantic pilasters of the encircling walls, and even partly obscured by the monu-mental portico, are awe-inspiring in their massive grandeur, and in themselves make up a monument of cunningly contrived parts. Externally, however, S. Peter's owes half its majesty to the manner in which it sits enthroned above its vast entrance piazza (650 ft wide), with its grouped fountains and central obelisk, which is guarded by those noble colonnades whose proportions are on such a generous scale that they are not dwarfed even by the huge Order of the façade on which they abut. No other city has accorded such a wide-swept approach to its Cathedral Church, no other architect could have conceived a design of greater nobility; this colonnade-encircled piazza of Bernini is, if one may say so, the greatest of all atriums before the greatest of all churches in Christendom.

DOMENICO FONTANA (1543–1607), born near Lake Lugano in Lombardy, came to Rome in 1563, where he received many commissions, including that for his share in S. Peter's, referred to above. He laid out new streets and places, with

A. S. Peter, Rome: aerial view from E. showing Vatican on right, with covered approach from Castle of S. Angelo (1506–1626; colonnades 1655–7). See p. 714

B. S. Peter, Rome: interior

S. PETER : ROME

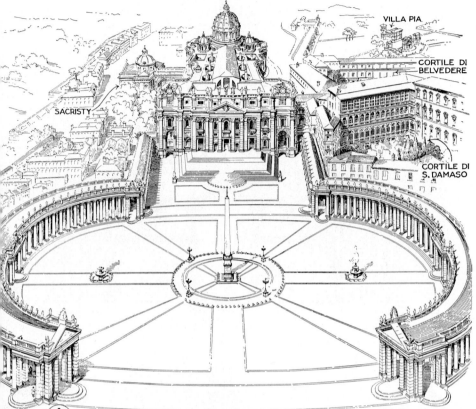

VILLA PIA

CORTILE DI
BELVEDERE

SACRISTY

CORTILE DI
S. DAMASO

(A) BIRD'S-EYE VIEW OF S. PETER AND THE VATICAN

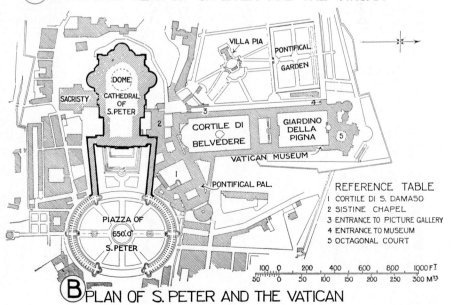

VILLA PIA

PONTIFICAL
GARDEN

SACRISTY

DOME

CATHEDRAL
OF
S. PETER

3

2

4

CORTILE DI

BELVEDERE

GIARDINO
DELLA
PIGNA

5

VATICAN MUSEUM

PONTIFICAL PAL.

I

PIAZZA OF
650'.0
S. PETER

REFERENCE TABLE
1 CORTILE DI S. DAMASO
2 SISTINE CHAPEL
3 ENTRANCE TO PICTURE GALLERY
4 ENTRANCE TO MUSEUM
5 OCTAGONAL COURT

100 0   200   400   600   800   1000 F^T
50   0   50   100 150 200 250 300 M^{TS}

(B) PLAN OF S. PETER AND THE VATICAN

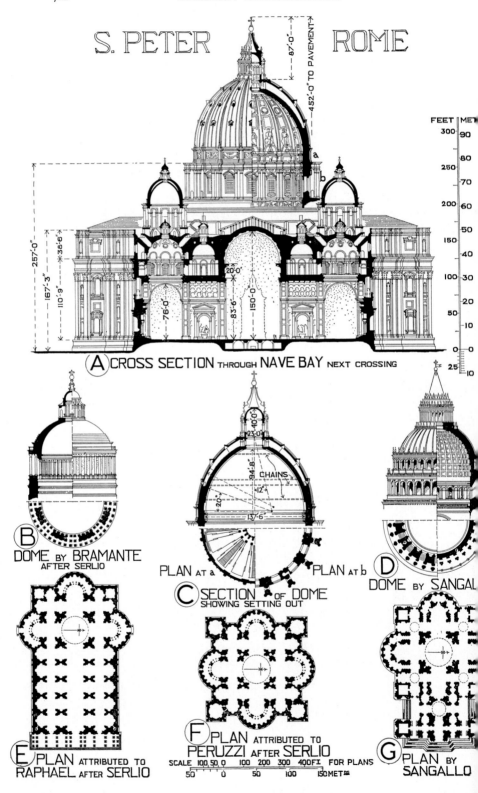

S. PETER   ROME

87'-0"
452'-0" TO PAVEMENT

FEET | MET
300 | 90
80
250 | 70
200 | 60
50
150 | 40
100 | 30
20
50 | 10
0 | 0
25 | 10

257'-0"
167'-3"
110'-9"
38'-6"
20'-0"
76'-0"
83'-6"
150'-0"

a
b

Ⓐ CROSS SECTION THROUGH NAVE BAY NEXT CROSSING

Ⓑ DOME BY BRAMANTE
AFTER SERLIO

40'-0"
23'-0"
94'-8"
CHAINS
12'
20'
13'-6"

PLAN AT a   PLAN AT b

Ⓒ SECTION OF DOME
SHOWING SETTING OUT

Ⓓ DOME BY SANGAL

Ⓔ PLAN ATTRIBUTED TO
RAPHAEL AFTER SERLIO

Ⓕ PLAN ATTRIBUTED TO
PERUZZI AFTER SERLIO

SCALE 100,50, 0   100   200   300   400 FT   FOR PLANS
50   0   50   100   150 METRES

Ⓖ PLAN BY
SANGALLO

S. PETER : ROME

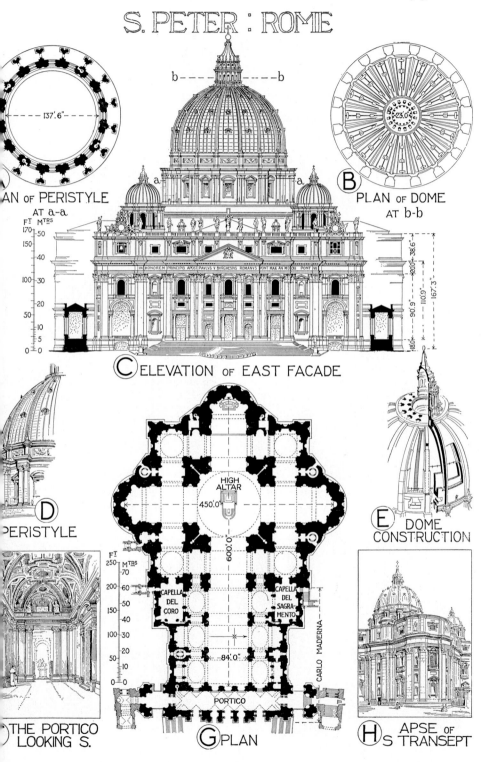

PLAN OF PERISTYLE
AT a-a

137'.6"

(B) PLAN OF DOME
AT b-b

23'.0"

(C) ELEVATION OF EAST FACADE

IN HONOREM PRINCIPIS APOST PAVLVS V BVRGHESIVS ROMANVS PONT MAX AN MDCXII PONT VII

420'.0"—386'.6"
167'.3"
110'.9"
90'.9"
18'.0"

(D) PERISTYLE

(E) DOME CONSTRUCTION

HIGH ALTAR
450'.0"
600'.0"

CAPELLA DEL CORO
CAPELLA DEL SAGRAMENTO

84'.0"

CARLO MADERNA

PORTICO

THE PORTICO LOOKING S.

(G) PLAN

(H) APSE OF S TRANSEPT

A. General view, west side   B. Entrance block, west side

Palazzo Barberini, Rome (1628–38). See p. 725

C. Madonna di S. Luca, Bologna
(1723–57). See p. 729

D. Palazzo Marino, Milan:
cortile (1558–60). See p. 688

E. S. Maria Maggiore, Rome:
façade (1743). See p. 729

F. Palazzo Borghese, Rome: cortile (c. 1590).
See opposite page

their ornaments and fountains, for the latter collaborating with his brother, Giovanni (1540–1614), a distinguished water-engineer. Towards the end of the century he moved to Naples, where he designed the Royal Palace (1592). Architecturally, his work is not greatly distinguished, and he represents the last stages of the Proto-Baroque in Rome.

The **Palazzo del Laterano, Rome** (1586) (pp. 664, 706F), erected by Fontana on the site of the former palace, was, after being an orphan asylum, turned into a museum in 1843. The buildings are arranged round a court, and the astylar façade is a simple and tame version of the Palazzo Farnese treatment.

BAROQUE

CARLO MADERNA (1556–1629), also from Lake Lugano, came early to Rome and was trained under his uncle, Domenico Fontana. He is the chief figure of the early Baroque in Rome. His architecture has a vigour and robustness superior to that of his immediate predecessors (Michelangelo excluded), as is evident in the main work of his active life, the lengthening of S. Peter's.

S. Susanna, Rome (1597–1603) (p. 697B), has a façade virtually devoid of windows, their place being taken by enframed niches, comprised of two tiers of superimposed Corinthian Orders, expressed in crisply-projecting pilasters except on the centre bays of the lower tier, where attached columns appear. The decorative interest is built up to centre strongly on the entrance doorway, the bay spacings being progressively increased in width towards it, and advanced in planes. The crowning, balustraded pediment over the nave is reflected in a lesser pediment breaking the lower cornice, and in others of segmental form serving to emphasize the upper and lower axial openings The rich reiteration of features, as here in the theme of the pediments and in the clustered Orders, is typical Baroque practice.

The **Palazzo Barberini, Rome** (1628–38) (p. 724A, B), was only started the year before Maderna's death, but externally at least, was executed closely according to his designs by Bernini, with Borromini serving under him in a subordinate capacity: some novel features of the internal planning are due to Bernini. The plan of the palace is unusual for Rome, as it has no courtyard, and takes an 'H' shape, as, however, had been customary for some time for villas. The three-storey main façade is strongly rhythmical, like most Roman palaces, but unlike the majority is stylar, of fairly orthodox 'Roman Order' design except on the top floor, where there are overlaid pilasters, their lines carried up into the entablature, while the seven windows are treated in perspective.

FLAMINIO PONZIO (1560–1613), another Lombard, was an excellent designer, though less advanced in his style than his contemporary, Maderna.

S. Sebastiano fuori le mura, Rome (1608–13) (p. 727A), completed by Vasanzio, has a chastely severe façade, of which the lower storey has arches standing on paired columns, a motif appearing also in the courtyard of the **Palazzo Borghese, Rome,** begun in 1590 by Martino Lunghi the Elder and finished by Vasanzio; and again at a later time (1634–6) in Bianco's Palazzo dell' Università at Genoa (p. 691). Ponzio's **Fontana Paola, Rome** (1612) (p. 753H) is one of the city's finest monuments.

GIOVANNI LORENZO BERNINI (1598–1680) represents the Roman Baroque at its peak. Born in Naples, he was brought to Rome at a tender age (c. 1604), for his father was a sculptor of repute and followed his art in Florence, Naples and Rome in turn. In Rome, the father, Pietro Bernini (1562–1629) was the creator of the 'Barcaccia' (c. 1629), a boat-shaped fountain in the Piazza di Spagna, Rome, which attractively complements the spectacular 'Spanish Steps' (p. 730A). The son quickly achieved renown and social esteem. Primarily a sculptor, he was brilliant too as an architect and painter; being a facile and prodigious worker he executed a host of varied commissions in his long life, virtually all of them in and around Rome. His one and only foreign excursion was a short and abortive visit to Paris (1665) (p. 774). Much of Bernini's finest architectural as well as sculpturesque work was done for S. Peter's, where his colonnades for the piazza are world-famous (pp. 720A, 721A). Besides buildings, he designed very many altar pieces and also fountains, such as the 'Fountain of the Four Rivers' (1647–52) in the Piazza Navona, Rome.

S. Andrea del Quirinale, Rome (1658–70) (p. 727B), is the best known of Bernini's churches, each of them small, but widely imitated later on. The exterior demonstrates the essential simplicity of Bernini's effects. The protruding vestibule comprises a pair of overlaid plain Corinthian pilasters, with pedimented entablature above, enclosing an archway and a semicircular two-columned porch, on which is a large, sculptured coat of arms. The church behind is a domed ellipse, 80 ft by 55 ft across, with the main axis at right angles to the approach, and from this centralized space open eight radiating chapels, making, with the entrance and sanctuary, ten recesses embedded in the very thick walls. The scheme thus is similar to that of the ancient Pantheon, Rome (p. 199); and the likeness is still more close in the case of his **S. Maria dell' Assunta, Ariccia, Rome** (1662–4), which has a domed circular plan, with eight radiating recesses in the walls. Another church at **Castel Gandolfo, Rome** (1658–61), has a simple Greek-cross plan, with a pendentived dome over the crossing.

The **Palazzo Odescalchi, Rome** (1664–) (p. 706D), has a stylar main block with a giant Corinthian pilastered Order embracing the two upper floors, in a composition which has the broad simplicity typical of Bernini. Large consoles bestride the entablature frieze, and they are paired over the line of the pilasters. The length of the central façade was doubled from the original seven bays by additions made in 1745 by Salvi and Vanvitelli.

The **Palazzo Montecitorio, Rome** (begun 1650), was completed by Carlo Fontana (1634–1714) several decades later, but much on the lines Bernini had planned.

The **Scala Regia, Rome** (1663–6) (p. 715C), a magnificent monumental stairway approach to the Vatican, lies adjacent to the portico of S. Peter's, from which there is also an approach (p. 723G). It is celebrated for its remarkable perspective effects.

FRANCESCO BORROMINI (1599–1667), born near Como and at first a sculptor, came to Rome about 1614 and there received training under Carlo Maderna and Bernini. In temperament he was introspective and intense, and his architecture is as tortuous and involved as Bernini's is direct and fundamentally simple. He died by suicide.

S. Carlo alle Quattro Fontane, Rome (1638–41, façade 1665–7) (p. 727C), shows ingenious planning to meet the difficulties of a small and cramped site. Borromini here discards the typical Renaissance plan made up of clearly demarcated geometrical elements and adopts a scheme which, although resolving itself ultimately into an elliptical pendentived dome running east to west, begins at wall level internally as an undulated Greek cross, made up of four concave lobes passing into one another in convex curves. Undulating plan curves appear on the west front too, and henceforward Baroque architecture repeatedly takes advantage of this kind of device.

S. Ivo della Sapienza, Rome (1642–50) (p. 727D), the church of the University, which for the rest had been built by Giacomo della Porta in 1576, is another instance of the bizarre planning of Borromini, having a centralized plan contained by six lobes, of which three are semicircular and the alternate ones shaped as half-hexagons; Corinthian pilasters line the inner walls, and from their entablature springs a steep dome, faithfully retaining the plan shape internally, but masked

A. S. Sebastiano fuori le mura, Rome
(1608–13). See p. 725

B. S. Andrea del Quirinale (1658–70).
See p. 726

C. S. Carlo alle Quattro Fontane, Rome
(1638–41; façade 1665–7). See p. 726

D. S. Ivo della Sapienza, Rome: from
cortile (1642–50). See p. 726

A. Fountain (1648–51) and S. Agnese
(1652–), Rome. See p. 729

B. S. Maria della Pace, Rome: façade
(1656–7). See p. 729

c. S. Maria di Monte Santo and S. Maria dei Miracoli, Rome (1662–79).
See p. 729

externally by a six-lobed cupola and hexagonal lantern terminating in a corkscrew spire.

S. Agnese, Rome (1652–) (p. 728A), facing the Piazza Navona, was begun by Rainaldi, continued by Borromini from 1653–5 and completed by others by 1666. Owing to the circumstances, the plan is comparatively restrained, but the splendid and impressive composition, with recessed front, twin campanili and commanding dome is largely due to Borromini.

PIETRO DA CORTONA (1596–1669), distinguished painter and architect, was of the same generation as Bernini and Borromini; his early architecture had great vigour and originality, but became more commonplace in later life. He carried out very many commissions, both ecclesiastical and domestic.

S. Maria della Pace, Rome, the church to which Bramante had added the cloister (p. 753E), was rebuilt by Cortona, with a fine façade and semicircular portico (1656–7) (p. 728B) which well represent the vigorous modelling of this architect's schemes. He obtains forceful expression by the interplay of convex and concave plan forms at large and at small scale, or by advancing and receding planes, while securing richness by a lavish use of columns and pilasters. He rarely employed the giant Order, but expressed his buildings in distinct tiers. Similar characteristics appear in his **SS. Martina and Luca, Rome** (1634–47) and the façade of **S. Maria in Via Lata, Rome** (1658–62).

CARLO RAINALDI (1611–91), another High Baroque architect, is of only slightly less importance than the three last named. His extensive church work includes the commencement of S. Agnese, Rome, mentioned above, and the reconstruction (1673) of the east end of the old Basilica of S. Maria Maggiore, Rome, a very fine scheme.

S. Maria di Monte Santo and S. Maria dei Miracoli, Rome (1662–79) (p. 728C), are twin churches by Rainaldi dividing three main roads of central Rome as they leave the Piazza del Popolo, skilfully planned to present a fine civic effect towards the square. As there is a difference in width of their sites, the plans are not identical, and to give the illusion of symmetry externally, the central space and covering dome of S. Maria di Monte Santo are made elliptical in the depth of the church, while in the other church they are based on a circular plan. Both domes have faceted drums externally. When approaching completion, Bernini was given charge of the Monte Santo church.

CARLO DOTTI (1670–1759) represents the eighteenth-century Late Baroque at Bologna, in the north of the Papal territories, where the **Madonna di S. Luca** (1723–57) (p. 724C), a finely-massed, hill-top pilgrimage church outside the city, is his masterpiece. In its circumstances it resembles the Superga, Turin (p. 694A).

ALESSANDRO SPECCHI (1668–1729) was an able civic designer who, among other works, began the delightful **Scala di Spagna, Rome** ('Spanish Steps') (1721–5) (p. 730A), connecting in cleverly-varied curvilinear flights and landings the Piazza di Spagna with SS. Trinità de' Monti. It was, however, FRANCESCO DE SANCTIS (1693–1740) who took over in 1723 and completed the design.

ALESSANDRO GALILEI (1691–1737) carried out the principal façade of **S. Giovanni in Laterano, Rome** (1733–6) (p. 736B), and as this was entrusted to him as the result of an important architectural competition, it should well represent the standard of taste of the day.

NICOLA SALVI (1697–1751) has claims to fame for his **Fontana di Trevi, Rome** (1732–62) (pp. 730B, 754D), finished by Pannini.

FERDINANDO FUGA (1699–1780–), the designer of the entrance façade of **S. Maria Maggiore, Rome** (1743) (p. 724E), was the last notable Baroque architect of Rome.

A. Scala di Spagna (Spanish Steps), Rome (1721–5). See p. 725

B. Fontana di Trevi, Rome (1732–62). See p. 729

VENICE

EARLY RENAISSANCE

PIETRO LOMBARDO (1435–1515) was one of a family who impressed their personality upon the architecture of the sea-girt city, where the Renaissance arrived much later than in Florence.

The **Doge's Palace, Venice,** commenced in the Mediaeval period (p. 607), was continued at this time. The Cortile (p. 733) was undertaken by Antonio Rizzo from about 1485, continued by Pietro Lombardo from 1499–1511, and completed by Antonio Scarpagnino in 1545–50. The Cortile façades are transitional in retaining series of pointed arcades, but are otherwise quite Renaissance in character (p. 733B, C, E), especially the upper tier of the south face of the small Court of the Senators (p. 733C). Inside the main entrance (Porta della Carta) is the famous 'Giants' Staircase (Scala dei Giganti) (1485–9), flanked by Sansovino's figures of Mars and Neptune (p. 733A, B). The Ducal Palace is equally renowned for its external Gothic arcades (p. 611) and its sumptuously-enriched apartments, with their elaborate chimney-pieces (p. 757J) and stucco-encrusted walls and ceilings enriched with paintings by Veronese and Tintoretto and many other famous artists. The **Bridge of Sighs** (c. 1595) (p. 733D), connecting the Doge's Palace and the prison, is a romantic external feature, with its elliptical arch, rusticated pilasters, and heraldic devices.

The **Palazzo Corner Spinelli, Venice** (c. 1480) (p. 734B), which may be by one of the Lombardi family, is a delightful example of the Early Renaissance, and has some fine apartments. The symmetrical elevation; the dignified axial entrance from the Grand Canal; the balconied windows, so disposed as to give extra light to the large rooms reaching the centre of the façade; the strong angle treatment; all are traditional features in Venice, carried on from the Mediaeval period (p. 612B, E).

The **Palazzo Vendramini, Venice** (1481) (p. 734), ascribed to Pietro Lombardo, has the customary three-floored scheme and window arrangement, but is stylar, the attached Corinthian Order, with varied designs for the capitals, being used for each floor (p. 734E, G). The top entablature is made abnormally deep so as to serve as a fitting termination for the whole front, and, as usual in Venetian palaces, the full architectural treatment is confined to the main façade. The bifurcated, traceried windows (p. 734F), retaining a Mediaeval note, are typical of the Early Renaissance in Venetia. The charming balconies (p. 734G) still retain the miniature columns in place of the true baluster by this time usual in Italy elsewhere.

S. Maria dei Miracoli, Venice (1481–9) (p. 735), designed by Pietro Lombardo, is a marvel of marble work, both within and without. This miniature church has an aisleless nave covered internally by a deep segmental wooden roof with gilded panels, and with a non-concentric semicircular roof showing externally. The recessed sanctuary and the choir over the sacristy are approached by a wide flight of steps, flanked by marble balustrades and twin pulpits, while the altar is enclosed with beautiful pierced screenwork (p. 758H). Above the sanctuary is a small pendentived dome with a shallow, windowed drum. The east end, with its adjacent circular staircase carried up as a domed turret, and the lead-covered, external timber dome over the sanctuary, forms a delightful composition as seen from the nearby canal. The walls of the church are faced internally and externally with coloured marbles. The exterior (p. 735A), although clothing a one-storeyed structure, has two stages of superimposed pilasters, the upper as a blind arcade recalling Mediaeval treatment, while the roof runs through on the west front to a semicircular pediment, such as is seen at S. Zaccaria and the Scuola di S. Marco (p. 739C), probably borrowed from the Byzantines, with whom it represented the exterior of their vaults.

S. Zaccaria, Venice (1458–1515), and **S. Giobbe, Venice** (1451–93), are other early examples which have many interesting features, and show much the same character as the work of the Lombardi.

FRA GIOCONDO (1435–1515), a native of Verona, in later life worked in Rome, where for the two years before his death he was associated with the work at S. Peter's (p. 717).

The **Palazzo del Consiglio, Verona** (1476–92) (p. 744H), is notable for the delicate arcade, with columns directly supporting arches, after the manner of the Foundling Hospital, Florence (p. 677), but stiffened with a pilaster midway. The upper tier has paired segmental-headed windows of a Venetian type, and panelled arabesque decoration.

S. Maria dei Miracoli, Brescia (1488–) (p. 689B), was designed by Mastro Jacopo, but work continued slowly, and the scheme was altered in 1522. The delicately-sculptured marble façade of the earlier portion included a remarkably ornate porch.

S. Salvatore, Venice (1506–34), by Tullio Lombardo, a son of the famous Pietro, and Giorgio Spavento, has a Baroque façade (1663) and a plan somewhat similar to Alberti's S. Andrea, Mantua (p. 679J), but with a nave covered by two large domes, repeating, precisely, the dome over the crossing. In this manner of covering the church, the Byzantine influence is strongly apparent.

The **Scuola di S. Marco, Venice** (1485–95) (p. 739C), now the City Hospital, by Martino Lombardo, has a façade which echoes that of S. Mark. The ground storey has Corinthian pilasters between which are panels bearing some curious perspective reliefs. These are by Tullio Lombardo, and bear witness to the intense interest of artists in the science of perspective at this period, evidenced also in Bramante's S. Satiro, Milan (p. 696). The pediment over the doorway and those serving as cresting, again are semicircular, and bear acroteria decorations at base and apex.

S. Giorgio dei Greci, Venice (1538–), in which Sante Lombardo had a part, is a graceful little building in the style of the Early period, except the façade, which is mature Renaissance. It has an aisleless plan (p. 735G), somewhat resembling S. Maria dei Miracoli (p. 735B), and a triapsal sanctuary (p. 735G). A dome is placed centrally over the nave (p. 735H), while the exterior (p. 735F) has a rather unusual treatment, terminating in three pediments, and the group is completed with a lofty campanile (1587).

HIGH RENAISSANCE AND PROTO-BAROQUE

MICHELE SANMICHELE (1484–1559), born at Verona, was trained in Rome from the age of sixteen. He acquired distinction as a military engineer, and after 1527 was employed by the Venetian Republic in the design of fortifications. His work in architecture consequently has great vigour, and he often makes use of rustication, sometimes on the Orders themselves. His originality was not unduly restrained by observance of Roman precedent. The gateways of Verona, the **Porta Nuova** (1533–40) and the **Porta del Palio** (1542–55) (p. 746A) are excellent instances of his bold treatments.

The **Palazzo Bevilacqua, Verona** (1527–) (p. 744J), has rustications carrying across the pilasters on the ground storey and spirally-fluted Corinthian attached columns on the upper tier, arranged in alternating spacings suggestive of the Roman 'triumphal arch' motif. These features of the upper floor, and the smaller arched openings capped by alternating triangular and segmental-headed pediments, all

DOGE'S PALACE : VENICE

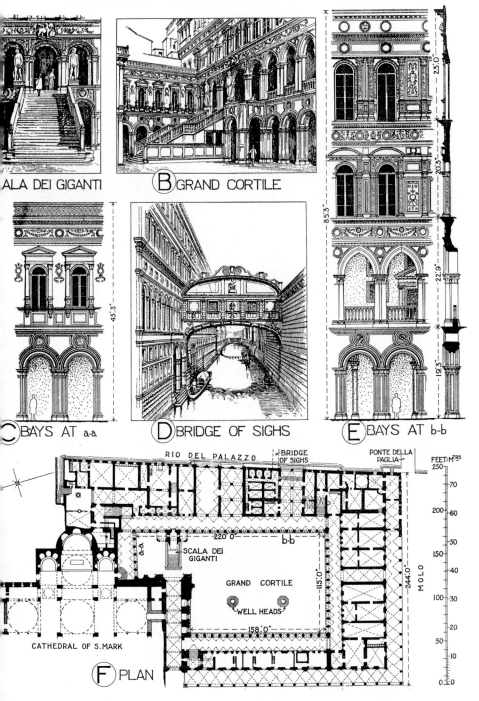

ALA DEI GIGANTI

B GRAND CORTILE

C BAYS AT a-a

D BRIDGE OF SIGHS

E BAYS AT b-b

25.0'

20.5'

85.3'

22.9'

19.3'

RIO DEL PALAZZO   BRIDGE OF SIGHS   PONTE DELLA PAGLIA

220.0'   b-b

a-a

SCALA DEI GIGANTI

GRAND CORTILE

115.0'

WELL HEADS

158.0'

244.0'

MOLO

CATHEDRAL OF S.MARK

F PLAN

FEET M TRS
250
200   70
         60
150   50
         40
100   30
         20
50   10
0   0

PAL. PESARO VENICE

PAL. CORNER SPINELLI: VENICE

PAL CORNER DELL CA' GRANDE: VENICI

(A)

(B)

(C)

PALAZZO VENDRAMINI: VENICE

(E) ORDERS TO FIRST & SEC^ND FLOORS

8 4"
16 5'
4 0'
17 4"

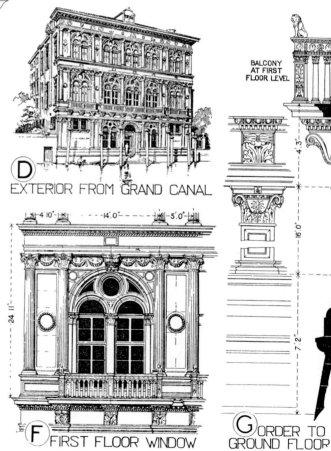

(D) EXTERIOR FROM GRAND CANAL

4'.10" — 14'.0" — 5'.0"

24 II"

(F) FIRST FLOOR WINDOW

BALCONY AT FIRST FLOOR LEVEL

4'.3"
16'.0"
7'.2"

(G) ORDER TO GROUND FLOOR

S. MARIA DEI MIRACOLI : VENICE

FEET METRES
100 30
90
80 25
70 20
60
50 15
40
30 10
20 5
10
0 0

A EXTERIOR FROM S.W.

B PLAN

CANAL

106'0"

32'7"

C INTERIOR
LOOKING INTO SANCTUARY

FT M^{TS}
50 15
40 10
30 5
20
10
0 0

37.5"

46.3"

D TRANS. SECTION

E LONGITUDINAL SECTION

S. GIORGIO DEI GRECI : VENICE

36.0"

102.0"

86.6"

52.0"

F EXTERIOR FROM N.W.

G PLAN

H LONGITUDINAL SECTION

A. S. Giorgio Maggiore, Venice (1565–1610). See p. 738

B. S. Giovanni in Laterano, Rome: façade (1733–6). See p. 729

have direct precedents in Roman arches still existing in the city, but the sculptured spandrels and keystones are his own innovations.

The **Palazzo Pompeii, Verona** (1530–) (p. 744), is a stately composition on axial lines, with a simple arched portal leading to a cortile. A rusticated basement, with arched windows, supports the 'piano nobile', with its fluted Doric columns, tall semicircular-headed windows and carved masks on keystones (p. 744C).

The **Palazzo Grimani, Venice** (1556–) (p. 745), facing the Grand Canal, is Sanmichele's greatest work. The plan is most cleverly contrived on an irregular island site with three large openings to the columned vestibule and long hall, off which are the staircases. The symmetrical façade, 90 ft long and 97 ft high, has superimposed Corinthian Orders, the lower comprising two storeys and the whole bound together with a striking balcony stretching from end to end. By doubling the Order to demarcate the end windows, the customary Venetian fenestration is preserved. A crowning entablature, 8 ft 8 ins high, is proportioned to the full height of the façade.

The **Palazzo dei Diamanti, Verona** (completed 1555) (p. 744G), has a façade showing some influence of Sanmichele, with faceted rustications, whence the name.

The **Gran Guardia Vecchia, Verona** (1610–) (p. 744), for public meetings, is the work of Domenico Curtoni, nephew and pupil of Sanmichele, and is more purely Classical than any of the buildings of the uncle. The façade, over 285 ft long, has a rusticated ground storey with semicircular arches, and an upper tier graced with a stately line of coupled Doric columns, surmounted by an entablature, while the centre is emphasized by an upper storey.

JACOPO SANSOVINO (1486–1570), sculptor and architect, born in Florence and trained there and in Rome, settled in Venice in 1527, where all his most important work is to be found. He was among the first to react from the strict Classical rule, and shows himself a skilful assimilator, borrowing ideas from Peruzzi, Sanmichele and other contemporaries and blending them cleverly in a unique manner.

The **Zecca, Venice** (1536–) has a peculiar treatment of column rustication, giving a severe appearance in keeping with its purpose as a mint.

The **Library of S. Mark, Venice** (1536–53) (pp. 611A, 740) is the most outstanding of the buildings by Sansovino, finished with magnificent sculptural grace. It has arcades of superimposed Ionic over Doric Orders, the upper embracing minor Ionic columns sustaining the window arches. The use of a deep, windowed, frieze in the upper entablature (p. 740B, D) gives the necessary extra importance to allow it to command the whole height of the façade, while the rich ornament of reclining figures in the arch spandrels and of cherubs and festoons in the upper frieze, remains firmly subservient to the architectural lines. The adjacent building, facing into the Piazza di S. Marco, rising one storey higher than the Library, was commenced by Scamozzi in 1584. This and the corresponding structures on the opposite side of the Piazza once were a series of residences for the nine 'Procurators', the chief officials of the Republic after the Doge.

The **Palazzo Corner della Ca' Grande, Venice** (1537–56) (p. 734C) has excellent proportions and stands on an imposing site fronting the Grand Canal. The lower part is rusticated and has three central openings flanked by windows in two tiers, while the two upper storeys are faced with paired Ionic and Corinthian Orders, embracing circular-headed windows. The windowed frieze is used again, but the arrangement of the windows has now become completely regular.

The **Loggetta, Venice** (1540–) (p. 757H), at the base of the great Campanile of S. Mark, is a light and graceful structure with detached Corinthian columns arranged in Sansovino's favourite 'triumphal arch' disposition, with a high attic and balustrade over. It is richly adorned with sculptures.

ANDREA PALLADIO (1508–80), the most influential architect of the whole Renaissance, was born in Padua and at first trained as a mason. Moving to Vicenza about 1524, his second home, where so much of his work was to be done, he secured the patronage of a connoisseur, with whom, after 1540, the date on which he first appears as an architect, he twice voyaged to Rome and made the intensive studies of ancient remains which led eventually to the publication of his famous book *I quattro libri dell' Architettura*. The results of his Classical research can be traced in his designs for buildings both in Venice and Vicenza. They were unfortunately mostly in mean materials, such as brick faced with stucco, and the success he achieved is an instance of how genius can produce works of art out of commonplace materials. Some of his buildings were never completed, or were finished by others, but the publication of the designs in his book, first issued in Venice in 1570, and since published in every country in Europe, has had a far greater influence on architecture than have his buildings; especially in England, where Palladio had an ardent disciple in Inigo Jones (p. 870), who published an annotated edition of his book (now in Worcester College, Oxford).

The **Palazzo Chiericati** (designed 1550, completed *c*. 1580), **Palazzo Thiene** (1556), **Palazzo Valmarana** (1566) (p. 742D), **Palazzo Barbarano** (1570), **Palazzo Capitanio** (1571), and **Casa del Diavolo** (1571) (p. 742G) at Vicenza, are some of the palaces exhibiting rusticated lower storeys supporting an Order often carried through the height of a building to give unity of design. He also built very many splendid villas in the Venetian countryside.

The **Teatro Olimpico, Vicenza** (1580–4), with a permanent stage built in perspective, is an interesting building, designed by Palladio but completed by Scamozzi (p. 693B), and inspired by ancient Roman theatres.

The **Basilica, Vicenza** (1549) (p. 741), is famous for its Renaissance arcades added by Palladio to the Mediaeval structure erected in 1444. The design was won in competition in 1545, and completed 1614. The plan (p. 741E) shows the large Mediaeval hall, 173 ft by 68 ft, with its supporting piers which gave the lines for the Renaissance piers of the surrounding arcades, while the transverse section (p. 741C) shows the upper floor, which regulated the height of the surrounding Orders. The arcades showing the cross-vaults and the twin columns supporting the arches are very impressive (p. 741F). Palladio had to adjust the arcades as an outer husk to the width and height of the Gothic building. The end bays on each façade were unrestricted in width, so Palladio made them narrower in order to give an effect of strength at the angles, as had been previously done by the Greeks, e.g. the Parthenon (p. 94). These arcades (p. 741B), in fine hard stone which has beautifully weathered, consist of superimposed Doric and Ionic Orders which, under the main entablature, frame intervening arches supported on smaller free-standing twin columns, and there are circular openings in the spandrels. This grouping and combination of columns and arches has been termed the 'Palladian motif', and is exceedingly effective, especially when seen in conjunction with the slender campanile alongside (p. 741D).

The **Villa Capra, Vicenza** (1567–) (p. 742), known also as the Rotonda, is a square building with pillared portico on each face, leading to a central circular hall of which only the low dome appears externally above the tiled roof, which is hipped from the angles of the main building. This design was an important departure, and caught the popular taste. It was utilized by Lord Burlington at Chiswick (p. 936B) and by Colin Campbell at Mereworth Castle, Kent (936A, 966G), and has often been copied both in England and on the Continent.

S. Giorgio Maggiore, Venice (1565–) (pp. 736A, 743), has a cruciform plan with apsidal transepts. The interior has piers faced with Corinthian columns and the

A. Exterior   B. Interior
S. Maria della Salute, Venice (1631–82). See p. 747

C. The Scuola di San Marco, Venice, from S. (1485–95). See p. 732

LIBRARY of S.MARK: VENICE

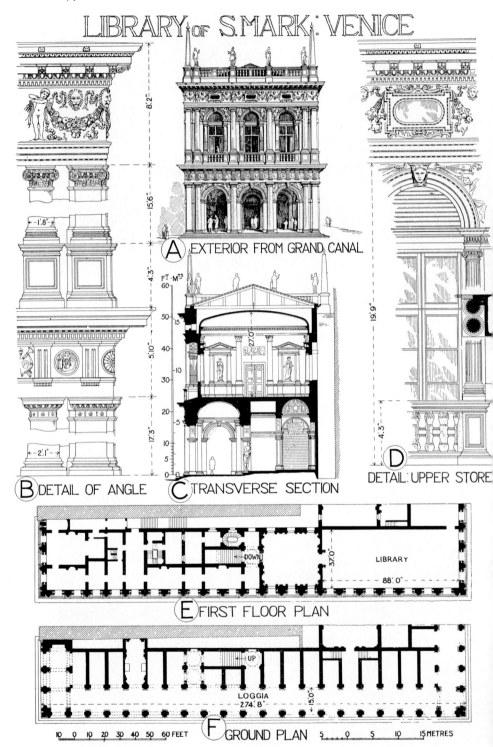

Ⓐ EXTERIOR FROM GRAND CANAL

Ⓑ DETAIL OF ANGLE　Ⓒ TRANSVERSE SECTION

Ⓓ DETAIL: UPPER STORE

Ⓔ FIRST FLOOR PLAN

LIBRARY

Ⓕ GROUND PLAN

LOGGIA

10 0 10 20 30 40 50 60 FEET　　　5 0 5 10 15 METRES

THE BASILICA : VICENZA

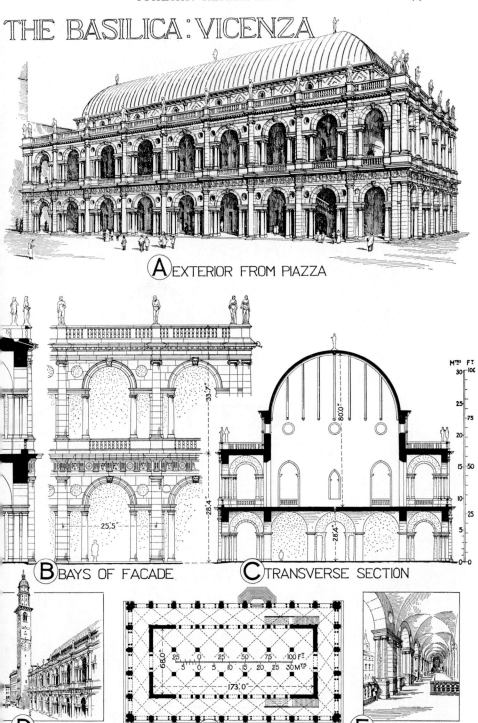

(A) EXTERIOR FROM PIAZZA

(B) BAYS OF FACADE

(C) TRANSVERSE SECTION

(D) SKETCH

(E) PLAN

(F) UPPER ARCADE

VILLA CAPRA : VICENZA

Ⓐ EXTERIOR

Ⓑ PLAN

Ⓒ SECTION

AS DESIGNED

45.8'

35.0'

32.6'

FEET METR
70 20
60
50 15
40
30 10
20 5
10
0 0

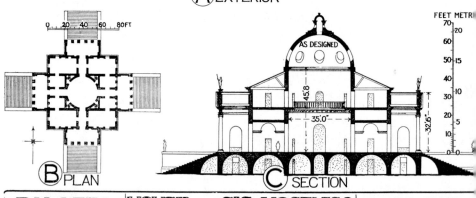

PALAZZO VALMARANA VICENZA

Ⓓ EXTERIOR

HOUSE FOR SIG. MOCENIGO
ON THE BRENTA   (NOT EXECUTED)

Ⓔ VIEW

50   0   50   100 150 200 FT
10 0 10 20 30 40 50 60 MTRS

HALL

87.6'
CORTILE

STABLES   STABLES

GALLERY

225.0'

Ⓕ PLAN

CASA DEL DIAVOLO VICENZA

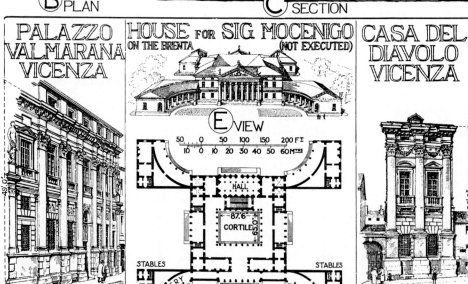

66.0'

Ⓖ PART EXECUTED

S. GIORGIO MAGGIORE : VENICE

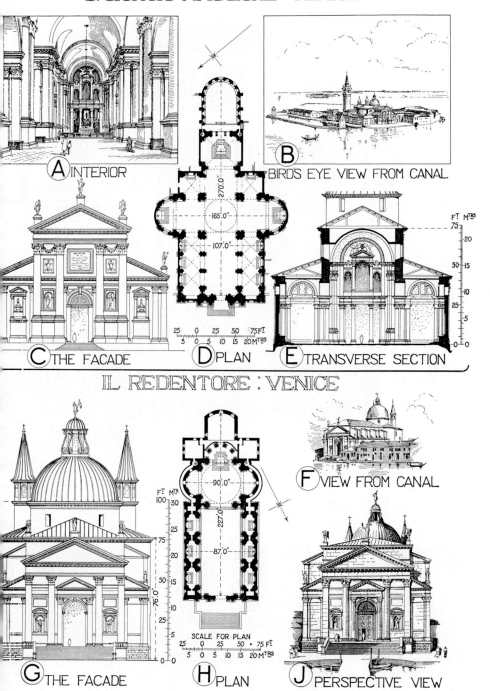

(A) INTERIOR

(B) BIRD'S EYE VIEW FROM CANAL

(C) THE FACADE

(D) PLAN

25 0 25 50 75 FT
5 0 5 10 15 20 M TRS

(E) TRANSVERSE SECTION

270.0"
165.0"
107.0"

FT M TRS
75
50
25
0

20
15
10
5
0

IL REDENTORE : VENICE

(F) VIEW FROM CANAL

(G) THE FACADE

(H) PLAN

(J) PERSPECTIVE VIEW

90.0"
227.0"
87.0"
76.0"

FT M TR
100 30
75
50 15
25
0 0

SCALE FOR PLAN
25 0 25 50 . 75 FT
5 0 5 10 15 20 M TRS

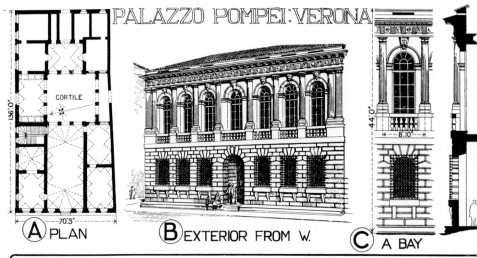

PALAZZO POMPEI : VERONA

Ⓐ PLAN

Ⓑ EXTERIOR FROM W.

Ⓒ A BAY

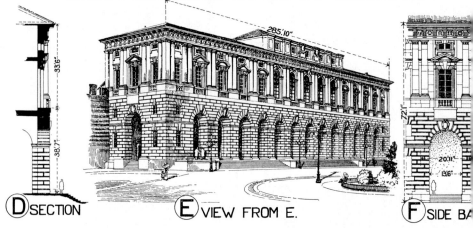

GRAN GUARDIA VECCHIA : VERONA

Ⓓ SECTION

Ⓔ VIEW FROM E.

Ⓕ SIDE BA

OTHER PALACES AT VERONA

Ⓖ PAL. DEI DIAMANTI

Ⓗ PALAZZO DEL CONSIGLIO

Ⓙ PAL. BEVILACQU

PAL. GRIMANI : VENICE

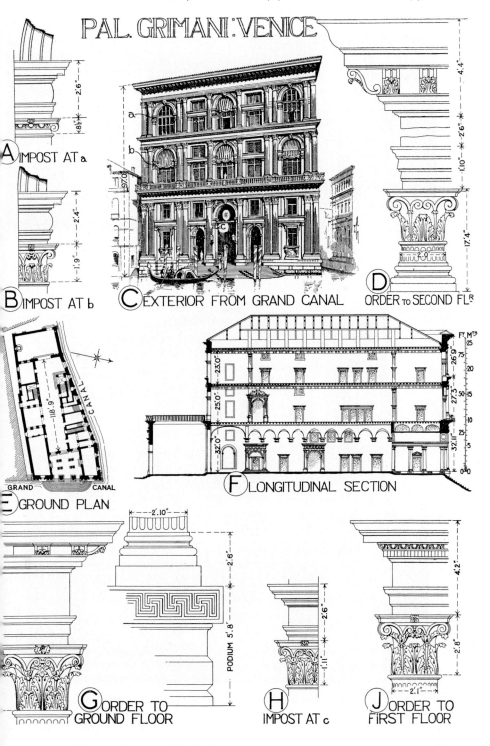

A IMPOST AT a

B IMPOST AT b

C EXTERIOR FROM GRAND CANAL

D ORDER TO SECOND FL.R

E GROUND PLAN

F LONGITUDINAL SECTION

G ORDER TO GROUND FLOOR

H IMPOST AT c

J ORDER TO FIRST FLOOR

A. The Porta del Palio, Verona (1542–55). See p. 732

B. Palazzo Rezzonico, Venice (1667–1756). See opposite page

façade, completed by Scamozzi (1602–10), shows the adaptation of Classic Orders to a church of the basilican plan. The church, with pedimented façade, dome, turrets, and campanile, stands picturesquely on an island framed in by the waters of the Lagoon (p. 743B).

Il Redentore, Venice (1577–92) (p. 743), is similar in plan, but there are side chapels in lieu of aisles. In the façade the principal and subsidiary Orders start from the same base, and the aisles are fronted with half-pediments. This church shows how impossible it is to judge a building from a geometrical drawing only, for in a near view (p. 743J) the dome over the crossing is dwarfed by the long arm of the nave, as in S. Peter, Rome.

BAROQUE

BALDASSARE LONGHENA (1598–1682), a pupil of Scamozzi and contemporary with Bernini, was by far the most distinguished Venetian architect of the period. He continued and developed the architectural traditions of the city.

S. Maria della Salute, Venice (1631–82) (p. 739A, B), groups up most effectively with the Dogana (Custom House) (1676) on the Grand Canal, and is sufficient to stamp the architect as a man of genius. The church is octagonal in form, with a central space, 65 ft in diameter, with Corinthian columns in the angles (p. 739B), and the spacious surrounding ambulatory and radiating chapels make it one of the largest aisled, polygonal churches. The circular dome with high drum is connected to the outer walls by scrolled buttresses which contribute much to the effect (p. 739A). The second dome with its flanking turrets over the wide chancel adds to the picturesqueness of this majestic group, which, throned upon its measured steps above the waters of the canal, is the apotheosis of the Baroque style in Venice.

The Palazzo Pesaro, Venice (1663–79) (p. 734A) was not finished in Longhena's lifetime and the top floor was added by Gaspari (1710). It is similar to the Palazzo Corner della Ca' Grande (p. 734C) of 126 years previously, but the columns are fully detached and combined with minor Orders carrying the window archivolts. Also, there is here a return to the traditional demarcation of the central group and the flank windows of the main façade. The ground storey rustications and the too-profuse sculptured ornament of the added top floor give a spiky effect.

The Palazzo Rezzonico, Venice (1667–) (p. 746B) again was finished after Longhena's death, the top floor being added by Massari in 1752–6. Except that the decorative columns are single rather than coupled, it bears a still closer resemblance to Sansovino's Palazzo Corner della Ca' Grande, having a regular disposition of windows across the façade, and the same serene air. In this case there is an attached Order on the ground storey too, the column shafts, as well as the walls, being rusticated.

COMPARATIVE ANALYSIS

(A comparative table of the essential differences between Gothic and Renaissance is given on p. 661, and between Italian and French Renaissance on p. 799. The following analysis concerns the regional distinctions in Italian Renaissance architecture insofar as they continue to survive: in the Baroque period, architectural style becomes more uniform and the characteristics are given on p. 659.)

PLANS

Florence. Symmetry and compactness of plan, adapted to town rather than country dwellings. Staircases, not axially placed, are enclosed by walls and roofed by barrel vaults (pp. 681F, 685G). Churches are either of basilican type, planned for domical-vaulted aisles and timber-roofed naves (pp. 676G, 679C) or have Byzantine-type eastern end combined with extended western arm, planned for vaults over arms and pendentived dome over crossing. Genoese palaces, planned on falling sites, have axial stair approaches through rear arcaded courts (p. 690C), while some churches are longitudinal and others are Greek-cross type fitted within a square (p. 682D).

Rome. Palace plans become more formal and grand (pp. 705G, 710A, 711D, 718E). Curvilinear elements are introduced (pp. 710A, D, 711D), and stairs may take a circular or elliptical form, as in the Barberini, Corsini and Braschi palaces, and at Caprarola (p. 711C). The Gesù church (p. 704D) established a common type, but centralized plans were also used for churches; the old Roman type of dome over a circular space (p. 700A) and the dome on pendentives over a square space (p. 704A, D) were both used.

Venice. Palace plans compact and rectilinear, with court where space permitted, from which staircases would then arise (p. 733F). Straight fronts to the canals were the rule for palaces (p. 745E) and on the main entrance front there was normally a deep central apartment on each floor, marked on upper floors by banded windows (p. 734A, B, D). The villas of Palladio set new standards in free and gracious planning (p. 742B, F). Early churches simple and aisleless (p. 735B, G), but developed plans usually longitudinal, with Byzantine-type 'centralized space' at east end (p. 743H). S. Maria della Salute unusual in having an ambulatory around its centralized plan, and a picturesque aspiring composition (p. 739A). Church naves were planned for vaults, domes or flat ceilings (pp. 735B, G, 743D, H).

WALLS

Florence. Walls are severe and frequently astylar, but varied surface treatment supplies character. Tiers are masked by string courses and a great crowning cornice is a notable feature (pp. 680A, E, F, 681B, 685B). Genoese and Milanese palaces show an early breakaway in Proto-Baroque (pp. 686B, 724D).

Rome. In High Renaissance palaces, walls are frequently screened with pilasters both single and coupled, on each upper storey (pp. 699A, 710B, F, H, 711A) and later, the pilasters may be carried through two stories (pp. 718A, F, 721A); but generally, the Roman Baroque palace is astylar and only church façades are profusely ornamented with the Orders (pp. 724E, 728B).

Venice. Walls usually have the Orders superimposed in tiers (pp. 734, 740A, 741A), and marble encrustation is common, medallions, lozenges and other motifs of coloured marble often appearing as points of special interest in friezes or centrally in panels (pp. 733C, E, 734B, D, F, 739C). From the time of Palladio and his contemporaries, the giant Order frequently appears (pp. 742D, E, G, 743C, G).

OPENINGS

Florence. Arcades have arches resting directly on columns, with or without a piece of entablature (pp. 676L, 679B, 681C). Doorways are small and severe yet imposing (p. 749G, J). The doorways at Genoa have triangular and segmental pediments (p. 759D, E), while another treatment has a subsidiary architrave (p. 759J). Windows are of three types: (*a*) 'Arcade' type with central column and round arches, as in the Palazzi Riccardi (p. 681G), Strozzi (p. 685H), and Quaratesi (p. 749D); (*b*) 'Architrave' type with cornice, as in the Palazzo Gondi, or with consoles, as in the Palazzi Pitti (p. 749F) and Riccardi (p. 681E); (*c*) 'Order' type with columns and entablature, as in the Palazzo Pandolfini (p. 756).

Rome. Arcades have arches supported on piers faced with columns or pilasters, as in S. Maria della Pace (p. 753E) and the Palazzo Farnese (p. 705F), based on the

A. CAPITAL IN CORTILE
PAL. GONDI : FLORENCE

B. CAPITAL AND BRACKETS
THE BADIA DI FIESOLE : NR FLORENCE

C. PILASTER CAPITAL
S. SPIRITO : FLORENCE

D. WINDOW IN CORTILE
PAL. QUARATESI : FLORENCE

E. NICHE : NATL MUS : FLORENCE

F. WINDOW AND FOUNTAIN
PALAZZO PITTI : FLORENCE

G. DOORWAY
S. CROCE : FLORENCE

H. CHIMNEY PIECE
NATIONAL MUS : FLORENCE

J. PORCH
S. ALESSANDRO : LUCCA

A TABERNACLE
S. CROCE : FLORENCE

A' FRIEZE : PAL. VECCHIO : FLORENCE

B CANTORIA (SINGING GALLERY)
MUSEUM OF S. MARIA DEL FIORE
FLORENCE

C HOLY WATER STO[UP]
SIENA CATHEDR[AL]

D 'LAVABO'
S. M. NOVELLA
FLORENCE

E ALTAR-PIECE : S. CROCE : FLORENCE

F PULPIT : S. M. NOVEL[LA]
FLORENCE

G BRACKET TO PULPIT
S. CROCE : FLORENCE

H RELI- QUARY
S. SALVA- DORE D'
OGNISSANTI : FLORENCE.

J BALUSTRADE TO PULP[IT]
SIENA CATHEDRAL

Colosseum façade. Doorways are flanked by columns (pp. 699A, 753F, G), consoles (pp. 699A, 703D), or rusticated blocks (pp. 705C, 753D). Windows have semi-circular arches enclosed in mouldings forming a square frame with spandrels (pp. 699E, 753C), or are flanked by columns (p. 753A, B), or have architraves and side consoles (p. 710G).

Venice. Arcades have round arches resting on columns (pp. 733C, E, 744H), or on piers faced with columns (pp. 740A, 741B, 743A, 757H). Doorways are flanked by columns and pilasters supporting cornice and semicircular or triangular pediment (p. 757A, C) or are enclosed in rusticated blocks (pp. 734A, 744B), while sometimes, as at Verona, they have architraves and side consoles (p. 759L). Windows are large with semi-Gothic tracery (p. 734B, F) or are flanked by columns (p. 757D), some-times supporting round arches with carved spandrels (pp. 734A, C, 740D).

Roofs

Florence. Low, tiled, roofs are sometimes visible above cornices (pp. 680, 681B, 685B). Domes were favourite features in churches (pp. 676, 679). Raking vaults to staircases and waggon or cross-vaults are general, both frescoed and coffered (pp. 676A, 681C, 690D).

Rome. Roofs are rarely visible (p. 699A) and often hidden by balustrades (p. 718A, B, F). Domes on high drums and crowned with lanterns are usual in churches (pp. 700B, 704B, H). Vaults were either coffered in stucco or painted, after the style of the newly excavated Baths of Titus (pp. 703A, J, 705H, 723F).

Venice. Roofs with balustrades are frequent (p. 740A). Vaulted ceilings of halls, staircases, and churches were elaboratedly moulded in plaster and frescoed (p. 735C), while timber ceilings are a feature in palaces. Domes in churches are grouped with towers (pp. 735F, 739A, 743B, F). In Milan and other north Italian cities the low internal cupola was often covered by a lofty structure in diminishing stages, as at the Certosa, Pavia (pp. 617F, 686A), and S. Maria delle Grazie, Milan (p. 698A, B).

Columns

Florence. The Orders, not at first in general use for façades, frequently supported the arches, both in 'cortile' (pp. 681C, 690D, 698H) and church arcades (pp. 676L, 679B).

Rome. The Orders, either single or coupled, were at first superimposed (pp. 699A, 710H), but later one great Order frequently included the whole height of the build-ing (pp. 710J, 718B). They regulated not only the height of balustrades, but the spacing and size of windows.

Venice. Projecting columns in successive tiers with entablatures, often broken back to the wall, were used (p. 734), while buildings by Sansovino and Palladio show a more correct and formal treatment (pp. 740A, 741, 742).

Mouldings

Florence. The few and simple mouldings of string courses were slight in projection so as to throw into relief the crowning cornice, designed on Classic models (pp. 681A, 685F), as are also the pedimented door-heads at Genoa (p. 759A, C). Mould-ings of ornamental features—consoles, capitals, corbels, niches, and brackets—exhibit refinement of line (pp. 682A, 749, 750), while coffered ceilings were of great elaboration, as at Genoa (p. 759G).

Rome. Classic mouldings from ancient Roman buildings naturally served as models which were closely followed (p. 700J), although new combinations were introduced by Michelangelo and his disciples (p. 705A). The mouldings of balconies, doorways, and tombs are all Classical in treatment (pp. 753, 754).

Venice. Mouldings were influenced by local Byzantine and Gothic art, and were extremely refined and original. Mouldings of pedestals, doorways, entablatures, and capitals are frequently carved with intricate ornament (pp. 734E, G, 740B, D, 745, 758).

ORNAMENT

The special character of Renaissance ornament has been mentioned (p. 664).

Florence. Florentine ornament is well illustrated in the sculptured frieze (p. 750J), coffered ceilings (p. 759G), pilaster (p. 759K), pilaster capitals (pp. 749C, 759H), capitals (p. 749A, B), chimney-piece (p. 749H), consoles or corbels (pp. 749J, 750G), niche (p. 749E), tabernacle (p. 750A), holy-water stoup (p. 750C), singing-gallery (p. 750B), lavabos (pp. 750D, 759F), altar-piece (p. 750E), pulpit (p. 750F), balustrade (p. 750J), angle lantern and link holder (p. 685A, C), and reliquary (p. 750H), many of which were delicately carved with pagan motifs of infant genii, fruit, flowers, and masks, while heraldic shields contrast with plain wall surfaces. The traditional school of fresco painting by Cimabue and Giotto was influenced by the discovery of ancient Roman paintings. The coloured bas-reliefs of Luca della Robbia and his school are specially characteristic of Florentine art at this period.

Rome. Sculpture was refined in treatment and naturally followed Classical precedent. Roman ornament generally can be studied from the capital (p. 699C), fountains (pp. 753H, 754F, H), the Triclinium (p. 753J), singing-gallery (p. 754G), monuments (p. 754J, K, L), candelabra (p. 754C, E), and fonts (p. 754A, B), and the Baroque treatment is seen in the Fontana di Trevi (pp. 730B, 754D), and the altar in the Gesù church (p. 704G). The unearthing of the Baths of Titus, with their frescoes, gave an impetus to the traditional art of painting in tempera on plastic surfaces, which was carried out on a large scale by Raphael, Giulio Romano, and Michelangelo, until it reached its zenith in the Sistine Chapel, Rome.

Venice. Sculpture is both beautiful and exuberant and even competes with the actual architectural features. The Colleoni Monument, Venice (1481) (pp. 606A, 757G), is one of the most famous in the world, with a lofty pedestal embellished with columns, surmounted by the bronze equestrian statue by Verrocchio.

Sculpture was much influenced by the various preceding styles and by a Venetian love of display, as seen in the statue niche (p. 757F), balcony (p. 757B), monument (p. 758D), chimney-piece (p. 757J), carved panel (p. 758E), balustrade (p. 758H), altar (p. 758F), candelabrum (p. 758C), flagstaff standard (p. 758A), capital (p. 758B), and carved ornament (p. 758G, J). The colour-loving Venetians clothed their walls internally with large pictures of subjects both sacred and profane, especially of the triumphs of their city; or else sheathed them in brilliant panels of many-coloured marbles from the shores of the Adriatic.

REFERENCE BOOKS
GENERAL

ALBERTI, L. B. *De re aedificatoria*, or *I dieci libri de l'architettura*. Florence, 1485. English trans. by J. Leoni, entitled *Architecture in Ten Books*. 3 vols. 1726.

ANDERSON, W. J., and STRATTON, A. *The Architecture of the Renaissance in Italy*. London, 1927.

ARGAN, G. C. *L'architettura in Italia*. Milan, 1957.

BRIGGS, M. S. *Baroque Architecture*. London, 1913.

BURCKHARDT, J. *Geschichte der Renaissance in Italien*. Stuttgart, 1912.

DURM, J. *Baukunst der Renaissance in Italien*. 1914.

FLETCHER, BANISTER. *Andrea Palladio: his Life and Works*. London, 1902.

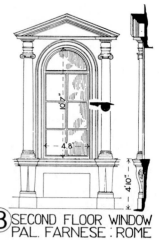

A FIRST FLOOR WINDOW PAL. FARNESE : ROME

C BALCONY WINDOW : PAL. DELLA CANCELLERIA : ROME

B SECOND FLOOR WINDOW PAL. FARNESE : ROME

D DOORWAY : PAL. GAGNATI MONTEPULCIANO

E ARCADE IN CLOISTER S. MARIA DELLA PACE : ROME

F DOORWAY : PALAZZO SCIARRA : ROME

G DOORWAY SACRATI : FERRARA

H FONTANA PAOLA : ROME

J TRICLINIUM OF LEO III : ROME

A FONT: SS. VINCENZO ED ANASTASIO: ROME

B FONT: S. ONOFRIO ROME

C CANDELABRUM S. ANDREA DELLA VALLE: ROME

D SCULPTURED GROUP ON PARAPET FONTANA DI TREVI: ROME

E CANDELABRU S. ANDREA DELL VALLE ROM

F FONTANA DELLE TARTARUGHE: ROME

G CANTORIA: SISTINE CHAPEL PALAZZO VATICANO: ROME

H FONTANA DE TRITONE: ROME

J THE BONSI MONT S. GREGORIO MAGNO: ROME

K TOMB OF PIETRO RIARIO SS. APOSTOLI: ROME

L MONT TO PIETRO C NARNI CATHEDRA

GROMORT, G. *Italian Renaissance Architecture.* Trans. by G. F. Waters, London, 1922.
JACKSON, SIR T. G. *The Renaissance of Roman Architecture.* Pt. I, *Italy.* London, 1921.
KINROSS, J. *Details from Italian Buildings.* Edinburgh, 1882.
OAKESHOTT, G. J. *Detail and Ornament of the Italian Renaissance.* London, 1888.
RICCI, C. *Architettura barocca in Italia.* Turin, 1922.
SCOTT, GEOFFREY. *The Architecture of Humanism.* London, 1924.
SERLIO, S. *I cinque libri d'architettura.* English trans. by R. Peake, *The Five Books of Architecture by Sebastian Serly.* 1611.
VASARI, G. *Lives of the most eminent Painters, Sculptors, and Architects.* 1897.
WITTKOWER, R. *Art and Architecture in Italy; 1600–1750.* Pelican History of Art, 1958.

FLORENTINE RENAISSANCE

CARLI, E. *Brunelleschi.* Milan, 1952.
GRANDJEAN DE MONTIGNY, A. H. V., et FAMIN, A. *Architecture toscane.* Paris, 1874.
RASCHDORFF, J. C. *Toscana.* Berlin, 1888.
RUGGIERI, F. *Scelti de architettura della Città di Firenze.* Florence, 1738.
STEGMANN, D. von, und GEYMULLER, H. von. *Die Architektur der Renaissance in Toscana.* 12 vols. Munich, 1909.

THE RENAISSANCE IN MILAN, TURIN AND GENOA

BARONI, C. *L'architettura da Bramante al Ricchino.* Milan, 1941.
BRIZIO, A. M. *L'architettura barocca in Piemonte.* Turin, 1953.
CALLET, F., et LESUEUR, J. B. C. *Architecture italienne: édifices publics et particuliers de Turin et Milan.* Paris, 1855.
CARDEN, R. W. *The City of Genoa.* London, 1908.
DURELLI, G. and F. *La Certosa di Pavia.* 1853.
GAUTHIER, M. P. *Les plus beaux édifices de la ville Gênes.* 2 vols. Paris, 1818.
GROSSO, O. *Portali e palazzi di Genova.* Milan, 19—.
GUARINI, G. *Architettura civile.* Turin, 1737.
PARAVICINI, T. V. *Die Renaissance Architektur der Lombardei.* Dresden, 1878.
PASSANTI, M. *Architettura in Piemonte.* Turin, 1945.
PORTOGHESI, P. *Guarino Guarini.* Milan, 1956.
REINHARDT, T. *Genua.* Berlin, 1886.
ROVERE, L., VIALE, V., and BRINCKMANN, A. E. *Filippo Juvarra.* Milan, 1937.
RUBENS, P. P. *Palazzi antichi e moderni di Genova.* Antwerp, 1663.

ROMAN RENAISSANCE

BOROMINI, F. *Opera della chiesa e fabbrica . . . di Roma.* 1720.
BRIGGS, M. S. *Baroque Architecture.* London, 1913.
CHIERICI, G. *Bramante.* Milan, 1954.
COLASANTI, A. *Case e palazzi barocchi di Roma.* Milan, 19—.
DONATI, C. *Carlo Maderno.* Lugano, 1957.
FOKKER, T. H. *Roman Baroque Art.* 2 vols. Oxford, 1938.
FONTANA, G. *Raccolta delle chiese di Roma.* 4 vols. Rome, 1855.
LETAROUILLY, P. M. *Édifices de Rome moderne.* 4 vols. Paris, 1868.
—. *Le Vatican et la basilique de Saint-Pierre de Rome.* 2 vols. Paris, 1882.
MACCARI, E. *Il Palazzo di Caprarola.* Rome, 1870.
PALLADIO, A. *I quattro libri dell' architettura.* Venice, 1570. The best English editions are those by Leoni (1715) and Ware (1738).
PERCIER, C., et FONTAINE, P. F. L. *Choix des plus célèbres maisons de plaisance de Rome et de ses environs.* Paris, 1809.
PEROTTI, M. V. *Borromini.* Milan, 1951.
RICCI, C. *Baroque Architecture and Sculpture in Italy.* London, 1912.
ROSSI, D. de. *Studio d'architettura civile della città de Roma.* 3 vols. Rome, 1720–1.
SCAMOZZI, O. B. *Fabbriche e i disegni di Andrea Palladio.* 4 vols. Vicenza, 1776–83.
STRACK, H. *Baudenkmaeler Roms des XV–XIX Jahrhunderts.* Berlin. 1891.
SUYS, T. F., et HAUDEBOURT, L. P. *Palais Massimi à Rome.* Paris, 1818.

Venetian Renaissance

CHIERICI, G. *Palladio.* Turin, 1952.

CICOGNARA, CONTE F. L. *Le fabbriche e i monumenti conspicui di Venezia.* 2 vols. Venice, 1838–40.

FLETCHER, BANISTER. *Andrea Palladio: his Life and Works.* London, 1902.

HAUPT, A. *Palast-architektur von Ober-Italien und Toscana—Verona.* Berlin, 1908.

LEONI, G. *The Architecture of Andrea Palladio.* London, 1715, 1721, 1742.

PAOLETTI, P. *L'architettura e la scultura del Rinascimento in Venezia.* 3 vols. Venice, 1893.

PIOZZA, A. M. D. *Palladio.* Vicenza, 1943.

RASCHDORFF, O. *Palast-architektur von Ober-Italien und Toscana—Venedig.* Berlin, 1903.

SCHMIDT, O. *Vicenza.* Vienna, 1898.

SEMENZATO, C. *L'architettura di Baldassare Longhena.* Padua, 1954.

Palazzo Pandolfini, Florence (1520–27). See p. 707

A DOORWAY
S. ZACCARIA : VENICE

32.10
19.4

B BALCONY : PALAZZO
FRANCHINI : VERONA

C DOORWAY . SCUOLA
DI S. ROCCO : VENICE

35.5"

D WINDOW : PAL.
REGIO : VENICE

19.3

136.9

SHOPS SHOPS
SHOPS

SHOPS SHOPS
SHOPS

91.0
BLOCK
PLAN

E THE RIALTO BRIDGE
VENICE

F STATUE - NICHE : PAL
CORNARO : VENICE

17.8

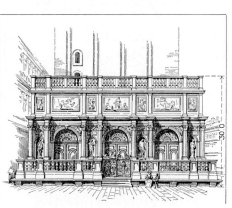

G MONUMENT TO GEN.
COLLEONI : VENICE

24.8"

H THE LOGETTA : VENICE

30.0

J CHIMNEY - PIECE
DUCAL PALACE
VENICE

8.5"

A BRONZE STANDARD
PIAZZA OF S. MARK: VENICE

B CAPITAL: S.M. DEI
MIRACOLI: VENICE

C BRONZE CANDELABR
S. ANTONIO: PADU

D MONT OF P. BERNARDO
THE FRARI CH: VENICE

E PANEL: S.M. DEI MIRACOLI: VENICE

F ALTAR OF S. GIAC
S. MARK: VENI

G PORTION OF DOORWAY
ORFANI AI GESUATI: VENICE

H BALUSTRADE: S.M. DEI MIRACOLI: VENICE

J PORTION OF VENDRAMIN M
SS. GIOVANNI E PAOLO: VEN

ANGLE OF CORNICE AT a

C ANGLE OF CORNICE AT b

B PLAN LOOKING UP AT y-y

D DOORWAY: PAL. BALBARO GENOA

E DOORWAY: PAL. CAREGA: GENOA

F LAVABO OLD CONVENT GENOA

SECTION THRO' COFFERS

G COFFERED CEILING: VILLA CAMBIASO IN ALBARO

H TYPICAL CAP.

J DOORWAY GENOA

K PILASTER VILLA CAMBIASO

L DOORWAY VERONA

GROUND LINE

A. Château d'Azay-le-Rideau (1518–27). See p. 773

B. Château de Chenonceaux (1515–23; bridge 1556–9; gallery over bridge 1576)
See p. 773

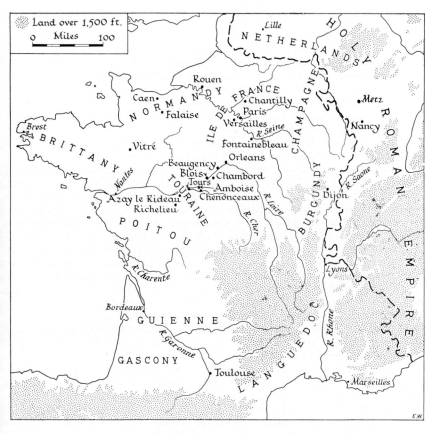

France in the sixteenth century

XXI. FRENCH RENAISSANCE

(fifteenth–nineteenth century)

INFLUENCES

GEOGRAPHICAL. France had, since the Romanesque and Gothic periods (pp. 335, 529), become one united kingdom, with Paris as the centre, from which the new Renaissance influence radiated to all parts of the country. This new geographical condition conduced to a homogeneous development within her extended boundaries, in striking contrast to the variety displayed at this period in the independent city-states of Italy. The distance of Paris from the centre of the Renaissance movement in Italy helped to delay its adoption in France for some seventy-five years or more.

GEOLOGICAL. We have already seen in considering the Romanesque and

Gothic periods (pp. 336, 530) that throughout France there was good building stone, easily worked; so much so that Paris, in which many of the finest buildings were erected under the influence of the now powerful court, is consequently a city of stone, just as, under different geological conditions, London is a city of brick. Iron, wrought and cast, came into use as a building material shortly after 1780.

CLIMATIC. The climate, as in previous periods (pp. 336, 530), asserted its influence on architecture in demanding a continuance of large windows, high-pitched roofs, and lofty chimneys, which differentiated Renaissance architecture in France from that in Italy, the land of its birth.

RELIGIOUS. The Reformation obtained little hold in France, and ecclesiastical polity remained much the same until the end of the eighteenth century. The supply of Gothic churches proved adequate for the needs of the population in the early part of the period, and therefore, as in England, few churches were then erected. From 1558 to the end of the century the country was distracted by religious wars between Huguenots and Catholics, and the Massacre of S. Bartholomew in 1572 drove many of the best Huguenot craftsmen into England. This emigration was further increased by the revocation of the Edict of Nantes in 1685. The chief influence on ecclesiastical architecture in France during later Renaissance times came from the powerful order of Jesuits, which, having received Papal approval in 1540, spread over Europe in the wake of the Reformation and built great churches in France designed for preaching to large congregations, with the object of refuting Reformation heresies. The Revolution of 1789 was antipathetic to religion, but Catholicism thereafter reasserted itself with renewed vigour.

SOCIAL. Paris, as the capital of the newly consolidated kingdom of France and as the centre of the brilliant court of Francis I, attained pre-eminence in art and literature. This resulted in the adoption of one national architectural style which emanated from Paris and the schools in the vicinity; while the valley of the Loire became a highway along which, in response to new social conditions, the famous châteaux of kings and courtiers sprang up and formed models for other parts of the country. This influence was largely augmented by the presence of a number of Italian artists at the court and in the so-called 'schools', established first at Amboise by Charles VIII, and afterwards at Tours, Blois and, most importantly, Fontainebleau. Notable among the Italian artists were the following, the length of residence in France being given in parenthesis after each name: Giuliano da Sangallo (1495; a brief visit only) (pp. 678, 717) and Fra Giocondo (1495–1505) (p. 732), neither of whom has left much trace of his stay; Domenico da Cortona, known as Boccadoro (1495; 1549), pupil of Giuliano da Sangallo, a woodworker who only emerged as an architect in 1519; the great Leonardo da Vinci (1516–19), who died at Amboise in the latter year; Giovanni Battista di Giacopo, known as Il Rosso (1530–40) and Francesco Primaticcio (1532–70) (p. 707), both being highly important in introducing Proto-Baroque or 'Mannerist' architectural practices, chiefly decorative, into France; Benvenuto Cellini (1537, and again, 1538–45), celebrated goldsmith and sculptor; G. B. Vignola (1541–3) (p. 708) and Sebastiano Serlio (1541–54), the latter having a profound influence in France rather by his writings than his architecture. These, and other artists, aided by Italian craftsmen, did much to further the spread of the Renaissance in the country. The kingly power was gradually becoming absolute, owing largely to the policy of Cardinal Richelieu and his successor, Mazarin, in the reign of Louis XIII (1610–43), so that Louis XIV (1643–1715) could declare with truth 'L'Etat c'est moi'. He was the great patron of the later Renaissance in France, and the palaces of the Louvre and Versailles are monuments of his lavish expenditure on architecture and the decorative arts. Under Louis XV (1715–74) the accumulated evils of despotism, bad government, and the

A. Château de Blois from N.W. (1508–1640). See pp. 770, 780

B. Château de Chambord from N. (1519–47). See p. 773

A. The Châtelet, Chantilly (*c.* 1560). See p. 774

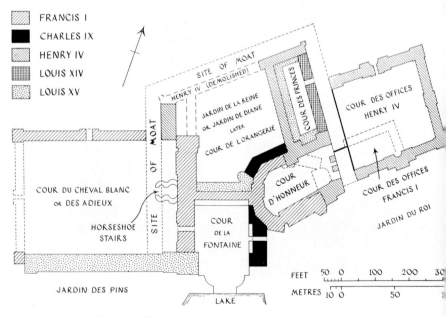

FRANCIS I
CHARLES IX
HENRY IV
LOUIS XIV
LOUIS XV

SITE OF MOAT
HENRY IV (DEMOLISHED)

SITE OF MOAT

JARDIN DE LA REINE
OR JARDIN DE DIANE
LATER
COUR DE L'ORANGERIE

COUR DES PRINCES

COUR DES OFFICES
HENRY IV

COUR DU CHEVAL BLANC
OR DES ADIEUX

HORSESHOE
STAIRS

COUR
D'HONNEUR

COUR DES OFFICES
FRANCIS I

COUR
DE LA
FONTAINE

JARDIN DU ROI

JARDIN DES PINS

LAKE

FEET 50 0   100   200   30
METRES 10 0   50

B. Palais de Fontainebleau: plan showing dates of erection

selfishness of the aristocracy had already become pronounced, when Voltaire and Rousseau voiced enlightened criticism in their writings, which prepared the way for the Revolution of 1789, when all architectural development was arrested until about 1794. In the interim, there was quite a little destruction and defacement of existing monuments. Development was resumed thereafter, new trends showing themselves in response to the changed social conditions. Patronage passed from the hands of the aristocracy to the ruling class of the new régime, which had tastes of a coarser and more pretentious kind. Ambitions mounted, however, and many new architectural works were carried out: Napoleon I carried on the work of beautifying Paris. The Restoration of the monarchy fostered fresh tendencies once again, but while these were intensifying, the current practices in architecture continued to prevail with diminishing support until about 1830.

HISTORICAL. The chief factor in the process of building up the Kingdom of France was the struggle to expel the English, inspired by Joan of Arc's leadership (1429–31) and culminating in the expulsion of the English in 1453. A new national feeling was then created, which, as in other countries under similar conditions, gave a great impetus to architecture, and resulted in the erection of many fine buildings, which have since been held worthy to rank as national monuments. During the first half of the sixteenth century Italy became the battlefield of Europe, for in 1494 Charles VIII of France marched through Italy to claim the Kingdom of Naples, and in 1508 Louis XII joined the League of Cambrai against Venice, when Florence became the ally of France. Francis I also invaded Italy to substantiate his claim to the duchy of Milan, but was defeated and taken prisoner at the battle of Pavia, 1525. In these wars the French kings, while failing in their actual object, were brought into contact with the older civilization of Italy and were thus drawn into the Renaissance movement. Following the disturbances caused by the religious wars of the second half of the sixteenth century, there began a long period of firm government commencing with the reign of Henry IV (1589), first of the Bourbon dynasty, which endured for some two hundred years. France then achieved an unprecedented unity, power and splendour, establishing a prestige in Europe which was not secured without civil and religious tribulations and military and diplomatic clashes with her neighbours. The long reign of Louis XIV (1643–1715) marked the zenith. The advent of Louis XV (1715) heralded a decline, culminating in the Revolution of 1789; this being succeeded by republican governments soon in aggressive conflict with England and the majority of the European states. Napoleon Bonaparte emerged as an omnipotent national figure, establishing an Empire (1804–14) by feats of arms; but, facing reverses and the defeat of his marshals in France, abdicated and retired to the island of Elba. He returned again in 1815 to lead a brief but brilliant campaign against his country's foes, only to meet disaster at the hands of Wellington at Waterloo in the same year. Bourbons (Louis XVIII and Charles X) reigned again until 1830.

ARCHITECTURAL CHARACTER

The architectural character of the Renaissance in Europe has already been described (p. 656). The style in France, which took root about seventy-five years later than in Italy, may be divided into three periods:

(a) *The Early Period* (1494–1589 or sixteenth century), comprising the latter part of the reign of Charles VIII (1483–98), beginning with his campaign through Italy against Naples, and the reigns of Louis XII (1498–1515), Francis I (1515–47), Henry II (1547–59), Francis II (1559–60), Charles IX (1560–74), and Henry III (1574–89). The special character of this transitional period lies in the combination of Gothic and Renaissance features to form a picturesque ensemble, and is best understood by noting how it differs from Italian Renaissance. Thus in Italy a return to Classic forms took place, though there was variety in the disposition of revived architectural features (p. 656); whereas in France there was a period of transition, during which Renaissance details were grafted on to such Gothic features as flying buttresses and pinnacles (p. 796A). In Italy the principal buildings were erected in towns, such as Florence, Rome, Venice, and Genoa, as palaces for popes, prelates, and nobles (pp. 690, 705, 734, 756); while the principal buildings in France were castles in the country round Paris and on the Loire for the king and his courtiers (pp. 760, 763, 767, 781). In Italy, moreover, the influence of ancient Rome is apparent in the Classical treatment of detail and ornament, while the influence of Rome was naturally less manifest in France than in Italy, and the influence of traditional Gothic craftsmanship was pronounced. Then, too, in Italy the predominant characteristics are stateliness and a tendency to Classical horizontality (p. 699A), but in France the salient features are picturesqueness and a tendency to Gothic verticality (p. 763B). Early buildings of the period in Italy were principally churches, in consequence of the comparatively small number erected in the Middle Ages, although there are also many Italian palaces of this epoch. Early buildings in France were principally châteaux for the nobility, as sufficient churches of the Middle Ages already existed.

Even before 1494 there were one or two instances of Renaissance architecture constructed in France, but they were wholly by Italians and evoked no French response. Through the majority of the reign of Francis I (to *c.* 1535), the French Renaissance was based upon the school of Amboise, which followed Lombard precedents; new buildings sometimes were designed in the general sense by the Italians, but mostly the Italians contributed the superficial effects to structures in the charge of distinguished French master-masons. After *c.* 1535 the school of Fontainebleau became the more prominent, and the Roman Renaissance provided the chief inspiration. Already the High Renaissance stage had been passed in Italy, and the character of architecture then in vogue was a moderately orthodox Classicism mingled with variously extreme instances of the Proto-Baroque. Primaticcio, in particular, carried the Mannerist decorative architectural arts of Rome via Mantua to Fontainebleau (p. 707). In this second phase too, Frenchmen were at length beginning to produce their own national version of the Renaissance style, the chief personalities being Jean Goujon (*c.* 1505–*c.* 1568), sculptor and architect Pierre Lescot (*c.* 1510–78); Philibert de l'Orme (*c.* 1512–70), a man of great ingenuity in construction and planning; Jean Bullant (*c.* 1520–78); and Jacques Androuet du Cerceau the Elder (*c.* 1520–85). It is significant that each of these visited Rome at some time in his career, usually in its earlier stages.

(*b*) *The Classical Period* (1589–1715 or seventeenth century) comprising the reigns of Henry IV (1589–1610), Louis XIII (1610–43), and Louis XIV (1643–1715). The period is notable for the dignity, sobriety and masculine quality of its foremost buildings, resulting from the subordination of plan, composition and detail to the unity of the whole, and the clarity and simplicity with which the elements were used. Ornament, though somewhat coarse, is vigorous and reasonably restrained. Influences from Italy on the one hand and the Low Countries on the other are for the most part tempered by French taste, and the Baroque is chiefly of importance in imparting grandeur of ideas in architectural and civic design and in garden planning, the latter art making great strides. Very few buildings, and those mostly ecclesiastical, are readily recognizable as Baroque from their external effects, and the extreme forms of Baroque are rare indeed; when they do appear, they usually are due directly to Italian or Flemish inspiration. Though exteriors become

A. Palais de Fontainebleau: Cour du Cheval-Blanc (1528–40 and later). See p. 774

B. Palais de Fontainebleau from the lake

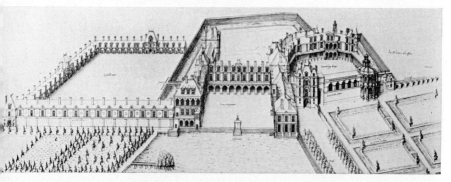

c. Palais de Fontainebleau looking N.: drawing by J. A. Du Cerceau

A. Palais de Fontainebleau: Galerie de François Ier (1533–40). See p. 774

B. Palais de Fontainebleau: Galerie de Henri II (*c.* 1540, decorations *c.* 1552–).
See p. 774

Classical and straightforward, interior decoration remains rich and luxuriant. It is here that foreign Proto-Baroque and Baroque influences play an important part, though again, the outcome of the amalgam is characteristically French. In the earlier part of the period brick is much favoured as a building material, usually in conjunction with stone or stucco used for quoins and dressings and for *chaînes*, which in lieu of pilasters, rise vertically between the string-mouldings and cornice so as to form wall-panels (pp. 782B, 784B), these often having central framed ornaments or niches or being infilled with patterned brickwork. Windows grow increasingly large, and ride up into the steep roofs as dormers, while stone mullions and transoms tend to give place to wood. There is much play with rustication, on the Orders themselves when these appear; sometimes the Orders enframe dormers, as well as the windows aligned vertically below. Roofs at first mostly are steep and treated in separate pavilion units, and the 'mansard' roof of two different slopes is popular, but as the period develops, unified pitched roofs or flat roofs become increasingly common. The Orders figure much more frequently in the second half of the period, normally superimposed in the typical French manner, but with a little recourse to the giant Order. The Orders become much more strictly Classical in proportions and detail than formerly, and this relative simplicity of exterior design accentuates the contrast with interior decoration, which is brilliantly profuse in fanciful scrolls, nymphs, wreaths and shells, carried out in stucco and papier-mâché, forms of ornament also consistently applied to furniture and fittings. This was the great age of Renaissance architecture in France. The principal architects of the period are the accomplished Salomon de Brosse (*c.* 1562–1626), best known for his Palais du Luxembourg; Jacques Lemercier (1585–1654), François Mansart (1598–1666) and Louis Le Vau (1612–70), the latter three largely responsible for the inception of true Classicism; François Derand (1588–1644), architect of the Society of Jesus and designer of the church of SS. Paul and Louis, Paris; Claude Perrault (1613–88), whose most famous work is the east front of the Louvre; André Le Nôtre (1613–1700), France's outstanding garden architect; Charles Lebrun (1619–90), skilful interior designer; and Jules Hardouin Mansart (1646–1708), celebrated particularly for his church of the Invalides, Paris, and the Chapel at Versailles, his later output showing a Baroque tendency.

(c) *The Late Period* (1715–1830 or eighteenth century), comprising the reigns of Louis XV (1715–74) and Louis XVI (1774–92) and the subsequent period of rapid political change, embracing the ascendancy of Napoleon Bonaparte, concluding with the reign of Charles X (1824–30). Architecturally, three stylistic phases may be distinguished. The first two are usually identified with the names of the sovereigns Louis XV and XVI, but in fact overlap considerably; the third is known as that of the 'Empire', approximately from 1790–1830. In the first phase there is a descent from the Classical grandeur of the previous, Louis XIV, era, towards a relative intimacy of effect, particularly marked in domestic planning and in interior decoration. Very many modest residences and town 'hôtels' were erected in which comfort and convenience were considered far more important than chilly dignity. Rooms were planned for independent approach rather than in sequence, now being interlocked in compact arrangements with many devices of circular, oval, curvilinear or polygonal shape to facilitate compression and produce diverting visual effects. Double-depth or deep, squarish plans became normal. Internal corners of apartments sometimes were rounded, and occasionally walls followed sinuous curves on plan, this type of planning being the especial forte of J. A. Meissonnier, whose work in general was that of an extreme form of Baroque known as Rococo, a term applicable to much of the interior decoration of the day. Though profuse, interior ornament is in the main cheerful, light and delicate, following a variety of

2B

H.O.A.

differing 'styles' or modes of composition and expression. Yet externally, except in church architecture, where near-Baroque instances occasionally occur, architecture became more simple but at the same time less Classically pure, the Orders often being substituted by scratchy *chaînes* of rustication and parched ornament in domestic buildings, while windows grew larger still, often absorbing the greater part of the wall. About the middle of the eighteenth century a romantic tendency made itself felt, leading to a return to the sober Classicism of Louis XIV's time and, more importantly, to a growing respect for the monuments of antiquity, stimulated by discoveries at Herculaneum (1719) and Pompeii (1748) and other sites in Italy, Asia Minor and Greece. Measured drawings and 'restorations' of ancient remains appeared in increasing volume. The puristic reaction was anti-Baroque and anti-Rococo, yet was more effective in cleansing exterior architecture of superfluities than in materially reducing the richness of interiors, which became austere and refined rather than simple, while new decorative motifs were drawn from widely divergent sources; from the art of neighbouring countries, the Orient, Egypt, or from France's own antecedents as well as from Classical antiquity. Classicism, however, chiefly gained the day in the 'Empire' phase, when a frigid formality was the keynote, Graeco-Roman coalescing with Egyptian motifs to produce a distinctively French national decorative style. Externally, it was Roman character that was chiefly favoured, only slightly tinctured with the Greek; in France the Greek and the Gothic Revivals never achieved the popularity that they did in early nineteenth-century England. Constructively, cast and wrought iron were exploited from the late eighteenth century, a dome and bridges having been erected in the material before 1810. Among the notable architects of the Late period are Jacques Jules Gabriel (1667–1742); Germain Boffrand (1667–1754); Juste Aurèle Meissonnier (1693–1750), Italian born, notorious for his eccentric Rococo decorative style; Jean Nicolas Servandoni (1695–1766), also Italian, designer of the S. Sulpice, Paris, façade; Jacques François Blondel (1705–74), more famous than his namesake, N. F. Blondel, of almost a century previously, as a writer and teacher, author of *Cours d'architecture*, an influential theoretical work; Jacques Germain Soufflot (1713–80), whose studies of Roman and Greek monuments in Italy produced their effects on his Panthéon, Paris; Etiénne Louis Boullée (1728–99) and Claude Nicholas Ledoux (1736–1806), each responsible for several fine houses and fertile of progressive ideas; Jacques Denis Antoine (1733–1801), designer of the Hôtel des Monnaies, Paris; Jean Francis Chalgrin (1739–1811), best remembered for his scheme for the famous Arc de Triomphe; Bernard Poyet (1742–1824) author of the frontispiece to the Chambre des Députés, Paris; the inseparables Charles Percier (1764–1838) and Pierre F. L. Fontaine (1762–1853), joint designers of the Arc du Carrousel, Paris, and virtual inventors of the 'Empire' decorative style; and Pierre-Alexandre Vignon (1763–1828), known for his Madeleine church, Paris.

EXAMPLES

SECULAR ARCHITECTURE

The **Château de Blois** (1498–1524 and later) (pp. 763A, 771), begun in the thirteenth century (p. 555), was continued (1498–1504) by Louis XII in an addition to the east wing which shows very little Renaissance influence, and by Francis I shortly afterwards (1515–24), being finally completed (1635–8) by François Mansart for Gaston d'Orléans in the reign of Louis XIII. The buildings belonging to these successive periods are grouped around an irregular quadrangle (p. 771B, E), with central entrance, enriched with statuary, through the Louis XII block. The façades

CHATEAU DE BLOIS

A TAIRCASE TOWER
(FRANCIS I)

B BIRD'S-EYE VIEW

C STAIRCASE TOWER (FRANCIS I)
AT ✕

■ 13ᵀᴴ CENTURY
▨ 15ᵀᴴ CENTURY
▧ LOUIS XII(1498–1504)
▨ FRANCIS I(1515–1524)
▦ GASTON D'ORLEANS
   (1635–1638)

ENTRANCE

E PLAN

50 0   50 100 150 200 Fᵀ
10 0 10 20 30 40 50 60 Mᵀˢ

D HIMNEY STACK (FRANCIS I)

F CHIMNEY-PIECE (FRANCIS I)

CHATEAU DE BURY

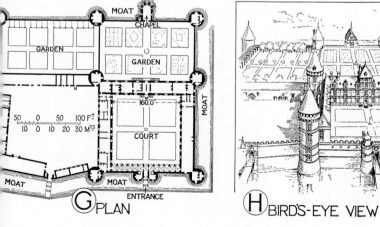

MOAT
CHAPEL
GARDEN
GARDEN
160.0
MOAT
COURT
50 0   50 100 Fᵀ
10 0 10 20 30 Mᵀˢ
MOAT
MOAT
ENTRANCE

G PLAN

H BIRD'S-EYE VIEW (RESTORED)

CHATEAU DE CHAMBORD

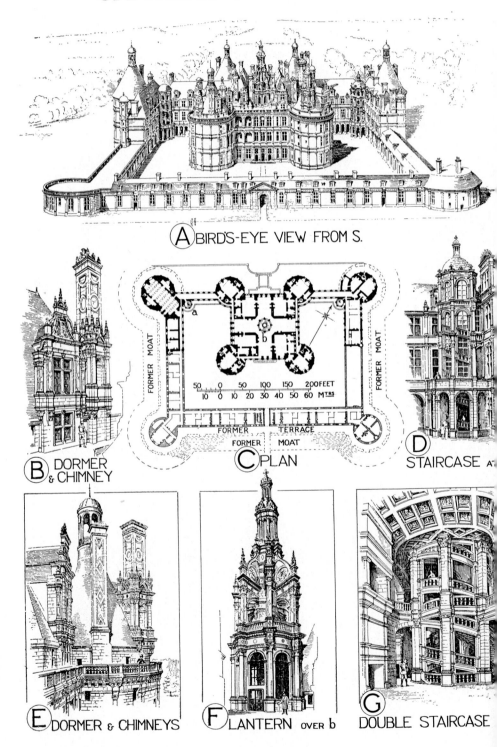

A BIRD'S-EYE VIEW FROM S.

B DORMER & CHIMNEY

C PLAN

FORMER MOAT

FORMER MOAT

50   0   50   100   150   200 FEET
10   0   10 20 30 40 50 60 MTRS

FORMER TERRACE

FORMER MOAT

D STAIRCASE A

E DORMER & CHIMNEYS

F LANTERN over b

G DOUBLE STAIRCASE

of the time of Francis I have windows with panelled instead of moulded mullions (p. 771C), ornate crowning cornices, and carved roof dormers and chimney stacks (p. 771D), which together make a pleasing and characteristic combination, further enhanced by the famous spiral staircase of Francis I in its open tower (p. 771C), in which the letter F and the Salamander, emblems of Francis I, are introduced as heraldic decoration among the carving on the balustrades and vault bosses. The staircase (p. 771A) has a beautiful architectural treatment, founded on the Mediaeval corkscrew stair (p. 558E), similar to a spiral shell. The chimney-pieces (p. 771F), with columns, niches, and carving are ornate, and show that internal fittings were elaborated more than in the Gothic period. The part by Gaston d'Orléans was designed by François Mansart, and its stately formality forms a contrast with the Early Renaissance work of the time of Francis I (p. 771B).

The **Château de Bury** (1520) (p. 771), a few miles from Blois, but now in ruins, consisted of a large square court fronted by a screen wall, one storey high, with internal colonnade and terminated by circular towers. The central entrance is contained between minor circular towers. The courtyard is flanked by two-storeyed wings containing servants' apartments on one side and offices and stabling on the other, connected with the three-storeyed 'corps de logis'—the block forming the residence of the family. Beyond this main building was the walled garden with the chapel at the centre of the further side facing the garden entrance of the house. In French country houses of this period, of which the Château de Bury is typical, the internal court, originally designed for security, was retained; whereas in England, after the time of Henry VII, the closed court had become an exception. This description applies also to French town houses even up to recent times, with modifications dependent on site and local conditions.

The **Château de Chambord** (1519-47) (pp. 763B, 772), designed by an Italian architect, Domenico da Cortona—though much modified by French masons—is the most famous in the Loire district. It is semi-fortified in character and has a plan reminiscent of a Mediaeval 'concentric' castle, being made up of two rectangles one within the other, but with the façade of the smaller on the same line as that of the outer court, which thus protects it on three sides, while the fourth is protected by the moat (p. 772C). This inner block or 'donjon', 220 ft square, corresponds to the keep of an English castle, and has four lofty halls on each floor, finished by elliptical barrel vaulting (p. 772G); at the junction of these halls is the world-famous double spiral staircase, by which people can ascend and descend simultaneously without being visible to each other. It is built up in a cage of stone (p. 772G), crowned with a storeyed lantern which forms the central feature of the exterior (pp. 763B, 772A, F). There is much waste of space, as rectangular rooms are formed in the circular towers. This remarkable pile has many Gothic features clothed with Renaissance detail, and a vertical Gothic effect is produced by wall pilasters with unique carved capitals (p. 803C, F), and angle towers with domes or with conical roofs (p. 772A); while the high-pitched roof with ornate dormers (p. 803H) and lofty chimneys (p. 772B, E) make the variegated skyline of this Early French Renaissance building (p. 763B). It may be contrasted with the palace at Caprarola by Vignola (p. 708).

The **Château de Chenonceaux** (1515-23) (p. 760B) stands on piles in the River Cher, and was originally a simple rectangular block with typical entrance doorway (p. 803G), and steep roof crowded with the conical tops of angle turrets, dormers and chimney stacks, but was picturesquely extended (1556-9) by Philibert de l'Orme by a five-arched covered bridge reaching across the Cher, to which an upper gallery was added (1576) by Jean Bullant in a much more ornate style.

The **Château d'Azay-le-Rideau** (1518-27) (p. 760A) is an attractive building, built on an island, with similar characteristics to the original at Chenonceaux, yet with the features much more sedately disposed. It retains a heavy machicolated cornice of Mediaeval type.

Other châteaux in transitional style are those of **Ecouen** (1531–8), to which the north wing was added (*c.* 1555) by Jean Bullant, and three mostly carried out by the master-mason, Pierre Chambiges (d. 1544); **S. Germain-en-Laye, La Muette,** and **Challuau,** all much of the same date (1539–49) but of which only S. Germain survives. There are also **Ancy-le-Franc** (*c.* 1546), designed by Serlio and much modified in the course of erection, the **Châtelet, Chantilly** (*c.* 1560) (p. 764A), in Jean Bullant's typical Proto-Baroque manner, and **Verneuil-sur-Oise** (1565–*c.* 1590), an extraordinarily perverse building by the elder Du Cerceau.

The **Palais de Fontainebleau** (1528–40) (pp. 764B, 767, 768), by the master-mason Gilles Le Breton for Francis I, has subsequent alterations by Primaticcio (1568) and others which account for its irregular plan. Unlike the Château de Blois, the exterior is remarkably ineffective in composition, and the palace depends for its attraction on the courts (pp. 764B, 767C), formal gardens, terraces, lakes, and radiating vistas, while the chief interest lies in the architectural features of the interior (p. 803A, B, D, E) and in the sumptuous saloons (p. 768A, B) decorated by Rosso, Primaticcio and later masters. The type of mural decoration practised here by the Italians, of boldly-modelled stucco varied with painted panels, had tremendous repercussions in Western Europe, particularly in the case of the modelled strapwork originated by Rosso in the Galerie de François Ier. The gallery is itself the earliest 'long gallery' surviving of those numerous examples found in the early Renaissance of France, England, Scotland and elsewhere.

The **Palais du Louvre, Paris** (1546–1878) (pp. 775–7), continued in course of construction from the time of Francis I to Napoleon III in the nineteenth century, and thus exhibits a complete history of the progressive stages of French Renaissance art carried out in successive periods (p. 775E). The Louvre, together with the Tuileries, constituted one of the most imposing palaces in Europe, and enclosed an area of over 45 acres. Pierre Lescot was employed by Francis I to design a palace in the new style on the site of the old Gothic château which occupied the south-west quarter of the present court, and he commenced the west side of the Renaissance palace (1546) (p. 775E). The façade of this early design consists of two storeys with Corinthian and Composite pilasters surmounted by an attic storey, and is enriched with beautiful sculptured detail by Jean Goujon (pp. 775A, B, 776A). Catherine de' Medici continued Lescot's design round the south of the court, and conceived the idea of connecting the Louvre and the Palais des Tuileries by a gallery along the Seine, a scheme which was not completed till some 300 years later. Henry IV, who was the last monarch to live in the Louvre, instructed Du Cerceau to erect (1600–9) the gallery facing the Seine, in which pilasters including two storeys were surmounted by alternately triangular and segmental pediments (p. 790C), remodelled under Napoleon III (1860–5). Louis XIII, with Cardinal Richelieu, enlarged the original scheme, and in 1624 the north and east sides of the old château were pulled down. Lemercier then commenced the present court, which, measuring 400 ft square, is four times the area of the Mediaeval court, but he only completed (1624–54) the north-west part, including the Pavillon de l'Horloge, which became the centre of the enlarged façade on the west. Louis XIV, with Cardinal Mazarin, commissioned Louis Le Vau to complete the north, east, and south sides of the enlarged court (1650–64), and with his minister, Colbert, employed Claude Perrault to erect (1667–74) the eastern external colonnade, after consideration of designs by several other notable French architects and even of two famous Italian Baroque masters, Carlo Rainaldi (p. 729) and the great Lorenzo Bernini (p. 725) the latter travelling to Paris (1665) specially for the purpose of presenting his

THE LOUVRE PARIS

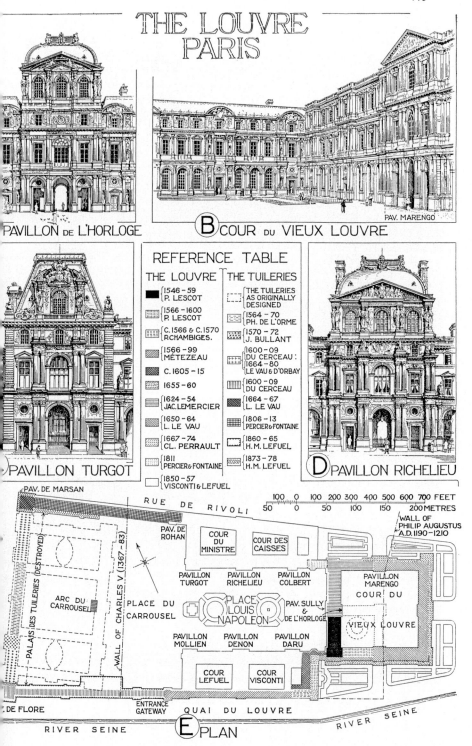

PAVILLON DE L'HORLOGE

B COUR DU VIEUX LOUVRE

PAV. MARENGO

PAVILLON TURGOT

REFERENCE TABLE

THE LOUVRE	THE TUILERIES
1546 - 59 P. LESCOT	THE TUILERIES AS ORIGINALLY DESIGNED
1566 -1600 P. LESCOT	1564 - 70 PH. DE L'ORME
C. 1566 & C.1570 P.CHAMBIGES.	1570 - 72 J. BULLANT
1566 -99 MÉTEZEAU	1600 - 09 DU CERCEAU: 1664 - 80 LE VAU & D'ORBAY
C. 1605 - 15	
1655 - 60	1600 - 09 DU CERCEAU
1624 - 54 JAC.LEMERCIER	1664 - 67 L. LE VAU
1650 - 64 L. LE VAU	1806 - 13 PERCIER & FONTAINE
1667 - 74 CL. PERRAULT	1860 - 65 H.M. LEFUEL
1811 PERCIER & FONTAINE	1873 - 78 H.M. LEFUEL
1850 - 57 VISCONTI & LEFUEL	

D PAVILLON RICHELIEU

E PLAN

PAV. DE MARSAN

RUE DE RIVOLI

100 0 100 200 300 400 500 600 700 FEET
50 0 50 100 150 200 METRES

WALL OF PHILIP AUGUSTUS A.D. 1190-1210

PAV. DE ROHAN

COUR DU MINISTRE

COUR DES CAISSES

PAVILLON TURGOT

PAVILLON RICHELIEU

PAVILLON COLBERT

PAVILLON MARENGO

COUR DU

VIEUX LOUVRE

ARC DU CARROUSEL

PLACE DU CARROUSEL

PLACE LOUIS NAPOLEON

PAV. SULLY & DE L'HORLOGE

PALAIS DES TUILERIES (DESTROYED)

WALL OF CHARLES V (1367 - 83)

PAVILLON MOLLIEN

PAVILLON DENON

PAVILLON DARU

COUR LEFUEL

COUR VISCONTI

. DE FLORE

ENTRANCE GATEWAY

QUAI DU LOUVRE

RIVER SEINE

RIVER SEINE

A. The Louvre, Paris: courtyard façade, with Pavillon de l'Horloge (1546–1654).
See p. 774

B. The Louvre, Paris: east façade (1667–70). See p. 779

A. Palais du Louvre, Paris: Galerie d'Apollon (decorated by Le Brun 1662).
See p. 779

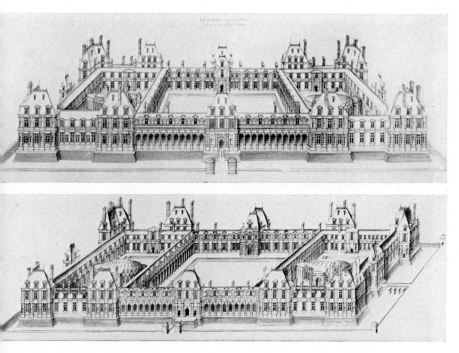

B. Palais des Tuileries, Paris (destroyed): drawings by J. A. Du Cerceau made in 1579.
(*Above*) view from W.; (*below*) view from E. See p. 779

A. Hôtel de Ville, Beaugency:
façade (1526). See p. 779

B. Maison Milsand, Dijon (c. 1561).
Upper part of façade. See p. 780

C. Hôtel d'Assezat, Toulouse: courtyard
façade (1555). See p. 779

D. Hôtel Lamoignon, Paris (1584).
See p. 780

schemes. The selected design by Perrault owes not a little to Le Vau, who was associated with him in the project. This eastern façade (p. 776B) is of a much more monumental character than the court façades. It is 600 ft in length, and consists of a solid-looking basement which supports a colonnade of coupled Corinthian columns, stretching between the pedimented centre-piece and the side wings, instead of the usual and more effective pavilion blocks. A pilaster treatment is carried round part of the north and south external façades. As Perrault's design was higher than the portions already erected, a third Order was now substituted for the attic storey on the east side and on the eastern half of north and south sides of the court, which, as completed with the three storeys of Orders (p. 775B), contrasts with the portion with two storeys and an attic as designed by Lescot. The courtyard of the Ospedale Maggiore, Milan (p. 698G, H), with its open arcades, is the only one in Italy that is comparable to the completed court of the Louvre, which has arcading in the French version on the wall surfaces.

In 1675 the work was suspended, as Louis XIV was directing his energies to his palace at Versailles, and very little appears to have been done to the building until Napoleon I employed Percier and Fontaine to continue the Order to the third storey on the western half of the north and south sides of the court, and a small portion at the north-east angle of the Place Louis Napoléon. Between 1806 and 1813 the same architects commenced the north wing from the Pavillon de Marsan to the Pavillon de Rohan, to connect the Louvre to the Palais des Tuileries, but this wing lost its significance when the latter was destroyed in 1871.

The later nineteenth-century history of these twin palaces may be conveniently added here. Napoleon III conceived the idea of effecting a satisfactory junction between the Louvre and the Tuileries, and in order to mask the converging sides of the connecting wings he employed (1850-7) Visconti and Lefuel to erect the building known as the 'Nouveau Louvre' on the north and south of the Place Louis Napoléon (p. 793B). Lefuel refaced (1860-78) the Pavillon de Flore and the adjacent wing towards the Seine, and also the Pavillon de Marsan and a small portion adjacent, and at the same time the facing of the north wing fronting the Rue de Rivoli was taken in hand. The Pavillon de l'Horloge (pp. 775A, 776A), designed by Lemercier, is a fine composition, obviously derived from the high towers of the Mediaeval period, and gave the keynote for the subsequent Pavillon Turgot (p. 775C) and the Pavillon Richelieu (p. 775D).

The sumptuous interiors (p. 777A) for which the Louvre is famous, are replete with decorations by all the best painters of the day.

The **Palais des Tuileries, Paris** (1564-1680) (pp. 775E, 777B), was commenced for Catherine de' Medici by Philibert de l'Orme, who only erected a domical central pavilion, flanked by low wings (1564-70). A wing was added (1570-92) by Jean Bullant, and further extensions were begun by Du Cerceau the Younger (1600-9), but not completed till 1680 by Le Vau and D'Orbay. The Palace was rich in historical associations, especially in connection with the overthrow of the French monarchy in 1792, and from the time of Napoleon I, who erected the Arc du Carrousel to serve as a monumental entrance, it was the constant residence of the French rulers, till its destruction in 1871. There is a small portion of the façade still preserved in the Tuileries gardens.

There are also throughout France numerous Early Renaissance buildings, such as the **House of Agnès Sorel, Orleans** (c. 1520), the later portion of the **Hôtel de Bourgtheroulde, Rouen** (1501-37) (pp. 554A, 559), the **Hôtel de Ville, Orleans** (1503-13) and a much humbler one of very similar design, the **Hôtel de Ville, Beaugency** (1526) (p. 778A), a beautiful instance of municipal architecture. More mature in character are the **Hôtel d'Assezat, Toulouse** (1555) (p. 778C), by an able local architect, Nicholas Bachelier, an advanced design of tiered, paired columns embracing shallow, windowed arcades; the **Maison Milsand, Dijon** (*c.* 1561) (p. 778B), by Hugues Sambin, its façade bearing an abundance of surface ornament; and the **Hôtel Lamoignon, Paris** (1584) (p. 778D), by Baptiste du Cerceau, instancing the use at this time of the giant Order.

The account given above of the Louvre and the Tuileries has carried us beyond the Classical period, to which we now turn.

The **Palais du Luxembourg, Paris** (1615–24) (p. 781E, F), was erected for Marie de' Medici by Salomon de Brosse, the most able architect of the century, in a bold and simple style designedly echoing Ammanati's rusticated garden façade to the Palazzo Pitti, Florence (p. 680D), but is superior to it. The plan (p. 781E) and composition admirably typify the French hôtel, consisting of a one-storeyed entrance screen with 'porte-cochère', two-storeyed side wings for service and stabling, and the three-storeyed 'corps de logis', forming a court, 240 ft by 190 ft. The palace is now used as the Senate House. De Brosse also built the **Château de Coulommiers** (1613–) (ruined), of similar character and plan and almost equally attractive, and the **Château de Blerancourt** (1614–19) (destroyed), which lacked wings to the forecourt.

The **Château de Richelieu** (1631–7), south-west of Tours, a vast scheme by Lemercier, survives only in a few small elements, but there still exists the walled town of Richelieu (p. 782A) by Lemercier which the Cardinal at the same time caused to be built in replacement of the former village. The 'gridiron' plan of streets and squares was filled out with appropriate buildings and houses of brick with stone dressings. The town, though small, always has been over-large for its functions.

The **Château de Maisons,** near Paris (1642–6) (p. 781A–D), is one of the most pleasantly harmonious of all the châteaux. It was designed by François Mansart on a symmetrical E-plan with central entrance and twin oval-shaped side vestibules. It is notable externally for the effective use of the Classic Orders and the high roofs, with prominent chimney stacks, of the three pavilions, and internally for the refinement of detail of the balustraded stairs, carved chimney-pieces and ornamental ceilings. The same fine quality as at Maisons is notable in the Orleans wing at Blois (p. 763A) which Mansart had added to the Château a little earlier (1635–8). Before this again, he had built the **Château de Balleroy** (1626–36) (p. 782B), an excellent composition in brick with stone dressings.

The **Château of Vaux-le-Vicomte** (1657–61), by Louis Le Vau, with its magnificent formal gardens, is one of the most spectacular in France. There are no wings, only a balustrade, to define the forecourt, and the apartments are consolidated in a double-depth arrangement in a symmetrical composite block, of which the transverse axis is strongly accentuated by a colonnaded entrance vestibule on the forecourt side leading directly to a grand oval saloon dominating the garden front, capped with a dome and lantern consorting awkwardly with the steeply-pitched roofs of the broad angle turrets. Flat pilasters rise through the two main storeys, enframing large windows differentiated to stress the 'piano nobile'.

The **Palais de Versailles** (1661–1756) (pp. 783, 784A) was built for Louis XIV by Le Vau, who designed a palace round the old hunting château (1624–6) erected by de Brosse for Louis XIII. Louis XIV later employed Jules Hardouin Mansart to extend the palace north and south, so as to form a building of over a quarter of a mile long. Other portions were added (1756) by Gabriel for Louis XV. The park façade (p. 783A), has a rusticated ground storey supporting an Order of pilasters, high attic and balustrade, producing a monotonous effect with unbroken skyline. The sumptuous apartments form in themselves a veritable museum of the decorative art of the period. The magnificent 'Galerie des Glaces' (p. 783B), by Mansart, is 240 ft by 34 ft and 43 ft high, and may be compared with the Galerie d'Apollon

CHATEAU DE MAISONS: NEAR PARIS

Ⓐ ENTRANCE FACADE

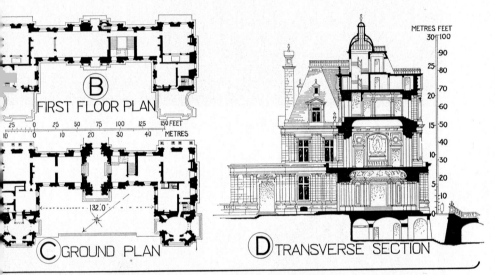

Ⓑ FIRST FLOOR PLAN

25 0   25   50   75   100 125   150 FEET
10 0   10   20   30   40   METRES

Ⓒ GROUND PLAN

132.0

Ⓓ TRANSVERSE SECTION

METRES FEET
30 100
90
25 80
70
20 60
15 50
40
10 30
20
5 10
0

PALAIS DU LUXEMBOURG: PARIS

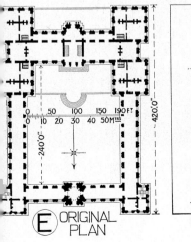

420.0"

240.0"

0   50   100   150   190 FT
0   10   20   30   40 50 MTRS

Ⓔ ORIGINAL PLAN

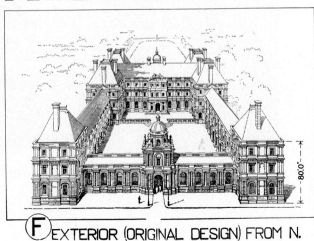

80.0"

Ⓕ EXTERIOR (ORIGINAL DESIGN) FROM N.

A. Town of Richelieu (1631–7). See p. 780

B. Château of Balleroy (1626–36). See p. 780

A. Palais de Versailles: park façade (1661–1756). See p. 780

B. Palais de Versailles: Galerie des Glaces (1678–84). See p. 780

C. Palais de Versailles: the entrance façade

A. Palais de Versailles: aerial view from the park (1661–1756). See p. 785

B. Place des Vosges, Paris (1605–12). See p. 785

at the Louvre (p. 777A). Decorated by Le Brun in 1680, its walls are ornamented with Corinthian pilasters of green marble, supporting an entablature surmounted by trophies, and a fine ornamental vault with painted panels representing the apotheosis of 'Le Roi Soleil'. This royal residence is typical of the period to which it belongs, both in the magnitude of its lay-out and in the enormous expenditure in money and labour which it involved. The magnificent formal gardens laid out by Le Nôtre, on axial lines cleverly manipulated to give vistas of avenues and water canals, are liberally adorned with fountains, terraces, and arbours, set off with statues and vases in the Antique style (p. 788D, F). This ostentatious palace and pleasure garden was at once the expression of the irresponsible extravagance of 'Le Grand Monarque' and the aggravation of popular discontent.

Among the very many important urban dwellings constructed during the Classical period, especially in Paris, seat of the highly-centralized government of the country, are those built around the **Place des Vosges, Paris** (1605–12) (p. 784B), perhaps by Claude Chastillon, in a comprehensive scheme of private 'hôtels' fronting the arcaded square, forming an excellent example of the early (Henry IV) brick and stone style; also, the **Hôtel de Sully, Paris** (1624–9) (p. 786A), by Jean du Cerceau, dignified in scale and proportions but over-elaborated with the coarse ornament typical of the day; the **Hôtel Lambert, Paris** (1640–) (p. 786B), by Louis Le Vau, exhibiting the Classical character and restraint of the later phase of the period; and the **Place Vendôme, Paris** (1698–) (p. 787A), by J. H. Mansart, another group of private dwellings organized into a fine, unified Classical scheme, comprising a giant Order over a rusticated arcaded basement. Triumphal arches include the single-arched **Porte S. Denis, Paris** (1671–4) (p. 786C), by Nicholas François Blondel and the sculptor Michel Anguier, while among public buildings there is the **Collège des Quatre Nations, Paris** (1662), by Louis Le Vau, Classical in detail but Baroque in its bold conception.

In the Late period, châteaux and town houses at first follow the preceding trends, whilst showing an increasingly simple yet less pure external style, ornament being concentrated at nodal points. Keynotes are intimacy of scale; compact planning, leading to an abandonment of the courtyard approach in châteaux; and the development of many varieties of rich and delicate interior decoration. About mid-century, Antiquarianism begins to show positive and widespread effects.

The **Petit Trianon, Versailles** (1762–8) (pp. 788A, 789A), erected by J. A. Gabriel for Louis XV, who presented it to Madame du Barry, is the most superb piece of domestic architecture of the century. It has a gracious air, resulting from the clarity of its ordonnance and the sedate proportions. Though wholly contemporary in expression, it recalls ancient Roman architecture at its best. The south front (p. 788A) has a basement treated with the smooth-faced rustication of the day, while the ashlar of the upper floors is ornamented with flat, Corinthian pilasters rising through two stages between architraved windows differentiated in height to accentuate the 'piano nobile'. As the plan is nearly square, the four façades are similar, except that there are no pilasters on the eastern front, and on the western, they are substituted by columns. The building is related to an exquisite formal-garden setting by quadrant wing-walls and terraced staircases. The saloon (p. 789A) also is typical of the period, with its panelled walls, large mirrors, double doors, consoled chimney-piece, coved ceiling, and elaborate chandelier, while the chairs and the table with its Hermes legs complete this interesting interior.

The **Hôtel de Brunoy, Paris** (1772), by E. L. Boullée, and the **Hôtel de Thélusson, Paris** (1780: destroyed), by C. N. Ledoux show most strongly the archaeological reversion to ancient precedents, though still at this time many town residences continued to follow French national traditions in design.

A. Hôtel de Sully, Paris (1624–9). See p. 785

B. Hôtel Lambert, Paris: court (1640–).
See p. 785

c. Porte S. Denis, Paris (1671–4).
See p. 785

A. Place Vendôme, Paris (1698–). See p. 785

Civic scheme, Nancy: Place Stanislas looking N. to Place du Gouvernement (1750–7).
See p. 791

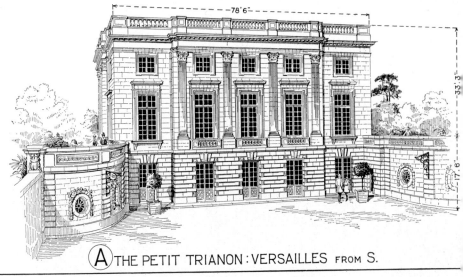

Ⓐ THE PETIT TRIANON : VERSAILLES FROM S.

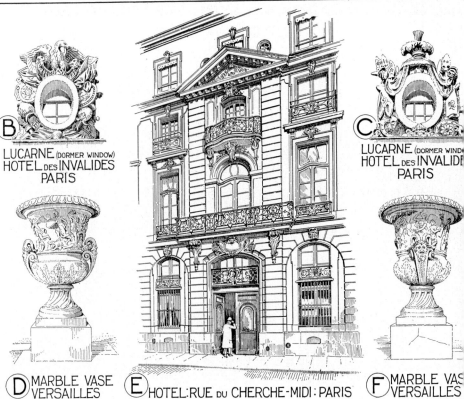

Ⓑ LUCARNE (DORMER WINDOW)
HOTEL DES INVALIDES
PARIS

Ⓒ LUCARNE (DORMER WIND)
HOTEL DES INVALIDE
PARIS

Ⓓ MARBLE VASE
VERSAILLES

Ⓔ HOTEL : RUE DU CHERCHE-MIDI : PARIS

Ⓕ MARBLE VAS
VERSAILLES

Ⓐ SALON: THE PETIT TRIANON: VERSAILLES

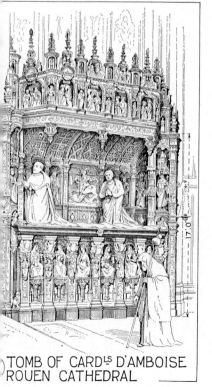

TOMB OF CARDᴸˢ D'AMBOISE
ROUEN CATHEDRAL

Ⓒ TOMB OF LOUIS XII
S. DENIS CATHEDRAL

A. Palaces in Place de la Concorde, Paris: angle pavilions (1753–70). See p. 791

B. Hôtel des Monnaies, Paris: centre block (1771–5). See p. 791

c. Palais du Louvre: gallery facing Seine Du Cerceau (since refaced) and Pavillon Flore (1600–9). See pp. 774, 791

The **Place Louis XV,** now **Place Stanislas, Nancy,** a city formerly the capital of Lorraine, formed part of an ambitious civic scheme laid out (1750–7) (p. 787B) by the architect Emmanuel Héré de Corny (1705–63), linking with two small 'hôtels' built earlier by G. Boffrand and with the Governor's Palace so as to form a series of squares of varying shape and character. The Place Stanislas, nearly square, is surrounded by public buildings which on the north side turn outwards to bridge a moat and frame a vista passing successively through a triumphal arch and the long Place de la Carrière, the latter flanked symmetrically by Boffrand's two hôtels and rows of simple terraced houses, to close on the Place du Gouvernement and Governor's Palace lying transversely at the northern end. Hemicycle screens bind the façade of the Governor's Palace to the northern ends of the terraced houses, and the Place de la Carrière is attractively laid out with alleys of trees and embellished with balustrades and statues. The principal buildings have that simple ordonnance yet rich detail which is found at an earlier time in the rest of France.

The **Place de la Concorde, Paris** (1753–70), by J. A. Gabriel, has twin palaces on the north side (p. 790A), now turned to other uses, which in their impressive monumental character evidence the sobering influence of archaeological research; as also do the **École Militaire, Paris** (1752–), by the same architect, the **Hôtel des Monnaies (Mint), Paris** (1771–5) (p. 790B), by J. D. Antoine and the **Palais de Justice, Paris** (rebuilt 1776), by J. D. Antoine and others.

The **Chambre des Députés, Paris,** south of the Place de la Concorde, received its dodecastyle (twelve-columned) portico (1807; architect, B. Poyet) (p. 794A) in the final (Empire) phase of the Late period. This façade shows the uncompromising Classical severity common in important monuments at that time. The whole composition is based on Roman principles, and comprises a broad flight of steps, flanked by statuary, preceding a temple-like pedimented front standing forward of plain wings decorated only with slight angle pilasters and isolated ornamental panels. The windowless walls are textured with plain-faced rustication.

At the Louvre, Paris, as mentioned on p. 779, the architects Percier and Fontaine erected the wing to the north of the Place du Carrousel (1806–13) (p. 775E), of which the design was in the nature of an antiquarian exercise since it followed closely that of the west end of the south wing of the same building, facing the Quai du Louvre, built by Du Cerceau in 1600–9 (pp. 775E, 790C) but subsequently refaced. Percier and Fontaine also were the designers of the **Arc du Carrousel** (1806) (pp. 775E, 779, 793B), standing nearby, this more definitely archaeological since it fairly closely reproduced the Arch of Septimius Severus, Rome (p. 224), and at the imperial residences were responsible for much restoration and interior decoration in the 'Empire' style, of which they were the principal creators. Another arch, having a greater fame, is the **Arc de Triomphe de l'Etoile, Paris** (p. 793A) (1806–36), by Chalgrin and others, a more original design and less obviously related to ancient models.

ECCLESIASTICAL ARCHITECTURE

The earliest indications of Renaissance in France, as in England, occur in sepulchral monuments, pulpits, portals, and fittings of existing Gothic churches, such as the **Tomb of Louis XII** (1515) in S. Denis Cathedral (p. 789C), the **Tomb of the Cardinals d'Amboise, Rouen** (1522) (p. 789B), the **portals of La Trinité, Falaise,** the **Château de Vitré pulpit** (p. 794C) and the apsidal chapels of S. **Pierre, Caen** (1528–45) (p. 794B).

S. Etienne du Mont, Paris (1517–60) (p. 795A, B), has nave piers crowned with

Doric-like capitals supporting ribbed vaulting, and there is an unusual ambulatory above the nave arcade. The famous Jubé or rood screen (*c.* 1545) (p. 795A), probably by Philibert de l'Orme, has double staircases with ornate balustrades of Renaissance detail. The screen was extended across the aisles in 1606. The centre of the façade, added 1610–25, has an entrance doorway framed with Composite columns, supporting an entablature and sculptured pediment. Above is a circular window with quasi-Gothic tracery, crowned with a steep-pitched gable to the nave, while beyond is a lofty tower.

     S. Eustache, Paris (1532–89) (p. 796A), not completed till 1654, may have been designed with the aid of the Italian-born Domenico da Cortona (p. 762). It is planned like a five-aisled Mediaeval church with apsidal end, high roofs, window tracery, flying buttress, pinnacles, and deeply-recessed portals, all clothed with Renaissance detail, and is a remarkable evidence of how the Mediaeval plan lingered on into the Renaissance period. The west front dates from 1772–87.

     S. Gervais, Paris (1616–21) (p. 795C), a façade added to the Late Gothic church by Salomon de Brosse, has three tiers of coupled columns of the Doric, Ionic and Corinthian Orders arranged to give the direct straightforward expression which is typical of this architect's work. It is the earliest wholly Classical church façade of importance of the French Renaissance.

     SS. Paul and Louis, Paris (1625–34) (p. 796B), by François Derand, built as the church of the Jesuit College, has the type of plan and richness of effect usually associated with Jesuit churches. Like S. Gervais, it is unusual, however, in having three tiers of Orders in its façade, which in the multiplication of its lines and features and abundant ornament is as nearly Baroque as is achieved in France, save for a few special exceptions. The dome is one of the earliest in Paris.

     The **Church of the Sorbonne, Paris** (1635–42) (p. 796C), designed for Cardinal Richelieu by Lemercier, bears evidence of the architect's long training in Rome, being much in the manner of the late Proto-Baroque there, yet having the restraint typical of the French Classical period as a whole, ornament being effectively subordinated to the comprehensive architectural effect. The plan has a double-axis symmetry, the crossing crowned with a fine dome, 40 ft in diameter. The façade has superimposed Orders, only the lower being in the round, and finishes above with an unbroken pediment, while the aisles are linked to the nave by extended scrolls.

     The **Church of the Val de Grâce, Paris** (1645–67), begun by François Mansart, formerly attached to a monastery, now forms part of the Military Hospital. Lemercier took over the work when Mansart was dismissed in 1646, and the design of the upper part is due to him. It is for this reason that the exterior (p. 797A) has some resemblance to the Church of the Sorbonne, though it is bolder and more successfully composed. It has a fine projecting portal, by Mansart, and the aisles are connected to the nave by vigorous scrolled consoles, while in the distance rises Lemercier's massive and ornate dome, retained by sixteen buttresses faced with pilasters and capped with inverted consoles above the serrated entablature. The interior, with wide nave flanked by piers faced with Corinthian pilasters, vaulted roof and dome (56 ft diameter), and the saucer-domed aisles, undoubtedly influenced Sir Christopher Wren in his design for S. Paul's, London (p. 906).

     S. Sulpice, Paris (p. 797B), was commenced in 1646 but the scheme was refashioned by Le Vau in 1655, while others took a hand before the body of the church was finished in 1745. It is a church of vast size, with no less than eighteen chapels, and with domical vaulting borne by Corinthian columns. The famous façade (1733–49) (p. 797B), designed by Servandoni, is 205 ft wide and forms a great two-storeyed narthex screen with superimposed Doric and Ionic Orders flanked by towers, the northernmost having been finished by Chalgrin in 1777–88.

A. Arc de Triomphe de l'Etoile, Paris (1806–36). See p. 791

Pavillon
de Rohan
↓

Pavillon
Turgot
↓

Pavillon Pavillon
Richelieu Colbert
↓   ↓

Pavillon
Sully
↓

de
nphe →
ousel

↑
Site of Palais des Tuileries

B. Palais du Louvre, Paris: from the Pavillon de Flore (1546–1878). See p. 779

A. Chambre des Députés, Paris: frontispiece (1807). See p. 791

B. S. Pierre, Caen: apsidal chapels   C. Château de Vitré: external pulpit
(1528–45). See p. 791   (16th cent.). See p. 791

a. S. Etienne du Mont, Paris (1517; façade 1610–25): showing jubé (c. 1545; screens across aisles 1606–). See p. 791

b. S. Etienne du Mont, Paris (1517–1560; centre of façade 1610–25).

c. Church of S. Gervais, Paris (1616–21). See p. 792

A. S. Eustache, Paris (1532–89). See p. 792

B. Church of SS. Paul and Louis, Paris (1625–34). See p. 792

C. Church of the Sorbonne, Paris (1635–42). See p. 792

Church of the Val de Grâce, Paris (1645–1667). See p. 792

B. S. Sulpice, Paris (façade 1733–49; except N. tower 1777–88). See p. 792

C. The Panthéon, Paris: interior looking towards apse (1757–c. 1790). See p. 799

D. The Dome of the Invalides, Paris (1680–91). See p. 799

A. The Panthéon, Paris (1757–c. 1790). See opposite page

B. The Madeleine, Paris (1806–42). See opposite page

The **Dome of the Invalides, Paris** (1680–91) (pp. 797D, 800A–C), by J. H. Mansart, completed the scheme of the Hôtel des Invalides undertaken by Bruant during the years 1670–7, and is one of the most impressive Renaissance domes in France (p. 797D). It has an internal diameter of 90 ft 9 ins, and is placed over the centre of a Greek-cross plan, resting on four piers in which openings lead by steps to four angle chapels (p. 800B) which fill in the angles of the cross, making a square of 198 ft externally. It has a high drum with coupled columns and lofty windows, and the dome proper is triple in construction (p. 800C). The inner dome, 175 ft high, has a wide central opening, through which are seen the painted decorations of the middle dome, lighted by windows at its base. The external dome is framed of timber covered with lead, and crowned by a high lantern and cross, rising to a height of 350 ft. The construction differs considerably from that of S. Paul's, London (pp. 906, 912), where an intermediate brick cone supports the external stone lantern.

The **Panthéon, Paris** (1757–90) (pp. 797C, 798A, 800D–F), erected from designs by Soufflot, has a fine portico with unusual arrangement of columns leading to the main building, which is a Greek cross on plan (p. 800D). The four piers which support the central dome were originally so slight as to threaten the stability of the structure, and were afterwards strengthened by Rondelet. The dome, 69 ft in diameter, is triple in construction (p. 800E), as in the Invalides, but has an outer dome of stone covered with lead (p. 798A). The interior (p. 797C) owes much of its elegance to the unusually slender piers, the fine Corinthian columns, and the large clear-story windows, invisible externally (p. 800F), surmounted by the domical vaulting. The general effect is enhanced by the coloured frescoes of foremost French artists. The exterior (p. 798A) is striking by reason of its magnificent hexastyle portico of Corinthian columns, thrown into relief by the unbroken, windowless walls, whose only decoration is a continuous entablature with carved festoons. The graceful dome is somewhat marred by the appearance of weakness in the free-standing columns round the lofty drum—a defect avoided by the unerring genius of Wren in designing the dome of S. Paul's Cathedral (p. 906).

The **Madeleine, Paris** (1806–42) (p. 798B), designed by Vignon in imitation of an octastyle peripteral Roman temple, 350 ft by 147 ft, has a 'cella' or nave divided into three bays, covered by saucer domes with central openings for lighting the church, which has a most impressive interior, while the apse at the sanctuary end has a semi-dome. The imposing exterior depends largely for its effect upon its island site, which is further accentuated by the podium, 23 ft high, on which the building stands, and by the magnificent rise of the approach up the wide expanse of steps. The Corinthian columns of the grand surrounding peristyle are built up in thin drums, the joints of which somewhat confuse the lines of the fluting. This peristyle supports an entablature in which the architrave is formed of voussoirs instead of a series of horizontal lintels, and the principal pediment has a sculptured tympanum.

COMPARATIVE ANALYSIS

(A comparative analysis of essential differences between Gothic and Renaissance architecture is given on p. 660. The architectural character of Italian and French Renaissance architecture has been considered (pp. 671, 765), and a Comparative Table of the two styles is here given.)

ITALIAN RENAISSANCE	FRENCH RENAISSANCE
PLANS. Severe Classic disposition rendered necessary by the narrow streets of Florence and Rome and the confining waterways of Venice (pp. 685G, 745E).	PLANS. The irregularity peculiar to Gothic buildings was occasionally retained as suitable to the exigencies of the country-side (p. 771E).

DOME OF THE INVALIDES: PARIS

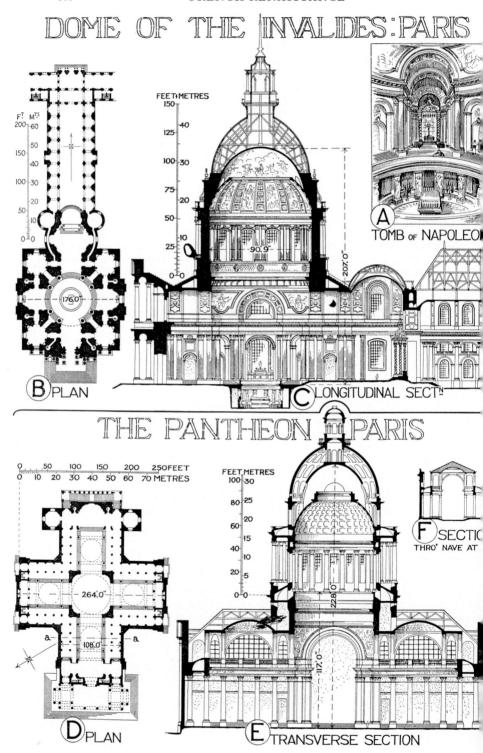

FEET METRES

F.T   M.T.S

TOMB OF NAPOLEON

B PLAN

C LONGITUDINAL SECT.N

THE PANTHEON: PARIS

D PLAN

E TRANSVERSE SECTION

F SECTION
THRO' NAVE AT

ITALIAN RENAISSANCE

A 'cortile' or central open court is generally surrounded by a colonnade or arcade supporting the main walls to give ampler space for the important rooms of the 'piano nobile' (pp. 681, 705, 733).

WALLS. A city palace, as in Florence, Rome, and Venice, is principally seen from the street, and the architectural features were often only applied to the street façade. Straight façades, varied by Orders, arcades, and windows, were crowned by a deep cornice (pp. 685, 734, 756). Attics are rare, but an open top storey (belvedere) is a feature. Brickwork was used in large masses with ashlar facings, also stone and marble, while ornament was confined to windows or Orders. Later buildings are often faced with stucco (p. 680F).

OPENINGS. Arcades, both in cortile and piazza, continued in use, as indeed had been the custom since the time of the Romans, affording shelter from the fierce rays of the southern sun. Symmetry, rather than convenience, determined the position of doors and windows (pp. 681, 705), round which ornament was concentrated, thus throwing these features into prominence. In Baroque palaces a return was often made to the astylar treatment, when elaboration of detail marked door and window frames. The attic was unusual and the top windows were often set in a deep frieze or between consoles supporting the main cornice (p. 740A).

ROOFS. Flat or low-pitched roofs are usual and roofs play no part in the design of buildings in narrow streets where they could not be seen, and even chimneys were masked, except at Venice (pp. 680, 734, 756). In the early period tiled roofs extended over the great cornice, but were hidden in many later buildings by the balustrade (pp. 718, 740A). Domes gave skyline to churches (pp. 679, 698, 704, 720, 739A).

COLUMNS. Pilasters, whether plain or carved with foliage, were used for their architectural importance as 'Orders' and panel decoration was often omitted (pp. 699, 706D, 718, 742D).

An 'Order' often included two or more storeys, while in churches a single Order

2C

FRENCH RENAISSANCE

The typical town-house plan has a court enclosed on one side by the 'corps de logis', flanked on either side by lower wings and cut off from the street by a screen wall (p. 781E, F).

WALLS. A country château is seen on all sides, and picturesque grouping from every point of view was therefore sought (pp. 763B, 772A). The gables and prominent stone dormers of the early period (pp. 763B, 772, 803H) gradually gave place to pedimented and balustraded façades (pp. 776A, 781A). Pavilions crowned with steep independent roofs mark the centre and ends of façades (pp. 775C, 781A, F). Stone was the chief material, sometimes combined with red brick (p. 782A).

OPENINGS. Arcades were not usual, owing to the northern climate. Doors of the early period often show Mediaeval influence and are much elaborated (p. 803G), but later are frequently treated plainly (p. 804F, K). Gothic mullions and transoms continued, though changed in detail (pp. 763B, 771C, 803H). Windows were often superimposed, but with the use of the Orders horizontal lines of the entablature prevailed (pp. 776A, 804D, K). Symmetry was so much considered that when there was a mezzanine floor with windows (p. 804K), similar windows were added in the upper part of main apartments adjoining. The attic was a favourite feature, often with circular windows ('œils-de-bœuf'), as at the Hôtel des Invalides, Paris (p. 788B, C).

ROOFS. High roofs are usual with dormer windows and lofty chimney stacks which give a picturesque skyline from a distance (pp. 763B, 771D, 772B, E). The 'mansard' roof (see Glossary), which gave more internal space, was favoured; while pavilions with independent roofs assumed the importance of towers (pp. 767A, 775, 776A, 781A). Domes were employed in churches of the later period (pp. 796C, 797A, D).

COLUMNS. Pilasters, lozenge-panelled or carved with foliage, were used to ornament quasi-Gothic features, as at Chambord, where slate in the panels gives variety (p. 803G, H).

A separate 'Order' was usually given to each storey, according to the practice of

ITALIAN RENAISSANCE

is the rule, as introduced by Palladio (pp. 706D, 718, 743).

MOULDINGS. Mouldings of heavy crowning cornices followed Roman models, although showing much originality. String courses between stories have only slight projection to give value to the top cornice, but the details of each Order were used in full (pp. 749, 753, 758).

ORNAMENT (pp. 749, 750, 754, 758, 759). Fresco and modelled plaster were much employed and in quite a few cases the two were combined, as in the arabesques of Raphael. Frescoes were, however, sometimes out of scale with the architecture, and therefore deficient in decorative value. Later stucco work suffered in the same way and Venice has some extraordinary examples of its abuse. Interiors generally in the later period were unduly regulated by the features of Classic temple architecture without relation to requirements. Sculpture tended increasingly to encroach upon the architectural lines of buildings, particularly in the Baroque period, when, however, considerable originality is displayed, especially in the fountains of Rome (pp. 753, 754). Characteristic ornament is seen in panels (p. 758E, H), capitals (pp. 749A, B, C, 758B, 759H), balconies (pp. 734G, 753C, D, F, G, 757B), chimney-pieces (pp. 749H, 757J), consoles (pp. 749B, 750G), ceilings (p. 759G), monuments (pp. 754J, L, 757G, 758D), and entablatures (pp. 758G, J, 759A, C).

FRENCH RENAISSANCE

Vignola (pp. 763, 767, 775, 776A, 781A, 783A).

MOULDINGS. Gothic influence pervaded the early period and combinations of Classic and Mediaeval mouldings were often used. Some cornices have unusually small members, while later mouldings gradually developed a distinctive character (pp. 803, 804).

ORNAMENT (pp. 771F, 783B, 803, 804). Gothic wood panelling continued into the early period, and was often splendidly carved with arabesques, as at Blois; whereas in later work the scale suggested by the material was gradually lost. Heraldry was much used in the early period (p. 771C, D, F). The Raphael style of decoration, introduced by Italian artists, as at Fontainebleau (p. 768), has continued to influence French art. Tapestry and hangings were superseded by the Louis XIV style of wood, papier-mâché, and stucco decoration in white and gold, which was also applied to furniture and every accessory, and thus gives fitness and unity to the interiors. Sculpture acquired increasing importance, and figure sculpture of great excellence appears in harmonious relationship with architecture. Other ornament is seen in panels (p. 803D, E), capitals (p. 803A, B, C, F), balconies (p. 804B), vases (p. 804C), keystones (p. 804A, H), consoles (p. 804E), walls and ceilings (p. 804G), fountains (p. 804J), and entablatures (p. 804L).

REFERENCE BOOKS

ARNOTT, J. A., and WILSON, J. Le Petit Trianon, Versailles. Edinburgh, 1907.

AUBERT, M., and VERNIER, G. L'Architecture francaise. 1941.

BERTY, A. La Renaissance monumentale en France. 2 vols. Paris, 1864.

BLOMFIELD, R. A History of French Architecture 1494 to 1661. 2 vols. London, 1911.

—. A History of French Architecture 1661–1774. 2 vols. London, 1921.

BLONDEL, J. F. L'Architecture francaise (known as the 'Grand Blondel'). 4 vols. folio. Paris, 1752–6.

BLUNT, A. Francois Mansart. London, 1941.

—. Art and Architecture in France, 1500–1700. Pelican History of Art, 1953.

BRIERE, G. Le chateau de Versailles: architecture et decoration. 2 vols. Paris, 19—.

CONTET, F., et VACQUIER, J. Les vieux hôtels de Paris. 20 vols. Paris, 1913.

DALY. Motifs historiques d'architecture et de sculpture. 2 vols. Paris, 1870.

—. Motifs historiques: decorations interieures. 2 vols. Paris, 1880.

DESHAIRS, L. Le Petit Trianon et le Grand Trianon. 2 vols. Paris.

DU CERCEAU, J. A. Les plus Excellents Bastiments de France. 2 vols. Paris, 1868–70.

GANAY, E. de. Chateaux de France. Paris, 1948–50.

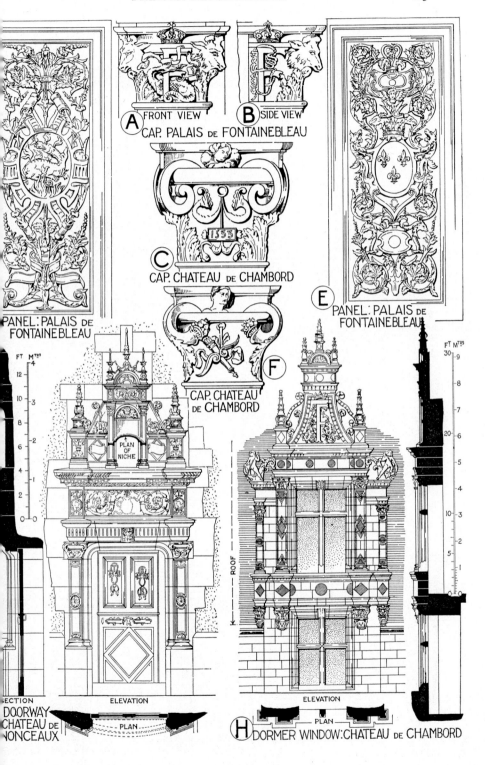

PANEL: PALAIS DE FONTAINEBLEAU

A FRONT VIEW B SIDE VIEW
CAP. PALAIS DE FONTAINEBLEAU

C CAP. CHATEAU DE CHAMBORD

1553

F CAP. CHATEAU DE CHAMBORD

E PANEL: PALAIS DE FONTAINEBLEAU

FT MTRS
12 4
10 3
8   2
6
4   1
2
0   0

PLAN OF NICHE

SECTION ELEVATION
DOORWAY CHATEAU DE MONCEAUX PLAN

ROOF

ELEVATION

FT MTRS
30 9
    8
    7
20 6
    5
    4
10 3
    2
5   1
    0

H DORMER WINDOW: CHATEAU DE CHAMBORD PLAN

(A) KEY STONE (LOUIS XV)

SIDE ← | (B) BALCONY (LOUIS XIV) PARIS | SECTION

(C) LEAD VASE — PAL DE V SAIL

(D) DORMER WINDOW (LOUIS XV) LYCEE NAPOLEON: PARIS

SIDE VIEW

14'-8"

(E) CONSOLE (LOUIS XV) PARIS

8'0"

(F) DOORWAY (LOUIS XV)

9'.9"

(G) LOUIS QUATORZE STYLE OF DECORATION

(H) KEY STONE (LOUI

SIDE ELEVATION

CONSOLE

39'-10"

15'6"

SECTION   ELEVATION

(J) FOUNTAIN (LOUIS XV) PARIS

PLAN

(K) DOOR & WINDOW (LOUIS XVI) PARIS

9'6"

SECTION

(L) CORNICE & BALUSTRADE (LC

SECTI

GEBELIN, F. *Les Chateaux de la Loire*. Paris, 1927.
—. *Les Chateaux de la Renaissance*. Paris, 1927.
—. *Le style Renaissance en France*. Paris, 1942.
GEYMULLER, H. von. *Die Baukunst der Renaissance in Frankreich. (Handbuch der Architectur)*. 2 vols. Stuttgart, 1898–1901.
Grands Palais de France: (1) *Palais du Louvre et des Tuileries*, 4 vols.
                  (2) *Versailles*, par Pierre de Nolhac, 2 vols.
                  (3) *Les Trianons*. par P. de Nolhac, 4 vols.
                  (4) *Fontainebleau*, par Louis Dimier, 2 vols.
                  (5) *Le Palais Royal*, 2 vols.
GROMORT, G. *Histoire abrégée de l'architecture de la Renaissance en France*. Paris, 1930.
GUEDY, HENRI. *Le Palais du Louvre, Paris*. Paris, 19—.
GUERINET, A. *L'Architecture francaise: extérieures, intérieures*. 12 vols. Paris, 19—.
GURLITT, C. *Die Baukunst Frankreichs*. 2 vols. 1900.
HAUTECOEUR, L. *L'Architecture francaise de la Renaissance à nos jours*. 1941.
—. *Histoire de l'architecture classique en France*. Paris, 1943.
JACKSON, SIR T. G. *Renaissance of Roman Architecture*. Pt. III, *France*. London, 1923.
KRAFFT et RANSONNETTE. *Plans . . . des plus belles Maisons . . . contrues à Paris*, etc. Paris, c. 1810.
LAVEDAN, P. *French Architecture*. Original French edition, 1944, trans., Pelican, 1956.
MARTIN, C. *La Renaissance en France*. 2 vols. Paris, 1910–12.
PALUSTRE, L. *La Renaissance en France*. 3 vols. Paris, 1879–85. (Not completed).
PFNOR, R. *Le Palais de Fontainebleau*. 3 vols. Paris, 1859–67.
PLANAT, P., et RUMLER, E. *Le style Louis XIV; XV; XVI*. 3 vols. Paris, 1911–14.
ROSENAU, H. *Boullée's Treatise on Architecture*. 1953.
ROUSSEL, J. Monographs on *Fontaineableu, Blois*, and *Versailles et Trianons*. Paris, 19—.
ROUYER, E. *La Renaissance de Francois I à Louis XIII*. Paris.
—., et DARCEL, A. *L'art architectural en France*. 2 vols. Paris, 1863–6.
SAUVAGEOT, C. *Palais, chateaux, hôtels et maisons de France*. 4 vols. Paris, 1867.
VACQUIER, J. *Les anciens chateaux de France*. 11 vols. Paris, 19—.
VERDIER, A., et CATTOIS, F. P. *L'architecture civile et domestique*. 2 vols. Paris, 1858.
VITRY, P. *Hôtels et maisons de la Renaissance francaise*. 3 vols. Paris, 1911–12.
WARD, W. H. *Architecture of the Renaissance in France, 1495-1830*. 2 vols. London, 1926.
—. *French Chateaux and Gardens in the Sixteenth Century*. Illustrated by facsimiles of original drawings by J. A. du Cerceau. London, 1909.

Germany in the Renaissance period

XXII. GERMAN RENAISSANCE

(sixteenth–nineteenth century)

INFLUENCES

GEOGRAPHICAL. The central position in Europe of the country inhabited by the
Teutonic peoples enabled it to receive Renaissance art from Italy on the south and
from France on the west; while, as the states in this great tract of country were
independent, there could be no central and unifying influence as in France. The
distance from the headquarters of the new movement resulted in deferring its introduction till some 125 years later than in Italy. The states of Prussia, Hanover,
Saxony, Bavaria, Würtemberg, and Baden, together with Silesia, Bohemia and
Austria, were widely scattered as to latitude and longitude, and were distinguished
by different geographical conditions of seaboard, rivers, and mountains, and this
differentiated the architecture of the various districts, as in previous periods (pp.
353, 583).

GEOLOGICAL. The geological conditions naturally remained the same as during
Romanesque and Gothic times (pp. 354, 583). Timber, brick, and stone continued
to give their own character to the architecture, according to their local use; thus
moulded and ornamental brickwork was used in great variety in the alluvial plains
of the north, while varieties of stone and timber are used according to locality and
produce consequent differences.

CLIMATIC. As in previous periods (pp. 354, 583), climate affected architecture,
and the revived Classic forms were modified from those in use in Italy to suit a
more northern temperature; thus windows still continued to be large, roofs to be

steep to throw off snow, and chimneys, necessary for heating in a cold climate, to be prominent features.

RELIGIOUS. Martin Luther (1483–1546) towers above all others as the dominating figure of the Reformation in Germany, and the day in 1517 on which he nailed to the church door in Wittenberg his famous theses against indulgences inaugurated a revolution in the religious life of Germany which culminated when Luther publicly burnt the Bull of Excommunication issued against him by the Pope. Luther's choice of High German for the translation of the Bible led to its adoption as the basis of the literary language of Germany, and it is significant that this literary aspect of the Reformation coincides with the Renaissance 'Humanist' movement in German universities. A decree of the Diet of Speyer (1529), forbidding ecclesiastical changes, called forth the protest from Luther and his adherents which originated the name of Protestant. This was followed in 1530 by the Confession of Augsburg and by the Schmalkaldic League of Protestant princes and cities for mutual defence against the House of Hapsburg. The stress and turmoil in religious thought of this period of upheaval allowed little opportunity for the erection of new churches, but it resulted in the transformation of those of previous periods to meet the needs of the reformed religion, in the ritual of which preaching became a powerful factor, and necessitated that increased space for seated congregations which brought about the introduction of galleries. Thus the reformers adapted old churches, while Catholics had no need to build new ones. The strife between Protestants and Catholics and dissensions between Lutherans, Zwinglians and Calvinists were finally followed by the counter-Reformation, which was reinforced by the arrival of the Jesuits in Germany and by the counter-blast to Protestantism of the decrees of the Council of Trent (1563).

SOCIAL. Germany was at this time composed of divers margravates, palatinates, electorates, duchies, ecclesiastical states, and imperial cities, subject to the different reigning houses of Hapsburg, Hohenzollern, Wittelsbach, and Wettin. It is therefore manifest that there could not be the same cohesion as in France, but much diversity and rivalry in social life and institutions, which also made for a corresponding diversity in artistic development. The Middle Ages had come to an end. The Holy Roman Empire was no longer predominant. Feudalism began to disappear; gunpowder changed military methods, and bands of mercenaries often replaced feudal troops. There were also various internal influences at work, such as the power of the great trading towns of the Hanseatic League, the position of the Guilds in civic government, and the attempt of the peasants to secure their freedom. The principal Renaissance factor was the influence of the universities, notably of Heidelberg, the chief seat of the Humanist movement. This was further strengthened by the invention of printing, while in the eighteenth century the literary works of Winckelmann, Goethe, and others aroused interest in the architecture of ancient Greece.

HISTORICAL. The succession of Charles V (Charles I of Spain) to the possessions of the Houses of Castile, Aragon, and Burgundy, as well as to the Low Countries, marks the beginning of German Renaissance. In 1516 he gained the two Sicilies, and on the death of Maximilian in 1519 he became, as Emperor, the most powerful ruler of his day. Various invasions by the Turks between the years 1529 and 1562 further complicated matters in Germany, increased the difficulties of the House of Hapsburg, and were inimical to architectural activities. The wars of Charles V and the Catholics against the Protestant princes (1547–55) were brought to an end by the Peace of Augsburg, which allowed each state to set up what religion it pleased, but made no provision for individuals who were of different religion from that of the prevailing government. This resulted in persecutions and culminated in the famous 'Thirty Years' War' (1618–48) between Catholic and Protestant princes. Frederick, the Elector Palatine, son-in-law of James I of England, Christian IV of Denmark and Gustavus Adolphus of Sweden fought on the Protestant side. France also took part in the war under Cardinals Richelieu and Mazarin, and when the Peace of Westphalia (1648) brought the long struggle to an end, the war had ruined the position of Germany, depleted her population, and left France the leading nation in Europe. These wars not only arrested the development of architecture during the period of their actual prosecution, but also retarded building activities for some time after the conclusion of peace. In the latter part of the seventeenth century many German princes allied themselves with Louis XIV, until the rise of the House of Hohenzollern, when the Elector Frederick III was crowned Frederick I, King of Prussia (1701). His son Frederick II ('the Great') raised Prussia to predominance among the German states, a position which it lost in the Napoleonic era but regained after 1815.

ARCHITECTURAL CHARACTER

The general character of Renaissance architecture in Europe has been dealt with as a whole, with regard to those features which are common to it in all countries (p. 656). The style was introduced into Germany at first through France and the Low Countries, as the Alps were a considerable barrier to easy transmission from Italy, appearing only about 1550, roughly one hundred and twenty five years after the inception in Italy, the parent country. Approximately, the successive periods were: (a) Early Renaissance (1550–1600), chiefly consisting of the introduction of Renaissance elements into Gothic buildings or of additions to them, though some examples, such as the Heinrichsbau, Heidelburg, are of great size; (b) Proto-Baroque (1600–1660), in which Italian architects themselves carried the Renaissance from north Italy to Switzerland, Austria and Germany, while native architects began successfully to emulate them and produce national versions of the style; (c) the Baroque (1660–1710), in which architects, principally of native origin but who often had received part of their training in Rome or elsewhere in Italy, brought German architecture to a splendid culmination; (d) the Rococo (1710–1760), an extension of the Baroque period wherein architecture and decoration show great refinement and technical mastery but less vigour and force; and (e) the Antiquarian (1760–1830), in which there is a progressive return to ancient classical models, the Greek Revival being a manifestation within and somewhat beyond the period 1790–1830. Broadly speaking, the greatest works of the German Renaissance lie in the hundred years 1660–1760, i.e., the Baroque period, including the Rococo. In no other part of Europe outside Italy was there so joyous and picturesque a flowering of Renaissance architecture, and indeed, the Baroque of Austria and neighbouring Bavaria and Bohemia appears as a natural, superlative, culmination of the Italian Renaissance, intimately related to and an outgrowth of the Baroque of Rome and Lombardy. The German Baroque thoroughly permeated town and countryside, much as did Georgian architecture in England. It suited the people, peasant and patrician alike, in its intensely visual appeal; the rich profusion of ornamentation in church interiors was not wilful display but told the Bible story much as hieroglyphs, mural reliefs or stained glass had carried the religious message in other times and climes. Church and palace interiors sometimes may appear over-ornate, even gaudy, to western eyes, but the opulent magnificence that frequently resulted was a direct response to social, religious and political circumstances, and just as spontaneous as the gaiety universally manifested in peasant art. Ornamentation was deliberate and purposeful, and had a greater part to play in ecclesiastical,

HEIDELBERG CASTLE

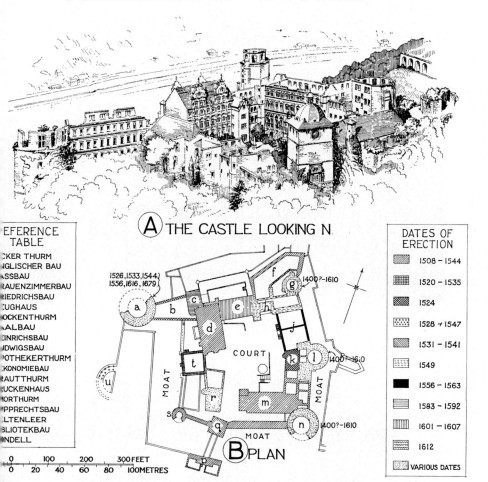

Ⓐ THE CASTLE LOOKING N.

DATES OF
ERECTION

▨	1508 – 1544
▦	1520 – 1535
▨	1524
░	1528 – 1547
▨	1531 – 1541
░	1549
■	1556 – 1563
▤	1583 – 1592
▥	1601 – 1607
▧	1612
░	VARIOUS DATES

1526,1533,1544,
1556,1616,1679

1400?-1610

COURT

MOAT

1400?-16.0

MOAT

1400?-1610

MOAT

0   100   200   300 FEET
0   20   40   60   80   100 METRES

Ⓑ PLAN

Ⓒ HEINRICHSBAU

SAAL BAU

Ⓓ FRIEDRICHSBAU

A. The Rathaus, Heilbronn (1535–96). See p. 811

B. The Loggia, Waldstein Palace, Prague (1621–30). See p. 812

particularly Jesuit, buildings than in secular architecture, which was relatively plain, except in the case of mansions and country residences, where it was appropriate to gracious living. Notable Baroque architects were Johann Bernhard Fischer von Erlach (1656–1723), also a sculptor and writer on architectural history, who trained under Carlo Fontana (p. 726) in Rome and worked principally in Vienna, and Jakob Prandtauer (1660–1726), designer of the monastery at Melk, an architectural masterpiece (p. 819B, C). A generation later came a group of almost precisely identical age: the brothers Asam (Cosmas Damian, 1686–1739, and Egid Quirin, 1692–1750), gifted fresco painters and stuccoists who also practised as architects; Balthasar Neumann (1687–1753), the most brilliant of the group; Lukas von Hildebrandt (1688–1745), who began as a military engineer but whose buildings nevertheless are cheerfully lively in mien; the Dientzenhofer family, native to Bavaria, six persons, working principally in Prague, and of whom Christopher and Kilian Ignaz (1689–1751) were perhaps the most distinguished; and Johann Michael Fischer (1692–1766), second in ability only to Neumann among south German architects.

EXAMPLES

(West German historical buildings suffered severely in the 1939–45 war. Some of the examples to be named were lost or severely damaged, as will be stated. In some cases they have since been repaired or rebuilt.)

SECULAR ARCHITECTURE

Heidelberg Castle (1531–1612) (p. 809) well exemplifies progressive developments of the Early Renaissance in the various additions to the Mediaeval castle (p. 809B). The later of them suffer from over-ornamentation. There is a great watch tower (1531–41) and an irregular court around which are grouped the Renaissance buildings (p. 809A). The Saulbau (1549) in the north-east corner shows Gothic features mingled with those of the incoming Renaissance: this is relatively plain (p. 809D). The Heinrichsbau (1556–63), long ago fallen into a ruined state, has superimposed Ionic and Corinthian pilasters and half-columns, two-light windows showing Venetian affinities, and symbolic statues in niches (pp. 809C, 824A, C). The Friedrichsbau (1601–7), on the north side, is more mature in design, again showing borrowings from early Venetian Renaissance in the round-headed traceried windows of the ground floor and the two tiers of pedimented two-light windows above them, while two picturesque windowed and scrolled gables and a steep roof indicate some slight retention of native Mediaeval traits (p. 809D). Niches containing statues of the Counts Palatine are distributed on each of the tiers (pp. 809D, 824B).

The **Rathaus, Heilbronn** (1535–96) (p. 810A) (severely damaged), is an attractive and quaint building still essentially Gothic in character. Its arcade of stumpy columns encloses a market, and side steps lead up to the upper storeys; while a central panel bears the signs of the zodiac and a clock with figures and a bell; the steep roof has three stages of dormer windows and an open turret.

The **Gewandhaus, Brunswick,** the body of which is Gothic, has an eastern façade (1592) (p. 813B) illustrating typical north-German early Renaissance characteristics, introduced via the Low Countries rather than directly from Italy. An arcade of three-centred arches is surmounted by three storeys of Ionic, Corinthian and Composite three-quarter columns, and above rises an immense gable of four storeys of Hermes pilasters, so much used in Elizabethan architecture, framed in by the customary side-scrolls of the stepped gables of the period.

The **Rathaus Portico, Cologne** (1569–71) (p. 813E) (destroyed) designed by

W. Wernickel, was an exquisite structure remarkably advanced for its day, showing marked north Italian traits. An arcade of semicircular arches with free-standing Corinthian columns was surmounted on the first storey by slightly-pointed arches flanked by Composite columns, while Gothic tradition was also evident in a 'rib-and-panel' vault within. The crestings and steep roof similarly showed mixed Mediaeval and Lombard Renaissance ideas.

The **Pellerhaus, Nuremberg** (1605) (p. 813D) (destroyed), one of the finest examples of the earlier Renaissance in the city, was of Proto-Baroque design externally, the influence of the stucco medium being clearly apparent in the busy ornament lavishly used in its upper parts. The main dispositions, however, were still of the native type, resembling Belgian practice rather than Italian, tiers of large windows rising into a stepped and scrolled gable ornamented with pinnacles and a sculptural centre-piece at the apex. The basement and the pilasters of the lower two window tiers were rusticated, while the gable windows were divided by Hermes pilasters.

The **Zeughaus, Danzig** (1605) (p. 813A) (destroyed), a good example of the brick architecture of the north, showed kinship with Belgian Early Renaissance, and was indeed designed by a Flemish architect, Anton van Obbergen. The tall, mullioned-and-transomed windows were of the plain early type, ornament being confined to doorways and to local features, except on the third storey, broken into scrolled and pinnacled gables and enlivened with strapwork decoration.

The **Rathaus, Bremen** (façade 1612–) (p. 813C) is mainly Gothic (1405–10). The chief frontage has a light arcade, large windows, central and side scroll gables and many statues.

The **Loggia, Waldstein Palace, Prague** (1621–30) (p. 810B) by Antonio and Pietro Spezza, is of Italian design, like the palace as a whole. Paired Tuscan-Doric columns support the triple arches of the porch in a gracious scheme showing expert knowledge of the classical elements. The fenestration is Proto-Baroque, as are the subsidiary details, while the stucco decorations are the work of the famous Genoese architect, Bartolomeo Bianco (p. 688).

The **Troja Palace, Prague** (1679–96) (p. 814A), by J. B. Mathey, is a fine instance of the Baroque period, a restrained design of a single giant Order, the lines of the Composite pilasters being carried into the entablature as far as the bed-mould of the cornice. The central intercolumniation is wider than the rest. While the façade proper has a Palladian dignity and simplicity, a profusion of rich sculptural detail is concentrated about the upper and lower portals and the double, horse-shoe, staircase giving access to the 'piano nobile'.

The **Palace of the Hungarian Guard, Vienna** (1710–12) (p. 825A) by J. B. Fischer von Erlach, is one of a considerable number of works by this celebrated architect. A giant Order of paired Composite pilasters stands over a horizontally-rusticated basement storey; the decoration is rich, but is not allowed anywhere to intrude upon the main elements of the architectural composition. While the modelling of the chief masses is vigorous, the modelling of the detail is finer and shallower than in typical Baroque architecture, and in fact tends towards the Rococo expression. Other notable secular buildings by Fischer von Erlach are the **Clam Gallas Palace, Prague** (1701–12), the **Ministry of the Interior, Vienna** (1716) and the **Schwarzenberg Palace, Vienna** (1705–20), while he collaborated with Lukas von Hildebrandt in the design of the **Ministry of Finance, Vienna** (1702–10).

The **Kinsky Palace, Vienna** (1709–13) (p. 813F) (half-ruined), by Lukas von Hildebrandt, is very representative of this architect's style. The windowed frieze in the main entablature is an interesting feature.

A. The Zeughaus, Danzig (1605).
See p. 812

B. The Gewandhaus,
Brunswick (1592).
See p. 811

C. The Rathaus, Bremen (1612).
See p. 812

D. The Pellerhaus, Nuremberg
(1605). See p. 812

E. The Rathaus, Cologne: Renaissance
portico (1569-71). See p. 811

F. The Kinsky Palace, Vienna
(1707-13). See p. 812

A. The Troja Palace, Prague: garden front (1679–96). See p. 812

B. The Zwinger, Dresden (1711–22). See p. 817

C. The Schloss, Karlsruhe (1751–6). See p. 817

A. The Brandenberg Gate, Berlin (1789-93). See p. 817

B. The Neumünster, Würzburg
(1710-19). See p. 818

c. The Frauenkirche, Dresden
(1726-40). See p. 818

A. The Upper Belvedere, Vienna (1721–4). See p. 817

B. The Theatine Church, Munich (1663–90). See p. 817

The **Belvedere, Vienna** (1693–1724), a summer residence, is one of Hildebrandt's most famous works. It has an upper (1721–4) (p. 816A) and a lower palace, and splendid gardens stretching between.

The **Zwinger, Dresden** (1711–22) (p. 814B) (badly damaged), by M. D. Poppelmann (1662–1736), is one of the most curious and bizarre constructions of the German Renaissance, built as a resort for the princely court for pageants, festivals and tournaments, structures of one and two storeys being arranged around an open enclosure. The entrance is particularly extravagant, seething with a congestion of columns, pilasters, fragmented entablatures and incoherent ornament, crowned with a bulbous, crested 'helm'.

The **Schloss, Karlsruhe** (1751–6 and later) (p. 814C) (badly damaged) has a fan-shaped plan which determines the arrangement of the whole town, laid out earlier in the century with thirty-two streets radiating from it.

The **Brandenburg Gate, Berlin** (1789–93) (p. 814C) (damaged), by C. G. Langhans, is in Greek Revival style and imitates the Propylaea at Athens (p. 142); it illustrates the Antiquarian trend of the later part of the century notable in Europe as a whole. The Glyptotek, Pinacothek and Propylaea, all in Munich, and the Walhalla, Regensburg, were designed by Klenze (1784–1864); the New Theatre, the Museum and the Polytechnic School, Berlin, by the architect Schinkel (1781–1841).

ECCLESIASTICAL ARCHITECTURE

There were few new churches in the sixteenth century. **S. Michael, Munich** (1583–97) was one of the earliest to show Renaissance features: already by this time Italian architecture was on the verge of the Baroque.

The **Marienkirche, Wolfenbüttel** (1608–23) is an essentially Gothic structure, adorned with quite unassimilated Proto-Baroque detail concentrated strongly in stepped and scrolled gables ranged together on the two long sides.

The **Church, Bückeburg** (1613) (p. 819A) has an extravagantly ornate Proto-Baroque west front, but the windows still are Gothic: the interior has Corinthian columns supporting a pointed arcade and rib-and-panel vault.

The **Cathedral, Salzburg** (1614–28) by Santino Solari, an Italian, and the Jesuit churches at **Dillingen** (1610–17), **Mindelheim** (1625–6), **Vienna** (1627–31) and **Innsbruck** (1627–40) were among the first to be expressed wholly in the Renaissance manner.

The **Theatine Church, Munich** (1663–90) (p. 816B) is an instance of the developed Baroque style. It is based upon the church of S. Andrea della Valle at Rome. The west façade has two tiers of Orders, the aisles being linked to the nave by swept buttresses, while twin western towers rise through three storeys of Orders to oddly coarse scroll-buttressed helms. The features are not as vigorously modelled as in contemporary Italian Baroque, nor is the focal emphasis on the west door so strongly marked. A lanterned dome over the crossing completes the impressive scheme.

The **Monastery, Melk** (1702–14) (p. 819B, C) by Jakob Prandtauer, is one of the most striking monuments of the Baroque period. The abbey buildings mount in stages at the crest of a steep-sided rocky ridge, riding high above the wood-fringed river Danube; western towers with helms of intriguing profile serve as foil to the softly-moulded contours of the crowning dome. The grand effect arises principally from the disposition of the building-masses on the rising site. Ornament is used sparingly in the most effective locations, and the abbey main buildings are relatively severe. There are other great monasteries at **S. Florian** (1686–1715), near Vienna, to which Jakob Prandtauer contributed after 1708, and **Klosterneuburg** (c. 1750), where the church is an old foundation of 1136.

Brevnov Monastery Church, Prague (1710–15) (p. 820A) by Christopher

Dientzenhofer is a splendid illustration of what Baroque architects could achieve without recourse to elaborate ornamentation. This modest building has most of the Baroque qualities, showing play with richly curved forms in plan, elevation and detail, varied expressions of condition and spacing of the Orders and the vigorous modelling of masses which distinguishes the Baroque proper from its later manifestation, the Rococo.

S. Nicholas, Prague (1703–52) (p. 821C, D), the finest Baroque church in the city, has a nave designed by Christopher Dientzenhofer (1703–11) (p. 821D) of which the interior has all the dramatic power of which the style was capable. Giant clustered pilasters are set diagonally to form an arcade embracing aisle and clerestory in such wise as to produce an undulated vault which, with the help of its painted decoration, seems less to contain than to free the upper space and open up the heavens. Most of the architectural lines are curvilinear; the voids seem to interweave, the lesser into the greater, and the whole effect is one of swirling movement totally different from the serene static character of Palladian architecture.

The Neumünster, Würzburg (façade, 1710–19) (p. 815B) is a truly Baroque design in its concave modelling, clustered and variously-disposed Orders and vigorous and dramatic effect.

Karlskirche, Vienna (1716–37) (p. 820B), by J. B. Fischer von Erlach, is this famous architect's masterpiece, finished after his death. In some respects it resembles S. Agnese, Rome. The hexastyle entrance porch leads up to a mighty dome, and the nave façade has quadrant links with scroll-topped, symmetrical angle pavilions beyond mighty replicas of Trajan's column at Rome (p. 228). The composition is grand and impressive, yet this instance of Fischer von Erlach's later architecture is quieter and shallower in modelling than his earlier work, thus partaking more of the Rococo than the true Baroque quality.

The Church of the Holy Ghost, Munich (1724–30) (p. 821A, B) by J. G. Ettenhofer, itself a rebuilding of an earlier hall-church, was extended westwards by three bays in 1885 and the west front re-fashioned after the former design. The Rococo interior is essentially the work of the brothers Asam.

The Frauenkirche, Dresden (1726–40) (p. 815C) (destroyed) was the prime example of eighteenth-century Protestant church architecture. It had a highly centralized plan, contained within a square of 140 ft side. The stone dome was oval, about 75 ft across, and so excessively stilted as to appear slightly onion-shaped. The strong modelling and pyramidal arrangement made a powerful composition.

S. Paulin, Trier (1732–54) (p. 825B) by Balthasar Neumann, is one of a number of fine works by this distinguished architect. It is an aisleless church, high in proportions, with a helm-topped axial western tower and an eastern apse. Internally (p. 825B) it is aglow with colour and lively with the play of form; clustered pilastered piers, some with sinuous cornices, contrast effectively with the relatively plain walls, while the compartmented domical vaults are enriched with refined stuccowork and brilliant frescoes. The columned and coroneted baldachino, the elaborately fretted woodwork and metalwork of the fittings, all contribute to the general unity of effect.

S. John Nepomuk, Munich (1733–5) by the brothers Asam, a small church designed and built by the architects at their own expense, is a very representative example of the Rococo phase of Baroque architecture.

S. Michael, Berg-am-Laim, Munich (1738–51) (pp. 822A, B), by J. M. Fischer, has a west front typical of many of the period, a bow-fronted, convex-faced nave being flanked by tall, staged and helm-crested western towers. The Abbey Church, Ottobeuren (1748–67), by the same architect, has a similarly-arranged west front,

A. The Church, Bückeburg (1613).
See p. 817

See p. 817

B. The Monastery, Melk (1702–14).
See p. 817

See p. 817

C. The Monastery, Melk: interior of church

A. Brevnov Monastery Church, Prague (1710–15). See p. 817

B. Karlskirche, Vienna (1716–37). See p. 818

A. Entrance front   B. Interior

The Church of the Holy Ghost, Munich (1724–30). See p. 818

C. Entrance front   D. Interior (1703–11)

S. Nicholas, Prague (1673–1752). See p. 818

A. West front   B. Interior

S. Michael, Berg-am-Laim (1738–51). See p. 818

C. West front   D. Interior

The Church, Vierzehnheiligen (1743–72). See p. 823

as also has the pilgrimage **Church at Vierzehnheiligen** (1744–72) (p. 822C, D) by Neumann, and **S. Gallen Cathedral** (1755–86) in neighbouring Switzerland, by Peter Thumb.

COMPARATIVE ANALYSIS

PLANS. The internal courtyard of the Mediaeval period is progressively less favoured, except where demanded in town houses, dwellings, large and small, being increasingly planned for the maximum enjoyment of external light and air. Church plans, as in Italy, vary between the longitudinal and centralized types, with the latter gaining in favour, particularly in the Baroque period.

WALLS. Wall surfaces, whether in brick, stone or stucco, commonly were relieved by Orders to each storey (pp. 809C, D, 813B, D, E), though there was some recourse to the giant Order in the Baroque period (pp. 813F, 820A). The traditional steep gables, stepped and scrolled (p. 813A, B, D), continued in the early period but were generally eliminated thereafter. In Baroque churches, walls locally curved on plan were quite often employed to diversify the building masses (pp. 815B, 820A, 821A, C, D, 822A).

OPENINGS. Arcades occasionally appear in the early period (p. 813C, E) but are not a favourite feature. Windows remain large, and at first are mullioned as in the Gothic period (p. 809C, D), and at this time may appear in ornamental roof gables (p. 824E). Ornamental surrounds to windows are crude in the early period (p. 824G), but are attuned to the design as a whole as experience ripens, following a similar development to that in Italy. Doorways commonly are made a special point of elaboration in secular architecture (pp. 813F, 814A), but are not so strongly emphasized in church west façades as in the Baroque of Italy (pp. 815B, 821A).

ROOFS. Large steep roofs with many storeys that were a feature of the Gothic period continue into the Early Renaissance (p. 810A), but lose quite a little of their importance later on, the pitch becoming flatter or the roofs half-concealed behind parapets (pp. 813F, 814A, 825A).

COLUMNS. The Orders were freely employed as decorative adjuncts at all times (pp. 809C, D, 813B–F), at first with novel designs for the capitals (p. 824D, F) but afterwards with orthodox detail (p. 816B). Clustered columns or pilasters or combinations of both were a feature of Baroque architecture (p. 821A–D), and sometimes pilasters were diagonally aligned (p. 821D). In Baroque buildings generally, the Orders were used for decorative effect rather than with due concern for their structural significance.

MOULDINGS. Mouldings were characterized by boldness and vigour rather than refinement in the early period (p. 824) and sometimes show the survival of Gothic practices, even to the retention of interpenetration of mouldings, but as time elapsed these were discarded in favour of the more correct profiles of the Italian Renaissance.

ORNAMENT. Sculpture of a fanciful and grotesque character ran riot in the mid-sixteenth century (p. 824H), especially at Heidelberg Castle, where Italian influence mingles with the native Gothic tradition (pp. 809C, D, 824A, B, C). Proto-Baroque sculptural ornament was more orderly, but still often excessive and involved, comprised largely either of strapwork or naturalistic motifs of sinuous or convoluted foliage tending to impair the clearness of the architectural lines (p. 813D). The Orders still were not fully understood, Gothic elements occasionally surviving (pp. 813C, 819A). In the Baroque and Rococo periods ornament was brought fully into subjection, and all the visual arts, sculpture, stucco decoration, fresco painting and wood and metal work were used in complete harmony one with the other (pp. 819C,

A WINDOWS & NICHE with DIANA:
HEINRICHSBAU, HEIDELBERG CASTLE

B CHARLES THE GREAT:
FRIEDRICHSBAU,
HEIDELBERG CASTLE

C WINDOWS & NICHE
with SATURN: HEINRICHSB
HEIDELBERG CAS

D CAPITAL·
FOUNT-
AIN OF
S.JEAN·
FREIBURG
SWITZ.

E GABLE HEILBRONN

F CAPITAL. FOUNTAIN OF
SAMARITAN: FREIBURG: SWIT

G WINDOW·ERFURT

H CARTOUCHE·HEILBRONN

J DOORWAY
S.MICHEL: MUNICH

821B, D, 822B, D), ornament becoming more refined but less robust as time passed (pp. 810B, 814A, 819C, 822B).

REFERENCE BOOKS

BENZ, R. *Deutscher Barock*. Stuttgart, 1949.
BOURKE, J. *Baroque Churches of Central Europe*. London, 1958.
BRIGGS, M. S. *Baroque Architecture*. London, 1913.
FREY, D. *Johann Bernhard Fischer von Erlach*. Vienna, 1923.
FRITSCH, K. E. O. *Denkmaeler Deutscher Renaissance*. 4 vols. Berlin, 1891.
GRIMSCHITZ, B. *Johann Lukas von Hildebrandt*. Vienna, 1923.
HAUPT, A. *Baukunst der Renaissance in Frankreich und Deutschland*. 1923.
LAMBERT, A., und STAHL, E. *Motive der Deutschen Architektur*. 2 vols. Stuttgart, 1890–3.
LANCHESTER, H. V. *Fischer von Erlach*. London, 1924.
MENCL, V. *Onze cent années d'architecture en Tchécoslovaque*. Prague, 1957.
ORTWEIN, A. *Deutsche Renaissance*. 9 vols. Leipzig, 1871–88.
PFNOR, R. *Monographie du Chateau d'Heidelberg*. Paris, 1859.
PLICKA, K. introduction by BRIGGS, M. S. *City of Baroque and Gothic*. London, 1946.
POPP, H. *Die Architektur der Barock und Rokokozeit in Deutschland*. Stuttgart, 1924.
POWELL, N. *From Baroque to Rococo—an Introduction to Austrian and German Architecture from 1580–1790*. London, 1959.
SITWELL, S. *German Baroque Art*. London, 1927.
WOLFFLIN, H. *Renaissance und Barock*. Munich, 1907.

A. Palace of the Hungarian Guard, Vienna (1710–12). See p. 812

B. S. Paulin, Trier (1732–54). See p. 818

A. The Town Hall, Enkhuizen (1686–8). See p. 835

B. The Royal Library, The Hague (1735). See p. 835

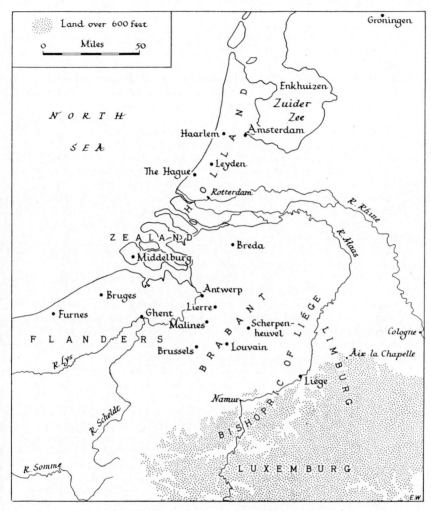

The Low Countries in the seventeenth century

XXIII. BELGIAN AND DUTCH RENAISSANCE

(sixteenth–nineteenth century)

INFLUENCES

GEOGRAPHICAL. The Netherlands is a term which formerly embraced the whole of the Netherlands (Holland) and Belgium. The physical similarity of the low-lying parts did not result in the maintenance of a firm political unity, chiefly owing to the intrusion of external powers, to which Belgium was the more susceptible, being related to Spain up to 1700, and afterwards to Austria and for short periods to France, while Holland formed a republic from 1588–1795. Belgium enjoyed the greater prosperity in the sixteenth century and Holland in the seventeenth, both declining in the eighteenth. The movement of power and commerce from the Mediterranean to the Atlantic and northern seas of Europe placed the Low Countries in a favourable central position to share in the new sea power, trade, world exploration and colonial expansion; at the same time they were directly in the path of conflicts between the major powers. The period opens with Antwerp, following the decay of Bruges due to the silting up of her waterways, as the richest city and greatest port in northern Europe. After the establishment of the Dutch Republic (1588) the ports of Zeeland, the Zuider Zee, and especially of Amsterdam and Rotterdam, rose to supremacy. Through them and through constant warfare the Dutch developed as an energetic and courageous seafaring nation, with extensive trade and colonial possessions. In the seventeenth century the Dutch began their great engineering feats of draining and reclaiming land, of building polders, dykes and canals, and erecting windmills for pumping water, for all of which they have long been famous.

GEOLOGICAL. Stone and marbles, because they were readily available, and brick continued to be the chief building materials of Belgium, together with the timber of the Ardennes which the craftsmen used with such skill and flourish, especially in the exuberant mature architecture of the seventeenth century. In Holland, bricks made from her clay soil largely created her relatively sober national architecture, and by the seventeenth century the influence of this was felt in England, Denmark and Sweden. The ever-present proximity of water and the clear, cool light deriving from it gave qualities to Dutch architecture which have been made familiar by the paintings of Vermeer, de Hoogh and others.

CLIMATIC. In addition to the remarks on p. 570, it should be noted that there are two main climatic zones in the Low Countries, the one relating to the highlands of eastern Belgium and Dutch Limburg, which share the characteristics of continental France and Germany, and the other to the low-lying parts of the Flemish and Dutch coastal areas. The architecture of Holland is greatly influenced by its sea-girt, river intersected and low-lying, fen character, where the frequent driving rains, the winds and clear light produced a simplicity of façade and large windows, with compositions conceived in terms of planes rather than sculptural form. Such circumstances apply less strongly to lowland Belgium, and scarcely at all to its eastern parts.

RELIGIOUS. The ideals of Luther and Calvin were received early in the Low Countries, where many accepted them, especially in the north and east, but, since Charles V and Philip II, rulers during the greater part of the sixteenth century, regarded the Catholic Church and the State as indivisible, Protestants were persecuted. However, the revolt and war against the Spanish was, in the end, as much a war between the interests of the burghers and those of the ruling aristocracy as it was a question of religion: indeed the Protestant Prince of Orange led armies which included a minority of Catholics. Most of the Dutch living south of the Rhine and Meuse remained Catholic, though without political power. Belgium remained almost wholly Catholic and followed the lead of Rome in church building, wherein as elsewhere, the Baroque style was favoured by the Jesuits. The Dutch, after first adapting and even copying the old churches and setting an enormous pulpit halfway along the side of the nave, arranging pews to face it, experimented with a variety of central plans which were developed to suit the reformed religion and national taste. Some were sufficiently important to be the probable basis for certain of Wren's churches.

A. The Town Hall (1561–6) and Guild Houses, Grand' Place, Antwerp. See p. 832

B. Guild Houses, Grand' Place, Brussels (1690–1752). See p. 832

SOCIAL. During the sixteenth century, power and wealth in the Low Countries were mainly in the south (Belgium), the Court residing at Brussels or Malines, while trade was concentrated on Antwerp. After the independence of the Dutch provinces (1588) the interests and histories of Belgium and Holland diverged. For Belgium a crushing blow came in 1648, when Antwerp, the great art centre of northern Europe and city of Rubens, lost control of the Scheldt and her trade rapidly dwindled. The result was catastrophic, since there were no other good ports in the south. For a short time, within the period of Austrian Rule in the eighteenth century, prosperity revived, but Belgium remained poor compared with Holland, a country of landed nobility, burghers and peasants.

As the prosperity of the south waned, the fortunes of the north grew and reached a climax in the 'Golden' seventeenth century, with the Dutch Republic as a great European power; the power of wealth through trade—though seldom political power—was largely in the hands of the burgher class, principally of the provinces of Holland and Zeeland. Yet although a Republic, its rulers were Princes with a Court and aristocratic ministers looking to France for a lead in taste and fashions. The burghers followed the Court in its patronage of art, and their houses were richly decorated and furnished, giving a lively market for the many artists of this great period of Dutch art. The prosperity of the seventeenth century did not last and, by comparison, the next century was one of consolidation, and later, of stagnation. At the end of the eighteenth century the power of the Dutch middle class triumphed briefly, as it did in Belgium too, but almost at once (1794–5) both countries temporarily lost their independence to France; they were then united from 1815–30, at which latter date Belgium became a separate monarchy.

HISTORICAL. Through the marriage of the Emperor Maximilian with Mary of Burgundy all of the Low Countries from Groningen to the Somme became a Hapsburg domain. Hence, on the abdication of Charles V in 1555, both Dutch and Belgians came under the fanatically rigid rule of Philip II of Spain (1556–98). A long and bitter revolt, led by William the Silent, Prince of Orange (1533–84), was ruthlessly opposed by the Duke of Alva's forces, but in 1588 the northern Dutch provinces, with Zeeland, declared their independence, and this was recognized by France and England in 1596.

The seventeenth century in Belgium was not a peaceful one, and, with the decay of Antwerp's trade in mid-century her prosperity suffered greatly. In the eighteenth century, Spanish authority was followed by a period of French rule (1700–06), and under the Treaty of Utrecht (1713) the country passed to Austria. Later, it became involved in the struggle against Louis XV's ambitions (1740–48), only to be returned to Austrian rule. In 1789 there was an internal revolt, and soon after came occupation by the French Revolutionary Forces (1794), this a prelude to her absorption into Napoleon's Empire.

Holland, though equally plagued by wars in the seventeenth century, became a great naval power and maritime trading nation with overseas colonies. So great was this prosperity that it survived almost to the end of the next century, despite further major wars, and finally, a middle-class revolt. The shrunken and ramshackle Batavian Republic which followed received French acquiescence in 1795 (consolidated 1798), but expired in 1806 when Napoleon decided to make his brother Louis, King of Holland, and in 1810 Dutch independence was eclipsed for a while when Holland became a French province.

The Kingdom of the Netherlands, including Belgium, Holland and Luxembourg, was created in 1815 with William I of Orange as its head. The rule of the Dutch king was unwise, and the situation so disadvantageous to the Belgians that they revolted and became a separate kingdom in 1830; Luxembourg too was made independent.

ARCHITECTURAL CHARACTER

The general character of Renaissance architecture in Europe has already been described (p. 656). The Early Renaissance becomes notable in the Low Countries about 1515, at first in the southern zone, which continued to enjoy a prodigious prosperity, the factors at work on this Belgian architecture producing that same rich and often extravagantly ornate expression, and that same zest for ornamentation, that had created the Brabantine Gothic. To some extent the nature of this style can be explained by the circumstance of the distance from the Italian source, and Spanish, French and German influence during transmission, but its strong individuality is mainly due to national conditions and characteristics. It is rich externally and internally, is rarely grand in scale and, as befits the northern clime, windows in domestic work are even larger than the French and may occupy almost as much space as wall. Architectural details progressively assume a more authentic Italian character, but methods of composition and decoration are in a variety of ways unique. The Early Renaissance was centred on Flanders and Brabant, and at first, pseudo-classical detail was applied to Gothic forms. The Parma Palace (now the Palais de Justice) at Malines (1503) was perhaps the first instance in Northern Europe; but more typical is the Old Chancellery, Bruges (1530–35) (p. 833A). Several Italians were then working in the Low Countries, Donato di Boni on the fortifications of Antwerp (1543) and Tommaso Vincidor at Breda Castle (1536). Antwerp was the chief centre, with its great school of painters and sculptors who were often also architects. There, Pieter Coecke van Aalst (1502–50) published translations of Alberti and Serlio, and Cornelius Floris (or de Vriendt) (1504–75) established a style with his Town Hall (p. 829A). This style was widely spread by the books of Hans Vredeman de Vries (1527–1606) throughout northern Europe. The Early Renaissance of Belgium continued to the end of the sixteenth century, though owing to political reasons little was done in the last thirty years. The northern provinces (Holland) followed the southern lead, but at a little distance of time, since they were as yet economically less robust, but from the first, Dutch architecture was simpler and more restrained. It was the books of Vredeman de Vries and the example of the Antwerp Town Hall that guided Lieven de Key (1560–1627), Flemish refugee, in designing the buildings in Holland that first soundly established the Renaissance there (p. 839G).

For the seventeenth century and later it is essential to speak separately of Belgium and Holland. Belgium progressed with its individualistic interpretation of the Italian Proto-Baroque flourishing at that time, to a style which may be described as Baroque, though it is more profuse and less bold and grand than its Italian counterpart; apart from Jesuit and other church architecture which affords a closer parallel. The best period of the Belgian version of the Baroque falls in the first half of the seventeenth century, after which it loses some of its virility though none of its exuberance; and with the eighteenth, shows in its decoration the influence of Austrian and French Rococo, while from the mid-century it took the Antiquarian turn notable also in Italy, France and England. Towards the end of the same century, occasional Greek Revival manifestations appeared. Meanwhile, Dutch architecture took a substantially different course. Lieven de Key and Hendrik de Keyser (1565–1621) developed the early Dutch style, usually plainer than the Belgian, until c. 1625 when it matured in a 'Palladian' phase of considerable dignity and quality, the principal exponents being Jacob van Campen (1595–1657) and Pieter Post (1608–69). The Palladian phase passed about 1670, merging easily into another of some twenty years' duration of positive austerity, external decoration being almost wholly excluded. Next, Daniel Marot (1661–1752), a Huguenot refugee, introduced the masculine style of Louis XIV to the Dutch court, effective in influencing interior decoration rather than architecture proper, and thenceforward French fashions continued to be followed, though with sober external expression and bold and effective planning. As in France and England in the eighteenth century, plain exteriors often belie lavish but tasteful interior decoration. Minor and provincial architecture remained more strongly Dutch. Eighteenth-century architects of note were P. de Swart (1709–72) in Holland and J-P. van Baurscheit the Younger (1699–1768) in Belgium.

EXAMPLES

BELGIAN SECULAR ARCHITECTURE

The **Chancellery (Maison de l'Ancien Greffe), Bruges** (1535) (p. 833A), a town house, has seemingly precocious Baroque qualities which are in fact due to the perpetuation of the Flamboyant Gothic spirit. It has a two-storeyed façade with quasi-Doric Orders, mullioned and transomed windows, and central gable with side-scrolls, crockets and figures.

The **Musée Plantin-Moretus, Antwerp** (1550) (p. 833C), once the house of Christopher Plantin, printer to Philip II, is more authentically Classical, and in its extent and character illustrates the opulence and social status of a highly successful Flemish burgher.

The **Town Hall, Antwerp** (1561–66) (p. 829A), by Cornelius Floris (or de Vriendt), the most distinguished architect and sculptor of the century in the Netherlands, as already mentioned (p. 831) is an important prototype of Belgian Early Renaissance, signalling the conclusion of the experimental stage. It has superimposed Orders between closely-spaced large windows, a rusticated basement storey and a galleried upper storey. While in the main straightforward and plain, its centre-piece is highly characteristic of the phase, with its freely manipulated classical detail and generous use of plastic ornament.

The **Guild Houses, Grand' Place, Brussels** (p. 829B), erected by various guilds, Archers (1691), Shipmasters (1697), Carpenters (1697), Printers (1697), Mercers (1699), Butchers (1720), Brewers (1752), Tailors and Painters, are late Belgian-Baroque and Rococo fantasies which with their serried gable fronts and large window areas follow types established by the late-sixteenth century **Guild Houses in the Grand' Place, Antwerp** (p. 829A), and indicate the wealth of Flemish and Brabantine guilds of craftsmen and tradesmen.

The **Hotel d'Ansembourg, Liége** (1740) (p. 833B), now a museum, is an example of French fashions in Belgium, while the **Town Hall, Lierre** (1740) (p. 833D), by J-P. van Baurscheit, is similarly an instance of the Rococo period.

The **Place Royale, Brussels** (late eighteenth cent.) (p. 834B), together with the Rue Royale, by Barnabé Guimard, a Frenchman, show the Antiquarian trend in evidence at this time. Guimard was also the designer of the church of **S. Jacques sur Coudenberg** (1773–6) in the Place Royale (p. 834B).

DUTCH SECULAR ARCHITECTURE

The **Town Hall, Leyden** (1594) (p. 839D, G), by Lieven de Key, a religious refugee from Antwerp, owes something of its inspiration to Antwerp Town Hall, but is especially noteworthy as an example of the strapwork, fretwork and other petty ornament (p. 839G) typical of the Early Renaissance in the Netherlands generally, and popularized there as in Germany and Elizabethan and Jacobean England (p.

A. The Old Chancellery,
Bruges (1535). See p. 832

B. The Hôtel d'Ansembourg, Liége (1740).
See p. 832

C. The Musée Plantin-
Moretus, Antwerp (1550).
See p. 832

D. The Town Hall, Lierre (1740).
See p. 832

E. The Trippenhuis, Amsterdam
(1662). See p. 835

F. The Mauritshuis, The Hague (1633).
See p. 835

A. The Royal Palace, Amsterdam (1662). See p. 835

B. The Place Royale, Brussels (c. 1776). See p. 832

869) by the books of Vredeman de Vries, principally those appearing in 1565 and 1568. The Butchers' Hall, Haarlem (1602), also by de Key, again has the profusion of pseudo-Classical detail normal to the Netherlands Early Renaissance.

The **Mauritshuis, The Hague** (1633) (p. 833F), built by van Campen and Pieter Post for Prince Maurice of Nassau, instances the Dutch Palladian phase in its flattened temple-like front in a harmonious façadal treatment of brick and stone. Buildings of this class may have influenced Hugh May's Eltham House, Kent (p. 906), and hence the tradition which succeeded it in Georgian England. The **Cloth Hall, Leyden** (1640), by Arent van 's-Gravensande, is a further example of Dutch Palladianism.

The **Royal Palace, Amsterdam** (originally the Town Hall) (1648–65) (p. 834A), by Jacob van Campen, is a major example of Dutch civic architecture on an unusually large scale. Its style is Palladian in the sense that it is of clear, simple ordonnance with no important departures from strict Classical rule and that there is no intrusion of ornament on to the architectural lines. There is, however, a greater freedom in the design of an open cupola-turret over the central, shallowly-projecting pavilion of the two-tiered pilastered façade, standing on a low basement storey, and the crowning pediment has an infilling of petty sculpture.

No. 460, Singel, Amsterdam (1662), by J. Vingboons, is representative of a type of tall, narrow house in that city, usually adorned with the Classic Orders, in the development of which first de Keyser and then the Vingboons played an important part. The **Trippenhuis, Amsterdam** (1662) (p. 833E), also by J. Vingboons, is a larger example of such houses for the merchant class.

The **Town Hall, Enkhuizen** (1686–88) (p. 826A), by Stevin Vennecool, represents the later stage of the Palladian phase, achieving a soft plastic quality despite its being almost completely devoid of decoration.

No. 8, Lange Vijverberg, The Hague (1715) (p. 840), by Daniel Marot, a Frenchman, is of undecorated, Italianate character inclining to the Baroque, but the building now used as the **Royal Library, The Hague** (1735) (p. 826B), also by Marot, shows in its Rococo ornament the influence of French taste upon the Dutch court.

The **Town Hall, Groningen** (1774–92, built 1802–10), by J. O. Husley, belongs to the Antiquarian phase.

BELGIAN ECCLESIASTICAL ARCHITECTURE

The **Church at Scherpenheuvel** (near Louvain) (1607) (p. 837C), by Wenzel Coeberger, was the earliest centrally-planned and domed church in the Low Countries, and is among the exceptions in Belgium to the basilical 'altar' churches normal there. Its style is Proto-Baroque.

S. Pierre, Ghent (1629–1749), **S. Michel, Louvain** (1650–70) (p. 837A) and the tower of **S. Charles, Antwerp** (1620), all by Pieter Huyssens, who belonged to the Jesuit Order, typify the Catholic Baroque style in Belgium. In its west façade, with its superimposed Ionic and Composite columns, broken pediments and enormous side scrolls masking the aisle roofs, S. Michel shows a close approach to the Baroque of Rome, except that its portal is mean and less focal than it would be there, while the banded Orders show some French influence and the ornament has native, Netherlands, characteristics.

DUTCH ECCLESIASTICAL ARCHITECTURE

The **West Church, Amsterdam** (1620–30), by Hendrik de Keyser, is Classical in decoration though its form is based on Gothic precedent adapted to Protestant needs. Its dominant tower (1638), with that of the **South Church** (1614) also by

Keyser, are among the best examples in Holland of the adaptation of the native Gothic tradition to classical themes and elements, this development beginning with de Key's towers (p. 839D, E), which have an affinity with those of Wren's City churches (p. 913). The **North Church, Amsterdam** (1620), a further church by de Keyser, has a Greek Cross plan typical of the Dutch, central-space 'pulpit' churches.

The **New Church, Haarlem** (1645–9) (p. 837B), by van Campen, has the Greek-Cross-in-square plan popular in Holland, the arms of the cross being covered by wooden barrel vaults meeting at a cross vault, the corner squares by flat ceilings —a scheme similar to S. Martin's, Ludgate, London (p. 914) by Wren. The Baroque elongated church normal to Belgium is occasionally represented in Holland, as in the **New Church, The Hague** (1649–56) (p. 837D), by P. Noorwits and B. van Bassen, the plan being made up of two interlocking squares with six projecting apsidal bays.

The **East Church, Middelburg** (1647–67), by Frans Drijfhout and Pieter Post, centrally-planned, has some resemblance to the Scherpenheuvel church in the Belgian zone; the **Marekerk, Leyden** (1639–49), by 's-Gravensande, though smaller, is more original and refined.

COMPARATIVE ANALYSIS

PLANS. At first the Mediaeval church plan was retained, but adapted by Protestants to new forms of worship. In Belgium, from the early seventeenth century, the Jesuit and other Baroque types were used, while in Holland a variety of centralized or semi-centralized plans on a small scale were the subject of Protestant experiment. Civic buildings and large houses used the central block and balanced wing forms, while the medium-sized house and smaller civic buildings were usually in simple square or rectangular forms; town houses had narrow street fronts but were of great depth, often with inner courts and light-wells.

WALLS. Walls, usually decorated with Orders, were in stone in the Belgium inland areas, and for major buildings nearly everywhere, but in Holland and coastal Belgium brick, with stone dressings, was the chief material. Gables, stepped or enriched with scrolls and other devices (pp. 829A, B, 833A, C, 838C) were common, and often had projecting beams for hoists. Due to the dull northern climate, window areas were large and tended to dwarf the Orders; in town façades, especially in Holland, the ratio of window to solid was high, and made possible by foundational piling solely under the side walls, so that the street front was little else than a screen.

OPENINGS. Arcades were unusual, due to lack of strong sunlight, but appeared under Italian influence in the early period, for example at the Musée Plantin-Moretus, Antwerp (p. 833C), and Breda Castle. Doorways were tall and richly decorated (p. 838E, D), often with huge fanlights; entrances had steps, and perrons were common. The large, tall and narrow windows were of the transom-and-mullion type, except in Holland after the middle of the sixteenth century when the sash window (perhaps a Dutch invention) was introduced—it fell into comparative disuse by the end of the next century.

COLUMNS. The early use of the Orders was characterized by the grotesque distortions favoured by Floris and de Vries (p. 838K), until the true Renaissance Orders became common after the second quarter of the sixteenth century; in Belgium they produced a sculptural-plastic effect, but often in Holland the effect was very flat.

MOULDINGS. As in Mediaeval times the mouldings tended to be heavier than in Italy, probably to compensate for the lack of strong shadows. Nevertheless, fine

S. Michel, Louvain (1650–
1670). See p. 835

B. The New Church, Haarlem (1645–9).
See p. 836

The Church at Scherpenheuvel
(1607). See p. 835

D. The New Church, The Hague (1649–56).
See p. 836

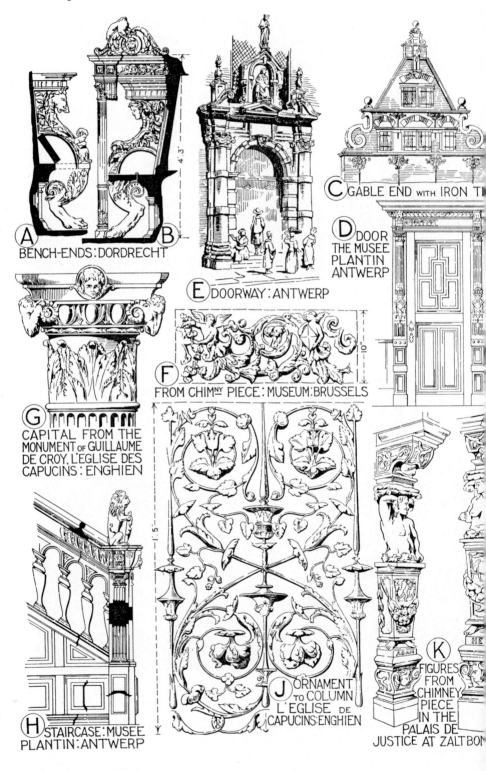

A. BENCH-ENDS: DORDRECHT

B.

C. GABLE END WITH IRON T

D. DOOR THE MUSEE PLANTIN ANTWERP

E. DOORWAY: ANTWERP

F. FROM CHIMNY PIECE: MUSEUM: BRUSSELS

G. CAPITAL FROM THE MONUMENT OF GUILLAUME DE CROY, L'EGLISE DES CAPUCINS: ENGHIEN

H. STAIRCASE: MUSEE PLANTIN: ANTWERP

J. ORNAMENT TO COLUMN L'EGLISE DE CAPUCINS: ENGHIEN

K. FIGURES FROM CHIMNEY PIECE IN THE PALAIS DE JUSTICE AT ZALTBON

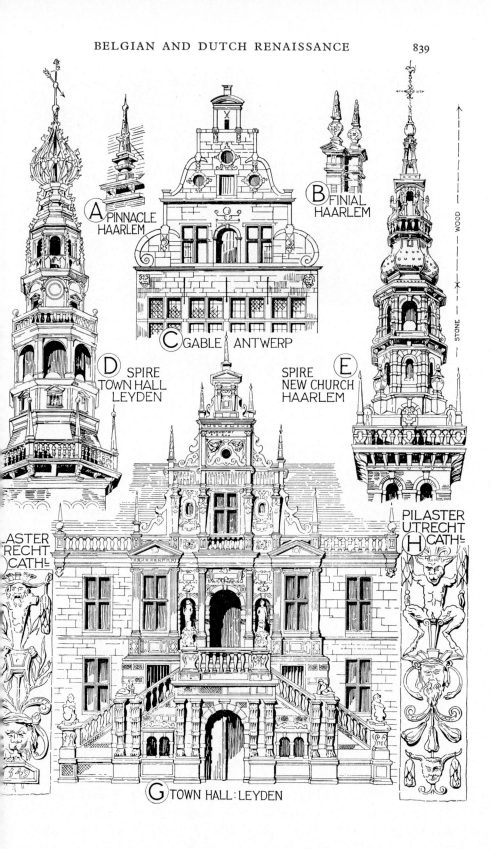

A PINNACLE HAARLEM

B FINIAL HAARLEM

C GABLE ANTWERP

D SPIRE TOWN HALL LEYDEN

E SPIRE NEW CHURCH HAARLEM

WOOD

STONE

PILASTER UTRECHT CATHL

ASTER RECHT CATHL

G TOWN HALL: LEYDEN

A. Staircase B. Landing on second floor

No. 8, Lange Vijverberg, The Hague (1715). See p. 835

craftsmanship, mostly originating from Antwerp, produced excellent work in stone, marble, wood and metals throughout the Netherlands.

ORNAMENT. In Belgium, the Catholic religion encouraged richness in decoration, and gave ample opportunity for its display in churches, where the altars and fittings were extravagantly ornate. In Dutch Protestant churches—often in contrast with their general sobriety—screens, benches (p. 838A), pulpits, organ cases and stained glass were richly designed. In houses of all sizes, great prosperity was reflected in the richness of the interiors in all periods; in Holland, often again in contrast with the plain exteriors. Chimney pieces (p. 838F, K) in the Early Renaissance were major fields for ornate extravagance, but during the sixteenth century, taste, though often still exuberant, saw that ornament was more widely and evenly distributed—in plaster ceilings, panelling, painted walls and ceilings, staircase balustrades (p. 838H), and fittings.

REFERENCE BOOKS

BURKE, G. L. *The Making of Dutch Towns*. London, 1956.

EDWARDS, T. *Belgium and Luxembourg*. London, 1951.

FOCKEMA ANDREAE, S. J. and others. *Duizend Jaar Bouwen in Nederland*. Vol. ii. Amsterdam, 1957.

GEYL, P. *The Revolt of the Netherlands, 1555–1609*. London, 1958.

MINISTRY OF EDUCATION, ARTS AND SCIENCES. *Guide to Dutch Art*. The Hague, 1953.

NIJHOFF, M. *La Belgique monumentale*. The Hague, 1915.

OZINGA, M. D. *De Protestansche Kerkenbouw in Nederland*. Amsterdam, 1929.

PLUYM, W. van der. *Vijf eeuwen Binnenhuis en Meubels in Nederland*. Amsterdam, 1954.

SITWELL, S. *The Netherlands*. London, 1948.

SLUYTERMAN, K. *Old Interiors in Belgium*. The Hague, 1908.

—. *Ancient Interiors in Belgium*. The Hague, 1915.

VRIEND, J. J. *De Bouwkunst van ons Land*. Amsterdam, 1949.

YERBURY, F. R. *Old Domestic Architecture in Holland*. London, 1924.

YSENDYCK, J. J. van. *Documents classiques de l'art dans les Pays-Bas*. 5 vols. Antwerp, 1954.

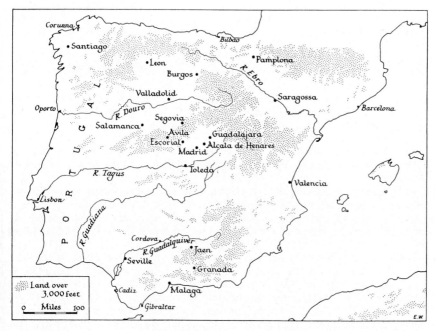

Spain in the seventeenth century

XXIV. SPANISH RENAISSANCE

(sixteenth–nineteenth century)

See p. 1126 for Spanish architecture in the Americas.

INFLUENCES

GEOGRAPHICAL. Spain, in the Mediaeval period (p. 635), could well be geographically considered as 'the Peninsula' and merely as a country in the extreme south-
west of Europe. It was far otherwise in the Renaissance period, when her prestige
and power had been increased and extended by the discovery of the New World,
which, together with the vast hereditary possessions and the military conquests of
the Spanish monarchy, established Spain as the leading country in Europe. Her
dominions, under the Emperor Charles V, included the Netherlands and parts of
Germany, till, after eighty years of strife, they shrank again in Europe under the
Peace of Westphalia (1648). But there remained those partly tropical lands,
the Spanish colonies of South America—Mexico, Peru, and Chile—which were so
naturally allied in many aspects with the sunny Spain of Europe. In these exotic
lands Spanish architects had the widest scope for the exercise of their flamboyant
genius.

GEOLOGICAL. In continuation of previous practice (p. 635), granite was much
used, as in the Escorial where its hard severe nature had much to do with the grim

aspect of that building; while stone and the semi-marbles in which the country abounds were in general use. Brick was employed with stone in bonding courses, mainly in former Moorish centres, such as Toledo, and the iron ore of the northern mountains gave an impetus to the development of decorative ironwork, such as the 'rejas' (p. 862).

CLIMATIC. The climate varies, as stated in Chapter XVIII (p. 636), from severe winter cold on the high central table-lands to tropical summer heat in the south, and, owing to the general sunny character of the Peninsula, there is a prevalence of small windows, flat roofs, and open 'patios', or courtyards. In many of the new Spanish colonies in America, the climate was not unlike that of Spain, and was thus favourable to the reproduction there of similar architectural features to those of Spain. The effects aimed at by the Baroque style were peculiarly adapted to the clear air, intense sunlight and strong shadows of Spain and many parts of Spanish America.

RELIGIOUS. The Reformation obtained no hold whatever in Spain, for the religious and racial struggle between Christianity and Islam formed a bond of union amongst all Christians, and so left little opportunity for Christian internecine strife. The final expulsion of the Moors, after the fall of Granada (1492), resulted in a revival of ecclesiastical building, and many fine Renaissance churches were erected in the hitherto Moorish districts. Spain was the birthplace of Ignatius Loyola, the founder of the Society of Jesus, which received Papal recognition in 1540, and the religious zeal of this order is responsible for many magnificent Baroque churches and convents throughout the country.

SOCIAL. Goths from North Europe and Moors from North Africa were potent elements in the mixed population of Spain, and these warring influences are visible in the architecture. The marriage (1469) of Ferdinand of Aragon and Isabella of Castile—designated 'The Catholic Sovereigns' by the Holy See, 1497—began that fusion of the different states which resulted in the consolidation of the Kingdom of Spain. In 1512 Ferdinand conquered the Kingdom of Navarre, which was incorporated with Castile, and thus the whole of Spain was joined under one rule, and during the annexation of Portugal (1580–1640) the Spanish Kingdom covered the whole peninsula. Under the despotism of Philip II Jews and heretics were persistently persecuted. Under Philip III (1598–1621) the Moriscos (Moorish converts to Christianity) were driven out of the country, and this proved a great loss, both in handicrafts and commerce, to Southern Spain, for their industry had largely contributed to its prosperity. After the invasion by Napoleon, internal revolutions followed which have not been favourable to architecture.

HISTORICAL. In the latter part of the fifteenth century the power of Spain gradually increased until, under the Emperor Charles V (1516–56), it became the chief power in Europe. The Turkish occupation of the Levant, which closed the usual trade routes to the East, had promoted that spirit of maritime enterprise in Spain and Portugal which led to the great discoveries of new lands in the West and thus brought increased riches to the Peninsula. In 1487 Diaz discovered the Cape of Good Hope; in 1492 Columbus discovered the West Indies, and in 1497–9 the continent of America, bringing consequent riches to Spain. In 1497 Vasco da Gama carried Portuguese trade to India. The extent of the Spanish dominions in Europe was due to a succession of marriages, as a result of which the Emperor Charles V reigned over Spain, the Netherlands, Sardinia, Sicily, Naples, Franche-Comté, Milan and Germany, and he added by conquest Mexico, Peru, Chile, and Central America, before he abdicated (1555) the most powerful Emperor since Charlemagne. This vast empire was held together by his skill in government and by the excellence of the Spanish army, of which the infantry was the finest in Europe. Philip II

A. The Palace, Guadalajara (1480–92). See p. 846

B. The Casa de las Conchas, Salamanca (1512–14). See p. 846

A. The University, Salamanca (façade 1514–1529). See p. 846

B. Casa de Ayuntamiento, Seville: detail façade (1527–64). See p. 846

C. The University, Alcalá de Henares (1537–53). See p. 846

checked the power of the Turks in 1571 by winning the great naval battle of Lepanto, but his harsh and despotic rule alienated the Netherlands; while the expedition against England ended in the defeat of the Armada in 1588. Provinces were gradually lost, until in 1659 the power of Spain was shattered by the Peace of the Pyrenees. The war of the Spanish succession (1701–14), terminated by the Peace of Utrecht, resulted in the loss of Gibraltar as well as of the Spanish dominions in Italy and the Netherlands. At the commencement of the nineteenth century Napoleon's invasion led to an outburst of national resistance, when, with the powerful aid of the armies of Great Britain under Wellington, the French were finally driven out of Spain after the battle of Vittoria (1813), and during the Peninsular War the Spanish colonies in America had revolted and were eventually recognized as independent.

ARCHITECTURAL CHARACTER

Renaissance Spain was heir to two civilizations, Muslim and Christian, and not herself possessing much political and cultural unity, particularly in the Christian regions, tended to conservatism while being at the same time locally susceptible to external influences. Hence, although in general the Renaissance advanced by stages similar to those in other European countries, there was considerable diversity in the manner of expression and in the rates of progression in different parts of the country. Individualism was strongly marked. Keeping these matters in view, the Renaissance may be divided into four tolerably distinct phases, determined by the characteristics predominant in the different periods.

The Early Period (1492–1556), which begins with the fall of Granada, is notable for the grafting of Renaissance details on to Gothic forms, and was influenced by the exuberant fancy of Moorish art. Thus there had been produced by this time a style as rich and poetic as any in Europe, commonly known as the Plateresque (*plateria*=silverwork), from the minuteness of its detail and its similarity to silversmiths' work which itself had received a great impetus through the importation of precious metals from the New World. The Plateresque is extremely florid and decoratively involved, and has its fundamentally Gothic versions, carrying on until mid-sixteenth century, as well as those in which Renaissance detail substantially appears.

The Classical Period (1556–1650) was marked by a closer adherence to Italian Renaissance art, and under the influence of the sculptor Alonso Berruguete (*c.* 1488–1561) and the notable architect Juan de Herrera (*c.* 1530–97), who had visited both Flanders (1547–51) and Italy (1551–9), for a while took a more classical and austere turn.

The Baroque Period (1650–1750) was characterized by a reaction from the correct and frigid formalism observed by Herrera and his followers. As in the earlier phases of the Renaissance there was no single version to which all designers of the day adhered, but several, and among them one which is considered as being peculiarly Spanish in its extraordinary virility, opulence and disregard of strict classical rules. While the earlier Baroque examples show some relationship to Lombard, Central Italian or Neapolitan precedents, a fantastically extravagant expression, the 'Churrigueresque', developed in the late seventeenth century and continued to mid-eighteenth; due to a family of architects led by José de Churriguera (1665–1725,) though he was not himself the most extreme of the exponents of the style. There were also followers, including the brilliant Narciso Tomé, active between 1715–42, whose work, however, is mainly sculptural. The Spanish Churrigueresque is well seen in the Cathedral of Santiago de Compostela (west front, 1738–49) (p. 858B) several buildings at Seville, at Valladolid, and above all at Salamanca. The style inspired many buildings in the Spanish colonies. French and Italian fashions intruded strongly into Spain in the eighteenth century.

The Antiquarian Period (1750–1830). As in general in Central and Western Europe, architecture turned more and more towards ancient classical models at this time.

EXAMPLES

SECULAR ARCHITECTURE

The **Palace, Guadalajara** (1480–92) (destroyed, 1936) (pp. 647, 843A) and the **Collegio de San Gregorio, Valladolid** (1488–96) have patios with Moorish, Gothic and Renaissance detail of the transition period.

The **Casa de las Conchas, Salamanca** (1512–14) (p. 843B) takes its name from the curious treatment of its façade, which is covered with carved scallop shells. The windows are few in number; the small lower ones are guarded with grilles of elaborate Moorish ironwork, while the upper ones have carved panels in lieu of balconies and are enriched with heraldic carvings.

The **University façade, Salamanca** (1514–29) (p. 844A) is a masterpiece of Plateresque design, of admirable craftsmanship and embodying, within a Gothic frame, a number of Italianate motifs such as amorini, panelled pilasters infilled with arabesques, portrait roundels and candelabra as well as the arms of Ferdinand and Isabella and of Charles V, all embedded in a wealth of surface ornament of Moorish inspiration.

The **Casa de Ayuntamiento, Seville** (1527–64) (p. 844B), designed by Diego de Riano (active 1517–34), has a symmetrical front of two and three storeys fully ornamented with the Orders, spaced into bays by single or paired pilasters or on the upper storeys by attached columns treated as candelabra. The design is very reminiscent of Italian Lombard architecture, of mixed Early and Proto-Baroque character, but has the excessive elaboration stamping it as Plateresque.

The **University façade, Alcala de Henares** (1537–53) (p. 844C), by Rodrigo Gil de Hontanon (*c.* 1505–77), whose earlier work was Gothic, has the characteristically ornate centre-piece and paucity of windows, except for an arcaded third-storey window series bracketing the greater part of the front. The main, first-floor, windows have side scrolls, excessive enframements and iron grilles (p. 860D), while the angle treatment and pinnacles strike a Gothic note. Nearby is the **Archbishop's Palace,** its staircase and fine 'patio' being by Alonso de Covarrubias (1488–1570), the patio having spreading bracket capitals.

The **Casa de Miranda, Burgos** (1543) (p. 847B) has a noted two-storey patio with bracket capitals to the columns, so usual in Spain.

The **Casa Polentina, Avila** (*c.* 1550) (p. 854B) also has an attractive patio, the columns on each of two storeys carrying bracket capitals and richly-carved architraves, and having heraldic shields above the capitals.

The **Alcazar, Toledo** (*c.* 1537–53) (pp. 848A, 854A), a castle of mixed Moorish and Gothic character, was remodelled by Alonso de Covarrubias for Charles V. It was largely destroyed in the Civil War (1936–9). The well-designed patio (p. 848A) had superimposed Corinthian columns in light arcades of the Early Italian type, the arches standing upon the column caps, and like the façade which formed a new front to the old castle (p. 854A), was not richly sculptured, since the material was granite. The central entrance was flanked by Ionic columns surmounted by statues, and the elaborate overdoor had a panel carved with the arms of Charles V. The first storey windows of the façade, with iron balconies, were set off by plain walling.

A. Palace of Charles V, Granada (1527–68): detail of façade. See p. 851

B. Casa de Miranda, Burgos (1543). See p. 846

C. Palace of Charles V, Granada: central court

A. The Alcazar, Toledo: the patio (*c.* 1537–53). See p. 846

B. Casa de los Guzmanes, Leon (1560). See p. 852

A. The Tavera Hospital, Toledo: façade (1542–79). See p. 851

B. Tavera Hospital, Toledo: patio

A. The Casa Lonja, Seville: the patio (1583–98). See p. 852

B. The University, Valladolid: façade (1715–). See p. 852

while the top storey had an unusual rusticated treatment, with a small Order on pedestals, surmounted by a flat balustraded roof.

The **Palace of Charles V, Granada** (1527–68) (p. 847A, C), adjoining the Alhambra (p. 1233), was designed by Pedro Machuca (active 1517–50) and continued after his death by his son Luis. It equates with the Italian High Renaissance in character, and is thoroughly classical in spirit. It is a square mass of building about 200 ft each way, enclosing a fine, majestic open circular patio. The external façades are two storeys in height, the lower of which has rusticated Doric columns, except in the centre-piece, where they are fluted, and the upper has Ionic columns (p. 847A). In both storeys there are circular windows above the main ones, to light mezzanine floors, their place being taken by sculptured panels on the centre-piece. It is built in golden-coloured stone. The circular patio (p. 847C) is a grand architectural conception, 100 ft in diameter, with superimposed Doric and Ionic colonnades, and forms the chief feature of this monumental building, which, however, was never completed for occupation.

The **Tavera Hospital, Toledo** (1542–79) (p. 849), designed by Bartolomé de Bustamente (c. 1500–70) is again strongly Italianate and unusually restrained for Spanish Renaissance architecture. It has a rectangular plan, 350 ft long, and a powerfully severe façade, with vigorously protruding rusticated quoins at the angles of the building and around the sparse windows, in addition to channelled rustications covering the two principal storeys as a whole (p. 849A). There is, however, the usual Spanish centre-piece, rising through three tiers. The patio (p. 849B), with its two storeys of graceful arcades, Ionic over Doric, is as classically faultless as any Florentine Renaissance cortile, apart from the varied span of the arches.

The **Escorial** (1559–84) (pp. 853, 859A, B, 861A), about thirty miles from Madrid, was commenced by Juan Bautista de Toledo (d. 1567) for Philip II, but in 1572 Juan de Herrera was given charge of the work. This austere group of buildings on a lonely site, 675 ft by 685 ft, consists of monastery, college, church, and palace with state apartments (p. 853B). The grand entrance in the centre of the west front opens into the 'Patio de los Reyes', which, lying between the great courts of the monastery and the college, forms the atrium of the church, the latter measuring 330 ft by 210 ft. To the right of the atrium is the monastery, with its four courts, each 60 ft square, surrounded with arcades in three storeys, beyond which is the 'Patio de los Evangelistas'. To the left of the atrium is the college, with its four courts, and beyond this the great court of the palace is connected with the state apartments, which project behind the church and make the plan into the form of a gridiron. The church is similar in type to S. Maria di Carignano, Genoa (p. 688), and shows Italian influence on the work of Herrera, but the Spanish character is seen in the position of the choir over a vaulted vestibule at the west end, which shortens the long arm of the Latin cross, so that the main building is a Greek cross on plan. The simple church façade (p. 859A) has noble Doric columns, surmounted by granite figures of the Kings of Judah, and the windows between the statues light the raised choir within. The interior (p. 859B) is cold, but impressive by reason of its simplicity, and the granite walls are in strong contrast to the frescoed vaults, while the magnificent reredos, with its quiet blending of colour, further emphasizes the general subdued effect. This world-famous pile owes much of its character to the yellowish-grey granite of which it is built, both within and without, a material which imposed restraint upon the architect, and may indeed have accorded with the ascetic taste of Philip II. The external façades, five storeys high (p. 853A), are in great blocks of granite, of such a size that the door architraves are in one stone, 10 ft high, and there is no attempt at window grouping, as in the Alcazar façade (p. 854A), and openings generally are devoid of ornament. The external effect of the Escorial is remarkably dignified, with its plain façades and angle towers, the whole group culminating in the great western towers of the church and its central dome, 312 ft in height. The impressiveness of this group of buildings, grand in its severity (p. 861A), is enhanced by the lonely austerity of its mountain background.

The **Casa de los Guzmanes, Leon** (*c.* 1560) (p. 848B) is a representative building of the Classical period, the architectural elements being used with discretion and restraint. The special Spanish note is struck by the angle pavilions—normal to domestic architecture—the columned doorway flanked by statues, small windows protected by iron grilles, and continuous arcaded upper storey in the deep shadow of wide-spreading eaves.

The **Casa Lonja, Seville** (1583–98) (p. 850A), from designs by Herrera, shows in its patio of Ionic-over-Doric arcades, in which the attached Orders enframe the arches in the Roman manner, the cold academic character widespread at this time.

The **Hospicio Provincial, Madrid** (1722–) provides in its portal (p. 857A), designed by Pedro Ribera (1683–1742), an instance of the Churrigueresque version of the Baroque. In secular architecture externally, it was often solely upon portals that this kind of almost riotous elaboration was concentrated, as again too, though with greater discipline, in the façade of the **University, Valladolid** (p. 850B), begun in 1715 by Narciso Tomé. The **Palace of the Marqués de Dos Aguas, Valencia** (1740–4) (p. 857B) shows a later development in which the tortuous and involved ornament around the openings has something of the character of a viscous efflorescence.

The **Royal Palace, La Granja, near Segovia** (1719–39) (p. 857C) has an eastern or garden façade built by foreign architects, the centre part (1735–9) from the designs of the Italian, Filippo Juvarra (p. 695); and this, having a giant Corinthian Order embracing the two main floors, has most of the qualities associated with Italian Baroque architecture. The splendid gardens were laid out between 1727–43. The **Royal Palace, Madrid** (1738–64) by the Italian, Sacchetti, similarly is in classical heavy Baroque style, having little distinctive Spanish character.

ECCLESIASTICAL ARCHITECTURE

S. Estéban, Salamanca (1524–1610) is mainly a Gothic building, influenced by Moorish art, but has a rich Plateresque western front: a great arch, with superimposed pilasters, half-columns and baluster shafts, encloses sculptured figures of saints in high canopied niches carried right across the elaborate façade, which is further enriched with heraldic shields and finished off with a truncated pediment.

Burgos Cathedral (pp. 637, 641A, 652B) is conspicuous externally by its magnificent central tower, added 1539–67, with quasi-Gothic windows and lofty angle pinnacles emphasizing the old Gothic tradition which lingers throughout. Internally, four massive circular piers, built after the collapse of the previous Gothic piers in 1539, support pointed arches, elaborate squinches, high octagonal drum, and the open-work vault or 'cimborio'. The Escalera Dorada (1519–23) in the north transept is a unique Plateresque feature of the interior.

Granada Cathedral (1528–63 and later) (p. 858C, D), undertaken by Diego de Siloe (*c.* 1495–1563), is one of the grandest Renaissance churches in southern Spain, and a remarkable example of the Plateresque period. The interior (p. 858D) is a translation of Seville Cathedral into the Renaissance style, and the great piers of the nave (completed between 1667–1703) are faced with the Classic Orders, while the radiating piers, supporting the dome of the circular 'Capilla Mayor', show an ingenious and novel treatment. The Capilla Real, to the south of the transept, is late

THE ESCORIAL: Nᴿ MADRID

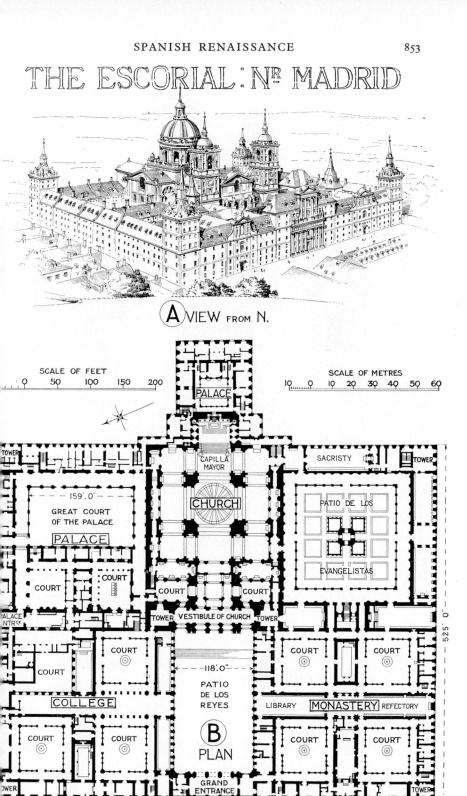

Ⓐ VIEW FROM N.

SCALE OF FEET
0   50   100   150   200

SCALE OF METRES
10   0   10   20   30   40   50   60

PALACE

TOWER

CAPILLA MAYOR

SACRISTY

TOWER

GREAT COURT OF THE PALACE

— 159'.0" —

CHURCH

PATIO DE LOS

PALACE

EVANGELISTAS

COURT

COURT

COURT

COURT

PALACE ENTR.ᶜᴱ

TOWER   VESTIBULE OF CHURCH   TOWER

COURT

COURT

COURT

COURT

— 118'.0" —

525'. 0"

COLLEGE

PATIO DE LOS REYES

LIBRARY   MONASTERY   REFECTORY

COURT

COURT

Ⓑ PLAN

COURT

COURT

TOWER

GRAND ENTRANCE

TOWER

COLLEGE ENTRANCE

— 675'.0" —

MONASTERY ENTRANCE

PLAZA   DEL   MONASTERIO

CAR·VRO. IMP. HISP. REX MDLI

Ⓐ CENTRAL PORTION OF N. FACADE: THE ALCAZAR: TOLEDO.

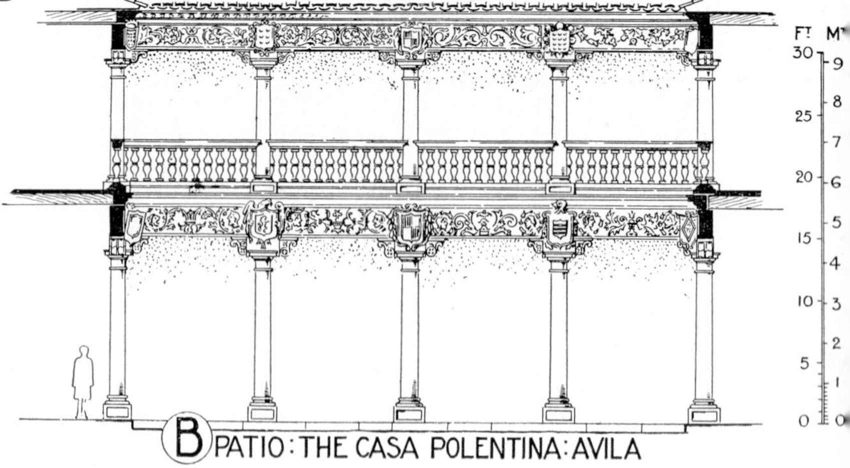

Ⓑ PATIO: THE CASA POLENTINA: AVILA

FT M
30 — 9
      8
25
      7
20 — 6
      5
15   4
10 — 3
      2
5   1
0 — 0

Gothic (1504–21) and earlier than the Cathedral itself. It is entered through a magnificent wrought-iron 'reja' and contains the famous tombs of Ferdinand and Isabella and other kings and queens of Spain. The unfinished west front shows a change of design, due to Alonso Cano (1601–1667) and erected 1667–1703: it is an instance of Baroque architecture, a type in which the use of the Orders is largely evaded (p. 858c).

Jaen Cathedral (1540–) is mainly of the Classical period but has an impressive Baroque west front and towers (1667–88) (p. 859c); **Malaga Cathedral** (1528–) continued in building into the eighteenth century, though without considerable departure from the early design.

Valladolid Cathedral (1580–) begun on the plans of Juan de Herrera, the Spanish Palladio, was never finished to his designs or it would have been just about as large as Seville, and among the largest cathedrals in the world. Nevertheless Herrera's design had great influence on other cathedrals in Spain and Spanish America. It was finished at a much reduced size in 1730–3, the upper part of the west front (p. 859D) being by Alberto Churriguera (1676–1750), whose style is here a vigorous Baroque, instead of having the intricacy usually found in the work of the Churriguera family of architects.

El Pilar Cathedral, Saragossa (begun 1677; extensively altered 1753–66) (p. 861B) has a rectangular plan similar to that of Herrera's Valladolid, with a fine enclosed western 'coro'. The exterior, as seen across the River Ebro, forms an imposing pile, of many domes, the two angle towers having been completed in modern times and the other two yet awaiting completion. The principal material is orange-brown brickwork, and the roofing is finished in colour-patterned tilework. Moorish influence is apparent.

The **Sacristy of la Cartuja (Charterhouse), Granada** (1727–64) (p. 858A) is famous as an extreme instance of Churrigueresque architecture, designed by F. Manuel Vasquez. The windows are at a high level and leave the walls free for the bizarre fretted plasterwork enclosing picture-panels and inlaid doors and cup-boards.

S. Francisco el Grande, Madrid (1761–84), built on the model of the Pantheon, Rome (p. 197), to contain the tombs of famous Spaniards, and the façade of **Pamplona Cathedral** (1780–83), severely formal in design, illustrate the Neo-Classical revival in the Antiquarian period.

COMPARATIVE ANALYSIS

(A comparative analysis of essential differences between Gothic and Renaissance architecture is given on pp. 660 ff.)

PLANS. In churches, wide naves are usual, and general largeness of scale is prevalent in the later rectangular churches, which are sometimes without aisles. A 'cimborio' (lantern or dome) is common at the crossing (p. 853B); transepts and apsidal chancels are usually shallow, and the ritual choir remains west of the transepts, as in many Spanish churches of the Gothic period. The patio (pp. 848A, 849B), or Spanish version of the Roman atrium and Italian cortile, is universal in houses, and is given even greater seclusion, doubtless due to Moorish influence; thus in Toledo only occasional glimpses of the patio can be obtained through doorways in jealously enclosing walls. Staircases, as in the transept of Burgos Cathedral (p. 852), are often on a grand scale. The spacious patio and broad staircase in the Casa Infanta, Saragossa, and the Alcazar, Toledo (p. 848A), make as picturesque and fanciful a group as any in Spain.

WALLS. Walls were usually of stone; granite was employed for the Escorial and in Madrid, while brickwork bonded with stone was used in the Moorish districts of Saragossa and Toledo. The arabesque parapets, as in the Palacio de Monterey, Salamanca, and the projecting timber cornices of the Saragossa palaces are both equally characteristic. The typical walls are plain below, with few openings, except the elaborate doorways, probably due to Moorish precedent, while the upper windows are accentuated by a wealth of ornament. The top storey is frequently designed as a continuous arcade (p. 848B), which with its deep shadow gives an impressive finish to the building. This served as an evening resort, much as did the flat parapeted roofs of the East. The internal walls of the great saloons of the early palaces are of plain stonework, ten or more feet in height, hung with tapestry. The steeples attached to the Cathedrals of Santiago de Compostela, Granada, Jaen (p. 859C), Malaga, Saragossa, and Carmona, are some of the many varieties of this feature to be found throughout Spain.

OPENINGS. Arcades were treated with lavish decoration, especially in the patios, as at Avila (p. 854B) and at Burgos (p. 847B), where they give special character to this central space. Doorways were important features, and, following Moorish tradition, were designed on a grand scale, as at Toledo and elsewhere (pp. 843, 844, 850B, 857A), probably due to the prominence given to gateways in Oriental countries. Windows are framed in richly carved stonework, and are flanked by small columns on corbels, and finished by a highly ornamental head (p. 860D). Ground-floor windows are frequently protected by those beautiful iron grilles for which Spanish craftsmen are renowned (p. 843B).

ROOFS. As in all hot countries, roofs with wide-spreading eaves are flat or of low pitch, and gables are rare (p. 843). Domes, both circular and octagonal, were used for churches (p. 861), and towers are frequently topped with domes or spires of fanciful design, such as the angle towers of the Escorial (p. 853). The large saloons in palaces sometimes have an internal upper gallery round the walls, carried on a projecting timber cornice of fanciful design, and suggestive of Moorish influence, as in the Audiencia, Valencia.

COLUMNS. Columns derived from the Roman 'Orders' were of varied types, with elaborate shafts, especially in the Plateresque style (p. 844A, B). They were either twisted or of baluster shape (p. 860D), frequently with wide-stretching bracket capitals, which acted as corbels to support the architrave, and were suggestive of forms used in timber work (pp. 126C, 847B). Later, owing to the influence of Herrera, columns of Classical correctness prevailed (pp. 847A, C, 850A, 859A), until replaced by the fanciful forms of the Baroque style, in which columns and entablatures were freely used as sculpturesque elements (p. 850B).

MOULDINGS. Throughout the earlier period mouldings reflect the Gothic tradition; they are small and refined, owing to the influence of the silversmiths' craft, and Moorish plasterwork, with its fineness of detail, seems to have served as a model for mouldings. Great richness was often produced by bringing the mouldings forward over the capitals, and this fluttering effect of many mitres gives great liveliness (p. 860).

ORNAMENT (p. 860). Ornament derives its special character from the mingling of Gothic, Moorish, and Renaissance elements in elaborate craftsmanship. 'Retablos' in alabaster, wood, or stone, peopled with life-size figures in architectural frames, are without doubt the finest decorative adjuncts to church interiors, where they often fill the width of the choir and rise to a great height, as at Burgos and elsewhere (pp. 641D, 859B). The tombs of Spanish grandees, rich with heraldic devices and portrait busts, offered opportunities for the display of the national love of ostentation (cf. p. 651E). Choir stalls are ornate, with carved misericords, baluster-shafts, elbow-rests, and canopies, as at S. Marcos, Leon, and Valladolid. The great

The Hospicio Provincial, Madrid: portal (1722–). See p. 852

B. The Palace of the Marqués de Dos Aguas, Valencia (1740–4). See p. 852

C. The Royal Palace, La Granja, near Segovia: garden façade (1735–9) See p. 852

A. The Sacristy, la Cartuja (Charterhouse), Granada (1727–64). See p. 855

B. The Cathedral of Santiago de Compostela: façade (1738–49). See p. 84

C. Façade (1667–1703)

D. Interior, looking W.

Granada Cathedral (1528–1703). See p. 852

A. Façade of church   B. Nave looking E.

The Escorial, near Madrid (1559–84). See p. 851

c. Jaen Cathedral: façade (1667–88).   D. Valladolid Cathedral: façade (lower
See p. 855   part 1580–; upper, 1730–3). See p. 855

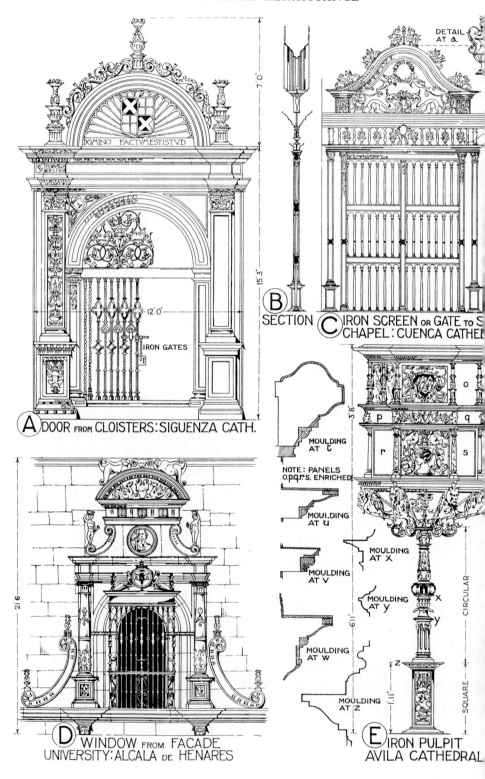

DOMINO FACTVMESTISTVD

7.0"

15.3"

12.0"

IRON GATES

B SECTION

DETAIL AT a

C IRON SCREEN or GATE to S
CHAPEL: CUENCA CATHE

A DOOR from CLOISTERS: SIGUENZA CATH.

MOULDING AT t

NOTE: PANELS
o,p,q,r,s. ENRICHED

MOULDING AT u

MOULDING AT v

MOULDING AT w

MOULDING AT x

MOULDING AT y

MOULDING AT z

o

p   q

r   s

3'8"

6'11"

1'11"

CIRCULAR

SQUARE

x

y

z

E IRON PULPIT
AVILA CATHEDRAL

21'6"

D WINDOW from FACADE
UNIVERSITY: ALCALA de HENARES

A. The Escorial, near Madrid (1559–84): south front. See p. 851

B. El Pilar Cathedral, Saragossa (1677–1766). See p. 855

wrought-iron screens, called 'rejas', of churches (p. 860B, C) and grilles of palace windows (pp. 843B, 860D) are among the most beautiful productions of Spanish craftsmanship, and everywhere show the influence of architectural forms, such as those in Seville Cathedral. The iron pulpit in Avila Cathedral in the Plateresque style (p. 860E), dating from 1525, of which the upper portion is wood plated with iron and gilded, is an instance of the importance attained by the metal-workers' craft, which also produced the elaborate armour of the period. Sculpture (pp. 850B, 859A) varied much in quality, and was sometimes coarse in execution, but the work of Berruguete, the Spanish Donatello, is refined, though it often fails to become an integral part of the building. The love for superficial ornament endures almost throughout the Renaissance period, and makes itself manifest in the various expressions of the Baroque which are found in the country, particularly in that known as the 'Churrigueresque', after the family of that name, who largely practised it (pp. 850B, 857A, 858A, B). Stained glass, at first influenced by Flemish work, was often heavy in colour, but the tile-work of southern Spain has the charm of its Moorish origin. Spanish churches are veritable museums for treasures of art, which have not, as often in other countries, been removed to public museums. Reliquaries, monstrances, bishops' crooks, candelabra, altar busts, and book-covers provided an opportunity for the workers in metal to exercise that meticulous treatment which even extended to architectural design so much as to have suggested the transference of the appellation of Plateresque from the ornament to the architecture.

REFERENCE BOOKS

BEVAN, B. *History of Spanish Architecture.* London, 1938.

BRIGGS, M. S. *Baroque Architecture.* London, 1913.

BYNE, A., and STAPLEY, M. *Provincial Houses in Spain.* New York, 1925.

CALZADA, A. *Historia de la arquitectura española.* Barcelona, 1933.

CHAMOSO LAMAS, M. *La arquitectura barroca en Galicia.* Madrid, 1955.

GALLEGO Y BURIN, A. *El barroco granadino.* Madrid, 1956.

HARVEY, J. *The Cathedrals of Spain.* London, 1957.

JUNGHÄNDEL, M., und GURLITT, C. *Die Baukunst Spaniens.* 2 vols. Dresden, 1889–93.

KUBLER, G. *Arquitectura española 1600–1800.* (Ars Hispaniae, XIV). Madrid, 1957.

—., and SORIA, M. *Art and Architecture in Spain and Portugal.* Pelican History of Art, 1959.

MAYER, A. L. *Architektur und Kunstgewerbe in Alt-Spanien.* Munich, 1920.

PRENTICE, A. N. *Renaissance Architecture and Ornament in Spain.* 1893.

SCHUBERT, O. *Geschichte der Barock in Spanien.* 1908.

SITWELL, S. *Spanish Baroque Art.* London, 1931.

UHDE, C. *Baudenkmaeler in Spanien und Portugal.* Berlin, 1889–92.

VILLA-AMIL, G. P. de. *España artistica y monumental.* 3 vols. Paris, 1842–50.

VILLIERS-STUART, C. M. *Spanish Gardens.* 1929.

WARING, J. B., and MACQUOID, T. R. *Examples of Architectural Art in Italy and Spain.* 1850.

WYATT, SIR M. DIGBY. *An Architect's Note-book in Spain.* 1872.

England in the Renaissance period

XXV. ENGLISH RENAISSANCE

(sixteenth–nineteenth century)

INFLUENCES

GEOGRAPHICAL. The island influence still continued, as in previous periods (p. 379), to produce those pronounced modifications which stamp all English architecture with an essentially national character. There is therefore no need for further reference to geographical influences, except insofar as their operation was affected, altered or arrested, by other considerations, such as the varying relations of England with Continental powers. Moreover, owing to the distance from Italy, the birth-place of Renaissance, England was the last country to fall under the influence of the new movement, which naturally reached this island by way of France and the Netherlands. The friendly relations which, at different times, marked our intercourse with these countries may be seen faithfully reflected in English architecture. The great wars, however, at the end of the eighteenth and beginning of the nineteenth century closed Continental travel to Englishmen, though contacts were at once renewed after 1815. Internal communications began to improve in Britain about the mid-eighteenth century, the first important step as regards good road-making having been taken by General George Wade in Scotland from 1726; the really important developments were due to Thomas Telford and James Loudon Macadam in the first quarter of the nineteenth century. Bridge-building necessarily improved at the same time. The peak period of canal and navigable inland waterway construction was between 1760 and 1800, and the extensive system created greatly facilitated the transport of heavy goods, including building materials, with the result that the surviving local character in minor architecture tended to disappear.

GEOLOGICAL. This influence has been considered in the Mediaeval period (p. 380), and, as one of the natural influences, it is continuous, and still gives a special character to the architecture of various districts; though other elements have modified its operation. Timber, for instance, gradually fell into disuse for building purposes, partly because of the growing scarcity of the material as forests were cleared for the needs of the rising population, or because of the risk of fire in crowded towns, but particularly because stone, and in due course, brick, provided more stable, permanent and weather-proof structures. Timber-frames, exposed externally, were still normal throughout Elizabethan times, and under various forms of external sheathing, such as plaster or tile-hanging, persisted in the smaller buildings of the countryside even until the opening of the nineteenth century in regions where building-stone was not readily available. In the latter regions, as in East Anglia, buildings of note not infrequently were being built in brickwork as early as c. 1500. Stone, however, was the natural successor to timber, and in favoured areas became usual in the seventeenth century. Inigo Jones first made use of Portland stone in his London buildings. Sir Christopher Wren also adopted it for his many churches and secular buildings, and it has been largely used up to the present day. Bath stone of the soft oolitic formation, which crosses England diagonally from Somerset to Lincoln, gives a charming character to the manor and other houses of these districts, just as the Yorkshire gritstone, which did not lend itself to carving, caused the adoption there of a plain and unornamented style. The geological map (p. 379) gives a rough indication of the building materials available in the different districts. By the eighteenth century, brick was becoming almost universal for domestic architecture and the less important classes of building. Bricks, thinner than today, were at first bonded irregularly in a loose form of 'English bond', but after mid-seventeenth century 'Flemish bond' became usual. Terra-cotta, introduced in the Tudor period, was not much used even for architectural details until Victorian times (p. 983). Roofing-tiles accompanied the use of bricks in the eastern and southern parts of the country, while stone slates or flags replaced thatch in the upland midland, western and northern regions. The employment of thin slates extended greatly after mid-eighteenth century, their distribution made practicable by the improvement of inland waterways and roads and the construction of canals. A consequence of the exploitation of mineral resources as the Industrial Revolution gathered force was the appearance of cast iron as a structural material, well before 1800.

CLIMATIC. The influence of climate was operative in the Renaissance as in former periods (p. 380). When the new style was introduced from Italy, the dull English climate caused it to be adapted to our northern use. In order to admit abundant light, large windows still continued, especially in the early period, in striking contrast to those of Italy. A growing desire for comfort, coinciding also with the more general use of coal as fuel in the reign of Charles I, brought about the introduction of a fireplace in each room; while chimneys continued, as in the Tudor period, to be prominent symmetrical features of the external design, instead of being disguised as in Italy.

RELIGIOUS. Early in the sixteenth century religious controversy was astir in the land, and the Reformation in religion coincided in England with the commencement of Renaissance in architecture. Abuses had crept into the Church, and the popes had failed to deal with them. The constant irritation which had existed between kings of England and popes of Rome had already been accentuated in England by the attitude taken up by Henry VIII, and the relation of the English Church to the Crown was finally settled by the Act of Supremacy (1559) in the reign of Elizabeth. When the monasteries, large and small, had been suppressed (1536–40), much of their property was distributed among the courtiers of Henry VIII. Monasteries either fell into ruin or, in a way characteristically English, emerged as national cathedrals; while others again were cleared away for the erection of country houses, or were even incorporated in the mansions of the new nobility. During this period men's minds were turned rather to Church reform than to church building. Moreover, the great church-building era of the Middle Ages had left an ample supply of churches, and not until the latter part of the seventeenth century was there a renewal of church building. In London especially, the Great Fire gave Sir Christopher Wren an opportunity of exercising his genius in the new style which, from an ecclesiastical point of view, was specially suitable for the preaching which formed so important a part in the Protestant service.

SOCIAL. At the time when the Renaissance came to England, not only had new social conditions been created, but national life was rich in every variety of social, artistic, and literary movement. The Renaissance, with its recognition of the inherent human right to the enjoyment of life, appealed strongly to a community which had thrown off ecclesiastical domination and was rapidly developing a free national and domestic life along secular lines. The Wars of the Roses (1454–85) had already decimated the old nobility, but expanding commerce was constantly supplying a new class of wealthy merchants and traders to take the place of the former feudal lords. The new men who, as we have seen, had acquired land—often from monastic establishments—now required houses suitable to their wealth and to the standing in the country which their enterprise and success in trade had conferred upon them. These then were the men who were ready to adopt the new style which, in its grandness of scale, exactly suited their ideas. Of this period it may also be said that 'knowledge spread from more to more'; for Caxton, with his printing press at Westminster (1477), had brought the hoarded knowledge of the privileged few within the reach of common humanity. The printed and picture book also served to make artists and craftsmen familiar with the plans and details of Classic buildings. An Englishman, John Shute, published the *First and Chief Groundes of Architecture* in 1563, this owing much to the writings of the Italian, Serlio; while the great work of Vitruvius, the ancient Roman architect, was also translated and circulated.

Foreign artists, imbued with Renaissance ideas, had already flocked to the court of Henry VIII, and to these were added, in the reign of Elizabeth, Flemish and German craftsmen, who settled principally in the eastern counties, and there influenced the style of the new mansions. Finally, the Massacre of S. Bartholomew's Day (1572) drove to England many skilled Huguenot craftsmen who contributed to the efficient execution of the new style in their new home. The changed social conditions, together with practical considerations resulting from new methods of warfare and the increasing use of gunpowder, had rendered the fortification of dwelling-houses useless. Thus the ancient castle had given way to the Tudor manor house, which in its turn was developed into the stately mansion of the Elizabethan and Jacobean periods. We have already seen the result of the suppression of the monasteries in the foundation of national cathedrals and in the erection of country houses; and yet another phase of national and local life, affected by the dissolution of monastic establishments, is seen in the growth of educational and philanthropic endowments. Both Henry VIII and Edward VI had devoted part of the monastic treasuries to the foundations of colleges and grammar schools, and thus some of the monastic funds continued in use for one of their original purposes, but no longer under the special control of the Church. The progressive development in domestic comfort and the increase in hospitality during the reign of Elizabeth (1558–1603) were responsible for an era remarkable for the erection of those great and commodious mansions which are still the special pride of England, and many important building schemes, as those of the ambitious Protector Somerset, cut short by his execution in 1552, had been initiated. It was also fashionable for young men to visit Italy, and thus Renaissance ideas were brought to England.

During the spacious days of Queen Elizabeth, literature bore no small part in influencing national architecture; for the writings of such literary giants as Spenser, Shakespeare, Bacon, and Sir Philip Sidney, with their constant reference to the themes and traditions of ancient Rome, could not fail to give a Classic tone to the buildings erected by men who were artists in stone as the others were artists in words. In all these combined and simultaneous activities we see a new national art in the making, under the influence of Italian and French Renaissance. During the reigns of James I and his son, English colonizing enterprise, which then surpassed that of any other country, led to the expansion of English trade, with a consequent further accession of numbers to the wealthy classes who, following the King's example, lived much in the country and there erected many stately houses. Though Charles I was a patron of art, the disturbed condition of the country during his ill-starred reign, culminating in the Civil War, arrested the progress of architecture, as exemplified in the abandonment of the great scheme for the projected Palace of Whitehall (p. 898). During the Stuart period the English colonies of North America and the West Indies exceeded all others in importance, and together with Indian and African trade established English overseas prestige. This growing trade also gave increased consideration to all questions of home commerce and a consequent greater importance to the trading classes.

In Charles II's reign the feudal system of knight-service was abolished. The revocation of the Edict of Nantes (1685) caused another influx of Huguenot craftsmen with their skill and trade secrets.

The Bank of England was established in 1694; the economic situation underwent a marked change, and the 'mercantile system' was concerned in securing a surplus of exports over imports, which naturally resulted in an increase of home manufactures. These conditions also created a further demand for houses for wool staplers and weavers, who challenged the supremacy of those in France and Holland. Agricultural industry was in a more thriving condition, and pauperism consequently decreased; while the settlement laws of the period helped to equalize the poor relief of different districts and to arrest vagrancy. There was a greater sense of security of living, which created better conditions for general architectural enterprise. It is difficult to realize that as late as the end of the eighteenth century there were still only some eight million inhabitants in England and Wales; while London, with almost a million, far exceeded any other town in size, and correspondingly influenced public opinion and national policy. Norwich, with its weaving and banking community, and Bristol, with its West India trade and sugar refining, were next in importance to the capital. The increase of population in London did not, however, induce the City to extend its boundaries, and thus a new town grew up to the westward, which gave a further opportunity to Renaissance architects, in addition to that which had been afforded by the Great Fire in the City in 1666. The general increase in wealth and the rise in the standard of comfort are seen in the number of plain comfortable Georgian houses of our country towns.

In the nineteenth century further changes in social conditions are reflected in a breaking away from tradition in architecture, and many minds turned restlessly for inspiration to past styles, which they applied to the new buildings required for the various needs of an increasing population. Nineteenth-century developments after 1830 are referred to later (Ch. XXVI, p. 982).

HISTORICAL. Henry VIII had been firmly established on the English throne, and the security of his position at home enabled him to interest himself in affairs on the Continent, and his famous meeting with Francis I on the Field of the Cloth of Gold in 1520, with all its resplendent accessories, resulted in attracting foreign artists to his court, and they largely determined the manner of the adoption of the Renaissance style in England, alike in architecture, sculpture, and painting. Henry VIII usually was on friendly terms with his brother monarchs, but would brook no interference from Rome with his royal prerogative. He handed on this legacy of political and religious freedom to his son, Edward VI; but the position was temporarily changed during the reign of Mary who, through her marriage with Philip II, was under Spanish influence, though it did not extend much beyond her own immediate surroundings. A similar foreign influence had been at work in Scotland, and there French architectural features were popularized, as at George Heriot's Hospital, Edinburgh (p. 525), owing to the alliance of France and Scotland under James IV (1488–1513).

The accession of Elizabeth brought in widely different elements, and the defeat of the Spanish Armada (1588) not only heralded the decline of Spanish power in Europe, but also further established the independent position of England, and gave an extended scope to her national genius, both in politics and art. This was the period of Hawkins, Drake, Frobisher, and Raleigh, when great discoveries were made in the New World. The sense of security and the prosperity which followed the defeat of Spain found material expression in the splendid mansion-building of the period.

The Stuarts brought England into closer touch with the Continent, more especially with France and Italy. James I was not only a disciple of the new learning, but was also a patron of Inigo Jones, the great English architect who studied in Italy and introduced the Palladian Renaissance into England, notably in his design for the Banqueting House, Whitehall (p. 898). Charles I inaugurated a period marked by an amazing intermingling of intrigue, politics, and war, when the King found himself embroiled both with France and Spain. These conditions were depicted in architecture, painting, and the minor crafts, which were fostered by the fine artistic sense of the King; but the Civil War arrested progress in architecture. The Commonwealth, with the social upheaval consequent upon a new form of government, together with the reaction represented by Puritanism, overshadowed general historic influences. It was essentially a period when the connection between England and the Continent was marked rather by the power of Cromwell in asserting the position of England than by the operation of foreign influences upon English art. Charles II had lived at the court of Louis XIV, and there imbibed French ideas in art, which were introduced into England at the Restoration and continued in force till the Great Rebellion and the flight of James II (1688). William of Orange brought over those Dutch influences which were so long predominant in English domestic architecture. He introduced into his new kingdom those substantial red brick houses, with the formal gardens and water-ways which make up the landscape of Holland, and which form such conspicuous features at his Hampton Court Palace. The later Stuart period had seen the carrying trade of the world transferred from Holland to England, while English victories over the French, followed by the Peace of Utrecht (1713), secured to England the chief trade of Europe and made her rich enough to build up a navy which gave her supremacy at sea, both over France and Holland. England still depended largely on the manufactured products of those countries, but Huguenot weavers from France helped our workmen in the towns to develop their industries, and engineers from Holland taught our agriculturists to convert swampy fenlands into corn-growing country. Thus there was an increase in general prosperity which naturally produced a still further demand for more and better dwelling-houses.

The reigns of Queen Anne and the four Georges saw Dutch influence on architecture gradually anglicized, and the houses that were now built were of that convenient and comfortable type known as Queen Anne and Georgian, well suited to the needs of the increasing middle classes, both in town and country.

The French Revolution (1789) was the outcome in one country of a spirit of revolt general in all countries, which in England led to the breaking up alike of stereotyped social conventions and of continuous tradition in architecture, and this has resulted in that revival of past styles which is the special characteristic of nineteenth-century architecture (Ch. XXVI, p. 982).

ARCHITECTURAL CHARACTER

We have already studied the general architectural character of the Renaissance in Europe (p. 656), and traced its gradual adoption in different countries to suit different nationalities. From Italy, where it had its origin about 1400, the Renaissance movement travelled to the sister Latin country of France; to Germany, which, through the universities, welcomed the new movement; to the Netherlands, and to Spain. Not until a century after its birth in Florence did it make its first appearance in England in the famous Tomb of Henry VII (1509) (p. 879A), which was a tentative display of a style which afterwards secured a firm footing, as suitable for the magnificent country mansions and stately town houses of the substantial professional and trading families which were rapidly forming England's new nobility.

English Renaissance architecture may be divided as follows:

Early Renaissance $\begin{cases} \text{Elizabethan} & (1558–1603) \text{ (pp. 868, 878)} \\ \text{Jacobean} & (1603–25) \quad \text{ (pp. 869, 885)} \end{cases}$

Late Renaissance $\begin{cases} \text{Stuart} & (1625–1702) \text{ (pp. 870, 897)} \\ \text{Georgian} & (1702–1830) \text{ (pp. 872, 928)} \end{cases}$

The architectural character of Early and Late Renaissance will now be traced through successive periods, displaying a more or less persistent continuity of style with variety in detail, and the reader is referred to the Comparative Analysis (p. 964) for the characteristic features in each period.

EARLY RENAISSANCE

Elizabethan Architecture. The reign of Elizabeth (1558–1603) witnessed the establishment of the Renaissance style in England. Elizabethan architecture, which followed the Tudor, was a transition style with Gothic features and Renaissance detail, and in this respect it bears the same relation to fully developed English Renaissance as the style of Francis I does to fully developed French Renaissance.

But in character it was quite individual, fundamentally still Mediaeval yet affected superficially by influences which had been transmuted in the course of their passage from the source in Italy. Italian or French books on architecture, notably the writings of the Italian, Sebastiano Serlio (1475–1552), in various editions, had some importance, but particularly, the Renaissance influences reached England from Flanders, which at the time was practising a decoratively-exaggerated style of 'strapwork' and grotesques mainly based on the work of the Italian stuccoists, such as Il Rosso and Primaticcio at Fontainebleau (p. 774). As we have seen, Antwerp was a highly important commercial and artistic centre at this period, and from that locality and neighbouring Germany came not only architectural pattern books of various kinds but also craftsmen and artisans displaced by political disturbances or religious persecution. The zeal for church building in the Middle Ages in England had provided churches which remained sufficient for popular needs, and thus Elizabethan architecture was secular rather than ecclesiastical in its nature, and was the outcome of the needs of a time when powerful statesmen, successful merchants, and the enriched gentry required mansions suitable to their new position, and these were built in England, as in France, mainly in the country, in contrast to the churches and palaces of the cities in Italy. These great houses were not designed comprehensively by a single person but were rather the conceptions jointly of the owner and his chosen master-craftsmen (for large buildings, the chief was usually a mason), and subordinate specialist craftsmen might be employed to execute decorative features like entrance-doorways, porticoes, fireplaces, staircases and panelling, to their own designs. The mansions displayed many new combinations of features. Externally, towers, gables, parapets, balustrades, and chimney-stacks produced an effective skyline, and walls were enlivened by oriel and bay-windows with mullions and transoms (p. 880), while internally the same style applied to fittings, furniture, and decoration, made for repose, dignity, and uniformity (p. 977). Elizabethan mansions looked outwards rather than inwards towards courtyards as in the Mediaeval period, so that there now could be formal settings related to each front, a forecourt, perhaps with decorative gateway and angle pavilions, on the entrance side, and on the others, formal gardens with beds of plants arranged in intricate geometrical knots and a central fountain marking converging paths, or balustraded terraces, topiary gardens and walks, or terraces and orchards.

Jacobean Architecture. The architecture of the reign of James I (1603–25) inherited Elizabethan traditions; but as Roman literature and models became better known, a subtle change crept in, and the sober regularity of Classic columns and entablatures gradually supplanted the quaint irregularity of Elizabethan architecture, although the main lines of the design were much the same in both periods (p. 892). There was a greater tendency, now, for new structures to be designed by a single hand. Buildings still continued to be for domestic rather than religious use, and thus the style developed along lines suited to popular needs, with considerable latitude in detail and ornament, not only for buildings, but also for fittings and furniture, which now became more abundant in quantity and more decorative in quality, and were supplied both for mansions and churches (p. 977). As in the Elizabethan period, it was in the screens, pulpits, and monuments, which were freely added to Mediaeval churches, that Jacobean art found its outlet in ecclesiastical architecture, and much of the human interest of English Gothic churches is due to the historical continuity supplied by these Jacobean monuments (p. 976).

The drawings collected by John Thorpe (1563–1654) and Huntingdon Smithson (died 1648), the former collection now being preserved in Sir John Soane's Museum and the latter at the R.I.B.A., London, are very informative about the houses of the period *c.* 1570–1633. The buildings represented are not by any means all their own personal designs, but in many cases represent the work of others. There were two notable generations of Thorpes and three of Smithsons. Thomas Thorpe (died 1596) probably was the principal mason and virtual designer of Kirby Hall, Northants (p. 881), while his son John, a land surveyor and officer of the King's works, made drawings of notable contemporary structures without himself contributing any buildings of special merit. Robert Smithson (c. 1536–1614) was an outstanding figure. Probably the chief mason-designer of Longleat House, Wilts (p. 881), he was certainly the architect of Wollaton Hall, Notts (p. 881), his chief work, and importantly concerned with Hardwick Hall, Derbyshire (p. 882) and other great houses in the Midlands, besides originating plans for smaller houses which became established types. His son John (d. 1634) designed Bolsover Castle, Derbyshire (p. 886), and he with his son, Huntingdon Smithson, made important additions to the same building later on.

LATE RENAISSANCE

Stuart Architecture. The term 'Stuart' is used for the architecture of Charles I (1625–49), the Commonwealth (1649–60), Charles II (1660–85), James II (1685–8), and William and Mary (1689–1702).

The period readily falls into two phases, dominated respectively by two great personalities, Inigo Jones and Sir Christopher Wren: but in the first, lasting to about 1660, the majority of buildings showed little response to the striking innovations of Inigo Jones in his courtly circles, and maintained a consistent trend on the basis of the Jacobean. The designers mostly were working masters of the respective crafts, rising from the ranks of the masons, carpenters or bricklayers. The latter term may today suggest a more lowly social status than was sometimes attained by the more gifted of such master-craftsmen. Influences still came mainly via the Netherlands, but also from France; the former were evidenced at this time by the so-called 'Dutch gables', shaped with ogee parapets crowned with semicircular or triangular pediments (p. 907C). Brickwork, very often with stone dressings, became increasingly popular as the century advanced, and stone and brick mullions progressively gave place to wooden windows. Notable master-masons were Nicholas Stone (1586–1647), who received part of his training in Amsterdam; the younger Smithsons, still working in this phase; and, among master-bricklayers, Peter Mills (1600–70). In the second or 'Wren' phase of the period, from c. 1660 onwards, the national character of English architecture was becoming more firmly established, in commonplace buildings as well as in those of prime importance. Dutch influences, now much more authentically Classical, were reinforced towards the end of the century, while increased travel brought a surer knowledge of French practices and genuine Italian precedents. By this time Italy had nearly passed the peak of the Baroque. Thus it will be seen that in the Stuart period the influences upon English architecture became increasingly complex, and they remained so in the next, the Georgian period. Development throughout the Late Renaissance was importantly determined by the fortunes, training and preferences of distinguished individuals referred to in the short notices which follow.

Inigo Jones (1573–1652) was a man of dominating personality and brilliance who produced an architecture which was far in advance of that of his contemporaries, so much so that its revolutionary nature was not at once fully recognized, and it was only after his death that its importance began fully to be appreciated. His prolonged studies in Italy, more especially of the works of Palladio but also of contemporary Italian architecture as well as the antique, caused him to become an ardent disciple of the Italian Renaissance style. Born of an undistinguished London family, he apparently had first visited Italy about 1601, and emerges in 1605 as the designer of costumes and scenery for court masques, an activity which he continued until the outbreak of the Civil War. It is known that he visited Paris in 1609, and had an important nineteen-months further tour in Italy in 1613–14 in the retinue of the Earl of Arundel. His attractive personality, together with his skill and ingenuity in stage-craft, seem to have brought him favour, for in 1611 he was appointed Surveyor to Prince Henry, and in 1613, Surveyor of the King's Works. Yet it was only in the latter year that his notable work in architecture began. His principal buildings are mentioned on pp. 898–905. A pupil and assistant of Inigo Jones from 1628 to 1652 was John Webb (1611–72), who naturally absorbed his master's ideas; Webb's own personality emerges in a small number of houses which he erected on his own account after c. 1648. His greatest work and only public building was the King Charles block at Greenwich (p. 898). Sir Roger Pratt (1620–85) spent six years studying on the Continent (1643–9) and brought back ideas directly from Italy. He knew Jones, who served as adviser for the first of the five considerable houses which represented Pratt's total architectural output, all completed before 1672, and shared Jones's taste for architecture as interpreted by the Italian writers, Palladio, Serlio and Scamozzi; thus being similarly in advance of the general run of practice of the day. Pratt secured his knighthood for his services as one of the three Royal Commissioners appointed for the control of the city after the Great Fire of London of 1666, the other two being Hugh May and Sir Christopher Wren. Hugh May (1622–84) is less readily classed with the Inigo Jones group, as his architecture had a Dutch inclination, due to his strong contacts with Holland, which at this time was practising its own brick-and-stone interpretation of Palladianism.

Sir Christopher Wren (1632–1723) was the supreme figure of the second phase of the Stuart period. Scholar, mathematician, astronomer, his scientific training at Oxford developed his constructive power, and largely counterbalanced his lack of early architectural training; for he did not start the study and practice of architecture until somewhat late in life, when in 1663 he was made a member of the Commission for the repair of S. Paul's Cathedral. In the same year he was asked to prepare a design for Pembroke College Chapel, Cambridge (p. 906). As Inigo Jones had come under Italian, so Sir Christopher Wren came under French influence. He was in Paris in 1665, when the Palais du Louvre was in course of extension, and he then became associated with the group of architects and artists, such as Bernini (the great Italian master of the Baroque, invited to Paris by Louis XIV to prepare a design for the Louvre), Mansart, Louis le Vau and others, and he not only studied Renaissance buildings in Paris but also saw the royal and other chateaux in the surrounding country: he may have visited the Netherlands. As he never went to Italy, the force of this French influence was further accentuated, and, moreover, his royal patron, Charles II, had been an exile at the French court, and had there imbibed similar ideas. The destructive ravages of the Great Fire of London (1666) offered Wren an immediate opportunity for practising his art on a grand scale in the rebuilding of S. Paul's and the city churches, although it was found not possible to put into execution his plan for the rebuilding of the City of London. As mentioned earlier, Wren was one of three Royal Commissioners charged to consider the problems of rebuilding the city after the Fire, and one outcome of their recommendations was an Act (1667) which laid down standards for the new houses, which were to be in brick and follow one or other of three types, each with specified wall-thicknesses and floor-heights. These prescriptions had ramifications in other cities and towns. In 1669, Wren was appointed Surveyor-General of the King's Works. Apart from his activities at the palaces at Hampton Court (p. 914) and Greenwich (p. 928), Wren does not appear to have been responsible for much domestic building, and such as survive of his lesser houses show some influence of the mature Dutch style, like domestic architecture in general in the country. Wren had, in an unusual degree, the power of adapting his designs so as to secure the best results from the financial means at his disposal, and as has been said, his 'designs are mixed with brains'; for he produced his effects, not by expensive elaboration, but by careful proportion of the various parts, by concentration of ornament in the most telling position, or by one outstanding feature in the design. His buildings, too, owe much of their character to the use of Portland stone, which proved to have such good weathering properties; while in his domestic buildings, and some of his city churches, he made an effective use of brick with stone dressings, as at Hampton Court and S. Benet, Paul's Wharf, London. Whether in the graded greys of quarried stone or in the warm reds of hand-made bricks, Wren's buildings seem native to the site for which they were designed, and his influence was of the greatest importance to subsequent developments. His principal buildings are referred to and are illustrated later (pp. 906, 908–28). Wren's work is individual, but its character in the later stages gave rise to a brief phase of English Baroque, this spanning the thirty or so years concluding about 1725. As the main buildings of this nature were in course of erection in the early eighteenth century, the phase may be regarded as introductory to Georgian architecture.

Georgian Architecture. Under this title is classed the architecture of the reigns of Anne (1702–14), George I (1714–27), George II (1727–60), George III (1760–1820), George IV (1820–30).

Reference has been made to the English Baroque, the rare examples of which fall mainly between 1695–1725; Georgian architecture in general otherwise may be divided into two phases, the Anglo-Palladian and the Antiquarian, the latter commencing about 1750 and comprehending almost completely the so-called 'Greek Revival' and the formative stages of the 'Gothic Revival'—which only matured in Victorian times—as well as a variety of other manifestations of a developing retrospective outlook.

As to the English Baroque; we have seen that the arrival of the Renaissance in England was much belated and its nature transformed by practice in the countries through which it had passed from the fountain-head in Italy, as well as by circumstances in England itself. Yet as there was always some direct intercourse between England and Italy, increasing as time passed, and published works which gave fairly recent accounts of what was transpiring at the source, the influences on England were bound to be somewhat confused, the more recent being superficially imposed upon those of longer standing, already partly or wholly assimilated. In Italy, the 'High' Baroque of *c.* 1625–75 had been passed, and though in the main it was little to the English taste it would have been remarkable if it had not been reflected in some degree. A comparatively early response is shown in the south porch of S. Mary the Virgin, Oxford (1637) (p. 396c), with its twisted columns and broken pediment. It is not known who designed it, but the mason was a John Jackson. Besides the echoes in the later works of Wren and in those of William Talman (1650–1719), who built Thoresby House, Notts (1671; destroyed by fire, 1745), of remarkably advanced character, and the south and east fronts of Chatsworth House, Derbyshire (1687–96), famous for its art treasures and grounds laid out by Paxton, the English Baroque appears outstandingly in the architecture of three great personalities, and, to a diminished extent, in some few buildings designed by admiring followers. The three were Vanbrugh, Hawksmoor and Archer.

Sir John Vanbrugh (1664–1726) was a writer of dramas as well as a designer of palaces, besides being a military officer, a wit and a courtier, who became Controller of the Royal Works (1702). Monumentality is the keynote of his architecture.

His was a personal, not recognizably Italian, interpretation of the Baroque, depending on plasticity of mass; that is, a bold advance or recession of parts, or 'movement' as it was called. At least as regards the detail a good deal of the eventual character of his buildings must have been due to Nicholas Hawksmoor (1661–1736), for Vanbrugh turned abruptly to architecture, and Hawksmoor was his distinguished assistant from the outset, already possessing highly-developed practical abilities, for previously he had been a right-hand man to Sir Christopher Wren from the age of about eighteen. Hawksmoor assisted Wren with the city churches, and again at Greenwich Hospital, where he was Clerk of Works or Assistant Surveyor for his whole life after 1698. He also did important work on his own account, including six London churches, some buildings at Oxford and Cambridge, and designs for the western towers of Westminster Abbey (1734) (pp. 424, 663A), completed after his death. Hawksmoor's varied interpretations of the Baroque seem to have been based partly on Wren and partly on books; he was much interested in antiquity. Thomas Archer (c. 1668–1743), designer of a small number of churches and houses, studied for four years on the Continent. His buildings are the closest approximation to the Italian Baroque ever achieved in England, showing a leaning in taste towards Borromini (p. 726). Archer influenced provincial vernacular building, particularly in Somerset, Dorset and Devon, as in the work of the Bastard brothers (John, 1688–1770; William, c. 1689–1766) at Blandford, Dorset, in the rebuilding of the town after a disastrous fire in 1731. Outside the London region there was little new church building, and thus so much the less room for the Baroque to take hold: we have seen that, in Italy, churches were the chief vehicle for the more florid expressions of the style. In the eighteenth century, domestic architecture continued to be the chief type of building, though there was an expansion in public building too. The spread of wealth brought fewer opulent great houses but many more of comparatively modest dimensions, sited in the attractive parts of the countryside or at the fringes of towns, while the smaller houses reached new standards of comfort and convenience, and even cottages passed into permanent, solidly-built form.

The English phase of the Baroque, acclimatized and restrained though it was, was short-lived and already being supplanted by a 'Palladian' phase before it had run its course. The change is illustrated by the professional career of James Gibbs (1683–1774), born near Aberdeen, who, having travelled extensively on the Continent and studied under Carlo Fontana (p. 726) in Rome, returned to England in 1709, imbued with the Baroque. In this vein he built S. Mary-le-Strand, London (1714–17) (p. 949), but thereafter his very great output of building was accommodated to the prevailing Palladian mode, which from about 1710 to 1750 came to affect building comprehensively in the country down to the most modest dwelling. Gibbs himself contributed to the diffusion of Palladian principles in his many writings, of which the principal was *Rules for Drawing the Several Parts of Architecture* (1732), used as a copy-book by builders not only in England but also in America. Foundational in the Palladian movement was a growing recognition of the virtues of the buildings of Inigo Jones, together with the influence of books such as the *Vitruvius Britannicus* (1717 and 1725) of the Scot, Colin Campbell (d. 1729), architect of a score of houses between 1712–27, and a new edition (1715–16) of Palladio's *I quattro libri dell' Architettura*, by Giacomo Leoni (1686–1746)—a Venetian working in England—under the title of *The Architecture of A. Palladio*.

Palladio's restrained Classicism was readily adaptable to the English taste. Its most influential advocate was the Earl of Burlington (1694–1753), who in the part he played typifies the interest now displayed in architecture by the social *élite*. Attracted by Colin Campbell's *Vitruvius Britannicus*, Burlington visited Italy a second time in 1719 expressly for the study of Palladio's architecture, particularly that at Vicenza (p. 738). He was accompanied on his return by William Kent (*c.* 1685–1748), who long had been studying in Italy as a painter-stuccoist and who turned architect under Burlington's patronage from about 1732. Lord Burlington at first employed Campbell's services for the buildings he undertook, but after about 1721 began himself to assume the position of designer, with or without the help of Campbell, Kent and others, but with Henry Flitcroft (1697–1769) as his personal assistant. After *c.* 1729, Flitcroft designed a number of houses and one or two churches in his own right, including S. Giles-in-the-Fields, London. Kent is worthy of his fame as a decorator, and as a prolific architect is celebrated especially for his Horse Guards building, Whitehall (p. 956). He is almost more famous as a landscape architect, for he headed a revolt against the formal garden, which had been customary through the seventeenth century, in favour of informal, 'natural' landscape settings calculated to lend pungent contrast to the strict lines of Palladian-type dwellings. Another protégé of Burlington was Isaac Ware (d. 1766), whose fame rests mainly on his writings; he made his own translation of Palladio, published a collection of *Designs of Inigo Jones and Others* and, much more important, *The Complete Body of Architecture*. The two latter went through several editions, and became much-used copy-books. Important, too, as a writer, was John Vardy (d. 1765). There was a veritable flood of such books at this period, laying down the standard parts of the Orders, ostensibly according to the revered masters, Alberti, Palladio, Jones, etc., giving ranges of designs for doorways, windows, fireplaces and other features and reproducing buildings designed by famous contemporary personages; not, of course, excluding the works of the author himself, where forthcoming, for the books of the eighteenth century served as a chief means of advertisement. Books were directed now, not solely towards the informed patrician or connoisseur, but increasingly towards the master-builder, the working craftsman, artisan and even gardener, like those of 'William Halfpenny', an alias for Michael Hoare (d. 1755) and Batty Langley (1696–1751), both of whom were enormously prolific writers. Langley's *The Builder's Jewel, or the Youth's Instructor, and Workman's Remembrancer* (1746), and *New Principles of Gardening* (1728) are typical. He attracted much ridicule by attempting to standardize Gothic elements into Orders in his book *Gothic Architecture improved by Rules and Proportions* (1742), a topic significant of a coming change in the trend of architectural development. Of this same generation was Roger Morris (1695–1749), designer of the famous Palladian bridge at Wilton House, Wilts (1736) (p. 905).

Palladianism thus entered the bloodstream of the architecture of England, and also of Scotland, Ireland and even North America, at the lowest level variously producing charming, bizarre or crude effects. England was never so completely unanimous in the whole Renaissance. Formal Palladian principles were applied not alone to individual buildings but to the relationship of buildings one to another in schemes of civic design. The work of the Woods at their native town of Bath (John the elder, 1704–54; John the younger, 1728–81) serves as an illustration, and demonstrates the link between successive generations of designers practising Palladian principles. There, town houses were drawn together to afford collectively a 'palatial' effect. The Circus, Bath, begun 1754 by the elder Wood and completed by the younger, and the Royal Crescent (1767–75) by the latter, are famous instances (p. 946A). Notable London architects at this time were Sir Robert Taylor (1714–88), who began as a sculptor and studied in Rome, and James Paine (1716–89), each enjoying a very large practice. It was said that they 'divided the practice of the profession between them until Robert Adam entered the lists', though in fact, John Carr (1723–1807), a provincial architect, of York, only a few years younger, was equally if not more prolific of country houses. This sweeping extension of the employment of architects, who now began to engage pupils, indicates a consolidation of the profession as well as the revivification and enlargement of the gentry, due to the incipient industrialization of the country, while urban nucleation proceeded apace and brought demands for an increasing number of public buildings. The luxury of internal decoration in dwellings, often contrasted with grandly simple exteriors, bears witness to the influx of wealth from fresh sources. Landscape art reached its climax in the work of Lancelot Brown (1716–83), known as 'Capability' Brown from his habitual reference to the capabilities of the site and grounds of a mansion for the purposes of his art. He designed very many gardens and converted old formal gardens into the new style, besides in his later days adventuring in architectural design.

While Palladian architecture proceeded, a new trend became clearly apparent about mid-century: there had been signs long before of an Antiquarian movement, which was on the one hand romantic and trivial, and on the other archaeological. Indeed Palladianism itself was in some sense a reversion to practices of an earlier time, but now, designers began to turn to more distant architectural antecedents, to the Gothic and to ancient Rome and to Greece. The Roman grafted itself almost imperceptibly on to the Palladian—one important outcome was the 'Adam' manner —and to a less extent so did the Greek, though the latter and the Gothic emerged as plainly recognizable 'styles' after the end of the century. Each of the latter styles, as also some quaint interpretations of the Chinese and Indian, was superficial rather than fundamental, and building plans remained essentially Renaissance in character. Gothic architecture had never been wholly abandoned: Wren, Vanbrugh, Kent and others occasionally had produced their personal versions of it, usually, but not invariably, to match existing structures, while country builders in stone-producing districts like the Cotswolds might continue to preserve the old traditions uninterruptedly. The new tendency of mid-eighteenth century was a deliberate looking-back to bygone times. Whimsical, decorative 'Gothick' was popularized particularly by Horace Walpole (1717–97), 4th Earl of Orford, who from 1747 to 1776 progressively extended and decorated his house at Twickenham, which he named Strawberry Hill (p. 944A), in Gothic conceits. Sanderson Millar (1717–80) was another amateur with kindred tastes, who, however, was himself the actual designer of one or two buildings in the new Gothic mode.

Books, French, German and British, particularly those reporting archaeological investigations, were important in stimulating the various antiquarian movements; like Robert Wood's (1716–71) *Ruins of Palmyra*, published in 1753, and his *Ruins of Baalbec* (1757); or the series due to James Stuart (1713–88) and Nicholas Revett (1720–1804), beginning some years after their visit to Greece with *The Antiquities of Athens* in 1762. Both Stuart and Revett did a little designing in full-blooded Greek style, but their volumes, appearing intermittently over a long span of years, had much the greater influence.

The famous Robert Adam (1728–92) emulated Stuart and Revett. He left his native Scotland for Italy in 1754, studying in Paris on the way, and after a long period centred on Rome, where he met Piranesi, the accomplished draughtsman and etcher, whose imaginative restorations of Roman monuments are world-renowned. Adam went with a small party to Dalmatia in 1757, where he made the measurements which led to the publication of his *Ruins of the Palace of Diocletian at Spalatro* (now Split) in 1764. He returned to England in 1758 to found with his brother James an enormous practice, advertising it very soon with the first two volumes of his *Works in Architecture of Robert and James Adam* (1773, 1779). Adam's light and gracious style owed little to the Palace of Diocletian, and was due to his discreet selection among Roman precedents and the Italian Renaissance interpretations of them, particularly of methods of stucco ornamentation. He captured the Greek Hellenistic spirit in Roman work, and justly claimed to have introduced depth of 'movement' and a calculated variety of effect in his buildings, inside as well as out. Sir William Chambers (1723–96), on the other hand, abhorred his rival Adam's light style, and practised a robust and correct Classicism tinctured with the contemporary French; for he too, studied abroad for a considerable period. Not only did he visit the nearer European countries, including a five-years stay in Italy (1750–5), but in his earlier days had twice been to China. An outcome of the latter voyages was a book on *Design of Chinese Buildings, etc.* (1757). Of more far-reaching importance was his *Treatise on Civil Architecture* (1759), enlarged in subsequent editions. The range and quality of Chambers's architectural work vied with that of the Adams.

The 'Grand Tour' on the Continent became a regular procedure, followed by Robert Mylne (1734–1811), another Scottish architect, who also gained an extensive practice, and, a decade later (1762–8), by James Wyatt (1746–1813), a much more colourful personality. Wyatt's Classical style had a strong resemblance to that of Adam, of which the latter complained; like Adam and others of his predecessors and contemporaries, some of his country houses were Gothic, but whereas theirs were usually Classical conceptions tricked out with battlements, turrets and towers, Wyatt's were imaginative decorative creations in the succession of Walpole's Strawberry Hill. A growing respect at this time for the old Mediaeval buildings led to a general move for their repair, and Wyatt got into trouble with knowledgeab!e antiquarians for his too-drastic 'improvements' to several of the great cathedrals; Salisbury, Lichfield, Hereford and Durham. A lesser light practising a frail and decorative Gothic was the provincial architect, Francis Hiorne, of Warwick (1744–89) (p. 950). The better-known contemporaries of Wyatt include the younger George Dance (1741–1825), most of whose work, often highly original and sometimes showing a strong Greek note, has been destroyed or drastically remodelled; Thomas Cooley (1740–84) and James Gandon (1742–1823), the latter a pupil of Sir William Chambers, both famous for their Dublin buildings; Thomas Hardwick (1752–1829), another pupil and somewhat colourless follower of Sir William Chambers; and Henry Holland (1745–1806), son-in-law of 'Capability' Brown, whose style was the now-current 'Graeco-Roman'. Humphrey Repton (1752–1818), has more importance in the history of landscape art than in that of architecture, being a designer of 'Picturesque' gardens in which trees and other natural features were disciplined informally in a rolling sward; sometimes he himself designed the related mansions also, at others he deputed the latter function to his collaborator, John Nash, who struck a new note by introducing the informality of the Picturesque into the buildings too.

John Nash (1752–1835) is an outstanding figure. He acquired extensive commissions and the royal favour, and designed many mansions as well as civic schemes, and some churches and public buildings. In his day the English Renaissance movement came to a close, succumbing to the rising tide of stylistic revivalism, to which Nash himself contributed. A brilliant if superficial designer, with grand ideas, his urban style was mostly Neo-Classical, a compound of the notions of his contemporaries, cleverly organized on Picturesque lines. Hard plaster stucco was his favourite medium, in which at relatively low cost his external effects were secured. But he also worked in the Gothic, and some of his houses, villas and estate cottages were informal versions of this or were pretentiously based on English vernacular homesteads. He even essayed the 'Hindoo' at the Royal Pavilion, Brighton (p. 947D), with internal decorations veering to the Chinese. Much of an age with Nash was Sir John Soane (1753–1837), following the Neo-Classical expression with many personal idiosyncrasies. His interiors had fine and remarkable qualities, yet externally, his innovations were not invariably successful. The uncertainties of his style illustrate this period of change. He made the famous collection of models, casts, drawings and fragments of ancient architecture in his house in Lincoln's Inn Fields, which he left to the nation as a museum.

The work of the next generation of architects falls almost wholly in the early nineteenth century, and much of it after the Napoleonic wars; it tends more definitely to be revivalist, either Greek or Gothic, though some maintains the older cast. Despite a number of eighteenth-century precursors, both the Greek and the Gothic Revivals were only consolidated about 1805, and neither gained real force until after 1815. Meantime, books on Greek architectural precedents continued to appear, while antiquaries such as the draughtsmen John Carter (1748–1817) and A. C. Pugin (1762–1832) made faithful drawings of Mediaeval monuments which gave greater authority to the Gothic Revival. Thomas Rickman (1776–1841) was the author of a momentous book *An Attempt to Discriminate the Styles of English Architecture from the Conquest to the Reformation* (1817) which did much to turn the Gothic Revival from a wayward caprice into a definite and protracted movement. He himself built only three Classical churches, but some fifty-seven in the Gothic, all in the provinces, including four 'iron' churches at Liverpool, of which S. George's (1812–14) was said at the time to be 'nearly the first iron church erected in the kingdom; the framework of the windows, doors, pillars, groins, roofs, pulpit and ornamental enrichments are of cast iron'. Other early adherents to the Gothic Revival now were John Shaw (1776–1832), designer of S. Dunstan-in-the-West, Fleet Street, London (1831) (p. 954D), with a fine steeple; James Savage (1779–1852), author of S. Luke, Chelsea (1820) (p. 954C); Francis Goodwin (1784–1835), who built a number of churches in the provinces; and Francis Bedford (1784–1858), whose work, a few churches, is mostly in London. Each of these built in the Classical style too, still strongly favoured for public buildings; Goodwin's Old Manchester Town Hall (demolished 1912), in Greek Revival style, was especially fine.

The Greek Revival had passed its best by *c.* 1830, and by 1840 was definitely dead in England, though it lingered in Scotland until after mid-century. William Wilkins (1778–1839), designer of University College, London (1827–8) (p. 961B) and the National Gallery (1834–8) (p. 961A) was a notable figure, practising the style extensively from about 1806 onwards. He, and Sir Robert Smirke (1781–1867), a prolific though not particularly gifted architect, who used the Greek principally for public buildings such as the British Museum (1823–47) (p. 962D), had both undertaken Continental tours and studied architecture in Greece and South Italy, and thus their work has an archaeological correctness of detail. Wilkins was the author of *Antiquities of Magna Graecia* (1807) and several other writings on archaeological themes. Among the chief provincial architects adopting the Greek Revival importantly were David Hamilton (1768–1843) of Glasgow, John Foulston (1772–1842) of Plymouth, John Foster (1786–1846) of Liverpool, and Thomas Hamilton (1785–1858) and W. H. Playfair (1789–1857) of Edinburgh. In London, a slightly younger group included H. W. Inwood (1794–1843), who, with his father, William Inwood (*c.* 1771–1843), designed several churches of varying merit, including, however, S. Pancras Church, London (1819–22) (p. 954B), the finest ecclesiastical building of the whole Revival. He studied in Greece and published a book on the subject of the Erechtheion and other Greek remains (1827). In the Greek character were also certain of the earlier buildings of Decimus Burton (1800–81), whose triple archway at Hyde Park Corner, London, is famous (1825–46) (p. 962E), and of Sir Charles Barry (1795–1860), whose best design of the type was the Royal Manchester Institution building (1824–35) (p. 1022A), now the City Art Gallery.

By no means all architecture fell into the Greek or Gothic Revival categories. Sober Graeco-Roman continued to be a popular expression, the Georgian succession reached its final phase in the spare and refined delicacy of many a suburban or town house or terrace, while some buildings were so mixed in their characteristics as to defy classification. Architects might betray leanings in a particular direction, but changed freely from one expression to another as seemed to them best to meet the occasion. The scholarly and much-travelled Professor C. R. Cockerell (1788–1863), despite the extent of his archaeological knowledge, was no exception; he at times practised the Gothic, and in the Classical, had his own personal vein, favouring Graeco-Roman rather than Adam character while admitting some influence from contemporary French architecture. His buildings have quality of detail. Contemporary with him was John Dobson (1787–1867) of Newcastle-on-Tyne, who built up a considerable practice in north-east England, and designed the lay-out of the expanding city. While his public buildings were Classical, in his country mansions and churches he was among the first to introduce the Gothic into that region.

Churches in general were the more likely to be expressed in Gothic. Apart from a flurry of Classical works in the later seventeen-eighties and early nineties there had been comparatively little church building in the forty years before 1810; but by 1820 activity had become intense, partly as a result of the Church Building Act of 1818, which devoted a million pounds to contributions to the building of cheap churches and chapels to serve the fresh congregations of expanding towns. The aged John Nash and Sir John Soane, and the much younger Sir Robert Smirke, were advisers to the Commissioners discharging the Act, and each himself built one or two churches. By 1837 the 'Commissioner' churches totalled about 230, and the advance of the Gothic is indicated by the fact that scarcely a fifth of these were in the Classical styles. The Greek Revival was especially favoured in the London area at the outset, the provinces meanwhile having turned in force to the Gothic, but after 1827 the fashion passed and the very few churches afterwards built in the Greek style were almost all in the provinces. Classical churches of any sort became rare after 1827; but whatever the style externally, plans followed Classical lines. Being for congregational worship, they usually were simple rectangular boxes, lacking transepts or chancels, and had galleries inside. Nearly all had an axial 'western' tower, spire, cupola or bell-turret, unlike Victorian churches (Ch. XXVI), of which the towers normally were asymmetrically placed. For cheapness, they were mostly of brick with stone dressings. Churches built under private auspices ordinarily were much more costly and lavishly finished.

EXAMPLES

EARLY RENAISSANCE

(ELIZABETHAN ARCHITECTURE, 1558–1603)

MONUMENTS, TOMBS, AND FITTINGS

The early Renaissance was heralded by a number of smaller monuments and fittings erected in existing churches, as in other countries (pp. 976, 977M).

The **Culpepper Tomb, Goudhurst** (p. 976C), the **wall tablets at Peterhouse, Cambridge** (p. 976J), and also **All Hallows, Barking, London** (p. 976G), the **pulpit, North Cray** (p. 976A), and the **chapel screen, Charterhouse** (p. 976B), are examples of many features found in churches throughout the country, while the **stalls, King's College, Cambridge** (1531–5) (p. 977M), are amongst the earliest examples of the newly introduced style.

Westminster Abbey. Tomb
Henry VII (1509) and his
een (1503). See pp. 868, 881

B. Montacute House, Somerset (1580–99).
See p. 881

Knole House, Kent: stair-
case (1605). See p. 881

D. Canons Ashby, Northants (1584 with additions).
See p. 882

E. Burghley House, Northants (1577–87). See p. 881

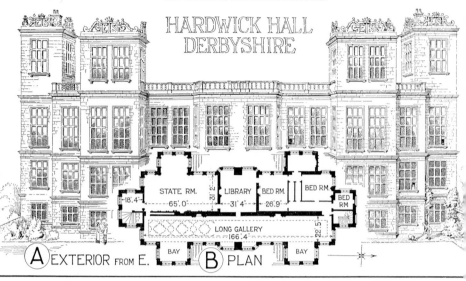

HARDWICK HALL DERBYSHIRE

STATE RM. — 65'0" — LIBRARY — 31'4" — BED RM. — 26'9" — BED RM. — BED RM.

18'4"

LONG GALLERY — 166'4"

22'5"

BAY

BAY

Ⓐ EXTERIOR FROM E.   Ⓑ PLAN

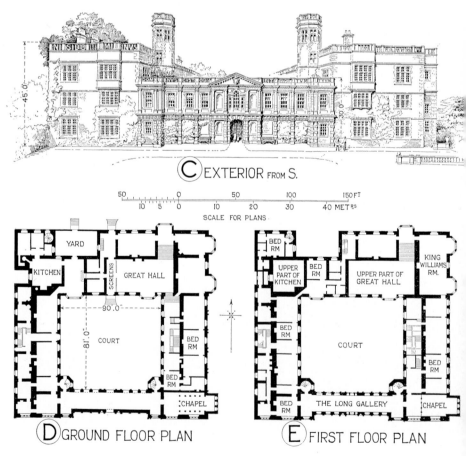

CASTLE ASHBY : NORTHANTS

45'0"   30'0"

Ⓒ EXTERIOR FROM S.

SCALE FOR PLANS

50   0   50   100   150 FT
10 5 0   10   20   30   40 METRS

YARD

KITCHEN   SCREENS   GREAT HALL

90'0"

81'0"   COURT   BED RM.

BED RM.

CHAPEL

Ⓓ GROUND FLOOR PLAN

BED RM   UPPER PART OF KITCHEN   BED RM   UPPER PART OF GREAT HALL   KING WILLIAMS RM.

BED RM

COURT   BED RM

BED RM   THE LONG GALLERY   CHAPEL

Ⓔ FIRST FLOOR PLAN

The **Tomb of Henry VII** (1509) (pp. 427, 868, 879A), in Westminster Abbey, by Torrigiani, is an early and exquisite example of Renaissance art. It is a black marble table tomb, with angle Corinthian pilasters, between which are the royal arms, while above are winged cherubs and recumbent life-like effigies of Henry VII and his queen, enclosed in a Chantry Chapel with fine Gothic screen by Ducheman (p. 428). Other monuments and fittings are referred to under Ornament, p. 974.

ELIZABETHAN MANSIONS

Well-known Elizabethan mansions are: **Charlecote, Warwickshire** (1558); **Loseley Park, Surrey** (1562–8) (p. 887A); **Longleat House, Wilts** (1567–80) (p. 965D) probably by Robert Smithson; **Kirby Hall, Northants** (1570–5) (pp. 888A, 905), perhaps by Thomas Thorpe; **Penshurst Place, Kent** (portion) (1570–85) (p. 449); **Burghley House, Northants** (1577–87) (pp. 965A, 969B); **Montacute House, Somerset** (1580–99) (pp. 879B, 965B); **Wollaton Hall, Notts** (1580–8) (pp. 883A, 965C), by Robert Smithson; **Longford Castle, Wilts** (1580) (p. 965E); **Haddon Hall, Derbyshire** (long gallery) (1567–84) (pp. 452, 884A); **Westwood Park, Worcester** (1590); **Bramhall Hall, Cheshire** (Additions 1590–1600) (p. 459); **Hinchingbrooke Hall, Hunts** (1602) (p. 969C); **Sizergh Castle, Westmorland** (1558–75), enlarged in this period, and **Lower Walterstone, Dorset** (1568).

These mansions show a general similarity in their arrangement with those of the Jacobean period, and so we give here detailed descriptions of the plan and usual features, which were evolved from those of the Tudor period (p. 452). The smaller mansions had a central hall flanked at one end by kitchen and offices, and at the other by withdrawing- and living-rooms; while the larger type was quadrangular with similar accommodation, but with additional rooms grouped round the court, and with a gatehouse in the centre of the entrance side, as at Oxburgh Hall (p. 450K), Compton Wynyates (p. 458C), and Sutton Place (p. 458G). Elizabethan and Jacobean architects adhered to the Tudor plan for smaller mansions, but they evolved the E-shaped plan from the quadrangular plan by omitting one side, as at Hatfield, thus admitting sunlight and air (p. 965F), and for this reason one side of the court at Caius College, Cambridge, was removed. The H-shaped plan was used also in this period (p. 964). The gatehouse often became a detached building, as at Burton Agnes, Yorkshire; Charlecote; Cranborne, Dorset (p. 897), and Stanway, Gloucestershire. Features, such as the great hall, grand staircase, and long gallery, are common to the typical houses mentioned above. As houses began to look outwards, instead of into courts, surrounding gardens developed, on formal lines.

The Great Hall (pp. 880D, 965) still retained its central position, but became more than ever a hall of state, connecting the various parts of the mansion. The walls were cased internally in oak panelling to a height of 8 or 10 ft, surmounted by ancestral portraits, armour, and trophies of the chase. The fireplace, with its huge dog-grate, was an elaborate feature flanked by columns, while above were ranged heraldic devices of the owners. The hall was covered either by an open timber roof, as that over the Middle Temple Hall (pp. 500H, 888C), or with elaborately moulded plaster panels (p. 891B). At the entrance end the carved oak screen supported the minstrels' gallery (p. 887B) and screened off the kitchen department beyond; while at the other end of the hall was the lofty bay window and raised dais, from which were reached the living-rooms of the family. A similar arrangement of plan was adopted in the colleges of Oxford (p. 891C) and Cambridge, and the Inns of Court, London, as Gray's Inn Hall (p. 888B) and Middle Temple Hall (p. 888C).

The Grand Staircase, as at Knole House (p. 879C), Aston Hall, and Blickling Hall (p. 975B, C), with carved newels and pierced balustrades, and usually adjacent to the hall, forms a dignified approach to the rooms above, and its prominence as a feature is in marked contrast with the inconvenient corkscrew stairs of the Mediaeval period.

The Long Gallery (pp. 880B, E, 884A, 965) is perhaps the most striking feature of an Elizabethan mansion, with ornamental chimney-pieces, panelled or tapestried walls, large mullioned windows, and modelled plaster ceiling. Long, low, and narrow, though varied as at Haddon by room-like bays (p. 884A), the gallery often ran the whole length of the upper floor of the house and connected the wings on either side of the central hall (p. 965F). Its original purpose is somewhat doubtful; it may have been designed merely as a connecting corridor, as a covered promenade, or as a 'picture gallery' which was also used to display the art treasures which it had now become the fashion to collect; or it may even have been designed to serve all three purposes. It would almost seem as if the aristocracy of Elizabethan times in England rivalled one another in the length of their galleries, even as did the nobility of Mediaeval Italy in the height of their towers (p. 624). Some of the finest of these galleries are: Haddon Hall (1567–84) (p. 884A), 109 ft by 18 ft; Montacute House (1580–99), 170 ft by 20 ft, and Hardwick Hall (1590–7) (pp. 880B, 884B), 166 ft by 22 ft.

The Withdrawing-room or 'solar' of previous times was often elaborately finished with carved chimney-pieces and panelled walls, as at Loseley Park, Surrey (1562–68) (p. 887A), Crewe Hall, Cheshire (1636) and Stockton House, Wiltshire (1610) (p. 975A), where it even rivalled a long gallery in treatment.

Bedrooms were multiplied and were often elaborate, as at Sizergh Castle, and a private chapel was frequently incorporated in the building (p. 965D, F).

Hardwick Hall, Derbyshire (1590–7) (pp. 880, 884B), by Robert Smithson, is unusual in plan (p. 880B), consisting of a rectangular block with projecting bays. The exterior is famous for its large mullioned and transomed windows, giving rise to the saying 'Hardwick Hall, more glass than wall', while bay-windows, carried up as towers, relieve the skyline and are terminated by open scroll-work with the initials 'E.S.' for Elizabeth, Countess of Shrewsbury, known as 'Bess of Hardwick'.

Castle Ashby, Northants (1572–) (p. 880), added to from time to time, is situated on high ground, and was originally in the form of a three-sided court, which included the great hall (60 ft by 30 ft), with screens, bay-window, and staircase turrets. The lettered balustrade displays the words 'Nisi Dominus ædificaverit', etc. (Ps. cxxvii). The fourth side (*c.* 1635), with the long gallery (91 ft by 15 ft 6 ins), attributed to Inigo Jones, illustrates the difference between the Elizabethan and Later Renaissance styles (p. 880C).

Canons Ashby, Northants (1584) (p. 879D), is an Elizabethan house with an internal court showing Tudor influence, and with Jacobean additions.

ELIZABETHAN COLLEGES

During the Mediaeval period many colleges had been founded at the universities (p. 473), and as the day of the pious founder had not yet passed, new colleges were still endowed both at Oxford and Cambridge. These were, of course, built in the Elizabethan style, which retained many Gothic features; while additions were also made to Mediaeval colleges. Thus revival of learning and Renaissance in architecture went hand in hand in the old universities. At **Cambridge** there is **Emmanuel College** (1584), with its dignified façade; the beautiful little **Gate of Honour, Caius College** (1572–3) (p. 895B), designed by the founder, Dr Caius; **Nevile's Court, Trinity College** (1593–1615) (p. 922A), and new quadrangles to **Sidney Sussex College** (1596–8) and **S. John's College** (1598–1602) (p. 473), by Ralph Simons. At **Oxford** there is a fine example of Renaissance work in **Jesus College**

A. Wollaton Hall, Notts: aerial view from S. (1580–8). See p. 881

B. Blickling Hall, Norfolk: aerial view from W. (1626). See p. 886

A. Haddon Hall, Derbyshire: long gallery (1567–84). See p. 881

B. Hardwick Hall, Derbyshire: long gallery (1590–7). See p. 882

(1571) by Holt. Other colleges and additions at both universities belong to the later periods (pp. 886, 963). Among the **Inns of Court, London, Gray's Inn Hall** (1556–60) (p. 888B), **The Temple** (p. 889A), with its church, halls, libraries, chambers, and the famous **Middle Temple Hall** (p. 888C), with its magnificent hammer-beam roof (1562–70) (p. 500H), partly date from this period. Much damage was caused at Gray's Inn and the Temple by enemy action in 1941–5.

ELIZABETHAN SCHOOLS

The reign of Elizabeth saw the beginning of many schools, such as Repton (1556), Merchant Taylors (1561), Highgate (1565), Rugby (1567), Harrow (1572), and Uppingham (1584), and some had joint founders, as at Wakefield, Ashbourne, and Sandwich. The **Charterhouse** (1611) (p. 889B) and Dulwich School (1619) both started under James I. The Commonwealth fostered old schools and established new ones, notably in Wales, at Cardiff, Carnarvon, and Denbigh; while the Restoration period proved anti-educational. Subsequent to the Restoration period, education saw a new development in the increase of elementary schools for the poor, and over one hundred such schools were established in London in Queen Anne's reign; the Blue Coat School was founded at Hertford (1683) on the model of Christ's Hospital, London, while the Foundling Hospital, London (destroyed), received its charter in 1739.

ELIZABETHAN TOWN HOUSES

Many interesting houses were built, not only in London, but also in country towns; for in days of slow and difficult travelling by coach, many of the landed gentry, especially in parts remote from London, found it convenient to have their town residences close at hand. York, Chester, Shrewsbury, Ludlow, Coventry, Canterbury, Exeter, Truro, and many another town bear testimony to the fine design and craftsmanship of the houses of this period. In London there remain, in spite of the Great Fire, the half-timber building of Staple Inn (1581), with its fine hall and hammer-beam roof, and portions of the **Charterhouse** (p. 889B), including the great hall (1571, mutilated by war damage), added by the Duke of Norfolk; while the façade of Sir Paul Pindar's House (1600) is now preserved in the Victoria and Albert Museum, as is also a panelled room from the Palace of Bromley-by-Bow (1606), which, with its plaster ceiling (p. 977B), recalls the glories of such palatial buildings although it actually dates from the Jacobean period.

EARLY RENAISSANCE
(JACOBEAN ARCHITECTURE, 1603–25)
JACOBEAN MANSIONS

The great era of mansion building, which had commenced under Elizabeth, continued in the reign of James I.

Hatfield House, Herts (1607–11) (pp. 890B, C, 891A, B, 965F), built for Robert, first Earl of Salisbury, stands pre-eminent among many noble piles of this period in displaying the special characteristics and elaboration of treatment considered suitable for the country mansion of a nobleman. The house is E-shaped in plan (p. 965F), with central hall and projecting symmetrical wings, and is set off by formal gardens, designed with the same care as is displayed in the planning of the house itself (p. 890B). The entrance front, 225 ft long, is of daringly plain brickwork with stone mullioned windows, relieved by a projecting central entrance (p. 890C); while the bay-windows of the wings are taken up as small lateral towers, and the building is finished by a flat roof and balustrade and dominated by a central clock-turret. The south front (pp. 890B, 891A) is much more ornate in treatment, with Doric, Ionic, and Corinthian Orders superimposed to form a centre-piece flanked by an arcaded ground storey, mullioned windows and pierced parapet. The two-storeyed hall (p. 891B), with mullioned windows, minstrels' gallery, and modelled plaster ceiling, is a Renaissance development of the traditional Mediaeval hall, but there is an unusual connecting gallery at the dais end. The long gallery, chapel, grand staircase, and suites of private rooms all contribute to the completeness of this Jacobean mansion, designed, at least in part, by Robert Lyming, who was also the designer of the whole of Blickling Hall (see below).

Holland House, Kensington (1607) (p. 892), erected for Sir Walter Cope and afterwards inherited by the Earl of Holland, was the residence of many famous men. It was burnt out in 1940. The plan (p. 892B, C) was H-shaped, with entrance at one end, as at Bramshill (p. 965G), and arcades on the south bordering a fine terrace (p. 892A). The central porch, carried up as a tower with an ogee roof, was flanked by bay-windows and by curved gables. The entrance had been intended to be central on the south front, and the change to the east side required an encroachment on one of the arcades. The doorway (p. 892D) and the typical chimney-piece and oak-panelled walls in the White Parlour (p. 892E) are noticeable features.

Bramshill House, Hants (1605–12) (pp. 893A, 965G, 969A, D, J) was designed for Lord Zouche. Its unusual plan (p. 965G), partly due to an older building, is of the H-type, with entrance through an arcaded porch (p. 893A) direct into the hall, which thus loses its feudal character, but still retains the dais. An odd feature is the long narrow internal area. The long gallery (130 ft long), the terrace with its arcades (p. 969J), and the oriel window (pp. 893A, 969A) are among the many beautiful features of this building.

Blickling Hall, Norfolk (1626) (pp. 881, 883B, 965J, 969G, 975B, C, F) by Robert Lyming, is in brick and stone, usual in Norfolk, and the plan resembles that of Bramshill. It has two small internal courts, the outer court giving entrance to the hall, which is a thoroughfare room, as at Aston Hall (p. 965H); at the external angles of the building are square towers. The principal entrance (p. 969G), reached across the moat, has an arched opening with carved spandrels, framed with Doric columns and entablature, surmounted by the arms of Sir Henry Hobart. The staircase (p. 975B, C), rearranged in its present position in 1770, with the upper part in two opposite flights—unusual in this period—has boldly carved newels surmounted by figures, and an arched balustrade. The chimney-piece (p. 975F) has flanking pilasters diminishing towards the base and surmounted by Hermes figures which frame heraldic devices.

Other Jacobean mansions are: **Chastleton House, Oxon** (1603–14); **Audley End, Essex** (1603–16) (pp. 887B, 894A, 977A), by Bernard Johnson; **Knole House, Kent** (1605) (pp. 879C, 890A) (re-modelled); **Charlton House, Wilts** (1607); **Stockton House, Wilts** (1610) (p. 975A); **Aston Hall, Warwickshire** (1618–35) (pp. 965H, 977C); **Bolsover Castle, Derbyshire** (1612–), by John Smithson, which has later additions made (1629–33) by John and his son, Huntingdon Smithson; **Quenby Hall, Leicestershire** (–1621); and **Charlton House, Kent** (1607–12) (p. 894D).

JACOBEAN COLLEGES

This period saw a number of additions to colleges both at Oxford and Cambridge, which are of the greatest interest.

The **Bodleian Library, Oxford** (1613–36) (pp. 475A, 895A), formerly the Old Schools, attributed to Thomas Holt (d. 1624), is a conspicuous instance of the

A. Loseley Park, Surrey: drawing room (1562–8). See p. 882

B. Audley End, Essex: hall (1603–16). See opposite page

A. Kirby Hall, Northants: courtyard (1570–5). See p. 881

B. Gray's Inn Hall: interior (1556–60). See p. 885

C. Middle Temple Hall, London; interior (1562–70). See p. 885

A. The Temple, London: aerial view in 1938. See pp. 885, 928

1. Middle Temple Library
2. Garden Court
3. Fountain Court
4. Middle Temple Hall
5. New Court
6. Essex Court
7. Hare Court
8. Pump Court
9. Elm Court
10. Crown Office Row
11. Inner Temple Hall and
    Library
12. Temple Church
13. Master's House
14. Tanfield Court
15. King's Bench Walk
16. Paper Buildings
17. Middle Temple Lane

Many of these buildings were destroyed in the war of 1939–45

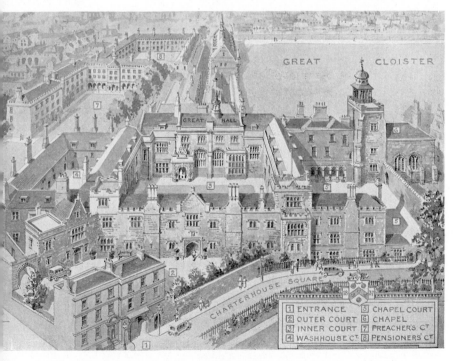

1 ENTRANCE   5 CHAPEL COURT
2 OUTER COURT 6 CHAPEL
3 INNER COURT 7 PREACHER'S CT
4 WASHHOUSE CT 8 PENSIONERS' CT

B. The Charterhouse, London: aerial view from S. (1545–71 and later).
See p. 885

A. Knole House, Kent: aerial view from S. (1605). See p. 886

B. Hatfield House, Herts: aerial view from S.E. See p. 885

C. Hatfield House: entrance (N.) façade (1607–11)

A. Hatfield House, Herts: south façade (1607–11). See p. 886

B. Hatfield House, Herts: hall (1607–1611). See p. 886

C. Wadham College, Oxford: hall (1610–1613). See p. 897

HOLLAND HOUSE : KENSINGTON

Ⓐ SOUTH FRONT AS EXISTING IN A.D. 1837

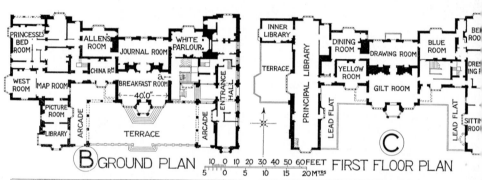

Ⓑ GROUND PLAN

PRINCESSES BED ROOM
ALLENS ROOM
JOURNAL ROOM
WHITE PARLOUR
CHINA Rᴹ
WEST ROOM
MAP ROOM
BREAKFAST ROOM
40'.0"
ENTRANCE HALL
PICTURE ROOM
LIBRARY
ARCADE
TERRACE
ARCADE

Ⓒ FIRST FLOOR PLAN

INNER LIBRARY
DINING ROOM
DRAWING ROOM
BLUE ROOM
BEᴰ ROOᴹ
TERRACE
PRINCIPAL LIBRARY
YELLOW ROOM
DRESSING Rᴹ
GILT ROOM
LEAD FLAT
LEAD FLAT
SITTIᴺ ROOᴹ

10 0 10 20 30 40 50 60 FEET
5   0   5   10   15   20 Mᵀᴿˢ

Ⓓ DOORWAY AT a (ON PLAN)

Ⓔ CHIMNEY PIECE IN WHITE PARLOU

A. Bramshill, Hants: entrance (S.W.) front (1605–12). See p. 886

B. Old Market Hall, Shrewsbury (1595). See p. 897

A. Audley End, Essex (1603–16). See p. 886

B. Fountains Hall, Yorkshire (1611). See p. 897

C. S. Peter's Hospital, Bristol (1610). See p. 897

D. Charlton House, Kent: west façade (1607–12). See p. 886

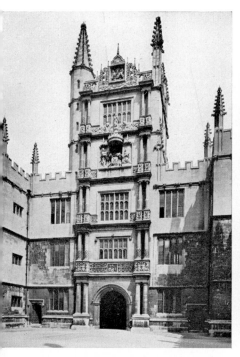

A. Tower of the Bodleian Library, Oxford (1613–36). See p. 886

B. Gate of Honour, Caius College, Cambridge (1572–3). See p. 882

C. Library (additions c. 1600–24)

D. Frontispiece (1610).

Merton College, Oxford. See p. 897

A. Queen's House, Greenwich: the Great Saloon (1616–35). See p. 898

B. The Banqueting House, Whitehall, London: west façade (1619–22). See p. 898

work of the period, for the tower over the gateway is a curious but effective mixture of traditional Gothic and new Renaissance, with mullioned windows and canopied niches flanked by the five Orders of architecture, one above the other; while the whole is capped by Gothic pinnacles.

Thomas Holt is equally dubiously credited with several other works at the older University at this time. At **Merton College** he is said to have designed the entrance, with superimposed Orders (1610) (p. 895D), and library (p. 895C); **Wadham College,** frontispiece of 'Orders' (1610–13), and fine hall (p. 891C), besides additions to Oriel and Jesus Colleges (1612). Pembroke College (1624) is certainly by another hand. At Cambridge the quadrangle of **Clare College** (1638–) is later than our period.

JACOBEAN MANOR HOUSES

Mediaeval manor houses supplied a good ground-work for Jacobean architects to elaborate with Renaissance additions and fittings, such as we see in South Wraxall Manor, Wilts (p. 452), and Cranborne Manor House, Dorset (1601–12)—a Tudor building with a Jacobean casing; while **Fountains Hall, Yorkshire** (1611) (p. 894B), is a complete example, built largely with material from the Mediaeval abbot's house (p. 430).

JACOBEAN TOWN HOUSES

The building known as **S. Peter's Hospital, Bristol** (1610, totally destroyed in the war of 1939–45) (p. 894C), was a fine half-timbered house of this period, with over-hanging upper stories and panelled 'Court Room' with carved chimney-piece and modelled plaster ceilings.

JACOBEAN MARKET HALLS

Market halls, as at **Shrewsbury** (1595) (p. 893B) and Chipping Campden (1627), are frequently built of stone or brick, while the Market Hall, Wymondham, Norfolk (1617), is a half-timbered example.

JACOBEAN HOSPITALS AND ALMSHOUSES

The need for hospitals and almshouses, which had already been recognized in the Mediaeval period (p. 479), became greater after the Dissolution of the Monasteries, and many hospitals were erected in this period.

The Whitgift Hospital, Croydon (1596–9), with its fine quadrangle, common hall, and living-rooms, still carries on the uses for which it was founded. Sackville College, East Grinstead (1619), Weekley Hospital, Northants (1611), Chipping Campden Hospital (1612), Trinity Hospital, Greenwich (1613), Trinity Hospital, Castle Rising (1614), Eyre's Hospital, Salisbury (1617), Abbot's Hospital, Guildford (1619), and somewhat later, Berkeley Hospital, Worcester, are a few of these buildings which have a similar arrangement of hall, kitchen, chapel, and rooms for the inmates.

LATE RENAISSANCE
(STUART, 1625–1702)

The architecture of this period is seen in the work of two of England's greatest architects—Inigo Jones (p. 870) and Sir Christopher Wren (pp. 871, 906)—and their best-known buildings will now be described.

INIGO JONES (1573–1652) (p. 870).

The court masques (1605–40) of the time of James I and Charles I, for which Inigo Jones designed the scenery (p. 871), showed his intimate acquaintance with

Italian Renaissance architecture, and he was thus able to practise the art tentatively while applying his knowledge to actual buildings.

The **Banqueting House, Whitehall, London** (1619–22) (pp. 896B, 899), was erected by Inigo Jones on the site of the old Jacobean Banqueting House burnt down in 1619. It was afterwards intended by John Webb, Inigo Jones's talented pupil, to incorporate this Banqueting House in a design for a royal palace which is shown on the plan (p. 899B). This palace-scheme would have formed one of the grandest architectural conceptions of the Renaissance in England, both in extent and in the finely adjusted proportions of its various parts (p. 899A). The complete plan of the palace (p. 899B), with its seven courts, shows the position the Banqueting House would have occupied on the Grand Court (800 ft by 400 ft), twice the size of the court of the Louvre, Paris (p. 775E); across its intended site now runs the thoroughfare of Whitehall. The façades of the Banqueting House (pp. 896B, 899C), 75 ft 6 ins high have a rusticated lower storey and two upper storeys, each with an Order in which no two adjacent columns are uniformly treated, except those in the centre. The lower windows have pediments, alternately triangular and segmental, and the upper windows have straight cornices; while festoons and masks under the upper frieze suggest the feasting and revelry associated with the idea of a royal banqueting hall. The severely Classic treatment here employed for the first time in England was the natural result of Inigo Jones's study of the correct Palladian architecture of Italy, and it constituted nothing less than an architectural revolution following directly, as it did, on the free and picturesque Jacobean architecture. This noble building has a fine interior occupying the entire height, with a gallery at the level of the upper order (p. 899D). It was converted into a Chapel Royal by George I, and in 1894 it became the Museum of the Royal United Service Institution.

The **Queen's House, Greenwich** (1616–35) (pp. 900, 901) (now National Maritime Museum), by Inigo Jones for the Queen of James I, shows the influence of Palladian architecture. It has a great central galleried saloon (p. 896A) and well-balanced façade with rusticated ground storey and central Ionic loggia, flanked by plain wings—a model for many later houses.

Greenwich Hospital had its commencement as a palace by the erection of 'King Charles's Block' designed 1663–7 by John Webb, the pupil of Inigo Jones. The façade (p. 901F) has a lofty Corinthian Order and chaste Classic details showing a close study of Inigo Jones's work, and recalls a similar treatment by Michelangelo on the Capitol at Rome (p. 718B). The building was completed as a Hospital by Sir Christopher Wren, who included the Queen's House and King Charles's Block in one grand symmetrical scheme (pp. 900, 901, 928).

York Water-Gate, London (1626) (p. 902A, B, C) appears to have been designed by Sir Balthazar Gerbier (c. 1591–1667) as an element in the scheme for York House, residence of the Duke of Buckingham. It was executed by the master-mason, Nicholas Stone, to form the river entrance, in days when the Thames was used as a highway for the pleasure barges of the nobility, but it now stands isolated in the Embankment gardens. This is a charming little piece of monumental architecture, with rusticated masonry and Tuscan Order surmounted by a pediment with armorial bearings flanked by 'lions couchants'.

S. Paul, Covent Garden, London (1631–5) (p. 902G, H, J), was designed by Inigo Jones to be the 'handsomest barn in England', for he was told by the Earl of Bedford to erect a church as simple and inexpensive as a barn, and he here showed, in the Tuscan portico, wide-spreading eaves and simple pediment, how it was possible to produce dignity by the simplest means. Actually, the present building is merely a close copy, for the original was burnt in 1795 and rebuilt by Thomas

WHITEHALL PALACE : LONDON

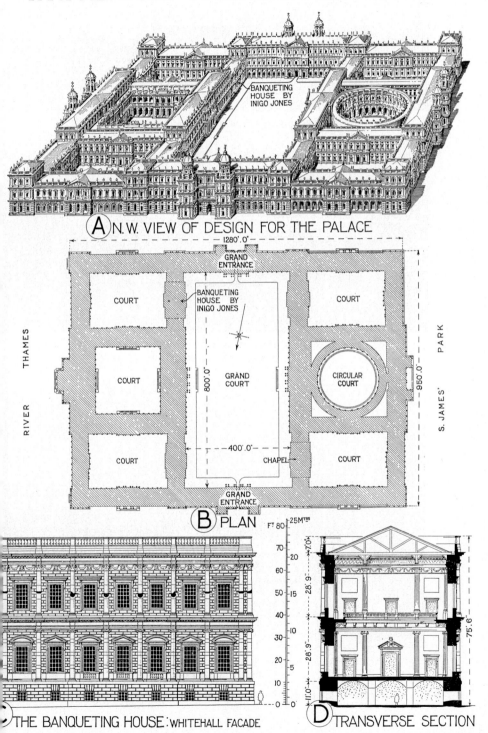

BANQUETING
HOUSE BY
INIGO JONES

Ⓐ N.W. VIEW OF DESIGN FOR THE PALACE

1280'.0"

GRAND
ENTRANCE

COURT

BANQUETING
HOUSE BY
INIGO JONES

COURT

THAMES

COURT

GRAND
COURT

800'.0"

CIRCULAR
COURT

950'.0"

RIVER

S. JAMES' PARK

COURT

400'.0"

CHAPEL

COURT

GRAND
ENTRANCE

Ⓑ PLAN

Ⓒ THE BANQUETING HOUSE : WHITEHALL FACADE

Ⓓ TRANSVERSE SECTION

FT 80 25 MTRS
70   20
60   47'.0"
50   15   28'.9"
40   10
30   28'.9"   75'.6"
20   5
10
0   0   11'.0"

A. The Queen's House (1616–35): north façade

B. The Royal Hospital (1663–1814) from the river (N.), with the Queen's House in the background

C. The Royal Hospital from the South, with the Queen's House in the foreground

Greenwich: the Royal Hospital and the Queen's House. See pp. 898, 928

ROYAL HOSPITAL ⚓ GREENWICH

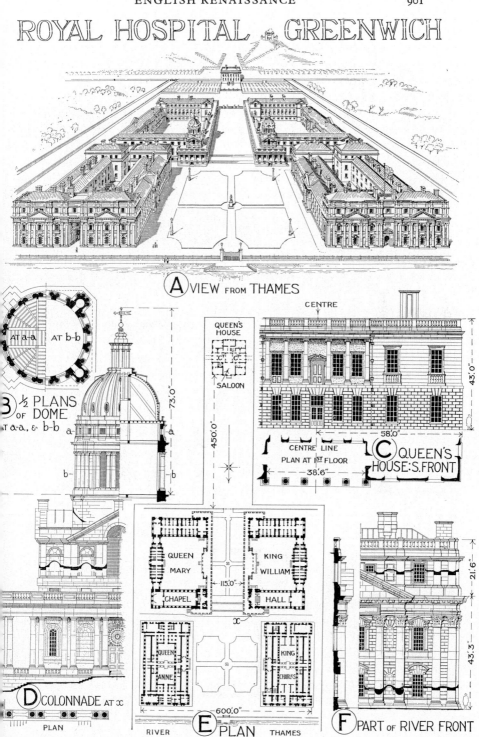

A VIEW FROM THAMES

B ½ PLANS OF DOME AT a-a, & b-b

AT a-a   AT b-b

QUEEN'S HOUSE

SALOON

CENTRE

C QUEEN'S HOUSE: S. FRONT

CENTRE LINE
PLAN AT 1ST FLOOR

43'0"
58'0"
38'6"
73'0"
450'0"

D COLONNADE AT x

PLAN

QUEEN MARY   KING WILLIAM

CHAPEL   HALL

QUEEN ANNE   KING CHARLES

115'0"

600'0"

RIVER   E PLAN   THAMES

F PART OF RIVER FRONT

21'6"
43'3"

YORK WATER-GATE LONDON

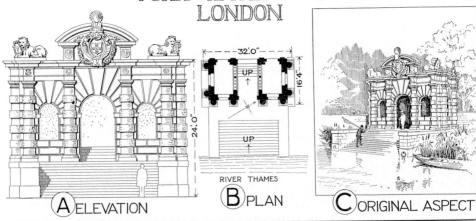

Ⓐ ELEVATION   Ⓑ PLAN   Ⓒ ORIGINAL ASPECT

THE COVERED BRIDGE : WILTON

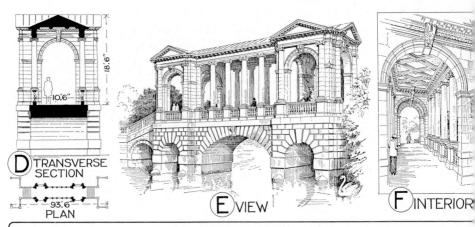

Ⓓ TRANSVERSE SECTION / PLAN   Ⓔ VIEW   Ⓕ INTERIOR

S. PAUL, COVENT GARDEN : LONDON

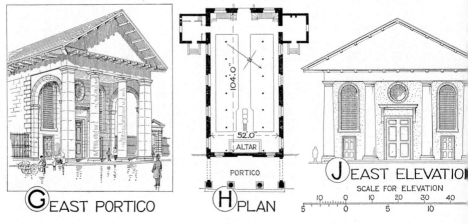

Ⓖ EAST PORTICO   Ⓗ PLAN   Ⓙ EAST ELEVATION

SCALE FOR ELEVATION

A. Wilton House, Wilts: south façade (1647–9). See p. 905

B. Saloon   C. Entrance façade

Coleshill, Berks (1650–2): destroyed by fire 1952. See p. 905

D. Eltham House, Kent: the staircase (1664). See p. 906   E. Belton House, Lincs. (1685–8). See p. 905

Ⓐ STAIRCASE : ASHBURNHAM HOUSE : LOND.　　Ⓑ CHIMNEY PIECE : STOKE HALL : DERBYSH

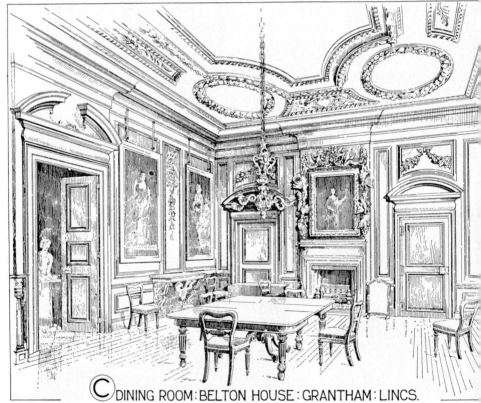

Ⓒ DINING ROOM : BELTON HOUSE : GRANTHAM : LINCS.

Hardwick (1752–1829) in 1795–8. The church was part of a scheme for Covent Garden—which soon began to develop in a small way as a market—standing on the west side of the square, which for the rest was lined with uniform terraced houses, arcaded on the ground floor, the whole forming the earliest instance in London of this class of civic planning. The houses, too, have been replaced, in a character different from the original.

Stoke Bruerne Park, Northants (1629–35) (p. 966N), by Inigo Jones, consisted of a central block containing the living-rooms connected by quadrant wings for library and chapel—a Palladian type of plan which influenced the larger Georgian houses (p. 931). Of the impossibly large number of further houses and other buildings ascribed to Inigo Jones there is probability for **Chevening Place, Kent** (1630) (p. 966H), much altered, and for **Wilton House, Wilts** (additions, 1647–9) (p. 903A), in the grounds of which is the later, very fine ornamental Palladian Bridge (1736) (p. 902D, E, F), by Roger Morris, imitated afterwards at Prior Park, Bath (p. 935D) and Stowe, Bucks. Rather less likelihood of Jones's authorship attaches to **Raynham Hall, Norfolk** (1635–8) (pp. 907C, 940E), though this, at least, plainly has been built under his influence; **Kirby Hall, Northants** (additions, 1638–40) (p. 881); **Lindsay House, Lincoln's Inn Fields** (1640); and **Barber-Surgeons' Hall** (1636) (destroyed). The Marlborough Chapel in S. James's Palace, London (1623–7) (altered later) is among his earliest designs.

Ashburnham House, Westminster (–1662) probably by John Webb (1611–72), pupil and assistant of Inigo Jones from 1628–52, is notable for its fine staircases (pp. 904A, 971J).

Coleshill House, Berks (1650–62) (pp. 903B, C, 937), by Sir Roger Pratt in consultation with Inigo Jones, was a work of fine quality representative of the small output of this able designer. It was destroyed by fire in 1952.

Belton House, Grantham (1685–8) (pp. 903E, 904C, 966B), built by the mason William Stanton (1639–1705) for Sir John Brownlow, very strongly shows the influence of the domestic designs of Sir Roger Pratt. It is of the H-type plan (p. 966B) double depth in the centre, with central steps leading to the hall and rooms on the principal floor. There is a main staircase to the right of the hall, and in each wing service stairs from the kitchen in the basement. The exterior (p. 903E) has a projecting pedimented centre, hipped roofs, dormers, belvedere, and central turret. The dining-room (p. 904C) has a Late Renaissance decorative treatment with walls panelled from floor to ceiling, doors with large panels and pediments, and chimney-piece surmounted by elaborately carved birds, fruit and flowers probably by the famous woodcarver Grinling Gibbons (1648–1720), while the plaster ceiling has a fine geometrical design.

Groombridge Place, Kent (late seventeenth century) (pp. 907B, 966F) is similar in many respects to Belton House, having an H-type plan and a central hall serving as a thoroughfare room, although the entrance is across one end, in the old tradition. Externally it has the same essentially English character. It is reached by a bridge across the moat (p. 907B), and is of red brick with sash windows, divided by stout bars, with Ionic portico, hipped roofs, dormers, and tower-like chimney stacks.

Honington Hall, Warwickshire (c. 1685; with later additions) (p. 907A) is another example of an opulent country house of the period, of brick with stone dressings, projecting wings and hipped, low-pitched roof.

Thorpe Hall, Northants (1653–6) (pp. 907D, 966M) is reminiscent of Chevening Place in its deep rectangular plan and of both this and Coleshill House in its external character. But it is by no means equal to either in quality, and is indeed a coarser rendering of the type, suited to the average country house and soon in popular favour. It was designed by Peter Mills (*c.* 1600–1670), a master-bricklayer of London who attained considerable repute as a surveyor and architect.

Eltham House, Kent (1664) (pp. 903D, 966E), designed by Hugh May (1622–84), Paymaster (Surveyor) to the King's Works from 1660 to 1668, externally evidences the influence of a Palladianism which had recently developed in Holland, where he had resided. He also erected some buildings at Cornbury House, Oxfordshire (1663–8) and did some remodelling at Windsor Castle (1675–83), besides designing Berkeley House, Piccadilly (1665) and Cassiobury Park, Herts (*c.* 1677–80).

SIR CHRISTOPHER WREN (1632–1723) (p. 871).

Pembroke College Chapel, Cambridge (1663–5), designed for his uncle, the Bishop of Ely, was Wren's first essay in architecture, and though a daring innovation, shows restraint in design, with its Corinthian pilasters, central window flanked by niches, and hexagonal cupola (p. 908A, B, 971A).

S. Paul's Cathedral, London (1675–1710) (frontispiece, pp. 663B, 908–12, 915A, B, 925), occupying the site of the Mediaeval cathedral destroyed in the Great Fire, is Wren's masterpiece. The first design, of which there is a model in the north triforium, was a Greek cross in plan, with projecting vestibule (p. 910A, B), but the influence of the clergy, who desired a long nave and choir suitable for ritual, finally caused the selection of a Latin cross or Mediaeval type of plan (p. 910D). The interior has a length of 463 ft including apse, a breadth including aisles of 101 ft, and an area of about 64,000 square ft. This plan, in which Wren wisely so spread the weight of the structure that in the crypt solids and voids are approximately equal, consists of a great central space at the crossing suitable for vast congregations, like Ely Cathedral, crowned by a dome painted by Sir James Thornhill; choir and nave in three bays, north and south transepts with semicircular porticoes, and projecting western portico of coupled columns. The western bay of the nave is, unlike the other bay's square on plan, and is flanked by chapels, which project externally. This bay (p. 910D) has coupled columns supporting lateral arches, through the northern of which is visible the Chapel of S. Dunstan, with its fine columnar screen of carved woodwork. The piers of the nave (pp. 909B, 910C) are fronted with Corinthian pilasters, entablature, and attic which conceals the triforium, while the nave is crowned by ingeniously designed saucer-like domes, 91 ft high (p. 658F–J), beneath which the clear-story windows (not visible from the exterior) (pp. 908C, 909B, 910, 911F) have lunette vaults. The choir is enriched with fine stalls and organ case by Grinling Gibbons, and beautiful hammered iron gates by Tijou, while it terminates in the modern reredos, the vaulting being decorated by Sir William Richmond with coloured glass mosaics. The dome (pp. 908C, 909B, 910C, D) and its support presented a complicated structural problem (p. 912). The dome is carried on eight piers, and is 112 ft in diameter at the base of the high drum, at the level of the Whispering Gallery, diminishing to 101 ft at the top of the drum, and is of triple construction. The inner dome of brick, 18 ins thick, has its eye 214 ft 3 ins above the floor, while the intermediate conical dome, of brick 18 ins thick, strengthened by a double chain of iron (pp. 911E, 912A), supports the stone lantern, ball, and cross; besides which the outer dome also rests on this intermediate cone and is formed of timber covered with lead (pp. 910C, 911E). Eight openings are formed in the summit of the outer dome to admit light to the inner dome (p. 911D, E) (cf. dome of the Panthéon, Paris (p. 800E).

The vaulted crypt, extending under the whole church, is the last resting place of many famous men, including Nelson, Wellington and Wren himself.

The exterior is exceedingly effective and groups well with the central dome. The façades have two Orders, the lower Corinthian and the upper Composite, totalling

A. Honington Hall, Warwickshire (*c.* 1685). See p. 905

B. Groombridge Place, Kent (late 17th cent.). See p. 905

C. Raynham Hall, Norfolk (1635–8).
See p. 905

D. Thorpe Hall, Northants
(1653–6). See p. 905

A. Façade   B. Interior
Pembroke College Chapel, Cambridge (1663–5). See p. 906

C. The crossing   D. South transept
S. Paul's Cathedral, London (1675–1710). See p. 906

A. Aerial view from S.W.

B. Nave looking E.
S. Paul's Cathedral, London (1675–1710). See p. 906

S. PAUL : LONDON

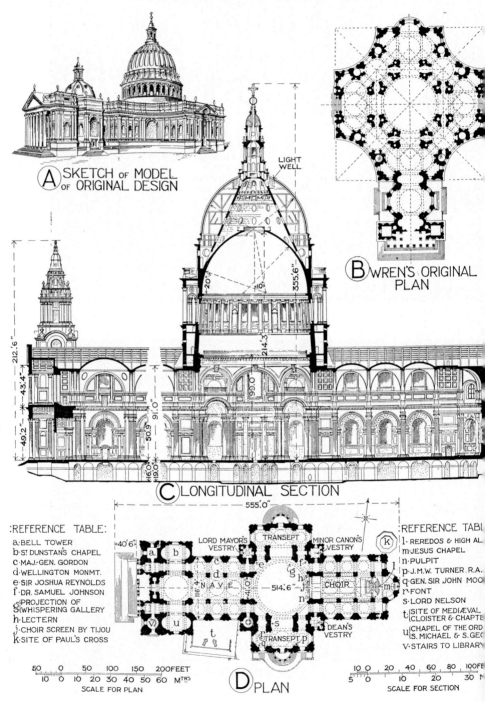

Ⓐ SKETCH OF MODEL OF ORIGINAL DESIGN

Ⓑ WREN'S ORIGINAL PLAN

Ⓒ LONGITUDINAL SECTION

LIGHT WELL

Ⓓ PLAN

:REFERENCE TABLE:
a·BELL TOWER
b·S⸀ DUNSTAN'S CHAPEL
c·MAJ.·GEN. GORDON
d·WELLINGTON MONMT.
e·SIR JOSHUA REYNOLDS
f·DR. SAMUEL JOHNSON
g·{PROJECTION OF WHISPERING GALLERY
h·LECTERN
j·CHOIR SCREEN BY TIJOU
k·SITE OF PAUL'S CROSS

:REFERENCE TABL⸀
l· REREDOS & HIGH AL⸀
m·JESUS CHAPEL
n·PULPIT
p·J.M.W. TURNER.R.A.
q·GEN. SIR JOHN MOO⸀
r·FONT
s·LORD NELSON
t·{SITE OF MEDIÆVAL CLOISTER & CHAPTE⸀
u·{CHAPEL OF THE ORD⸀ S. MICHAEL & S.GE⸀
v·STAIRS TO LIBRAR⸀

LORD MAYOR'S VESTRY
TRANSEPT
MINOR CANON'S VESTRY
CHOIR
DEAN'S VESTRY
TRANSEPT
NAVE

555.0"
514.6"
40.6"

50   0   50   100   150   200 FEET
10   0   10   20   30   40   50   60 M⸀ᴿˢ
SCALE FOR PLAN

10 0   20   40   60   80   100 FE⸀
5   0   10   20   30 M⸀
SCALE FOR SECTION

212.6"
43.4"
49.2"
91.0"
50.9"
16.0"
19.0"
99.0"
214.3"
355.6"
20°

S. PAUL · LONDON

366'.0" TO PAVEMENT

PERISTYLE

67.0"

53.0"

PLAN OF PERISTYLE

212.6"

Ⓑ SUGGESTED OPENING IN SCREEN WALL TO SHOW FLYING BUTTRESS

43'.4"

49'.2"

Ⓓ WEST ELEVATION

WELLS TO INTERIOR ONE

ESTIMATED WEIGHT OF LANTERN 850 TONS

1'.6"

1'.6"

WREN'S CHAIN

110'.6"

47'.0"

91'.0"

41'.0"

58'2"

16'.0"

43'.4"

59'.2"

Ⓕ SECTION THRO' NAVE LOOKING W.

SECTIONAL VIEW OF DOME

25   0   25   50   75   100 FEET
10   0   10   20   30 METRES

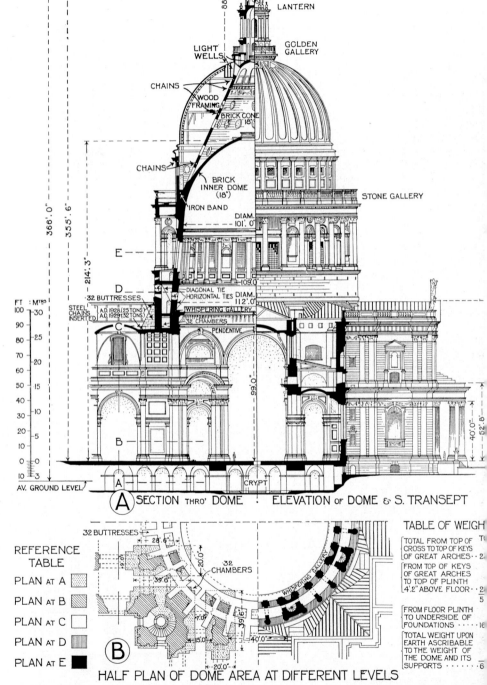

S. PAUL'S CATHEDRAL

LANTERN

LIGHT WELLS

GOLDEN GALLERY

CHAINS

WOOD FRAMING

BRICK CONE (18")

CHAINS

BRICK INNER DOME (18")

STONE GALLERY

IRON BAND

DIAM. 101'. 0"

E ————— 109.0"

DIAGONAL TIE

D ————— HORIZONTAL TIES DIAM. 112'.0"

32 BUTTRESSES

STEEL CHAINS INSERTED A.D. 1928 (25 TONS) A.D. 1929 (32 TONS)

WHISPERING GALLERY

32 CHAMBERS

C

PENDENTIVE

99.0"

B

A CRYPT

AV. GROUND LEVEL

FT : M^{TRS}

100 —30

90 —25

80

70 —20

60

50 —15

40 —10

30

20 —5

10

0 —0

10 —3

366'. 0" 355'. 6" 214'. 3" 86'. 0"

40'.0" 52'.8"

A SECTION THRO' DOME · ELEVATION OF DOME & S. TRANSEPT

REFERENCE TABLE

PLAN AT A

PLAN AT B

PLAN AT C

PLAN AT D

PLAN AT E

32 BUTTRESSES

28'.6"

20.0"

39.6"

32 CHAMBERS

7'.0"

39.6"

15.0"

40.0"

20.0"

WHISPERING GALLERY

B HALF PLAN OF DOME AREA AT DIFFERENT LEVELS

TABLE OF WEIGH

TOTAL FROM TOP OF CROSS TO TOP OF KEYS OF GREAT ARCHES·· 2

FROM TOP OF KEYS OF GREAT ARCHES TO TOP OF PLINTH 4'.2" ABOVE FLOOR · 2 5

FROM FLOOR PLINTH TO UNDERSIDE OF FOUNDATIONS ····· 18

TOTAL WEIGHT UPON EARTH ASCRIBABLE TO THE WEIGHT OF THE DOME AND ITS SUPPORTS ····· 6

The calculations in the Table of Weights are those made by Mr J. E. Drower for the S. Pau
Commission. The thrusting weight of the inner and outer drums of the dome is extended over a lar
area by means of the thirty-two radiating buttresses, assisted at a lower level by the four great an
bastions. Various cracks in the masonry having appeared, a sum of £400,000 was collected publi
between the years 1914–30 and expended on strengthening the eight piers carrying the dome, the fo
surrounding bastions, and the insertion of chains in the great triple dome itself, as shown in this secti

110 ft 6 ins in height (p. 911F). The aisles are only one storey high, so the part above them is a screen-wall introduced to give dignity and to act as a counterweight to the flying buttresses concealed behind it, which receive the thrust of the nave vault. Considerable criticism has been directed against this screen wall, which is said to be a sham, since the space behind it is unroofed, and a suggestion is here put forward (p. 911B) that such objections might be removed if the wall were pierced with openings so as to show the flying buttresses behind. The western façade, 177 ft wide (frontispiece, p. 911D), approached by a broad flight of steps which give scale to the building, has a central two-storeyed portico of coupled Corinthian and Composite columns superimposed, surmounted by a pediment sculptured with the Conversion of S. Paul. The portico is flanked by two beautifully proportioned taper-ing steeples, which are pleasing features in the design, 212 ft 6 ins high above the nave floor, that on the left containing bells and that on the right the clock, while the fine semicircular porticoes to the transepts are notable (p. 908D). The external dome (frontispiece, p. 909A) is probably the finest in Europe, for the projecting masses of masonry at the meeting of nave and transepts, forming the vestries and stairs to dome, express support from the ground upwards (pp. 663B, 910D). The peristyle round the drum, with an external diameter of about 139 ft 6 ins, is particularly effective with threequarter columns attached to radiating buttress-walls; while as every fourth intercolumniation is filled with masonry, there is an appearance of strength and solidity lacking in the Panthéon, Paris. Above the colonnade is the 'Stone Gallery', and attic supporting the dome, which is crowned with lantern, ball, and cross, weighing 850 tons, rising to a height of 366 ft above the pavement.

There are some striking contrasts in the history of the building of the great metropolitan cathedral and that of S. Peter, Rome (p. 714). S. Paul's, London, had one architect and one master mason, and was built in 35 years, during the episco-pate of one bishop; while S. Peter's, Rome, had 13 successive architects and numerous master-masons, and the building extended over 100 years, during the pontificates of 20 popes.

The **London City Churches** (pp. 916, 925, 926), 52 in number, designed 1670–1711 by Wren in the Renaissance style to replace those destroyed by the Great Fire, are models of simplicity and restraint in treatment. Many have been destroyed or war-damaged but the towers and steeples still remaining make London City one of the most picturesque in the world, and form a unique setting to the great cathedral. Many are most skilfully planned on cramped and awkward sites (p. 916), and are among the first churches actually designed to meet the requirements of Protestant worship, in which a central preaching-space usurps the nave and aisles suitable for the processions of Roman Catholic ritual, while galleries were frequently added.

S. Stephen, Walbrook (1672–9, damaged in 1941) (pp. 917, 925M), is famous for original and ingenious planning which produces a wonderful effect within a limited area. Enclosed in a rectangle are sixteen columns, of which eight are arranged in a circle to carry a central cupola, with the judicious disposition of single-columns so as to produce a church with five aisles. The fine pulpit (p. 921E), organ (p. 917E) and reredos (p. 917F) are typical of Grinling Gibbons's influence.

S. Mary-le-Bow, Cheapside (1670–3, much damaged in 1941) (pp. 915C, 916G, 919, 925R), is specially notable not only for 'Bow Bells', but for its graceful Renais-sance steeple (completed 1680), the masterpiece of that particular type which Wren may be said to have evolved. With the Gothic spire as his prototype, he surmounted a square tower with a pyramidal spire in receding stages of encircling columns, all unified by a clever use of inverted consoles.

S. Bride, Fleet Street (1671–8, gutted 1940) (pp. 915D, 918, 919, 920B), has a similar though less successful steeple (1701–3), in which the absence of the inverted consoles gives a telescopic effect to the series of columned stages.

S. Martin, Ludgate (1677–84) (pp. 916D, 924A, 925D), has an interior with four Corinthian columns to the central vault, but is best known for its beautiful little steeple, consisting of a square tower connected by side scrolls to the façade and surmounted by an octagonal stage with timber spire and weather vane, all grouping well with views of S. Paul's Cathedral.

S. Clement Danes, Strand (1680–2) (pp. 920C, 924B) (gutted 1941, restored 1958) which has a graceful spire in diminishing stages added by Gibbs in 1719–20, and S. James, Piccadilly (1682–4) (pp. 918, 920A) (much damaged 1941, restored 1952) are remarkable for their two-storeyed aisles in which galleries are supported by square piers surmounted by Corinthian columns and a barrel-vaulted roof, intersected by semi-cylindrical vaults at right angles over the gallery bays (p. 918C).

S. Mary Abchurch (1681–6) (pp. 916A, 921B) (damaged, 1940) is a square church in a cramped position with the dome on pendentives as a principal feature, while the steeple is neither fine nor well placed; but the Grinling Gibbons altarpiece and the excellent organ case, pulpit and pews help to produce an attractive interior, which even appears spacious under its painted dome.

S. Mildred, Bread Street (1677–83) (destroyed, 1941) was a rectangle in three compartments with central dome on pendentives, and was quite a gem in the perfection of its parts and in the beauty of its carved woodwork.

S. Lawrence Jewry (1671–7) (pp. 916B, 921C); S. Benetfink (1670–3) (p. 916C) (destroyed, 1842); S. Mary-at-Hill (1670–6) (pp. 916E, 921A), a vaulted and domed church formed into a cross by four columns; S. Anne and S. Agnes (1677–80, steeple c. 1714) (p. 916F); S. Swithin, Cannon Street (1677–85) (p. 916H) (gutted, 1941); Christ Church, Newgate Street (1677–87, steeple 1704) (p. 916J) (gutted, 1940), and S. Magnus-the-Martyr, London Bridge (1671–6, steeple 1705) (pp. 916K, 920D), all show Wren's subtle adaptation of plan to site.

S. Alban, Wood Street (1682–5) (wrecked, 1940); S. Dunstan in the East (1670–1, steeple 1697–9) (gutted, 1941); S. Mary Aldermary (1681–2, tower 1702–44) (p 925G) and S. Michael, Cornhill (1670–2, tower completed by Hawksmoor 1718–22) (p. 925J), offer examples of his treatment of Gothic towers and spires.

Wren designed a number of collegiate buildings in Oxford and Cambridge which display his peculiar power of adapting the design to meet the exigencies both of site and purpose. At Oxford there is the Sheldonian Theatre (1664–9) (pp. 475A, 925X) designed after the Theatre of Marcellus with roof on the lines of a velarium, since altered, while the Library, Queen's College (1693–6) (pp. 922C, 959C), the Tom Tower, Christ Church (1682) (p. 925S) and the Garden Quadrangle, Trinity College (1668, north wing; 1682, west wing; 1728, south wing) exhibit Wren's mastery of design. The Old Ashmolean Museum (1679–83) (p. 475A) was designed by T. Wood under Wren's influence. The designer of Trinity College Chapel, Oxford (1691–4) (p. 922B) is not definitely known. At Cambridge, in addition to Pembroke College Chapel (p. 906), there are Emmanuel College Chapel (1668–73), and Trinity College Library (1676–84) (pp. 921F, 922A, 925Z).

Among Wren's secular works are the Monument, London (1671–6) (p. 925H), to commemorate the Great Fire of 1666; the Fountain Court and garden façades (1689–94) of Hampton Court Palace (pp. 459, 923A, 925U) which have been described in connection with the Tudor portion of Henry VIII (p. 459); Chelsea Hospital (1682–91) (pp. 923B, C, 925I) with its fine chapel (p. 923C); Marlborough House, Pall Mall (1709–11); additions to Kensington Palace (1690–1704); and the

A. Bishop's Throne and stalls   B. S. aisle looking W.
S. Paul's Cathedral, London (1675–1710). See p. 906

C. S. Mary-le-Bow, Cheapside, London   D. S. Bride, Fleet Street, London (1671–8):
(1670–3): steeple (1680). See p. 913   steeple (1701–3). See p. 913

WREN'S CITY CHURCHES

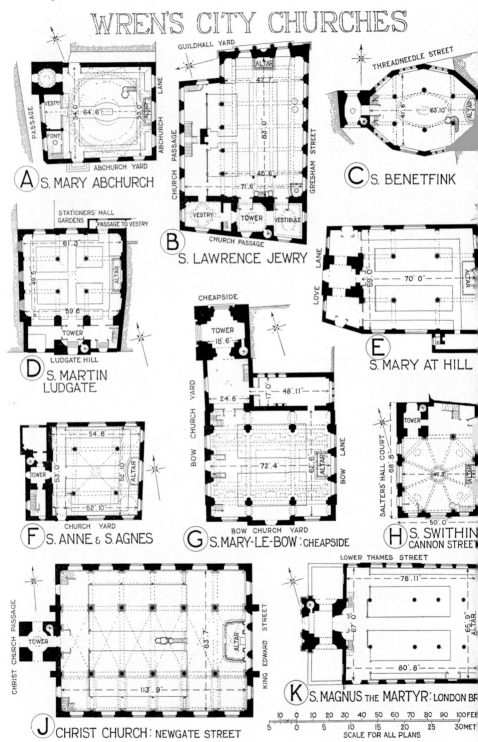

A S. MARY ABCHURCH

B S. LAWRENCE JEWRY

C S. BENETFINK

D S. MARTIN LUDGATE

E S. MARY AT HILL

F S. ANNE & S. AGNES

G S. MARY-LE-BOW : CHEAPSIDE

H S. SWITHIN CANNON STREET

J CHRIST CHURCH : NEWGATE STREET

K S. MAGNUS THE MARTYR : LONDON BR

SCALE FOR ALL PLANS

S. STEPHEN, WALBROOK: LONDON

(A) INTERIOR LOOKING S.W.

(B) SKETCH OF STEEPLE

(C) SECTION a-a

(D) PLAN

(E) INTERIOR WEST DOOR & ORGAN

(F) THE REREDOS

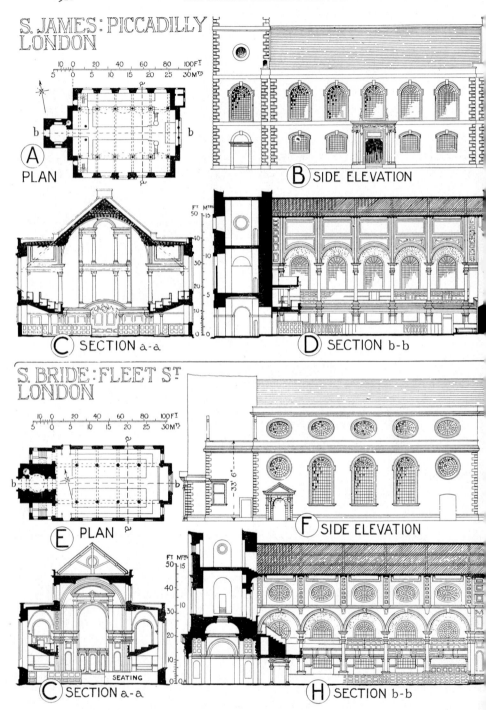

S. JAMES: PICCADILLY LONDON

10 0 20 40 60 80 100 FT
5 0 5 10 15 20 25 30 MTS

(A) PLAN

(B) SIDE ELEVATION

(C) SECTION a-a

FT MTRS
50 15
40
30 10
20 5
10
0 0

(D) SECTION b-b

S. BRIDE: FLEET ST. LONDON

10 0 20 40 60 80 100 FT
5 0 5 10 15 20 25 30 MTS

(E) PLAN

(F) SIDE ELEVATION

—33′ 6″—

FT MTRS
50 15
40
30 10
20 5
10
0 0

(C) SECTION a-a

SEATING

FT MTRS
50 15
40
30 10
20 5
10
0 0

(H) SECTION b-b

S. MARY LE BOW
LONDON

PLAN AT a

PLAN AT b

HEIGHT &
THRUST
OF UPPER
PORTION
TAKEN BY
INVERTED
TRUSSES

a
b

c

d

e

f

25'.9"
STAIRS

18'.3"

33'.10"
17'.9"
19'.0"
104'.6"

111'.7"

FT MTRS
100 — 30
90
80 — 25
70 — 20
60
50 — 15
40
30 — 10
20
10 — 5
0 — 0

S. BRIDE
LONDON

PLAN AT g

PLAN AT h

103'.8"

226'.11"

g
h

j

k

l

CORBELS
OR
PENDEN-
TIVES

m

20'.10"

16'.0"

A SECTION   B ELEVATION   C ELEVATION   D SECTION

20'.6"

E PLAN AT f

½ PLAN
AT c

½ PLAN
AT d

½ PLAN
AT e

½ PLAN
AT j

½ PLAN
AT k

½ PLAN
AT l

19'.1"

F PLAN AT m

A. S. James, Piccadilly, London: interior looking W. (1682–4). See p. 914

B. S. Bride, Fleet Street, London: interio looking E. (1671–8). See p. 913

C. S. Clement Danes, Strand, London: interior looking W. (1680–2). See p. 914

D. S. Magnus-the-Martyr, London Bridge interior looking E. (1671–6). See p. 914

A. S. Mary-at-Hill, London
(1670–6). See p. 914

B. S. Mary Abchurch, London (1681–6).
See p. 914

C. S. Lawrence Jewry,
London (1671–7):
vestry. See pp. 914, 974

D. The Banqueting Hall (Orangery), Kensington
Gardens, London (1704). See p. 928

E. S. Stephen, Walbrook,
London (1672–9):
pulpit. See p. 913

F. Trinity College, Cambridge: library
(1676–84). See p. 914

A. Trinity College, Cambridge: Nevile's Court, looking towards the Library
(1676–84). See pp. 882, 914

B. Trinity College Chapel, Oxford
(1691–4). See p. 914

C. Queen's College, Oxford: library
(1693–6). See p. 914

A. Hampton Court Palace: aerial view from S.E. See pp. 459, 914

B. Portico   C. Chapel
Royal Hospital, Chelsea (1682–91). See p. 914

A. S. Martin, Ludgate, London
(1677–84). See p. 914

B. S. Clement Danes, London
(Tower 1680–2, steeple 1719–20).
See p. 914

C. Custom House, King's Lynn
(1683). See p. 928

D. Temple Bar, Strand, London:
looking E. (1672). See p. 928

Buildings by Sir Christopher Wren: an imaginative composition made by C. R. Cockerell in 1841. (See pp. 871, 906 and overleaf.) Not all these buildings are now ascribed to Wren

A. S. Paul's Cathedral
B. Christ Ch., Newgate St.
C. S. Bride, Fleet Street
D. S. Martin, Ludgate

E. Greenwich Hospital
F. Winchester Palace
G. S. Mary Aldermary
H. The Monument, London
I. Chelsea Hospital

J. S. Michael, Cornhill
K. S. Margaret, Lothbury
L. S. Magnus, London Bridge
M. S. Stephen, Walbrook

N. S. Dunstan in the East
P. S. Augustine, Watling St.
Q. S. Edmund, Lombard St.
R. S. Mary-le-Bow, Cheapside
V. S. Michael Paternoster
    Royal

S. Tom Tower, Oxford
T. S. Nicholas Cole Abbey
U. Hampton Court Palace

W. Temple Bar
X. Sheldonian Theatre, Oxford
Y. S. Mary Somerset (Tower)
Z. Library, Trinity College,
    Cambridge

Complete outline key to the buildings by Sir Christopher Wren shown on the previous page. Not all these buildings are now ascribed to Wren

1. S. Paul's Cathedral	13. S. Peter's, Cornhill	24. Tower of Edem	34. Doctors' Commons	44. S. Michael's, Cornhill	55. Old Mansion House,
2. Chichester	14. S. Michael's, Wood Street	25. S. Michael, Queenhithe	35. Temple Bar	45. S. George's, Botolph Lane	Cheapside
3. St. Bride's Church	15. All Hallow's, Bread Street	26. Laurence Pountney Hill	36. S. Margaret Pattens	46. Morden College	56. S. Matthew's, Friday St.
4. Westminster Abbey	16. S. Michael, Queenhithe	27. S. James's, Piccadilly	37. S. Mary Aldermary	47. Old Custom House	57. S. James's, Garlick Hill
5. S. Vedast, Foster Lane	17. Marlborough House	28. S. Benet, Paul's Wharf	38. S. Mary-le-Bow	48. Chelsea Hospital	58. Sheldonian Theatre
6. Christ's Church	18. S. Martin's, Ludgate	29. Buckingham House	39. Great Pillar or Monument	49. S. Margaret's, Lothbury	59. Trinity College Chapel,
7 & 8. All Souls, Oxford	19. Royal Hospital, Greenwich	30. Hampton Court Palace	40. Greenwich	50. Christ Church, Oxford	Oxford
9. S. Benets, Gracechurch	20. Winchester Palace	31. S. Nicholas, Cole Abbey	Observatory	51. S. Edmund the King	60. S. Mary Somerset
10. Christ's Hospital	21. S. Dunstan's in the East	32. Colonnade, Hampton	41. S. Anthony, Watling St.	52. College of Physicians	61. Trinity College Library,
11. S. Bartholomew	22. S. Lawrence, Jewry	Court	42. S. Alban's, Wood Street	53. S. Austin	Cambridge
12. S. Magnus-the-Martyr	23. S. Stephen, Walbrook	33. S. Michael Royal	43. S. Andrew's, Holborn	54. S. Benetfink	62. Doctors' Commons

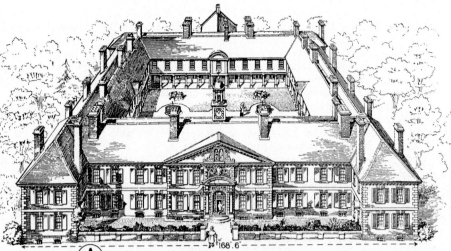

Ⓐ MORDEN COLLEGE : BLACKHEATH : KENT

Ⓑ BUTTER MARKET NARD CASTLE : DURHAM

Ⓒ GARDEN HOUSE POUNDISFORD PARK : SOM.

Ⓓ BUTTER MARKET BUNGAY : SUFFOLK

Ⓔ TOWN HALL : MONMOUTH

Ⓕ TOWN HALL : ABINGDON : BERKS

Greenwich Observatory (1675–6). There is no evidence that he designed **Temple Bar, London** (1672) (pp. 924D, 925W), (now at Theobald's Park, Herts), commonly ascribed to him, which was built by two master-masons, Thomas Knight and Joshua Marshall; and he was only indirectly concerned with the **Orangery, Kensington Gardens** (1704) (p. 921D), probably designed by Vanbrugh (p. 872). Again, there is no documentary proof that Wren had directly anything to do with **Morden College, Blackheath** (1694) (pp. 927A, 966K).

Greenwich Hospital (1696–1715) (pp. 898, 900, 901, 925E) is a magnificent palace scheme devised by Wren to include the Queen's House and King Charles's Block, respectively by Inigo Jones and John Webb (p. 898), with which he incorporated the great court and Queen Anne's Block, and the two intermediate blocks of King William and Queen Mary with the Hall, Chapel, two majestic domes, and fine colonnades.

Winchester Palace (1683–5) (p. 925F), designed by Wren, was left unfinished at the death of Charles II, and burnt down in 1894.

Middle Temple, London; the cloisters in Pump Court (1680–1) (pp. 885, 889A8) (destroyed 1941) were from Wren's design.

Wren appears to have done very little domestic work of modest scale, despite the substantial number of town and country mansions loosely attributed to him. Thus in this connection the course of the Renaissance owed nothing much to his influence, though it was considerable in other directions.

Abingdon Town Hall (1677–80) (p. 927F), with its open market and assembly-room over, is a bold design with pilasters including two storeys, of a character strongly suggesting the influence of Wren.

The **Custom House, King's Lynn** (1683) (p. 924C), by Henry Bell (1653–1717), is an example of effective grouping.

Guildford Town Hall (1682) (p. 971C) is a bold and picturesque building of the period, partly vernacular in that it retains timber-frame structure, with carved brackets supporting the overhanging storey; above are large pedimented windows separated by pilasters, consoled cornice, hexagonal turret and projecting clock with wrought-iron stays.

LATE RENAISSANCE
(GEORGIAN, 1702–1830)

As stated under Architectural Character (p. 872), there was some appearance of an English form of the Baroque between the years 1695–1725, but otherwise the Georgian period may be divided into two phases, Anglo-Palladian, to about 1750, overlapping with the Antiquarian phase thereafter, the latter marked principally by the 'Adam' manner but in which designers tended increasingly to turn to differing ancient models and after 1800 produced not only the 'Regency', natural successor of the Adam style, but also the 'Greek Revival', an early stage of the 'Gothic Revival' (sometimes denoted by the contemporary spelling of 'Gothick'), and certain other expressions.

GEORGIAN HOUSES

We have seen that the course of Renaissance architecture depended largely upon the preferences of individual designers. So far as domestic architecture is concerned, the Low Countries still had continued mainly to be favoured in the Stuart period, influences proceeding therefrom through trade, political expatriates or pattern books. But about 1630 Dutch architecture itself changed to a straightforward Palladianism, expressed in brick with stone dressings, reflected in England after the Restoration in 1660. These fresh influences were in turn assimilated, and

CASTLE HOWARD : YORKSHIRE

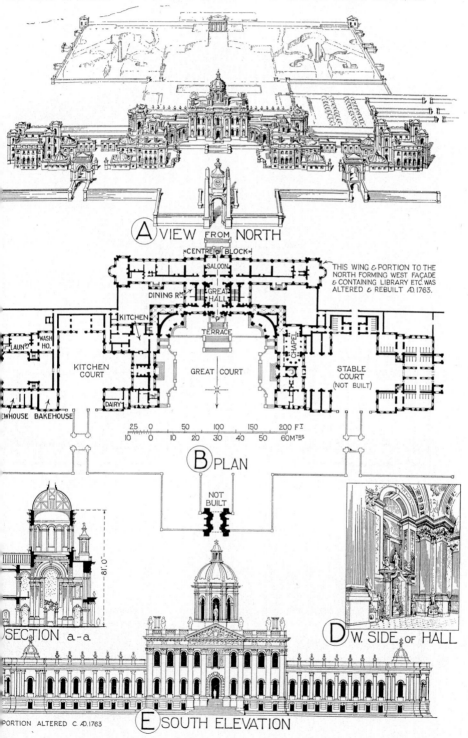

Ⓐ VIEW FROM NORTH

CENTRE ⌀ BLOCK
SALOON

THIS WING & PORTION TO THE
NORTH FORMING WEST FAÇADE
& CONTAINING LIBRARY ETC. WAS
ALTERED & REBUILT AD. 1763.

DINING RM
GREAT HALL

KITCHEN

WASH HO.

LAUN?

TERRACE

CHAPEL

KITCHEN COURT

GREAT COURT

STABLE COURT (NOT BUILT)

DAIRY

EWHOUSE BAKEHOUSE

25 0   50   100   150   200 Fᵀ
10 0   10   20   30   40   50   60Mᵀᴿˢ

Ⓑ PLAN

NOT BUILT

18'.0"

SECTION a-a

Ⓓ W. SIDE of HALL

PORTION ALTERED C. AD.1763

Ⓔ SOUTH ELEVATION

BLENHEIM PALACE : OXON

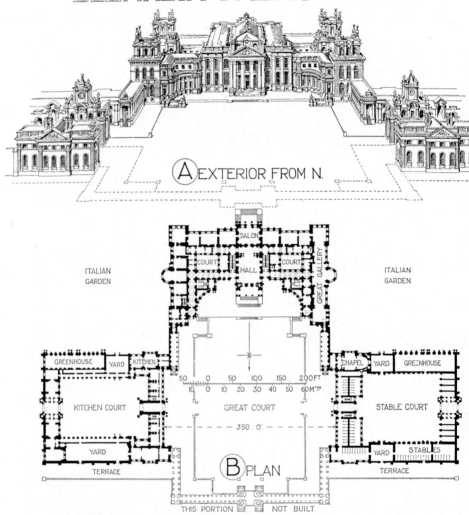

Ⓐ EXTERIOR FROM N.

ITALIAN GARDEN

ITALIAN GARDEN

SALON

COURT

HALL

COURT

GREAT GALLERY

GREENHOUSE   YARD   KITCHEN

CHAPEL   YARD   GREENHOUSE

KITCHEN COURT

STABLE COURT

50   0   50   100   150   200 FT

10   0   10   20   30   40   50   60 M.TRS

GREAT COURT

YARD

YARD   STABLES

— 350·0 —

TERRACE

Ⓑ PLAN

TERRACE

THIS PORTION   NOT BUILT

Ⓒ GREAT HALL

Ⓓ EXTERIOR FROM S.E.

by the present period an English national character was being firmly established. There was a great expansion in domestic building. Mansions for the aristocracy grew more numerous, if progressively less grand in scale, but the really significant increase was in the houses of the middle and inferior classes. Already before 1800, villas were being erected on the fringes of towns, and even humble cottages mostly had achieved lasting form. In towns, terrace building in rows, a mark of the Industrial Revolution, became an increasingly common practice, in turn for the rich, the citizen proper, and at length, the artisan and labourer.

Eighteenth-century mansions were of two types, essentially similar, and differing chiefly in their scale and pretensions.

(a) *The central block with wings.* This type of plan now begins to denote the greatest houses, in place of the more modest E- and H-shaped plans of the previous period. It is a type deriving from Palladio, first used in England at Stoke Bruerne Park, Northants, by Inigo Jones (p. 905); it remains popular until towards the end of the eighteenth century. The central block has a basement storey, not necessarily below ground, often containing kitchen and domestic offices. The principal floor, with its columned portico, reached by imposing external steps, was devoted to the hall, grand staircase, saloon, and reception rooms, which were usually of noble proportions. On either side, colonnades, quite often quadrant in form, connected the central block to the wings, which sometimes contained the chapel, library, kitchens, and stables. All the component parts, whether central block, pedimented portico, wings, or colonnades, were designed to give scale and dignity expressing the greatness of England's noble families.

Castle Howard, Yorkshire (1699–1712) (p. 929), by Sir John Vanbrugh, an outstanding figure of the English Baroque, assisted by Nicholas Hawksmoor, is a stately palace (p. 929A) possessing many of the general features already alluded to, with a total length of 660 ft. Externally, it has that boldness of advance and recession and the richness of expression which are the hall-marks of the Baroque in whatever country it is found, though here the total effect is somewhat massive and ponderous, as critics of the time were not slow to point out. The plan (p. 929B) shows a central block, with north entrance to the great hall, 34 ft square, which is crowned by a dome and flanked by staircases. The saloon beyond, on the central axis, faces the garden, and on either side are the principal rooms. Curved arcades connect the main building with the stable court on the west and the kitchen court on the east. The hall (p. 929C, D) forms a stately vestibule, with its Composite Order, statues in niches, and arched openings admitting light from the central dome to the main staircases. The **Mausoleum** in the grounds, with its circular plan and external periphery of Doric columns (1729–) was designed by Hawksmoor working alone, he himself having the same Baroque preferences.

Blenheim Palace, Oxfordshire (1705–20) (pp. 930, 933A, 934A) by Sir John Vanbrugh, is again Baroque and the most monumental mansion in England. It was given by the nation to the first Duke of Marlborough. The plan (p. 930B) (850 ft long) is designed on axial lines in which symmetry rather than convenience is aimed at. A bold entrance gate led to a great court, three acres in extent, beyond which is the central block, with hall, saloon, internal courts for light, and numerous corridors, while on the west is the great gallery, 180 ft by 22 ft. Right and left on the entrance façade are quadrants and colonnades which connect the main building to the kitchen and stable courts. The great hall (p. 930C), 70 ft long by 45 ft wide and 67 ft high, forms a worthy approach to the saloon and state apartments. The exterior (p. 930A), with its imposing Corinthian portico, embraces two storeys, flanked by quadrants, and there are four angle turrets to the main structure, all set amidst fine formal gardens. The garden façade, 320 ft long, is more delicate in treatment than the ponderous but imposing entrance façade, satirized by the Rev. Abel Evans, an Oxford don, in his reference to Vanbrugh.

> Lie heavy on him earth, for he
> Laid many a heavy load on thee.

Seaton Delaval, Northumberland (1720–8) (p. 934B, D), by Sir John Vanbrugh, is a smaller but splendid example of English Baroque, in which bold use is made of rustication, extended to the shafts of the Doric Order in the porticoes. The building was gutted by fire in 1822. The wings here again flank a great forecourt, having the kitchen and stable courts on their outer sides.

Holkham Hall, Norfolk (1734–) (pp. 934E, 966J), designed by William Kent in collaboration with Lord Burlington and the owner, Thomas Coke, Earl of Leicester, but executed by Matthew Brettingham (1699–1769), is a representative mansion of Palladian character in the present class. Unlike Vanbrugh's principal houses, the plan (p. 966J) shows no deliberate framing of the entrance court by the wings, which here number four instead of two and give symmetrical elevations on all four fronts. A grand feature of the central block is the hall, adorned by Ionic colonnades which turn in an apse to enclose an axial flight of steps rising to the 'piano nobile' or principal floor; the chief apartments include a stately gallery of three related rooms. Externally (p. 934E) on the south front is the inevitable Palladian portico, while the angles of the main block are raised by attic stories into pavilions, each of which has as a chief feature a 'Venetian' window (p. 970C), of a type deriving from the so-called 'Palladian motif' (p. 738). The elevations in general are typically Palladian in that considerable play of form is contrived by simple means of advance and recession of the planes, which mostly comprise local symmetrical and focalized features though subordinated to the general composition: there is little recourse to identical rhythms in the fenestration as a means of binding the elements visually together. The similarity of the Holkham exterior to that of the Horse Guards, Whitehall (p. 958A), also by Kent, is noteworthy.

Other Palladian mansions with wing blocks are **Ditchley, Oxon** (1720–5) by James Gibbs, who formerly had been an exponent of the Baroque; **Moor Park, Herts** (c. 1720), by Sir James Thornhill (1675–1734), of which the wings were rebuilt by Robert Adam in 1763 and demolished c. 1785; **Houghton Hall, Norfolk** (1722–6) (p. 935B) by Colin Campbell; **Prior Park, Bath** (1735–48) (pp. 933B, 935D), by John Wood the elder, the grounds of which contain a delightful version of the Palladian bridge (perhaps by 'Capability' Brown, c. 1765) originated by Roger Morris at Wilton House, Wilts (p. 905); **Wentworth Woodhouse, Yorkshire,** as remodelled from the dull and tasteless designs of Henry Flitcroft, c. 1735; **Buckland House, Berks** (1755–7) (p. 966L), by John Wood the younger, which has a central block on the model of his father's Prior Park, Bath, with corridors right and left leading to the octagonal chapel and library; and **Harewood House, Yorkshire** (1759–71) (p. 936E), by John Carr of York, which in some sense is transitional to the next phase, since substantial amendments by Robert Adam were incorporated in the design, and Adam was responsible for the interior. John Carr designed and built the adjacent Harewood village.

Kedleston Hall, Derbyshire (pp. 936C, D, 939) was designed by James Paine and its erection supervised by Matthew Brettingham between 1757–61, but Robert and James Adam succeeded them and completed the work, including the south front, the saloon, and the interior decoration as a whole (c. 1765–70). It is thus, like Harewood House, Yorkshire, partly Palladian, yet in many respects the whole building exhibits the Antiquarian tendency. The plan (p. 939D) consists of a central block, 135 ft by 105 ft, having on its principal floor the great hall, 66 ft by 42 ft, and

A. Blenheim Palace, Oxfordshire: aerial view from S.W. (1705–20). See p. 931

B. Prior Park, Bath: view from E. (1735–48). See opposite page

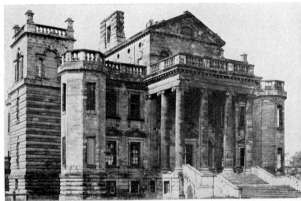

A. Blenheim Palace,
Oxfordshire (1705–20):
gateway in east wing.
See p. 931

B. Seaton Delaval, Northumberland: south front
(c. 1720–8). See p. 932

C. Flint Cottage, Box Hill,
Surrey (18th cent.). See p. 938

D. Seaton Delaval, Northumberland: north front.
See p. 932

E. Holkham Hall, Norfolk: south front (1734–). See p. 932

A. Stowe House, Buckingham: south front (1771–9). See p. 937

B. Houghton Hall, Norfolk (1722–6). See p. 932

C. Heaton Hall, Lancashire (1772–). See p. 937

D. Prior Park, Bath: the Mansion (1735–48) with Palladian Bridge (c. 1765) in foreground. See pp. 932, 979

A. Mereworth Castle, Kent (1722–5).
See p. 938

B. Chiswick House, Chiswick, Middlese
(1725–). See p. 938

C. Aerial view from S.W.

D. Hall (1765–70)

Kedleston Hall, Derbyshire (1757–70). See p. 932

E. Harewood House, Yorks: aerial view from S. (1759–71). See p. 932

saloon on the central axis, with drawing-room and other apartments on either side. Quadrant corridors connect the main building with the kitchen and private wings, the southern wings, which would have completed a general likeness to the Holkham Hall, Norfolk, plan, were not carried out. The hall (pp. 936D, 939C, E) is a most imposing apartment, being the whole height of the mansion and having the appearance of an ancient basilica, with colonnades of alabaster Corinthian columns, 25 ft high, surmounted by a coved ceiling in the Adam style, while the walls have statue niches. The drawing-room is a fine example of Adam's style. The general lay-out (p. 939A) shows the usual basement storey, the external steps to the principal floor, with its fine Corinthian portico, and on either side are the wings, which being lower, give scale and importance to the central block. The south front (p. 939B), by Adam, is treated in lighter vein with curved steps to the garden.

Further examples of the mansion with linked wings in the second half of the eighteenth century, during which time the type was becoming rare, are **Mersham-le-Hatch, Kent** (1762–5), by Robert Adam, for once wholly from his designs, for so many of his country domestic works were remodellings; **Wardour Castle, Wilts** (1770–6), in James Paine's half Palladian style; **Heaton Hall, Lancashire** (1772) (p. 935C), and **Castlecoole, Co. Fermanagh, Ireland** (1790–7), both by James Wyatt, rival of Adam; and **Stowe House, Buckingham**, where the south front (1771–9) (p. 935A) was a remodelling from the designs of Robert Adam, carried out by J. B. Borra and others. The grounds of Stowe, where the famous 'Capability' Brown first developed his art as a landscape gardener, are exceedingly rich in garden temples and other ornamental buildings, variously by Sir John Vanbrugh, James Gibbs, William Kent and Giacomo Leoni, who each contributed a number. Ornamental garden buildings, including bridges, arches, grottoes and the like, were normal embellishments of the grounds of eighteenth-century mansions of whatever type (pp. 902D–F, 929A, 935D, 980D, G). The **Garden House, Poundisford Park** (c. 1675) (p. 927C) near Taunton, Somerset, is an earlier homely and pleasing example.

(b) *The simple block plan.* This type of plan was very generally employed for eighteenth-century houses both in town and country, in which the hall and staircase occupy the centre, while the rooms are compactly disposed on either side. It was developed from the square or oblong block of the previous period as in the **Queen's House, Greenwich** (p. 901E), **Chevening** (p. 966H), **Coleshill** (p. 966C) and **Thorpe Hall** (p. 966M). In the same succession is the simple **Moot House, Downton** (1650, remodelled 1720) (p. 941A), with brick walls, stone quoins, pedimented central feature, sash windows and wooden cornice, crowned with a hipped roof. Early eighteenth-century examples built as a whole are **Eagle House, Mitcham, Surrey** (c. 1700) (p. 941B); **Mompasson House, Salisbury** (1701) (pp. 941C, 966A, 971B,L) and **Fenton House, Hampstead** (p. 966D). **Swan House, Chichester** (1711) (p. 940A) is characteristic of the smaller Georgian houses of the middle classes, with a basement for kitchen, stores and servants' quarters. Such eighteenth-century houses sometimes have stone but usually brick walling of neat, fine-jointed brickwork in Flemish bond, which universally replaces English bond except in certain parts of the north. Projecting angle quoins of stone or brick tend to disappear, but frequently are substituted by flush quoins in brickwork of a second colour. Symmetrically disposed sash windows, at first with heavy sash-bars, are normal for all but cottages, where casements often are retained, and there are columned or architecturally enframed doorways, bold crowning cornices, dormered and hipped roofs of which the pitch grows more flat as thin slates come into general use, and large chimney stacks, which continue for some time to be a feature of the more ostentatious designs. The type lingered on for many decades, with only moderate changes of external detail, which nevertheless is regularly significant of the passage of time, while there were similar progressive developments in internal planning. Every old provincial town furnishes examples of these quiet and dignified houses, often now occupied by professional men. Innovations of whatever character took time to pass down from the more opulent houses to the smallest, so that a lapse of more than twenty-five years might occur in the process.

Flint Cottage, near Box Hill, Surrey (p. 934C) is a typical example of the smallest type of house above the cottage scale, of an almost standard character found in all parts of the country.

Turning again to the principal houses, source of the innovations which determined the trend of development of the lesser dwellings just referred to, we find the Palladian movement affecting the compact type in the earlier part of the century.

Mereworth Castle, Kent (*c.* 1722–5) (pp. 936A, 966G), by Colin Campbell, is based very closely on the Villa Capra at Vicenza (p. 742), by Palladio, whose precepts the English Palladian followed with slavish zeal. The elevations are the same on all four fronts, and the principal apartments are ranged around a great circular hall, 35 ft in diameter, crowned by a dome which commands the whole composition. Chimney flues ascend the shell of the dome, and meagre circular windows afford the only natural light which the hall receives. The kitchen and offices are in the basement, which is only partially below ground. Two separate pavilions flank the main entrance front, the one containing bedrooms and the other stables.

Chiswick House, Chiswick (1725–) (p. 936B), by Lord Burlington and William Kent, is a second and better version of the Villa Capra, Vicenza, having again the raised 'podium' sustaining the principal apartments, these ranged around a high, domed hall, the dome being octagonal and having arched windows in the drum. This type of plan is not well suited to the English climate, but was also followed in **Nuthall Temple, Notts,** a house designed by Thomas Wright in 1754 (demolished 1923). Chiswick House has only one grand portico and impressive flights of entrance steps.

Wrotham Park, South Mimms, Middlesex (*c.* 1754) by Isaac Ware, and **Spencer House, London** (1756–65) by John Vardy, are later and less extreme examples of the English Palladian style.

The **Casino at Marino,** near Dublin (p. 970E) designed by Sir William Chambers in 1759 and built in 1769, is a dwelling in miniature, neatly contained in a Greek-cross plan. The design was originally intended for an end pavilion at Harewood House, Yorkshire, and is a fine early example of the Antiquarian phase.

From mid-century onwards, a small but increasing proportion of houses show departures from the compact rectilinear plan, being looser or even asymmetrical, particularly those which ape non-Classical models. **Strawberry Hill, Twickenham** (p. 944A), 'Gothick' plaything of Horace Walpole (p. 875), an accretion from 1747–1776 in which a number of designers had a hand, is of this class, as also is a hall (1753–5) at **Lacock Abbey, Wilts,** by Sanderson Millar, another instance of flimsy Gothic.

Syon House, Isleworth, Middlesex, a square-planned Jacobean house remodelled 1762–9 by Robert Adam, affords some of the finest instances of his methods of interior decoration (p. 942A, B), while **Osterley Park, Middlesex** (p. 942C), a similar remodelling (1761–80) by the brothers Adam, and **Luton Hoo, Beds** (1768–75), wholly built by Robert but reconstructed in later times, are other examples of Adam domestic works. Later houses of the same class include **Althorp, Northants** (p. 944C), reconstructed internally and cased externally (1787–9) in white 'mathematical tiles' (these are brick-tiles nailed to timber, brick, stone or flint walls through a flange which is hidden when the tiles are mortared into position, giving a

KEDLESTON HALL : DERBYSHIRE

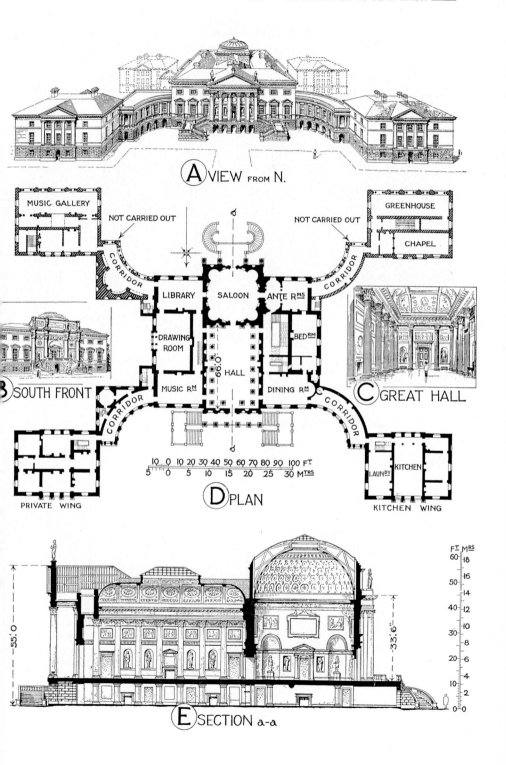

Ⓐ VIEW FROM N.

MUSIC GALLERY

NOT CARRIED OUT

CORRIDOR

GREENHOUSE

NOT CARRIED OUT

CHAPEL

CORRIDOR

LIBRARY   SALOON   ANTE Rᴹˢ

BED Rᴹ

DRAWING ROOM

66.0

HALL

Ⓑ SOUTH FRONT

MUSIC Rᴹ   DINING Rᴹ

Ⓒ GREAT HALL

CORRIDOR

CORRIDOR

PRIVATE WING

10 0 10 20 30 40 50 60 70 80 90 100 Fᵀ
5 0 5 10 15 20 25 30 Mᵀᴿˢ

Ⓓ PLAN

LAUNDʸ KITCHEN

KITCHEN WING

55.0

33.6"

Fᵀ Mᴿˢ
60 18
50 16
   14
40 12
   10
30 8
20 6
   4
10 2
0 0

Ⓔ SECTION a-a

A SWAN HOUSE: CHICHESTER

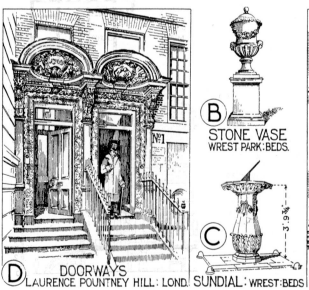

D DOORWAYS
LAURENCE POUNTNEY HILL: LOND.

B STONE VASE
WREST PARK: BEDS.

C SUNDIAL: WREST: BEDS

E DOORWAY
RAYNHAM HALL: NORFOLK

A. The Moot House, Downton,
Wilts (1650; remodelled 1720).
See p. 937

B. Eagle House, Mitcham, Surrey
(c. 1700). See p. 937

C. Mompasson House, Salisbury (1701). See p. 937

A. Ante-room to hall   B. Long gallery

Syon House, Middlesex (1762–9). See p. 938

C. Osterley Park, Middlesex (c. 1575; remodelled 1761–80). See p. 938

A. Home House, 20, Portman Sq., London: music room (1775–7). See p. 949

B. Heveningham Hall, Suffolk: saloon (1788–99). See p. 948

A. Strawberry Hill, Twickenham (1747–76). See p. 938

C. Althorp, Northants: house recased in white brick-tile (1787–9). See p. 938

B. Ashridge Park, Herts (1803–13): hall and staircase. See p. 948

D. Cronkhill, Salop (c. 1802). See p. 948

A. Fonthill Abbey, Wiltshire (1796–1807). See p. 948

B. Culzean Castle, Ayrshire (1777–90). See p. 948

A. Bath, Somerset: aerial view showing Circus and Royal Crescent (1754–75).
See pp. 874, 948

B. The Mansion House, London (1739–52). See p. 948

oane Museum, London
1812-13). See p. 949

B. Cumberland Terrace, Regent's Park, London (c. 1827).
See p. 949

. Ely House, London
(c. 1772). See p. 948

D. Royal Pavilion, Brighton (1815–21): centre part of E. front.
See p. 948

very convincing cheap imitation of brickwork), by Henry Holland; **Heveningham Hall, Suffolk** (1778–99), begun by Sir Robert Taylor and completed after his death by James Wyatt, which shows Wyatt's interior decoration at its best (p. 943B) and as being very similar to that of Adam; **Dodington Park, Glos** (1798–1808), by James Wyatt, designed in a style tinctured with the Greek, then coming into popular favour; and **Stratton Park, Hants,** comprehensively remodelled in 1803–6 by George Dance II, wholly in Greek Revival mode.

Meanwhile there were further stages of advance towards the Gothic Revival, in houses often less compact in plan than those of Classical design, or even deliberately irregular. Such are **Downton Castle, Shropshire** (1774–8), by Richard Payne Knight, forerunner of the Picturesque movement which affected all styles from about twenty years later; **Culzean Castle, Ayrshire** (1777–90) (p. 945B) a massive symmetrical structure by Robert Adam; **Luscombe Castle, Devonshire** (1800–4), by John Nash, of more intimate and varied character; and **Lowther Castle, Westmorland** (1806–11), by Sir Robert Smirke, all in towered, castellated Gothic, a type of design which remained popular for country houses for several decades after 1790. More ornate, yet a definite improvement upon Strawberry Hill, were **Lee Priory, Kent** (1783–90); **Fonthill Abbey, Wilts** (1796–1807) (p. 945A), a brilliantly romantic pile of cruciform plan with wide-flung arms, but so flimsily constructed that the central tower, 278 ft high, collapsed in 1807; and **Ashridge Park, Herts** (1803–13) (p. 944C), all three from the designs of James Wyatt. **Eaton Hall, Cheshire** (1804–12, remodelled 1870), by William Porden, was a remarkably elaborate and spiky version of the Gothic, with traceried windows, ornamental battlements, and pinnacled buttresses and angle turrets. Extraordinarily decorative were two mansions in 'Indian' style, **Sezincote House, Glos** (c. 1803–15) by S. P. Cockerell and the **Royal Pavilion, Brighton** (1815–21) (p. 947D), an extensive remodelling by John Nash, with wonderfully rich interior decorations of a Chinese character eked out with Gothic. John Nash also was largely instrumental in bringing sophistication to cottage architecture, and in developing the Picturesque manner in urban and suburban villas, variously using the vernacular, Gothic or Italianate styles. **Cronkhill, Salop** (c. 1802) (p. 944D), is an instance of the last.

GEORGIAN TOWN HOUSES

Restrictions of site did not usually permit the town house to have the extended treatment practicable in the country, and though circumstances sometimes allowed them to be freestanding, the house confined between others was now the most common.

Among town houses of Palladian character, the **Mansion House, London** (1739–52) (p. 946B), by George Dance I, is exceptional in that it was built as a mayoral residence to be occupied during terms of office, and thus has the qualities of a public building. **No. 44, Berkeley Square, London** (1742–4), by William Kent, a terrace house, developed in depth, is more representative. The idea of organizing terrace houses in palatial or unified schemes became widespread at this time. The Woods, father and son, created their splendid frontages at **Bath** (p. 946A); **Queen Square,** north side (1729–), **South Parade** (1743–) and the famous **Circus** (1754–) by John Wood I, and the **Royal Crescent** (1767–75) by John Wood II. The **Crescent, Buxton, Derbyshire** (1779–81), by John Carr of York, followed the Woods' inspiration. Palladianism continued to be popular for town houses well into the second half of the century. **Chesterfield House, South Audley Street, London** (1766, demolished 1937), by Isaac Ware, and **Ely House, Dover Street, London** (1772) (p. 947C), by Sir Robert Taylor, with its well-contrived and dignified front, are instances.

The Antiquarian phase is represented by many fine houses, including a number in London by Robert Adam: **Lansdowne House, Berkeley Square** (1762–8, now altered), **No. 20, S. James's Square** (1772–4), **Apsley House, Piccadilly** (c. 1775, also altered) and **Home House, No. 20, Portman Square** (1775–7; now the Courtauld Institute) with some splendid interior decoration (p. 943A). Adam also carried out a considerable venture at the **Adelphi, London** (1768–72), a speculative undertaking which failed and of which very little now is left, and a scheme for **Charlotte Square, Edinburgh** (1791, built 1792–1807). Henry Holland developed **Hans Town, Chelsea** (1771–), covering a number of streets, but of which only a house or two remain, and built individual houses such as **Carlton House, Pall Mall, London** (1783–5, demolished 1827) and **Dover House, Whitehall** (1787). **No. 13, Lincoln's Inn Fields** (1812–13) (p. 947A), by Sir John Soane, is now the Soane Museum, housing a collection of drawings, antiquities and works of art which he left to the nation. The most extensive work of the whole career of the prolific John Nash was his grand scheme of civic design for frontages extending through Regent St., London, to Regent's Park. The **Quadrant, Regent Street** (1818–20) was rebuilt between 1906–23, but much remains of the terraces of houses (1821–30) facing the Park, one of the best being **Cumberland Terrace** (c. 1827) (p. 947B).

Georgian Churches

A number of churches of this period were designed by followers of Wren, whose influence was paramount, with central space and surrounding galleries, suitable for the preaching requirements of the Protestant faith. The first to be noted are several having a character as nearly approaching the Baroque as was ever achieved in ecclesiastical architecture in Renaissance England.

S. Mary Woolnoth, London (1716–26) (p. 951A), by Nicholas Hawksmoor, who had been assistant both to Wren and Vanbrugh, is remarkable for its fortress-like rusticated façade and curious oblong tower with Composite columns surmounted by two low turrets, forming a very original treatment. It was one of six built by him under the Act of 1711 for the erection of fifty new churches (only a dozen materialized), others of his being **S. Alphege, Greenwich** (1712–14, later steeple); **S. Anne, Limehouse** (1712–14, restored 1851) (p. 951D); **S. George-in-the-East** (1715–23, gutted 1941); **S. George, Bloomsbury** (1720–30) (p. 951B), with a pyramidal spire; and **Christ Church, Spitalfields** (1723–9) (p. 951C), having a lofty and unusual steeple. **S. Philip, Birmingham** (1709–25) (p. 952A), now the Cathedral, instances the strong Baroque leanings of its gifted designer, Thomas Archer. The much-weathered western tower, with its concave sides, is unique in the country. A chancel was added in 1883–4. Similar though less pungent qualities are observable in two of the 'fifty churches' by Archer; **S. Paul, Deptford** (1712–30), a compact, centralized structure with a western spire and a columned semicircular porch embracing its base, and **S. John, Westminster** (1714–28, gutted 1742 and again in 1941), a less attractive composition. The influence of Archer was traceable in **S. Paul, Sheffield** (1720–1, demolished 1937), by John Platt I, an attractive composition with a western tower completed by a nephew, John Platt II, in 1769.

S. Mary-le-Strand, London (1714–17) (p. 952B), by James Gibbs, another of the 'fifty churches', shows evidence of his studies in Rome, where he had been a pupil of Carlo Fontana (pp. 726, 873), but although it is florid it is not of thorough-paced Baroque character. Situated conspicuously on an island site in the Strand, it is notable for its fine general proportions, with façades of superimposed Ionic and Corinthian Orders, a semicircular portico and storeyed western steeple, oblong on plan.

S. George, Hanover Square, London (1712–25) (p. 952C), by John James, yet another of the 'fifty churches', is progressive in many ways while being massive and indecisively Baroque in external character. Its ponderous Corinthian portico, 70 ft long, serves as a shelter in connection with the numerous weddings solemnized within. Here for the first time is found a steeple rising from the roof, without apparent support from the ground. **S. Martin-in-the-Fields, London** (1722–6) (p. 952D), by James Gibbs, shows the developing mature manner of the architect after he had tempered his Baroque inclinations and adopted a more orthodox style, based on the characteristic work of Wren yet paying deference to current English-Palladian trends. Here, all the rich architectural features are a logical expression of the plan. A straightforward rectangular building, roofed from end to end, it has a great Corinthian portico approached by a broad flight of steps and a western steeple of singular beauty. Gibbs also designed (1719–20) the upper part of the steeple of Wren's **S. Clement Danes** (p. 914).

S. Giles-in-the-Fields, London (1731–4), is by Henry Flitcroft, protégé of Lord Burlington, the architect being both designer and contractor for the building. It is an impoverished version of S. Martin-in-the-Fields, except that its steeple is at the side and not on the axis at the west.

Mistley Church, Essex (1776, demolished 1870 except for its twin east and west towers) (p. 953A), by Robert Adam, was one of the remarkably few wholly new churches built in the latter part of the century. Expressed in typical Adam manner, it had a quite unorthodox composition with balancing towers at east and west ends and an axial southern Doric-columned entrance portico.

Other churches about this time were **All Hallows-on-the-wall, London** (1765–7), by George Dance II, having admirable internal detail; **All Saints, Newcastle-upon-Tyne** (–1796), by David Stephenson (b. 1757) and **S. Chad, Shrewsbury** (1790–2) (p. 953C), by George Stewart (d. 1806), the latter two with circular naves and storeyed western towers.

Tetbury Church, Gloucestershire (rebuilt 1777–81, except steeple) (p. 953B), by Francis Hiorne, is one of the precursors of the Gothic Revival. The nave is dull externally but internally amazingly light and delicate, with slender piers of lapping timbers which carry nothing but a timber shell-vault, for the roof is supported from the side walls.

S. George, Liverpool (1812–14), by Thomas Rickman is the earliest of about forty-seven churches built by this influential author-architect, all in the provinces and all but three being in the revived Gothic style. Here, as in other cases, he used cast iron extensively for the structural and decorative elements.

S. Marylebone Parish Church, London (1813–18) (p. 954A), by Thomas Hardwick, was the first London church of importance in the new century. A dignified hexastyle pedimented portico, said to be 'after the Pantheon', fronts a transverse vestibule and stair block carrying a double-tiered, domed spire over a rusticated base. Inside are galleries carried on cast-iron pillars, and there are two vestries set angle-wise to frame the altar, behind which is a mahogany reredos screen, ornamented with Ionic pilasters, carrying the organ. Originally there were private galleries at the sides of the organ, fitted with fireplaces, but these were altered to normal open galleries in 1826.

S. Pancras, London (1819–22) (p. 954B), by William Inwood and his father H. W. Inwood, is the best-known example of the Greek Revival, a fine design based very closely upon the Erechtheion at Athens (p. 133). It has a hexastyle portico, vestries resembling the Caryatid porch and an axial western steeple which is a two-storeyed version of the Tower of the Winds, Athens (p. 140). By the same architects is the less-striking **All Saints, Camden Town** (1822–4), also in Greek Revival style.

A. S. Mary Woolnoth, London
(1716–26). See p. 949

B. S. George, Bloomsbury, London
(1720–30). See p. 949

C. Christ Church, Spitalfields, (1723–9).
See p. 949

D. S. Anne, Limehouse
(1712–14). See p. 949

A. S. Philip, Birmingham (1709–25).
See p. 949

B. S. Mary-le-Strand, London
(1714–17). See p. 949

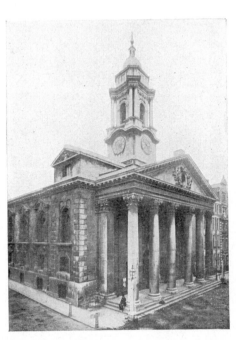

C. S. George, Hanover Square, London
(1712–25). See p. 949

D. S. Martin-in-the-Fields, London
(1722–6). See p. 950

A. Mistley Church, Essex (1776, partly demolished 1870). From an old photograph.
See p. 950

B. Tetbury Church, Glos. (1777–81).
See p. 950

C. S. Chad, Shrewsbury (1790–2).
See p. 950

A. S. Marylebone Parish Church, London (1813–18). See p. 950

B. S. Pancras, London (1819–22). See p. 950

c. S. Luke, Chelsea (1820–4). See p. 955

D. S. Dunstan-in-the-West, London (1831–3). See p. 955

All Souls, Langham Place, London (1822–5), by John Nash, is one of about 230 churches built under the Church Building Act of 1818, devoting one million pounds to providing churches to serve the new populations of expanding towns. It is a simple Bath stone box, of Classical design, elaborated by a western circular Ionic portico from which springs a sharp conical spire, itself having a ring of Corinthian columns at its base, concentric with the portico below but of a reduced diameter.

S. George, Camberwell (1822–4), by Francis Bedford, and **S. Mark, Kennington** (1822–4), by D. R. Roper assisted by A. B. Clayton, are typical churches built for the Commissioners administering the Act of 1818, here expressed in the Greek Revival style, which was strongly favoured in the London area in the years 1821–7, but rarely used thereafter; they are simple rectangular boxes with western, Doric, porticoes and axial, storeyed western towers riding the ridge, over the vestibule.

S. Mary, Wyndham Place, London (1822–4, remodelled internally 1874), by Sir Robert Smirke, has a semicircular columned Ionic portico in a sober Classical style, like the same architect's **S. Philip, Salford, Lancashire** (1822–5, altered 1895).

S. Luke, Chelsea (1820–4) (p. 954C), by James Savage, is the earliest—and one of the best—Commissioner churches in London in the Gothic Revival style, having a nave and aisles forming the usual plain rectangular composition and with an axial tower which here visually reaches the ground to contain the principal portal of the western entrance porch. It is unusual for its class in having vaults over the nave, with flying buttresses spanning the aisles. **Holy Trinity, Bordesley, Birmingham** (1820–3), by Francis Goodwin, is a provincial example without a tower.

S. Dunstan-in-the-West, Fleet Street, London (1831–3) (p. 954D), by John Shaw I and his son, John Shaw II, not a Commissioner church, shows a fine treatment of a town church with a steeple in imitation of 'Boston Stump'.

GEORGIAN PUBLIC BUILDINGS

Civic, social, government, and collegiate requirements had all to be provided for during this period. **Town Halls** arose, as at Liverpool (1748–55), by John Wood and son of Bath, at Monmouth, where the Shire Hall (1724) (p. 927E) is a well-balanced building, and at Salisbury, where the Council House (1788–95) is from the designs of Sir Robert Taylor though executed after his death by his pupil W. Pilkington; **Exchanges,** as at Rochester (1766) (p. 957A), Bristol (1741–3), by John Wood I, and Liverpool (1749–95), also by John Wood I but burned and rebuilt (1795–1802) by John Foster, a portico being added in 1811; **Law Courts,** as the 'Four Courts', Dublin (1776–1802, damaged 1922) (p. 957B), by Thomas Cooley and James Gandon; **Custom Houses,** as in London (1813–17) (p. 957D), by David Laing, partly rebuilt by Sir Robert Smirke in 1825, and Dublin (1781–91, damaged 1921) (p. 957E), by James Gandon; **Prisons,** such as Newgate (1770–8, demolished 1902) (p. 958D), by George Dance II; **Hospitals,** such as S. Bartholomew's (1730–, gateway of 1702 by E. Strong), by James Gibbs, S. Luke's Hospital (1782–4), by George Dance II. Many **Banks** were erected in this period throughout the country.

The Bank of England, London (1788–1833), by Sir John Soane, is unique by reason of its windowless façades in which he employed the Corinthian Order as used for the Temple at Tivoli (p. 194), while he obtained light and shade by columned recesses. It was reconstructed (1930–40) by Sir Herbert Baker, rising to a much greater height than formerly, though within the original shell of Soane's façades.

The Banking House, No. 70, Lombard St., London (c. 1756), later the Pelican Life Assurance Office, now demolished, was a scholarly building.

The **Butter Markets,** Barnard Castle (1747) (p. 927B), Bungay (1789) (p. 927D), and Ludlow, are examples of the civic buildings on a smaller scale which abound throughout the country towns, and show the full corporate and commercial life of the period.

Clubs and similar social institutions developed greatly in the period, particularly in the latter part. **The Assembly Rooms, York** (1731-2) (p. 958C), by Lord Burlington, is a fine example of Anglo-Palladian art; the entrance front was re-modelled in 1828 by J. P. Pritchett and W. Watson. Clubs were developed from coffee-houses, which originally were almost indistinguishable from private houses. Examples in London are Almack's Club, S. James's (1764-5, demolished 1863), by Robert Mylne; **Boodle's Club** (1775) (p. 957C), by John Crunden; the Royal Society of Arts (1772-4), by Robert Adam; Brooks's Club (1776-8), by Henry Holland; the 'Pantheon', Oxford St. (1770-2), by James Wyatt, a famous fashion-able resort, eventually demolished (c. 1936) after much reconstruction and change of function; United University Club (1822-6, demolished 1902), by William Wilkins and J. P. Deering; United Service Club (1827, altered later), by John Nash; Athenaeum Club (1827-30, attic 1899), by Decimus Burton; and the **Travellers' Club** (1829-31), by Sir Charles Barry (p. 1019), which, as it heralded a Renaissance Revival in England, may best be considered in the following chapter. Barry was also the architect of the Royal Manchester Institution of Fine Arts building (1824-35), now the City Art Gallery, a notable instance of the Greek Revival (p. 1021E). Clubs multiplied in all cities and large towns.

Theatres were liable to rapid change, often due to fire, as Covent Garden, Lon-don (1732), by E. Shepherd, reconstructed (1792) by Henry Holland, rebuilt after a fire (1809-10) by Robert Smirke and A. Copland, and again rebuilt after fire (1857-8) by E. M. Barry; also Drury Lane theatre, London (1672-4), by Wren, refronted (1775-6) by Robert Adam, rebuilt (1791-4) by Henry Holland, rebuilt after fire (1811-12) by B. D. Wyatt, altered (1822) by Samuel Beazley. Beazley (1786-1851) was responsible for much other theatre building in London, and theatres at Bir-mingham (Royal, 1820), Dublin (Royal, 1821, burned 1880), Leamington (Royal Music Hall, 1821) and abroad in South America, Belgium and India.

Hospitals and Almshouses still continued to reflect the wishes of the pious founders, as we have seen in **Morden College, Blackheath** (1694) (p. 928). Many of these buildings date from the seventeenth century, and amongst them may be mentioned Smyth's Almshouses, Lewisham (1664), Bromley College, Kent (1666), Corsham Almshouses (1668), **College of Matrons, Salisbury** (1682) (p. 958B), Trinity Almshouses, Mile End, London (1695), Trinity Almshouses, Salisbury (1702), Fishmongers' Almshouses, Yarmouth (1702), and Somerset Hospital, Petworth (1748).

Government Buildings of the period in London include the Old Admiralty, Whitehall (1723-6), by Thomas Ripley, and its enclosing street screen (1759-61), by Robert Adam; the Treasury Buildings (façade to S. James's Park) (1734-6), and **Horse Guards** (1750-8) (p. 958A), from designs by Kent. The Register House, Edinburgh (1774-92), is by Robert Adam.

Somerset House, London (1776-86, east and west wings completed 1834 and 1856) (p. 960A), by Sir William Chambers, is a grand and dignified building, with a river façade, 600 ft long, in which rusticated walls carry a Corinthian Order rising through two stories, pleasingly relieved by colonnades which emphasize the open courts.

The British Museum, London (1823-47) (p. 962D) by Sir Robert Smirke, con-tinued in building into the Victorian era. Its southern front has an octastyle pedi-mented portico and projecting wings, around which the portico is continued.

Corn Exchange, Rochester
(1766). See p. 955

B. 'Four Courts', Dublin (1776–1802).
See p. 955

Boodle's Club, London
(1775–6). See p. 956

D. The Custom House, London (1813–17).
See p. 955

E. The Custom House, Dublin (1781–91). See p. 955

A. The Horse Guards, Whitehall, London: west façade (1750–8). See p. 956

B. College of Matrons, Salisbury(1682). See p. 956

C. Assembly Rooms, York (1731–2). See p. 956

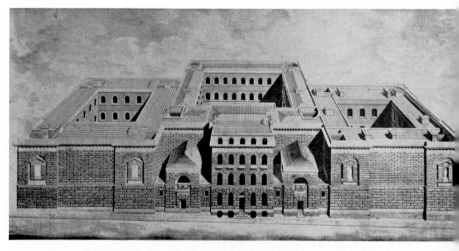

D. Newgate Prison, London (1770–8, demolished 1902). See p. 955

A. Radcliffe Library, Oxford (1737–49). See p. 963

B. Queen's College, Oxford (1709–38): gateway. See p. 963

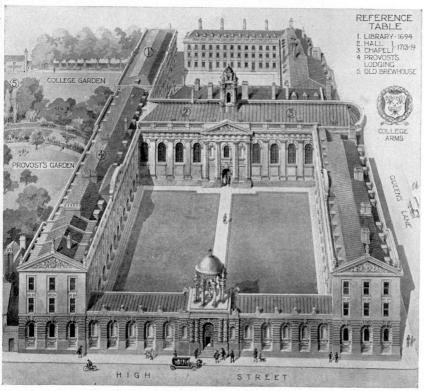

C. Queen's College, Oxford (1709–38): Library by Wren (1693–6). See p. 963

A. Somerset House, London (1776–86): north side of quadrangle (*top*), and waterfront. See p. 956

B. Senate House, Cambridge (1722–30). See p. 963

A. The National Gallery, Trafalgar Square, London (1834–8). See p. 963

B. University College, London (1827–8). See p. 963

A. Radcliffe Observatory, Oxford
(1772–94). See p. 963

B. The Old University Library, Cambridge
(1754–8). See p. 963

C. Guildhall, Worcester
(1721–3). See p. 964

D. The British Museum (1823–47).
See p. 956

E. Triple Archway, Hyde Park Corner, London (c. 1825). See p. 963

The massive and impressive scale of the Greek Ionic Order is impaired by over-reiteration of the columns. The domed reading room, 140 ft in diameter, was added (1854–7) by Sydney Smirke. The General Post Office (1824–9), by the same architect, also a Greek Revival building in the Ionic Order, was demolished in 1912.

The National Gallery, London (1834–8) (p. 961A), by William Wilkins, occupies a magnificent position in Trafalgar Square, which it fails to command, in spite of its excellent detail. Its southern façade is much broken into pavilions and parts, which insufficiently subscribe to the central octastyle Corinthian portico, pedimented and crowned with an inadequate dome, while the principal floor is raised upon a high podium, which appears to diminish the effective height.

Ornamental buildings in London include the Marble Arch (c. 1825), by John Nash, built to front the architect's half-realized scheme for Buckingham Palace, and moved to its present position at the north-east corner of Hyde Park in 1847. Also connected with the scheme for Buckingham Palace was the arch on Constitution Hill (1828), a composition by Decimus Burton similar to the Arch of Titus, Rome (p. 222), in the Composite Order. It is not now in its original position, its alignment having been changed in 1883 from one axial with the nearby magnificent **Ionic screen at Hyde Park** south-east corner (c. 1825) (p. 962E), a Greek Revival masterpiece which Decimus Burton had intended to be a complementary feature.

Collegiate buildings received many important additions, and numerous effective examples of the period are to be seen in the universities.

The Radcliffe Library, Oxford (1737–49) (pp. 475A, 959A), by J. Gibbs—probably his finest work—is monumental in character, with a rusticated sixteen-sided ground storey, having alternately pedimented arch openings and niches, while the upper portion is circular, 100 ft in diam., with two storeys of windows and niches included in one Order of coupled Corinthian columns, supporting entablature and balustrade, behind which a high drum with eight buttresses supports the lead-covered dome.

Queen's College, Oxford (1709–38) (pp. 475A, 959B), by Nicholas Hawksmoor, a pupil of Wren, is a fine example of a late Renaissance college with its quadrangle, hall, and chapel, and the library designed by Wren (p. 922) with a dignified Order. The gateway (p. 959B, C) is an effective composition with an archway flanked by Tuscan columns and entablature, surmounted by an open cupola, enclosing a statue of Queen Caroline.

The **Clarendon Building, Oxford** (1712–15) (p. 475A), by Hawksmoor, is a pleasing structure with a fine Doric portico.

The **Senate House, Cambridge** (1722–30) (pp. 475B, 960B), is by James Gibbs. Two storeys are included in a single Order of Corinthian pilasters, coupled at ends, and centre-piece of four half-columns surmounted by a sculptured pediment, flanked by balustrades, while the sash windows of the ground storey are headed by alternately triangular and segmental pediments, the upper windows being round-headed. The whole has a unity of composition and is rich yet reposeful in effect.

Among collegiate buildings of this period may be mentioned: at **Oxford** (p. 475A), Worcester College (planned c. 1720, Hawksmoor participating), the **Radcliffe Observatory** (1772–94) (p. 962A), by Henry Keene and James Wyatt, and the North Quadrangle, All Souls College (1715–40), by Hawksmoor. At **Cambridge** (p. 475B), the **Old University Library** (1754–8) (p. 962B), by Stephen Wright, and Downing College (1807–20), an early instance of the Greek Revival by Wilkins. Trinity College, Dublin (1752–98), was altered by Chambers, and Edinburgh University (1789–91) is substantially by Robert Adam, completed (1815–34) by W. H. Playfair. **University College, London** (1827–8) (p. 961B), by William Wilkins, assisted by J. P. Deering, is a fine Greek Revival design with an axial Corinthian portico with

2H

dome over (destroyed 1941, rebuilt 1950), elevated on a high podium and approached by grand flights of steps.

The **Guildhall, Worcester** (1721–3) (p. 962C), by Thos. White, is a fine civic example, while the **Guildhall, High Wycombe** (1757) by Henry Keene, is an interesting building of which there are many in English country towns by provincial architects whose names and works are now becoming more generally known.

Bridges of architectural character, as Pulteney Bridge, Bath (1769–74), by Robert Adam; Richmond Bridge (1774–7) and Kew Bridge (1783–9, rebuilt 1903), both designed by James Paine, now joined up the busy districts on either side of the Thames and other bridges of this period are at Chertsey and Walton. Waterloo Bridge (1811–17, demolished 1938), designed by John Rennie, showed the influence of the Greek Revival.

The bridge at Coalbrookdale, Shropshire (1777–9), designed by T. F. Pritchard, spanning about 100 ft, was the first cast-iron bridge built in England, and very many bridges of iron and stone were built in connection with road and canal developments (and for railways, after the opening of the Stockton and Darlington Railroad in 1825) by John Rennie (1761–1821), Thomas Telford (1757–1834), first President of the Institution of Civil Engineers (1820), and others, as well as dock and harbour works and warehouses. **S. Katherine's Docks, London** (1827–8) (p. 982), by Telford, is one of the best examples.

COMPARATIVE ANALYSIS

(A comparative analysis of essential differences between Gothic and Renaissance Architecture is given on p. 661.)

This comparative analysis covers Early Renaissance (Elizabethan and Jacobean) and Late Renaissance (Stuart and Georgian), as tabulated, p. 868.

PLANS

Early Renaissance. House plans are often E- or H-shaped (p. 965) with central entrance and two side wings, as at Montacute (p. 965B), Bramshill (p. 965G), Aston Hall (p. 965H), Hatfield (p. 965F), and Audley End. Plans are sometimes quadrangular, as at Burghley (p. 965A), Longleat (p. 965D), Wollaton (pp. 883A, 965C), and Castle Ashby (p. 880D). Occasionally plans are of a fanciful shape, as at Longford Castle (p. 965E). Hardwick Hall (p. 880B) is a rectangular block with large projecting bays. Such buildings as Knole, Penshurst (p. 449E), and Haddon (p. 449H) are of irregular plan, and are additions to previous Gothic houses. Internal courts for lighting are sometimes employed, as at Blickling (p. 965J) and Chastleton House, Oxfordshire. Characteristic features are the great hall (p. 887B), broad staircase (pp. 879C, 975B, C), and long gallery (p. 884A, B). Broad terraces with balustrades (p. 969D, F) raised above the garden level and wide flights of steps are charming features; while the gardens were often laid out in a formal manner, as at Holland House (p. 892A), Montacute, Longford, Blickling (p. 883B), and Hatfield (p. 890B).

Late Renaissance. Plans are now marked by regularity and even by exaggerated symmetry, which aimed at uniting the various parts in an imposing façade (p. 966). The square type of plan sometimes had a central saloon, as at the Queen's House, Greenwich (pp. 900A, 901E), and Chiswick House (p. 938), and Mereworth (p. 966G). The oblong type was usually divided into three, of which the centre third was occupied by hall, saloon, and stairs, as at Chevening (p. 966H) and Coleshill (p. 966C), or a broad cross-belt containing stairs divided the principal rooms, as at Thorpe Hall (p. 966M) and Eltham (p. 966E). The Italian 'piano nobile' was adopted

EARLY RENAISSANCE PLANS
(ELIZABETHAN & JACOBEAN)

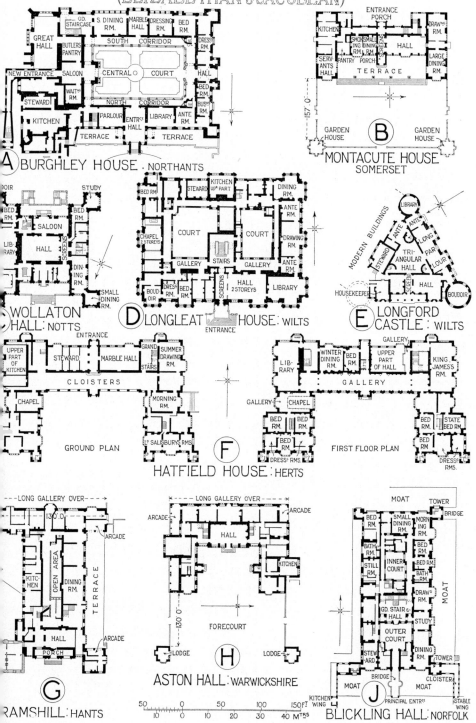

A BURGHLEY HOUSE · NORTHANTS

B MONTACUTE HOUSE SOMERSET

D LONGLEAT HOUSE · WILTS

E LONGFORD CASTLE · WILTS

WOLLATON HALL · NOTTS

GROUND PLAN — HATFIELD HOUSE · HERTS — FIRST FLOOR PLAN — **F**

G RAMSHILL · HANTS

H ASTON HALL · WARWICKSHIRE

J BLICKLING HALL · NORFOLK

LATE RENAISSANCE PLANS
(STUART & GEORGIAN)

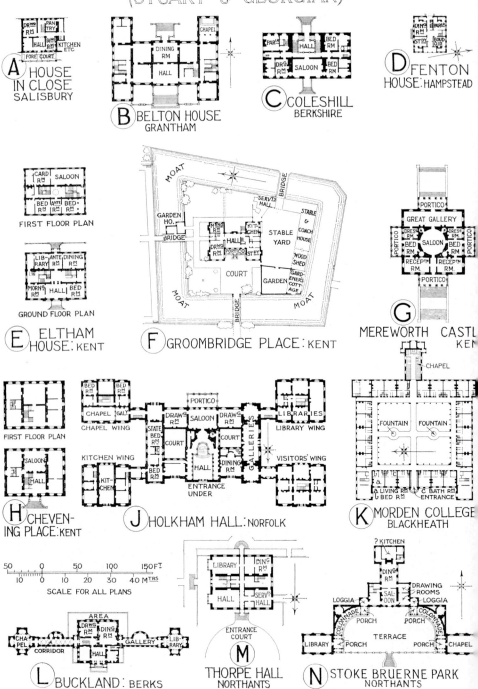

A HOUSE IN CLOSE SALISBURY

B BELTON HOUSE GRANTHAM

C COLESHILL BERKSHIRE

D FENTON HOUSE: HAMPSTEAD

E ELTHAM HOUSE: KENT

FIRST FLOOR PLAN

GROUND FLOOR PLAN

F GROOMBRIDGE PLACE: KENT

G MEREWORTH CASTLE KENT

H CHEVENING PLACE: KENT

FIRST FLOOR PLAN

J HOLKHAM HALL: NORFOLK

K MORDEN COLLEGE BLACKHEATH

SCALE FOR ALL PLANS
50   0   50   100   150 FT
10   0   10   20   30   40 MTRS

L BUCKLAND: BERKS

M THORPE HALL NORTHANTS

N STOKE BRUERNE PARK NORTHANTS

for many country houses (pp. 903E, 929A, E, 930A, D, 939A, B) with basement, not necessarily below ground, for cellarage and kitchen offices, while the principal rooms are approached either by a great external staircase with a portico (pp. 903E, 929A, E, 930A, D, 939A) or by an internal stair from the basement. The larger houses have quadrant colonnades to detached wings (pp. 929A, 930B, 933B, 939A, D, 966N). Octagonal, circular, and elliptical-shaped apartments became increasingly common, but are not indicated externally (p. 966G, J, L, N). Staircases, as at Ashburnham House (pp. 904A, 971J), well-designed, with stout newels, variously treated balusters, and consoled step-ends (pp. 903D, 971L), are a most characteristic feature of the period. Corridors gradually superseded the 'thoroughfare' system of planning (p. 452), and added much to the convenience and privacy of houses. The Jacobean gallery survived in a modified form, as at Castle Howard (p. 929B), Chatsworth, Holkham (p. 966J), and Blenheim (p. 930B), while fine formal gardens are seen at Hampton Court (p. 923A), Blenheim (p. 933A) and Harewood House (p. 936E). Towards the close of the period informal domestic planning was attaining favour, not only for Gothic Revival and other non-Classical designs (pp. 944A, 947D) but also for certain of the Italianate 'villas' springing up around towns (p. 944D).

WALLS

Early Renaissance. Façades, both in brick and stone, are picturesque in character and often marked by a free use of the Classic 'Orders' one above the other, as at Hatfield (p. 891A), the Bodleian Library, Oxford (p. 895A), Kirby Hall (p. 888A), and Holland House (p. 892A). Gables are often of scroll-work, due to foreign influence, and their general outlines are governed by the roof-slope (pp. 888A, 892A), while parapets are balustraded (p. 880A) or pierced with letters or characteristic patterns (pp. 880C, 891A). Chimney stacks, either of cut brickwork or stone, follow Tudor traditions; the shafts are carried up boldly above the roof and are sometimes disguised as columns, as at Burghley (p. 969B) and Kirby (p. 888A), and owing to their prominence on the skyline they play an important part in the design, thus differentiating it from Italian and approximating it to French treatment. Walls were frequently finished internally with panelling or wainscoting, with framing often joined by a 'mason's mitre' (see Glossary), in small divisions of uniform size, as at Stockton House (p. 975A), Hatfield (p. 891B), Knole (p. 879C), Haddon (p. 884A), Crewe Hall, and Sizergh.

Late Renaissance. Walls continued to be of stone, but in the less important buildings the prevalence of timber led to many disastrous fires in towns and villages (Fire of London, 1666) and popularized the use of brickwork, e.g. Belton House (p. 903E) and Groombridge Place (p. 907B). Wall angles were frequently emphasized by raised blocks or quoins, as at Swan (Dodo) House (p. 940A), which in brick buildings were often of stone (p. 941A), as also were the window architraves. The walls of Georgian houses are often terminated with well-designed cornices in brick (p. 940A), stone (p. 941C), or wood (pp. 941A, 971D, E), which, when painted white in conjunction with the window-frames, give pleasant relief to the façades, especially when of red brickwork. Plain ashlar wall surfaces served to throw into relief the ornate stonework of porticoes and windows (pp. 901C, 935B): stucco, to simulate the effect of stone, became prevalent after *c.* 1774 and especially in Regency times (p. 947B). Pediments and hipped roofs take the place of gables (pp. 903E, 935B), and chimneys are often hidden behind parapets, and thus the design approximates more in this respect to Italian Renaissance. The panelling of internal walls now generally extended in houses from floor to ceiling, and the wall surface was divided into dado, large panels, and moulded cornice, which gives a finished appearance and sense of comfort, as at Belton House (p. 904C), the Orangery, Kensington (pp. 921D, 971K), and the vestries of many city churches, as S. Lawrence Jewry (p. 921C).

OPENINGS

Early Renaissance. Arcades were introduced into the larger houses, such as Hatfield (p. 891A), Bramshill (p. 969J), and Holland House, Kensington (p. 892A). Doorways are always important features, as at S. Catherine's Court (p. 969H), and are sometimes elaborate in design, flanked by columns (pp. 888A, 891A, 895A, B) and are an evidence of the hospitality of the times, which is expressed in the couplet at Montacute House:

> Through this wide opening gate
> None come too early, none return too late.

Windows still resembled those of the Tudor period with vertical mullions, horizontal transoms, and leaded glass (pp. 880A, 888A, C, 892A). They became flat-headed instead of arched, to suit the level ceilings of dwelling-rooms. Projecting oriel windows, as at Bramshill (pp. 893A, 969A), and bay-windows were also used and give light and shade to façades, as at Hardwick Hall (p. 880A), Longleat, Holland House (p. 892A), Hinchingbrooke Hall (p. 969C), and Kirby Hall (p. 888A).

Late Renaissance. Arcades, formed of columns of correct Classic proportions, are familiar features of this period, especially in the larger mansions, such as Blenheim (p. 930A) and Castle Howard (p. 929A). Arcades with superimposed Orders, under the influence of Palladio, became systematized (p. 970K), as were also superimposed colonnades (p. 970G), and various other combinations were used by Sir William Chambers (p. 970D, F, J). Doorways became more formal in design, owing to the influence of Palladio (p. 903E), and many treatments became standardized (pp. 970B, 980A, C). The doorways of Georgian houses are often special features of the façades, showing variety of treatment, and are sometimes provided with shell hoods (pp. 940D, 971G). Gateways, frequently filled in with wrought-iron gates, are flanked by well-proportioned piers of stone crowned with balls, sculptured figures, or armorial bearings (pp. 902A, 940A), and rustication was frequently employed (p. 970A). Windows, although sometimes still following the Early Renaissance pattern, commonly became smaller, mullions and transoms being used in a four-light window arrangement of stone or wood such as that at Wolvesey Palace, Winchester (p. 971H), until, about 1660, sash windows were introduced (pp. 903E, 940A), often replacing the older four-light type in existing buildings. These sash windows, placed almost flush with the outer face of the walls (p. 971F), were painted white and form a pleasant colour scheme when flanked by green shutters, which contrast with the red brickwork commonly in use. The openings were surrounded by moulded architraves and frequently surmounted by a pediment (pp. 899C, 936A, B), while larger openings were often formed in three divisions, as in Italy (p. 741)—a treatment much favoured by the Brothers Adam (pp. 957C, 970C, 980B). In later practice, as a precaution against fire, sash windows often were set back behind a $4\frac{1}{2}$ ins reveal (pp. 942C, 944D). Many old door and window types were unconvincingly revived in the 'Gothick' of the Antiquarian phase (pp. 944A, 945A).

ROOFS

Early Renaissance. Steep sloping roofs, sometimes covered with tiles or stone slabs, were still used (p. 893B), as well as flat lead-covered roofs, and sometimes both occur together (pp. 880, 883A, 888A, 892A). Roofs were fronted with gables of the Gothic type, as well as with low pediments of Classic origin, even in the same

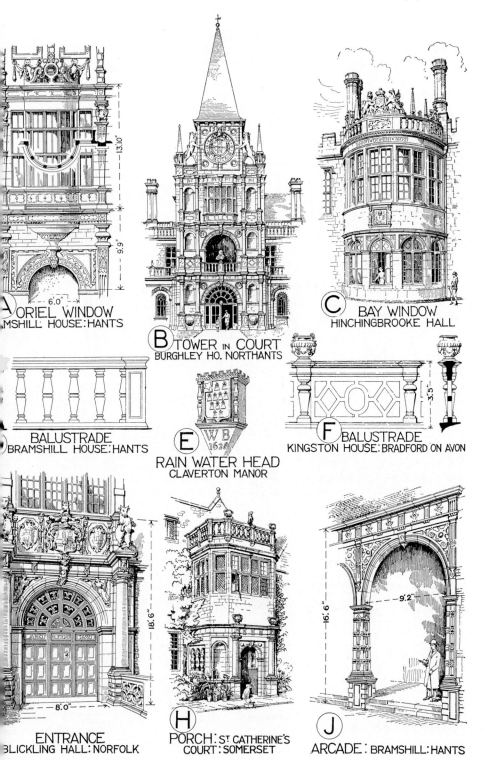

A. ORIEL WINDOW
BRAMSHILL HOUSE : HANTS
13.10"   9.9"   6.0"

B. TOWER IN COURT
BURGHLEY HO. NORTHANTS

C. BAY WINDOW
HINCHINGBROOKE HALL

D. BALUSTRADE
BRAMSHILL HOUSE : HANTS

E. RAIN WATER HEAD
CLAVERTON MANOR
W B 1628

F. BALUSTRADE
KINGSTON HOUSE : BRADFORD ON AVON
3.5"

ENTRANCE
BLICKLING HALL : NORFOLK
18.6"   8.0"

H. PORCH : ST CATHERINE'S
COURT : SOMERSET

J. ARCADE : BRAMSHILL : HANTS
16.6"   9.2"

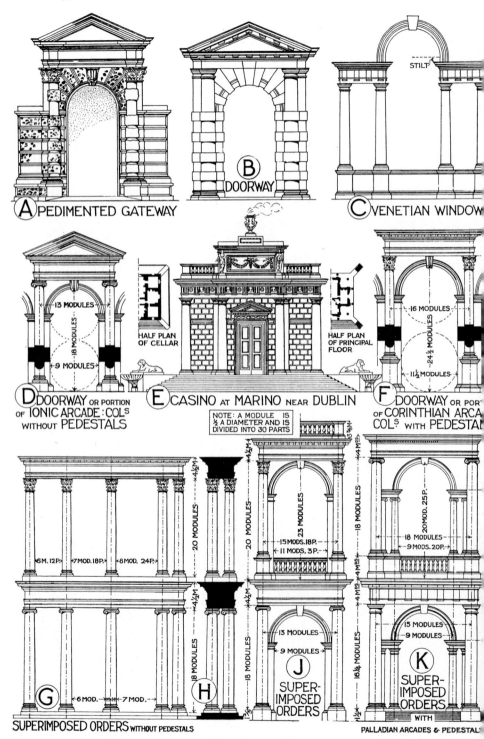

Ⓐ PEDIMENTED GATEWAY

Ⓑ DOORWAY

Ⓒ VENETIAN WINDOW

Ⓓ DOORWAY OR PORTION OF IONIC ARCADE : COLˢ WITHOUT PEDESTALS

13 MODULES
18 MODULES
9 MODULES

HALF PLAN OF CELLAR

Ⓔ CASINO AT MARINO NEAR DUBLIN

HALF PLAN OF PRINCIPAL FLOOR

NOTE: A MODULE IS ½ A DIAMETER AND IS DIVIDED INTO 30 PARTS

Ⓕ DOORWAY OR POR OF CORINTHIAN ARCA COLˢ WITH PEDESTAL

16 MODULES
24½ MODULES
11½ MODULES

Ⓖ SUPERIMPOSED ORDERS WITHOUT PEDESTALS

6M. 12P.
7 MOD. 18 P.
8 MOD. 24 P.
20 MODULES
4½ M
18 MODULES
4½ M
6 MOD.
7 MOD.

Ⓗ

20 MODULES
4½ M
18 MODULES
4½ M

Ⓙ SUPER-IMPOSED ORDERS

15 MODS. 18 P.
11 MODS. 3 P.
23 MODULES
13 MODULES
9 MODULES

Ⓚ SUPER-IMPOSED ORDERS WITH

18 MODULES
4 M
16½ MODULES
4 M
20 MOD. 25 P.
18 MODULES
9 MODS. 20 P.
15 MODULES
9 MODULES

PALLADIAN ARCADES & PEDESTAL

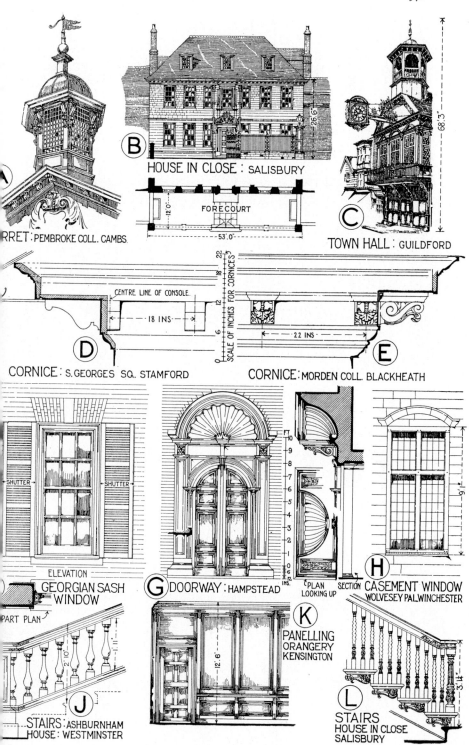

TURRET: PEMBROKE COLL. CAMBS.

B — HOUSE IN CLOSE : SALISBURY

FORECOURT

C — TOWN HALL : GUILDFORD

D — CORNICE : S. GEORGES SQ. STAMFORD

CENTRE LINE OF CONSOLE.

18 INS

SCALE OF INCHES FOR CORNICES

22 INS

E — CORNICE : MORDEN COLL. BLACKHEATH

SHUTTER SHUTTER

ELEVATION

GEORGIAN SASH WINDOW

PART PLAN

G — DOORWAY : HAMPSTEAD

PLAN LOOKING UP

SECTION

H — CASEMENT WINDOW WOLVESEY PAL. WINCHESTER

K — PANELLING ORANGERY KENSINGTON

J — STAIRS : ASHBURNHAM HOUSE : WESTMINSTER

L — STAIRS HOUSE IN CLOSE SALISBURY

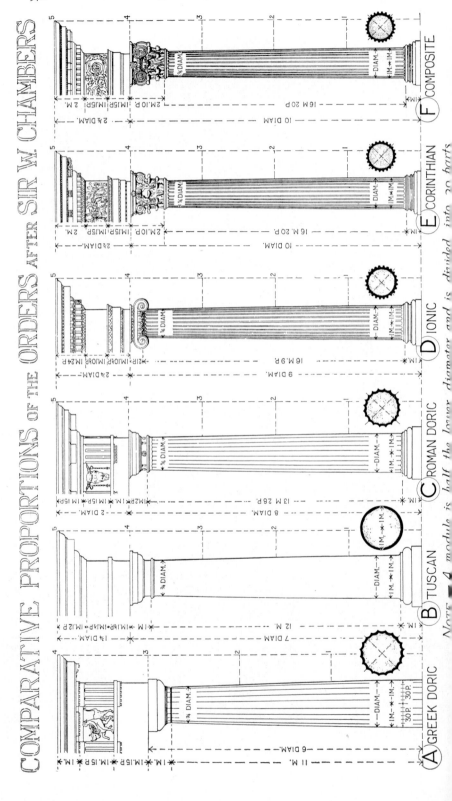

COMPARATIVE PROPORTIONS of the ORDERS after SIR W. CHAMBERS

A GREEK DORIC   B TUSCAN   C ROMAN DORIC   D IONIC   E CORINTHIAN   F COMPOSITE

Note — A module is half the lower diameter and is divided into 30 parts

building, and this is one of the many instances of reluctance to break with tradition (p. 892A). Balustrades in great variety—arcaded, columned, pierced, or battlemented —were favourite features evolved from those of the Gothic period (p. 969B, C, F, H).

Late Renaissance. Sloping roofs were frequently 'hipped' and without gables, because the cornice was now the characteristic feature of the building and gables were therefore inappropriate, while dormer windows now took the place of the windows in the gables of the Jacobean period (pp. 903E, 907B, 940A, 941A). A low-pitched pediment (p. 936B) sometimes outlined the ends of sloping roofs, in contrast to the steep gables of the early period (p. 902G). The upper part of the roof was often formed as a lead flat, surrounded by a balustrade and surmounted by a turret with a domical roof (p. 903E). Balustrades played an important part in the general design, and partly concealed the flat-pitched roofs behind them (pp. 929, 930, 939). Domes and cupolas were much in vogue (p. 971A, C), while splendid steeples, initiated by Sir Christopher Wren, rival and even surpass Mediaeval spires in their fanciful storeyed outlines (p. 925).

COLUMNS

Early Renaissance. The columns of the five Orders of architecture, as standardized by the Romans, were reintroduced, and indeed form the outstanding features of the Renaissance style; so that all five Orders were sometimes superimposed, as in the Bodleian Library, Oxford (p. 895A), and four Orders occur at Merton College, Oxford (p. 895D). They were employed in all parts of the building, externally in porches, gables, and even in chimney stacks (pp. 888A, 891A), and internally in panelling, doorways, and fireplaces (p. 892D, E). These columns, both circular and square, were as yet seldom correct, either in design or proportion, while pilasters, banded with strapwork or prismatic ornament (p. 969J), often tapered towards the base like the 'Hermes' columns, which were also now used, especially in the design of hall screens and elaborate chimney-pieces (p. 887). Pedestals also received similar ornamentation.

Late Renaissance. The Orders of architecture now lost the naïve incorrectness of proportion and detail which characterized them in the early period. After Inigo Jones's visits to Italy and his study of Palladio's buildings, columns, as in the Banqueting House (p. 899C), and other buildings (p. 902), were more strictly designed according to the proportions laid down by that autocrat of architecture. Full scope was afforded for the display of the Orders in the spacious porticoes of churches (frontispiece), country mansions (pp. 929, 930, 936B, 939), and public buildings (pp. 959A, B, 960), and they were often carried through two or more storeys to give an effect of unity, as at Greenwich Hospital (p. 901A, F). Columns and pilasters are also the prevailing features of the Renaissance monuments introduced into Gothic churches, while panelling, doorways, and chimney-pieces of interiors conform to the same columnar style (p. 904). The canons governing proportions, first promulgated by Vitruvius and further systematized by Palladio, were again formulated by Sir William Chambers, who was generally accepted by English architects as the authority on this subject (pp. 970, 972). The Greek Orders affected design considerably in the later eighteenth century, and were used exclusively in buildings of Greek Revival character in the early nineteenth century.

MOULDINGS

Early Renaissance. Mouldings once again reverted to Roman forms as applied to the bases and capitals of columns and their entablatures (pp. 164, 165), but naturally displayed considerable variety, due to lingering Gothic influence. They were often coarse in outline, but became more refined when used in wood panelling or plaster ceilings (p. 884). Bold convex mouldings, banded and decorated with strapwork (p. 892D, E), characterize many Jacobean chimney-pieces as well as monuments and tombs.

Late Renaissance. Mouldings, like other features, became more strictly Classical in form and, as the stock-in-trade of every craftsman, they admitted of little variety in design (pp. 164, 165). Mouldings in general, whether in stone, wood, or plaster, became bolder, and the large 'ogee' moulding was the one chiefly in use round fireplaces and panels (pp. 904, 940).

ORNAMENT

Early Renaissance (pp. 976, 977). The carved ornament of the Early Renaissance period is often a strange mixture of Gothic and Renaissance forms, and this transitional treatment gives it a special interest. 'Strap' ornament, now much employed in all materials, received its name from its resemblance to leather straps interlaced in geometrical patterns, attached to the background as if by nails or rivets (p. 977C, E). It appears on pilasters, as at Hatfield (p. 891A), on piers, spandrels, and plaster ceilings, as at Bromley (p. 977B), and in friezes, as at Yarmouth (p. 977E) and Aston Hall (p. 977C). Carved figures of mythological personages, and of grotesques, such as satyrs and fauns, are further evidence of Classic influence, while heraldry was freely employed (pp. 969B, C, G, 977D). Interiors owe much of their finished character to the carved wainscot panelling, wide stairs with carved newels (pp. 879C, 975C, E), chimney-pieces, as at Blickling Hall (p. 975F), and Holland House (p. 892E), wall tapestries, and modelled plaster ceilings, as at Audley End (p. 977A), developed from the rib and panel type of the Tudor period (p. 510). Renaissance features also pervaded every branch of the allied arts and crafts, as in the following examples: the monuments to Elizabeth (1604) and Mary, Queen of Scots, in Westminster Abbey; the tomb of Lord Burghley (1598) (p. 976E); the Culpepper Tomb, Goudhurst (p. 976C); the chapel screen at the Charterhouse (p. 976B); the doorway in Broughton Castle (1599) (p. 975D); the bookcase at Pembroke College, Cambridge (p. 976D); the throne and stalls in the Convocation Room, Oxford (1639) (p. 976F); the pulpit in North Cray Church, Kent (p. 976A); the rain-water head from Claverton Manor (p. 969E); a cistern (p. 976H); the tablets in Peterhouse Chapel, Cambridge (p. 976J), and All Hallows, Barking (p. 976G); the entrance porch (p. 969G) and chimney-piece at Blickling Hall (p. 975F); while the style was also applied to the furniture, such as chairs (p. 977K), chests, tables (p. 977G), stools (p. 977F), table settles (p. 977J), cupboards (p. 977H, N), and bedsteads (p. 977L).

Late Renaissance (pp. 978, 980). The carved ornament of the later period is an anglicized version of the fully developed Italian Renaissance, from which all trace of Gothic influence disappeared as Classic tradition reasserted itself. The style of Louis XIV naturally affected decorative art in England; while later on the brothers Adam show the effect of the simpler Classic tradition on their designs (p. 943A), also adopted by their followers and imitators (p. 943B). The pulpits, fonts, and panelled vestries are characteristic and striking features of Wren's city churches (p. 921C, E). Interiors are characterized by large wall panels (p. 904C), often containing family portraits, which also appear over chimney-pieces which otherwise became simpler in treatment (p. 904B). Plaster ceilings are boldly set out in squares, ovals, or circles, framed in by mouldings, on which fruits and flowers are modelled in high relief (pp. 903B, 904A, C). Walls and ceilings were sometimes painted, as those by Verrio and Sir James Thornhill at Blenheim Palace and Hampton Court, and S. Paul's Cathedral. Renaissance features, now more sedate in type, were reproduced in all decorative features, such as the archway at Wilton (p. 980D) by Sir William Chambers, the gate piers (p. 980G) by Inigo Jones, the circular window (p. 980E) by

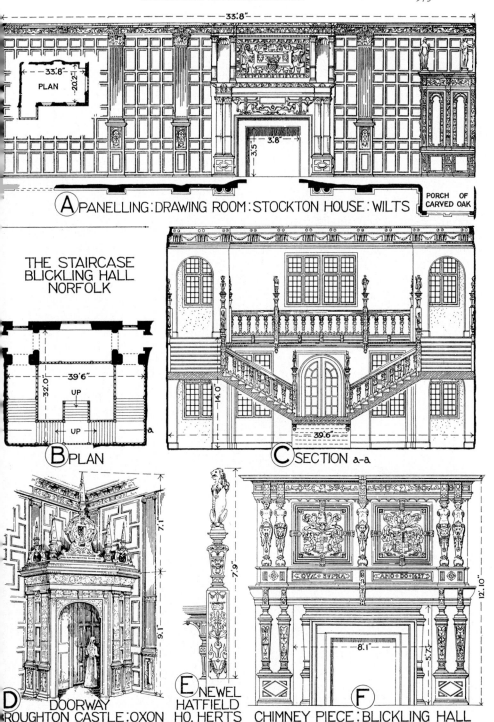

PLAN
33.8"
20.2"

33.8"

3.5

3.8"

A PANELLING: DRAWING ROOM: STOCKTON HOUSE: WILTS

PORCH OF CARVED OAK

THE STAIRCASE BLICKLING HALL NORFOLK

39'6"
32.0"
UP
UP
a

B PLAN

14.0

39.6

C SECTION a-a

7.1

9.1

D DOORWAY ROUGHTON CASTLE: OXON

7.9

E NEWEL HATFIELD HO. HERTS

QVÆ SVPRA · ANO DO 1627

12.10

8.1

5.7

F CHIMNEY PIECE: BLICKLING HALL

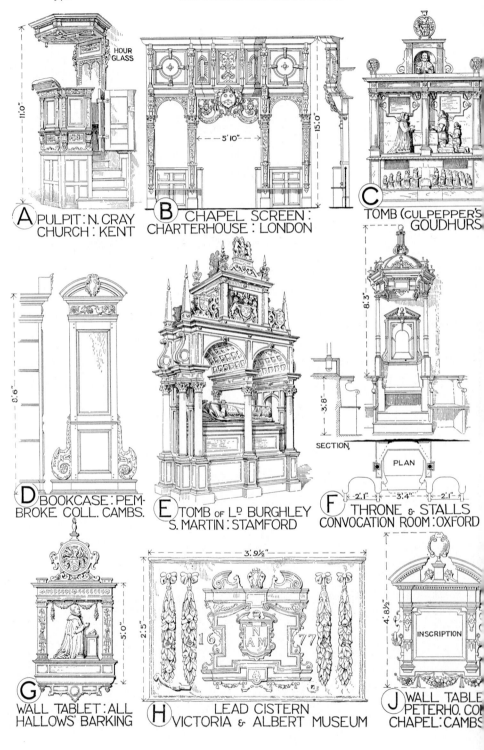

A PULPIT: N. CRAY CHURCH: KENT

HOUR GLASS

11.0"

B CHAPEL SCREEN: CHARTERHOUSE: LONDON

5' 10"

15.0"

C TOMB (CULPEPPER'S GOUDHURS

D BOOKCASE: PEMBROKE COLL. CAMBS.

8.6"

E TOMB OF LD BURGHLEY S. MARTIN: STAMFORD

F THRONE & STALLS CONVOCATION ROOM: OXFORD

8.3"

3.8"

SECTION

PLAN

2.1"   3.4"   2.1"

G WALL TABLET: ALL HALLOWS' BARKING

5.0"

H LEAD CISTERN VICTORIA & ALBERT MUSEUM

3' 9½"

2' 5"

16   N A M   77

J WALL TABLE PETERHO. CO CHAPEL: CAMBS

INSCRIPTION

4' 8½"

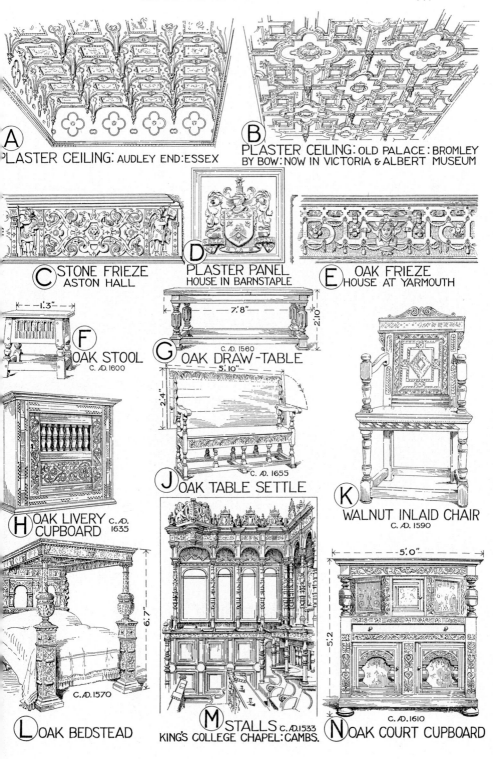

A PLASTER CEILING: AUDLEY END: ESSEX

B PLASTER CEILING: OLD PALACE: BROMLEY BY BOW: NOW IN VICTORIA & ALBERT MUSEUM

C STONE FRIEZE ASTON HALL

D PLASTER PANEL HOUSE IN BARNSTAPLE

E OAK FRIEZE HOUSE AT YARMOUTH

F OAK STOOL C. AD. 1600

G OAK DRAW-TABLE C. AD. 1560

J OAK TABLE SETTLE C. AD. 1655

K WALNUT INLAID CHAIR C. AD. 1590

H OAK LIVERY CUPBOARD C. AD. 1635

L OAK BEDSTEAD C. AD. 1570

M STALLS C. AD. 1533 KING'S COLLEGE CHAPEL: CAMBS.

N OAK COURT CUPBOARD C. AD. 1610

LATER RENAISSANCE FURNITURE

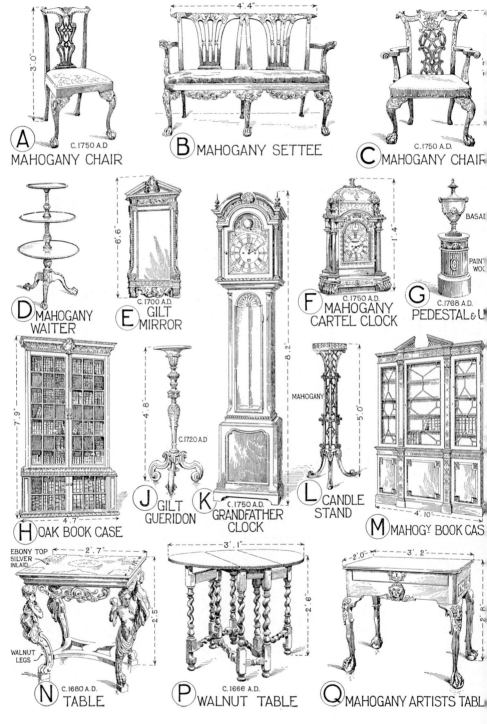

A MAHOGANY CHAIR — C. 1750 A.D — 3'.0"

B MAHOGANY SETTEE — 4'.4"

C MAHOGANY CHAIR — C. 1750 A.D.

D MAHOGANY WAITER

E GILT MIRROR — C. 1700 A.D. — 6'.6"

F MAHOGANY CARTEL CLOCK — C. 1750 A.D. — 1'.4"

G PEDESTAL & U — C. 1768 A.D. — BASAL / PAINT WOO

H OAK BOOK CASE — 7'.9" — 4'.7"

J GILT GUERIDON — 4'.8" — C. 1720 A.D.

K GRANDFATHER CLOCK — C. 1750 A.D. — 8'.2"

L CANDLE STAND — MAHOGANY — 5'.0"

M MAHOGY BOOK CAS — 4'.10

N TABLE — EBONY TOP SILVER INLAID — 2'.7" — 2'.5" — WALNUT LEGS — C. 1680 A.D.

P WALNUT TABLE — 3'.1" — 2'.6" — C. 1666 A.D.

Q MAHOGANY ARTISTS TABL — 2'.0" — 3'.2" — 2'.8"

Gibbs, the typical chimney-pieces (p. 980H, K) by Gibbs; in the numerous wall tablets of the period (p. 980F) and in monuments, such as that of the Duke of New-castle in Westminster Abbey (p. 980J); in casinos, such as that near Dublin (p. 970E), and covered bridges, as in Prior Park, Bath (p. 935D), and Wilton (p. 902E), and in buildings resembling Roman temples, as the famous temples in Kew Gardens by Chambers, which were introduced into the formal gardens, the latter usually decorated with ornamental vases and sundials (p. 940B, C). Houses owe much of their interest to their beautiful fittings and furniture by Chippendale, Hepplewhite, Sheraton, and their followers. Chairs (p. 978A, C), settees (p. 978B), tables (p. 978N, P, Q), waiters (p. 978D), book-cases (p. 978H, M), clocks (p. 978F, K), mirrors (p. 978E), candlestands (p. 978L), gueridon (p. 978J) and pedestals (p. 978G) all help to give a comfortable feeling to houses of this period.

REFERENCE BOOKS

EARLY RENAISSANCE (ELIZABETHAN AND JACOBEAN) AND GENERAL WORKS

AMBLER, L. *Old Halls and Manor Houses of Yorkshire.* London, 1913.
DAWBER, E. G. *Old Cottages and Farmhouses in Kent and Sussex.* London, 1900.
—. *Old Cottages in the Cotswold District.* London, 1904.
FOX, SIR C., and LORD RAGLAN. *Monmouthshire Houses.* 3 vols. Cardiff, 1951–4.
GOTCH, J. A. *Architecture of the Renaissance in England.* 2 vols. London, 1891–4.
—. *Early Renaissance Architecture in England.* London, 1914.
—. *The Growth of the English House.* London, 1928.
GREEN, W. CURTIS. *Old Cottages and Farmhouses in Surrey.* London, 1908.
JACKSON, SIR T. G. *The Renaissance of Roman Architecture.* Pt. II. England, 1928.
NASH, J. *Mansions of England in the Olden Time.* 4 vols. London, 1839–49.
OLIVER, B. *Old Houses and Village Buildings in East Anglia.* London, 1912.
PARKINSON, J., and OULD, E. A. *Old Cottages, Farmhouses and other Half-timber Buildings of Shropshire, Herefordshire and Cheshire.* London, 1904.
RICHARDSON, C. J. *Old English Mansions.* London, 1841–8.
SHAW, H. *Details of Elizabethan Architecture.* London, 1839.
SHUFFREY, L. A. *The English Fireplace to the XIXth Century.* London, 1912.
SHUTE, J. *First and Chief Groundes of Architecture.* 1563 (the first English book on the Orders). Repr. London, 1912.
STRATTON, A. *The English Interior to the XIXth Century.* London, 1920.
SUMMERSON, SIR J. *Architecture in Britain, 1530–1830.* Pelican History of Art, 1953.
TANNER, H. *Interior Woodwork of the XVI–XVIIIth Centuries.* London, 1902.
Thorpe Collection of original drawings in the Soane Museum.
TIPPING, H. A. *English Homes: Period III (1558–1649).* 2 vols, London, 1922, 1927.

LATE RENAISSANCE (STUART AND GEORGIAN)

ADAM, R. and J. *Works in Architecture.* 3 vols. London, 1773–1822.
BELCHER, J., and MACARTNEY, M. E. *Later Renaissance Architecture in England.* 2 vols. London, 1897–1901.
BEVERIDGE, T. J. *English Renaissance Woodwork, 1660–1760.* London, 1921.
BIRCH, G. H. *London Churches of the XVIIth and XVIIIth Centuries.* London, 1896.
BLOMFIELD, R. *A History of Renaissance Architecture in England.* 2 vols. London, 1897: and abridged edition, London, 1900.
BULTON, A. T. *The Architecture of R. and J. Adam.* 2 vols. 1922.
BRIGGS, M. S. *Baroque Architecture.* London, 1913.
—. *Wren the Incomparable.* London, 1953.
BRITTON, J., and PUGIN, A. *Public Buildings of London.* 2 vols. London, 1825–8.
CLARK, K. *The Gothic Revival.* 2nd ed. London, 1950.
CLAYTON, J. *Parochial Churches of Sir Christopher Wren.* London, 1848–9.
COBB, G. *The Old Churches of London.* London, 1941.

A DOORWAY: TYPE WITH RUSTICATED ARCHITRAVE

B TYPICAL WINDOW BY KENT HORSE GUARDS LONDON

C DOORWAY: WITH RUSTICA ¾ IONIC C

D ARCH WILTON 9'.1" KEY PLAN 25'.0"

E TYPICAL CIRCU WINDOW: S.MARTIN: LON

F MONUMENT TO SIR JOHN BRIDGMAN ASTON: WARWICKSHIRE
INSCRIPTION

G GATE PIERS 10'.0"

H CHIMNEY PIECE BY GIBBS
FRAME FOR PICTURE

J MON.MT TO DUKE OF NEWCASTLE WESTMINSTER ABBEY
30'.0" ABOVE GROUND

K CHIMNEY PIECE BY GIBBS
FRAME FOR PICTURE

COLVIN, H. M. *Biographical Dictionary of English Architects 1660–1840*. London, 1954.
—. 'Gothick survival and Gothick revival'. *Arch. Review*, 1948.
DALE, A. *James Wyatt, Architect*. 1936.
DUTTON, R. *The English Country House*. London, 1935.
—. *The English Interior*. London, 1948.
FIELD, H., and BUNNEY, M. *English Domestic Architecture of the XVIIth and XVIIIth Centuries*. London, 1905.
GIBBS, J. *Book of Architecture*. London, 1728.
GOTCH, J. A. *The English Home from Charles I to George IV*. London, 1919.
—. *Inigo Jones*. London, 1928.
HUSSEY, C. *The Picturesque*. London, 1924.
JONES, INIGO. *Designs*. published by W. Kent, 2 vols. 1770.
JOURDAIN, M. *English Decoration and Furniture, 1760–1820*. London, 1922.
—. *English Decorative Plasterwork of the Renaissance*. London, 1926.
—. *The Work of William Kent*. London, 1948.
KNOOP, D., and JONES, G. P. *The London Mason in the 17th Century*. Manchester, 1935.
LEES-MILNE, J. *The Age of Adam*. London, 1947.
LENYGON, F. *Decoration in England from 1660–1770*. London, 1927.
MACARTNEY, M. *English Houses and Gardens*. London, 1908.
POLEY, A. F. E. *St. Paul's Cathedral, London*. 1927.
RAMSEY, S. C. *Small Houses of the Late Georgian Period*. 2 vols. London, 1919–23.
REDDAWAY, T. F. *The Rebuilding of London after the Great Fire*. London, 1940.
RICHARDSON, SIR A. E. *Monumental Classic Architecture in Great Britain*. London, 1914.
—. *Georgian England*. London, 1931.
—. *The Smaller English House, 1660–1830*. London, 1925.
—., and GILL, C. L. *London Houses, 1660–1820*. London, 1911.
R.I.B.A. *Sir Christopher Wren: Bicentenary Memorial Volume*. London, 1923.
SMALL, T., and WOODBRIDGE, C. *Houses of Wren and Early Georgian Periods*. London, 1928.
STRATTON, A. *The Life of Sir Christopher Wren*. Liverpool, 1897.
STROUD, D. *Henry Holland*. London, 1950.
—. *Capability Brown*. London, 1950.
SUMMERSON, SIR J. *John Nash*. London, 1935.
—. *Georgian London*. London, 1945.
—. *Sir John Soane*. London, 1952.
—. *Sir Christopher Wren*. London, 1953.
SWARBRICK, J. *Robert Adam and his Brothers*. London, 1915.
TIPPING, H. A. *English Homes: Periods IV, V, VI, 1649–1820*. 4 vols. London, 1920–8.
TRIGGS, H. INIGO. *Formal Gardens in England and Scotland*. London, 1902.
—., and TANNER, H. *Some Architectural Works of Inigo Jones*. London, 1901.
Vitruvius Britannicus, by Campbell, Woolfe and Gandon. 5 vols. London, 1715–71.
WALPOLE SOCIETY. vol. XII (1923–4). *Designs by Inigo Jones for Masques and Plays at Court*. Oxford.
WARE, I. *Complete Body of Architecture*. London, 1756.
WHIFFEN, M. *Stuart and Georgian Churches outside London*. London, 1947–8.
—. *Thomas Archer*. London, 1950.
WHISTLER, L. *Sir John Vanburgh*. London, 1938.
WREN, C. and S. *Parentalia*. London, 1750.
WREN SOCIETY. Publications, vols. I–XX. 1924–43.

S. Katherine's Docks, London (1827–8). See p. 964

XXVI. NINETEENTH AND TWENTIETH CENTURY ARCHITECTURE IN GREAT BRITAIN

(1830 to present day)

INFLUENCES

GEOGRAPHICAL. The great wars of the end of the eighteenth and the beginning of the nineteenth century had closed Continental travel for a while to British people, yet left Britain with an enhanced prestige and a clear lead in the economic field. Trade with foreign and Empire countries developed apace, and brought far-ranging contacts and a miscellany of influences, faithfully reflected in her architecture, from all parts of the world. Not until the latter part of the nineteenth century did European countries, with Germany in the lead, seriously challenge her commercial supremacy. Factors of greatest importance to her emergence as the world's leading industrial power were the vast improvements made in the means of transport and communication. Internally in Britain, a canal system, totalling some 2,300 miles and linking the rising ports and chief manufacturing centres, had been cut between 1755–1827, while the main roads, so reconditioned after 1815 on the principles of the engineers John L. Macadam (1756–1836) and Thomas Telford that they brought about the great coaching era of 1820–36, were almost immediately surpassed in economic importance by the mesh of railways, laid out principally between 1825–50, thrusting to all vital parts of the realm. In 1834 highways passed into the charge of local authorities, and turnpikes began to disappear. Complementing these developments was that of the steamship, driven by paddle and then by screw-propeller; the old wooden walls were supplanted by iron hulls from 1821, and by 1840 the steamship was in regular ocean service, vastly shortening international communications. Very much later came the automobile, around 1900, and the aeroplane, in progress of development in the early twentieth century but of little commercial importance until after the war of 1914–18.

GEOLOGICAL. As in preceding periods, indigenous materials, brick, tile, terra-cotta, stone, and such little building-timber as the country now produced, continued to be used, but with the difference that facile transport allowed hitherto uneconomical sources to be tapped and permitted ready distribution of the products wherever they might be required. An outcome was that vernacular architecture by 1850 had finally lost the last vestiges of regional character. Methods of processing or manufacture of materials too were improved on mass-production lines: thin slates of a range of uniform sizes supplanted the rough, thick slates of 'random' sizes (i.e. courses diminishing in dimension from the eaves to the ridge of a roof), while machine-made bricks and tiles, with meticulous dimensions and hard, shiny surfaces, laid with tight joints, became everywhere common in the second half of the nineteenth century. Bricks of different colours—yellow, black, blue and white— were manufactured, tiles similarly of various hues, and were popularized in the polychromatic architecture of William Butterfield (p. 990) and others after mid-nineteenth century. Terra-cotta came back into favour about the same time, and was extensively employed in urban buildings in the last quarter of the century. Polychrome faience was a special mark of 'Art Nouveau' (p. 991), and in extensive use from about 1895 to the start of the war of 1914–18. Apart from minor structures and occasional small houses in the south-eastern part of England, genuinely historical timber-frame building ceased entirely (after c. 1600 it nearly always had been sheathed over with plaster, stucco, tile-hanging or weather-boarding), though half-timber was revived in the influential work of Norman Shaw (p. 991). Due to the enormous building programme of a rising industrial nation, great quantities of wood nevertheless were needed, and since 1850 more than nine-tenths of the supply, chiefly softwood, has been imported. As labour costs increased, stone progressively gave way to brick as a principal walling material, as it had been doing already in previous centuries, and in the last quarter of the nineteenth century brick invaded even the larger monuments in towns.

Of tremendous importance was the advent of structural iron. Britain has a wealth of ore and the fuel to process it, and in the nineteenth century began to produce it in great quantities. Employed for utilitarian structures, such as bridges, since c. 1770, and for very many decorative adjuncts to architecture, the techniques had so far developed by the railway era that great arched iron-and-glass roofs could be thrown over the new stations in the principal towns and cities, and the Great Exhibition of 1851 was housed in a structure wholly of this character (p. 1041). Pre-fabricated cast-iron houses and other buildings even were exported about this period to various parts of the Empire. A remarkably advanced completely iron-framed structure, a large boatstore, survives at the Royal Naval Dockyard at Sheerness, built 1858–60 (p. 1042). Systematic steel-framed building, however, had to await the commercial exploitation of the mass-produced commodity in the eighteen-nineties, and the first English wholly steel-framed building of architectural consequence dates only from 1905, later than in America or the European continent. Reinforced-concrete framing was first used in the country about the same time, again later than abroad.

CLIMATIC. In building design, methods of combating climatic variations developed in the second half of the nineteenth century, and by its end, central heating and ventilation of buildings were conducted on scientific lines. Direct heating by open fires, with various fuels, remained in favour for individual houses for a much longer period than in flats or public, commercial and industrial buildings in general, and still is by no means superseded. Gas lighting, introduced in 1792, had become normal by 1850; electric lighting, known by 1846, was in general use by the eighteen-nineties, and many improvements followed, including the introduction of the fluorescent lamp in 1938. The systematic heating of buildings facilitated the enlargement of window areas—liable to make rooms cold—needful in the dull climate and smoky towns, and in Modern architecture after 1930 increasing advantage was taken of the fact. Already in the second half of the nineteenth century, the dim light in the close-built streets had led designers to contrive such additional glass areas as the revived Classical or Mediaeval stylar systems then fashionable would permit.

RELIGIOUS. In the earlier part of the period there was a further breaking off from the established church (the Church of Scotland is Presbyterian) of various sects, which together with the proliferating older groups of nonconformists occasioned the need for innumerable places of worship, in addition to the old English parish churches, in the towns and villages throughout the country. By the middle of the nineteenth century the church-going population in England was as much Nonconformist as Anglican, and this approximate equality persists, matched by the membership of the Roman Catholic church. Above all, the need for new churches was due to the greatly enlarged population, strongly concentrated in the industrialized tracts. No obstacle was placed in the way of faiths brought to England's shores in the wake of foreign trade, and sacred buildings of many exotic creeds were erected in the principal cities and towns.

In Church of England circles there was formed in 1839 the Cambridge Camden Society, the activities of which were to have a profound effect upon forms of religious practice as well as upon the design of church buildings. It published a series of pamphlets and, in 1841, a magazine entitled the *Ecclesiologist*, which at first were concerned with matters of the nature and meaning of ecclesiastical architecture and the care and management of the ancient churches—which in many cases were ill-kept, misused or in abject disrepair—but soon turned to questions of doctrine and the advocacy of the restoration of ancient rubrical usage. Critical comments were made upon the design of new churches, and despite spirited protests from some quarters that Protestant principles were being endangered, had the effect of restoring to church design all the main parts and features which had been normal to churches of the Middle Ages. This was a tremendous change, for as the 'Commissioner' churches built under the Act of 1818 so strongly demonstrate (p. 878), all that had been considered requisite previously were pewed and galleried preaching boxes, lacking transepts, chancel, rood screen, altar and sedilia, devoid of symbolic ornamental and ritualistic trappings. After mid-century, it was the nonconformist rather than the anglican churches that retained the protestant austerity. An almost contemporary foundation to the Cambridge Camden Society was that of the 'Oxford Society for promoting the study of Gothic architecture', which developed in a similar way, both attracting highly influential support. A further outcome of their activity was the extraordinary number of restorations of ancient churches that came to be carried out, so that scarcely any in the realm fully retained its pristine form.

SOCIAL. The consequences of the change from an agricultural to a dominantly industrial economy were profound. The rapidly-increasing population was strongly concentrated in towns, these thus expanding at an enormous rate and much too hastily for any organized town planning until the nineteenth century was well advanced. In the physical as well as the economic sense, life centred around factories, warehouses and nodes of commerce. For the many, conditions were wretched indeed; for the relatively few, great wealth accrued. Business men rather than the aristocracy were the overlords. Reformers endeavoured to mitigate the lot of the unfortunates and the masses; order began to emerge from chaos and, at length, the industrial population as a whole began to share the benefits of the very great advances made in pure and applied science. By the twentieth century the gap between the lowest and the highest social strata had considerably narrowed, and in recent decades is less than it has ever been in past history, all classes now enjoying a remarkably high standard of living.

The nineteenth century surpassed all its predecessors in the variety of its discoveries, most of them related to the developing industrial, economic and social patterns. Invention mounted on invention, and very great material progress was made, though at some considerable expense of the finer cultural values, aesthetic perceptions in particular growing gravely blunted. Among the innumerable series of practical inventions some of the more relevant may be cited (some, regarding long-distance transport, heating, lighting and ventilation already have been noted). Photography, practicable from 1839, advanced via the dry-plate (1874) and celluloid film (1889) to public cinematography in 1905, sound track being added in 1926. Telegraph (1837), telephone (1878) and phonograph, the gramophone, wireless telegraphy (c. 1896) and television; in the medical field, x-rays and the employment of radium; all indicate unprecedented progress along the lines of applied science. The wire rope came into use about mid-nineteenth century; the lift, developed after 1852, was driven at first by steam or gas, then hydraulically, and from the eighteen-eighties by electricity. For local transport there were the bicycle (1867); the tramway (1860), started in Birkenhead by an American, George Francis Train (1829–1904), greatly developed between 1868–73 and electrified 1900–14, now practically obsolete; the motor-bus, which superseded the horse-bus in the years before 1914; and the underground railway (London, 1860–3; electrified partly in 1890, mainly in 1903–6).

Education, at first much neglected, was affected by the Public Schools Commission (1863) and the School Enquiry Reports (1868), and the Elementary Education Act of 1870 opened a better era for general education and started well-governed schools, free from religious tests. Since 1902, educational institutions, like others of public interest, have passed under a democratic charge, and there is now a free ladder through primary and secondary schools to the universities.

In the eighteenth century the greater and older established schools, such as Eton, Winchester, and Westminster, had attracted students away from the grammar schools, some of which were for a time reduced to the status of elementary schools. In the nineteenth century many important public schools were founded, such as the Colleges of Cheltenham (1841), Clifton (1862), Haileybury (1862), Lancing (1848), Marlborough (1843), Malvern (1863), Radley (1847), Rossall (1844) and Wellington (1859).

Many novel types of building sprang up in the period, such as Mechanics' Institutes—intended for adult education—which flourished briefly between 1824–50; museums, provided by generous benefactors, associated with learned societies or maintained by local authorities after the first Museum Act of 1845; public libraries, due to the Public Libraries Act; town halls, after the Municipal Corporation Act, 1835; and cinemas, of which there was at least one in each large town by 1916 and over 4,500 in the United Kingdom by 1953. Besides these, there were markets, hospitals, benevolent institutions, swimming baths, exhibition halls,

technical colleges, art galleries, very many types of factory and industrial establishment, railway and bus stations, aerodromes, and shops, stores and offices. Offices,
known as 'counting-houses' by the earlier merchants, traders and manufacturers,
were needed in vastly greater number than formerly, while shops similarly expanded tremendously in quantity. Multiple shop businesses, chain stores and
department stores were under development from the beginning of the period, but
in their present form their history commences in the second half of the nineteenth
century. Terrace housing was the principal nineteenth century expedient in towns,
with single or paired houses on the outskirts. Flats, though usual in Scottish cities
were not popular in England until quite recent times, having latterly been adopted
extensively by local authorities because of land-shortage problems. The Town
Planning Acts since 1909 have influenced recent developments and produced
striking results in the laying out of 'garden cities' and new, satellite, towns.

HISTORICAL. After the turmoil of the Napoleonic wars, England enjoyed a
protracted period of economic prosperity, which opened up facilities for travel, for
the intensification of overseas trade and the consolidation and expansion of her
colonies. The Industrial Revolution affected western Europe in general, and the
development of pure and applied science gave a lead over the countries farther afield
which occasioned the widespread diffusion of European civilization. The abrupt
rise in the population and other factors encouraged emigration, and flourishing
colonies absorbed the ideas of the mother countries no less than their manufactured
commodities. The new freedom for travel gave unprecedented opportunities too,
for the study of past architectural styles, and encouraged the growth of revivalism,
which is so conspicuous a feature of western-European nineteenth-century
architecture: for whereas in previous centuries architecture had developed on
traditional lines, industrialization represented so violent a change and proceeded so
rapidly that the development of building outpaced the capacity to find an appropriate aesthetic expression for it. It was not until the twentieth century that a
machine-age architecture was evolved.

The course of British architecture was undisturbed by the distant Crimean war
(1854–6), the Indian Mutiny (1857) or the Boer war (1899–1902), and little by the
Franco-Prussian war (1870–1) on the Continent; but World War I (1914–19) was a
conflict which halted progress completely. Hardly had recovery taken place before
a serious economic depression ensued, and it was only after 1932 that the threads
were once more effectively taken up. Then again, World War II (1939–45) brought
a protracted pause, and for some years afterwards Britain's building resources had
to be concentrated mainly on particular types of buildings—housing and schools—
under national control, before architecture could be given free rein to shape its
Modern course.

ARCHITECTURAL CHARACTER

The period opens at 1830, and the rest of the nineteenth century is marked by the
'Battle of the Styles'; i.e., between Classic and Gothic, the varieties of each that
were practised growing increasingly numerous and ever more eclectically confused.
Completely alien styles also were sporadically introduced. The issue was at its most
acute around the 1860's. By 1900, the Classic almost had triumphed again, but
meanwhile fresh trends were shaping: an 'Arts and Crafts' movement led to 'Art
Nouveau' at the turn of the century, the benefits of which were experienced on the
European continent rather than in Britain, and it was there that 'Modern' architecture evolved. British architecture after the death of Queen Victoria (1901) became
considerably more rational than it had been, but was still traditional in complexion

until about 1930, when Continental influence at length began to turn it into the Modern path.

British nineteenth-century architecture after 1830 may be considered as 'Victorian' (William IV, 1830–7; Victoria, 1837–1901) and divided into three phases: (A) Early Victorian, 1830–50; (B) High Victorian, 1850–75; and (C) Late Victorian, 1875–1901. These will be examined in turn, and (D) Twentieth Century architecture thereafter.

(A). The various types of 'Antiquarian' expression prevalent in the earlier part of the nineteenth century have been considered in the previous chapter (p. 877). In monumental architecture, Greek Revival and Graeco-Roman had been particularly important. The Greek Revival had passed its peak in the eighteen-twenties; but certain of the exponents mentioned previously remained productive in the present period, including Sir Robert Smirke, Thomas Hamilton and W. H. Playfair of Edinburgh, and John Dobson of Newcastle-upon-Tyne. Yet to be noted are the younger Hardwick, Philip (1792–1870), and a Scot, Alexander Thomson (1817–75), known as 'Greek' Thomson, who at Glasgow belatedly produced some extremely fine instances of the style. Other architects of the older generation, mentioned before, were Professor C. R. Cockerell (p. 878) and Decimus Burton (p. 877), and there was also George Basevi (1795–1845), an English architect despite his name and a pupil of Sir John Soane, these continuing to produce fine work of a Graeco-Roman character nearly to the middle of the century. With them must be included a much younger man, Harvey L. Elmes (1815–47), who died at so early an age that he has little more than the one splendid building to his credit, S. George's Hall, Liverpool (p. 1020). With these latter personalities monumental Graeco-Roman architecture came virtually to an end in England.

Sir Charles Barry (pp. 877, 956) is yet another of those born in the previous century who continues to be of high importance in the present period. His Greek Revival Royal Manchester Institution building has been referred to already (p. 956), as also has his Travellers' Club, London (1829–31) (p. 956), but we must recur to the latter here for it was a building which confirmed his reputation, and moreover it was in the Italian High Renaissance style, a new departure in revivalism so far as urban architecture is concerned, although it had been presaged in villa design and in the simple Brunswick Chapel (now S. Andrews), Hove, built by Barry in 1827–8. A book was published on the subject of the Travellers' Club in 1839. The building at once turned the attention of designers to the Italian High Renaissance source. In earlier life, Barry had had useful professional training before he spent three years (1817–20) in extensive travel in Italy, Greece, Turkey, Asia Minor and Egypt, but none of these latter studies was of immediate advantage, as on setting up in practice on his return, his earliest works were 'Commissioner' and other Gothic Revival churches. The best of these was S. Peter, Brighton (1824–8) won in competition in 1823. After the Travellers', Barry also built the Reform Club (1837–41) and the Athenaeum, Manchester (1837–9). But it was in the course of a busy practice that he carried out, in Tudor Gothic, the work for which he is the most famous, the Houses of Parliament or Westminster New Palace, London (1840–c. 1860) (p. 1022D). This now is a much loved building, but it is significant too in having given sanction to the use of revived Mediaeval architecture for public buildings. The medley of old buildings that had constituted the earlier palace mostly had been burnt down in 1834; and as the Westminster Hall had been saved, it was decided that the new structure ought to be 'either Gothic or Elizabethan'. A two-stage competition was held in 1835–6, ninety-seven designs being submitted and four offered to the scrutiny of William IV, who chose Barry's.

Barry was aided in the competition and in the early stages of erection by the

youthful Augustus Welby Northmore Pugin (1812–52), who contributed his un-
rivalled knowledge of Mediaeval decorative detail and skill in design in these
terms; he was one of the most brilliant and picturesque figures of the Gothic
Revival, outstanding even when measured against any of the whole group of remarkable personalities born in the same decade as himself, which included not only
Elmes and Alexander Thomson already referred to, but Gilbert Scott, William
Butterfield, J. L. Pearson and John Ruskin, destined to be leaders in the High
Gothic period. Son of an architectural draughtsman who himself influenced the
course of the Gothic Revival through the volumes of drawings that he published, an
even more superb and facile draughtsman than his parent, A. W. N. Pugin was a
high-strung, fanatically intense person who drove himself to insanity and death with
his unremitting labours. He developed a passionate interest in church architecture
and religious affairs, becoming a fierce controversialist on ritual and the proprieties
of church design. His writings, notably his *Contrasts*, published in 1838, comparing most unfavourably the buildings of the day with those of the Middle Ages,
and *The True Principles of Pointed or Christian Architecture* of 1841, were of
tremendous importance in securing popular favour for the Gothic style. It was he
and the ecclesiologists of the Oxford Movement and the Cambridge Camden
Society (p. 984) who sought to restore the fervour of faith and the self-denying
spirit which were the foundations of the artistic creations of the Middle Ages. This
study of Mediaeval church building inaugurated a new era in the Gothic Revival,
and had the effect of converting churches from the preaching boxes that they had
become, once again into meaningful, articulated structures possessing all the parts,
adornments and fittings deemed to have been customary in former times. Pugin
erected over sixty-five churches in the United Kingdom, and many in the colonies,
besides convents, monasteries, mansions and schools.

Other architects active at this time were Edward Blore (1787–1879), who completed Buckingham Palace (1846), begun by John Nash (later refaced by Sir Aston
Webb), and restored various castles, cathedrals and churches, besides building
houses and many new churches; Antony Salvin (1799–1881), pupil of John Nash,
an authority on Mediaeval military architecture and restorer of many old castles,
as well as an able designer of churches and country mansions; and Benjamin Ferrey
(1810–80), biographer of the Pugins, father and son, but not particularly distinguished in his practice.

Urban architecture in general soon followed Barry's Italian Renaissance lead,
and many new buildings were modelled on Italian palaces. Like Barry's, these were
at first usually astylar, but afterwards, the stylar exemplars began to receive attention, particularly those with Orders in superimposed tiers, or with stylar tiers over
rusticated basement storeys, for the giant Order was not greatly favoured. Whatever
the type, there was a strong tendency to descent in scale, for to gain greater natural
light, as was necessary in northern urban conditions, compared with the Italian,
windows were made proportionally larger, and already by 1850 façades began to have
a crowded, busy and bitty air. In the countryside, countless unassuming residences
and farmhouses continued to be built, but the castles and mansions of the social
élite frequently were remodelled or new residences created. When a Mediaeval
nucleus existed, its character usually was reasonably well preserved in any alterations or extensions, but sometimes such remodellings were carried out in 'Tudor'
or the 'Jacobethan' style which was still at this time normal for new residences,
though used with considerably greater archaeological verisimilitude than in the
previous period. ('Jacobethan' is a modern term telescoping 'Elizabethan' and
'Jacobean', two historical architectural styles which are not very dissimilar and
which usually are indistinguishable in nineteenth-century revivalism). In the

eighteen-forties, the Renaissance Revival and Puginesque Gothic made themselves felt.

This was the period of greatest activity in railway building, but the railway stations up and down the country conformed to the prevailing styles, without any special distinction apart from one or two of the greater terminals; and in those it was mainly the workaday rear parts that bore the innovations. Great progress had been made in the constructive use of cast iron since the later eighteenth century. Beginning with an iron bridge at Coalbrookdale in 1777–9, facility in the use of the material developed apace, and bridges of many types, for roads, canals and, at length, railways, were used in ever greater numbers and increasing spans. The emphasis was upon utility, and while many were sightly and even impressive by reason of their dimensions and the confident skill to which they bore witness, they were rarely deliberate architectural conceptions. Large-span roofs in wood and glass, then iron and glass, arose in the railway developments, and again were usually utilitarian. These remarkable technical advances were due to the early engineers: Thomas Telford (1757–1834); John Rennie (1761–1821); George Stephenson (1781–1848) and son Robert (1803–59); Sir William Fairbarn (1789–1874); and I. K. Brunel (1806–59). Yet at the same time iron, and iron and glass in combination, were reaching recognition as normal building or decorative materials. Cast-iron pillars and beams appeared in mills by 1800, with filler joists supporting jack-arches of fire-resisting brick or tile, or the pillars supported church galleries and roofs. Decoratively, iron was used extensively in the Regency period for such as balconies, awnings, window grilles, and even for vaulting, as in the Gothic Revival conservatory added to Carlton House, London by Thomas Hopper in 1811–12 (p. 1022B). As already noted, iron was extensively used in Rickman's churches both decoratively and constructively (p. 877), but the great era for cast iron, eked out with wrought iron where tensional stresses were to be anticipated, was that towards the end of the present Early Victorian period and the beginning of the next. Constructional ironwork in buildings was usually internal and hidden from sight, as in the case of roof principals, but there are great station halls, conservatories, and exhibition halls extant to show the courage with which the material was employed. The Crystal Palace (p. 1041) by Sir Joseph Paxton, was one of the most remarkable feats. It was a little later (1854–7) that the domed, circular reading room, framed wholly in metal, was added to the British Museum (p. 956) by Sydney Smirke (1799–1877), brother of Sir Robert. The unreliability of cast iron as manufactured at this time, and its behaviour in the case of fire, discouraged new adventures in the structural use of ferrous metals until after the commercial exploitation of steel in the last decade of the century, though cast and wrought iron continued to be extensively employed in all the established connections. Terra-cotta came back into popularity, re-introduced in 1846 by Edmund Sharpe (1809–77).

(B). High Victorian architecture, in the period 1850–75, is characterized by the spread of the Gothic Revival into virtually every architectural field. Anglican churches were almost exclusively in this style, though nonconformist churches and chapels often preserved the Classical expression and almost invariably their meeting-house arrangements. Precedent having been established by the Houses of Parliament, public buildings as well as domestic, commercial and even industrial, increasingly succumbed to the Gothic, and whatever was not Gothic—and there was still a great deal—was mostly Renaissance Revival, this astylar for the most part, made up of serried tiers of large windows with one or other of the types of architrave enframement which historicism permitted. In commercial buildings especially, windows tended to expand at the expense of the enframing wall, the device of the mock arcade becoming an increasingly popular expedient.

The symbolic figure of the High Victorian Period is Sir George Gilbert Scott (1811–78), younger son of a clergyman, who, after initial training, was at first in practice with a partner, W. B. Moffat, during the years 1834–45, the firm gaining commissions for as many as fifty workhouses in this period—these arising from the Poor Law Act of 1834—as well as others for new churches. The churches were mostly undistinguished, but meantime Scott was gaining in archaeological knowledge as well as developing his undoubted business ability and professional capacity, which were superior to his artistic talent, though he himself had every confidence in it. He was an industrious, tenacious and devout person, insatiable in building up the enormous practice that came to be his. His reputation was made when in 1844 he won an international competition for S. Nicholas' Church (Nikolaikirche) at Hamburg (p. 1081A). Thereafter he had a hand in some seven hundred and thirty buildings, including a great many new or restored churches, thirty-nine of the latter being of cathedral status. As a restorer he was almost as drastic as James Wyatt (p. 876), imposing his own favourite Decorated Gothic wherever possible. He was essentially a Gothicist, having no enthusiasm for classical architecture.

Not an architect but extremely influential in relation to the Gothic Revival was John Ruskin (1819–1900), social reformer, critic, writer and lecturer on art and architecture. Well to do, imperious, deeply religious, brilliant and intense, his reason became impaired at the end of his long life. At first concerned in his writings with the relationship between art and morals, he extended his exposition into the field of architecture, especially in two of his many books, *The Seven Lamps of Architecture* (1849) and *The Stones of Venice* (1851 and 1853). In the earlier of the two, he advocated that instead of striving for novelty or searching for a new style, as architects were doing, they should fix upon *one* style and stick to it whether for secular or church architecture, and proposed four alternatives: Pisan Romanesque; Early Gothic of the Western Italian Republic; Venetian Gothic; or 'English earliest decorated'. At this time his own choice fell upon the last, but later (1851), he veered to the Venetian Gothic. His counsels were immediately followed; not scrupulously, for to many, they appeared to give sanction to northern Italian Mediaeval architecture in general. Polychrome striated patterning with stone, coloured bricks, marble or terra-cotta; squat cylindrical columns with bunchy, foliated capitals; bifurcated windows with non-concentric extradoses and pied voussoirs; marble sheathing; ornamental medallions and lozenges; billet mouldings; all soon became part of the regular Gothic Revival stock-in-trade.

As to polychromy, Ruskin may have been anticipated by William Butterfield (1814–1900), the most original designer of the period, who in his All Saints' church, Margaret St., London (1849–59) (p. 1008) had used stripes and patterns of black brick upon red brickwork, and stone bands on the spire, while internally rich permanent polychrome patterns in the nave arcade spandrels and chancel arch were contrived by the same method. Up to this time, his ecclesiastical work had been orthodox revived Gothic, but in a number of his later schemes the polychromy is still more sharply accentuated. He liked stark colours and harsh, angular forms. Other Gothicists of note were R. C. Carpenter (1812–55), who died young, and J. L. Pearson (1817–97), expert on vaulting, who restored and built many churches in discreet style. Rather younger, born in the twenties, were G. F. Bodley (1827–1907), brought up in the Scott tradition, but influenced to some extent by French Gothic; and William Burges (1827–81) very much more so, almost completely drawing his inspiration from French sources. More important was George Edmund Street (1824–1881), who spent five years in Scott's office before setting up in practice in 1849. Highly successful in church building both at home and abroad, restorer of five cathedrals and author of two books, *Brick and Marble in North Italy* (1855) and

Gothic Architecture in Spain (1865), he is best known for his Law Courts, London (p. 1025), won in competition in 1866 but not finished until after his death. Reputedly this was the last notable public building in revived Gothic; but there were later ones in the provinces. Yet the style was declining, and architects born in the thirties mostly turned away from it in their later careers. One of these was Alfred Waterhouse (1830–1905).

Of considerable significance was the talented William Morris (1834–96), not an architect but a designer, who brought a fresh outlook in decorative design, establishing in 1861 a firm for the manufacture of furniture, fabrics, wall-papers and other furnishings. In 1884 he founded the Art Workers' Guild, and in 1877, the Society for the Protection of Ancient Buildings. He also took a leading part in the Arts and Crafts Movement, initiated in 1887. As early as 1859 he had commissioned a house at Bexley Heath, Kent (p. 999), built for him by Philip Webb (1834–96), which represents a new trend, towards simplicity and away from the extravagances of contemporary historicism. Though it still has the flavour of the Gothic Revival it marks a move in the direction of the 'functional' architecture of the twentieth century. A similar restraint had appeared a decade earlier in the work of George Devey (1820–86), who built a great many country houses, and contemporaneously in that of W. Eden Nesfield (1835–98), which instead has a 'Queene Anne' character, later developed strongly in the individualistic architecture of Norman Shaw (1831–1912), who became extremely influential in the Late Victorian period. To the same train of development belongs also the output of E. W. Godwin (1833–86). At Liverpool are two remarkably advanced commercial buildings of the sixties by Peter Ellis (d. 1884) (p. 1047), quite unhistorical in design and wholly framed in cast iron.

(C). In the Late Victorian period, while the principal mode was the so-called Queen Anne, popularized by Norman Shaw, the range of historical sources tapped by designers broadened almost to include every known style. Old favourites variously strongly maintained their appeal, while others came freshly into favour, notably, towards the end of the century, Romanesque, Byzantine and Baroque, while Flemish Early Renaissance became a special favourite for buildings in terra-cotta, a material never more extensively employed than at this time. There was, however, progressively less concern with historical accuracy, and progressively more with the quest for novelty and for architectural expressions more in keeping with the age. On the one hand the outcome was an enhanced eclecticism, elements of different styles being blended or combined in the one building, and on the other, the sporadic appearance of new motifs for which there was no historical precedent, or even of whole buildings conceived in a new spirit. In the latter, attempts were made to design buildings rationally rather than to cast them in bygone moulds, and to allow ornament to proceed naturally from structure. The invigorating influences produced the Arts and Crafts Movement mentioned previously, yet as also we have seen, were equally if less obviously at work upon domestic, commercial and industrial architecture. In turn, the Arts and Crafts Movement generated 'Art Nouveau', a decorative movement of such vitality that for a brief span of years, from about 1892 to 1905, it assumed the consequence of an architectural phase. This was almost wholly Continental European, thoroughpaced British examples being relatively few. In Britain, a principal exponent was Charles Rennie Mackintosh (1868–1928) of Glasgow, in his own day more famous on the Continent than at home. Despite the seeming contradiction, Art Nouveau, even at its most extravagant, was part and parcel of the same rationalistic movement as was affecting the work of progressive architects in general. It clearly expresses antipathy towards historic ornament, and as events in Continental Europe were later to show, represents a positive step in the development of the 'organic' architecture of modern times; for what is not so obvious is that the external exuberance masks a transformation taking place in spatial planning and a growing appreciation of the aesthetic virtues of simple geometrical forms. When the excessive ornamentation was stripped away, as happened in due course, the potentialities of the essential structural forms became more fully apparent and were seized upon and developed. That story, however, belongs to a following chapter (p. 1062 ff.).

In Britain, logical planning and simple, direct expression already has been substantially achieved in at least one class of building. The houses by Webb, Shaw and Godwin were variously strongly reminiscent of the historic styles (Godwin's interiors were influenced by Japanese Art); others, by younger men like A. H. Mackmurdo (1851–1941) and W. R. Lethaby (1857–1931) somewhat less so, while the best of those of Charles Francis Annesley Voysey (1857–1941) show scarcely a trace. Voysey thus stands out very importantly in the train of evolution of the progressive architecture of today. A Yorkshireman, he had at one time been assistant to George Devey (p. 991), beginning his own practice in 1882, this chiefly concerned with houses of modest dimensions. All these personalities carried considerable influence upon the Continent, but over the turn of the century none more so than Voysey and Mackintosh, earlier named. Another who achieved direct simplicity in his best houses was Edgar Wood (1860–1935), though these are more obviously related than Voysey's to Art Nouveau. Baillie Scott (1865–1945) and George Walton (1867–1933) are others who continued to build homely dwellings into the new century.

British Art Nouveau was very much more subdued than the Continental mode: indeed it is impossible to draw any strict line between it and the preceding Arts and Crafts movement. Both had some effect upon buildings of all classes, whatever their type of expression, be it Gothic, Classic or Romanesque Revival, sometimes inducing a comparative simplicity or a note of asymmetry, though usually only traceable in the dressings and ornament. C. H. Townsend (1850–1928) was more adventurous than most in introducing the new spirit into urban building, and Edward S. Prior (1852–1932), pupil of Norman Shaw, was original in most of his work, which at the height of his career was strongly infused with Art Nouveau feeling. Prior was the author of *History of Gothic Art in England* (1900) and *Cathedral Builders in England* (1905). The majority of buildings remained firmly 'old style', pretentious, fussy and crowded with detail, like interiors in general at this time, which were never more overloaded with knick-knackery. Notable for their fine Gothic designs were Basil Champneys (1842–1920) and John Francis Bentley (1839–1902), the latter far better known, however, for his last and greatest work, Westminster (R.C.) Cathedral (p. 1011). For Neo-Baroque, in a brief phase overlapping the end of the century, there is John Belcher (1841–1913), author of *Essentials in Architecture* (1907), a book on architectural theory which takes up the principles defined by Ruskin in 1849; and the brilliant Edwin Alfred Rickards (1872–1920) while a partner in the distinguished firm of Lanchester, Stewart (d. 1904) and Rickards. Alfred Waterhouse did some of his best work in the period. Norman Shaw, also active throughout and beyond the period, was not consistent in the character he imparted to his buildings. Some of his earliest houses were responsible for the 'half-timber' vogue still tenuously surviving in suburban residences today. His churches and urban structures have excellent quality and many innovations, while being eclectic or strongly based on one or other of the historic styles.

(D). After the Victorian era, Britain lost its lead in most architectural matters. For long, the U.S.A., France and other Continental manufacturing countries had been vying with her in technological developments, and in the second half of the nineteenth century had been keeping a generally similar pace, innovations being

A. Highclere Castle, Hampshire (1842–4). See p. 996

B. Cliveden, Buckinghamshire (1849–51). See p. 996

A. Bridgewater House, London
(1847–57). See p. 996

B. Pugin House, Ramsgate
(1841–3). See p. 996

C. Scarisbrick Hall, Lancs (1837–52).
See p. 996

D. Castle Coch, Cardiff (18
hall. See p. 999

E. The Vicarage, S. Saviour's, Coalpitheath,
Gloucestershire (1844–5). See p. 996

F. Adcote, Shropshire (1877
See p. 999

due sometimes to one nation and sometimes to another. Now, in the early twentieth century, it was Continental Europe that assumed the role of pioneer, in architectural design as well as in constructional method.

Up to the war of 1914–18, architecture in Britain merely maintained the trends noted in connection with the previous, Late Victorian, phase; and after that war, before economic recovery could fully take place came the depression centred around 1932. Revivalism remained paramount, the various modes so blended or loosely interpreted as almost to defy definition except as 'Free Classic' or—for churches—'Free Gothic'. Commercial buildings became higher and their window areas expanded still more, as they could well do, since the steel frame, supporting the masonry shell rather than buried within it as was normal with the cast- and wrought-iron frames quite extensively used in the previous phase, came into use about the beginning of the century. The first steel-framed building of this nature in London is reputed to have been the Ritz Hotel (1905–6), by the architects Mewés and Davies, and it is perhaps significant that the first of these, Charles Mewés (1858–1947), was a Frenchman, of international reputation. (However, the method already had been used in the U.S.A. by W. Le B. Jenney as early as 1883–5, in the early stages of development of the sky-scraper (see p. 1152)). The advent of reinforced concrete, the most significant building material of the twentieth century, was delayed by restrictive building regulations, and the initial appearance of the material in a building of importance was in the extensions to the General Post Office, London (1907), by Sir Henry Tanner. There were, of course, quite a few individual buildings of merit erected during the period, and two architects in particular, Sir Edwin Lutyens (1869–1944), whose work included buildings in Delhi, Washington and Rome, and Sir Giles Gilbert Scott (1880–1960), grandson of Sir George Gilbert Scott of mid-nineteenth century fame, had their own admirable personal interpretations of traditional architecture, the one favouring Neo-Classic and the other Neo-Gothic. Lutyen's first commission was in 1887 and Scott's in 1903, both being active through most of the first half of the century. Sir Robert Lorimer (1864–1929), Scottish architect, completed much of his best-known work within the period. Notable for his domestic architecture and far more for his sterling contributions to Town Planning was Sir Raymond Unwin (1863–1940), author of *Town Planning in Practice*.

Between the World Wars I and II taste and the economic depression at first occasioned an architecture of stripped Classicism, or its Gothic parallel, but by the nineteen-thirties, the Modern architecture evolved on the Continent was beginning to be understood and emulated (the nature of this architecture will be more fully explained in Chapter XXVIII). The British architects, and those from the Commonwealth working in Britain, who first practised it included Wells Coates (1895–1958), E. Maxwell Fry (b. 1899), A. D. Connell (b. 1901), B. R. Ward (b. 1902), C. A. Lucas (b. 1906) and F. R. S. Yorke (b. 1906). They were joined by certain distinguished foreigners, most of whom stayed in Britain only a few years; B. Lubetkin (b. 1901), of Russian birth, Erich Mendelsohn (p. 1068), Walter Gropius (p. 1066) and Marcel Breuer (p. 1159), coming from Germany, and Serge Chermayeff (b. 1900). Most buildings, however, remained essentially traditional until after World War II when, after the country had recuperated, Modern architecture expanded rapidly and is now ascendant in all classes of structure.

EXAMPLES

DOMESTIC BUILDINGS

In the Early Victorian period (1830–50), revivalist classical architecture turned from 'Antiquarian' to Italian High Renaissance character, while the Gothicists generally favoured what was known as 'Tudor', which was in fact mostly freely imitative of the Elizabethan and Jacobean English phases, and is sometimes therefore known today as 'Jacobethan'.

Harlaxton Hall, Lincolnshire (1834–55) (p. 1004A), by Antony Salvin, is a picturesque, strongly-modelled and ornate mansion, reasonably authentic in its 'Jacobethan' detail. By the same architect was **Scotney Castle, Kent** (1837–40), a much plainer but pleasant building.

Highclere Castle, Hampshire (1842–4) (p. 993A) is a refacing by Sir Charles Barry of an existing mansion. Also 'Jacobethan', it is formal and severe in its modelling if not in its detail. It is a four-square block with serried two-light transomed windows in three tiers, demarcated by pilastered Orders and crowned by pinnacled pierced parapets. Angle towers rise a storey higher, and a massive principal tower rises in further stages to command the whole.

Bridgewater House, London (1847–57) (p. 994A), a town house of grand scale by Sir Charles Barry, is in the Renaissance Revival mode he first introduced in his Travellers' Club (pp. 956, 987, 1019). The house is arranged around a high, galleried central hall (in lieu of the Italian 'cortile'), and has some splendidly-decorated formal apartments on the 'piano nobile'. It is astylar, with regularly-spaced consoled segmental-pedimented windows over a rusticated basement. There are bolder rustications at the building's angles, their lines carried up above the cornice by chimney stacks. The second floor windows are set in the deep, panelled frieze of a bold, astragal-type entablature, with balustrade over.

Cliveden, Buckinghamshire (1849–51) (p. 993B), a stately country house by Barry, stands very graciously on a raised terrace, its astylar, arcaded basement storey extended into colonnaded short wings. Above, rhythmically-spaced Ionic pilasters closely embrace a range of consoled triangular-pedimented tall windows, these having smaller windows above them.

Scarisbrick Hall, Lancashire (1837–52) (p. 994C), by A. W. N. Pugin, Gothic enthusiast, was completed by his son, E. W. Pugin, between 1860–8. Its attractive picturesque grouping may have been deliberate, but the building incorporates some Mediaeval remains which already had been partially restored in 1814. The son's work was principally at the east end, including the upper part of the inordinately high tower, and that of the parent mainly in the centre, around the hall proper. Pugin's extraordinary decorative ability gave the Gothic Revival a new turn.

The **House at Ramsgate, Kent** (1841–3) (p. 994B), built for himself by Pugin in his own version of the Gothic (he had built an earlier residence, of eccentric design, S. Marie's Grange, near Salisbury, in 1835–6, which he had occupied for the previous five years), is of flint on the road elevation, with stone dressings, and grey-yellow brickwork for the toothed quoins and for the walling elsewhere. Notable features are the studied asymmetry, the steep, barge-boarded gables and the general informality of the arrangements. Only the more important windows have label-moulds, transomes and traceried heads, and there is a first-floor oriel of timber of quite unorthodox design.

The **Vicarage, S. Saviour's, Coalpitheath, Gloucestershire** (1844–5) (p. 994E), an early design by William Butterfield, is a freely-planned composition of stone rubble with ashlar dressings. The main rooms are reached from the living-hall, as was normal in the traditional yeoman's house. The roofs, which have gable parapets, are steep, and there are casually-disposed angle-buttresses as well as a square, shallow bay.

High Victorian domestic architecture (1850–75) still included many 'Jacobethan' buildings, but the phase is particularly notable for the expansion of the Gothic Revival at the expense of the Classical, and the beginning of a rational movement in

A. The Red House, Bexley Heath, Kent (1859–60). See p. 999

B. Glen Andred, Groombridge, Sussex (1866–7). See p. 999

A. Alford House, London (1872).
See p. 999

B. 196, Queen's Gate, Londo
(1875). See p. 1000

C. 170, Queen's Gate, London (1888).
See p. 999

D. Old Swan House, Londo
(1876). See p. 999

E. The Pastures, North Luffenham, Rutland
(1901). See p. 1000

F. 180, Queen's Gate, L
don (1885). See p. 100

which interest in homely craftsmanship and the inherent qualities of building materials tended to replace the prevailing fashionable preoccupation with ostentatious stylar display.

The **Red House, Bexley Heath, Kent** (1859–60) (p. 997A) built by Philip Webb for William Morris, sociologist and decorative designer, so named because of its materials, red brick and tiles, represents a striking change from the normal pretentious and heavily stylized dwelling of the period. Although its high-pitched roofs and occasional pointed arches are faintly reminiscent of English Mediaeval architecture, it is informal and novel in its arrangements, intimately domestic in appearance and convenient to the requirements of the day.

Another fine brick and tile-roofed house by Webb is **Smeaton Manor, Yorkshire** (1877–9), much more formal but equally direct, simple and unadorned, deriving its qualities from the materials, neat arrangement and excellent proportions.

Glen Andred, Groombridge, Sussex (1866–7) (p. 997B), was the first wholly personal design by Norman Shaw, though he was at that time still in partnership (to 1868) with W. Eden Nesfield. Shaw's style was not as yet fully formed, and the effect is somewhat restless, due to the crowding of certain of the features and the use of tile-hanging on the upper part of the house. Yet the house has an honesty of expression which compares favourably with the products of most of his fellow architects. In it there are hints of the so-called 'Queen Anne' style which he was later to make so popular. Much more romantic is his **Leys Wood, Groombridge** (1868–9), a large brick and partly tile-hung structure arranged around three sides of a court, embodying Mediaeval motifs, including half-timber elements. Half-timber appears also in a number of houses that followed: **Grim's Dyke, near Harrow** (1872); **Wispers, Midhurst, Sussex** (1875); and **Pierrepont, Farnham, Surrey** (1876). In these and several others Shaw's indebtedness to late Mediaeval and Elizabethan architecture is patent, whether the main materials be brick, timber or stone. In the last material is **Adcote, Shropshire** (1877) (p. 994F).

Alford House, London (1872) (p. 998A), by Sir M. D. Wyatt, evidences French 'Second Empire' influence (p. 1063) upon English architecture at this time, evident in Classic design, as here, as well as in Gothic. This town house is of brick with luxuriant terra-cotta dressings and a mansard roof.

Cardiff Castle (1865) and **Castle Coch, near Cardiff** (1875) were reconstructed for the Marquess of Bute at the dates given, the architect being William Burges, in an extraordinarily fantastic personal version of the Gothic Revival, flavoured with French and oriental notions (p. 994D). The profusion of detail and ornament is representative of Late Victorian architecture in general, even if these particular concoctions are unique to Burges.

Late Victorian domestic architecture is generally more restless and congested than at any other time, bygone styles of whatever country being ransacked for novel ideas. A coarse Gothic Revivalism survived longer in domestic than in public architecture, especially among the lesser dwellings, before succumbing to one or other of the Classical modes. For the larger residences the 'Queen Anne' and Flemish Renaissance became particularly popular, and the best versions were relatively simple and had qualities expressive of their own time. Towards the end of the period, and beyond, quite a few houses were affected in greater or less degree by Art Nouveau.

Old Swan House, Chelsea (1876) (p. 998D) by Norman Shaw, is a dignified brick mansion the design of which owes quite a little to historical Georgian architecture, yet is original in many ways. The cantilevered upper portion is carried upon an iron frame. Shaw's **No. 170, Queen's Gate, London** (1888)

(p. 998c), square-built, plain and unadorned save for stone quoins and shutters to the triple tiers of sash windows, is more truly 'Queen Anne', while his **No. 196, Queen's Gate, London** (1875) (p. 998b), wholly of brick, rising in five twin-pilastered storeys to a scrolled, windowed and pedimented gable had a considerable influence upon the domestic architecture of the time. Another example, again of brick and with an arcaded angle porch, is **No. 180, Queen's Gate, London** (1885) (p. 998f). In 1876–7 Shaw laid out Bedford Park, London, an early experiment in suburban planning, and he and several other well-known architects, including E. W. Godwin, built modest and pleasant houses there, mostly in the Queen Anne vein. An earlier nineteenth-century venture in town-planning had been the industrial village of Saltaire, Yorkshire (1851–3) in relation to a mill built for Sir Titus Salt by William Fairbarn; and it was followed in 1888 by the model industrial town of Port Sunlight, near Chester. All these were greatly admired on the Continent.

The **Forster House, Bedford Park** (1891) (p. 1001b) by C. F. A. Voysey, was one of the first in which a definite breakaway was made from traditional conceptions. As nearly as possible the house was reduced to its elemental components, presenting externally its white stuccoed fronts with low, casement windows disposed informally to the greatest internal advantage. The plan is neat and compact and the general air of the house 'cottage' and comfortable. The topmost of the three tiers formed a studio. The wide eaves, supported at intervals by light iron stays, the canopied entrance door and the tapering chimney stacks are features which were to become popular in English Art Nouveau. Similar in style but larger and low-crouching, a style made familiar by countless imitations, are **Broadleys, Gill Head, Windermere** (1898–9) (p. 1001a), with three bow-windows of two storeys penetrating a low Westmorland-slated dormered roof, and **The Orchard, Chorley Wood, Herts** (1899), the latter having shallow sloping buttresses at the principal end of the long rectangle of the house. Others, long, low, with ranges of casement windows of a varying number of lights, white walls and stone-slated roofs, gabled or hipped, extended into the next century, **The Pastures, North Luffen-ham, Rutland** (1901) (p. 998e), **The Homestead, Frinton, Essex** (1905) and S. **Winifred's Quarry, Coombe Down, near Bath** (1909) being further examples. A feature of certain of Voysey's houses was the large and comfortable living-hall, the stair at **The Orchard** rising informally out of it (p. 1002a).

The **Barn, Exmouth, Devonshire** (1896) (p. 1003a), by E. S. Prior, has an approximately symmetrical blunted-V-shaped plan, entered in the inner angle. In character it is dominantly Art Nouveau, the composition having little or no historical allusion. The house has varied floor levels, walls of local stone textured and patterned and in part stuccoed or tile-hung, tiled steep roofs forming a complex geometrical pattern, large cylindrical chimney stalks tapering slightly to lidded caps which have side outlets between stone balls, and extensive transomed windows on the terraced garden front. Part of the hall rises through two storeys. Somewhat similar in plan is his **Home Place, Kelling, Norfolk** (1904) (p. 1003b), an elaborate symmetrical composition with splay wings, the main entrance here being upon one outer flank. The generously-large, axially placed hall again goes through two storeys. Prior's obsession with wall patterning and the use of miscellaneous local materials here gives the house an extraordinarily garish and restless air, bricks of various colours being used to diversify the flint-built walls. The numerous prominent chimney stalks are vaguely Elizabethan in their intricate detail.

Up to the Great War of 1914–19, the previous Classical trends were maintained, though dwellings became plainer than they had been. Gothic Revivalism concluded, and the promise held out by the Arts and Crafts Movement and Art Nouveau faded: the new functional or 'Modern' architecture, developed on the Continent,

A. Broadleys, Gillhead, Windermere (1898–9). See p. 1000

B. The Forster House, Bedford Park, London (1891). See p. 1000

C. Exterior

D. Entrance hall

Hill House, Helensburgh, Dumbartonshire (1902–3). See p. 1007

E. Upmeads, Stafford (1908). See p. 1007

F. Derngate, Northants (1916). See p. 1007

A. The Orchard, Chorley Wood, Herts (1899): hall. See p. 1000

B. Hous' Hill, Nitshill, Glasgow (c. 1906): music room. See p. 1007

A. The Barn, Exmouth, Devonshire (1896). See p. 1000

B. Home Place, Kelling, Norfolk (1904). See p. 1000

A. Harlaxton Hall, Lincolnshire (1834–55). See p. 996

B. Deanery Garden, Sonning, Berks (1900–1). See p. 1007

C. Temple Dinsley, Herts (1909). See p. 1007

A. Sun House, Hampstead, London (1935). See p. 1007

B. House near Halland, Sussex (1938). See p. 1007

A. Highpoint 1, Highgate, London
(1934–5). See p. 1008

B. House in Newton Road, Pad(
ton (1939). See p. 1007

c. Belem Tower, Sefton Park, Liverpool
(1958–9). See p. 1008

D. Alton Estate, Wandsworth, Londo
(1954–6). See p. 1008

made little or no progress before *c*. 1930, and even in the post-wars period Britain has remained somewhat in arrears. Yet under its influence historicism consistently diminished and today the practices opposed to Modernism can only be summed up loosely as 'traditional'.

Hill House, Helensburgh, Dumbartonshire (1902–3) (p. 1001C, D) is one of several houses by C. R. Mackintosh, the most distinguished of the few Britons who practised architectural Art Nouveau. It has a similar directness and homely character to Voysey's houses, with white walls, informally disposed casement windows and an absence of historic ornament, though here the composition is tinged with a Scottish 'Baronial' flavour. The house embodies innovations in interior design (p. 1001D), as also does the same architect's **Hous' Hill, Nitshill, Glasgow** (*c*. 1906), where the Music Room (p. 1002B) shows his extraordinary sense of volume and spatial values.

No. 78, Derngate, Northampton (1916) (p. 1001F), an alteration and extension of an existing terrace house by C. R. Mackintosh, is a remarkable anticipation, unique for Britain, of the Modern architecture of the future, with its forthright geometrical composition, white walls, enclosed balcony, plain vertical balusters and, in general, genuine structural expression, unencumbered with ornament.

Upmeads, Stafford (1908) (p. 1001E), by Edgar Wood, has a symmetrical front, unadorned, parapeted brick walls, flat roof and plain casement windows so arranged as to accentuate the stone entrance porch and centre feature. Like other houses by the same architect, it is in most respects a progressive design showing Art Nouveau traits and a tendency towards functional expression.

Hampstead Garden suburb (begun 1906), Letchworth Garden City (begun 1903) and Welwyn Garden City (begun 1920), the latter two following the principles laid down by Sir Ebenezer Howard (1850–1928), founder (1899) of the Garden City Movement, were important developments in which modest, neatly-designed dwellings were set in pleasant, green surroundings. Howard's principles were adapted for the governmental policy embodied in the New Towns Act of 1944.

The **Deanery Garden, Sonning, Berks** (1900–1) (p. 1004B) is one of the many fine works of Sir Edwin Lutyens. His designs regularly were based upon tradition but invariably infused with fresh, contemporary feeling. He used building materials —brick, terra-cotta or stone—with the greatest attention to their natural properties, and paid scrupulous attention to detail. Many of his designs follow historical vernacular styles, though some, like **Temple Dinsley, Herts** (1909) (p. 1004C) have the character and qualities of the historical greater houses. Others by him are **Marsh Court, Stockbridge** (1901); **Heathcote, Ilkley** (1906); **Gledstone Hall, Skipton** (1923); and some at the Hampstead Garden suburb (1907–9).

The **Sun House, Hampstead, London** (1935) (p. 1005A), by E. Maxwell Fry, is an early instance of English 'Modern' domestic architecture. The flat roof, white walls, metal-and-glass ribbon windows, metal handrails, balustrades and gates, concrete canopies and balconies, all are significant features. The main rooms on the first floor have a virtually unimpeded glass wall, while the bedroom windows are appropriately reduced in height. The house is attractive in its play of form and contrast of solid and void, and needs no ornament to enhance its domestic virtues. Other notable late inter-war examples are a further **House at Hampstead** (1938), by Connell, Ward and Lucas, a **House near Halland, Sussex** (1938) (p. 1005B), by Serge Chermayeff, a simple, two-floored, timber box-frame structure standing in park-like spacious grounds, and an urban **House in Newton Road, Paddington, London** (1939) (p. 1006B) by Denys Lasdun, which has the service quarters on the ground floor, together with a garage, the living rooms and bedrooms respectively on the first and second floors and a studio and balcony on the top floor. Only the south (entrance) front of the latter is in concrete, the rear walls being in eleven-inch brickwork.

Highpoint I, Highgate, London (1934–5) (p. 1006A), by Tecton, is an eight-storey group of flats, standing on pillars or 'pilotis', made up of wings thrown outwards to catch the sun and air. There are generous windows and balconies on each storey, and the flat roof is turned to useful account.

Since World War II flats have been a much more common form of civic housing than formerly in cities and large towns, complementing housing schemes of the normal two-floored types. Among the many fine flat blocks erected in the post-wars period are the **Spa Green Estate, London** (1949) by Tecton; the **Churchill Gardens Development, Pimlico, London** (1951) by Powell and Moya; the **Tower Block, Harlow New Town** (1951) by Frederick Gibberd; the **Belem Tower, Sefton Park, Liverpool** (1958–9) (p. 1006C) by Ronald Bradbury; and the **Alton Estate, Wandsworth, London** (1954–6) (p. 1006D) by H. Bennett, Sir J. L. Martin, R. H. Matthew, H. J. Whitfield Lewis and others.

CHURCHES

S. Wilfred, Hulme, Manchester (1839–42), by A. W. N. Pugin, largely of red brick, was designed in accordance with the architect's ecclesiological principles, and was described by him in his book *The Present State of Ecclesiastic Architecture in England*. It differs from the average 'Commissioner' Gothic Revival church of the preceding period in having separately articulated parts—nave, aisles and south porch, together with eastern lateral chapels divided from the aisles and chancel by ornamentally-painted screens. It was to have had an asymmetrical tower at the north-west corner, which would have made it the first Revival church to depart from the axial principle, but funds gave out before it was built. Intended to demonstrate that a Gothic 'correct' church need not be more costly than a classical one, it is in fact mean and pinched and of little architectural merit.

S. Giles, Cheadle, Staffs (1841–6) (p. 1009A), by Pugin, is stone built and finely finished. Its composition profits by the presence of a commanding axial western tower and spire. Not unduly ornamented outside, its interior retains all the rich furnishings and polychromatic painted decoration that the designer intended.

S. Giles, Camberwell Church Street, London (1842–4) (p. 1009B), by Scott and Moffatt, the commission for which was won in competition before George Gilbert Scott had set up on his own account, is a large stone structure seating 1,500 persons. Cruciform in plan, it rises to an impressive, spire-crowned central tower over 200 ft high, the spire patterned in dressings of a lighter-coloured stone, which give a somewhat disturbing effect. Designed in Geometrical Gothic style, it demonstrated Scott's powers and also provided a model for certain of his own later churches as well as for those of fellow architects. Other notable Gothic Revival churches, slightly later in date, are **S. Paul, Brighton** (1846–8), by R. C. Carpenter; **S. Stephen, Rochester Row, London** (1847–50), by Benjamin Ferrey; and **Holy Trinity, Bessborough Gardens, London** (1849–52), by J. L. Pearson.

All Saints, Margaret Street, London (1849–59) (p. 1009C), by William Butterfield, was the first and most outstanding of the High Victorian churches. It stands on a cramped site, with a parsonage and choir school adjacent. It was built by public subscription as a model church of the Camden Society. Typical of Butterfield are the harsh angularity of the forms, the hard-faced enduring materials and the strident 'constructional polychromy' found externally and internally. Vaguely, the design was based upon the 'Middle Pointed' or fourteenth-century Gothic, this being the popular model of the day. The façades and the high and rather narrow tower, turning abruptly to an octagonal spire, are banded and patterned

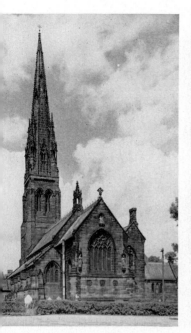

S. Giles, Cheadle, Staffs (1841–6).
See p. 1008

B. S. Giles, Camberwell Church Street, London
(1842–4). See p. 1008

. Church, Choir School and Parsonage   D. Interior: nave and chancel
All Saints, Margaret Street, London (1849–59). See p. 1008

A. Truro Cathedral, Cornwall (1880–).
See opposite page

B. The Chapel, Lancing College, Sussex
(1854–). See opposite page

C. Keble College, Oxford: chapel (1873–6). See opposite page

with black brick on bright red, the spire being further varied with stone (p. 1009C). Inside, there are geometrical patterns and frescoes on the walls, ornament brilliant in the varied colours of marble, alabaster, brick and glazed tiles, stained glass windows and gilded ironwork and woodwork (p. 1009D). The church had its critics, but was enormously influential. Constructional polychromy became a mark of the High Victorian period. Among many other churches by Butterfield are **Keble College Chapel, Oxford** (1873-6) (p. 1010C), and **S. James, Baldersby, Yorkshire** (1856), a fine composition upon an unencumbered site, with a dominating spire located asymmetrically over the south porch.

The **Chapel, Lancing College, Sussex** (1854-) (p. 1010B), by R. C. Carpenter, had been barely commenced at the architect's death in 1855, like the college of which it forms a part. The grand asymmetrical west-end tower he intended was never carried out. The chapel evidently owes something to French influence, as it has soaring proportions and double flying-buttresses externally, spanning the aisles, though not at the half-octagonal east end, where the aisles are not carried round.

The **Caledonia Road Free Church, Glasgow** (1856-7) (p. 1013A), by Alexander Thomson, is an admirable if belated example of the Greek Revival, this style having survived much longer in Scotland than in England. However, it has the asymmetrical western tower normal to High Victorian Gothic, an impressively massive structure terminating rather weakly above an open belfry in an inset, heavily-corniced attic. The hexastyle west porch, of faultless Classical proportions, is raised upon a high podium adorned only with lateral entrance doors. Two other Presbyterian churches by Thomson, also in Greek Revival style, are in S. Vincent Street (1859) and Queen's Park (1867), Glasgow.

Truro Cathedral, Cornwall (1880-) (p. 1010A) by J. L. Pearson, was not wholly completed at his death and was continued by his son. A granite structure, it is typical of the architect's style; grand, plain and bold. He was expert in vaulting, not often used in churches in his time. There are spired central and western towers, and powerful vertical emphasis is given to the transept fronts and east end.

Westminster (R.C.) Cathedral (1895-1903) (p. 1013B, C), by J. F. Bentley, was based upon Byzantine precedents for the practical reason that in this particular style the main structure could be finished reasonably quickly and the internal decorative veneers applied afterwards when the church had been put into service. That process has actually been followed. There is a spacious nave, 60 ft wide, covered by three pendentived domes, 112 ft above the floor to the crown, flanked by aisles with side chapels—or, in the case of the easternmost dome, by transepts— bringing the full width to 98 ft (p. 1013C). A fourth, slightly smaller, dome covers the sanctuary and choir, and the full length to the apse is 342 ft. The grey-brown bricks of the walls are being progressively sheathed with similar marbles to those used in S. Sophia (p. 280), chapel by chapel, and the vaults covered with mosaics. Over the altar is a white marble baldachino supported on yellow marble columns. Externally (p. 1013B), the brick walls are patterned horizontally with stone, and near the N.W. angle rises the sheer campanile known as S. Edward's tower.

Liverpool Cathedral (1903-) (p. 1014A, B) by Sir Giles Gilbert Scott, who won the commission by competition at the early age of twenty-two, is still incomplete, though it has now progressed from the east end westwards well beyond the central tower. It is in many ways original but essentially is in Free Gothic style of the Decorated period. It is untraditional in having a double-axis symmetry—apart from relatively minor masses at the east end—dominated by a great central tower (p. 1014A), on either side of which lie double transepts. The spaces between the double transepts are bridged over by arches to form northern and southern porches. The material mostly is red sandstone, the vaults being covered by upper roofs of reinforced concrete. The eventual floor area will be about 100,000 square ft, greater than any existing cathedral in England (S. Paul, London, is 63,000 sq. ft), the internal length being 480 ft and the width, including the aisles, 87 ft, the vaults rising to 173 ft.

S. Andrew, Roker, near Sunderland (1906) (p. 1015), the masterpiece of E. S. Prior and a great testimony to his interest in the qualities of building materials, is a fine, strong and masculine Free Gothic church with many Art Nouveau characteristics, standing on an elevated site commanding the neighbouring coastline. Insofar as it is Revivalist, it is eclectic, combining Norman and Gothic traits. The massive walls flanking the nave, this 43 ft wide and 105 ft long, are pierced by shallow aisles in their 7 ft 6 in thickness, the inner faces of the splayed piers demarcating the lateral windows being carried on paired 'Norman' pillars of original design; from their lintels spring diaphragm pointed arches supporting the open roof (p. 1015C). The arches spanning the short transepts are splayed inwards to embrace the choir space and to connect with the narrow chancel, 24 ft wide, above which is a dignified tower, with hexagonal angle turrets (p. 1015B). The mullions and embryonic tracery of the ample windows are powerfully strong, admirably in keeping with the whole vigorous design. The fitting, furnishings and decoration were contributed by persons eminent in the Arts and Crafts movement.

S. Jude, Hampstead Garden Suburb (1910) (p. 1014C), by Sir Edwin Lutyens, is eclectic, but the historically-discordant elements are handled in the designer's unfailingly brilliant fashion to form a most agreeable composition. Latin cross in plan, a central tower with open belfry and crowning spire dominates the massing, and a vast pitched roof, similarly of Mediaeval aspect, broken by tall dormer windows, sweeps down almost to the ground over the aisles, though for the rest the design is of Classical, Renaissance, character.

The **Church of the Annunciation, Old Quebec Street, London** (1912) (p. 1016A), by Sir Walter Tapper, is one of the best examples of late Gothic Revivalism. It has few novel features, but is a dignified structure, of brick with stone dressings, of excellent proportions.

The **War Memorial Chapel, Charterhouse School** (1922-6) (p. 1016B) by Sir Giles Gilbert Scott, is in the Gothic Revival mode yet has refreshingly original dispositions. Rectangular in plan and high-proportioned, the severity of the longitudinal walls is relieved by angle turrets and tall, slot-windows in buttress-like projections.

S. Nicholas, Burnage, Manchester (1931) (p. 1016C), by Welch, Cachemaille-Day and Lander, instances the endeavours being made at this time to break away from revivalism and to secure the right qualities by contemporary methods and materials. The interior effects are contrived by simple means: the wall openings are skilfully disposed, certain of the pillars within them being left in exposed brickwork, the walls otherwise being finished in tinted plaster; the Lady Chapel, partitioned off by a metal grille, is raised above the sacristy and vestries; and below is the altar, against the brick-faced podium wall. Very important to the effect is the panelled, darkly-coloured wall-board ceiling. Equally original for the period is **S. Saviour, Eltham, Kent** (1932) (p. 1016D), by the same architects.

The **Cathedral, Guildford** (1936-) (p. 1017A), by Sir Edward Maufe, the subject of a competition, still is only partially completed. Traditional in its cruciform, central-towered composition, and Gothic Revival in theme, it is extremely broad and bold in scale, the massive simplicity of the towering brick walls contrasting powerfully with the traceried tall windows.

The **Cathedral, Coventry** (1951-62) (p. 1018), by Sir Basil Spence, the major ecclesiastical building of the post-wars period, lies on a N.S. axis at right angles

A. Caledonia Road Free Church, Glasgow (1856–7). See p. 1011

B. Westminster Cathedral (1895–1903): exterior from south-east. See p. 1011

C. Westminster Cathedral: interior from west

A. Central tower from south   B. Interior: bay below tower

Liverpool Cathedral (1903–). See p. 1011

c. S. Jude, Hampstead Garden Suburb, London (1910). See p. 1012

A. Exterior from S.W.

B. East front, showing tower
over chancel

C. Interior, looking east

S. Andrew, Roker (1906). See p. 1012

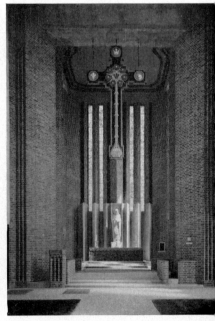

A. Church of the Annunciation, Old Quebec Street, London (1912). See p. 1012

B. War Memorial Chapel, Charterhouse School, Surrey (1922–6). See p. 1012

C. S. Nicholas, Burnage, Manchester (1931): interior. See p. 1012

D. S. Saviour, Eltham, Kent (1932): interior. See p. 1012

A. Guildford Cathedral, west front (1936–). See p. 1012

B. Church at Tile Hill, Coventry (1957). See p. 1019

A. Interior looking north

B. East side and Chapel of Christ
the Servant

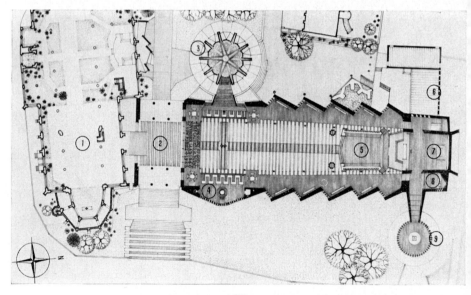

c. Plan

1, Ruins of old cathedral.   2, Entrance porch.   3, Chapel of Unity.
4, Baptistry.   5, Chancel.   6, Refectory.   7, Lady Chapel.
8, Chapel of Christ in Gethsemane.   9, Chapel of Christ the Servant.

Coventry Cathedral (1951–62). See p. 1012

to the former church, of which the spired tower and ruined walls are being preserved to form a ceremonial approach to the new cathedral, which otherwise is reached from an adjacent double-sided porch astride the axis. The Cathedral is a modern version of a hall-church, 250 ft long by 80 ft wide, the high-proportioned nave and aisles being divided by slender, downward-tapering pillars, fanning out at the head into a faceted vault, pierced with decorative patterns (p. 1018A). The side walls are formed in oblique short sections, joined by tall stained-glass windows running the full height, which throw the incoming light towards the altar. Behind the altar is the Lady Chapel, the rear wall of which is clothed with a vast tapestry. A 'Chapel of Unity', of circular plan, projects westward near the entrance end, and a smaller, circular, 'Chapel of Christ the Servant' lies beyond the east side of the Lady Chapel.

The **Church at Tile Hill, Coventry** (1957) (p. 1017B), by Sir Basil Spence, is one of three churches built to serve a new community. It is a simple rectangle, walled in 'no-fines' concrete, the low, open timber roof being sustained on concrete frames. The latter afford the only decorative relief to the body of the church internally, apart from the entrance door, small side windows and tall, lattice-framed windows which admit a flood of light on either side of the altar, illuminating a fine tapestry filling most of the east wall. Adjacent to the church is a church hall and a concrete, openwork belfry.

PUBLIC BUILDINGS

The **Travellers' Club, Pall Mall, London** (1829–31) (p. 1021A, B), by Sir Charles Barry, initiated the Renaissance Revival in England. The two-storey façade (p. 1021A) is astylar, with toothed angle-quoins, regular architecturally-enframed windows—those of the upper floor being of the aedicule type—and a console-corniced, asymmetrically-placed doorway. The storeys are divided by an ornamental string, and there is a crowning astragal cornice. The main features are said to have been derived from Raphael's Palazzo Pandolfini at Florence (p. 756). On the garden front (p. 1021B) the windows have a Venetian grouping, those of the first floor being round-headed and those of the lower square-headed and ornamentally rusticated.

The **Reform Club, Pall Mall, London** (1838–40) (p. 1021C, D), by Barry, adjoins his Travellers' Club and is similar in design but has a central doorway and is larger and three-storeyed, the upper range over the regular, aedicule, windows being embraced in the astragal frieze below the main cornice. Barry's **Athenaeum, Manchester** (1837–39), actually the earlier of the two, is a further variant upon the same 'palazzo' theme.

The **Fitzwilliam Museum, Cambridge** (1837–47) (p. 1022C), by George Basevi and C. R. Cockerell, is a fine flourish of the departing 'Antiquarian' mode, still continuing in this period in the more monumental work of a few architects. Cockerell continued the work after the death of Basevi in 1845. The building is vigorous in modelling but coarser in detail than Neo-Classical monuments of the first quarter of the century. The façade comprises a giant Corinthian portico extended into pilastered, buttress-like wings.

Westminster New Palace (Houses of Parliament), London (1840–60) (p. 1022D), by Sir Charles Barry, with the assistance of A. W. N. Pugin, is Neo-Tudor in decorative detail although axial and classical in plan. The plan is in some respects asymmetrical, partly in order to accommodate Westminster Hall, which had survived the fire of 1834. Substantially, the architectural dispositions are Barry's and the busy detail Pugin's. The buildings extend along the Thames side a distance of rather more than 900 ft, the river terrace being on the east side, where the front is symmetrical, ending in angle pavilions. The formal approach from the west or landward side is via S. Stephen's Porch, which also gives access to Westminster Hall and delivers into the Central Hall, where a cross-axis leads south to the House of Lords and north to the House of Commons. Subsidiary suites of chambers are arranged around a series of courts. In the S.W. corner rises the massive Victoria Tower, 336 ft high, and at the northern end is the Clock Tower, 316 ft in height, the clock faces of which are 23 ft across, wherein is a 13-ton bell, 'Big Ben'. There is a further 'Middle Tower' or spired lantern over the Central Hall, rising to 300 ft in height. This great complex of buildings, with its wonderfully intricate Tudor detail, had great influence upon the course of the Gothic Revival, though during the long period of its building Tudor Gothic largely went out of fashion in favour of fourteenth century precedents.

The **Ashmolean Museum (University Galleries) and Taylor Institution, Oxford** (1841–5) (p. 1021E), by C. R. Cockerell, a confirmed classicist, is an extensive, southward-facing building breaking forward at the ends into wings. It is ornamented with a giant Ionic Order, pilastered mostly but with slightly-freestanding or attached columns at the principal points. The monumental qualities are most apparent on the east front of the east wing (p. 1021E), where the Order is the Ionic of the Temple of Apollo Epicurius at Bassae (p. 124), with its extraordinarily deep capitals, which Cockerell had himself studied in Greece in his youth. The entablature returns above the columns, which carry only statues.

S. George's Hall, Liverpool (1842–54) (p. 1023C), was the outcome of a competition won by the youthful H. L. Elmes in 1839. After his untimely death in 1847, the work was continued successively by Sir Robert Rawlinson and C. R. Cockerell, who each made their contributions to this, the most splendid monument of the century. The main axis of this Classical building runs north-south, and the two long fronts are essentially symmetrical; the south short front has an octastyle porch and the north is rounded and faced with attached columns. The overall dimensions are 420 ft by 140 ft wide, the centre portion being occupied by the Great Hall, and the two wings by court rooms. The principal front is the east, where a grand portico of sixteen Graeco-Roman Corinthian columns matches the length of the Hall.

The **Royal College of Physicians, Edinburgh** (1850–4) (p. 1021F), by Thomas Hamilton, has a Graeco-Roman façade with an entrance porch flanked with columns of the type of those of the Tower of the Winds, Athens (p. 140).

The **National Gallery of Scotland, Edinburgh** (1850–4) (p. 1023A), by William H. Playfair (1789–1857), is a monumental building in Ionic Greek Revival style. Among other important buildings in the city Playfair also designed the **Royal Institution** (1833–6) (p. 1023B), in a cumbrous version of the Greek Doric.

The **University Museum, Oxford** (1855–9) (p. 1024A, B), by Sir Thomas Deane (1792–1871) and Benjamin Woodward (1815–61), is a landmark of Victorian High Gothic architecture, regarded by Eastlake as 'one of the first fruits of Mr. Ruskin's teaching'. The main front (p. 1024A) has a narrow, steeply-roofed central feature, containing the entrance door, flanked by two-storey wings in which there are regularly-spaced windows of Italian Gothic type. In the steep roofs of the wings there are triangular dormers in two series, the upper extremely small. The walls are of cream-coloured Bath stone, with inset marbles around the doorway head and upper-window arches, and the roofs are patterned in purple and grey-green slates. Internally, there is a quadrangle roofed with iron and glass (p. 1024B), the ironwork decoratively 'Gothicised' with elaborate ornament. The roof is carried upon clustered and banded iron pillars, from which spring arcade ribs and steeply-pointed transverse ribs, the latter reaching to the apex of the glazed, pitched roof. As the covered quadrangle is itself walled about by polychrome arcades, the total effect

A. Pall Mall front (*right*)   B. Garden front

The Travellers' Club, Pall Mall, London (1829–31). See p. 1019

c. Exterior   D. Saloon

The Reform Club, Pall Mall, London (1838–40). See p. 1019

E. The Taylor Institution, Oxford (1841–5): east front. See p. 1020   F. Royal College of Physicians, Edinburgh (1850–4). See p. 1020

A. Royal Manchester Institution Building (1824–35), now the City Art Gallery.
See pp. 877, 956, 987

B. Carlton House, London:
conservatory (1811–12).
See p. 989

C. The Fitzwilliam Museum, Cambridge (1837–47)
See p. 1019

D. Westminster Palace, London (1840–60). See p. 1019

A. The National Gallery of Scotland, Edinburgh (1850–4). See p. 1020

B. The Royal Scottish Institution Buildings, Edinburgh (1833–6). See p. 1020

C. S. George's Hall, Liverpool (1842–54). See p. 1020

A. The University Museum, Oxford (1855–9). See p. 1020

B. The University Museum, Oxford:
interior

C. The Albert Memorial, London
(1863–72). See p. 1025

is extremely busy and ill-calculated to afford effective contrast with the exhibits.

The **Foreign Office, London** (1860–75) (p. 1027A), by Sir George Gilbert Scott, is in Neo-Renaissance, High Victorian style. It has no great merit, being irresolute and diffuse, perhaps for the reason that Scott was here obliged to adopt the Classical style against his will by the Prime Minister, Lord Palmerston, who abhorred the Gothic. Scott adapted his rejected Gothic designs to serve for the hotel buildings fronting S. Pancras station (p. 1039D).

The **Albert Memorial, London** (1863–72) (p. 1024C), by Scott, marks the zenith of the Gothic Revival and is its best known and most representative monument. The seated figure of the Prince is covered by a pointed-arched spired canopy of vari-coloured marbles, adorned with numerous free-standing sculptures and a bas-relief of 178 famous artists around the base, the whole monument standing on a high flight of steps. The total height is 175 ft, higher by five feet than the **Nelson Column in Trafalgar Square, London,** erected in 1843 from the designs of William Railton (1803–77) (the lions were added in 1867). The Albert Memorial had been the subject of a competition held in 1862, won by Scott, and in the same year Thomas Worthington won a similar competition for the **Albert Memorial, Manchester** (p. 1028A), producing a design which bears a remarkable likeness, though it is simpler and of English rather than Continental Gothic inspiration. Which was the prototype is not clear.

The **Assize Courts, Manchester** (1859–64), by Alfred Waterhouse, were irreparably damaged in World War II and demolished in 1959. It was by this building, won in competition, that Waterhouse first made his name. After its completion, it was said to 'unite considerable artistic merit with unusual advantages in regard to plan and internal arrangement'. A symmetrical two-storey building, over a windowed basement, with an arcaded central entrance block, slightly-projecting angle pavilions and a bell-tower rising axially behind, it was typical High Victorian Gothic in its admixture of English, Lombard and French characteristics, the latter shown especially in the high-pitched and pavilioned roofs. Of somewhat similar character is Waterhouse's **Town Hall, Manchester** (1868–77) (p. 1028A), placed fourth as regards its 'thirteenth century Gothic' elevations in the two-stage competition concluded in 1867, but deemed much superior to others 'in the supply of light, the facility of ventilation, the ease of access and the general excellence of the plan'. Waterhouse was also the architect of the Gothic **Owens College (University), Manchester** (1870–1902). In his **Natural History Museum, South Kensington, London** (1879–80), he turned to the Romanesque.

The **Town Hall, Congleton, Cheshire** (1864–7) (p. 1029B) by E. W. Godwin, is in Italian Gothic style. It is a two-storeyed scheme, arcaded below, with a central machicolated and battlemented tower rising vertically from the façade. A modest and pleasant building, it is much superior to his larger, asymmetrical and elevationally-congested **Town Hall, Northampton** (1861–4), otherwise of similar character. 'Constructional polychromy' is employed in both buildings.

The **Law Courts, London** (1874–82) (p. 1028B), by G. E. Street, one of the last important buildings to be erected in the Gothic style, is a huge, vigorously modelled and romantic composition, attractive but inconvenient.

New Scotland Yard, London (1887–8) (p. 1027B), by Norman Shaw, is a well-known building in which the lower storeys are wholly stone-faced and the upper of brick with stone horizontal striations. At the angles there are domed turrets reminiscent of Scottish castle architecture, and the steep, dormered roofs finish in gables on the front, their apices embellished with architecturally-enframed decorative niches. In the latter and the elaborate asymmetrically-placed doorway there is something of the vigorous character of the English Baroque.

The **Rylands Library, Deansgate, Manchester** (1890–9) (p. 1029A), by Basil Champneys, is a splendid if belated example of secular Gothic Revival. It is a much lighter and more gracious Gothic than was normal in the High Victorian period, the richly-ornamented centre-piece and the great bay-windows of the recessed upper stage contrasting effectively with the relatively plain walls on the lower flanks, in which deep, traceried windows are set in studied asymmetry. For the materials and the craftsmanship in stone, wood and metal, no expense was spared.

The **School of Art, Glasgow** (1897–1909) (p. 1030A, B, C) by C. R. Mackintosh, is one of the few examples in Britain of Art Nouveau, being almost completely novel in its forms and evidencing only the barest trace of historicism. It faces north and was built in stages, the eastern half in 1897–9 (p. 1030A), and most of the remainder in 1907–9, after some modifications of the original design which affected the west end, the rear and the interior. Most dramatic is the west end (p. 1030B), which anticipated developments on the Continent by more than a decade, being comparable with some of the work of de Klerk and Kramer (p. 1067) at Amsterdam. Still more striking are some of the interior effects, especially the library (p. 1030C), which shows a remarkable feeling for spatial values, evidenced also in the architect's commercial and domestic interiors (pp. 1001D, 1002B).

The **Whitechapel Art Gallery, London** (1897–9) (p.1030D), by C. H. Townsend (1850–1928), has a façade of Art Nouveau character in which a very large dual portal is placed asymmetrically in the composition, the remaining features, too, having novel dispositions and treatment. Local asymmetry of features became a fashionable practice in the following decade, and may be seen also in the centre-piece of the Glasgow School of Art (p. 1030A): it led eventually to the comprehensive asymmetry common in Modern architecture.

The **Town Hall, Colchester** (1898–1902) (p. 1029C), by J. Belcher (1841–1913), is a fine example of Neo-Baroque, of which there are quite a few notable instances of about this period, including the **City Hall and Law Courts, Cardiff** (1897–1906) (p. 1031B) and the **Methodist Central Hall, Westminster** (1906–12), both by Lanchester and Rickards.

The **London County Hall** (1912–22) (p. 1031A), by Ralph Knott (1878–1929), is a Thames-side building of strong Free-Classical design showing some French influence.

New Delhi, India (1913–30) (p. 1031C), a great administrative centre laid out by Sir Edwin Lutyens, who also designed the Government Buildings there, is a scheme of far greater splendour than any carried out during the same period in Britain. The city plan follows classical axial principles and is connected with old Delhi, seven miles distant. It has an axis running east and west two miles in length, flanked by lawns and canals, at the foot of which is the colossal All India War Memorial Arch, and to the westward lies an open space ornamented with six fountains. Off this, to the north, lies the circular Council Chamber, by Sir Herbert Baker (1862–1946). The axis, continuing westward between the two Secretariats designed by Baker, leads up to the principal monument of the new city, the President's House (1920–31), a splendid building of enormous size. The general view (p. 1031C) indicates this magnificent lay-out in which Indian architectural motifs with domes and minarets are bound together in a design almost western in character.

The **Cenotaph, Whitehall, London** (1920) (p. 1032C), by Lutyens, is the principal instance of great numbers of memorials erected to commemorate the Fallen in World War I, and which served as prototype for many of the others. An annual service of remembrance is conducted there on the Sunday nearest to Armistice Day (November 11th). It is a tall, simple monument of Portland stone, of Classical character, mounting in slightly receding stages to a tomb-shaped terminal.

A. The Foreign Office, London (1860–75). See p. 1025

B. New Scotland Yard, London (1887–8). See p. 1025

A. The Town Hall, Manchester (1868–77) with Albert Memorial on left. See p. 1025

B. The Law Courts, London (1874–82). See p. 1025

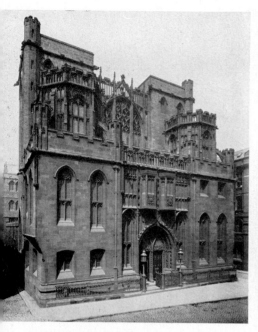

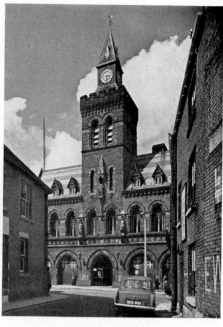

A. The Rylands Library, Manchester
(1890–9). See p. 1026

B. The Town Hall, Congleton, Cheshire
(1864–7). See p. 1025

C. Town Hall, Colchester (1898–1902).
See p. 1026

D. The Municipal Buildings, Norwich
(1938). See p. 1035

A. North front (1897–9)   B. West end (1907–9)

The School of Art, Glasgow (1897–1909). See p. 1026

C. School of Art, Glasgow: D. The Whitechapel Art Gallery, Lond
    the library (1907–9).   (1897–9). See p. 1026

A. London County, Hall, Westminster (1912–22). See p. 1026

B. Cardiff Civic Centre: Aerial View. See p. 1026
Law Courts (*left*) and City Hall (*centre*), 1897–1906; National Museum of
Wales (*right*), 1910–27

C. New Delhi: Aerial View looking W. (1913–30). See p. 1026

A. The Bank of England, London (1788–1833) with upper portion added,
1923–33. See p. 1035

B. R.I.B.A. Building, London (1932–1934). See p. 1035

C. The Cenotaph, Whitehall, London (1920). See p. 1026

D. The City Hall, Swansea (1930–4). See p. 1035

A. The Senate House, University of London (1933–9). See p. 1035

B. The Royal Corinthian Yacht Club, Burnham-on-Crouch,
Essex (1930). See p. 1035

C. The Pentley Park Primary School, Welwyn, Herts (1948–50).
See p. 1035

A. Impington Village College, Cambs (1936). See p. 1035

B. The Day Nursery, Garston, Herts (1951–2). See p. 1035

c. The Finsbury Health Centre, London (1938–9). See p. 1035

The **Bank of England, London** (1923–33) (p. 1032A). Additions were made at this time by Sir Herbert Baker in the form of a new block rising in the rear of Soane's façades, with a columned centre feature projecting from it towards the street line.

The **City Hall, Swansea** (1930–4) (p. 1032D) by Sir Percy Thomas (b. 1883), the **Municipal Buildings, Norwich** (1938) (p. 1029D) by C. H. James and Roland Pierce and the **R.I.B.A. Building, Portland Place, London** (1932–4) (p. 1032B) by G. Grey Wornum (1888–1957) are leading instances of traditional classical design in an aesthetically-economical and refreshed mode, current in the later inter-wars period.

The **Senate House, London University** (1933–9) (p. 1033A) by Charles Holden (1875–1960), consists of two large four- and five-storey rectangular blocks, 248 ft by 166 ft, joined together by a massive tower, 120 ft wide at the base and 210 ft high. Forecourts on the east and west sides of the tower lead to a vestibule in its base, above which are the libraries and stack rooms. The southern block contains the administrative rooms and the northern certain other University elements. All the walls are load-bearing, being of stone-faced brickwork, although there is a steel frame in the tower to take the weight of the book stacks. In elevational character the building is not very dissimilar to the London Passenger Transport Building, Westminster (p. 1048), by the firm of which Charles Holden was a member.

The **Royal Corinthian Yacht Club, Burnham-on-Crouch, Essex** (1930) (p. 1033B) by Joseph Emberton, is one of the earliest English buildings of its class to attain a non-stylistic expression, the south front towards the river Crouch being wholly functional and comprising tiers of deep balconies with continuous ribbon windows behind. Of steel-framed construction, the walls of the main block are of stucco-faced cavity brickwork.

Impington Village College, Cambridgeshire (1936) (p. 1034A) by E. Maxwell Fry (b. 1899) and Walter Gropius, the latter having reached England from Germany in 1934 (p. 1066), represents a new departure in school design. An attractively informal and mainly one-storey structure, it caters for adult education whilst also serving the normal purpose of a school.

The **Finsbury Health Centre, London** (1938–9) (p. 1034C) by Tecton, is unaffectedly symmetrical in mass arrangement, having been designed to fulfil its purpose in a thoroughly efficient and economical manner. A 'Modern' design in the full sense, it has a concrete frame and façades faced with glazed tiles, the windows of the two-storey wing blocks being linked vertically with opaque glass panels.

In the years following the Second World War the national policy for new building was concentrated strongly on the erection of schools and dwellings, and many fine, yet economical, schools were erected.

The **Pentley Park Primary School, Welwyn Garden City, Herts** (1948–50) (p. 1033C) by C. H. Aslin (1893–1959), the County Architect, instances the trend in post-wars schools design for younger children, away from institutional formality and towards a domestic intimacy of scale and character. Full advantage is here taken of an undulating wooded site: the buildings cannot be viewed comprehensively. The individually-arranged classrooms are generously lighted and the walls are of pre-cast concrete slabs on a light steel frame. The **Day Nursery, Garston, Herts** (1951–2) (p. 1034B) by Aslin, admirably fulfils similar objectives. The structure is a light steel frame, the supports being within the thin walls of metal and glass and laminated plaster, these protected above by a deep fascia of fluted asbestos. The **Hallfield Primary School, Paddington, London** (1955) (p. 1037A), by Drake and Lasdun, is another possessing excellent qualities. Built on a well-treed site, its concrete buildings are diversified in character and shape, presenting many intriguing and attractive facets.

The **Royal Festival Hall, London** (–1951) (p. 1037B), by R. H. Matthew, Sir J. L. Martin, Peter Moro and Edwin Williams, prepared for the 'South Bank' Exhibition of that year, brought an entirely new kind of architecture to the Thames river front. Its principal contents are a large auditorium to seat 3,000, primarily for orchestral and choral concerts, and a smaller hall for recitals, chamber music, ballet and the like, but also there are the attendant promenades, foyers and refreshment bars and a spacious restaurant—this facing the river—an exhibition gallery and meeting rooms, together with all the requisite ancillary accommodation for the respective elements. The structural frame is of reinforced concrete, and the auditorium is suspended above a grand foyer approach. There are no solid load-bearing walls, all the work being done by reinforced-concrete pillars, the interior partitions and outer sheath being of glass and metal or light materials. The whole endeavour was to make it a gay, cheerful and sparklingly-refreshing building. The exterior successfully fulfils this objective and expresses the nature of the construction, which plainly appears as a sheath upon a caged frame. Patterns are contrived in the sheathing by the disposition of the window and void areas, and the terraced setting, with diverting look-out features inclining over the river bank, and made gay with slender masts, adds further variety to the total effect.

Industrial and Commercial Buildings

The **Royal Arcade, Newcastle-upon-Tyne** (1831–2) (p. 1038A), probably from the designs of John Dobson, was a part of the town-planning enterprises of Richard Grainger and Dobson, carried out from *c.* 1824 onwards, which gave the streets of the city centre their fine complexion. The arcade leads through a building block which architecturally has the same tasteful Greek Revival character as many others forming part of the scheme, the Monument of Lysicrates (p. 139) here having provided the inspiration for the Corinthian capitals used for the attached columns forming the upper part of the external façade, though the entrances and the arcade itself are Doric. The arcade was designed to provide professional and commercial premises, and is arranged in a series of bays with circular glass-and-iron top lights standing over pendentives. John Dobson also designed the monumental **Central Station, Newcastle-upon-Tyne** (1846–50).

The **Entrance Screen, Euston Station, London** (1835–7) (p. 1038C) by Philip Hardwick, was at first the only frontispiece to the then very simple building which comprised the station. Four pavilions stood side by side, and centrally between them was an enormous and impressive Doric Gateway (p. 1038C, destroyed 1962) which originally led to elongated porticoes flanking the approach way, where arriving passengers might descend from their carriages. In their thoroughpaced Greek garb, the screen and gateway represented an already departing fashion in the metropolis. Behind them the present **Station Buildings, Euston** (1846–9), again by Philip Hardwick, assisted by his son, P. C. Hardwick (1822–92), are Graeco-Roman. The Great Hall (p. 1038D) is particularly impressive.

The **Sun Fire Office, Threadneedle Street, London** (1841–2), by Professor C. R. Cockerell, with its three-storeyed rusticated façades, stylar only on the top floor, is nearer to the new Italian Renaissance 'palazzo' mode than the majority of Cockerell's monumental buildings, for he usually adhered in these to a bold Graeco-Roman character. In 1833 he had become architect to the Bank of England in succession to Sir John Soane, and made alterations there in 1834–5 and again in 1845, whilst also building several branch banks in the principal cities: **Plymouth** (1835); **Bristol** (1844–6) (p. 1039A); **Manchester** (1845–6); and **Liverpool** (1845–58) (p. 1039B). They are similar, both in the composition of their strongly-modelled façades and in the classical elements they comprise. Commonly a

A. The Hallfield Primary School, Paddington, London (1955).
See p. 1035

B. The Royal Festival Hall, London (–1951). See p. 1036

A. The Royal Arcade, Newcastle-upon-Tyne (1831–2). See p. 1036

B. The Coal Exchange, Lower Thames Str London: interior (1846–9). See p. 1041

C. Entrance Gateway, Euston Station, London (1835–7). See p. 1036

D. Great Hall, Euston Station, London (1846–9). See p. 1036

Bristol branch, Bank of England (1844–6).
See p. 1036

B. Liverpool branch, Bank of England
(1845–58). See p. 1036

c. Bank (now Williams Deacons), S. Ann's
Square, Manchester (1848–9). See p. 1041

D. S. Pancras Station, London (1866–71).
See p. 1042

A. The Conservatory, Chatsworth, Derbyshire (1836–40). See p. 1041

B. The Palm House, Royal Botanic Gardens, Kew (1845–7). See p. 1041

C. King's Cross Station, London (1851–2). Original state. See p. 1042

Greek- or Roman-Doric attached Order brackets the lower storeys and above them is an attic storey in which at least one of the windows is round-arched, the whole crowned by a pediment. Each design is in fact eclectic, the Greek and Roman elements being combined rather than fused, and Renaissance and Baroque elements are here and there introduced.

The **Bank** (now **Williams Deacons) S. Ann's Square, Manchester** (1848–9) (p. 1039C), by J. E. Gregan (1813–55), is representative of classical architecture in the Early Victorian period in being of Italian Renaissance 'Palazzo' style. Standing at the angle of the square, it has a rusticated ground floor storey with Palladian windows, pedimented aedicule windows on the first floor and square-headed windows on the second floor, these last being in the frieze of an astragal cornice. The upper tiers are ashlar finished except that there are rusticated toothed quoins at the building angles. The entrance doorway is placed in a one-storey structure which links the bank proper with a rear building, of brick with stone dressings, forming part of the same scheme.

The **Conservatory, Chatsworth, Derbyshire** (1836–40; demolished 1920) (p. 1040A), was an early venture in iron and glass by the gardener-architect Joseph Paxton, assisted by Decimus Burton, in the grounds of this sixteenth and late seventeenth-century mansion (p. 872). It was not the first of its kind, except in its extraordinary magnitude, being 277 ft long, and 123 ft wide, rising to a height of 67 ft in the form of a double vault, one cloister vault being raised upon another. The glass ridge-and-furrow sections anticipated those of the famous Crystal Palace.

The **Palm House, Royal Botanic Gardens, Kew** (1845–7) (p. 1040B), by Decimus Burton and Richard Turner, resembles the Chatsworth design in its central part—except that all the glass follows the vault section precisely, and that it is crowned by a shallow, continuous apex feature—but has extended wings of slightly ovoid section, rounded at the ends, again bearing the continuous apex feature. The central portion spans 106 ft and rises 62 ft; the wings 56 ft for a height of 33 ft. Kew is substantially smaller than Chatsworth in the floor area covered, yet makes a much more handsome structure.

The **Coal Exchange, Lower Thames Street, London** (1846–9, scheduled for demolition) (p. 1038B), by J. B. Bunning (1802–63), was a corner block presenting Italian Renaissance façades linked by a be-columned tower over the angle entrance. It was notable for its internal iron-framed glass dome over the circular court, the dome being 60 ft in diameter and 74 ft high, with cantilevered access balconies serving each of its three upper tiers. The whole structure, walls and dome, was metal-framed, and no masonry at all appeared. A comparable domical building is the **Reading Room, British Museum** (1854–7), added there by Sydney Smirke, the structure similarly being of iron but of much greater dimensions, the room being 140 ft across and 106 ft high.

The **Crystal Palace, London** (1850–1) (p. 1043), by Sir Joseph Paxton, was the most remarkable building of the High Victorian period. Originally erected in Hyde Park, to house the Great Exhibition of 1851, it was moved to Sydenham in 1852–4 and destroyed by fire in 1936. The idea of holding a great exhibition was conceived in 1849, and public subscriptions invited. An international competition was launched in 1850 and 245 designs were received. On the score of cost and the time needful to complete, all were set aside in favour of an idea of Paxton's, after an attempt to combine the best features of the more promising of the competition designs in a single official project. The working drawings were hurriedly prepared in a seven week period after the contract actually had been let in August 1850, and the structure was wholly completed nine months later, May 1st 1851. Paxton's idea, arising from his experience at Chatsworth and elsewhere, was a giant conservatory.

In cross section the building somewhat resembled a double-aisled basilica, rising in three tiers, the lowest 408 ft wide, the next (the inner aisles) 264 ft and the nave or topmost, 120 ft. However, the 'aisles' and 'nave' were divided from one another by tiered open galleries 24 ft wide, so that the actual span of the 'nave' was only 72 ft (the same as its height). Symbolically, the total width was made up of fifty-one of the 8 ft-wide bay units, and the length was 1,848 ft, this being as near to 1,851 as the 8 ft-units would allow. The roofs were supported by openwork horizontal girders carrying Paxton's favourite ridge-and-furrow glazing. About the middle of the length a 'transept' was introduced, as a last-minute modification of the working design, to allow the enclosure of a growing tree. The transept had the same width as the nave but was barrel-vaulted. In this colossal project of prefabricated building, requiring vast quantities of iron and glass and other materials as well as scrupulous organization to allow the work to be completed in so short a time, Paxton had as engineer-associates Sir Charles Fox (1810–74) and his partner, while Owen Jones (1809–74), author of the well-known book *Grammar of Ornament* (1856), was responsible for the decoration. Changes were made when the Palace was re-erected at Sydenham, the nave then being given a barrel roof, like the transepts (p. 1043B).

King's Cross Station, London (1851–2) (p. 1040C), by Lewis Cubitt (1799–?), has an entrance façade which is part and parcel of the station sheds behind, reflecting them in a pair of vast brick arches in receding orders, with a clock-tower rising on a buttress-like mass between. Before the station acquired the untidy medley of miscellaneous structures in front of it, there could be seen the triple-arcaded porticoes below each of the great arched windows which lent a Roman scale and dignity to the unassuming composition. The two iron-and-glass barrel vaults over the tracks are carried on laminated-timber arches rising 72 ft to bridge the 105 ft spans.

Paddington Station, London is of interest principally for its station sheds (1852–4) by the celebrated engineer, I. K. Brunel and the architect M. D. Wyatt (1820–77), the rich and fussy 'High Victorian' Great Western Hotel forming the frontispiece (1851–3) being an independent conception by P. C. Hardwick. The sheds are of three spans totalling 238 ft, the centre one being wider than the others. Each of the coverings is carried on semi-elliptical wrought-iron ribs, without principals, glazed only over the central third. The three are joined together by cross vaults at two points in the length.

S. Pancras Station, London, like Paddington, was conceived independently of the (former) Midland Hotel and offices which front it. The shed (1863–5), by the engineer W. H. Barlow (1812–1902), is the largest and most spectacular of the High Victorian period, being a single span of 243 ft, rising 100 ft high in a slightly pointed arch. The total length is 700 ft. At the base the arched vault is secured by 3 ins diameter rods under the platforms. The **Hotel and Station block** (1866–71) (p. 1039D), by Sir George Gilbert Scott, is the prime example of High Victorian secular Gothic. Won in competition in 1865, the building allowed free rein to Scott's predilection for the style. The frowning frontages rise through tiers of crowded pointed-arched openings to a steeply-pitched roof busy with jagged dormers, massive chimney-stalks and soaring pinnacled and spired towers.

The **Warehouse, Jamaica Street, Glasgow** (1855) (p. 1044A), with its cast-iron façades, illustrates the great popularity of the material about this time. Iron was economical of floor space and allowed virtually continuous runs of large windows. The small scale of the parts and the extended repetition of a single motif are typical of the period.

The **Boatstore, Royal Naval Dockyard, Sheerness** (1858–60) (p. 1045), by

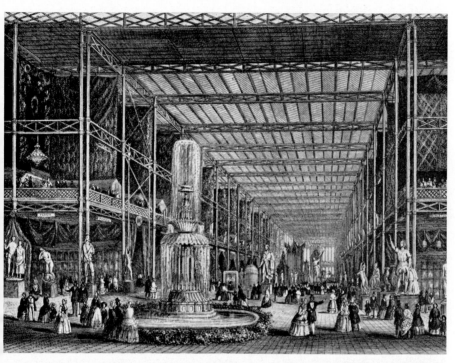

A. The Crystal Palace at completion in Hyde Park, London (1850–1): interior

B. Revised structure, re-erected (1852–4) at Sydenham, London

The Crystal Palace, London. See p. 1041

A. Warehouse, Jamaica Street,
Glasgow (1855). See p. 1042

B. Oriel Chambers, Liverpool
(1864–5). See p. 1047

C. Deller's Café, Exeter (1900): destroyed. See p. 1047

A. Boatstore, Royal Naval Dockyard, Sheerness (1858–60). See p. 1042

B. Boatstore, Royal Naval Dockyard, Sheerness: interior

A. The Piccadilly Hotel, London
(1905–8). See p. 1047

B. The Horticultural Hall, London
(1923–6). See p. 1047

C. The Eagle Insurance
Building, Birmingham (1900).
See p. 1047

D. The Shakespeare Memorial Theatre, Stratford-on-Avon
(1928–34): river front, with later additions.
See p. 1047

G. T. Greene, who from 1850–64 was Director of Engineering and Architectural Works to the Admiralty, is among the earliest known tiered iron-framed buildings, particularly advanced in the details of its construction. Being a utilitarian building, the external panels could be lightly infilled with sheeting. It is 210 ft long and 135 ft wide, arranged internally as a top-lit 'nave' running the whole length of the building, and double 'aisles' on each side with floors at each of the four storeys. The stanchions already have the 'H' section which came regularly to be adopted later on.

Oriel Chambers, Liverpool (1864–5) (p. 1044B), by Peter Ellis, is another remarkably advanced building for the period, both in construction and architectural character. It has a complete cast-iron frame, stone cladded on the front in thin stone piers, between which are iron frames carrying delicately-detailed shallow oriels in each panel. There is little or no historical allusion in the forms employed, save a suggestion of collegiate Gothic in the cresting. **No. 16, Cook Street, Liverpool** (*c.* 1866), also by Ellis, is of similar construction and equally original.

The **Eagle Insurance Building, Birmingham** (1900) (p. 1046C), by W. R. Lethaby and J. L. Ball, has a façade which shows a little influence of Art Nouveau and the Romanesque Revival but is superior to many buildings of the day in the quality of its design and the honesty of expression. The upper storeys have large efficient windows between stout piers capped with powerfully-moulded strings, that at the top being undulated to suggest alternating segmental and triangular pediments, each with an indented billet moulding supplanting the lower member. The attic is decorated with slightly-projecting roundels. The ground storey has an enormous five-light transomed window, awkwardly truncated at pavement level, flanked by symmetrical doorways with paired windows and small ornamental panels over them.

Deller's Café, Exeter (1900, destroyed) (p. 1044C); the **Ingram Street** (1901) and the **Willow** (1904) **Tea-rooms, Glasgow,** the latter two by C. R. Mackintosh, are among the few genuine instances in Britain of Art Nouveau.

The **Piccadilly Hotel, London** (1905–8) (p. 1046A), by R. Norman Shaw, was the architect's last major work. It is one of the best instances of the Neo-Baroque mode which, along with other expressions, was current over the turn of the century. A series of grand, vigorously-rusticated arches embodies shops at pavement level, and together with a shallow balconied tier immediately over serves as a podium for an open Ionic colonnade, linking pavilions behind which rises the main mass of the building.

The **Ritz Hotel** (1905–6), the **'Morning Post' Building** (1906, altered) and **Kodak House** (1910), **London,** the first two by Mewés and Davies and the last by Burnet, Tait and Lorne, are early instances, for Britain, of the use of the complete steel frame.

The **Midland Bank, Piccadilly** (1922) and **Britannic House, Finsbury Circus** (1922–4) **London,** by Sir Edwin Lutyens; and the **Wolseley Building—** now **Barclay's Bank—Piccadilly, London** (1921–2), by Curtis Green, are among the best instances of modulated historicism in the early inter-wars period.

The **Royal Horticultural Hall, London** (1923–6) (p. 1046B), by J. Murray Easton (b. 1889) and Sir Howard Robertson (b. 1888) shows development towards Modern architecture, particularly in the internal arrangements. Tall, diaphragm arches span the hall and support a series of concrete flat decks, stepped inwards concentrically with the arches and connected vertically with ribbon windows, diminishing in height towards the top of the hall. The deck above the apex has a cone-shaped top light in each bay. Heating is by hot water pipes embedded in the ceiling-decks, an early instance of the method of heating from above.

The **Shakespeare Memorial Theatre, Stratford-on-Avon** (1928–34) (p. 1046D), by Scott, Chesterton and Shepherd, was the outcome of a competition won in 1928 by Elizabeth Scott. A café and restaurant were added on the river front a few years later. Brick is the main material, chosen to harmonize with the architectural character of the small town, and a gracious and dignified effect is contrived without recourse to historical sources for inspiration for the features and detail.

The **London Passenger Transport Building, Westminster** (1929) (p. 1049A) by Adams, Holden and Pearson, has an external character rooted in classicism but so simplified as to exclude the customary detail almost completely. The massing is cleverly contrived along the diagonals of the site, thus obviating courts and giving the maximum amount of natural light; it builds up pyramidally to a height presaging the high city blocks of the future.

The **Boots Chemical Factory, Beeston, Notts** (1930–2) (p. 1049B), by Sir Owen Williams, is not particularly attractive but employs on a vast scale the 'mushroom' type of concrete construction first used on the Continent by Robert Maillart in 1908 (p. 1066). The supporting concrete pillars swell outwards at the top on each storey in a form like an inverted pyramid and support a continuous slab floor. No supports are needed at the margins of the building, so the windows can, if need be, rise in continuous horizontal ribbons, stiffened by the protruding edges of the concrete floors.

The **Penguin Pool, Regent's Park Zoo, London** (1933–5) (p. 1050C), by B. Lubetkin, is a spatial adventure in form which was among the earliest wholly modern designs to be executed in Britain, demonstrating that even the most improbable subjects are capable of yielding high-quality architecture. The somewhat earlier **Gorilla House** (1933) there has comparable virtues.

The **'Daily Express' Offices, Fleet Street, London** (c. 1933) (p. 1049C), by Ellis and Clarke, with Sir Owen Williams, is a concrete-framed building with horizontal 'ribbon' windows and a facing, most unusual for the period, of polished black glass, the joints of the sheets being covered with strips of silver-coloured metal. The colours give the reverse from the normal effect of dark openings in comparatively light walls, throwing the metal strips into visual prominence and giving the building a surprisingly cheerful effect, despite the sombre facing materials. There is a similar *Daily Express* building at Manchester.

The **De la Warr Pavilion, Bexhill, Sussex** (1935), by Erich Mendelsohn and Serge Chermayeff, is a contribution to British architecture by two distinguished foreigners, conveying a distinctly Continental and progressive air. The long body of the hall, its sheer white walls perfectly plain apart from a circular, decorative inscription, forms a striking contrast with the semicircular bay (p. 1049D) at the restaurant end, busy in interest with its tiers of balconies and translucent walls through which the convolutions of the ascending staircase can be seen.

The **Peter Jones Store, Sloane Square, London** (1935–6) (p. 1050A), by William Crabtree, J. A. Slater and A. H. Moberly, with Sir Charles Reilly as consultant, gains much of its attractiveness from the undulations of its façade and the close-spaced vertical ribs which counter the insistence of the long, horizontal windows. An incisive crowning member gains in effectiveness by the recession of the storey immediately below it, giving a band of deep shadow.

The **Brynmawr Rubber Factory, South Wales** (1945–51) (p. 1053A), by the Architects' Co-Partnership, with Ove Arup and Partners, Consulting Engineers, is a large industrial scheme covering almost three acres, in which the main factory area is roofed by nine concrete shell-domes, each of a rectangular plan, 85 ft by 62 ft clear span, arranged in a three-by-three block and standing on pillars at the corners. The general ceiling level is 14 ft above the floor, raised higher locally by shallow segmental domes, $3\frac{1}{2}$ ins thick, sufficiently spaced apart to allow clear-storey

. The London Passenger Transport
Building, Westminster (1929).
See p. 1048

B. The Boots Chemical Factory, Beeston,
Notts (1930–2). See p. 1048

C. *Daily Express* offices, Fleet Street,
London (*c.* 1933). See p. 1048

D. The De la Warr pavilion, Bexhill, Sussex
(1935). See p. 1048

A. The Peter Jones store, Sloane Square, London (1935–6). See p. 1048

B. Office building, 93–7 New Cavendish Street, London (1955–7). See p. 1051

C. The Penguin Pool, Regent's Park Zoo, London (1933–5). See p. 1048

lighting through the lunettes below the domes. The external effect is sightly and the interior impressive.

The **'South Bank' Exhibition, London** (1951) (p. 1053B), for which Sir Hugh Casson was the Director of Architecture, was an important event in the history of British Architecture as it served to popularize the Modern movement, none of the exhibition buildings showing a trace of historicism and all being light, graceful and gay. Very many able architects and designers contributed. The whole site was planned on informal lines and enlivened with flowers, trees, shrubs, water gardens, garden ornaments, statuary and variegated pavings. Numerous fresh ideas were evolved which since have passed into general currency. The Royal Festival Hall (p. 1036) formed a part of the Exhibition and from the first was intended to remain as a permanent building.

The **Office Building, 93–7, New Cavendish Street, London** (1955–7) (p. 1050B) by Gollins, Melvin, Ward and Partners, is a well-proportioned and attractively simple edifice of reinforced concrete, comprehensively curtained with glass, opaque blue-grey in the aprons, in white frames.

COMPARATIVE ANALYSIS

PLANS. Early Victorian secular urban buildings, such as houses, clubs, learned societies' rooms, and public buildings, usually followed a rectangular, Italian 'palazzo' plan, the larger having central open or covered courtyards (pp. 994A, 1021A–D). Later, the same principle was maintained, but cramped urban conditions necessitated many individualistic arrangements, and courtyards usually were abandoned for all but the largest structures, small internal light-wells serving to light such as staircases, lavatories and minor rooms (p. 998B, D). Plans of public buildings, needing rooms of very varied dimensions and uses, grew increasingly complex, and often were made more so by the bays, oriels and other projections from the peripheral walls demanded by the various stylistic expressions adopted for the façades (pp. 1028A, B, 1029A). For factories, mills, warehouses and similar buildings, however, the aim was to provide as much free floor space as possible over large areas, and for these cast-iron pillars were used for the internal supports from the beginning of the century. Top-light was a device often called into service. In the twentieth century similar conditions still obtained in urban building, and the specifics adopted remained much the same, save that frontages were less broken than formerly. By far the greater proportion of nineteenth-century dwellings were terrace houses, and these are specially distinctive of the Industrial Revolution, being very rare before the late eighteenth century. In the earliest terrace houses for the working classes, the individual house plans often repeated exactly, but soon they were arranged in reflected pairs, chiefly to economize in the construction of chimneys. In the twentieth century, terrace houses for a time passed out of fashion, the detached or semi-detached suburban residences becoming the common form of dwelling. Flats, never popular in England previously, are for various reasons now becoming more frequent, for whatever social class (p. 1006A, C, D).

The larger Early Victorian country houses also were frequently of the compact 'palazzo' plan, though if of 'manorial' or 'castellated' character more often were picturesquely irregular (p. 994C), like villas in general. Those of moderate dimensions lacked a centre court, and in arrangement resembled the 'simple block plan' of the Georgian period (type (b), p. 937), rooms being arranged on either side of a longitudinal spine wall, the hall and staircase placed centrally on one long front (p. 993B). Later, this type of domestic plan acquired a far more irregular and individualistic outline, and there commonly were service-quarter appendages

(p. 997B). In general, the houses of the middle classes were never more tortuously complicated than in the Late Victorian period. In the twentieth century they became more simple and regular again (pp. 1001E, 1005A, B); and since World War II even the most luxurious have become quite modest in size, due to the lack of domestic servants, forcing reliance upon labour-saving appliances.

Anglican churches no longer remained the simple galleried boxes they for so long had been, but recovered the articulated form of the Mediaeval church, with nave, aisles, chancel, lady-chapel, south-porch, etc., coherently expressed (p. 1009A, B); and any tower or spire, instead of being invariably axial was frequently placed asymmetrically at the west end (p. 1013A). Nonconformist churches mostly remained of the older type, but certain of the more important followed the same course as the Anglican. Roman Catholic churches, too, followed suit, except that Byzantine forms of plan were occasionally favoured (p. 1013B, C). Recent small churches, built for new communities, for economic reasons are often extremely simple and follow unorthodox lines (p. 1017B).

WALLS. Nineteenth-century façades typically were highly ornate, imitative of bygone classical or Mediaeval styles (pp. 1028, 1039). Classical façades passed from a relatively straightforward 'palazzo' character (pp. 1021A, C, 1039C), through a busier and much less coherent phase (p. 1027A) to a semblance of the Baroque (p. 1046A). Neo-mediaeval secular façades were not prevalent before the High Victorian period, and were commonly even more restless than their classical counterparts, romantic asymmetry being popular (p. 1039D). Italian, French and other Continental influences added a number of exotic features to the regular stock-in-trade. The Romanesque found some favour at the end of the century (p. 1046C). In domestic work the principal styles, (other than the 'palazzo' style, practised contemporaneously) were the Tudor or 'Jacobethan' (pp. 993A, 1004A), passing to a 'Queen Anne' style (p. 998C, D) and thence to an imitation of Flemish Early Renaissance. At the turn of the century there was a brief flourish of English Art Nouveau (p. 1003A). In the twentieth century all the various surviving expressions underwent a process of simplification, the decorative and stylistic features being reduced to a minimum and much more reliance than formerly placed upon the effects to be gained from the simple geometry of the masses and parts (p. 1001E). In Modern architecture after c. 1930 reference to the historical styles ceased completely (p. 1005A, B).

Throughout the whole period, the chief walling materials were brick and stone, brick still gaining ground compared with stone. In the High Victorian phase the two were admixed decoratively, bricks of different colours being worked into patterns with marbles and stone (p. 1009C, D). This practice was known as 'constructional polychromy', since the colours were inherent in the materials themselves, and not applied superficially. It lent itself particularly to the Neo-Gothic, voussoirs of arches being of alternate colours (p. 1024A), but was used in other styles too in the following phase (pp. 1013B, 1027B). Mock half-timber was introduced in the eighteen-sixties, and left a trail for many decades. Nearly always nineteenth-century walls were 'load-bearing' (sustaining the weight of floors and roof), but some use was made of cast-iron framing, sometimes embedded in the walls and sometimes free-standing (p. 1044A, B); and after 1906 steel-framed and then concrete-framed structures became increasingly common for the larger urban structures. Frames are now almost invariably employed. In framed structure loads are carried by the frames and the walls are merely weather-proofing panels; consequently walls may be substituted by thin metal-and-glass screens, with suitable insulating materials behind the parts not used as windows (pp. 1034C, 1050B). 'Curtain walling' is a modern expedient in which a metal-and-glass screen passes

A. The Brynmawr Rubber Factory, South Wales (1945–51). See p. 1048

B. South Bank Exhibition, London (1951), general view. See p. 1051

comprehensively over the face of storeyed steel- or concrete-framed structures, in lieu of solid walls (p. 1050B).

OPENINGS. During the nineteenth century and until World War I, openings were treated in the manner appropriate to the particular revived style adopted. Apart from Graeco-Roman designs of the Early Victorian phase (pp. 1021E, 1023C, 1039A, B) and the Baroque interlude at the end of the century (pp. 1029C, 1046A), colonnades and the giant Order did not often appear. On the other hand, tiered arcaded windows were popular in the second half of the century as a means of admitting the maximum possible light to urban buildings. On cast-iron buildings this device often was used almost exclusively (pp. 1043B, 1044A). In the 'palazzo' (p. 994A) and 'Queen Anne' (p. 998C, D) styles, tall sash or four-light casement windows were usual, sometimes with astragals to give them the genuine historical air, though it was wholly practicable to dispense with them wherever desired, as was often the case with the less pretentious buildings. Mullioned-and-transomed or traceried casement windows accompanied the Tudor, High Gothic and similar expressions, tracery appearing even in secular Gothic buildings in the High Victorian phase (p. 1024A) and to some extent in the next (p. 1029A). In Neo-Gothic churches, mullioned and traceried windows were, of course, normal. Bays and oriels appeared in virtually every revived style. Top light metal-and-glass windows were increasingly employed, and were almost indispensable for such as station-sheds, factories and similar one-storey extensive buildings (p. 1046B). Windows of early steel-framed commercial buildings frequently were drawn together by metal aprons to form large vertical panels between the Classical columns or piers masking the stanchions. In general in the early twentieth century, the decorative enframements normal to historical windows were either highly simplified or wholly suppressed (p. 1032B, D), and in Modern architecture windows are always clean cut, whether they stand singly or form long 'ribbons' of metal and glass (p. 1005A). Also, astragals are dispensed with, windows only being subdivided as necessary for stability or to accommodate opening lights. Large, unimpeded glass areas are a leading modern objective (p. 1034B).

ROOFS. These in the nineteenth century were as varied as the architectural styles employed, and for the most part followed the appropriate historical precedent in each case. 'Jacobethan', Neo-Gothic and Flemish-inspired buildings have the serrated silhouettes endowed by steep ornamental gables, dormers, pinnacles, turrets and chimney-pieces (p. 1004A), while the Classical buildings have low-pitched or even flat roofs. All styles however—but especially the Gothic—were to some extent affected by French influence in the High Victorian period, the roofs in such cases being mansarded (p. 998A) or very steeply-pitched and perhaps divided into separate pavilions. Neo-Gothic houses and villas are today often ridiculed for their excessively diverse and ragged character, the straggling plans with their numerous excrescences being reflected in the tumultuous roofs, crested with spiky ridge-tiles and broken with pretentious dormers, tall ornamental chimney stacks and the inevitable turret or belvedere. Polychromy usually renders the effect still more disturbing, for roofs frequently were covered in colour-patterned slates or tiles to match the constructional polychromy of the walls (p. 1024A). In early twentieth century urban architecture roofs usually were unobtrusive, if not actually flat (p. 1032B, D). Since World War II the flat roof has been ubiquitous (p. 1050B), save only for churches, suburban houses and large-span structures (pp. 1037B, 1053A).

COLUMNS. These were used throughout the nineteenth and early twentieth centuries much in accordance with historical precedent, the customary proportions and parts being maintained (pp. 1023A–C, 1031A). When in cast iron they necessarily were abnormally slender, and the detail was rather coarse, as also was the case when the material was terra-cotta. From *c.* 1906–*c.* 1930 the Orders were used on steel-framed buildings, raising very difficult constructional problems, as columns and entablatures coincided with the main members of the frames, and had to be hung on to them by devious means. Columns of the historical types became rare in the inter-wars period and disappeared almost completely after World War II.

MOULDINGS. As with columns, these reproduced the respective prototypes fairly faithfully, so long as historicism lasted. One of the objects of the Arts and Crafts and Art Nouveau movements was to simplify or evade them, or to invent substitutes (p. 1030A, B). A similar objective was implicit in the Neo-Romanesque, this a further manifestation arising towards the end of the nineteenth century, for the Romanesque is a broad and bold style, in which mouldings are very few and simple (p. 1046C). In many buildings about this time openings often were shorn of their customary enframements or label moulds, or decorative variety was obtained by exploiting the texture and colour of brick and stone rather than by employing the time-honoured architectural elements (p. 1004B, C). In domestic architecture at least, almost total success was achieved in evading mouldings by C. F. A. Voysey (p. 992), although his method of composing buildings remained largely traditional (p. 1001A, B). The process of simplifying or evading mouldings continued in much of the work of the earlier twentieth century, and is complete in the Modern architecture dating from after *c.* 1930 (p. 1006B).

ORNAMENT. Interior decoration gravely deteriorated in the nineteenth century. Ornament became coarse and excessive. The more expensive High Victorian Gothic churches were lavishly finished, the inner walls covered with frescoes or a constructional polychromy of coloured bricks, marbles and mosaic, the windows rich with stained glass and the fittings opulently elaborate in their wood, iron and brass. Colour everywhere and not a square yard of plain wall to lend eye-resting relief (p. 1009D). Secular interiors suffered much in the same way, and great play was made with fashionable cast iron (p. 1024B). By the Late Victorian period, when taste reached its lowest ebb, ornament in domestic fabrics, furniture and fittings had become chaotically profuse, due to the ease with which machinery could reproduce patterns (p. 994D). The Arts and Crafts Movement, which had the object of reviving the handicrafts, and Art Nouveau, did much to reverse the trend. Interiors by Voysey (p. 1002A) show a restrained homely quality, and those by Mackintosh (pp. 1001D, 1030C) a wholly fresh approach, the forms used being quite novel and conceived in three-dimensional terms. Little further progress was made in the early twentieth century, except in moderating previous excesses, until in the inter-wars period Continental ideas in furniture and furnishings began to reach Britain. Taste in interior decoration today favours straightforward, rational and comfortable furniture and uncrowded effects in bright, cheerful and chaste settings.

Externally, the descent of artistic values was less strongly marked. In the Classical revived systems at least, tradition was reasonably closely observed, applied ornament mostly being limited to the customary locations. The Neo-Gothic was more susceptible to over-elaboration. High Victorian Gothic churches were sometimes nearly as elaborate outside as in (p. 1009C), and secular buildings freely ornamented at every practicable point of their restless, romantic surfaces (p. 1028). The most significant and representative monument of the period is the Albert Memorial, London (p. 1024C). At the end of the century, Art Nouveau was characterized decoratively by its polychrome ceramics, ironwork, mural displays and stone and wood carving, the ornament being based on plant forms (p. 1044C). Thereafter, as historicism waned, so did the practice of ornamenting buildings in whatsoever way, other than by occasional judiciously-disposed sculptures, symbols or advertisements

(p. 1037B), reliance for the rest being placed upon the decorative values of the materials employed and uniform tints of applied colour.

REFERENCE BOOKS

BARRY, A. *The Life and Works of Sir C. Barry.* London, 1867.

BLOMFIELD, SIR R. *Memoirs of an Architect.* London, 1932.

—. *Richard Norman Shaw.* London, 1940.

BUTLER, A. S. G. *The Architecture of Sir Edwin Lutyens.* 3 vols. London, 1948.

CASSON, SIR H. *Introduction to Victorian Architecture.* London, 1948.

CLARK, SIR K. *The Gothic Revival.* 2nd edition. London, 1950.

CLARKE, B. F. L. *Church Builders of the Nineteenth Century.* London, 1938.

DANNATT, T. *Modern Architecture in Britain.* Introduction by Summerson, Sir J. London, 1959.

DRUMMOND, A. L. *The Church Architecture of Protestantism.* 1934.

EASTLAKE, C. L. *A History of the Gothic Revival in England.* London, 1872.

FAIRBARN, SIR W. *On the Application of Cast and Wrought Iron to Building Purposes.* 4th ed. 1870. London, 1854.

FERGUSSON, J. *History of the Modern Styles of Architecture.* London, 1862.

GLOAG, J., and BRIDGWATER, D. *A History of Cast Iron in Architecture.* London, 1948.

GOODHART-RENDEL, H. S. *English Architecture since the Regency.* London, 1953.

GRILLET, C. *Edward Prior.* Architectural Review, November, 1952.

HARBRON, D. *Amphion, or the Nineteenth Century.* Toronto and London, 1930.

—. *The Conscious Stone* (Life of E. W. Godwin). London, 1949.

HEARN, A. *The Methodist Church Builds Again.* 1946.

HITCHCOCK, H. R. *Early Victorian Architecture in Britain.* 2 vols. London, 1954.

HOLME, C. G. (Ed.). Introduction by Bucknell, L. H. *Industrial Architecture.* London, 1935.

HOWARTH, T. *Charles Rennie Mackintosh and the Modern Movement.* London, 1952.

HUSSEY, C. *The Picturesque.* London, 1927.

—. *The Life of Sir Edwin Lutyens.* London, 1948.

JONES, J. BRANDON. 'C.F.A. Voysey', *Journal of the Architectural Association*, 1957.

JONES, R. P. *Nonconformist Church Architecture.* 1914.

LETHABY, W. *Philip Webb and his Work.* London, 1935.

MADSON, S. T. *Sources of Art Nouveau.* Oslo and New York, 1956.

MCGRATH, R., and FROST, A. C. *Glass in Architecture and Decoration.* London, 1937.

MARÉ, ERIC de. *The Functional Tradition.* Architectural Review, July, 1952.

MILLS, E. *The New Architecture in Great Britain, 1946–53.* London, 1953.

MUTHESIUS, H. *Das englische Haus.* 3 vols. Berlin, 1904–5.

PULLAN, A. *Architectural Designs of William Burges.* 2 vols. London, 1883–7.

RICHARDS, J. M. *The Functional Tradition in Early Industrial Buildings.* London, 1958.

RICHARDSON, SIR A. E. *Monumental Classic Architecture in Great Britain and Ireland during the XVIIIth and XIXth Centuries.* London, 1914.

R.I.B.A. *One Hundred Years of British Architecture, 1851–1951.* London, 1951.

SCOTT, SIR G. G. *Personal and Professional Recollections by the Late Sir George Gilbert Scott.* London, 1879.

SCOTT-MONCRIEFF, W. *John Francis Bentley.* London, 1924.

STREET, A. E. *Memoir of George Edward Street.* London, 1888.

SUMMERSON, SIR J. N. *Architecture in England since Wren.* 2nd ed. London, 1948.

—. *Heavenly Mansions.* London, 1949.

—. *Ten Years of British Architecture.* London, 1956.

TRAPPES-LOMAX, M. *Pugin, a Mediaeval Victorian.* London, 1932.

TURNOR, R. *Nineteenth Century Architecture in Britain.* London, 1950.

—. *The Smaller English House, 1500–1939.* London, 1952.

YORKE, F. R. S. *The Modern House in England.* 8th ed. London, 1957.

See also the list in Chapter XXVIII (Nineteenth and Twentieth Century Architecture in Continental Europe).

The Burgher Watch House, Cape Town (1755–). See p. 1058

XXVII. ARCHITECTURE OF SOUTH AFRICA, AUSTRALIA AND NEW ZEALAND

THE architectural development of these countries has followed a pattern not dissimilar to that of the Americas (p. 1119) and may be considered as passing through four comparable stages: (1) *Indigenous,* during which building activity was limited to primitive native forms; (2) *Colonial,* during which buildings followed prototypes in the homeland of the British and European colonists but were modified by climatic factors, the labour obtainable and the materials available; (3) *National,* extending from the time that the countries being considered here attained independent architectural status, generally speaking in the latter part of the nineteenth century, and (4) *Modern,* from about 1930.

SOUTH AFRICA

In 1487 Bartholomew Diaz rounded the Cape of Good Hope, marking this important exploit by erecting a commemorative pillar at the spot now known as Lüderitz Bay, and ten years later Vasco da Gama, en route for India, landed on the site of modern Durban. Cape Town was founded by the Dutchman, Jan van Riebeck, in 1650 and from that time Dutch influence in the Cape area has been strong. In

1795 Cape Colony was annexed by Britain to be joined during the nineteenth century by other provinces. Uneasiness between the Dutch (or Boer) element and the British was evident until the conclusion of the South African War (1899–1902). In 1909 the British South Africa Act established the present-day Union of South Africa.

Colonial buildings in areas of Dutch influence had much in common with contemporary examples in Holland (p. 827). Flemish gables, often of a curvilinear form, decorated with scrolls and 'strapwork' (p. 839), are found in surviving seventeenth- and eighteenth-century examples, while some eighteenth-century work incorporates charming Rococo details. Brick and stucco were popular building materials, and thatch, tiles and shingles were used for roofs.

Examples of Dutch colonial work in South Africa include: **Burgher Watch House, Cape Town** (1755–) (p. 1057); **Lutheran Parsonage, Cape Town** (*c.* 1780); **Government House, Cape Town** (1682; much altered 1798–; considerable later additions); **Rhone, Groot Drakenstein** (1795–); **Groot Constantia** (1691; rebuilt *c.* 1780); **Groot Schuur** (restored by H. Baker in 1898); and the **Koopman de Wet House, Cape Town** (*c.* 1790).

Early in the present century there was a popular revival of the Dutch Colonial style for domestic work, but at that time most public buildings were designed in the academic Classical idiom currently fashionable in England. Sir Herbert Baker (1862–1946) was responsible for the **Government Building, Pretoria** and **Bloemfontein** and Sir Edwin Lutyens (p. 995) designed the **Art Gallery, Johannesburg.**

Today South African architecture reflects the stylistic revolution of the 1930's (p. 995) and her cities provide examples of excellent modern work, making full use of the most recent technical advances.

AUSTRALIA AND NEW ZEALAND

Discovered by the Portuguese navigator, Luis de Torres, in 1606, systematic European settlement of Australia was delayed until after Captain James Cook took possession of New South Wales in the name of the British Crown in 1770. The colony was founded initially as a penal settlement but in 1793 it was opened to free immigration. The city of Sydney was founded in 1788 and Melbourne in 1835, and throughout the nineteenth century the story of modern Australia unfolded, characterized by the pioneering spirit of the settlers and their descendants. Although New Zealand had been annexed by Cook in 1770, this was disavowed by the British Government and it was not until 1840 that the country was formally adopted by Britain. Wellington was founded in 1839, Auckland in 1840 and Canterbury in 1850.

The first important Australian architect was Francis Greenway (1777–1837). Trained in England by John Nash (p. 876), he was transported to Australia in 1814 on being convicted of forgery. Here he became Government Architect and carried out a number of important buildings in Sydney, among them **S. James's Church** (–1824) since altered, and **Fort Macquarie** (1817–), now demolished.

The work of Greenway and his contemporaries is comparable with that of the English 'Regency' (*c.* 1811–30), often making use of Greek motifs and sometimes Gothic. Some buildings, however, show a continuation of the older 'Georgian' tradition, **S. Luke's Church, Liverpool** (1819) and **S. Matthew's Church, Windsor** (1817), both by Francis Greenway, among them. **Hyde Park Barracks, Sydney** (1817), by the same architect, but since altered, is Palladian in its layout, while Greenway's **Stables, Government House, Sydney** (1817), now the Conservatorium of Music, provides an example of Regency 'castellated' architecture.

Generally, early nineteenth-century domestic buildings were low, often of one storey only, with wide, spreading eaves. Covered, colonnaded verandahs were popular features, sometimes contained under the main roof of a building and often displaying great sensitivity in their elegant columnar supports. Lace-like iron-work, imported from England until the establishment of the Russell foundries at Sydney *c.* 1843, became popular for railings and screens. Although the first colonial structures were of timber, the use of stone and brick (the latter often stucco-faced) soon became general, while for roofs, generally of a low pitch, tiles, wood shingles and corrugated iron were employed.

In the second half of the nineteenth century, Australian and New Zealand architecture again moved parallel with that of Britain. Among numerous examples the following should be noted: **The Houses of Parliament, Melbourne** (1856–1880) by J. C. Knight and Peter Kerr, a monumental, classical building, surmounted by a stately cupola; **The Treasury Buildings, Melbourne** (–1862) by J. Clark, also in the classical manner; **The Church of S. John the Evangelist, Toorak** (1860–73) by W. W. Wardell (1823–1900) in the English Gothic style and the same architect's great **Catholic Cathedral of S. Patrick, Melbourne** (1860–1939), also Gothic but of a continental European character. **The Catholic Cathedral, Adelaide** (1870–) is based on designs prepared by A. W. N. Pugin (p. 988), while the **Anglican Cathedral, Melbourne** (1850–1934) was designed by William Butterfield (p. 990). **S. John's Anglican Cathedral, Brisbane** (1901–) was carried out by F. L. Pearson to the designs of his father, J. L. Pearson (p. 990).

The **Public Library, Melbourne** (1909–1913) by Messrs. Bates, Peebles and Smart, provides a significant and early example of reinforced-concrete construction in its great dome, measuring 115 ft in diameter.

Today the architectural activity of the two countries is of a high order and immense in scope, and Australian and New Zealand architects are making contributions of an international nature in all fields of building. In Melbourne alone, between 1955 and 1958, thirty major city buildings were completed, an indication of the general architectural activity.

REFERENCE BOOKS

SOUTH AFRICA

BAKER, Sir H. *Architecture and Personalities*. London, 1944.
FAIRBRIDGE, D. *Historic Houses of South Africa*. London, 1922.
PEARSE, G. E. *The Cape of Good Hope 1652–1833: An account of its buildings and the life of its people*. Pretoria, 1956.
—. *Eighteenth-century Architecture in South Africa*. London, 1933.

AUSTRALIA AND NEW ZEALAND

BALLANTYNE, J. *Homes and Homesteads in the Land of Plenty: A Handbook of Victoria as a field for emigration*. Melbourne, 1871.
BEIERS, S. *Homes of Australia*. Sydney, 1948.
BOYD, R. *Australia's Home*. Carlton, 1952.
CASEY, M., and others. *Early Melbourne Architecture, 1840–1888*. Melbourne, 1953.
ELLIS, M. H. *Francis Greenway: His Life and Times*. Sydney, 1953. (Revised edition.)
HERMAN, M. *The Architecture of Victorian Sydney*. Sydney, 1956.
—. *The Early Australian Architects and Their Work*. Sydney, 1954.
SHARLAND, M. *Stones of a Century* (about Tasmania). Hobart, 1952.
TURNBULL, C., and JACK, K. *The Charm of Hobart*. Sydney, 1949.

Aircraft hangar, Orbetello, Italy (1939–40). See p. 1111

XXVIII. NINETEENTH AND TWENTIETH-CENTURY ARCHITECTURE IN CONTINENTAL EUROPE

(*c.* 1830 to present day)

INFLUENCES

GEOGRAPHICAL. The developments which took place in European architecture in the nineteenth and twentieth centuries were bound up with the progress of industrialization. Circumstances favoured the western, non-Mediterranean countries. They possessed good soil, suited to intensive agriculture, and for this reason already were well-populated; they enjoyed admirable central locations to profit by rapidly-expanding world trade, between the European hinterland on the one hand and the Atlantic seaboard on the other; and certain among them were rich in the essential minerals, coal and iron. Northern Italy and Scandinavia were on the fringes of this favoured zone. Best circumstanced of all were Northern France and Germany, for it was chiefly there that the best coal measures lay. Outside the favoured zone, other areas were relatively retarded, in architecture clinging longer to late-Renaissance practices.

GEOLOGICAL. The direct significance of geology in relation to architecture diminished during the period. Excellent transport, by canal, river, sea, road or rail made it practicable to distribute natural materials widely, even internationally, thus mitigating if not actually eliminating the sharp differences of regional practice which formerly had existed. Vernacular architecture at least, had almost completely lost its distinctively varied local character by the opening of the period. Then too, manufactured or processed materials, with their dependable qualities and relative cheapness, came to be preferred to natural products. Brick, terra-cotta and tiles gained in popularity at the expense of stone, even in stone-producing districts. The advent of reinforced concrete, a twentieth-century material, further depressed the demand for stone, except for the best qualities, used sparingly for wall facings. Iron, the 'new' material adopted widely in the nineteenth century, though circumscribed in origin was freely distributed once its virtues had become recognized for the strong, space-saving structural framing of buildings. Steel, designed and used in accordance with scientific formulae, offered even greater advantages, and still competes today with reinforced concrete as an economical medium for load-bearing structural frameworks. Similarly, modern factory-made synthetic materials have a universal range of distribution.

CLIMATIC. Climatic differences, ranging very widely between the different countries, continued to produce their various effects upon architecture, but in diminishing degree, owing to the measures which progressively were developed to overcome the drawbacks of climatic extremes. Old direct methods of 'space-heating' by wood, peat, charcoal or coal, in fireplaces or stoves, long continued, and in the lesser domestic buildings still to some extent remain in use today. However, the distribution of coal improved enormously in the industrial period, and made possible the development of heating by the circulation of hot water or steam throughout a building, while heating by circulated hot air, known from Roman times (p. 205), followed new lines. Fuels for heat and light included the derivatives of coal (coke and gas—town gas came into use early in the nineteenth century), while oil and electricity are popular twentieth-century means. Empiricism in heating and ventilation gave way to scientific method towards the end of the nineteenth century. Most buildings now have circulatory systems distributing controlled heat from a central point, providing hot water too, and 'district heating' is sometimes applied to whole groups of houses or associated buildings. By such means and by insulating devices the rigours of cold seasons or climates can be largely overcome, and in hot seasons or climates similar methods can be utilized for the cooling of buildings and the refrigeration of perishables. Gas lighting, normal by mid-nineteenth century, was generally replaced by electric lighting in the twentieth; both of these very considerably enhanced the attractions of indoor life.

RELIGIOUS. On the whole, the period was marked by religious tolerance, and Roman Catholics, Protestants and their sects built churches according to their needs, foreign communities also being provided for. Demand for new churches arose from the swollen populations, concentrated principally in the industrialized towns. In the twentieth century there has been a move towards reunion among certain of the various non-papal denominations. Early in the nineteenth century many countries took steps towards the secularization of education, which thereafter became the responsibility of the state.

SOCIAL. Social changes were immense, owing to the rapid progress of industrialization, which affected the principal countries comprehensively, and all in some degree. Populations grew most intensively in the broad geographical belt extending eastwards of the English Channel. The greater part of the industrial population was concentrated in towns, and quite a number of new towns arose in locations favourable for industry. Concentration created a demand for many fresh types of social institution, as well as causing old ones to divide into sub-types Marketing, entertainment, sports, welfare, education, medical, public transport, local government and other service buildings were needed in quantity, besides commercial and industrial premises. A greater proportion of everyday life necessarily was spent indoors, whether for employment or leisure, and buildings responded to this circumstance, becoming not only vastly more numerous and varied but also generally more convenient, amply serviced and commodious; though not without very great initial difficulties in the early days of industrial expansion, before suitable methods and techniques of planning and design had been developed. A feature of the period was the acceleration of the levelling of the social classes, continuing at the present time, which progressively reduced the requirement for great houses while expanding the need for homes for the middle and, particularly, the lower groups, these in turn tending to merge their standards of space and quality. Domestic building in repetitive units, whether singly, in pairs or in terraces or flats, is a special mark of the industrial period, affecting the lesser dwellings at all times.

HISTORICAL. The reconstruction of Europe which followed the congress of the Great Powers at Vienna in 1814–15, laid down state boundaries which in the concern for the balance of power took too little account of national feeling and thus occasioned wars and disturbances thenceforward to 1880. In 1814, union was enforced between Norway and Sweden and in 1815 between Holland and Belgium, while in Italy, Austria recovered Lombardy and annexed Venetia. Germany, however, emerged more nearly unified than formerly, Prussia being the dominant power. Between the two dates 1815–80 came the independence of Greece and Belgium (1830); the disintegration of the Ottoman Empire and the emergence of a number of minor states in the Balkan peninsula; the union of Italy by stages between 1859–70; and the consolidation of the German Empire, completed 1871. Norway and Sweden agreed to a separation in 1905. The aftermath of the First World War of 1914–19 was the readjustment of eastern territories to produce Finland, Poland and intervening states and the emergence of Czechoslovakia and Yugoslavia at the expense of a reconstituted Austria-Hungary, thereafter divided. The Second World War of 1939–45 occasioned a political division of Germany into East and West States, with different ideological allegiances.

ARCHITECTURAL CHARACTER

It has been shown earlier, in the respective chapters on Renaissance Architecture, that the Antiquarian phase of *c.* 1750–1830 was common to European countries in general. At first this retrospective architecture recalled anew the Ancient Roman, but soon was increasingly tinctured with the Greek, in Germany to the extent that, as in England, a proportion of buildings of the early nineteenth century can readily be classed as 'Greek Revival'. In France, classicism remained mainly Roman, developing highly individual and sometimes austere traits before turning instead towards the Italian Renaissance, about the end of the Antiquarian phase. Gothic Revivalism was merely tentative in France and at this time in Germany too, and negligible in other continental European countries. The adherence of France to classicism throughout the century was in some part due to her unique system of art education, adopted in 1666 and extended to architecture some fifty years later, by which winners of the Prix de Rome competitions rounded off their training by a period of years of study at the French Academy in Rome (from 1725–1800 the Academy occupied the Palazzo Salviati, and from 1801 onwards the Villa Medici, Rome (p. 713)). From 1806 the architectural designs made in the École des Beaux-Arts competitions were published, and had an important influence on French taste, and thus on that of other countries, for Italy herself, Spain, the Low Countries and Germany—apart from her deep interest in Greek architecture—tended to follow the French lead. Another French institution which helped to shape progressive ideas in the first three decades of the nineteenth century was the École Polytechnique, founded 1794, which looked upon architectural matters from the engineering side.

The 'nineteenth and twentieth-century' period, considered here as beginning at 1830, may be regarded as falling into two phases, the one from 1830 to 1900 and the other from 1900 to the present; for although historicism remained the keynote down to the First World War of 1914–19, and is not entirely defunct at the present day, the development of 'Organic' or 'Modern' architecture is consistently traceable on the Continent from about 1900.

Period 1830–c. 1900. Continental revivalism, like the British, became less and less academic, drawing ideas and motifs from past styles yet with a decreasing regard for the faithful reproduction of them; in quite a few respects it proceeded upon its own impetus, evolving characteristic arrangements which had no counterpart in past history. France led the fashions, except that Germany had a strongly competitive influence in Central and Northern Europe through the first half century. Italian Renaissance classicism, modified in the respective countries by their own historical interpretations of it, superseded the Roman or Greek between 1830–50, and it is this Neo-Renaissance mode, or that of the Neo-Baroque into which it developed, which characterizes most Continental architecture through the century. Gothic revivalism made some headway in France, almost exclusively for ecclesiastical buildings, and also in Germany, whereas there was very little in other countries.

Where necessary for particular investigation, terms convenient for reference to Continental architecture as a whole may be taken from French history, since it was that country that exercised the principal influence through most of the period. These accord fairly closely with those used for the British (p. 987). The French 'July Monarchy' (1830–48) accords approximately with the British 'Early Victorian' (1830–50), and the 'Second Empire' (1848–70) with the British 'High Victorian' (1850–75). The French 'Third Republic' (1870–1914) covers British 'Late Victorian' (1875–1900) and the ensuing years to the First World War. The 'July Monarchy' was a transitional phase, mainly Neo-Renaissance, the 'Second Empire' a High Neo-Renaissance phase—marked by a return to mansard and pavilion roofs —and the 'Third Republic', Neo-Baroque. These are very broad generalizations, as there were distinct time-lags in the countries remote from the French and German chief centres of influence: also, eclecticism was on the increase throughout the period, and there was no great consistency, anywhere, in the developments.

Though much nineteenth-century architecture was dull, extravagantly ornate, coarse or downright ugly, there were many quite fine monuments. The momentous developments however, were those made in the planning of buildings or in technique, in direct response to the now-prevailing industrial economy Especially in France, numerous courageous experiments were undertaken to discover means of covering greater spaces and erecting higher and fire-resisting buildings with the maximum efficiency. Among the available materials, most of which could now be produced and transported in great quantities, the newest was iron, and its possibilities were explored with the utmost zeal, just as in Britain. Constructionally, iron was at first used mainly as a fire-resisting roofing material; with it J.-V. Louis (1731–1800) had roofed the Théâtre Français, Paris, in 1786–90, and afterwards, bridges, pavilions, galleries, market-halls, glass-houses and other mainly-iron structures were built in abundance. Then, in the present period, Henri Labrouste (1801–75) produced his extraordinarily brilliant Library of S. Geneviève, Paris (1843–50)

(p. 1085) as fine and original in the architecture of its stone exterior shell as in its cast- and wrought-iron complete inner frame, this last an innovation for a public building. He followed this with the National Library, Paris (1862–8) (p. 1085), embodying further developments. Meanwhile, Britain's Crystal Palace (p. 1041) had stimulated emulation, and at the first International Exhibition, Paris, of 1855, there was built a masonry-buttressed glass-and-iron vaulted hall of 158 ft span. At a similar International Exhibition in Vienna held in 1873, there was an iron cupola no less than 350 ft across, the largest of the century. A different kind of innovation was that represented by a chocolate factory at Noisiel-sur-Marne, near Paris (1871–2) (p. 1103), probably the first true skeleton-framed building in France. It indicates a new, anti-traditional trend in several ways, including the idea of supporting a building entirely upon its structural frame, the walls becoming merely a weather-resistant sheathing or 'cladding'. It was influential, as it secured the commendation of Eugène Emmanuel Viollet-le-Duc (1814–79), architect, a famous and prolific writer, known particularly for his *Dictionnaire Raisonné de l'Architecture Française du 11ᵉ au 16ᵉ Siècle* (1854–61) and *Entretiens sur l'Architecture* (1863), and for his numerous restorations, considered nowadays to have been over-drastic, of some of the greatest of France's mediaeval monuments (p. 549).

Bridges, railway stations, industrial structures and yet more international exhibitions in Paris in 1867, 1878 and 1889 provided opportunities for the exploitation of structural iron. That of 1889 was remarkable not only for the gigantic Halle des Machines (p. 1103) but also for that symbol of Paris, the Eiffel Tower (1887–9). 984 ft high, the best-known work of the engineer Gustave Eiffel (1832–1923), Eiffel also designed the entrance building of the 1878 Paris Exhibition (p. 1103). largely of metal and glass and highly ornate, comprising a long rhythm of rectangular bays marked at the middle and ends by prominent domed pavilions penetrated by enormous lunette arches. Such dispositions and features were to remain popular with the École des Beaux-Arts and typical of French architecture until the end of the century, as is instanced by the Petit Palais, Paris (1897–1900) (p. 1092B), which repeats the arrangement, including the domed pavilions, abutted—in the centre— by similar great arches. The difference, however, is that the Petit Palais is of stone and of that distinctive Neo-Baroque character representative of the generality of French major buildings of its period.

Yet towards the end of the century, an increasing proportion of buildings, particularly those in which iron played an important part, were in process of shedding Classical traits and developing a free, naturalistic decoration which presaged international Art Nouveau. A new material too, was coming to the fore—reinforced concrete. Mass concrete, an artificial material of sand, shingle and cement, mixed with water and allowed to set, already had been used for a number of buildings, in the form of building-blocks or cast *in situ* within containing 'formwork'; and at the same time experiments had been proceeding towards strengthening concrete with iron, so disposed within the concrete as to resist tensional stresses, against which the material is weak, to complement its very great ability to resist compression. Mathematical as well as practical problems were involved. French invention achieved a narrow lead over British, German and American, and in 1892, François Hennebique (1842–1921) produced and rapidly exploited a complete system of reinforced concrete, this closely followed by many other proprietary systems. Used initially for industrial projects, the first building of architectural consequence was a church, S. Jean de Montmartre, Paris (1897–1905) (p. 1080), by Anatole de Baudot (1836–1915).

Thus by the last decade of the century, the several lines of architectural development had reached an important stage. They then began to converge, and lead more or less directly towards 'Modern' architecture as understood today. In tectonics there were reinforced concrete, the steel frame and ferro-vitreous construction of the older kind, while in the polite realm the British Arts and Crafts cleansing movement was on the point of inspiring and giving way to Continental Art Nouveau. The latter, known in France as 'Le Modern Style', in Germany and Austria as the 'Jugendstil' and in Italy as the 'Stile Liberty', is deemed to have begun in Brussels with the house No. 6, Rue Paul-Émile Janson (1892–3), by the Belgian, Victor Horta; though less abruptly than is usually contended as there had been quite a few portents, some of them already noted. The earlier work of Antoni Gaudí (1852–1926) at Barcelona, Spain, especially the Palazzo Guell (1885–9) (p. 1071) is to be reckoned among the anticipations of the style, if not actually its real beginning. France adopted the style with enthusiasm. In Holland, where Hendrick P. Berlage (1856–1934) was the leader, the extremes of Art Nouveau were almost unknown, and the country progressed to a rational architecture, usually expressed in the native brick, that was substantially her own.

Period c. 1900 to present day. Being essentially a decorative movement, Art Nouveau was characterized principally by its flowing, attenuated and sinuous naturalistic ornament, often profuse, concentrated particularly at corners of openings or junctions of features, or other telling points, and by the repudiation of historic forms. Curvilinear motifs abounded, and were either lineal or plastic according to the material, and polychromy was favoured. The lineal expression was well-suited to ferro-vitreous buildings, and thus to department stores, of which a number were constructed in Paris and other cities at this time, and to light structures like underground stations, arcades, pavilions and kiosks. Houses and urban buildings in general were less amenable externally, normally being in stone or brick, but could express the style in ceramic tiles, mosaic, carved, painted or plaster ornament or in the ironwork of grilles, balconies and railings; or again, elements of the façades could themselves be moulded, as in the extraordinarily bizarre later work of Gaudí (p. 1072). The movement affected Germany and Austria almost immediately, and the contacts with the English Arts and Crafts were direct and strong. Early exponents in Germany were August Endell (1871–1925) and Henri van de Velde (1863–1957), the latter a Belgian who moved to Berlin in 1899. In Vienna, artists formed a 'Sezession' away from the old-fashioned Academy, and adopted Art Nouveau. Otto Wagner (1841–1918) and J. M. Olbrich (1867–1908) were principal figures. There, taste was less extreme than at Brussels or Paris, as is indicated by the fact that Mackintosh of Glasgow (p. 991), whose manner of Art Nouveau design was relatively economical, was invited to contribute the decoration of a room for the Sezession's exhibition of 1900 : already he had exhibited at Munich, Germany, in 1898. The distinguished Austrian-born Adolf Loos (1870–1933), showed his advanced ideas by declaring himself against all ornament of whatever nature, as early as 1897/8. Yet it was several years later before the tide of opinion began to turn in favour of machine art rather than the handicrafts approach favoured by Arts and Crafts partisans, and led to the formation of 'Werkbund' associations devoted to stimulating quality in industrial work, the German founded in 1907, the Austrian 1910, the Swiss 1913 and the Swedish 1910–17. The English 'Design and Industries Association' of 1915 was launched upon the inspiration of the German Werkbund. In sympathy with the new ideal, teaching in German and Austrian art schools was fundamentally reorientated, and progressive designers appointed to direct them. In Germany were Peter Behrens (1868–1938) at Düsseldorf, Hans Poelzig (1869–1936) at Breslau, Bruno Paul (1874–1954) at Berlin and Van de Velde at Weimar, while Josef Hoffman (1870–1956) became Professor of Architecture in Vienna.

In continental Europe as a whole, the greatest names of the period 1900–16 are those of Perret, Behrens and Loos, respectively French, German and Austrian. Auguste Perret (1874–1954), not previously mentioned, as he played no great part in Art Nouveau, began practice about 1895, and throughout much of his long career devoted himself single-mindedly to the advancement of the technique and art of reinforced concrete. He quickly appreciated that reinforced concrete should be used, like timber, on the frame-and-panel method—the frame, outlining the building, serving to carry all the weight—and was the architect of the earliest secular building in the material to have its structure expressed visibly in a logical and sightly manner (1903) (p. 1072). He continued to produce significant architecture in the inter-war and post-war periods, this always showing a respect for Classical principles of design. Behrens was important in disseminating the machine-age style. His work developed from the later stages of Art Nouveau into a clean and direct expression of orderly structure, and showed that industrial as well as public, ecclesiastical and domestic buildings could have fine architectural qualities. Loos unswervingly followed his own precepts, excluding ornament completely and deriving his architectural effects solely from the necessary tectonic forms. It was in his domestic work that modern architecture first reached maturity (1910). Progress in steel and reinforced concrete construction continued. Tony Garnier (1867–1948) achieved with steel a span of 262 ft in a hall for the cattle market and abattoirs at Lyons (1913), and Max Berg (b. 1870) the glazed dome of 213 ft diameter of the Centennial Hall at Breslau (1912–13) (p. 1097) with reinforced concrete. The latter has massive radial and concentric ribs almost of masonry proportions. Eugene Freyssinet (b. 1879) used concrete far more economically in his impressive parabolic-vaulted airship hangar at Orly, near Paris (1916) (p. 1106A), destroyed in the Second World War, which in the thin zig-zag section of its enormous ribs inaugurated the principle of the 'folded slab', a principle widely adopted later on. Another engineer, the Swiss, Robert Maillart (1872–1940), employed the 'flat slab' method in his splendidly-simple bridge designs (p. 1108), the first in 1906, or in the case of tiered buildings, used the slab in conjunction with pillar supports in an arrangement known as 'mushroom' construction (1908). However, the parabolic vault, folded slab and slab-and-pillar or mushroom types of reinforced concrete construction did not come into general use until the inter-war period, the normal early system being that of the simple box-frame outlining the space to be enclosed.

Four outstanding personalities of the inter-war period and later are Walter Gropius (b. 1883), Mies van der Rohe (b. 1886), Le Corbusier (b. 1887) and J. J. P. Oud (b. 1890). Actually, the German-born Gropius already had designed notable buildings before 1914, including one, the Fagus Factory at Aldfeld-an-der-Leine (1911–14) (p. 1104), in collaboration with Adolf Meyer (d. 1925), which has a near equivalent of the modern 'curtain-wall', this a glazed framework suspended across the face of a building in front of the various floors and inner dividing partitions. The idea already had been current from the 1890's in America, and the first true example is said to be that of the Hallidie Building, San Francisco, completed in 1918 (p. 1156). In 1919 Gropius succeeded Van de Velde at Weimar, where he founded the 'Bauhaus', developing a form of training intended to relate art and architecture with machine-age daily life. In 1925 Gropius moved to Dessau, and re-established the Bauhaus there, erecting a new building (1925–6) (p. 1094) to house the school, based on his own advanced principles. His book *The New Architecture and the Bauhaus* (1935) explained his system, which had an international influence. From 1934–7 he was in England, and subsequently lived in the U.S.A.

Van der Rohe, also German and similarly influenced by Behrens, became the Director of the Dessau Bauhaus in 1930, but went to America in 1937. His personal interpretation of Modern architecture had matured by 1919. In a competition in that year, he essayed a glass-sheathed, twenty-storey Berlin skyscraper and in 1920–1, a model of another, thirty storeys high, designed as a cluster of interpenetrating circularly-planned elements sustained by an inner steel skeleton supporting cantilevered floors, the whole entirely glass-faced. These towers anticipated by very many years his forty-storey Seagram Building, New York (1956–7) built in collaboration with P. C. Johnson, planned as a simple, colossal rectangular block (p. 1163). All his mature work has a refreshing simplicity, the respective structural materials being used frankly according to their nature. Externally, glass is used extensively, and normally he adheres to the rectangular frame, while interior accommodation is contrived by freely-disposed light partitions, interwoven with the inner pillars of the structural frame.

'Le Corbusier' (a pseudonym of Charles-Edouard Jeanneret), of Swiss birth but whose work has centred in France, has dominated the European scene for many years. In his formative period he worked both with Perret in Paris and Behrens in Berlin; and being himself a painter, he was receptive to ideas from contemporary Cubist painting. His earlier interests were in domestic work, and his philosophy at that time—the early 1920's—is summed up in his dictum that 'the house is a machine to live in'. This was intended to imply not that a dwelling need not be attractive, but that it should be attractive, diverting and efficient. A prolific writer, his books, particularly *Vers une Architecture* (1923—English translation 1927) had enormous influence. He advocated that the structural frame should be separately identified from the space-enclosing walls, that a house should be lifted on pillars ('pilotis') so that the garden might spread under it; that roofs should be flat, capable of use as a garden, as pitched roofs were intrusive on the cubic or rectilineal idea; that the interior accommodation should be freely planned, each floor according to the need, since all loading could be taken by the structural frame. The latter was not a new notion, for Perret had conceived it in 1903, nor (apart from the 'pilotis') were the others, but collectively they constituted a fresh conception, entirely opposed to the traditional principles still generally obtaining. The relatively thin enveloping walls could have continuous bands of horizontal windows. From houses, Le Corbusier went on to produce buildings of virtually all principal classes and schemes for town-planning, ever provoking international curiosity and controversy yet ultimately securing general confidence in the tenability of his many stimulating ideas.

J. J. P. Oud is representative of Holland at this time as Berlage had been in the pre-1914 period. Gropius and Le Corbusier both were influenced by contemporary painting in their formative years, and so was Oud, having been a member of the important Dutch 'De Stijl' group of abstract artists, formed in 1917, whose tenets concerned the manipulation of geometrical forms: architecturally, they rejected the rigid enclosure of buildings in their enveloping walls in favour of the free interplay of spatial volumes. Oud softened the jagged asperities of the early architectural ventures of the group and developed a clean, sedate style, markedly horizontal in stress but with emphasis on the sheer wall, rather than upon the banded windows. Another coming under the influence of 'De Stijl' was W. M. Dudok (b. 1884) designer of many fine buildings, who, however, went less quickly and less far towards Modern architectural principles, and chose to work almost exclusively in brickwork, thus allying himself to some extent with an Amsterdam group of architects who exploited fine brickwork, the traditional material of Holland, in a dramatic and romantic manner. Notable among the latter were Michael de Klerk (1884–1924) and P. L. Kramer (b. 1884). Yet Holland's greatest building of the period is the Van Nelle Factory, Rotterdam (1927–30) (p. 1104), by J. A. Brinckmann and L. C. van der Vlugt (b. 1894): it is unique for its day in the measure of its fulfilment of modern principles.

Thus the new architecture grew in Europe. France, Germany, Austria and Holland, the countries where it originated, have been mentioned, though by no means all the famous men who contributed to its development. One other, at least, should be mentioned: Erich Mendelsohn (1887–1953), a pioneer German who left his own country for England in 1933, spent the years 1934–8 in Palestine and then settled in the U.S.A. Then too, there were architects of considerable stature in other European countries. In Sweden, Ragnar Ostberg (1866–1945) produced his romantically beautiful Stockholm City Hall (1911–23) (p. 1093), and Ivar Tengbom (b. 1878) likewise showed that the traditional mode could vie in brilliance with the new, as pursued so effectively by Sven Markelius (b. 1889) or again by Erik Gunnar Asplund (1885–1940), who effected the transition from historicism superbly in his own professional span. Asplund helped by his example to quicken the pace in Denmark too, for there, Neo-Classicism held sway almost to 1930. Finland came into the picture fairly early, due to the endeavours of Elial Saarinen (1873–1950), though he settled in the U.S.A. after 1923. After him Alvar Aalto (b. 1898) was the dominant Finnish figure. Under Viennese influence pre-wars Italy made tentative steps towards Modernism in the visionary schemes of Antonio Sant' Elia (1888–1917), but no real beginning until the formation in 1927 of 'Gruppo 7', this once again an association of progressive artists and designers such as had led the revolt against revivalism in so many other countries. Fascism, then in the ascendant, tolerated the Modern movement, but the new architecture developed in the late inter-war period was largely impersonal, apart from the fact that Pier Luigi Nervi (b. 1891) already had begun his remarkably distinguished career, and produced impressive monuments.

After the Second World War, the new architecture extended rapidly in Europe, while under its influence the buildings still designed on traditional lines tended to shed stylistic ornament and mouldings and to share its directness and simplicity. Steel and reinforced concrete frames became common for all but the smallest structures. Multifarious fresh departures were made in the servicing and equipment of buildings and in the methods of cladding and weather-proofing. Synthetic materials played a large part in these developments. In the field of structure, 'shell' vaulting offered—and continues to offer—the greatest opportunities for architectural exploitation. Long ago, Perret and Freyssinet separately had appreciated that the need for bulk is greatly diminished when reinforced concrete is used for arched vaults, particularly those of parabolic section, since the stresses then are mainly compressional, with a consequent considerable saving in the load to be supported. In domes, the conditions are especially favourable, as was discovered by Walter Bauersfeld in 1922. After experiments, the first sizeable shell-dome was constructed at Jena, Germany, in 1925, spanning 82 ft, with the concrete no more than $2\frac{3}{8}$ ins thick. An octagonal dome at Basle market hall spans 197 ft, at a thickness of $3\frac{1}{8}$ ins. After hemispherical domes, segmental domes and then barrel vaults were essayed, the latter sometimes running with the length and sometimes in a series, side by side, across a hall; and with these too, enormous unobstructed spans were at length achieved. Sometimes the transverse barrel vaults were allowed to protrude beyond their seating on the longitudinal walls, cantilevered to provide a serrated crest or awning. In the case of all these types there were problems of stiffness to be resolved, for arches or vaults, however light, exert thrust, which has to be buttressed, contained or countered.

Before the War of 1939–45, the shell vault was used mainly for purely utilitarian structures; it was in the post-war world that it emerged definitely as a reputable feature in polite architecture, and remarkable feats have been accomplished with it, great roofs striding almost from the ground in varying degrees of geometrical

A. Rue de Rivoli (west), Paris (1811–35).
See p. 1071

B. No. 11, Rue de Milan,
Paris (c. 1860). See p. 1071

c. The Palazzo Güell, Barcelona (1885–9).
See p. 1071

D. No. 6, Rue Paul-Émile
Janson, Brussels (1892–3):
staircase. See p. 1071

E. Workers' Houses, Hook of Holland (1926–7).
See p. 1075

F. Apartment House, Rue
Raynouard, Paris (1929–32).
See p. 1079

A. The Majolica House, Vienna (c. 1898).
See p. 1072

B. The Casa Battló, Barcelona
(1905–7). See p. 1072

C. The Casa Milá, Barcelona (1905–10). See p. 1072

simplicity or complexity. Thus the curvilinear note has been restored again to organic architecture, after decades of rectilineal modernism, bringing with it a charm, even delicacy, hitherto frequently lacking. A vast new field still remains only partially explored. However, it is not only in reinforced concrete that further potentialities have been discovered, for steel, while remaining the most suitable structural material for the framing of high 'sky-scraper' and other cellular buildings, is now often used over great halls in unified 'space-frame' arrangements, composed in three dimensions instead of as a series of principals or trusses supporting longitudinal members (purlins, etc.) on the age-old method. Then too, it has been discovered that the natural deficiencies of timber can be overcome by lamination, the glueing together of many overlapping layers of the material to provide beams and arches of calculable capacities vastly beyond the range of timber in its natural state. Glass, which plays so large a part in current architecture also has been developed so as to remove many of the former deficiencies and present a variety of new properties.

Many of the notable architects practising in the inter-war period continued active in the post-war phase, though, as we have seen, quite a number of the more famous had left Europe for the U.S.A., where economic and other circumstances have been more propitious for architecture. In France, Perret maintained for the rest of his lifetime his devotion to reinforced concrete; and his zeal for prefabrication still further accentuated the reticulated air, which together with the Classical dispositions always remained a mark of his authorship. Factory prefabrication, allowing speedy erection upon the site, steadily increased in Europe, and in France in 1960 accounted for about five per cent of the total building production. Le Corbusier remains France's outstanding figure, with an international reputation and an intercontinental practice, while Nervi similarly retains his place in the forefront of Italian architecture and engineering. In all countries, the younger generation of designers has adopted organic architecture enthusiastically, and new leaders are in the process of emerging from a host of gifted practitioners.

EXAMPLES

DOMESTIC BUILDINGS

The Houses, Rue de Rivoli (west), Paris (1811–35) (p. 1069A), by Percier and Fontaine, have five storeys, the lowest arcaded and the upper a mansard, and illustrate the quiet classicism of the 'Empire' style at the opening of the present period. The **'Nouveau Louvre' extensions, Paris** (1850–7) (pp. 775C, D, E, 793B), by Visconti and Lefuel, show a far richer Neo-Baroque. In European cities and large towns, flats had become the chief type of dwelling: the **Flat-block, No. 11, Rue de Milan, Paris** (c. 1860) (p. 1069B), by A.-F. Mortier, has a typical Neo-Baroque façade, fine and vigorous but crowded with features and with scarcely a trace of unrelieved wall.

The **Palazzo Güell, Barcelona, Spain** (1885–9) (p. 1069C), by Antoni Gaudí, is indicative of a revolt against historicism and presages Art Nouveau. The building presents many novelties. The first floor is cantilevered, and the twin portals are parabolic, infilled with iron grilles, which at the top make a very rich filigree of swirling and convoluted forms. Between the portals is an elaborate heraldic ornament over a small, grilled window. Neither the heraldic ornament nor that at the door-heads is precisely symmetrical. There are more iron grilles in the series of first-floor windows, divided by simple post-mullions. In the whole of this part of the composition there is scarcely any recognizable historical feature.

No. 6, Rue Paul-Émile Janson, Brussels (1892–3) (p. 1069D) by Victor

Horta, is accounted the first house and the first complete building in full-fledged Art Nouveau. It is narrow-fronted and deep, the rooms planned rather more freely than normal and with some exploitation of floor levels. The façade is unexciting but novel for its day, being almost wholly non-traditional: the main element is an oriel segmental bay, with metal mullions and window-heads and decorative ironwork balustrades. The new character is much more evident internally (p. 1069D) particularly in the stair-hall and salon, where iron work is used lavishly both for the structure and for free-flowing, plant-like ornament in linear intertwinings. Ornament of similar character springs from the angles of the walls, which otherwise are refreshingly plain and simple.

The **Majolica House, Vienna** (c. 1898) (p. 1070A), a block of flats by Otto Wagner, has a six-storey façade ornamented on the upper part with a rich floral pattern worked in coloured tiles, and delicate ironwork elsewhere. The simple dignity of effect contrasts with the florid character of contemporary expressions of Art Nouveau in the western countries of Europe.

The **Casa Battló, Barcelona** (1905-7) (p. 1070B), by Antoni Gaudí, instances the bizarre mature manner of this Catalan architect. The stone dressings of the lower façade are modelled plastically into ovoid and sinuous shapes, echoed in the metal upper balustrades, while the wall surfaces around the rectangular upper windows are studded with coloured glass fragments. The **Casa Milá, Barcelona** (1905-10) (p. 1070C), a block of flats, also by Gaudí, is even more extraordinary in that its stone façades undulate to enclose an irregular mesh of polygonal rooms, on two alike and none with right-angled corners. The external walls are swept into heavy brows over the tiers of roll-edged, round-angled windows, and the ironwork of the balconies resembles tangles of brushwood. Gaudí's Art Nouveau is exceptional in being dominantly plastic, for elsewhere it is mainly planar, with linear adjuncts and decorations.

The **Apartment-block, No. 25b, Rue Franklin, Paris** (1903) (p. 1073A), by Auguste Perret, is the earliest instance of frank architectural expression of reinforced concrete framed construction in an important secular building. The block is trapped between other frontages, and to avoid internal light wells, the centre of the façade is deeply recessed, the wings at the same time having projecting bays. The concrete is faced externally with ceramic slabs, plain where the essential frame was to be expressed and around the windows, but ornamented with floral or pebble patterns on the non-load-bearing panels between. Ceramic tiles were a usual method of facing concrete at this time, but the floriated decoration is one of the few concessions made in the building to the still-fashionable Art Nouveau. Glass bricks, invented about 1890, were used on the staircase outer wall at the rear. The floor loads are taken upon internal pillars instead of the dividing walls, and this innovation had an important influence upon later domestic architecture.

The **Stocklet House, Brussels** (1905-11) (p. 1073B), by Josef Hoffmann, is an opulent asymmetrically-composed mansion, lavishly marbled internally and elegant externally, with white walls patterned by rhythms of neat windows. A feature much imitated later on is the tall staircase window running the full height of the house, accentuating the vertical lines of the dominant tower.

The **Steiner House, Vienna** (1910) (p. 1073C), by Adolf Loos, is the first wholly Modern dwelling. It is strictly functional, the designer being strongly opposed to ornament in whatever form. Elevationally it is symmetrical and flat-roofed, its plain white walls broken by stark windows devoid even of the hitherto normal astragals, yet carefully proportioned to give a balance and restfulness to the whole façade.

The **Dageraad Housing Estate, Amsterdam** (1918-23), by Piet Kramer, is represented by the tenement blocks erected in 1922-3 (p. 1073D), which show the

B. The Stocklet House, Brussels (1905–11).
See p. 1072

A. Apartment Block, No. 25b, Rue
Franklin, Paris (1903). See p. 1072

C. The Steiner House, Vienna (1910–). See p. 1072

D. The Dageraad Housing Eastate
Amsterdam (1922–23). See p. 1072

E. Group of Flats, Henriette Ronnerplein,
Amsterdam (1920–2). See p. 1075

A. The Villa 'Les Terraces', Garches, near Paris (1926–7). See opposite page

B. The Villa Savoye, Poissy, S. et O., France (1928–31). See opposite page

clever and ornamental treatment of fine brickwork evidenced by the Amsterdam school of architects at this time. The block of **Flats on the Henriette Ronnerplein, Amsterdam** (1920–2) (p. 1073E) by Michel de Klerk, offers a further example.

The **Workers' Houses, Hook of Holland** (1926–7) (p. 1069E) by J. J. P. Oud, comprising two terraces, represent the Dutch Rotterdam school, more genuinely functional and progressive than the foregoing. The white façades are linked by long balconies which curve to form canopies over shops at the ends. The plinths are of yellow brick, and colour is applied to some of the wood and the iron elements.

The **Villa 'Les Terraces' at Garches, near Paris** (1926–7) (p. 1074A) by Le Corbusier and Pierre Jeanneret (b. 1896—Le Corbusier's cousin, who practised with him until 1943) is the most famous of the many houses by this celebrated architect, and embodies his principles. There are two main floors, the first floor providing the kitchen and living accommodation and the second the bedrooms. The ground or entrance floor includes the garage and remaining domestic offices, while the roof has terrace gardens, a guest suite and servants' bedroom quarters. As a whole, the villa forms a rectangle, the concrete floors being carried on the end walls and upon sparse internal pillars, but projecting forward on the two long sides as cantilevers, so that none of the main structural supports is visible in the long horizontal 'ribbon' windows. Since there are no internal load-bearing walls the accommodation could be freely planned, differing on each floor. The living floor is treated as a single lightly-divided space, the elements being demarcated by doorless and movable curved or straight partitions. Each main floor includes a covered garden, that of the first floor being related to the external garden by a projecting terrace, supported on a squat round column, and a flight of steps.

The **Villa Savoye, Poissy, S. et O., France** (1928–31) (p. 1074B) follows similar principles to 'Les Terraces', but differs in design. The main floor is raised upon 'pilotis', approached by a dog-legged long ramp or inclined way instead of a stair-case. Most of the accommodation is on the first floor, which also includes a large covered terrace. Above, there is a roof garden, with curvilinear screens to the access stair and small pavilions. The ground floor is cored by a spacious, round-fronted hall, from which the ramp leads, and also accommodates servants' quarters, a guest suite and a large garage for three cars. The upper floors are cantilevered at the two ends, but on the sides of the rectangular house-block the pillar supports pass immediately behind the first-floor wall-screens, the latter pierced by almost continuous horizontal ribbon windows.

Other interesting houses of about the same date were those built for their own occupation by Walter Gropius at Dessau (1926) and Erich Mendelsohn at Berlin (1929).

The **Tugendhat House, Brno, Czechoslovakia** (1930) (p. 1076) by Ludwig Mies van der Rohe, is celebrated for its gracious effects in internal open planning. The house stands on a southern steep slope, and is entered from the top partial storey, which contains the entrance hall, bedrooms and guest suite, besides the garage block at the west end. The stair descends to the main floor, of which an area of about 80 ft by 40 ft is lightly divided into study, living room, dining room, and pantry areas by free-standing partitions (p. 1076B). One of the screens is of pale onyx marble, and another, forming a semicircle around the dining space, is of ebony, while the steel pillars supporting the upper floor are finished in chrome bronze. The service quarters project outwards to the west. The continuous great windows on the cantilevered south and east sides of the block may be lowered electrically into the storage basement which elevates the main floor above the terrace and hillside. Externally (p. 1076A), the house has that grand elegance which regularly distinguishes the work of the designer.

A. The Tugendhat House, Brno (1930): exterior. See p. 1075

B. The Tugendhat House, Brno: interior

A. The Swiss Hostel, Cité Universitaire, Paris (1931–2). See p. 1079

B. The Stockholm Exhibition, 1930. See p. 1111

The Unité d'Habitation, Marseilles (1946–52). See opposite page

The **Swiss Hostel, Cité Universitaire, Paris** (1931-2) (p. 1077A) by Le Corbusier, is a dormitory block standing impressively upon enormous double 'pilotis' of concrete which leave the site almost completely open at ground level. Above, the building is steel-framed, faced with concrete slabs, with bands of large windows facing south-west to light the single-banked study-bedrooms. The ends of the block are devoid of windows, as also is the concave north-east face of a rear wing which juts out to contain the communal rooms.

The **Apartment Block, 51-5, Rue Raynouard, Paris** (1929-32) (p. 1069F) by Auguste Perret, contrived on an awkward wedge-shaped site, is very representative of this architect's mature style, of which the distinguishing traits are the emphasis of the vertical and horizontal lines of the reinforced-concrete frame, the use of pre-cast infilling slabs between, the upright, traditional form of the windows and the Classical symmetry and character of the features. Together, these give a busy, reticulated effect.

In post-war Europe, though many fine houses have been constructed, they contribute no particularly new principle: the main developments have been in great housing schemes, especially of flat-blocks.

The **Unité d'Habitation, Marseilles** (1946-52) (p. 1078) by Le Corbusier, is an enormous apartment block designed to house a complete community. It stands on massive coupled 'pilotis', and is concrete framed, faced with prefabri-cated slabs or units. Near the centre of the height is a floor devoted to shops and communal services, complemented by other facilities on the roof—swimming bath, gymnasium, nursery school and play and sun-bathing areas. The apartments are ingeniously interlocked between front and back of the block so that each dwelling can occupy a floor and a half of height, including a two-storey living room. Covering the front and back faces of the block are concrete frames, which shield the rooms from glare and provide balconies on both fronts to each dwelling.

CHURCHES

The Gothic Revival, never as important on the Continent as in England, affected church building more strongly than it did other types. In France and Germany it found some favour during the period of the July Monarchy (1830–48), replacing the Neo-Classic, and a good deal more in that of the Second Empire (1848–70), though mostly for the restoration, completion or extension of existing cathedrals and churches. The rest of Europe was variously strongly affected, roughly accord-ing to the distance from the two main centres. English contemporary architecture had a not inconsiderable influence. Representative Continental churches are: **S. Clotilde, Paris** (1846–57); the **Petrikirche** (1843–9) and the **Nikolaikirche** (1845–63) (p. 1081A), **Hamburg,** the latter built from the winning competition designs of Sir G. G. Scott (p. 990); the **Votivkirche, Vienna** (1856–79) (p. 1081C), a rich and attractive composition with twin western spires, also from a competition design, by H. von Ferstel; **S. Denys de l'Estrée, S. Denis, Seine, France** (1864–7), by the influential restorer and writer, Viollet-le-Duc; and the very large **Fünfhaus Parish Church, Vienna** (1868–75), by F. von Schmidt, a domed, centralized com-position with two western spires.

S. Eugène, Paris (1854–5) (p. 1081D), by L.-A. Boileau (1812–96) is France's first iron-framed church, much of the detail being in that material too. The interior, with its slender, single-shafted arcades, is well-lit, spacious and elegant. Other 'iron' churches are **S. Eugène, Le Vesinet, S. et O.,** (1863), by Boileau; **S. Augustin, Paris** (1860–7) by Victor Baltard (1805–74); and **Notre Dame du Travail, Paris** (1899–1901), by Anstruc.

The **Church of the Sacré Cœur, Paris,** begun 1875–7 on the plans of Paul Abadie (1812–84) and largely completed before the end of the century, though not wholly finished until 1919, famous as a landmark, stands with its cluster of gleaming white domes on the heights of Montmartre; it reflects Byzantine influence through the medium of the Mediaeval S. Front, Perigueux (p. 290).

S. Jean de Montmartre, Paris (1897–1905) (p. 1081B), by Anatole de Baudot, is the first building of major architectural importance to have been designed in reinforced concrete, though the architect already had completed some houses and a school in the material. In the system used, the compression elements were of reinforced brickwork and the tensional elements of reinforced cement, without a stone aggregate. The design is Mediaeval in general complexion, yet with many novel forms and with considerable play externally and internally with interlaced arches, those of the inner gallery being decorated with mosaics.

The **Church of the Sagrada Familia, Barcelona** (crypt 1882–91; chevet, 1887–1891; transept façade designed 1891–1903 and built 1903–26) (p. 1082A), by Antoni Gaudí, who took over the work in 1884, still largely unfinished, is just as fantastic as others of this architect's principal buildings. The 'south transept' façade (the church is abnormally orientated), comprises a trio of steeply-gabled, deeply-recessed porches, the two lesser ones on the flanks corresponding to the transept aisles, dominated by four skittle-shaped openwork spires. The porches are profusely ornamented with sculptured naturalistic floral and figure ornament which, although in stonework, has the effect of having been modelled in soft, melting snow. Enormous faceted finials, studded with broken coloured tiles, cap the four towers. The inner arcades were to have been inclined towards one another and were intended to give the semblance of weird, angular trees, stark branches reaching upwards to sustain a stalactite vault over the nave and flat roofs over the double aisles, again with stalactites, between which scores of circular 'eyes' would admit shafts of daylight. Art Nouveau was never more dramatic, plastic or eccentric.

The **Grundvig Church, Copenhagen** (designed 1913, completed 1921–6) (p. 1082D) by P. W. Jensen Klint (1853–1930), has an impressively-composed western front which well represents progressive architecture of its day yet retains something of the traditional Baltic flavour. Indeed the vertical grooving and the 'crow-steps' of the tripartite gable recall the brick fourteenth-century church at Ystad, on the southern tip of Sweden, in the area which once belonged to Denmark. The traditional note is present too in the admirable **Engelbrekt Church, Stockholm** (1908–14) (p. 1082B) by L. I. Wahlman, which has a brick parabolic vault, and the equally fine **Högalid Church, Stockholm, Sweden** (1918–23) (p. 1082C) by Ivar Tengbom.

The **Church of Notre Dame, Le Raincy, S. et O.** (1922–3) (p. 1083A, B) by Auguste Perret, is the first in which reinforced concrete finds direct architectural expression. The simple, single-aisled 'hall-church' plan, 185 ft by 63 ft wide, is formed by four rows of slender, vertically-reeded tapering pillars, 37 ft high, supporting a flat segmental concrete vault, 2 ins thick, over the nave, and transverse shallow segmental vaults over the bays of the aisles. Being so thin, the nave vault is stiffened by transverse fins protruding above the vault, themselves covered by large, curved tiles. The church floor falls towards the east. The slight walls clasp the outer lines of columns, and are constructed of pre-cast concrete elements forming trellis-like 'claustra', glazed with stained glass to their full height over a plain dado. There is a shallow segmental apse at the east end, and the chancel is raised 5 ft above a basement containing vestries and sacristies, eastward of a flight of steps extending across the church. At the west end, where there is an organ gallery, a tower rises from cruciform pillars, each compounded of four columns

A. The Nikolaikirche, Hamburg (1845–63). See pp. 990, 1079

B. S. Jean de Montmartre, Paris (1897–1905). See p. 1080

C. The Votivkirche, Vienna (1856–1879). See p. 1079

D. S. Eugène, Paris (1854–5). See p. 1079

A. Church of the Sagrada Familia, Barcelona: 'south' transept (1903–26) seen from the inner side. See p. 1080

B. The Engelbrekt Church, Stockholm (1908–14). See p. 1080

c. The Högalid Church, Stockholm (1918–23). See p. 1080

D. The Grundvig Church, Copenhagen (1921–6). See p. 1080

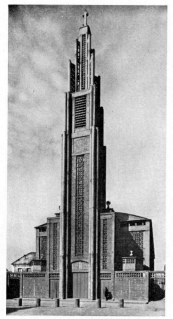

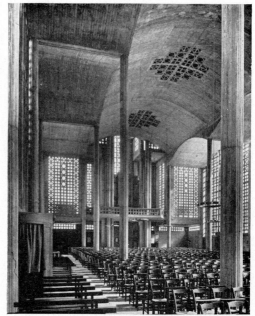

A. Exterior   B. Interior, looking W.

The Church of Notre Dame, Le Raincy, S. et O. (1922–3). See p. 1080

C. S. Antonius, Basel (1926–7). See p. 1085

A. The Chapel of Notre Dame, Ronchamp, Haute Sâone
(1950–5). See p. 1085

B. S. Thérèse, Montmagny, S. et O. (1925–6).
See p. 1085

C. The Steel Church, Presse, Cologne
(1928). See p. 1085

similar to those supporting the vaults. Externally (p. 1083A), the tower rises 140 ft, and has clustered angle-shafts which are inset in stages towards the top, resulting in a weak, inconclusive finish. All the structural concrete in the church is left as it came from the formwork, without facing. **S. Thérèse, Montmagny, S. et O.** (1925–6) (p. 1084B), by Perret, is a similar if less attractive church.

S. Antonius, Basel, Switzerland (1926–7) (p. 1083C) by Karl Moser (1860–1936) owes its inspiration to the Le Raincy church. It is plainer and much less subtle, its square, tall pillars supporting a concrete barrel vault over the nave and flat ceilings over the narrow aisles, these coverings being heavily ribbed into square coffers. Its tower, on the other hand, is more successful than Perret's.

The **Steel Church, Presse, Cologne** (1928) (p. 1084C), by Otto Bartning (b. 1883), with steel and glass walls, and **S. Matthew, Düsseldorf** (1930–1), by Wach and Roskotten, are other interesting examples of the inter-war period.

Since the Second World War, traditional character in church design has been almost entirely abandoned, yet the many new churches built have been extraordinarily diverse in the nature of their plans, structural systems, forms of construction and materials, having little in common one with another.

The **Chapel of Notre Dame, Ronchamp, Haute Saône** (1950–5) (p. 1084A), by Le Corbusier, is a surprisingly plastic and sculptural work for this advocate of functional precision in architecture. Standing on the crest of a hill, the chapel is compact and massively walled, the south wall battered inwards and containing an intriguing pattern of slot windows of varying dimensions and proportions, some square and inert, others with vertical or horizontal trends. Round, soft-contoured angle towers contain minor chapels, and with the help of a south-eastern great spur-buttress sustain a billowing roof, sweeping outwards and upwards to form an enormous canopy. On the east wall is an outdoor pulpit. Internally, the deep-set, jewel-like splay-jambed windows send shafts of richly-coloured light across the crepuscular gloom, while at the wall top a thin band of light demarcates wall from roof, the latter being slightly elevated on metal supports.

PUBLIC BUILDINGS

The **Library of S. Geneviève, Paris** (designed 1843, built 1845–50) (p. 1087) by Henri Labrouste, is a significant building in several ways. It is a fine design externally, within its Neo-Renaissance astylar terms (p. 1087A); is the first French library to be designed as an individual building; and inside the stone shell it has a complete iron frame running from bottom to top of the building, including a metal double roof. The outer iron pillars, however, are embedded in the thickness of the masonry walls. It is a long, rectangular building, 263 ft by 75 ft, with a rear projection containing a double staircase. The lofty main floor stands above a shallow ground floor, and is covered by two longitudinal barrel vaults, with iron decorative arch-ribs, supported centrally by a line of slender metal columns (p. 1087B). Between the vault ribs the panels are of thin, reinforced plaster. A metal, low-pitched upper roof spans the full width of the building. The building served as a model for the Boston Public Library, U.S.A. (p. 1151).

The **Thorwaldsen Museum, Copenhagen** (1839–48) by M. G. B. Bindesbøll (1800–56), and the **Opera House, Hanover** (1845–52), by G. F. L. Laves (1789–1864) are approximately contemporary with Labrouste's building, the first a refined astylar design following the still-continuing German Greek-Revival mode, the other an elaborately correct version of stylar Italian High Renaissance, with a slightly French cast.

The **National Library, Paris** (1862–8) (p. 1088), by Labrouste, shows further structural advances. The reading room (p. 1088A) is covered with pendentived simple domes of terra-cotta, nine in all, with 'eyes' for top light at the crown, supported by twelve slim columns, arranged in four rows, the outer columns standing close to the walls. The vaults, arch-soffits and the wall faces above book-stack level are ornamented with delicate decorations. Adjacent is the Stack Room (p. 1088B), formed of tiers of top-lighted stacks with openwork metal floors, to allow the light to pass through (p. 1088C), flanking a central space bridged at intervals by communicating passages. This light and airy arrangement foreshadows twentieth-century developments.

The **Opera House, Paris** (1861–74) (p. 1089), is the architectural masterpiece of Charles Garnier. Though commenced in the 'Second Empire' period it establishes a type of Neo-Baroque which is typically French. Opulent to a degree far beyond modern taste, it shows supreme skill in the handling of the age-old Classical elements. The façade (p. 1089A) has monolithic coupled columns, with a lesser Order threaded through, the flanking pavilions being crowned with segmental pediments; and under the entablature are circular windows and portrait busts. Above is a bold attic storey sculptured with festoons and gilded masks, while beyond is seen the low dome over the auditorium. The ornate treatment of the interior is indicated by the imposing *escalier d'honneur* (p. 1089C) and the sumptuous foyer (p. 1089B).

The **Opera House, Cologne** (1870–2) (p. 1090B), by J. Raschdorf (1825–1914), a building of modest dimensions, destroyed in the 1939–45 war, had French Neo-Baroque affinities, recognisable in the steep mansard roof, the 'lucarne' or dormer windows and the disposition and nature of the highly-decorative pavilion-like features on the otherwise astylar façades.

The **Palais de Justice, Brussels** (1866–83) (p. 1090A), by Joseph Poelaert (1817–79), stands weightily on a height overlooking the city, and builds up pyra-midally to a massive central tower. Vast, heavy, and coarse in its ragged, over-crowded Classical rhythms, it compares very unfavourably with the brilliantly-ornate Paris Opera House.

The **Rijksmuseum, Amsterdam** (1877–85) (p. 1091A), by P. H. J. Cuijpers (1827–1921), has French massing, with steep roofs which are pyramidal over the end pavilions and the twin towers flanking the entrance feature, but emulates sixteenth-century transitional Gothic in its detail. The **Town Hall, Copenhagen** (1893–1902) (p. 1091B), by Martin Nyrop (1849–1923) is similar in emulating transi-tional Gothic but is a compact block, of finer and more original design.

The **Victor Emanuel II Monument, Rome** (1885–1911) (p. 1092A), on the slope of the Capitol, was designed in 1884 by Giuseppe Sacconi (1854–1905) and completed by others after his death. It consists of a vast platform with a terrace supporting an equestrian statue of the king, backed by columns 50 ft high and having a total height of over 200 ft. French Beaux-Arts influence is apparent. Of facile Neo-Baroque design, it dwarfs its surroundings and is vulgarly over-rich.

The **Petit Palais, Paris** (1897–1900) (p. 1092B), an art gallery, by Charles Girault, was designed for the International Exhibition of 1900, along with the neighbouring Grand Palais and the Pont Alexandre III. It has a finely-balanced trapezoidal plan and a Neo-Baroque exterior which is among the best of the day, much imitated abroad. Between the end and central domed pavilions, the latter abutted by an imposing entrance portal, are regular Ionic colonnades standing on a shallow, windowed basement. Ornament and sculpture are fittingly disposed. Internally, two subsidiary semicircular staircases are in reinforced concrete, an early and suc-cessful experiment.

A. The Library of S. Geneviève, Paris (1845–50). See p. 1085

B. The Library of S. Geneviève, Paris: reading room

A. Reading room

B. Stack room   C. Detail of stacks

The National Library, Paris (1862–8). See p. 1085

A. Façade

B. Foyer   C. Grand staircase: upper flight

The Opera House, Paris (1861–74). See p. 1086

A. Palais de Justice, Brussels (1866–83). See p. 1086

B. The Opera House, Cologne (1870–2). See p. 1086

A. The Rijksmuseum, Amsterdam (1877–85). See p. 1086

B. The Town Hall, Copenhagen (1893–1902). See p. 1086

A. The Victor Emanuel II Monument, Rome (1885–1911). See p. 1086

B. The Petit Palais, Paris (1897–1900). See p. 1086

The **Stock Exchange, Amsterdam** (1898–1903) (p. 1095A) by H. P. Berlage, the commission for which was won in competition, brought the architect widespread renown beyond his own country. It is of red brick with limited stone dressings, and shows that honesty and simplicity of expression which marks the trend towards true Modern architecture. Internally, the glass and metal roof is frankly exposed, as also are the brick and stone of the galleried tiers rising from the hall floor. The style throughout, has Romanesque associations, as has also the **Diamond Workers' Union Building, Amsterdam** (1899–1900) (p. 1118) by the same architect. The exuberance of Art Nouveau was not favoured in Holland, and the Romanesque, unaffectedly robust and direct, offered a suitable vehicle for the designer's aspirations. A similar recourse to this style is found in England and the U.S.A. at about the same period.

The **Post Office Savings Bank, Vienna** (1904–6) (p. 1095B), by Otto Wagner, marks a further step towards the new architecture. The architect had been a follower of Art Nouveau, and the interior still retains in the semi-elliptical form of its metal and glass roof a trace of the lightness associated with that style, but otherwise bears no readily-identifiable historical associations, the character proceeding solely from the essential structure.

The **City Hall, Stockholm** (1911–23) (p. 1096), by Ragnar Ostberg, is the last important romantically-traditional Swedish building, wonderfully rich, spectacular and impressive. Though eclectic, motifs being drawn from many historical sources, it is composed with remarkable skill and striking originality, so much so that it was considered 'modern' in its day and widely imitated abroad. It stands on the lakeside (p. 1096A), its south and east sides towards the water, and is arranged as a slightly wedge-shaped rectangular block around two unequal courts, the larger open at ground level by arcades towards the broad, lakeside terrace, resplendent with gardens, fountains and statues. The building material is red brick, with sparing stone dressings. At the south-east corner rises a dominant tower, with inward-sloping sides, sheer brickwork for 230 ft and 354 ft to the apex above the openwork cylindrical lantern and its delicate, three-crowns terminal. The principal chambers are on the first floor, the largest being the Assembly Room or 'Golden Chamber' (p. 1096B), magnificent with mural mosaics, dividing the two courts and approached by an open ceremonial staircase from the smaller court, covered over to form the 'Blue Hall'. The Council Chamber occupies the middle of the south side.

The **Champs-Élysées Theatre, Paris** (1911) (p. 1106B) was in the first place designed by Henri van de Velde, but as completed is almost wholly due to the Perret brothers. It is of reinforced concrete, faced externally with thin slabs of marble. Internally, the actual structural frame determines the essentials of the effect, the concrete merely being covered with plaster. The building has the Classical dispositions and character normal to Auguste Perret's work, but in the foyer seems even more than usually austere, lacking colour and having little decoration apart from the balustrades and low-relief panels. The façades, with relief sculpture by Bourdelle, are a modification of Van de Velde's original design.

The **Centennial Hall, Breslau** (1912–13) (p. 1097), by Max Berg, one of the most daring structures erected before the First World War, is covered by a vast concrete dome (p. 1097B), 213 ft diameter, springing from the ground, its upper part comprising a series of heavy radial ribs, serving to carry tiers of continuous windows, which mask the dome externally and give it the much lighter appearance of a stepped cupola. Here, reinforced-concrete structure itself makes the design. The approach and entrance porches however, are fashioned into slender colonnades of Classical complexion (p. 1097A).

The **Einstein Tower, Potsdam, near Berlin** (1920–1) (p. 1099B), by Erich Mendelsohn, an observatory and astrophysical laboratory, is a wholly plastic expression, completely devoid of historical allusions, its forms being symbolic of optical instruments. Designed for poured concrete, it is actually executed in cement-covered brickwork.

The **City Library, Stockholm** (1924-7) (p. 1099A), by E. Gunnar Asplund, has a high cylindrical lending hall rising above a contrasting rectilinear arrangement of lesser apartments, the whole making a very dignified, reticent composition, showing only the barest trace of Classical historical allusion.

The **Bauhaus, Dessau** (1925-6) (p. 1098A, C), by Walter Gropius, was erected to provide studio-dormitories, assembly and dining-hall, workshops, administrative and social rooms and the school of design for this famous pioneer establishment, and is itself expressive of the Bauhaus aims of uniting art with industrial production. The design consolidates the new developments made in architecture up to this time. The various elements of the accommodation are linked together into an asymmetrical composition, the living quarters projecting towards the rear. The three upper of the four floors of the workshop block are cantilevered, and sheathed with a metal-and-glass curtain, while the administrative wing has long, horizontal ribbon windows. Between them is a two-floored link standing over a wide bridge, and towards the rear the projecting hostel wing presents a pattern of wide windows joined to individual cantilevered balconies (p. 1098A). Throughout, the flat-roofed elements are designed with the utmost regard for their respective functions, yet manipulated in mass and detail to present an attractive composition.

The **Vondelschool, Hilversum** (1926) (p. 1098D), by W. M. Dudok, is one of his many buildings, including other schools, at this new town, south-east of Amsterdam, founded shortly before the First World War, of which he was appointed chief architect. The Vondelschool—which received an extension at the entrance end in 1931—is very characteristic of his mature style, which still echoes his early contact with the 'De Stijl' group of artists (p. 1067). Like the architects Klerk and Kramer and the Amsterdam group in general, he adheres to fine brickwork as his principal medium, but unlike them avoids fanciful effects, instead giving his buildings a serene dignity, stressing the horizontal lines and opposing the restfulness of large plain areas of brickwork to the pungent rhythms of long, banded windows. There is usually an element of cubism in his compositions, as is plainer to see in his **Town Hall, Hilversum** (1929) (p. 1098B), and they are normally asymmetrical, their essential horizontality being compensated by a strong tower or vertical feature.

The **Tuberculosis Sanatorium, Paimio, Finland** (1929-33) (p. 1099C), by Alvar Aalto, is an early and advanced demonstration of the adaptation of modern structural resources to the design of hospitals. Of reinforced concrete, this large establishment is freely and openly planned, the various units receiving the ideal orientation for each of them, the wings thus running on different alignments. The material permits widely-projecting balconies, ample windows, and light, cheerful appearance.

The **Casa del Popolo, Como** (1932-6) (p. 1101A) by Guiseppe Terragni (1904-1943), a member of the original 'Gruppo 7', shows Italian Modern architecture too to have reached maturity about this time. Finely finished and studiously proportioned, this reinforced-concrete building achieves a distinctively Mediterranean character.

The **Musée de l'Art Moderne, Paris** (p. 1100A) by A. Aubert and others, and the **Palais de Chaillot, Paris** (p. 1100B), were designed for the International Exhibition of 1937. Both are attractive, with admirably designed settings and fine sculptural and garden embellishments, yet are essentially traditional, the Classical ancestry being plainly visible.

A. The Stock Exchange, Amsterdam (1898–1903). See p. 1093

B. The Post Office Savings Bank, Vienna (1904–6). See p. 1093

A. Exterior

B. The Golden Chamber

The City Hall, Stockholm (1911–23). See p. 1093

A. Exterior

B. Interior

Centennial Hall, Breslau (1912–13). See p. 1093

A. The Bauhaus, Dessau:
Hostel wing. See p. 1094

B. The Town Hall, Hilversum (1929).
See p. 1094

c. The Bauhaus, Dessau (1925–6). See p. 1094

D. The Vondelschool, Hilversum (1926 and (*right*) 1931). See p. 1094

A. The City Library, Stockholm (1924–7). See p. 1094

B. The Einstein Tower, Potsdam (1920–1). See p. 1093

C. The Tuberculosis Sanatorium, Paimio, Finland (1929–33). See p. 1094

A. The Musée de l'Art Moderne, Paris (1937). See p. 1094

B. The Palais de Chaillot, Paris (1937). See p. 1094

A. The Casa del Popolo, Como (1932–6). See p. 1094

B. The Musée des Travaux Publics, Paris (1938–). See p. 1103

C. Garage, Rue de Ponthieu, Paris (1905–6). See p. 1104

A. The Palazzetto dello Sport, Rome (1956–7). See opposite page

B. The Palazzo dello Sport, Rome (1959). See opposite page

C. The Palazzo dello Sport, Rome: interior

The **Musée des Travaux Publics, Paris** (1938–) (p. 1101B), an office of works museum in reinforced concrete by Auguste Perret, was still not quite finished at his death. It stands on a wedge-shaped island site, entered at the narrow end, where the entrance vestibule surrounds a semicircular auditorium. The composition is symmetrical about the long axis, and the design clearly bears Perret's personal stamp, being conceived throughout on Classical lines. The elements of the design, however, are carefully attuned to the material, both in the decorative and structural sense. Externally there are concrete colonnades, their shafts tapering downwards for logical reasons, and these correspond with similar columns internally, together carrying the load of the coffered ceiling and superstructure, the thin outer walls carrying nothing but their own weight.

The **Palazzetto dello Sport, Rome** (1956–7) (p. 1102A), by P. L. Nervi and Annibale Vitellozzi, is of circular plan, 200 ft diameter, covered by a shell-concrete shallow dome with a rippled edge, the thrusts at the base taken by forked flying buttresses. The stadium was designed to accommodate about 5,000 spectators and to serve the Olympic Games of 1960. It was made of pre-fabricated elements, the dome proper having been erected in the space of forty days. The much larger **Palazzo dello Sport, Rome** (1959) (p. 1102B, C), also by Nervi and for the 1960 Olympic Games, is again circular and domed, capable of accommodating 15,000 people in three tiers of seats, one of them descending below ground level, along with the arena (p. 1102C). The construction and method of lighting are similar, there being a large central 'eye' and peripheral vertical windows near the base. Externally it differs in having a surrounding open, skeletal colonnade (p. 1102B).

INDUSTRIAL AND COMMERCIAL BUILDINGS

The **Galleria Vittorio Emanuele, Milan** (1865–77) (p. 1105A), by G. Mengoni (1829–77), is one of the many iron-and-glass-roofed arcades that have been built since the late eighteenth century, mainly in France and England. It is a very large and ambitious project, arranged on a cruciform plan, broadening out to a domed octagon at the intersection. The style of the façades is Classical, bordering on the Neo-Baroque.

The **Chocolate Factory, Noisiel-sur-Marne, near Paris** (1871–2) (p. 1105B), by Jules Saulnier, is thought to be the earliest skeleton-framed building in France. It stands upon massive stone piers over the river Marne, borne upon iron double girders which carry an iron frame comprehending the floors and pitched roof. The upright stanchions and diagonal braces show externally, the panels infilled with wooden tiles bearing a polychromatic floral pattern.

The **Entrance Pavilion, International Exhibition, Paris, 1878** (p. 1105D) (destroyed), by Gustave Eiffel, showed iron and glass used with full architectural pretensions externally. There was here more glass than wall, the reverse from traditional building and an anticipation of Modern architecture. The domed central and end pavilions had large glazed lunettes, one on the centre pavilion being projected downwards to form a dominating portal. The glazed, projecting canopies over the lateral terraces in front of the building were a further innovation.

The **Halle des Machines, International Exhibition, Paris, 1889** (p. 1105F) (destroyed 1910), by the engineer Contamin (1840–93) and the architect F. Dutert (1845–1906), was a remarkable building, spanning 375 ft, 1,400 ft long and 150 ft high, consisting of steel principals forming four-centred arches, hinged at the apex and at the base, where they tapered to their bearings. The principals were steel-braced longitudinally and the building was completely glazed. For the same exhibition was built the celebrated **Eiffel Tower**, 984 ft high, named after the designer.

The **Metro Station, Place Bastille, Paris** (1900) (p. 1105E), by Hector Guimard (1867–1943), is one of the minor iron-and-glass constructions which well illustrate the characteristics of Art Nouveau. The linear expression of the metal, curved, sinuous or convoluted wherever structure allowed; the naturalistic, vegetable-like nature of the ornament; the lack of imposts on arches, as here on the dual, horse-shoe entrance; and the exclusion of historical references, are all significant of the style. Art Nouveau denied tradition; the Arts and Crafts respected it.

The **Samaritaine Department Store, Paris** (1905–6) (p. 1105C), by F. Jourdain (1847–1935), is of a class of commercial establishment which in France had its beginnings early in the nineteenth century, and from the nature of the enterprise lent itself readily to external expression in metal and glass. The Samaritaine is thoroughpaced Art Nouveau. The knots of metal foliage swirl sinuously over the functional structure, softening the strictness of its lines, aided in this object by bold patterns of coloured faience, filling the unglazed panels.

The **Garage, Rue de Ponthieu, Paris** (1905–6) (p. 1101C) by Perret, contrasts markedly with the foregoing. It is of reinforced concrete, totally unadorned, a direct expression of the functional structure, organized to present a fine, orderly and appropriate effect.

The **Turbine Factory, Berlin** (1909) (p. 1107A), by Peter Behrens, is important in having shown that industrial buildings can make good architecture solely by meticulous organization of the structure and materials, without recourse to orna-ment or other non-essentials. Great windows provide the flood of light needful, set between steel uprights, exposed externally, to which the metal roof principals are framed, and taper downwards onto hinged base-plates. Apart from the metal and glass the walls are of concrete, with horizontal striations on the angle masses.

The **Railway Station, Stuttgart** (begun 1914, completed 1919–27) (p. 1107B) by P. Bonatz and F. E. Scholer, is a fine, masculine design, based on tradition but stripped of superfluous ornament, great decorative value being secured from the rusticated stonework.

The **Fagus Factory, Alfeld-an-der-Leine** (1911–14) (p. 1110B), by Walter Gropius and Adolf Meyer, is of brick, but on the main fronts tall windows project beyond the intervening piers and give the impression of continuous curtain walls, an impression heightened by the use of angle windows. Though there are actually three floors of height, the intermediate floors are concealed behind opaque panels in the window frames.

The **Airship Hangar, Orly, near Paris** (1916) (p. 1106A) (destroyed), by the engineer Freyssinet, was a remarkable concrete vault, parabolic in section, com-prised of a thin skin of reinforced concrete given stiffness and strength by being undulated to form great ribs, lattices of window apertures being formed on the backs of the ribs.

The **Salginatobel Bridge, Switzerland** (1929–30) (p. 1108A) by Robert Maillart, is one of the many fine reinforced-concrete bridges by this distinguished engineer, which gain their elegance and beauty from the functional simplicity of the means employed, here a curved slab supporting a flat one, other slabs spanning between them vertically.

The **Market Hall, Leipzig** (1928) (p. 1108B) by Deschinger and Ritter, is covered by two octagonal shell-concrete domes of 248 ft span, $3\frac{1}{2}$ ins thick. The earliest shell-concrete dome was that of the Jena Planetarium (1923), spanning 82 ft.

The **Van Nelle Factory, Rotterdam** (1927–30) (p. 1109A), by J. A. Brinkmann and L. C. van der Vlugt, architects not otherwise especially known, for a firm of tobacco, tea and coffee merchants, is Holland's finest Modern building of the first half of the century. Of reinforced concrete, the main eight-storey block is in

A. The Galleria Vittorio
Emanuele, Milan (1865–77).
See p. 1103

B. The Chocolate factory, Noisiel-sur-Marne, near
Paris (1871–2). See p. 1103

c. The Samaritaine Department Store, Paris (1905–6).
See p. 1104

D. The Entrance Pavilion, International Exhibition,
Paris, 1878. See p. 1103

E. The Metro Station,
Place Bastille, Paris (1900).
See p. 1104

F. The Halle des Machines, Paris (1889).
See p. 1103

A. Airship Hangar, Orly, near Paris (1916). See p. 1104

B. The Champs–Elysées Theatre, Paris (1911). See p. 1093

A. Turbine Factory, Berlin (1909). See p. 1104

B. The Railway Station, Stuttgart (1914–27). See p. 1104

A. The Salginatobel Bridge, Switzerland (1929–30). See p. 1104

B. The Market Hall, Leipzig (1928). See p. 1104

A. The Van Nelle factory, Rotterdam (1927–30). See p. 1104

B. The Station, Amstel Suburb, Amsterdam (1939). See p. 1111

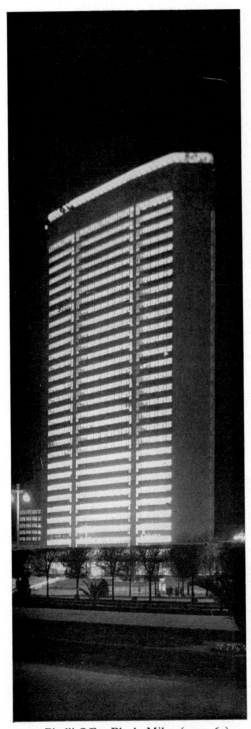

B. The Fagus factory, Alfeld-an-der-Lei
(1911–14). See p. 1104

A. Pirelli Office Block, Milan (1957–60).
See p. 1111

C. Exhibition Hall, Turin: interior (194
1949). See p. 1111

'mushroom' construction (a system used by Maillart as early as 1908), the respective floors being carried on internal pillars which fan outwards at the top, the outer walls being non-load bearing and supported by the floors. Externally, the horizontal ribbon windows are admirably balanced by the flow of form of the projecting tower blocks, and afford an effective contrast of panels of plain wall. Linked to the main block is a less high wing which sweeps on a pleasant curve.

The **Stockholm Exhibition, 1930** (p. 1077B), by Gunnar Asplund, admirably illustrates the capacity of modern architectural forms, aided by colour, to produce gay, graceful and delicate effects.

The **Station, Amstel suburb, Amsterdam** (1939) (p. 1109B), by H. G. J. Schelling, is an attractive, economical structure built of brick, with very large panels of glass on the two long sides, and a low-pitched roof.

The **Aircraft Hangars** (1935 and 1939-40) (p. 1060) (destroyed) which were located on various sites, several of a standard type designed by P. L. Nervi, 330 ft by 135 ft internally, involved a three-dimensional conception of structure, a segmental barrel vault of pre-cast reinforced-concrete ribs forming a diagonal lattice being sustained on only six buttressing supports. The lower edges of the hipped roof were stiffened by triangular 'space-frames' on the open side.

The **Exhibition Hall, Turin** (1948-9) (p. 1110C), by P. L. Nervi, is the larger and slightly the earlier of two constructed there, and is a rectangular building of 312 ft span, bridged by a segmental vault of concrete springing from the ground. Forked buttresses fan into ribs near the base, and these support corrugations of 8 ft interval carrying pre-cast shell units 2 ins thick, braced by fins and embodying shallow, strip windows. This remarkable structure took only eight months to build.

The **Stazione Termini, Rome** (1947-51) (p. 1113), by E. Montuori and associates, includes a vast concourse, of imposing simplicity, fronting a 'slab' office block with narrow, horizontal ribbon windows. The concourse ceiling, finished in white glass mosaic, stands on multiple slender pillars of granite-faced concrete, and undulates in logical accord with the stresses resisted; the latter are asymmetrical, since the ceiling continues externally to form a great, cantilevered canopy over the entrance front, ending in a thin fascia slab.

The **Jespersen Office Block, Copenhagen** (1956) (p. 1117), by Arne Jacobsen, has a façade of ultimate simplicity, a curtain wall fronting cantilevered floors being divided uniformly into panels. Each of the windows reproduces the proportions of the block as a whole. The opaque panels underneath the ribbon windows are differentiated from them solely by change of colour.

The **Pirelli Office Block, Milan** (1957-60) (p. 1110A), by P. L. Nervi, Gio Ponti and others, with its thirty-two storeys above ground, towers to such a height as to constitute a skyscraper. Skyscrapers are as yet fairly few in Europe, though they are commonplace in America. In all European cities there has been a general tendency since the Second World War for commercial and apartment buildings to reach far greater heights than ever before.

COMPARATIVE ANALYSIS

PLANS

Nineteenth Century. The common form of town dwelling became the flat block (p. 1069B), often preserving the 'hotel', courtyard, arrangement (p. 788E) but generally becoming larger and higher than formerly, though in Paris height was restricted to 65 ft, above which further tiers had to be set back in stages. Rooms were not ordinarily assigned to particular uses until the later part of the period. Public building plans continued mostly to follow traditional Classic formulae, but necessarily became more extensive and complex in response to social developments, while building types proliferated for similar reasons. Office blocks, commercial undertakings and department stores developed apace, factories became even more numerous on the outskirts of towns and the railways created new nodes of attraction around the station locations. Church plans varied little from the old, except in being derived from several different historical traditions.

Twentieth Century. The former tendencies continued, but increasingly were affected by the development of framed structure, which from beginnings in the nineteenth century became commonplace after 1900 and preponderated after about 1930. Thus wall thicknesses became progressively lighter—the steel or concrete pillars or 'stanchions' being at first embedded in the walls—and at length might be no more than thin, insulating veneers (p. 1074A, B). Solid internal walls similarly tended to disappear, substituted by light partitions, all load being taken by relatively slender pillars (p. 1076B). In some constructional systems the pillars could be wholly internal, floors being cantilevered from them towards the thin façades (p. 1109A). The 'free plan' affected all classes of building, including individual houses (pp. 1074, 1076), though despite occasional exceptions (p. 1083A, B) churches followed old patterns until after the Second World War, since when they have become excessively varied in their dispositions, based on a wide range of geometrical or asymmetrical patterns. In general, symmetry dominates nineteenth-century planning and asymmetry that of the twentieth. The development of heating systems, distributing heat from a single point, largely removed the need for fireplaces and their flues, these being a serious obstacle to free planning.

WALLS

Nineteenth Century. Solid, load-bearing walls remained normal, constructed of the various traditional materials. Brick, of variegated colours, terra-cotta and faience tiles were favoured in the second half of the century, especially towards its end. Polychrome faience was almost a hall-mark of Art Nouveau (p. 1070A). Though metal stanchions, when used, were usually embedded in external walls throughout the century, there were occasional iron and glass façades (p. 1105D), popular for department stores at and beyond its end (p. 1105C) and for many types of minor structure (p. 1105E). Generally, walls were increasingly loaded with architectural features, the Classical system being the most favoured (pp. 1089A, 1092A), progressing from Neo-Renaissance (p. 1087A) to Neo-Baroque (p. 1092B), though with less and less faithfulness to the historical prototypes. Except for churches (p. 1081A, C), the Gothic Revival played no great part.

Twentieth Century. With the advent of systematic framed structure in steel and reinforced concrete in the opening years of the century, walls began to lose their chief function of supporting floors and roof. In the early stages of realization of this circumstance, the walls, still solid, were partly or wholly carried on the frame, but the exterior effects gave little or no evidence of the fact, still being designed as though they were performing their time-honoured tasks to the full, dressed in reminiscence of one or other of the various kinds of traditional attire (p. 1107B). Elevations did, however, become more and more simple. Perret, in France in 1903, was the first to give a just external expression to the frame (p. 1073A), though it was a long time before he was extensively followed. He stressed the frame and reduced the wall to infilling panels (see also p. 1069F). This kind of construction is still quite valid, and many are the kinds of materials that have been used for the infilling, some traditional and some new; though the problem always has been partially solved since some of the space normally is needed for windows. A next stage of development was to remove this sheathing or 'cladding' from direct association with the outer stanchions, placing it instead either just outside them (p. 1101B) or just inside

A. Exterior

B. Concourse

The Stazione Termini, Rome (1947–51). See p. 1111

(p. 1083B, left); or alternatively, extending the floors as cantilevers and placing the thin walls between them as continuous horizontal strips (p. 1109A, curved block), or covering the whole face of the building with a continuous 'curtain' (p. 1117) supported at the floor lines or even hung from the top. In all these latter cases the screening walls needed no greater thickness or stiffness than was necessary for weather protection and their own support. Metal became usual for the light wall-framings, though timber often was equally practicable. The infillings of such frames could either be glass, transparent or opaque, or other suitable light and tough material, natural or synthetic.

OPENINGS

Nineteenth Century. Since façades mainly were traditional in complexion, windows and other openings were organized on age-old lines, with their customary types of enframement. Yet as eclecticism increased and architecture in general became less academic, non-Mediterranean countries sought to gain more natural light than strict Classic precedent permitted, and enlarged window areas by various devices, whilst still retaining a semblance of the style represented. Thus pseudo-arcades (p. 1087A) and pseudo-colonnades (pp. 1089A, 1092B), infilled with windows, were common features. Business and commercial establishments had a greater need for light than had apartment houses, and at the end of the century and the beginning of the next, non-domestic stylar façades already sometimes had more window than wall, the stylar elements surviving only in a few tortured fragments. Exhibition buildings in metal and glass had shown the way (p. 1105D). As methods of glass-making advanced, larger and larger areas of unobstructed opening became practicable, and window bars were no longer necessary. It was particularly its advantage in offering large window areas that gave the iron-and-glass façade its popularity for shopping stores (p. 1105C). Iron-and-glass arcades (p. 1105A), roofs, awnings, porches, conservatories and similar structures offered this facility to the full (p. 1105E).

Twentieth Century. Openings maintained their traditional aspect, as modified in the previous century, wherever load-bearing wall construction continued to be used or imitated, save that under the general movement towards simplicity they lost their elaborate enframements almost completely, and became much more regular in their mutual dispositions (pp. 1073B, E, 1099A, 1107B). The framed building, once the frame is expressed, produces its own kind of effect, paralleled to some extent in old timber buildings, where long 'ribbon' ranges of windows had sometimes appeared; but in the main, framed buildings, whether 'cladded' in local panels (pp. 1069F, 1073A), horizontally between floors (p. 1109A), vertically between stanchions (p. 1110B) or covered comprehensively by 'curtain' walls (p. 1117) have little precedent in history and inevitably visually dissociate themselves from it. The fact took time to reach public acceptance. Generally speaking, Modern architecture is a framework lightly infilled or sheathed with a protective covering—a skin having little depth (p. 1074A, B)—quite the opposite from the traditional massive, load-bearing walls, through which shadow-creating openings are cut deeply through the solid. Thus openings in walls are much less strongly differentiated from wall than formerly (p. 1117). Very large, totally unobstructed windows can be provided when needed. Traditional building normally presents more wall than window; Modern architecture readily may have more window than wall.

ROOFS

Nineteenth Century. These normally were pitched, usually steeply, though in an eclectic age much depended upon the style being more or less faithfully represented.

The mansard, complete with ornate dormer windows, was a common 'Second Empire' (1848–70) feature (p. 1090B) in Europe, and the roofs then and later often were broken into pavilions, accentuated centrally and at angles or ends either pyramidally (p. 1091A) or in square or circular domes (p. 1092B). In iron construction the domes might be of iron and glass (p. 1105D), which in any case were materials extensively used for arcades (p. 1105A) and for coverings over courts, light-wells and inner apartments where only roof-light was possible. Mansard roofs, with dormers, were useful over urban frontages above the limits of permissible vertical height, and were continued into the next century.

Twentieth Century. Pitched roofs, high or low, were a normal counterpart of northern European traditional-style building, and so were frequently used where old-style building was perpetuated (p. 1073E). But in the new architecture, particularly the domestic, the pitched roof was considered inadmissible, at least while ideas were shaping (pp. 1074, 1076). Also, in houses and flats (p. 1078) the roof was looked upon as a proper part of the usable accommodation, and must therefore be flat. In the case of large halls, however, it would be difficult to achieve a wide span without recourse to a trussed roof or a vault. Great spans already had been achieved with metal in the nineteenth century (p. 1105F), and developments in the twentieth with that material were principally refinements upon types already known. Reinforced concrete introduced fresh opportunities. Mostly its advantages were offset by weight and expense (p. 1097B), until, from already long-standing isolated precedents, shell-concrete, only two or three inches thick, was rediscovered and systematically exploited. A whole range of possibilities for shell-vaults was opened up, beginning with the dome—which has naturally a high degree of stiffness resulting from its shape (p. 1108B)—and extending to types capable of covering large rectangular compartments, which however, required stiffening as well as buttressing against the thrusts accumulating towards the base (p. 1060). An early precedent (p. 1106A) had shown that stiffening could be contrived by corrugating the shell of domes or rectangular vaults in 'waves' or folds (pp. 1102A, B, 1110C). Vaults, whatever their thickness, give rise to stresses and strains appropriate to their shape, and the difference between shell-vaults and their Roman or Mediaeval antecedents lies in the vastly reduced weight, their homogeneity and their capacity, up to a limited point, to contain their own resistance against tensional as well as compressional stresses. So far, large-span shell-vaults normally have been made to spring at or near the ground, so that they might be the more readily buttressed or contained (p. 1102A).

COLUMNS

Nineteenth Century. The Orders, where appearing, were used for the most part in the time-honoured ways (pp. 1089A, 1092B). Even when converted into cast iron (pp. 1087B, 1088A) they approximated to the ancient norms as nearly as possible, except in being vastly more slender, whether in their shafts, archivolts or entablatures. Gothic shafts similarly were closely imitated in iron (p. 1081D). Cast-iron columns led to iron building-frames and these to steel and reinforced-concrete frames, the latter only at the turn of the century. Iron or concrete pillars had the merit of strength and economy of space, obviating internal walls as a means of support for upper floors in cases where strict room division was unnecessary or undesirable.

Twentieth Century. The Orders began to disappear from buildings, and by the inter-war period became quite rare. In the process they often became much simplified, or were substituted by abjectly plain pillars or arcades (pp. 1100A, B, 1107B). With the spread of framed construction in steel or reinforced concrete, internal pillar supports came to be relied upon even when room division was necessary, for the reason that building thereby became a straightforward unified process and partitions could be added at the finishing stage of operations, varied as necessary from floor to floor. The method was applied to houses (p. 1076B) and flats (p. 1073A) as well as to public (p. 1101B), commercial and industrial building. Pillars (stanchions) normally carried beams and the beams the floors, but in 'mushroom' construction, first used in a Zurich factory in 1908, the concrete stanchions are shaped like an inverted cone at the top, carrying a beamless floor forming a uniformly thick concrete slab (p. 1109A: main building).

MOULDINGS

Nineteenth Century. These followed historical precedent fairly faithfully, whether Classical or Mediaeval. In the later decades attempts were made to abandon historicism and to invent a new style, resulting in occasional unprecedented profiles or the drastic revision or simplification of old ones (p. 1069C). Such endeavours had their climax in Art Nouveau, which continued for a few years into the next century, wherein mouldings were either substituted by sinewy, seaweed-like trailing forms, turned into knots at extremities and building angles, or were fundamentally Classical or Mediaeval but so drastically revised as to be scarcely recognisable (p. 1105C). Also, curvilinear brackets and scrolled ironwork were greatly favoured (p. 1105C, E). Alternatively, mouldings were dispensed with in favour of soft, plastic surface modelling (pp. 1070B, C, 1082A).

Twentieth Century. The aftermath of Art Nouveau was a restrained historicism, in which mouldings played a decreasing part (p. 1096A, B). Such mouldings as were retained were sparsely distributed and confined to a few telling elements, or were merely simple projections (p. 1099A). The modernists, led by Adolf Loos, rejected mouldings completely after about 1910 (p. 1073C), and in the inter-war period architects in general mostly abandoned them.

ORNAMENT

Nineteenth Century. Ornament followed historical precedents, though becoming smaller in scale, more confused and less tasteful than the prototypes (p. 1089B, C). Unadorned structural ironwork was not considered to be admissible to polite architecture, and so had to be ornamented (p. 1088A). Art Nouveau ornament took many exotic forms (pp. 1069D, 1070C, 1082A, 1105E), and polychrome faience was a feature (pp. 1070A, 1105C).

Twentieth Century. Apart from the initial continuance of preceeding practices, ornament virtually disappeared, since it was deliberately excluded from the new architecture just as firmly as mouldings were refused. In theory, effects were to be contrived solely by the manipulation of the constructional elements (pp. 1078, 1109A) and by the exploitation of the colour and texture of the materials used. In practice, ornamental patterns have sometimes been admitted (pp. 1083A, B, 1084B), and polychrome effects often are used nowadays, obtained by panelling with different-coloured synthetic materials (p. 1117) or by the calculated use of attractive facing materials to concrete structure. Mosaics, heraldry, stained glass (p. 1084A), decorative painting and sculpture are sometimes employed.

REFERENCE BOOKS

BANHAM, R. *Theory and Design in the First Machine Age.* London, 1960.
BILL, M. *Ludwig Mies van der Rohe.* Milan, 1955.
BRESSET, M. *Gustave Eiffel, 1832–1923.* Milan, 1957.

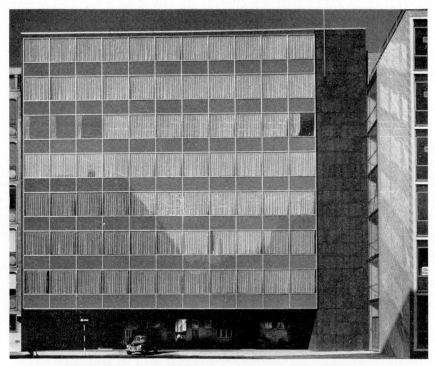

The Jespersen Office block, Copenhagen (1956). See p. 1111

COLLINS, PETER. *Concrete, The Vision of a New Architecture.* London, 1959.
DORFLES, G. *L'Architettura moderna.* Milan, 1954.
FISKER, K., and YERBURY, F. R. *Modern Danish Architecture.* London, 1927.
GIEDION, S. *Space, Time and Architecture.* 3rd edition. London, 1954.
—. *Walter Gropius.* London, 1954.
GROPIUS, W. *Internationale Architektur.* Munich, 1925.
—. *The New Architecture and the Bauhaus.* New York, 1936.
HITCHCOCK, H. R. *Gaudí.* New York, 1957.
—. *Architecture, Nineteenth and Twentieth Centuries.* Harmondsworth, 1958.
HOEBER, F. *Peter Behrens.* Munich, 1913.
HUXTABLE, A. L. *Pier Luigi Nervi.* New York, 1960.
JAFFÉ, H. L. C. *De Stijl, 1917–1931.* London, 1956.
JOEDICKE, J. *A History of Modern Architecture.* Trans. J. C. Palmes. London, 1959.
KAUFMANN, E. *Von Ledoux bis Le Corbusier.* Vienna, 1933.
KIDDER SMITH, G. E. *Italy Builds.* London, 1955.
—. *Sweden Builds.* London, 1950.
—. *Switzerland Builds.* London, 1950.
LABÒ, G. *Alvar Aalto.* Milan, 1948.
LE CORBUSIER. *Towards a New Architecture.* Trans. F. Etchells. London, 1947.
MARTINELL, C. *Antonio Gaudí.* Milan, 1955.
MCGRATH, R. *Twentieth Century Houses.* London, 1934.
MIERAS, J., and YERBURY, F. *Dutch Architecture of the XXth Century.* London, 1926.
MÜNZ, H. *Adolf Loos.* Milan, 1956.
OUD, J. J. P. *Holländische Architektur.* Munich, 1926.
PAGANI, C. *Architettura italiana oggi.* Milan, 1955.

PAPADAKI, S. (ed.) *Le Corbusier: Architect, Painter, Writer*. New York, 1948.
PEVSNER, N. *Pioneers of the Modern Movement*. London, 1936. Revised edition, *Pioneers of Modern Design*, Penguin Books, Harmondsworth, 1960.
RICHARDS, J. M. *An Introduction to Modern Architecture*. Harmondsworth, 1940.
ROTH, A. *The New Architecture*. Zurich, 1940.
SARTORIS, A. *Gli elementi dell' architettura funzionale*. 2nd edition. Milan, 1935.
—. *Introduzione alla Architettura Moderna*. Milan, 1949.
SCHMALENBACH, F. *Jugendstil*. Wurzburg, 1935.
SWEENEY, J. J., and SERT, J. L. *Antoni Gaudí*. London, 1960.
WHITTICK, A. *European Architecture in the Twentieth Century*. 2 vols. London, 1950–3.
YERBURY, F. R. *Modern Dutch Buildings*. London, 1931.
ZEVI, B. *Storia dell' architettura moderna*. 3rd edition. Turin, 1955.
—*Gunnar Asplund*. Milan, 1948.

The Diamond Workers' Union Building, Amsterdam (1899–1900).
See p. 1093

Falling Water, Pennsylvania (1936–7). See p. 1156

XXIX. ARCHITECTURE OF
THE AMERICAS
(*c.* 500 B.C. to the present day)

INFLUENCES

GEOGRAPHICAL. The position of the American continent has been an important factor in its architectural development. Separated by vast oceans from the cradles of civilization in the Near and Middle East, the cultures of its peoples advanced comparatively slowly until the sixteenth century when the first European settlements were established in the continent. The discovery of America, or more narrowly the West Indies, by Christopher Columbus (1446–1506) in 1492 radically altered the rate and pattern of progress, and from that time the links between the Old and New Worlds have been strong. Internal geographical conditions have also helped to determine the history of the continent. For obvious reasons, the first colonial centres were established on or near the coast; and mountain ranges, the more important of which all run in a north-south direction, controlled the areas and rate of settlement. Down the western side of the continent runs a great ridge of mountains, the Rockies of North America and the Andes of South America, to the west of which, between the mountains and the Pacific, lie narrow coastal plains. To the east of the mountains lie, in South America, the jungle forests of the Amazon basin

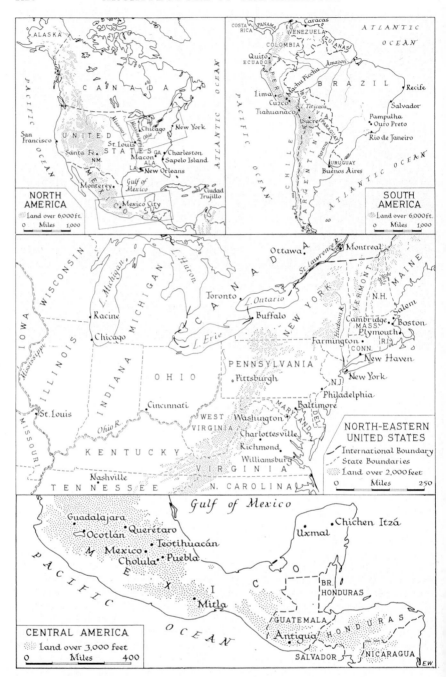

The American Continent

and, further south, the plains of Argentina, while in North America there are vast plains, drained by the Mississippi and Missouri Rivers, cradling the Great Lakes complex and extending from the Gulf of Mexico to Hudson Bay. In North America, to the east of the plains is another important range of mountains, the Appalachians, while the Brazilian Highlands lie in a similar position in South America. Between the eastern mountains and the Atlantic runs a coastal plain which in North America was roughly the extent of the British American colonies.

GEOLOGICAL. The search for precious metals has played an important part in the development of the Americas. Their appetites whetted by tales of mineral wealth, the Spanish sent out expeditions to Peru and Mexico, and later to what are now New Mexico, California and Arizona. In the nineteenth century, various 'gold rushes' contributed to the development of remote areas of North America. The pre-Columbian civilizations of Peru and Mexico made good use of the excellent building stones available in these regions, and this tradition was maintained and extended by the Spanish colonists. The North American Indians, being largely nomadic, did not develop a building tradition comparable with that of Mexico, and European settlers in North America built mainly in timber—unlimited supplies of which were readily available from the vast tracts of virgin forest—and later in brick, but only rarely in stone. It was not until the nineteenth century, with the development of railway and canal transport, that the excellent building stones of North America were fully exploited. Limestones, sandstones and granites are all to be found, but specific reference should be made to three particular building stones, all from the eastern part of the U.S.A.: Quincey Granite, used in the Bunker Hill Monument, Charlestown, Mass. (1825–43) and other buildings; Pennsylvanian Marble, popular in nineteenth-century Philadelphia; and Brown Stone, widely used in New York. Coal and iron ore are to be found in Pennsylvania, Ohio and other areas, and this has accounted for the development of cities like Pittsburgh, Cincinnati and Baltimore, while in more recent times the presence of oil under Texas and neighbouring states has contributed much to their wealth and thus affected their building activity.

CLIMATIC. Throughout the continent, the climate varies enormously, from the almost arctic conditions of Alaska to the tropics of Brazil. The temperate climate of the north-eastern part of what is now the U.S.A. and parts of Canada has helped the industrial and commercial development of these areas, while the west coast of North America provides a delightful climate, in California similar to that of the Mediterranean region. In the southern part of North America, the climate is warm and humid, ideal for the cultivation of crops like cotton and tobacco but somewhat enervating as far as human activity is concerned. Despite bitter winters and torrid summers, the central plains of North America are extremely fertile and also healthy, but in the south-west the climate is hot and dry and there are wide areas of desert. In the Panama region tropical conditions prevail, as they do in the northern and central parts of South America. In Peru, the altitude of the Andes affords pleasanter conditions, while further south in the plains of Argentina a more temperate climate is found.

RELIGIOUS. Highly organized religions existed among the pre-Columbian peoples of Central and South America, centred upon the worship of natural objects and phenomena—mountains, clouds, rain, earthquakes, the sun, moon, stars, etc.— and incorporating a form of confession of sins. Among the Aztecs of Mexico, the Sun God was the most important deity, while the Inca pantheon had as its chief god, Viracocha, the Creator. Aztec religion incorporated human sacrifice of a particularly repellent nature, the heart being plucked out of the still-living victim. Both Peruvian and Mexican religions were controlled by powerful priesthoods and each was based on a strict moral code.

In the sixteenth century, Spanish colonists brought with them the religion of their mother country as did the Portuguese in the case of Brazil, so that Latin America is predominantly Catholic. Various Orders of friars—the Franciscans, Dominicans, Augustinians and Mercedarians—played a considerable part in the cultural as well as the religious development of South America and Mexico. Later the Jesuits and Carmelites made a great contribution, particularly the former whose power and enlightenment were such as to disturb the somewhat reactionary local administrations, with the result that the Order was expelled from Brazil in 1759 and from the Spanish colonies in 1767. In the early seventeenth century it was estimated that 70,000 churches had been built and 500 monasteries founded in Latin America.

In North America, the religious pattern was again determined by the beliefs of the settlers, which here varied widely. Thus Virginia, the first British colony, was Anglican; while (since their settlers had left England for reasons of conscience) Massachusetts was Puritan, Pennsylvania Quaker and Maryland Catholic. Areas settled by the French tended to be Catholic. Because of this diversity of belief, North America developed a tradition of toleration, unknown in Europe until fairly recent times.

SOCIAL. Social organization was highly developed in the pre-Columbian civilizations of Peru and Mexico. The Aztec Empire of Mexico flourished under a military theocracy of priest-warriors, while in Peru, under the Incas, government was carried out by a series of provincial councils, each with an Inca nobleman as adminstrator and each responsible to the Emperor in Cuzco, the capital of the Empire. Both the Inca and Aztec civilizations planned and built fine cities and showed considerable prowess in civil engineering by constructing excellent paved roads, necessitating in the case of the Incas, tunnelling through the rock of the Andes.

Soon after their establishment, the Spanish colonies in the New World were divided into two viceroyalties, that of New Spain, set up in 1535, embracing Mexico and Central America with its capital at Mexico City, and that of Peru (1544) with its capital at Lima. In 1717 the viceroyalty of New Granada, covering what are now Colombia, Venezuela and Equador, was established, while in 1776 the viceroyalty of Rio de la Plata came into being, embracing Argentina, Bolivia, Paraguay and Uruguay. Portuguese possessions in the continent were limited to Brazil.

Each of the viceroyalties was in the charge of a viceroy who had supreme authority over all civil and military matters, and governed virtually as an absolute ruler in the name of the Spanish king. Of almost equal importance was the Church already referred to.

By the early seventeenth century, a fine road system had been set up in Latin America, the 'Camino Real', in part following roads laid by the pre-Columbian Indians. In their building and road-making use was made by the 'conquistadores' and their successors of Indian labour which was also employed, often under appalling conditions, for work in factories producing wool and cotton goods, and on plantations. In 1501 the first slaves were introduced from Africa, and by 1560 it was estimated that there were 100,000 negro slaves in Latin America.

Education was not overlooked, and a royal decree ordered that every village in the Spanish Empire was to have its own school, while the universities of Mexico and Lima were established in 1553 and 1576 respectively. Life in both Lima and Mexico City could be luxurious, and equalled that in the great capitals of Europe until the decline of Spanish fortunes.

Turning to North America, the pre-colonial societies were infinitely more primitive than those of the Aztecs and Incas and were organized on a tribal basis. With the development of the colonies came a social pattern very different from that in Latin America, due largely to the character of the colonists, who were settlers rather than colonizers in the sense of the 'conquistadores'. In colonial Virginia, for instance, government was divided between the governor, representing the British Crown, and the House of Burgesses, representing the people of the colony, who thus had a measure of independence with the advantage of British protection. Each colony was a distinct entity and this has, in a sense, been perpetuated in the democratic system of the U.S.A., which retains a separate legislature for each state in the union although, in addition, each state is represented in the U.S. Federal or central Government.

Education received consideration in the colonies at an early date, and in 1636 Harvard, the oldest university in North America, was founded. In 1693 a royal charter was granted for the foundation of William and Mary College at Williamsburg, while Brown, Princeton and Yale Universities were all founded in the eighteenth century, prior to the Revolution of 1775.

Many colonial centres, like Boston, Philadelphia and Williamsburg, although hardly the compeers of Lima and Mexico City, were delightful towns and possessed all the amenities for gracious living in eighteenth-century terms. A less pleasant aspect of society was the plantation and slave system of the cotton and tobacco-growing areas of the South. It should be borne in mind, however, that this was as much an economic phenomenon as a social one, and that many plantation owners were benevolent and humane masters. Nevertheless, the principle of slavery was in direct opposition to the ideals of freedom and equality, strongly cherished by the new country which came into being after the War of Independence; this was one reason for the tragic Civil War which broke out in 1861 between the Northern States (whose economy did not depend upon slavery and who could therefore afford to oppose it) and the Southern States, and in which the former were victorious.

Today the U.S.A. stands as a great world power, characterized by her commercial prosperity and championship of democratic government. Her vigour may in part be accounted for by the racial variety of her population. English, Scots, Irish, Germans, Italians, Poles and many of other nationalities have, as immigrants to a land of promise and opportunity, contributed much to her spiritual, cultural and technical development.

Canada, governed by a democratic Parliament modelled on that of Great Britain, has much in common with her neighbour to the south, and with the backing of her own vast natural resources is developing economically and culturally at a prodigious rate.

HISTORICAL. The background of the early 'native' civilizations of the Americas is often obscure, but we have seen that in Mexico and Peru they were of a high order. Indeed the Spanish conquest of these areas took years to bring about, even with the aid of the horse, gunpowder and steel weapons, none of which was known to the Indians. With regard to Mexico and Central America, pre-Columbian civilization may be divided into three main phases: (i) Mayan (c. 500 B.C.–c. A.D. 800); (ii) Toltec (from about the time of Christ to c. 1200); (iii) Aztec (c. 1200–1519). In Peru, the Inca Empire became established in the early fifteenth century, with its capital at Cuzco, although a highly developed culture with considerable building skill had existed from perhaps as early as 300 B.C. In North America the picture is more confused because of the nomadic nature of most of the tribes, but recently, interesting movements among the Pueblo Indians of the south-west of what is now the U.S.A. have been traced. Between c. A.D. 600 and c. 1100 these tribes erected permanent fortified villages on the flat-topped outcrops ('mesas') which characterize this region, but later, for reasons as yet unknown, the villages were abandoned and new settlements were made in and at the bases of canyon walls in the same area.

Following the discovery of the New World by Columbus there were numerous exploratory voyages, among them Magellan's discovery of a south-west passage from the Atlantic to the Pacific round Cape Horn (1520); Cabral's voyage on which he touched Brazil (1500); and Frobisher's journeys to Labrador (the first in 1576). In addition there were specific campaigns of colonization: Hernan Cortes in Mexico (1519) and Francisco Pizarro in Peru (1532). In 1528, Panfilio de Narvaez led a Spanish expedition to Florida; in 1534 Jacques Cartier explored the S. Lawrence River and staked a claim for France in what is now Canada; in 1583 Sir Humphrey Gilbert landed at S. John, Newfoundland (discovered by John Cabot in 1497), while in 1585, Sir Walter Raleigh landed on the coast of Virginia.

In 1607 Jamestown, the first important British settlement in the New World, was founded, and thirteen years later the Pilgrim Fathers sailed in the famous *Mayflower* from Plymouth, England, to establish Plymouth in what is now Massachusetts. New Amsterdam, on Manhattan Island, was founded by the Dutch in 1626, to be taken by the English in 1664, when it became New York. The year 1638 saw the founding of a Swedish colony on the Delaware River, and 1668 the establishment of the Hudson Bay Company, dealing in furs and skins from the Hudson Bay region of Canada. In 1682 the English Quaker, William Penn, founded Pennsylvania. Later, the Mississippi was explored by the French, moving south from their Canadian settlements, and bases were established by them on the Gulf of Mexico at Biloxi (1699), Mobile (1702) and New Orleans (1718), while S. Louis was founded by a French merchant in 1764.

By 1755 the spheres of influence of European nations within the New World were roughly as follows: Portugal, whose main empire lay in the Far East, was limited to Brazil under the ruling of Pope Alexander VI who, in 1494, had divided the new discoveries of the world between Spain and Portugal on a longitudinal basis; Spain possessed Mexico, Central and South America (excluding Brazil) and what are now Texas, California, Arizona, New Mexico and Florida; the English colonies comprised virtually the whole of the eastern seaboard of North America, and the holdings of the Hudson Bay Company in Canada were vast; French settlements were centred along the S. Lawrence River, in the Great Lakes region and in the central plains of the U.S.A. down to and including the Mississippi delta.

For obvious reasons there was considerable rivalry between the British and French over their respective claims in North America, but a more important event occurred in 1775, with the revolt of the British colonies against the mother country. A year previously, the first Continental Congress, a gathering of representatives of all the British colonies (except Georgia), met in Philadelphia to discuss their relationship with England, particularly with regard to taxation and trade. This move was precipitated through the decision of the British Government to close the port of Boston after the famous 'Boston Tea Party' (where angry Bostonians had refused to permit the landing of three shiploads of tea on which the colonists were to pay what they considered to be an unfair tax). In 1775 the first shot of the Revolution was fired, and the following year, with the adoption by the thirteen colonies of the Declaration of Independence—the most important document in the history of the U.S.A.—the Revolution became the American War of Independence. Peace came in 1783 and with it recognition of the independent status of the nucleus of the modern U.S.A.

From this point the history of the U.S.A. is one of expansion, principally westwards—the romantic era of the covered waggon. Certain areas were ceded by Britain in 1783; in 1803 the central region of the country—the 'Louisiana Purchase' —was absorbed and in 1819, Florida. Oregon Territory was ceded by Britain in 1846, extensive areas by Mexico in 1848, while Texas was annexed in 1845. Minor adjustments were made to the border between Canada and the U.S.A. in 1818, and a small area of Mexican territory—the 'Gadsden Purchase'—was added to the country in 1853.

The countries of South America gained their independence in the nineteenth century when the various viceroyalties of Portugal and Spain were terminated; Brazil (1806), New Granada and Rio de la Plata (1810), Peru (1817) and New Spain (1821).

Canada, which had remained loyal to Britain throughout the American War of Independence, was faced with her own internal problems, springing from the existence of two distinct cultures within her boundaries—the French and the English—but these were largely overcome in 1791 by the creation of two separate provinces, Lower Canada (fundamentally French) and Upper Canada. In 1840 responsible government by an elected assembly was granted to the country, the British governor assuming a purely legal and symbolic role, while in 1867, with the passing of the British North-America Act, the country achieved full Dominion status which it retains within the British Commonwealth today, and its own Parliament and Ministries were set up at Ottawa on the lines of those at Westminster. Finally, the original provinces of Ontario and Quebec were joined by New Brunswick, Nova Scotia, Manitoba, British Columbia, Saskatchewan and Alberta to form modern Canada.

ARCHITECTURAL CHARACTER

The architecture of the Americas may be conveniently considered as passing through four main phases: (i) Indigenous (c. 500 B.C.–A.D. sixteenth century); (ii) Colonial (sixteenth–nineteenth century); (iii) National (nineteenth century–c. 1930); (iv) Modern.

INDIGENOUS PHASE (c. 500 B.C.–A.D. sixteenth century). Although in North America permanent buildings of this phase, extending from earliest times to the establishment of European settlements in the sixteenth and seventeenth centuries, were rare owing to the nomadic nature of most of the tribes, a vigorous building tradition of a high order obtained in Mexico and Peru. In North America permanent building seems to have been restricted to the Pueblo Indians of the southwest part of what is now the U.S.A., but this was of a comparatively primitive order, using rubble and sun-dried clay. In Mexico religious buildings were the most important structures and great truncated pyramids were built by the Mayans, Toltecs and Aztecs (pp. 1128, 1129). The latter were generally built up in 'adobe' or sun-dried brick, and then faced with stone slabs, sometimes richly carved in low relief or coated with lime-plaster and painted (p. 1128). Masonry was finely dressed and laid in courses, but the staggering of vertical joints was ignored and thus walls tended to be weak in bonding. The round arch and barrel vault were unknown, but the corbelled arch and vault (limited to spans of 15–20 ft) were used. Roofs were constructed of logs or corbelled vaults. Formal planning was appreciated, and Toltec and Aztec cities were laid out on grand lines (p. 1131). Stone columns were used by the Toltecs (p. 1128). Temples, generally sited on great pyramidal bases, were windowless, and in all buildings wall-openings were kept to a minimum. Stone surfaces were carved in intricate designs, often incorporating formalized representations of serpents, warriors, tigers and eagles (p. 1128). In Peru the most important building work was in fortified towns (p. 1131), where a high standard was attained in coursed and polygonal masonry, the stones being rubbed down and fitted together with great precision. Round burial towers, predating the Inca Empire, are to be found in Bolivia (p. 1131). As in Mexico, adobe brick was used as well as the corbelled arch and vault.

COLONIAL PHASE (sixteenth–nineteenth century). Extending from the time of European settlement to that of independent national status, this phase varied in duration from one area to another; in Latin America, from the early sixteenth century to the early nineteenth century; in North America from the early seventeenth century to the late eighteenth century in the case of the U.S.A., and in Canada to the mid-nineteenth century. In general the architecture of a particular area mirrored that of the homeland of the colonizers or settlers of that area, with modifications occasioned by climate, the types of building material obtainable and the quality of labour available. Thus in seventeenth-century New England building followed the pattern of English weather-boarded, heavy timber-frame prototypes (p. 1131), while in eighteenth-century Virginia we find a 'Georgian' architecture, often almost indistinguishable from that of eighteenth-century England (p. 1132). Colonial architecture of Latin America followed the pattern of Spanish and Portuguese work. Early examples show derivation from Spanish Mediaeval prototypes (p. 1135), and Moorish influences (p. 1139) are apparent. The Plateresque, Churrigueresque, Baroque and Antiquarian phases of the architecture of the Spanish homeland are all mirrored in the work of Spanish America (pp. 1135, 1139). Architecture of Portuguese Brazil in the second half of the eighteenth century had much in common with the Rococo of Central Europe (p. 1136).

NATIONAL PHASE (nineteenth century–c. 1930). This phase followed the shaking-off by an area of its colonial ties with European powers, although it must be emphasized that European influence in architecture and other matters remained strong throughout the continent. In South and Central America and Mexico conditions were somewhat unstable following the collapse of the Portuguese and Spanish Empires and it is only in the present century that these areas have achieved independent architectural maturity. In the nineteenth century there was a tendency to rely on foreign architects, particularly French, and notable examples of their work are the **Itamaratí Palace, Rio de Janeiro** (1851–4) by J. M. J. Rebelo; the **Customs House, Rio de Janeiro** (1826) by A. J. V. Grandjean de Montigny (1776–1850); and work in Santiago by C. F. Brunet-Debaines (1799–1855), all of which are unequivocally French in character. The nineteenth century saw the establishment of schools of architecture in Latin America based on the French École des Beaux-Arts, and these have had an important influence on architecture.

In Canada there was a similar situation, and architecture was strongly influenced by trends in England until comparatively recently.

In the U.S.A. on the other hand, a conscious striving for a truly 'national' architecture became evident soon after the War of Independence (1776–83), and the architecture of the National Phase in the U.S.A. can best be followed if it is considered under three sub-headings:

(a) Post-colonial Period, c. 1790–c. 1815
(b) First Eclectic Period, c. 1815–c. 1860
(c) Second Eclectic Period, c. 1860–c. 1930

(a) *Post-colonial Period* (c. 1790–c. 1815). Architecture of this period moved away from the English Georgian idiom which had become established along the eastern seaboard of the country. Neo-Classic elements were introduced (p. 1147) and, while there was influence from the English architects the Adam brothers (p. 875) and John Soane (p. 876), American architects tended to look more to France for inspiration.

(b) *First Eclectic Period* (c. 1815–c. 1860). During this period the revived Greek style was predominant (p. 1143), receiving a more whole-hearted acceptance than in England (p. 877) and developing specifically American characteristics. The Gothic

(p. 1144) and Egyptian (p. 1148) styles found some popularity but, compared with the Greek Revival, these were minor streams, and the American Gothic Revival did not develop the strength of the parallel movement in Britain (pp. 875, 877, 986).

The type of timber-framing known as the 'balloon-frame' came into use during this period (c. 1830) and revolutionized timber construction. Requiring relatively unskilled labour and obviating the elaborate joints of the traditional heavy timber structures built in colonial times, the balloon-frame has played an important part in American architecture and is still widely used in modern domestic work. As its name suggests, rather than relying on an essentially post-and-lintel construction, the balloon-frame owes its strength to its walls, roof, etc., as diaphragms. Comparatively light timber sections are employed which are nailed together, floor and ceiling joists acting as ties, the whole being stiffened by the external timber sheathing.

As in Britain and Europe (pp. 983, 1061) the period saw considerable developments in the use of cast-iron as a building material (pp. 1121, 1152).

(c) *Second Eclectic Period* (c. 1860–c. 1930). American architecture achieved international significance during this period and followed two main streams. The first, related to the Gothic Revival and initiated as a Romanesque Revival with H. H. Richardson (1838–86) as its first important exponent (pp. 1143, 1147), gained considerable momentum and reached a wonderful vigour and vitality in the work of Louis Sullivan (1856–1924) (p. 1155). In some respects the movement in its later stages can be equated with that of the Arts and Crafts in Britain (p. 991) and it culminated in the work of Frank Lloyd Wright (1867–1959) (pp. 1143, 1144).

The second stream was more academic in character. Influenced by the École des Beaux-Arts in Paris, its architecture was inspired by the great periods of the past, the Italian (p. 1143) and French Renaissance (p. 1143), Ancient Greek (p. 1151) and Roman (p. 1156) and Late Gothic (p. 1147).

Two important and influential exhibitions belong to this period: the **Centennial Exposition** (Philadelphia, 1876) and the **World's Columbian Exposition** (Chicago, 1893). The Classical buildings and formal layout of the latter did much to reinforce the popularity of the academic architectural stream.

The period is noteworthy for its structural experiment and achievement. The skyscraper, often regarded as America's greatest single contribution to architectural development, was a product of this phase and its development was closely related to that of metal frame-construction, the non-load-bearing 'curtain' wall and the lift or elevator.

The period saw also the establishment of many schools of architecture in the U.S.A., the first being that at Massachusetts Institute of Technology, founded in 1865.

MODERN ARCHITECTURE (from c. 1930). The architectural contribution of the Americas since c. 1930 has been of great significance. Not only the U.S.A., but also Canada, Mexico and the countries of South America have produced notable buildings which have had considerable influence throughout the world. In the case of the U.S.A., with the rise of German Nazism in the 1930's, some of the great leaders of European architecture sought asylum there (Walter Gropius (p. 1066), Erich Mendelsohn (p. 1068) and Ludwig Mies van der Rohe (p. 1066) among them), and these, both as teachers and practitioners, have had a profound effect on American architecture. In addition distinguished architects, like Alvar Aalto (p. 1068) from Finland, have been invited to undertake commissions in the country (p. 1159), while the growing prosperity of the U.S.A., helped rather than hindered by the 1939–45 War, has encouraged building activity. Furthermore, and this is true of the Americas generally, public acceptance of 'modern' architecture has been very much more wholehearted than in the older continent of Europe and healthy experiment, both technical and aesthetic, has been widespread.

In Mexico and South America the greatest contribution has been in reinforced-concrete building, and work in these areas is often characterized by its daring structural forms (pp. 1160, 1163). The use of colour is also noteworthy, often in a modern adaptation of the old 'azulejos' tradition (p. 1160), and in Mexico whole façades are sometimes treated as rich mosaic mural decorations (p. 1160).

There are notable examples of reinforced-concrete building in North America also, but there the steel-frame is more widely used. Important work has been done in the U.S.A. in the development of prefabrication techniques, particularly in respect of curtain walling (pp. 1127, 1163) and in site organization related to large industrial and commercial buildings, while in respect of building services (heating, lighting, etc.) American architects hold an unrivalled position.

EXAMPLES

INDIGENOUS PHASE

(*c.* 500 B.C.–A.D. sixteenth century)

MEXICO AND CENTRAL AMERICA

The **House of the Dwarf, Uxmal** (*c.* A.D. 700), an example of late Mayan work, was a large rectangular structure built around a central court on a 20 ft high stone base. Internally the rooms were spanned with corbelled stone vaults, while externally the building, particularly its central entrance, was richly decorated with low-relief carving. Entrances were square-headed and the walls windowless.

The **Pyramid of the Sun, San Juan Teotihuacán** (*c.* A.D. 800) (p. 1129D) was part of a great ceremonial complex of temple buildings planned on axial lines. A truncated pyramid, it rose from a base more than 700 ft square to a height of 216 ft in four stages, marked by terraces around the structure, the slope of each stage being varied to accentuate further the mass of the pyramid. A facing of brightly-coloured, plastered stone slabs covered the adobe brick core of the structure which was surmounted by a shrine dedicated to the Sun God.

The **Temple Pyramid, Xochicalco** (*c.* A.D. 800) (p. 1129A), was faced with stone slabs intricately carved with a design of interwining snakes, human figures and symbolic devices.

The **Great Pyramid, Cholula** (commenced *c.* A.D. 125), the greatest of all the Mexican pyramids, was built over a long period. Today it is overgrown with vegetation and crowned by a Spanish colonial church.

The **Pyramid Temple, Tenayuca** (*c.* A.D. 1270) (p. 1129B) went through a series of reconstructions, the last in 1507. It rises to a height of 50 ft from a base measuring 140 ft square. Three faces of the pyramid were carved with a design incorporating serpents, probably related to the Aztec calendar (there were 52 years in the Aztec cycle and on each of the carved faces of the pyramid there were 52 serpents): the fourth side is formed as a double stairway which led originally to twin temples on the truncated summit of the structure.

The **Ball Court and Observatory, Chichen Itzá** (*c.* A.D. 1200) show evidence of Toltec craftsmanship and are characterized by the fine quality of their masonry, laid in courses but in some instances indefinitely bonded. The observatory is particularly interesting and provides an example of a circular plan form.

The **Hall of the Monoliths, Mitla** (*c.* A.D. 1100) (p. 1129E) is one of the most important surviving buildings in the sacred city, the name of which is derived from the Aztec for 'place of the dead'. Approached by a flight of steps, the building stands on a mound and is entered through three square-headed openings. Externally the façade is decorated with panels of carved geometric ornament. Internally the hall

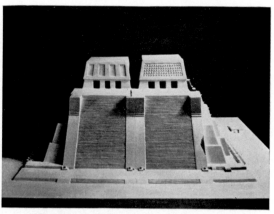

The Temple Pyramid, Xochicalco
(c. 800): Detail. See p. 1128

B. The Pyramid Temple, Tenayuca (c. 1270):
model of restoration. See p. 1128

c. The Gateway of the Sun, Tiahuanaco
(c. 500–1000). See p. 1131

D. The Pyramid of the Sun, San Juan Teotihuacán (c. 800). See p. 1128

E. The Ruins of Mitla (c. 1100).
See p. 1128

F. Tenochtitlán in 1519. See p. 1131

A. San Geronimo de Taos, New Mexico (*c.* 1540). See p. 1131

B. Machu Picchu (*c.* 1500). See p. 1131

measures 125 ft by 23 ft and has six 14-ft high, tapered porphyry columns (each of 3-ft diameter) on its centre line, thus breaking the span of the roof which was probably of timber.

At **Tenochtitlán** (p. 1129F), the Aztec island capital set in Lake Texcoco and now the site of modern Mexico City, there were many fine buildings. **The Palace of Montezuma**, the Aztec Emperor at the time of the Spanish conquest, was a particularly fine work and incorporated patios, terraces, zoological gardens and numerous apartments decorated with woven fabrics, leather and carved, sweet-scented woods.

PERU AND THE ANDES REGION

The **Gateway of the Sun, Tiahuanaco** (c. A.D. 500–1000) (p. 1129C) is a fine example of pre-Inca work. Two immense slabs of stone carry a great andesite lintel, 10 ft deep and weighing approximately 10 tons, richly carved and surmounted by a carved head of Viracocha.

Burial Towers, Bolivia (A.D. 1000–1440) also pre-date the Inca Empire but show highly developed masonry techniques. These circular tombs or 'chullpas' are constructed in finely laid polygonal masonry.

Cuzco (after 1200), the Inca capital, has fine walls of coursed, black andesite masonry, apparently quarried at least nine miles from the city.

The **Fort of Sacsahuamán** (c. 1475) provides another example of the building and engineering prowess of the Incas in its superb cyclopean masonry walls overlooking the neighbouring city of Cuzco.

Machu Picchu (c. 1500) (p. 1130B), a late Inca hillside town, is dramatically sited above the Urubamba River and has wide stairways, terraces and battered defensive walls constructed in coursed and polygonal masonry.

NORTH AMERICA

Cliff Dwellings, Frijoles Canyon, New Mexico (c. A.D. 1300). Dwellings here were either natural or man-made caves, linked by terraces constructed of rubble and adobe and approached by ladders. Other examples can be seen in Mesa Verde National Park, Colorado.

San Geronimo de Taos, N.M. (c. 1540) (p. 1130A), despite more recent additions, retains its original character. Rectangular adobe dwellings are piled together to make a five-storey complex, the flat roofs, constructed of tree-trunks, forming a series of stepped terraces. Outer rooms, often receiving light only from their entrances, provide living accomodation, while the inner rooms are used as stores. Originally, for defensive reasons, dwellings at ground level were without doors and access was by ladder to roof level.

COLONIAL PHASE
(sixteenth–nineteenth century)

DOMESTIC BUILDINGS

Capen House, Topsfield, Massachusetts (1683) (p. 1133A), an excellent example of seventeenth-century colonial architecture in New England, is of heavy timber-frame construction, the first floor and gables being carried forward as 'jetties' as in antecedent English examples, while the central, clustered brick chimney is reminiscent of similar features in England. Externally, the house is clad in weather-boarding and has a wood shingle roof. Internal walls and partitions are faced with vertical boarding, beams are left exposed and decoration is sparse, being confined to such details as the stair balusters. Windows are small, leaded casements. The ground floor is divided into two rooms by a central brick core, incorporating two fireplaces back-to-back. An entrance lobby is at one end of the brick core, from which a staircase leads to the upper floor. Other houses of a similar character are: **Whipple House, Ipswich, Mass.** (1639); **Scotch-Boardman House, Saugus, Mass.** (1651); **Fairbanks House, Dedham, Mass.** (*c.* 1637); **Whitman House, Farmington, Connecticut** (1664); **Paul Revere House, Boston, Mass.** (*c.* 1676); **John Ward House, Salem, Mass.** (1684); **House of the Seven Gables, Salem, Mass.** (*c.* 1670).

Bacon's Castle, Surry County, Virginia (*c.* 1655) (p. 1133E) is cruciform in plan. Built in brick, with its curved Flemish gables, high clustered chimneys and Classical details in the brickwork over its entrance, the house has much in common with Jacobean examples in England.

Abraham Ackerman House, Hackensack, N.J. (1704) shows Dutch influence. Its roof is of the 'gambrel' or mansard type with widely projecting eaves, covered in wood shingles, as also are the gables and dormer cheeks. The walls of the ground floor are of roughly-dressed, coursed masonry. Other houses showing Dutch influence are: **Dyckman House, New York, N.Y.** (*c.* 1783); **Terheun House, Hackensack, N.J.** (*c.* 1709); **Vreeland House, Englewood, N.J.** (1818) and **Jan Ditmars House, Brooklyn, N.Y.** (*c.* 1700).

Parlange, Pointe Coupée Parish, Louisiana (1750) (p. 1133B), a French plantation house, has an open, colonnaded verandah running round the house on both floors, a feature providing protection from the hot sun and heavy rains of the area. The high-pitched, hipped roof is covered in shingles and, because of the dampness of the site, the ground floor is constructed of brick, although the first floor is of timber. Other examples showing a similar character are: **Connelly's Tavern, Nachez, Mississippi** (*c.* 1795); **Keller Mansion, St. Charles Parish, La.** (*c.* 1801).

Westover, Charles City County, Va. (*c.* 1730–4) (p. 1133C), one of the most distinguished eighteenth-century Virginian plantation houses, has a close affinity with English Georgian work. A seven-bay brick structure of two storeys, there are further rooms in the steeply-pitched hipped roof, which is punctuated with elegant dormer windows. The central entrance to the main front is accentuated by a baroque-like broken pediment, finely carved in Portland stone, probably shipped specially from England for this purpose. The house is flanked symmetrically by (though originally not physically linked with) two minor structures, one providing kitchen and servants' quarters, the other serving as the plantation office. Internally the house has finely proportioned rooms, with their superbly executed details ranking with the best contemporary work of the mother country. Some ceilings have applied designs, cast in composition and almost certainly imported from England where they were currently fashionable.

Other colonial houses of Georgian character are: **Mount Pleasant, Philadelphia** (1761–2), built in stuccoed rubble, its stone details probably derived from a contemporary English pattern book like those of Batty Langley (p. 874), has a low-pitched, lead-covered roof, truncated to form a flat terrace or deck, a feature of many American houses of this period known as a 'captain's walk'; **Miles Brewton House, Charleston, South Carolina** (1765–9) has a fine two-storeyed pedimented, colonnaded porch and similar features are to be found at **Shirley, Charles City County, Va.** (*c.* 1769), **Drayton Hall, S.C.** (1738–42) (p. 1133D) and in Thomas Jefferson's first design for his own house, **Monticello, near Charlottesville, Va.** (1770–5).

Brandon, Prince George County, Va. (*c.* 1765) has a more monumental plan arrangement showing Palladian influence, and the house is flanked on either side by minor buildings to which it is joined by low linking elements. A similar plan

Capen House, Topsfield, Massachusetts
(1683). See p. 1131

B. Parlange, Pointe Coupée Parish, Louisiana
(1750). See p. 1132

c. Westover, Charles City County, Virginia (c. 1730–34). See p. 1132

D. Drayton Hall, South Carolina (1738–42).
See p. 1132

E. Bacon's Castle, Surry County, Virginia (c. 1655). See p. 1132

A. Ecala Palace, Querétaro (c. 1785).
See p. 1135

B. São Pedro dos Clérigos,
Recife (1729–). See p. 1136

C. Mercedarian Monastery, Quito (c. 1630).
See p. 1136

D. The Sanctuary, Ocotlán
(c. 1745). See p. 1136

E. The Cathedral, Mexico City (1563–1667).
See p. 1135

F. Casa del Alfeñique, Puebla
(c. 1780). See p. 1135

arrangement is found at **Mount Vernon, Fairfax County, Va.** (1757–87), **Mount Airy, Richmond County, Va.** (1758–62), **Tulip Hill, Anne Arundel County, Maryland** (*c.* 1756) and the **Hammond-Harwood House, Annapolis, Md.** (1773–4).

The **Ecala Palace, Querétaro, Mexico** (*c.* 1785) (p. 1134A), with its richly decorated façade, heavy Baroque pediments over the first-floor windows with their lace-like wrought iron balconies, deep, arcaded loggia on the ground floor and, under the roof cornice, a wide frieze of blue and white tiles, provides a fine example of a Spanish colonial palace.

The **Casa del Alfeñique, Puebla, Mexico** (*c.* 1780) (p. 1134F) is particularly noteworthy on account of its lavish use of 'azulejos' (glazed tiles) as a facing. Its façade is covered with large, octagonal, unglazed, red tiles and chequered with smaller, white glazed tiles, decorated with blue flowers.

Other important houses in colonial Latin America are: **Torre Tagle Palace, Lima, Peru** (*c.* 1730) showing pronounced Moro-Spanish characteristics; **Quinta de Presa, Lima, Peru** (1766), with its pink colour-washed, adobe walls, evocative of Austrian Rococo work; and the **Saldanha Palace, Salvador, Brazil** (*c.* 1720) with a richly carved entrance incorporating flanking caryatids.

RELIGIOUS BUILDINGS

The **Cathedral, Santo Domingo (now Ciudad Trujillo), Dominican Republic** (1521–41), an important example of the use of late Gothic forms in colonial architecture, has chevet and lateral chapels, and Gothic ribbed vaulting over its square nave bays. The west façade is in the Plateresque style.

The **Cathedral, Mexico City** (1563–1667) (p. 1134E) replaced an earlier primitive, flat-roofed structure (1525–). The building shows a curious mingling of Baroque and more severely Classical features. With three aisles to both nave and chancel, and rows of side chapels filling the length of the building on both sides, the church measures 177 ft in width and is 387 ft long. The nave and shallow transepts are covered by barrel vaults pierced by lunettes, while each bay of the side aisles is domed. The clustered piers of the nave are each made up of four engaged Roman-Doric columns, the fluting of which is continued round the nave arches. Externally, the west façade is flanked by twin towers rising 203 ft, but these and the remainder of the elevational detail (carried out in buff-coloured limestone with statues and other detail in white marble, to the designs of José Damiàn Ortiz de Castro) date from 1786 and are Neo-Classic in character. The present dome and lantern and some of the decorative work on the west front are by Manuel Tolsa, and date from the early nineteenth century.

The **Cathedral, Lima, Peru** (1543–51; altered and enlarged *c.* 1570–; rebuilt *c.* 1750–) provides a fascinating story of the battle against earthquakes. After the collapse of the original stone vaults in the early seventeenth century, these were rebuilt in brick. Further earthquakes caused the latter to be replaced by vaults of wood, reed and plaster in the mid-eighteenth century and this form of construction has been retained for various later rebuildings. Externally, the church with its twin west towers and enriched central entrance bay (although heavily restored in 1940) retains original work by the sculptor Juan Martínez de Arrona (1562–1635) and, despite its Baroque flavour, has much in common with the work of Juan de Herrera, architect of the Escorial (p. 851).

Among numerous examples, the following Latin American colonial religious buildings are particularly noteworthy: the **Cathedral, Puebla, Mexico** (1562–1664); the **Cathedral, Monterrey, Mexico** (1630–1800); **Mercedarian Monastery and Cloister, Cuzco, Peru** (1650–69); **Mercedarian Cloister, Mexico City**

(1634–); **Mercedarian Monastery, Quito, Ecuador** (*c.* 1630–) (p. 1134C) and **College of San Francisco Javier, Sucre, Bolivia** (*c.* 1624–).

São Pedro dos Clérigos, Recife, Brazil (1729–) (p. 1134B) by Ferreira Jacome is an example of Portuguese colonial work. Characterized by the tall, elegant proportions of its west front, the church is generally evocative of mid-European baroque. The same qualities are seen in the churches of the **Rosário** (1725–77) and **Santo Antonio** (1750–3), both at Recife.

The **Sanctuary, Ocotlán, Mexico** (*c.* 1745–) (p. 1134D), marking a famous pilgrimage site, has a façade of gleaming white stucco shaped into fantastic Churrigueresque forms, flanked by slender twin towers covered with bright red tiles in a scale-like pattern. The interior is equally rich, much of its carving being by the eighteenth-century Indian sculptor, Francisco Miguel.

The **Church and Convent of San Estevan, Ácoma, N.M.** (*c.* 1640) (p. 1137A) provides an example of a Spanish colonial mission centre, and was built by local Indian labour from a mixture of rubble and adobe brick. The flat roof is formed from dressed tree-trunks carried internally on richly carved timber brackets. Squat twin bell-towers flank the entrance façade, and the church receives natural light from only the entrance, two very small windows and a transverse clear-story between the roof of the nave and the higher ceiling of the sanctuary, the latter flooding the altar and its richly-painted reredos with bright light.

Other similar examples are: **San José, Laguna, N.M.** (1699–1706) and the church at **Ranchos de Taos, N.M.** (1772).

S. Luke's Church, Smithfield, Va. (1682–) (p. 1137C) shows the influence of English Mediaeval parish churches. Built in brick, the church consists of a simple, rectangular nave with a squat, square tower at the west end. The gables to the nave have stepped parapets reminiscent of Dutch work, while the side walls are strengthened by mediaeval-like buttresses. With their crudely-formed brick tracery, the windows also indicate a Mediaeval prototype.

Bruton Parish Church, Williamsburg, Va. (1711–15) (p. 1137E), a simple brick structure of cruciform plan, has round-headed windows lighting the nave and transepts and an internal west gallery. The square west tower was added in 1769; this is surmounted by a timber steeple, a much-simplified version of an English eighteenth-century spire like that by Gibbs at S. Martin's-in-the-Fields, London (p. 950).

S. Michael's Church, Charleston, S.C. (1752–61) (p. 1137B), a beautiful example of a fully-developed English colonial church in the style of James Gibbs, has a classical entrance portico, surmounted by an elegant timber steeple built up of a series of diminishing octagonal drums with pilasters, entablatures and arched openings to each stage, all reminiscent of S. Martin's-in-the-Fields, London, (p. 950). The main body of the church is of stuccoed brick; there is a gallery around three sides of the interior, carried on timber Ionic columns.

Christ Church (Old North), Boston, Mass. (1723), a simple brick building with an internal gallery and box-pews, has a square western tower surmounted by a timber steeple, a simplified version, perhaps, of that of Wren's S. Dunstan-in-the-East (1693) (p. 914).

King's Chapel, Boston, Mass. (1749–54) (p. 1137D), a stone church, considerably grander than most English colonial examples with an unpedimented Ionic portico surmounted by a square tower (the latter uncompleted); **Christ Church, Cambridge, Mass.** (1759–61) built in timber; and **Touro Synagogue, Newport, Rhode Island** (1759–63) were all designed by Peter Harrison (1716–75), an English sea-captain from York.

The **First Baptist Meeting House, Providence, R.I.** (1774–5); **Christ**

A. San Estevan, Ácoma, New Mexico (c. 1640). See p. 1136

B. S. Michael's Church, Charleston, South Carolina (1752–61). See p. 1136

C. S. Luke's Church, Smithfield, Virginia (1682–). See p. 1136

D. King's Chapel, Boston, Massachusetts (1749–54): interior. See p. 1136

E. Bruton Parish Church, Williamsburg, Virginia (1711–15). See p. 1136

A. The Governor's Palace, Santa Fé, New Mexico (1610–14). See p. 1139

B. Independence Hall, Philadelphia (1731–91). See p. 1140

C. The Cabildo, New Orleans, Louisiana
(1795–). See p. 1139

D. The White House, Washington, D.C. (1792–1829). See p. 1140

Church, Philadelphia, Pennsylvania (1727–54) and S. Paul's Chapel, New York, N.Y. (1764–6) are other important examples of English colonial churches and show the influence of the work of Wren and, more particularly, James Gibbs through his *Book of Architecture* (1728) and his other publications (p. 873).

EDUCATIONAL, CIVIC AND PUBLIC BUILDINGS

The **Governmental Palace, Guadalajara, Mexico** (1751–75), by Nicholas Enriquez del Castillo and José Conique, presents a rich mixture of Churrigueresque, Baroque and Neo-Mudéjar elements, while the patio of the **University, Antigua, Guatemala** (rebuilt in 1763) is an important example of Neo-Mudéjar design in Latin America.

The **Real Cabildo (Town Hall), Antigua, Guatemala** (1743–), an example of the more strictly Classical style favoured for colonial government buildings at this time, has arcaded loggias to both floors of its nine-bay façade.

The **Vizcaínas, (formerly Colegio de San Ignacio), Mexico City** (1734–53) by Pedro Bueno, a school for poor girls, is a good example of the current idiom for public buildings in Spanish America, while the **Cabildo (Town Hall), New Orleans, La.** (1795–) (p. 1138C), built to house the Spanish administrative council during its period of control in this area, shows the academic trend of late eighteenth-century Spanish design. The open arcaded ground floor, the arcaded first floor with its pilasters, the central pedimented feature, the weight and richness of the stone detail and the academic use of classical motifs, relate the building closely to contemporary Spanish work. The mansard roof was a later addition (*c.* 1850).

The **Penitentiary, Ouro Preto, Brazil** (1784–8) by Francisco Pinto de Abreu, combined the functions of town hall and prison, and despite its purpose, has a Rococo elegance in its façade.

The **Governor's Palace, Santa Fé, N.M.** (1610–14) (p. 1138A) was the dominating building in the original walled 'presidio' or administrative enclosure of this outpost of the Spanish Empire. The building, a long single-storeyed structure, constructed by local Indian labour in adobe brick, is approached from the 'plaza' of Santa Fé through an open loggia or 'portal' running the length of the palace and terminated at each end by simple adobe pavilions. The flat roof of the building is formed of round logs, supported along the portal by crude columns, hewn from whole tree trunks, with carved bracket-heads.

The **Governor's Palace, San Antonio, Texas** (1749), built in stone, with fine wrought-iron window grilles, possessed a ballroom and grand reception rooms overlooking its internal patio, and evinces the high standard of life even in remote parts of the Spanish Empire.

William and Mary College, Williamsburg, Va. (1695–1702) may have been designed by Sir Christopher Wren in his capacity of Royal Surveyor of England. If this were so, the drawings provided by Wren must have been largely diagrammatic, for records state that they were 'adapted to the nature of the country by the gentlemen there'. The plan is U-shaped, the three-storeyed central block containing classrooms, while two projecting wings house, respectively, the college chapel and refectory. On the west side of the building, an open arcaded loggia extends between the two projecting wings. The building is Georgian in character, its central block surmounted by an elegant cupola.

Harvard University, Cambridge, Mass., founded as Harvard College in 1636, is the oldest university in the U.S.A. Nothing remains of the first buildings, constructed largely of timber, but the following are important: **Massachusetts Hall** (1718–20); **Holden Chapel** (1742–4); **Hollis Hall** (1762–3); and **Harvard Hall** (1764–6), with its pedimented gables, full cornice and comparatively massive cupola, representing an early attempt to introduce a more monumental character into North American collegiate architecture.

Other important colonial university buildings include: **Nassau Hall, Princeton University, N.J.** (1754–6) (much altered); **University Hall, Brown University, Providence, R.I.,** (1770–1) and **Connecticut Hall, Yale University, New Haven, Conn.** (1750–2).

The **Capitol, Williamsburg, Va.** (1701–5; rebuilding completed 1934) (p. 1141A) is an accurate reconstruction of the Capitol as it was completed in 1705. The latter was replaced after a fire in 1747 by another building, in turn burned down in 1832. The plan is H-shaped, one of the two apsidal-ended wings providing accommodation for the House of Burgesses, while the other housed the General Courtroom on the ground floor, with the Governor's Council Chamber above. The entrance is through a central linking block which, on the ground floor, takes the form of an open arcaded loggia and, on the first floor, housed a conference room for joint meetings between the Governor's Council and members of the House of Burgesses. Built of brick and basically Georgian in character, the building shows the effect of climate on architectural style; because of the heat of the Virginian summers the proportion of solid to void is considerably higher than in English examples. The open entrance loggia, permitting the free circulation of air, is similarly explained.

The **Governor's Palace, Williamsburg, Va.** (1706–20; reconstructed 1932) is a particularly fine piece of Georgian design, evocative of the work of Wren. With its magnificent gardens and fine ballroom (a later addition) it provides evidence of the sophistication of life in early eighteenth-century Virginia.

Independence Hall, Philadelphia, Pa. (1731–91) (p. 1138B) was the scene of the signing of the Declaration of Independence on July 4th, 1776, and is therefore a monument of great significance to Americans. Work on the State House, as it was called, commenced in 1731, and the central block was completed by 1745. The tower with its fine steeple was built 1750–3; becoming unsound, this was demolished in 1781 and rebuilt on the original lines by William Strickland in 1832. The two-storeyed flanking buildings, connected with the central block by arcaded links, were erected in 1736 and 1739 respectively and have recently been restored. In 1789 and 1791 further buildings were added, completing the seven-unit complex and providing a civic centre perhaps unequalled in eighteenth-century America. The buildings, essentially Georgian in character, are in brick with white stone quoins and other dressings. The central block is surmounted by a balustraded roof-deck, above which rises the tower and its elaborate timber lantern, a rich piece of design forming one of the finest Georgian towers in America or Britain.

Carpenters Hall, Philadelphia, Pa. (1770–1), built as the headquarters of the 'Carpenters Company', i.e. the master carpenters, of Philadelphia, is a simple Georgian building of cruciform plan, its four gables being treated as pediments. A timber lantern surmounts the building which to Americans is of particular importance, since it was here that the First Continental Congress gathered on September 5th, 1774.

Province House, Halifax, Nova Scotia (1811–18) by John Merrick, a simple sturdy Classical building in stone, is strongly evocative of English Georgian work and set the pattern for other English administrative buildings in Canada.

NATIONAL PHASE

(nineteenth century–*c*. 1930)

DOMESTIC BUILDINGS

The **White House, Washington, D.C.** (1792–1829) (p. 1138D), the official residence of the Presidents of the U.S.A., was designed by James Hoban (*c*. 1762–1831),

A. The Capitol, Williamsburg, Virginia (1701–5). See p. 1140

B. Monticello, nr. Charlottesville, Virginia (1770–1808). See p. 1143

A. Trinity Church, Boston, Massachusetts (1872–7). See p. 1147

B. Belle Grove, nr. White Castle, Louisiana (1857).
See p. 1143

c. Biltmore, Ashville, North Carolina (1890–5). See p. 1143

D. Stoughton House, Cambridge, Massachusetts
(1882–3). See p. 1143

E. Robie House, Woodlawn Avenue
Chicago (1908–9). See p. 1144

an Irish architect, in the English Palladian style. After damage sustained in the War of 1812, it was restored by B. H. Latrobe and further considerable restoration has been carried out in the present century.

Monticello, nr. Charlottesville, Va. (1770–5; remodelled 1796–1808) (p. 1141B) was designed by Thomas Jefferson (1743–1826), third President of the U.S.A., for his own use. The first house, an elegant example of colonial Georgian, was completely remodelled in a free and imaginative Palladian manner (1796–1808).

Tontine Crescent, Boston, Mass. (1793–) by Charles Bullfinch (1763–1844), an example of terrace or, as they are often termed in America, 'row' houses has much in common with contemporary English work of the same type. Fine examples of early nineteenth-century brick terrace houses are also to be found in Philadelphia, again similar to English prototypes. A more monumental terrace is the brownstone **Colonnade Row, New York** (1832) by A. J. Davis (1803–92), where a screen of Corinthian columns rises through two storeys from above the rusticated ground floor.

Arlington, Va. (nr. Washington, D.C.), (1802–), at one time the home of General Robert E. Lee, is an interesting example of a Greek Revival mansion, particularly in the great hexastyle Doric Portico (added 1826), with its squat, sturdy order.

Other major Greek Revival houses are: **South End House, Sapelo Island, Georgia** (1810–12), a fine and unusual example, especially interesting in that its walls are made from 'tabby' (concrete made from oyster shells); **Gaineswood, Demopolis, Alabama** (1842–9), a large house reminiscent of the domestic work of Decimus Burton in England (p. 877); The **Hermitage, Nashville, Tennessee** (1819; rebuilt 1835), a characteristic example of a Tennessee plantation house with six Corinthian columns rising through two storeys across its main front, thus providing covered loggias at ground- and first-floor levels; **Polk Mansion, Rattle and Snap, Ten.** (c. 1845) with a grand, pedimented tetrastyle Corinthian portico projecting from its main front and rising through the building's two storeys; **Ralph Small House, Macon, Ga.** (c. 1835), a typical plantation house of the area, with a simple double-storeyed unpedimented hexastyle Doric portico; and **Belle Grove, near White Castle, La.** (1857) (p. 1142B) a particularly grand example with 75 rooms and a superb portico with the Corinthian capitals of its columns carved in cypress wood.

Vanderbilt Mansion, 5th Avenue, New York (1879–81) was designed by R. M. Hunt (1827–95), the first American architect to be trained at the École des Beaux-Arts in Paris, in the style of an early French Renaissance château. An example of the academic stream of late nineteenth-century American architecture, it provided a prototype for other buildings, among them **Biltmore, Ashville, N.C.** (1890–5) (p. 1142C), also by Hunt.

Villard Houses, New York (1883–5) by McKim, Mead and White (C. F. McKim (1849–1909), W. R. Mead (1848–1928) and Stamford White (1856–1906), are in brown stone and were based on 'palazzi' of the Italian High Renaissance.

Stoughton House, Cambridge, Mass. (1882–3) (p. 1142D) by H. H. Richardson (1838–86) is a timber-framed house, its walls clad externally with wood shingles. Although by no means representative of Richardson at his greatest, the house provides an important example of the so-called 'Shingle Style'. An external cladding of wood shingles over a timber frame became a popular device in domestic building during the second half of the nineteenth century. Internally, the plan arrangement shows a loosening and foreshadows the free plan, to be developed later by Frank Lloyd Wright.

Winslow House, River Forest, Illinois (1893), the first important work of

Frank Lloyd Wright (1869–1959), is a simple structure, basically symmetrical, but its hipped roof, wide projecting eaves and emphatic horizontal lines foreshadow the architect's later work and what was to become known as the 'Prairie House'.

Robie House, Chicago, Ill. (1908–9) (p. 1142E), also by Wright, is dominated externally by its strong horizontal lines which seem to make it almost one with the land on which it is built. Constructed of fine, small brick with low-pitched hipped roofs, the house is planned in an open and informal manner, interesting use being made of changes of level internally.

Other important houses of this period by Wright are: **Willitts House, Highland Park, Ill.** (1902); **Ross House, Delavan Lake, Wis.** (1902) and **Coonley House, Riverside, Ill.** (1908).

Gamble House, Pasadena, California (1908–9) by C. S. Greene (1868–1957) and H. M. Greene (b. 1870) has much in common with the work of Wright in its sympathetic use of natural materials and, owes something also to the vernacular tradition of the west coast of America.

RELIGIOUS BUILDINGS

The **Catholic Cathedral, Baltimore, Md.** (1805–21), probably the most important work of Benjamin H. Latrobe (1764–1820), was the first major Roman Catholic Cathedral in the U.S. The plan is in the form of a Latin cross; over the crossing there is a great, coffered Pantheon-like dome (more than 60 ft in diameter) while the nave is roofed by lesser saucer domes. Internally, the building is characterized by a wide spaciousness and is reminiscent of the work of Sir John Soane (p. 876) and of contemporary French examples. Externally, it has a fine pedimented portico (intended in the original design but added only in 1863), flanked by twin west towers, while the main dome springs from an octagonal drum.

Notre Dame, Montreal, Quebec (1824–43) by James O'Donnell (1774–1830), an important early Canadian Gothic Revival building, has twin west towers and a triple-arched west entrance. Somewhat naïve in its detail, which is derived mainly from English sources, it originally had double internal galleries. The interior was completely remodelled c. 1870.

S. Andrew's Presbyterian Church, Niagara-on-the-Lake, Ontario (1831) is a rare example of the Greek Revival in Canada. A simple brick building, its 'west end' takes the form of a Greek Doric hexastyle temple-front and is surmounted by a timber cupola and spire.

Trinity Church, New York (1839–46) by Richard Upjohn (1802–78), now dwarfed by the commercial buildings of the modern city, was the third church of this name on the site. Comparable with the better examples of Gothic Revival Commissioners' Churches in nineteenth-century England (p. 878), it is in the Decorated style and in its day was the most important Gothic Revival building in the U.S.

Grace Church, New York (1843–6) and **S. Patrick's Cathedral, New York** (1858–79) were both by James Renwick Jr. (1818–95) and are important examples of American Gothic Revival architecture. The former was based on English examples, while the latter has continental sources.

The **Church of the Assumption, Montreal, Quebec** (1863–5) by Victor Bourgeau (1809–88), with elegant twin west towers, is a charming example based on Baroque prototypes, while the **Church of Notre-Dame-de-Grâce, Montreal** (–1851) by John Ostell (1813–92) provides another example of the Baroque Revival which found favour for churches in this area in the mid-nineteenth century.

The **Cathedral of S. James, Montreal, Quebec** (1875–85), designed by Joseph Michaud (1822–1902) and Victor Bourgeau, was (at the direction of the Bishop of Montreal) based on the Cathedral of S. Peter, Rome (p. 714). Despite

A. The State Capitol, Richmond, Virginia (1789–98). See p. 1147

B. The Episcopal Cathedral of S. John the Divine, New York
(commenced 1892; remodelled 1910). See p. 1147

A. The United States Capitol, Washington, D.C. (1792–1867). See p. 1147

B. The City Hall, Philadelphia (1874–1901). See p. 1151

great differences in scale, the west façade, the dome and general plan arrangement are clearly derived from S. Peter's. Nevertheless, the church possesses its own strong and specifically Canadian character.

The **Episcopal Cathedral of S. John the Divine, New York** (p. 1145B), was originally designed in the Romanesque style (1892) by Heins (1860–1907) and Lafarge (1862–1938) who completed the choir in 1907. It was remodelled (commencing 1910) by Cram, Goodhue and Ferguson, in a mixture of Late English and French Gothic, and five aisles, together with a double clear-story, great central tower, twin west towers and eastern chevet termination were incorporated.

Trinity Church, Boston, Mass. (1872–7) (p. 1142A), by H. H. Richardson, is one of the key monuments of American architecture. The design, chosen in competition, although basically Romanesque in character is handled in a masterful and imaginative way and established Richardson's reputation. A Greek cross in plan, the building is dominated by a square central tower with round corner turrets, and is constructed mainly of red granite, the rock-faced texture of which is exploited. Internal decoration in encaustic colour was carried out by J. Lafarge, while the west porch was added in 1897 to the designs of Shepley, Rutan and Coolidge.

Unity Temple, Oak Park, Ill. (1905–7) by Frank Lloyd Wright, is characterized by the sturdy simplicity of its external massing, on which the design relies rather than eclectic detail. In the building, as in all his work, the architect displayed a knowledge of and sympathy with the natural qualities of materials, which are here exploited both externally (in the pebble-faced concrete of the walls) and internally (in the sand-lime plaster work and natural timber details).

EDUCATIONAL, CIVIC AND PUBLIC BUILDINGS

The **State Capitol, Richmond, Va.** (1789–98) (p. 1145A) by Thomas Jefferson, was based on a Roman temple prototype, the Maison Carrée, Nîmes (p. 188). An Ionic order was used by Jefferson, while for the fenestration of the 'cella' he had recourse to Palladian formulae. The building may be regarded as the first truly Neo-Classic monument in the U.S. and, heralding the equivalent of the European Antiquarian phase (p. 875), had much influence on later American buildings. Classical temple forms, both Greek and Roman, were adapted for banks, schools and other buildings, accommodation being sometimes somewhat ruthlessly crammed into the 'cella' in order to retain, at all costs, the external lines of the antique form. The appendages to the flanks of the Richmond Capitol are additions dating from the early years of the present century.

The **State House, Boston, Mass.** (1795–1808), by Charles Bullfinch, shows the influence of French and English Neo-Classicism in its elevational treatment, particularly in the projecting central feature, with its simple arcade at entrance level and colonnaded loggia above, and in the Adam-like detail of the windows at the extremities of the main façade. The building is surmounted by a dome, a feature to be incorporated in later American governmental buildings.

The **United States Capitol, Washington, D.C.** (1792–1867), (p. 1146A) seat of the United States Government, has become, with its great crowning dome, one of the world's best-known buildings. The first building, erected to the designs of Dr. William Thornton (1761–1828), an amateur architect from England, was planned on Palladian lines with a central rotunda; this has survived in essentials, despite numerous modifications and additions. Thornton's work, in which he was assisted by a French architect, E. S. Hallet, was continued by B. H. Latrobe, who had been trained in England as a pupil under Samuel Pepys Cockerell (1754–1827) (p. 948). After the War of 1812, Latrobe was responsible for rebuilding the structure (1815–17), badly damaged by the British. Charles Bullfinch continued the work which was completed in 1829. Between 1851 and 1867 extensive additions were made by Thomas Ustick Walter (1804–88), who was responsible for the flanking wings and great dome over the central rotunda; the latter, replacing an earlier Pantheon-like dome, was constructed largely of cast iron and has an internal diameter of 98 ft and a total height of 222 ft.

The **University of Virginia, Charlottesville, Va.** (1817–26), was designed by Thomas Jefferson with the assistance of Thornton and Latrobe as an 'academical village'. Set in the plain overlooked by Jefferson's own home, Monticello (p. 1143), it established a pattern followed by other later American universities in their campus layouts. The plan consists of a wide, rectangular, tree-lined open space, on each of the longer sides of which are ranged five double-storeyed pavilions with classical, columned porticoes. These house teaching staff and lecture rooms and are linked to one another by low colonnades from which open the students' rooms. The central space is terminated at one end by the university library (modelled on the Roman Pantheon), burned down in the early part of the present century and rebuilt by Messrs. McKim, Mead and White. Behind the ranges of teaching and living accommodation and separated from them by gardens, accommodation was provided for the slaves whom the students brought to the university as personal servants. Each of the buildings in the scheme was intended to illustrate some famous classical work, and thus provide architectural exemplars to the students.

Founders' Hall, Girard College, Philadelphia, Pa. (1833–47) by T. U. Walter, is in the form of a giant, peripteral octastyle Corinthian temple, and in the grandeur of its conception is an important monument of the Greek Revival in America.

The **County Record Office, Charleston, S.C.** (1822–3), the **Patent Office** (1836–40) and the **Treasury Building** (1836–42), **Washington, D.C.** by Robert Mills (1781–1855) were all designed as 'fire-proof' buildings, making extensive use of vaulted construction. Like most work by Mills, they are characterized by their constructional ingenuity and vigorous and highly personal interpretation of the Greek style.

City Prison (The Tombs), New York (1838) by John Haviland (1792–1852), was in the Egyptian style, while the same architect's **Eastern State Penitentiary, Philadelphia, Pa.** (1821–35), planned with radiating cell blocks, was regarded in its day as a model prison.

Washington Monument, Washington, D.C. (1836–84), a slender 555 ft high obelisk in white granite, designed by Robert Mills as a monument to the great general of the War of Independence, was when completed the highest structure in the world.

The **Smithsonian Institution, Washington, D.C.** (1847–55), by James Renwick Jr., is a romantic and picturesque structure in the Norman style.

University College, Toronto, Ontario (1856–8) by W. C. Cumberland (1821–1881) is an essay in the Romanesque style comparable with the Smithsonian Institution.

The **National Academy of Design, New York** (1862–5) (p. 1149C), by P. B. Wight (1838–1925), Venetian Gothic in style and making full use of polychrome masonry patterning, shows the influence of the writings of John Ruskin.

The **Pennsylvania Academy of the Fine Arts, Philadelphia, Penn.** (1871–1876) by Frank Furness (1839–1912), a highly individualistic building, makes imaginative use of forms of diverse stylistic origin and polychromatic masonry. Its architect is of particular interest for he employed the young Louis Sullivan as an assistant in his office in Chestnut Street, Philadelphia. The **Provident Trust Company Building, Philadelphia** (1879) is another characteristic building by Furness.

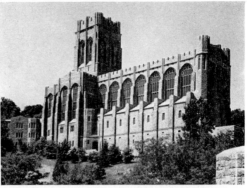

A. The Lincoln Memorial, Washington, D.C. (1911–22). See p. 1151

B. The Chapel, U.S. Military Academy, West Point, New York (1904). See p. 1151

The National Academy of Design, New York (1862–5). See p. 1148

D. The Temple of Scottish Rite, Washington, D.C. (1916). See p. 1151

E. The Public Library, Boston, Massachusetts (1887–93). See p. 1151

A. Merchants' Exchange, Philadelphia (1832–4).
See p. 1152

B. The Larkin Soap Building, Buffal
New York (1904–5). See p. 1155

C. The Second Leiter Building, Chicago (1889–90).
See p. 1155

D. The Schlesinger-Mayer Stor
Chicago (1899–1904). See p. 115

E. The Auditorium Building, Chicago (1886–9).
See p. 1152

F. Wainwright Building, S
Louis, Missouri (1890–1).
See p. 1155

Dominion Parliament Buildings, Ottawa, Ontario (1861–7) (p. 1275), by Thomas Fuller (1822–98), an English architect who moved to Canada in 1856, and F. W. Stent, provided a superb example of Victorian Gothic with an ebullient silhouette of towers, pinnacles and crestings. Most of the original buildings were destroyed by fire in 1916 and the present structure (largely based on the original but lacking much of its decorative richness) and the soaring neo-Gothic **Peace Tower** (1919–) were designed by J. A. Pearson (1867–1940) and J. O. Marchand (1873–1936).

The **City Hall, Philadelphia, Pa.** (1874–1901) (p. 1146B), by John McArthur (1823–90), in the French Second Empire style (p. 1063), provides an example of fashions prevailing in the late nineteenth century. Its central tower (512 ft) is crowned by a 37 ft-high bronze statue of William Penn, the founder of the city.

The **Public Library, Boston, Mass.** (1887–93) (p. 1149E) by McKim, Mead and White is a beautifully detailed building, representative of the best in the academic stream of late nineteenth and early twentieth-century architecture in America. Elevationally it is based on the Library of S. Geneviève, Paris, (1843–50) (p. 1085) by Henri Labrouste.

The **Public Library, New York,** (1897–1910) by J. M. Carrére (1859–1911) and Thomas Hastings (1860–1929) is also noteworthy as another example of academic Classical architecture.

The **Lincoln Memorial, Washington, D.C.** (1911–22) (p. 1149A), by Henry Bacon (1866–1924), is in the form of an unpedimented Greek Doric peripteral temple, set on a high podium and surmounted by a simple attic. Executed in white marble, its detail is superlatively refined and in its scholarship and execution marks a peak in academic architecture.

The **Temple of Scottish Rite, Washington, D.C.** (–1916) (p. 1149D), a masonic temple designed by John Russell Pope (1874–1937), is in the same tradition as the Lincoln Memorial. Externally, it takes the form of a reconstruction of the Mausoleum at Halicarnassus (p. 148).

The **Chapel** (p. 1149B) **and Post Headquarters, U.S. Military Academy, West Point, N.Y.** (1904–), romantically sited on a steep escarpment overlooking the Hudson River, are the work of Cram, Goodhue and Ferguson, and provide examples of academic architecture in the Gothic style.

The **Allegheny County Courthouse and Gaol, Pittsburgh, Pa.** (1884–7), by H. H. Richardson, is a fine and vigorous piece of work which, despite its overtly Romanesque character, is indicative of the virility of a rising movement. The building relies largely on the inherent qualities of the materials in which it is constructed and these are exploited in an imaginative yet highly disciplined manner, particularly the great, rock-faced slabs of granite forming the jail walls.

The **City Hall, Toronto, Ontario** (1890) by E. J. Lennox (1856–1933) has a sturdy, Romanesque character and owes much to the work of H. H. Richardson, particularly his Allegheny County Court House, Pittsburgh (above).

COMMERCIAL AND INDUSTRIAL BUILDINGS

The **Second Bank of the U.S. (Old Customs House), Philadelphia, Pa.** (1817–24) by W. Strickland, carried out in brick and white Pennsylvanian marble, was the result of an open architectural competition. With octastyle Doric porticoes to the front and rear, modelled on those of the Athenian Parthenon (p. 119), the building is rectangular in plan. Internally the central banking hall, with its fine barrel-vaulted ceiling springing from Ionic colonnades, is particularly fine.

The **Providence Arcade, Providence, R.I.** (1828), by James Bucklin (1801–90) and Russell Warren (1783–1860), provides, as in European arcades, a covered avenue for business premises, and is entered from either end through superbly detailed Ionic columnar screens carried out in granite. Internally the arcade is lighted by skylights, while the first-floor premises are entered from elegant iron balconies.

Merchants' Exchange, Philadelphia, Pa. (1832–4) (p. 1150A), by William Strickland, is in the Greek Revival style and is noteworthy for the grand, apsidal treatment of its rear elevation, enriched externally by a screen of Corinthian columns rising from first-floor level through two storeys, and crowned by a cupola based on the Choragic Monument of Lysicrates, Athens (p. 139).

The **Farmers' and Mechanics' Bank, Pottsville, Pa.** (1830), by John Haviland, is important since it was probably the first building in America to make use of a cast-iron façade. Here iron sheets, moulded to simulate masonry, were fixed to a brick backing; but later pre-fabricated iron units were to be used for complete structures.

James Bogardus (1800–74) played an important part in the development of this type of construction, which he employed in many buildings, among them his own factory, New York (1848–9); **Laing Stores, New York** (1849); and **Harper Bros. Printing Works, New York** (1854). He also put forward an adventurous scheme for the **New York Exhibition Building** (1853) but this was not realized. Other buildings using the same constructional technique were the **Penn Mutual Life Insurance Building, Philadelphia, Pa.** (1850–1) by G. P. Cummings, and some particularly fine examples in the dock area of S. Louis, Mo. (*c.* 1850–*c.* 1880) (p. 1153A).

The **A. T. Stewart Store (later Wanamaker's Store), New York, N.Y.** (1862; burned 1956) by John Kellum (1807–71), was another noteworthy example of iron construction using pre-fabricated units. Elevationally the building was made up of repeated bays, each of its five floors being treated as a 'Renaissance' arcade or, in the case of the ground floor, colonnade. Internally the building was framed with iron stanchions (cast in the form of Classical columns) and girders.

The **Montauk Building, Chicago, Ill.** (1881–2), by D. H. Burnham (1846–1912) and J. W. Root (1850–91), the first of a series of extremely important buildings in Chicago, made use of spread foundations to carry its ten-storey load-bearing walls and heralded the advent of the sky-scraper.

The **Home Insurance Co. Office Building, Chicago, Ill.** (1883–5) by W. Le B. Jenney (1832–1907) and W. B. Mundie (1893–1939), a ten-storey building, was the first in Chicago to make use of a metal skeleton carrying the walls as opposed to load-bearing walls.

The **Marshall Field Wholesale Warehouse, Chicago, Ill.** (1885–7) (p. 1170), by H. H. Richardson, had seven storeys and was of load-bearing wall construction. A remarkably powerful design, with its great arched openings and the vigorous texture of its masonry, it had considerable influence on later buildings in Chicago and elsewhere.

The **Tacoma Building, Chicago, Ill.** (1887–8) by W. Holabird (1854–1923) and M. Roche (1855–1927) also had its external walls carried by a metal skeleton.

The **Auditorium Building, Chicago, Ill.** (1886–9) (p. 1150E) by Dankmar Adler (1844–1900) and Louis Sullivan (1856–1924) combines an opera house with hotel and office accommodation and owes much of its external character to Richardson's Marshall Field Warehouse (p. 1170). Ten storeys high, it is of load-bearing wall construction built on spread foundations. Settlement has occurred to one side of the structure, in the tower which rises nearly 100 ft higher than the main building. Internally, the details are of a high order, many showing a Byzantine character and some probably designed by Frank Lloyd Wright, who entered Sullivan's office in 1887 as a draughtsman.

A. Cast-iron façade, S. Louis, Missouri (c. 1850). See p. 1152

B. The Gage Building, Chicago (*right*) (1898–9). See p. 1155

C. The Monadnock Building, Chicago (1891). See p. 1155

D. The Reliance Building, Chicago (1890–4). See p. 1155

E. Woolworth Building, New York (1911–13). See p. 1155

A. Rockefeller Centre, New York (1931–9). See p. 1156

B. Pennsylvania Railroad Station, New York
(1906–10): main concourse. See p. 1156

C. Empire State Building, New
York (1930–2). See p. 1156

The **Monadnock Building, Chicago, Ill.** (1891–) (p. 1153C) by Burnham and Root has sixteen storeys and is of load-bearing wall construction. The building derives distinction from the simplicity of its elevational treatment and was the last tall building in Chicago for which load-bearing walls were employed.

The **Second Leiter Building, Chicago, Ill.** (1889–90) (p. 1150C) (now occupied by Messrs. Sears Roebuck) by W. Le B. Jenney, is an eight-storey metal-framed building with a simple and effective elevational treatment, the stone façade reading as a sheath over the internal metal structure.

The **Reliance Building, Chicago, Ill.** (1890; extended 1894) (p. 1153D), by Burnham and Root, was originally built as a four-storeyed structure but was later extended to thirteen floors. The terra-cotta facing to the metal frame was reduced to a minimum and in its simple yet carefully-detailed elevation the building marks an important advance in sky-scraper design.

The **Gage Building, Chicago, Ill.** (1898–9) (p. 1153B) by Louis Sullivan and Holabird and Roche, is a three-bay, eight-storey framed structure, and fore-shadows the elevational treatment of the Schlesinger-Mayer Store.

The **Schlesinger-Mayer Store (now Carson, Pirie, Scott and Co.), Chicago, Ill.** (1899–1904) (p. 1150D) by Louis Sullivan, was perhaps the architect's crowning achievement. Originally a nine-storey structure, a twelve-storey section was added in 1903–4 and further additions were made in 1906 by D. H. Burnham, following Sullivan's original design. The building was originally crowned by a rich over-hanging cornice (recently removed). The white terra-cotta facing to the building's steel frame truthfully follows its structure, and horizontal lines are emphasized. The ground and first floors have cast-iron friezes richly decorated in low relief, providing first-rate examples of Sullivan's decorative work, to some extent sug-gestive of European Art Nouveau.

The **Wainwright Building, S. Louis, Mo.** (1890–1) (p. 1150F) by Louis Sul-livan, a ten-storey steel-framed building, provided an excellent answer to the eleva-tion problem of the sky-scraper. Vertical members of the frame are emphasized externally as brick piers, and the building is capped by a deep, richly decorated frieze, pierced by circular windows lighting the top floor, while the recessed panels between floors are similarly decorated.

The **Guaranty (now Prudential) Building, Buffalo, N.Y.** (1894–5), also by Adler and Sullivan is similar in general character to the Wainwright Building but rises through thirteen floors and is faced externally in terra-cotta.

The **Larkin Soap Co. Building, Buffalo, N.Y.** (1904–5: destroyed) (p. 1150B), by Frank Lloyd Wright, was designed around a great central circulation court, lit from the roof and sides by windows sealed from noise and dirt. Offices were approached from galleries around the court, borne on brick piers. Externally, the building was characterized by the simplicity and scale of its massing, which relied entirely on the relation of a few clearly articulated forms.

The **National Farmers' Bank, Owatonna, Minnesota** (1907–8), a virile and characteristic building by Louis Sullivan, is particularly noteworthy for its inventive decorative detail and the bold geometry of its simple but powerful forms.

The **Woolworth Building, New York** (1911–13) (p. 1153E), by Cass Gilbert (1859–1934), 792 ft high with fifty-two storeys, was carried out in the Gothic style. It is an important landmark in the story of high building.

Soon after the completion of the Woolworth Building, the New York City Zoning Ordinance (1916) became law. This had a profound effect on the form of New York sky-scrapers which, for reasons of light and ventilation, were now required to have certain minimum set-backs, related to their height. The effects of the ordinance can be seen in J. M. Howells' (b. 1868) **Panhellenic House** (–1928), with 27 storeys, and more clearly in the **Empire State Building** (1930–2) (p. 1154C) by Shreve, Lamb and Harmon, which rises through 85 storeys and is the highest office block in the world.

Later Chicago buildings to be noted include: **Tribune Tower** (1923–5) a newspaper office block by J. M. Howells and Raymond Hood (1881–1934). In the Gothic style, the sky-scraper was the result of an architectural competition in which Eliel Saarinen and Walter Gropius also took part. **Palmolive Building** (1929) and **333 North Michigan Avenue** (1928) are both by Holabird and Root and provide interesting examples of Chicago sky-scrapers of the 1920's.

Rockefeller Centre, New York (1931–9) (p. 1154A) by Henry Hofmeister, H. W. Corbett and Raymond Hood in collaboration with others, is a complex of buildings set amid a series of related open spaces. The focus of the centre is the R.C.A. Building, 850 ft high with 70 storeys, a sheer slab-like structure with its vertical lines strongly emphasized. Around it are grouped 13 lesser buildings, including the **Time and Life Building** (36 storeys); **International Building** (41 storeys) and a six-storey garage.

Among numerous examples of railway stations, the following are particularly important: **Grand Central Station, New York** (1903–13), by Reed and Stem (later replaced by Warren and Wetmore), provides a fine example of American academic architecture, particularly in its great concourse. Based on antique Roman sources, it shows the influence of the École des Beaux-Arts. **Pennsylvania Railroad Station, New York** (1906–10) (p. 1154B), by McKim, Mead and White, is in the same tradition. Overtly based on Roman 'thermae' designs, its concourse, both in scale and detail, recalls the central hall of the Baths of Caracalla, Rome (p. 204D).

The **Hallidie Building, San Francisco, California** (1918) (p. 1171), by W. J. Polk (1867–1924) was remarkably prophetic of techniques to become widely used 40 years later. The main façade is in the form of a great, glass 'curtain', broken only by the grid of the horizontal and vertical glazing members and enriched at its crown and base by bands of intricate, fretted metal-work. Behind, and free from the glass 'curtain', rise the main structural supports of the building.

MODERN ARCHITECTURE

DOMESTIC BUILDINGS

Falling Water, Pa. (1936–7) (p. 1119), by Frank Lloyd Wright, is constructed of stone and reinforced concrete. The free plan makes good use of level changes and in its woodland site, its structure partly cantilevered over a waterfall, the house presents a superbly balanced composition of rectilinear masses. **Friedman House, Pleasantville, N.Y.** (1948–9), by the same architect, is based in plan on circular forms and built mainly in rubble walling, with mushroom-like concrete roofs over the circular elements. Circular plan forms are used also in the same architect's **Jacobs House, Middleton, Wisconsin** (1948) and the **David J. Wright House, nr. Phoenix, Arizona** (1952).

Farnsworth House, nr. Plano, Ill. (1950) (p. 1157A), by Ludwig Mies van der Rohe, is remarkable for the simplicity of its form and the precision of its detail. The plan of this flat-roofed, single-storey building is rectangular, with a central core (comprising bathrooms, heating plant and a fire-place) around which space flows freely, the various areas for eating, sleeping, etc. being indicated simply by partitions and fittings which do not connect with the ceiling. Structurally the house is a cage of white-painted welded steel (with large areas glazed in plate glass) carried on a concrete slab, lifted above the ground on low supports.

A. Farnsworth House, nr. Plano, Illinois (1950). See p. 1156

B. Chemistry Building, Illinois Institute of Technology, Chicago (1946).
See p. 1159

Nos. 845–60 Lake Shore Drive, Chicago (1949–51). See opposite page

Nos. 845-60 Lake Shore Drive, Chicago, Ill. (1949–51) (p. 1158), two 26-storey blocks of flats by Mies van der Rohe, are characteristic examples of his work. Like great glazed cages of steel, lifted from the ground on 'pilotis' at entrance level, the services, lifts, etc., are contained in a central core, thus permitting completely glazed elevations. The designs rely on the careful proportioning of the rectangular grid formed by vertical and horizontal structural steel members and refinement of detail. Between the main vertical structural members, intermediate uncased steel I-sections are introduced, running the height of the building and stiffening the structure.

Promontory Apartments, Chicago, Ill. (1949), also by Mies van der Rohe, are 22 storeys high and of reinforced concrete construction, vertical structural members being emphasized externally. The plan is U-shaped and consists of two self-sufficient blocks, each with its own lifts and staircase, joined as one. The detail is severe but carefully considered.

Among numerous examples of first-rate domestic work, the following are particularly noteworthy: Houses at Wayland, Mass. (1940) and Lincoln, Mass. (1938) by Walter Gropius (p. 1127) and Marcel Breuer (b. 1902); work by Richard Neutra (b. 1892); Boissonas House, New Canaan, Conn. (1955–6) and R. S. Davis House, Wayzata, Minnesota (1954) by Philip Johnson (b. 1906).

Among interesting examples of domestic architecture in South America are: Parque Guinle Flats, Rio de Janeiro (1948–54) by Lúcio Costa (b. 1902), the designer of Brasilia, the new Brazilian city; and blocks of flats (1954) in the Cerro Piloto Housing Estate, Caracas, Venezuela, by Guido Bermudez. Built of reinforced concrete and making good use of colour, in the liveliness of their conception these represent characteristic examples of modern South American design.

RELIGIOUS AND EDUCATIONAL BUILDINGS

Illinois Institute of Technology, Chicago, Ill. (1939–) (p. 1157B). In 1939, a year after settling in the U.S., Mies van der Rohe was commissioned to design an entire campus layout together with its buildings. Work is still progressing, but of the 24 buildings making up the scheme many have been completed, including Crown Hall, housing the School of Architecture, (1956); Administration Building (1944); Chemical Engineering and Metallurgy Building (1949); Mineral and Metal Research Building (1943); the Alumni Memorial Hall (1946) and the Chemistry Building (1946) (p. 1157B). Like all Mies van der Rohe's work, the beauty of these buildings lies in their proportions, refined and appropriate detail and first-rate craftsmanship. Exposed structural steel (painted black), large areas of glass reflecting the trees and landscaping of the campus, and a buff-coloured brick are the basic materials used in the scheme. Internal planning is generally open, particularly in the Alumni Memorial Hall and Crown Hall, the main floor of the latter being completely unimpeded by walls or partitions.

Baker House (Dormitory Block), Massachusetts Institute of Technology, Cambridge, Mass. (1947–9), by Alvar Aalto (p. 1127), has a serpentine plan and is carried out in a rich, red brick, the walls punched with simple but finely-detailed windows on its six residential floors. Overlooking the Charles River, it is a particularly delightful building.

The Graduate Centre, Harvard University, Cambridge, Mass. (1949–50) (p. 1161B), by Walter Gropius and his associates, is a fine and characteristic example of the former's work. Seven dormitories, housing altogether some 300 students, and the Commons Building form the scheme which, although basically in two loose courts, is informal in layout and most attractively landscaped. The higher dormitory buildings have reinforced concrete frames and the predominant facing material is a yellowish brick. Horizontal lines are emphasized, particularly in the Commons Building the interior of which is enriched with works by Hans Arp and others.

The **Auditorium Building, Massachusetts Institute of Technology, Cambridge, Mass.** (1952–5) (p. 1253), by Eero Saarinen (b. 1910) is noteworthy for its great shell-concrete roof, springing from the ground at three points like a billowing sail, the three elevations being glazed up to the soffit of the shell.

University City, Mexico (1950–) (p. 1161A) is a vast complex of buildings mainly constructed in reinforced concrete. Particularly notable are the **Olympic Stadium** (1951–2) by A. P. Salacios (b. 1909) and others, and the **Central Library** (1951–3) by Juan O'Gorman and others. The latter is dominated by a massive tower housing the library stacks and covered in brilliant mosaic, incorporating decorative and symbolic devices from the pre-Columbian civilizations of Mexico.

University City, Rio de Janeiro, was initially planned by Le Corbusier in 1936; work is progressing under Jorge Moreira (b. 1904).

The **Church of São Francisco, Pampulha, Brazil** (1943) (p. 1161C), by Oscar Niemeyer (b. 1901), an example of (perhaps excessive) virtuosity in reinforced concrete, is roofed by a series of concrete vaults. Its flank walls are faced with murals in 'azulejos' and to one side there is a concrete bell-tower, tapering towards its base.

The **Chapel, Illinois Institute of Technology, Chicago, Ill.** (1950), by Mies van der Rohe, is a simple, box-like structure in black-painted steel and buff brick, its west end entirely glazed.

Marial Chapel, Lac Bouchette, Quebec (1952) by Henri Tremblay is intended to form part of a larger church. Billowing shell-concrete vaults are used in interesting juxtaposition to solid rubble walls.

The **Chapel, Massachusetts Institute of Technology, Cambridge, Mass.** (1954–5), by Eero Saarinen, is in the form of a cylinder of beautifully-laid, rich red brick rising on low arches from a shallow pool, through which diffused and flickering light enters the building. In addition, partially-baffled light enters from above, producing a most effective atmosphere.

COMMERCIAL, INDUSTRIAL AND GOVERNMENTAL BUILDINGS

The **Johnson Wax Co. Buildings, Racine, Wis.** (1936–49) (p. 1162A) by Frank Lloyd Wright, consist of two main units, the **Administration Building** (1936–9) and the **Laboratory Tower** (1946–9). Carried out principally in red brick, the buildings are characterized by the plasticity of their forms, generated by the curvilinear plan shapes. The interior of the Administration Building presents a forest of reinforced-concrete mushroom columns, with elegant shafts tapering towards bases set in steel shoes and surmounted by wide, circular concrete discs. The interstices between the discs are glazed with glass tubes laid in patterns through which light filters, providing an unusually dramatic effect. The Laboratory Tower is constructed on what Wright called the 'tap-root' principle, a massive concrete core with deep foundations providing a structural spine for the building and anchorage for the floors which are cantilevered from it. The external walls carried by the floors are merely screens giving protection from the elements: they consist of brick and glazing (made up from horizontal glass tubes) which wrap around the building in wide alternating bands.

The **General Motors Technical Institute, Warren, Michigan** (1946–55) (p. 1162B), by Eliel Saarinen (p. 1068) and his son, Eero Saarinen, a complex of twenty-five laboratory and other technical buildings, grouped about a formal lake, is comparable with the work of Mies van der Rohe in the clear-cut precision of its forms. Stainless steel, black oxidized aluminium, glass and brightly-coloured glazed brick are used in the buildings, which admirably express their functions.

A. University City, Mexico : Central Library (1951–3). See opposite page

B. The Graduate Centre, Harvard University, Cambridge,
Massachusetts (1949–50). See p. 1159

C. São Francisco, Pampulha (1943). See opposite page

A. The Johnson Wax Buildings, Racine, Wisconsin (1936–49). See p. 1160

B. General Motors Technical Institute, Warren, Michigan (1946–55).
See p. 1160

Lever House, New York (1952) (p. 1165C),by Gordon Bunshaft (b. 1909) of the firm of Skidmore, Owings and Merrill, is a fine example of a modern office block. Completely sheathed in glass and stainless steel curtain-walling, a sheer slab block rises from a low structure mounted on pilotis, through which one enters a small patio, a delightful oasis in busy Park Avenue.

The **Seagram Building, New York** (1956–8), by Mies van der Rohe and Philip Johnson, is another notable sky-scraper office block, clad externally in glass and bronze.

The **Alcoa Building, Pittsburgh, Pa.** (1952), by W. K. Harrison (1895–) and Max Abramovitz (1908–), is an instance in which the structural frame of the sky-scraper is sheathed in pre-fabricated, pressed aluminium panels with relatively small window areas.

The **United Nations Headquarters, New York,** (1947–50) (p. 1165A), was designed with the advice of an international committee including Le Corbusier, Oscar Niemeyer and Sir Howard Robertson, with Harrison and Abramovitz of New York as executive architects. Sited by the East River, the scheme is dominated by the towering slab block of the Secretariat Building which, with its narrow end walls rising like sheer white cliffs and its longer sides clad in glass curtain walling, has had considerable influence on subsequent high buildings throughout the world.

The **Ministry of Education and Health, Rio de Janeiro** (1937–42) (p. 1165B), was designed by Lúcio Costa (b. 1902) and Oscar Niemeyer (b. 1901) with Le Corbusier as consultant. A sky-scraper in reinforced concrete borne on pilotis, the deep reveals of the building's vertical structural members, aided by horizontal louvres, control sunlight and provide an example of the influence of climate on modern architecture.

The **Edificio Polar, Caracas, Venezuela** (1953–4), by M. Vegas Pacheco (b. 1926) and J. M. Galia, has a fifteen-storey tower rising above a lower structure and shows strong influence of the work of Mies van der Rohe.

COMPARATIVE ANALYSIS

PLANS

Indigenous Phase. Normally rectangular, although there are circular examples in Bolivia (p. 1131) and at Chichen Itzá (p. 1128), plans were largely controlled by roofing spans (p. 1130A). The central courtyard or 'patio' was a common feature in Mexico and Central America for larger domestic work (p. 1129F).

Colonial Phase. Plans followed prototypes in the homeland of the settlers of a particular area. In Latin America the patio, often surrounded by arcaded covered walks, was normal in monastic, collegiate and large domestic buildings (p. 1134C) and arcaded loggias were sometimes used for entrances, etc. (p. 1134A). Seventeenth-century houses in New England followed plans found in English vernacular work of the same period (p. 1133A) while later, in the eighteenth century, plans conformed to Palladian principles (Brandon, p. 1132) or were based on English Georgian examples (p. 1133C), with modifications, in the way of open loggias and similar features, occasioned by climate (p. 1141A). In the southern part of North America colonnaded verandahs were popular—sometimes on both storeys of a building (p. 1133D) and sometimes encircling a building on all sides (p. 1133B).

National Phase. For important buildings in Latin America the principles of the École des Beaux-Arts were usually followed, since most major works were carried out by either French architects or by architects trained in France (p. 1126). In North America, there was a general acceptance of Neo-Classic plan forms (p. 1146A) but Palladian principles were adhered to, in some cases until quite late in the nine-teenth century. During the last three decades of the nineteenth century, more informal, 'open' planning developed, particularly in domestic work (p. 1142D), while the acceptance of the metal frame for multi-storeyed buildings permitted greater freedom in the plan arrangements of office and similar buildings (p. 1150C).

Modern Architecture. With the development of steel and reinforced-concrete construction and the vast spans which it is now possible to achieve, structure is no longer as important a controlling factor as in the past. It is possible to roof large buildings with one unbroken span (p. 1161C). For multi-cellular buildings, a steel or reinforced-concrete frame is general, the plan on each floor being controlled merely by the constructional grid (p. 1165). Framed buildings can be raised completely from the ground on 'pilotis', thus providing the equivalent of a covered loggia at ground level (p. 1158), while flat roofs can be utilized as roof gardens or as recreation spaces. By incorporating all services—lifts, stairs, plumbing, heating equipment, etc.— within a central core, it is now possible to free external walls from the elevational restrictions imposed in earlier times. This form of planning has been widely adopted, not only for multi-storeyed buildings (p. 1158) but also for comparatively small domestic work (p. 1157A).

WALLS

Indigenous Phase. In Peru important buildings and defensive walls were constructed of polygonal and coursed masonry of a high standard (p. 1130B). In Mexico and Central America, in the construction of the great truncated pyramids, limestone slabs, often carved and sometimes plastered, were used as a facing to a rubble and adobe brick core (p. 1129D). Less important buildings were constructed of adobe brick and/or timber (p. 1130A).

Colonial Phase. In Latin America the existing stone and adobe traditions were continued and developed by the Spaniards. Coloured, glazed tiles were a popular facing material (p. 1134F), while colour-wash on stucco was also used, the latter technique finding particular favour with the Portuguese in Brazil (p. 1134B). Wall-treatments generally followed fashions in Spain and Portugal.

In North America weather-boarding on heavy timber framing was used in seventeenth-century colonial work (p. 1133A), but a fine brick-building tradition developed in Virginia and spread along the eastern seaboard (p. 1133E) although timber building remained popular (steeple, p. 1137B). In the seventeenth century there are instances of work related to Jacobean prototypes (p. 1133E) while in the eighteenth century, in the English colonies, façades were almost always Georgian in character (p. 1133C).

National Phase. Wall treatments were dictated by the style adopted for a particular building—Greek, Egyptian, Gothic, Italian Renaissance, etc.—but materials provided an important modifying influence. In their adaptation to timber buildings, the historical styles acquired a new and often specifically 'American' character; while stylistic elements were retained, details were simplified as the limitations of materials and craftsmanship demanded. For the cast-iron façades popular in mid-nineteenth-century America, the Italian Renaissance style was frequently used, since this could be readily adapted to a repetitive bay-system, essential for the economic casting of iron units (p. 1153A).

In the latter part of the nineteenth century, the intrinsic qualities of walling materials tended to be exploited and, in some cases, buildings rely on this rather than eclectic detail for their character (p. 1150F). With the development of metal-frame construction, the wall as such tended to disappear, to be replaced sometimes by piers expressing the vertical members of the frame (p. 1153B) and sometimes by an elevational grid following the lines of the structural skeleton (p. 1153D), in both cases with light, non-load-bearing panels between the structural members.

A. The United Nations Headquarters, New York (1947–50): the Secretariat Block.
See p. 1163

B. The Ministry of Education and Health,
Rio de Janeiro (1937–42). See p. 1163

c. Lever House, New York (1952).
See p. 1163

Modern Architecture. Technological developments have made it possible for the 'wall' to become merely a skin of glass, sheet-metal or similar material, protecting the structure and the inside of the building from the elements but playing no part in the stability of the building (p. 1165C). In some cases floors are cantilevered out from the line of the structural supports and the wall becomes a screen, carried separately on each projecting floor (p. 1162A). Although the structural role of the wall has altered radically, traditional walling methods are still used for decorative effect and a slab of brickwork or rubble walling is sometimes introduced into a modern building to provide an accent in its elevational design.

OPENINGS

Indigenous Phase. Openings were kept to a minimum and were invariably square-headed, spanned either by timber or stone lintels (p. 1129). Sometimes stone lintels were carved (p. 1129C, E).

Colonial Phase. Generally, openings followed the pattern of those in the homeland of the colonizers, and both arched and square-headed forms were used. In Spanish colonial work, Gothic, Neo-Mudéjar, Renaissance and Baroque treatments can be found (p. 1134). As in the Iberian peninsula, decorative iron grilles were sometimes incorporated (p. 1134F). In English colonial work, for churches and similar buildings, arched windows were general (p. 1137B, D, E) and there is an example of the use of Gothic forms in a seventeenth-century Virginian church (p. 1137C). In domestic work, seventeenth-century examples have leaded casement windows, but in the eighteenth century the typical 'double-square' Georgian sliding-sash window with glazing bars became usual (p. 1133D). In the late eighteenth century there are examples of the use of the pointed arch for windows, a development of the current English 'Gothick' fashion (p. 875). For doorways, typical Georgian treatments are found and a pediment, often supported by flanking pilasters, was an accepted means of enrichment to entrances (p. 1133C). A classical portico, often of two storeys (p. 1133D), was a common feature for larger houses in the south-eastern part of North America. Sometimes derived from Palladian prototypes, this feature developed specifically American associations and its use continued well into the nineteenth century (p. 1142B).

National Phase. The design of openings was dictated by the style adopted for a particular building. In the early part of the nineteenth century, windows often continued the Georgian tradition, since there were not always convenient precedents in the styles adopted (p. 1150A). In the later decades of the century with the Romanesque Revival, arched openings, often of great power, were used (p. 1170), but for framed buildings, square-headed openings provided the most logical solution (p. 1153B, D).

Modern Architecture. With structural developments and advances in glass manufacture, it is no longer always possible to assess buildings in terms of 'solid and void', and a complete elevation may now be glazed (p. 1165C). Generally, openings are rectangular and rely for their effect almost entirely upon their proportions (p. 1157B). With air-conditioning and modern artificial lighting techniques, if required, a building may be windowless, or conversely its façades may be entirely of glass with entrance doors in the same material.

ROOFS

Indigenous Phase. Timber logs, sometimes plastered with adobe, were used, as was the corbelled vault. Spans were limited to about 20 ft and roofs were generally flat, often being used as terraces (p. 1130A). Pitched roofs covered in thatch were employed for peasant dwellings in Aztec Mexico.

Colonial Phase. While existing local techniques were adopted and developed, the

Spanish and Portuguese also introduced their own methods of roofing. The Gothic vault (p. 1135), the dome (p. 1134E), and the pitched roof are all found in colonial Latin America. In North America the pitched roof was in general use. In seventeenth-century English work, roofs were normally gabled and of a steep pitch (p. 1133A) but during the eighteenth century lower pitches became popular. The hipped roof seems to have been more common than the gabled roof in the eighteenth century (partly because it was more economical) and sometimes the roof was truncated to form a balustraded roof-deck (p. 1132). Where gables were built, they were often treated as classical pediments (p. 1133D). In Dutch colonial work, the mansard (or gambrel) roof was used (p. 1132). For churches and civic buildings in the English colonies, steeples and cupolas in the manner of Wren and Gibbs were common (p. 1137B). Roofs were frequently punctuated by dormer windows (p. 1133C).

National Phase. As with other features, the forms of roofs were largely dictated by the styles employed for buildings. Tiles, wood shingles, lead and asphalt were all used as coverings. Although Gothic Revival buildings required a steeply-pitched roof for reasons of stylistic character, broadly speaking, American architects seem to have favoured a lower pitch wherever this could be used. At the end of the nineteenth century this apparently inherent bias towards the low pitch became manifest with great power and an infusion of oriental character in the work of Frank Lloyd Wright (p. 1142E). The development of the metal frame encouraged the acceptance of the flat roof (p. 1153B, D), although, throughout the century, minor structures (generally in timber) employed, for reasons of economy, a flat or mono-pitch roof, an upstanding timber façade providing a parapet on the main elevations.

Modern Architecture. Roofs can take a wide variety of forms. The low-pitched roof, in the manner of Frank Lloyd Wright, is still popular in the U.S.A. for domestic work. Although for large steel- or reinforced-concrete-framed buildings the flat roof is generally adopted, for buildings like churches and auditoria more plastic forms find favour (p. 1161C).

COLUMNS

Indigenous Phase. Stone and timber columns were used in order to reduce roofing spans, but architecture of this phase is essentially of a mass-wall type rather than columnar (p. 1129).

Colonial Phase. In the Latin-American colonies columns were based on European prototypes generally (p. 1134), although there are examples which show a curious intermingling of native and Spanish features (p. 1138A). In North America, columns were based on prototypes in England, Palladian exemplars or copied from eighteenth-century English architectural pattern-books (p. 1133C, D).

National Phase. The design of columns was, of course, directly related to the style of a building, and the architect was assisted by an increasing number of publications giving details not only of the Classical Orders, but of Gothic, Egyptian and Muslim architecture. The use of cast-iron tended to affect the proportions of columns, and although iron columns were frequently enriched with Greek, Roman and Renaissance capitals and bases, they seldom had any relation to the proportions of their prototypes (p. 1153A). In the work of the Academic stream towards the close of the National Phase, considerable care was taken with the design of columns, which followed as closely as possible their historical sources (p. 1149A, D). In the work of Richardson and his followers, although broadly speaking Romanesque in character, considerable inventiveness was often displayed in the design of capitals, etc. (p. 1142A).

Modern Architecture. Today, columns are usually expressed frankly as structural supports and little or no attempt is made at enrichment or at incorporating the traditional divisions of base, shaft and capital. In the work of some architects, steel I-sections are left exposed as an integral feature of a design (p. 1157B), but normally fire regulations require steel structural members to be protected by a concrete or similar covering. Concrete columns are sometimes tapered towards their bases, as in the Administration Building of the Johnson Wax Co., Racine, Wis. (p. 1160).

MOULDINGS

Indigenous Phase. Mouldings were extremely severe, normally of a rectangular section and used in the manner of string courses (p. 1129A, C, E). In Mexico there are examples of the use of moulding similar to the Egyptian 'gorge' (pp. 55J, 1129A).

Colonial Phase. In Latin America, mouldings followed the pattern of contemporary Spanish and Portuguese work at home, modified by the materials and labour available in the colonies (p. 1134). In North America, in the English colonies, prototypes were provided by seventeenth and eighteenth-century English examples, often through the medium of pattern-books. While seventeenth-century examples are often crude, a remarkably high degree of refinement was achieved in eighteenth-century work (particularly in timber), sometimes of a higher standard than its equivalent in England (pp. 1137B, D, 1138B).

National Phase. Mouldings followed those belonging to the particular style adopted for a building (pp. 1142A, B, C, 1146). A simplification of mouldings is often apparent, for example in Greek Revival timber buildings and cast-iron work, necessitated by questions of economy and the materials employed (p. 1153A). Towards the end of the nineteenth century considerable originality is found in the work of designers like Richardson, Sullivan and Wright where, although still often inspired by historical precedent, simplicity and clarity become the keynotes (p. 1150F). In the work of more academic architects, like Hunt, Bacon and McKim, Mead and White, mouldings often achieved the perfection of the Classical and Renaissance examples from which they were copied (p. 1149A, D, E).

Modern Architecture. Mouldings as such are rarely used today but their equivalents are to be found, for example, in the section of a handrail or the detailing of the nosings to a staircase and it is through the careful and sensitive design of elements such as these that the modern architect enriches and humanizes his buildings (pp. 1157, 1161B, 1162B).

ORNAMENT

Indigenous Phase. Often, bold, abstract geometric shapes were carved in the stone facing slabs to the pyramids of Central America and Mexico (p. 1129), and sometimes conventionalized forms—warriors, wild animals, serpents and gods— were incorporated (p. 1129A, C). The carved stone slabs could be covered with plaster and coloured.

Colonial Phase. Spanish and Portuguese forms were used in Latin America (p. 1134) sometimes combined with existing Indian decorative devices. In North America, ornament was sparse in early colonial work, but, in the eighteenth century, it reached standards comparable with those in the mother country which provided prototypes. In the mid-eighteenth century, ornate designs, cast in 'composition' and imported from England, were used in some buildings, where they were applied to walls and ceilings (cf. Westover, p. 1132). Timber details— panelling, fireplace surrounds, doors and doorways—were often particularly fine. Towards the end of the eighteenth century there is evidence of influence from the work of the Adam brothers in internal ornamental work.

National Phase. Ornament was dictated by the precedents of the style adopted for a building but since appropriate prototypes did not always exist—e.g. for fireplaces, ceilings and wall treatments—there were inventive adaptations of Greek, Egyptian and Gothic motifs in many instances. In the later nineteenth century, in addition to the whole gamut of the decorative vocabularies of the historical styles, the influence of European Art Nouveau is evident (p. 1150D).

Modern Architecture. For the enrichment of their buildings modern architects have tended to rely on the inherent qualities of materials (p. 1161B). In Latin America, 'azulejos' and 'brise soleil' have been exploited to produce exciting effects of colour and texture (pp. 1161C, 1165B), while in North America interesting use has been made of brightly-coloured glazed bricks (p. 1162B), moulded sheet metal (cf. the Alcoa Building, p. 1163) and even glass tubing (p. 1162A). Recently, North American architects have been seeking additional enrichment to their buildings by pierced screens, in metal or concrete, used as non-structural claddings, features closely related to the 'brise soleil' of the tropical areas of South America.

REFERENCE BOOKS

GENERAL WORKS

GIEDION, S. *Space, Time and Architecture.* 3rd Edition, Cambridge (Mass.), 1954.
GOODWIN, P. L. *Brazil Builds.* New York, 1953.
GOWANS, A. *Looking at Architecture in Canada.* Toronto, 1958.
HAMLIN, T. F. *The American Spirit in Architecture.* New Haven, 1926.
JACKSON, H. *New York Architecture, 1650–1952.* New York, 1952.
KIMBALL, F. *American Architecture.* Indianapolis, 1928.
LARKIN, O. W. *Art and Life in America.* New York, 1949.
ROOS, F. J. *Writings on Early American Architecture.* Columbus, 1943.
SANFORD, T. E. *The Story of Architecture in Mexico.* New York, 1947.
TALLMADGE, T. *The Story of Architecture in America.* 1928.

INDIGENOUS PHASE

BINGHAM, H. *Machu Picchu, a Citadel of the Incas.* New Haven, 1930.
KINGSBOROUGH, Lord. *Antiquities of Mexico.* 9 vols., 1930–48.
KUBLER, G. *Cuzco; Reconstruction of the Town and Restoration of the Monuments.* Unesco (Paris), 1952.
MASON, J. A. *The Ancient Civilizations of Peru.* Penguin Books, Harmondsworth, 1957.
MEANS, P. A. *Ancient Civilizations of the Andes.* 1931.
PETERSON, F. *Ancient Mexico.* 1959.
PRESCOTT, W. H. *History of the Conquest of Peru.* 1847.
—. *History of the Conquest of Mexico.* 1850.
TOTTEN, G. O. *Maya Architecture.* Washington, 1926.
VAILLANT, G. C. *The Aztecs of Mexico.* 1944. Penguin Books, Harmondsworth, 1955.

COLONIAL PHASE

BAZIN, G. *L'Architecture réligieuse baroque au Brésil.* 2 vols., Paris, 1956–8.
BRIDENBAUGH, C. *Peter Harrison, First American Architect.* Chapel Hill, 1949.
BRIGGS, M. S. *Homes of the Pilgrim Fathers in America, 1620–1685.* London, 1932.
FORMAN, H. C. *Architecture of the Old South; The Medieval Style, 1585–1850.* Cambridge (Mass.), 1948.
JOHNSTON, F. B. and WATERMAN, T. T. *The Early Architecture of North Carolina.* Chapel Hill, 1941.
KELEMEN, P. *Baroque and Rococo in Latin America.* New York, 1951.
KELLY, J. F. *The Early Domestic Architecture of Connecticut.* New Haven, 1924.
KIMBALL, F. *Domestic Architecture of the American Colonies and of the Early Republic.* New York, 1922.
KUBLER, G. *Mexican Architecture in the Sixteenth Century.* 2 vols., New Haven, 1948.
LIVERMORE, H. V. (Ed.) *Portugal and Brazil: An Introduction.* Oxford, 1953.
MORRISON, H. *Early American Architecture.* New York, 1952.
NAVARRO, J. G. *Religious Architecture in Quito.* New York, 1945.

The Marshall Field Wholesale Warehouse, Chicago
(1885–7). See p. 1152

NEWCOMB, R. *Spanish-Colonial Architecture in the United States*. New York, 1937.
—. *Architecture in Old Kentucky*. Urbana (Ill.), 1953.
SANTOS, P. F. *O Barroco e o Jesuítico na Arquitetura do Brasil*. Rio de Janeiro, 1951.
WATERMAN, T. T. *Domestic Colonial Architecture in Tidewater Virginia*. New York, 1932.
—. *The Mansions of Virginia*. Chapel Hill, 1946.
—. *The Dwellings of Colonial America*. Chapel Hill, 1950.
WETHEY, H. E. *Colonial Architecture and Sculpture in Peru*. Cambridge (Mass.), 1949.
WHIFFEN, M. *The Public Buildings of Colonial Williamsburg*. Williamsburg, 1958.

NATIONAL PHASE
BOSSOM, A. C. *Building to the Skies*. London, 1934.
CONDIT, C. *The Rise of the Skyscraper*. Chicago, 1952.
FRARY, I. T. *Early Homes of Ohio*. Richmond, 1936.
HAMLIN, T. F. *Greek Revival Architecture in America*. New York, 1944.
HITCHCOCK, H. R. *The Architecture of H. H. Richardson and his Times*. New York, 1936.

NEWCOMB, R. *Architecture of the Old North-West Territory*. Chicago, 1950.
RANDALL, F. *History of the Development of Building Construction in Chicago*. Urbana (Ill.) 1949.
SCULLY, V. J. *The Shingle Style*. New Haven, 1955.
SULLIVAN, L. H. *The Autobiography of an Idea*. New York, 1949.
TALLMADGE, T. *Architecture in Old Chicago*. Chicago, 1941.
WHITE, T. (Ed.) *Philadelphia in the Nineteenth Century*. Philadelphia, 1953.

Monographs on individual architects:
GALLAGHER, H. M. P. *Robert Mills*. New York, 1935.

The Hallidie Building, San Francisco (1918). See p. 1156

GILCHRIST, A. A. *William Strickland: Architect and Engineer*. Philadelphia, 1950.
HAMLIN, T. F. *Benjamin Henry Latrobe*. New York, 1955.
HITCHCOCK, H. R. *In the Nature of Materials*. New York, 1942. (on Frank Lloyd Wright)
KIMBALL, F. *Thomas Jefferson, Architect*. Boston, 1916.
MAGGINIS, C. *The Work of Cram and Ferguson, Architects*. New York, 1929.
Monograph of the Work of McKim, Mead and White. 4 vols., New York, 1915–25.
MORRISON, H. *Louis Sullivan*. New York, 1952.
NEWTON, R. H. *Town and Davis: Architects*. New York, 1942.
NORTH, A. T. *Raymond M. Hood*. New York, 1931.
PLACE, C. *Charles Bullfinch: Architect and Citizen*. Boston, 1925.
REILLY, C. H. *McKim, Mead and White*. London, 1924.
UPJOHN, E. *Richard Upjohn: Architect and Churchman*. New York, 1939.
WRIGHT, F. L. *An Autobiography*. New York, 1945.

MODERN ARCHITECTURE

HITCHCOCK, H. R., and DREXLER, A. *Built in the U.S.A.: Post-war Architecture*. New York, 1952.
HITCHCOCK, H. R. *Latin American Architecture since 1945*. New York, 1955.
MINDLIN, H. E. *Modern Architecture in Brazil*. Rio de Janeiro, 1956.
MUMFORD, L. *Roots of Contemporary American Architecture*. New York, 1952.
MYERS, I. E. *Mexico's Modern Architecture*. New York, 1952.
MCCALLUM, I. *Architecture U.S.A*. London, 1959.

Monographs on individual architects:
CHRIST-JANER, A. *Eliel Saarinen*. Chicago, 1948.
GIEDION, S. *Walter Gropius*. London, 1954.
JOHNSON, P. *Mies van der Rohe*. 2nd Edition, New York, 1953.
PAPADAKI, S. *The Work of Oscar Niemeyer*. New York, 1950.
—. *Oscar Niemeyer: Work in Progress*. New York, 1956.
ZEVI, B. *Richard Neutra*. Milan, 1954.

The following periodicals contain important articles, particularly on individual architects and buildings:
Journal of the Society of Architectural Historians; Architectural Review; Architectural Record; Forum; Pencil Points.

PART II

Architecture in the East

INTRODUCTION

FROM the very ancient architectures of Egypt and Mesopotamia we have been able to trace, through the rise and fall of successive styles, a continuous development trending towards the West, fanning from the Mediterranean and then expanding in the train of colonization from Europe to the outer Western World. It remains to give some account of the succession in the East. There, modern archaeology has located two further ancient nodes or cradles of civilization, the one in the basin of the River Indus in North West India, now in Pakistan, and the other on the middle reaches of the Hwang Ho (Yellow River) and Yangtze-Kiang, China. Applying once again the tests of the resort to town-building and the use of writing, both are less old than the cultures of either Egypt or Mesopotamia. They were each substantially independent of other chief centres, though that of the Indus had contacts with and a somewhat similar ancestry to the Sumerian, being related by events on the fringes of the Persian plateau which lies between. The Indus region, a zone along the river greater in extent than the British Isles, was settled after 3000 B.C., and in the enormously long period c. 2500–1500 B.C., displayed an advanced civilization quite comparable with that of contemporary Mesopotamia. It collapsed with the Aryan invasion of c. 1500–1000 B.C., but left its important mark on the Hindu civilization which succeeded. How architecture developed thereafter in the Indian peninsula a following account will show; in its ultimate scope it embraced the lands to the east from Burma down to the Malayan archipelago, and missionaries and merchants carried its influences to China and even Japan. The foundational Chinese culture, in its turn, bloomed in the Shang period (c. 1766–1122 B.C.) after long stages of growth dating back to the third millennium. It spread eastward to the river plains; and so to South China. Relatively, civilization in Japan was much belated, and can scarcely be put before the middle of the first millennium B.C. Substantially, its architecture derived from China, but was nevertheless extremely consistent and conservative in character. From time to time, as history marched, influences of varying importance reached these several countries from the West, as equally they traversed in the reverse direction; but the development which had the most profound consequences of all was that of the Muslim dominion, which from beginnings in Arabia in the seventh century A.D., bracketed East and West and established a religious faith which has continued to span them from that time. Yet since its consequence has been the greater to the Eastern World, Muslim architecture is included with the present group of styles.

In the case of the three old civilizations, Indian, Chinese and Japanese, the architectural treatment in the following pages begins at the much later stages when the surviving evidence becomes adequate to show continuity. The Muslim, based on previously-developed architectures, springs almost fully fledged.

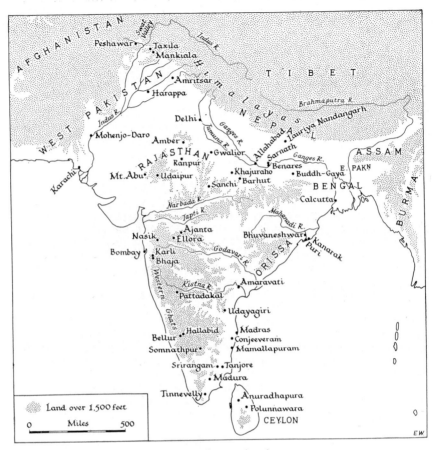

The Indian peninsula

XXX. ARCHITECTURE IN INDIA
AND PAKISTAN

(HINDU, BUDDHIST AND JAIN)*

(*Circa* 300 B.C. to present day)

INFLUENCES

GEOGRAPHICAL. India and Pakistan, together with the outlying countries of
Afghanistan, Burma, and Indo-China, form the southern fringe of Asia. The main
triangular peninsula, comprising the first two countries, is about fifteen times the

* Although the main developments in Hindu, Buddhist and Jain architecture took place
within the Indo-Pakistan sub-continent, there were important Buddhist centres in
Afghanistan, and there were equally important later developments in Burma and Indo-
China. For Muslim architecture in the sub-continent, see Chapter XXXIII, p. 1222.

size of Great Britain. On the north, a barrier is formed by high mountain ranges stretching from the Hindu Kush in the west, through the Pamirs, Karakorams, and the Himalayas to the mountains of Sikang in China, in the east. On the east, south, and west, the area is bounded by the sea. In the earliest times, influences entered the area mainly from Central Asia through the passes of the north-west and north-east: there was also a strong tide of influence from Persia and the Middle East, which came through what is now Baluchistan. Good harbours along the coast are few; intercourse by sea was, therefore, less important in early days, although by the first century A.D., there was a thriving maritime trade with the Roman Empire. The great rivers in the north, the Indus and Ganges and their tributaries, provided trade ways, and many of the area's most important cities were founded along them. Delhi, the 'Rome' of India, on the River Jumuna, has been the capital of India, at various times, over a period of a thousand years: around it still are the remains of at least seven separate 'cities' scattered over nearly fifty square miles. Its importance was due to its commanding position at the junction of the four trade routes from the Lower Ganges, the Hindu Kush, the Indus Valley, and the Gulf of Cambay. The chief commercial city of Pakistan is Karachi, a port founded in the eighteenth century and the sea gateway to the Indus Valley. Excavations at Mohenjodaro and Harappa, and in Rajasthan, indicate close links between the so-called 'Indus Valley culture' and ancient Mesopotamia. It is only in the south and east of the peninsula that the stream of influences seems to have been unimportant, in spite of Roman trading stations on the coast of the Bay of Bengal.

GEOLOGICAL. The lack of building stone along the Indus and Ganges Valleys, and the easily available timber which was floated down the rivers from the mountains have influenced architecture in the area from the earliest times. In the north, architectural forms, at least until the eighteenth century A.D., tended to be simply the translation into stone of carpentry techniques. There is good white marble in Rajasthan, widely used in Mogul buildings, and fine red and cream sandstone from the neighbourhood of Agra; generally speaking, however, these are used mainly as facing materials for rubble walling behind. In the centre and south, the 'trap' and granite of the Deccan and the volcanic potstone of Hallabid made their own contributions to the development of regional characteristics. In the Western Ghats, the horizontal rock strata which rise in perpendicular cliffs, made possible the rock-cut sanctuaries of Karli (p. 1181A), Ajanta (p. 1181B), and Elephanta (p. 1185B). At Mamallapuram and Ellora (p. 1185A) rock-cut temples, known as 'Raths', were hewn out of amygdaloidal trap formations. As far as timber is concerned, hard teak is found in Burma and in the eastern and western coastal mountains. An excellent softwood, deodar, is found abundantly in the northern mountain ranges; shisham, a hardwood somewhat inferior to teak, grows everywhere in the river valleys of the north. In the riverine plains of Bengal, Uttar Pradesh, and the Punjab, the alluvial soil makes good bricks which were, and are, used extensively in these areas. Terracotta has been used from the earliest times; the ease with which the plastic clay can be pressed into moulds or carved, before firing, may be responsible (together with the traditions of wood-carving), for the exuberance of decoration in subsequent periods. Lime for building was obtained by burning limestone, shells, and kankar, a nodular form of impure lime found in the river valleys.

CLIMATIC. Although slightly more than half the area lies within the Tropic of Cancer, the climate varies widely. In the east, there is a small variation of temperature between summer and winter, a very heavy rainfall in the monsoon season (May to August), and a moderate rainfall throughout the year. This produces a climate generally warm and humid, but not excessively hot. In the bulk of the peninsula, the temperature is fairly equable throughout the year, but the distinction between dry and wet seasons is more clearly marked. In the plains of the north, temperatures rise high in the summer months (May to July) and drop markedly about the winter solstice. The rainy season comes later than in the east, and is shorter. The general character of the climate is dry, with a cooler winter. In the north-west, the hot season and the cold season are nearly equal in length, the former being severe (temperatures rising to 120° F), and the latter also sharp with night-frosts and sleet: the summer rainy season is short and late, and the winter rains are more marked than in the Gangetic Plain. This great variation of climate has less general effect on architecture than might be expected, as protection against heat, even in the north-west, seems to have received more attention than winter comfort. Pierced, or latticed, windows to exclude sunlight and heat are general: and canals, reservoirs and tanks, for ceremonial use, for irrigation, and for comfort, are features of all important religious and secular buildings. The high angle of the sun over much of the area, and the frequency of sunny days, may well have helped to produce the characteristic external carved decoration which takes much of its effect from the contrasts of light and shade. The flat roof, for summer sleeping, is almost universal except in the east, where the need to deal with heavy and continuous rain produced steeply-pitched roofs. Major climatic changes have taken place at least in some parts of the area in historic times: excavations at Mohenjodaro, for example, clearly indicate that the Lower Indus Valley, now largely semi-desert, once supported the rich animal and vegetable life normally associated with tropical jungles. This may explain, in part, the replacement of wood by stone as a basic building material.

RELIGIOUS. In these lands, religion impinges more strongly and continually on everyday life than is normal in the West. The basic doctrines of Hinduism have been modified by the impact of Buddhism and Jainism, which are both, fundamentally, non-conformist sects of Hinduism. The former sect has moved much further from the parent doctrine than the latter, and has now largely disappeared from the country of its origins, although there are Buddhist communities in East Pakistan. Jainism still attracts many devotees in India.

Hindu. The Hindu religion seems to have evolved from a combination of the faiths of the indigenous Dravidians and the Aryan invaders: the Dravidian cult of 'bhakti' (devotion to an incarnation, and so to images) modifying the Aryan preference for abstract principles. These Aryan principles are incorporated in the 'Rig-Veda', a series of hymns composed some time between 1500–800 B.C. About the beginning of the Christian era, the Vedic gods were superseded by the trinity ('Trimurti') of modern Hinduism: Vishnu, the preserver; Siva, the destroyer; and Brahma (the prime being of the trinity), soul and creator of the universe. Vishnu and Siva appear in various forms ('avatars') and for this reason the triune aspect of Hinduism has often been misrepresented as multiple idol worship. Hindu worship is essentially an individual act, and except on certain specified occasions communal worship is foreign to it. This has produced the basic difference between the Hindu temple, and the Muslim mosque (p. 1226).

From the earliest days of Hinduism, an orthodox Hindu's daily life has been governed by religious practice in its minutest details. Any major occasion demands the services of one of the Brahman priesthood, who alone have the authority to officiate. Before the advent of Buddhism, the Brahman caste had thus so concentrated power in their own hands that this early period of Hinduism is known as the Brahmanical period, and the Brahman abuse of their powers produced the challenges of both the Buddhists and the Jains.

Buddhist. Siddartha, or Gautama Buddha, was born about 563 B.C. on the borders of Nepal. He belonged to the princely Kshatriya caste, who had obvious reasons to dispute Brahman domination. Buddha's basic doctrine was that salvation, being attainable by the individual's actions, was within the reach of all regardless of caste, and did not depend on Brahmanical intercession. It followed that the Buddhist religious buildings became concentrated in monasteries (where the contemplative life could be lived in communion with fellow spirits), and in shrines where relics of those who had achieved salvation ('nirvana') were deposited. These shrines took the form of 'stupas', or domical mounds which, grouped with their rails, gateways, processional paths, and crowning 'umbrellas', came to be regarded as symbols of the universe. The monasteries became places of international pilgrimage and dissemination of learning. With the passage of time, the original asceticism of Buddha's doctrines became modified, and pictorial sculpture revived the idolatry which had originally been forbidden. Buddhism declined in India after the seventh century A.D., but has revived strongly in Burma, and the Far East.

Jain. Jainism was traditionally founded by Mahavira (roughly a contemporary with Buddha) who was himself a Brahman. The goal is salvation through successive re-births, the ideal being rigid asceticism and the avoidance of injury to every living creature, which might be some soul in the process of purification. Jain temples differ little in essentials from the normal Hindu temple, but are distinguished by the extraordinary richness and complexity of their sculptural ornament. Mahavira and twenty-four other saints who had achieved salvation before him are worshipped, sometimes in the form of the animals which are attributed to each of them.

The Muslim religion and the forms in architecture to which it gave rise are considered in Chapter XXXIII, Muslim Architecture (e.g. India and Pakistan, p. 1238).

SOCIAL. Some religious implications of the organization of society into castes have already been indicated, and these divisions still remain clearly marked in spite of recent efforts to break them down. Apart from forming social divisions into classes, the caste system had a racial significance in that Brahmans and Kshatriyas claimed descent from the Sanskrit-speaking Aryan invaders, the Vaisyas were held to be of mixed blood and could therefore lay no claim to racial aristocracy, and the Sudras were the defeated aboriginals. Apart from these, there was a large Muslim population claiming descent from Arab and Persian invaders, but in fact drawn mainly from converts to Islam: these were mostly concentrated in what is now Pakistan. The sub-continent cannot be considered as an entity either socially or artistically, for there is as great a divergence of language, social custom, climate, and ethnographic type as may be found within Europe from Scandinavia to the Mediterranean: thus a simple picture of architectural development is impossible. Ordinary domestic buildings of any great age do not exist; wealth, until very recently, was concentrated in the hands of feudal landlords who built palaces for themselves or temples for their gods. In an order where life on earth is looked upon mainly as a preparation for something more enduring after death, it is not surprising that temples are more important monuments than palaces.

HISTORICAL. The earliest defined civilization in the sub-continent is that of the so-called 'Indus Valley culture' (2500–1500 B.C.), which was related to the Sumerian cultures of the Middle East. The most famous excavated sites of this period are those at Mohenjodaro (in Sind) and Harappa (about a hundred miles south of Lahore); but recent excavations in the Rajasthan area of India indicate that this civilization was more widely spread than its present name indicates. All remains discovered so far are archaeological rather than architectural, and therefore are not included in the present account.

Successive incursions, military and economic, into the area from 2000 B.C. until the nineteenth century A.D., brought art and architecture into contact with many influences; Persian, Graeco-Roman, Sassanian, Portuguese, French, and English.

The strength of these varied considerably: the first three exercised a deep influence, the fourth and fifth more purely local ones, and the last, again a strong one. Between the periods of internal weakness marking these incursions, indigenous empires and kingdoms rose and declined. From the point of view of the Hindu, Buddhist and Jain cultures, the most important of these were:

(a) The Mauryan Buddhist Empire in the north, founded c. 300 B.C. on the remains of Alexander the Great's short-lived 'empire'. Cultural influences from Sassanian Persia (e.g. the Persepolitan type of memorial pillar or 'lath' erected by Asoka) are indicated by the descriptions by a Chinese pilgrim in A.D. 400 of the wooden palace of Asoka at Pataliputra, then still surviving.

(b) The Bactrian Buddhist kingdoms of Gandhara and Sialkot in the north-west, breaking away from the Mauryan Empire in about 200 B.C. Close cultural affinities with the Graeco-Roman world existed, probably through trade with Africa and Asia Minor.

(c) The more orthodox Hindu Andhra and Sunga kingdoms in Central and South India, from about 185 B.C. These areas were less under external influences, and their art was more indigenous in character. Presumably this also applied to their buildings, though none survive.

(d) The Kushan Empire, founded by a tribe of Central Asian nomads in the north-west, and in existence for the first three centuries of the Christian era. The greatest ruler was Kanishka (c. A.D. 78), whose capital was at Peshawar. This period shows a great cultural influx from Alexandria, Syria, and China. There are 'architectural' remains of this period in the excavated city of Sirkap (Taxila), and rock-cut shrines with important architectural detail at Bamiyan in Afghanistan.

(e) The Gupta Empire, embracing the northern areas from the Jumuna River in the west to Assam in the east, and south to the Narbadda River. During this period (fourth to sixth century A.D.), there was maritime expansion to the Far East, carrying with it artistic influences which flowered later in Cambodia and similar places. To this phase belong the earliest substantial architectural remains that survive.

(f) In the south, four orthodox Hindu states were successively dominant: the Cholas, from the late tenth to the thirteenth century A.D., whose power reached into Burma and Ceylon; the Hoysalas in Mysore, more or less contemporary with the Cholas; the kingdom of Vijayanagar, south of the Kistna River, founded in the first half of the fourteenth century and destroyed in 1565; and the Nayak dynasty of Madura, of the seventeenth and eighteenth centuries.

After the middle of the eighteenth century, the disintegration of the Mogul Empire in the north, and the Hindu states in the south, combined with the arrival of European fashions through France and England, virtually put an end to any further development of Hindu architecture. Some self-conscious attempts at a 'revival' since 1947, when India and Pakistan became sovereign states, have produced nothing of importance.

ARCHITECTURAL CHARACTER

(1) *Buddhist* (300 B.C.–A.D. 320). The major examples are in the north-west (i.e. the old Bactrian kingdoms) and in the mountains of the Western Ghats above Bombay. The main characteristic of Buddhist shrines (as opposed to those of the Hindus and Jains) is that they are all designed for congregational use. Monasteries, meeting halls ('chaityas'), and stupa shrines are all planned to accommodate large groups of worshippers. In the rock-cut chaityas of the Western Ghats, the main forms and the details of the wooden prototype buildings, now vanished, have been preserved.

Decorative detail is used more in the Western classical tradition—to emphasize structure—than in Hindu and Jain buildings, where it conceals structure like a jungle growth. This is even more noticeable in the north-west, where near-replicas of Hellenistic buildings occur (e.g. the Zoroastrian temple at Jhaulian, Taxila), and where both Corinthian and Ionic Orders occur in a distorted, but plainly recognizable, form. Virtually no secular buildings remain, but the excavated parts of the city of Sirkap (Taxila) (*fl.* 200 B.C.–A.D. 200), show a city neatly laid out on a rectangular grid and dominated by an 'acropolis' containing a monastery and stupa. The acropolis appears again in other civil settlements, such as Mingaora (Swat state).

(2) *Jain* (A.D. 1000–1300). Jain temples are found over most of the area, but mainly in the northern central part of the peninsula. There were revivals of architectural activity in the fifteenth century A.D., but the work from this period has little life and shows no real development. The main difference between the Jain and the Hindu temple is the lighter and more elegant character of the former. The Jains, also, paid particular attention to the siting and environment of their monuments. Although both Hindu and Jain temples are basically enclosed shrines introduced by a more open porch, specifically Jain are ceilings in the form of flat domes, and stonework so elaborately carved that it often loses all its own character and can rather be compared to petrified foliage.

(3) *Hindu.* Hindu temples may be roughly grouped into three types, although these are not clear cut and a hard division cannot be assumed.

(*a*) Northern Indian: A.D. 600 to the present.

(*b*) Central Indian: A.D. 1000 to 1300.*

(*c*) South Indian (Dravidian): A.D. 625 to 1750.

In all types, the fundamental plan consists of a small unlit shrine called the 'garbhagriha', crowned with the spire-shaped 'sikhara', and introduced by one or more porch-like halls ('mandapas') used for religious dancing and music. This form seems to have evolved about the fourth century A.D. The sanctuary as a whole is the 'vimana'. Except in the south, the vimana is seldom designed to take a congregation of worshippers; its entire self becomes an object of worship. This explains the importance attached to the sculptural decoration of the exterior, and also the sanctity traditionally ascribed by Hindus to the art and to the practitioners of temple building. The vertical sikhara makes a very marked contrast with the low, flat roof-lines of the average Indian village, and proclaims the holy place as unmistakably as does the church-tower in the English countryside. In (*a*), the Northern Indian temple, the sikhara is very dominant: it is conical in form, with convex curved sides; and there is normally a finial ('kalasa') of vase or 'melon' form. The 'mandap' or porch-hall is usually more or less enclosed with walls or screens. The general plan form of the vimana is a combination of simple rectangles. Temples of (*b*), the Central Indian type, combine features of the Northern (e.g. the sikhara) with those of the Dravidian (e.g. the stellate plan form). Generally speaking, temples of this type are more florid and exuberant in form and decoration than those of the north. In (*c*), Dravidian temples, the form of the spire becomes a flatter pyramid with straight or (later) concave sides: the term 'sikhara' in this type is given only to the top storey of the spire, which becomes much elaborated and follows either the Buddhist stupa or chaitya form (pp. 1181A, 1193B). These crowning spires are often grouped in miniature repetitions round the lower stages of the building. Peculiar to the later Dravidian temples are the many-columned halls, tanks, and courtyards surrounding the inner sanctuary. Between these courtyards

* This type is sometimes called 'Chalukyan', but misleadingly, as the Chalukya dynasty had ceased to rule by A.D. 750.

are gigantic gateway towers ('gopurams') which replace the sikhara as the dominating features of the temple group (p. 1190A). The intention of this arrangement is to
heighten the emotional impact of the approach to the shrine, and to display the
wealth and power of the temple and its servants. The sculptural and decorative
details are of little importance compared with those of earlier temples: compare
the dry, lifeless carving in the **Temple at Tarputry** (seventeenth century A.D.) (p.
1190B) with that at Bellur (twelfth century A.D.) (p. 1189B).

EXAMPLES

1. BUDDHIST ARCHITECTURE
(300 B.C.–A.D. 320)

(1) *Stambhas* or *Laths*. These are monumental pillars, standing free without any
structural function. Inscriptions were carved on the shaft. The capital, which was
usually Persepolitan in form (cf. p. 78), was crowned with animal supporters
bearing the Buddhist 'chakra' or 'wheel of the law'. The emblem of the Republic
of India is the capital of the 'stambha' at **Sarnath**. There are others at **Allahabad,**
and at **Lauriya Nandangarh** in Nepal (p. 1186A).

(2) *Stupas*. The most important group of these domical mounds is at **Sanchi** in
the former state of Bhopal. The **Great Stupa** here dates, in its present form, from
the end of the first century B.C., and preserves its stone enclosing railings (pp.
1182A, 1194E) and the four ceremonial gateways ('toranas') (p. 1194A) at the cardinal
points of the compass. These ancillary features must have been common to all
important stupas. The toranas resemble the Chinese 'pai-lou' (p. 1205) and the
Japanese 'torii' (p. 1218). At the base of the stupa is a processional path above a
platform 14 ft high. The stupa is of solid brickwork, 106 ft in diameter and 42 ft
high. Originally, it was faced with stone, and the crowning feature was a three-
tiered stone 'umbrella', similar to that still in place (though damaged) on the stupa
within the hall at **Karli** (p. 1181A). Other important stupas are at **Barhut** (second
century A.D.), and **Amaravati** (A.D. 200).*

There are many lesser stupas throughout north-west Pakistan; at **Mankiala** near
Rawalpindi, at **Taxila,** and in the **Khyber Pass.** The great stupa built by Kanishka
at Shah-ji-ki-Dheri, on the outskirts of **Peshawar,** has disappeared, but it was
carefully described by Chinese pilgrims of the sixth century as rising to a height
of 700 ft (including the wooden superstructure). Excavations on its site in 1908
revealed an important bronze relic casket (now in Peshawar Museum), decorated
with debased Hellenistic motives, and signed by the Greek-named maker, Agesilas.

(3) *Chaityas* or Assembly Halls. No free-standing chaityas of any importance
remain, but rock-cut examples at **Bhaja** (250 B.C.), **Nasik** (129 B.C.), **Karli, Ellora,**
and **Ajanta,** show clearly the form of the original structure (p. 1181A). The latest of
these dates from A.D. 250. The plan consists of an apsidal-ended hall with closely-
spaced pillars at each side, forming aisles. A stupa shrine is placed in the apse,
furthest from the entrance. The roofs are semicircular in section, and ribs representing the original timber members of the prototypes are cut from the rock. The
façade normally contains, above a low entrance portico, a horseshoe-shaped window filled with rock-cut or wooden tracery (p. 1181B).

The **Chaitya, Karli** (78 B.C.) (p. 1181A), is 126 ft long, and the height and width
are 45 ft. The Persepolitan-type columns are octagonal, and the capitals are formed
by pairs of elephants. The roof ribs, in this case, are actually of wood, inserted
after the roof was cut. A fine lath, crowned with four lions, stands at the entrance
of this chaitya.

* Many sculptured panels from Amaravati are in the British Museum, and a full-size
reproduction of the Sanchi railings is in the Indian Museum, South Kensington.

A. The Chaitya, Karli: interior (78 B.C.). See opposite page

B. The Chaitya, Ajanta: façade (c. A.D. 250). See opposite page

A. The Great Stupa, Sanchi, from E. (late 1st cent. B.C.) See p. 1180

B. Monastery at Takht-i-Bhai (A.D. 3rd cent.). See p. 1183

(4) *Viharas* or Monasteries. Most of the existing viharas are in the north-west of Pakistan and in Afghanistan. There are several fine remains round **Taxila** (second century B.C. to second century A.D.) and near **Mingaora** in the Swat valley. That at **Takht-i-Bhai** (p. 1182B) is typical of these. A number of simple cells are ranged round a quadrangle; the main stupa is placed adjoining this quadrangle in a second courtyard which is crowded with smaller votive stupas. There are several larger chambers for assembly or dining. All roofs have disappeared—they were of wood and thatch, or tile—as has most of the painted stucco with which the masonry was originally faced. Apart from that on the stupas and their bases, there seems to have been little carved ornament on buildings. The Corinthian column appears frequently in miniature in the carved aedicules on stupa bases, and also as full-sized fragments detached from their original contexts. The Buddhist monastery at **Nalanda** (Bengal) which flourished in the seventh century A.D., represents the last phase. It was of great size, and could more properly be described as a university. A stupa excavated there retains little of the Graeco-Roman characteristics of the earlier types: the simple rectangular base has developed into a four-storeyed rectangular tower, topped by a drum supporting a flat saucer-dome—all that remains of the hemispherical stupa-mound.

There are rock-cut viharas adjoining some of the chaitya caves, notably at **Bhaja** (second century B.C.): they consist of a simple group of cells without any adornment.

There are major Buddhist remains in Ceylon, particularly at **Anuradhapura** and **Polunnawara**, which were the capital cities from the first to the eighth and the eighth to the thirteenth century respectively. In Java, there is a great stupa at **Barobudar,** which represents the culmination of the conception of the stupa as representing the cosmos. The Singhalese stupas are remarkable for their size, one being 370 ft in diameter. The ornament has a lively elegance which is lacking in the Buddhist buildings of the north-west.

2. JAIN ARCHITECTURE
(A.D. 1000–1300)

The most important group of Jain temples is at **Mount Abu** (p. 1184A), below the peak of this name at the south-western end of the Aravalli range in Rajasthan. Typical of this group is the **Dilwarra Temple** (1032) (p. 1184B), built of white marble. There is a large portico-hall, the columns of which are crowned with bracket capitals, carrying the raking struts which are peculiarities of Jain building. The interior of the corbelled dome roof is so highly carved that the marble assumes the character of lacework. In common with the majority of Jain temples, the artistic quality of the carved ornament falls short of the technical achievement.

The **Temple, Ranpur** (1439), on the side of the Aravalli Mountains in Rajasthan, gives the completest picture of a Jain monument. It stands on a high substructure some 200 ft square, surrounded by eighty-six cells, each of which is covered by a sikhara-shaped roof. There are five shrines, one at each angle of that in the centre, with four open light courts between. Twenty domes, 21 ft in diameter, supported on over four hundred columns, are placed symmetrically in groups of five round the angle shrines. The central dome of each group is three storeys high and 36 ft in diameter. The domes are all formed in the usual way, of horizontally-corbelled courses of masonry elaborately carved. The multiple repetition of parts, and the virtuosity of the craftsmanship, are typical of Jain temples in general.

A. The Jain temples, Mount Abu (1000–1300). See p. 1183

B. Dilwarra Temple, Mount Abu: interior (1032). See p. 1183

A. The Rath, Ellora (750–950). See p. 1188

B. Rock-cut temple, Elephanta: interior (9th cent.). See p. 1191

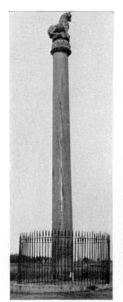

A (*left*). The Lath (Lion column), Lauriya Nandangarh (243 B.C.). See p. 1180

B (*right*). The Parasuramesvara Temple, Bhuvaneshwar (750). See p. 1187

C. Hindu Temple, Amber (1000–1200). See p. 1188

At **Udayagiri** in Orissa, are several rock-cut Jain viharas dating from the second and first century B.C. These are irregular in plan, but are interesting in that they reproduce in their sculptured façades, structural details of vanished buildings of that period.

3. HINDU ARCHITECTURE

(*a*) *Northern Indian* (A.D. 600 to the present).

Temples in **Orissa** (800–1200) on the east coast, form a series which presents the finest examples of this type. The typical plan is square; the lofty sikhara covering the 'garbha-griha' or shrine has convex curved sides, the mandap or porch-hall is without columns, and has a lower, stepped roof. Each façade has rectangular projections in the centre, which become triangular in plan in later examples. The elaborate gateways and enclosures of Dravidian temples are entirely missing. Of these Orissa temples, the best known are at **Bhuvaneshwar** (p. 1186B). The strong contrast between the emphatic vertical lines of the sikhara and the horizontality of the mandap is softened by the horizontal lines of sculpture, each separated by an incised band, running round the former: these, from a distance, produce an effect reminiscent of rustication. The melon-shaped finial is particularly dominant, and increases in importance as the type develops.

The **Black Pagoda, Kanarak** (thirteenth century) (p. 1194C, D) is the ruin of a huge, uncompleted temple to the sun. The cell was never raised above its basement courses. The mandap is so large as to be a virtual assembly hall, and it has been suggested that the problem of supporting the weight of the sikhara, which would have been 200 ft high if it were in normal relation with the mandap, was the main reason for the building's incompletion. The sculptured decoration is arranged to form horizontal bands running round the mass of the building (as in the Bhuvaneshwar temples), but all on a proportionately larger scale.

The **Kandarya Mahadev Temple, Khajuraho,** (*c.* 1000) (p. 1190D), is typical of a large group of temples in Central India. There is a series of mandaps leading to the garbha-griha, but the whole is grouped on one, firmly defined, base. This, together with the strong horizontals of both sculptured and architectural details, and the carefully considered relationship of the ascending sikhara roof, produce a satisfying unity in the whole mass. The verticals are dominant, but the skilful counterpoint of horizontals prevents monotony. The sides of the main sikhara are enriched by miniature reflections of the whole spire: a common feature in Dravidian temples. There are nearly a thousand figures on the temple, half life-size, and all of a uniformly high artistic standard.

The **Sas Bahu Temple, Gwalior,** (1093) (p. 1189A), belongs to the same group as the temples at Khajuraho. Like the Black Pagoda, it comprises only the mandap, the garbha-griha having vanished. Although more complex in detail than the Orissa temples, the same feeling of horizontality (to contrast with the vertical sikhara) is present, and the same low-pitched pyramidal roof. The canopied balconies found at Khajuraho (p. 1190D) are here developed into features of major importance.

Other temples of this type are the **Jagannath Temple, Puri** (1174), and those at **Pattadakal** (700) near the west coast; **Chandravati** (ninth century) in Rajasthan; **Baroli,** (ninth century) (p. 1190C); and **Udaipur,** Rajasthan (eleventh century).

The **Golden Temple of the Sikhs, Amritsar,** (1766) is very strongly influenced by Mogul buildings: it consists of a hall to hold congregations at the reading of the sacred books, standing in an artificial lake surrounded by older ancillary buildings.

The **Birla Temple, New Delhi** (1938–) is an attempt to translate traditional forms into contemporary idioms in reinforced concrete.

There are many palaces, architecturally the most important being in Rajasthan, dating from the fifteenth century onwards. These were largely influenced by the Mogul palaces at Agra, Delhi, and Lahore. The city of **Jaipur** was laid out in the eighteenth century when the ruler moved his seat from the ancient fortress of Amber, and is a charming composition of rose-pink stucco-faced buildings laid out in an orderly fashion around the ruler's palace. There are two towers at **Chitor,** also in Rajasthan, commemorating victorious battles there. These, in their stellate plans, perhaps owe something to the much older towers at Ghazni in Afghanistan, but the top storey is a purely Hindu composition of projecting balconies and flat pyramidal roofs, reminiscent (in miniature) of the Sas Bahu Temple at Gwalior.

(b) *Central Indian* (A.D. 1000–1300).

The **Temple, Amber** (1000–1200) (p. 1186C) illustrates the difficulty of making stylistic divisions of Hindu architecture; for although the building belongs in type to those of Central India, it is situated in Rajasthan and surrounded by later secular buildings of the type mentioned in the previous section (a). The mandap (perhaps added in the sixteenth century) might, in fact, be mistaken for a Mogul pavilion. The sikhara, however, has the elaborate stellate plan, small finial, and elaboration of architectural (as distinct from sculptural) decoration typical of examples such as Hallabid in Mysore.

The **Hoysaleswara Temple, Hallabid** (1141–1182) (p. 1193A) consists of unfinished twin temples standing side by side on a terrace 5 ft high, with detached, pillared porches. The walls are covered with friezes of extremely elaborate carving, 700 ft long, of elephants, lions, horsemen, geese, and scenes of the conquest of Ceylon. The window openings are filled with elaborately pierced marble slabs.

The **Great Temple, Bellur** (1117) (pp. 1189B, 1194J), has the typical star-shaped garbha-griha and an elaborately pillared mandap, all covered with highly ornate carvings.

The **Temple, Somnathpur** (1268), like that at Hallabid, has more than one shrine: in this case there are three, radiating from a central hall. The sikharas have not the emphatic vertical lines of the Northern temples, and the horizontal bands of carving are more marked. On the other hand, the domical top storey, found in Dravidian types, is absent.

The carved detail of all these temples, particularly of those at Hallabid and Somnathpur has more affinity to the richness of Singhalese work than to the more restrained 'classicism' of Northern sculpture.

(c) *South Indian* (Dravidian) (A.D. 625–1750).

At **Mamallapuram,** near Madras, a series of huge granite rocks was carved into small temples or 'Raths' between 625–674. They are reproductions in solid rock of vanished prototypes; although so early, they contain all the fundamentals of the fully developed Dravidian type, including the domed (stupa-shaped) crowning storey to the sikhara. There is also a chaitya-type roof, and a pyramidal thatch-like roof on a square base; all these are cut in the rocks.

The rock-cut **Temple, Ellora** (750–950) (p. 1185A), stands free within a huge artificial basin in the mountain side, 290 ft long and 150 ft wide. The whole temple stands on a podium 25 ft high to raise it above the basin floor. All the familiar elements are present: the garbha-griha, the mandap, and a detached shrine in front of the latter for the Siva bull-image. The mandap is larger than those in

A. The Sas Bahu Temple in the Fort, Gwalior (1093). See p. 1187

B. Great Temple, Bellur, from E. (1117). See p. 1188

A. The Gopuram, Madura (1623). See p. 1191

B. Old Temple, Tarputry: portion of entrance (17th cent.). See p. 1180

C. Column and temples, Baroli (9th cent.). See p. 1187

D. Kandarya Mahadev Temple, Khajuraho (c. 1000). See p. 1187

Northern temples, and indicates what was to follow later at Madura. The pillars are typically Dravidian, seen in their latest form in the rock-cut temples on **Elephanta** island in Bombay harbour (ninth century) (p. 1185B). The heavy, curved cornice is also typical of this class, and re-appears for a thousand years.

The **Temple, Conjeeveram,** Vellore, is early eighth century. The garbha-griha is enclosed with a courtyard wall containing gateways crowned with hull-shaped structures; these are a clear forecast of the great eighteenth-century gopurams at Madura and elsewhere. The form of the sikharas is based on that of the largest Rath at Mamallapuram.

The **Great Temple, Tanjore,** (1000) (p. 1193B), is 180 ft long, and the sikhara of thirteen storeys is 190 ft high. The form of the crowning member of the tower, a single stone weighing 80 tons, is based on the Buddhist stupa. The basic forms are used repeatedly in the decoration of the tower: this, and the very beautiful proportions, produce a feeling of great repose.

The later temples, such as those at **Madura** (1623) (p. 1190A), **Srirangam** (seventeenth century) (p. 1194F), and **Tinnevelly,** in spite of their apparent complexity, preserve the simple fundamentals of the traditional plan. But the garbha-griha and its sikhara are dwarfed by the successive giant gopurams (there are fifteen of these gateway towers at Srirangam), and the small mandap has developed into a series of huge halls, reminiscent of Egyptian hypostyle halls, containing forests of columns; at Madura, there are over 2,000 of them.

COMPARATIVE ANALYSIS

PLANS

Buddhist. Rock-cut 'chaityas', based on vanished prototypes, consist of apsidal-ended assembly halls. Free-standing columns down each side and round the apse form an aisle or ambulatory. The entrance, and lighting, is from the end opposite to the apse, which is occupied by a domical mound or 'stupa'. 'Viharas' (monasteries) consist of a quadrangle surrounded by a verandah on to which simple square cells open. Adjacent to this 'cloister' was the courtyard containing the main stupa, which was usually crowded with smaller votive stupas. Communal rooms, like dining halls and kitchens, adjoined the cloister as the site allowed. Major stupas were surrounded by a raised processional path, enclosed by a stone railing (pp. 1182A, 1194E), containing four gates (p. 1194A) at the cardinal points. These, with the stupa itself, symbolized the cosmos (p. 1182A).

Jain. The central shrine, covered by a dome or spire, is introduced by a pillared portico, usually in the form of an octagon set within a square (p. 1194B). There are thus twelve pillars supporting the roof, which is formed of successively diminishing squares, laid diagonally to each other. Although Jain temples are seldom simple units (cf. Ranpur, p. 1183), the most elaborate examples are but a multiplication of the basic form.

Hindu. The small, dark, shrine, and the more open porch which introduces it, are the basic elements, to which may be added an enclosure with gateways. The shrine is crowned with a spire, and the portico with a lower roof. These elements are seen at their simplest at Kanarak (p. 1194D) or Baroli (p. 1190C). In their most elaborate form, they are found at Srirangam and Madura (p. 1190A). Tanks for ritual ablution are the only fresh features in the latter. Variations of the simple plan are such as those at Brindaban (p. 1194G) where accommodation was necessary for crowds of pilgrims, and at Bellur (p. 1194J) where the mandap has become a theatre for ritual dances.

WALLS

Buddhist walls in the north-west of Pakistan are built of stone blocks, dressed to a fair face on the outside surfaces, but not squared along the sides. The interstices are filled with much smaller fragments of stone, firmly wedging the large blocks. All appear to have been laid dry, and were probably originally thickly rendered with lime stucco.

Hindu and *Jain* walls are of simpler ashlar masonry, often laid without mortar. There is a general tendency to cover walls externally with a texture of sculptured ornament. Walls are often thicker than structurally necessary; either because of an intention to build for eternity, or from a lack of instinct for the techniques of masonry buildings.

OPENINGS

Buddhist. The gateways of the Sanchi stupa (pp. 1182A, 1194A), are peculiar to this style. The horseshoe arch became adopted in later Hindu buildings, but it probably derived from the shape of the gable wall of the chaitya hall (p. 1181B). It was never built as a true arch, and would appear to derive from wooden prototypes. When used as the light source for the chaitya, the opening was screened by a wooden trellis to filter the sunlight (this has disappeared from the façade at Ajanta). In the north-west, and in Kashmir, openings were either square-headed or filled with trefoil or ogival arch forms. These latter, however, were formed by corbelling and not with voussoirs.

Jain. Openings are normally square-headed. In pillared porches, stone architraves rest on bracket capitals; the square openings were often modified by the insertion of sloping struts, producing a triangular head to the openings (pp. 1181B, 1194B). These struts evidently derive from a timber form, and appear in a few Muslim buildings of the Emperor Akbar's reign (cf. p. 1242) as a deliberate eccentricity. An extension of the bracket capital is often applied to wall openings, lintels being supported by brackets built out into horizontal courses. This feature also appears in buildings of Akbar's period.

Hindu. Square-headed openings are usual, but they are often modified (as in Jain openings) by the introduction of corbelled brackets at the corners to reduce the span of the lintel. Buildings of the Central Indian type have pierced window slabs, as at Bellur (p. 1189B) and Hallabid (p. 1193A). These pierced slabs are distinctive of this type, though somewhat reminiscent of Muslim treatment.

ROOFS

Buddhist. Although no structural roof of the period survives, the rock-cut chaityas and raths at Mamallapuram, as well as paintings at Ajanta and the descriptions of Chinese pilgrims, clearly show that roof structures were of wood, covered normally with thatch. In Kashmir, there are a few surviving examples of steeply-pitched pyramidal roofs of stone, on square buildings, but it seems likely that these were masonry reproductions of wooden originals: a very similar type of wooden structure may still be found in temples in the remoter parts of the Kangra Valley in the Himalayas.

Jain. The shrine was covered by flat domes (p. 1184A) or by what was virtually a Hindu sikhara. In either case, the construction was of successively diminishing courses of stone. In the case of the flat dome, these courses were either laid diagonally each to the next (p. 1194B), or, in the larger examples, in circular courses laid horizontally and gradually diminishing in diameter (cf. the Treasury of Atreus,

A. The Hoysaleswara Temple, Hallabid: doorway (1141–1182). See p. 1188

B. The Great Temple, Tanjore (1000). See p. 1191

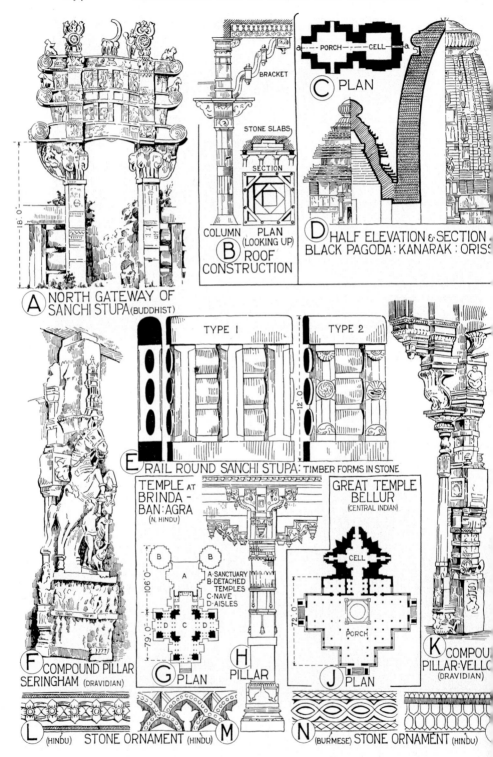

A NORTH GATEWAY OF SANCHI STUPA (BUDDHIST)

B COLUMN PLAN (LOOKING UP) ROOF CONSTRUCTION

BRACKET

STONE SLABS

SECTION

C PLAN

PORCH — CELL

D HALF ELEVATION & SECTION BLACK PAGODA : KANARAK : ORISS

E RAIL ROUND SANCHI STUPA : TIMBER FORMS IN STONE

TYPE 1

TYPE 2

F COMPOUND PILLAR SERINGHAM (DRAVIDIAN)

TEMPLE AT BRINDA-BAN : AGRA (N. HINDU)

A · SANCTUARY
B · DETACHED TEMPLES
C · NAVE
D · AISLES

G PLAN

H PILLAR

GREAT TEMPLE BELLUR (CENTRAL INDIAN)

CELL

PORCH

J PLAN

K COMPOU PILLAR : VELLO (DRAVIDIAN)

L (HINDU) STONE ORNAMENT (HINDU) M

N (BURMESE) STONE ORNAMENT (HINDU)

Mycenae, p. 101). The concentric rings are elaborately carved, and the single cap stone at the apex of the dome is often developed as a pendant.

Hindu. Roofs are either steeply-tapering sikharas formed of horizontal courses of stone (p. 1190D), or flatter pyramidal coverings to the mandap. In the latter case, the span is often reduced either by the introduction of wide-spreading brackets above the column capital, or by successive corbels as in Jain buildings. The vault never seems to have been used at any period, however large the building, except in an isolated and late case at Agra, which was under the direct influence of the many Mogul buildings near-by.

COLUMNS

Buddhist. Buddhist columns are of two types, those based on Persepolitan models (such as the laths), and those derived from Graeco-Roman origins. The former have circular or octagonal shafts (p. 1186A) with bell-shaped capitals: these carry animal supporters, either for the roof or (as in the case of laths) for the symbol of the law. The bases shaped like inverted vases seem to be an indigenous development; it has been suggested that they derive from stone or earthenware sockets to protect the wooden columns from the attacks of water and insects. The Graeco-Roman type may be rectangular in plan (as a pilaster), fluted, and crowned with Corinthian or Composite type capitals (cf. pp. 191, 224G). More rarely, this type may be circular, unfluted, and with an Ionic cap (cf. p. 160C, D), as at Jhaulian, Taxila.

Jain. Columns are much used, and very elaborately decorated. As at Mount Abu, there may be prominent corbels below the capital to support the struts, and the capital itself may carry corbels to support the roof beams, thus producing an effect of superimposed capitals. In neither Jain nor Hindu columns is there any standardization of 'Orders' as in Greek or Roman work.

Hindu. The column at Baroli (p. 1190C) shows many characteristics of the Hindu column; the deeply cut bell-form capital (cf. Elephanta, p. 1185B), the garland decoration below the capital, the chain-and-bell ornament modulating the transition from the circular to polygonal shaft section, the four apsuras (female divinities) below, and finally the heavy base with its deep-cut mouldings. As already pointed out, the typical Hindu column does not exist, but this is a good example of an often-found type. In Dravidian temples, the heavy cushion capital often appears, (p. 1185A). In later periods decoration becomes so lavish that the column loses its identity as a supporting member (p. 1194F, K), and assumes the character of free-standing sculpture (cf. Greek caryatids, p. 136).

MOULDINGS

In all three styles, mouldings have a bulbous character, often heavily undercut. The height and brightness of the sun produce strong shadow lines, and any subtlety of moulding would be lost. In Buddhist Graeco-Bactrian mouldings, in particular, the lack of refinement is noticeable when compared with their Greek or Roman originals. A moulding made by overlapping rectangular slabs is often used. In other cases, a semicircular openwork moulding, like basketwork, and also the torus, are found. The double convex shape, into which the cross-pieces of Buddhist railings are cut, forms horizontal bands of light and shade, taking the place of mouldings (p. 1194E).

ORNAMENT

In marked contrast to Hindu and Jain ornament, Buddhist ornament is restrained both in character and extent, although in later periods and outlying places (such as Ceylon, Indo-China and Java) it became almost Hindu in its exuberance. In the Bactrian work of the north-west, familiar Hellenistic motives (such as garlands carried by cupids, gryphons, and acanthus ornaments) are combined with more exotic ones, like the double-headed eagle, elephants, and flying divinities. In the Central Indian monuments (e.g. Sanchi, and Ajanta) the indigenous love of ornament asserts itself more strongly: the female figure in its most voluptuous form is often used, with an apparent disregard for Buddhist rules of asceticism. A female holding the bough of a tree in an upraised hand, which becomes a familiar figure in later periods, first appears in Buddhist work: the origins of the motive are mysterious, and have been attributed severally to Alexandrian Egypt, and to Scythian Central Asia. Painted wall decoration was widely used, and ranged from purely architectural forms to the very elaborate and beautiful 'genre' paintings on the cave walls at Ajanta, which provide invaluable social and architectural records of the period. Jain and Hindu ornament, in contrast on the one hand to the severely classical restraint of the Buddhist north-west, and on the other to the highly-stylized decoration of the Muslims (p. 1249), is immensely exuberant, and based on an appreciation of human and animal forms in their most sensual manifestations. At its best, this sculpture is highly emotive and very beautiful; but it too easily descends, first into sheer virtuosity, and thence into mechanical repetition. Much of the highly elaborate Jain sculpture is an example of this. In the earlier, and finest, examples (e.g. Hallabid) the sculptured ornament, although keeping its vitality and interest, is perfectly related to the buildings it adorns. But this is rare, and more often the building is little more than a support for a completely dominant cloak of decoration.

REFERENCE BOOKS

ACHARYA, P. K. *A Dictionary of Indian Architecture*. London, 1927.

BROWN, P. *Indian Architecture, Buddhist and Hindu*. Bombay, 1942.

Cambridge History of India. 6 vols., 1922.

CODRINGTON, K. DE B. *Ancient India*. London, 1926.

COHN, W. *Indische Plastik*. Berlin, 1923.

COOMARASWAMY, A. K. *History of Indian and Indonesian Art*. New York, 1927.

CUNNINGHAM, SIR A. *Archaeological Survey of India*, 23 vols. (2 vols. Cunningham only, 1762–5). Simla and Calcutta, 1871–87.

DE FOREST, L. *Indian Domestic Architecture*. Boston, 1885.

DEY, MUKUL. *My Pilgrimages to Ajanta and Bagh*. London, 1925.

FERGUSSON, J. *Picturesque Illustrations of the Ancient Architecture of Hindostan*. London, 1848.

—. *Illustrations of the Rock-cut Temples of India*. London, 1845.

—. *Architecture of Ahmedabad*. London, 1866.

—. *History of Indian and Eastern Architecture*. 2 vols., revised by Jas. Burgess and R. Phene Spiers. London, 1910.

GANGOLY, O. C. *Indian Architecture*. 2nd ed. Calcutta, 1946.

HAVELL, E. B. *The Ancient and Mediaeval Architecture of India*. London, 1915.

KRAMRISCH, S. *The Hindu Temple*. Bombay, 1948.

LA ROCHE. *Indische Baukunst*. 6 vols. Berlin, 1921–2.

LE BON, G. *Les Monuments de l'Inde*. Paris, 1893.

LE MAY, R. *Buddhist Art in Siam*. London, 1938.

Marg, Bombay. Articles by various writers from 1947 onwards.

MARSHALL, SIR J. *Taxila*. 3 vols. Cambridge, 1951.

MORELAND, W. H., and CHATTERJEE, SIR A. C. *A Short History of the Indian People*. London, 1936.

RICHARDSON, A. E., and CORFIATO, H. *The Art of Architecture*. Revised ed., London, 1946.

ROWLAND, B. *The Art and Architecture of India: Buddhist, Hindu, Jain*. Pelican History of Art, 1953.

SMITH, V. A. *A History of Fine Art in India and Ceylon*. 2nd ed. revised by K. de B. Codrington. Oxford, 1930.

WHEELER, SIR M. *Rome Beyond the Imperial Frontiers*. London, 1954.

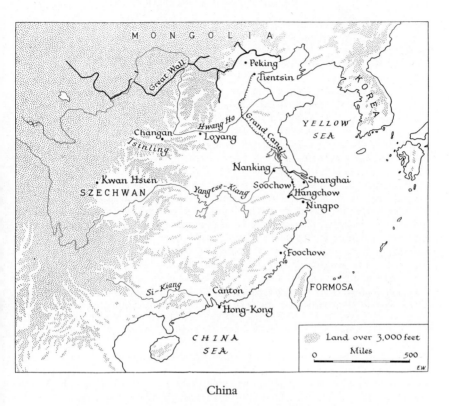

China

XXXI. CHINESE ARCHITECTURE

(Third century B.C. to present day)

INFLUENCES

GEOGRAPHICAL. The Republic of China, comprising twenty-two provinces and the three autonomous regions of Tibet, Inner Mongolia, and Sinkiang-Uigur, covers an area larger than the whole of Europe and equal to nearly one-thirteenth of the total land area of the world. The great bulk of transport in South China is still carried on inland waterways as it has been for centuries, including the great rivers Yangtze and Si Kiang, and their tributaries supplemented by canals; the Grand Canal from Tientsin to Hangchow, about 600 miles long, at one time a dominant waterway, has deteriorated in recent years. Wheeled transport supersedes water transport north of the Tsinling Mountains, and has done so ever since the development of the 'Silk Road' from Changan 1,500 miles to Balkh in Afghanistan at the time of Pan Ch'ao (A.D. 32–102). A programme of railway construction was commenced in the twentieth century and continued in the 1930's with the construction of great trunk lines in the north, while in July 1956 the great Paochi-Chengtu railway, 420 miles long, was completed. The country is mountainous, with extensive fertile valleys in the middle and south-east, and great plains in the north. There are many excellent harbours, which have promoted the development of Western influence in China, particularly during the past two hundred years.

GEOLOGICAL. Coal is widely distributed, but the country is deficient in iron and petroleum; in the south tin, copper, zinc, antimony, tungsten, manganese, and mercury are abundant. The soil in the north is chiefly loess and alluvium with a marked absence of trees; further south on the west of the Yangtze gorges there are many pine trees, chestnuts and maples. Red sandstone is characteristic of Szechwan, where the dominant trees are nanmu, paulownia, catalpa, and broussonetia, the paper mulberry tree. South of the Tsinling the bamboo tree is cultivated extensively. Sedimentary rocks exist in South West China on the high plateau, and jungle vegetation is prolific in the valleys. The mulberry tree, which has no direct influence on architecture as a structural timber, created the ancient and prosperous silk industry which initiated Chinese contacts with the Western World at the time the Roman Empire was at its height. Timber is the principal material in Chinese architecture; bamboo, pine, and the Persea nanmu, the tallest and straightest of all the trees in China; it was floated down the Yangtze River in trunks to serve as columns in palaces and temples in Peking. Bricks from the clay of the river plains were also used, as well as limestone and sandstone; but brick and stone were never considered as important as timber. A standard work on architecture, *Ying Tsao Fa Shih* (*The Method of Architecture*) published by Imperial order in the year A.D. 1103 refers only to stonework as a material fit for use in thresholds, stairs, balusters, engineering works, etc., and disregards brick altogether. Roofs were covered with clay tiles, coloured and glazed with symbolic colours, black, red, azure, white and yellow.

CLIMATE. The mountain ranges leave the north unprotected from the cold strong winter winds from Mongolia, which, sweeping down from Asia produce severe winters with an average January temperature in Peking of 23·5° F. Further south it is warmer, and the winter temperature is equivalent to an English summer. Because the country extends from latitude 45° to latitude 20° north of the equator, it experiences a range of climate varying from extreme cold to almost tropical. The north-east and south-westerly monsoons sweep across the country in summer and winter, yielding the heaviest rainfall in the summer, averaging from 40 to 60 ins per year. These climatic conditions are partly responsible for the characteristic Chinese roof with its accentuated curved eaves. Heating of buildings was often provided by charcoal burners without flues or fire-places; beds were heated with burning charcoal.

RELIGIOUS. The main religious and ethical influences in China have been Confucianism (Confucius, 551–479 B.C.), Taoism, and Buddhism. Confucianism was a code of social conduct and a philosophy of life; it was not a religion as we understand it; it laid stress on the family and ancestor worship; it was a doctrine of the 'Middle Way'. Taoism attempted to transcend Confucianism and was founded at about the same time, probably by Lao Tzŭ in the fourth to the third century B.C. It encompassed mysticism and superstition and was readily combined with Buddhism when that religion spread to China from India in the second century A.D. by way of the three trade routes from India. By the first century A.D., Buddhist monks and laymen were living in China, and a Buddhist temple was built at Anhui in A.D. 190. It developed rapidly after the downfall of the Han (A.D. 221) and exerted a great influence on architectural expression. The combination of Confucianism, Taoism, and Buddhism has produced conceptions of the universe and beliefs about the future closely allied with superstition, astrology and necromancy which have controlled the planning of society and of cities as well as of the design of buildings. A pseudo-science, 'fêng shui', evolved, which was based on a belief that forces exist in every locality which act on all types of buildings, towns and cities, for good or ill, and sites were chosen or adapted accordingly. With the impact of the West, starting with the Jesuit mission in 1582, Christian influence gradually developed and is a potent factor in China today. Confucianism has gradually disintegrated and ancestor worship has declined.

SOCIAL. As Chinese archaeology is still in its infancy there is very little positive evidence about prehistoric China, but it is certain that there existed a culture between the Stone and the Bronze Age. Researches into records of solar eclipses and other astronomical phenomena recorded by the Chinese, indicate dates ranging from 3253 B.C. to 2127 B.C. as the earliest authentic historical records, but their complicated system of chronology combined with confused and scanty records makes it difficult to establish accurate dates until about 720 B.C. Before that time dynastic history is legendary and includes the Emperor Fu-hsi (2852 B.C.) who, it is claimed, evolved social order out of chaos. Fu-hsi was followed by Shên Nung, who introduced agricultural implements and discovered medicine. He was succeeded by Huang Ti, the Yellow Emperor, who consolidated the Empire, enlarged its boundaries, and introduced extensive reform and social improvements. Of a succession of emperors that followed, the most outstanding was the great Yao who, with his successor Shun, stands at the dawn of Chinese history as a model of all wisdom and sovereign virtue. The dynasties Hsia (2205–1766 B.C.), Shang or Yin (1766–1122 B.C.) followed, until the Chou (1122 B.C.) and first Emperor Wu Wang, started an era of great expansion of culture and territory; but expansion brought disintegration; the power of central government declined and feudalism flourished, resulting in the break-down of the Empire into a number of warring states similar in many respects to Europe in the Middle Ages. This deterioration resulted in the emergence of thinkers and the expansion of thought and schools of philosophy. Confucius sought to bring a new order by his code of ethics and education, with emphasis on the sanctity of the family and filial piety. Contemporary with Confucius was Lao Tzǔ, reputed founder of Taoism, who offered a doctrine of universal love as his solution to social disorder. There were other philosophers of vigorous thought, but the Chou dynasty, which meantime had survived in an effete form and with much-shrunken dominions, continued to decline until it disappeared and was replaced by the Ch'in (255–206 B.C.), the fourth emperor of which, Shih Huang Ti, styled himself the First Emperor, and founded a new and homogeneous empire on the ruins of the old feudal system. He divided the Empire into thirty-six provinces, and built a vast palace by forced labour at Hsien Yang; he also constructed by forced and convict labour fortifications including part of the Great Wall. He suppressed opposition and criticism by destroying records of all opposing ideas and doctrines, and imposed his will by harsh discipline. He built roads, extended canals, and laid the foundations of a great Empire, which found full expression in the succeeding dynasty, the Han (206 B.C.–A.D. 220) which so developed the economic and cultural state of the Empire that at the time of the Emperor Kuang Wu Ti, it vied with the Roman Empire of Hadrian as the most powerful state on the face of the earth. During this time trade routes were developed and commerce in silk, cloth, furs, rhubarb, and cinnamon was carried on extensively with the Roman Empire, Persia, India and other Asiatic countries. There was an exchange of ideas, an influx of foreign culture, and the introduction of Buddhism. Confucianism and Taoism were revived, and the capital was moved first to Changan and thence to Loyang. But the dynasty weakened and the Han was followed by three and a half centuries of disunion, until the Empire was reunited in the T'ang (A.D. 618–907) when, under the leadership of the second

Emperor T'ai Tsung, it became more powerful than before. Foreign traders came by land and sea, and Chinese goods were on sale in Baghdad; Nestorian Christians, Jews, Muslims, and Persians were seen in the streets of Canton. But the Chinese were forbidden by Imperial rescript from going abroad, and their architecture consequently suffered little influence from the expansion of trade. Buddhism reached its peak and stimulated the arts and influenced architectural form; painting probably reached the highest point in Chinese history with an emphasis on calligraphy and the use of the brush. Printing was introduced; books printed in 868 have been found in the grottoes of Tun-huang, and the first book on architecture was issued in 1103. The Sung dynasty followed the T'ang, with capitals at K'aifêng and Hangchow; from 960–1279 the cultural developments of the T'ang were maintained, but the dynasty succumbed to the military superiority of Kublai the Mongol, who founded the Yüan (Mongol) dynasty which flourished until A.D. 1368. The Grand Canal was completed, and Chinese influence spread further west as a result of the exploration of Marco Polo. With the collapse of the Mongol Empire in 1368 there was an anti-foreign wave, and with the pre-eminently Chinese dynasty of the Ming (1368–1644) foreign trade and influence deteriorated. The first Ming Emperor established his capital at Nanking (southern capital), and his successor Yung Lo founded the northern capital Peking, and laid out the city as one of the outstanding architectural conceptions of the world. The ban on foreigners was lifted, and penetration by Jesuit missionaries initiated a subsequent invasion of Western culture and ideas which eventually transformed the social structure of the Empire. Manchus overthrew the Ming, and established the Ch'ing dynasty in 1644, and this gave way to the Republic in 1912. The outstanding feature of the Ch'ing is the increasing Western influence and the gradual but insistent infiltration of Western traders. To the Chinese the Westerners were barbarians, and their ideas and influence were strongly resisted; but since the formation of the Republic and the establishment of a different system of education largely influenced by America, the old culture and philosophies have given way to Western methods and industrialization has become firmly established. The construction of roads, railways, schools, factories, housing, and welfare buildings now occupies the major part of the Chinese building programme, constructed by Western methods and design. This transformation has been accelerated by the People's Republic of China, so that whereas in Sinkiang in 1949 there were 14 factories with less than 4,000 workers, there were 400 factories and more than 58,000 workers in 1957, and this is typical of the whole of China.

HISTORICAL. The early history of China is indistinguishable from the legends of the Emperors, who were identified with various progressive steps in civilization. The Chou dynasty is said to have waged war in the tenth century B.C. against the barbarians from the north. During the Ch'in dynasty (255–206 B.C.) Shih Huang Ti, the 'First Emperor' (246–210 B.C.) built part of the Great Wall against barbarian invasions. The earlier (Western) Han dynasty (206 B.C.–A.D. 25) sent Chinese ambassadors to Western Asia, discovered India and made Eastern Turkestan a Chinese colony. In the time of the Later (Eastern) Han dynasty (A.D. 25–220), Emperor Ming Ti extended the Empire and Buddhism was introduced from India. During the reign of Ssŭ Ma-Yen of the Tsin dynasty (A.D. 265–420) the Emperor Diocletian sent ambassadors to China (A.D. 284). T'ai-Tsung (A.D. 627–649) of the T'ang dynasty (A.D. 618–907) purchased the alliance of the Turks, just as the Emperor Justinian had done in A.D. 558, and regained Eastern Persia up to the Caspian Sea. Ambassadors from Persia and Constantinople went on a mission to the Emperor in 645. During the Sung dynasty (960–1280) China was engaged in war with the conquering Mongols, which left her under the Mongol heel for 88 years. Under the Emperor Shih Tsu (Kublai) (1280–94) of the Mongol or Yüan dynasty (1280–1368), China reached her greatest extent and with the exception of Hindustan, Arabia, and Western Asia, all the Mongol princes as far as the Dnieper were her tributaries. Hung-Wu, the first Emperor of the Ming dynasty (1368–1644), conquered the Mongols and established his capital at Nanking, but his successor removed it to Peking, the present capital, in 1403. The Ch'ing (Manchu) dynasty, which lasted from 1644 until the establishment of the Republic (1912), introduced the shaved head and pigtail as emblems of Tartar sovereignty. K'ang Hsi (1661–1721) added Tibet to the Empire and published the Dictionary of the Chinese language. Ch'ien Lung (1735–95) invaded Burma, Cochin-China, and Nepal, and crushed the Muslim rebellion. He received Lord Macartney as first ambassador of George III. In 1840 war was declared by England against China, and this marks the beginning of active European intervention. In 1873 foreign ministers obtained the right of audience with the Emperor, and in 1912 the Chinese Republic adopted the calendar of Western Europe. A period of internal strife and disunity followed and the interference of foreign powers accelerated China's disintegration. China joined the Allies in the First World War, but took little part in the conflict. In 1937 a life and death struggle opened with Japan, and in 1941 China declared war with Japan and became a member of the allied nations in the Second World War. In 1949 the Nationalist government collapsed, the Communists seized control, and the People's Republic of China was proclaimed. The Nationalists, evacuating to Formosa under Chiang Kai-shek, still sought to recover the support and sympathy of the Chinese on the mainland, but with little or no success.

ARCHITECTURAL CHARACTER

The architecture of China is a faithful index of her civilization, for both were practically stationary for many centuries. Of the fine arts as understood in the West, only painting was recognized by the Chinese; sculpture, architecture, and the crafts were regarded as artisan work. The art was poetic rather than material; the Chinese revelled in the beauty of nature and had little feeling for architectural design, which they held subservient to human needs. Chinese architecture, though subject to Buddhist and Muslim influence, held its own as an indigenous style from the early centuries until the present day; there has been no distinction between sacred and secular architecture, and temples, tombs, public buildings, and private houses, whether great or small, all follow the same plan.

The roof was the chief feature, supported on timber uprights and independent of the walls, which were often as useless for support as were the large traceried windows of the European Gothic style. The great Temple of Heaven at Peking was dignified by a triple roof of blue tiles, and this use of bright colours, applied in the form of glazed tiles and porcelain, is a characteristic of Chinese buildings; the colours were symbolic of Chinese rites. 'Pai-lous' or gateways, of stone and wood, derived from Indian 'toranas', are features of Chinese architecture and, like many others, were only erected by government permission. Towers in stone, square like those in the Great Wall, are of early date, and show influence of Mesopotamia in the use of arch and vault. The pagoda, the most typical Chinese building, is usually octagonal in plan, with thirteen storeys and repeated roofs, highly coloured, and with upturned eaves. The Chinese built chiefly in timber; brick and timber were sometimes combined, and stone was reserved for special structures and parts of buildings. The Chinese had little religious zeal, and therefore few great temples;

no territorial aristocracy and therefore no noble country houses; little pride of living and therefore no town mansions, while their domestic architecture was trammelled by sumptuary laws to mark the social status of the owner.

EXAMPLES

TEMPLES

The **Temple of Heaven, (Ch'i Nien Tien), Peking** (A.D. 1420), circular and triple-roofed, with roofs covered with deep cobalt-blue glazed tiles, dominates the Ch'i Ku T'an or altar of prayer for grain, open to the sky with three tiers of marble steps and balustrades. The temple, facing south, is 99 ft high with the upper roof supported by four gigantic columns, and the lower roofs by twelve columns, all straight trunks of nanmu trees. Originally founded by Ch'ien Lung (A.D. 1420) it was rebuilt correctly in every detail in recent years. To the south is the **Great Altar of Heaven,** the most sacred of all Chinese religious structures, consisting of marble terraces and nine circles of nine marble stones symbolizing Chinese numerical philosophy. There are other single-roofed temples, of which one is 'Hall of Central Peace', and another the **Temple of Agriculture** (p. 1204D). In all these circular buildings there is the characteristic bracket frieze under the widely projecting eaves.

The **Temple of Honan, Canton,** (p. 1204N) is a typical Buddhist temple, enclosed by a wall with gateway, porch, ante-chapel, successive halls, and sanctuary with the idol, and seats for the monks, with a 'dagoba', offices and kitchens beyond.

The **Temple of the Sleeping Buddha, near Peking,** built of brick in two storeys, is unusual in having circular-headed windows in a clear-storey as well as in the ground storey. The columns are faced with glazed bricks, and between them are niches with the statue of Buddha; the roof has an elaborate cresting with finials and flamboyant dragons (p. 1203A).

Most Chinese temples, however, are of the simple T'ing type as exemplified in the **Sacrificial Hall of Yung Lo** (fifteenth century A.D.) near Peking, consisting of a concave roof on uprights, covered with brilliant coloured tiles, yellow at the temple of the earth, red at the temple of the sun, bluish-white at the temple of the moon. There are monastery temples containing the image of the Buddhist triad—just as in England there were monastic churches—surrounded by a wall and approached through the typical 'pai-lou' or gateway. The whole monastic group consists of temple, 'dagoba' or relic shrine, bell-tower, pagoda, library, and dwellings for the monks. There are also ancestral temples such as the Confucian Temple in the Kuo Tzu Chien, Peking, and mosques which resemble the Buddhist temples.

PAGODAS

The pagodas (t'ai), derived from Indian prototypes, are distributed in considerable numbers over the country and form the most important structures in the temple enclosures (pp. 1203B, 1204E). They vary from three to fifteen storeys in height, the number being uneven in every case and very often thirteen, sometimes with staircases to each floor, and were probably originally constructed in timber; those that remain are mostly of brick, the timber structures having perished. Pagodas had formerly a religious significance, but those erected latterly are secular in character and are sometimes monuments to victory; they are often associated with fêng-shui to insure good fortune. They are frequently polygonal in plan and the roof slopes to each storey, and are elaborately ornamented.

The **Pagoda, Sung Yüeh Ssŭ, Honan** (c. A.D. 523), is the oldest pagoda still

A. Temple of the Sleeping Buddha, in the Summer Palace, near Peking. See p. 1202

Typical Chinese pagoda. See p. 1202   c. A typical pai-lou. See p. 1205

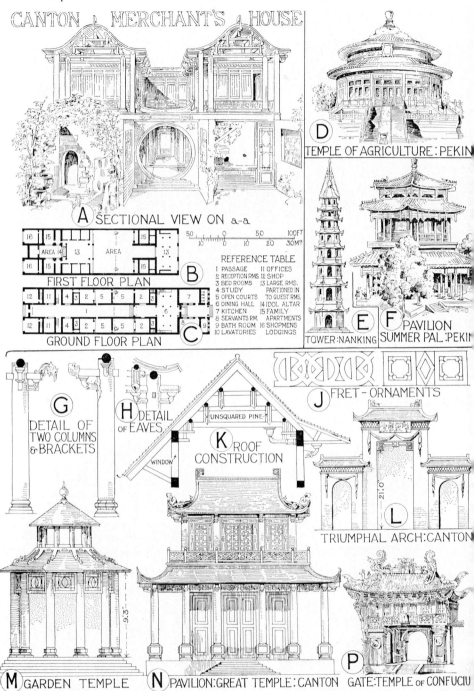

CANTON MERCHANT'S HOUSE

A SECTIONAL VIEW ON a-a

D TEMPLE OF AGRICULTURE : PEKIN

B FIRST FLOOR PLAN

C GROUND FLOOR PLAN

REFERENCE TABLE
1 PASSAGE
2 RECEPTION RMS.
3 BED ROOMS
4 STUDY
5 OPEN COURTS
6 DINING HALL
7 KITCHEN
8 SERVANTS RM.
9 BATH ROOM
10 LAVATORIES
11 OFFICES
12 SHOP
13 LARGE RMS.
　PARTIONED IN
　TO GUEST RMS.
14 IDOL. ALTAR
15 FAMILY
　APARTMENTS
16 SHOPMENS
　LODGINGS

E TOWER : NANKING

F PAVILION SUMMER PAL : PEKIN

G DETAIL OF TWO COLUMNS & BRACKETS

H DETAIL OF EAVES

J FRET - ORNAMENTS

K ROOF CONSTRUCTION
UNSQUARED PINE
WINDOW

L TRIUMPHAL ARCH : CANTON

M GARDEN TEMPLE

N PAVILION : GREAT TEMPLE : CANTON

P GATE : TEMPLE OF CONFUCIU

standing in China; constructed of brick and mud on an octagonal base, it rises to a height of about 90 ft in fifteen blind storeys.

The **Porcelain Pagoda, Yüan Ming Yüan, near Peking,** is a fine example of glazed faience after the style of the famous porcelain pagoda at Nanking (p. 1204E) which was destroyed by the Taiping rebels in A.D. 1854. The whole of the brick walls and projecting roof eaves are clothed in coloured porcelain tiles, glazed in five colours, deep purplish-blue, rich green, yellow, sang de boeuf red, and turquoise-blue, which were intended to suggest the five jewels of Buddhist paradise. Conspicuous amongst many other pagodas are the Pa Li Chuan Pagoda, near Peking (thirteenth century A.D.) of thirteen storeys; the Nan t'a at Fang Shan, Chih-li (eleventh century A.D.) of eleven storeys; the Pei t'a at Fang Shan, Chih-li (eighth century A.D.); the pagoda at Ling Kuang Ssŭ, near Peking (seventh century A.D.) of thirteen storeys, built of brick upon stone foundations; and others at Hangchow, and Foochow, where the White Pagoda of seven storeys dominates the town. There are the Great Pagoda, the Twin Pen Pagodas—reputed to be 1,000 years old—and the Ink Pagoda, 120 ft high, all at Soochow, and others at Shanghai, Ningpo, Nanking and Peking. There is a somewhat lifeless example in Kew Gardens designed by Sir William Chambers, and there are models in the Indian Museum, South Kensington.

PAI-LOUS

The pai-lous of China (p. 1203C) bear a family resemblance to the toranas of India (cf. the Sanchi stupa, p. 1180) and the torii of Japan, and were erected by special authority as memorials to deceased persons of distinction. They were constructed of wood or stone and have one or three openings, formed by posts supporting horizontal rails bearing an inscription and often crowned with bold projecting roofs of symbolical coloured tiles. The pai-lou which spans the avenue leading to the **Temple of the Sleeping Buddha,** near Peking, is a magnificent example with three arches in sculptured marble, separated by vermilion stucco walls with panelled faience enamelled in yellow, green and blue, in the centre of which is the inscribed marble tablet. The all-timber pai-lou at the lake of the Summer Palace, Peking, is a characteristic example of another form of pai-lou which marks the entrance to a sacred or beautiful place; the marble pai-lou at the **Altar of Heaven, Peking,** shows the type of structure which is one of the most salient features of Chinese architectural design, upon which was lavished all possible richness of decoration.

TOMBS

Tombs, though associated with ancestor-worship and therefore sacred, are not of great architectural value because the pai-lous were the real memorial monuments. Tombs are sometimes cone-shaped mounds surrounded by stones, sometimes cut in the rock or designed in the hillside, with a horseshoe back in stone sloping to the front and covered with symbolic carvings, while mythical animals guard the entrance.

The **Tombs of the Ming Dynasty** (A.D. 1368–1644),north of Peking, are entered through triumphal gateways or pai-lous of white marble and along an avenue a mile in length, flanked by thirty-two large monolithic figures (12 ft high) of camels, horses, priests, elephants, lions and griffins. Each of the thirteen tombs consists of an earthen mound, half a mile in circumference, supported by a retaining wall 20 ft high, and they seem to be founded on such monuments as the Sanchi stupa in India (p. 1180).

The **Tomb of Yung-lo, Peking** (A.D. 1425), consists of a tumulus, surrounded by a crested wall with a three-storeyed tower, two entrance gateways, and an ancestral hall of the T'ing type in the entrance court.

PALACES

Imperial palaces and official residences were erected as isolated, one-storeyed pavilions resembling temples in general design, and crowned with the typical roof, but these detached buildings are not imposing as are the large homogeneous palaces of Europe.

The **Imperial Palace, Peking,** situated in the centre of the 'Forbidden City', has three vast halls, all similar in design, of magnificent proportions and resplendent in oriental decoration. The 'Tai Ho Tien' Hall of Highest Peace (A.D. 1602) is the most important, with terraces and open verandahs, and is formed of nave and aisles, parallel to the façade, separated by great columns, with the Imperial dais at the centre. A Pavilion (p. 1204F) of the Summer Palace, Peking, destroyed A.D. 1860, gives an idea of some of the smaller buildings. Within the enclosing wall there were residences for emperor and officers of state, and the groups of buildings were set amidst pleasure gardens, lakes and grottoes on a magnificent scale.

HOUSES

Houses, generally of one storey like the temples, are constructed with timber supports, filled in with brickwork (p. 1201). The building regulations not only govern the dimensions, but also the number of columns, and thus had a marked effect on the plan and arrangement of Chinese houses; for, while the Emperor had his hall of nine bays, a prince was restricted to seven, a mandarin to five and an ordinary citizen to three bays. Roofs are of a steep pitch with boldly projecting eaves and highly ornamented ridges of coloured and glazed tiles, with the angles turned up and finished with grotesque animals or fantastic ornament. The roof-framing in bamboo and other wood is frequently painted red, green or blue. The houses owe much of their character to their environment of gardens planned to suggest a natural landscape, elaborated with fountains, artificial rocks, woodland scenery, lakes, flower-beds, hanging plants, bridges, watercourses, stepping-stones, and garden temples (p. 1204M). Town houses of importance are also made up of a collection of isolated pavilions, surrounded by gardens. There are three principal divisions, viz.: (a) vestibule or porter's lodge on the street; (b) audience chamber and family rooms; (c) kitchen and servants' rooms (p. 1204A, B, C).

BRIDGES

Bridges form conspicuous features in a country of rivers and waterways, and constitute the main architectural characteristic of the Chinese landscape; it has been estimated that there are about twelve bridges per square mile in many parts of the country, and about two and a half million altogether. They are of various types of construction and design, pontoon bridges, wooden truss bridges, stone bridges, arched bridges of brick and stone, cantilever bridges and suspension bridges. Pontoon bridges have been in use since the beginning of recorded history, a well-known example being that at Ningpo. Nearly as old as the pontoon bridge is the wooden truss bridge, and in the densely-forested mountainous districts of the country there are countless examples of this form of construction. In the area around the Yangtze delta, where natural stone is plentiful, bridges built of granite are numerous; the Chinese bridge-builders used this material to its maximum ability, allowing no margin for safety. Stone truss bridges in spans less than 14–16 ft, and 6–10 ft high above the water were the cheapest form of construction for narrow canals. They were also used for wider spans, such as the 'Bridge of 10,000 Ages', Foochow, built A.D. 1323, 1,270 ft long and 14 ft 6 ins wide, with thirty-five intermediate piers and thirty-six spans; the 'Bridge of 10,000 Times Peace', at Tsienchowfu, built during the Sung Dynasty, is 3,780 ft long and 16 ft wide, with forty-seven spans. Normally, however, bridges of great length were arched; the arch is never skew, and the abutments are nearly always vertical; the arch stones are cut to fit each other exactly but are not radiating voussoirs. Mortar was seldom used either in the arch, abutments or foundations. Arches were usually circular, but pointed arches were sometimes used, as in a bridge at Yachowfu, Szechwan. The 'Jewel Belt' bridge, near Soochow, has fifty-three arches, all semicircular; the 'camel-back' bridge at the Summer Palace, Peking, has a pointed arch. In those parts of the country where tree trunks were easily obtainable, cantilever construction was popular; this incorporated stone abutments supporting piled up cantilevered wooden trunks which carried the horizontal roadway. In Western China, the use of bamboo rope encouraged the construction of suspension bridges with granite abutments and wooden intermediate supports with bamboo ropes; at Kwan Hsien there is a bridge of this kind 700 ft long, with its longest span 200 ft by 9 ft wide, which is carried by ten bamboo cables each $6\frac{1}{2}$ ins in diameter. The bamboo ropes have a breaking load of 26,000 lbs. per sq. in. The Yangtze River Bridge (A.D. 1957), is one of the world's largest bridges, of 5,480 ft total length with a clearance above the water level of 59 ft, constructed of concrete piers with a double-decker steel-and-concrete decking. It was commenced in A.D. 1955 and completed twenty-six months later.

THE GREAT WALL OF CHINA

The 'Great Wall' (214 B.C.) (p. 1197), the most famous of ancient Chinese building undertakings, is 1,400 miles long, 20 to 30 ft high, 25 ft thick at the base, sloping to 15 ft at the top. There are square towers at intervals in this immense mileage of masonry which, like Hadrian's Wall in Britain, follows the contours of the country, climbs mountain tops, descends deep gorges, strides across lofty table-lands, and spans wide rivers, like a huge serpent wrought in brick and stone. Recent investigations of the brick arches in the Wall have led to the conclusion that the Wall was originally an earth embankment faced with stone at a later date and that the brick arches in the passages and the watch towers originate from A.D. 1368, when the whole Wall was thoroughly repaired.

MODERN BUILDINGS

Since 1949, a vast number of new buildings have been erected in China; in Peking alone the total floor area of new buildings amounts to over 150 million sq. ft, including commercial buildings, industrial buildings, schools and colleges, hospitals, hotels, cinemas and theatres and housing. These buildings show a complete departure from Chinese tradition and exhibit (with a few exceptions) an unimaginative adaptation of Western Renaissance revival in concrete and stone. The Peking Institute of Iron and Steel Technology, in symmetrical blocks of three and four storeys, flat-roofed, with uniformly distributed windows in unrelieved façades, is typical. The Chinese People's Political Consultative Conference Assembly Hall has an entrance with three huge arched openings, with attached columns on the supporting piers terminating in crude capitals. Blocks of four-storeyed flats are similar to those to be found anywhere in the West, and it is only in a few buildings such as the Asian Students' Sanitorium that any semblance of Chinese individuality can be found.

COMPARATIVE ANALYSIS

PLANS. Buddhist temples resemble those of India, consisting of successive open courts and porticoes with kitchens, refectories, and sleeping cells for the priests. The normal type consists of three lofty pavilions of one storey, with parallel open timber roofs, approached by broad flights of steps, gateways, and bridges. Houses, like temples, face south; the front door opens into a courtyard with rooms on either side and a hall at the end, followed by another and often by a third or women's court with garden beyond; while all windows, as in French fortified châteaux, face inwards.

WALLS. Stone is employed in important edifices, but ordinary building materials are brick and timber. Most Chinese buildings of wood are raised on a stone or brick platform as a protection against damp. Bricks sometimes have a glazed coloured surface and walls are also faced with glazed tiles or majolica. Walls are often constructed hollow, as described by Sir William Chambers, thus saving material and effecting a more equable temperature in the house. The 't'ais' or 'pagodas' are mostly of brick covered with highly-coloured glazed tiles or marble, and vary from three to fifteen storeys, each reduced in height and provided with projecting roof (pp. 1203B, 1204E). The veranda or portico of wooden columns is a special feature of dwelling-houses (p. 1204N).

OPENINGS. Doorways are square-headed, but varied in outline by fretted pendants from the horizontal timbers. 'Pai-lous' are distinctive Chinese gateways (p. 1203C), sometimes as entrances to temples and tombs, sometimes as monuments to the deceased, and sometimes they stand across a street. Their construction is timber in origin, and they consist of two or more upright posts with horizontal frieze, making one, two, or three openings, sometimes surmounted by a series of brackets like those under the temple eaves. Windows are of similar form, suiting the rectangular framing of timber posts or lashing together of bamboos (p. 1210). They are frequently filled in with the lining of the oyster shell, which is as transparent as talc and admits an effective subdued light. Rice paper was also used instead of glass in windows.

ROOFS. The roof is the principal feature of the building, and contrasts strongly with the Greek, Roman, and Renaissance styles, in which there is often an evident endeavour to hide the roof, whereas the Chinese roof-ridges are laden with elaborate ornamental cresting and the up-tilted angles are finished off with fantastic dragons and grotesque ornament. It is considered a sign of dignity to place roofs one over the other, and this system also serves to protect the interior from extremes of heat and cold. The framing of the characteristic T'ing roof with 'I'rimoya' gables is of open timber construction and is supported on wooden posts independent of the enclosing walls (pp. 1203, 1204). Roofs, which are concave in section, are generally covered with enamelled tiles of S shape (pantiles) set in mortar, which is also used to form cover-joints as a protection from the driving winds (p. 1210). The roof-framing consists of a system of trusses in rigid rectangles (not triangles as in Europe) formed of bamboos held together by wooden tenons, and thus the weight of the roof acts vertically and no oblique thrust comes on the walls (p. 1204H, K). The lightness and strength of bamboo were important factors in influencing a system of construction quite different from the framed European roof-truss. The connection between the roof and the pillars which sustain it is often strengthened by brackets, and the soffits are often divided into square or octagonal coffers by means of raised ribs with brass socketings at their intersection.

COLUMNS. Chinese building procedure as applied to columns is peculiar, and is the reverse of that in other countries; for instead of first raising the columns and

framing the superstructure upon them, the Chinese first made the framework of
the roof and that determined the position of the columns, which were often of
nanmu wood, while the rigidity of the framework and roof-beams was relied on to
keep the columns in position on the stone foundations; in short, instead of putting
the roof on the columns, they put the columns under the roof (p. 1204G, M, N). It
was therefore essential that the roof-beams should be tenoned direct at the various
heights into the shaft, without the intervention of a second member or capital,
which was therefore omitted, but the roof-beams were supported by brackets, often
multiplied in number and ornate in character. Chinese columns, whether for
temples, pai-lous, palaces, or houses, are unique, for in all other styles the capital
is one of the most important of architectural features. Columns, whether free-
standing, as in palace halls, or carried up as an integral part of the wall, were without capitals, and were bound direct to the roof-beams of the rectangular-framed
roof which press vertically down on them, and thus columns and roofs are the chief
features of the T'ing type of building, in which the walls are of no constructive
value.

MOULDINGS. In China, where roof and columns are the chief architectural
features, and where building is generally in brick or timber and much of the ornament is in glazed tiles, mouldings play a small part in decoration. In fact, here as
in other styles where wall tiling came in, mouldings went out. They are seen in the
cyma and ovolo of the bronze bases of timber pillars, but as there are no capitals
they do not appear again in the columns; simple mouldings, however, occur in the
compound brackets supporting the roof timbers, which are chiefly treated with
grotesque carving. They are also used in the panelled railing round temple enclosures,
but in the temples and pagodas the chief relief is found in the boldly projecting
uplifted eaves of the superimposed roofs (pp. 1203, 1204).

ORNAMENT (p. 1204). Chinese ornament expresses national characteristics. All
Eastern nations appear to have a natural instinct for colour, and the Chinese are no
exception. Colour schemes form an integral part of Chinese architecture; roofs are
covered with brightly glazed tiles in symbolic colours, while the outstanding ridges
and hips are emphasized with highly coloured dragons, fishes, and grotesque figures
in glazed terra-cotta. Coloured ornament is applied to buildings in the form of
enamelled glazed tiles, painted woodwork, landscape and figure subjects. The
Chinese excel in the minor arts, in silk- and cotton-weaving, in carvings of wood
and ivory, and in porcelain ware. The Chinese national sense for art found its outlet not in architecture, but in painting, of which from early times there were several
great schools. The Chinese were past masters in the use of the brush, with which
they produced a wonderful fineness of line, as is seen in their calligraphy, for which
they used a soft brush instead of a hard stylo. Thus it was that their decoration in
architecture took the form of colour applied to surfaces on which were painted
landscapes, birds, and flowers. The Buddhist religion encouraged their love of
mystery and symbolism, and the great yellow dragon and the tiger were freely
introduced into decorative colour schemes.

REFERENCE BOOKS

ALLOM, T., and WRIGHT, G. N. *The Chinese Empire*. Illustrated. 2 vols., 1858–9.
BOERSCHMANN, E. *Die Baukunst und religiöse Kultur der Chinesen*. Berlin, 1911.
—. *Chinesische Architektur*. 2 vols., Berlin, 1926.
BUSHELL, STEPHEN W. *Chinese Art*. London, 1924.
CHAMBERS, SIR W. *Designs of Chinese Buildings*. London, 1757.
CHI, TSUI. *A Short History of Chinese Civilisation*. London, 1942.
DOUGLAS, R. K. *Society in China*. London, 1894.

EDKINS, J. *Chinese Architecture*. Shanghai, 1890.
FUGL-MEYER, H. *Chinese Bridges*. Shanghai, 1937.
GEIL, W. E. *Eighteen Capitals of China*. London, 1911.
GRATTAN, F. M. *Notes upon the Architecture of China*. London, 1894.
HILDEBRAND, H. *Der Tempel Ta-chüeh-sy bei Peking*. Berlin, 1897.
JONES, O. *Examples of Chinese Ornament*. London, 1867.
LATOURETTE, K. S. *The Chinese Civilisation*. New York, 1941.
MÜNSTERBERG, O. *Chinesische Kunst-geschichte*. 2 vols., Esslingen, 1910–12.
PALÉOLOGUE, M. *L'Art chinois*. Paris, 1887.
SIRÉN, O. *The Imperial Palaces of Peking*. 3 vols., Paris, 1926.
—. *The Walls and Gates of Peking*. London, 1924.
TOKIWA, D., and SEKINO, T. *Buddhist Monuments in China*. Tokyo, 1930.

Temple at Canton. See p. 1208 (under ROOFS)

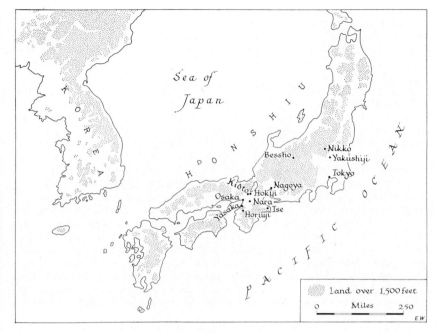

Japan

XXXII. JAPANESE ARCHITECTURE

(Sixth century A.D. to present day)

INFLUENCES

GEOGRAPHICAL. Japan, with its principal island, Honshiu, and attendant islands to north and south, lies off the eastern coast of Asia, from which it is separated by the Sea of Japan. The eastern shores of Japan are bounded by the Pacific Ocean. Geographically Japan has many points of resemblance to Great Britain; both lie opposite populous continents with indented coast-lines providing excellent harbours; both are at the head of important trade routes and across international lines of communication. Japan and Great Britain also lie in the path of warm ocean currents, which tend to produce equable temperatures.

GEOLOGICAL. The prevalence of earthquakes in Japan has had a profound effect upon building development. Practically the whole of Japan is rugged hill country, and some four-fifths of the entire area is occupied by forests and wild vegetation. The land however, is one of very great natural beauty. There is probably a greater diversity of trees than in any other country. Bamboo is plentiful, and extensively used in building. Stone is mainly of volcanic origin and unstratified. Granites and porphyries are well represented, but there is a dearth of lime and sandstone. Stone is used for foundation work, or in polygonal form for the lower portions of walling, upon which would be erected an upper timber structure.

CLIMATIC. Japan is influenced by a cold airstream from Asia in winter, and by the incursion of warm moist air from the Pacific in the summer. The mountainous nature of the country, in conjunction with the prevailing airstreams, conduces to exceptionally heavy rainfall, particularly in the summer. Houses, wherever possible, face south and deeply projecting eaves are provided to give protection against the sun, while high courtyard walls screen the northern aspect from the cold winds of winter. In summer, portable partitions forming house fronts are removed, leaving the dwellings quite open to the breezes.

RELIGIOUS. Shintô was the Chinese name for the indigenous polydemonism which existed in Japan before the introduction of Buddhism. While Shintôism was without any well-defined moral code, it did lay great stress upon ancestor and nature worship. Image worship or elaborate temple buildings were uncalled for. The native Shintô faith was profoundly affected by Buddhism, introduced from the Chinese mainland about A.D. 550. Buddhism encouraged the erection of temples, and its mystic symbolism inspired the artistic Japanese temperament to the production of countless images of every possible size and fantastic form. The priesthood contributed greatly to the development of the country, even in road construction and bridge building, which by aiding communication between isolated localities greatly helped the unification of the country and strengthened the influence of the priesthood. Buddhism gradually became the paramount religious influence, but Shintôism was never extinguished, and in course of time was grafted upon the Buddhist faith. In relatively modern times Shintôism regained predominance, and by its tenets largely contributed to the fervent Japanese nationalism displayed in recent history.

SOCIAL. Japan can be credited with a degree of civilization even before the true historic period, which commenced about A.D. 400, when Chinese culture was introduced through Korea. Early written records, the Kojiki, a 'Record of Ancient Matters' (A.D. 712), and the Nihongi, the 'Japanese Chronicle' (A.D. 720), commence chronology with the Emperor Jimmu, who is reputed to have united Japan in 660 B.C. By A.D. 500 the Japanese had become a distinctive race of people, but at a primitive state of development, with the population divided into isolated communities ruled by chieftains. These conditions led to intrigue among the rulers, superstition became rampant and abuses flourished. During the Suiko period (A.D. 552–645), Buddhism became firmly established and the nation tended to become a bureaucratic state with Chinese laws and ceremonial. The Mikado, as the most powerful chieftain, acquired certain prerogatives with which he eventually acquired full domination over the nation. It is reputed that by about 600, more than four hundred Buddhist temples had been erected. Nara became the capital in 710, and the city was laid out with nine gates, a palace and seven great temples. When Kiôto became the capital in 794, the arts of domestic architecture and landscape gardening made great strides. Through many vicissitudes and in the face of open aggression, Buddhism gained in strength and fortified monasteries multiplied. Feudalism, at its height in the thirteenth century, recognized three groups— the Emperor and nobles, the Shoguns with the military caste, and the people. Under the Tokugawa dynasty (1603–1868), the divine descent of the Emperor was emphasized and actively promulgated. After continual strife, which at times resulted in a full civil war, the last of the Shoguns resigned in 1867. A constitution was formed in 1890 which eventually recognized the rights of the people. The representative government which emerged laid the foundations of the subsequent progressive position of Japan.

HISTORICAL. The early history of Japan is obscure, while later records for the main part are both vague and unreliable. The Japanese, however, date back an unbroken line of Mikados to the Emperor Jimmu, reputed to have ascended the throne in 660 B.C. There is clear evidence of Chinese influence as early as the seventh century of our era. The Japanese have at all times tended towards a self-imposed isolationism, with exclusion of all foreign intercourse. Overseas trade was a government monopoly; thus there was no incentive for individual enterprise in foreign commerce. Some intercourse was established with Korea and China as early as the eighth century A.D., but it was not until 1543 that the Portuguese discovered and began trading with Japan. This was the first direct contact that the Japanese had with peoples of the Western World. Christianity was introduced in 1549 by S. Francis Xavier, but this missionary effort led to many conflicts. Envoys from Japan visited Europe in 1582. Korea was invaded by the Japanese in 1592. Despite these tentative contacts with the outer world, Japan reverted to isolationism and in 1614 all foreign priests were expelled. The Spaniards were driven out in 1624, and the Portuguese in 1638. Christianity was finally interdicted on the departure of the Portuguese, and then for a period of almost 200 years, Japan was closed to the outside world. Commercial treaties with America and European countries were, however, entered into in 1854, when Japan felt the effects of American enterprise and English institutions. Following these contacts came wars with China and Russia, while in 1914 Japan joined the alliance against Germany; but in 1941 she sided with the Axis powers.

ARCHITECTURAL CHARACTER

The architecture of Japan was largely derived from China, but at all times maintained its own special characteristics of lightness and delicacy. Refinement in Japanese architecture, combined with minuteness in carving and decoration, are particularly noticeable in timber construction, where cumulative skill and artistry of generations of craftsmen render work in timber akin to fine joinery. Notable are the dominant roofs, which form a striking contrast with practice in the Middle East and India, where flat terrace roofs predominate. The roofs of Japan, with exquisite curvature and exotic decoration, are supported upon a succession of simple or compound brackets which are striking features (p. 1216K). The conventional arrangement of these brackets produces what are known as 'orders'. Japanese temples, which were inspired by Chinese influence, do not rely upon monotonous repetition of similar features as in China but owe much of their distinctive character to a well-balanced symmetry of component parts. Interiors are largely dependent upon the justly world-famous decorative art of Japan. Decoration, with lavish use of gold lacquer and brilliant colouring, can cover both walls and ceilings, and is particularly suited to the subdued lighting of temple buildings. Minor details—gateways, torii, belfries, summer-houses and garden treatment—are all imbued with a characteristic national feeling and contribute to the formation of delightful settings for many buildings.

EXAMPLES

TEMPLES

Buddhist Temples at Hôriuji, Nara, and Nikkô, like other examples, underwent little change from Chinese prototypes. The mountainous character of the country made it possible to utilize natural terraces for temple sites, instead of having to rely upon artificial, built-up platforms which are the rule in China. In Japan, avenues of trees, and rows of standard lanterns in both stone and bronze, produce picturesque and imposing effects in conjunction with buildings when viewed against the sombre background of wooded landscape. Generally, temples comprise isolated structures within concentric enclosures, the outer enclosure formed by a low wall, the second as a promenade for priests, and the third enclosing the main temple building surrounded by a lofty, roofed screen wall. Temples are invariably raised upon a stone foundation to a height of approximately 5 ft, and the sanctuary is reached by steps leading to a veranda covered by the projecting roof of the temple in the centre, a typical example being the **Temple of Miyo-Jin-Kanda, Tokyo** (p. 1216A). In 1949, fire destroyed the main portion of the Temple at Hôriuji, but this has now been faithfully restored to its original form; an example of Japanese reverence for tradition. Mortuary temples of the Shoguns at Tokyo are regarded as ranking among the more famous buildings of Japan.

The **Buddhist Temple of Hommonji, near Tokyo,** has a two-storey gateway and a reliquary, a library, reception hall and rooms for priests, besides a pagoda. Tiles were used for roofing of Buddhist temples, instead of the thatch customary on Shintô shrines.

The **Shintô shrine of Kamiji-Yama, in Isé** (p. 1220), comprises a series of single-storeyed buildings typical of other Shintô structures. While these shrines are commonly considered as being of little architectural importance, they are significant as contributing to the picturesque element in the Japanese scene. The shrines in Isé offer another example of the national homage to tradition, for despite the fact that they are entirely rebuilt during the course of every twenty years, the shrines today remain exact replicas of original structures.

The **Kurodani Temple, Kiôto** (p. 1215A), is noted for its beautiful garden, and is surrounded by a cemetery with typical monuments.

PAGODAS

Pagodas followed in the wake of Buddhistic influence from China, but those now standing mainly date from the seventeenth century, and are adjuncts of important temples. They are square in plan, mostly five-storeyed and about 150 ft in height. In construction, they are virtually suspended around a central timber post, thus providing a measure of stability against earthquake shock. The ground storey contains images and shrines, while the upper storeys serve as 'belvederes'. There are wide projecting roofs to each storey, and the subtle curvature distinguishes them from comparable Chinese examples.

The **Pagoda, Hôriuji,** is the earliest example remaining, and is reputed to have been built by Koreans in 607. This pagoda is supported by a great central post, 100 ft high and 3 ft square at the base, the whole being surmounted by a curious finial, decorated with metal rings and bells.

The **Pagoda, Hokiji** (646), is a particularly beautiful example, and while probably constructed by a Japanese master, it clearly follows the Korean tradition.

The three-storeyed **Pagoda, Yakushiji,** was built only a little later; 680. This is notable not only because it comprises three storeys, but also because it is one of the earliest works by native builders. It is more graceful than the Korean-inspired examples, and introduces the truly national style.

The **Pagoda, Bessho,** is a four-storeyed octagonal structure, while the **Tenno-ji Pagoda, Osaka** (p. 1216G) and the **Pagoda, Yasaka** (1618) (p. 1215B), are fine examples of five-storeyed pagodas.

TOMBS

Reverence for the dead has at all times led to the erection of large and small monuments. Apart from the tombs of the Shoguns, Tokyo, which are world-famous, the **Tomb of Ieyasu, Nikkô,** is typical of the larger mausoleum. Flights of steps

A. Kurodani Temple, Kiôto. See opposite page

B. Pagoda, Yasaka (1618). See opposite page

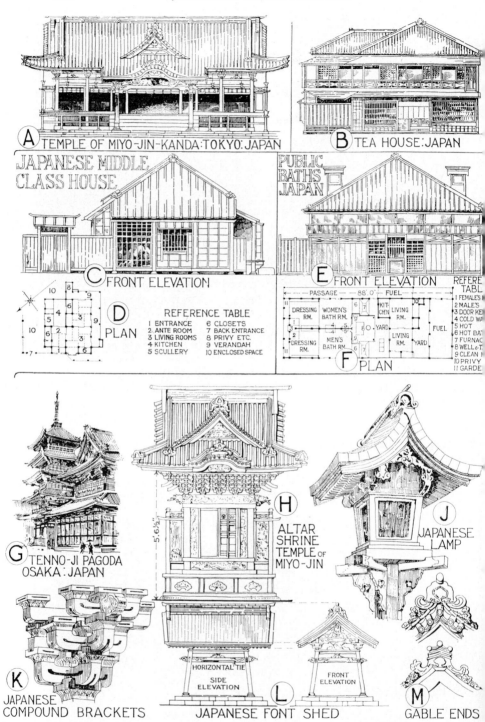

A TEMPLE OF MIYO-JIN-KANDA:TOKYO:JAPAN

B TEA HOUSE:JAPAN

JAPANESE MIDDLE CLASS HOUSE

C FRONT ELEVATION

D PLAN

PUBLIC BATHS JAPAN

E FRONT ELEVATION

F PLAN

REFERENCE TABLE

1 ENTRANCE	6 CLOSETS
2 ANTE ROOM	7 BACK ENTRANCE
3 LIVING ROOMS	8 PRIVY ETC.
4 KITCHEN	9 VERANDAH
5 SCULLERY	10 ENCLOSED SPACE

PASSAGE — 88'.0" — FUEL

DRESSING RM. — WOMEN'S BATH RM. — KIT-CHEN — LIVING RM. — YARD — FUEL

DRESSING RM. — MEN'S BATH RM. — LIVING RM. — YARD

REFERE TABL
1 FEMALE'S
2 MALE'S
3 DOOR KE
4 COLD WA
5 HOT
6 HOT BAT
7 FURNAC
8 WELL&T.
9 CLEAN
10 PRIVY
11 GARDE

G TENNO-JI PAGODA OSAKA:JAPAN

H ALTAR SHRINE TEMPLE OF MIYO-JIN

5'-6½"

HORIZONTAL TIE

SIDE ELEVATION

J JAPANESE LAMP

K JAPANESE COMPOUND BRACKETS

L JAPANESE FONT SHED

FRONT ELEVATION

M GABLE ENDS

make an imposing entry to the mortuary chapel and tomb chambers. Besides these structures there are priests' chambers, store houses, and a pagoda. The whole is contained within a triple enclosure, with three 'pai-lou'-style entrances. This tomb, however, belongs to a late period (seventeenth century), and is an example of decadence in design, through over-elaboration with ornamentation tending to lose all restraint and constructive meaning (p. 1221).

PALACES

The Imperial palaces were of a simple type, consisting of a principal hall, joined by corridors to three separate pavilions for the family of the Emperor. From the sixteenth century, palaces were protected by walls of masonry, often formed with a batter, concave on the external face, and with tilted quoin stones, to resist earthquake shocks. A moat invariably encircled the walls.

The **Imperial Palace, Nára,** (eighth century) is the focal point of the city, being situated at the end of a central avenue possessing four parallel streets on either side, crossed by others at right angles—evidence of considered town planning and indicating Chinese inspiration.

When the capital was removed to Kiôto in 794, this city too was carefully planned, but on an even more sumptuous scale, being formed with a series of rectangular blocks for buildings similar to many modern American cities.

The **Mikado's Palace, Kiôto,** is a typical example, comprising one-storey buildings covered with temple-style roofing, which instead of having one uniform slope has gables in what is known as the 'I'rimoya' style. The pavilions overlook splendid gardens, and are connected by covered corridors. Pavilions are divided internally into rooms by sliding screens 7 ft high, and as in smaller houses, the rooms are reached by an exterior veranda. Room sizes are governed by the number of floor mats, which for Imperial palaces measure 7 ft by 3 ft 6 ins. The residential block is about 100 ft by 60 ft and can be divided into fourteen separate rooms, including a throne room with the Imperial dais, and the Mikado's sleeping apartment.

The **Palaces of the Shoguns** reflect the feudal conditions which prevailed in a later period (1603–1868), and were protected by moats and fortified enclosures like so many of the mediaeval castles of England. They offer a grim reminder of the civil strife which ravaged the country at the time of their erection.

The **Kinkaku-ji** and **Ginkaku-ji, Kiôto** (c. 1600), are examples of particularly charming garden pavilions. Originally covered with gold and silver leaf, they represent the Japanese delight in brilliant ornamentation, which ran to excess in a later period.

HOUSES

Timber construction, and consequent fire risks, led to development of the detached pavilion treatment for larger houses. A typical middle-class dwelling, except where a central court is introduced, is planned as a simple rectangle (p. 1216c, D), usually one-storey high, with entrance, ante-room, living rooms, kitchen (with scullery), store rooms, and garden. A separate small fire-resisting structure, with clay walling, known as a 'go-down', is built for the storage of valuables. The size and shape of rooms are dependent upon the number of floor mats, each 6 ft by 3 ft, required to cover the floor areas. Walling is formed by light timber vertical posts and horizontal members covered with weather boarding. Interior partitions are formed with light movable timber frames, with infilling of stout translucent paper, 6 ft in height, the friezes above being plastered or wood-lined. Screens can be slid aside, allowing maximum flexibility of interior arrangement, while exterior veranda partitions can be likewise rearranged or removed. No distinction is made between living and sleeping apartments. Two main reception rooms form a suite, the second a step higher than the first and having two alcoves or 'tokonamas', a special feature of Japanese houses, used to display a flower arrangement or a selected art treasure. Thatched roofs are employed in rural areas, steeply pitched to ward off heavy rains. Tiled roofing is more common in built-up areas, to give protection from fire. Chimneys are unnecessary, as charcoal braziers are the usual source of domestic heating. In some larger houses, European influence has led to the erection of a separate wing with rooms in the 'Western' style.

INNS AND BATH-HOUSES

The typical Japanese inn closely resembles the large private house, but it is invariably planned round a central courtyard. In larger examples, upper floors are provided with connecting galleries on the principle developed in London during mediaeval and later times. The **Shukin-ro, Nagoya,** is an excellent example of Japanese practice.

Appreciation of the importance of personal hygiene is strongly marked in the Japanese character. A typical public bath-house is illustrated (p. 1216E, F).

TEA-HOUSES

Tea-houses (p. 1216B) were developed in the Kamakura period (1185–1335) as a result of the aesthetic doctrine of Zen Buddhism, which permeated Japanese thought and resulted in the 'tea-ceremony', garden cultivation and flower arrangement. They represent a most exclusive Japanese social institution and were the resort of the sophisticated and fashionable world. In no sense can they be identified with a normal public restaurant. Tea-houses are maintained solely for the cult of the tea-drinking ceremony, associated with contemplation and appreciation of the Arts. Typically indigenous in style, tea-houses are normally on a small and dainty scale, the size regulated by mats, often down to a single-mat room, only 6 ft by 3 ft. Always there is the inevitable recess or tokonama. Architecturally, the greatest care is lavished on these small structures, while no detail of lighting, ventilation or decoration is neglected. The entry for guests is usually approached by stepping stones through a pleasure garden with tastefully-arranged flower beds. Decorative stone lanterns, skill in landscaping with trees and watercourses, contrive to form a delightful setting to the small central fane dedicated to the tea-drinking ceremony.

COMPARATIVE ANALYSIS

PLANS. Shintô temples can be distinguished from Buddhist by the characteristic 'torii' or gateways formed by upright posts supporting two or more horizontal beams, under which, it was considered, worshippers must pass for prayers to be effectual. Japanese houses are entered through a vestibule and have a veranda, living, dining and guest rooms with the necessary recess for display of flowers and art treasures. There are rooms for host and hostess, but no bedrooms in the usual sense. Any room can be made a sleeping chamber by spreading a mattress on the floor. Light movable screens form interior partitions, and when removed, permit the entire house to be open to the garden. Maximum flexibility in planning is characteristic of Japanese dwellings. Rooms are regulated in size by floor mats or 'tatami' used as floor coverings, and measuring one 'ken', about 6 ft, by a 'half-ken'. Imperial or royal mats, only, are a little larger. Japanese houses owe much of their bright and cheerful character to simplicity of design, consummate skill in both selection and working of materials, as well as to well-chosen garden settings. Night illumination by decorative Japanese lanterns produces effects of exquisite beauty.

WALLS. Most houses are constructed of wood-framing with wood or stout paper infilling, which in an earthquake shock is much safer than stone or brick construction. Temple walling is a strictly trabeated arrangement of timber posts and rails dividing surfaces into regular oblong spaces, filled in with plaster, boarding or carved and painted panels (p. 1216A). Light is introduced principally through doorways. A system of cornice-bracketing in both simple and complex forms is one of the most characteristic features of Japanese buildings (p. 1216K). Standardized arrangements of this bracketing constitute various 'orders'. Immediately above the pillars or columns is a highly-decorated frieze, and above this, the bracketing consists of a series of projecting wooden corbels supporting horizontal members and rafters with decorated faces, thus allowing the roof to overhang the wall, often by as much as 8 ft. The disposition of columns, posts, brackets, and rafters forming the cornice is in accordance with well-recognized modules of measurement. Intercolumniation is governed by the 'ken', and a rough assessment of spacing would be one 'ken' for small and two 'ken' for large structures. Buildings are stilted upon stone piles to a height which would ensure timber being above ground water during the rainy season. The undersides of beams are frequently cambered to avoid any impression of sagging, while piers and columns are given a refined entasis and frequently an inward inclination to mitigate the effects of earthquake shocks.

OPENINGS. Owing to the great projection of roofs over exterior walls, there is little direct natural light and the greater part of the light which reaches interiors is reflected from the ground. Window-openings are filled with timber trellis and provided with wooden shutters externally, and paper—usually rice-paper—in light sashes, internally. In all cases, exterior walling is extremely thin; columns receive the main load from the roof and wall panels are entirely non-structural. While Shintô temples are approached through torii, Buddhist foundations are entered through an elaborate two-storeyed gateway, surmounted by a muniment room and covered by an ornate roof.

ROOFS. While Japanese roofs bear a general resemblance to Chinese, they are as a rule simpler in treatment and possess more subtlety and refinement in outline, having some intangible quality which stamps them as indubitably Japanese (p. 1216A). The upper part of the roof is terminated by a gable placed vertically above the end walls, known as an 'I'rimoya' gable, while the lower part of the main roof is carried round the ends of the building in a hipped form (p. 1216A, H). Roof coverings can be thatch, shingles or tiles. Thatched roofs often have a prominent ridge of tiles with an exaggerated cresting, or the ridge may be of stout bamboos, tied with blackened rope and terminated with finials. Tiled roofs have flattish and roll tiles alternately, while cover tiles, often of decorative form, are used to mask joints at the eaves. Ridges and hips are made up of layers of tiles set in mortar, finished with large moulded tile cappings and crestings. A lower roof, known as 'hisashi', is sometimes projected below the eaves of the main roof. Hollowed bamboos are used to form roof gutters and down pipes. Gable ends often have cusped barge-boards with pendants (p. 1216H, J, M). Curved brackets ('Kumo-Hijiki') adorn the underside of the overhanging eaves. The subtle curvature of barge-boards and brackets has been compared to the shapes of certain cloud formations, and the resemblance is such as to indicate an inherent appreciation of natural beauty in the minds of the craftsmen.

COLUMNS. Columns, which followed the Chinese form, are conspicuous in Japanese temples and in façades to palaces and gateways. Temples usually have a columned loggia, either round three sides or forming a façade to the main building. Frequently there is a portico over the approach steps which rests upon timber columns, held together at the top by horizontal tie beams. In large temples and halls, the interior columns are provided with elaborate compound bracketing to support the roof. Intercolumniation is regulated by the standard of measurement known as the 'ken', which is divided into twenty parts, termed minutes, and each minute being again divided into a further twenty-two parts or seconds of space. Columns, when square, are panelled and when round or octagonal are reeded and often richly lacquered. Even when plain, columns are objects of beauty, as timber was split by wedges and smoothed with a spear-shaped plane known as a 'Yariganna', which left a very beautiful non-mechanical finish.

MOULDINGS. Circumstances which led to a comparative absence of mouldings in Chinese architecture, apply also to Japanese work. Wall surfaces were admired for their own intrinsic beauty, and emphasis by surrounding mouldings was not required. The plain cyma and ovolo were introduced in column bases, but as there are no capitals they do not appear as decoration to the head of a column.

ORNAMENTS. Carved and coloured panels formed in enclosure walls, in projecting eaves to roofs, and in the 'ramma' or pierced ventilators below cornices are characteristic. In friezes, panels in high relief occur, representing cloud forms and objects of natural beauty—the chrysanthemum, the stork and pine tree being typical subjects for motifs, which invariably carried a symbolic significance. Ornamental brass caps, usually gilded for preservation, are frequently fixed to the ends of projecting timbers and over connections in wood to hide open joints which may occur through shrinkage. Embossed gilded metalwork is also freely applied to gables and pendants. Colour decoration, introduced from China in the sixth century, is applied to both exteriors and interiors of Japanese temples. Beams, brackets, carvings and flat surfaces are picked out in gilding and bright colours—blue, green, purple, madder and vermilion—the last a particularly beautiful colour when subjected to weathering. Wall paintings frequently appear upon a gold ground, and usually depict animal forms, birds, insects and flowers. Supporting pillars are usually black, red or gold. Lacquering is extensively employed, and is applied with consummate skill. Subjects for decoration are birds, trees attended by idealistic mountain, cloud and water forms. Frequently, natural objects are combined with

The Sacred Shintô Shrine of Kamiji-Yama in Isé. See p. 1214

Main Entrance Gate to Temple at Nikkô. See p. 1217

the weird and grotesque, resulting in a curious mixture of realistic and symbolic forms. Despite rigid conventions and disregard of perspective, Japanese genius for pure decoration has contrived to invest all major works of every period with vitality and dramatic presentation. The Japanese are noted too, for their meticulous treatment of detail. All the accessories of architectural design, lacquer work, ivory carving, enamels, faience and bronzes vie with each other in minute accuracy and softness of colour. While inspired by the Chinese, the Japanese are unsurpassed in whatever branch of artistic expression they employ, with the possible exceptions only of Chinese painting and porcelain of the finest periods.

REFERENCE BOOKS

CRAM, RALPH ADAMS. *Impressions of Japanese Architecture and the Allied Arts*. New York, 1905.
HARADA, JIRO. *The Lesson of Japanese Architecture*. London, 1936.
HUISH, M. B. *Japan and its Art*. London, 1912.
KISHIDA, HIDETO. *Japanese Architecture*. Tokyo, 1935.
MINAMOTO, H. *An Illustrated History of Japanese Art*. Kiôto, 1935.
PAINE, R. T., and SOPER, A. *The Art and Architecture of Japan*. Pelican History of Art, 1957.
SADLER, ARTHUR L. *A Short History of Japanese Architecture*. Sydney, 1941.
SANSOM, G. B. *Japan, A Short Cultural History*. New York, 1943.
SOPER, A. *The Evolution of Buddhist Architecture in Japan*. Princeton, U.S.A., 1942.

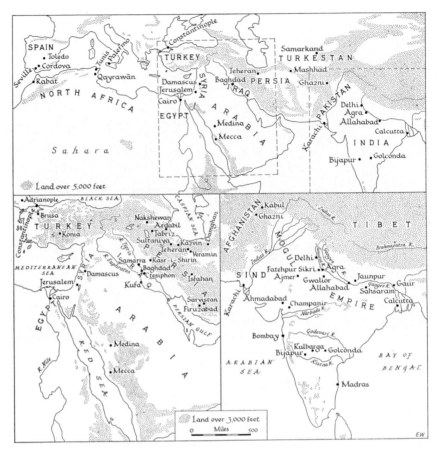

The Muslim World

XXXIII. MUSLIM ARCHITECTURE*

(seventh century to present day)

INFLUENCES

GEOGRAPHICAL. Arabia, Persia (Iran), Mesopotamia (Iraq), Syria, Palestine, Egypt, North Africa and Spain were successively conquered, wholly or partially, by the Arabs during the seventh and eighth centuries; and were then subjected to

* This style of architecture is known by many names: 'Arab' or 'Arabian' because it was first evolved by the Arabs; 'Muhammadan' (also spelt 'Mohammedan' or 'Mahometan') because it was used by the followers of the prophet Muhammad (or Mohammed or Mahomet), who founded the religion of Islam; 'Muslim' (or 'Moslem') because those followers were called Muslims (or Moslems); 'Islamic' (for the same reason); and 'Saracenic', a name of Greek origin, applied by the Romans and afterwards by the Crusaders to

the influence of Islam, the religion preached by Muhammad and his followers. Muslim architecture therefore differs from that of ancient Rome, in that it was the product of a religion rather than of a country, whereas Roman architecture everywhere reveals the influence of a nation rather than of a religion. Muslim architecture, though exhibiting local divergences in treatment and detail, had many distinctive features which are found in all countries ruled or influenced by the Arabs.

GEOLOGICAL. Building methods and even architectural style were affected by the great variation between the materials—marble, stone, brick, timber, plaster —available in the different countries. Domes, for instance, were either of brick covered externally with plaster or faience (as in Persia and Mesopotamia), or of stone (as in Egypt and parts of India and Persia), or occasionally of timber. Particularly fine limestone was available from quarries near Cairo, and red sandstone in parts of India. Plaster ornament reached a high level of intricacy and beauty in Egypt, Spain, and elsewhere.

CLIMATIC. The Muslim dominions, at their greatest extent (see map) lay mainly between the twentieth and forty-fifth parallels of latitude, south and east of the Mediterranean; so that the range of climate was not quite so great as in the Roman Empire at its maximum; and the consequent influence of climate upon architectural design was not so varied in the different regions. In all the Muslim countries, because of the glare of the sun, sheltering arcades were provided, and windows were small. Moreover, window-openings were usually filled with geometrical lattice-work in marble or plaster, or with intricate wooden lattices (*mashrabiyya*). In India, especially, the flat roofs of mosques were provided with widespreading eaves. In dwelling-houses, the flat roofs—protected by a parapet ensuring privacy—formed a welcome resort in the cool of the evening.

RELIGIOUS. The Muslim faith was the last of the three great religions which have risen from among the Semitic nations, and its essence is contained in the words from the Koran: 'There is no God but Allah, and Muhammad is his prophet'. The Koran is a compilation of the utterances of Muhammad (*c.* 571– 632) which purported to reveal the word of God; it shows many traces of the influence of the Bible, the Apocryphal Gospels and the Talmud. After Muhammad's death, the supreme spiritual and temporal direction of Islam was exercised by a succession of Caliphs ('successors' or 'deputies') who were at first chosen from amongst his own companions but from 661 were hereditary dynastic rulers established at Damascus and later at Baghdad and Cordova. The Caliphs, and also the rulers or governors who effectively controlled major regions of the Muslim world on their behalf, were responsible for directing the enormous amount of religious building in their domains, and this individual influence led to marked differences in the plan and architectural details of the religious buildings, i.e. mosques. The order and development of the plan and arrangement of the mosque are treated below (p. 1245). In certain passages of the Koran, and in some of the other writings that contain his precepts, Muhammad forbade the representation of human, animal and other natural forms in art—apparently as an austere reaction from the excessive devotion to sculptured and painted images by Christians, as represented by the Byzantine Church of his own day—his greatest enemy. Hence the lavish decoration of Muslim mosques at all periods consists either of elaborate interlacing and geometrical patterns, often of great beauty, or of conventionalized foliage and ornamental lettering, mainly texts from the Koran.

Because Muslims were fatalists, they regarded the present as more important

the nomad Arab tribes of the deserts of Egypt and Western Asia. In North Africa, it is sometimes called the 'Moorish' style after the Moors; in Turkey its earlier stages are called 'Seljuk' and its later stages 'Ottoman', after Turkish dynasties; in India its later phases are called 'Mughal' or 'Mogul' after a line of emperors, all as explained hereafter.

than the future, and were content to build their houses of relatively flimsy materials; but, on the whole, the structural soundness and fine craftsmanship of their mosques and tombs is far better than some prejudiced writers have admitted. Indeed, among the most magnificent of their buildings are the great tomb-mosques erected by rich and despotic rulers. Many of these are mentioned hereafter.

SOCIAL. The wild Arabs who surged over so large a part of the then civilized world in the seventh and eighth centuries A.D. had no knowledge of architecture or any of the arts; so that in each country that they occupied they made use of the traditional skill of the vanquished people—Christians and others—as explained later. Most of those countries, and especially those hitherto ruled by the Byzantine Emperor, had an advanced civilization, in which the richer people enjoyed a considerable degree of luxury. As the Arab invaders became settled, they adopted in their palaces and dwelling-houses many of the social habits of the Near Eastern nations, notably the seclusion of the women's apartments (harim). Their houses had blank exterior walls, with a single entrance guarded by a door-keeper (bawwab or boab). The various rooms were grouped around an inner courtyard (hosh). Certain rooms were open to male visitors, but, throughout the 'unchanging East', the women's quarters were isolated up to the late nineteenth century A.D., since when the emancipation of women has reached many Muslim countries. In small town-houses, the harim was usually placed on an upper floor, and the windows opening on to the street were filled with wooden lattices which provided shade and ventilation, enabling the women of the household to look down on to the street while themselves remaining invisible. Muslim social life in the Middle Ages is well pictured in The Arabian Nights, a composite production first compiled in Baghdad under Harun ar-Rashid (786–809), but much altered by editors or contributors in Cairo many centuries later. Another famous book, the Rubaiyat of Omar Khayyam (1075–1125)—the great Persian poet, philosopher, astronomer and mathematician—sheds much light upon Persian social life and ideas in his own day.

HISTORICAL. Muslim chronology dates from 622, the year of the Hijra (or Hegira), when Muhammad fled from Mecca to Medina in Arabia. The invasion of the adjoining countries by his Arab followers, under the first Caliphs, began about ten years later; and continued till c. 750. The seat of the Caliphate was transferred from Medina to Kufa in Mesopotamia, and then to Damascus, which remained the capital of the Muslim world until it was superseded by Baghdad.

Persia (see p. 65) was subjugated during 632–41 by the Caliph Omar. The Umayyad Caliphs of Damascus governed it till they were overthrown in 750 by the descendants of Abbas (uncle of Muhammad) who established the Abbasid Dynasty. Their new capital of Baghdad (in modern Iraq), founded in 762, became an important centre of art and science under the Caliph Harun ar-Rashid (786–809), but was sacked and burnt by the Mongols in 1258.

Syria, including Palestine, was conquered during 632–9, and in c. 639 a primitive mosque was built near the site of the later magnificent 'Dome of the Rock' at Jerusalem, the erection of which began c. 685. When the Crusaders entered Palestine four centuries afterwards, they took back with them to Europe many Muslim notions about architecture which influenced our castles and our Gothic churches. Parts of Syria and Palestine were governed by the Crusaders for many years, but they—as well as the Muslim sultans of Egypt who ruled the rest of the country—were vanquished by the Ottoman Turks in 1516, and the latter remained in possession up to the end of the First World War.

Egypt fell to the Arabs in 640, and a mosque was built c. 642 at Fustat, south of the present great city of Cairo, which was founded more than two centuries later. Egypt was ruled by dynasties of Muslim princes or sultans till 1517, when it was conquered by the Ottoman Turks. After a period of semi-independence from the early eighteenth century to the First World War, it became an independent kingdom in 1922 and a republic in 1952.

North Africa was conquered in 647–709, and a primitive mosque was founded at Qayrawān *c.* 670. The Muslim architecture of the North African countries from Egypt to the Atlantic—comprising modern Cyrenaica, Libya, Tunisia, Algeria, and Morocco—is commonly called 'Moorish', and in France these countries are known by the convenient name of 'Moghreb'. In 711, the Arab armies invaded Southern *Spain*, and founded the fortress of Gibraltar. An independent Western Caliphate was established at Cordova (Córdoba) in 758, and a magnificent mosque there was begun in 785–6. After much fighting with the Christians during the fourteenth to the fifteenth century, the Moors were finally defeated in 1492. Though that date marks their expulsion from Spain, they had left many important buildings in the country, and these too are known as 'Moorish' architecture. For a time, the Moors also ruled *Sicily* (*c.* 827–1061), where a few examples remain showing their influence upon later Romanesque and Gothic buildings.

Turkey, originally the core of the Byzantine or East Roman Empire, with its capital at Constantinople (Istanbul), was conquered in part by the Muslim Seljuk Dynasty, who, during the eleventh to the twelfth century gradually invaded Asia Minor, via Baghdad, from their home in Central Asia. They established their capital at Konia, where they erected a number of mosques and other fine buildings. This dynasty ended shortly after 1300, and was followed by the Ottoman Turks, another warlike tribe from Central Asia, who established their capital at Brusa (now Bursa), built many handsome mosques there, and captured Constantinople in 1453. Turkish rule continued under sultans till 1923, when a republic was established, with its capital at Ankara; but the area of Turkey is now small compared with the vast extent of its empire in the past.

India was first invaded in 1001–27 by Muslim armies coming from Ghazni (then in Persia), who established a sultanate at Delhi in 1206. Here a great mosque had already been built in 1193–8 by a victorious Muslim general. This Pathan dynasty ruled the whole of North India; but, after the death of Muhammad Shah I in 1316, there gradually arose other independent states with capitals at Jaunpur, Ahmadābād, Mandu, Gaur, Kulbarga, Golconda, Bijapur and elsewhere. The Mogul or Mughal Empire (1526–1857), founded by Babar, consolidated the Muslim dominions by the gradual absorption of these petty kingdoms. Akbar the Great (1556–1605) first removed his capital from Delhi to Agra, and afterwards founded Fatehpur-Sikri as the new capital. In these three cities are to be found the most famous buildings of the period. Shāh Jahān (1628–58) raised the Mogul Empire to its highest pitch of power and magnificence. He erected in North India many splendid memorials of his dynasty, such as the Tāj Mahal and the Pearl Mosque at Agra and the Jami Masjid and the Palace at Delhi. He was deposed in 1658 by his third son Aurangzeb who reigned till his death in 1707, the date at which the Mogul period may be said to have ended. Meanwhile the influence of the East India Company, political as well as commercial, steadily increased, and British rule was established by royal proclamation in 1858. In 1947, India was divided into the Republic of India and the Dominion of Pakistan.

ARCHITECTURAL CHARACTER

The character of Muslim architecture varied a great deal in each region, because of the differing cultures of the inhabitants and the existing local tradition. The followers of the Prophet, simple soldiers, carried their faith into many lands but had no architectural style of their own to accompany it. Thus they were content to adopt each local style that they found, modifying it mainly in distinctive ornamental details, but also introducing several important new features of plan and structure. The mosque was an entirely novel type of building, originally devised by Muhammad in Arabia in a very rudimentary form. (Its subsequent evolution is described on p. 1245). The earliest examples have a large open courtyard surrounded by colonnades or arcades carrying flat roofs. A later but still early innovation was the minaret, a tower from the top of which a priest chanted the call to prayer, in deliberate distinction from the bell-tower used by Christians. The columns used for the colonnades were generally rifled from Roman temples; but the arches that replaced them were of a type that became characteristic of Muslim architecture all over the world and in all periods. The two-centred pointed arch, a device known in ancient Assyria (p. 86) and employed again in Syria just before the Muslim conquests, was brought into use as early as the eighth century by the Muslims in Mesopotamia (Iraq), and forms a notable feature in the great mosque of Ibn Tūlūn at Cairo (876–9), centuries before it appeared in France or England. Sometimes these arches were stilted (10 on p. 1256), sometimes were prolonged below their springing to form a 'pointed horseshoe' (8). A 'round horseshoe' type is a semicircular arch prolonged below the springing (9). Another form, the four-centred or 'Persian' type (17), closely resembles our so-called 'Tudor' arch, which it antedates by many centuries. At a later date, cusped or foliated arches (24–7) were introduced long before they appeared in England.

Domes of stone or brick were largely used for mosques and tombs (pp. 1243A, 1244A). They normally rose from a square substructure, and the transition from square to circle, hitherto achieved either by means of a spherical pendentive, as used in Byzantine architecture (p. 277), or a squinch-arch (see Glossary), was usually solved by the Muslims with the aid of tiers of stalactites—rows of upright pointed niches. So popular did this feature become among Muslim architects that it came to be introduced for purely decorative purposes on ornamental details, just as miniature buttresses are represented on wooden chancel-screens in our Late-Gothic churches. Surface-decoration in relief is applied to the exteriors of stone domes in Cairo, while in Persia domes are covered with brilliantly coloured faience or with metal. (For further description of Muslim ornament, see p. 1249.)

EXAMPLES

a. Arabia.   e. Persia (Iran), Turkestan, and Meso-
b. Syria and Palestine.   potamia (Iraq).
c. Egypt.   f. Turkey.
d. North Africa, Spain, etc.   g. India and Pakistan.

a. ARABIA

Arabia was the cradle of Islam, which sprang up there among nomads who had no permanent architecture. All that Muhammad required of them was that they should pray at stated times, wherever they might find themselves, whether journeying across the desert, minding their flocks, or resting on the house-top; and that

A. The Dome of the Rock, Jerusalem (685–91). See p. 1229

B. The Great Mosque, Damascus (c. 706–15). See p. 1229

A. Mosque of Ibn Tūlūn, Cairo:
interior arcades (876–9).
See p. 1229

B. Mosque of Qā'it Bay *extra
muros*, Cairo (1468–96).
Detail of dome. See p. 1230

c. Interior courtyard　　　　　D. Principal apartment
House of Jamāl ad-dīn az-Zahabi, Cairo (1637). See p. 1230

when they prayed they should turn towards the holy shrine at Mecca. For this simple ritual, no man-made temple was essential. The Kaaba at Mecca, the holiest spot in the world, was its focus, and was an object of veneration long before Muhammad founded Islam, but it has no architectural merit. It is simply a small plain rectangular structure. The imposing mosque which now surrounds it is mainly a building of the sixteenth century, and contains nothing from Muhammad's day. When he fled from Mecca in 622 to **Medina**, some 200 miles away, he planned a house which became the prototype of all succeeding mosques. It was merely a square enclosure surrounded by walls of mud-brick. Some part of it, presumably the north portion where he said his prayers, was roofed over, the roof being flat and constructed of palm trunks and branches covered with mud. The congregation in prayer faced the Holy City of Jerusalem and that direction (*qibla*) was somehow indicated for worshippers. In 624 Mecca became the focus for prayer, as it still remains all over the Muslim world. In this primitive mosque at Medina, there was nothing approaching architectural planning or design.

b. SYRIA AND PALESTINE

Although Syria was conquered by the Muslims in 632–9, nothing remains of the first mosque that they built in **Jerusalem** in *c.* 639. It stood in the temple enclosure, near the Sacred Rock, and apparently on the site of the **Mosque of al-Aqsā**, which has since been rebuilt several times. This locality had long been venerated, for here had stood successively the Altar of David, Solomon's Temple, the later temple erected by the Jews on returning from exile, Herod's Temple (destroyed A.D. 70), and Hadrian's Temple of Jupiter. From the Sacred Rock, legend asserts that Muhammad ascended to Heaven at his death in 632; and it was over the Rock that the Caliph Omar or Umar built the magnificent '**Dome of the Rock**' in 685–91 (p. 1227A), as a place of pilgrimage rather than as a mosque for the worship of a large congregation. It was an entirely new type of Muslim building, an annular rotunda of late-Roman or Byzantine type. (Its fine mosaics and external faience are later additions.)

The **Great Mosque, Damascus** (*c.* 706–15) (p. 1227B), built by the Caliph Walid, presents many problems, for it stands in the middle of an enormous Roman temenos, a colonnaded enclosure measuring 1,263 by 1,002 ft, in which was once a large temple, transformed into a Christian church in 379. The mosque enclosure is much smaller than the temenos, and its southern portion is a huge roofed structure, 446 by 121 ft, with aisles and a transept like a Christian church, but open towards the courtyard. It is uncertain how far this plan was suggested by the arrangement of the preceding church. The arcade towards the courtyard has tall 'round horseshoe' arches rising from square piers. There is a 'mihrab' (niche indicating the direction of Mecca) and some handsome minarets of later date.

c. EGYPT

The **Mosque of Amr, Fustat** (near Cairo), built *c.* 642 by the Arab general of that name after the invasion of Egypt two years earlier, has a large square open court with a fountain in the centre, for ritual ablutions. The surrounding arcades are single on the entrance-wall facing the mihrab, triple on the two flank walls, and six in number on the mihrab or sanctuary side. The arches are carried on antique columns rifled from Roman ruins. Unfortunately, this mosque has been so often altered that there is no certainty that much of it is original.

The **Mosque of Ibn Tūlūn, Cairo** (876–9) (pp. 1228A, 1232A, B) is of similar plan, but of much more original architecture. The Governor of Cairo who built it had been educated at Samarra in Iraq (p. 1235) where brick pointed arches and arcades had been used; and he introduced these in his mosque at Cairo, in lofty arcades. The parapets of the mosque are pierced ornamentally; there is an extraordinary and hideous spiral minaret (also found at Samarra), and a large amount of delicate and attractive conventional ornament in stucco, including the original mihrab and window-lattices. Apart from its great size (about 532 ft square), this mosque, ruined though it now is, forms one of the great landmarks of Muslim architecture.

The **Mosque of Al-Azhar, Cairo** (979 onwards) is the first notable building of the Fatimid Dynasty, which ruled Egypt from 969–1171 and was so called after Muhammad's daughter Fatima. It is a very large building, planned like Ibn Tūlūn's mosque for the worship of great congregations, but has served for centuries as the religious university of Cairo, and still accommodates thousands of students. Altered again and again since its first foundation, the building is most picturesque; although most of the columns supporting its arcades are from Christian churches, its Muslim features are striking.

The **Mosque of Al-Hakim** (990–1012) and the small one of **Al-Aqmar** (1085) are other important Fatimid monuments in Cairo. To the same period belong three fine gateways in the city walls (1087–91). The magnificent **Citadel of Cairo**, commenced c. 1171, is due to Saladin, whose figure looms so large in the history of the Crusaders and who founded the Ayyubid Dynasty which ruled Egypt and Palestine from 1171–1250. It is now realized that the Crusaders acquired much of their knowledge of fortification from their 'Saracen' foes in Egypt and the Holy Land. None of Saladin's mosques in Cairo have survived, but there are a large number in excellent preservation from the period of the Mamlūk rulers who governed Egypt from 1250 until the Turkish conquest in 1517. Among them may be mentioned the large **Mosque of Baybars I** (1266–9); the **Mosque and Mausoleum and Hospital of Qalāwūn** (1284–5), showing a definite kinship with European Gothic architecture; the enormous **Mosque and Mausoleum of Sultan Hasan** (1356–63) (p. 1232C, D), with four colossal arch recesses around a square central court; and with walls rising 100 ft and rich decorations; the **Mosque and Mausoleum of Sultan Barkūk**, outside the city (1399–1412), with its handsome domes and pair of minarets (p. 1251); the **Mosque of Mu'ayyad** (1415); and the two **Mosques of Qā'it Bay** (1468–96) (pp. 1228B, 1231A, B), one inside and one outside the city walls. All these later examples are roofed over, not being congregational mosques with a large central open court; and all are most elaborately decorated. Apart from mosques, of which hundreds exist in Cairo alone, many palaces were built, but hardly a trace of them remains. Cairo possesses, however, several handsome dwelling-houses of the thirteenth to the seventeenth century (p. 1228C, D), notably the so-called **Bayt al-Qady** (1495), a beautiful building.

After the Turkish conquest of Egypt in 1516, architecture took its cue from Constantinople and was of inferior quality. For Egyptian examples of this Turkish period, see 'Turkey' (p. 1237). From the seventeenth century onwards, European influence made itself apparent.

d. NORTH AFRICA AND SPAIN

After the Muslim conquest of North Africa and Spain in the seventh to the eighth century, and the establishment of the Western Caliphate at Cordova in 760, mosque building proceeded rapidly. As in Egypt, extensive use was made of antique marble and stone columns. Domes, which in Egypt, Persia, and India usually

A. Exterior   B. Mihrab and Mimbar

Mosque of Qā'it Bay *extra muros*, Cairo (*c.* 1468–96). See p. 1230

C. Mosque, Cordova: interior   D. Alhambra, Granada: stalactite capital

(786 and later). See p. 1233   (1334–91). See p. 1233

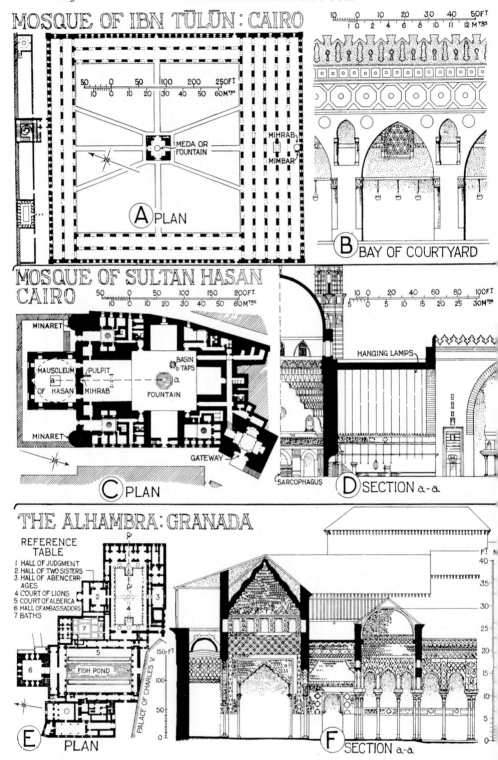

MOSQUE OF IBN TŪLŪN: CAIRO

MEDA OR FOUNTAIN

MIHRAB

MIMBAR

Ⓐ PLAN

Ⓑ BAY OF COURTYARD

MOSQUE OF SULTAN HASAN CAIRO

MINARET

MAUSOLEUM OF HASAN

PULPIT

MIHRAB

BASIN & TAPS

FOUNTAIN

MINARET

GATEWAY

Ⓒ PLAN

HANGING LAMPS

SARCOPHAGUS

Ⓓ SECTION a-a

THE ALHAMBRA: GRANADA

REFERENCE TABLE
1 HALL OF JUDGMENT
2 HALL OF TWO SISTERS
3 HALL OF ABENCERR-
  AGES
4 COURT OF LIONS
5 COURT OF ALBERCA
6 HALL OF AMBASSADORS
7 BATHS

FISH POND

PALACE OF CHARLES V.

Ⓔ PLAN

Ⓕ SECTION a-a

indicate a tomb-mosque or mausoleum, were seldom used in these 'Moorish' countries and were generally small; but, like all other parts of the mosque, were lavishly decorated internally.

The **Great Mosque, Qayrawān, near Tunis,** was probably founded in 670. It contains the earliest known example of a minaret, recorded to have been built *c.* 724–7 during the caliphate of Hisham (724–43). This is a huge and clumsy tower with 'battered' (tapering) walls, crowned with battlements. The mosque itself is very large, and of congregational type, with an oblong courtyard which is not quite rectangular. The covered arcades are three bays deep on the north-west, two bays on north-east and south-west, and ten bays on the south-east, where there is a small dome over the mihrab. The minaret is in the centre of the south front. The arches of the arcades are stilted and slightly pointed. This mosque has been altered and partly rebuilt again and again, but remains a fine example.

The **Mosque of Zaytunah, Tunis** (founded 732) is also of the congregational type, with stilted arches supported on antique columns. As in many other Muslim buildings, wooden tie-rods are fixed at the spring of the arches, probably to counteract the effect of earthquakes.

Other notable examples in North Africa are the Great Mosques of Algiers (1018), Tlemcen and Sfax.

In Spain, the **Great Mosque, Cordova** (p. 1231C) was begun in 786 by the Caliph Abd ar-Rahman, but was more than doubled in area during the tenth century. Its original form, however, may still be traced. It was a congregational mosque with a very deep sanctuary, consisting of eleven aisles separated by arcades, each carried on twenty antique columns. This sanctuary was so lofty that ordinary horseshoe arches, resting on the available columns, were not adequate for such a height. A second range of arches was therefore added above them, and the resultant complication is restless and disturbing (p. 1231C). If piers of brick or stone had been introduced, as at Ibn Tūlūn's mosque at Cairo, instead of 1,200 antique columns, this effect might have been avoided. In 1238 the mosque was converted into a Christian church and became the Cathedral of Cordova, but is still known as *La Mezquita*. It is of enormous size, measuring 585 ft by 410 ft. Of this total area, about two-thirds is roofed as described above, the northern third being an open court, the *Patio de los Naranjos*. The whole interior is finely decorated with coloured marbles and precious stones.

S. Cristo de la Luz, Toledo was originally a mosque, built in 960, but became a Christian church in 1186.

Among the famous minarets in North Africa and Spain are the **Kutubiyya, Marrakesh,** in Morocco (1169–84), the **Minaret of Hasan, Rabat,** also in Morocco (1178–84), and the **Giralda, Seville** (1184–96). All these are lofty square towers, but the belfry added to the Giralda in 1568 deprived it of much of its original grace.

Among Muslim secular monuments, the **Alcázar, Seville** (Arabic *al-kasr* = the castle), chiefly built in 1350–69 but much altered since and badly restored in the nineteenth century, is the finest example of a palace in the so-called 'Mudéjar' style (i.e. erected by Muslims for Christians). Begun by Pedro the Cruel with the aid of craftsmen lent by the Sultan of Granada, it contains a wealth of delicate ornament.

The Alhambra, Granada is a vast red castle (Arabic *al-hamra* = the red), built on a ridge above the city. It includes a complex of buildings dating from the twelfth to the sixteenth century; but the most famous and notable among them is the Moorish palace which was chiefly erected by Yusuf I (1334–54) and Muhammad V (1354–91). It is the last purely Muslim building in Spain, and one of the most richly decorated pleasure-houses in the world. The plan (p. 1232E) includes two oblong courts at right angles to each other. The elaborate Court of the Lions, 115 ft by 66 ft, is surrounded by columns with stalactite capitals, supporting wooden arcading decorated in stucco (p. 1231D). At the eastern end of the court is the Hall of Judgement (p. 1232F), and on either side are the smaller Halls of the Two Sisters and of the Abencerrajes, with roofs formed of stuccoed vaults. The Court of the Alberca, 138 ft by 74 ft, has a two-storeyed arcade on the south; and, on the north, in the massive Tower of Comares, is the Hall of the Ambassadors, 35 ft square, crowned with a polygonal dome, and having deeply-recessed windows giving fine views of the city below. The profuse decoration of all the principal rooms consists chiefly of a dado of coloured enamelled tiles on the walls, and of most elaborate ornament above, modelled in plaster and coloured. This plaster or stucco ornament displays the features characteristic of all Muslim architecture—geometrical interlacings, stalactites, bands of decorative lettering, conventionalized foliage; but nowhere else in the Muslim world was so much of the decoration carried out in so impermanent a medium as plaster; and the Alhambra is largely responsible for the common belief that all 'Saracenic' architecture is flimsy and unsubstantial. It must be added that the fountains and gardens within the palace add greatly to its charm.

Sicily, at that time a part of the Byzantine Empire, was invaded by the Moors in 827, and Palermo became their capital. Gradually the whole island was conquered. The Normans who had settled in Southern Italy, invaded Sicily under Robert and Roger Guiscard in 1061; and completed their conquest by 1090. Roger's second son was crowned King of Sicily at Palermo in 1130. Muslim influence is apparent in many churches and palaces in Palermo, especially in the use of the horseshoe arch, stalactite pendentives, and decorative inscriptions.

e. PERSIA (Iran), TURKESTAN, AND MESOPOTAMIA (Iraq)

The Arab armies conquered Persia from the Sassanian kings in 632–41, and built a primitive mosque at Kufa in 638. Under the Sassanian dynasty (226–641), a number of important brick buildings had been erected, including the great palaces of Firuzabad, Sarvistan, Ctesiphon, and Kasr-i-Shirin, from which the Muslims learned much about vaults and domes. They also employed Persian architects. From 661–750, Persia was ruled by the Umayyad caliphs of Damascus; then, in 750, the Abbasid line of caliphs was established, and reached its apogee during the reign of Harun ar-Rashid (786–809), whose grandfather, Mansur, had laid out the new city of Baghdad in 762. In 962, a Turkish governor from Ghazni (in modern Afghanistan) usurped the throne, but this Ghaznavid dynasty was superseded in 1037 by two brothers from Turkestan, sons of a shepherd named Seljuk. The Seljuk (Turkish) dynasty, reference to which is made under Turkey (p. 1237), lasted till 1300 and moved the capital from Baghdad to Rayy. Mongol invasions, under Jenghiz Khan in 1220 and Hulagu Khan in 1258, laid Persia waste and destroyed most of the buildings in Baghdad and elsewhere. Another disastrous invasion by Timur ('Tamerlane') occurred in 1380. He had been born in Samarkand, where he established his capital and erected some notable buildings. His 'Timurid' dynasty endured until 1500, and was followed by the Safavid rulers (1502–1736) who made their capital at Isfahan and enriched it with many fine mosques and palaces.

The **Mosque at Kufa** (638) was of the congregational type, with a large open court, and a sanctuary (*liwan*) which had a flat roof supported on antique columns.

The **Great Mosque, Baghdad** (764) has been so often altered and rebuilt that hardly anything of its original form remains. Other mosques of the late eighth and early ninth centuries, all in ruins, are at Ukhaidir, Rakka, Abu Dulaf, and Samarra—all in Mesopotamia (Iraq).

The **Malwiyya Mosque, Samarra** (847) is of the congregational type with spacious open court surrounded by porticoes, that on the Mecca side being the deepest and forming the sanctuary. The porticoes have flat roofs, carried on brick piers, not on palm-trunks or antique columns. The lofty external walls have several towers. There is a curious spiral minaret, and windows with cusped or foliated heads. Ibn Tūlūn, whose famous mosque at Cairo has already been described (p. 1229), was educated at Samarra, and certainly borrowed many features from it, including the ugly spiral minaret.

The small **Mosque at Nāyin,** in Persia (early tenth century) is the oldest in that country of which any considerable portion remains. It has shallow brick domes on brick piers, 'Persian' arches, and stucco decoration. The domed **Tombs of Pir i-Alamdar** (1026) and **Chihl Duktaran** (1054) at **Damghan** are mausolea used for private prayer, and each is therefore provided with a mihrab. Later examples of note are the **Tombs of Mumine Khatun** (1186) and of **Yusuf ibn-Kutayyir** (1162), both at **Nakhshewan.**

The **Tomb of Khudabanda Khān, Sultāniya** (1320) is the next important monument, as architecture naturally languished during the Mongol invasions. It is an enormous octagonal structure in brick with eight minarets, now mostly fallen. The roof consists of a steeply-pointed double dome, measuring over 80 ft in diameter and 150 ft high internally. The whole building is faced with glazed bricks and tiles, a fashion derived from ancient times in Persia.

Timur embellished his new capital at **Samarkand** with many notable monuments during the years preceding his death in 1405. His own mausoleum, the so-called **Gur Amir** ('Prince's Tomb', 1386–1404) (p. 1236B), is octagonal externally, square internally, with a curious and slightly swelling dome rising from a tall drum. He also built the **Tomb of Shāh Zinda** (1392–1434) and the **Madrasa of Bibi Khanum** (1389–1403), which has eight minarets. These, together with some later buildings, including the large **Mosque of Ulugh Beg** (*c.* 1430), make Samarkand a perfect museum of Persian art.

The **Blue Mosque, Tabrīz** (*c.* 1437–67), so called from the fine blue tiles with which it was covered, but now ruined, is still a notable building; as is the **Mosque of Shaykh Safi, Ardabil,** also of the fifteenth century. The **Friday Mosque, Veramin** (1322–26) is sadly ruined.

The city of **Mashhad** contains a group of buildings which attract an enormous number of pilgrims annually. The finest of these is the **Mosque of Gawhar Shad** (1418) (p. 1236A), a Persian princess, and provides perhaps the best example of coloured tile decoration in all Persia. The Shrine of the Imām Riza consists of a congeries of mosques, mausolea, etc., and attracts pilgrims because here was buried Harun ar-Rashid himself in 809, and also his successor as Caliph, the Imām Ali-ar-Riza of Mecca, in 811. The **Tomb of the Imām Riza,** with a helm-shaped dome covered with gold, is, however, a building of 1607.

During the seventeenth and the early eighteenth century, **Isfahan** became the most important architectural centre in Persia. It contains over 200 mosques and colleges. Of these, the old **Masjid-i-Juma** ('Friday mosque' or congregational mosque, as opposed to a tomb-mosque or mausoleum used only for private prayers) was founded in 760, much enlarged *c.* 1080 and further enlarged in the seventeenth to the eighteenth century Shāh Abbas I, who ruled over Persia from 1587–1629, laid out Isfahan on monumental lines, thus providing almost the only

A. Mosque of Gawhar Shad, Mashhad (1418). See p. 1235

B. The Gur Amir ('Prince's Tomb'), Samarkand (1386–1404). See p. 1235

known example of early town-planning in an Oriental city. The central feature is the Maidan-i-Shāh (= 'Royal Square'). On the east of that vast space stands the small but beautiful **Mosque of Lutfullah**, the Shāh's father-in-law; on the west, a great gateway, with the dainty little pavilion known as the **Chihil Sutun** behind it; on the north the entrance to the Great Bazaar; and on the south the Masjid-i-Shāh (= 'Royal Mosque'). Round the remainder of the square run arcades, two storeys high. The **Masjid-i-Shāh** (1612–27) does not lie parallel with the Maidan, but obliquely, so that its orientation with Mecca is preserved, yet this peculiarity is not perceptible from the Maidan. Through a magnificent portal, 90 ft high, one passes into a vestibule and thence into one of the four great porches or recesses placed centrally on each side of the courtyard. Through the porch opposite, one enters the sanctuary containing the mihrab. The dome and the slender cylindrical minarets are covered with glazed tiles or bricks.

f. TURKEY

Long before the Ottoman Turks captured Constantinople (Istanbul) in 1453, they had been erecting mosques and other buildings elsewhere. The Seljuk Turks who had invaded and subjugated Persia in 1037 (p. 1234) gradually extended their dominions westwards into Asia Minor, hitherto ruled by the Byzantine Emperor; and, after making their headquarters at Nicaea for some time, established their capital at Konia—the ancient Iconium—in 1097, after Nicaea had fallen to the Crusaders. Here the Seljuks employed Persian craftsmen to design and build for them numerous mosques and palaces. The dynasty of Seljuk sultans of Konia ended c. 1300, when they were superseded by the Ottoman Turks who had come, like them, from Central Asia and had hitherto accepted Seljuk suzerainty. Brusa, in Asia Minor, became the first Ottoman capital, and here again the Turkish invaders relied heavily upon Persian tradition in building their new mosques and other buildings. After Constantinople fell in 1453, the great Byzantine church of S. Sophia was adopted as the model for future Turkish mosques; but many Persian details, and especially the tall pencil-shaped minarets, came to be incorporated in Turkish architecture, not only in Turkey itself but in Egypt and Syria (conquered in 1516), and in some of the Balkan countries which remained in Turkish hands up to the nineteenth and twentieth century.

In **Konia** all the principal monuments are of the thirteenth century: viz. the great **Mosque of Ala ad-Din** (1221) which dominates the city; the domed **Karatay Mosque** (1251), formerly used for religious instruction and now a museum; the **Ince Minar** (= 'Slender Minaret', 1265–7); the **Mausoleum of Meylama**, the mystical poet (d. 1273), with a curious fluted cupola covered with glazed tiles; the **Mosque of Sirceli** (1242); and the **Mosque of Energhe** (1258 or 1269).

In **Brusa** the chief early Ottoman buildings are the **Ulu Jami** (= 'Great Mosque', 1379–1414); the **Muradiye** (1414); the **Yesil Jami** (= 'Green Mosque', 1424); and the **Yilderim Jami** (1389–1402).

When **Constantinople** was conquered by the Turks in 1453, S. Sophia was soon converted into a mosque and furnished with minarets. Six very large new mosques were erected during the next two hundred years, viz.: the **Mosque of Muhammad II, the Conqueror** (1463–9); the **Mosque of Bayazid** (1497–1505); the **Selimiye** (1520–6); the **Suleymāniye** (1550–7) (p. 1239A); the **Mosque of Sultan Ahmed** (1607–14); and the **Yeni Valide** (1615–1663). The **Suleymāniye** was designed by the architect Sinān, as was the splendid **Selimiye** (1570–4) at **Adrianople**, now 'Edirne'.

Outside Turkey itself, many mosques of Turkish type were erected, e.g. the **Tekkiya or Dervish Mosque, Damascus** (1516); the **Mosque of Sinān Pasha** (1571), **Bulak**, near Cairo; the **Mosque of Al Malika Safiyya, Cairo** (1610); and the huge **Mosque of Muhammad Ali** in the **Citadel, Cairo** (1824–57), with its tall pencil-shaped minarets. Among other features common to nearly all Ottoman mosques are spherical domes on pendentives, and apses covered with semidomes, following S. Sophia. In many examples, the decoration is rich and profuse, though it deteriorated during the eighteenth century.

Turkish domestic architecture resembled that of other Muslim countries, but was often flimsily constructed of wood and was therefore liable to fire. Overhanging windows filled with wooden lattices, inner courtyards, the rigid seclusion of women, and graceful interior decoration with glazed tiles are normal features. Well-designed fountains are found in many streets, also in the courtyards of mosques and large houses (p. 1239B). In **Damascus,** many fine mansions, e.g. the **House of Abdalla Pāshā,** date from the Turkish period; as does the **Khan Asad Pāshā.**

g. INDIA AND PAKISTAN

Muslim architecture entered Northern India from Persia via Afghanistan in the twelfth century. A previous invasion of 712 had established a small Muslim colony in Sind, but it soon expired and left no architectural remains of any importance. It was in *c.* 962 that a Turkish slave from Turkestan had established a small principality at Ghazni. He raided the Punjab in 987 and founded the Ghaznavid dynasty. His son Mahmud, succeeding him in 997, made Ghazni a place of some importance until it was sacked by a rival chieftain in *c.* 1150. A contemporary chronicler wrote that 'the capital was . . . ornamented with mosques, porches, fountains, aqueducts, reservoirs and cisterns, beyond any city of the East'. The scanty remains of all this glory show that the buildings of Ghazni were essentially Persian, owing nothing to Hindu India.

In 1193, a later ruler of Ghazni, Mahmud the Ghori, with his general, Qutb ad-Dīn, conquered Northern India and established a new capital at Delhi. This date marks the real beginning of Muslim architecture in India. From 1193–1554 the Pathan dynasty ruled a large part of the country, excluding a number of important principalities.

The **Mosque of the Quwwat al-Islam** (= 'Might of Islam'), **Delhi** (1198) was erected on the site of a Hindu temple and originally measured about 210 ft by 150 ft externally on plan, the inner courtyard being 142 ft by 108 ft. The sanctuary (which in India is, naturally, on the west as that is the side towards Mecca), had an arcaded façade; but, as this Persian feature was unfamiliar to Hindu craftsmen, they used projecting courses to form the arches, instead of proper voussoirs. Here, as in most subsequent Muslim buildings in India, one can distinguish Persian from Hindu forms. The founder's son and successor Altamsh proceeded in about 1225 to enlarge the mosque; and also built the large and clumsy minaret, 238 ft high, known as the **Qutb Minar.** Its tapered form and its fluting are both derived from Persian examples, and it has tiers of stalactites under its galleries. The neighbouring **Tomb of Altamsh** (1235) is a fine specimen of nearly pure Persian design.

The **Great Mosque, Ajmer** (*c.* 1200) is of the congregational type, and has an imposing arcade of Persian arches, but these are unscientifically constructed.

The Mongol invasions of the thirteenth century interrupted building in India, as in Persia. The **Alai Darwaza** (1310), a noble gateway in the mosque at Delhi, combines Persian and Hindu features. The **Adina Mosque, Gaur,** in

A. The Suleymaniye, Constantinople (Istanbul) (1550–7). See p. 1237

B. Fountain in court of S. Sophia, Constantinople (Istanbul).
See opposite page

A. Tomb of Humāyūn, Old Delhi (1565). See p. 1242

B. The Dīwān-i-'Am, Agra Fort, from S.W. (1628–58). See p. 1245

C. The Dīwān-i-Khāss, Fatehpur-Sikri (1569–75). See p. 1242

D. The Tāj Mahal, Agra: Great Gateway to garden court (1630–53). See p. 1245

Bengal (c. 1360) and the **Jami Masjid, Kulbarga** or Gulbarga (fourteenth century) are both notable for the enormous number of their small domes, which in the latter mosque cover the whole area, 216 ft by 176 ft.

The **Jami Masjid** (=congregational mosque or 'Great Mosque'), **Jaunpur** (1438–78), has its court surrounded by five-aisled colonnades, of which the inner and outer rows are of double columns with bracket-capitals supporting a roof of flat slabs in the Hindu method. The great arched portals show the usual mixture of Hindu and Persian elements. The interior domes and roofs are beautiful in design and colour.

The **Jami Masjid, Mandu** (1405–54) has a square courtyard enclosed by arcades, each of eleven pointed arches supported on red sandstone piers and roofed with numerous domes.

Ahmadābād, capital of the kingdom of Gujarat, was the most important architectural centre during the fifteenth century. The **Jami Masjid** (c. 1411–24) is a huge mosque which shows the combination of Muslim pointed arches with Hindu trabeated construction. The sanctuary on the Mecca side has two hundred and sixty columns supporting fifteen symmetrically-placed stone domes, all built up of horizontally projecting courses in Hindu fashion. The smaller mosques at Ahmadābād are those of **Muhafiz Khān, Sidi Sayyid,** and **Rānī Sipārī**—all in the same mixed style. In Ahmadābād are also the fine **Tombs of Sayyid Usman** (1460) and of **Sayyid Mubarak** (1484).

The **Jami Masjid, Champanīr** (1500–8), one of the largest and most imposing mosques in India, has a spacious court, a many-domed sanctuary, and two minarets flanking the central entrance gateway.

In 1526, Babar, the Mongol King of Kabul, defeated the great army of the Sultan of Delhi at Panipat, and inaugurated the Mogul or Mughal dynasty which may be considered to have lasted up to the death of the emperor Aurangzeb in 1707. The buildings of this period are more definitely Persian than Hindu in character, though Hindu features were freely used.

The **Tomb of Sher Shāh, Sahsarām** (1540–45) is built on a platform, with four angle-pavilions, in the middle of an artificial lake. It is octagonal on plan, with a deep gallery round the central tomb-chamber, which is crowned by a dome 71 ft in diameter. Small domed octagonal kiosks are grouped round the central dome.

The **Mosque of Sher Shāh, Delhi** (1541), without courtyard or minarets, is simple in design, and a prototype of others to follow. It measures 168 ft by 145 ft, and has five entrance portals with depressed pointed arches, and panelled piers inlaid with coloured marbles. The façade is crowned with a carved cresting, behind which rises the single central dome.

At **Bijapur,** capital of an independent kingdom which was not added to the Mogul Empire till 1686, a remarkable outburst of monumental building took place between 1565 and 1686. The principal buildings include the unfinished **Jami Masjid** (c. 1576) (p. 1247G, H), a great mosque measuring 330 ft by 260 ft, roofed with a number of small domes over square compartments, and a central dome 57 ft in diameter supported on interlacing pointed arches—a remarkable example of Muslim skill in construction. The fine group of buildings known as the **Ibrāhīm Rauza, Bijapur** (1626–33), includes the tombs of Ibrāhīm II and his family, and a fine mosque, in a courtyard which was once a royal garden embellished with kiosks and fountains, all enclosed within a wall with a lofty portal. The Mausoleum of Mahmūd, Ibrāhīm's successor, commonly called the **Gol Gombaz, Bijapur** (1636–59) is a bold and magnificent building with a dome nearly 125 ft in diameter, supported on a gallery formed by intersecting pendentive arches, a method devised to counteract the outward thrust of the dome, as used in the **Jami Masjid, Bijapur.**

The noble **Tomb of Humāyūn, Delhi** (1565) (p. 1240A) the next Mogul building to be mentioned, was erected by the widow of the Emperor Humāyūn during the reign of his son, the great Emperor Akbar. Surrounded by a formal garden, it stands on a vast platform of red sandstone, 22 ft high, with arches in white marble. From this base rises the domed tomb itself, 156 ft square and 125 ft high. This great block, though square on plan, consists in fact of a central domed octagon buttressed by four octagonal towers. It is faced with red sandstone, picked out with white marble, and the dome itself is faced with white marble. It is of double construction and is slightly bulbous in form, thus introducing into India for the first time a feature characteristic of late work in Persia and Samarkand, whence its architect presumably came. This great building is generally regarded as the pro-totype of the Tāj Mahal (p. 1245).

The **Tomb of Muhammad Ghaus, Gwalior** (1562), in a city famous for its fine craftsmanship, is 100 ft square on plan externally, with hexagonal domed towers at each corner, and a central dome carried on pointed arches. The gallery has a screen of exquisitely pierced tracery.

The city of **Fatehpur-Sikri,** near Agra, was founded by the Emperor Akbar in 1569, and was the seat of his court till c. 1585. It was formally planned and splendidly built but is now in ruins. The **Jami Masjid** (pp. 1243A, 1247C) has an immense courtyard, 433 ft by 366 ft, surrounded by arcaded cloisters and entered by a magnificent gateway, the **Buland Darwaza** (= 'high gateway'), which is 130 ft high, plus a flight of steps 42 ft high. Though its huge recessed portal, with a wide rectangular frame of flat ornament, is essentially Persian in character, the kiosks (*chatris*) on its roof give it an Indian flavour. The **Dīwān-i-Khāss** (1569–75) (p. 1240C) was Akbar's private audience chamber. The walls are lined with precious stones. The flat ceiling is supported by a central pillar with an intricately bracketed capital (p. 1240C) carrying the Emperor's throne. From this capital four stone bridges radiate to the four corners of the hall, where his four ministers sat. The **Tomb of Salīm Chishtī** (1571–80) (pp. 1243B, 1247D, E) is a domed square chamber lit by windows with geometrical tracery, and has over-elaborate brackets under the eaves.

The great **Palace of Akbar, Allahābād** (1583) is now an arsenal, and the only remaining portion is the square Zenāna Hall, with a roof carried on sixty-four columns in eight rows, these columns having elaborate bracket-capitals.

The **Mausoleum of Akbar, Sikandra,** near Agra (1593–1613) is unique among the tombs of India. A massive gateway of red sandstone, inlaid with white marble, leads into the garden surrounding the four-storeyed pyramidal tomb en-circled by an arcaded cloister with angle-pavilions and a domed entrance-portal. From this terrace rise three more in succession, each diminishing in size. On the topmost terrace, surrounded by dazzling marble trellis-work, is Akbar's cenotaph, raised high above his tomb beneath.

The huge **Palace, Delhi** (1639–48), within the Fort, has been much altered but still displays a great deal of the work of Shāh Jahān (1628–58), who carried out much important building at Delhi and Agra. The palace occupied a space of c. 1,600 ft by c. 3,200 ft, entered by a lofty gateway and containing many courts, halls, baths and gardens. It was all laid out with great splendour on formal lines.

The **Jami Masjid, Delhi** (1644–58), also built by Shāh Jahān, has a fine courtyard 325 ft square, and two minarets 130 ft high. It is raised on a lofty base-ment and entered by three handsome gateways. These features, together with its

A. The Jami Masjid, Fatehpur-Sikri: western side of court
(1569–85). See opposite page

B. Tomb of Salīm Chishtī, Fatehpur-Sikri (1571–80). See opposite page

A. General view of Mausoleum

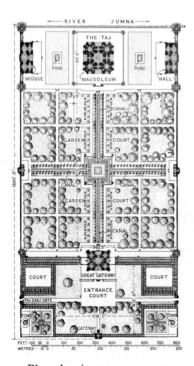

B. Plan showing entrance court,   c. Marble screen enclosing tombs.
gateway, garden court and
Mausoleum

The Tāj Mahal, Agra (1630–53). See opposite page

domes and angle-towers, make its external appearance much more attractive than most Indian mosques.

The **Motī Masjid** (= 'Pearl Mosque'), **Agra** (1646–53) forms part of the Palace. It is an elegant three-domed marble building facing on to a court 150 ft square, adorned with kiosks or *chatris*. It was one of Shāh Jahān's additions to the Palace, which also included the **Nagina Masjid** in the women's quarters, the **Dīwān-i-Khāss** or private audience-hall (1637), and the noble **Dīwān-i-Am** or public audience-hall, measuring 208 ft by 76 ft (p. 1240B).

The **Tāj Mahal, Agra** (1630–53) (pp. 1244, 1247A, B) was, however, Shāh Jahān's greatest building, and indeed one of the greatest buildings in the world, erected to the memory of his favourite wife, Mumtaz-i-Mahal, Persian by descent. The Mausoleum itself is 186 ft square, with canted angles, and has a central inner dome 80 ft high and 58 ft in diameter, surmounted by an outer dome nearly 200 ft high (p. 1247B). Around this central dome are two-storeyed aisles, and at each angle is a small dome. The entrance-portal in the centre of each side is of the usual recessed type, crowned with a four-centred arch set in a square frame. The actual tombs of Shāh Jahān and his queen are enclosed in a marble screen of incredible elaboration and delicacy, possibly erected after Shāh Jahān's death. The interior of the Mausoleum is dimly lit through pierced marble lattices, which provide a most impressive half-light, just sufficient to enable a visitor to see the amazing beauty of the inlaid marble decoration of the walls. The Mausoleum stands on a marble platform 313 ft square and 22 ft high. At each corner is a white marble minaret 137 ft high. This platform is surrounded by an outer court, 880 ft by 440 ft, on one side of which is a great gateway. The approach to the Tāj from the bank of the Jumuna River is along a water-course or canal, lined with cypresses. The reflections of these trees, the minarets, and the domed Mausoleum enhance a splendid view.

Shāh Jahān was deposed in 1658 by his third son Aurangzeb, whose buildings were inferior in character to those of his father. They included the **Motī Masjid, Delhi** (1659), with delicate marble decoration. From that date onwards the Mogul tradition continued right through the seventeenth and the eighteenth century with diminished vigour, and was imitated by the Mahratta rulers of India; but it may be said to have reached its real end when the Mogul dynasty expired at the death of Aurangzeb in 1707. Moreover, by that time, European influence was making itself felt in Indian architecture.

COMPARATIVE ANALYSIS

PLANS. Throughout the history of Muslim architecture, the principal type of building was the mosque (Arabic *masjid* = 'place of prostration'). The 'congregational mosque' or 'Friday mosque' (*Jami Masjid*) was used—especially on Friday, the Muslim Sabbath—for public or congregational worship, as opposed to private prayer which was enjoined upon Muslims at stated hours several times a day, wherever they might be. Such mosques normally had a large open court (*sahn*) corresponding to the Early Christian *atrium*, and surrounded by arcades or colonnades (*līwānāt*, plural of *līwān*) affording protection from the sun (pp. 1232A, 1247C). The līwān on the side facing Mecca was of greater depth than the other three, and constituted the sanctuary. In the middle of the wall towards Mecca, the *qibla* or direction for prayer (i.e. towards Mecca) was indicated by a niche (the *mihrab*). By the side of the niche stood the pulpit (*minbar* or *mimbar*) (p. 1231B), and a reading-desk (*dikka*) from which the priest (imām) read passages from the Koran and intoned the prayers. A portion of the sanctuary was often enclosed by a screen (*maqsūra*), corresponding to a Christian chancel-screen. One or more tall towers, 'minarets' (Arabic *manāra*) were invariably provided, from which the 'muezzin' (Arabic *muadhdhin*) chanted the call to prayer at prescribed times. All the above requisites apply to a modern mosque. On the centre of the open court stood a fountain (*fawwāra*), often sheltered by a dome, for ritual ablution.

Another type of mosque was the *Madrasa* or collegiate mosque, e.g. the Madrasa or Mosque of Sultan Hasan at Cairo (p. 1232C, D), which is cruciform on plan, the central portion being open to the sky. The four arms of the cross are spanned by enormous pointed vaults; and behind the mihrab is the founder's tomb crowned with a dome, a most unusual arrangement. A third type of mosque, the tomb-mosque, is sometimes entirely covered with domes, vaults, or flat roofs, and may be used for private prayer.

The khāns (caravanserais or inns for travellers and merchants) in large cities such as Cairo, Damascus, and Constantinople (where there are said to have been 180) were large buildings, usually planned around an open courtyard. The lower storey provided stabling for camels, etc.; the upper storeys contained rooms for merchants and their goods. The Khān Asad Pāshā, Damascus, is a particularly fine example.

Dwelling-houses were planned in the normal Oriental fashion, with the principal rooms grouped around an internal courtyard, often adorned with a fountain. The windows facing the street are small, and strongly barred in the lower storeys. Those above often overhang and have wooden lattices (p. 1248C). The women's quarters (*harīm*) in all Muslim houses are carefully secluded from the portions accessible to male visitors.

WALLS. Walls were of brick or stone according to locality, and were often covered with delicate surface ornament in plaster, precious stones or glazed tiles (p. 1249). At the Alhambra, Granada, walls have a dado of glazed tiles 4 ft high; above this are geometrical patterns in plaster. The horizontal bonding of walls in alternate courses of light and dark stone (p. 1231A) is a fashion borrowed from the Byzantines. External walls of mosques are often crowned with bold cresting (pp. 1231A, 1232B, 1243A, 1248N) or stalactites instead of a cornice. In Mogul architecture, walls were sometimes crowned with rows of small kiosks (*chatris*) (p. 1243A, B).

OPENINGS. Arcades were largely used to provide shade from the sun. Five main types of arches were used: (*a*) the two-centred pointed arch, without mouldings (p. 1248K); (*b*) the four-centred or 'Persian' arch, resembling the English 'Tudor' arch (p. 1256 No. 17); (*c*) the pointed horseshoe arch (p. 1256 No. 8); (*d*) the round horseshoe (pp. 1231C, 1248L, 1256 No. 6); (*e*) the ogee arch (p. 1256 Nos. 28, 29); the multifoil or cusped arch (pp. 1231C, 1240B, 1248M, 1256 No. 7). In some of the earliest mosques, arches rest on antique Roman columns (p. 1231C); and in a few late examples, specially-made columns are used, but piers are more general (p. 1232A, B). Wooden beams or iron rods are occasionally fixed as ties across the springing of arches, partly as a precaution against earthquakes. The various types of arches mentioned above are also used over door-openings and windows. In some of the later Cairo mosques, the voussoirs of arches are of alternating colours and are interlocked joggles which form a counterchange pattern (pp. 1231B, C, 1248E). Partly because all woodwork shrinks in excessive heat, doors are divided into very small panels forming a geometrical pattern, with elaborate mouldings and inlay (p. 1247F). Windows are usually small, to suit the hot climate, occasionally grouped together, and generally filled with elaborate stone or marble or stucco tracery (*qamariyya*) in the case of mosques, or with wooden lattices (*mashrabiyya*) in the case of houses. Glass was occasionally used from the thirteenth century onwards; the coloured glass windows in the Dome of the Rock at Jerusalem were inserted in 1528.

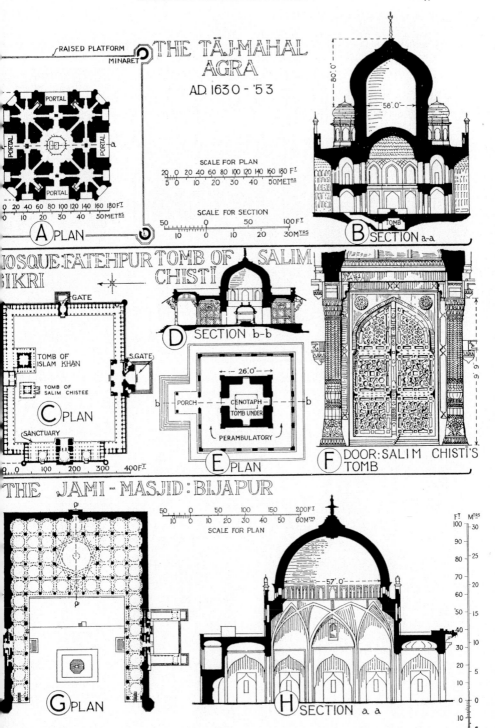

RAISED PLATFORM
MINARET

THE TĀJ·MAHAL
AGRA

A.D. 1630 - '53

PORTAL

PORTAL

PORTAL

PORTAL

PORTAL

a

SCALE FOR PLAN

20 0 20 40 60 80 100 120 140 160 180 FT
5 0 10 20 30 40 50METRS

SCALE FOR SECTION

50 0 50 100FT
10 0 10 20 30MTRS

0 20 40 60 80 100 120 140 160 180FT
0 10 20 30 40 50METRS

(A) PLAN

80'·0"

58'·0"

TOMB

(B) SECTION a-a

MOSQUE·FATEHPUR
SIKRI

TOMB OF SALIM
CHISTĪ

GATE

TOMB OF
ISLAM KHAN

TOMB OF
SALIM CHISTEE

S.GATE

(C) PLAN

SANCTUARY

0 100 200 300 400FT

(D) SECTION b-b

26'·0"

b

PORCH

CENOTAPH

TOMB UNDER

b

PERAMBULATORY

(E) PLAN

9'·6"

(F) DOOR: SALIM CHISTI'S
TOMB

THE JAMI·MASJID: BIJAPUR

50 0 50 100 150 200FT
10 0 10 20 30 40 60MTRS

SCALE FOR PLAN

57'·0"

FT MTRS
100 30

90
80 25

70
60 20

'50 15

40
30 10

20
5
10

0 0

10

5

(G) PLAN

(H) SECTION a a

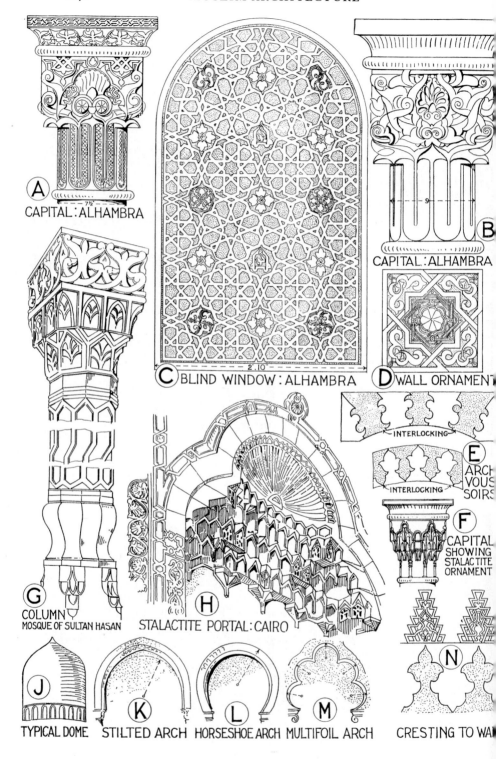

CAPITAL: ALHAMBRA (A)

CAPITAL: ALHAMBRA (B)

(C) BLIND WINDOW: ALHAMBRA

(D) WALL ORNAMENT

INTERLOCKING

INTERLOCKING

(E) ARCH VOUSSOIRS

(F) CAPITAL SHOWING STALACTITE ORNAMENT

(G) COLUMN MOSQUE OF SULTAN HASAN

(H) STALACTITE PORTAL: CAIRO

(N)

(J) TYPICAL DOME

(K) STILTED ARCH

(L) HORSESHOE ARCH

(M) MULTIFOIL ARCH

CRESTING TO WALL

ROOFS. Roofs were normally either flat or domed; but pointed vaults were also used occasionally. Flat roofs were mainly constructed of palm-trunks or other timber, covered with clay or mortar reinforced with palm-branches. In India, flat roofs of corbelled stone slabs repeated an older tradition from Jain temples. Flat ceilings were often richly decorated: at the Alhambra much of this decoration is of coloured stucco. Domes were very widely used in Muslim mosques and tombs. They are seldom, if ever, spherical as in Byzantine architecture; seldom bulbous, as commonly believed; very occasionally saucer-shaped, as in Gujarat; but for the most part are slightly pointed. Only in later examples, and in the eastern of the Muslim countries, is there a slight pinching-in of the dome at its base foreshadowing the bulbous Tartar or 'onion' domes of Russia and the Central European Baroque style.

Domes are usually of stone in Egypt and in parts of Persia and India, of brick elsewhere. A few examples are of double construction. In Cairo especially, where fine limestone was readily available, their exterior was decorated with elaborate geometrical carved ornament—either to mitigate the glare of the sun on such large surfaces, or in sheer exuberance. Fluted or ribbed domes are characteristic of parts of Persia and Turkestan. Domes are almost invariably placed on square compartments; but, unlike the Byzantine type which rests upon smooth pendentives, the typical dome pendentive is formed of tiers or rows of small arches known as 'stalactites' (p. 1232D).

COLUMNS. Ready-made columns, from old Roman and Byzantine buildings in the locality, were often utilized for colonnades of mosques, and as they are of various designs they naturally produce an incongruous and haphazard effect, very much as in some Early Christian churches. The new columns designed by Muslim architects were founded on old models varied with Muslim ornament (p. 1248G). The columns in the Alhambra, Spain, are very slender, 12 diameters in height, surmounted by capitals (p. 1248A, B), with long necking and square upper portion carved with stalactite ornament (pp. 1231D, 1248F). Above this singular capital rises again a square post, like an elongated dosseret-block, carved with geometric and arabesque ornament, and against its sides abut the springings of the stilted arches carried on stalactite brackets resembling the stalactite capitals below (pp. 1231D, 1232F). In India, local Hindu influence produced a short, stunted pier quite Eastern in character, and also a variety of columns founded on Jain models, with cubiform capitals and deep abacus-block, while two-thirds of the way up the shaft start curious brackets or serpent-like struts which appear to support the outstanding beam of the roof (p. 1243B).

MOULDINGS. Mouldings are unimportant in Muslim architecture, and usually consist of small flat bands as a capping to a dado or around doors and window-openings. Where cornices might be expected, e.g. to crown a façade, rows of stalactites are generally employed, beneath an ornamental pierced parapet (p. 1231A, B, D).

ORNAMENT (p. 1248). Ornament in general was restricted, as far as 'motif' was concerned, by passages from the Koran prohibiting the representation of natural forms. Thus Muslim ornament is in sharp contrast to the elaborate naturalistic sculpture of a Greek temple, a Roman triumphal arch, or the façade of a Gothic cathedral. The Muslims, debarred from imitating natural forms, devised and perfected a system of decoration in which geometry was a ruling factor; and covered their principal buildings, inside and out, with geometrical interlacing patterns, sometimes enhanced and enriched with gorgeous colouring, and thus producing a brilliant surface resembling a carpet (p. 1248D). The term 'arabesque' (=Arab-like) seems to have been originally coined in the eighteenth century to describe this form of Muslim geometrical ornament; but in modern scholarly usage is applied only to Renaissance panels decorated with conventional foliage, figures, and emblems.

Among different types of Muslim surface ornament are: (*a*) Mnemonic inscriptions or texts', consisting of extracts from the Koran, either in the stiff characters known as 'Kufic' and so called from their origin at Kufa; or in the more flowing Nashki alphabet, equally old in origin. In either case, the letters are intertwined with conventional foliage to form ornamental bands or panels (p. 1231D), and may well have inspired our Late-Gothic texts in churches. (*b*) Superimposed ornament, made up of conventional designs in different planes, in which one scheme of design forms the background to the one over it, enhancing the intricacy of detail beloved of Muslim craftsmen (p. 1231D). (*c*) Stalactite ornament, already mentioned (p. 1249), devised primarily to decorate the pendentives of domes (p. 1232D, F) but afterwards applied decoratively to door-heads (p. 1248H), capitals (pp. 1231D, 1248F) and other features.

The *mashrabiyya* grilles in windows were formed of wooden bobbins, framed together in geometrical patterns, and are of great delicacy, originality and beauty. The pulpit (*mimbar*) in the mosque was richly ornamented with panelling, carving and inlay; while the adjoining prayer-niche (*mihrab*), as being the focal point of worship, was gorgeously treated with joggled voussoirs, stalactite ornament, and inlay. A fine example exists in the mosque of Qā'it Bay at Cairo (p. 1231B).

Taken as a whole, ornament forms an exceptionally important part of Muslim architecture. It varies greatly in form, treatment, and colour, while restricted everywhere by the prohibitions of the Koran. To our modern eyes, this style seems to present an effect of restlessness, a striving after excess, in contrast with the Greek spirit which recognized perfection in simplicity and was content to let a fine line tell its own tale. In Muslim architecture generally—but especially in India and at the Alhambra, rather than in Persia and Cairo—we find intricacy rather than simplicity. There are brackets of such tortured forms as to be structurally useless; crestings of pierced and carved marble as delicate as lace-work (p. 1248N); surface panels inlaid with the precious stones of the jeweller as well as with the coloured marbles of the sculptor; geometrical polychrome patterns of labyrinthine design (pp. 1231C, 1243A). To these features must be added the distinctive stalactite ornament, monotonously repeated.

It is now generally admitted that European Gothic architecture owes a substantial debt to Islamic prototypes, many of which became familiar to the Crusaders in Egypt, Palestine and Syria. Some of the skill in building brick vaults which the Muslim craftsmen of Persia had inherited from their Sassanian forebears seems to have reached Europe from those countries, as certainly did many notions of military architecture such as the 'crooked entrance', crenellation, and machicolation. On the other hand, many details probably transmitted by the Crusaders to Europe appear to have been originally borrowed by the Muslims from their Byzantine foes, e.g. the use of striped façades, which are common in Cairo as in Pisa and Genoa—both of which cities were in touch with the Levant; this practice may as easily have been borrowed from Constantinople as from Cairo. Engaged shafts built into the angles of brick piers were used in pre-Muslim buildings, and the Muslims must have transmitted them to the West.

More important is the very early Muslim use of the two-centred pointed arch—centuries before it appeared in Europe—and also the four-centred (or 'Persian' or 'depressed' or 'Tudor') arch—hundreds of years before England adopted it. Ogee and cusped (or foliated) arches appear to have had the same origin. The graceful form of the Cairene minaret, diminished in stages, may well have influenced the designers of Renaissance *campanili* in Italy, to say nothing of Wren's steeples. The dainty wooden *mashrabiyya* of Muslim houses was copied in metal on several grilles of English churches. Beautiful inscriptions in Kufic lettering may have affected the design of Late-Gothic inscriptions; and ornamental parapets surely reached us from the Islamic countries.

Almost the first person to suggest the possible kinship between Gothic and Muslim architecture was Wren, who, in attempting to summarize the history of Westminster Abbey wrote (in 1713) that: 'This we now call the Gothick Manner of Architecture . . . tho' the Goths were rather Destroyers than Builders; I think it should with more Reason be called the Saracen style; for those People wanted neither Arts nor Learning'. This surmise, daring indeed when it was made, has since been proved reasonable by modern scholarship.

REFERENCE BOOKS

BELL, G. L. *Palace and Mosque at Ukhaidir*. London, 1914.
BOURGOIN, J. *Les Arts arabes*. Paris, 1873.
BRIGGS, M. S. *Muhammadan Architecture in Egypt and Palestine*. Oxford, 1924.
BROWN, P. *Indian Architecture: The Islamic Period*. Bombay, 1942.
CALVERT, A. *Moorish Remains in Spain*. London, 1906.
COHN-WIENER, E. *Turan: Islamische Baukunst in Mittelasien*. Berlin, 1930.
COSTE, P. *Architecture arabe . . . du Caire*. 2 vols., Paris, 1837–9.
CRESWELL, K. A. C. *Early Muslim Architecture*. 2 vols., Oxford, 1932–40.
—. *The Muslim Architecture of Egypt*. Vol. i, Oxford, 1952.
—. *A Short Account of Early Muslim Architecture*. London, 1958.
DIEZ, E. *Die Kunst der Islamischen Völker*. Berlin, 1917.
—. *Islamische Baukunst in Churasan*. Hagen, 1923.
EGLI, E. *Sinan* [Turkish architect]. Zurich , Stuttgart, 1954.
FERGUSSON, J. *History of Indian and Eastern Architecture*. 2 vols., London, 1910.
FRANZ, J. *Die Baukunst des Islam*. Darmstadt, 1887.
GAYET, A. *L'Art arabe*. Paris, 1893.
—. *L'Art persan*. Paris, 1895.
HAVELL, E. B. *Indian Architecture*. 2nd ed., London, 1927.
JONES, O. *Plans and Details of the Alhambra*. 2 vols., London, 1845.

Tomb-Mosque of Sultan Barkūk *extra muros*, Cairo
(1399–1412). See p. 1230

JUNGHÄNDEL, M. *Die Baukunst Spaniens* [vol. i, Moorish Work]. Dresden, 1893.

KUHNEL, E. *Maurische Kunst*. Berlin, 1924.

MARÇAIS, G. *L'Architecture musulmane d'Occident* [North Africa, etc.]. Paris, 1954.

MAYER, L. A. *Islamic Architects and their Works*. Geneva, 1956.

POPE, A. U. *A Survey of Persian Art*. 6 vols. [vol. ii, pp. 897–1246, Architecture of the Islamic Period]. London, 1939.

PRISSE D'AVENNES, E. *L'Art arabe . . . du Caire*. 3 vols., Paris, 1877.

RICHMOND, E. T. *The Dome of the Rock in Jerusalem*. Oxford, 1924.

—. *Moslem Architecture*. Royal Asiatic Society, 1926.

RIVOIRA, G. T. *Moslem Architecture*. Oxford, 1918.

SALADIN, H. *Manuel d'art musulman* (vol. i, *Architecture*). Paris, 1907.

SARRE, F. *Denkmäler persischer Baukunst*. 2 vols., Berlin, 1901–10.

TARCHI, U. *L'Architettura musulmana in Egitto*. Turin, 1922–3.

TERRY, J. *Indo-Islamic Architecture*. London, 1955.

The Auditorium Building, Massachusetts Institute of Technology,
Cambridge, Massachusetts (1952–5). See p. 1160

GENERAL REFERENCE BOOKS

N.B. Lists relating to special periods are given at the end of each chapter.

Architectural Association Sketch Book. Folio. 1867–1918.
ATKINSON, R., and BAGENAL, H. *Theory and Elements of architecture.* Vol. I. Pt. I.
London, 1926.
BRIGGS, M. S. *Concise Encyclopaedia of architecture.* 1959.
Cambridge Ancient History. 12 vols. 1924–39; *Mediaeval History.* 8 vols. 1911–36; *Modern History.* 14 vols. 1902–12 (New edition in progress, 1957–).
CHOISY, A. *Histoire de l'architecture.* 2 vols. Paris, 1899.
CUMMINGS, C. A. *A History of Architecture in Italy.* 2 vols., Boston and New York, 1901.
DEHIO, G., and BEZOLD, G. V. *Die Kirchliche Baukunst des Abendlandes.* Folio. 1884.
Dictionary of Architecture, issued by the Architectural Publication Society. With Detached
Essays and Illustrations. 6 vols., folio., London, 1848–92.
DURAND, J. N. L. *Parallèle des Edifices de tout genre.* Paris, 1800.
FERGUSSON, J. *History of Architecture.* 6 vols., London, 1893, etc.
GAILHABAUD, J. *L'architecture du V au XVII siècle.* 5 vols., folio and 4to, 1869–72.
—. *Monuments anciens et modernes.* Paris, 1850.
GARDINER, A. H. *Outline of English Architecture.* 3rd edition. 1949.
GODFREY, W. H. *A History of Architecture in London.* 1911.
GWILT, J. *Encyclopaedia of Architecture.* London, 1900.
HAMLIN, A. D. F. *Text Book of History of Architecture.* New York, 1896.
—. *A History of Ornament.* 2 vols., New York, 1916.
HAMLIN, T. *Architecture through the Ages.* New York, 1941.
Handbuch der Architektur. Stuttgart.
HARVEY, J. *The Gothic World.* London, 1950.
JONES, O. *Grammar of Ornament.* London, Folio, 1856; and 4to, 1868.
KIMBALL, F., and EDGELL, G. H. *A History of Architecture.* New York, 1920.

KUGLER, F. *Geschichte der Baukunst.* 5 vols. Stuttgart, 1859–72. Continued by Burckhardt, Lubke and Gurlitt as *Geschichte der neuern Baukunst.* 4 vols. 1887–1911.

LAVEDAN, P. *French Architecture.* 1944, English trans., Penguin Books, Harmondsworth, 1956.

LETHABY, W. R. *Architecture.* London, 1912.

LLOYD, N. *A History of English Brickwork.* London and New York, 1925.

——. *A History of the English House.* London and New York, 1931.

MILIZIA, F. *Lives of Celebrated Architects.* 2 vols., London, 1826.

MUMFORD, L. *The Culture of Cities.* London, 1938.

——. *Technics and Civilization.* London, 1934.

PARKER, J. *Glossary of Terms used in Architecture.* 3 vols. 1850.

PERROT, G., and CHIPIEZ, C. *History of Ancient Art.* 12 vols. 1883–94.

PEVSNER, N. *The Buildings of England.* A series of guide books, by counties, from 1951.

——. *An Outline of European Architecture.* 5th (Penguin) ed., 1957.

QUENNELL, M., and C. H. B. *A History of Everyday Things, 1066–1942.* 4 parts. 1918–42.

RICHARDSON, A. E., and CORFIATO, H. O. *The Art of Architecture.* London, 1938.

Royal Institute of British Architects' Transactions. 1836 et seq.

SCOTT-MONCRIEFF, G. *The Stones of Scotland.* London, 1938.

SIMPSON, F. M. *A History of Architectural Development.* 3 vols., London, 1905–11. Revised edition in 5 vols.:

    I. Plommer, Hugh. *Ancient and Classical Architecture.* London, 1956.

    II. Stewart, Cecil. *Early Christian, Byzantine and Romanesque Architecture.* London, 1954

SINGER, C., HOLMYARD, E. J., HALL, A. R., with WILLIAMS, T. I. for vols. ii-v, editors. *A History of Technology.* 5 vols. 1954-.

STATHAM, H. H. *A Short Critical History of Architecture.* 3rd ed., London, 1950.

STURGIS, R. *A Dictionary of Architecture.* 3 vols. New York, 1901.

STURGIS, R., and FROTHINGHAM, A. L. *History of Architecture.* 4 vols., New York, 1916.

TOY, S. *A History of Fortification from 3,000 B.C. to A.D. 1700.* London, 1955.

VAN DER MEER, F. *Atlas of Western Civilization.* Trans. Birrell, T. A. Amsterdam, 2nd ed., 1960

VASARI, G. *Lives of the most Eminent Painters, Sculptors and Architects.* Edited by Blashfield. 4 vols., New York, 1897.

VIOLLET-LE-DUC, E. E. *Dictionnaire de l'architecture.* 10 vols., Paris, 1859.

——. *Lectures on Architecture.* 2 vols., London, 1877–81.

VITRUVIUS, MARCUS POLLIO. *The Ten Books on Architecture,* Trans. M. H. Morgan, Harvard University Press, 1914.

WATERHOUSE, P. L., and CORDINGLEY, R. A. *The Story of Architecture.* 3rd ed., London, 1950.

Various articles in the *Encyclopaedia Britannica* and *Chambers' Encyclopaedia* dealing with Architecture may be referred to with interest. Articles on aspects of architectural history appear from time to time in various journals, such as the *Journal of the Royal Institute of British Architects,* the *Journal of the Warburg and Courtauld Institutes,* the *Architectural Review, Architectural History, Journal of the Society of Architectural Historians* and the *Art Bulletin.*

First Church of Christ Scientist, Berkeley, California (1912)
Architect: Bernard R. Maybeck (1862–1957)

GLOSSARY OF ARCHITECTURAL TERMS

Abacus (Lat. *abacus* = table, tablet). A slab forming the crowning member of a capital. In Greek Doric, square without chamfer or moulding (pp. 110A, 113, 160A). In Greek Ionic, thinner with ovolo moulding only (p. 160C). In Roman Ionic and Corinthian, the sides are hollowed on plan and have the angles cut off (pp. 160F, 189J, 246D). In Romanesque, the abacus is deeper but projects less and is moulded with rounds and hollows, or merely chamfered on the lower edge (pp. 503B, C, E, 504A, B). In Gothic, the circular or octagonal abacus was favoured in England (pp. 503L, Q, U, 504), while the square or octagonal abacus is a French feature (p. 567A, C).

Abutment. Solid masonry which resists the lateral pressure of an arch (pp. 277, 369).

Acanthus. A plant whose leaves, conventionally treated, form the lower portions of the Corinthian capital (pp. 138, 156, 162A, 246D).

Acropolis (Gk., upper city). Most ancient Greek cities were on hills, the citadel on the summit being known as the Acropolis, containing the principal temples and treasure-houses (p. 104).

Acroteria (Gk., summits or extremities). Blocks resting on the vertex and lower extremities of the pediment to support statuary or ornaments (pp. 117A, B, C, D, 122B, D, 157B).

Adyton or **Adytum.** The most sacred room of a Greek temple. Usually approached from the naos by a doorway (pp. 109H, 124E).

Aedicule (Lat. *aedicula* = a little house). A small temple-like arrangement originally

COMPARATIVE ARCHES

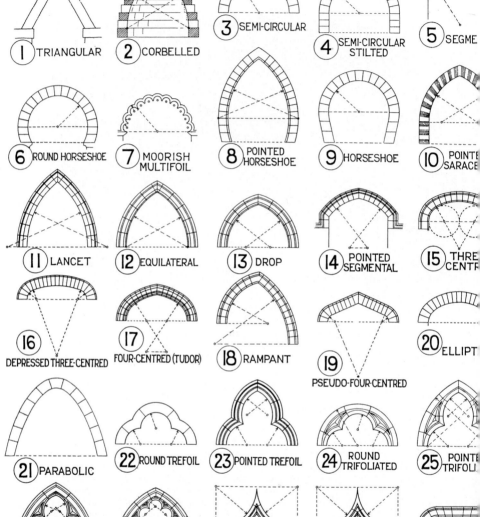

(1) TRIANGULAR

(2) CORBELLED

(3) SEMI-CIRCULAR

(4) SEMI-CIRCULAR STILTED

(5) SEGME.

(6) ROUND HORSESHOE

(7) MOORISH MULTIFOIL

(8) POINTED HORSESHOE

(9) HORSESHOE

(10) POINTE SARACE

(11) LANCET

(12) EQUILATERAL

(13) DROP

(14) POINTED SEGMENTAL

(15) THRE CENTF

(16) DEPRESSED THREE-CENTRED

(17) FOUR-CENTRED (TUDOR)

(18) RAMPANT

(19) PSEUDO-FOUR-CENTRED

(20) ELLIPT

(21) PARABOLIC

(22) ROUND TREFOIL

(23) POINTED TREFOIL

(24) ROUND TRIFOLIATED

(25) POINTE TRIFOLI

(26) CINQUEFOIL

(27) MULTIFOIL

(28) OGEE

(29) OGEE

(30) PSEUDO-THREE-CE

METHOD OF SETTING OUT THE VOUSSOIRS

(31) FLAT OR STRAIGHT

(32) ITALIAN POINTED

(33) VENETIAN

(34) FLORENTINE

(35) SHOULDER

limited to shrines but which became a common motif in the Classical system: columns or pilasters carry a pedimented entablature and enframe a niche or a window. The term 'tabernacle' sometimes is used to convey a similar meaning (pp. 249D, 716B, 756, 757D, F, 1021A).

Agora. The Greek equivalent of the Roman forum, a place of open-air assembly or market (p. 105A).

Aisles (Lat. *ala* = wing). Lateral divisions parallel with the nave in a basilica or church (pp. 259, 264J, 560, 910D).

Alure (Fr. *aller* = to go). An alley, walk or passage. A gallery behind a parapet (pp. 436A, 438).

Ambo (Gk. *ambōn* = a stage, a pulpit). A raised pulpit from which the Epistle and the Gospel were read (pp. 255C, H, K, 256A).

Ambry (or **Aumbry**). A cupboard or recess in a church to contain sacred vessels (p. 630H).

Amorino (pl. **amorini**). Diminutive of Amor, the Roman god of love, identified with the Greek Eros. Amorini were usually represented by Renaissance artists as cherubs or juvenile angels. (pp. 740B, 749G, 750A, D, E, 768A).

Amphi-prostyle. A temple with portico at both ends (pp. 109D, 132A).

Ancones (Gk., elbow or hollow). Consoles on either side of a doorway supporting a cornice (p. 159D, E). Also, projections left on blocks of stone such as drums of columns for use in hoisting and setting in position (p. 110G).

Annulet (Lat. *annulus* = a ring). A small flat fillet encircling a column. It is several times repeated under the ovolo or echinus of the Doric Capital (pp. 110A, 113, 972A).

Anta (plural antæ). A pilaster terminating the side wall of a Greek temple, with base and capital differing from those of adjacent columns; also seen in Egyptian temples (*see* Pilaster) (pp. 55L, 109, 120E, G, J, 132B, E, F, 163L).

Antefixæ (Lat. *ante* = before + *figo* = I fix). Ornamental blocks, fixed vertically at regular intervals along the lower edge of a roof, to cover the ends of tiles (pp. 110H, 117E, G, 134A, 163C).

Anthemion (Gk., a flower). A term given to honeysuckle or palmette ornament of several varieties, in cornices, neckings of Ionic capitals and elsewhere in Greek and Roman architecture (pp. 126R, S, 157G, 159D, E, 163A, C, D, 164G).

Antiquarian. The term is applied to a phase of change in Western European Renaissance architecture (p. 660), lasting from the eighteen-fifties to about 1830, wherein renewed inspiration was sought from ancient Greek and Roman and from Mediaeval architecture. The more concrete manifestations of the Antiquarian movement were the Greek and Gothic Revivals (q.q.v.), both continuing further into the nineteenth century. These Revivals were more strongly marked in some countries than in others.

Apophyge (Gk., a flying off). The cavetto or concave sweep at the top and bottom of the column shaft connecting it with the fillet (pp. 126R, S, 127C, 160B, 165R, 195B, 972B).

Apse (Lat., an arch). The circular or multangular termination of a church sanctuary, first applied to a Roman basilica. The apse is a Continental feature, and contrasts with the square termination of English Gothic churches (pp. 200, 255J, K, 256A, 259C, E, 264A, D, J, K, 269, 273, 281D, G, 322, 330E, F, G, 334C, E, F, 355, 356, 391A, 424D, 491C, D, E, 561, 698B, D, E, 723G, H, 910C, D).

Apteral (Gk., without wings). A term applied to a temple without columns on the sides (p. 109A–D).

Arabesque. Surface decoration, light and fanciful in character, much used by Arabian artists, in elaborate continuations of lines. Applied also to the combinations of flowing lines interwoven with flowers, fruit, and figures as used by Renaissance artists (pp. 758E, 838J).

Aræostyle. A term used when the space between two columns is more than three diameters (p. 113A).

Arcade. A range of arches supported on piers or columns, attached to or detached from the wall (pp. 166, 269, 391, 422B, 611, 720B).

Arch (Lat. *arcus* = an arc of a curve, an arch). A structure of wedge-shaped blocks over an opening, so disposed as to hold together when supported only from the sides. Various forms are shown on the opposite page.

Architrave (Gk., chief beam). The beam or lowest division of the entablature, which extends from column to column (pp. 110A, 144B, 160, 972). The term is also applied to the moulded frame round a door or window (pp. 159, 267R, 759J, L).

Archivolt. The mouldings on the face

of an arch, and following its contour (pp. 203A, 223B, F, 224, 350K).

Arris. The sharp edge formed by the meeting of two surfaces (pp. 113E, 160A, 165J).

Art Nouveau (Fr., new art). A decorative movement in European architecture heralded in the eighteen-eighties (p. 1069C) and flourishing strongly in the period 1893–1907. Its particular characteristics were a flowing and sinuous naturalistic ornament and avoidance of historical architectural traits. The style went under other names in certain European countries: Le Modern Style (France); Jugendstil (Germany and Austria); and Stile Liberty (Italy) (pp. 1065, 1069D, 1070B, C, 1105C, E).

Ashlar. Masonry of smooth squared stones in regular courses, in contradistinction to rubble work (pp. 132E, F, 798A).

Astragal (Gk., knuckle-bone). A small semicircular moulding, often ornamented with a bead or reel (p. 164B). Torus is the name applied to large mouldings of similar section (p. 164L).

Astylar. A treatment of a façade without columns (pp. 681, 685).

Atlantes. Carved male figures serving as pillars, also called Telamones (p. 114J).

Atrium. A highly important apartment in a Roman house, forming an entrance hall or court, the roof open to the sky in the centre (p. 234A, B, D, F). Sometimes the rim of the roof aperture (compluvium) was supported by four or more columns. In Early Christian and later architecture, a forecourt (pp. 259C, E, 260C, 281G, 285C).

Attic. A term first applied in the Renaissance period to the upper storey of a building above the main cornice; also applied to rooms in a roof (pp. 223B, F, 224, 742A, D).

Attic base. A base to a Classic column, so named by Vitruvius, and formed of upper and lower torus and scotia joined by fillets, and the most usual of all column bases (pp. 135B, 165H, S).

Aureole (Lat. *aurum* = gold). A quadrangular, circular, or elliptic halo or frame surrounding the figure of Christ, the Virgin, or certain saints. Also known as the Mandorla or Vesica Piscis (q.v.). When a circular halo envelops only the head, it is called a Nimbus.

Bailey. Open area or court of a fortified castle (pp. 440C, 441A, 442E, L).

Baldachino. A canopy supported by columns, generally placed over an altar or tomb, also known as a 'ciborium' (pp. 256, 263, 720B).

Ball-flower. The ornament of Decorated Gothic architecture (p. 508P), possibly from a flower form or a horse-bell.

Baluster. A pillar or column supporting a handrail or coping, a series of such being called a balustrade (pp. 740A, 741A, 750J, 880A, C, 957D, 960B, 962A, 969D, 971J, L, 980B).

Baptistery. A separate building to contain a font, for the baptismal rite (pp. 313A, 314B, E–G, 321C).

Barbican. An outwork of a mediaeva castle, of which the object was to protect a drawbridge or the entrance (p. 441C, D).

Barge board. A board fixed to the verge of a pitched roof (p. 456A).

Baroque (Fr. *bizarre* = fantastic or irregular). A term applied to design during the late Renaissance period (from 1600 to 1760 in Italy), after the stages of learning and experiment had been passed and Renaissance architecture had reached a characteristic, non-Roman expression; rich, bold and vital. A description is given on p. 659 (pp. 693C, 697A, B, 727, 728, 730, 739A, B, 821C, D).

Bartizan. A small, overhanging turret (p. 487E).

Base (Gk. *basis* = that on which one stands). The lower portion of any structure or architectural feature.

Basement. The lowest stage of a building; also applied to an underground storey (pp. 899C, 903E).

Basilica (Gk. *basileus* = a king). A hall for the administration of justice (p. 200).

Batter. A term applied to a wall with an inclined face (pp. 38E, 47, 51, 1084A).

Battlement. A parapet having a series of indentations or embrasures, between which are raised portions known as merlons (pp. 455A, 484J, 511D–F).

Bays. Compartments into which the nave or roof of a building is divided (pp. 369, 494, 495, 909B). The term is also used for projecting windows (pp. 455A, 456A, 458B).

Bead. A small cylindrical moulding often carved with an ornament resembling a string of beads (pp. 164B, 165P, Q) (*see* Astragal).

Beak-head. A Norman enrichment like a bird's head and beak (p. 508D).

Belfry (Old Fr. *berfrei* = a tower—not connected with 'bell'). A term generally applied to the upper room in a tower in which the bells are hung, and thus often to the tower itself (pp. 259D, 264, 314, 325A, 431D, E, 579C, 611A, 615A, 628D).

Belvedere (Ital. = beautiful view). A roofed but open-sided structure affording an extensive view, usually located at the roof-top of a dwelling but sometimes an independent building on an eminence in a landscape or formal garden (pp. 680F, 706E).

Bema (Gk., a raised platform). A raised stage reserved for the clergy in Early Christian churches; it forms the germ of the transept when expanded laterally in later architecture (p. 259C, E).

Billet. A Norman moulding of short cylinders or square pieces at regular intervals (p. 508A).

Boss (Fr. *bosse* = lump or knob). A projecting ornament at the intersection of the ribs of ceilings, whether vaulted or flat. The term is also applied to the carved ends of weather-mouldings of doors and windows. Bosses are often carved with great delicacy, with heads of angels, flowers, or foliage (pp. 399C–G, 400C, 422C, 468, 471H, 512J–M, 566A, C).

Bouleuterion. A Greek Senate building or council house (p. 105).

Bowtell (supposed to be so called from its resemblance to an arrow shaft or bolt). A Norman convex moulding (usually three-quarters of a circle in section) applied to an angle—a form of roll moulding (p. 508B, C, E, G, H, K, L).

Pointed bowtell, a roll moulding in which two faces meet in a blunt arris (p. 508H, K).

Brace. In framed structure, a subsidiary member placed near and across the angle of two main members in order to stiffen them, as in carpentry roofs (p. 486J).

Brace-moulding. See bracket-moulding.

Bracket. A projecting member to support a weight, generally formed with scrolls or volutes; when carrying the upper members of a cornice, brackets are generally termed Modillions or Consoles (*see also* Ancones) (pp. 191B, C, 700J, 749B, 750G, 753C, 971D, E).

Bracket Moulding (also called 'brace' or 'double ogee'). A late Gothic moulding consisting of two ogee mouldings with convex faces adjoining, resembling a printer's 'brace' or bracket (p. 507V).

Brise Soleil (Fr., sun shield). A screen to break the glare of sunshine upon windows. In recent architecture such screens often take the form of louvres, and are usually made a permanent and effective part of the architecture (p. 1165B).

Broach Spire. An octagonal spire rising without a parapet above a tower, with pyramidal forms at the angles of the tower, as in Early English churches (p. 492A).

Buttress (Old Fr. *bouter* = to bear against). A mass of masonry built against a wall to resist the pressure of an arch or vault. The development is noted in each style (p. 497). A flying buttress is an arch starting from a detached pier and abutting against a wall to take the thrust of the vaulting (pp. 369, 497, 532C, 539A, 544E, 564A, B).

Byzantine Architecture. The style evolved at Constantinople (Byzantium, now Istanbul) in the fifth century (p. 271), and still the style of the Eastern or Greek Church.

Cable. A Norman moulding enrichment like a twisted rope (p. 455G).

Caisson (*see* Coffer).

Caldarium or **Calidarium.** A chamber with hot water baths in a Roman baths building (*see also* **Tepidarium** *and* **Frigidarium**) (pp. 203B, 204B, 207D).

Camber. Slight rise or upward curve of an otherwise horizontal structure.

Cames. Slender strips of lead, grooved at the sides for the reception of pieces of glass, in casement, stained glass and other types of window (p. 510).

Campanile (It. *campana* = bell). An Italian name for a bell-tower, generally detached from the main building (pp. 259D, 264B, F, 314, 325A, 628D, 611A, 615A).

Canephoræ (Gk., basket-carriers). Sculptured female figures bearing baskets on their heads (p. 157D).

Canopy. A covering over a niche or a tomb (pp. 415C, 472G, K, L, 517D, E, F, N, 581A, 631B, C, G, 650B).

Capital (Lat. *caput* = head). The crowning feature of a column or pilaster (pp. 55, 127, 138, 162, 191, 195, 503, 504, 972).

Caryatids. Sculptured female figures used as columns or supports (pp. 135A, 136, 157J).

Casement. A wide hollow used in late Gothic (pp. 498P, 507W, X), so called as it encased bunches of foliage.

Casement window. A window of which the opening lights are hinged at the side and open in the manner of a door (pp. 484G, L, 969H).

Casino. A summer- or garden-house of ornamental character (pp. 715B, 970E).

Castellation. Fortifying a house and providing it with battlements.

Caulicoli (Lat. *caulis* = a stalk). The eight stalks supporting the volutes in the Corinthian capital (pp. 138, 162A, 191, 246D).

Cavetto (It., from Lat. *cavus* = hollow). A simple concave moulding (p. 164D).

Cella (Lat.). The chief apartment of a temple, where the image of a god stood. (pp. 189, 190G, 192).

Cenotaph (Gk., an empty tomb). A sepulchral monument to a person buried elsewhere (pp. 220H, 1032C).

Chaînes (Fr. *chaîne* = a chain). Vertical strips of rusticated masonry rising between the horizontal string-mouldings and cornice of a building, and so dividing the façades into bays or panels (p. 782B, 784B). A popular mode of wall-ornamentation in French seventeenth-century domestic architecture (p. 769).

Chamfer (Fr. *chanfrein* = channel). A diagonal cutting off of an arris formed by two surfaces meeting at an angle. Hollow chamfer, the same but concave in form, like the cavetto.

Chancel (Lat. *cancellus* = a screen). The space for clergy and choir, separated by a screen from the body of the church (pp. 424D, 431C, 491, 910D).

Chantry (Fr. *chanter*, to sing). A small chapel, usually attached to a church, endowed with lands or by other means, for the maintenance of priests to sing or say mass for the donor or such as he may appoint (p. 472).

Chapels. Places for worship, in churches, in honour of particular saints. Sometimes erected as separate buildings (pp. 424D, 426, 468, 469, 470, 471).

Chapter House (Lat. *capitulum* = council). The place of assembly for abbot, prior and members of a monastery for the transaction of business, and often reached from the cloisters, as at Westminster (p. 424D). In England, it was usually polygonal on plan, with a vault resting on a central pillar, e.g. Lincoln (pp. 396B, 410F), Wells (p. 412J), Westminster (p. 422C). It was sometimes oblong, as at Canterbury (p. 411B).

Chatri (Hindi, *chatta* = umbrella). An umbrella-shaped cupola (p. 1243A, B).

Chevet (Fr. *chef* = head). A term applied to a circular or polygonal apse when surrounded by an ambulatory, off which are chapels (pp. 424D, 544G, 560B, 561).

Chevron (Fr., rafter). A zigzag moulding used in Norman architecture, and so called from a pair of rafters, which give this form (pp. 499A, 508C).

Choir (*see* Chancel).

Ciborium (*see* Baldachino).

Cimborio. The Spanish term for a lantern or raised structure above a roof through which light is admitted into the interior (pp. 637B, 641D, 650D, F).

Cinquefoil (Fr. *cinque feuilles* = five leaves). In tracery an arrangement of five foils or openings, terminating in cusps (*see* Cusp).

Cladding. An outer veneer of various materials applied to a building façade (p. 1064).

Classic, Classical. The architecture originating in ancient Greece and Rome, the rules and forms of which were largely revived in the Renaissance in Europe and elsewhere. **Classicism,** a classic idiom or style.

Claustra. A term which had some currency in the late nineteenth and early twentieth century to describe panels, pierced with geometrical designs, as employed by the French architect, Auguste Perret (1874–1954) in certain of his reinforced-concrete buildings (pp. 1083A, B, 1084B).

Clear-story, clere-story, clearstory or **clerestory** (probably from Fr. *clair* = light). An upper stage in a building with windows above adjacent roofs; especially applied to this feature in a church (pp. 40B, F, 41A, 122J, 200, 207A, 369, 658, 663, 911F).

Clepsydra (Gk., a stealing away of water). A water-clock or instrument for measuring time by the discharge of water through a small opening (p. 141F–H).

Cloisters (Lat. *claustrum* = a secluded place). Covered passages round an open space or garth, connecting the church to the chapter house, refectory, and other parts of the monastery. They were generally, as at Westminster, south of the nave and west of the transept, probably to secure sunlight and warmth (pp. 424D, 425A, 560A, 679D).

Coemeteria. Underground burial places, in ancient Rome often taking the form of vaults each containing a number of interments in funerary receptacles (p. 217).

Coffers. Sunk panels, caissons or lacunaria formed in ceilings, vaults, and domes (pp. 110B, 165P, 177J, 191B, C, 196B, 759G).

Colonnade. A range of columns (pp. 171, 190A, 721A, 1023C).

Column (Lat. *columna* = a post). A vertical support, generally consisting of base, circular shaft, and spreading capital (pp. 41A, 46B, 55, 76B, D, 160, 972).

Compartment. A division or separate part of a building or of an element of a building (*see* **Bays** *and* **Severy**).

Composite. An Order employed by the Romans, with a capital composed of the upper part of the Ionic and the lower part of the Corinthian (pp. 223G, 224G, 244, 972).

Conoid. Having the form of a cone. The term is usually applied to the lower part of a Mediaeval vault where the ribs converge against the outer wall and form an approximation of an inverted half-cone or half pyramid (p. 399D, E, F, H).

Console (*see* Bracket).

Coping. The capping or covering to a wall (pp. 388A, 940A).

Corbel (Fr. *corbel* = a raven, hence a beak-like projection). A block of stone, often elaborately carved or moulded, projecting from a wall, supporting the beams of a roof, floor, vault, or other feature (pp. 211A, 231A, 260K, M, 330D, 512N–Q).

Corbel Table. A plain piece of projecting wall supported by a range of corbels and forming a parapet, generally crowned by a coping (pp. 332H, 350C, G, 511A, B, C).

Corinthian. The third Order of Greek architecture (pp. 137, 138, 160E, F, 972E).

Cornice (Fr. *corniche*). In Classic or Renaissance architecture, the crowning or upper portion of the entablature, also used as the term for any crowning projection (pp. 110A, 160, 191, 246B, 681A).

Coro (Sp.). Choir. In Spain the choir usually occupied two or more bays of the nave, the *Capilla Mayor* (comprising sanctuary, high altar and presbytery) filling the east end (pp. 637D, 649B, D). Rejas (q.v.) often served as dividing screens.

Corona. The square projection in the upper part of a cornice, having a deep vertical face, generally plain, and with its soffit or under surface recessed so as to form a 'drip', which prevents water from running down the building (pp. 165A, N, 191, 971E).

Cortile. The Italian name for the internal court, surrounded by an arcade, in a palace or other edifice (pp. 680C, 685G, 690C, D, 699B, D, 733B, F).

Cove, coving. A large hollow, forming part of an arch in section, joining the walls and ceilings of a room. Often decorated with coffering or other enrichment (pp. 936D, 939C, E (left)).

Credence. A small table or shelf near the altar, on which the elements were placed (p. 519K).

Crenellation (Old Fr. *crenel*, a notch). An opening in the upper part of a parapet. Furnished with 'crenelles', or indentations (pp. 454B, 484J). In Britain, a licence to crenellate was necessary before houses could be fortified.

Crepidoma. The steps forming the base of a columned Greek temple (pp. 103A, 110A, 116A, 118B, 135A, 136).

Cresting (Old Fr. *creste* = crest or summit). A light repeated ornament, incised or perforated, carried along the top of a wall or roof (pp. 74E, 511J, K, 1248N).

Crocket (Fr. *croc* = a hook). In Gothic architecture a projecting block or spur of stone carved with foliage to decorate the raking lines formed by angles of spires and canopies (pp. 492, 498F, 511E, N–T, 512F, H, 566J, 630C, H).

Cross. The symbol of Christianity, generally placed on the summit of a gable and in other prominent positions. It is often contained in a circle, and in the fourteenth and fifteenth centuries is richly floriated and of complicated forms (pp. 252B, 260B, E, 267, 287, 294, 359, 396D, 512, 516C, L, 572, 663B, 722).

Crossing. Area at the intersection of nave, chancel and transepts (pp. 395A, 431C, 560).

Crown-post. A post standing upright on the tie-beam of a timber roof and by means of struts or braces giving support to a central collar-purlin and adjacent rafters (p. 446E) but not reaching the apex of a roof, as in the case of a king-post (q.v.).

Crucks. Pairs of timbers, arched together and based near the ground, erected to form principals for the support of the roof and walls of timber-framed small houses (p. 467B): in use in the western half of England until the sixteenth century or later.

Crypt (Gk. *kryptos* = hidden). A space entirely or partly under a building; in churches generally beneath the chancel and used for burial in early times (pp. 260A, 322A, 426F, 722A, 911F).

Crypto-porticus (Lat. concealed or enclosed portico). A passage way wholly or mainly below ground (pp. 48B, 51B, 1023B).

Cunei (Lat. *cuneus* = wedge). The wedge-shaped sections into which seats are divided by radiating passages in ancient theatres (p. 145).

Cupola (Lat. *cupa* = cup). A spherical roof, placed like an inverted cup over a circular, square, or multangular apartment (pp. 195H, 196A, 460A, 679, 700, 704, 720, 739, 743B, G, 800E, 927, 959A, B). (*See* **Dome**).

Curtain. In modern architecture, a glazed wood or metal frame suspended on the face of a building in lieu of a solid, load-bearing wall (pp. 1051B, 1117).

Curtain wall. In mediaeval architecture, the wall surrounding a courtyard: usually interrupted by towers at intervals (pp. 436A, B, 439A, 441C).

Cusp (Lat. *cuspis* = a point). The point formed by the intersection of the foils in Gothic tracery (pp. 499, 515F, G, M, 1256).

Cyma (Lat. *cyma* = wave or billow). A moulding with an outline of two contrary curves—either the cyma recta or cyma reversa (pp. 164G, H, 165Q).

Cymatium. The crowning member of a cornice generally in the form of a cyma, so called from its contour resembling that of a wave (p. 144B).

Dado. The portion of a pedestal between its base and cornice (p. 976E). A term also applied to the lower portions of walls when decorated separately (p. 904C).

Daïs. A raised platform at the end of a Mediæval hall, where the master dined apart from his retainers. The term is now applied to any raised portion of an apartment (p. 449C).

Decastyle. A portico of ten columns (p. 109N).

Decorated. The second of the three divisions of English architecture, which was prevalent during the fourteenth century (p. 393).

Demi-columns. Columns semi-sunk into a wall.

Dentils (Lat. *dentes* = teeth). Tooth-like blocks in Ionic and Corinthian cornices (pp. 127E, F, 160D, 164J, 165N, P, 191C, 246B).

Diaper. A term probably derived from tapestry hangings of Ypres, and applied to any small pattern, such as lozenges or

squares, repeated continuously over the wall surface, as in the spandrels of the nave arcades in Westminster Abbey (pp. 422B, 511B, 566H).

Diastyle. A term used when the space between two columns is three diameters (p. 113A).

Diazoma. A horizontal passage dividing upper and lower levels of seats in an ancient theatre or amphitheatre (p. 145).

Die. The part of a podium or pedestal between its cap-mould and base (pp. 189, 224). (*See* **Dado**).

Dipteral (Gk. *dipteros* = double-winged). A temple having a double range of columns on each of its sides (p. 109A).

Distyle-in-antis. A portico with two columns between antae (p. 109A).

Dodecastyle. A portico of twelve columns (rare).

Dog-tooth. An ornament resembling a row of teeth specially occurring in Early English buildings (p. 508L, M).

Dome (It. *duomo* = a cathedral, from Lat. *domus* = a house). The custom in Italy was to erect cupolas over churches, and the word 'dome' has passed in English and French from the building to this form of roof (*see* **Cupola**).

Donjon. *See* **Keep**.

Doric. The simplest Order of Greek architecture (pp. 108, 110, 113, 116).

Dormer. A window in a sloping roof, usually that of a sleeping-apartment, hence the name (pp. 760, 763B, 767, 771B, H, 772E, 783C, 784B, 788B, C, 803H).

Dosseret. A deep block sometimes placed above a Byzantine capital (pp. 252B, 267E, 285D, 300B–E) in order to support the wide voussoirs of the arch above. Sometimes held to be a survival of the piece of entablature similarly placed in Roman architecture (pp. 177J, L, 200C, F).

Dripstone. In Gothic architecture, the projecting moulding over the heads of doorways, windows, and archways to throw off rain; also known as 'hood-moulding' or, when rectangular, a 'label' (pp. 495G, J, L, 498).

Dromos. A long, uncovered narrow passage leading to an underground tholos or chamber tomb (p. 100B, C).

Drum. The upright part below a dome cr cupola, in which windows might be placed to light the central area of a building (p. 658C).

Early English. The first of the three

divisions of English Gothic architecture, prevalent during the thirteenth century (p. 390).

Eaves. The lower part of a roof projecting beyond the face of the wall (pp. 332H, 435A, C, 456B, 464A, B, F, 552A).

Echinus (Gk. *echinos* = sea-urchin). The term applied to the convex or projecting moulding, resembling the shell of a sea-urchin, which supports the abacus of the Greek Doric capital; sometimes painted with the egg and dart ornament (pp. 110A, 113).

Elizabethan. A term applied to English Early Renaissance architecture of the period 1558–1603 (p. 868).

Embrasure. An opening in a parapet between two merlons; (pp. 442A, C, 450G, 454B, 484J), the inward splaying of a door or window (p. 446G, K).

Encaustic. The art of mural painting in any way in which heat is used to fix the colours (p. 179). **Encaustic tiles;** ornamental tiles of different clays, producing colour patterns after burning. Used in the Middle Ages and revived in the nineteenth century.

English Bond. Brickwork arranged in alternate courses of stretchers and headers.

Enneastyle. A portico of nine columns (p. 109K).

Entablature. The upper part of an Order of architecture, comprising architrave, frieze, and cornice, supported by a colonnade (pp. 110, 144B, 160, 972).

Entasis (Gk., distension). A swelling or curving outwards along the outline of a column shaft, designed to counteract the optical illusion which gives a shaft bounded by straight lines the appearance of curving inwards (p. 95D).

Entresol (*see* **Mezzanine**).

Ephebeion (Ephebeum). An important room connected with an ancient Greek or Roman gymnasium, or with the gymnasium element of a baths building (pp. 203B, 207D, H).

Epinaos (*see* **Opisthodomos**).

Eustyle. A term used when the space between two columns is $2\frac{1}{4}$ diameters (p. 113A).

Exedra (Gk., out-door seat). In Greek buildings, a recess or alcove with raised seat where the disputations of the learned took place. The Romans applied the term to any semicircular or rectangular recess with benches, and it is also applied

to an apse or niche in a church (pp. 190C, 193D, F, 199B, 203B, 207D, 281G).

Extrados (Lat. *extra* = without + *dorsum* = back). The outer curve of an arch.

Façade. The face or elevation of a building (pp. 122B, 232A, 403, 690A).

Faience. Glazed earthenware, often ornamented, used for pottery or for building. Originally made at Faenza in Italy from about 1300 (pp. 676A, D, 1223, 1226).

Fan Vault. A system of vaulting peculiar to the Perpendicular period, in which all ribs have the same curve, and resemble the framework of a fan (pp. 398, 399H, 426C, E).

Fascia (Lat. *facies* = face). A vertical face of little projection, usually found in the architrave of the entablature of an Order. The architrave of the Ionic and Corinthian Orders is divided into two or more such bands (pp. 157J, 160D–F, 191C).

Also, a board or plate covering the end of roof rafters.

Feretory (Lat. *ferre* = to carry). A shrine for relics designed to be carried in processions (p. 581D).

Fielded panels. Panels of which the surface projects in front of the enclosing frame.

Fillet. A small flat band between mouldings to separate them from each other; also the uppermost member of a cornice (p. 164A).

Finial (Lat. *finis* = end). The upper portion of a pinnacle, bench-end, or other architectural feature (pp. 450C, 461D, 512E–H, 556).

Flamboyant (Fr. *flambeau* = flame). Tracery in which the bars of stonework form long wavy divisions like flames (p. 563D).

Flèche (Fr., arrow). A term applied to a slender wooden spire rising from a roof (p. 564C, H).

Flemish Bond. Brickwork arranged in alternate headers and stretchers in the same course.

Fluting. The vertical channelling on the shaft of a column (pp. 144B, 165F, J, K, M).

Flying Buttress (*see* **Buttress**).

Foil (Lat. *folium* = leaf). Each of the small arc openings in Gothic tracery separated by cusps. Trefoil, quatrefoil, cinquefoil, etc., signify the number of foils (p. 1256).

Formeret. In a Mediæval vault, the half-rib against the wall, known in England as the 'wall rib' (p. 373C).

Formwork. Temporary casing of woodwork, within which concrete is moulded.

Forum. A Roman public open space, for social, civic or market purposes. There was at least one in every Roman town (pp. 182, 185, 190C, 226).

Fresco (It. *fresco* = fresh). The term originally applied to painting on a wall while the plaster is wet, but is often used for any wall painting not in oil colours. Other processes are called 'tempera' or 'encaustic', etc. (pp. 179, 247).

Fret (Old Fr. *frettes* = grating). An ornament in Classic or Renaissance architecture consisting of an assemblage of straight lines intersecting at right angles, and of various patterns (pp. 163F, 745G). Sometimes referred to as the **Key Pattern.**

Frieze (It. *fregio* = ornament). The middle division of the Classic entablature (pp. 110A, 120N, 160, 163H, 351J, L) (*see* **Zoophorus**).

Frigidarium. An apartment in a Roman baths building, equipped with a large, cold bath (pp. 203, 204A, B, C, 207B, D) (*see also* **Caldarium** *and* **Tepidarium**).

Gable. The triangular portion of a wall, between the enclosing lines of a sloping roof. In Classic architecture it is called a pediment (pp. 387E, K, M, 403A, 450, 456B, 458).

Galilee. A porch used as a chapel for penitents, etc., in some Mediæval churches. The origin of the term is conjectural. Some derive it from the Latin *galeria*, a long porticus or porch. Others suppose that the verse in S. Mark xvi, 7, 'He goeth before you into Galilee: there shall ye see him,' suggests a meeting-place, and hence the name. Examples at Ely (p. 410A), Lincoln (p. 410F), and Durham (p. 411E).

Gallery. A communicating passage or wide corridor for pictures and statues (pp. 884A, 965F). An internal and external feature in Mediæval buildings (p. 355A, C). An upper storey for seats in a church (pp. 264A, C, D, E, 281D, G, 282B, 918).

Gargoyle (Lat. *gurges* = whirlpool). A projecting water-spout grotesquely carved to throw off water from the roof (pp. 511L, M, 566B).

Georgian. A term applied to English Late Renaissance architecture of the period 1702–1830 (p. 868).

Glyph (Gk., a groove). A carved vertical channel (*see* Triglyph).

Glyptotheca (Gk. *glypton* = carving + *theke* = repository). A building to contain sculpture.

Gothic. The name generally given to the pointed style of Mediæval architecture prevalent in Western Europe from the thirteenth to the fifteenth century (p. 367).

Gothic Revival. A manifestation first evident in the late eighteenth century (p. 660), but belonging principally to the nineteenth. The countries most affected were England (pp. 875, 986), France and Germany (p. 1063) and, less strongly, the U.S.A. (p. 1127).

Greek Revival. Like the Gothic Revival (q.v.), this had its beginnings in the late eighteenth century (p. 660). In England it culminated in the eighteen-twenties and had concluded by 1840 (later in Scotland), while in France it similarly was at its most evident in the early nineteenth century (p. 770). In Germany it endured to mid-nineteenth century) (p. 1062). In the U.S.A. it was the especial characteristic of the architecture of the period 1815–60 (p. 1126).

Groin. The curved arris formed by the intersection of vaulting surfaces (pp. 177M, 207A, 370B, D, 373A, B, D, 399A).

Guilloche. A circular interlaced ornament like network, frequently used to ornament the 'torus' moulding (p. 164L).

Guttæ (Lat. *gutta* = drop). Small cones under the triglyphs and mutules of the Doric entablature (pp. 110A, 120M).

Gymnasium (Gymnasion). In ancient Greece, a place for physical exercises and training, including running, larger than the palaestra (q.v.).

Hagioscope (Gk. *hagios* = sacred + *skopein* = to view). An oblique opening in a Mediæval church wall to give a view of the altar, and sometimes known as a 'squint' (p. 491E).

Half-timber Building. A structure formed of timber posts, rails, and struts, and interspaces filled with brick or other material, and sometimes plastered (pp. 456B, 462C, 464, 478J, K, 484, 485, 595A, C).

Hall church. Church in which nave and aisles are of, or approximate to, equal height (pp. 388B, 591C, 1083B).

Hammer-beam Roof. A late Gothic form of roof without a direct tie, the finest example being in Westminster Hall (pp. 434, 435F, H, K, L, 500E, G, H).

Hearth-money; Hearth-penny. A tax on hearths existing in England from the Conquest, sanctioned by Parliament in 1672/3 and abandoned 1689.

Hecatompedon (Gk., a hundred-foot temple). The name given to the naos of the Parthenon, Athens (pp. 119, 122G), inherited from a former temple of 566 B.C. upon the site, of which the length was exactly 100 Doric feet (1 Doric foot = 12·88 ins) and the width 50 Doric feet. The original Hecatompedon temple was demolished in 490–488 B.C. to make way for the Older Parthenon, destroyed by the Persians in 480 B.C. when only partly completed.

Helix (Gk., a spiral or tendril). One of the 16 spirals or small volutes (helices) under the abacus of a Corinthian capital (pp. 138, 162A, 191C, D, 195B, 199E, 246D).

Helm. A bulbous termination to the top of a tower. The type is found principally in central and eastern Europe (pp. 816B, 819B, 822A, C).

Helm Roof. The type of roof in which four faces rest diagonally between the gables and converge at the top (pp. 355C, 362K, 387E).

Henostyle-in-antis. A portico with one column between antae.

Heptastyle. A temple having seven columns on the front (p. 109G).

Hermes. A Greek deity. A bust (Hermes, Herm or Term) on a square pedestal instead of a human body, used in Classic times along highways and to mark boundaries, and decoratively in Roman and Renaissance times (pp. 759K, 975F).

Heroum. In Greek architecture, a small shrine or chapel dedicated to a semi-deified person or to the memory of a mortal.

Hexastyle. A portico having a row of six columns (pp. 109J, 116A, 118, 377B).

Hieron (Gk., a holy place). The whole of the sacred enclosure surrounding a temple, as at Epidauros (pp. 105B, 106B).

Hippodrome. In ancient Greece, a course for horse and chariot racing, the equivalent of the Roman circus (p. 216A, D).

Hood Moulding (see **Dripstone**).

Hoop-tie Principle. A method developed in the Renaissance period, by which a pieced ring of timber, or a metal chain or hoop, binds the lower part of a dome or cupola to prevent splitting outwards or to minimise the burden on external buttresses having a similar purpose (pp. 616C, 722C, 912A).

Hypæthral (Gk., under the sky). A building or temple without a roof or with a central space open to the sky (pp. 38E, H, 122E, F, K, 141N, 199A).

Hypocaust (Lat. *hypocaustum* = a fire chamber). A system of ducts by which heat from the furnace was distributed throughout the building (p. 203).

Hypogeum. In ancient times, all parts of a building undergound.

Hypostyle (Gk. *hypo* = under + Lat. *stylus* = pillar). A pillared hall in which the roof rests on columns. Applied to the many-columned halls of Egyptian temples (pp. 38E, G, 40F, G, 41).

Hypotrachelion (Gk., under the neck). The channels or grooves beneath the trachelion at the junction of capital and shaft of a column (p. 113) (see **Trachelion**).

Iconostas. A screen between nave and chancel of a Byzantine church (pp. 286B, 300L).

Imbrex. In classical architecture, a roofing cover tile over the joint between flat or hollow tiles (p. 110H, 181H).

Imbrication. An overlapping, as of one row of scalloped roofing tiles breaking joint with the next, after the manner of the scales of a pine cone (pp. 141A, 754K).

Impluvium. In Greek and Roman houses, a shallow tank under the Compluvium, or opening in the roof of an atrium (p. 234B).

Impost (Lat. *imponere* = to lay upon). The member, usually formed of mouldings, on which an arch rests (pp. 207A, 223, 224, 256A, 498).

Indent. A notch. **Indented moulding.** A moulding cut in the form of zig-zag pointed notches (p. 504B—abacus of left capital).

Intarsia. In furniture, a decorative inlay of various materials in another, usually wood.

Intercolumniation. The space between the columns (pp. 113A, 970G).

Intrados (Lat. *intra* = within + *dorsum* = back). The inner curve of an arch.

Ionic. The second Order of Greek architecture (pp. 125, 126, 127, 130, 132, 134, 160, 972).

Jacobean. A term applied to English Early Renaissance architecture of the period 1603–25 (p. 868).

Jambs (Fr. *jambe* = leg). The sides of doors and windows (pp. 159, 498). The portion exposed outside the window-frame is the 'reveal'.

Jubé (Fr.). The equivalent of the English rood-screen between nave and chancel (p. 795A).

Keel Moulding. A moulding like the keel of a ship formed of two ogee curves meeting in a sharp arris (p. 507J, K); used rounded in form in the fifteenth century. The word 'keel' is also applied to the ogee form of arch (p. 1256, Nos. 28, 29).

Keep. The inner Great Tower or Donjon of a castle (pp. 436D, E, 440A, B, 442L, 445B, D, E, F).

Keystone. The central stone of a semicircular arch, sometimes sculptured (pp. 223A, B, C, F, M, 224, 970, 1256).

King-post. A vertical post extending from the ridge to the centre of the tie-beam below (pp. 264A, 321B, 433, 435B, E).

Label (*see* **Dripstone**).

Laconicum. A dry sweating room in a Roman baths building.

Lacunaria (*see* **Coffer**).

Lancet Arch. A sharp pointed arch, resembling a lancet, chiefly in use during the early English Period (pp. 388A, 415D, 424A, B, 499B, C, 1256).

Lantern. A construction, such as a tower, at the crossing of a church, rising above the neighbouring roofs and glazed at the sides (pp. 375, 408A).

Lararium. A room or niche in a Roman house, in which the effigies of the household gods (Lares) were placed (p. 232E).

Later. A Roman unburnt brick.

Lich Gate (A.-Sax. *lic* = body). A covered gateway to a churchyard, forming a resting-place for a coffin where portion of the burial service is often read.

Lierne (Fr. *lien* = tie). A short intermediate rib in Gothic vaulting which does not rise from the impost and is not a ridge rib (pp. 398, 399F, G).

Linenfold. A type of relief ornament, imitating folded linen, carved on the face of individual timber panels. Popular in the late 15th and the 16th century (p. 461J).

Lintel. The horizontal timber or stone, also known as the architrave, that spans an opening (pp. 46B, 48B, 54H, J, 116, 144B, 146A).

Loggia. A gallery behind an open arcade or colonnade (pp. 611, 703, 710F, 744H, 892A, B).

Louvre. A series of inclined slats in a vertical frame, allowing ventilation without admitting rain. A roof ventilator embodying the principle. Sometimes applied to roof ventilators in general (p. 449A).

Lozenge. Diamond-shape.

Lunette (Fr. *lune* = moon). A semicircular window or wall-panel let into the inner base of a concave vault or dome (p. 658F).

Lych gate (*see* **Lich gate**).

Machicolation (Fr. *mache* = melted matter + *coulis* = flowing). A projecting wall or parapet allowing floor openings, through which molten lead, pitch, stones, etc., were dropped on an enemy below (pp. 445C, H, 552B, C, 612H, 625A).

Maeander. Running ornament in the form of a fret or key pattern (p. 163F).

Mandorla (It., almond) (*see* **Aureole**).

Mannerism. A term of recent invention coined to describe the characteristics of the output of Italian Renaissance architects of the period 1530–1600, who, after the long period occupied in imbibing Roman classical rules chose to work in a relaxed nonconformist style (p. 671). Architecture of this character (pp. 682D, 686B, 706B, 709A, 716A, B, 724D), which in fact is common to the European Renaissance as a whole, is for that reason herein distinguished as 'Proto-Baroque' (pp. 660, 671), the Baroque being the ultimate outcome (pp. 659–60, 671–2).

Mansard Roof. A roof with steep lower slope and flatter upper portion, named after Mansart (pp. 1032A, 1138C). Also known as a 'gambrel' roof.

Marquise (Fr.). A projecting canopy over an entrance door, often of metal and glass (p. 1105C, E).

Masons' Mitre. The treatment in masonry and sometimes in joinery for mouldings meeting at right angles, when the diagonal mitre thus formed does not coincide with the joint, but is worked on the face of the one piece which is carried straight through and simply butts on the other (pp. 159D, E, 267R).

Mastaba. An ancient Egyptian, rectangular, flat-topped, funerary mound, with battered (sloping) sides, covering a burial chamber below ground (p. 24A–G). As royal tombs, mastabas preceded the great pyramids of the third to sixth dynasties.

Mediaeval. A term taken to comprehend the Romanesque and Gothic periods of architectural development.

Megaron. The principal room of an Aegean house (p. 99C).

Merlon. The upstanding part of an embattled parapet, between two 'crenelles' or embrasure openings (pp. 454B, 484J).

Metope (Gk. *meta* = between + *ope* = an opening). The space between Doric triglyphs, sometimes left open in ancient examples; afterwards applied to the carved slab (pp. 110A, 118B, 120A, C, M, 144B, 163K, M).

Mezzanine. An intermediate floor formed within a lofty storey (Fr. *entresol*) (p. 804K).

Misericord (Lat. *misericordia* = pity). A hinged seat, made to turn up to afford support to a standing person, and with underside frequently grotesquely carved (pp. 517H–K, 596H).

Mitre. The term applied, especially in joinery, to the diagonal joint formed by the meeting of two mouldings at right angles (pp. 519E, F, 971K).

Modillions (*see* **Bracket**).

Module (Lat. *modulus* = measure). A measure of proportion, by which the parts of a Classic Order or building are regulated, being usually the semi-diameter of a column immediately above its base, which is divided into thirty parts or minutes (pp. 113, 160, 970, 972).

Monopteral. A temple, usually circular, consisting of columns only.

Mosaic. Decorative surfaces formed by small cubes of stone, glass, and marble; much used in Hellenistic, Roman and later times for floors and wall decoration (pp. 179, 249, 252, 256, 266, 267, 269, 291B, 292, 332K).

Motte. The earthen conical mound of a castle; usually has a related **Bailey**, this a courtyard or ward (p. 441A).

Mouldings (Lat. *modulari* = to be measured). The contours given to projecting members (pp. 155, 164, 165, 507, 508).

Mudéjar. A Spanish Muslim under Christian rule. A vernacular style of Spanish architecture, particularly of Aragon and Castile, of the twelfth to the sixteenth century, blending Muslim and Christian characteristics: its influence survived into the seventeenth century (p. 1233). **Neo-Mudéjar.** A perpetuation or revival of features of the style in the Colonial phase (sixteenth–nineteenth century) in Latin America (pp. 1139, 1166).

Mullions. Vertical members dividing windows into different numbers of lights (pp. 456B, 458B, 499).

Mutules. Projecting inclined blocks in the Doric cornices, derived from the ends of wooden beams (pp. 110, 111, 113, 120M, 244).

Naos (Gk., dwelling). The principal chamber in a Greek temple, containing the statue of the deity (pp. 107, 109, 117, 122).

Narthex. A long arcaded porch forming an entrance into a Christian basilican church, originally appropriated to penitents (pp. 255K, 259C, E, 264J, 278B, F, 281G).

Naumachia (Gk., a battle of ships). A lake for the exhibition of sea fights, encircled by seats for spectators; sometimes refers to the spectacle itself.

Nave (Gk. *naos* = dwelling, or more probably Lat. *navis* = ship). The ship was the symbol of the Church, in which the faithful are borne safely over the sea of life to the haven of eternity. The term is applied to the western limb of a church, as opposed to the choir; also to the central aisle of the basilican, Mediæval, or Renaissance church, as opposed to the side aisles (pp. 255K, 259C, E, 369C, 424D, 560A, B, 910D).

Necking. The space between the astragal of the shaft and the commencement of the capital proper in the Roman Doric (pp. 699C, 972).

Necropolis. A town of the dead: a burial ground (p. 183).

Newel. (1) The central shaft, round which wind the steps of a circular staircase; (2) also applied to the post into which the handrail is framed (pp. 771A, 838H, 903D, 904A, 971J, L, 975C, E).

Niche (It. *nicchio* = shell). A recess in a wall hollowed like a shell for the reception of a statue or ornament (pp. 192J, L, 193B, D, 195H, J, 403, 757F).

Nimbus (Lat., bright cloud). A circular halo (*see* **Aureole**).

Norman. The style, also termed English Romanesque, of the 11th and 12th centuries (pp. 390, 391A, 392B, 494A–D).

Nymphæum (literally a sanctuary of the nymphs). A building in Classic architecture for plants, flowers, and running water, ornamented with statues (pp. 206, 285A, B).

Obelisk. A tall pillar of square section tapering upwards and ending in a pyramid (pp. 49, 664).

Octastyle. A portico with a range of eight columns (pp. 103, 109H, M, 377C).

Odeion (Gk., music-room). A building, resembling a Greek theatre, designed for musical contests (pp. 103B, 104C).

Oecus. The main room of a Greek house, the successor of the Aegean megaron (p. 238A).

Ogee. A moulding made up of a convex and concave curve. Also applied to an arch of similar shape (pp. 164H, 1256).

Ogivale (Fr., pointed). The term given to Gothic architecture in France (p. 534).

Opaion. A Greek term for a clearstory or top light.

Opisthodomos (Gr., a back room). The rear porch of a temple. (pp. 117H, 122G).

Opus (pl. Opera). A work.

Opus Alexandrinum (Lat., Alexandrian work). Mosaics inlaid in a stone or marble paving (p. 267Q).

Opus incertum, — quadratum, — reticulatum, — testaceum, etc. (*see* p. 175).

Order. An Order in architecture signifies a column, with base (usually), shaft, and capital, together with the entablature which it supports (pp. 160, 972). Also applied to each ring of voussoirs in a Mediæval arch (p. 507).

Ordonnance (Fr.). The disposition of the parts of a building.

Oriel. A window corbelled out from the face of a wall by means of projecting stones (pp. 450D, 460F, 485D).

Orthostates. In Greek architecture, a course of large squared stones at the base of a wall (pp. 120G, J, 132C, E, F).

Ovolo. A convex moulding much used in Classic and Renaissance architecture, often carved with the egg and dart or egg and tongue (pp. 164F, 165L, Q, 750G).

Palæstra (Gk. *palaistra* = wrestling school). A public building for the training of athletes (pp. 105B, 148).

Palladian motif. An arched opening flanked by two smaller, square-headed openings (p. 741).

Palmette (*see* **Anthemion**).

Panel. A compartment, sunk or raised, in walls, ceilings, doors, wainscoting, etc. (pp. 159A, 246F, 461J, 519, 904, 971K, 977D) (*see also* **Coffer**).

Parapet (Lat. *parare* = to guard + *pectus* = breast). The portion of wall above the roof-gutter, sometimes battlemented; also applied to the same feature, rising breast-high, in balconies, platforms, and bridges (pp. 245, 334, 449A, 511A–F, 552B, C, 663, 690, 1023C).

Parclose Screen (Old Fr. *parclose* = an enclosure). A screen enclosing a chapel, as a shelter from draughts, or to prevent distraction to worshippers; also applied to the screen around a tomb or shrine (p. 516A).

Pargetting (pargeting, parging). External ornamental plasterwork having raised, indented or tooled patterns; used from Tudor times onward chiefly in East Anglia and the south-east.

Pastas or **Prostas.** A vestibule in front of a Greek house, with a part of one side open to a forecourt (p. 153B).

Pateræ. Flat circular ornaments which resemble the Classical saucers used for wine in sacrificial libations (pp. 159D, E, 163D, G, J).

Patio. A Spanish arcaded or colonnaded courtyard, similar to an Italian cortile (pp. 646A, B, 847B, C, 848A, 849B, 850A, 853B).

Pavimentum (Lat. *pavire* = to ram down). A pavement formed by pieces of tile, marble, stone, flints, or other material set in cement and consolidated by beating down with a rammer (pp. 249H, K, L, M).

Pedestal. A support for a column, statue or vase. It usually consists of a base, die and cornice or cap-mould (pp. 224A, B, C, F, H, J, 970C, F, J, K).

Pediment. In Classic architecture, a triangular piece of wall above the entablature, enclosed by raking cornices (pp. 110A, 116A, 130A). In Renaissance architecture used for any roof end, whether triangular, broken or semicircular (pp. Frontis., 903E, 1023A, B, C). In Gothic, such features are known as gables.

Pendentive. The term applied to the triangular curved overhanging surface by means of which a circular dome is supported over a square or polygonal compartment (pp. 80H, 177N, 277, 281C, 285, 291B, 658, 909B, 917).

Pentastyle. A temple front of five columns.

Peribolus (Gk. *peribole* = an enclosing). The enclosing wall or colonnade surrounding a temenos or sacred enclosure, and hence sometimes applied to the enclosure itself (pp. 130A, 190A, C, 192B).

Peripteral. A term applied to an edifice surrounded by a single range of columns (p. 109E, F, H, K, M, N).

Peristyle. A range of columns surrounding a court or temple (pp. 116, 118B, 130, 190, 195, 663B, 700B, 721A).

Perpendicular. A phase of English Gothic evolved from the Decorated style, and prevalent during the fifteenth and sixteenth centuries (pp. 391B, 393, 495L, M).

Perron (Fr.). A landing or platform outside the portal of a domestic or public building, approached in a dignified way by a single or double flight of steps (p. 833D).

Piano nobile (It., noble floor). The principal floor of an Italian palace, raised one floor above ground level and containing the principal social apartments (pp. 703E, 711B, D).

Piazza (It.). A public open place, square or market place, surrounded by buildings: may vary in shape and in civic purpose (pp. 611D, 718, 721).

Picturesque. The term is used in a specialized sense to describe one of the attitudes of taste towards architecture and landscape gardening in the late eighteenth and early nineteenth century (c. 1785–1835): buildings and landscape were to have the controlled informality of a picture. Influential publications of the period were *An Essay on the Picturesque* (1794) by Sir Uvedale Price and *An Enquiry into the Changes of Taste in Landscape Gardening* by Humphrey Repton (p. 876).

Pier (Lat. *petra* = rock). A mass of masonry, as distinct from a column, from which an arch springs, in an arcade or bridge; also applied to the wall between doors and windows (pp. 166, 214A, 238, 245, 351K, 909B, 960A). The term is sometimes given to a pillar in Gothic architecture (pp. 422B, 503).

Pilaster. A rectangular feature in the shape of a pillar, but projecting only about one-sixth of its breadth from a wall, and the same design as the Order with which it is used (*see* Anta) (pp. 160F, 196B, 690, 776, 960, 1023C).

Pilotis (Fr., stilts). Posts on an unenclosed ground floor carrying a raised building (pp. 1008, 1074B, 1077A, 1078).

Pinacotheca (Gk., picture gallery). A building to contain painted pictures (p. 142H).

Pinnacle. In Gothic architecture, a small turret-like termination on the top of buttresses, parapets, or elsewhere, often ornamented with bunches of foliage called crockets (pp. 369, 403, 418A, 426A, 511E, 686A, 739C, 819A, 1022D).

Piscina (Lat., a reservoir of water). A stone basin in a niche near the altar, to receive the water in which the priest rinses the chalice (p. 515E–H). A term also applied to the tank or fountain in Roman baths (pp. 203A, 207B).

Pitch of Roof. The inclination or angle of its surface to the horizon.

Plan. The representation of the shape of a building showing the general distribution of its parts on the ground (pp. 40G, 74H, 109, 203B, 231B, 259C, 281G, 560, 723G, 775E, 899B).

Plateresque (Sp., *plateria* = silverwork). A phase of the Early Period of Spanish Architecture of the later fifteenth and early sixteenth century, an intricate style named after its likeness to silverwork (p. 845).

Plinth. The lowest square member of the base of a column; also applied to the projecting stepped or moulded base of any building (pp. 127E, F, 199E, 377D, 388A).

Plough-share Twist. The irregular or winding surface in a vault, resembling a plough-share, where the wall ribs, owing to the position of the clear-story windows, start at a higher level than the other ribs (p. 373C).

Podium. A continuous pedestal; also the enclosing platform of the arena of an amphitheatre (pp. 171A, 189, 190, 211B, 798B, 1023C).

Poppy-head (Lat. *puppis* = poop or raised stern of a ship). The ornamental termination to a bench-end, frequently carved with fleur-de-lis, animals, or figures (p. 517B, C, G).

Portcullis (Fr. *porte* = a gate; *coulisse* = a groove). A heavy lattice grating of timber or iron, sliding in vertical grooves in the jambs of a portal of a defended building.

Portico. A colonnaded space forming an entrance or vestibule, with a roof supported on at least one side by columns (pp. Frontis., 103, 190F, 798B, 813E, 902G, 1023C).

Posticum. The Latin term for the rear porch of a temple (*see* **Opisthodomus**) (p. 117H).

Presbytery (Lat. *presbyter* = elder). The space at the eastern end of a church for the clergy, but often applied to the whole sanctuary (pp. 410–13, 424D, 560).

Priory. A monastic establishment presided over by a prior, who was often subordinate to an abbot (p. 402).

Pronaos. The part of a temple in front

of the naos, often synonymous with portico (pp. 109, 122G).

Propylæum (pl. **Propylæa**) (Gk., a front portal). An important entrance gateway or vestibule, in front of a sacred enclosure, as at Athens, Priene, Sunium, and Eleusis (pp. 103C, 104, 142).

Proscenium (Gk., *proskenion*). In ancient Greek theatres, a colonnade standing in front of the scene building (*skene*), the top of which eventually became the stage (*logeion* = a speaking place): thus all of the stage works in front of the ornamental back-stage. Nowadays, the term means only the frontispiece of the stage.

Prostyle (Gk., a column in front). An open portico of columns standing in front of a building (pp. 109C, D, 134B).

Prytaneion (**Prytaneum**). The public hall and state dining room of a Greek city (p. 105B).

Pseudo-dipteral (Gk., false doublewinged). A temple which is planned as a dipteral building, i.e. two columns in depth around the naos, but from which the inner range is omitted (p. 109L).

Pseudo-peripteral (Gk., falsely peripteral). A temple lacking a pteroma and having the flank columns attached to the temple walls (pp. 109G, 189A–C).

Pteroma (Gk., a wing). The space between the lateral walls of the naos of a temple and the peristyle columns (p. 109).

Pulpitum (Lat.). A stone gallery or rood-loft (q.v.) over the entrance to the choir of a cathedral or church (Fr. Jubé, p. 795A).

Pulvinated (Lat., a cushion). A term applied to a frieze whose face is convex in profile (pp. 159C, 195H, J, 745A, B).

Purlin. A horizontal beam in a roof, resting on the principal rafters and supporting the common rafters and roof covering (p. 500D–F).

Pycnostyle (Gk., close columned). A term given when the space between two columns is 1½ diameters (p. 113A).

Pylon (Gk., a gateway). A term applied to the mass of masonry with central opening, forming a monumental entrance to Egyptian temples (pp. 47, 51A).

Quadrangle. A broad enclosure or court, defined by buildings (pp. 478A, C, 480A, B, D, F).

Quadriga. A four-horsed chariot, in sculptured form, often surmounting a monument (pp. 149, 223F, 224F, 1092A).

Quatrefoil (Fr. *quatre feuilles* = four leaves). In tracery, a panel divided by cusps into four leaf-shaped openings (pp. 499D, 511D, F).

Quirk. A sharp V-shaped incision in a moulding, such as that flanking the Norman bowtell (pp. 498B, 507B, E).

Quoin (Fr. *coin* = angle). A term generally applied to the corner-stones at the angles of buildings and hence to the angle itself (pp. 756, 940A).

Rampart. Defensive earthen bank surrounding a castle, fortress or fortified city (p. 441A). May have a stone parapet.

Rebate. A rectangular sinking, channel or groove cut longitudinally in a piece of timber in order to receive the edge of another, or a recess in the jambs of an opening to receive a door or window (pp. 942C, 944D).

Reeding. A series of convex mouldings of equal width, side by side: the inverse of fluting (pp. 55J, 74F). The fluting of the lower third of column shafts was sometimes infilled with reeds to strengthen them against damage (p. 196B).

Refectory. The dining-hall in a monastery, convent, or college (pp. 308, 402, 424D, 432C, 476).

Regula (Lat., a rule). The short band, under the triglyphs, beneath the tenia of the Doric entablature, and to which the guttæ are attached (pp. 110A, 113, 120M, 144B).

Reja (Sp.). An ornate iron grille or screen, a characteristic feature of Spanish church interiors (pp. 637B, 860B, C).

Reliquary. A light portable receptacle for sacred relics (pp. 630B, 750H).

Renaissance (Fr., a new birth). The term applied to the reintroduction of Classic architecture all over Europe, in the fifteenth and sixteenth centuries (p. 654).

Rendering. Plaster or stucco applied to an external wall; a first coat of plaster internally.

Reredos. The screen, or ornamental work, rising behind the altar. The reredoses in Manchester, S. Albans, and Durham Cathedrals are carved structures reaching nearly to the roof (pp. 420G, 425D, 581C, 631H, K, 638A, 641D, 750E, 909B).

Respond. A half-pillar at end of an arcade.

Retable. A ledge or shelf behind an altar for holding vases or candles. The

Spanish **retablo** (p. 638A) is a sumptuously ornate form of reredos (above).

Retro-choir. The parts of a large church behind the high altar (pp. 410D, 412G, J).

Reveal. The surface at right angles to the face of a wall, at the side of an opening cut through it; known as a 'splay' when cut diagonally. Especially applied to the part outside the window-frame (pp. 942C, 944D).

Rib. A projecting band on a ceiling, vault, or elsewhere (pp. 370, 373, 399, 461C, 507E, L, U, Y, 884, 887, 959A, 977A, B).

Ridge. The apex of a sloping roof, running from end to end (pp. 117A, 132H, 259A, 388A, 418A, 432A, 532C, 539A).

Ringhiera. A balcony on the main front of an Italian Mediæval town-hall from which governmental decrees might be proclaimed or public addresses delivered by the magistrates (p. 330D).

Rococo (Fr. *rocaille* = rock-work). A term applied to a type of Renaissance ornament in which rock-like forms, fantastic scrolls, and crimped shells are worked up together in a profusion and confusion of detail often without organic coherence, but presenting a lavish display of decoration (pp. 804, 825B). A later development of the Baroque.

Roll Moulding. A plain round moulding (p. 55J). In Mediæval architecture, sometimes known as the Bowtell (p. 507B, C, D).

Romanesque. The name given to the style of architecture, founded on Roman architecture, and prevalent in Western Europe from the ninth to the twelfth century (p. 303).

Rood Loft (A.-Sax., rod, hence cross or crucifix). A raised gallery over the rood screen (p. 516C, D), a name given to the chancel screen when it supports the 'rood or large cross erected in many churches in Mediæval times (p. 516L). It was reached by stairs in the chancel wall (p. 516F, G), and was also used as a gallery for minstrels and singers on festival days.

Rose Window (*see* **Wheel Window**).

Rostrum (Lat., the prow of a ship). The plural 'rostra' denoted the raised tribune in the Forum Romanum, from which orators addressed the people, and was so called because decorated with the prows of ships taken in war (p. 171) as were rostral columns (p. 228).

Rotonda. A round building.

Rubble. Stone walling of rough, undressed stones.

Rustication. A method of forming stonework with roughened surfaces and recessed joints, principally employed in Renaissance buildings (pp. 681, 685, 902A, 970A).

Sanctuary. A holy or consecrated place. The most sacred part of a church or temple (pp. 410D, 411F, 424D).

Sarcophagus. Richly carved coffin (pp. 150G, H, 181C, 267H, 300J).

Scena (Gr. *skene*). The back scene of an ancient theatre (p. 145D, F).

Scotia (Gk. *skotia* = darkness). The concave moulding between the two torus mouldings in the base of a column, throwing a deep shadow (pp. 164E, 165H, T).

Screen. A partition or enclosure of iron, stone, or wood, often carved; when separating choir from nave, it is termed the choir screen. The Latin cancellus (screen), corrupted to 'chancel', primarily used for the enclosing object, was afterwards applied to the space which it enclosed (pp. 291B, 392B, 516B, 581E, 595B).

Scroll Moulding. A kind of moulding, so called from its resemblance to a scroll of paper, the end of which projects over the other part (p. 507M).

Section (Lat. *sectus* = cut). A term used to express the representation of a building cut by a vertical plane, so as to show the construction. The term is also applied in the same way to any solid (pp. 32, 38, 117E, F, 199A, 281D, E, 416E, 910C).

Sedilia (Lat., seat). The seats for the priests, generally of masonry, formed in the wall on the south side of the chancel (p. 515K, M, N, P).

Severy. A compartment or bay of a vault (pp. 369C, F, 370F, H).

Sgraffito (It., scratched). A method of decoration by which an upper coat of white stucco is partially cut away to expose a dark undercoat and so form a design (pp. 680F, 684—Pal. Guadagni).

Shaft. The portion of a column between base and capital (p. 110A, 160, 972); also applied in Mediæval architecture to a small column, as in a clustered pier, supporting a vaulting rib (pp. 388B, 503).

Shrine. A sacred place or object, e.g. a receptacle for relics (p. 581D).

Soffit. The ceiling or underside of any architectural member (pp. 120M, 138G,

190D, 191B, C, 224A, E, 426C, D, 705A, 759B, G, 977A, B).

Solar (Lat. *solarium* = a sunny place or balcony). A Mediæval term for an upper chamber, usually the private room of the owner (pp. 442E, 446E, F).

Span. The distance between the supports of an arch, roof, or beam.

Spandrel. The triangular space enclosed by the curve of an arch, a vertical line from its springing, and a horizontal line through its apex (pp. 223B, D, E, F, 267E, 351M, 416D, 498M).

Specus. The duct or channel of a Roman aqueduct, usually rectangular in section and lined with a waterproofing of successive coatings of hydraulic cement. Ducts were covered by stone slabs or by arched vaults and, where necessary, were partially or wholly cut through rock (p. 216E).

Spina. The spine wall down the centre of an ancient hippodrome or circus, around which the contestants turned (p. 216A, D).

Spire (A.-Sax. *spir* = a stalk). The tapering termination of a tower in Gothic or Renaissance architecture, which was the result of elongating an ordinary pyramidal or conical roof (pp. 415B, 419B, 431, 492, 540A, 547A, 548D, 572D, 590B, 591A, C, 637E, 919).

Splay (short form of 'display', cf. 'reveal'). The diagonal surface formed by the cutting away of a wall, as when an opening is wider inside than out or conversely.

Springer. The lowest unit or voussoir of an arch, occurring just above the springing line.

Squinch Arches. Arches placed diagonally at the internal angles of towers to bring them from the square to support the octagonal spire (pp. 322A, D, 431E, 638A, 641D).

Stalls. Divisions with fixed seats for the clergy and choir, often elaborately carved, with projecting elbows, 'misericords', and overhanging canopies. The bishop's seat is called the 'throne' (pp. 417B, 418B, 517D, E, F, G, 596H, 651C, 977M).

Starling. The pointed mass of masonry projecting from the pier of a bridge, for breaking the force of the water, hence known also as a 'cutwater' (p. 487H–M).

Steeple. The term applied to a tower crowned by a spire (pp. 431A, 917B, C, 919).

Stele. An upright slab forming a Greek

tombstone or carrying an inscription (pp. 157G, 163D).

Stilted Arch. An arch having its springing line higher than the line of impost mouldings, to which it is connected by vertical pieces of walling or stilts (pp. 391A, 424B, 1256).

Stoa. In Greek architecture, a portico or detached colonnade, corresponding with the Latin 'porticus' and the Italian 'portico' (pp. 104C, 132K).

Storey (pl. **Storeys**). The space between two floors.

Strapwork. A type of relief ornament or cresting resembling studded leather straps, arranged in geometrical and sometimes interlaced patterns; much used in the Early Renaissance architecture of England and the Low countries (pp. 839G, 969A, J, 976B, E, 977B, C, E).

String Course. A moulding or projecting course running horizontally along the face of a building (pp. 196A, 387C, E, L, M, P, 681A, 685B, 880A, C, 895A, 917C).

Stuart. A term applied to English Late Renaissance architecture of the period 1625–1702 (p. 868).

Stucco (It.). A fine quality of plaster, much used in Roman and Renaissance architecture for ornamental modelled work in low relief (pp. 219B, C, 715B, C, 768A). In England, it was extensively employed in the late eighteenth and early nineteenth century as an economical medium for the modelling of external architectural features, in lieu of stone (p. 947B).

Stupa or **Tope.** A mound forming a Buddhist sacred monument (p. 1182A).

Stylobate. In Classic architecture, the upper step forming a platform on which a colonnade is placed (pp. 110A, 116A, 118B). Collectively, the three steps of a Greek Doric temple constitute a crepidoma.

Sudatorium. The sweating room in a Roman baths building (p. 203B).

Systyle. A term used when the space between two columns is two diameters (p. 113A).

Tabernacle. A recess or receptacle—usually above an altar—to contain the eucharistic Host (p. 581A), and is also applied to a niche or arched canopy (p. 515J, L). 'Tabernacle work' is the name given to elaborately carved niche and canopy work (pp. 517D, E, F, 581).

Tegula. The Latin term for a large flat tile (pp. 110E, H, 181H).

Telamones (*see* **Atlantes**).

Temenos. A sacred precinct in which stood a temple or other sanctuary (pp. 48A, 103B, 105B, 106).

Tempera (It.). In painting, the same as distemper.

Tempietto. A small temple. The term is usually reserved for Renaissance and later buildings of an ornamental character, compact circular or temple-like structures erected in the parks and gardens of country houses. The most famous instance, however, is the small, colonnaded circular chapel by Bramante in the cloisters of S. Pietro in Montorio, Rome, a prime example of the Italian High Renaissance (p. 700A–C).

Tenia or **Taenia.** The band or fillet forming the upper member of the Doric architrave (pp. 110A, 144B).

Tepidarium. An apartment in a Roman baths building equipped with warm baths (pp. 203B, 204B) (*see* **Caldarium** *and* **Frigidarium**).

Terra-cotta. Earth baked or burnt in moulds for use in building construction and decoration, harder in quality than brick.

Tessera. A small cube of stone, glass, or marble, used in making mosaics.

Tetrastyle. A portico of four columns (pp. 109C, D, 132A, C, D, 135B, 377D).

Tholos. The dome (cupola) of a circular building, hence applied to the building itself (pp. 100A, B, E, 109E).

Thrust. The force exerted by inclined rafters or beams against a wall, or obliquely by the weight of an arch, vault or dome.

Tie-bar. A beam, bar or rod which ties parts of a building together, and is subjected to tensile strain. Sometimes of wood, but usually of metal. Tie-bars are especially notable in Byzantine, Italian Gothic and Renaissance architecture to stiffen arcades or to contain the outward thrust of vaults (pp. 268B, 277N, 282A, B, 601B, 606C, 611C, 615B, C, 622B, 628F, 735C).

Tierceron. An intermediate rib between the main ribs of a Gothic vault (p. 399D, E).

Tope (*see* **Stupa**).

Torus (Lat., a swelling). A large convex moulding, used principally in the bases of columns (pp. 141M, 164L, 165H, S) (*see* **Astragal**).

Trabeated (Lat. *trabs* = a beam). A style of architecture such as the Greek, in which the beam forms the constructive feature (pp. 38, 40, 41A, 46B, 48B, 51B, 110, 116, 118B, 130A, 135A, 144B).

Tracery. The ornamental pattern-work in stone, filling the upper part of a Gothic window; it may be either 'plate' or 'bar' tracery. 'Plate' tracery appears to have been cut out of a plate of stone, with special reference to the shape of the lights, whereas 'bar' tracery was designed principally for the pleasing forms produced by combinations of geometrical figures. It is also applied to work of the same character in wood panelling (pp. 499, 516, 519H, 563, 598, 602B, 626C, 628A, B).

Trachelion. The neck of a Greek Doric column, between the annulets and the grooves or hypotrachelion (p. 113).

Transept. The part of a cruciform church, projecting at right angles to the main building (pp. 410–13, 425B, 431C, 560, 910D).

Transoms. The horizontal divisions or cross-bars of windows (pp. 499D, M, 803H, 888).

Trefoil (Fr. *trois feuilles* = three leaves). A term applied to this distribution in Gothic tracery (pp. 499D, E, H, 515F, G, L, M, 1256).

Triclinium. A Roman dining room with couches on three sides (p. 234B).

Triforium (Lat. *tres* = three + *fores* = openings). The space between the sloping roof over the aisle and the aisle vaulting. The term was first applied to the Norman arcades at Canterbury which had triple openings towards the nave, and was afterwards used for any passages and galleries in this position. It occurs in large churches only, and, from having no windows to the open air, is often called a 'blind-storey' (pp. 369C, F, 414E, 424B, 494, 495).

Triglyphs (Gk., three channels). Blocks with vertical channels which form a distinguishing feature in the frieze of the Doric entablature (pp. 110A, E, 120M, 160A, B, 972A, C).

Tristyle-in-antis. A portico having three columns between antae.

Tudor. A term applied to English Late Gothic architecture of the period 1485–1558 (p. 389).

Turrets. Small towers, often containing stairs, and forming special features in Mediæval buildings (pp. 436D, 445H, 460A, 461B, 470A).

Tympanum. The triangular surface

bounded by the sloping and horizontal cornices of a pediment (pp. 110A, 116A, 196A, 902G); also the space enclosed between the lintel and the arch of a Mediæval doorway (pp. 351B, 567D).

Undercroft. In Mediæval architecture, vaulted chambers upon which the principal rooms are sometimes raised (p. 442J).

Vault. An arched covering in stone or brick over any building (pp. 74J, 80M, 177, 192G, 200F, 207A, H, 370, 373, 399).

Velarium. A great awning drawn over Roman theatres and amphitheatres to protect spectators against the sun (p. 211B).

Vesica Piscis (Lat., bladder of a fish). A pointed oval form, so called from its shape (p. 351B) (*see* **Aureole**).

Vestibule. An ante-room to a larger apartment of a building (pp. 203B, 207F, 690C, 703C, H).

Volute (Lat. *voluta* = scroll). The scroll or spiral occurring in Ionic, Corinthian, and Composite capitals (pp. 126, 127, 162A, 165D, 191D, 223G, 224G, 246D).

Voussoirs. The truncated wedge-shaped blocks forming an arch (pp. 373A, B, D, 1256).

Wave Moulding. A typical moulding of the Decorated period consisting of a slight convexity flanked by hollows (p. 507P, R, S).

Weathering. The slope given to off-sets to buttresses and the upper surface of cornices and mouldings, to throw off rain (pp. 199A, 388A, 497, 744C).

Westblock. A multistorey gallery at the west end of some German and Netherlandish churches, surmounted by towers or turrets.

Wheel Window. A circular window, whose mullions converge like the spokes of a wheel (pp. 325A, 414A, C, 532A, 543, 563E, H, 628A).

Window-tax. A tax levied in Britain from 1695–1851 upon all house windows above six.

Ziggurat or Ziqqarat. A high pyramidal staged tower, of which the angles were orientated to the cardinal points, which formed an important element in ancient Mesopotamian temple complexes. An especially sacred ceremony took place annually at the top of the ziggurat in an 'upper temple' having the form of a shrine or bower. The number of stages rose from one to seven in the course of time, and in the Assyrian version the stages were developed into a continuous inclined ramp, circulating the four sides in turn (pp. 68, 71A, 72A, 74A, E, G, H).

Zoophorus. A frieze in which reliefs of animals are introduced, as in the portico of the Theseion and the Panathenaic frieze on the naos wall of the Parthenon (pp. 120N, 163H).

Parliament Building, Ottawa, Ontario (1861–7). See p. 1151

INDEX

EXPLANATORY NOTE

Page numbers in **bold** type are main references.
Page numbers within square brackets [ ] refer to illustrations.
Bis, ter, or *quater* after a page number means that the subject is mentioned *two, three* or *four times* on that page.
(i) or (ii) after a page number indicates the first or second column on that page.

For explanation of symbols used see p. 1275

For explanation of symbols used see p. 1275

Brickwork (*cont.*)

1011, 1012, 1055; Byzantine, 272, **276**, 280; Egyptian, 13–14, **22**, 50; English Mediaeval, **380**, 444, 451, 459, 469, 473; English Renaissance, **864**, 870, 872, 937, 938, 967; Etruscan, 173; French, 549, **769**, 1080; German, **354**, 358, 364, **583**, 587, 588, 594, 806, 1094; Indian, 1175; Italian, 312, 600, 603, 607 *ter*, 613, 801 (i); Roman, 168, 175–6, 198, 202, 218, 221, 276, 636 [177D]; Spanish, **636**, 855 *bis*; West Asiatic, **61**, 66

Bridge:

Alcantara, 222, **239**; of Augustus, Rimini, 239 [245C]; Avignon, 347, 549; Aylesford, 489 [487M]; Coombe Bisset, 489 [488C]; Crowland, 489 [487J]; East Farleigh, 489 [488D]; Kirkby Lonsdale, 489 [487K]; Old London, 489 [487L]; Prior Park, 905, **932** [935D]; Saintes, 222; of Sighs, Venice, 731 [733D]; Stopham, 489 [487H]; Stowe, 905; of Ten Thousand Ages, Foochow, 1207; of Ten Thousand Times Peace, Tsienchowfu, 1207; Wakefield, 489; Warkworth, 489; Wilton, **905**, **932** [902D–F]; Yangtse River, 1207

Bridges:

British, 989; Chinese, 1206–7; English Mediaeval, 489 [487H–M, 488C, D]; French, **347**, 773 [760B]; Georgian, 964; iron, **964**, 989; Italian, **608**, 624; many-arched, 239, 489; Palladian, **905**, 932 [902D–F, 935D]; Roman, 222, **236**, **239** [238B, C, 241E, 245A, B, 634A]; single-arched, 239; Spanish, 644 [645B]; Swiss, 1104 [1108A]

Bridgewater House, London, 996 [994A]

Bridgman, Sir John, monument to, Aston [980F]

Bridlington Priory (Yorks.), mouldings [507M]; piers [503K, 504E]

Bridport, Bishop, his tomb at Salisbury, 509 [472B]

Brighton: Royal Pavilion, 876, **948** [947D]; S. Paul, 1008; S. Peter, 987

Brinckmann, J. A. (*archt.*), 1067, 1104

Brisbane (Australia), S. John's Anglican Cathedral, 1059

Bristol (Glos.):

Bank of England, 1036 [1039A]; Colston's House, 469 [464H]; Exchange, 955; Mayor's Chapel [512Q]; S. Mary Redcliffe [399G]; S. Peter's Hospital, 897 [894C]

Bristol Cathedral, **405**, 587

Chapter House, 405 [413K]; Elder Lady Chapel, 393, 405, **469** [413K]; model of [409A]; monastic foundation of, 402; plan of [413K]; vaulting of, 398 [399F]

Britannic House, London, 1047

British Museum, London, 877, **956** [962D]; Reading Room, 963, 987, **1041**

British Museum (*cont.*)

Aegean antiquities in, 102; Assyrian antiquities in, 64, 73 *bis*, 87 [72B, 84J]; Buddhist antiquities in, 1180; Early Christian antiquities in, 266; Egyptian antiquities in, 19, 57; Etruscan antiquities in, 180, 183 *bis* [181D, E, H]; Greek antiquities in, 123 *bis*, 125, 129, 131, 133, 137, 148, 151 *ter*; Mediaeval objects in, 509

British 19th and 20th century architecture, 982–1056

analysis, 1051–6; Art Nouveau, 991–2; character, 986–95; columns, **1054–5**, 1012, 1047; commercial and industrial buildings, **1036–51**, 1054; domestic buildings, 995–1008; Early Victorian, 987–9; ecclesiastical, 1008–19; examples, 995–1051; Gothic Revival, 986–95; Greek Revival, 987; High Victorian, 989–91; influences upon, 982–6; Late Victorian, **991–2**, 995, 999; mouldings, 1055

openings, 1054; ornament, 1055–6; plans, 1051–4; public buildings, 1019–1036; Queen Anne style, 991; roofs, 1054; Twentieth century era, 992–5; walls, 1052

Brixworth Church, Northampton, 390, 489

Brno (Czechoslovakia), Tugendhat House, 1075 [1076]

Broach spire, 490 *bis*, **1259** [492A]

Broadleys, Gill Head, Windermere, 1000 [1001A]

'Brochs' (*ancient Scottish forts*), 521

Broletto, Monza, 608 [330D]

Brooklyn (N.Y.), Jan Ditmars House, 1132

Bromley-by-Bow Old Palace, London, **885**, 974 [977B]

Bromley College (Kent), 956

Brooks's Club, London, 956

Brosse, Salomon de (*archt.*), 687, 769, **780** *ter*, 792

Brou (France), tomb of Philibert [567F]

Broughton Castle (Oxon.), doorway, 974 [975D]

Brown, Lancelot ('Capability') (*landscape gardener*), **875**, 876, 932, 937

Brown stone, 1121, 1143

Brown University, Providence (R.I.), University Hall, 1140

Browne's Hospital, Stamford, 479 [480H–K]

Bruant, Libéral (*archt.*), 799

Bruges (Belgium):

Chapelle du Saint-Sang, 574; Cloth Hall, 577 [579C]; Guild Houses, 570; Hospital, 582 [581D]; Notre Dame, 574; Old Chancellery, 831, **832** [833A]; S. Ursula shrine, 582 [581D]; Town Hall, 570, **577** [579F]

Brunel, I. K. (*engineer*), **989**, 1042

For explanation of symbols used see p. 1275

For explanation of symbols used see p. 1275

For explanation of symbols used see p. 1275

For explanation of symbols used see p. 1275

For explanation of symbols used see p. 1275

For explanation of symbols used see p. 1275

For explanation of symbols used see p. **1275**

For explanation of symbols used see p. 1275

For explanation of symbols used see p. 1275

For explanation of symbols used see p. 1275

For explanation of symbols used see p. 1275

For explanation of symbols used see p. 1275

For explanation of symbols used see p. 1275

For explanation of symbols used see p. 1275

For explanation of symbols used see p. 1275

For explanation of symbols used see p. 1275

For explanation of symbols used see p. 1275

Pagodas: Chinese, 1201, **1202-5**, 1208 [1203B, 1204E]; Japanese, 1214
'Pai-lous' (*gateways*): Chinese, 1180, 1201, 1202, **1205** bis, 1208 [1203C]; Japanese, 1217, 1219
Paimio (Finland), Tuberculosis Sanatorium, 1094 [1099C]
Paine, James (*archt.*), 874, 932, 937, 964
Palace (*see also* Palazzo):
Alcázar, Seville, 1233; Archbishop's, Alcalá, 846; Croydon, 452; Lambeth, 393, 394; Palermo, 624 bis [626C, J]; Artaxerxes II, Susa, 75; Ashurbanipal, Nineveh, 73; Ashurnasirpal II, Nimroud, 64, 73 [71A]; Augustus, Rome, 227 [232E]; Bishop's, Alcalá, 648 [646G]
Bishop's, Wells, 452; Blenheim, **931-2**, 967 [930, 933A, 934A]; Bromley-by-Bow, **885**, 974 [977B]; Buckingham, London, 963, 988
de Chaillot, Paris, 1094 [1100B]; Charles V's, Granada, 851 [847A, C]; Clam Gallas, Prague, 812; Crystal, London, 1041-2 [1043]; Ctesiphon, 79 [80L-P]; Cyrus the Great, Pasargadae, 75
Darius I, Persepolis, **75**, 78 [76C]; Darius I, Susa, 75 [76F, G]; Diocletian, Spalato, 194, **229-30**, 875 [231]; Doge's, Venice, *see* Doge's Palace; Domitian, Rome, 227, **229** [232E]; Ducal, Guadalajara, **647**, 846 [646A, 843A]; Ducal, Gubbio, 695; Ducal, Urbino, 695 [675B]
Eltham, 437 [500G]; Esarhaddon, Nimroud, 64, 73 [71A]; Esarhaddon, Nineveh, 64; Feruz-abad, 79 [80A-F]; Fontainebleau, **774**, 802 (ii) [764B, 767-8, 803A, B, D, E]; Furstenburg, Innsbruck [592F]
Governor's, Nancy, 791; Hampton Court, 380, 394, 437, **459**, **463**, 496, 502, 510, 914, 967, 974 [460, 461C, E, 923A, 925U]; Hungarian Guard, Vienna, 812 [825B]; Kensington, 914; Kinsky, Vienna, 812 [813F]
Louvre, 762, 769, **774**, **779**, 780, 785, **791**, 871, 880, 898 [775-7, 793B]; Luxembourg, 769, **780** [781E, F]; Marqués de Dos Aguas, Valencia, 852 [857B, C]; Minos, King, at Knossos, 98 [99B]; Montezuma, at Mexico City, 1131
Persepolis, **75**, 78 [76C, 77A]; Petit, Paris, 1064, **1086** [1092B]; Phaestos, 98; Royal, Madrid, 852; S. James's, London, 394 [461A, 462B]; San Antonio, 1139; Santa Fé, 1139 [1138A]; Sargon II, Khorsabad, 64, **73-5** [71B, 74]; Sarvistan, 79 [80G-K]; Schwarzenberg, Vienna, 812 [813F]; Sennacherib, Nineveh, 64, 73
Tiryns, **98**, 101 [99C]; Troja, Prague, 812 [814A]; Tuileries, Paris, 774, **779** [775E, 777B]; Versailles, 762, **780**, **785** [783, 784A, 788D, F, 804C]; Waldstein, Prague, 812 [810B]; Wells, Bishop's 452; Westminster, 451, *see also* Westminster Hall; Whitehall, London, 866,

Palace (*cont.*)
898 [899]; Williamsburg, 1140; Winchester, 928 [925F]; Wolvesey, 968 [971H]; of Xerxes, Persepolis, 75, 78 [76C]
Palaces:
Aegean, 97, **98-101** [99, 100H]; Assyrian, **73**, 371 [71A, B, 74]; Chinese, 1206; Italian, 748, *see also* Palazzo; Japanese, 1217; Rajasthan, 1188; Renaissance, 213; Roman, 8, 169, **227**, **229-230** [231-2]; Rome's, 673; Syrian, 85; West Asiatic, 64, 70, 73, **75**, **79** [71A, 72, 74, 80]
Palacio de la Audiencia, Barcelona, 644
Palacio de Monterey, Salamanca, 956
Palacios, A. P. (*archt.*), 1160
Palaestra, Greek, 148; Roman, 202
Palais de Justice: Brussels, 1086 [1090A]; Malines, 831; Paris, 791; Rouen, **555**, 559 [556B, 558B]; Zaltbommel [838K]
Palatine Hill, Rome, Palaces on, 227 [232]
Palazzetto dello Sport, Rome, 1103 [1102A]
Palazzo:
Albergati, Bologna, 702; Barbarano, Vicenza, 738; Barberini, Rome, **725**, 748 [724A, B]; Bargello, Florence, 623; Bevilacqua, Verona, 732 [744J]; Borghese, Rome, 691, **725** [724F]; Braschi, Rome, 748
Ca d'Oro, Venice, 608 [612C]; della Cancelleria, Rome, **696**, **701** [699, 753C]; Capitanio, Vicenza, 738; Carega, Genoa [759E]; Carignano, Turin, 695 [694B]; Cavalli, Venice, 608; Chiericati, Vicenza, 738; del Commune, Verona [628D]; dei Conservatori, Rome, 714 [718D, E]; del Consiglio, Verona, 664 (ii), **732** [744H]; Contarini-Fasan, Venice, 608; Contucci, Montepulciano, 702; Cornaro, Venice [757F]; Corner della Ca' Grande, Venice, **737**, 747 bis [734C]; Corner Spinelli, Venice, 731 [734B]; Corsini, Rome, 748
dei Diamanti, Verona, 737 [744G]; Durazzo-Pallavicini, Genoa, 691 [689D]; Episcopio, Pienza, 684
Farnese, Caprarola, **708**, 748 [711]; Farnese, Rome, 217, **702**, 725, 748 [705, 753A, B]; Farsetti, Venice, 324; Foscari, Venice, 608; Franchini, Verona [757B]
Gambaro, Genoa [759D]; Gondi, Florence, 748 [749A]; Grimani, Venice, 737 [745]; Guadagni, Florence, 685 [680F]; Güell, Barcelona, 1065, **1071** [1069C]; del Laterano, Rome, 725 [664, 706F]
Marino, Milan, **688**, 691 [724D]; Massimi, Rome, 673, **702** [703]; Micheletti, Lucca, 687 [689C]; Montecitorio, Rome, 726; Municipale, Genoa, **688**, 691 [690]; del Municipio, Perugia, 623; Odescalchi, Rome, 726 [706D]
Pandolfini, Florence, **707**, 748, 1019 [756]; Pazzi, Florence, *see* Quaratesi; Pesaro, Venice, 747 [734A]; Piccolomini,

For explanation of symbols used see p. 1275

For explanation of symbols used see p. 1275

For explanation of symbols used see p. 1275

For explanation of symbols used see p. 1275

For explanation of symbols used see p. 1275

For explanation of symbols used see p. 1275

For explanation of symbols used see p. 1275

For explanation of symbols used see p. 1275

For explanation of symbols used see p. 1275

For explanation of symbols used see p. 1275

For explanation of symbols used see p. 1275

For explanation of symbols used see p. 1275

For explanation of symbols used see p. 1275

For explanation of symbols used see p. 1275

For explanation of symbols used see p. 1275

For explanation of symbols used see p. 1275

For explanation of symbols used see p. 1275

For explanation of symbols used see p. 1275

For explanation of symbols used see p. 1275

For explanation of symbols used see p. 1275

For explanation of symbols used see p. 1275

For explanation of symbols used see p. 1275

For explanation of symbols used see p. 1275

For explanation of symbols used see p. 1275